Dresible

Dreamweaver® MX Bible

Joseph W. Lowery

Wiley Publishing, Inc.

Dreamweaver® MX Bible

Published by
Wiley Publishing, Inc.
10475 Crosspoint Boulevard
Indianapolis, IN 46256
www.wiley.com

Copyright © 2002 by Wiley Publishing, Inc., Indianapolis, Indiana

Library of Congress Control Number: 2002108095

ISBN: 0-7645-4931-6

Manufactured in the United States of America

10 9 8 7 6 5 4 3 2

1B/QX/QY/QS/IN

Published simultaneously in Canada

For general information on our other products and services or to obtain technical support, please contact our Customer Care Department within the U.S. at (800) 762-2974, outside the U.S. at (317) 572-3993 or fax (317) 572-4002.

Wiley also publishes its books in a variety of electronic formats. Some content that appears in print may not be available in electronic books.

About the Author

Joseph Lowery has been writing about computers and new technology since 1981. He is the author of the previous editions of *Dreamweaver Bible* and *Fireworks Bible* as well as *Buying Online For Dummies* (all published by Wiley). He recently co-wrote a book on Flash with designer Hillman Curtis and has also written books on HTML and using the Internet for business. His books are international bestsellers, having sold more than 300,000 copies worldwide in ten different languages. Joe is also a consultant and trainer and has presented at Seybold in both Boston and San Francisco, Macromedia UCON in the U.S. and Europe, and at ThunderLizard's Web World. As a partner in Deva Associates, Ltd., Joe developed the Deva Tools for Dreamweaver set of navigational extensions. Joe and his wife, dancer/choreographer Debra Wanner, have a daughter, Margot.

About the Contributors

Lisa Boesen spent eleven years as a systems programmer — working with, learning from, and being inspired by some of the most impressive people in the computer industry. This background in computer science and her experience as both a software developer and an end user perfectly suited her to step into the role of technical writer in 1993. As a specialist in online documentation, Lisa has consulted with a wide variety of clients, designing, writing, and implementing their online documentation in formats that include WinHelp, Adobe Acrobat, and HTML. Most recently, Lisa has focused on developing training materials to teach others about her favorite Web authoring tool, Dreamweaver.

Rick Scott has worked as a technical writer, programmer, tester, layout artist, instructor, multimedia developer, Web site designer, philologist, linguist, composer, performer, failed screenwriter, (marginally) successful novelist, and devout neopagan herbalist. What draws him to technical writing is the great and good joy of creating Order from Chaos.

Daniel Short never planned to be a Web designer, it just happened. He started out in the Army tearing apart computers and eventually began putting together Web sites. Dan is a devoted Macromedian (and Team Macromedia volunteer) and uses almost the entire Macromedia Web Design Suite, including Fireworks and Macromedia Flash. He's been doing the Web gig since the end of 1998 and has had great luck building his Web design business through Web Shorts Site Design. Dan helps maintain several HTML and Dreamweaver reference sites including DreamweaverFAQ.com, for which he created the style changer and all ASP functionality, including the Snippets Exchange. Dan has also written articles for several resource sites, including AListApart.com, run by Jeffrey Zeldman, and Spider Food.net, run by J.K. Bowman. Dan is a contributing author for *Dreamweaver MX Magic* (published by New Riders).

About the Technical Editors

Angela C. Buraglia spent six years as an independent film makeup artist before realizing that she wanted a career that would allow her to start a family and stay home with her husband and child. In an effort to give back to the Macromedia Dreamweaver newsgroup community that helped and encouraged her in her new career, she founded DreamweaverFAQ. com. Although she only intended to be a Web developer, life's path has led her to become that and more. In addition to her contribution to this book, Angela is also a contributing author for *Dreamweaver MX Magic* (published by New Riders) and *ColdFusion MX Web Application Construction Kit* (published by Macromedia Press). Currently, Angela is also a Team Macromedia volunteer for Dreamweaver. Angela's future plans are to continue developing DreamweaverFAQ.com, to build and sell Dreamweaver extensions, to give presentations at conferences, and perhaps to become involved in new book projects. Long gone are the days of applying makeup; now Angela applies behaviors and CSS to Web sites and — most importantly — is home with her little boy.

Marc Garner runs sixtyeight, a UK-based Web design and development company (www. sixtyeight.co.uk). He has over 15 years experience in the creative design industry, with the last 6 years devoted to Web design and application development. Marc has provided organizations with Macintosh training in major graphics and Internet software packages. In addition, he was the Macintosh technical editor for *Dreamweaver MX Weekend Crash Course*, also published by Wiley. Away from the studio, Marc can be found painting with Aimee or playing trains with Curtis.

Jon Parkhurst's Internet quest began when he was handed MPI's Web site in 1995. As he delved further into the underbelly of the Net, he soon became lost with the endless lines of code-crunching minions. In 1996, Jon began doing contract work under CDC Digital (www.cdcdigital.com) and continued until 2000. Jon currently works as the head of the E-Commerce Department at Unimark, Inc. (www.unimark.com) and contracts under NetNucleus.org. During the workday, he can typically be found peppering the Macromedia newsgroups as a volunteer Team Macromedia Member. During his off hours, he can be found administering his main personal site, IdentityOutpost.com, or hiking through the foothills of Missouri with his two kids.

Credits

Acquisitions Editor
Carol Sheehan

Senior Project Editor
Jodi Jensen

Lead Technical Editor
Angela Buraglia

Technical Editors
Marc Garner
Jon Parkhurst

Development Editors
Erik Dafforn
Susan Hobbs

Copy Editors
Mary Lagu
Luann Rouff

Editorial Manager
Mary Beth Wakefield

**Vice President and
Executive Group Publisher**
Richard Swadley

**Vice President and
Executive Publisher**
Bob Ipsen

Executive Editorial Director
Mary Bednarek

Project Coordinator
Erin Smith

Graphics and Production Specialists
Beth Brooks
Sean Decker
Melanie DesJardins
Stephanie D. Jumper
Heather Pope
Betty Schulte
Jeremey Unger

Quality Control Technician
Laura Albert
David Faust

Permissions Editor
Carmen Krikorian

Media Development Specialist
Angela Denny

Proofreading and Indexing
TECHBOOKS Production Services

Cover Image
Murder By Design

For my father, William W. Lowery, 1920-2002.
Love you, Dad.

Foreword

Things were starting to become predictable.

Like clockwork, Macromedia has dutifully updated the world's leading Web development environment annually since the original Dreamweaver 1 release in December, 1997. It was getting to the point where you could plan family events around it: "The new Dreamweaver is out. Time to start the holiday shopping!" This tradition continued through December 2000 when I joined the Dreamweaver team.

Then, all at once, everything changed. The nature and scope of Web development changed. Suddenly the newspapers weren't just reporting that www.milkshakedelivery.com had wasted its $100 million in venture capital and filed for bankruptcy. The entire technical sector of the economy was looking bleak. Stalwarts like IBM and Cisco were suddenly laying people off. Web-related projects were put on hold across the board; it was as if the Web was put on standby. People began to question the hype that had been generated the last couple years. Was the Web here to stay?

The Dreamweaver team watched all this and decided it was time to take a step back and rethink what Dreamweaver was all about. Another yearly update simply wasn't going to cut it this time. We used the downturn in the economy as an opportunity to batten down the hatches, prolong the development cycle, and try to really do something big. The next version of Dreamweaver couldn't be about just incremental improvements and new features. It had to fundamentally change, just as the Web development landscape had fundamentally changed. We knew the Web was here to stay, but there was no doubt that things were different; and with change comes opportunity.

It turns out that we were literally surrounded by opportunities. With ColdFusion as part of the product portfolio, we had an opportunity to bring the power of Web application development to every static HTML designer out there. With the release of .NET, we had the chance to take the power of a new platform and make it readily usable by mere mortals. With the settling of standards, we could lead developers into creating next-generation sites using CSS2, XML, and XHTML to allow them to be maintained and expanded for years to come. With the advent of Web services, we had the opportunity to let developers add sophisticated functionality to their sites without learning Java or C#. And with the convergence of the Web development workforce, we had the potential to produce a single tool that all members of a Web development team could use to get their jobs done, whether it was visually oriented, code-centric, or some combination thereof.

We seized on all these opportunities with Dreamweaver MX and, in the end, produced a totally new Web-development environment. What you may not realize is that Joe Lowery was with us just about every step of the way. We do our best to get customer feedback throughout the development cycle, and Joe has always been great at providing this input. Whether filing bug reports, contributing to newsgroups, or sending e-mails about feature requests and ideas, Joe is a constant source of real-world feedback for us. And that comes through in his writing. Joe uses the products he writes about day in and day out, and that makes all the difference. With a product as different and new as Dreamweaver MX, I'm not sure which is more difficult: building an application or describing it. Either way, Joe shows how to use the most significant release of Dreamweaver since version 1 to solve real-world development problems. I hope you enjoy using Dreamweaver as much as we enjoyed creating it.

David Deming
Product Manager, Dreamweaver
Macromedia, Inc.

Preface

Dreamweaver MX stands at the center of a complex series of overlapping worlds. In one realm, we have designers of static Web pages looking to expand their knowledge base into data-driven sites. Over there, you'll find application developers — some savvy in Active Server Pages and ASP.NET, some in ColdFusion, and some others in JavaServer Pages and PHP — anxious to develop for the Internet. There's a spectrum of experience in both camps that runs the gamut from eager novice to experienced professional. Then there's yet another group of prospective Web craftsmen and artists who want to do it all and are looking for a place to start. Dreamweaver MX is the one program robust enough for them all, and *Dreamweaver MX Bible* is your guidebook to all its features and capabilities.

What's in a name? In the case of Macromedia's Dreamweaver MX, you'll find one of the most appropriate product names around. Web page design is a blend of art and craft; whether you're a deadline-driven professional or a vision-filled amateur, you'll find that the Dreamweaver underpinnings of this tool provide an intuitive way to make your Web visions a reality. Dreamweaver implies development, and Dreamweaver MX excels at producing multifaceted Web pages that bring content locked in a data store to the surface.

To use this book, you need only two items: the Dreamweaver software and a desire to make cutting-edge Web pages. (Actually, you don't even need Dreamweaver to begin; the CD-ROM that accompanies this book contains a trial version.) From quick design prototyping to ongoing Web site management, Dreamweaver automates and simplifies much of a Webmaster's workload. Dreamweaver is not only the first Web authoring tool to bring the ease of visual editing to an HTML-code–oriented world, it also brings a point-and-click interface to complex coding whether server-side or client-side. The *Dreamweaver MX Bible* is designed to help you master every nuance of the program. Are you building multipage Web applications? Are you creating a straightforward layout with the visual editor? Do you need to extend Dreamweaver's capabilities by building your own custom objects? With Dreamweaver and this book, you can weave your dreams into reality for the entire world to experience.

What's New in Dreamweaver MX

Since its inception, Dreamweaver has strived to serve two masters: professional Web developers, savvy in technique and used to hand-coding, and beginning designers looking to overcome their lack of HTML and JavaScript expertise. Dreamweaver MX attempts to continue the balancing act of satisfying the two different markets — and, in large part, succeeds. Innovations in Dreamweaver MX can be categorized into three areas: layout and design, code editing, and Web-application building.

Enhanced layout features

Perhaps the most obvious new feature is Dreamweaver's totally redesigned workspace. Panels are now docked together and, if the Windows-only MDI mode is used, documents appear in a single window. The redesigned look and feel matches other Macromedia products in the MX line: Fireworks, Flash, and soon, FreeHand. This common user interface smoothes out the workflows and aids productivity.

Dreamweaver also revamped the underlying architecture of how documents and sites work together and, in the process, made it far easier to work with different types of Web documents. The New Document feature now allows you to pick from 36 different standard formats — and, better still, you can add your own. Macromedia also includes a wide variety of basic page layouts: everything from text-based pages to product catalogs.

Dreamweaver honed its cutting edge a little finer with enhanced Cascading Style Sheet (CSS) support — both on the coding and the rendering side. The CSS Panel has been given a full makeover and now offers split functionality for easier editing and applying of styles. Design Time Style Sheets is another new feature, which incorporates CSS design with dynamic application power.

If you're a template user, you'll also find a lot more flexibility available to you. In addition to editable regions, templates may now have repeating regions or optional regions. Repeating regions are used to increase or decrease the rows in a table while keeping the table structure intact. Optional regions can hide or display any elements on a page — like an "On Sale Now" graphic — at design time.

Code editing improvements

The most far-reaching change to Dreamweaver's coding environment is under the hood, so to speak. Dreamweaver MX completely revitalized its coding architecture by tying each page type to a customizable set of tags known as a *tag library*. This enhancement gives Dreamweaver users the power to create HTML, XHTML, ASP, ColdFusion, XML pages, and more with equal ease. Macromedia also provides an easy-to-use editor for managing existing tag libraries and adding new ones.

Some of the more resonant repercussions of Dreamweaver's underlying tag library structure are of particular use to hand-coders. On demand, Dreamweaver provides hints for both tags and their attributes. This enables very rapid code development. The tag libraries are also responsible for Dreamweaver's code completion system — you'll never forget to close a tag again!

Two other new features are geared to ramp up code production. The Snippets panel keeps commonly used blocks of code within easy reach — and, of course, you can add your own code and manage the categories however you choose. The Tag inspector serves double-duty by first exposing all the page elements in a collapsible tree structure, and second by allowing all the attributes of any selected element to be directly edited.

Web application advancements

Dreamweaver's connectivity greatly expands in Dreamweaver MX. In addition to supporting ASP (in both JavaScript and VBScript), JSP, and ColdFusion, Dreamweaver now writes ASP.NET (in either C# or VBScript) and PHP code with equal aplomb. Macromedia has even developed some custom ASP.NET tags to speed development.

Given Macromedia's merger with Allaire, you might expect a greater integration between Dreamweaver and ColdFusion—and you'll get it in Dreamweaver MX. In addition to a major overhaul of the server behavior code so that it's more familiar to ColdFusion developers, Dreamweaver now boasts a direct connection to a new feature in ColdFusion MX: ColdFusion Components. Components can be written, applied, and even inspected from within Dreamweaver.

One of the hottest trends in Web application development is known as Web services. Web services are a form of distributed application—and Dreamweaver lets you build pages that can access Web services and display the required information.

Dreamweaver appeals to both the expert and the novice Web designer. Although the program is extraordinarily powerful, it's also fairly intuitive. Nonetheless, designers new to the Web often find the entire process overwhelming—understandably so. To give folks a bird's-eye view of the overall use of Dreamweaver in Web site design and production, this edition includes a Quick Start in Chapter 2. In this chapter, you'll see how one designer—yours truly—works with Dreamweaver in every aspect of building Web pages and constructing a site.

Who Should Read This Book?

Dreamweaver attracts a wide range of Web developers. Because it's the first Web authoring tool that doesn't rewrite original code, veteran designers are drawn to using Dreamweaver as their first visual editor. Because it also automates complicated effects, beginning Web designers are interested in Dreamweaver's power and performance. *Dreamweaver MX Bible* addresses the full spectrum of Web professionals, providing basic information on HTML if you're just starting, as well as advanced tips and tricks for seasoned pros. Moreover, this book is a complete reference for everyone working with Dreamweaver on a daily basis.

What Hardware and Software Do You Need?

Dreamweaver MX Bible includes coverage of Dreamweaver MX. If you don't own a copy of the program, you can use the trial version on this book's CD-ROM. Written to be platform-independent, this book covers both the Macintosh and Windows versions of Dreamweaver MX.

Macintosh

Macromedia recommends the following minimum requirements for running Dreamweaver on a Macintosh:

- ✦ Macintosh PowerPC (G3 or higher recommended)
- ✦ Mac OS 9.1 or higher or Mac OS 10.1 or higher
- ✦ 96MB of available RAM
- ✦ 275MB of available disk space
- ✦ 256-color monitor capable of 800 × 600 resolution (OS X requires thousands of colors)
- ✦ CD-ROM drive

Windows

Macromedia recommends the following minimum requirements for running Dreamweaver on a Windows system:

+ Intel Pentium II processor, 300MHz or equivalent

+ Windows 98, ME, NT, 2000, or XP

+ 96MB of available RAM

+ 275MB of available disk space

+ 256-color monitor capable of 800 × 600 resolution

+ CD-ROM drive

Note   These are the minimum requirements. As with all graphics-based design tools, more capability is definitely better for using Dreamweaver, especially in terms of memory and processor speed.

How This Book Is Organized

Dreamweaver MX Bible can take you from raw beginner to full-fledged professional if read cover to cover. However, you're more likely to read each section as needed, taking the necessary information and coming back later. To facilitate this approach, *Dreamweaver MX Bible* is divided into seven major task-oriented parts. After you're familiar with Dreamweaver, feel free to skip around the book, using it as a reference guide as you build up your own knowledge base.

The early chapters present the basics, and all chapters contain clearly written steps for the tasks you need to perform. In later chapters, you encounter sections labeled Dreamweaver Techniques. *Dreamweaver Techniques* are step-by-step instructions for accomplishing specific Web designer tasks — for example, building an image map that uses rollovers, or eliminating underlines from hyperlinks through Cascading Style Sheets. Naturally, you can also use the Dreamweaver Techniques as stepping stones for your own explorations into Web page creation.

If you're running Dreamweaver while reading this book, don't forget to use the CD-ROM. An integral element of the book, the accompanying CD-ROM offers a vast number of additional Dreamweaver server behaviors, objects, commands, and other extensions in addition to relevant code from the book.

Part I: Dreamweaver MX Basics

Part I begins with an overview of Dreamweaver's philosophy and design. To get the most out of the program, you need to understand the key advantages it offers over other authoring programs and the deficiencies that it addresses. Part I takes you all the way to setting up your first site. In Chapter 2, you'll get an overview of the Web development process as a quick start to Dreamweaver. The other opening chapters give you a full reference to the Dreamweaver interface and all of its customizable features.

Part II: Web Design and Layout

Although Dreamweaver is partly a visual design tool, its roots derive from the language of the Web: HTML. Part II gives you a solid foundation in the basics of HTML, even if you've never seen code, as well as showing you how to get the most out of Dreamweaver's code environment with any language. The three fundamentals of static Web pages are text, images, and links. You explore how to incorporate these elements to their fullest extent in Chapters 7, 8, and 9, respectively. Chapter 10 examines the various uses of tables — from a clear presentation of data to organizing entire Web pages. Here you learn how to use Dreamweaver's visual table editing capabilities to resize and reshape your HTML tables quickly. Forms are an essential element in dynamic Web page design — you'll learn all about them in Chapter 11. Chapter 12 examines another fundamental HTML option: lists. You study the list in all of its forms: numbered lists, bulleted lists, definition lists, nested lists, and more.

Chapter 13 is devoted to image maps and shows how to use Dreamweaver's built-in Image Map tools to create client-side image maps. The chapter also explains how you can build server-side image maps and demonstrates a revised technique for creating image map rollovers. Chapter 14 investigates the somewhat complex world of frames — and shows how Dreamweaver has greatly simplified the task of building and managing these multifile creations, particularly with the new Frame objects. You also learn how to handle more advanced design tasks such as updating multiple frames with just one click.

Part III: Incorporating Dynamic Data

Chapter 15 begins an in-depth investigation of Dreamweaver's power to create dynamic Web pages by describing how to set up your basic connections and recordsets. Chapter 16 explains how to insert text from a data source on to your Web page and how to format it once it's incorporated. You'll also see how to relate other Web page elements — such as images, Flash movies, and other media files — to a data source. Chapter 17 continues the exploration by delving into Dreamweaver's powerful Repeat Region server behavior as well as discussing techniques for hiding and showing your data at will.

One of Dreamweaver's most useful features, the Live Data Preview, is explored extensively in Chapter 18. Chapter 19 enters the world of multipage applications and explains how variables and other data can be passed from one page to another.

Part IV: Dynamic HTML and Dreamweaver

Dynamic HTML brought a new world of promises to Web designers — promises that went largely unfulfilled until Dreamweaver was released. Part IV of the *Dreamweaver MX Bible* examines this brave new world of pixel-perfect positioning, layers that fly in and then disappear as if by magic, and Web sites that can change their look and feel at the click of a mouse.

Chapter 20 takes a detailed look at the elegance of Cascading Style Sheets and offers techniques for accomplishing the most frequently requested tasks, such as creating an external style sheet. Many of the advantages of Dynamic HTML come from the use of layers, which enable absolute positioning of page elements, visibility control, and a sense of depth. You discover how to handle all these layer capabilities and more in Chapter 21. Chapter 22 focuses on timelines, which have the potential to take your Web page into the fourth dimension. The chapter concludes with a blow-by-blow description of how to create a multiscreen slide show, complete with layers that fly in and out on command. Chapter 23 offers an in-depth look at the capabilities of Dreamweaver behaviors. Each standard behavior is covered in detail with step-by-step instructions.

Part V: Adding Multimedia Elements

In recent years, the Web has moved from a relatively static display of text and simple images to a full-blown multimedia circus with streaming video, background music, and interactive animations. Part V contains the power tools for incorporating various media files into your Web site.

Graphics remain the key medium on the Web today, and Macromedia's Fireworks is a top-notch graphics generator. Chapter 24 delves into methods for incorporating Fireworks graphics — with all the requisite rollover and other code intact. Special focus is given to the Dreamweaver-to-Fireworks communication link and how your Web production efforts can benefit from it.

In addition to Dreamweaver, Macromedia is perhaps best known for one other contribution to Web multimedia: Flash. Chapter 25 explores the possibilities offered by incorporating Flash and Shockwave movies into Dreamweaver-designed Web pages and includes everything you need to know about configuring MIME types. You also find step-by-step instructions for building Shockwave inline controls and playing Shockwave movies in frame-based Web pages, as well as how to add Flash buttons and Flash text.

Chapter 26 covers digital video in its many forms: downloadable AVI files, streaming RealVideo displays, and panoramic QuickTime movies. Chapter 27 focuses on digital audio, with coverage of standard WAV and MIDI sound files as well as the newer streaming audio formats, like MP3.

Part VI: Enhancing Web Site Management and Workflow in Dreamweaver

Although Web page design gets all the glory, Web site management pays the bills. In Part VI, you see how Dreamweaver makes this essential part of any Webmaster's day easier to handle. Chapter 28 starts off the section with a look at the use of Dreamweaver Templates and how they can speed up production while ensuring a unified look and feel across your Web site. Chapter 29 covers the Library, which can significantly reduce any Webmaster's workload by providing reusable — and updateable — page elements. Chapter 30 describes Dreamweaver's built-in tools for maintaining cross- and backward-browser compatibility. A Dreamweaver Technique demonstrates a browser-checking Web page that automatically directs users to appropriate links.

Until now, individual Web developers have been stymied when attempting to integrate Dreamweaver into a team development environment. File locking was all too easily subverted, allowing revisions to be inadvertently overwritten, site reports were limited in scope and output only to HTML, and, worst of all, version control was nonexistent. Dreamweaver MX addresses all these concerns while laying a foundation for future connectivity. In Chapter 31, you see how you can tie Dreamweaver into an existing Visual SourceSafe or WebDAV version control system. Other new features covered include custom file view columns and enhanced Design Notes accessibility.

I can't think of any new technology on the Web that has so quickly gained the widespread acceptance that XML has. In a nutshell, XML (short for eXtensible Markup Language) enables you to create your own custom tags that make the most sense for your business or profession. Although XML doesn't enjoy full browser support as of this writing, it's only a matter of time — and little time at that. Chapter 32 shows you how to apply this fast-approaching technology of tomorrow in Dreamweaver today.

Part VII: Extending Dreamweaver

Dreamweaver is a program with extensive capabilities for expanding its own power. Chapter 33 explores the brave new world of Dreamweaver extensibility, with complete coverage of using and building commands as well as custom tags, translators, floaters, and C-level Extensions. With its own set of objects and behaviors, Dreamweaver complements HTML's extensibility. Chapter 34 shows you how you can use the built-in objects to accomplish most of your Web page layout chores quickly and efficiently — and when you're ready for increased automation, the chapter explains how to build your own custom objects. If you're JavaScript-savvy, Chapter 35 gives you the material you need to construct your own client-side behaviors and reduce your day-to-day workload. Finally, Chapter 36 examines server behaviors, describing every standard one in detail and then exploring the use of the Server Behavior Builder, Dreamweaver's tool for creating custom server behaviors.

Appendix

The appendix describes the contents of the CD-ROM that accompanies this book. Throughout this book, whenever you encounter a reference to files or programs on the CD-ROM, please check this appendix for more information.

Conventions Used in This Book

I use the following conventions throughout this book.

Windows and Macintosh conventions

Because *Dreamweaver MX Bible* is a cross-platform book, it gives instructions for both Windows and Macintosh users when keystrokes for a particular task differ. Throughout this book, the Windows keystrokes are given first; the Macintosh are given second in parentheses, as follows:

> To undo an action, press Ctrl+Z (Command+Z).

The first action instructs Windows users to press the Ctrl and Z keys in combination, and the second action (in parentheses) instructs Macintosh users to press the Command and Z keys together.

Key combinations

When you are instructed to press two or more keys simultaneously, each key in the combination is separated by a plus sign. For example:

> Ctrl+Alt+T (Command+Option+T)

The preceding tells you to press the three listed keys for your system at the same time. You can also hold down one or more keys and then press the final key. Release all the keys at the same time.

Mouse instructions

When instructed to *click* an item, move the mouse pointer to the specified item and click the mouse button once. Windows users use the left mouse button unless otherwise instructed. *Double-click* means clicking the mouse button twice in rapid succession.

When instructed to *select* or *choose* an item, you may click it once as previously described. If you are selecting text or multiple objects, click the mouse button once, press Shift, and then move the mouse to a new location and click again. The color of the selected item or items inverts to indicate the selection. To clear the selection, click once anywhere on the Web page.

Menu commands

When instructed to select a command from a menu, you see the menu and the command separated by an arrow symbol. For example, when instructed to execute the Open command from the File menu, you see the notation File ➪ Open. Some menus use submenus, in which case you see an arrow for each submenu, as follows: Insert ➪ Form Object ➪ Text Field.

Typographical conventions

I use *italic* type for new terms and for emphasis and **boldface** type for text that you need to type directly from the computer keyboard.

Code

A special typeface indicates HTML or other code, as demonstrated in the following example:

```
<html>
<head>
<title>Untitled Document</title>
</head>
<body bgcolor="#FFFFFF">
</body>
</html>
```

This code font is also used within paragraphs to designate HTML tags, attributes, and values such as <body>, bgcolor, and #FFFFFF. All HTML tags are presented in lowercase, as written by Dreamweaver, although browsers are not generally case-sensitive in terms of HTML.

The code continuation character (↩) at the end of a code line indicates that the line is too long to fit within the margins of the printed book. You should continue typing the next line of code before pressing the Enter (Return) key.

Navigating This Book

Various signposts and icons are located throughout *Dreamweaver MX Bible* for your assistance. Each chapter begins with an overview of its information and ends with a quick summary.

Icons appear in the text to indicate important or especially helpful items. Here's a list of the icons and their functions:

Tip Tips provide you with extra knowledge that separates the novice from the pro.

 Note Notes provide additional or critical information and technical data on the current topic.

 New Feature Sections marked with a New Feature icon detail an innovation introduced in Dreamweaver MX.

 Cross-Reference Cross-Reference icons indicate places where you can find more information on a particular topic.

 Caution The Caution icon is your warning of a potential problem or pitfall.

 On the CD-ROM The On the CD-ROM icon indicates that the accompanying CD-ROM contains a related file in the given folder. See the appendix for more information about where to locate specific items.

Further Information

You can find more help for specific problems and questions by investigating several Web sites. Macromedia's own Dreamweaver Web site is the best place to start:

    www.macromedia.com/software/Dreamweaver/

I heartily recommend that you visit and participate in the official Dreamweaver newsgroup:

    news://forums.macromedia.com/macromedia.Dreamweaver

You can also e-mail me:

    jlowery@idest.com

I can't promise instantaneous turnaround, but I answer all my mail to the best of my abilities.

Acknowledgments

When it became known what a tremendous program Dreamweaver MX had become, I knew I needed a tremendous team to do it justice. Luckily, I found one. My contributors, Lisa Boesen, Dan Short, and Rick Scott, all did what I think was a superb job in bringing *Dreamweaver MX Bible* to life — and they did it in record time, under enormous pressure.

Making sure that we all got it right were the technical editors, Angela Buraglia, Jon Parkhurst, and Marc Garner. As lead technical editor, Angela — who you might know as the guiding light behind DWFaq.com — brought a keen eye and just the right edge of care. A big virtual hug and some very real rounds for everyone the next time we get together.

Macromedia has been wonderfully supportive of my efforts to bring out the most detailed *Bible* possible. I can only imagine the collective groan that goes up when yet another e-mailed question from me — with a deadline, no less — arrives. Warm thanks and heartfelt appreciation to Sho Kuwamoto, Alain Dumesney, Heidi Bauer Williams, and all the other Dreamweaver engineers and techs who opened up their brains for me to pick. I'd also like to single out the Dreamweaver Technical Support staff, whose answers to users' queries have been tremendous sources of information. And who's that in the back of the room? Macromedia management — in the form of David Mendels, Beth Davis, David Deming, Susan Morrow, Matt Brown, and others — has opened many, many doors to me and should stand up and take a bow. And, finally, I and the rest of the Dreamweaver community are beholden to Kevin Lynch and Paul Madar for their vision and hard work in bringing this dream home.

To me, there's no higher compliment than to be told that I know my business. Well, the folks I work with at Wiley sure know their business: Acquisitions Editor Carol Sheehan, Senior Project Editor Jodi Jensen, and all the additional support staff. And to someone whose business is to know my business, a double thank you with a cherry on top for my agent, Laura Belt, of Adler & Robin Books.

One last note of appreciation — for all the people who took a chance with some of their hard-earned money and bought the previous editions of this book. That small sound you hear in the background is me applauding you as thanks for your support. I hope my efforts continue to be worthy.

Contents at a Glance

Contents

Part II: Web Design and Layout · 215

Part III: Incorporating Dynamic Data   501

Part IV: Dynamic HTML and Dreamweaver 625

Dreamweaver MX Basics

Introducing Dreamweaver MX

Dreamweaver MX, by Macromedia, is a professional Web site development program for creating static pages and dynamic Web applications. Among its many distinctions, Dreamweaver was the first Web authoring tool capable of addressing multiple server models, making it equally easy for developers of ASP, ColdFusion, or JavaServer Pages to use. In its latest incarnation, Dreamweaver MX has re-invented itself with a new user interface and a broader focus; in addition to creating straight HTML pages, Dreamweaver is also suitable for coding a wide range of Web formats including JavaScript, XML, and ActionScript to name a few.

Dreamweaver is truly a tool designed by Web developers for Web developers. Designed from the ground up to work the way professional Web designers do, Dreamweaver speeds site construction and streamlines site maintenance. This chapter describes the philosophical underpinnings of the program and provides a sense of how Dreamweaver blends traditional HTML and other Web languages with cutting-edge server-side techniques. You also learn some of the advanced features that Dreamweaver offers to help you manage a Web site.

The Dynamic World of Dreamweaver

Dreamweaver is a program very much rooted in the real world. Web applications are developed for a variety of different server models, and Dreamweaver writes code for the most pervasive ones. The real world is also a changing world, and Dreamweaver's extensible architecture opens the door for custom or third-party server models as well.

Moreover, Dreamweaver recognizes the real-world problem of incompatible browser commands and addresses the problem by producing code that is compatible across browsers. Dreamweaver includes browser-specific HTML validation so you can see how your existing or new code works in a particular browser.

Dreamweaver MX extends the real-world concept to the workplace. Features such as the Assets panel streamline the production and maintenance process on large Web sites. The advanced Design view makes it possible to quickly structure whole pages during the production stage, while maintaining backward compatibility with browsers when the pages are published. Dreamweaver's Commands capability enables Web designers to automate their most difficult Web creations, and its Server Behavior Builder permits often-used custom code to be easily inserted.

Connecting to the world's data

Connectivity is more than a buzzword in Dreamweaver; it's an underlying concept. Dreamweaver makes it possible to connect to any data source supported by the most widely used application servers: ASP, ASP.NET, ColdFusion, PHP, and JSP. Moreover, the actual connection type is quite flexible; developers may opt for a connection that is easier to implement but less robust or one that requires slightly more server-side savvy and offers greater scalability. Dreamweaver even offers a choice of languages for a number of applications servers, as shown in Figure 1-1.

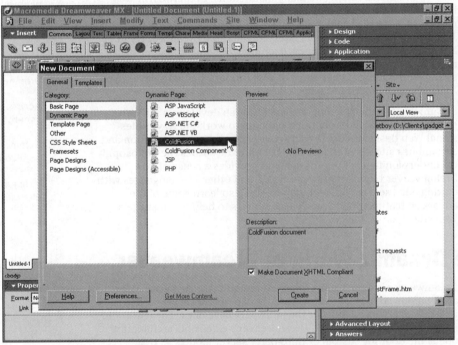

Figure 1-1: Get a jump start on building your Web pages by choosing a page — and the corresponding tags — from Dreamweaver's extensive collection.

Dreamweaver accesses standard recordsets — a subset of a database — as well as more sophisticated data sources, such as session or application variables and stored procedures. Through their implementation of cookies and server-side code, Web applications designed in Dreamweaver may track visitors or deny them entrance.

You'll also find support in Dreamweaver for high-end technologies such as Web services, JavaBeans, and ColdFusion components. Dreamweaver allows you to introspect elements of all technologies, enabling coders to quick grasp the syntax, methods, and functions required.

True data representation

One truly innovative feature of Dreamweaver integrates the actual data requested with the Web page—while still in the design phase. Dreamweaver's Live Data view sends the page-in-process to the application server to depict records from the data source within the page, as shown in Figure 1-2. All elements on the page remain editable in Live Data view; you can even alter the dynamic data's formatting and see those changes instantly applied. Live Data view shortens the work cycle by showing the designer exactly what the user will see. In addition, the page may be viewed under different conditions through the Live Data Settings feature.

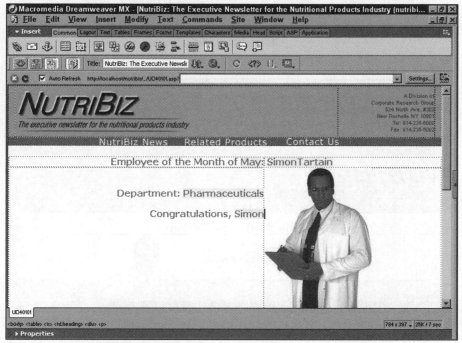

Figure 1-2: When in Live Data view, you can edit the Web page to accommodate the actual data used, as highlighted here.

Integrated visual and text editors

In the early days of the World Wide Web, most developers "hand-coded" their Web pages using simple text editors such as Notepad and SimpleText. The second generation of Web authoring tools brought visual design or WYSIWYG ("what you see is what you get") editors to market. What these products furnished in ease of layout, they lacked in completeness of code. Professional Web developers found they still needed to hand-code their Web pages, even with the most sophisticated WYSIWYG editor.

Dreamweaver acknowledges this reality and has integrated a superb visual editor with its browser-like Document view. You can work graphically in Design view, or programmatically in Code view. You even have the option of a split-screen view, which shows Design view and

Code view simultaneously. Figure 1-3 shows Dreamweaver's visual editor and code editor working together. Any change made in the Design view is reflected in the Code view and vice versa. If you prefer to work with a code editor you're more familiar with, Dreamweaver enables you to work with any text editor. Moreover, the program includes two of the best: a full-version of HomeSite for Microsoft Windows developers and a trial version of BBEdit for Macintosh developers. Dreamweaver enables a natural, dynamic flow between the visual and code editors.

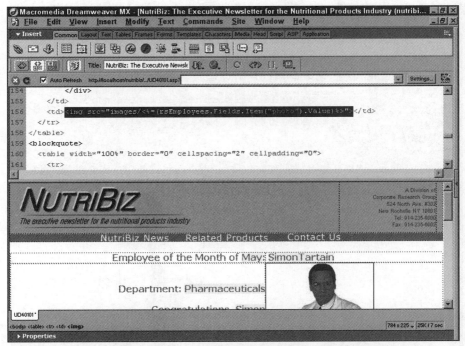

Figure 1-3: Dreamweaver enables you to work with a visual WYSIWYG editor and a code editor simultaneously.

Dreamweaver further tightens the integration between the visual design and the underlying code with the Quick Tag Editor. Web designers frequently need to adjust the HTML code minutely—changing an attribute here or adding a single tag there. The Quick Tag Editor, which appears as a small pop-up window in the Design view, makes these code tweaks quick and easy.

World-class code editing

Coding is integrally tied to Web page development, and Dreamweaver's coding environment is second-to-none. If you're hand-coding, you'll appreciate the code completion feature and Code Hints (shown in Figure 1-4). Not only do these features speed development of HTML pages, but Dreamweaver's underlying Tag Libraries extend their use to the full range of other code formats such as JavaScript, ActionScript, and XML.

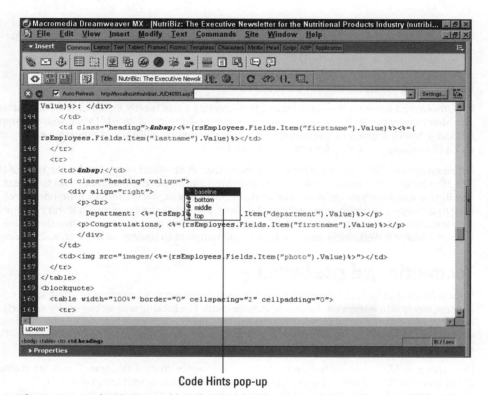

Code Hints pop-up

Figure 1-4: Code Hints speed hand-coding by displaying all the attributes available for a specific tag.

Dreamweaver's Code view is easy on the eyes as well with syntax coloring that can be turned off and on at will. To get around the page quickly, use either the standard line numbering facility or the advanced Code Navigation feature; Code Navigation lists all the functions found on a page and instantly jumps to that code when a function is selected.

New Feature

Veterans and novices alike will find Dreamweaver's Tag Chooser and Tag Inspector indispensable. As the name implies, the Tag Chooser allows the coder to select the desired tag from a full list of tags in the various Web markup languages including HTML, CFML, PHP, ASP, ASP.NET, and more. The Tag Inspector displays a detailed tree of all the tags on your page, as well as an editable list of any selected tag's attributes for quick modification.

Code is far more than just a series of individual tags, of course. Dreamweaver's Snippets panel stores the most commonly used sections of code just a drag-and-drop away. Dreamweaver comes with hundreds of snippets ready to use—and gives you the ability to add your own at any time.

Roundtrip HTML

Most Web authoring programs modify any code that passes through their system—inserting returns, removing indents, adding `<meta>` tags, uppercasing commands, and so forth. Dreamweaver's programmers understand and respect the fact that all Web developers have their own particular coding styles. An underlying concept, Roundtrip HTML, ensures that you can move back and forth between the visual editor and any HTML text editor without your code being rewritten.

Web site maintenance tools

Dreamweaver's creators also understand that creating a site is only a part of the Webmaster's job. Maintaining the Web site can be an ongoing, time-consuming chore. Dreamweaver simplifies the job with a group of site management tools, including a library of repeating elements and a file-locking capability for easy team updates.

In Dreamweaver, Web site maintenance is easier than ever — and very visual. Take note of the Site Map feature that enables you to view your Web site structure at a glance and to access any file for modification. Links are updated automatically or, if a file moves from one directory to another, are under user control. Moreover, not only can you access a library of repeating elements to be inserted in the page, you can also define templates to control the entire look and feel of a Web site — and modify a single template to update all the pages sitewide.

Team-oriented site building

Until now, individual Web developers have been stymied when attempting to integrate Dreamweaver into a team development environment. File-locking was all too easily subverted, enabling revisions to be inadvertently overwritten; site reports were limited in scope and only output to HTML; and, most notable of all, version control was nonexistent. Dreamweaver MX addresses all these concerns while laying a foundation for future connectivity.

Dreamweaver MX supports two industry-standard source control systems: Visual SourceSafe (VSS) and WebDAV. Connecting to a Visual SourceSafe server is well integrated into Dreamweaver; simply define the VSS server as your remote site and add the necessary connection information. WebDAV, although perhaps less well known than VSS, offers an equally powerful and more available content-management solution. More important, Macromedia has developed the source-control solution as a system architecture, enabling other third-party content management or version control developers to use Dreamweaver as their front end.

New Feature   ColdFusion developers have long enjoyed the benefits of RDS, short for Remote Development Services, and now, RDS connectivity has been added to Dreamweaver. Through RDS, teams of developers can work on the same site stored on a remote server.

Extensible architecture also underlies Dreamweaver's site reporting facility. Dreamweaver ships with the capability to generate reports on usability issues such as missing Alt text or workflow concerns such as showing who has what files checked out. However, users can also develop custom reports on a project-by-project basis.

The Dreamweaver Interface

When creating a Web page, Webmasters do two things repeatedly: They insert an element — whether text, image, or layer — and then they modify it. Dreamweaver excels at such Web page creation. The Dreamweaver workspace combines a series of windows, panels, and inspectors to make the process as fluid as possible, thereby speeding up the Webmaster's work.

Choice of environments

For the first time, Dreamweaver MX offers developers a choice of design environments. The classic floating panel interface is available for both Windows and Macintosh users, and Windows users have the option of selecting an integrated workspace.

New Feature

The new integrated workspace, available for Windows users, utilizes a Multiple Document Interface (MDI) that keeps all the open documents and panels together in one application window. There are two flavors of the MDI workspace: the default with panels grouped on the right and HomeSite style, with panels on the left. As shown in Figure 1-5, you switch from one workspace to another in Preferences.

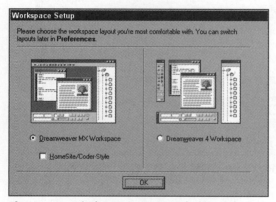

Figure 1-5: Windows users get a choice of design environments in Dreamweaver MX.

Note

When using the Dreamweaver MX workspace, it is highly recommended that your monitor resolution be set for 1024x768 or higher. Lower resolutions, I find, do not offer sufficient space for the Document window.

Easy text entry

Although much of the World Wide Web's glitz comes from multimedia elements such as images and sound, Web pages are primarily a text-based medium. Dreamweaver recognizes this and makes the text cursor the default tool. To add text, just click in Dreamweaver's main workspace — the Document window — and start typing. As shown in Figure 1-6, the Text Property inspector even enables you to change characteristics of the text, such as the size, font, position, or color by assigning a Cascading Style Sheet (CSS) style; you can also use regular HTML tags if you prefer.

Drag-and-drop data fields

It's one thing to make a connection to a data source; it's quite another to actually insert the dynamic data in the proper place on the Web page. Dreamweaver makes drag-and-drop easy with the Bindings panel. All the available data sources for a page are displayed in an expandable tree outline in the Bindings panel, as shown in Figure 1-7. An instance of any dynamic field displayed in the panel may be inserted on the page by either dropping it into place or by using the Insert button.

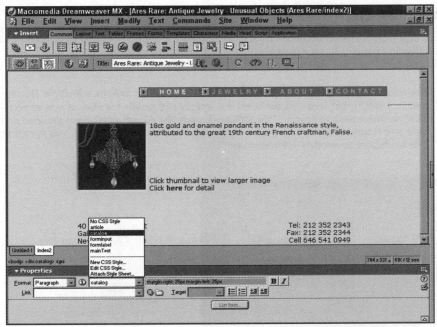

Figure 1-6: Use the Text Property inspector to change the format of the selected text with CSS or straight HTML tags.

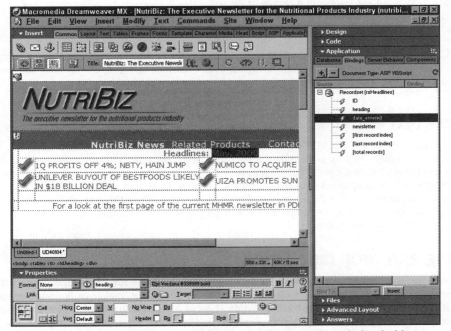

Figure 1-7: Drag any field from the Bindings panel onto a selected placeholder phrase to quickly turn a static page into a dynamic one.

One-stop object modification

You can select Web page elements other than text from the Insert bar. Adding a picture to a Web page is as easy as clicking the Image icon from the Insert bar. Dreamweaver asks you to select the file for the image, and your image appears in your current cursor position. After your graphic is onscreen, selecting it brings up the appropriate Property inspector to enable you to make modifications. The same technique holds true for any other inserted element — from horizontal rules to Shockwave movies.

Accessing and managing resources

One standout addition to Dreamweaver's interface is the Assets panel, shown in Figure 1-8. The Assets panel gathers all the various elements used in an individual site: images, background and text colors, external URLs, included scripts, Flash movies, Shockwave content, and QuickTime media, as well as Dreamweaver templates and library items. Sizeable thumbnails of graphics and media are displayed in the preview pane of the Assets panel — you can even play Flash, Shockwave, and QuickTime elements in preview before dragging them onto the page. Moreover, often-used resources can be listed in a Favorites category, distinguishing them from the rest of the assets found in the site.

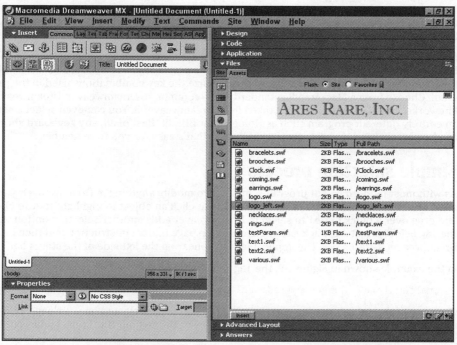

Figure 1-8: You can preview a Flash movie with the Assets panel before placing it on the Dreamweaver page.

Complete custom environment

Dreamweaver enables you to customize your workspace to suit yourself. A handy Launcher opens and closes various windows, panels, and inspectors, all of which are movable. Just drag them wherever you want them onscreen. Want to see your page by itself? You can hide all windows at the touch of a function button; press it again, and your controls are revealed.

Dreamweaver's customization capabilities extend even further. If you find that you are repeatedly inserting something, such as a QuickTime video or WAV sound file, you can add that element to your Insert bar. Dreamweaver even enables you to add a specific element—a Home button, for example—to the Insert bar. In fact, you can add entire categories of objects if you like. Moreover, Dreamweaver MX exposes the entire menu structure for customization—you can not only change keyboard shortcuts, but also add custom menus.

 Cross-Reference   For more information about customizing your Insert bar, see Chapter 34.

Managing keyboard shortcuts

Keyboard shortcuts are great in theory: Just press a key combination to activate an essential feature. Unfortunately, in reality, there are too many essential features, too few single-purpose keys on the keyboard, and (most important), too few brain cells to retain all the widely varied keyboard combinations from all the programs the working designer must master.

Macromedia has taken steps to ease keyboard-shortcut overload across its entire product line, and Dreamweaver's no exception. Dreamweaver now offers a Keyboard Shortcut Editor that enables you to both standardize and customize the key combinations used in the program. Choose from a Macromedia standard set—common to Dreamweaver, Dreamweaver, Fireworks, and Flash—or use a set taken from Dreamweaver 3. You can even select a set from an entirely different program such as HomeSite or BBEdit. Best of all, any keyboard shortcut can be personalized to represent a combination that's easy for you to remember.

Simple selection process

As with most modern layout programs, in order to modify anything in Dreamweaver, you must select it first. The usual process for this is to click an object to highlight it or to click and drag over a block of text to select it. Dreamweaver adds another selection option with the Tag Selector feature. Click anywhere on a Web page under construction and then look at Dreamweaver's status bar. The applicable tags appear on the left side of the status bar.

In the example shown in Figure 1-9, the Tag Selector shows

```
<mm:template> <body> <mm:editable> <div.catalog> <table> <tr> <td> <p>
```

Click one of these tags, and the corresponding elements are selected on your page, ready for modification. The Tag Selector is a terrific time-saver; throughout this book, I point out how you can use it under various circumstances.

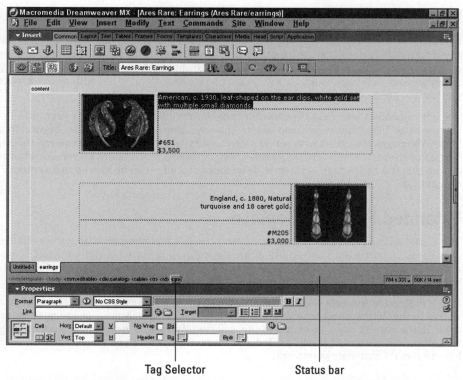

Tag Selector   Status bar

Figure 1-9: Choosing the <p> tag in Dreamweaver's Tag Selector is a quick and easy way to highlight the current paragraph on your Web page.

Enhanced layout options

Dreamweaver works much more like a desktop publishing program than do many other visual HTML editors. Today's browser capabilities permit images and text to be placed in specific locations on the Web page — a concept known as *absolute positioning*. To enable you to take full advantage of this power, Dreamweaver includes both rulers and grids. You can specify the type of measurement to be used (inches, pixels, or centimeters), as well as the spacing and appearance of the grid lines. You can even have objects snap to the grid for easy alignment.

Dreamweaver has always made it easy for designers new to the Web to build nice-looking interactive Web pages without having to know HTML. Dreamweaver MX expands on that theme with Layout view. Layout view enables designers to draw tables and cells directly on the screen for positioning content. Once drawn, cells can be modified by dragging borders or moving the entire cell. Nested tables may also be included.

Cross-Reference   To find out more about absolute positioning, see Chapter 29; you can learn more about Layout view in Chapter 10.

Plugin media preview

In order for a browser to display anything beyond standard format graphics, a plugin is generally required. Plugins extend the capability of most browsers to show animations, play music, or even explore 3D worlds. Dreamweaver is one of the first Web authoring tools to enable you to design your Web page with an active plugin playing the extended file; with all other systems, you have to preview your page in a browser to see the active content.

The active content feature in Dreamweaver enables the playback of plugins such as Macromedia Flash, Shockwave, and others. However, this feature extends far beyond that. Many Web pages are coded with server-side *includes*, which traditionally required the page to be viewed through a Web server. Dreamweaver translates much of the server-side information so that the entire page — server-side includes and all — can be viewed in its entirety at design time.

Extended Find and Replace

The Web is a fluid medium. Pages are constantly in flux, and because changes are relatively easy to effect, corrections and additions are the norm. Quite often, a Web designer needs to update or alter an existing page — or series of pages. Dreamweaver's enhanced Find and Replace feature is a real power tool when it comes to making modifications.

Find and Replace works in the Document window, whether in Design view or Code view, as well as in the Code inspector to alter code and regular content. Moreover, changes are applicable to the current page, the working site, selected Web pages, or an entire folder of pages, regardless of the number. Complex Find and Replace queries can be stored and retrieved later to further automate your work.

Up-to-Date Code Standards

Most Web pages are created in HyperText Markup Language (HTML). This programming language — really a series of tags that modify a text file — is standardized by an organization known as the World Wide Web Consortium, or W3C (www.w3.org). Each new release of HTML incorporates an enhanced set of commands and features. The current version, HTML 4, is recognized by the majority of browsers in use today. Dreamweaver writes clear, easy-to-follow, real-world, browser-compatible HTML 4 code whenever you insert or modify an element in the visual editor.

Cutting-edge CSS support

Support for Cascading Style Sheets (CSS) has been steadily growing among browsers, and Dreamweaver has greatly enhanced its own support in response. In addition to enhanced rendering in the Design view for advanced CSS effects such as backgrounds and positioning, Dreamweaver has made it far simpler to apply CSS from the ground up. A handy toggle on the Property inspector allows the designer to switch between HTML and CSS tags with a single click.

New Feature   The CSS Styles panel has also had a complete make-over in Dreamweaver MX, as shown in Figure 1-10. Now editing a CSS style is just as easy as applying one. When in Edit CSS mode, the CSS Styles panel displays all the current styles — both internal and external — with detailed characteristics. Double-click on any style to modify it.

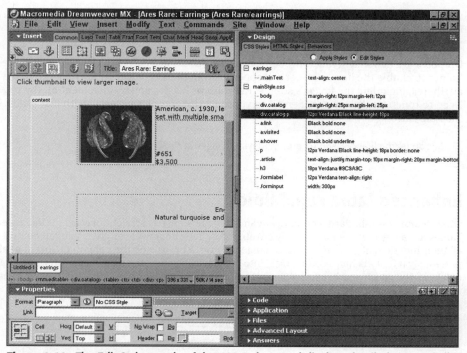

Figure 1-10: The Edit Styles mode of the CSS Styles panel displays detailed views of all the styles connected to the current page.

Addressing accessibility

Accessibility is an issue of great concern to many Web developers. Increasingly, many designers labor under a mandate to produce accessible sites, especially in consideration of Section 508 of the Federal Rehabilitation Act. To help designers create accessible pages, Dreamweaver MX optionally displays additional attributes for key Web page objects such as tables, forms, images, media, and frames. These attributes — like summary for the `<table>` tag — are always available through the Tag Inspector when enabled through Dreamweaver Preferences.

In addition, Dreamweaver MX, as a tool, is far more accessible than previous versions. A number of screen readers, including JAWS for Windows and Window Eyes, are supported. Furthermore, the entire Dreamweaver interface may be navigated without using the mouse.

Straightforward text and graphics support

Text is a basic building block of any Web page, and Dreamweaver makes formatting your text a snap. After you've inserted your text, either by typing it directly or pasting it from another program, you can change its appearance. You can use the generic HTML formats, such as the H1 through H6 headings and their relative sizes, or you can use font families and exact point sizes.

Cross-Reference　Chapter 7 shows you how to work with text in Dreamweaver.

Additional text support in Dreamweaver enables you to add both numbered and bulleted lists to your Web page. The Text Property inspector provides buttons for both kinds of lists as well as easy alignment control. Some elements, including lists, offer extended options. In Dreamweaver, clicking the Property inspector's Expander arrow opens a section from which you can access additional controls.

Graphics are handled in much the same easy-to-use manner. Select the image or its place-holder to enable the Image Property inspector. From there, you can modify any available attributes, including the image's source, its width or height, and its alignment on the page. Need to touch up your image? Send it to your favorite graphics program with just a click of the Edit button.

Cross-Reference You learn all about adding and modifying images in Chapter 8.

Enhanced table capabilities

Other features — standard, yet more advanced — are similarly straightforward in Dreamweaver. Tables are a key component in today's Web pages, and Dreamweaver gives you full control over all their functionality. Dreamweaver changes the work of resizing the column or row of a table, previously a tedious hand-coding task, into an easy click-and-drag motion. Likewise, you can delete all the width and height values from a table with the click of a button. Figure 1-11 shows the Table Property inspector, which centralizes many of these options in Dreamweaver.

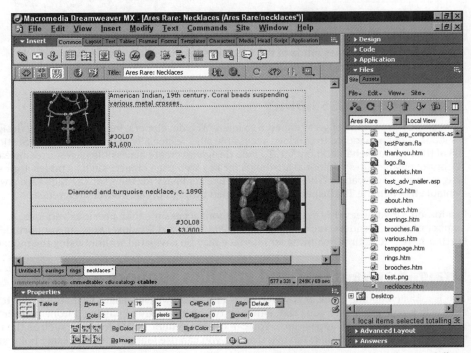

Figure 1-11: The Table Property inspector is just one of Dreamweaver's paths to a full range of control over the appearance of your table.

Tables are flexible in Dreamweaver. Font changes can be applied to any number of selected cells, rows, or columns. Standard commands enable you to automatically format or sort a table as well.

Easy form entry

Forms, the basic vehicle for Web page data exchange, are just as easy to implement as tables in Dreamweaver. Switch to the Forms category of the Insert bar and insert any of the available elements: text boxes, radio buttons, checkboxes, and even drop-down or scrolling lists. With the Validate Form behavior, you can easily specify any field as a required field and even check to ensure that the requested type of information has been entered.

Click-and-drag frame setup

Frames, which enable separate Web pages to be viewed on a single screen, are often considered one of the most difficult HTML techniques to master. Dreamweaver employs a click-and-drag method for establishing your frame outlines. After you've set up your frame structure, open the Frames panel (see Figure 1-12) to select any frame and modify it with the Property inspector. Dreamweaver writes the necessary code for linking all the HTML files in a frameset, no matter how many Web pages are used. Dreamweaver keeps frame creation simple with the Frames category of the Insert bar.

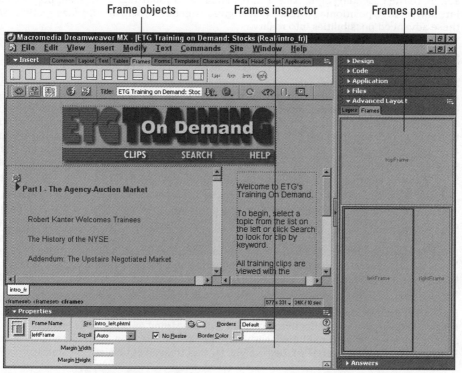

Figure 1-12: In Dreamweaver, you use the Frames panel to choose which frame you want to modify through the Property inspector.

For more information about creating frame-based Web pages, see Chapter 14.

Multimedia enhancements

Dreamweaver enables you to drop in any number of multimedia extensions, plugins, applets, or controls. Just click the appropriate button on the Insert bar and modify with the Property inspector. Two multimedia elements, Shockwave movies and Flash files — both from Macromedia — warrant special consideration in Macromedia's Dreamweaver. When you insert either of these objects, Dreamweaver automatically includes the necessary HTML code to ensure the widest browser acceptance, and you can edit all the respective properties.

Dreamweaver fully supports the wide range of multimedia output through custom objects that enable complex images, audio, and presentations to be easily inserted and displayed in Web pages.

Next-Generation Features

Dreamweaver was among the first Web authoring tools to work with the capabilities brought in by the 4.0 generation of browsers. Both Netscape Communicator 4+ and Microsoft Internet Explorer 4+ include variations of Dynamic HTML (DHTML). Moreover, both of these browsers adhere to the Cascading Style Sheet (CSS) standards to some degree, with support for absolute and relative positioning. Dreamweaver gives Web developers an interface that translates these advanced possibilities into reality.

Flash and Fireworks integration

Dreamweaver MX has upped the ante for integration with Macromedia's graphics engine, Fireworks. Now, images derived from Fireworks are identified as such, both in the Property inspector and in the Assets panel. Graphics may be optimized to alter the file size, cropping, transparency, or many other aspects right from within Fireworks. If more extensive modification is required, selecting the Edit button sends the graphic back to Fireworks. More impressively, sliced images — maintained as a borderless table in HTML — may be edited in their entirety. Fireworks even respects HTML alterations to a degree, such as changes to URLs or converting an image slice to a text block. This degree of integration lends an amazing fluidity to the workflow.

Just as Dreamweaver behaviors may add JavaScript interactivity to a page without the developer knowing JavaScript, the Flash objects offer the potential for including highly attractive navigation elements without mastering that vector-based animation program. Two different types of Flash objects are available: Flash buttons and Flash text. A Flash button is actually a Macromedia Generator template with full animation and sound capabilities. Because it's a template, the layout artist may customize it with text and a link. Dreamweaver ships with numerous examples, but anyone with Flash 5 can create his own template.

Flash text, on the other hand, does not handle any animation other than a simple color rollover. However, it is an effective way to include a heading or other page element in a specific font — a far better solution, with more market penetration, than materializing from Dynamic HTML. Moreover, Flash text weighs far less than an equivalent GIF image.

New Feature

Perhaps the coolest Dreamweaver-Flash feature yet is the most basic. As with Fireworks, Flash movies can now be sent to be edited directly from within Dreamweaver. After your editing operation is completed in Flash, just select Done (Figure 1-13), and your revised movie is republished and inserted back into Dreamweaver.

Figure 1-13: Dreamweaver provides a direct connection for editing Flash movies.

Server-side behaviors

The driving forces behind Dreamweaver's Web application creation are its server behaviors. A *server behavior* is code written in a language understood by the particular server model that is executed on the server. Dreamweaver comes standard with a wide variety of useful server behaviors, ranging from one that replicates records on a page to another that restricts access to a page.

Server behaviors are applied and managed from the Server Behaviors panel, shown in Figure 1-14. Unlike the Bindings panel, from which fields are dragged onto the page, the main area of the Server Behaviors panel indicates which server behaviors have been inserted into the page. If the server behavior has user-defined parameters, they may be altered by double-clicking the entry in the Server Behaviors panel.

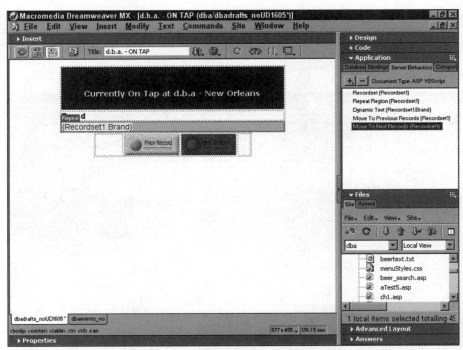

Figure 1-14: Quickly identify the page elements affected by a server behavior by selecting the entry in the Server Behaviors panel.

Roundtrip XML

A new type of markup language has excited a wide cross-section of Web designers, intranet developers, and corporate users. XML, which stands for eXtensible Markup Language, has piqued the interest of many because of its underlying customizable nature. With XML, tags are created to describe the use of the information, rather than its appearance.

Dreamweaver is capable of exporting and importing XML tags, no matter what the tag definition. You can also create, modify, and validate XML files in Dreamweaver. As XML grows in popularity, Dreamweaver is ready to handle the work.

3D layers

One particular Dynamic HTML feature enables Dreamweaver to be called "the first 3D Web authoring tool." Until Dynamic HTML, Web pages existed on a two-dimensional plane — images and text could only be placed side by side. Dreamweaver supports control of Dynamic HTML layers, meaning that objects can be placed in front of or behind other objects. Layers can contain text, graphics, links, and controls — you can even nest one layer inside another.

You create a layer in Dreamweaver by clicking the Draw Layer button on the Insert bar. Once created, layers can be positioned anywhere on the page by clicking and dragging the selection handle. As with other Dreamweaver objects, you can modify a layer through the Property inspector.

See Chapter 21 for detailed information about using layers in Dreamweaver.

Animated objects

Objects in layers can be positioned anywhere on the Web page under construction, and they can also be moved when the page is viewed. Dreamweaver takes this capability and adds its Timelines panel, becoming a 4D Web authoring tool! The Timelines panel, shown in Figure 1-15, is designed along the lines of Macromedia's world-class multimedia creation program, Director. With timelines, you can control a layer's position, size, 3D placement, and even visibility on a frame-by-frame basis. With Dreamweaver, you no longer have to plot a layer's path on a timeline—now you can just draw it using the Record Path of the Layer feature.

Figure 1-15: Use the Timelines panel to animate objects in layers using Dreamweaver's advanced Dynamic HTML features.

Dynamic style updates

Dreamweaver completely supports the Cascading Style Sheet (CSS) specification agreed upon by the World Wide Web Consortium. CSS gives Web designers more flexible control over almost every element on their Web pages. Dreamweaver applies CSS capabilities as if they were styles in a word processor. For example, you can make all the <h1> tags blue, italic, and put them in small caps. If your site's color scheme changes, you can make all the <h1> tags red—and you can do this throughout your Web site with one command. Dreamweaver gives you style control over type, background, blocks, boxes, borders, lists, and positioning.

Dreamweaver enables you to change styles online as well as offline. By linking a CSS change to a user-driven event such as moving the mouse, text can be highlighted or de-emphasized, screen areas can light up, and figures can even be animated. Moreover, it can all be done without repeated trips to the server or huge file downloads.

Cross-Reference   Details about using Cascading Style Sheets begin in Chapter 20.

JavaScript behaviors

Through the development of JavaScript behaviors, Dreamweaver combines the power of JavaScript with the ease of a point-and-click interface. A *behavior* is defined as a combination of an event and an action—whenever your Web page user does something that causes something else to happen, that's a behavior. What makes behaviors extremely useful is that they require no programming whatsoever.

Behaviors are JavaScript-based, and this is significant because JavaScript is supported to varying degrees by existing browsers. Dreamweaver has simplified the task of identifying which JavaScript command works with a particular browser. You simply select the Web page element that you want to use to control the action, and open the Behaviors panel. As shown in Figure 1-16, Dreamweaver enables you to pick a JavaScript command that works with all browsers, a subset of browsers, or one browser in particular. Next, you choose from a full list of available actions, such as go to a URL, play a sound, pop up a message, or start an animation. You can also assign multiple actions and even determine when they occur.

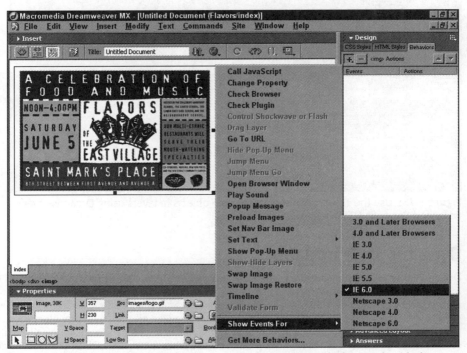

Figure 1-16: Dreamweaver offers only the JavaScript commands that work with the browser you specify.

For complete details about working with JavaScript behaviors, see Chapter 23.

Program Extensibility

One of Dreamweaver's primary strengths is its extensibility. Virtually no two Web sites are alike, either in their design or execution. With such a tremendous variety of results, the more flexible a Web authoring tool, the more useful it is to a wider group of designers. When it was introduced, Dreamweaver broke new ground with objects and behaviors that were easily customizable. Now, Dreamweaver lengthens its lead with custom floaters, commands, translators, and Property inspectors. The basic underpinnings of Dreamweaver can even be extended with the C-Level Extensibility options.

Dreamweaver's extensibility continues to grow—now, custom toolbars have been added to the mix. Look for new toolbars on the Macromedia Dreamweaver Exchange, which you can get to by choosing Help ➪ Dreamweaver Exchange.

Objects and behaviors

In Dreamweaver parlance, an *object* is a bit of HTML code that represents a specific image or HTML tag, such as a `<table>` or a `<form>`. Dreamweaver's objects are completely open to user customization, or even out-and-out creation. For example, if you'd rather import structured data into a table without a border instead of with the standard 1-pixel border, you can easily make that modification to the Insert Tabular Data object file—right from within Dreamweaver—and every subsequent table is similarly inserted. Objects are accessed from the Insert bar as well as through the menus.

Objects are a terrific timesaving device, essentially enabling you to drop in significant blocks of HTML code at the click of a mouse. Likewise, Dreamweaver behaviors enable even novice Web designers to insert complex JavaScript functions designed to propel the pages to the cutting edge. Dreamweaver ships with a full array of standard behaviors—but that's only the tip of the behavior iceberg. Because behaviors are also customizable and can be built by anyone with a working knowledge of JavaScript, many Dreamweaver designers have created custom behaviors and made them publicly available.

You can find a large assortment of custom objects, behaviors, and commands on the CD-ROM that accompanies this book.

Server Behavior Builder

Server behaviors are key to Dreamweaver's success as a Web application authoring tool. Although Dreamweaver provides a full palette of server behaviors for handling many of the required tasks, the needs of Web developers are too diverse and numerous to be able to supply a server behavior for every occasion. Enter Dreamweaver's Server Behavior Builder, shown in Figure 1-17, a terrific tool for creating custom server behaviors.

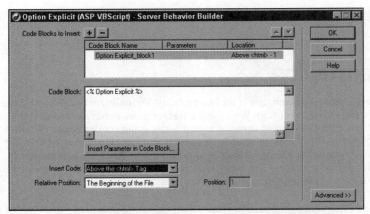

Figure 1-17: With the Server Behavior Builder, you can create a new behavior from the ground up or modify an existing behavior.

The Server Behavior Builder is engineered to handle a wide range of circumstances. Some server behaviors may be encapsulated in a single line of code repeated verbatim, whereas others require multiple blocks of programming involving several user-supplied parameters — you can construct almost any kind of code with the Server Behavior Builder. After the custom server behavior is created, it may be applied and modified just like any of the standard Dreamweaver server behaviors.

Commands and floating panels

Objects and behaviors are great ways to help build the final result of a Web page, but what about automating the work of producing that page? Dreamweaver employs commands to modify the existing page and streamline production. A great example is the Sort Table command, standard with Dreamweaver. If you've ever had to sort a large table by hand — meticulously moving data, one row at a time — you can appreciate the power of commands the first time you alphabetize or otherwise re-sort a table using this option.

Commands hold a great promise — they are, in effect, more powerful than either objects or behaviors combined. In fact, some of the more complex objects, such as the Rollover Image object, are actually commands. Commands can also extract information sitewide and offer a powerful programmable language within Dreamweaver.

Creating a Dreamweaver command is now easier than ever, thanks to the History panel. Aside from displaying every action you undertake as you build your Web page, the History panel enables you to select any number of those actions and save them as a command. Your new command is instantly available to be called from the menu whenever you need it.

After only a few moments with Dreamweaver, you become accustomed to its use of floating panels. In Dreamweaver MX, you can create custom floating panels. These custom panels can show existing resources or provide a whole new interface for modifying an HTML element.

Adjustable Insert bars

The tabbed Insert bar is more than just a new look for Dreamweaver. Now, at a glance, designers can quickly see all the available object categories and switch to them with a single click. More important — from an extensibility standpoint — new categories may be developed and integrated into the Dreamweaver workspace on a contextual basis. In other words, if you create a category for SMIL, you can set the preferences so that it displays only when an SMIL file is being worked on.

Custom tags, translators, and Property inspectors

In Dreamweaver, almost every part of the user interface can be customized — including the tags themselves. New tags and how they should be formatted can easily be added via the Tag Library Editor; entire tag sets represented by DTDs can even be imported. After you've developed your custom third-party tags, you can display and modify their current properties with a custom Property inspector. Moreover, if your custom tags include content not typically shown in Dreamweaver's Document window, a custom translator can be built, enabling the content to be displayed.

Programs such as Dreamweaver are generally built in the programming language called C or C++, which must be compiled before it is used. Generally, the basic functions of a C program are frozen solid; there's no way that you can extend them. This is not the case with Dreamweaver, however. Dreamweaver offers a C-Level Extensibility that permits programmers to create libraries to install new functionality into the program. Translators, for example, generally rely on new C libraries to enable content to be displayed in Dreamweaver that could not be shown otherwise. Companies can use the C-Level Extensibility feature to integrate Dreamweaver into their existing workflow and maximize productivity.

Automation Enhancements

Web site design is the dream job; Web site production is the reality. After a design has been finalized, its execution can become repetitive and burdensome. Dreamweaver offers a number of ways to automate the production work, keeping the look of the Web pages consistent — with minimum work required.

Rapid application development with Application objects

Although it's true that almost every active Web site has one or more unique situations that require some custom coding, it's equally true that the same type of Web application is used repeatedly. It's hard to find an e-commerce–enabled site that doesn't use some variation of the master-detail Web application in which a search returns a list of matches (the master page), each of which links to a page with more information (the detail page). Likewise, every intranet administration application requires the capability to add, edit, and remove records. To speed the development of these types of applications, Dreamweaver includes a series of Application objects, some of which reduce a 20-step operation to a single dialog box, like the one shown in Figure 1-18.

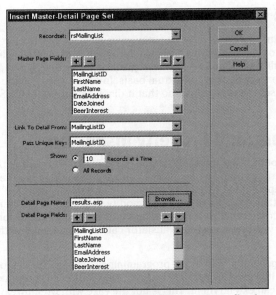

Figure 1-18: The Master-Detail Page Set Application object provides rapid development for a common Web application.

Here are some of the Application objects that come standard with Dreamweaver:

✦ Dynamic Table

✦ Master Detail Page Set

✦ Recordset Navigation Bar

✦ Recordset Navigation Status

✦ Record Insertion Form

✦ Record Update Form

Although they vary in complexity, all are guaranteed timesavers. In addition to creating pages as needed, Application objects can also insert dynamic data and apply server behaviors.

Applying HTML Styles

Designers in every field depend on the consistency and flexibility of styles. Until recently, the only styles available to Web designers came through a Cascading Style Sheet (CSS). Although CSS is, for many, an ideal solution, numerous clients are hesitant to authorize its use for fear of alienating users with older browsers that don't support CSS. The Dreamweaver engineers have come up with a solution that maintains backward compatibility while simplifying text formatting: HTML Styles.

The HTML Styles panel enables you to define, manage, and apply any combination of text formatting. You can apply your new style to either a selection or an entire paragraph—and styles can be defined either to add formatting to the existing tags or to replace them. Although redefining an existing HTML Style does not cause text to update, HTML Styles are sitewide and can be used to enforce a consistent look and feel without CSS limitations.

Importing office documents

Much of the Web's content originates from other sources—in-house documents produced by a word processor or spreadsheet program. Dreamweaver bridges the gap between the offline and online world with two useful import features: Import Word HTML and Import Tabular Data.

Microsoft Word, perhaps the premier word processor, is great at creating and storing word processing documents but not so accomplished at outputting standard HTML. An HTML file derived from Word is, to put it mildly, bloated with extraneous and repetitive code. Dreamweaver's Import Word HTML feature strips out the unnecessary code and even permits you to format the code as you format your other Dreamweaver files. The Import Word HTML command offers a wide-range of options for cleaning up the code.

Of course, not all Web content derives from word processing documents—databases and spreadsheets are the other two legs of the modern office software triangle. With the Import Tabular Data command, Dreamweaver offers the capability to incorporate data from any source that can export structured text files. Just save your spreadsheet or database as a comma, tab, or otherwise delimited file and bring it directly into Dreamweaver in the table style of your choice.

Reference panel

Even the most advanced coder needs to refer to a reference when including seldom-used HTML tags or arcane JavaScript functions. Dreamweaver includes a built-in reference with HTML, JavaScript, and Cascading Style Sheet details. Taken from O'Reilly's *Dynamic HTML: The Definitive Reference,* by Danny Goodman, Dreamweaver's guide is context-sensitive; highlight a tag or function in Code view and press Shift+F1 to get a breakdown on syntax and browser compatibility.

New Feature The reference panel has been expanded in Dreamweaver MX. In addition to the resources already noted, you'll find a ColdFusion Markup Language reference from Macromedia, as well as its Sitespring Project Site Tag Reference. UsableNet has contributed a valuable guide to accessibility issues, and two new guides from Wrox are onboard—one for ASP 3.0 and one for JSP.

History panel

The repetitiveness of building a Web site is often a matter of repeatedly entering the same series of commands. You might, for example, need to add a vertical margin of 10 pixels and a horizontal margin of 5 around most, but not all, of the images on a page. Rather than selecting each image and then repeatedly entering these values in the Property inspector, you can now enter the values once and then save that action as a command.

The feature that brings this degree of automation to Dreamweaver is found in the History panel. The History panel shows each step taken by a designer as the page is developed. Although this visual display is great for complex, multilevel undo actions, the capability to save any number of your steps as an instantly available command is truly timesaving.

Site Management Tools

Long after your killer Web site is launched, you'll find yourself continually updating and revising it. For this reason, site management tools are as important as site creation tools to a Web authoring program. Dreamweaver delivers on both counts.

Object libraries

In addition to site management functions that have become traditional, such as FTP publishing, Dreamweaver adds a whole new class of functionality called *libraries*. One of the truisms of Web page development is that if you repeat an element across your site, you're sure to have to change it — on every page. Dreamweaver libraries eliminate that drudgery. You can define almost anything as a Library element: a paragraph of text, an image, a link, a table, a form, a Java applet, an ActiveX control, and so on. Just choose the item and open the Library category of Assets (see Figure 1-19). After you've created the Library entry, you can reuse it throughout your Web site. Each Web site can have its own library, and you can copy entries from one library to another.

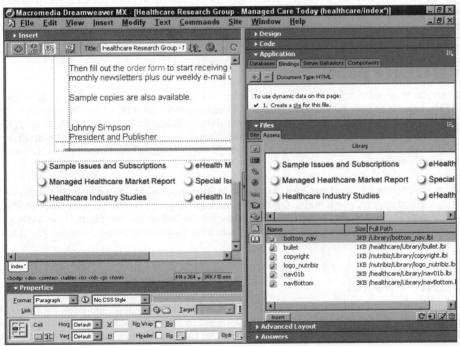

Figure 1-19: Use Dreamweaver's Library feature to simplify the task of updating elements repeated across many Web pages.

Being able to include "boilerplate" Web elements is one issue, being able to update them across the site simultaneously is quite another! You can easily change a Library entry through the Library panel. After the change is complete, Dreamweaver detects the modification and asks if you want to update your site. Imagine updating copyright information across a 400+ page Web site in the wink of an eye, and you start to understand the power of Dreamweaver libraries.

To find out more about making sitewide changes with Library items, see Chapter 29.

Super-charged templates

The more your Web site grows, the more you'll find yourself using the same basic format for different pages. Dreamweaver enables the use of Web page templates to standardize the look and feel of a Web site and to cut down on the repetitive work of creating new pages. A Dreamweaver template can hold the basic structure for the page—an image embedded in the background, a navigation bar along the left side, or a set-width table in the center for holding the main text, for example—with as many elements predefined as possible.

Dreamweaver templates are far more than just molds for creating pages, however. Basically, templates work with a series of locked and editable regions. To update an entire site based on a template, all you have to do is alter one or more of the template's locked regions. Naturally, Dreamweaver enables you to save any template that you create in the same folder, so that your own templates, too, are accessible through the Templates category of the Assets panel. (You can find more about using and creating templates in Chapter 28.)

Dreamweaver templates are much more than just editable and uneditable regions, however. Now, Dreamweaver gives the designer a much higher degree of control with such features as repeating regions—which, for example, allow a table row to be repeated as many times as needed but constrain the other areas of a table. You're also able to hide and show areas of a page conditionally with optional regions, shown in Figure 1-20. Dreamweaver's template power extends to nested templates, so that changes can ripple down through a series of locked and editable regions.

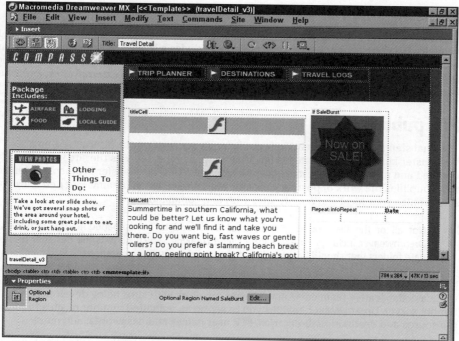

Figure 1-20: This template contains editable, repeating, and optional regions.

Browser targeting

Browser targeting is another site management innovation from Dreamweaver. One of the major steps in any site development project is to test the Web pages in various browsers to look for inconsistencies and invalid code. Dreamweaver's Browser Targeting function enables you to check your HTML against any existing browser's profile. Dreamweaver includes predefined profiles for several browsers, and you can create a profile for any browser you'd like to check.

 Cross-Reference   To learn how you can set up your own profile for Browser Targeting, see Chapter 30.

You can also preview your Web page in any number of browsers. Dreamweaver enables you to specify primary and secondary browsers that can display your page at the press of a function key. You can install up to 18 other browsers for previewing your Web page. The entire list of browsers is available through the Preview in Browser command under the File menu.

Converting Web pages

Although Web site designers may have access to the latest HTML tools and browsers, much of the public uses older, more limited versions of browsers. Dreamweaver gives you the power to build Web pages with the high-end capabilities of fourth-generation browsers — and then convert those pages so that older browsers can also read what you've created. Moreover, you can take previously designed Web pages that use tables and "upgrade" them to take advantage of the latest HTML features with the Tables to Layers command. Dreamweaver goes a long way toward helping you bridge the gap between browser versions.

Verifying links

Web sites are ever-evolving entities. Maintaining valid connections and links amid all that diversity is a constant challenge. Dreamweaver includes a built-in link checker so you can verify the links on a page, in a directory, or across your entire site. The Link Checker quickly shows you which files have broken links, which files have links to external sites, and which files may have been "orphaned" (so that no other file connects with them).

FTP publishing

The final step in Web page creation is publishing your page on the Internet. As any Webmaster knows, this final step is one that happens repeatedly as the site is continually updated and maintained. Dreamweaver includes an FTP (File Transfer Protocol) publisher that simplifies the work of posting your site. More importantly, Dreamweaver enables you to synchronize your local and remote sites with one command.

 New Feature   Not all of the files found in your local site need to be uploaded to the remote site. Dreamweaver includes a new feature called cloaking, which permits the designer to designate folders that should be excluding during synchronization operations.

You can work with sites originating from a local folder, such as one on your own hard drive. Or, in a collaborative team environment, you can work with sites being developed on a remote server. Dreamweaver enables you to set up an unlimited number of sites to include the source and destination directories, FTP user names and passwords, and more.

The Dreamweaver Site panel, shown in Figure 1-21, is a visual interface in which you can click and drag files or select a number of files and transfer them with the Get and Put buttons. You can even set the preferences so the system automatically disconnects after remaining idle for a user-definable period of time.

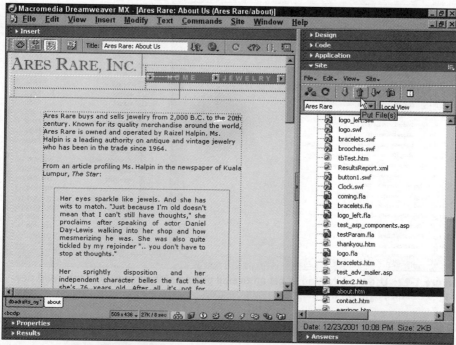

Figure 1-21: The FTP Site panel enables you to publish your Web site directly from within Dreamweaver to your application server.

Site map

Web sites can quickly outgrow the stage in which the designer can keep all the linked pages in mind. Dreamweaver includes a visual aid in the Web site management toolbox: the Site Map. With the Site Map, the Web designer can see how the entire Web site is structured. However, you can use the Site Map to do far more than just visualize the Web.

The Site Map, shown in Figure 1-22, can be used to establish the structure of the Web site in addition to viewing it. New pages can be created, and links can be added, modified, or deleted. In fact, the Site Map is so powerful, it becomes a site manager as well.

File check in/check out

On larger Web projects, more than one person is usually responsible for creation and daily upkeep of the site. An editor may need to include the latest company press release, or a graphic artist may have to upload a photo of the newest product—all on the same page. To avoid conflicts with overlapping updates, Dreamweaver has devised a system under which Web pages can be marked as "checked out" and locked to prevent any other corrections until the file is once again "checked in."

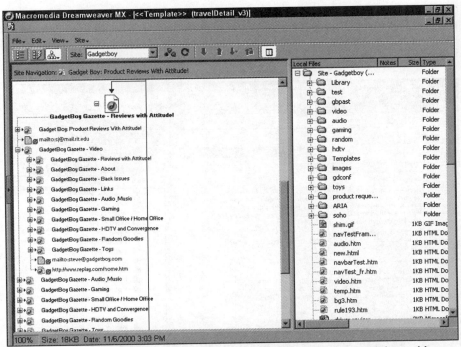

Figure 1-22: Use the Site Map to get an overall picture of your site — and then add new pages or links, right on the map.

Dreamweaver places a green checkmark over a file's icon in the Site Files window when you have checked it out and a red checkmark if another member of your team has checked it out. In addition, so you won't have to guess who that team member is, Dreamweaver displays the name of the person next to the filename. You can also keep track of who last checked out a particular Web page (or image) — Dreamweaver keeps an ongoing log listing the file, person, and date and time of the check-out.

Summary

Building any Web site — whether static or dynamic — is half craft and half art, and Dreamweaver is the perfect tool for blending these often dueling disciplines. Dreamweaver's visual editor enables quick and artful page creation, and at the same time, its integrated text editors offer the detail-oriented focus required by programmers. Dreamweaver's key features include the following:

✦ Dreamweaver works the way professional Web developers do, with integrated visual and text editors. Dreamweaver won't convert your code when it's used with preexisting Web pages.

✦ It supports HTML standard commands with easy entry and editing of text, graphics, tables, and multimedia elements.

✦ Dreamweaver provides straightforward yet robust connectivity to data sources and access to the most popular server models.

✦ It makes cutting-edge features, such as Dynamic HTML and Cascading Style Sheets, easy to use.

✦ A super-charged editor features advanced options like code completion and Code Hints.

✦ With Dreamweaver's Live Data view, you can construct your page while viewing the actual data to be displayed in the online application.

✦ Dreamweaver offers you a variety of reusable server behaviors, JavaScript behaviors, object libraries, commands, Application objects, and templates to streamline your Web page creation.

✦ Enhanced templates are possible with optional and conditional regions.

✦ Dreamweaver's wide range of site management tools includes FTP publishing, with a file-locking capability that encourages team creation and maintenance, as well as a built-in Link Checker, cloaking capabilities and visual Site Map.

In the next chapter, you hit the ground running with a quick-start guide to Dreamweaver.

✦   ✦   ✦

QuickStart

Designing a Web site is a big job, and Dreamweaver is a big program; both can be overwhelming when you first approach them. If you're new to Web design in general or Dreamweaver in particular, the best way to learn either is to build several sample sites. I've found that working on a project—especially a project that has meaning—helps most people to absorb all the little details needed to be productive.

This chapter presents an overview of how I use Dreamweaver to begin to build a Web site. One of the hallmarks of any world-class software program, such as Dreamweaver, is its capability to be used in many ways by many different people. Don't get the idea that what follows is the only way to construct a site; it is, however, the basic methodology that I've used successfully.

If you are totally new to Web site creation or Dreamweaver, I recommend reading through the chapter in one sitting. You get an overview of both the process and the program. Throughout this chapter, you can find many cross-references to other sections of the book where step-by-step instructions are detailed. As you begin to build your sites, use this chapter as a jumping-off place to delve deeper into each topic.

Setting Up a Site

The first phase of designing a Web site is pure input. You need to gather as much information from your client as possible. Some of the information relates to the overall message of the Web site: its purpose, intended audience, and goals. Other information is more tangible: logos, textual content, data sources, and prior marketing materials. I've found that it's best to get as much information up front—in both categories—as possible.

Tip   Whenever possible, get your data—not just the data sources—in digital format; the images ideally should be in a format your graphics program can read, and the content in a standard word processing file. Your workflow will be greatly enhanced if you don't have to spend time re-creating logos or keying in faxed text.

For Web applications, data source design is just as important as page design. A well-designed data source may have a tremendous impact on Web site performance and scalability. Generally, the more a database is divided into discrete tables, the more flexible it is; the goal is to force the user to download only the necessary data.

Although you may not have complete control over how the site's databases and the like are structured, you should have a complete understanding of the fields used and the type of data stored within them. For example, if the links to product images are in URL format, such as `http:// www.idest.com/images/logoanim/logoanim.gif`, the code calling the dynamic link would be different than if the same field stored data as plain text, such as `/images/ logoanim/logoanim.gif`.

As you are sketching out design ideas for the look of the site (on paper and in your head), you can begin to set up the structure of the site on your computer system. Dreamweaver uses a folder on your hard drive as the local site root; when the site goes live on the Internet, the local site is mirrored on the Web server, also known as the *remote site*. Therefore, the very first physical step is to create a folder with the site or client name. All you need is a single folder to define a site in Dreamweaver, and you can begin building your Web site.

Note   As mentioned in Chapter 1, you can run Dreamweaver MX in two workspace modes: the "classic" Dreamweaver 4 mode or the new Dreamweaver MX mode. In Dreamweaver 4 mode, each document resides in its own window, and panels reside in floating windows. In Dreamweaver MX mode — which is supported by Windows only — all Document windows and panels reside in a single application window. Most of this book assumes that you are running in Dreamweaver MX mode.

Here's how you typically start:

1. Using the system file manager, create a folder on your local hard drive and give it a unique name, reflective of the client or site. If you are going to use a default images folder, create it also.

2. In Dreamweaver, open the Site panel by choosing the Show Site button from the Launcher (at the bottom right of the Dreamweaver window). Alternatively, you could select Site ➪ Site Files or use the keyboard shortcut F8.

3. Click the Expand/Collapse button to expand the Site panel view to that shown in Figure 2-1.

4. Choose Site ➪ New Site from the Site panel menu (or from the main Dreamweaver menu if you are *not* running Dreamweaver in its single-window MX mode).

   The Site Definition dialog box opens. Choose the Advanced tab if it is not already selected. If a prompt appears warning you that the root folder you have chosen is the same as the folder for another site, ignore it and click OK to continue.

5. In the Local Info category of the Site Definition dialog box, enter the name of the new site, its local root folder, default images folder (if applicable), and HTTP address in the appropriate fields.

6. In the Remote Info category, choose how you'll access your remote site: via a local area network, with FTP, with RDS, or using a source control protocol such as SourceSafe or WebDAV. Each option has its own settings to specify.

Expand/Collapse button

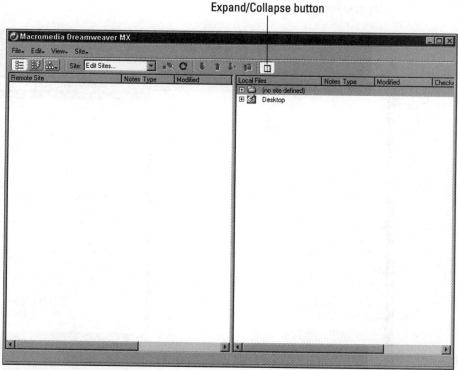

Figure 2-1: Use the expanded Site panel (shown here in Dreamweaver MX mode) to lay out the structure of your site.

7. If you are creating a Web application, in the Application Server category, select which of the various server models the site is to use. You should also define, at this time, whether the testing server is located locally or should be accessed via FTP.

8. In the Site Map Layout category, enter the name of your site home page, typically index.htm. You need to do this now, or Dreamweaver will not allow you to display a site map.

9. After you've successfully created your site and home page, choose Map and Files under the Site Map button to display the site in Site Map view, as shown in Figure 2-2.

Site Map button

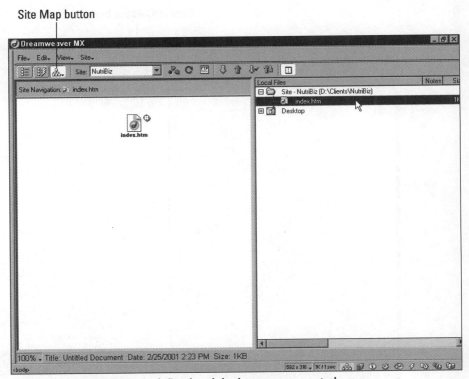

Figure 2-2: The Web site is defined and the home page created.

Cross-Reference A detailed breakdown of the process of defining a site can be found in Chapter 5.

After the site is initially defined, you have a folder and a home page, as shown in Figure 2-2. Dreamweaver's Site Map is not just a useful tool for maintaining a Web site; I recommend that you use it to develop the entire structure of your Web site before you begin adding content.

Using the techniques outlined in Chapter 5, you create new blank files, already linked to your home page. These new pages act as placeholders for content to come and help ease the building of the site by providing existing pages to link to and to preview the navigation of your site. To function properly, many of Dreamweaver's commands depend on a file being saved, so by prebuilding your site pages, you avoid unnecessary delays and warning dialog boxes. By the time you're finished, your Web site is beginning to take form, as you can see in Figure 2-3.

Note Although it's not necessary to create all the pages a site might use, I find it helpful to link the primary ones to the home page. Then, when I work on a section, such as Products, I use the Site window to create the pages in that division.

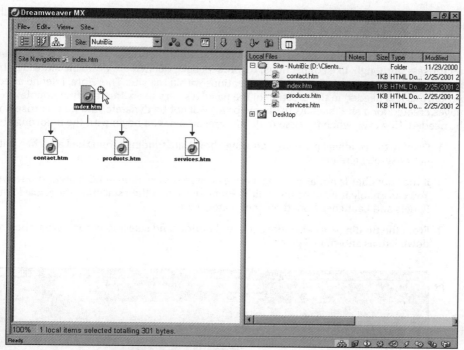

Figure 2-3: Dreamweaver's Site window is a valuable Web site prototyping tool.

Making the Data Source Connection

While not all sites are data-driven, pages with dynamic content have two basic requirements. First, it's necessary to establish a connection to a data source. A data source connection grants the Web application access to the database for reading and, perhaps, modifying or adding records. The second requirement for a dynamic page is to define one or more record-sets for that page. A recordset is a subset of the information in a data source, quite literally a set of the database's records. Recordsets may be limited by the number of fields they extract from a database, the range of data they use, or both.

Note   ColdFusion applications connect to their data sources through the ColdFusion Administrator; Windows users don't have to create a separate connection in Dreamweaver when building ColdFusion applications on a local development system.

Dreamweaver includes robust tools for fulfilling both dynamic page requirements. There are numerous ways to connect to a data source, and they vary according to the application server. For example, with ASP applications the simplest method is to specify the Data Source Name or DSN; a more involved method uses what are referred to as *connection strings*. Any defined connection is available from anywhere in the site, so I prefer to declare the connections I know I'll need right after defining the site. Following industry practice, I give each connection a unique name, each starting with the `conn` prefix; for example, `connEvents`.

Connections come in many flavors and can be established in a variety of ways. To find the way that works best for you, see Chapter 15.

After I've opened up a connection or two to my site's data sources, I'm able to begin defining recordsets. Although, like connections, recordsets once defined are available sitewide; they are generally applied to specific Web applications within the site. Therefore, I define a recordset only as it is needed in the creation of the page. It's very likely that the first couple of pages created for a site (such as the home page) will not be dynamic, and no recordsets will be needed. However, when it's time to define a recordset, you begin with the following steps:

1. Display the Bindings panel by choosing Show Data Bindings from the Launcher, if it's not onscreen already.

   If the Launcher is not already onscreen, be sure to turn it on — it's a great time-saver. You can enable it by choosing Edit ⇨ Preferences and then selecting the Show Icons in Panels and Launcher from the Panels category.

2. From the Bindings panel, choose the Add button, and select Recordset from the drop-down list, as shown in Figure 2-4.

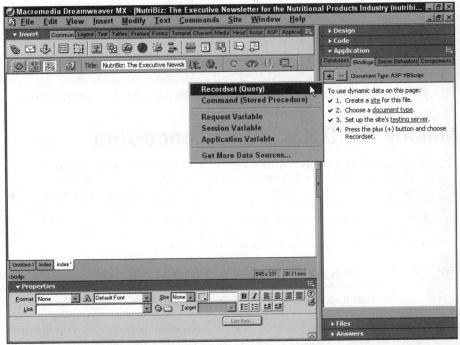

Figure 2-4: Recordsets are just one of the data sources available from the Bindings panel.

3. In the Recordset dialog box, give your recordset a unique name and specify the connection.

As with connections, the naming is up to you. Again, the conventional approach is to use a name starting with rs like rsEvents.

After the connection is chosen, Dreamweaver lists all the available tables within that data source.

4. Select the desired table and, if possible, limit the number of columns (also called *fields*) to be included in the recordset. Again, select only the columns you'll need.

5. Narrow the recordset further by choosing Filter options.

6. Optionally, you can sort your recordset by any column in the table in either an ascending or descending manner.

The preceding steps describe the process of defining a relatively simple recordset. By selecting Advanced from the Recordset dialog box, you can define more complex recordsets by entering the Structured Query Language (SQL) statements directly.

Cross-Reference   For a detailed description of data source connections and recordsets, see Chapter 15.

Home Page Layout

With the site's structure beginning to emerge, it's time to turn your attention to what most visitors see first at your Web site: the home page. Although any page can act as a doorway to your site, the home page is by far the most commonly used entrance. I like to start my design on the home page for another reason also — I frequently reuse core elements from the home page, such as the logo and navigation system, throughout the site. By setting these designs early — and getting approval for them — I can save myself a fair amount of work down the road while maintaining a consistent look and feel to the site.

Starting with the <head>

One of the most important sections of a Web page is also one of those most frequently — and wrongly — ignored: the <head> section. Under normal circumstances, the <head> area (as opposed to the <body>) is not seen, but its effect is enormous. The <head> section contains vital information about the page and the site itself, including the page's title, its description, and the keywords used to describe the page for search engines. Much of this information is contained in a page's <meta> tags. I like to add this information at the beginning of my Web site development, partly to get the chore out of the way, but primarily so I don't forget to do it! Dreamweaver offers an easy way to input <head> information:

1. Change the Title field in the Document toolbar from Untitled Document to whatever you'd like to appear in the browser title bar. Keep in mind that a page's title is an important factor in how most search engines rank a site.

2. Choose View ➪ Head Content from the main menu, or choose Head Content under the View Options button on the toolbar. The <head> section appears at the top of the Document window, as shown in Figure 2-5.

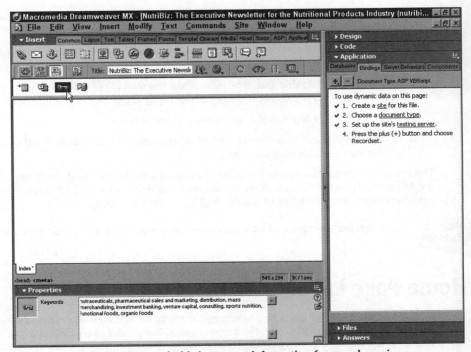

Figure 2-5: The <head> area holds important information for search engines.

3. From the Head panel of the Insert bar, insert both Keywords and a Description object and fill them out appropriately. I prefer my client to supply both the keywords and the description whenever possible. Naturally, they know their business and how best to market it.

Cross-Reference   For a detailed description of the <head> section and its various tags, turn to Chapter 6.

4. Close the Head Content view by deselecting that option under the View Options button of the toolbar.

Specifying page colors

I always begin a new page by entering its <head> content, and then using CSS or HTML to specify its background, text, and link colors. Though CSS is the more professional approach, I chose the convenience of using HTML to define the page's colors and margins through Dreamweaver's Page Properties dialog box, as shown in Figure 2-6. Choose Modify ➪ Page Properties to set these parameters. This is also the location for setting up a background image, if you're using one. It's not unusual for me to alter these settings several times in the home page design stage as I try out different looks, so I've memorized the keyboard shortcut Ctrl+J (Command+J).

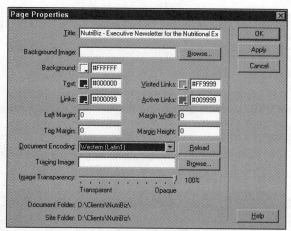

Figure 2-6: As an alternative to using the preferred CSS approach, you can set your page colors through the Page Properties dialog box.

Tip   Not sure about your color combinations? Dreamweaver has a useful command, Set Color Scheme, which contains background, text, and link color selections designed to work together. If you're a CSS devotee — and you should be, since many HTML attributes are now deprecated (that is, they should no longer be used) in favor of CSS rules — you can take the colors that Dreamweaver comes up with and embed them in the document's style sheet.

Initial graphic layout

Like many small-shop Web designers, I create the majority of the graphics for use on my pages myself, and the Dreamweaver/Fireworks Studio has been a major boon to my productivity. Typically, I create or modify the logo for the home page in Fireworks, while Dreamweaver is open, for instant placement and integration. Although the use of layers is always a possibility for placement, I prefer to lay out my pages with tables for most situations. Many designers new to the Web — especially those from a print background — prefer the exact positioning of layers and can use Dreamweaver's excellent layers-to-tables conversion features. The approach you use is up to you, but keep in mind that many clients still balk at using layers for fear of excluding visitors with older browsers.

Tip   Dreamweaver includes a feature that makes composing the basic layout of a page very straightforward: the Layout view.

Here's how a typical home page is developed using Layout view:

1. Start by creating a logo for the Web in your favorite graphics editor. Remember that Web graphics are of a particular format, usually GIF or JPEG with a screen resolution of 72 dpi. Although most Web page visitors' monitors display thousands of colors, it's still good practice to use Web-safe colors wherever possible.

Cross-Reference   An explanation of Web graphic formats and Web-safe colors can be found in Chapter 3.

2. In Dreamweaver, click the Layout View button in the Insert bar's Layout panel. With Layout view enabled, both the Draw Layout Cell and Draw Layout Table tools become available.

3. Select Draw Layout Cell and drag out the initial cell for holding the logo. Dreamweaver automatically creates a layout table — a borderless table the full width of your window — around the layout cell.

4. Select Draw Layout Cell again while pressing the Ctrl (Command) key to continuously draw out other layout cells for your navigational elements and any other upfront information, such as the company's name.

Although your layout is likely to be different from mine, in the example shown in Figure 2-7, I start with a three-row by one-column configuration and modify it as needed.

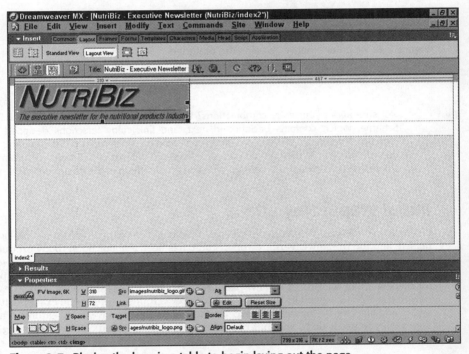

Figure 2-7: Placing the logo in a table to begin laying out the page.

Cross-Reference: A table is an important layout tool for Web designers. Chapter 10 shows you how to create and modify tables in Dreamweaver.

5. Place your logo in the layout cell by choosing Image from the Common panel of the Insert bar or dragging the graphic into place from the Assets panel.

6. Add background color to the table or rows, if desired, by picking a color from the Property inspector.

Using a table's background color features is a good, no-overhead way to add color to your page. Dreamweaver enables you to sample colors directly from the logo to begin to tie the page together graphically.

7. If desired, adjust the positioning of the logo by selecting the cell it resides in and using the Horz (align) option in the Property inspector.

I continue to add and modify elements to the logo area until I'm satisfied. In the case of this example site, I added right-justified contact information on one side of the table and then added navigation elements below the logo, as shown in Figure 2-8. I used a contrasting background color for the second smaller row to set off the navigation bar. Initially, the navigation bar is just text and not graphics; this enables me to prototype the page quickly, and I can always replace the text with images at a later date.

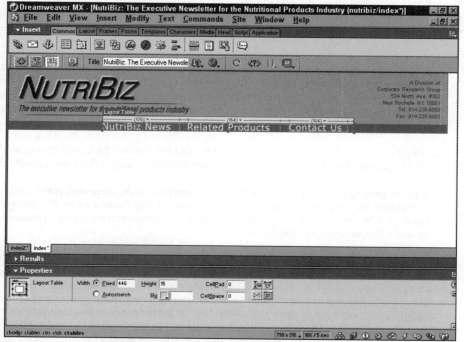

Figure 2-8: All the graphic elements are now in place in the logo area.

Note   One advantage of using tables instead of layers is that tables can adjust in width more consistently across browsers than layers can. If you set your tables to 100 percent width and use the Page Properties dialog box to change your page margins to zero, you can be sure the background color will stretch across the page, regardless of the user's browser window size.

Including Client Text

Now that your home page is beginning to attract some eyeballs with its graphic look, it is time to throw in some content to get the message across. Text from a client comes in many forms: from the headings and paragraphs of a marketing brochure to bulleted copy points written especially for the Web, and everything in between. Your job as a Web designer is to make it all flow together in a logical, attractive, understandable fashion.

Many print designers coming to the Internet are appalled at the lack of typographic control on the Web. Particular fonts are, for the most part, suggested, rather than specified, with alternatives always available. Sizes are often relative, and line spacing — outside of Cascading Style Sheets — is nonexistent. A typical first response is to render blocks of text into graphics to achieve exactly the look desired. In a word, don't. Graphics, unlike text, aren't searchable, and displaying text as graphics defeats much of the purpose of the Web. Moreover, large blocks of graphics can take a long time to download. It's far better to learn the ins and outs of HTML text and take advantage of its universality. Besides, Cascading Style Sheets (CSS) are increasingly a real option and give the Web designer almost as much control as the print designer.

To facilitate including client-generated text in my Web page designs, I often work with my word processing program and Dreamweaver open simultaneously. This arrangement enables me to quickly cut and paste text from one to the other.

Note   If you have a great deal of client text that's already formatted for inclusion on your page — and a copy of Microsoft Word — take advantage of Dreamweaver's Import Word HTML feature. When you run the command, Dreamweaver brings the Word-generated HTML document into a new page, and you can copy the needed sections (or all of it, if you like) and paste them directly into the home page. Dreamweaver preserves all the coding during the copy-and-paste operation.

I generally adopt a top-down approach when inserting text: I place the headings followed by the body copy. I can then try different heading sizes independently of the main paragraphs.

Tip   If you're copying multiple paragraphs from your word processing document, make sure your paragraphs are separated by two returns. When pasted into Dreamweaver, the paragraph breaks will be preserved. If you just have a single return between paragraphs, Dreamweaver converts the paragraphs to line breaks.

Although it depends on the design, I rarely let the text flow all the way across the page. If my page margins are set at zero — which they often are for the graphics I use — the text bumps right up against the edge of the browser window. I frequently use two techniques in combination. First, I place the text in a borderless table, set at 95 percent width or less and centered on the page. This technique ensures that some "air" or gutter-space is inserted on either side of my text, no matter how the browser window is sized. I'm also fond of the `<blockquote>` tag, which indents text by a browser-defined amount. You can access the `<blockquote>` tag by selecting your text and choosing the Text Indent button on the Property inspector. The text blocks on the example page shown in Figure 2-9 use both techniques.

Note   The `<blockquote>` tag is deprecated in favor of CSS. But, as with many deprecated — but still widely used — HTML tags, it is safe to use `<blockquote>`, particularly in non-mission-critical situations (such as, where failure of the tag will not cause the page to collapse into incomprehensibility).

I think that it's important to style your text in some fashion to maintain the desired look. Unless you specify the font, size, and color, you're at the mercy of your visitors' browser preferences — which can totally wreck your layout. You have two methods for defining text formatting: standard HTML tags and CSS. Whenever possible, I try to use CSS because of its greater degree of control and flexibility. With CSS, if a client doesn't like the color of body text I've chosen, or its size, I can modify it sitewide with one alteration. HTML tags, on the other hand, offer backward compatibility with three browsers. However, for most clients, the relatively small percentage of visitors still using the earlier browser versions is a fair trade-off for the power of CSS.

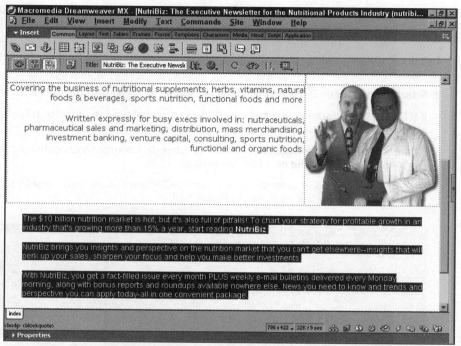

Figure 2-9: The text in the top paragraph is right-aligned within a centered table, whereas the text below is indented with the <blockquote> tag.

Note

Over the years, Web-page design has turned to CSS over HTML for many page layout and formatting tasks. Many HTML tags and attributes — such as <font>, <blockquote>, bgcolor, align (for <img> tags), and so on — have been declared as *deprecated* in favor of their CSS equivalents. If a tag or attribute is deprecated, it does not necessarily mean that you should never use it, rather, that you should gradually wean yourself from its use and turn, instead, to its CSS equivalent.

Cross-Reference

To get the full scope of what CSS can do for you and your Web sites, see Chapter 20.

Adding Dynamic Content

With the basic design of your page complete, you're ready to add some dynamic content. Dynamic content may take many forms, but text extracted from database fields is by far the most common. Dreamweaver enables you to drag and drop fields listed as a data source from the Bindings panel directly onto the page.

I prefer to create placeholders for my dynamic data during the design phase, rather than insert the fields as I'm building the page. This approach helps me complete a consistent design before I begin integrating the data source material. However, it's important to maintain a flexible design, as dynamically added data often varies in length from one record to the next.

You'll need to make sure that you have the recordset or other data source for the page under development properly defined, as described previously. After this task is handled, adding dynamic text and other content is very straightforward:

1. If the Bindings panel is not displayed onscreen, choose Show Data Bindings from the Launcher.

2. Select the text in the Document window that will be replaced with the dynamic data.

   If HTML or CSS formatting has been applied, you can make a more precise selection by using the Tag Selector, rather than dragging the mouse over the text.

3. If necessary, expand the defined recordset or other data source by choosing the plus (right-triangle) next to the data source heading.

4. Drag the desired field or other data item from the Bindings panel onto the selected text in the Document window, as shown in Figure 2-10.

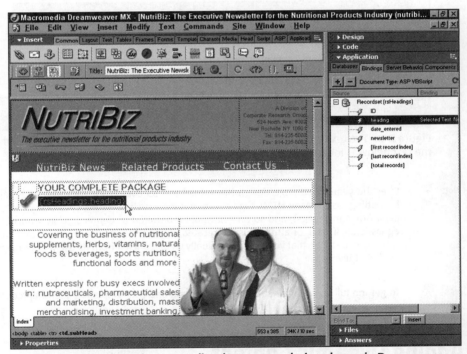

Figure 2-10: Drag dynamic content directly onto your designed page in Dreamweaver.

You can also select the field and then click the Insert button from the Bindings panel. I vary my technique depending on what type of static content is being replaced. It's often easier to use the Insert button for content in a complex table.

5. Certain types of data, such as currency and dates, may benefit from specific server-side formatting. You can choose a format by selecting the inserted data placeholder. Then, from the Bindings panel, choose the down arrow to the right of the Format column.

Note   You may need to widen your Bindings panel or use its horizontal scroll bar to see the Format column.

It's a good idea — and immediately gratifying — to use Dreamweaver's Live Data view early and often when designing with dynamic data. Often, adjustments to table-cell sizes are required in order to get the look you want with the actual data. Choose the Show Live Data View button on the toolbar to see your page with the desired information in place.

Cross-Reference   Including dynamic content is a key activity in Dreamweaver. For all the details you'll need for this operation, see Chapter 16.

Inserting Server Behaviors

As the name implies, a server behavior is code that is executed on the server. Technically, when you add any dynamic content from the Bindings panel, you have already inserted a server behavior. For example, if you drag the Event_Date field from the rsNY_Events recordset onto the page, the Server Behaviors panel displays Dynamic Text (rsNY_Events.Event_Date). Dreamweaver offers a wide range of server behaviors with the standard installation; additional ones may be added through the Extension Manager. Although server behaviors may be added at any time, I like to add them along with the dynamic content so that I can get a better sense of what the final page will look like.

The Server Behaviors panel is used for inserting, deleting, and managing server behaviors. Although all the server behaviors have dialog boxes specific to their needs, you use the same basic steps to insert any server behavior. The following steps illustrate how one of the most commonly used server behaviors, Repeat Region — which displays multiple records from a recordset on the same page — is used:

1. Choose Show Server Behaviors from the Launcher, if the Server Behaviors panel is not open.

2. Select the area in the Document window to which you'd like to apply the Repeat Region server behavior.

    Typically, the Repeat Region server behavior is applied to a table row or a series of paragraphs that include some dynamic content. For this example, I've selected a table row with a graphic bullet in one table cell and dynamic text in the other, as shown in Figure 2-11.

3. Select Add from the Server Behaviors panel and choose Repeat Region from the drop-down list.

4. In the Repeat Region dialog box, select the desired recordset from the list and choose whether to display all the available records or a set number of them.

    A Repeat Region (yourRecordset) item is added to the list in the Server Behaviors panel.

5. Choose the Show Live Data View button from the toolbar to see how your data looks on the page.

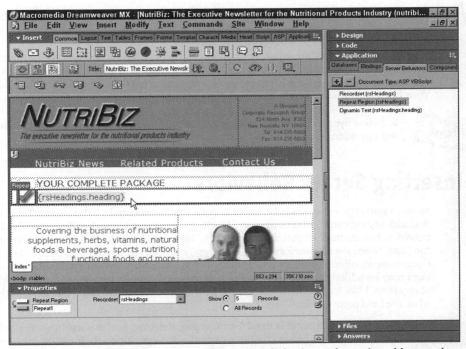

Figure 2-11: By applying the Repeat Region server behavior to the entire table row, the graphic bullet will repeat with each iteration of the dynamic text.

If the Invisible Elements option is enabled, the repeated data is displayed in a highlighted color. The highlighting indicates that this data is for display only and cannot be formatted. You can, however, alter the formatting of the first record in the repeat region, and the changes will be displayed in all the records if Refresh from the Live Data toolbar is selected.

Activating the Page with JavaScript

Study after study has proven that an engaged viewer remembers your message better than a passive viewer. One method of grabbing people's attention is to activate your Web page in some fashion, so that some element of the page reacts to the visitor's mouse movements. This reaction could be anything from a simple rollover to the complete rewriting of a frame. Activating a page typically requires a combination of HTML and JavaScript, frequently beyond the programming skill level — or interest — of the Web designer. Luckily, Dreamweaver makes such effects possible through client-side behaviors, which are executed in the user's browser, unlike server behaviors.

After I have the basic layout of a page accomplished, I go back and activate the page in a fitting manner. As with any effect, too many behaviors can be more distracting than attractive, and it's best to use them only when called for. At the very least, I typically use some form of rollover for the navigation bar, which is particularly feasible now with Dreamweaver's tighter integration with Fireworks. But even without Fireworks, Dreamweaver enables you to construct a complete multistate navigation bar, or you can use the Swap Image behavior to create your own. Here's one method of activating your page:

1. In Fireworks, or another graphics program, create a series of rollover buttons with one image for each state. You need at least two states (Up and Over), and you can use as many as four (Down and Over While Down).

2. In Dreamweaver, remove the temporary text links for the navigation bar.

3. If you've created your rollover buttons in Fireworks, you can choose Fireworks HTML from the Common panel of the Insert bar. Dreamweaver inserts a table of sliced images, complete with all the necessary code. In Figure 2-12, you can see the result of using the Fireworks HTML command to insert the rollover buttons Home, Newsletter, Products, and Contact.

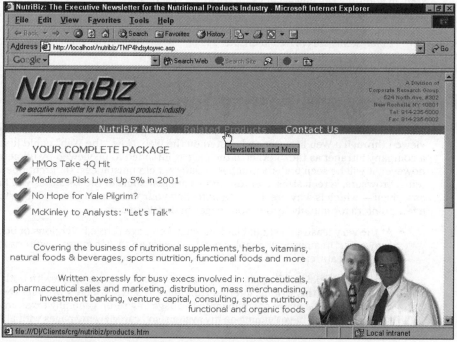

Figure 2-12: These three rollover buttons (NutriBiz News, Related Products, and Contact Us) were imported directly from Fireworks-generated HTML.

4. If you're working with separate images for the various rollover states, either use the Swap Image behavior or insert a Navigation Bar object. Either method enables you to select the separate images for your rollover states.

Cross-Reference All of Dreamweaver's standard behaviors are covered in Chapter 23; information on the Navigation Bar object can be found in Chapter 6.

When I'm using tables for my layouts, I tend to nest the table containing the navigation bar inside the cell of another table. If the outer table has a percentage-based width, say 95%, this technique results in a fluid design that resizes and realigns well to match the user's browser window width.

Tip　Another alternative, sure to give your page some pizzazz, is the Flash Button object. A Flash Button is a predesigned graphic template with animation that uses your specified text. Flash Button objects are great for quickly turning out a professional-quality navigation system. Because they are actually Flash animations, users must have the Flash Player plugin installed, which is very likely, since the vast majority of users are Flash-enabled.

After I've completed the initial elements of my page, I take advantage of one of Dreamweaver's key features: Library items. By turning my navigation bar into a Library item, I can easily reuse it on the same page and on every other page of the site. This technique keeps consistent elements on every page — an important consideration for design. Moreover, if I ever need to update the navigation system by changing a link or adding more buttons, I can do it in one step. In addition, Dreamweaver's Library items, if activated with behaviors, retain all the necessary code.

Cross-Reference　Library items are covered in Chapter 29.

Previewing and Posting Your Pages

No matter how beautiful or spectacular your home page design, it's not a Web page until it's viewed through a Web browser and posted on the Web. Now, "the Web" could just as easily be a company intranet as the Internet. If the page is intended to be viewed by numerous people, however, it will be seen under a number of different circumstances. Different operating systems, browsers, screen sizes, and resolutions are just some of the variables you have to take as a given — which is why previewing and testing your Web page is vitally important. Here are a few pointers for initially testing your pages in development:

✦ At the very least, you should look at your Web page through versions of both major browsers. Dreamweaver enables you to specify up to 20 browsers with its Preview in Browser feature; I currently have five available on my system.

✦ During the initial building phase, my routine is to preview my page with both my primary browser (as of this writing, Internet Explorer 5.5) and secondary browser (Netscape 6.2) whenever I add a major component to the page. My setup generally takes advantage of the Web server I have running on my system, so I can view my pages with all the dynamic content intact.

✦ Make it a point to resize the page several times to see how your layout is affected by different screen sizes. If a client has specified maximum browser compatibility as a site requirement, you should also look at the page under various screen resolutions.

✦ When a page is largely completed, I run Dreamweaver's Check Target Browsers command to make sure I'm not committing some grievous error. If incompatibilities appear — as they often do when checking the earliest browsers (as shown in Figure 2-13) — I have to decide whether to keep the offending tag or risk the page being visited by users with those browsers. To see which browsers are generating the specific error, choose Browser Report from the Results panel toolbar.

I also make it a habit to routinely check the Download Stats found in Dreamweaver's status bar. The Download Stats show the "weight" of a page — its file size and the download time at a set speed. By default, the speed is set for a 28.8 modem, but you can alter that in the Status Bar panel of Preferences. Keep in mind that the Download Stats include all the dependent files (images and other media) as well as the size of the page itself. Remember also that, due to the unpredictability of Internet traffic flow, these Download Stats are more "ballpark" than exact; use them as guidelines to estimate download times, not as 100% accurate predictors.

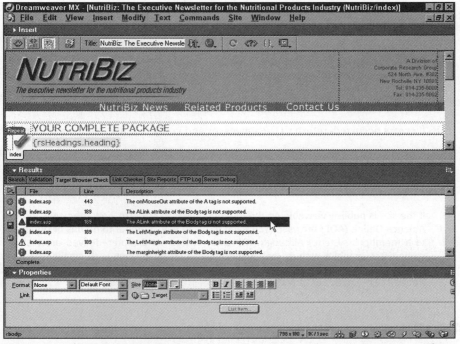

Figure 2-13: Errors from the Check Target Browsers command are not uncommon when checking early browser versions.

To ensure that all my ducks are in a row—and all my links are valid—I use the Check Links Sitewide command from the Site panel's drop-down Site menu. Not only does this give me a report of broken links, but it also displays orphaned files and offers a list of external links that I can verify from its report.

My final testing phase is always conducted online. Here's the procedure I use for uploading my site and testing it:

1. Choose Window ➪ Site to open the Site panel and expand the panel using the Expand/Collapse button (in Dreamweaver MX mode). By this time, I've already established a domain with an Internet host and edited my site definition to include the necessary FTP information.

2. Click the Connects to Remote Host button in the Site panel. Dreamweaver logs on to the remote system and displays the remote files in the Remote Site pane opposite the Local Site pane.

3. Select the HTML files for the completed Web pages.

4. Click the Put File(s) button.

5. By default, Dreamweaver asks if you'd like to include the dependent files; click Yes.

   Dreamweaver begins to transfer the HTML files as well as all dependent files. All necessary subfolders (connections, images, media) are created to replicate the local site structure on the remote site.

Note
If the Include Dependent Files dialog box does not appear, open Preferences and, in the Site category, select the Dependent Files: Prompt on Put/Check In option. Be aware that Dreamweaver does not always know to include files that are used within scripts; you might need to upload these files manually.

6. After the file transfer is complete, open a browser and connect to the URL for the site.

7. Navigate to every page and try all links and user actions, including rollovers. Note any "files not found" or other errors.

8. If errors occurred, return to Dreamweaver and verify the links for the problem files.

9. If necessary, repair the links and re-upload the HTML file. In most cases, you will not need to resend the dependent files.

10. Repeat Steps 6 through 9 with all available browsers and systems.

Tip
If the site is publicly viewable on the Internet, make an effort to view the pages through an America Online (AOL) browser. (You need to be an AOL member to do this or obtain access to a member's system.) Although AOL uses an Internet Explorer–derived browser, it also compresses graphics with its own algorithm and tends to open with smaller-than-normal windows. If you find problems, you might consult AOL's Webmaster Site at `http://webmaster.info.aol.com`.

Summary

Designing Web sites appeals to me because it engages both the left and right sides of my brain. Web site design is, at turns, both creative and pragmatic, and Dreamweaver balances that equation with grace. Although everyone works differently, try to keep the following points in mind as you're working:

✦ The more time spent in planning, the less time spent in revision. Get as much information as possible from the client before you begin designing.

✦ Use Dreamweaver's Site Map to prototype the site; the existing structure saves time as you begin to fill in the content.

✦ Work from the home page out. The home page is primarily used to succinctly express the client's message, and it often sets the tone for the entire site.

✦ Include some interactivity in your Web page. A static page may be beautiful to behold, but an active page enables the visitor to interact, and it leaves a more lasting impression.

✦ Preview your pages early and often during the development phase. It's far better to discover an incompatibility with the page half done than when you're doing a demonstration for the client.

In the next chapter, you get an in-depth tour of all Dreamweaver's features.

Touring Dreamweaver

♦ ♦ ♦ ♦

In This Chapter

Comparing workspace layouts

Working in the Document window

Accessing common commands on the toolbars

Inserting elements with the Insert bar

Modifying tag properties with the Property inspector

Working with dockable panels

Stepping through the menus

♦ ♦ ♦ ♦

Dreamweaver's user interface is efficient, powerful, and flexible. By offering a wide variety of customizable tools and controls, Dreamweaver helps you tailor its workspace to your specific preferences and needs, so you can focus on the task of creating your Web site. This chapter provides a detailed overview of the Dreamweaver workspace so you know where all the tools are when you need to use them.

Choosing a Workspace Layout

One of Dreamweaver's greatest strengths is its flexibility. The makers of Dreamweaver realize that not everyone works in the same way, and they have created a product that you can customize to maximize your efficiency. If you work in Windows, the first time you open Dreamweaver, you are presented with a major customization decision: You are asked to choose one of three Dreamweaver workspace layouts.

Note   Mac users are not offered a choice of workspace; the Mac always uses a variation of the Dreamweaver 4 workspace, described later in this section.

The first layout option is called the Dreamweaver MX workspace. Also referred to as the multiple-document interface, or the integrated workspace, this configuration enables you to open several documents within the same window. By default, Dreamweaver's many panels are organized into groups and docked on the right side of the window. The Dreamweaver MX workspace is illustrated in Figure 3-1.

A variation on the Dreamweaver MX workspace is the HomeSite/Coder Style option. This is similar to the Dreamweaver MX workspace, but the panels are docked on the left side of the window. With this option, when you first open documents, you are presented with the code for the document, rather than a view of the page that reflects what the page will look like when viewed in a browser. Figure 3-2 shows the HomeSite/Coder Style workspace layout.

Document toolbar

Insert bar

Menus   Property inspector   Document window (Design view)   Panels

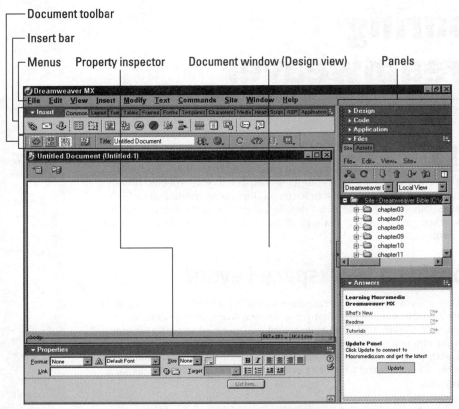

Figure 3-1: The Dreamweaver MX workspace places docked panel groups on the right.

The final layout option for Windows is called the Dreamweaver 4 workspace, and is shown in Figure 3-3. This workspace is similar to that used in previous versions of Dreamweaver. Each page opens in a separate window, and the tools appear in floating panels that you can position anywhere onscreen.

Why would you choose one workspace over another? Your decision could be based on many factors, including the size of your monitor, your work style, the content of your site, and the other HTML tools you've used in the past. For example, a user whose monitor is small or runs at a low screen resolution might experience the Dreamweaver MX layout as cramped, not leaving enough space for editing the document itself. Someone with a larger monitor might work more efficiently in the Dreamweaver MX workspace, where all the needed tools are visible on the screen at once. Users with more than one monitor might prefer the Dreamweaver 4 layout, so they could position the panels on one monitor and the Document window on another. Those who primarily work with the code might prefer the HomeSite/Coder Style workspace, while designers who develop their pages visually might choose one of the other layouts.

Collapsed Property inspector ⎯

Document toolbar ⎯

Menus   Panels   Document window (Code view)   Insert bar ⎯

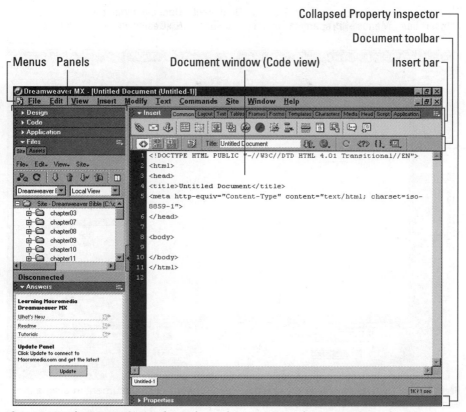

Figure 3-2: The HomeSite/Coder Style workspace opens documents in Code view, and docks panels on the left.

If you aren't sure which workspace will work best for you, don't worry; you aren't committed to your initial choice. You can alter your workspace at any time by choosing Edit ➪ Preferences, and clicking the Change Workspace button in the General category. You'll see the new workspace configuration the next time you start Dreamweaver.

Cross-Reference

You have numerous options for customizing Dreamweaver. Later in this chapter, you'll learn how to move the panels and toolbars, dock or float the panels, hide, show, or resize panels, and more. Chapter 4 systematically covers many additional customization options, referred to within Dreamweaver as *preferences*.

Caution

When you change workspaces, Dreamweaver will open with the default setup. Any customizations you have made, such as moving, resizing, or renaming panels, will be lost.

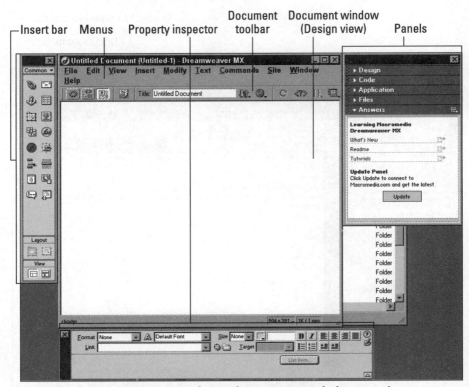

Figure 3-3: The Dreamweaver 4 workspace layout opens each document in a separate window, with tools arranged in separate floating panels.

Macintosh users are not offered a choice of workspace layout. The workspace for Macintosh users, shown in Figure 3-4, is a variation of the Dreamweaver 4 workspace on Windows. Like the Dreamweaver 4 workspace, each document opens in a separate window, and the tools are grouped into floating panels that can be docked to each other. On a Mac, however, the Dreamweaver menus appear in a separate menu bar, rather than within the window containing the document.

Note

A major difference between the Macintosh workspace and the Dreamweaver 4 workspace involves an important tool: the Insert bar. On Windows, the Insert bar for the Dreamweaver MX workspace works differently than for the Dreamweaver 4 workspace. Macintosh users can choose whether to use the Dreamweaver MX or Dreamweaver 4 configuration for the Insert bar. Refer to the section "Selecting from the Insert Bar" later in this chapter, for more information.

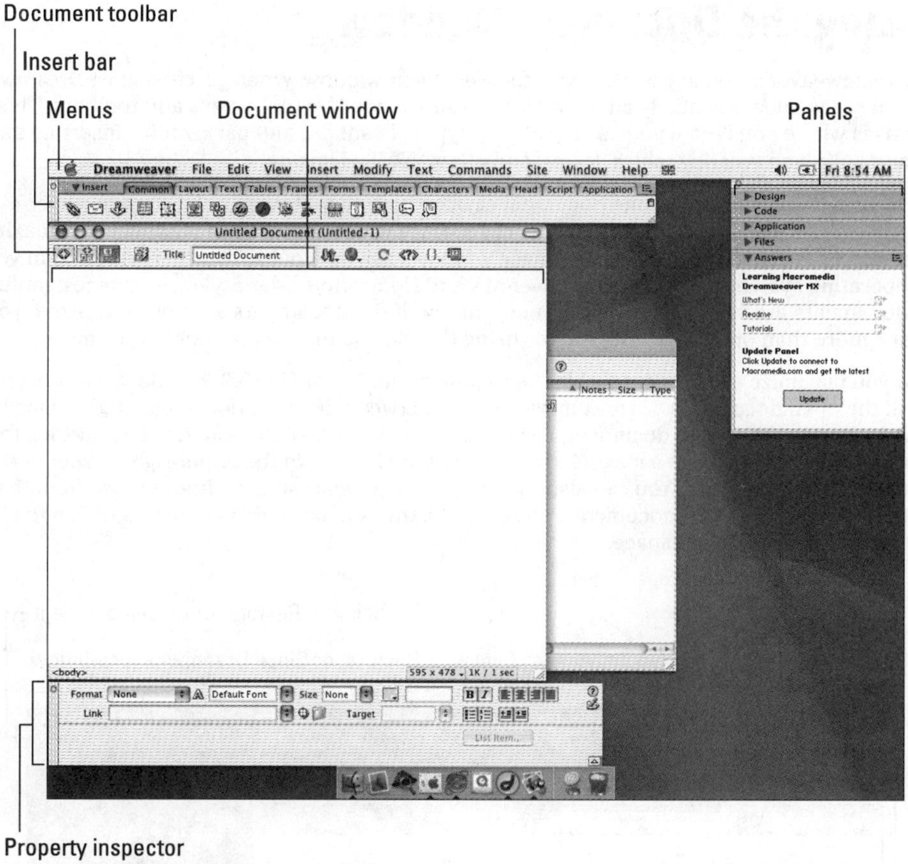

Document toolbar

Insert bar

Menus   Document window   Panels

Property inspector

Figure 3-4: The workspace for Macintosh users is similar to the Dreamweaver 4 workspace on Windows.

Figures 3-1, 3-2, 3-3, and 3-4 show that, although laid out differently on the screen, all of the workspaces are comprised of the same basic elements. For the most part, you work with those elements in the same way, regardless of workspace; the only major difference between the workspaces is the location of the tools onscreen. The basic elements of Dreamweaver include the following:

✦ Document window

✦ Toolbars

✦ Insert bar (In previous releases, this was called the Objects panel.)

✦ Property inspector

✦ Panels

✦ Menus

The rest of this chapter takes you on a tour of each of these basic interface elements.

Viewing the Document Window

Dreamweaver's primary work area is the Document window. When you first start Dreamweaver, you see what is essentially an empty canvas surrounded by tool panels and toolbars. This canvas is where you create your Web pages by typing headlines and paragraphs, inserting images and links, and creating tables, forms, and other HTML elements.

You can open more than one document at once in Dreamweaver. In the Dreamweaver 4 workspace, multiple documents open in separate windows. You can minimize and maximize, resize, move, and switch between these windows as you would any other windows in your operating system. In the Dreamweaver MX and HomeSite/Coder Style workspaces, multiple documents are viewed within the same window. If the documents are not maximized, you can see more than one document at once using the tile commands on the Window menu.

If you maximize a document within the Dreamweaver MX or HomeSite/Coder Style workspaces, all the open documents are maximized. Switch between the open documents by clicking the appropriate tab for the document, located near the bottom of the window. The buttons to minimize, restore, and close a maximized document are located in the upper-right corner of the Dreamweaver window. You can also right-click a document tab and choose Close from the context menu to close the document. Figure 3-5 illustrates maximized documents within the Dreamweaver MX workspace.

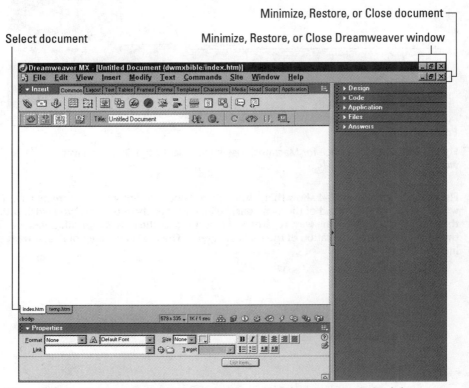

Figure 3-5: In the Dreamweaver MX workspace, switch between maximized documents using tabs.

Switching views in the Document window

Typical Web design tasks consist of visually creating your page in Dreamweaver, perhaps tweaking the underlying code to achieve the exact effect you desire, and making sure your Web application is performing as expected with Dreamweaver's Live Data view (if you are creating dynamic pages). You can do all of these things without ever leaving the Dreamweaver Document window, simply by switching the view of the page you are editing.

Design and Code views

Design view is the default view for the Dreamweaver MX and Dreamweaver 4 workspaces. In Design view, you can lay out your page visually. As your Web page begins to take shape, Design view shows you a close representation of how the page looks when viewed through a browser such as Netscape Communicator or Internet Explorer. You can even see active elements, such as QuickTime movies or Shockwave and Flash files, in your Web page as you're building it. You can switch to Design view with the View ⇨ Design menu command or by clicking the Show Design View button on the Document toolbar, described in the section "Accessing the Toolbars," later in this chapter.

As the name suggests, Code view displays the underlying code used to create the document, whether that is HTML, CSS style definitions, or JavaScript — whatever code is used to create your page is visible to you in Code view. If you are working in the HomeSite/Coder Style workspace, Code view is the default view, but you can also switch to Code view by choosing the View ⇨ Code menu command or by clicking the Show Code View button on the Document toolbar.

Tip You can choose View ⇨ Code and Design to split the Document window, so that both Code view and Design view are visible at the same time. You can also do this by clicking the Show Code and Design Views button on the Document toolbar.

When you switch document views, the switch applies to the currently active open document, and to any subsequent documents you open. It does not, however, change the view of other open documents.

Live Data view

If you are creating a Web application that includes dynamic elements from a database, Dreamweaver offers an alternate version of Design view for your page — Live Data view. In Live Data view, Dreamweaver displays your page with data from your data source. Toggle Live Data view on and off by choosing View ⇨ Live Data or by selecting the Live Data View button on the Document toolbar (as described later in this chapter). There's also a keyboard shortcut, Ctrl+Shift+R (Command+Shift+R), for enabling Live Data view.

Live Data view is one of Dreamweaver's key features. When you're in Live Data view, you can lay out your page — formatting text items, adjusting graphics, and modifying tables — while the actual data from your application is onscreen. The live data that Dreamweaver displays replaces data source placeholders such as {rs.employeeID} with the selected information pulled from the designated database's field, as shown in Figure 3-6.

Live Data view requires that a connection to a testing server, either local or remote, be properly established in the Site Definition dialog box. If Dreamweaver is unable to complete the connection, an error message appears with several possible solutions listed.

Cross-Reference Live Data view is extremely helpful in building your Web applications. Find out more about how to use this important feature in Chapter 18.

Live Data View button

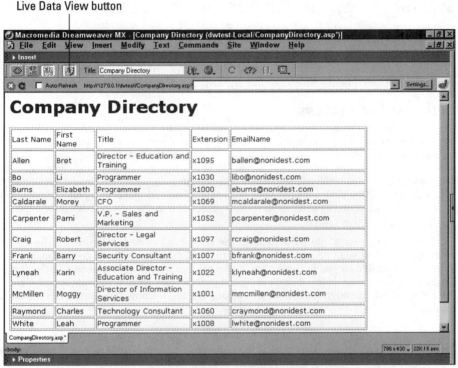

Figure 3-6: Live Data view lets you work on the Web page — altering the format and layout — while working with actual data from your application.

Working with the status bar

The status bar is found at the bottom of the Document window. Embedded here are four important tools: the Tag Selector, the Window Size pop-up menu, the Download Indicator, and the Launcher. These helpful status bar tools provide the Web designer with several timesaving utilities.

Tag Selector

The Tag Selector is an excellent example of Dreamweaver's elegant design approach. On the left side of the status bar, you see a listing of the current HTML tags. When you first open a blank page in Dreamweaver, you see only the <body> tag. If you type a line of text and then press Enter (Return), the paragraph tag <p> appears. Your cursor's position in the document determines which tags are displayed in the Tag Selector. The Tag Selector keeps continuous track of where you are in the HTML document by displaying the tags surrounding your current cursor position. This becomes especially important when you are building complex Web pages that use such features as nested tables.

As its name implies, the Tag Selector does more than just indicate a position in a document. Using the Tag Selector, you can quickly choose any of the elements surrounding your current cursor. Once an element is selected, you can modify or delete it. If you have the Property inspector (described later in this chapter) onscreen, choosing a different code from the Tag Selector makes the corresponding options available in the Property inspector.

Tip
If you want to quickly clear most of your HTML page, choose the `<body>` tag in the Tag Selector and press Delete. All graphics, text, and other elements you have inserted through the Document window will be erased. Left intact is any HTML code in the `<head>` section, including your title, `<meta>` tags, and any preliminary JavaScript. The `<body>` tag is also left intact.

In a more complex Web page section such as the one shown in Figure 3-7, the Tag Selector shows a wider variety of HTML tags. As you move your pointer over individual codes in the Tag Selector, they are highlighted; click one, and the code becomes bold. Tags are displayed from left to right in the Tag Selector — starting on the far left with the most inclusive (in this case, the `<body>` tag) and proceeding to the narrowest selection (here, the italic `<i>` tag) on the far right.

Tag Selector

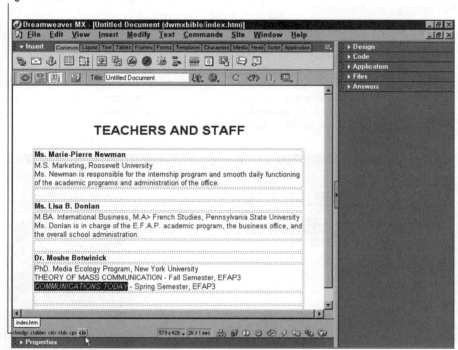

Figure 3-7: The Tag Selector enables you to highlight just the code you want. Here, selecting the `<i>` tag chooses only the italicized portion of the text.

As a Web page developer, you're constantly selecting elements in order to modify them. Rather than rely on the click-and-drag method to highlight an area — which often grabs unwanted sections of your code, such as `<font>` tags — use the Tag Selector to unerringly pick just the code you want. Dreamweaver's Tag Selector is a subtle but extremely useful tool that can speed up your work significantly.

Right-clicking (Control+clicking) an item in the Tag Selector displays a menu that contains several tag-editing commands. Using this menu in Design view, you can remove the tag or select a `class` or `id` attribute for the tag. From either Design view or Code view, you can also modify the tag by choosing Edit Tag from the context menu.

Window Size pop-up menu

The universality of the Internet enables virtually any type of computer system from anywhere in the world to access publicly available Web pages. Although this accessibility is a boon to global communication, it forces Web designers to be aware of how their creations look under various circumstances — especially different screen sizes.

The Window Size pop-up menu gives designers a sense of how their pages look on different monitors. Located just right of center on the status bar, the Window Size pop-up menu indicates the screen size of the current Document window, in pixels, in *width × height* format. If you resize your Document window, the Window Size indicator updates instantly. This indicator gives you an immediate check on the dimensions of the current page.

The Window Size pop-up menu goes beyond just telling you the size of your screen, however — it also enables you to quickly view your page through a wide variety of monitor sizes. Naturally, your monitor must be capable of displaying the larger screen dimensions before they can be selected.

To select a different screen size, click once on the expander arrow to the right of the displayed dimensions to display a menu listing the standard sizes, as shown in Figure 3-8. Click the desired size from the menu.

Note   If no sizes are listed in the status bar, you may be in Code view, described later in this chapter. Select View ➪ Design to gain access to the Window Size pop-up menu. If you can see the menu, but the options are disabled, your Document window is maximized (this happens only in the Dreamweaver MX integrated workspace).

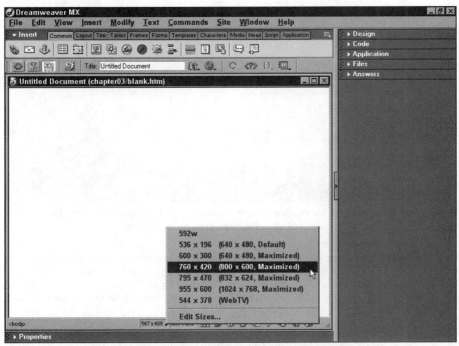

Figure 3-8: You can change your current screen size to any of seven standard sizes — or add your own custom sizes — with the Window Size pop-up menu.

The standard sizes, and their most common uses, are as follows:

✦ 592w

✦ 536 × 196 (640 × 480, Default)

✦ 600 × 300 (640 × 480, Maximized)

✦ 760 × 420 (800 × 600, Maximized)

✦ 795 × 470 (832 × 624, Maximized)

✦ 955 × 600 (1024 × 768, Maximized)

✦ 544 × 378 (WebTV)

The first option, 592w, is the only option that does not change the height as well as the width. Instead, this option uses the current window height and just alters the width.

Tip   You can set up your own custom screen settings by choosing Edit Sizes from the Window Size pop-up menu. This option opens the Status Bar category of the Preferences dialog box. Chapter 4 describes how to modify the pop-up list.

The dimensions offered by the Window Size pop-up menu describe the entire editable area of a page. The Document window has been carefully designed to match specifications set by the primary browsers. Both the left and right margins are the same width as both the Netscape and Microsoft browsers, and the status bar matches the height of the browser's bottom row as well. The height of any given browser environment depends on which toolbars are being used; however, Dreamweaver's menu bar is the same height as the browsers' menu bars.

Tip   If you want to compensate for the other browser user-interface elements, such as the toolbar and the Address bar (collectively called *chrome*), you can decrease the height of your Document window by approximately 72 pixels. Combined, Netscape Navigator's toolbar (44 pixels high) and Address bar (24 pixels high) at 68 pixels are slightly narrower than Internet Explorer's total chrome. Microsoft includes an additional bottom separator that adds 6 pixels to its other elements (toolbar, 42 pixels; and Address bar, 24) for a total of 72 pixels. Of course, with so many browser variables, the best design course is to leave some flexibility in your design.

Download Indicator

So, you've built your Web masterpiece, and you've just finished uploading the HTML, along with the 23 JPEGs, 8 audio files, and 3 Flash movies that make up the page. You open the page over the Internet and—surprise!—it takes five minutes to download. Okay, this example is a tad extreme, but every Web developer knows that opening a page from your hard drive and opening a page over the Internet are two vastly different experiences. Dreamweaver has taken the guesswork out of loading a page from the Web by providing the Download Indicator.

The Download Indicator is located to the right of the Window Size item on the status bar. As illustrated in Figure 3-9, Dreamweaver gives you two values, separated by a slash character:

✦ The cumulative size of the page, including all the associated graphics, plugins, and multimedia files, measured in kilobytes (K)

✦ The time it takes to download at a particular modem connection speed, measured in seconds (sec)

Tip You can check the download size of any individual graphic by selecting it and looking at the Property inspector—you can find the file size in kilobytes next to the thumbnail image on the left.

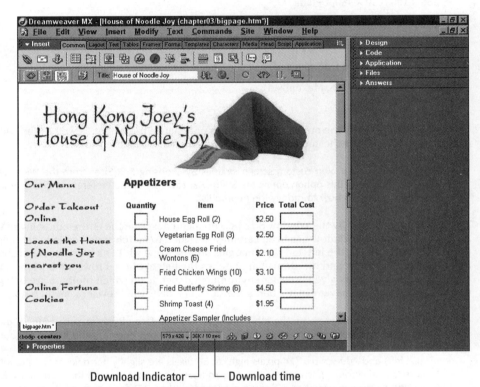

Download Indicator ⌐ └ Download time

Figure 3-9: Note the Download Indicator whenever you lay out a page with extensive graphics or other large multimedia files.

The Download Indicator is a handy real-world check. As you build your Web pages, it's a good practice to monitor your file's download size—both in kilobytes and seconds. As a Web designer, you ultimately have to decide what your audience will deem is worth the wait and what will have them reaching for that Stop button. For example, the graphic shown in Figure 3-9 is attractive, but at 36K, it's on the borderline of an acceptable size. Either the graphic should be resized or the colors reduced to lower the overall "weight" of the page.

 Cross-Reference Not everybody has the same modem connection. If you are working with an intranet or on a broadband site, you can set your connection speed far higher. Likewise, if your site gets a lot of traffic, you can lower the connection speed. Change the anticipated download speed through Dreamweaver's Preferences dialog box, as explained in Chapter 4.

Launcher

The final status bar tool is the Launcher. The Launcher enables you to quickly open the most commonly used Dreamweaver tool panels. A key feature of the Launcher is that it's completely customizable, so that you can gain quick access to the tools that you use most, and you can hide the tools you rarely need.

See Chapter 4 for details on customizing the Launcher to display the icons for your most frequently used tools.

The Launcher resides on the far right of the status bar. If you don't see the Launcher, you can display it by choosing Edit ➪ Preferences and in the Panels category, select the Show Icons in Panels and Launcher option. Likewise, you can hide the Launcher by clearing this option.

By default, the Launcher opens and closes the following panels, each of which handles a different aspect of the program:

✦ The Site panel handles all elements of publishing to the Web, as well as basic file maintenance such as moving and deleting folders.

✦ The Assets panel gives you access to the "assets" in your site—the objects that are the building blocks of your site, such as images, URLs, colors, and so on.

✦ The CSS Styles panel enables you to create and assign formatting styles to the content of your documents by using cascading style sheets.

✦ The Behaviors panel enables you to implement Dynamic HTML effects with relative ease, such as displaying a message box, changing the message in the browser status bar, or creating button rollover effects.

✦ The History panel shows the actions you've just taken in Dreamweaver, and enables you to undo or repeat any number of steps.

✦ The Bindings panel makes a variety of data sources available for your Web applications: database recordsets, form variables, session variables, server variables, and more.

✦ The Server Behaviors panel is the gateway for applying, modifying, and removing server-side scripts. Dreamweaver offers a number of standard server behaviors as well as the capability to construct your own with the Server Behavior Builder.

✦ The Components panel enables you to inspect and use ColdFusion, ASP.Net, or JavaServer Pages (JSP) components.

✦ The Databases panel lists any databases to which the site is connected. Using this panel, you can add, remove, or update database connections.

As with the Tag Selector, each one of the buttons in the Launcher lights up when the pointer passes over it, and it stays lit when selected. Selecting a button opens the panel. Clicking a Launcher button when a panel is already open has one of two effects. If the panel for the button is on top, the panel closes. If the panel is hidden behind another floating panel, the panel corresponding to the button is brought forward. Dreamweaver enables you to open multiple panels at the same time.

Accessing the Toolbars

Regardless of the job—whether it's hanging a picture or fixing a faucet—work goes faster when your tools are at your fingertips. The same principle holds true for Web site building: The easier it is to accomplish the most frequently required tasks, the more productive you'll be as a Web designer. Dreamweaver puts a number of repetitive tasks, such as previewing your page in a browser, just a function key away. However, there are far more necessary operations than there are function keys. In an effort to put needed functionality right up front, Dreamweaver incorporates two toolbars, Standard and Document, located across the top of the Document window. A third toolbar is available only when you are in Live Data view.

The Standard toolbar

When first enabled, the Standard toolbar appears across the top of the Dreamweaver window, whether you're in Design view or Code view. As shown in Figure 3-10, the Standard toolbar offers some of the most frequently used editing commands, familiar to you from any word processing program.

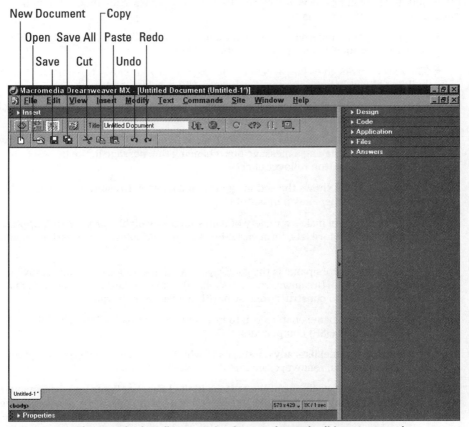

Figure 3-10: The Standard toolbar contains frequently used editing commands.

The first group of buttons you find on the Standard toolbar includes New Document, Open, and Save. These create a new document, open an existing document, and save the current document, respectively. The Save All button saves all open documents. The next set of buttons includes Cut, Copy, and Paste. These enable you to place a selected item on the clipboard, and paste it in another location. The final buttons on the Standard toolbar are the all-important Undo and Redo. Undo removes the effects of the last action you performed, and Redo repeats the most recent action or performs an undone action again.

The Standard toolbar itself is toggled on and off by choosing View ➪ Toolbars ➪ Standard. On Windows, you can reposition the Standard toolbar by clicking one of the separator bars between the toolbar buttons and then dragging. If you drag the standard toolbar away from the edge of the window, it becomes a floating toolbar. You can dock the standard toolbar by dragging it to the top or bottom edge of the window. On a Macintosh, the Standard toolbar cannot be repositioned.

The Document toolbar

The Document toolbar gives you quick access to commands that affect the entire document. Like the Standard toolbar, you can hide and show the Document toolbar with a menu command: View ➪ Toolbars ➪ Document. One of the Document toolbar's best features is the quick and easy access it offers to changing your Web page's title, as shown in Figure 3-11.

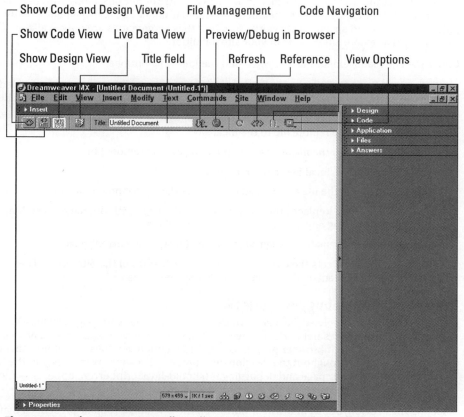

Figure 3-11: The Document toolbar offers easy access to an important element of a Web page, the title.

The first set of buttons in the Document toolbar is dedicated to the various views: Code, Code and Design, and Design. These buttons are mutually exclusive, as only one view can be shown at a time. To the right of the first three buttons is one more view-related button: Live Data view. As previously explained, when Live Data view is enabled, Dreamweaver sends your page to the testing server and incorporates the results in an editable format on the screen. When you switch to Live Data view, another toolbar becomes visible; this is described later in this chapter, in the section called "The Live Data toolbar."

Next to the Live Data View button is a text field for displaying and altering the title of your document. Dreamweaver, by default, titles every new page "Untitled Document." Not only is it considered bad form to keep this default title, search engines need a relevant title to properly index a site. To change a page title, enter the new text in the Title field and press Enter (Return) to confirm your modification.

Managing files

The File Management button, next to the Title field, contains Web publishing–related commands. While maintaining a Web site, you'll often be required to make small alterations such as changing a bit of text or rescaling an image. I prefer to post these changes as quickly as possible to get the work off my virtual desk. The Get and Put options, along with the Check In and Check Out options, found on the Document toolbar under File Management, greatly simplify the process and speed up my work. Note that these commands are only available if you have defined a remote site as part of your site definition.

Under the File Management button, you'll find the following options:

✦ **Turn off Read Only:** Unlocks the current file for editing. This command is enabled only if the current document is marked as read-only. (On the Macintosh, the Turn off Read Only option is called Unlock.)

✦ **Get:** Transfers the remote file to the local site.

✦ **Check Out:** Marks the file as checked out and gets the remote file.

✦ **Put:** Transfers the local file to the remote site.

✦ **Check In:** Marks the file as checked in and puts the file to the remote site.

✦ **Undo Check Out:** Replaces the local version of the page with the remote version, effectively undoing any changes made on the local file.

✦ **Design Notes:** Opens the Design Notes dialog box for the current page.

✦ **Locate in Site:** Selects the current page in the file listings of the Site panel. This command is only enabled if the current file has been saved.

Previewing and debugging your file

Although Dreamweaver gives you a good representation of what your page will look like when rendered in a browser, it's not perfect — even with Live Data view. There are so many variations among the different browser programs — not to mention versions — that you absolutely must test your page throughout the development process. Dreamweaver gives you the tools for both previewing your page and debugging it (should JavaScript errors appear) — and you can access those tools right from the Document toolbar.

Selecting the Preview/Debug in Browser button on the Document toolbar presents a dynamic list of available browsers. All of the browsers entered in Preferences appear first, with the primary and secondary browsers leading the list. After the preview commands, Dreamweaver displays debug options for all the supported browsers installed on the local system.

Note   Dreamweaver can preview in any browser you assign — however, the debugger only works with specific browsers. As of this writing, only Internet Explorer 4 and later and Netscape 4.x are supported.

The final entry under the toolbar's Preview/Debug in Browser button is Edit Browser List. When invoked, this command opens the Preview in Browser category of Preferences, enabling you to add, remove, or otherwise manage the browsers on your system in relation to Dreamweaver.

Cross-Reference See Chapter 4 for details about working with the Preview in Browser preferences.

Easy refresh and reference

The next two options on the Document toolbar are the Refresh button and the Reference button. Use the Refresh button when you've altered code directly in the Code view and you're ready to apply those changes in the Design view; this option is especially useful when the split-screen Code and Design view is in operation.

The Reference button opens the Reference panel, which contains reference documentation for HTML, JavaScript, style sheets, accessibility guidelines, and more. If a tag, attribute, JavaScript object, or CSS style rule is selected, choosing the Reference button causes the Reference panel to open to the pertinent entry.

Straightforward code navigation

Dreamweaver's code editor offers a number of key features for programming and debugging Web pages with increasingly complex JavaScript routines. Several of these features are grouped under the Code Navigation button found on the toolbar. One such feature is the capability to set *breakpoints*. Breakpoints are markers that temporarily halt the execution of the code when running the JavaScript Debugger. When the program execution is stopped, you can retrieve the current values of variables, and other information.

Although you can set breakpoints directly in the JavaScript Debugger, you can also set them in Dreamweaver's Code view. Position the cursor where you'd like the program to stop during debugging and choose Set Breakpoint from the Code Navigation button. After the first breakpoint is set, two additional commands are dynamically added: Remove Breakpoint and Remove All Breakpoints. Remove Breakpoint is only active when placed on the code line where a breakpoint was previously applied.

The remainder of the menu items under the Code Navigation button display JavaScript functions in the current page. Selecting any of these functions positions the cursor directly on that piece of code in Code view. This capability makes it easy to quickly move from function to function; it also tells you at a glance which functions are included in a page.

View options

View Options is a welcome but somewhat schizophrenic button found on the far right of the Document toolbar. The options that it makes available depend on the view mode currently employed. If, for example, you're in Design view and choose View Options, you're given the option to hide various visual aids, such as table borders or frame borders, individually or all at once. If, on the other hand, you're in Code view, View Options toggles code-oriented functions such as Word Wrap and Line Numbers. Best of all, if you're in the split-screen Code and Design view, you get both sets of view options! The view options (all of which act as toggles) under Design view are as follows:

✦ Hide All Visual Aids

✦ Visual Aids ⇨ Table Borders, Layer Borders, Frame Borders, Image Maps, and Invisible Elements

✦ Head Content

✦ Rulers

✦ Grid

✦ Tracing Image

✦ Design View on Top

When in Code view, the View Options are as follows:

✦ Word Wrap

✦ Line Numbers

✦ Highlight Invalid HTML

✦ Syntax Coloring

✦ Auto Indent

The Live Data toolbar

Dreamweaver's Live Data view has its own toolbar, shown in Figure 3-12. Enabling the Auto Refresh option forces Dreamweaver to update the data in the page whenever its data format is altered. For example, if you include a date field in your page, you might want to alter the format from something like March 31, 2002 to 31 March, 2002. The Auto Refresh option is particularly helpful when your data is enclosed by a Repeat Region server behavior. Auto Refresh, however, does not apply when the HTML formatting is modified; for example, making selected text bold or altering its color. To see the HTML format changes applied to all the Live Data, you'll need to select the Refresh button on the Live Data toolbar.

Live Data toolbar

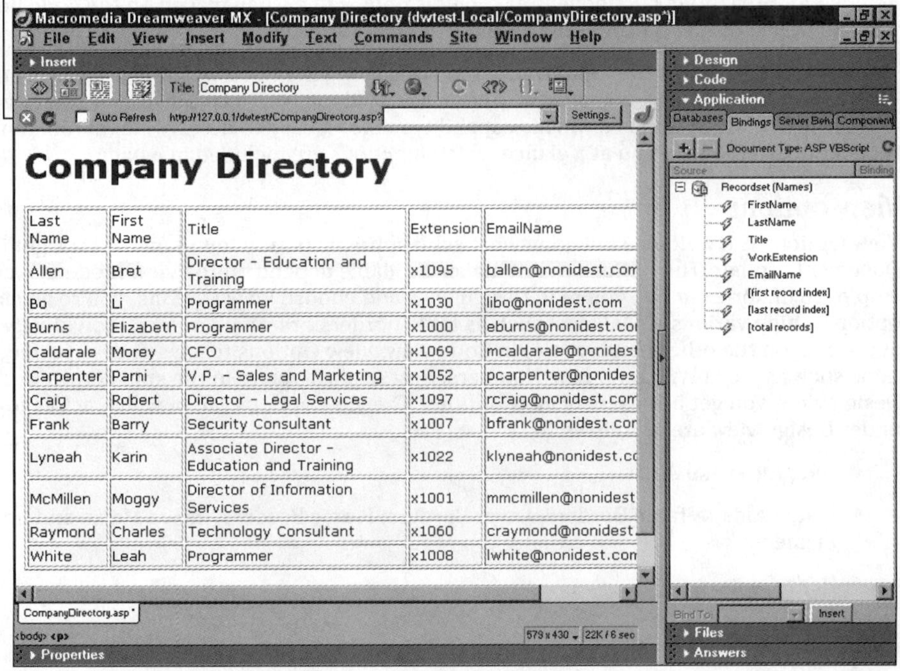

Figure 3-12: Live Data view has its own toolbar.

The Live Data toolbar also includes a field for entering URL parameters. This feature is handy when the dynamic content on your page requires an argument passed from a form or other method. By entering different values in the URL field, you can test your page under a variety of different data conditions.

Selecting from the Insert Bar

The Insert bar holds the items most frequently used — the primary colors, as it were — when designing Web pages. Everything from images to ActiveX plugins to HTML comments can be selected from the Insert bar. Figure 3-13 illustrates the Insert bar in the Dreamweaver MX workspace.

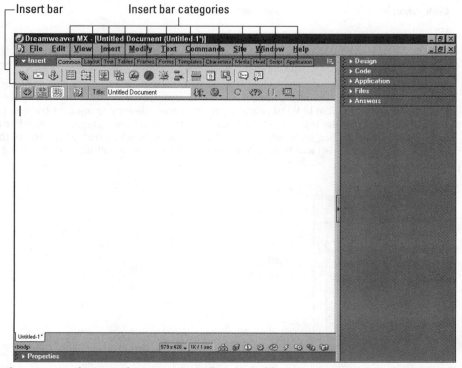

Figure 3-13: The Insert bar acts as a toolbox for holding your most commonly used Web page elements.

Cross-Reference The Insert bar is completely customizable — you can add your own favorite items and even set up how the Insert bar is organized. To learn how you can add custom Dreamweaver objects to the Insert bar, turn to Chapter 34.

The Insert bar is divided into separate categories of objects: Common, Layout, Text, Tables, Frames, Forms, Templates, Characters, Media, Head, Script and Application. Additional advanced categories are available for different types of server-side scripting languages: ASP, ASP.NET, CFML Basic, CFML Flow, CFML Advanced, JSP, and PHP. These advanced categories are available only when the currently open document is of the relevant file type, as determined by its file extension. Table 3-1 shows the file extensions related to each category.

Table 3-1: File Types for Advanced Categories

Insert Bar Category	Related File Extensions
ASP	.asp
ASP.NET	.aspx, .ascx
CFML Basic	.cfm, .cfc
CFML Flow	.cfm, .cfc
CFML Advanced	.cfm, .cfc
JSP	.jsp
PHP	.php, .php3

The initial view is of the Common category. In the Dreamweaver MX or HomeSite/Coder Style workspaces (only available in Windows), switch from one category to another by selecting the appropriate tab at the top of the Insert bar. To switch from one category to another in the Dreamweaver 4 workspace on Windows, select the small expander arrow at the top of the Insert bar (see Figure 3-14) and then choose an option from the resulting drop-down list.

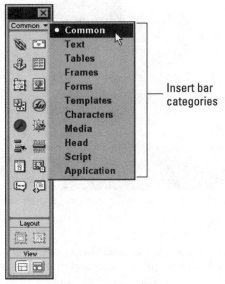

Insert bar categories

Figure 3-14: In the Dreamweaver 4 workspace, change categories in the Insert bar by clicking the expander arrow.

On a Macintosh, the appearance of the Insert bar depends on whether you have configured it to be horizontal or vertical. In the horizontal configuration, the categories on the Insert bar appear as tabs, like in the Dreamweaver MX workspace. In the vertical configuration, the Insert bar looks similar to that in the Windows Dreamweaver 4 workspace. Figure 3-15 illustrates both configurations of the Insert bar. To switch from the horizontal to the vertical orientation, click the Vertical Insert bar icon at the bottom of Insert bar. The Horizontal Insert bar icon for switching from the vertical to the horizontal configuration is on the right end of the Insert bar.

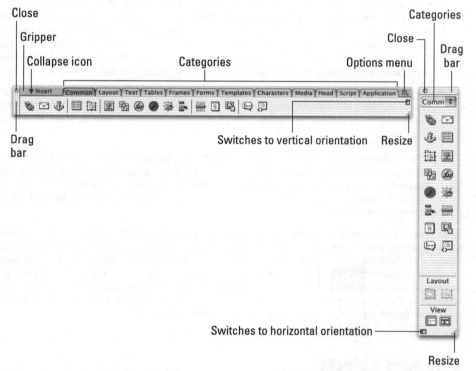

Figure 3-15: On a Macintosh, the Insert bar appears differently, depending on whether it is in its horizontal or vertical orientation.

If the Insert bar is not available when you first start Dreamweaver, you can enable it by choosing Window ➪ Insert or the keyboard shortcut, Ctrl+F2 (Command+F2). Likewise, choosing Window ➪ Insert (or the shortcut) again closes the Insert bar. On a Macintosh or in the Dreamweaver 4 workspace for Windows, you can also remove the Insert bar from your screen by clicking its Close button. In the Dreamweaver MX or HomeSite/Coder Style workspaces or when the Insert bar is in its horizontal orientation on Macintosh, you can choose Close Panel Group from the Options menu, located at the right of the Insert bar.

Tip   In the Dreamweaver MX and HomeSite/Coder Style workspaces, you can "window shade" the Insert bar by selecting the Collapse icon—the small triangle to the left of the toolbar name. Mac users can also do this by selecting the Collapse button.

To reposition the Insert bar, do one of the following:

✦ In the Dreamweaver 4 workspace on Windows, place your cursor over the drag bar at the top of the floating Insert bar and drag it to a new location. The Insert bar can be placed anywhere on the screen, not just over the Document window. Some Web designers like to size their Document window to a standard width that renders well across a variety of platforms and resolutions, and then place the Insert bar outside of that window so they have a clear canvas with which to work.

✦ In the Dreamweaver MX or HomeSite/Coder Style workspaces on Windows, the Insert bar can be docked at the top or bottom of the Dreamweaver window, or it can be undocked and treated as a floating panel. To move the Insert bar, first make sure the bar is not collapsed; then move the cursor over the gripper at the upper-left corner of the Insert bar, so that the cursor changes to a four-headed arrow and drag the Insert bar to the desired location. When it is floating, you can also move the Insert bar by clicking the drag bar and dragging, but the Insert bar can only be docked again using the gripper.

✦ On a Macintosh, you can move the Insert bar by clicking on the drag bar at the top (vertical configuration) or left (horizontal configuration) of the Insert bar and dragging to the desired location. When the Insert bar is oriented horizontally, you can also click and drag the gripper.

Tip

When the Insert bar is floating, you can dock other panels with it by dragging the tab of the panel onto the Insert bar. On a Macintosh or in the Dreamweaver MX or Coder/Coder Style workspaces, you can also drag the Insert bar on top of other panels, but only if they are floating. You cannot combine the Insert bar with panels that are already docked to the Dreamweaver window.

If the Insert bar is undocked, you can reshape it by positioning your pointer over the panel's border so that a double-headed arrow appears. Click and drag the rectangle into a new size or shape, and the icons within the Insert bar rearrange themselves to fit. If your resized Insert bar is too small to contain all the objects, a small scroll arrow is displayed. When you click the arrow, the Insert bar scrolls to show additional objects; at the same time, another arrow appears at the opposite side of the window to indicate more hidden objects. Mac users can resize the Insert bar only by dragging the lower-right corner.

The following sections describe each category in the Insert bar.

Common objects

The most frequently used HTML elements, aside from text, are accessible through the Common category of the Insert bar. Table 3-2 explains what each icon in the Common category represents.

Table 3-2: Common Category

Icon	Name	Description	Detailed Information
	Hyperlink	Use to Insert a link to another document	See Chapter 9
	Email Link	Inserts a text link that opens an e-mail form when selected	See Chapter 9
	Named Anchor	Inserts a target in a document, so that links can go to a particular place on a Web page	See Chapter 9

Icon	Name	Description	Detailed Information
	Insert Table	Creates a table at the cursor position	See Chapter 10
	Draw Layer	Enables you to drag out a layer of a specific size and shape at a specific location	See Chapter 21
	Image	Use for including any graphic (including animated GIFs) at the cursor position	See Chapter 8
	Image Placeholder	Visually reserves space in your document for an image file, which you can specify later	See Chapter 8
	Fireworks HTML	Inserts images and code generated by Fireworks	See Chapter 24
	Flash	Use to include a Flash movie	See Chapter 25
	Rollover Image	Inserts an image that changes into another image when the user's mouse moves over it	See Chapter 8
	Navigation Bar	Inserts a series of images with links used as buttons for navigation	See Chapter 8
	Horizontal Rule	Draws a line across the page at the cursor position	See Chapter 8
	Date	Inserts the current date in a user-selected format	See Chapter 7
	Tabular Data	Imports delimited data exported from a spreadsheet or database program and formats it as a table	See Chapter 10
	Comment	Places HTML comment tags inside your code; these comments are ignored by the browser	See Chapter 7
	Tag Chooser	Brings up a dialog box in which you can choose HTML or Scripting tags to enter at the text insertion point	See Chapter 6

Many of the common objects open a dialog box that enables you to browse for a file or specify parameters. If you prefer to enter all your information (including the necessary filenames) through the Property inspector or in Code view, you can turn off the automatic appearance of the dialog box for some objects when inserted through the Insert bar or the menus. Choose Edit ⇨ Preferences and, from the General category, clear the Show Dialog When Inserting Objects option. In the Common category, this option affects the Hyperlink, Email Link, Named Anchor, Insert Table, Image, Image Placeholder, and Flash objects.

Note Additional preferences settings, located in the Accessibility category of the Preferences dialog box, also cause dialog boxes to appear when you insert an object using the Insert bar. These accessibility dialog boxes appear even if the Show Dialog When Inserting Objects option is clear.

Layout objects

Use the Layout category of the Insert bar to work with tables and layers — objects that enable you to define the layout of your page. Dreamweaver offers you two ways to work with tables — Standard view, where you define the structure of a table using dialog boxes, menu commands, and the Property inspector, and Layout view, where you create tables and cells by drawing them. The Layout objects enable you to switch between Layout and Standard view, and create tables in either view.

In Windows, the Layout objects reside in a separate category only in the Dreamweaver MX and HomeSite/Coder Style workspaces. On a Macintosh, the Layout objects reside in a separate category only if the Insert bar is configured horizontally.

In the Dreamweaver 4 workspace on Windows or if the Insert bar is configured vertically on Macintosh, the same layout controls are available, but they are not grouped into a separate Layout category. Instead, the controls for switching between Standard and Layout view and for drawing Layout tables and cells are visible on the Insert bar for every category, as shown in Figure 3-16. The buttons for creating a table in Standard view and for drawing layers are available in the Common category of the Insert bar.

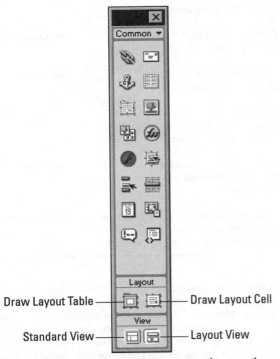

Draw Layout Table — Draw Layout Cell
Standard View — Layout View

Figure 3-16: In the Dreamweaver 4 workspace, the layout objects for working with Layout tables are visible in every category of the Insert bar.

Note Due to the visual nature of tables and layers, many of the objects in the Layout category can only be used in Design view.

Table 3-3 describes the Layout objects.

Table 3-3: Layout Category

Icon	Name	Description	Detailed Information
	Insert Table (Available in Dreamweaver MX and HomeSite/Coder Style workspaces for Windows, and when the Insert bar is in its horizontal configuration on a Macintosh)	Creates a table at the cursor position in either Code view or Design view. This button is not available in Layout view. If you are using the Dreamweaver 4 workspace for Windows, or if you are using a Macintosh with the Insert bar in its vertical configuration, this button can be found in the Common category.	See Chapter 10
	Draw Layer (Available in Dreamweaver MX and HomeSite/Coder Style workspaces for Windows, and when the Insert bar is in its horizontal configuration on a Macintosh)	Enables you to drag out a layer of a specific size and shape at a specific location. This button is not available in Layout view. If you are using the Dreamweaver 4 workspace for Windows, or if you are using a Macintosh with the Insert bar in its vertical configuration, this button can be found in the Common category.	See Chapter 21
Standard View	Standard view (For Dreamweaver MX and HomeSite/Coder Style workspaces in Windows or when the Insert bar is in its horizontal configuration on a Macintosh)	Switches the display of tables to Standard view, in which you create tables and cells using the menus, Table object, and Property inspector	See Chapter 10
	Standard view (For Dreamweaver 4 workspace in Windows or when the Insert bar is in its vertical configuration on a Macintosh)	Switches the display of tables to "Standard view," where you create tables and cells using the menus, Table object, and Property inspector. In the Dreamweaver 4 workspace (Windows) or if the Insert bar is in its vertical configuration (Macintosh), this button is available for every category.	See Chapter 10

Continued

Table 3-3: *(continued)*

Icon	Name	Description	Detailed Information
Layout View	Layout view (For Dreamweaver MX and HomeSite/Coder Style workspaces in Windows or when the Insert bar is in its horizontal configuration on a Macintosh)	Switches to a view of tables in which you can draw tables and cells by dragging the mouse	See Chapter 10
	Layout view (For Dreamweaver 4 workspace in Windows or when the Insert bar is in its vertical configuration on a Macintosh)	Switches to a view of tables in which you can draw tables and cells by dragging the mouse. In the Dreamweaver 4 workspace (Windows) or if the Insert bar is in its vertical configuration (Macintosh), this button is available for every category.	See Chapter 10
	Draw Layout Table	Enables you to drag the mouse to create a new table in a document. This object is only available in Layout view. In the Dreamweaver 4 workspace (Windows) or if the Insert bar is in its vertical configuration (Macintosh), this button is available for every category.	See Chapter 10
	Draw Layout Cell	Enables you to draw a cell within a table by dragging with the mouse. This object is only available in Layout view. In the Dreamweaver 4 workspace (Windows) or if the Insert bar is in its vertical configuration (Macintosh), this button is available for every category.	See Chapter 10

Text objects

The text objects represent the most commonly used text formatting HTML tags, such as those needed to emphasize text, change the font face, or create bulleted lists. Table 3-4 describes the objects you'll find in the Text category of the Insert bar.

The Text objects behave differently, depending on whether you are working in Design view or Code view. If you are working in Code view, Dreamweaver puts you in charge, and simply surrounds whatever text is selected with the appropriate HTML tags. If no text is selected, then the tag pair is inserted at the current text insertion point.

In Design view, selected text is also surrounded by the appropriate tag pair. But in some situations, Dreamweaver does more than blindly surround the selected text with the specified HTML tags. The following examples illustrate the additional processing that occurs in Design view:

✦ In Design view the Paragraph, Preformatted Text, Heading 1, Heading 2, and Heading 3 objects are treated as mutually exclusive. If you select text that is formatted as a Heading 1, and then you click the Heading 2 button on the Insert bar, Dreamweaver not only surrounds the selected text with `<h2></h2>` tags, but also removes the `<h1></h1>` tags that were there before. In Code view, Dreamweaver simply adds the `<h2></h2>` tags without automatically removing the `<h1></h1>` tags.

✦ When you select one or more paragraphs of text in Design view and then click the Unordered List button, Dreamweaver creates a bulleted list by inserting `<ul></ul>` tags around the selected text, as in Code view. But in Design view, Dreamweaver additionally converts each paragraph to be a separate item in that list by inserting the appropriate `<li></li>` tags. The same is true for Ordered lists and Definition lists.

In Design view, if no text is selected when you click a button in the Insert bar, no tags are added until you start typing. This feature helps prevent the inclusion of empty tag pairs within your document.

Table 3-4: Text Category

Icon	Name	Description	Detailed Information
	Font Tag Editor	Opens the Tag Editor dialog box for the `<font>` tag, where you can specify font choices, such as font face, size, and color	See Chapter 7
	Bold	Formats text as bold using either `<b></b>` or `<strong></strong>` tags. The tag used depends on a setting in the General category of the Preferences dialog box.	See Chapter 7
	Italic	Formats text as italic using `<i></i>` or `<em></em>` tags. The tag used depends on a setting in the General category of the Preferences dialog box.	See Chapter 7
	Strong	Formats text with strong emphasis, using `<strong></strong>` tags	See Chapter 7
	Emphasis	Adds emphasis to text using the `<em></em>` tag pair	See Chapter 7
	Paragraph	Creates a new paragraph by inserting the tags `<p></p>`	See Chapter 7
	Block Quote	Typically used to format long quotations, this inserts the tags `<blockquote></blockquote>`	See Chapter 7

Continued

Table 3-4: *(continued)*

Icon	Name	Description	Detailed Information
PRE	Preformatted Text	Inserts `<pre></pre>` tags, to indicate that the text should be displayed "as is," preserving spacing	See Chapter 7
h1	Heading 1	Formats text as a level 1 heading using the `<h1></h1>` tag pair	See Chapter 7
h2	Heading 2	Formats text as a level 2 heading using the `<h2></h2>` tag pair	See Chapter 7
h3	Heading 3	Formats text as a level 3 heading using the `<h3></h3>` tag pair	See Chapter 7
ul	Unordered List	Adds the code `<ul></ul>`, used to create a bulleted list	See Chapter 12
ol	Ordered List	Inserts `<ol></ol>` tags to create a numbered list	See Chapter 12
li	List Item	Inserts the tags `<li></li>`, used to denote an item within an ordered or unordered list	See Chapter 12
dl	Definition List	Adds the HTML code `<dl></dl>`, which is used to surround a definition list	See Chapter 12
dt	Definition Term	Inserts the `<dt></dt>` tags, which denote a term within a definition list	See Chapter 12
dd	Definition Description	Inserts a `<dd></dd>` pair, which marks the definition portion of a definition list entry	See Chapter 12
abbr.	Abbreviation	Opens a dialog box in which you can enter the full text for the abbreviation, before inserting the `<abbr></abbr>` tags	See Chapter 7
W3C	Acronym	Inserts `<acronym></acronym>` tags after opening a dialog box in which you can enter the expanded text of the acronym	See Chapter 7

Table objects

Primarily for use in Code view, the Tables category on the Insert bar provides quick access to the HTML tags used in defining tables. In Design view, only the Insert Table button is active in the Tables category of the Insert bar. The remaining objects are only available in Code view. In Design view, you can use instead the Layout objects on the Insert bar, the Property inspector, and the menus to work with tables. The objects in the Tables category are described in Table 3-5.

Table 3-5: Tables Category

Icon	Name	Description	Detailed Information
	Insert Table	Creates a table at the cursor position	See Chapter 10
tabl	Table Tag	Inserts just the `<table></table>` tags at the text insertion point or surrounding any selected text. Only available in Code view.	See Chapter 10
tr	Table Row	Inserts `<tr></tr>` tags at the text insertion point or surrounding selected text. The `<tr>` tag denotes a row within a table. Only available in Code view.	See Chapter 10
th	Table Header	Adds tags for a table header cell, `<th></th>`, at the text insertion point or around the selected text. Only available in Code view.	See Chapter 10
td	Table Data	Inserts `<td></td>` tags, which demark a cell within a table. The tags are added at the text insertion point or surrounding any selected text. Only available in Code view.	See Chapter 10
cap	Table Caption	Inserts `<caption></caption>` tags at the text insertion point or around any selected text. Only available in Code view.	See Chapter 10

Frames objects

In HTML terms, a *frame* is a collection of separate pages arranged on a single screen. Frames are contained within framesets. Because it involves multiple pages, creating a frameset can prove difficult for the novice designer. However, the process for making standard framesets is greatly simplified when using the Frames category objects. The most commonly used designs are now immediately available. Select any frame object, and the frameset is made, incorporating the existing page.

The blue, shaded area in the frame object icons indicates the frame in which the current page is placed when the frameset is created. For example, if you create a single page with the text "Table of Contents" and then choose the Top Frame object, "Table of Contents" is moved below the newly inserted top frame. All of the Frames category objects are described in Table 3-6.

Table 3-6: Frames Category

Icon	Name	Description	Detailed Information
	Left Frame	Inserts a blank frame to the left of the current page	See Chapter 14
	Right Frame	Inserts a blank frame to the right of the current page	See Chapter 14
	Top Frame	Inserts a blank frame above the current page	See Chapter 14
	Bottom Frame	Inserts a blank frame below the current page	See Chapter 14
	Bottom and Nested Left Frame	Makes a frameset with three frames; the bottom frame spans the width of the other frames. The current page is placed in the upper-right frame.	See Chapter 14
	Bottom and Nested Right Frame	Makes a frameset with three frames, with the bottom frame spanning the other frames. The current page appears in the upper-left frame.	See Chapter 14
	Left and Nested Bottom Frame	Opens a frameset with three frames. The left frame spans the other frames and Dreamweaver places the current page in the upper-right frame.	See Chapter 14
	Right and Nested Bottom Frame	Makes a frameset with three frames, with the right frame spanning the other frames. The current page is placed in the upper-left frame.	See Chapter 14
	Top and Bottom Frames	Inserts a three-frame frameset, with all frames spanning the width of the entire window. The current page goes in the center frame.	See Chapter 14
	Left and Nested Top Frames	Creates a frameset with three frames, with the left frame spanning the height of the other frames. Dreamweaver puts the current page in the lower-right frame.	See Chapter 14

Icon	Name	Description	Detailed Information
	Right and Nested Top Frames	Inserts a frameset with three frames, with the right frame spanning the height of the other frames. The current page is placed in the lower-left frame.	See Chapter 14
	Top and Nested Left Frames	Creates a frameset with three frames, with the upper frame spanning the width of the other frames. The current page is put in the lower-right frame.	See Chapter 14
	Top and Nested Right Frames	Inserts a frameset with three frames, with the top frame spanning the other frames. Dreamweaver inserts the current page in the lower-left frame.	See Chapter 14
fset	Frameset	Inserts the tags `<frameset>` `</frameset>` at the text insertion point or surrounding any selected text. Only available in Code view.	See Chapter 14
frm	Frame	Inserts the `<frame>` tag at the current text insertion point or around any selected text. Only available in Code view.	See Chapter 14
ifrm	Floating Frame	Inserts `<iframe></iframe>` tags to create a floating frame in the document. The tags are inserted at the current text insertion point or around the current selection. This object is available only in Code view.	See Chapter 14
	No Frames	Inserts the tags `<noframes>` `</noframes>`, which surround alternative content viewed in browsers that don't support frames. Only available in Code view.	See Chapter 14

Forms objects

The form is the primary method for implementing HTML interactivity. The Forms category of the Insert bar gives you the basic building blocks for creating your Web-based form. Table 3-7 describes each of the elements found in the Forms category.

Table 3-7: Forms Category

Icon	Name	Description	Detailed Information
	Form	Creates the overall HTML form structure at the cursor position. In Code view only, Dreamweaver wraps the `<form></form>` tags around any selected text.	See Chapter 11
	Text Field	Places a text box or a text area at the cursor position	See Chapter 11
	Hidden Field	Inserts an invisible field used for passing variables to a CGI or JavaScript program	See Chapter 11
	Textarea	Inserts a multiline text box	See Chapter 11
	Checkbox	Inserts a checkbox for selecting any number of options at the cursor position	See Chapter 11
	Radio Button	Inserts a radio button for making a single selection from a set of options at the cursor position	See Chapter 11
	Radio Group	Opens a dialog box in which you can define a group of related radio buttons	See Chapter 11
	List/Menu	Enables either a drop-down menu or a scrolling list at the cursor position	See Chapter 11
	Jump Menu	Opens a dialog box for building a pop-up menu that activates a link	See Chapter 11
	Image Field	Includes an image that can be used as a button	See Chapter 11
	File Field	Inserts a text box and Browse button for selecting a file to submit	See Chapter 11
	Button	Inserts a Submit, Reset, or user-definable button at the cursor position	See Chapter 11
	Label	Inserts a `<label></label>` tag pair in Code view. If you are in Design view, selecting this button automatically switches the Document window to Code and Design view before inserting the tags.	See Chapter 11
	Fieldset	Groups selected controls by inserting the tags `<fieldset></fieldset>`, with an optional legend	See Chapter 11

Template objects

Templates are special Dreamweaver documents that define the layout and visual design of a page. Once you've set up a template, you can create new pages based on that template, or apply the template to existing pages in your site. Pages based on a template inherit that template's design and layout. The objects in the Templates category of the Insert bar are described in Table 3-8.

Table 3-8: Templates Category

Icon	Name	Description	Detailed Information
	Make Template	Saves the current document as a template	See Chapter 28
	Make Nested Template	Makes a template based on another template	See Chapter 28
	Editable Region	Defines an area that can be modified in a document that is based on the template	See Chapter 28
	Optional Region	Delimits part of the template that may not appear within some of the documents that are based on the template	See Chapter 28
	Repeating Region	Defines structured content that may appear more than once within a document that is based on the template	See Chapter 28
	Editable Optional Region	Creates an area of optional content that may be modified in documents based on this template	See Chapter 28
	Repeating Table	Inserts a table with repeating editable rows into the template	See Chapter 28

Character objects

Certain special characters — such as the copyright symbol (©) — are represented in HTML by codes called *character entities*. In code, a character entity is either a name (such as © for the copyright symbol) or a number (©). Each character entity has its own unique code.

Dreamweaver eases the entry of these complex, hard-to-remember codes with the Characters category. The most commonly used characters are included as separate objects, and another button opens a dialog box with additional special characters from which to choose. Table 3-9 details the Characters category objects. The Characters category also contains objects for inserting a line break and a non-breaking space.

Table 3-9: Characters Category

Icon	Name	Description	Detailed Information
BR↵	Line Break	Inserts a ` ` tag that causes the line to wrap at the cursor position	See Chapter 7
⬇	Non-Breaking Space	Inserts a hard space at the current cursor position	See Chapter 6
"	Left Quote	Inserts the code for the opening curly double-quote symbol	See Chapter 6
"	Right Quote	Inserts the code for the closing curly double-quote symbol	See Chapter 6
—	Em Dash	Inserts the code for the em dash symbol	See Chapter 6
£	Pound	Inserts the code for the pound currency symbol	See Chapter 6
€	Euro	Inserts the code for the Euro currency symbol	See Chapter 6
¥	Yen	Inserts the code for the yen currency symbol	See Chapter 6
©	Copyright	Inserts the code for the copyright symbol	See Chapter 6
®	Registered Trademark	Inserts the code for the registered trademark symbol	See Chapter 6
TM	Trademark	Inserts the code for the trademark symbol	See Chapter 6
⌗	Other Character	Opens the dialog box for inserting special characters	See Chapter 6

Media objects

Part of HTML's power is its ability to go beyond its native capabilities by including special objects. Dreamweaver facilitates the inclusion of external elements — such as multimedia animations, Java applets, plugins and ActiveX controls — through the Media category of the

Insert bar. Some of these objects, such as Flash buttons, can be viewed directly in the Document window; for others, such as ActiveX controls, Dreamweaver inserts a placeholder in the page, but the actual content must be viewed in a browser. Table 3-10 details the Media objects.

Table 3-10: Media Category

Icon	Name	Description	Detailed Information
	Flash	Use to include a Flash movie	See Chapter 25
	Flash Button	Creates a Flash button	See Chapter 25
	Flash Text	Makes a Flash headline or other rollover text	See Chapter 25
	Shockwave	Use to include a Shockwave movie	See Chapter 25
	Applet	Includes a Java applet at the cursor position	See Chapter 6
	param	Inserts a `<param>` tag in Code view, used to specify settings within `<applet>` and `<object>` tags	See Chapter 6
	ActiveX	Inserts a placeholder for an ActiveX control at the cursor position, using the `<object>` tag	See Chapters 25 and 27
	Plugin	Use for including a file that requires a plugin	See Chapters 25, 26, and 27

Head objects

General document information—such as the title and any descriptive keywords about the page—are written into the `<head>` section of an HTML document. The Head category enables Web designers to drop in these bits of code in a handy object format. These objects insert `<meta>` tags with keywords for search engines; specify refresh times; and do many more tasks that affect a Web site's overall performance.

Although Dreamweaver enables you to see the `<head>` objects onscreen via the View ➪ Head Content menu option, you don't have to have the Head Content visible to drop in the objects. Simply click any of the objects detailed in Table 3-11, and a dialog box opens, prompting you for the needed information.

Table 3-11: Head Category

Icon	Name	Description	Detailed Information
	Meta	Includes document information usable by servers and browsers	See Chapter 6
	Keywords	Inserts keywords used by search engines to catalog the Web page	See Chapter 6
	Description	Provides a description of the current page	See Chapter 6
	Refresh	Sets a tag to refresh the current page or redirect the browser to another URL	See Chapter 6
	Base	Specifies the base address of the current document	See Chapter 6
	Link	Declares a relationship between the current document and another object or file	See Chapter 6

Script objects

Increasingly, documents on the Web are moving away from being simply a static presentation of text and images. Pages can be made dynamic by adding scripts to them; for example, Dreamweaver automatically adds JavaScript to pages to create rollover buttons and navigation bars. In fact, many Dreamweaver commands and behaviors insert pre-written scripts into your page. However, if you want to write your own scripts, the Script category can simplify this task. Table 3-12 describes the objects in the Script category.

Table 3-12: Script Category

Icon	Name	Description	Detailed Information
	Script	Inserts `<script></script>` tags, which enable you to add JavaScript or VBScript either directly or from a file	See Chapter 6
	Noscript	Inserts `<noscript></noscript>` tags in Code view, which surround content that displays in browsers that don't support scripting	See Chapter 6
	Server-Side Include	Inserts a directive that indicates to the server that another file should be displayed within the current document	See Chapter 29

> **Note**
>
> If the Show Dialog when Inserting Objects option is set in the General category of the Preferences dialog box, when you choose the Script or Server-Side Include objects, dialog boxes open to guide you in specifying relevant information. If the preferences option is clear, the dialog boxes do not appear.

Application objects

Although the layout of a Web page and the dynamic content that fills it may vary widely, many of the structures underlying basic Web applications remain the same. For example, the same basic code that is used to insert employee records into a Human Resources database may be used to add a new entry into a database that maintains a DVD collection. Dreamweaver removes much of the tedium of scripting common Web applications by supplying objects in the Application category of the Insert bar.

With a single Application object, you can build an entire Web application that displays a list of records, enables you to navigate through them, displays which records are currently onscreen, and links to another page with detailed information from a selected record. Dreamweaver's Application objects may be used separately or together. The Master Detail Page Set object, shown in Figure 3-17, includes two other Application objects: the Recordset Navigation Bar object and the Recordset Navigation Status object.

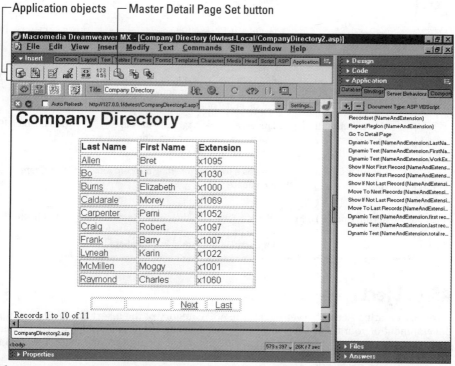

Figure 3-17: Common Web applications, such as the Master Detail Page Set, are created in one action with Dreamweaver's Application objects.

Application objects are particularly powerful when combined with Dreamweaver's template feature. It's possible, for example, to create a basic Master Detail Page Set with the Application object and then apply a template to give the page a specific look and feel, thereby integrating it into a site. The Application objects are outlined in Table 3-13.

Table 3-13: Application Category

Icon	Name	Description	Detailed Information
	Recordset	Opens a dialog box in which you can define the subset of data to be extracted from a database	See Chapter 15
	Repeated Region	Alters the selected dynamic area of the page so that data from more than one record is displayed on the page at a time	See Chapter 17
	Dynamic Table	Inserts a table in the document that is populated with data from a recordset you have defined	See Chapter 17
	Dynamic Text	Adds data from a recordset to the document	See Chapter 16
	Recordset Navigation Bar	Includes the server behavior for a text- or graphics-based navigation bar for moving among records	See Chapter 17
	Recordset Navigation Status	Adds a server behavior for showing which records are currently displayed out of a total number of records available	See Chapter 17
	Master Detail Page Set	Creates a master page with data in a repeated region and navigation elements, along with a detail page	See Chapter 19
	Record Insertion Form	Creates a form for inserting a record into a database	See Chapter 19
	Record Update Form	Places a table with the desired form fields on the page along with the server behavior for updating the record in a database	See Chapter 19

ASP objects

If you are creating Active Server Pages, the ASP category of the Insert bar can speed up the development of your code. Only available when the current document is named with an extension of .asp, this category contains the building blocks of an ASP page. Table 3-14 describes each of the objects in the ASP category.

Table 3-14: ASP Category

Icon	Name	Description
	Server Variable	Opens a dialog box in which you can choose one member of the server variables collection to reference in your code
#	Include	Inserts a #include statement for implementing a server-side include
<%	Code Block	Inserts the <% %> delimiters, used to enclose a code block
<%=	Output	Inserts the <%= %> delimiters, used to enclose an output statement
if	If	Inserts an If-Then conditional statement in the ASP code
else	Else	Inserts an Else statement in the ASP code
elsif	Else If	Inserts an ElseIf statement in the ASP code, used to create alternative conditions
end	End	Inserts the ASP code to signal the end of an If statement
	Response.Write	Inserts the statement for passing data from the server to the browser for display
	Trimmed Form Element	Inserts the code for trimming elements in a form
	Trimmed QueryString Element	Inserts the code for referencing trimmed elements in a QueryString collection
	Server.CreateObject	Adds the Server.CreateObject method, used to instantiate ASP components or scripting objects
	More Tags	Opens the Tag Chooser dialog box, giving you access to additional tags

ASP.NET objects

The ASP.NET category is only available on the Insert bar if the active document has a file extension of .aspx or .ascx. The objects in this category, described in Table 3-15, give you quick access to frequently referenced elements of an ASP.NET page.

Caution

There is a known issue in which the ASP.NET category of the Insert bar is not initially accessible with an open .aspx file. The problem occurs if your testing server is not set to one of the ASP.NET options or if you change an file to .aspx format by changing its extension rather than creating the file through Dreamweaver's New Document feature. To make the ASP.NET objects accessible, select the Document Type link on the Components panel and choose either ASP.NET C# or ASP.NET VB.

Table 3-15: ASP.NET Category

Icon	Name	Description
	Register Custom Tag	Inserts the code required to create custom tags, which you can use to implement new server behaviors
	Import Namespace	Adds the statement `<%@ Import Namespace="" %>` to your code
	Trimmed Form Element	Inserts the code for trimming elements in a form
	Trimmed QueryString Element	Inserts the code for referencing trimmed elements in a QueryString collection
	Runat Server	Inserts the code `runat="server"` at the current location
	Bound Data	Inserts the `<%# %>` delimiters for bound data
	Page_Load	Inserts a Page_Load subroutine
	asp:button	Inserts a .NET Form Control button in a form
	asp:checkbox	Inserts a .NET Form Control checkbox in a form
	asp:checkboxlist	Inserts a .NET Form Control for a checkbox list, a listing of a dataset as a series of checkboxes

Icon	Name	Description
	asp:dropdownlist	Inserts a .NET Form Control drop-down list in a form
	asp:imagebutton	Inserts a .NET Form Control graphical button in a form
	asp:label	Inserts a .NET Form Control label for an element in a form
	asp:listbox	Inserts a .NET Form Control list box in a form
	asp:radiobutton	Inserts a .NET Form Control single radio button in a form
	asp:radiobuttonlist	Inserts a .NET Form Control radio button list, a series of related radio buttons listed from a dataset
	asp:textbox	Inserts a .NET Form Control textbox in a form
	More Tags	Opens the Tag Chooser dialog box, giving you access to additional ASP.NET tags

CFML Basic objects

The CFML Basic category of the Insert bar gives you access to the most frequently used objects in the ColdFusion toolbox. This category is only available on the Insert bar if the active document has a file extension of .cfm or .cfc. Table 3-16 describes each object in the CFML Basic category.

Table 3-16: CFML Basic Category

Icon	Name	Description
	Server Variable	Opens a dialog box in which you can choose one member of the server variables collection to reference in your code
	cfquery	Opens the Tag Editor for the cfquery tag, which queries a data source

Continued

Table 3-16: *(continued)*

Icon	Name	Description
out	cfoutput	Opens the Tag Editor for specifying attributes of the `cfoutput` tag
	cfinsert	Opens the Tag Editor for specifying attributes of the `cfinsert` tag, for adding form data to a data source
	cfupdate	Opens the Tag Editor for specifying attributes of the `cfupdate` tag, for updating records in a data source
	cfinclude	Opens the Tag Editor for specifying attributes of the `cfinclude` tag, used to include a file in a ColdFusion page
	cflocation	Opens the Tag Editor, in which you can specify the file to open when the `cflocation` tag is processed
set	cfset	Inserts the `<cfset >` tag at the current location; used to set the value of a variable
!	cfparam	Opens the Tag Editor for the `<cfparam>` tag
`<!---`	Comment	Inserts the code for a comment
#...#	Surround with #	Inserts # characters around the selected text
	cfscript	Inserts `<cfscript></cfscript>` tags at the current location or around the selected text, designating a block of ColdFusion code

Tip   You can find detailed descriptions of the ColdFusion tags in the Reference panel. To view the ColdFusion documentation, select Window ➪ Reference, and then select Macromedia CFML Reference from the Book drop-down list.

CFML Flow objects

The CFML Flow category on the Insert bar includes objects for inserting ColdFusion markup tags that alter the flow of control through the code. These include tags for handling exceptions, such as error conditions, as well as tags for implementing conditional statements and looping. Table 3-17 describes the objects in the CFML Flow category.

Table 3-17: CFML Flow Category

Icon	Name	Description
	cftry	Inserts the `<cftry></cftry>` exception handling tags at the current location
	cfcatch	Opens the Tag Editor for the `<cfcatch></cfcatch>` tags, used to intercept and process an interruption in the program flow
	cfthrow	Opens the Tag Editor for `<cfthrow>`, which forces an interruption in the program flow
	cflock	Opens the Tag Editor for the `<cflock></cflock>` tag pair, used to serialize access to shared data
	cfswitch	Opens the Tag Editor for a `<cfswitch></cfswitch>` pair, where you can define the expression to be evaluated in the ColdFusion version of a Case statement
case	cfcase	Opens the Tag Editor for a `<cfcase></cfcase>` tag pair; these tags enclose the actions to be taken when the expression specified by `<cfswitch>` has a given value
def	cfdefaultcase	Inserts `<cfdefaultcase> </cfdefaultcase>` tags, which specify what action should be taken when the expression specified by the `<cfswitch>` tag has a value not specified in any `<cfcase>` tag
if	cfif	Inserts `<cfif ></cfif>` tags, used to indicate a conditional statement
else	cfelse	Inserts a `<cfelse>` tag, used to specify what actions are to be taken if the original condition from the associated `<cfif>` statement was not met
elsif	cfelseif	Inserts a `<cfelseif>` tag, used to implement alternative conditions
	cfloop	Opens the Tag Editor for the `<cfloop> </cfloop>` pair, which are used to repeat statements until some condition is met
	cfbreak	Inserts the `<cfbreak>` tag, used to exit a `<cfloop>` before the specified loop condition is met

CFML Advanced objects

The Insert bar's CFML Advanced category provides objects for ColdFusion tags that provide numerous advanced functions, many of which enable you to transfer files and data using a variety of protocols. The More Tags button also gives you access to ColdFusion tags not available elsewhere on the Insert bar. Table 3-18 describes the objects in the CFML Advanced category.

Table 3-18: CFML Advanced Category

Icon	Name	Description
	cfcookie	Opens the Tag Editor for the `<cfcookie>` tag, which is used to save cookies — small amounts of textual information — on the client's hard drive
	cfcontent	Opens the Tag Editor for the `<cfcontent>` tag, where you can specify the type of encoding used in the file
	cfheader	Opens the Tag Editor for you to specify `<cfheader>` tag attributes
	ColdFusion Page Encoding	Adds tags to specify page encoding and content type
	cfapplication	Opens the Tag Editor for the `<cfapplication>` tag, where you can specify session and application characteristics, such as timeout values
	cferror	Opens the Tag Editor for the `<cferror>` tag, which enables your code to define a particular page to display when an error occurs
	cfdirectory	Opens the Tag Editor for the `<cfdirectory>` tag, which enables your code to create, rename, delete, and obtain the contents of server directories
	cffile	Opens the Tag Editor for the `<cffile>` tag, which enables your code to read, write, update, copy, delete, upload, rename, and move server files
	cfmail	Opens the Tag Editor for the `<cfmail> </cfmail>` tag pair, which enables your code to send an e-mail message with dynamic content
	cfpop	Opens the Tag Editor for the `<cfpop>` tag, enabling you to read e-mail messages or message headers from the server, and to delete them
	cfhttp	Opens the Tag Editor for the `<cfhttp></cfhttp>` tag pair, enabling your code to upload files using HTTP protocol
	cfhttpparam	Opens the Tag Editor for the `<cfhttpparam>` tag, needed if the `method` specified in the `<cfhttp>` tag is `post`
	cfldap	Opens the Tag Editor for you to specify parameters for the `<cfldap>` tag, used to communicate with an LDAP server

Icon	Name	Description
	cfftp	Opens the Tag Editor for the `<cfftp>` tag, which your code can use to transfer files to and from an FTP server
	cfsearch	Opens the Tag Editor for the `<cfserach>` tag, which enables your code to search a collection
	cfindex	Opens the Tag Editor for the `<cfindex>` tag, which adds indexed entries to a pre-existing collection; this is required before the collection can be searched
	cfmodule	Opens the Tag Editor for the `<cfmodule>` tag, used to call a custom tag
	cfobject	Opens the Tag Editor for you to specify `<cfobject>` parameters
	cfchart	Opens the Tag Editor for a `<cfchart></cfchart>` tag pair, for graphically depicting data
	More Tags	Opens the Tag Chooser dialog box, which gives you access to additional ColdFusion tags

JSP objects

The JSP category on the Insert bar includes objects that aid in adding code specific to JavaServer Pages. This category is only visible when the currently active document has a file extension of `.jsp`. Table 3-19 describes the objects in the JSP category.

Table 3-19: JSP Category

Icon	Name	Description
	Page Directive	Inserts the code for a Page directive, `<%@ page %>`, at the current location in the document
	Include Directive	Inserts an Include directive, `<%@ include %>`, used to include either a static HTML page or another JSP page in the document
	Taglib Directive	Inserts the code to implement the Taglib directive, `<%@ taglib %>`, for working with custom tag libraries

Continued

Table 3-19: *(continued)*

Icon	Name	Description
`<%!`	JSP Declaration	Inserts the code for a JSP declaration, `<%!  %>`, which encloses the definitions for page-level variables and supporting methods
`<%`	JSP Scriptlet	Inserts the code `<%  %>`, used to delimit a block of Java code
`<%=`	JSP Expression	Inserts the code `<%=  %>`, used to enclose a Java expression, at the current location in the document or around the selected text
	JSP Use Bean	Opens the Tag Editor for the `<jsp:useBean />` tag, which is required before you can access a bean within a JSP page
	JSP Set Property	Opens the Tag Editor for the `<jsp:setProperty />` tag, which is used to store the value of a property
	JSP Get Property	Opens the Tag Editor for the `<jsp:getProperty />` tag, which retrieves the current value of a property
	JSP Include	Opens the Tag Editor for the `<jsp:include />` tag, which includes another static HTML page or JSP file at runtime
	JSP Forward	Opens the Tag Editor for the `<jsp:forward />` tag, which redirects a request to another JSP, servlet, or static HTML page
	JSP Params	Inserts the `<jsp:params></jsp:params>` tag pair at the current location in the document
	JSP Param	Opens the Tag Editor for the `<jsp:param />` tag, which is used to provide additional information for other tags, such as `jsp:include` and `jsp:forward`
	JSP Plugin	Opens the Tag Editor for the `<jsp:plugin />` tag, where you can specify a bean or Java applet to use
	JSP Comment	Inserts the code for a JSP comment
	More Tags	Opens the Tag Chooser dialog box, which gives you access to additional JSP tags

Tip   You can get information about JSP tags without leaving Dreamweaver. To view the JSP documentation, select Window ⇨ Reference, and then select Wrox JSP Reference from the Book drop-down list.

PHP objects

The PHP category of the Insert bar enables you to insert code used in the PHP server-side scripting language. This category is only available if you are working in a document with the extension of .php or .php3. Table 3-20 describes the PHP objects available in the Insert bar.

Table 3-20: PHP Category

Icon	Name	Description
	Form Variables	Inserts a reference to $HTTP_POST_VARS, used to retrieve form data passed using the Post method
	URL Variables	Inserts a reference to $HTTP_GET_VARS, used to retrieve information passed using the GET method
	Session Variables	Inserts a reference to $HTTP_SESSION_VARS, an array that contains session variables available to the script
	Cookie Variables	Inserts a reference to $HTTP_COOKIE_VARS, used to retrieve information passed to the script using cookies
	Include	Inserts code to include either a static HTML page or another PHP page in the document. During execution, if an error is encountered reading the included file, a warning is issued.
	Require	Inserts code to include either a static HTML page or another PHP page in the document. During execution, if an error is encountered reading the included file, a fatal error occurs.
	Code Block	Inserts the code <?php ?>, used to define a block of code, at the current location or surrounding selected text
	Echo	Inserts the code to output data
	Comment	Inserts the code for a PHP comment
	If	Inserts the tag used to conditionally execute code

Continued

Table 3-20: *(continued)*

Icon	Name	Description
else	Else	Inserts the tag used to indicate the actions taken when the conditions specified in the corresponding If statement are not met
	More Tags	Opens the Tag Chooser dialog box, which gives you access to additional PHP tags

Getting the Most Out of the Property Inspector

Dreamweaver's Property inspector is your primary tool for specifying an object's particulars. What exactly those particulars are — in HTML, they are known as *attributes* — depends on the object itself. The contents of the Property inspector vary depending on which object is selected. For example, click anywhere on a blank Web page, and the Property inspector shows text attributes for format, font name and size, and so on. If you click an image, the Property inspector displays a small thumbnail of the picture, and the image's attributes for height and width, image source, link, and alternative text. Figure 3-18 shows a Property inspector for an image with an attached hyperlink.

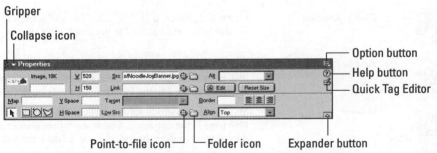

Figure 3-18: The Property inspector takes many forms, depending on which HTML element you select.

Manipulating the Property inspector

You can enable the Property inspector by choosing Window ➪ Properties or selecting the keyboard shortcut, Ctrl+F3 (Command+F3). As with the Insert bar, the Property inspector can be closed by selecting the Close button (only available if the Property inspector is floating), unchecking Window ➪ Properties, or choosing the keyboard shortcut again. You can also close the Property inspector by selecting Close Panel Group from the Options menu, which is accessed by clicking the Option button at the right of the Properties inspector title bar. On Macintosh OS9 and in the Dreamweaver MX or HomeSite/Coder Style workspaces on Windows, you can window shade the Property inspector so that only the title bar is left showing by clicking the collapse button on its window.

You can reposition the Property inspector in one of the following ways:

✦ If the Property inspector is floating, you can click and drag the drag bar that appears along the left edge of the window and move it to a new location, or — unlike the Insert bar — you can click and drag any open gray area in the floating inspector itself (on Windows only). This technique is handy for quickly moving the inspector aside, out of your way. When you move the floating inspector near the edge of the screen or near a window border, the Property inspector will snap to the edge of the window or screen.

✦ In the Dreamweaver MX and HomeSite/Coder Style workspaces, whether the inspector is docked or floating, you can move it by clicking on the gripper and dragging the inspector. In these workspaces, the Property inspector can be docked at the top or the bottom of the Dreamweaver window. If you move or resize the Dreamweaver window, the docked Property inspector will move with the window.

The Property inspector initially displays the most typical attributes for a given element. To see additional properties, click the expander arrow in the lower-right corner of the Property inspector. Virtually all the inserted objects have additional parameters that can be modified. Unless you're tight on screen real estate, it's a good idea to keep the Property inspector expanded so you can see all your options.

Tip   In addition to using the expander arrow, you can reveal (or hide) the expanded attributes by double-clicking any open gray area of the Property inspector.

Property inspector elements

Many of the attributes in the Property inspector are text boxes; just click in any one and enter the desired value. If a value already appears in the text box, whether a number or a name, double-click it (or click and drag over it) to highlight the information and then enter your new data — the old value is immediately replaced. You can see the effect your modification has had by pressing the Tab key to move to the next attribute or by clicking in the Document window.

Using the Quick Tag Editor, Dreamweaver enables you to make small additions to the code without switching to Code view. Located on the right of the Property inspector just below the Help button, the Quick Tag Editor pops open a small window to display the code for the currently selected tag. You can swiftly change attributes or add special parameters not found in the Property inspector.

For several attributes, the Property inspector also provides drop-down list boxes that offer a limited number of options from which you can choose. To open the drop-down list of available options, click the arrow button to the right of the list box. Then choose an option by highlighting it.

Tip   Some options on the Property inspector are a combination drop-down list and text box — you can select from available options or type in your own values. For example, when text is selected, the font name and size are combination list/text boxes.

If you see a folder icon next to a text box, you have the option of browsing for a filename on your local or networked drive, or manually inputting a filename. Clicking the folder opens a standard Open File dialog box (called Select File in Dreamweaver); after you've chosen your file and clicked OK (Open or Choose on Macintosh), Dreamweaver inputs the filename and any necessary path information in the correct attribute.

Dreamweaver enables you to quickly select an onscreen file (in either a Document window or the Site panel) as a link, with its Point to File icon, found next to the folder icon. Just click and drag the Point to File icon until it touches the file (or the filename from the Site panel) that you want to reference. The path is automatically written into the Link text box.

New Feature

For text objects, the Property inspector can toggle between two modes of operation — CSS and HTML modes. If you want to use cascading style sheets to style your text, click the Toggle HTML/CSS Mode icon, located to the right of the Format text box, to display controls for defining and assigning CSS styles to your text. If you would prefer to use HTML tags, such as `<font>`, to style and size your text, click the Toggle HTML/CSS Mode icon again. Figure 3-19 shows both versions of the Text Property inspector.

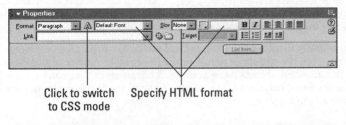

Click to switch to CSS mode   Specify HTML format

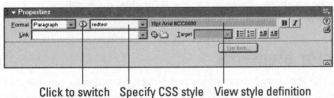

Click to switch to HTML mode   Specify CSS style   View style definition

Figure 3-19: Using the Text Property inspector, you can style text with HTML tags or with CSS styles.

Certain objects such as text, layers, and tables enable you to specify a color attribute. The Property inspector alerts you to these options with a small color box next to the text box. You can type in a color's name (such as "blue") or its six-figure hexadecimal value ("#3366FF"), or select the color box. Choosing the color box opens a color picker, shown in Figure 3-20, that displays the colors common to both the Netscape and Microsoft browsers — the so-called *browser-safe colors*. You can go outside of this range by clicking the System Color Picker icon in the upper-right corner of the color picker. This opens a full-range Color dialog box in which you can choose a color visually or enter its red, green, and blue values or its hue, saturation, and luminance values.

The color picker in Dreamweaver is very flexible. Not only can you choose from a series of color swatches, but you can also select any color onscreen with Dreamweaver's Eyedropper tool. The Eyedropper button has two modes: If you select Snap to Web Safe from the color picker's context menu, the Eyedropper snaps the selected color to its nearest Web-safe neighbor; if you deselect Snap to Web Safe, colors are sampled exactly. If you'd like to access the system color picker, the color wheel button opens it up for you. You can also use the Default Color tool, which deletes any color choice previously inserted. Finally, you can use the color picker's context menu to change the swatch set shown. By default, the Color Cubes view is shown, but you may also view swatches in a Continuous Tone configuration or in Windows OS, Macintosh OS, or Grayscale colors. Although the Web designer may not use these options may frequently, Macromedia standardized the color picker across its product line to make it easier to switch between applications.

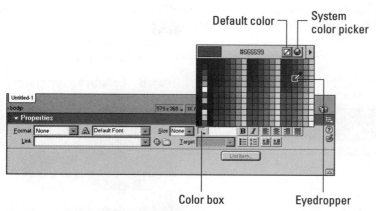

Figure 3-20: Dreamweaver's color picker enables you to choose from a wide selection of colors, from the palette or right off the desktop, with the Eyedropper tool.

Tip To close the color picker without selecting a color, click in the empty gray area at the top of the color picker.

In the Dreamweaver MX and HomeSite/Coder Style workspaces, the Property inspector also includes an Options menu. Open this context-sensitive menu by clicking the Options menu icon, located in the upper-right corner of the Property inspector. The commands on this menu vary depending on what type of object has been selected in the Document window. Some basic commands, however, are always available, regardless of what has been selected. These include the following:

    ✦ **Help:** Opens a Help topic for the current Property inspector

    ✦ **Rename Panel Group:** Enables you to rename the Property inspector

    ✦ **Close Panel Group:** Closes the Property inspector

Note Two additional commands that are typically available for panels, Group Properties With, and Maximize Panel Group, are disabled for the Property inspector. You cannot dock the Property inspector with other panels, and you cannot change the height of the Property inspector.

Another aspect of the Property inspector is worth noting: The circled question mark in the upper-right corner of the Property inspector is the Help button. Selecting this button invokes online Help and displays specific information about the particular Property inspector you're using.

Customizing Your Workspace with Dockable Panels

Dreamweaver is known for its powerful set of tools: behaviors, layers, timelines, and so much more. Dreamweaver presents its tools in a variety of panels, as shown in Figure 3-21. Panels can be combined into the same window; when grouped together in this way, each panel is displayed as a tab within the panel group. The panel groups can be floating or docked to each other. If you're using the Dreamweaver MX or HomeSite/Coder Style workspaces, the panel groups can also be docked within the Dreamweaver window.

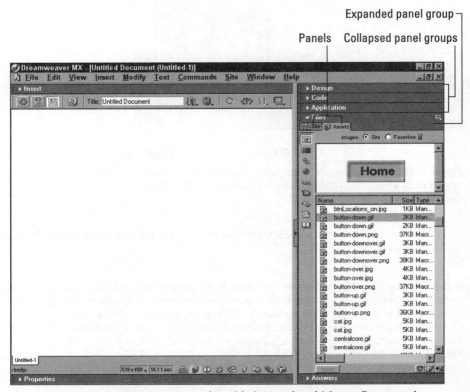

Figure 3-21: Dreamweaver's many tools reside in panels, which can float anywhere on the screen, or, in the Dreamweaver MX workspace, can be docked within the Document window.

Table 3-21 lists each of the panels available in Dreamweaver, along with a description and a cross-reference to chapters in this book that provide more information about the panel. It also lists a keyboard shortcut that you can use to open the panel. If the keyboard shortcut is different between Mac and Windows platforms, the Mac shortcut is listed in parentheses after the Windows shortcut.

Table 3-21: Dreamweaver Panels

Panel	Keyboard Shortcut	Description	Detailed Information
Answers	Alt+F1 (Option+F1)	Provides links to Dreamweaver documentation	See Chapter 1
CSS Styles	Shift+F11	Enables you to create external and embedded CSS style sheets	See Chapter 20

Panel	Keyboard Shortcut	Description	Detailed Information
HTML Styles	Ctrl+F11 (Command+F11)	Enables you to define, modify, delete, and apply HTML styles	See Chapter 7
Behaviors	Shift+F3	Enables you to create Dynamic HTML effects	See Chapter 23
Tag Inspector	F9	Displays a collapsible outline of the tags used on the current page, enabling you to quickly determine if tags are correctly nested, and to view and change tag attributes	See Chapter 6
Snippets	Shift+F9	Gives you access to prewritten snippets of code for common scenarios	See Chapter 6
Reference	Ctrl+Shift+F1 (Shift+F1)	Presents extensive reference documentation for HTML, CSS, JavaScript, accessibility guidelines, and a variety of server-side scripting languages	See Chapter 6
Databases	Ctrl+Shift+F10 (Command+Shift+F10)	Provides a bird's-eye view of all the connections currently defined for your site, enabling you to add new connections, browse tables, views, and stored procedures for each database, and add the necessary server side include to use that connection	See chapters in Part III
Bindings	Ctrl+F10 (Command+F10)	Enables you to create recordsets and datasets and display that information on your page. You can also bind data to tag attributes and form elements and set the formatting for dynamic elements.	See chapters in Part III
Server Behaviors	Ctrl+F9 (Command+F9)	Gives you access to prewritten server-side scripts that are used in applications. For example, you can use server behaviors to create, update, or delete records.	See Chapter 36
Components	Ctrl+F7 (Command+F7)	Enables you to quickly add new JavaBeans components (if you're using JSP) or Web Services (if you're using JSP or .NET), or ColdFusion components (if you're using ColdFusion). Setting up the JavaBeans or Web Service will give you full introspection to all the pieces of that component.	See Chapter 16

Continued

Table 3-21: *(continued)*

Panel	Keyboard Shortcut	Description	Detailed Information
Site	F8	Manages the files in your local, remote, and testing sites. (In the Dreamweaver 4 workspace, the Site panel behaves as a separate window, rather than as a panel.)	See Chapter 5
Assets	F11	Gives you access to many components that make up your site, including images, colors, URLs, Flash and Shockwave objects, movies, scripts, templates, and library items.	See the following: Images: Chapter 8 Colors: Chapter 7 URLs: Chapter 9 Flash: Chapter 25 Shockwave: Chapter 25 Movies: Chapter 26 Scripts: Chapter 6 Templates: Chapter 28 Library: Chapter 29
Search	Ctrl+Shift+F (Command+Shift+F)	Shows the results of a Find All request	See Chapter 7
Validation	Ctrl+Shift+F7 (Command+Shift+F7)	When you validate a document, the results are displayed in this panel	See Chapter 30
Target Browser Check	Ctrl+Shift+F8 (Command+Shift+F8)	Displays results of a target browser check	See Chapter 30
Link Checker	Ctrl+Shift+F9 (Command+Shift+F9)	Shows the results when you check for broken links within your site	See Chapter 9
Site Reports	Ctrl+Shift+F11 (Command+Shift+F11)	Displays the output from a variety of site reports	See Chapter 31
FTP Log	Ctrl+Shift+F12 (Command+Shift+F12)	Lists the results of FTP operations	See Chapter 5
Server Debug (Not available on Macintosh)	Ctrl+Shift+F5	Enables you to browse your page directly in Dreamweaver's Design window as if it were a Web browser. This is different from Live Data view because the page is not editable.	See Chapter 36
Code Inspector	F10	Provides an alternative to Code view, in a floating window	See Chapter 6
Frames	Shift+F2	Enables you to select and rename frames within a frameset	See Chapter 14

Panel	Keyboard Shortcut	Description	Detailed Information
History	Shift+F10	Tracks each change you make, enabling you to undo and redo multiple steps at a time	See Chapter 7
Layers	F2	Enables you to view and change some characteristics of layers	See Chapter 21
Sitespring	F7	Gives you instant access to all your Sitespring tasks in a separate panel inside Dreamweaver. Instead of logging on to the Sitespring site, you can update status information and check for new tasks without leaving your workspace.	See Chapter 31
Timelines	Alt+F9 (Option+F9)	Enables you to add and modify time-related Dynamic HTML effects, such as moving items across a page	See Chapter 22

Hiding and showing panels

With the large number of panels available in Dreamweaver, your workspace can become cluttered very quickly. To reduce the amount of screen real estate taken up by the individual panels, but still utilize their power, Dreamweaver enables you to group multiple panels in a single window. These groups of related panels are called, not surprisingly, *panel groups*. Whenever one panel is docked with another in a panel group, each panel becomes accessible by clicking its representative tab. Selecting the tab brings the panel to the front.

You can also display individual panels by using the keyboard shortcuts listed in Table 3-21, or by using commands in the Window menu; there is a separate command to open each panel. Finally, you can use one of the buttons in the status bar Launcher, described earlier in this chapter, to open the desired panel. Using any of these methods opens the panel or brings it to the top if it is hidden; if the panel is already on top, any of these actions will collapse the panel group so that only its title bar is showing.

Tip

One very important keyboard shortcut to remember is the F4 key, which hides all panels. This shortcut immediately clears the screen of everything except the basic Document window—the Insert bar, the Property inspector, all toolbars, and all panels are immediately hidden, enabling you to enter content in your pages without distraction. Pressing F4 again restores all the hidden tools.

In the Dreamweaver MX and HomeSite/Coder Style workspaces, the panel groups may be docked along the edges of the Dreamweaver window. In this situation, you can collapse all of the panel groups to maximize your work area by clicking the button that appears along the border of the panel area, as shown in Figure 3-22. This collapses only the panel groups docked on one edge of the screen, while leaving toolbars, floating panels, or even panels docked along a different edge of the window, intact.

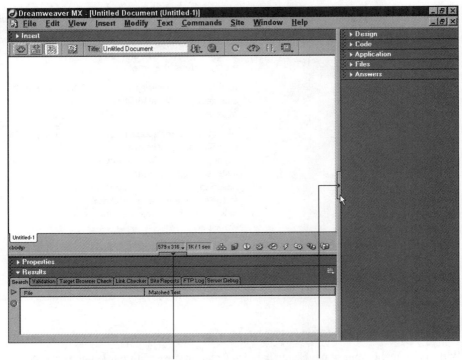

Click to collapse bottom panel area   Click to collapse right panel area

Figure 3-22: You can collapse all the panel groups along one edge of the screen with the click of a single button.

In any workspace, you can collapse an individual panel group so that just its title bar is showing. To do this, click the panel group name in the title bar, or click the small triangle next to the panel group name.

Tip

> To resize any floating panel, click and drag its borders. On the Mac, you can resize only by dragging the resize handle in the bottom-right corner of a window. If the panel groups are docked together, you can drag the border of the panel area to resize all the panel groups in that area.
>
> You can also right-click (Control+click) the title bar of the panel group or click the Options menu on the right of the title bar, and then select Maximize Panel Group from the drop-down list. This action expands the panel to the fullest possible height, but leaves the panel width unchanged.

Finally, if you want to close a panel group entirely so that even its title bar is not visible, click the Options menu located on the right of the title bar in an open panel group, and then select Close Panel Group from the drop-down list. You can also right-click (Control+click) in the title bar and then select Close Panel Group, even if the panel group is collapsed. The next time you open any panel within the group, the entire panel group will open automatically.

Note The Options menu also gives you access to Help for the currently displayed panel, and may contain additional commands specific to the panel that is open.

Customizing panel groups

Dreamweaver comes with related panels already combined into panel groups. However, you're not limited to the predefined panel groups. In fact, the panel groups are completely customizable, giving you optimum control over your workflow. Moving panels from one group to another, creating new groups, and renaming panel groups are straightforward operations. If you want, you can also remove little-used panels from groups and reorder the panels within a group.

To move a panel from one group to another, start by opening the panel you want to move; then right-click (Control+click) in the title bar of the panel group, point to Group <*panel*> With in the context menu, and click the name of the panel group where you want the panel to reside. The same command is available from the Options menu, accessed by clicking the icon at the right of an open panel group's title bar. This command removes the current panel from its original panel group, and adds the panel's tab to the right of the existing tabs in the target panel group.

Tip To reorder panels within a panel group, open the panel, right-click (Control+click) on the title bar of the panel group, point to Group <*panel*> With and then click the name of the current panel group. This moves the currently open panel to the right-most position in the group. By repeatedly moving panels within the current group, you can achieve the order you desire.

To create a new panel group, open a panel that you want to be in the new group. right-click (Control+click) in the title bar of the current panel group, and select Group <*panel*> With ⇨ New Panel Group. This creates a new, separate panel group that contains the removed panel. Initially, the name of the new panel group is the same as the panel name, but you can change it, as explained below. You can add other panels to your new panel group, using the method described previously; you'll find your new panel group name automatically shows up in the context menu for the panel group. You can also dock the new panel group with others, and in the Dreamweaver MX and HomeSite/Coder Style workspaces, you can dock the panel group within the Document window.

Note Some caveats apply when customizing panels. You cannot combine panels with the Insert bar or the Property inspector. Also, if you customize your panel groups and then change workspace layouts, your customizations will be lost.

Dreamweaver initially assigns a new panel group the same name as the first panel in the group. You can change this name — or the name of one of Dreamweaver's original panel groups — by choosing Rename Panel Group from the Options menu, accessed by clicking the icon at the right of an open panel group's title bar. The same command is available by right-clicking the panel group title bar.

How do you remove a panel from a panel group? First use the Group <*panel*> With ⇨ New Panel Group command on the Options menu to move the panel to its own group. Then close the panel group for the removed panel by right-clicking (Control+clicking) in the title bar and choosing Close Panel Group.

You can move a panel group by clicking the gripper icon in the panel group's title bar and dragging the window to any location on the screen, as shown in Figure 3-23.

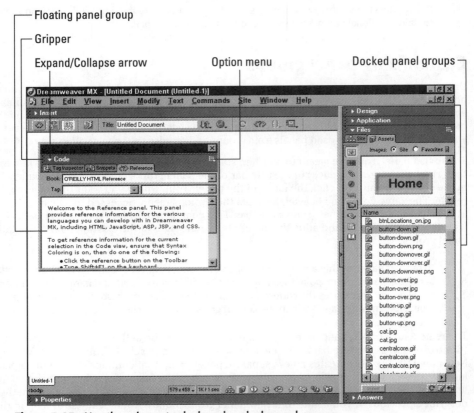

Figure 3-23: Use the gripper to dock and undock panel groups.

In the Dreamweaver 4 workspace, you can dock panel groups to each other, but you cannot dock them within the Document window. In the Dreamweaver MX and HomeSite/Coder Style workspaces, not only can you dock floating panel groups together, you can dock panel groups within the Dreamweaver window; when you move or resize the Dreamweaver window, the docked panels move too. To dock panel groups, drag the window by the gripper over another panel group, or to the edge of the window, until the outline of the window changes to indicate it is in position. When you release the mouse button, the panel group will be docked. Although you can move floating panels by dragging the title bar, panels can be docked only when you are dragging with the gripper.

Tip

In the Dreamweaver MX and HomeSite/Coder Style workspaces, you are not limited to having your panels on one edge of the window. You can dock panels to both the left and right sides of the screen at the same time, although this reduces your work area considerably unless you have a large monitor.

Accessing the Menus

Like many programs, Dreamweaver's menus duplicate most of the features accessible through panels. Certain features, however, are available only through the menus in the

Document window or through a corresponding keyboard shortcut. This section offers a reference guide to the menus when you need a particular feature or command. (Note to Windows users: The menus referred to here are those for the Document window and not the Site panel; the menu options particular to the Site panel are covered in Chapter 5.)

Tip　Almost every element placed in the Document window has a shortcut menu associated with it. To access a shortcut menu, right-click (Control+click) any area or object. The shortcut menus are context-sensitive and vary according to which object or area is selected. Using the shortcut menus can enhance your productivity tremendously.

The File menu

The File menu contains commands for file handling and overall site management. Table 3-22 describes the commands and their keyboard shortcuts.

Table 3-22: File Menu Commands

Command	Description	Windows	Macintosh
New	Opens the New Document dialog box, where you can specify the type of document to create	Ctrl+N	Command+N
Open	Displays the Open dialog box for opening an existing file	Ctrl+O	Command+O
Open in Frame	Opens an existing file in the selected frame	Ctrl+Shift+O	Command+Shift+O
Close	Closes the currently active open window	Ctrl+W or Ctrl+F4	Command+W
Save	Saves the current document, or displays the Save As dialog box for an unnamed document	Ctrl+S	Command+S
Save As	Displays the Save As dialog box before saving the document	Ctrl+Shift+S	Command+Shift+S
Save As Template	Stores the current document as a template in the Templates folder of the current site	N/A	N/A
Save Frameset	Saves a file describing the current frameset, or displays the Save As dialog box for an unnamed document. This command is available only if a frameset is selected in the Document window.	Ctrl+S	Command+S

Continued

Table 3-22: *(continued)*

Command	Description	Windows	Macintosh
Save Frameset As	Displays the Save As dialog box before saving the current frameset. This command is available only if a frameset is selected in the Document window.	Ctrl+Shift+S	Command+Shift+S
Save Frame	Saves the file in the currently selected frame, or displays the Save As dialog box for an unnamed document. This command is available only if a frame is active in the Document window.	Ctrl+S	Command+S
Save Frame As	Displays the Save As dialog box before saving the file for the currently selected frame. This command is available only if a frame is active in the Document window.	Ctrl+Shift+S	Command+Shift+S
Save Frame As Template	Stores the document in the currently selected frame as a template in the Templates folder of the current site. This command is available only if a frame is active in the Document window.	N/A	N/A
Save All	Saves all currently open documents	N/A	N/A
Revert	Loads the previously saved version of the current page. This command is available only if the current document has been changed since the last time it was saved.	N/A	N/A
Print Code	Opens the standard Print dialog box to print the code for the current document	Ctrl+P	Command+P
Import ➪ XML into Template	Creates a new document by inserting an XML file into the current template	N/A	N/A
Import ➪ Word HTML	Opens an HTML file saved in Microsoft Word and, optionally, cleans up the code	N/A	N/A
Import ➪ Tabular Data	Inserts a table derived from a file with delimited data	N/A	N/A

Command	Description	Windows	Macintosh
Export ➪ Template Data as XML	Saves the current template's editable regions as an XML file. This is available only if the current document is attached to a Dreamweaver template.	N/A	N/A
Export ➪ CSS Styles	Creates an external style sheet based on CSS styles defined in the current document. This is available only if styles have been defined in the document.	N/A	N/A
Export ➪ Table	Saves data in the currently selected table as a delimited text file	N/A	N/A
Convert ➪ 3.0 Browser Compatible	Creates a new Web page from the current document, optionally converting all layers to tables and converting any CSS styles to HTML markup	N/A	N/A
Convert ➪ XHTML	Changes the current document to use XHTML markup	N/A	N/A
Preview in Browser ➪ Your Browser List	Displays a list of browsers established in Preferences; choose one to preview the current page using that browser	F12 (Primary); Shift+F12 or Ctrl+F12 (Secondary)	Command+F12
Preview in Browser ➪ Edit Browser List	Displays the Preview in Browser category of Preferences, where the user can add, edit, or delete additional preview browsers	N/A	N/A
Debug in Browser ➪ Your Browser List	Displays a list of browsers established in Preferences; choose one to debug the current page using the JavaScript Debugger with that browser	Alt+F12 (Primary); Ctrl+Alt+F12 (Secondary)	Option+F12 (Primary); Command+ Option+F12 (Secondary)
Debug in Browser ➪ Edit Browser List	Displays the Preview in Browser category of Preferences, where the user can add, edit, or delete additional preview browsers	N/A	N/A
Check Page ➪ Check Accessibility	Checks the current document against accessibility guidelines and displays the results in the Site Reports panel. This command is available only in a document that has been saved.	N/A	N/A

Continued

Table 3-22: *(continued)*

Command	Description	Windows	Macintosh
Check Page ➪ Check Links	Verifies hypertext links for the current document and shows the results in the Link Checker panel	Shift+F8	Shift+F8
Check Page ➪ Check Target Browsers	Displays the Check Target Browsers dialog box, where the user can validate the current file against selected browser profiles	N/A	N/A
Check Page ➪ Validate Markup	Validates the current page against the code standard that you choose in the Validator category of the Preferences dialog box	Shift+F6	Shift+F6
Check Page ➪ Validate as XML	Validates an XML or XHTML document, displaying the results in the Validation panel	N/A	N/A
Design Notes	Displays the Design Notes dialog box for the current document	N/A	N/A
Your Last Opened Files	Displays the last four opened files; select any name to reopen the file	N/A	N/A
Exit (Quit)	Closes all open files and quits	Ctrl+Q or Alt+F4	Command+Q

The Edit menu

The Edit menu gives you the commands necessary to quickly modify your page — or recover from a devastating accident. Many of the commands (Cut, Copy, and Paste, for example) are standard in other programs; others, such as Paste HTML, are unique to Dreamweaver. Table 3-23 lists all of the commands found under the Edit menu.

Table 3-23: Edit Menu Commands

Command	Description	Windows	Macintosh
Undo	Reverses the last action; the number of times you can undo is determined by a Preferences setting	Ctrl+Z	Command+Z or Option+Backspace
Redo/Repeat	Repeats the last action or restores the effects of an action that was undone	Ctrl+Y	Command+Y or Command + Z

Command	Description	Windows	Macintosh
Cut	Places a copy of the current selection on the clipboard, and removes the selection from the current document	Ctrl+X	Command+X or Shift+Delete
Copy	Places a copy of the current selection on the clipboard, and leaves the selection in the current document	Ctrl+C	Command+C
Paste	Copies the clipboard to the current cursor position	Ctrl+V	Command+V
Clear	Removes the current selection from the document	Delete or Backspace	Delete or Backspace
Copy HTML	Copies the current selection onto the clipboard with the HTML codes	Ctrl+Shift+C	Command+Shift+C
Paste HTML	Pastes the current selection from the clipboard as HTML	Ctrl+Shift+V	Command+Shift+V
Select All	Highlights all the elements in the current document or frame	Ctrl+A	Command+A
Select Parent Tag	Chooses the tag surrounding the current selection	Ctrl+Shift+[	Command+[
Select Child	Chooses the first tag contained within the current selection	Ctrl+Shift+]	Command+]
Find and Replace	Displays the Find and Replace dialog box for locating items in and modifying one or more documents in the site	Ctrl+F	Command+F
Find Next (Find Again)	Repeats the previous Find operation	F3	Command+G
Go to Line	Moves the cursor to the start of the specified line (Command+comma) (Code view only)	Ctrl+G	Command+,
Show Code Hints	Presents a context-sensitive list of options for entering tags, attributes, or values within the code (Code view only)	Ctrl+Space	Command+Space
Indent Code	Indents selected code (Code view only)	Ctrl+Shift+>	Command+Shift+. (Command+Shift+ period)
Outdent Code	Removes indentations from selected code (Code view only)	Ctrl++Shift+<	Command+Shift+, (Command+Shift+ comma)

Continued

Table 3-23: *(continued)*

Command	Description	Windows	Macintosh
Balance Braces	Selects code within the nearest surrounding parentheses or braces (Code view only)	Ctrl+'	Command+' (Command+ apostrophe)
Set/Remove Breakpoint	Toggles the insertion and removal of a marker that stops the execution of JavaScript code, to aid in debugging (Code view only)	Ctrl+Alt+B	Command+ Option+B
Remove All Breakpoints	Eliminates all breakpoints previously set in the code (Code view only)	N/A	N/A
Repeating Entries ➪ Cut Repeating Entry/ Copy Repeating Entry/ Delete Repeating Entry	Cuts, copies, or removes the currently selected entry within a template's repeating region	N/A	N/A
Edit with External Editor (Editor is named in menu item once defined in Preferences)	Opens the current document in the External HTML Editor as defined in Preferences ➪ File Types/Editors	N/A	N/A
Tag Libraries	Opens the Tag Library Editor, where you can control how Dreamweaver works with and formats tags and their attributes	N/A	N/A
Keyboard Shortcuts	Opens the Keyboard Shortcuts dialog box to enable customization of the keyboard shortcuts	N/A	N/A
Preferences	Displays the Preferences dialog box, where you can customize many aspects of the Dreamweaver work environment	Ctrl+U	Command+U

The View menu

As you build your Web pages, you'll find that it's helpful to be able to turn certain features on and off. The View menu centralizes all these commands and switches between Design view and Code view. One of the handiest commands hides all the visual aids with a keyboard shortcut, Ctrl+Shift+I (Command+Shift+I). Table 3-24 describes each command under the View menu.

Table 3-24: View Menu Commands

Command	Description	Windows	Macintosh
Code	Displays the code for the current page	N/A	N/A
Design	Displays a view of the current page that is similar to what you would see when viewing it in a browser	N/A	N/A
Code and Design	Splits the view, showing Code and Design views simultaneously; also known as Split view	N/A	N/A
Switch Views	Switches between Design view and Code view, and activates the alternate view in Split view	Ctrl+`	Command+`
Refresh Design View	Applies changes made in Code view to Design view	F5	F5
Design View on Top	When selected, shows the Design view above the Code view	N/A	N/A
Server Debug (Windows only)	Displays a ColdFusion page in an internal browser for debugging	Crtl+Shift+G	N/A
Live Data	Processes the current page using the defined testing server, so that the actual data is visible in Design view	Ctrl+Shift+R	Command+Shift+R
Live Data Settings	Displays a dialog box for altering parameters passed to the current page	N/A	N/A
Head Content	Displays symbols for elements inserted in the `<head>` section of the current document	Ctrl+Shift+W	Command+Shift+W
Noscript Content	Displays any content enclosed within `<noscript></noscript>` tags, in addition to regular content	N/A	N/A
Table View ⇨ Standard View	Displays the Standard view in the Document window	Ctrl+Shift+F6	Command+Shift+F6
Table View ⇨ Layout View	Engages Layout view for creating layout cells and tables	Ctrl+F6	Command+F6
Table View ⇨ Show Layout Table Tabs	Shows outlines and tabs marking layout cells and tables	N/A	N/A
Visual Aids ⇨ Hide All	Toggles all the visual aids on or off	Ctrl+Shift+I	Command+Shift+I
Visual Aids ⇨ Table Borders	Displays or hides the border outlining a table	N/A	N/A

Continued

Table 3-24: *(continued)*

Command	Description	Windows	Macintosh
Visual Aids ⇨ Layer Borders	Toggles the border outlining an unselected layer	N/A	N/A
Visual Aids ⇨ Frame Borders	Displays/hides borders in a frameset	N/A	N/A
Visual Aids ⇨ Image Maps	Controls whether the hotspots for defined image maps are shown	N/A	N/A
Visual Aids ⇨ Invisible Elements	Displays or hides the symbols for certain HTML tags, which can be specified in the Preferences dialog box	N/A	N/A
Code View Options ⇨ Word Wrap	Determines whether lines automatically wrap in Code view	N/A	N/A
Code View Options ⇨ Line Numbers	Indicates whether line numbers are displayed in Code view	N/A	N/A
Code View Options ⇨ Highlight Invalid HTML	Determines whether invalid markup is highlighted in Code view	N/A	N/A
Code View Options ⇨ Syntax Coloring	Determines whether the code is displayed with color and other formatting defined in the Preferences dialog box	N/A	N/A
Code View Options ⇨ Auto Indent	Specifies whether the code is automatically indented	N/A	N/A
Rulers ⇨ Show	Displays the horizontal and vertical rulers	Ctrl+Alt+ R	Command+ Option+ R
Rulers ⇨ Reset Origin	Resets the rulers' 0,0 coordinates to the upper-left corner of the window	N/A	N/A
Rulers ⇨ Pixels/ Inches/Centimeters	Sets the rulers to a selected measurement system	N/A	N/A
Grid ⇨ Show Grid	Displays a background grid using the current settings	Ctrl+Alt+ G	Command+ Option+ G
Grid ⇨ Snap To Grid	Forces inserted objects to align with the nearest snap setting	Ctrl+Alt+ Shift+G	Command+ Option+ Shift+G
Grid ⇨ Settings	Displays the Grid Settings dialog box	N/A	N/A
Tracing Image ⇨ Show	Displays the image chosen as the Tracing Image according to the Page Properties settings	N/A	N/A
Tracing Image ⇨ Align with Selection	Aligns the top-left corner of the Tracing Image with the upper-left corner of the selected object	N/A	N/A

Command	Description	Windows	Macintosh
Tracing Image ⇨ Adjust Position	Enables the Tracing Image to be moved using the arrow keys or numerically	N/A	N/A
Tracing Image ⇨ Reset Position	Resets the position of the Tracing Image to the upper-left corner of the document	N/A	N/A
Tracing Image ⇨ Load	Displays the Open File dialog box for inserting the tracing image	N/A	N/A
Plugins ⇨ Play	Plays the selected plugin	Ctrl+Alt+P	Command+Option+P
Plugins ⇨ Stop	Stops the selected plugin from playing	Ctrl+Alt+X	Command+Option+X
Plugins ⇨ Play All	Plays all plugins on the current page	Ctrl+Alt+Shift+P	Command+Option+Shift+P
Plugins ⇨ Stop All	Stops all plugins on the current page from playing	Ctrl+Alt+Shift+X	Command+Option+Shift+X
Hide Panels	Hides or restores all open panels	F4	F4
Toolbars ⇨ Document	Toggles the Document toolbar to be visible or hidden	N/A	N/A
Toolbars ⇨ Standard	Toggles the Standard toolbar on and off	N/A	N/A

The Insert menu

The Insert menu contains the same items available through the Insert bar. In fact, if you add additional objects (as discussed in Chapter 34), you can see your objects listed on the Insert menu the next time you start Dreamweaver. All objects are inserted at the current cursor position. Table 3-25 lists the items available to be inserted in the standard version of Dreamweaver.

Table 3-25: Insert Menu Commands

Command	Description	Windows	Macintosh
Tag	Opens the Tag Chooser, where you can select a markup tag to insert at the current text insertion point	Ctrl+E	Command+E
Image	Opens the Insert Image dialog box, which enables you to input or browse for a graphics file	Ctrl+Alt+I	Command+Option+I
Image Placeholder	Reserves space on a page for an image to be specified later	N/A	N/A

Continued

Table 3-25: *(continued)*

Command	Description	Windows	Macintosh
Interactive Images ⇨ Rollover Image	Opens a dialog box for inserting a Rollover button	N/A	N/A
Interactive Images ⇨ Navigation Bar	Opens the Insert Navigation Bar dialog box for creating a series of Rollover buttons with links	N/A	N/A
Interactive Images ⇨ Flash Button	Inserts an animated button based on a Flash template	N/A	N/A
Interactive Images ⇨ Flash Text	Includes a Flash object for displaying rollover text	N/A	N/A
Interactive Images ⇨ Fireworks HTML	Imports HTML and JavaScript generated by Fireworks	N/A	N/A
Media ⇨ Flash	Inserts a specified Flash movie file	Ctrl+Alt+F	Command+ Option+F
Media ⇨ Shockwave	Inserts a specified Shockwave file into your page	Ctrl+Alt+D	Command+ Option+D
Media ⇨ Applet	Enables you to input or browse for a Java class source	N/A	N/A
Media ⇨ Plugin	Inserts a specified plugin into the document	N/A	N/A
Media ⇨ ActiveX	Inserts an ActiveX placeholder	N/A	N/A
Table	Creates a table	Ctrl+Alt+T	Command+ Option+T
Table Objects ⇨ Import Tabular Data	Creates a table derived from a file with delimited data	N/A	N/A
Table Objects ⇨ Table/ TR/TH/TD/Caption	Inserts the specified table-related markup tags at the text insertion point. Best used in Code view.	N/A	N/A
Layer	Inserts a layer of a preset size	N/A	N/A
Frames ⇨ Left/Right/Top/Bottom/ Bottom Nested Left/ Bottom Nested Right/ Left Nested Top/ Left Nested Bottom/ Right Nested Bottom/ Right Nested Top/ Top and Bottom/ Top Nested Left/ Top Nested Right	Inserts the selected frameset	N/A	N/A
Frames ⇨ Frameset/ Frame/Floating Frame/ No Frames	Inserts the selected frameset-related markup tags at the current position in your document. Best used in Code view.	N/A	N/A

Command	Description	Windows	Macintosh
Template Objects ⇨ Editable Region/ Optional Region/ Repeating Region/ Editable Optional Region/ Repeating Table	Inserts the selected type of region into a template file	N/A	N/A
Form	Creates the form structure on your Web page	N/A	N/A
Form Objects ⇨ Text Field/Textarea/ Button/Check Box/ Radio Button/ List-Menu/File Field/ Image Field/Hidden Field	Inserts the selected form object at the current cursor position	N/A	N/A
Form Objects ⇨ Radio Group	Creates a group of related radio buttons formatted as you specify	N/A	N/A
Form Objects ⇨ Jump Menu	Opens a dialog box for creating a list box with links	N/A	N/A
Form Objects ⇨ Fieldset	Inserts a `<fieldset></fieldset>` tag pair around the current selection or at the current cursor position if nothing is selected; used to group objects on a form	N/A	N/A
Form Objects ⇨ Label	Inserts `<label></label>` tags. Best used in Code view.	N/A	N/A
E-mail Link	Creates a mailto: link	N/A	N/A
Hyperlink	Inserts a text hyperlink into the page	N/A	N/A
Named Anchor	Inserts a named anchor at the current position	Ctrl+Alt+A	Command+ Option+A
Date	Inserts the current day, date, and time in a format of your choosing	N/A	N/A
Horizontal Rule	Inserts a horizontal line the width of the current window	N/A	N/A
Text Objects ⇨ Font	Inserts `<font></font>` tags in the document	N/A	N/A
Text Objects ⇨ Bold/Italic/Strong/Em	Creates the specified effect for selected text in Design view; in Code view, will also insert the appropriate empty tags if no text is selected	N/A	N/A

Continued

Table 3-25: *(continued)*

Command	Description	Windows	Macintosh
Text Objects ➪ Paragraph/Block Quote/ Preformatted Text/ H1/H2/H3	In Design view, converts the current block of text to the specified format; in Code view, inserts the appropriate tags around the selected text or as empty tags if nothing is selected	N/A	N/A
Text Objects ➪ Unordered List/ Ordered List	In Design view, converts the current block of text to an item in a list of the designated type; in Code view, inserts the opening and closing tags for the list at the current position or around the selected text	N/A	N/A
Text Objects ➪ List Item	Inserts $<li></li>$ tags at the current location or around the selected text	N/A	N/A
Text Objects ➪ Definition List	In Design view, converts the current block of text to a definition term within a definition list; in Code view, inserts the tags for a definition list	N/A	N/A
Text Objects ➪ Definition Term/ Definition	Formats the selected text as a term or definition in a definition list, or inserts empty tags for the term or definition if nothing is selected	N/A	N/A
Text Objects ➪ Abbreviation/Acronym	Inserts $<abbr>$ or $<acronym>$ tags around the current selection or at the text insertion point	N/A	N/A
Text Objects ➪ Comment	Inserts an HTML comment in the document	N/A	N/A
Script Objects ➪ Script	Opens a dialog box for you to insert JavaScript code in addition to alternate content for browsers that do not have scripting enabled	N/A	N/A
Script Objects ➪ Noscript	Opens a dialog box in which you can specify content that displays in browsers with scripting disabled	N/A	N/A
Script Objects ➪ Server-side Include	Opens the dialog box for inserting a server-side include file	N/A	N/A
Head Tags ➪ Meta/ Keywords/Description/ Refresh/Base/Link	Displays the appropriate dialog box for inserting the selected HTML tag in the $<head>$ section	N/A	N/A
Special Characters ➪ Line Break	Inserts a line break $ $ tag	Shift+Enter	Shift+Return

Command	Description	Windows	Macintosh
Special Characters ➪ Non-breaking Space	Inserts a hard space	Ctrl+Shift+ spacebar	Command+ Shift+ spacebar (or Option+ spacebar)
Special Characters ➪ Copyright/Registered/ Trademark/Pound/ Yen/Euro/Left Quote/ Right Quote/Em-Dash	Inserts the HTML code for the selected character entity	N/A	N/A
Special Characters ➪ Other	Opens the Insert Other Character dialog box to choose a special character	N/A	N/A
Application Objects ➪ Recordset	Opens a dialog box in which you can define the subset of data to be extracted from a database	N/A	N/A
Application Objects ➪ Dynamic Table	Inserts into the document a table that is populated with data from a recordset you have defined	N/A	N/A
Application Objects ➪ Dynamic Text	Adds data from a recordset to the document	N/A	N/A
Application Objects ➪ Recordset Navigation Bar	Inserts text- or graphic-based elements for controlling movement through a recordset	N/A	N/A
Application Objects ➪ Recordset Navigation Status	Displays which record(s) out of the current recordset are onscreen	N/A	N/A
Application Objects ➪ Repeated Region	Alters the selected dynamic area of the page so that data from more than one record is displayed on the page at a time	N/A	N/A
Application Objects ➪ Master Detail Page Set	Inserts the table of fields and server behaviors necessary for a Web application that displays a list of all records and links to details of selected records	N/A	N/A
Application Objects ➪ Record Insertion Form/ Record Update Form	Builds a form for inserting records into a data source or for modifying existing records in the datasource	N/A	N/A
ASP Objects ➪ Server Variables	Opens a dialog box in which you can choose the ASP server variable to insert	N/A	N/A
ASP Objects ➪ Include	Inserts a #include statement	N/A	N/A
ASP Objects ➪ Code Block/Output	Inserts the delimiters for a code block or output statement	N/A	N/A

Continued

Table 3-25: *(continued)*

Command	Description	Windows	Macintosh
ASP Objects ⇨ If/ElseIf/Else/End/ Response.Write/ Server.CreateObject	Inserts the specified statement in the ASP code	N/A	N/A
ASP Objects ⇨ Trimmed Form Element/Trimmed QueryString Element	Inserts code for referencing trimmed elements in a Form or QueryString collection	N/A	N/A
ASP.Net Objects ⇨ DataGrid/DataList	Adds customizable ASP.Net DataGrid or DataList controls	N/A	N/A
ASP.Net Objects ⇨ Bound Data	Inserts the code `<%# %>` at the text insertion point	N/A	N/A
ASP.Net Objects ⇨ Imported Namespace	Adds the statement `<%@ Import Namespace="" %>` to your code	N/A	N/A
ASP.Net Objects ⇨ Page Load	Inserts a Page_Load subroutine	N/A	N/A
ASP.Net Objects ⇨ Register Custom Tag	Inserts the code required to create custom tags, which you can develop to create new server behaviors	N/A	N/A
ASP.Net Objects ⇨ Runat Server	Inserts `runat="server"` at the current text insertion point	N/A	N/A
ASP.Net Objects ⇨ Trimmed Form Element/ Trimmed QueryString Element	Inserts the code for referencing trimmed elements in a Form or QueryString collection	N/A	N/A
ASP.Net Objects ⇨ asp:button/ asp:checkbox/ asp:checkboxlist/ asp:dropdownlist/ asp:imagebutton/ asp:label/asp:listbox/ asp:radiobutton/ asp:radiobuttonlist/ asp:textbox	Inserts the specified ASP.Net form object	N/A	N/A
ColdFusion Basic Objects ⇨ Server Variables	Opens a dialog box in which you can choose the server variable to insert	N/A	N/A
ColdFusion Basic Objects ⇨ CFQUERY/ CFOUTPUT/CFINSERT/ CFUPDATE/CFINCLUDE/ CFLOCATION/ CFSET/CFPARAM	Inserts the specified ColdFusion code at the text insertion point	N/A	N/A

Command	Description	Windows	Macintosh
ColdFusion Basic Objects ⇨ Comment	Inserts the ColdFusion code for a comment	N/A	N/A
ColdFusion Basic Objects ⇨ Surround with #	Inserts the characters ## around the selected text	N/A	N/A
ColdFusion Basic Objects ⇨ CFSCRIPT	Adds a `<cfscript> </cfscript>` tag pair	N/A	N/A
ColdFusion Flow Objects ⇨ CFTRY/ CFCATCH/CFTHROW/ CFLOCK/CFIF/ CFELSEIF/CFELSE/ CFSWITCH/CFCASE/ CFDEFAULTCASE/ CFLOOP/CFBREAK	Adds the specified ColdFusion tag at the current location	N/A	N/A
ColdFusion Advanced Objects ⇨ CFCOOKIE/ CFCONTENT/CFHEADER/ CFAPPLICATION/ CFERROR/CFDIRECTORY/ CFFILE/CFMAIL/CFPOP/ CFHTTP/CFHTTPPARAM/ CFLDAP/CFFTP/CFSEARCH/ CFINDEX/CFMODULE/ CFOBJECT/CFCHART/ CF Page Encoding	Adds the specified ColdFusion tag at the current location	N/A	N/A
JSP Objects ⇨ Page/ Include/TagLib/ Declaration/Scriptlet/ Expression/jsp:useBean/ jsp:setProperty/ jsp:getProperty/ jsp:include/jsp:forward/ jsp:params/jsp:param/ jsp:plugin/comment	Inserts the specified JSP tag(s) at the current location. When appropriate for the tag, the Tag Editor opens, enabling you to enter information about the tag.	N/A	N/A
PHP Objects ⇨ Form Variables/URL Variables/ Session Variables/ Cookie Variables/Include/ Require/Code Block/ Echo/Comment/If/ Else	Inserts the specified PHP code at the current location	N/A	N/A
Get More Objects	Connects to the Dreamweaver Online Resource Center	N/A	N/A

The Modify menu

Inserting objects is less than half the battle of creating a Web page. Most Web designers spend most of their time adjusting, experimenting with, and tweaking the various elements. The Modify menu lists all of Dreamweaver's commands for altering existing selections. Table 3-26 describes each of the Modify options.

Table 3-26: Modify Menu Commands

Command	Description	Windows	Macintosh
Page Properties	Opens the Page Properties dialog box	Ctrl+J	Command+J
Template Properties	For documents attached to a template, this command allows you to control optional content	N/A	N/A
Selection Properties	Displays and hides the Property inspector	Ctrl+Shift+J	Command+Shift+J
Edit Tag	Opens the Tag Editor for the current tag, where you can define values for tag attributes	N/A	N/A
Quick Tag Editor	Displays the Quick Tag Editor for the current selection; repeating the keyboard shortcut toggles between the three Quick Tag Editor modes	Ctrl+T	Command+T
Make Link	Presents the Select File dialog box for picking a linking file	Ctrl+L	Command+L
Remove Link	Deletes the current link	Ctrl+Shift+L	Command+Shift+L
Open Linked Page	Opens the linked page in Dreamweaver	N/A	N/A
Link Target ⇨ Default Target/_blank/ _parent/_self/_top	Selects the target for the current link	N/A	N/A
Link Target ⇨ Set	Enables you to name a target for the link	N/A	N/A
Table ⇨ Select Table	Highlights the entire table surrounding the current cursor position	N/A (Ctrl+A selects a single cell within a table)	N/A (Command+A selects a single cell within a table)
Table ⇨ Merge Cells	Merges selected cells using spans	Ctrl+Alt+M	Command+Option+M
Table ⇨ Split Cell	Splits cells into rows or columns	Ctrl+Alt+S	Command+Option+S
Table ⇨ Insert Row	Adds a new row above the current row	Ctrl+M	Command+M

Command	Description	Windows	Macintosh
Table ⇨ Insert Column	Adds a new column before the current column	Ctrl+Shift+A	Command+Shift+A
Table ⇨ Insert Rows or Columns	Opens a dialog box that enables multiple rows or columns to be inserted relative to the cursor position	N/A	N/A
Table ⇨ Delete Row	Removes the current row	Ctrl+Shift+M	Command+Shift+M
Table ⇨ Delete Column	Removes the current column	Ctrl+Shift+− (minus sign)	Command+Shift+− (minus sign)
Table ⇨ Increase Row Span/Increase Column Span/ Decrease Row Span/ Decrease Column Span	Increases or decreases by one row or column the span of the current cell	Ctrl+Shift+] (Increase Column Span); Ctrl+Shift+[(Decrease Column Span)	Command+Shift+] (Increase Column Span); Command+Shift+[(Decrease Column Span)
Table ⇨ Clear Cell Heights	Removes specified row height values for the entire selected table	N/A	N/A
Table ⇨ Clear Cell Widths	Removes specified column width values for the entire selected table	N/A	N/A
Table ⇨ Convert Widths to Pixels/Convert Widths to Percent	Changes column widths from a percentage to pixels, or vice versa, for the entire selected table	N/A	N/A
Table ⇨ Convert Heights to Pixels/Convert Heights to Percent	Changes row heights from percentage to pixels, or vice versa, for the entire selected table	N/A	N/A
Frameset ⇨ Edit No Frames Content	Opens a new window for content to be seen by browsers that do not support frames	N/A	N/A
Frameset ⇨ Split Frame Left/Split Frame Right/ Split Frame Up/ Split Frame Down	Moves the current frame in the specified direction, and adds a new frame opposite	N/A	N/A
Navigation Bar	Enables you to edit the selected navigation bar	N/A	N/A
Arrange ⇨ Bring to Front	Places selected layers or image map hotspots in front of other all other layers or hotspots	N/A	N/A
Arrange ⇨ Send to Back	Places selected layers or image map hotspots behind all other layers or hotspots	N/A	N/A

Continued

Table 3-26: *(continued)*

Command	Description	Windows	Macintosh
Arrange ⇨ Prevent Layer Overlaps	Stops newly created layers from overlapping	N/A	N/A
Align ⇨ Left	Aligns grouped layers or hotspots on the left edge	Ctrl+Shift+1	Command+ Shift+1 (use number pad keys)
Align ⇨ Right	Aligns grouped layers or hotspots on the right edge	Ctrl+Shift+3	Command+ Shift+3 (use number pad keys)
Align ⇨ Top	Aligns grouped layers or hotspots on the top edge	Ctrl+Shift+4	Command+ Shift+4 (use number pad keys)
Align ⇨ Bottom	Aligns grouped layers or hotspots on the bottom edge	Ctrl+Shift+6	Command+ Shift+6 (use number pad keys)
Align ⇨ Make Same Width	Changes the width of grouped layers or hotspots to that of the last selected layer	Ctrl+Shift+7	N/A
Align ⇨ Make Same Height	Changes the height of grouped layers or hotspots to that of the last selected layer	Ctrl+Shift+9	N/A
Convert ⇨ Tables to Layers	Places all content on the page in layers	N/A	N/A
Convert ⇨ Layers to Table	Places all content in layers in tables	N/A	N/A
Library ⇨ Add Object to Library	Opens the Library category of the Assets panel, and adds the selected object	Ctrl+Shift+B	Command+ Shift+B
Library ⇨ Update Current Page/ Update Pages	Replaces any modified Library items in the current page or current site	N/A	N/A
Templates ⇨ Export Without Markup	Exports the entire site to a separate folder, removing any template markup from files that were attached to templates in the original site	N/A	N/A
Templates ⇨ Apply Template to Page	Enables the selection of a template to be overlaid on the current page	N/A	N/A
Templates ⇨ Detach from Template	Breaks the link between the template and the current page	N/A	N/A
Templates ⇨ Open Attached Template	Opens the current template for editing	N/A	N/A
Templates ⇨ Check Template Syntax	Checks the structure of a template document for validity	N/A	N/A

Command	Description	Windows	Macintosh
Templates ⇨ Update Current Page	Automatically updates the page with template changes	N/A	N/A
Templates ⇨ Update Pages	Enables the updating of an entire site or of all pages using a particular template	N/A	N/A
Templates ⇨ Remove Template Markup	Removes the markup tags that designate an editable region, repeating region, and so on, for the current selection. This command is available only if the current selection includes template markup.	N/A	N/A
Templates ⇨ Repeating Entries ⇨ New Entry After Selection/New Entry Before Selection/ New Entry at End/ New Entry at Beginning	In a document based on a template, these commands add a new entry in a repeating region at the designated location	N/A	N/A
Templates ⇨ Repeating Entries ⇨ (No Repeating Entry Selected)/ Cut Repeating Entry/ Copy Repeating Entry/ Paste Repeating Entry/ Delete Repeating Entry	In a document based on a template, these commands will cut, copy, or delete a selected entry in a repeating region, or will paste a previously cut or copied entry. Note that the Paste command is only visible if an entry has been copied or cut.	N/A	N/A
Templates ⇨ Repeating Entries ⇨ Move ⇨ Up/Down/To Beginning/ To End	In a document that is based on a template, these commands move a selected entry within a repeating region to the designated location	N/A	N/A
Templates ⇨ Make Attribute Editable	Opens a dialog box in which you can specify an attribute of the current tag that can be changed in a document based on the template	N/A	N/A
Templates ⇨ No Editable Regions	Displayed in menu until editable regions are created and then replaced by editable region name	N/A	N/A
Timeline ⇨ Add Object to Timeline	Opens the Timelines panel and inserts the current image or layer	Ctrl+Alt+Shift+T	Command+ Option+Shift+T
Timeline ⇨ Add Behavior to Timeline	Opens the Timelines panel and inserts an onFrame event using the current frame	N/A	N/A
Timeline ⇨ Record Path of Layer	Plots the path of a dragged layer onto a timeline	N/A	N/A
Timeline ⇨ Add Keyframe	Inserts a keyframe at the current Playback Head position	F6	F6

Continued

Table 3-26: *(continued)*

Command	Description	Windows	Macintosh
Timeline ➪ Remove Keyframe	Deletes the currently selected keyframe	N/A	N/A
Timeline ➪ Change Object	Applies a timeline path to another object	N/A	N/A
Timeline ➪ Remove Object/ Remove Behavior	Deletes the currently selected object or behavior	N/A	N/A
Timeline ➪ Add Frame/ Remove Frame	Inserts or deletes a frame at the current Playback Head position	N/A	N/A
Timeline ➪ Add Timeline/ Remove Timeline/ Rename Timeline	Inserts an additional timeline, deletes the current timeline, or renames the current timeline	N/A	N/A

The Text menu

The Internet was initially an all-text medium, and despite all the multimedia development, the World Wide Web hasn't traveled far from these beginnings. The Text menu commands, described in Table 3-27, cover overall formatting as well as text-oriented functions such as spell checking.

Table 3-27: Text Menu Commands

Command	Description	Windows	Macintosh
Indent	Marks the selected text or the current paragraph with the `<blockquote>` tag to indent it	Ctrl+Alt+]	Command+ Option+]
Outdent	Removes a `<dir>` or `<blockquote>` surrounding the selected text or currently indented paragraph	Ctrl+Alt+[	Command+ Option+[
Paragraph Format ➪ None	Removes all HTML formatting tags surrounding the current selection	Ctrl+0 (zero)	Command+0 (zero)
Paragraph Format ➪ Paragraph	Converts the selected text to paragraph format	Ctrl+ Shift+P	Command+ Shift+P
Paragraph Format ➪ Heading 1–6	Changes the selected text to the specified heading format	Ctrl+1–6	Command+1–6
Paragraph Format ➪ Preformatted Text	Formats the selected text with a monospaced font and preserves whitespace	N/A	N/A
Align ➪ Left	Aligns the selected text to the left of the page, table, or layer	Ctrl+Alt+Shift+L	Command+ Option+Shift+L

Command	Description	Windows	Macintosh
Align ⇨ Center	Aligns the selected text to the center of the current page, table, or layer	Ctrl+Alt+Shift+C	Command+Option+Shift+C
Align ⇨ Right	Aligns the selected text to the right of the page, table, or layer	Ctrl+Alt+Shift+R	Command+Option+Shift+R
Align ⇨ Justify	Justifies text such that both the left and right margins are straight	Ctrl+Alt+Shift+J	Command+Option+Shift+J
List ⇨ None	Changes a list item into a paragraph	N/A	N/A
List ⇨ Unordered List	Makes the selected text into a bulleted list	N/A	N/A
List ⇨ Ordered List	Makes the selected text into a numbered list	N/A	N/A
List ⇨ Definition List	Converts the selected text into alternating definition terms and items	N/A	N/A
List ⇨ Properties	Opens the List Properties dialog box, where you can adjust the characteristics of the selected list	N/A	N/A
Font ⇨ Default	Changes the current selection to the default font	N/A	N/A
Font ⇨ Your Font List	Displays the fonts in your current font list; choose an entry in the list to apply those fonts to the selected text	N/A	N/A
Font ⇨ Edit Font List	Opens the Font List dialog box for adding or deleting fonts from the current list	N/A	N/A
Style ⇨ Bold	Makes the selected text bold, using either `<b></b>` or `<strong></strong>` coding, depending on a Preferences setting in the General category	Ctrl+B	Command+B
Style ⇨ Italic	Makes the selected text italic, using either `<i></i>` or `<em></em>` tags, depending on a Preferences setting	Ctrl+I	Command+I
Style ⇨ Underline	Underlines the selected text	N/A	N/A
Style ⇨ Strikethrough	Surrounds the selected text with the `<s></s>` tags for text with a line through it	N/A	N/A
Style ⇨ Teletype	Surrounds the selected text with the `<tt></tt>` tags for a monospaced font	N/A	N/A
Style ⇨ Emphasis	Surrounds the selected text with the `<em></em>` tags for slightly emphasized, usually italic, text	N/A	N/A

Continued

Table 3-27: *(continued)*

Command	Description	Windows	Macintosh
Style ➪ Strong	Surrounds the selected text with the `<strong></strong>` tags for more emphasized, usually bold, text	N/A	N/A
Style ➪ Code	Surrounds the selected text with HTML code for depicting programming code	N/A	N/A
Style ➪ Variable	Surrounds the selected text with HTML code for depicting a variable in programming, typically in italic	N/A	N/A
Style ➪ Sample/ Keyboard	Surrounds the selected text with HTML code for depicting monospaced fonts	N/A	N/A
Style ➪ Citation	Surrounds the selected text with HTML code for depicting cited text, usually in italic	N/A	N/A
Style ➪ Definition	Surrounds the selected text with HTML code for depicting a definition, usually in italic	N/A	N/A
Style ➪ Deleted	Surrounds the selected text with HTML code for depicting deleted text, typically using strikethrough	N/A	N/A
Style ➪ Inserted	Surrounds the selected text with HTML code for depicting inserted text, usually with underlining	N/A	N/A
HTML Styles ➪ Clear Selection Style	Removes text formatting tags around the current selection	N/A	N/A
HTML Styles ➪ Clear Paragraph Style	Removes text formatting tags for the paragraph containing the current selection	N/A	N/A
HTML Styles ➪ Your Style List	Lists the HTML styles defined for your site; select a style to apply it to the current selection	N/A	N/A
HTML Styles ➪ New Style	Displays the Define HTML Style dialog box to create a new text style	N/A	N/A
CSS Styles ➪ None/ Your Style List	Applies a user-defined style to selected text. The None option removes previously applied styles.	N/A	N/A
CSS Styles ➪ New CSS Style	Displays a dialog box for creating a new CSS style	N/A	N/A
CSS Styles ➪ Edit Style Sheet	Opens the Edit Style Sheet dialog box for adding, deleting, or modifying custom styles	Ctrl+Shift+E	Command+ Shift+E
CSS Styles ➪ Attach Style Sheet	Links a CSS file that you select to the current document	N/A	N/A

Command	Description	Windows	Macintosh
CSS Styles ⇨ Export CSS Styles	Exports CSS styles defined within the document to an external CSS file	N/A	N/A
CSS Styles ⇨ Design Time Style Sheets	Enables you to hide or show the effects of specific style sheets while you are editing in Dreamweaver	N/A	N/A
Size ⇨ Default / 1–7	Converts the selected text to the chosen font size	N/A	N/A
Size Change ⇨ +1 through +4	Increases the size of the selected text relative to the defined basefont size (the default is 3)	N/A	N/A
Size Change ⇨ −1 through −3	Decreases the size of the selected text relative to the defined basefont size (the default is 3)	N/A	N/A
Color	Opens the operating system's Color dialog box for altering the color of the selected or following text	N/A	N/A
Check Spelling	Opens the Spell Check dialog box	Shift+F7	Shift+F7

The Commands menu

Commands are user-definable code capable of affecting almost any tag, attribute, or item on the current page — or even the current site. Commands increase your productivity by automating many of the mundane, repetitive tasks in Web page creation.

Dreamweaver comes with several handy commands, but they are truly just the tip of the iceberg. Commands are written in a combination of HTML and JavaScript and can be created and modified by any capable JavaScript programmer.

The first few items on the Commands menu enable you to create, add, and manage custom commands. The additional items represent standard commands that come with Dreamweaver. If you add custom commands to Dreamweaver, they will also appear in this menu. Table 3-28 describes the standard items on the Commands menu.

Table 3-28: Commands Menu

Command	Description	Windows	Macintosh
Start/Stop Recording	Records the sequence of user commands; toggles with Stop Recording	Ctrl+Shift+X	Command+Shift+X
Play Recorded Command	Executes the last recorded command	N/A	N/A
Edit Command List	Opens the Edit Command List dialog box for arranging and deleting custom items from the Commands menu	N/A	N/A

Continued

Table 3-28: (continued)

Command	Description	Windows	Macintosh
Get More Commands	Connects to the Dreamweaver Online Resource Center	N/A	N/A
Manage Extensions	Opens the Extension Manager for installing and removing extensions	N/A	N/A
Apply Source Formatting/Apply Source Formatting to Selection	Structures the code for the current page according to the code color and formatting options specified in the Preferences dialog box	N/A	N/A
Clean Up HTML	Processes the current page according to various options for removing extraneous HTML	N/A	N/A
Clean Up Word HTML	Processes the current page according to various options for removing extraneous HTML inserted by Microsoft Word	N/A	N/A
Add/Remove Netscape Resize Fix	Inserts or deletes code to compensate for a bug affecting layers in Netscape 4+ browsers	N/A	N/A
Optimize Image in Fireworks	Displays the Optimize Image dialog box for processing images. Requires Fireworks 4 or later.	N/A	N/A
Create Web Photo Album	Uses Fireworks to make a thumbnail catalog of a folder of images. Requires Fireworks 4 or later.	N/A	N/A
Set Color Scheme	Selects a color scheme for the current page affecting background color, text color, and link colors	N/A	N/A
Format Table	Enables a predesigned format to be set on the current table	N/A	N/A
Sort Table	Sorts the current table alphabetically or numerically	N/A	N/A
Your Commands	Automatically lists new commands added to the Commands folder	N/A	N/A

Cross-Reference   Of the standard Dreamweaver commands, all but the first two are described in detail elsewhere in this book. Chapter 33 describes the Clean Up HTML command, and Chapter 7 includes information about Clean Up Word HTML. Chapter 21 explains how to use the Netscape Resize Fix. You can find information about the two Fireworks commands in Chapter 24, and a description of Set Color Scheme in Chapter 6. Chapter 10 covers the two table commands.

The Site menu

Web designers spend a good portion of their day directly interacting with a Web server: putting up new files, getting old ones, and generally maintaining the site. To ease the workflow, Dreamweaver groups site-management commands in their own menu. The Site menus are very different on the Windows and Macintosh platforms. In Windows, the most commonly used commands are listed in the Site menu in the Document window; additional commands are located on another menu on the Site panel. On Macintosh systems, the Dreamweaver window has a single Site menu containing all site-related commands, with no separate menu in the Site panel.

Because of the differences between Windows and Macintosh, the commands are listed in two different tables. All the commands found in the Document window Site menu on Windows are described in Table 3-29.

Table 3-29: Site Menu Commands (Windows)

Command	Description	Shortcut
Sites Files	Opens the Site panel if it is not already open. If the Site panel is collapsed to a single pane (Dreamweaver MX and HomeSite/Coder Style workspaces only), this command displays the Local view of the Site panel or hides the panel if it is already visible. If the Site panel is expanded (possible in any workspace), this command displays the Remote and Local views of the Site panel. If the panel is already open, the views change, but the panel will not close.	F8
Site Map	Opens the Site panel if it is not already open. If the Site panel is collapsed to a single pane (Dreamweaver MX and HomeSite/Coder Style workspaces only), this displays the Map view of the Site panel, or hides the panel if it is already visible. If the Site panel is expanded (possible in any workspace), this displays the Map and Local views of the Site panel. If the panel is already open, the views change, but the panel will not close.	Alt+F8
New Site	Presents the Site Definition dialog box for creating a new site	N/A
Edit Sites	Opens the Edit Sites dialog box, where you can choose an existing site definition to update, remove, duplicate, and so on.	N/A
Get	Transfers the selected files from the remote site to the local folder	Ctrl+Shift+D
Check Out	Transfers the selected files from the remote site to the local folder and marks the files on the remote site as checked out	Ctrl+Alt+Shift+D
Put	Transfers the selected files from the local folder to the remote site	Ctrl+Shift+U
Check In	Transfers the selected files from the local folder to the remote site and marks the files as checked in	Ctrl+Alt+Shift+U
Undo Check Out	Removes the Check Out designation on selected files	N/A

Continued

Table 3-29: *(continued)*

Command	Description	Shortcut
Locate in Site	Selects the current document in the current view (Local, Remote, or Testing Server) of the Site Files list	N/A
Reports	Opens the Reports dialog box for running the currently available interactive reports	N/A
Deploy Supporting Files	If you're using ASP.NET as your application server language, places supporting files in the correct folders on the testing server	N/A

The Macintosh Site menu is set up somewhat differently from the Windows version, although the functionality is the same. Table 3-30 details the Site menu for Macintosh systems.

Table 3-30: Site Menu Commands (Macintosh)

Command	Description	Shortcut
Site Files	Displays the Remote and Local views of the Site panel; opens the panel if it is not already visible.	F8
Site Map	Displays the Site Map and Local views of the Site panel. This opens the panel if it is not already visible.	Option+F8
New Site	Presents the Site Definition dialog box for creating a new site	N/A
Open Site ⇨ Your Site List	Displays a user-definable list of sites; when one is selected, the Site panel opens pointing to the selected site	N/A
Edit Sites	Displays the Site Information dialog box for setting up a new site, or for modifying or deleting an existing site	N/A
Connect	Connects to the current site online	N/A
Refresh	Refreshes the files list in the Site panel	F5
Site Files View ⇨ New File	Creates a new HTML file in the current site	Command+Shift+N
Site Files View ⇨ New Folder	Creates a new folder in the current site	Command+Shift+Option+N
Site Files View ⇨ Refresh Local	Rereads and displays the current local folder	Shift+F5
Site Files View ⇨ Refresh Remote	Rereads and displays the current remote folder	Option F5
Site Files View ⇨ Select Checked Out Files	Highlights files that have been checked out	N/A
Site Files View ⇨ Select Newer Local	Highlights files that have been modified locally but not transferred to the remote site	N/A

Command	Description	Shortcut
Site Map View ⇨ View as Root	Makes the selected file the starting point for the map	Command+Shift+R
Site Map View ⇨ Link to New File	Creates a new file and adds a link to the selected page	Command+Shift+N
Site Map View ⇨ Link to Existing File	Adds to the selected page a text link to an existing file	Command+Shift+K
Site Map View ⇨ Change Link	Selects a new page to use as a link (instead of the selected file) and updates the link	Command+L
Site Map View ⇨ Change Link Sitewide	Opens a dialog box that enables you to redefine the target of a link throughout the site	N/A
Site Map View ⇨ Remove Link	Deletes the selected link	Command+Shift+L
Site Map View ⇨ Show/Hide Link	Marks a file and all its dependent files as hidden or displayable	Command+Shift+Y
Site Map View ⇨ Open Source of Link	Opens the HTML file containing the selected link in Dreamweaver	N/A
Site Map View ⇨ New Home Page	Makes the selected file the starting point for the Site Map	N/A
Site Map View ⇨ Set as Home Page	Presents a Select File dialog box to choose a file that becomes the new starting point for the Site Map	N/A
Site Map View ⇨ Save Site Map ⇨ Save Site Map as PICT | JPEG	Stores the current Site Map as a graphic file in the chosen format	N/A
Site Map View ⇨ Show Files Marked as Hidden	Displays all hidden files, with the filename in italics	N/A
Site Map View ⇨ Show Dependent Files	Shows all the graphic and other additional files associated with the HTML pages	N/A
Site Map View ⇨ Show Page Titles	Displays icons identified by page titles instead of by filenames	Command+Shift+T
Site Map View ⇨ Layout	Opens the Layout dialog box, which determines the structure of the Site Map	N/A
Site Map View ⇨ Refresh Local	Redraws the Site Map	Shift+F5
Get	Transfers the selected files from the remote site to the local folder	Command+Shift+D
Check Out	Marks selected files on the remote site as checked out	Command+Shift+ Option+D

Continued

Table 3-30: *(continued)*

Command	Description	Shortcut
Put	Transfers the selected files from the local folder to the remote site	Command+Shift+U
Check In	Marks selected files as checked in	Command+Shift+Option+U
Undo Check Out	Removes the Check Out designation on selected files	N/A
Cloaking ➪ Cloak	Excludes the selected folders from various site operations, such as reporting, checking in and out, and template updating.	N/A
Cloaking ➪ Uncloak	Removes cloaking from the selected folder.	N/A
Cloaking ➪ Uncloak All	Removes cloaking from all files a.nd folders within the site	N/A
Cloaking ➪ Enable Cloaking	Enables or disables the ability to cloak files within the current site.	N/A
Cloaking ➪ Settings	Displays a dialog box that enables you to enable or disable cloaking, and to designate certain file types as being cloaked.	N/A
Open	Loads a selected file into Dreamweaver	Command+Shift+Option+O
Rename	Renames the selected file	N/A
Unlock	Makes selected read-only files accessible	N/A
Locate in Local Site	Selects the current document in the Local view of the Site Files list	N/A
Locate in Remote Site	Selects the current document in the Remote view of the Site Files list	N/A
Export	Exports the site definition as an XML file, so you can move it to another machine	N/A
Import	Imports a site definition	N/A
Reports	Opens the Reports dialog box for running the currently available interactive reports	N/A
Check Links Sitewide	Checks for broken links and unreferenced files throughout the site.	Command+F8
Change Link Sitewide	Opens a dialog box to specify a link to change	N/A
Synchronize	Transfers files between the local and remote sites so that the latest version of all selected files are on both sites	N/A
Recreate Site Cache	Rebuilds the Site Cache to enable quicker updates	N/A
Remove Connection Scripts	Deletes connection scripts found in the site	N/A

Command	Description	Shortcut
Deploy Supporting Files	Copies ASP.NET components to the testing server. This is used with the DataGrid, DataList, and DataSet components in the ASP.NET server model. You must deploy supporting files for your ASP.NET behaviors to function.	N/A
FTP Log	Opens the FTP Log window	N/A
Tool Tips	Enables long filenames or page titles to be displayed when passed over by the pointer	N/A

The Window menu

The Window menu manages both program and user-opened windows. Through this menu, described in Table 3-31, you can open, close, arrange, bring to the front, or hide all of the additional Dreamweaver screens.

Table 3-31: Window Menu Commands

Command	Description	Windows	Macintosh
Insert	Opens the Insert bar	Ctrl+F2	Command+F2
Properties	Shows the Property inspector for the currently selected item	Ctrl+F3	Command+F3
Answers	Toggles the display of the Answers panel	Alt+F1	Option+F1
CSS Styles	Opens the CSS Styles panel, for creating and assigning styles	Shift+F11	Shift+F11
HTML Styles	Displays the HTML Styles panel for creating and assigning HTML styles	Ctrl+F11	Command+F11
Behaviors	Shows the Behaviors panel	Shift+F3	Shift+F3
Tag Inspector	Displays the Tag Inspector panel	F9	F9
Snippets	Displays the Snippets panel	Shift+F9	Shift+F9
Reference	Displays the Reference panel	Ctrl+Shift+F1	Shift+F1
Databases	Displays the Databases panel	Ctrl+Shift+F10	Command+Shift+F10
Bindings	Shows the available data sources	Ctrl+F10	Command+F10
Server Behaviors	Displays and manages server-side behaviors	Ctrl+F9	Command+F9
Components	Displays the Components panel	Ctrl+F7	Command+F7
Site	Displays the Local view of the Site panel	F8	F8

Continued

Table 3-31: *(continued)*

Command	Description	Windows	Macintosh
Assets	Shows the various resources for the current site	F11	F11
Results ⇨ Search	Displays the Search panel, where you can run and see the results of a Find and Replace command	Ctrl+Shift+F	Command+Shift+F
Results ⇨ Validation	Displays the Validation panel	Ctrl+Shift+F7	Command+Shift+F7
Results ⇨ Target Browser Check	Displays a panel where you can run and see the results of a target browser check	Ctrl+Shift+F8	Command+Shift+F8
Results ⇨ Link Checker	Displays the Link Checker panel	Ctrl+Shift+F9	Command+Shift+F9
Results ⇨ Site Reports	Opens a panel where you can run and see the results of site reports	Ctrl+Shift+F11	Command+Shift+F11
Results ⇨ FTP Log	Displays the FTP log	Ctrl+Shift+F12	Command+Shift+F12
Results ⇨ Server Debug (Windows only)	Opens the Server Debug panel	Ctrl+Shift+F5	N/A
Others ⇨ Code inspector	Displays the Code inspector	F10	F10
Others ⇨ Frames	Opens the Frames panel	Shift+F2	Shift+F2
Others ⇨ History	Displays the History panel	Shift+F10	Shift+F10
Others ⇨ Layers	Opens the Layers panel	F2	F2
Others ⇨ Sitespring	Displays the Sitespring panel	F7	F7
Others ⇨ Timelines	Shows the Timelines panel	Alt+F9	Option+F9
Arrange Panels	Moves all open panels to preset positions	N/A	N/A
Show/Hide Panels	Displays/hides all open panels	F4	F4
Next Document (Macintosh only)	Brings the next open document to the front	N/A	Control+Tab
Previous Document (Macintosh only)	Brings the previous open document to the front	N/A	Control+Shift+Tab
Cascade (Windows only)	Arranges open documents so they overlap, but so their title bars are showing	N/A	N/A
Tile Horizontally/ Tile Vertically (Windows only)	Arranges open documents so every document is visible, displayed either horizontally or vertically	N/A	N/A
Your Open Windows	Displays a list of the currently open documents	N/A	N/A

Tip

The commands for Dreamweaver's various windows, panels, and inspectors are toggles. Select a command once to open the window; select it again to close it.

The Help menu

The final menu, the Help menu, offers access to Dreamweaver's excellent online Help, as well as special examples and lessons. Table 3-32 explains each of these useful options.

Table 3-32: Help Menu Commands

Command	Description	Windows	Macintosh
Welcome	Opens the Welcome overview that also displayed the first time you opened Dreamweaver	N/A	N/A
What's New	Displays the What's New section of the Welcome screen	N/A	N/A
Tutorials	Displays the available lessons in the online Help	N/A	N/A
Using Dreamweaver	Opens the Dreamweaver online Help system	F1	F1
Extending Dreamweaver	Opens the Extending Dreamweaver online documentation	N/A	N/A
Using ColdFusion	Opens the online Help for ColdFusion	Ctrl+F1	Command+F1
Reference	Opens the Reference panel to the selected code, if any	Shift+F1	Shift+F1
Dreamweaver Exchange	Connects to the Dreamweaver Online Resource Center	N/A	N/A
Manage Extensions	Opens the Extensions Manager for installing or removing extensions to Dreamweaver	N/A	N/A
Creating and Submitting Extensions	Opens the Help pages for using the Extension Manager to package extensions	N/A	N/A
Dreamweaver Support Center	Connects to Macromedia's Dreamweaver Support Center	N/A	N/A
Macromedia Online Forums	Connects to Macromedia's Online Forums page	N/A	N/A
Online Registration	Goes online to register your copy of Dreamweaver	N/A	N/A

Continued

Table 3-32: *(continued)*

Command	Description	Windows	Macintosh
Print Registration	Opens a product registration form that you can fill out, print, and mail	N/A	N/A
About Dreamweaver (Windows only)	Displays version information. On Macintosh, this information is available by choosing About Macromedia Dreamweaver MX from the Apple menu for OS9 or from the Dreamweaver menu on OSX.	N/A	N/A

Summary

In this chapter, you've observed Dreamweaver's power and had a look at its well-designed layout. From the Insert bar to the various customizable panels, Dreamweaver offers you an elegant, flexible workspace for creating next-generation Web sites.

✦ Windows users can choose from three basic workspace layouts: Dreamweaver MX, HomeSite/Coder Style, and Dreamweaver 4. The same basic tools are available in each layout; the primary differences involve where the panels are located, and whether the multiple documents can open in a single Document window.

✦ The Document window is your main canvas for visually designing your Dreamweaver Web pages. This window includes simple, powerful tools such as the Tag Selector and the status bar Launcher.

✦ Frequently used tools are available on Dreamweaver's various toolbars. The toolbars can be displayed or hidden, as you prefer.

✦ The Insert bar is Dreamweaver's toolbox. Completely customizable, the Insert bar holds the elements you need most often, grouped into useful categories.

✦ Dreamweaver's mechanism for assigning details and attributes to an HTML object is the Property inspector. The Property inspector is context-sensitive, and its options vary according to the object selected.

✦ Many of Dreamweaver's tools reside in dockable panels, which can be combined into panel groups. Panel groups can be docked or floated, hidden or shown.

✦ Dreamweaver's full-featured menus offer complete file manipulation, a wide range of insertable objects, the tools to modify them, and extensive online — and on-the-Web — help. Many menu items can be invoked through keyboard shortcuts.

In the next chapter, you learn how to customize Dreamweaver to work the way you work by establishing your own preferences for the program and its interface.

✦ ✦ ✦

Setting Your Preferences

Everyone works differently. Whether you need to conform to a corporate style sheet handed down from the powers that be or you think, "it just looks better that way," Dreamweaver offers you the flexibility to shape your Web page tools and your code output. This chapter describes the options available in Dreamweaver's Preferences and then details how you can instruct Dreamweaver to format your source code your way.

Customizing Your Environment

The vast majority of Dreamweaver's settings are controlled through the Preferences dialog box. You can open Preferences by choosing Edit ⇨ Preferences or by using the keyboard shortcut, Ctrl+U (Command+U). Within Preferences, you find 20 different subjects listed on the left side of the screen. As you switch from one category to another by selecting a name from the Category list, the options available for that category appear in the main area of the dialog box. This chapter covers all the options available in each category; the categories are grouped by function rather than by order of appearance in the Category list.

Most changes to Preferences take effect immediately after you close the window by clicking OK or the Close button. Only two preferences are not updated instantly:

✦ The Show Only Site Window on Startup option goes into effect the next you run Dreamweaver. Checking this option will disable the default blank document that comes up each time Dreamweaver starts.

✦ If you change your workspace from the General tab, you must restart Dreamweaver. Your workspace will be updated on the next running of Dreamweaver. (This option isn't available on the Macintosh; the Dreamweaver 4 Workspace is the only option for those users.)

General Preferences

Dreamweaver's General Preferences, shown in Figure 4-1, cover the program's appearance, user operation, and fundamental file settings. The appearance of the program's interface may seem to be a trivial matter, but Dreamweaver is a program for designers and coders — to whom work environment is extremely important. These user-operation options are based purely on how you, the user, work best. The following sections describe the various options available from this screen.

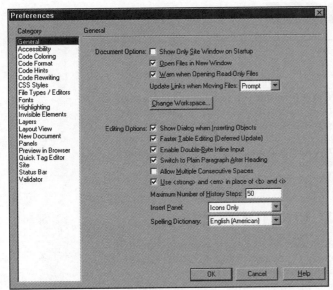

Figure 4-1: Dreamweaver's General Preferences enable you to change your program's appearance and certain overall operations.

Document Options

The first area of the General category, Document Options, determines how you work with HTML and other files.

> **Tip** In choosing all the preferences, including the General ones, you can work in two ways. If you are a seasoned Web designer, you probably want Dreamweaver to work in your established manner to minimize your learning curve. If you're just starting out as a Web-page creator, work with the default options for a while and then try other options. You should know right away which style works for you.

Show Only Site Window on Startup

Some Web designers prefer to use the Site panel as their "base of operations," rather than the Document window. For them, it's easier — particularly with many of Dreamweaver MX's new features — to construct and maintain their Web pages from the sitewide perspective offered through the Site panel. Dreamweaver offers you the option to begin a Web-authoring session using just the Site panel.

Selecting the Show Only Site Window on Startup option displays just the Site panel the next time you open Dreamweaver. The Site panel is shown with the configuration used the last time you had it open — with or without the Site Map enabled and with the various columns positioned in the same manner. To bring up the Document window, choose File ➪ New.

If you uncheck this option, Dreamweaver opens with a new blank document already open.

Open Files in New Window (Windows only)

Select the Open Files in New Window option when you need to have several Web pages open simultaneously. Alternatively, if you want to free up some of your system resources (such as memory) and you need only one Dreamweaver window, you can deselect this option.

Note If this option is not selected and changes are made to the current file, Dreamweaver asks if you'd like to save the current page when you attempt to load a new file. This option is not available on Macs.

Warn when Opening Read-Only Files

Read-only files have been locked to prevent accidental overwriting. Optionally, Dreamweaver can warn you when such a file is opened. The warning is actually more than just an alert, however. Dreamweaver provides an option on the warning dialog box to make the file writable, (or check it out if you're using the Check In/Check Out feature). Alternatively, you can just view the file.

Cross-Reference See Chapter 31 for more on the Check In/Check Out features.

New Feature Although Dreamweaver enables you to edit the file either way, if the document is still read-only when you save your changes, the Save As dialog box appears, and you are prompted to store the file under a new name.

Update Links

As your site grows in complexity, you'll find that keeping track of the various links is an increasingly difficult task. Dreamweaver has several enhanced features to help you manage links, and the Update Links option is one of them. Dreamweaver can check each link on a page when a file is moved—whether it is the Web page you're working on or one of the support files, such as an image, that goes on the page. The Update Links option determines how Dreamweaver reacts when it notes an altered link.

By default, the Update Links option is set to Prompt, which causes Dreamweaver to alert you to any link changes and requires you to verify the code alterations by selecting the Update button. To leave the files as they are, choose the Don't Update button. You can elect to have Dreamweaver automatically keep your pages up to date by selecting the Always option from the Update Links drop-down list. Finally, you can select the Never option, and Dreamweaver ignores the link changes necessary when you move, rename, or delete a file.

As a general rule, I keep my Update Links option set to Always. It is a very rare circumstance when I intentionally maintain a bad link on my Web page. Likewise, I recommend using the Never option with extreme caution.

Change Workspace

One of the best new features of Dreamweaver is the new user workspace, which allows you to work exactly the way you want to work. The new MDI (Multiple Document Interface) allows all the panels to be neatly docked on either side of the window. But moving to the new workspace can be quite a shock. If you prefer to work in the classic Dreamweaver floating panel mode, clicking Change Workspace allows you to switch to the new mode. You can also choose the default MX mode or the HomeSite mode.

Caution Changing modes in Dreamweaver requires you to restart the program for the new mode to take effect. Also, changing back and forth between modes removes any prior panel settings. So if you have your panels just the way you like them in MX mode and then switch to the Dreamweaver classic workspace, you lose your MX workspace settings. Switch modes carefully. The new MX workspace is not available on the Mac.

Editing options

The second main section of the General Preferences screen consists of numerous checkbox options you can turn on or off. Overall, these options fall into the user-interaction category, reflecting how you like to work. Take the Show Dialog when Inserting Objects option, for example. Some Web creators prefer to enter all their attributes at one time through the Property inspector and would rather not have the dialog boxes appear for every inserted object. Others want to get their file sources in immediately and modify the rest later. Your selection depends on how you want to work. The following sections describe various other options.

Show Dialog when Inserting Objects

By default, almost all the objects that Dreamweaver inserts — via either the Insert bar or the Insert menu — open an initial dialog box to gather needed information. In some cases, the dialog box enables you to input a URL or browse for a source file. Turning off the Show Dialog option causes Dreamweaver to insert a default-sized object, or a placeholder, for the object in this circumstance. You must then enter all attributes through the Property inspector.

Tip To selectively avoid the prompts, leave this option checked, but press Ctrl+click (Option+click) on an object to skip the prompt.

Faster Table Editing (Deferred Update)

When you enter text into a table, the current column width automatically expands whereas the other columns shrink correspondingly. If you're working with large tables, this updating process can slow your editing. Dreamweaver gives you a choice between faster input and instantaneous feedback.

When the Faster Table Editing preference is turned on, Dreamweaver updates the entire table only when you click outside the table or if you press Ctrl+spacebar (Command+spacebar). If you prefer to see the table form as you type, turn this option off.

Enable Double-Byte Inline Input

Some computer representations of languages, primarily Asian languages, require more raw descriptive power than others. The ideogram for "snow," for example, is far more complex than a four-letter word. These languages need twice the number of bytes per character and are known as *double-byte languages*. In versions of Dreamweaver before 2, all double-byte characters had to go through a separate text-input window, instead of directly into the Document window.

Dreamweaver now simplifies the page creation process for double-byte languages with the Enable Double-Byte Inline Input option. Once selected, this option enables double-byte characters to be entered directly into the Document window. To use the old method of inserting such characters, deselect this option.

Switch to Plain Paragraph After Heading

This might seem to be a small addition, but this new, nifty little feature is one of my favorites. In Dreamweaver 4, if you changed a line to a heading (such as <H1> or <H2>), pressing Enter closed the heading tag but the next line maintained the same heading style. Checking the

Switch to Plain Paragraph After Heading option changes the next line to a standard paragraph (<p>) tag.

New Feature — Use the Switch to Plain Paragraph after Heading to speed up your workflow. You'll almost always want a heading followed by a plain paragraph. This option gets rid of one more click of the mouse or shortcut key, making your workflow that much faster.

Allow Multiple Consecutive Spaces

Some designers prefer adding two spaces after every period, or they like to use multiple spaces to indent paragraphs to maintain a print-type appearance. In Dreamweaver 4 this spacing required pressing Ctrl+Shift+Space (Command+Shift+Space) to be able to add a   to the document. Check this option, and Dreamweaver will add the 's for you, without requiring the additional keyboard shortcut.

New Feature — This option may seem wonderful at first, but I'd recommend leaving it unchecked. Leaving a single space after a paragraph is the standard online and is even becoming standard practice in most print applications. (You'll find no double spaces in this little tome.) Enabling this option only encourages bad habits.

Use <strong> and <em> in place of <b> and <i>

In new HTML and XHTML standards, the <b> and <i> tags are deprecated, as they don't imply any structural significance to the text they surround. Many screen readers may even completely ignore the <b> and <i> tags. Check this box to use the more syntactically correct <strong> and <em> tags in their place.

New Feature — The new option to use <strong> and <em> tags will allow you to create more descriptive HTML code. This will benefit individuals using screen readers and make your code more syntactically correct, further separating style from content.

Maximum Number of History Steps

Almost every Dreamweaver action, except the mouse click, is listed in the History panel. These steps can be undone by moving the slider on the History panel or choosing Edit ⇨ Undo. A limit exists, however, to the number of steps that can be tracked. By default, the limit is set to 50.

Although 50 history steps are more than enough for most systems, you can alter this number by changing the Maximum Number of History Steps value. When the maximum number of history steps is exceeded, the oldest actions are wiped from memory and made unrecoverable. The history steps are not discarded when a file is saved.

Insert bar

Learning a new software program can be tough — just memorizing which icon means what can increase your learning curve. With Dreamweaver, you don't have to try to remember all the Insert symbols right off the bat. If you like, you can opt to have the names of the Insert symbols next to their icons — or even just the names themselves. You make this choice with the Insert bar option.

By default, the Insert bar is composed only of icons. When you pass your mouse over each one, a ToolTip appears that names the object. However, if you don't want to hunt for your object, you can select Icons and Text (or Text Only) from the Insert bar option. Whichever option you select, when you exit from Preferences, the Insert bar changes size and shape to accommodate the new format, as shown in Figure 4-2.

Figure 4-2: The Insert bar can display each object's name along with its icon.

Notice the small black down arrow in the lower left-hand corner. If the objects and their labels are too wide for the panel, you can click the down arrow to cycle through the objects not currently being displayed.

Spelling Dictionary

The Dictionary option enables you to select a spell-checking dictionary from any of those installed. In addition to the standard English-language version, which has 14 options—Danish, Dutch, English (American), English (British), English (Canadian), Finnish, French, German, Italian, Norwegian (Bokmal), Portugese (Brazilian), Portugese (Iberian), Spanish and Swedish—additional dictionaries exist online. As of this writing, dictionaries in the following other languages are also available: German, Spanish, Swedish, French, Italian, Brazilian-Portuguese, and Catalan. You can download these dictionaries from Macromedia's Dreamweaver Exchange at www.macromedia.com/support/dreamweaver/documentation/dictionary.html. After a dictionary is downloaded, save the .dat file in the Configuration\Dictionaries folder and restart Dreamweaver.

To select a different dictionary for spell checking, select the Dictionary option button and choose an item from the drop-down list. Dreamweaver also maintains a personal dictionary (although it's not visible on the list) to hold any words you want Dreamweaver to learn during the spell-checking process. So the next time you spell check a technical document, just click Add for each word Dreamweaver catches that you want it to remember. That word will them be added to the personal dictionary, and you'll never have to worry with it again.

Preferences for invisible elements

By their nature, all HTML markup tags remain unseen to one degree or another when presented for viewing through the browser. You may want to see certain elements while designing a page, however. For example, adjusting line spacing is a common task, and turning on the visibility of the line break tag `<br>` can help you understand the layout.

Dreamweaver enables you to control the visibility of 12 different codes, as well as of dynamic data and server-side includes—or rather their symbols, as shown in Figure 4-3. When, for example, a named anchor is inserted, Dreamweaver shows you a small gold shield with an anchor emblem. Not only does this shield indicate the anchor's position, but you can also manipulate the code with cut-and-paste or drag-and-drop techniques. Moreover, clicking a symbol opens the pertinent Property inspector and enables quick changes to the tag's attributes.

Tip   You can temporarily hide all invisible elements by deselecting View ➪ Visual Aids ➪ Invisible Elements.

The 12 items controlled through the Invisible Elements panel are as follows:

✦ Named Anchors

✦ Scripts

✦ Comments

- ✦ Line Breaks

- ✦ Client-Side Image Maps

- ✦ Embedded Styles

- ✦ Hidden Form Fields

- ✦ Form Delimiter

- ✦ Anchor Points for Layers

- ✦ Anchor Points for Aligned Elements

- ✦ Server Markup Tags (ASP, CFML)

- ✦ Nonvisual Server Markup Tags (ASP, CFML)

Most of the Invisible Elements options display or hide small symbols in Dreamweaver's visual Document window. Several options, however, show an outline or another type of highlight. Turning off Form Delimiter, for example, removes the dashed line that surrounds a form in the Document window.

Tip   You may have noticed that the ColdFusion tags and Active Server Page tags are combined into one symbol, Server Markup tags. Dreamweaver's capability to handle dynamic pages generated by databases makes these invisible elements essential. I generally leave the Nonvisual Server Markup Tags option unchecked as these icons flag server-side coding in the page and tend to interrupt the flow of the design.

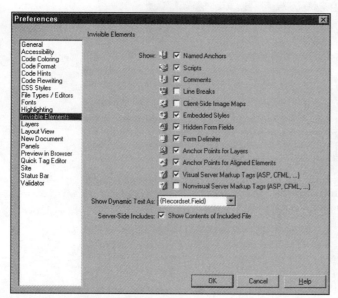

Figure 4-3: You can show or hide any or all of the 12 invisible elements listed in the Preferences dialog box and determine the appearance of recordset fields and includes.

Dreamweaver-developed pages often include references to *dynamic text*. Dynamic text is text that will be replaced by an entry from a recordset when the page is processed by the application server. Dreamweaver uses what is called *dot notation* in programming circles to fully display these names, such as {rsMaillist.EmailAddress}, enclosed in curly braces. When designing a page, the field names may be longer than the actual data, and the full dot notation becomes a visual hindrance rather than an aid. In these situations, you may want to use Dreamweaver's alternative dynamic text syntax, an empty pair of curly braces: { }. Enable this option from the Show Dynamic Text As drop-down list on the Invisible Elements panel.

When designing dynamic sites you may often use server-side includes to speed development and updates. Unfortunately, rendering these in the design window can often cause problems if you are conditionally including multiple files. Uncheck the Show Contents of Included Files to disable rendering your server-side includes.

Panels preferences

Although the various windows, panels, and inspectors are convenient, sometimes you just want a clear view of your document. The Panels category of Preferences enables you to choose which of Dreamweaver's accessory screens stay on top of the Document window. As shown in Figure 4-4, you can adjust 16 different elements. By default, they are all set to float above the Document window. One of the options, All Other Panels, controls the behavior of custom panels.

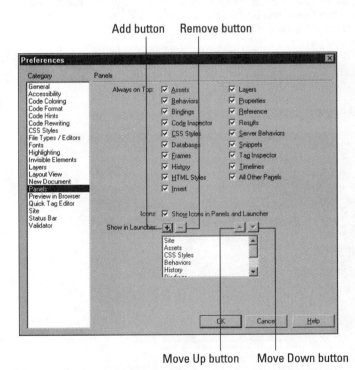

Figure 4-4: If you deselect any of the floating panel screens, they move behind the Document window.

Tip   You can use the Show/Hide Panel key to bring back any screen element that has gone behind the Document window. Just press F4.

If you prefer to use the Code inspector, rather than Code view, you might consider taking it off the "always on top" list. Then, after you've made your HTML code edits, click in the Document window. This sequence updates the visual document, incorporating any changes and simultaneously pushing the Code inspector behind the Document window. You can switch between the two views of your Web page by using the Ctrl+` (Command+`) key combination. The ` character is the grave accent paired with the tilde (˜) on the keyboard.

Show Icons in Panels and Launcher

Checking this option inserts small icons next to the Panel names in all your panels and displays the icons in the Launcher. I find the Launcher especially useful for one-click panel operation, so I recommend selecting this option. When used in combination with the Show Launcher feature, this option puts the panels you use most often right at your fingertips. However, if you're tight on screen real estate, leaving the option unselected makes it easier to view all the names of the different panels in a panel group.

Show in Launcher

The Launcher (both the floating panel and the status bar versions) displays a series of icons for quickly opening and closing various Dreamweaver panels and windows. The Launcher is completely customizable — you can add or remove icons for any of the available panels. Moreover, the order of their appearance is up to you.

To add a new icon to the Launcher, follow these steps:

1. Click the Add (+) button and choose an available floating panel from the drop-down list. The chosen panel is added to the end of the list, and the icon appears on the right of the Launcher.

2. You can reposition the icon by using the up and down arrows with the panel's name selected.

To remove an icon from the Launcher, select the panel in the list, and choose the Remove (–) button.

Tip   By default, Dreamweaver includes a minimum number of icons — nine — in the Launcher. I find that including several additional icons greatly enhances my workflow. I add the panels I use most frequently when designing a page, such as Layers, and remove the ones I don't access as often, such as Databases.

Highlighting preferences

Dreamweaver is extremely extensible — custom functions are better handled, server-side markup is more acceptable, and more third-party tags are supported. Many of these features depend on "hidden" capabilities that are not noticeable in the final HTML page. The Web designer, however, must take them into account. Dreamweaver employs user-selectable highlighting to mark areas on a Web page under construction.

The Highlighting panel of the Preferences dialog box, shown in Figure 4-5, enables you to choose the highlight color for seven different types of extended objects:

✦ Editable Regions

✦ Nested Editable regions

✦ Locked Regions

✦ Library Items

✦ Third-Party Tags

✦ Translated Live Data

✦ Untranslated Live Data

In each case, to choose a highlight color select the color swatch to open Dreamweaver's color picker. Then, use the Eyedropper to pick a color from the Web-safe palette or from the desktop. After you've chosen an appropriate color, be sure to select the related Show checkbox so that the highlighting is displayed.

Note   You can see the Locked Region highlighted in Templates only if you open the Code view; the Display view only highlights Editable Regions. You'll see the Live Data highlighting only while actually viewing your page in Live Data mode.

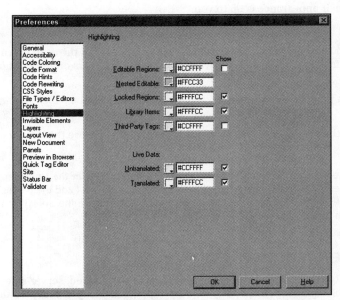

Figure 4-5: Use the Highlighting preferences to control how template regions, library items, and third-party tags appear in the Document window.

Quick Tag Editor preferences

The Quick Tag Editor is designed to bridge the gap between the visual layout and the underlying code. With the Quick Tag Editor, you can quickly edit a tag or wrap the selection in an entirely new tag without opening the Code inspector. The Quick Tag Editor pops open a small draggable window when invoked, and its preferences, shown in Figure 4-6, control the appearance and behavior of that window.

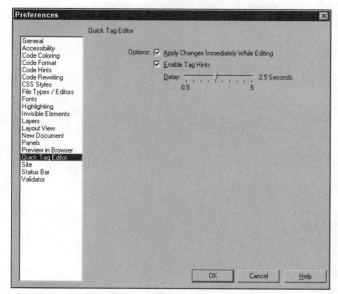

Figure 4-6: Adjust the Quick Tag Editor preferences to suit the way you like to add code to a page.

The Quick Tag Editor has three modes: Edit Tag, Insert HTML, and Wrap Tag. The first option, Apply Changes Immediately While Editing, affects only the Edit Tag mode. When this option is disabled, the Enter (Return) key must be pressed to confirm the edits. In the other two modes, you must always confirm your additions with the Enter (Return) key.

The second option, Enable Tag Hints, works in all three modes. A short time after the Quick Tag Editor is invoked, a list of possible tags appears. To reduce your typing, when the first letter of the tag is typed, the list scrolls to the tags starting with that letter. For example, if you want to wrap a `<blockquote>` tag around a paragraph, typing a *b* brings the list to the `<b>` (bold) tag; type the next letter, *l*, and the list scrolls to `<blockquote>` — at this point, all you have to do is press Enter (Return) to confirm your choice. The Tag Hints list does not appear at all if Enable Tag Hints is unchecked. You can also control the speed at which the Tag Hints list appears by moving the Delay slider; the range is from .5 seconds to 5 seconds.

Tip If you like using the Tag Hints list, set the Delay slider to 0.5 seconds; with that setting, the list pops up almost immediately and speeds up your work.

Status Bar preferences

The status bar is a handy collection of four different tool sets: the Tag Selector, the Window Size pop-up menu, the Connection Speed indicator, and the Launcher. The Status Bar category of the Preferences dialog box, shown in Figure 4-7, controls options for two of the four tools.

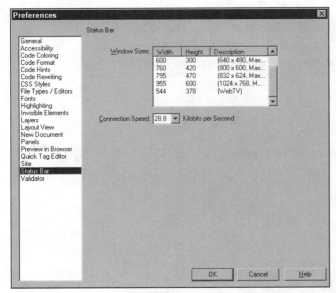

Figure 4-7: Use the Status Bar category to evaluate your real-world download times.

Window Size

The Window Size list at the top of the Status Bar category shows the current options for the Window Size pop-up menu. This list is completely user-editable and enables you to add new window sizes, modify existing dimensions, add descriptions, or delete rarely used measurements.

As discussed in Chapter 3, the Window Size pop-up is a Dreamweaver feature that enables you to instantly change your screen size so that you can view and build your page under different monitor conditions. To change any of the current dimensions, simply click the measurement you wish to alter and enter a new value. You can also change any description of the existing widths and heights by clicking in the Description column and entering your text. Although you can enter as much text as you like, it's not practical to enter more than about 15 to 20 characters. To enter a new set of dimensions in the Window Size list box, follow these steps:

1. From the Status Bar category of the Preferences dialog box, locate the last entry in the current list.

   If the last entry is not immediately available, use the vertical scroll bar to move to the end.

2. Click once in the Width column on the line below the last entry.

3. Enter the desired width of the new window size in pixels.

4. Press Tab to move to the Height column.

5. Enter the desired height for the new window size. Press Tab again.

6. Optionally, you can enter short descriptive text in the Description column. Press Tab when you're finished.

7. To continue adding new sizes, repeat Steps 2 through 6. Select OK when you finish.

Caution You don't have to enter the word *pixels* or the abbreviation *px* after your values in the Width and Height columns of the Window Size list box, but you can. If you enter any dimensions under 20, Dreamweaver converts the measurement to its smallest possible window size, 20 pixels.

Connection Speed

Dreamweaver understands that not all access speeds are created equal, so the Connection Speed option enables you to check the download time for your page (or the individual images) at a variety of rates. The Connection Speed setting evaluates the download statistics in the status bar. You can choose from seven preset connection speeds, all in kilobits per second: 14.4, 28.8, 33.6, 56, 64, 128, and 1,500. The lower speeds (14.4 through 33.6) represent older dial-up modem connection rates — if you are building a page for the mass market, you should consider selecting one of these slower rates. Although 56K modems are widespread on the market today, the true 56K connection is a rare occurrence. Use the 128 setting if your audience connects through an ISDN line. If you know that everyone will view your page through a direct LAN connection, change the connection speed to 1,500.

You are not limited to these preset settings. You can type any desired speed directly into the Connection Speed text box. You could, for example, specify a connection speed more often experienced in the real world, such as 23.3. If you find yourself designing for an audience using DSL or cable modems, change the Connection Speed to 150 or higher.

File Types/Editors preferences

Refinement is often the name of the game in Web design, and quick access to your favorite modification tools — whether you're modifying code, graphics, or other media — is one of Dreamweaver's key features. The File Types/Editors category, shown in Figure 4-8, is where you specify the program you want Dreamweaver to call for any file type you define.

Open in Code View

It's no longer just an HTML world — many other code types may be found on a Web designer's palette such as XML, XSL, or Perl. Dreamweaver's internal code is full-featured enough to handle a wide variety of code and, with the Open in Code View option, you can determine which types you'd like it to handle. By default, JavaScript (.js), text (.txt) and Active Server Application (.asa) files are automatically opened in Code view. Dreamweaver attempts to open any other selected file type in Design view.

If you find yourself hand-editing other file types, such as XML files, you can add their extension to the Open in Code View field. Separate extensions with a space and be sure to begin each one with a period.

Note Although Macintosh systems do not require extensions, you can still use the Open in Code View feature.

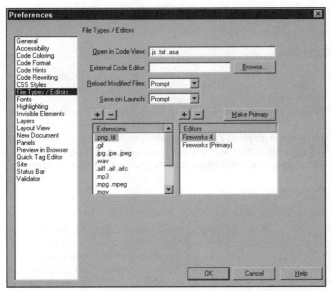

Figure 4-8: Assign your favorite HTML, graphics editors, and more through the newly extended File Types/Editors category of the Preferences dialog box.

External Code Editor preferences

Dreamweaver recognizes the importance of your choice of a text editor. Although Dreamweaver ships with two extremely robust code editors — as well as its excellent built-in code editor — you can opt to use any other program. To select your editor, enter the path in the External Code Editor text box or select the Browse (Choose) button to choose the appropriate executable file.

The two included editors, BBEdit for Macintosh and HomeSite for Windows, are integrated with Dreamweaver to varying degrees. Both of the editors can be called from within Dreamweaver, and both have "Dreamweaver" buttons for returning to the main program — switching between the editor and Dreamweaver automatically updates the page. Like Dreamweaver's internal HTML editor, BBEdit highlights the corresponding code to a selection made in Dreamweaver; this property does not, however, extend to HomeSite. You specify and control your external editor selection with the following options.

Enable BBEdit Integration (Macintosh only)

Dreamweaver for Macintosh ships with this option activated. If you prefer to use another editor or an older version of BBEdit that lacks the integration capabilities, deselect this option. Uncheck this box to enable the Browse to External Code Editors fields.

Reload Modified Files

The drop-down list for this setting offers three options for working with an external editor:

✦ **Prompt:** Detects when files are updated by another program and enables you to decide whether to update them within Dreamweaver.

✦ **Always:** Updates the file in Dreamweaver automatically when the file is changed in an outside program.

✦ **Never:** Assumes that you want to make all updates from within Dreamweaver yourself.

Personally, I prefer to have Dreamweaver always update my files. I find that it saves a couple of mouse clicks — not to mention time.

Save on Launch

Any external HTML editor — even the integrated HomeSite or BBEdit — opens and reads a previously saved file. Therefore, if you make any changes in Dreamweaver's visual editor and switch to your editor without saving, the editor shows only the most recently saved version. To control this function, you have three options:

✦ **Prompt:** Determines that unsaved changes have been made and asks you to save the file. If you do not, the external editor reverts to the last saved version.

✦ **Always:** Saves the file automatically before opening it in the external editor.

✦ **Never:** Disregards any changes made since the last save, and the external editor opens the previously saved file.

Here, again, as with Reload Modified Files, I prefer to always save my files when switching back and forth.

Tip

If you try to open a file that has never been saved in an external editor, Dreamweaver prompts you to save it regardless of your preference settings. If you opt not to save the file, the external editor is not opened because it has no saved file to display.

File Types Editor preferences

Dreamweaver has the capability to call an editor for any specified type of file at the touch of a button. For example, when you import a graphic, you often need to modify its color, size, shape, transparency, or another feature to make it work correctly on the Web page. Rather than force you to start your graphics program independently, load the image, make the changes, and resave the image, Dreamweaver enables you to send any selected image directly to your editor. After you've made your modifications and saved the file, the altered image appears automatically in Dreamweaver.

The capability to associate different file types with external editors applies to more than just images in Dreamweaver. You can link one or more editors to any type of media — images, audio, video, even specific kinds of code. The defined external editor is invoked when the file is double-clicked in the Site panel. Because the editors are assigned according to file extension, as opposed to media type, one editor can be assigned to GIF files and another to JPEGs. The selection is completely customizable.

Note

If you have the same file type both defined to Open in Code View and set up in the editor list, the file defaults to opening in Code view.

When a file is double-clicked in the Site panel, that file type's primary editor runs. Dreamweaver offers the capability to define multiple editors for any file extension. You might, for instance, prefer to open certain JPEGs in Fireworks and others in Photoshop. To choose an alternative editor, right-click (Control+click) the filename in the Site panel and select the desired program from the Open With menu option. The Open With option also enables you to browse for a program.

To assign an editor to an existing file type, follow these steps:

1. Select the file type from the Extensions list.

2. Click the Add (+) button above the Editors list. The Add External Editor dialog box opens.

3. Locate the application file of the editor and click Open when you're ready.

You can also select a shortcut or alias to the application.

4. If you want to select the editor as the primary editor, click Make Primary while the editor is highlighted.

To add a new file type, click the Add (+) button above the Extensions list and enter the file extension — including the period — in the field displayed at the bottom of the list. For multiple file extensions, separate each extension with a space, as shown here:

```
.doc .dot .rtf
```

Tip   Looking for a good almost-all-purpose media editor? The QuickTime Pro Player makes a great addition to Dreamweaver as the editor for AIFF, AU, WAV, MP3, AVI, MOV, animated GIF files, and others. The Pro Player is wonderful for quick edits and optimization, especially with sound files. It's available from the Apple Web site (`www.apple.com/quicktime`) for both platforms for around $30.

Finally, to remove an editor or a file extension, select it and click the Remove (–) button above the corresponding list. Note that removing a file extension also removes the associated editor.

Cross-Reference   Make sure that your graphics program is adept at handling the three graphic formats used on the Web: GIFs, JPEGs, and PNG images. Macromedia makes Fireworks, a graphics editor designed for the Web, which integrates nicely with Dreamweaver. In fact, it integrates so nicely that this book includes an entire chapter on it, Chapter 24.

New Document preferences

Dreamweaver has greatly improved the New Document interface. You can now quickly choose which type of document you want to create, as well as select from built-in page designs and CSS. The New Document dialog appears each time you press Control + N (Command + N) or choose File ⇨ New. Use the New Document preferences shown in Figure 4-9 to refine how you interact with this New Document dialog box.

Default Document Type

This list menu contains all the default document types in the New Document dialog box (File ⇨ New). Choose which document type you want to be the default for quickly creating new documents. If you design ASP applications more often than plain HTML files, just choose ASP VBScript or ASP JavaScript from the list menu. You can also choose templates, XML files, PHP files, and the list goes on.

Default Extension

You can define a default extension for each document type in Dreamweaver. This means that if your server requires all ASP files to have the .dan extension and all your ColdFusion pages to have the .joe extension, you can change the extension to fit your needs. Click the <u>document type XML file</u> link to open the Dreamweaver help system to the topic that explains manually editing the Document Type XML File.

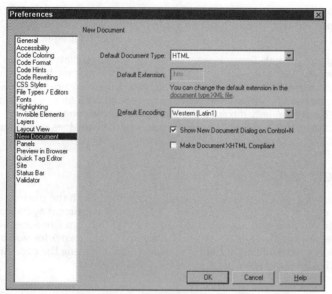

Figure 4-9: Choose your default document extensions, encoding, and HTML version.

Show New Document Dialog on Control+N

If you consistently use the same document type, uncheck this box to prevent the New Document dialog box from coming up when you press Ctrl+N (Command+N). This can measurably speed up creating new documents. Leave this box checked to see the New Document dialog box every time you create a new document.

Make Document XHTML-compliant

XHTML is the latest and greatest version of HTML. Fortunately, Dreamweaver can handle XHTML just as well as HTML. Checking this box will make every new document an XHTML document. This includes adding a DOCTYPE to each document and holding it to the more rigid XHTML standard.

More and more sites will be moving to XHTML in the near future. In most documents, coding for XHTML requires only a bit more care with opening and closing tags. I recommend building a few documents as XHTML to find out if it's something you can work with for your new sites.

See Chapter 6 for more on working with XHTML.

Adjusting Advanced Features

Evolution of the Web and its language, HTML, never ends. New features emerge, often from leading browser developers. A developer often introduces a feature similar to those marketed by his competitors but that works in a slightly different way. The HTML standards organization—

the World Wide Web Consortium, also known as the W3C—can then endorse one approach or introduce an entirely new method of reaching a similar goal. Eventually, one method usually wins the approval of the marketplace and becomes the accepted coding technique.

To permit the widest range of features, Dreamweaver enables you to designate how your code is written to accommodate the latest Web features: accessibility options, layers, and style sheets. The default preferences for these elements offer the highest degree of cross-browser and backward compatibility. If your Web pages are intended for a more specific audience, such as a Netscape Navigator–only intranet, Dreamweaver enables you to take advantage of a more specific feature set. Furthermore, Dreamweaver also gives you control over its Layout view, enabling you to set options globally or on a site-by-site basis.

Accessibility preferences

Dreamweaver offers much improved support for accessibility options. With the passing of the Section 508 statute (www.usdoj.gov/crt/508/508home.html), all government agencies are required to make their sites as accessible as possible (and making your own site accessible isn't such a bad idea). Dreamweaver will make that transition just a little easier for you by allowing you to manage which accessibility options you want to enable using the accessibility preferences, as shown in Figure 4-10.

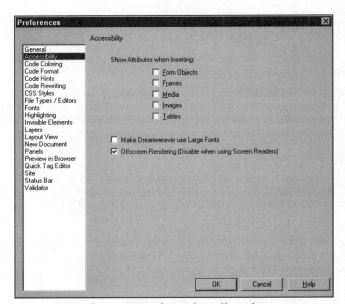

Figure 4-10: Choose to use larger fonts if you have poor vision or an ultra-high screen resolution. You can also choose the tags for which you want additional accessible options.

Show Attributes when Inserting

Check the box next to each tag you want to view additional accessible options for when inserting that object. If you check the box next to Tables, you'll get an expanded dialog the next time you insert a table into your page, as shown in Figure 4-11.

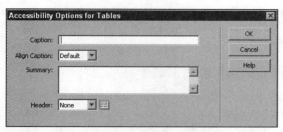

Figure 4-11: The Dreamweaver accessibility options offer a quick way to ensure that the most common tags have everything they need to meet Section 508 guidelines.

Inserting a table with the accessibility options enabled gives you a much wider range of options, including captions and summaries as well as choices about headers for rows, columns, neither, or both. The same holds true for forms, frames, media, and images.

Make Dreamweaver use Large Fonts

If you've got poor vision or an ultra-high resolution, Dreamweaver's small fonts in the Property inspector and throughout the panels can cause major problems when trying to design a site, much less make that site accessible. Turning on Large Fonts in Dreamweaver 4 led to disastrous effects throughout the program. Dreamweaver MX has vastly improved in this area, mainly due to Section 508 guidelines for software developers. Checking the option to use large fonts will require you to restart Dreamweaver.

Offscreen Rendering (Disable when using Screen Readers)

Dreamweaver uses double buffering (drawing into an offscreen bitmap before drawing to the screen) to prevent flickering. Unfortunately, this confuses screen readers, devices that help blind people use applications such as Dreamweaver. If you're using a screen reader, disable this option.

Layout View preferences

In Layout view, a column in a table may be set to automatically match the size of the browser window; if the window is resized, the column is stretched or shrunk accordingly. To maintain the structure of such tables and other complex layout devices, professional designers often include an added row on the top or bottom of the table. This additional row is sized to be 1 pixel high, with the same number of cells as the table itself. Within each cell (except for the resizable cell) is a transparent GIF image, sized to match the cell's dimensions. This image is sometimes called a *shim*—Dreamweaver refers to it as a *spacer*. One of the major functions of the Layout View category of Preferences is managing these spacers.

Dreamweaver automatically includes spacers if a column is set to Autostretch and the Autoinsert Spacers When Making Autostretch Tables option is selected, as it is by default (see Figure 4-12). If you decide not to include spacers, select Never. Which should you choose? I find that spacers definitely help; and, unless you have a compelling reason not to use them—such as a corporate edict, I'd advise you to go with the default option. Because a spacer is an actual graphic image, albeit a small one, you must include such a file in every site. Dreamweaver will create one for you if you like, or you can select an existing one. The option for creating or locating a spacer is offered when an autostretch table is designated.

However, if you'd prefer not to worry about spacers each time you create an autostretch table, you can preselect an existing image to use through the Layout View category of Preferences. This option is set on a sitewide basis.

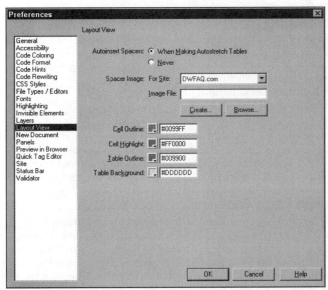

Figure 4-12: Spacers are used to maintain a table's complex layout; you can set which spacer is used on a site-by-site basis through the Layout View category of Preferences.

To set a spacer image for a site, follow these steps:

1. In the Layout View category of Preferences, choose the site to be affected from the Spacer Image For Site drop-down list.

2. If you do not have a transparent, single-pixel GIF image available, select Create.

   Dreamweaver opens the Save Spacer Image File As dialog box.

3. Select a location within your site to store the spacer file.

   If you like, you can also rename the file from spacer.gif to something else.

4. If a graphic on your site is using a transparent, single-pixel GIF image, select Browse (Choose) to locate the graphic.

   As noted earlier, Fireworks uses such a file, which is stored as shim.gif. If you have Fireworks-sliced images in your site, I recommend selecting shim.gif as your Dreamweaver spacer to reduce the number of files on the site.

The remaining options found under the Layout View category are concerned with the various colors used:

✦ **Cell Outline:** The color of the layout cell when it is selected; the default is bright blue.

✦ **Cell Highlight:** The color used to designate an unselected layout cell when the designer's mouse rolls over it; it is red by default.

✦ **Table Outline:** The color of the outline surrounding the entire table; the outline is initially set to dark green.

✦ **Table Background:** The color of the layout table where no layout cell has been drawn; a light gray is the default background color.

Should your site design make any of the colors unusable—if, for example, your page background is the same light gray as the default table background—you can alter the colors by selecting the color swatch and choosing a new color from the standard color picker.

Layers preferences

Aside from helping you control the underlying coding method for producing layers, Dreamweaver enables you to define the default layer. This capability is especially useful during a major production effort in which the Web development team must produce hundreds of layers spread over a Web site. Being able to specify in advance the initial size, color, background, and visibility saves numerous steps—each of which would have to be repeated for every layer. Figure 4-13 shows the layout of the Layers category of the Preferences dialog box.

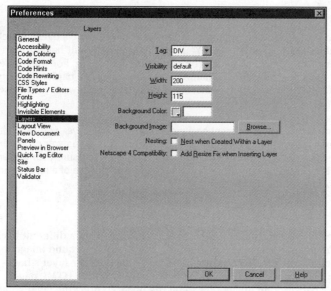

Figure 4-13: In the Layers category of Preferences, you can predetermine the structure of the default Dreamweaver layer.

The controls accessible through the Layers category are described in the following sections.

Tag

Select the arrow button to see the tags for the two HTML code methods for implementing layers: `<div>` and `<span>`. These two tags were developed by the W3C as part of their Cascading Style Sheets recommendation and are supported by both the Netscape and Microsoft 4.0 browsers. Dreamweaver uses the `<div>` tag for its default. Supported by both major 4.0 and later browsers, the `<div>` element offers the widest cross-browser compatibility.

Visibility

Layers can be either visible or hidden when the Web page is first loaded. A layer created using the default visibility option is always displayed initially; however, no specific information is written into the code. Selecting Visible forces Dreamweaver to include a visibility:visible line in your layer code. Likewise, if you select Hidden from the Visibility options, the layer is initially hidden.

Use the Inherit option when creating nested layers. Creating one layer inside another makes the outer layer the parent and the inner layer the child. If the parent layer is visible and the child layer is set to visibility:inherit, the child is also visible. This option makes it possible to affect the visibility of many layers with one command — hide the parent layer, and all the inheriting child layers disappear as well.

Width and Height

When you choose Draw Layer from the Insert bar, you drag out the size and shape of your layer. Choosing Insert ➪ Layer puts a layer of a default size and shape at your current cursor position. The Width and Height options enable you to set these defaults. Select the text boxes and type in your new values. Dreamweaver's default is a layer that is 200 pixels wide and 115 pixels high.

Background color

Layers can have their own background colors independent of the Web page's overall background color (which is set as a <body> attribute). You can define the default background color of any inserted layer through either the Insert menu or the Insert bar. For this preference setting, type a color, either by its standard name or as a hexadecimal triplet, directly into the text box. You can also click the color swatch to display the Dreamweaver browser-safe color picker.

Caution

Note that although you can specify a different background color for the layer, you can't alter the layer's default text and link colors (except on a layer-by-layer basis) as you can with a page. If your page and layer background colors are highly contrasting, be sure your text and links are readable in both environments. A similar caveat applies to the use of a layer's background image, as explained in the next section.

Background Image

Just as you can pick a specific background color for layers, you can select a different background image for layers. You can type a file source directly into the Background Image text box or select your file from a dialog box by clicking the Browse button. The layer's background image supersedes the layer background color, just as it does in the HTML page. Similarly, just as the page's background image tiles to fill the page, so does the layer's background image.

Nesting

The two best options regarding layers seem to be directly opposed: overlapping and nesting layers. You can design layers to appear one on top of another, or you can code layers so that they are within one another. Both techniques are valuable options, and Dreamweaver enables you to decide which one should be the overriding method.

If you are working primarily with nested layers and plan to use the inheritance facility, check the Nest when Created Within a Layer option. If your design entails a number of overlapping but independent layers, make sure this option is turned off. Regardless of your preference, you can reverse it on an individual basis by pressing the Ctrl (Command) key when drawing out your layers.

Netscape 4.x compatibility

Netscape 4.x has a particularly annoying problem when displaying Web pages with layers. When the user resizes the browser, all the CSS positioning information is lost — in other words, all your layers lose their exact positioning and typically align themselves on the left. The only solution is to force Netscape to reload the page after the browser has been resized.

When the Netscape 4 Compatibility option is enabled, Dreamweaver automatically includes a small JavaScript routine to handle the resizing problem. The code is inserted in the `<head>` section of the page when the first layer is added to the page. If additional layers are added, Dreamweaver is smart enough to realize that the workaround code has already been included and does not add more unnecessary code.

Many Web designers run into this problem as they begin to explore the possibilities of Dynamic HTML. Although the problem has been fixed with the release of Netscape 6, I highly recommend that you enable this option to prevent any problems with the large number of Netscape 4.x browsers still in use.

CSS Styles preferences

The CSS Styles category (see Figure 4-14) is entirely devoted to how your code is written. As specified by the W3C, CSS declarations — the specifications of a style — can be written in several ways. One method displays a series of items, separated by semicolons:

```
H1 {
   font-family: Arial, Helvetica, sans-serif;
   font-size: 12pt;
   line-height: 14pt;
   font-weight: bold;
}
```

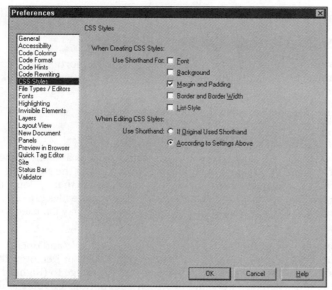

Figure 4-14: The CSS Styles category enables you to code the style sheet sections of your Web pages in a graphics-designer–friendly manner.

Certain properties (such as Font) have their own grouping shorthand, developed to be more readable to designers coming from a traditional print background. A second, "shorthand" method of rendering the preceding declaration follows:

```
H1 { font: bold 12px/14px Arial, Helvetica, sans-serif; }
```

With the CSS Styles category, you can enable the shorthand method for any or all the five different properties that permit it. Select any of the checkboxes under Use Shorthand For to have Dreamweaver write your style code in this fashion.

The second option on the CSS Styles category determines how Dreamweaver edits styles in previously coded pages. If you want to retain the format of the original page, click Use Shorthand If Original Used Shorthand. If you want Dreamweaver to write new code in the manner that you specify, select Use Shorthand According to Settings Above.

Caution   Although the leading varieties of the 4.0 and later browsers can read the style's shorthand with no difficulty, Internet Explorer 3.0 does not have this capability. IE3 is the only other mainstream browser that can claim support for Cascading Style Sheets, but it doesn't understand the shorthand form. If you want to maintain browser backward-compatibility, don't enable any of the shorthand options.

Making Online Connections

Dreamweaver's visual layout editor offers an approximation of your Web page's appearance in the real world of browsers — offline or online. After you've created the initial draft of your Web page, you should preview it through one or more browsers. And when your project nears completion, you should transfer the files to a server for online, real-time viewing and further testing through a File Transfer Protocol program (FTP). Dreamweaver gives you control over all these stages of Web-page development, through the Site and Preview in Browser categories.

Site preferences

As your Web site takes shape, you'll spend more time with the Site panel portion of Dreamweaver. The Site category, shown in Figure 4-15, enables you to customize the look-and-feel of your site, as well as to enter essential connection information.

The available Site preferences are described in the following sections.

Always Show Local/Remote Files on the Right/Left

The full-screen Site panel is divided into two panes: one showing local files and one showing remote files on the server. By default, Dreamweaver puts the local pane on the right and the remote pane on the left. However, Dreamweaver enables you to customize that option. Like many designers, I'm used to using other FTP programs in which the remote files are on the right and the local files on the left; Dreamweaver enables me to work the way I'm used to working.

To switch the layout of your expanded Site panel, switch to full-screen mode and open the Site preferences. Select the file location you want to change to (Local Files or Remote Files) from the Always Show drop-down list or select the panel you want to change to (Right or Left) from the "on the" drop-down list. Be careful not to switch both options or you end up where you started!

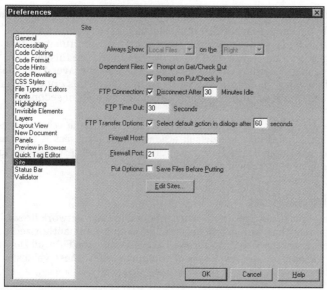

Figure 4-15: Options for Dreamweaver's Site panel are handled through the Site category.

Dependent files

Web pages are seldom just single HTML files. Any graphic — whether it's in the background, part of your main logo, or used on a navigational button — is uploaded as a separate file. The same is true for any additional multimedia add-ons such as audio or video files. If you've enabled File Check In/Check Out when defining your site, Dreamweaver can also track these so-called dependent files.

Enabling the Prompt checkboxes causes Dreamweaver to ask you if you'd like to move the dependent files when you transfer an HTML file. You can opt to show the dialog box for Get/Check Out, Put/Check In, or both.

Tip   You're not stuck with your Dependent Files choice. If you turn off the Dependent Files prompt, you can make it appear by pressing the Alt (Option) key while clicking the Get or Put button.

FTP Connection: Disconnect After __ Minutes Idle

You can easily forget you're online when you are busy modifying a page. You can set Dreamweaver to automatically disconnect you from an FTP site after a specified interval. The default is 30 minutes; if you want to set a different interval, you can select the FTP Connection value in the Disconnect After text box. Dreamweaver then asks if you want to continue to wait or to disconnect when the time limit is reached, but you can maintain your FTP connection regardless by deselecting this option.

FTP Time Out

Client-server communication is prone to glitches. Rather than hanging up your machine while trying to reach a server that is down or slow, Dreamweaver alerts you to an apparent problem after a set period. You can determine the number of seconds you want Dreamweaver to wait by altering the FTP Time Out value. The default is 60 seconds.

FTP Transfer Options: Select default action in dialogs after __ seconds

This is a handy new feature in Dreamweaver MX. I often start a large FTP process (like uploading an entire site) and then go for my morning blast of coffee. Unfortunately, this means that I sometimes miss a prompt, such as "Do you want to overwrite this file?" or "Do you want to upload all dependent files?" With earlier versions of Dreamweaver, I'd come back an hour later (I drink a lot of coffee) and nothing would be done. Check this option to have Dreamweaver accept the default action for the prompt after a set number of seconds.

This action is enabled by default, but be sure you know what the default values for most dialogs are before checking this box. The default action for uploading files is to include dependent files. If you have out-of-date files on your local machine, the latest awesome logo your graphic designer uploaded last night might be overwritten.

Firewall Host and Firewall Port

Dreamweaver enables users to access remote FTP servers outside their network firewalls. A firewall is a security component that protects the internal network from unauthorized outsiders, while enabling Internet access. To enable firewall access, enter the Firewall Host and External Port numbers in the appropriate text boxes; if you do not know these values, contact your network administrator.

If you're having trouble transferring files through the firewall via FTP, make sure the Use Firewall (in Preferences) option is enabled in the Site Definition dialog box. You can find the option on the Testing Server category.

Put options

Certain site operations, such as putting a file on the remote site, are now available in the Document window. It's common to make an edit to your page and then quickly choose the Site ⇨ Put command—without saving the file first. In this situation, Dreamweaver prompts you with a dialog box to save your changes. However, you can avoid the dialog box and automatically save the file by choosing the Save Files Before Putting option.

Edit Sites button

Dreamweaver now offers access to your site definitions from the Preferences dialog box. Just click the Edit Sites button to open the Edit Sites dialog box.

See Chapter 5 to learn how to use the site definitions.

Preview in Browser preferences

Browser testing is an essential stage of Web page development. Previewing your Web page within the environment of a particular browser gives you a more exact representation of how it looks when viewed online. Because each browser renders the HTML with slight differences, you should preview your work in several browsers. Dreamweaver enables you to select both a primary and secondary browser, which can both be called by pressing a function key. You can name up to 18 additional browsers through the Preview in Browser category shown in Figure 4-16. This list of preferences is also called when you choose File ⇨ Preview in Browser ⇨ Edit Browser List.

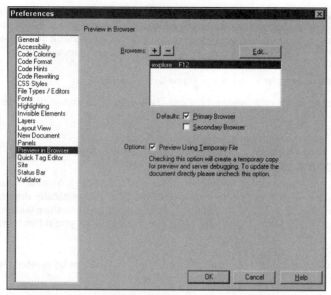

Figure 4-16: The Preview in Browser category lists browsers currently available for preview and enables you to modify the list.

To add a browser to your preview list, follow these steps:

1. Choose Edit ⇨ Preferences or press the keyboard shortcut, Ctrl+U (Command+U).

2. Select the Preview in Browser category.

3. Select the Add (+) button.

4. Enter the path to the browser file in the Path text box or click the Browse (Choose) button to pick the file from the Select Browser dialog box.

5. After you have selected your browser application, Dreamweaver fills in the Name field. You can alter this name if you wish.

6. If you want to designate this browser as your primary or secondary browser, select one of those checkboxes in the Defaults section.

7. Click OK when you have finished.

8. You can continue to add browsers (up to a total of 20) by following Steps 3 through 7. Click OK when you have finished.

After you've added a browser to your list, you can modify your selection by following these steps:

1. Open the Preview in Browser category and highlight the browser you want to alter.

2. Select the Edit button to get the Edit Browser dialog box.

3. After you've made your modifications, click OK to close the dialog box.

Tip You can quickly designate a browser as your primary or secondary previewing choice without going through the Edit screen. From the Preview in Browser category, select the desired browser and check either Primary Browser or Secondary Browser. Note that if you already have a primary or secondary browser defined, this action overrides your previous choice.

You can also easily remove a browser from your preview list:

1. Open the Preview in Browser category and choose the browser you want to delete from the list.

2. Select the Remove (–) button and click OK.

Preview Using Temporary File

By default, Dreamweaver uses temporary files for previewing your work in a browser. The temporary files generally have TMPXXXXX.html-type names and are automatically deleted when you quit Dreamweaver. Unselect this option and Dreamweaver previews the last saved file; if your file has been modified since the last save, Dreamweaver asks if you'd like to save the file.

Caution If Dreamweaver does not shut down normally, the temporary files will not be deleted. Feel free to remove them the next time you launch Dreamweaver.

Customizing Your Code

For all its multimedia flash and visual interactivity, the Web is based on code. The more you code, the more particular about your code you are likely to become. Achieving a consistent look-and-feel to your code enhances its readability and, thus, your productivity. In Dreamweaver, you can even design the HTML code that underlies a Web page's structure.

Every time you open a new document, the default Web page already has several key elements in place, such as the language in which the page is to be rendered. Dreamweaver also enables you to customize your work environment by selecting default fonts and even the colors of your HTML code.

Fonts preferences

In the Fonts category, shown in Figure 4-17, you can control the basic language of the fonts as seen by a user's browser and the fonts that you see when programming. The Default Encoding section enables you to choose Western-style fonts for Web pages to be rendered in English, one of the Asian languages — Japanese, Traditional Chinese, Simplified Chinese, or Korean — or another language, such as Cyrillic, Greek, or Icelandic Mac. Changing the Document Encoding in the Page Properties for a document will use the font sizes defined in these preferences.

Dreamweaver now offers 11 encoding options, as well as a generic Other category. Many of the encodings, such as Icelandic Mac, have platform-specific configurations. Be sure to examine all the options before you make a selection.

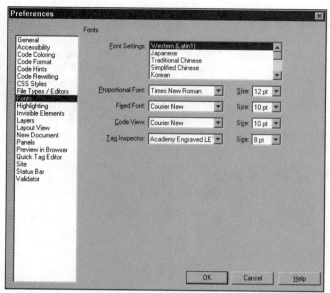

Figure 4-17: Use the Fonts category to set the font encoding for each Web page and the fonts you use when programming.

In the bottom portion of the Fonts category, you can alter the default font and size for four different fonts:

✦ **Proportional Font:** This font option sets the default font used in Dreamweaver's Document window to depict paragraphs, headings, and lists.

✦ **Fixed Font:** In a fixed font, every character is allocated the same width. Dreamweaver uses your chosen fixed font to depict preformatted-styled text.

✦ **Code View:** The Code View font is used by Dreamweaver's built-in text editor. You should probably use a monospaced font such as Courier or Monaco. A monospaced font makes it easy to count characters, which is often necessary when debugging your code.

✦ **Tag Inspector:** The Tag Inspector font is used by the Tag Inspector panel. The default font for the Tag Inspector is rather tiny, so you may want to increase the size here to make using the Tag Inspector a little more pleasant.

For all four font options, select your font by clicking the list and highlighting your choice of font. Change the font size by selecting the value in the Size text box or by typing in a new number.

Caution

Don't be misled into thinking that by changing your Proportional Font preference to Arial or another font, all your Web pages are automatically viewed in that typeface. Changing these font preferences affects only the default fonts that you see when developing the Web page; the default font that the user sees is controlled by the user's browser. To ensure that a different font is used, you have to specify it for any selected text through the Text Properties inspector.

Code Hints preferences

Dreamweaver now offers Code Hints similar to HomeSite and ColdFusion Studio. This makes working in Code view much more productive. You can now start typing a tag in Code view, and Dreamweaver shows you a list of available codes. Start typing **<b** and a list appears with <b> highlighted. Type **<bl** and <blockquote> is highlighted. After the tag you want is highlighted, just press Enter (Return) to insert the proper tag. But wait, there's more. The Code Hints also include all the available attributes for each tag, and when you add the closing > symbol, the matching closing tag is automatically inserted for you. The Code Hints preferences shown in Figure 4-18 determine how Code Hints work for you.

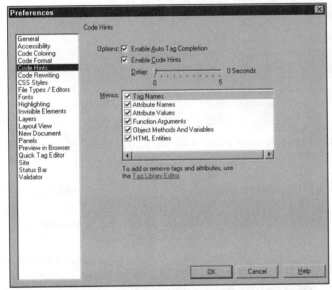

Figure 4-18: The Code Hints are among the most powerful new additions to the Dreamweaver workflow. Choose exactly how you want to put them to use.

Options: Enable Auto Tag Completion

Enabling Auto Tag Completion tells Dreamweaver to close all the tags you created while working in Code view. For example if I have Auto Tag Completion on and I type <b> into Code view, the corresponding </b> will be added as soon as I type the last > in the bold tag.

New Feature   Auto Tag Completion is one of my favorite new features in Dreamweaver, and it definitely keeps me from forgetting those pesky closing tags. I highly recommend leaving this option enabled at all times.

Options: Enable Code Hints

This checkbox determines whether you get the new Dreamweaver Code Hints. If you have this box enabled, you can set the delay before the Code Hints drop-down menu appears. I leave the delay set to 0 so that Code Hints display as soon as I start typing, as you can see in Figure 4-19.

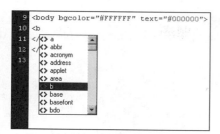

Figure 4-19: Code Hints make adding new tags to Code View a quick and pleasant experience.

Code Rewriting preferences

The exception to Dreamweaver's policy of not altering imported code occurs when HTML or other code is incorrectly structured. Dreamweaver automatically fixes tags that are nested in the wrong order or have additional, unnecessary closing tags — unless you tell Dreamweaver otherwise by setting up the Code Rewriting preferences accordingly (see Figure 4-20).

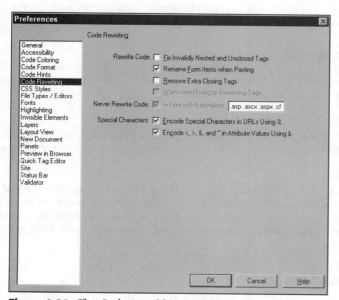

Figure 4-20: The Code Rewriting category can be used to protect nonstandard HTML from being automatically changed by Dreamweaver.

Dreamweaver accommodates many different types of markup languages, not just HTML, through the Never Rewrite Code in Files with Extensions option. Moreover, you can prevent Dreamweaver from encoding special characters, such as spaces, tildes, and ampersands, in URLs or attribute values. Dreamweaver is now extremely flexible. The following sections describe each of the options available through the Code Rewriting category.

Fix Invalidly Nested and Unclosed Tags

When enabled, this option repairs incorrectly placed tags. For example, if a file contains the following line:

```
<h3><b>Welcome to the Monkey House!</h3></b>
```

Dreamweaver rewrites it as follows:

```
<h3><b>Welcome to the Monkey House!</b></h3>
```

Open that same file with this option turned off, and Dreamweaver highlights the misplaced code in the Document window. Double-clicking the code brings up a window with a brief explanation.

Rename Form Items when Pasting

In general, static Web pages require each form element to be uniquely named; with this option selected, you can quickly insert a series of text fields with similar attributes and still be assured that they are individually named. However, with dynamic applications, the names may be supplied dynamically and you don't want to have that code overwritten. Unchecking this box prevents Dreamweaver from renaming all your form elements.

Remove Extra Closing Tags

When you're editing your code by hand, it's fairly easy to miss a closing tag. Dreamweaver cleans up such code if you enable the Remove Extra Closing Tags option. You may, for example, have the following line in a previously edited file:

```
<p>And now back to our show...</p></i>
```

Notice that the closing italic tag, `</i>`, has no matching opening partner. If you open this file in Dreamweaver with the Remove option enabled, Dreamweaver plucks out the offending `</i>`.

Tip   In some circumstances, you want to ensure that your pages remain as originally formatted. If you edit pages in Dreamweaver that have been preprocessed by a server unknown to Dreamweaver (prior to displaying the pages), make sure to disable both the Fix Invalidly Nested and Unclosed Tags option, where possible, and the Remove Extra Closing Tags option.

Warn when Fixing or Removing Tags

If you're editing a lot of Web pages created on another system, you should enable the Warn when Fixing or Removing Tags option. If this setting is turned on, Dreamweaver displays a list of changes that have been made to your code in the HTML Corrections dialog box. As you can see from Figure 4-21, the changes can be quite extensive when Dreamweaver opens what it regards as a poorly formatted page.

Caution   Remember that after you've enabled these Rewrite Code options, the fixes occur automatically. If this sequence happens to you by mistake, immediately close the file (without saving it!), disable the Code Rewriting preferences options, and reopen the document.

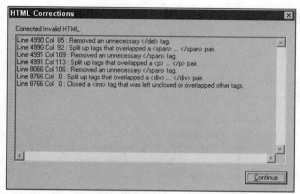

Figure 4-21: Dreamweaver can automatically catch and repair certain HTML errors. You can set Dreamweaver to send a report to the screen in the HTML Corrections dialog box.

Never Rewrite Code preferences

Many of the database connectivity programs, such as ColdFusion or Lasso, use proprietary tags embedded in a regular Web page to communicate with their servers. In previous versions, Dreamweaver often viewed these tags as invalid HTML and tried to correct them. Dreamweaver MX enables you to explicitly protect file types identified with a particular file extension.

To enter a new file type in the Never Rewrite Code options, select the In Files with Extensions field. Enter the file extension of the file type, including the period, at the end of the list. Be sure to separate your extensions from the others in the list with a space on either side.

Special Character preferences

In addition to the rewriting of proprietary tags, many middleware vendors faced another problem when trying to integrate with Dreamweaver. By default, earlier versions of Dreamweaver encoded all URLs so that they could be understood by Unix servers. The encoding converted all special characters to their decimal equivalents, preceded by a percent sign. Spaces became %20, tildes (~) became %7E, and ampersands were converted to &. Although this is valid for Unix servers, and helps to make the Dreamweaver code more universal, it can cause problems for many other types of application servers.

Dreamweaver gives you the option to disable the URL encoding, if necessary. Moreover, Dreamweaver also enables you to turn off encoding that is applied to special characters in the attributes of tags. This latter problem was particularly vexing because, although you could rewrite the attributes in the Code inspector, if you selected the element in the Document window with the Property inspector open, the attributes were encoded. Now you can prevent that from happening with the selection of a single checkbox.

In general, however, it's best to leave both of the Special Characters encoding options enabled unless you find your third-party tags being rewritten destructively.

Code Colors preferences

HTML code is a combination of the tags that structure the language and the text that provides the content. A Web page designer often has difficulty distinguishing swiftly between the two—and finding the right code to modify. Dreamweaver enables you to set color preferences for the code as it appears in Code view or the Code inspector. You can not only alter colors for the background, default tags, and text and general comments, but also specify certain tags to get certain colors.

New Feature   Dreamweaver now allows you to specify color coding for individual document types. If you want different code coloring in VBScript documents, HTML, and PHP documents, you can customize the coloring for each individually. The only color on the main dialog box is the default background color. This isn't the page background color, but the Code view background color.

To modify any of the elements for a specific document type, select the document type as illustrated in Figure 4-22, and click Edit Coloring Scheme.

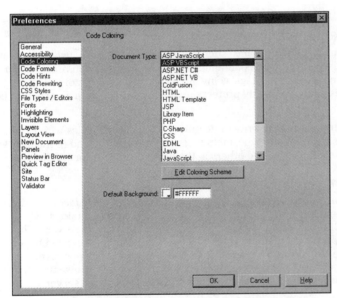

Figure 4-22: Use the Code Coloring category to custom color–code the HTML inspector.

After you click Edit Coloring Scheme you'll get the Edit Coloring Scheme for HTML dialog box, which enables you to change every facet of Dreamweaver's color coding, as shown in Figure 4-23.

The left-hand Styles for box contains every type of tag you could ever want to color. Just select a tag type and then select a color from any of the 216 displayed in the color picker or choose the small palette icon to select from the full range of colors available to your system. You can also click the Color Block and use the Eyedropper tool to pick a color from the Document window.

As you change colors, you'll see a preview of how your document will look in the Preview window.

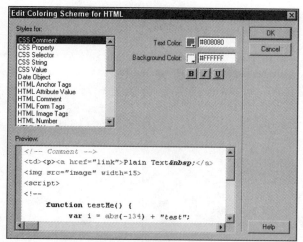

Figure 4-23: The Edit Coloring Scheme dialog box provides a method to completely customize the way you view your raw page code.

Code Format preferences

Dreamweaver includes a fantastic tool for customizing your HTML with the easy-to-use, point-and-click preferences category called Code Format. Most of your HTML code parameters can be controlled through the Code Format category.

In the Code Format category, you can also decide whether to use indentations — and if so, whether to use spaces or tabs and how many of each — or to turn off indents for major elements such as tables and frames. You can also globally control the case of your HTML tags and their attributes. As you can see in Figure 4-24, the Code Format category is full-featured.

To examine the available options in the Code Format category, separate them into four areas: indent control, line control, case control, and centering.

Indent control

Indenting your code generally makes it more readable. Dreamweaver defaults to indenting most HTML tags with two spaces, giving extra indentation grouping to tables and frames. All these parameters can be altered through the Code Format category of the Preferences dialog box.

The first indent option enables indenting, and you can switch from spaces to tabs. To permit indenting, make sure a checkmark is displayed in the Indent checkbox. If you prefer your code to be displayed flush left, turn off the Indent option altogether.

To use tabs instead of the default spaces, click the Use arrow button and select tabs from the drop-down list. If you anticipate transferring your code to a word-processing program for formatting and printing, you should use tabs; otherwise, stay with the default spaces.

Dreamweaver formats both tables and frames as special indentation groups. Within each of these structural elements, the related tags are indented (or nested) more than the initial two spaces. As you can see in Listing 4-1, each table row (<tr>) is indented within the table tag, and the table data tags (<td>) are nested within the table row.

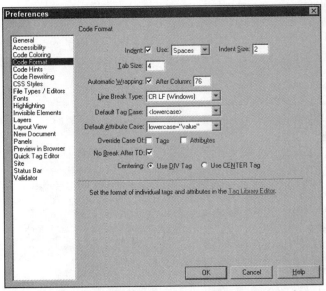

Figure 4-24: The Code Format category enables you to shape your HTML to your own specifications.

Listing 4-1: An indented code sample

```
<table border="1" width="75%">
  <tr>
    <td>Row 1, Column 1</td>
    <td>Row 1, Column 2</td>
    <td>Row 1, Column 3</td>
  </tr>
  <tr>
    <td>Row 2, Column 1</td>
    <td>Row 2, Column 2 </td>
    <td>Row 2, Column 3</td>
  </tr>
</table>
```

The other two items in the indent control section of Code Format preferences category are Indent Size and Tab Size. Change the value in Indent Size to establish the size of indents using spaces. To alter the size of tab indents, change the Tab Size value.

Line control

The browser is responsible for ultimately formatting an HTML page for viewing. This formatting includes wrapping text according to each user's screen size and the placement of the paragraph tags (<p>...</p>). Therefore, you control how your code wraps in your HTML editor. You can turn off the automatic wrapping feature or set it for a particular column through the Line Control options of the Code Format category.

To turn off the automatic word-wrapping capability, deselect Automatic Wrapping. When you are trying to debug your code and are looking for specific line numbers and character positions, enable this option. You can also set the specific column after which word wrapping should take effect. Be sure Automatic Wrapping is enabled and then type your new value in the After Column text box.

Tip   If you're using Code view or the Code inspector, selecting the Word Wrap option overrides the Automatic Wrapping setting in the Code Format category.

The Line Breaks setting determines which line break character is appended to each line of the page. Each of the major operating systems employs a different ending character: Macintosh uses a carriage return (CR), Unix uses a line feed (LF), and Windows uses both (CR LF). If you know the operating system for your remote server, choosing the corresponding line break character ensures that the file has the correct appearance when viewed online. Click the arrow button next to Line Breaks and select your system.

Caution   The operating system for your local development machine may be different from the operating system of your remote server. If so, using the Line Breaks option may cause your HTML to appear incorrect when viewed through a simple text editor (such as Notepad or vi). Dreamweaver's Code view and Code inspector, however, do render the code correctly.

Case control

Case of HTML tags is becoming more and more important. In XHTML, all tags and attribute names must be in lowercase. If you're coding in regular HTML, then case is only a personal preference among Web designers. That said, some Webmasters consider case a serious preference and insist on their codes being all uppercase, all lowercase, or a combination of uppercase and lowercase. Dreamweaver gives you control over the tags and attributes it creates, as well as over case conversion for files that Dreamweaver imports. The Dreamweaver default for both tags and attributes is lowercase.

Tip   Lowercase tags and attributes are also less fattening, according to the W3C. Files with lowercase tag names and attributes compress better and thus transmit faster.

You can also use Dreamweaver to standardize the letter case in tags of previously saved files. To alter imported files, select the Override Case Of Tags and/or the Override Case Of Attributes options. When enabled, these options enforce your choices made in the Case for Tags and Case for Attributes option boxes in any file Dreamweaver loads. Again, be sure to save your file to keep the changes.

New Feature   The No Break after TD checkbox makes sure that there is no line break after the `<td>` tag in your document. Putting a line break after the `<td>` can create some display anomalies in some browsers, such as unwanted space. I recommend leaving this one checked.

Centering

When an object—whether it's an image or text—is centered on a page, HTML tags are placed around the object (or objects) to indicate the alignment. Since the release of HTML 3.2, the `<center>` tag has been deprecated by the W3C in favor of using a `<div>` tag with an `align="center"` attribute. By default, Dreamweaver uses the officially preferred method of `<div align="center">`.

Many Web designers are partial to the older `<center>` tag and prefer to use it to align their objects. Dreamweaver offers a choice with the Centering option in the Code Format category.

To use the new method, select the Use DIV Tag option (the default). To switch to the older <center> method, select the Use CENTER Tag option. Although use of <center> has been officially discouraged, it is so widespread that all browsers continue to support it.

Cross-Reference   Not only can you customize your general code preferences, with Dreamweaver's Tag Library Editor you can modify all of the various tags individually – as well as import entire new tag sets. For details on how the Tag Library Editor works, see Chapter 33.

Validator preferences

Dreamweaver MX offers much improved Validator options, including the capability to validate against multiple HTML schemes and server-side languages. You can even choose which types of errors you'd like Dreamweaver to warn you about. In Figure 4-25, you'll see that you can choose just the specs you want to support.

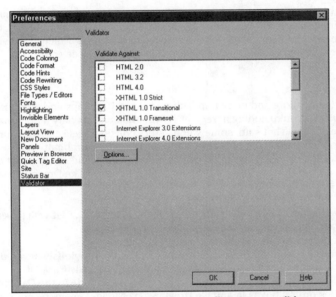

Figure 4-25: The Validator preferences allow you to validate against one or multiple HTML schemes or server-side languages.

The Validate Against list includes the following entries:

   ✦ HTML 2.0

   ✦ HTML 3.2

   ✦ HTML 4.0

   ✦ XHTML 1.0 Strict

- ✦ XHTML 1.0 Transitional
- ✦ XHTML 1.0 Frameset
- ✦ Internet Explorer 3.0 Extensions
- ✦ Internet Explorer 4.0 Extensions
- ✦ Netscape Navigator 3.0 Extensions
- ✦ Netscape Navigator 4.0 Extensions
- ✦ Basic ColdFusion
- ✦ ColdFusion 3.0
- ✦ ColdFusion 3.1
- ✦ ColdFusion 4.0
- ✦ ColdFusion 4.5
- ✦ ColdFusion 5.0
- ✦ ColdFusion 6.0
- ✦ Synchronized Multiple Integration Language (SMIL) 1.0
- ✦ Wireless Markup Language (WML)
- ✦ JavaServer Page Tags

Clicking Options allows you to choose which types of errors you want Dreamweaver to display and check for. The Display list includes Errors, Warnings, Custom Messages, and Nesting Errors. The Check For list includes High ASCII Errors, Quotes in Text, Line Spanning Quotes, and Entities in Text. All options are checked by default, as shown in Figure 4-26.

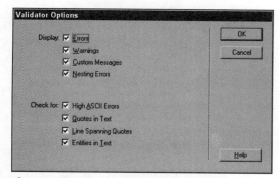

Figure 4-26: The Validator options allow you to choose exactly what you want the validator to check for.

Summary

Creating Web pages, like any design job, is easier when the tools fit your hands. Through Preferences and the Tag Library Editor, you can make Dreamweaver work the way you work.

✦ Dreamweaver enables you to customize your Web page design and HTML coding environment through a series of easy-to-use, point-and-click categories.

✦ You can decide how best to use cutting-edge features, such as layers and style sheets, depending on the degree of cross-browser and backward compatibility you need.

✦ Dreamweaver gives you plenty of elbow room for previewing and testing by providing for 20 selections on your browser list.

✦ Every aspect of code formatting can be modified using the Tag Library Editor, to the point of creating your own custom tag libraries. You can make alterations, from across-the-board case changes to tag-by-tag presentation, to define the way Dreamweaver writes your HTML code.

In the next chapter, you learn how to define a site in Dreamweaver.

✦   ✦   ✦

Setting Up a Site

Web sites — especially those integrating Web applications — are far more than collections of HTML documents. Every image — from the smallest navigational button to the largest image map — is a separate file that must be uploaded with your HTML page. Moreover, if you use any additional elements, such as an included script, background sound, digital video, or Java applet, their files must be transferred as well. To preview the Web site locally and view it properly on the Internet, you have to organize your material in a specific manner.

In Dreamweaver, the process of creating a site also involves developing Web applications in a particular server model. Dreamweaver is unique in its ability to author sites for a variety of server models. While it is feasible to mix pages developed for different server models, it's not really practical. Dreamweaver enables you to select one server model for each site.

Each time you begin developing a new site, you need to define several initial parameters, including the chosen server model, as described in this chapter (provided, of course, you are creating a dynamically driven site, such as a Web application). These steps lay the groundwork for Dreamweaver to properly link your local development site with your remote online site, as well as to link properly to your data sources (again, for dynamically driven sites). For those who are just starting to create Web sites, this chapter begins with a brief description of approaches to online design. The remainder of the chapter is devoted to the mechanics of setting up your site and basic file manipulation.

Planning Your Site

Planning in Web design, just as in any other design process, is essential. Not only will careful planning cut your development time considerably, but it makes it far easier to achieve a uniform look and feel for your Web site — making it friendlier and easier to use. This section briefly covers some of the basics of Web site design: what to focus on, what options to consider, and what pitfalls to avoid. If you are an established Web site developer who has covered this ground before, feel free to skip this section.

Primary considerations

Even before you choose the overarching structure for your site (as discussed in the following sections), you need to address the all-important issues of message, audience, and budget.

Deciding what you want to say

If I had to pick one overriding concern for Web site design, it would be to answer the following question: What are you trying to say? The clearer you are about your message, the more focused your Web site will be. To this end, I find it useful to try to state the purpose of the Web site in one sentence. "Creating the coolest Web site on the planet" doesn't count. Though it could be regarded as a goal, it's too open-ended to be useful. Here are some examples of clearly stated Web site concepts:

✦ "To provide the best small-business resource center focused on Macromedia software"

✦ "To chronicle the world's first voyage around the world by hot air balloon"

✦ "To advertise music lessons offered by a collective of keyboard teachers in New York City"

Targeting your audience

Right behind a site's concept — some would say neck-and-neck with it — is the site's audience. Who are you trying to reach? Quite often, a site's style is heavily influenced by a clear vision of the site's intended audience. Take, for example, Macromedia's monthly Edge newsletter (http://www.macromedia.com/newsletters/edge/flash/march2002/). The Edge is an excellent example of a site that is perfectly pitched toward its target; in this case, the intended audience is composed of professional developers and designers. Hence, you'll find the site snazzy but informative, and filled with exciting examples of cutting-edge programming techniques.

In contrast, a site that is devoted to mass-market e-commerce must work with a very different group in mind: shoppers. Everyone at one time or another falls into this category, so we're really talking about a state of mind, rather than a profession. Many shopping sites use a very straightforward page design — one that is easily maneuverable, comforting in its repetition, and where visitors can quickly find what they are looking for and — with as few impediments as possible — buy it.

Determining your resources

Unfortunately, Web sites aren't created in a vacuum. Virtually all development work happens under real-world constraints of some kind. A professional Web designer is accustomed to working within a budget. In fact, the term *budget* can apply to several concepts.

First, you have a monetary budget — how much is the client willing to spend? This translates into a combination of development time (for designers and programmers), materials (custom graphics, stock photos, and the like), and ongoing maintenance. You can build a large site with many pages that pulls dynamically from an internal database and requires very little hands-on upkeep. Alternatively, you can construct a small, graphics-intensive site that must be updated by hand weekly. It's entirely possible that both sites will end up costing the same.

Second, budget also applies to the amount of time you can afford to spend on any given project. The professional Web designer is quick to realize that time is an essential commodity. The resources needed when undertaking a showcase for yourself when you have no deadline are very different from those needed when contracting on June 30 for a job that must be ready to launch on July 4.

The third real-world budgetary item to consider is bandwidth. The Web, with faster modems and an improved infrastructure, is slowly shedding its image as the "World Wide Wait." However, many users are still stuck with slow modems, which means that Webmasters must keep a steady eye on a page's weight—how long it takes to download under the most typical modem rates. Of course, you can always decide to include that animated video masterpiece that takes 33 minutes to download on a 28.8 modem—you just can't expect anyone to wait to see it.

In conclusion, when you are trying to define your Web page, filter it through these three ideas: message, audience, and the various faces of the budget. The time spent visualizing your Web pages in these terms will be time decidedly well spent.

Design options

Many Web professionals borrow a technique used extensively in developing other mass-marketing forms: *storyboarding*. Storyboarding for the Web entails first diagramming the various pages in your site—much like the more traditional storyboarding in videos or filmmaking—and then detailing connections for the separate pages to form the overall site. How you connect the disparate pages determines how your visitors will navigate the completed Web site.

 Cross-Reference In addition to formulating a Web site design, Web application developers often need to be aware of how the data sources used by the site are structured. See Chapter 15 for a discussion of concerns and techniques in developing database layouts.

The following sections describe the basic navigational models. The Web designer should be familiar with them all because each one serves a different purpose, and they can be mixed and matched as needed.

The linear approach

Prior to the World Wide Web, most media formats were linear—that is, one image or page followed another in an unalterable sequence. In contrast, the Web and its interactive personality enable the user to jump from topic to topic. Nevertheless, you can still use a linear approach to a Web site and have one page appear after another, like a multimedia book.

The linear navigational model, shown in Figure 5-1, works well for computer-based training applications and other expository scenarios in which you want to tightly control the viewer's experience. Some Web designers use a linear-style entrance or exit from their main site, connected to a multilevel navigational model. With Dynamic HTML, you can achieve the effects of moving through several pages in a single page through layering.

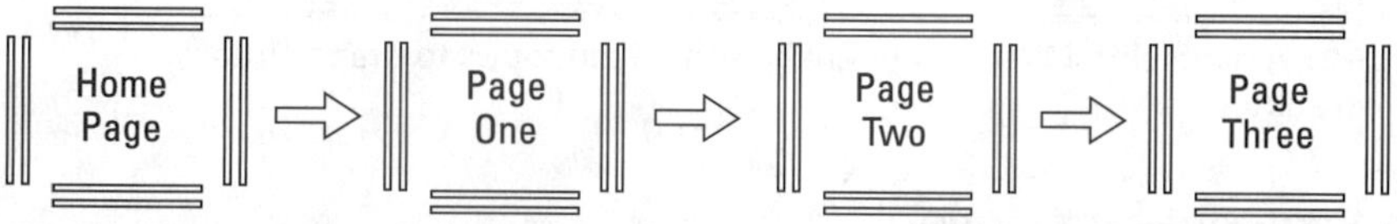

Home Page ⇒ Page One ⇒ Page Two ⇒ Page Three

Figure 5-1: The linear navigational model takes the visitor through a series of Web pages.

Caution Keep in mind that Web search engines can index the content of every page of your site separately. Each page of your site — not just your home page — becomes a potential independent entrance point. Therefore, make sure every page includes navigation buttons back to your home page, especially if you use a linear navigational model.

The hierarchical model

Hierarchical navigational models emerge from top-down designs. These start with one key concept that becomes your home page. From the home page, users branch off to several main pages; if needed, these main pages can, in turn, branch off into many separate pages. Everything flows from the home page; it's very much like a company's organizational chart, with the CEO on top followed by the various company divisions.

The hierarchical Web site, shown in Figure 5-2, is best known for maintaining a visitor's sense of place in the site. Some Web designers even depict the treelike structure as a navigation device and include each branch traveled as a link. This enables visitors to quickly retrace their steps, branch by branch, to investigate different routes.

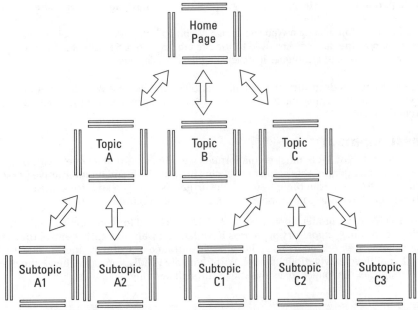

Figure 5-2: A hierarchical Web layout enables the main topics to branch into their own subtopics.

The spoke-and-hub model

Given the Web's flexible hyperlink structure, the spoke-and-hub navigational model works extremely well. The hub is, naturally, the site's home page. The spokes projecting out from the center connect to all the major pages in the site. This layout permits quick access to any key page in just two jumps — one jump always leading back to the hub/home page and one jump leading to a new direction. Figure 5-3 shows a typical spoke-and-hub structure for a Web site.

The main drawback to the spoke-and-hub structure is the required return to the home page. Many Web designers get around this limitation by using frames to make the first jump off the hub into a Web page; this way, the navigation bars are always available. This design also enables visitors using nonframes-capable browsers to take a different path.

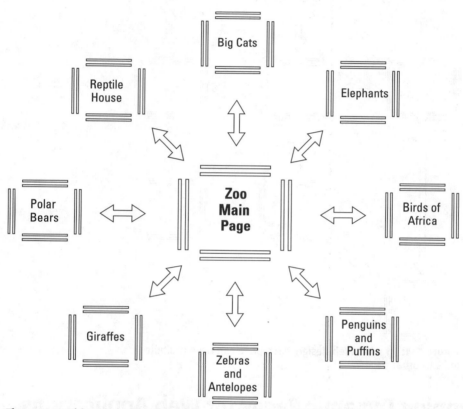

Figure 5-3: This storyboard diagram for a zoo's Web site shows how a spoke-and-hub navigational model might work.

The full Web design

The seemingly least structured approach for a Web site — full Web — takes the most advantage of the Web's hyperlink capabilities. This design enables virtually every page to connect to every other page. The full Web design, shown in Figure 5-4, works well for sites that are explorations of a particular topic, because the approach encourages visitors to experience the site according to their own needs, not based on the notions of any one designer. The danger in using full Web for your site design is that a visitor can literally get lost. As an escape hatch, many Web designers include a link to a clickable site map, especially for large-scale sites using this design.

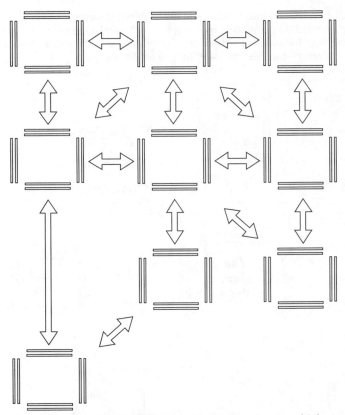

Figure 5-4: In a full Web design, each page can have multiple links to other pages.

Mapping Dynamic Pages for Web Applications

Many, if not most, Web applications require more than one Web page. One variation on a search engine, for example, would use the following:

✦ An entry page containing the form elements (text field, list boxes, and so on) that make up the search criteria

✦ A results page that displays the list of items matching the search criteria; each of the items typically provides a link to a detail page and more information

✦ A detail page (or pages) that provide more information—and are linked from the results page

✦ An error page, if the initial search criteria do not have any matches

The experienced Web developer maps out the structure for all the anticipated Web applications in the site before beginning the building process. In addition to providing a truer picture of the work involved, mapping the required pages highlights potentially redundant pages—for example, the same error page may be used throughout the site—and pinpoints areas that would benefit from dynamic data application. The Web application map can also serve as a workflow schematic that shows which pages are static HTML and could be built by an HTML designer with little or no coding experience (typically, the entry and error pages); and which pages are dynamic Web pages that require data-aware designers.

Defining a Site

Now that you've decided on a design and mapped your site, you're ready to set it up in Dreamweaver. When you define a site, you are telling Dreamweaver where to store your Web pages locally, where to transfer them to remotely, as well as the style of code in which to write them. Defining a site is an essential first step.

The Site Definition dialog box provides two operational modes: Basic and Advanced. In Basic mode, also known as the Site Definition wizard, you specify the bare essentials for editing, testing, and sharing your site files. In Advanced mode, you can specify all your site parameters, from the most basic down to the most obscure.

Using the Site Definition wizard

There are two main paths through the Site Definition wizard:

✦ One for sites that do not use a server technology — sites that contain no server-side code, just client-side HTML, JavaScript, and so on

✦ One for sites that use a server technology — sites that contain server-side code, such as ColdFusion, ASP, JSP, and so on

To keep things simple, I've written a separate procedure for each of these paths. So make sure to choose the correct path before you launch into your site definition!

Note   Using the Site Definition wizard to define a new site is a quick, convenient way to get a site off the ground. In some cases, however, it is not complete. Depending on the site, you might have to use the Advanced tab of the Site Definition dialog box to specify additional site options, such as testing server details, cloaking, and so on.

Defining a site that does not use a server technology

To use the Site Definition wizard to define a site that *does not* use a server technology (that is, a site that contains no server-side code), perform the following steps:

1. Choose Site ➪ New Site to open the Site Definition dialog box.

2. Select the Basic tab of the Site Definition wizard if it is not already selected. If a message appears informing you that the root folder you have chosen is the same as another folder, ignore it, and click OK to close the message box.

   In the What Would You Like To Name Your Site? field, enter a name to identify your site within Dreamweaver, as shown in Figure 5-5. Choose a descriptive name; spaces are fine, for example, mySite, my_site, My Site, and so on. To keep things simple, I recommend avoiding apostrophes, such as Joe's Site, joe's_site, and so on.

3. Click the Next button to move to the second page of the Wizard: Editing Files, Part 2.

   Select No to the prompt Do You Want to Work with A Server Technology?

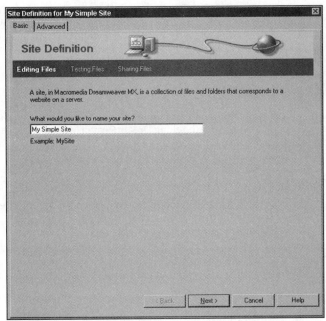

Figure 5-5: Use the Site Definition wizard to define a new site.

4. Click Next to move to the Editing Files, Part 3 page of the wizard.

   Select the appropriate option for How Do You Want to Work with Your Files During Development?: Edit Local Copies on My Computer Then Upload to Server When Ready, Edit Directly on Server Using Local Network, or Edit Directly on Server Using FTP or RDS.

   If you choose Edit Local Copies on My Computer, in the field Where on Your Computer Do You Want to Store Your Files?, create and/or specify the site's root folder on your local disk.

   If you choose Edit Directory on Server Using Local Network, in the field Where Are Your Files on The Network, create and/or specify the site's root folder on your network.

   If you choose Edit Directory on Server Using FTP or RDS, in the field Where on Your Computer Do You Want Dreamweaver to Store Local Copies of Your Files, create and/or specify the site's root folder on your local disk. Then check or uncheck the Automatically Upload Files to My Server Everytime I Save checkbox, depending on your preference.

5. Click Next to move to the Sharing Files page of the wizard.

Note   This page of the wizard does not appear if you chose Edit Directly on Server Using Local Network in Step 4.

   In the field How Do You Connect To Your Remote Server list box, select the appropriate option: FTP, Local/Network, RDS, SourceSafe Database, or WebDAV. If you do not know which option to choose, or if you want to specify your server connection type later, select None. (For more information on each of these options, turn to Dreamweaver's built-in help.)

Depending on the option you choose, a set of sub-options appears. Respond appropriately to these.

6. Click Next to move to the Sharing Files, Part 2 page of the wizard.

> **Note**
>
> This page of the wizard does not appear if you chose None in Step 5 or Edit Directly on Server Using Local Network in Step 4.

Select the appropriate option for the prompt Do You Want To Enable Checking In And Checking Out Files? Select Yes to ensure that different people cannot edit the same document at the same time. Select No if this is not a concern.

> **Caution**
>
> The Check In/Check Out system is a version-control system that is only effective if all members of the development team have the setting enabled. When someone has checked out a file, and you attempt to open it, Dreamweaver prompts you that the file is checked out. If someone on the team doesn't have Check In/Check Out enabled, however, they don't receive such a prompt. That person can open, edit, and upload the file, posing a potential version-control issue.

7. Click the Next button to move to the final, Summary page of the wizard.

   Review your selections; if necessary, use the Back button to change them.

8. When all is well, click Done (on the final, Summary page) to create your site.

   An alert box informs you that Dreamweaver is going to create a site cache, which will make various site operations faster.

9. In the Site panel, click the Expand/Collapse button to expand to remote/local pane view (this step assumes that you are running Dreamweaver in its single-window MX mode). In the Local Files pane (on the right, by default), Dreamweaver shows the local root folder for your newly defined site, and an icon—Desktop (Windows) or Computer (Macintosh)—to enable you to view all your local disks/folders/files. In the Remote Site pane (on the left, by default), Dreamweaver shows your remote folders/files (depending on your site definition, you might need to click the Connects To Remote Host button to show the remote folders/files).

Defining a site that uses a server technology

To use the Site Definition wizard to define a site that *uses* a server technology (that is, a site that contains server-side code), perform the following steps:

1. Choose Site ➪ New Site to open the Site Definition dialog box.

2. Select the Basic tab of the Site Definition wizard if it is not already selected. If a message appears informing you that the root folder you have chosen is the same as another folder, ignore it, and click OK to close the message box.

   In the What Would You Like To Name Your Site? field, enter a name to identify your site within Dreamweaver, as shown in Figure 5-5. Choose a descriptive name; spaces are fine, for example, mySite, my_site, My Site, and so on. To keep things nice and simple, I recommend avoiding apostrophes, such as Joe's Site, joe's_site, and so on.

3. Click Next to move to the second page of the Wizard: Editing Files, Part 2.

   Select Yes to the prompt Do You Want to Work with A Server Technology? Specify the server technology in the Which Server Technology? drop-down list: ColdFusion, ASP, JSP, and so on.

4. Click Next to move to the Editing Files, Part 3 page of the wizard.

   Select the appropriate option for How Do You Want to Work with Your Files During Development?: Edit and Test Locally, Edit Locally then Upload to Remote Testing Server, Edit Directly on Remote Testing Server using Local Network, or Edit Directly on Remote Testing Server Using FTP or RDS.

   If you choose either of the first two options, in the field Where On Your Computer Do You Want To Store Your Files?, create and/or specify the site's root folder on your local disk.

   If you choose Edit Directly on Remote Testing Server using Local Network, in the field Where are Your Files on the Network?, create and/or specify the site's root folder on your network.

   If you choose Edit Directly on Remote Testing Server Using FTP or RDS, in the field Where On Your Computer Do You Want Dreamweaver To Store Local Copies Of Your Files, create and/or specify the site's root folder on your local disk, and check or uncheck the Automatically Upload Files to My Server Everytime I Save checkbox, depending on your preference.

5. Click Next to move to the Testing Files page of the wizard. At this point, the Site Definition wizard branches off into several different subpaths, depending on the option you chose in Step 4.

Note Your Step 5 subpath might consist of one or several wizard pages. The thing to remember: All Step 5 subpaths eventually lead to Step 6's Summary page.

   Describing all possible subpaths would take several pages and be counterproductive to wade through. Fortunately, the options you must choose in each subpath are quite self-explanatory: the absolute URL of your remote site root (`http://hostname/path/filename`), the method you use to your remote server (such as FTP, Local/Network, or RDS), and so on.

Tip Remember: If you get confused or stuck, help is but a keypress (F1) or a mouse click (Help button) away.

   One option you might not be familiar with is: Do You Want To Enable Checking In And Checking Out Files? Select Yes to ensure that different people cannot edit the same document at the same time. Select No if this is not a concern.

6. When you have successfully worked through all your Step 5 subpaths, the final Summary page of the wizard appears.

   Review your selections, as listed in the Summary page; if necessary, use the Back button to change them.

7. When all is well, click Done to create your site.

   An alert box informs you that Dreamweaver is going to create a site cache, which will make various site operations faster. (Note: If the Don't Show Me This Message Again option is selected, this alert box does not appear.) Click OK to have Dreamweaver create your specified site.

8. In the Site panel, click the Expand/Collapse button to expand to remote/local pane view (this assumes you are running Dreamweaver in its single-window MX mode). In the Local Files pane (on the right, by default), Dreamweaver shows the local root folder for your newly defined site, and an icon—Desktop (Windows) or Computer (Macintosh)—to enable you to view all your local disks/folders/files. In the Remote Site pane (on the left, by default), Dreamweaver shows your remote folders/files (depending on your site definition, you might need to click the Connects To Remote Host button to show the remote folders/files).

Using Advanced mode

Advanced mode comprises seven categories of information: Local Info, Remote Info, Testing Server, Cloaking, Design Notes, Site Map Layout, and File View Columns. Note that only the first three categories—Local Info, Remote Info, and Testing Server—are essential for site definition.

Cross-Reference The other categories in the Site Definition dialog box Advanced mode (Cloaking, Design Notes, Site Map Layout, and File View Columns) are helpful for working in a team environment and for working visually with Dreamweaver's Site Map; more information on these features can be found later in this chapter and in Chapter 31.

There are three main steps to defining a site in Dreamweaver:

1. Locate the folder to be used for the local development site.

2. Enter the remote site information.

3. If you are creating a Web application, specify the testing server model to be used for the site.

Establishing local connections

Once your site is on your Web server and fully operational, the site consists of many files—server-side pages, plain HTML, graphics, and other media files—that make up the individual Web pages. All of these associated files are kept on the server in one folder, which may use one or more subfolders. This main folder is called the *remote site root*. In order for Dreamweaver to properly display your linked pages and embedded images—just as they are displayed online—the program creates a mirror of your remote site on your local development system. This primary mirror folder on your system is known as the *local site root*.

You must establish the local site root at the beginning of a project. This ensures that Dreamweaver duplicates the complete structure of the Web development site when it comes time to publish your pages to the Web. One of Dreamweaver's key site-management features enables you to select just the HTML pages for publication; Dreamweaver then automatically transfers all the associated files, creating any needed folders in the process. The mirror images of your local and remote site roots are critical to Dreamweaver's ability to expedite your workload in this way.

Tip If you do decide to transfer an existing Web site to a new Dreamweaver local site root, run Dreamweaver's Link Checker after you've consolidated all your files. In the Site panel, choose Site ➪ Check Links Sitewide or press the keyboard shortcut, Ctrl+F8 (Command+F8). The Link Checker informs you of broken links and orphan files.

To set up a local site root folder in Dreamweaver, follow these steps:

1. Select Site ➪ New Site from the main Dreamweaver menu. The Site Definition dialog box opens, as shown in Figure 5-6. If the Advanced tab is not already selected, please do so.

Note   If the root folder you have chosen is the same as another site folder, a prompt appears. If you have intentionally chosen the same folder, it's safe to ignore the warning and click OK to close it. However, using the same folder for multiple sites is not a typical practice, and it should only be undertaken by advanced users.

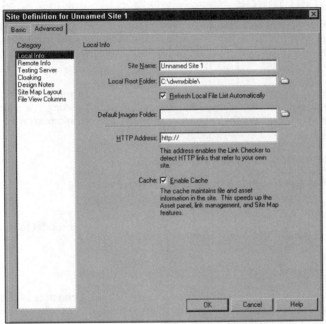

Figure 5-6: Set up your local site root through the Site Definition dialog box.

2. From the Local Info category, type a name for your site in the Site Name text box. This is the name that appears in the Sites drop-down list and the Edit Sites dialog box.

3. Specify the folder to serve as the local site root by either typing the pathname directly into the Local Root Folder text box or clicking the folder icon to open the Choose Local Root Folder dialog box. When you've made your choice there, click the Select button.

4. Leave the Refresh Local File List Automatically option selected. This option ensures that new files are automatically included in the list, and relieves you from having to select the Refresh command manually.

5. If your site is to have a dedicated images folder, specify it in the Default Images Folder text box. Note that your default images folder can have subfolders.

6. Enter the full URL for your site in the HTTP Address text box.

When checking links for your Web site, Dreamweaver uses the HTTP address to determine whether absolute links, such as www.idest.com/dreamweaver/index.htm, reference external files or files on your site.

7. For fastest performance, select the Enable Cache option. Having a site cache enables Dreamweaver to store information that makes certain key site tasks run faster, such as link updates.

Specifying the remote site

In addition to defining the local site root, you need to specify information pertaining to the remote site. The remote site may be a folder accessed through the local network or via FTP (File Transfer Protocol). If your remote site is located on the local network — in this arrangement, the remote site is often said to be on a *staging server* — all you need to do is select or create the particular folder to house the remote site. At the appropriate time, the network administrator or other designated person from the Information Technology department will export the files from the staging server to the Web or intranet server.

Many Dreamweaver developers have a Web server located on their development system, making it possible to have both the local and remote sites on the same machine.

If, on the other hand, you post your material to a remote site via FTP, you'll need various bits of information to complete the connection. In addition to the FTP host's name — used by Dreamweaver to find the server on the Internet — you'll also need, at a minimum, the user name and password to log on to the server. The host's technical support staff will provide you with this and any other necessary information.

Although it's entirely possible to develop your site locally without establishing a remote site root, it's not a recommended practice. Web sites require extensive testing in real-world settings — something that's just not possible with a local development setup. If you don't have the necessary information to establish a remote site root initially, you can still begin development locally; just be sure to transfer your files to your remote site and begin testing as soon as possible.

To enter the remote site information, follow these steps:

1. Continuing in the Site Definition dialog box, select the Remote Info category.

2. From the Access drop-down list, shown in Figure 5-7, choose the Web-server access description that applies to your site (FTP is shown in Figure 5-7):

   • **None:** Choose this option if your site is being developed locally and will not be uploaded to a Web server at this time.

   • **FTP:** Select this option if you connect to your Web server via File Transfer Protocol (FTP).

   • **Local/Network:** Select this option if you are running a local Web server and want to store your remote site on your local drive, or if your Web server is mounted as a network drive.

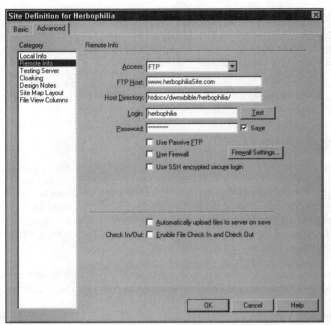

Figure 5-7: Choose whether your remote site is to be accessed via the local network or by FTP in the Remote Info panel.

3. If you selected None for access, skip the rest of this procedure and continue with the next section, adding application server details.

4. If you selected FTP for access, complete the following options:

   • **FTP Host:** This is the host name of the FTP connection for your Web server, usually in the form `ftp.sitename.com`. Do not include the full URL, such as `ftp://ftp.sitename.com`.

   • **Host Directory:** This is the directory in which publicly accessible documents are stored on the server. Typical host directory names are `www/public/docs/` and `public_html/`. Your remote site root folder will be a subfolder of the host directory. If you are unsure of the exact name of the host directory, check with your Web server administrator. Oftentimes, the FTP host connects to the correct directory automatically, and you can leave this field blank.

   • **Login:** This is the login name you have been assigned for access to the Web server.

   • **Password:** This is the password necessary for you to gain access to the Web server. Note that many servers are case-sensitive when it comes to logins and passwords!

   • **Save:** Dreamweaver automatically selects this option after you enter a password. Deselect it only if you and others access the server from the current system.

   • **Use Passive FTP:** Passive FTP establishes the FTP connection through the local software, rather than the server. Certain firewall configurations use passive FTP; check with your network administrator to see if you need it.

- **Use Firewall:** This option will be automatically selected if you've set the Preferences with the correct firewall host/port information (to access this information, click the Firewall Settings button).

- **Use SSH Encrypted Secure Login:** Choose this option to use SSH for secure FTP authentication and connection. Selecting the Use SSH encrypted secure login option opens a dialog box prompting you to download the PuTTY software from the Macromedia site. PuTTY is an SSH client that acts as an intermediary during a secure login from Dreamweaver.

   - **Test:** Once you've specified all your FTP parameters, you can use the Test button to verify that Dreamweaver can connect successfully to your Web server.

5. If you selected Local/Network for access, enter the name of the remote folder in the Remote Folder text box or click the folder icon to locate the folder. If you want to automatically update the remote file list (recommended), select the Refresh Remote File List Automatically option.

Adding Testing Server details

The final primary element for defining sites using the Advanced tab is supplying the server application information. One key aspect to Dreamweaver's power is its ability to create the same application for different server models using different scripting languages. The Live Data Preview—which enables designers to work with data directly from the data source—is another unique Dreamweaver feature. Settings in the Testing Server category of the Site Definition dialog box control both of these features. To set the Testing Server options, follow these steps:

1. Continuing in the Site Definition dialog box, choose the Testing Server category, as shown in Figure 5-8.

2. From the Server Model list, choose the application server to be used in this site: ASP JavaScript, ASP VBScript, ASP.NET C#, ASP.NET VB, ColdFusion, JSP, PHP MySQL, or None.

3. If you chose ColdFusion as your server model, the This Site Contains list becomes active. Choose the option that best describes the pages making up the site:

   - UltraDev 4 Pages Only

   - Dreamweaver MX Pages Only

   - Both Versions

4. To set the way in which you will connect with your testing server, choose FTP, Local/Network, or None from the Access list. If you choose None, Live Preview will not be available.

   The options for FTP and Local/Network are the same as those found in the Remote Info category.

 Tip   After selecting your options, it's always a good idea to select Test to make sure your connection is solid.

5. In the URL Prefix field, enter the HTTP address for the root folder on the testing server.

   If you're working locally, your URL Prefix is likely to start with `http://localhost/`.

6. Click OK to close the Site Definition dialog box.

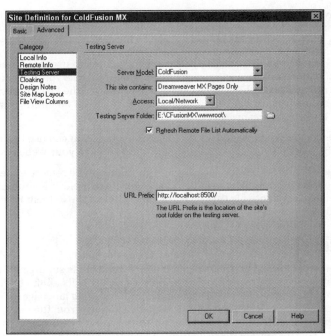

Figure 5-8: Before you can create any dynamic pages in Dreamweaver, you must choose a server model from the Testing Server category.

Dreamweaver doesn't save the site definition information until the program exits. If Dreamweaver should "unexpectedly quit"—the politically correct term for "crash"—any changes made to the Site Definition dialog box in the session will be lost.

Cloaking Site Folders

Dreamweaver MX supports *site cloaking*, which enables you to exclude (cloak) specified site folders from operations such as Put, Get, Check In/Out, Synchronize, and so on. (For a full list of cloaked operations, see the following paragraphs.) The site cloaking feature can save you a significant amount of upload/maintenance time. Suppose that you're working on a site that contains several dozen large MP3 files, all stored in a folder named mp3s. You can cloak the mp3s folder, so that when you put (upload) your site files at the end of the day, you don't end up re-putting all these mp3 files (which, most likely, haven't changed anyway).

A site's folder-cloaking settings are sticky; once you've specified them, Dreamweaver remembers them whenever you work on the site.

Cloaking folders

Cloaking excludes cloaked folders from the following operations:

✦ Put, Get

✦ Check In, Check Out

✦ Reports

✦ Select Newer Local, Select Newer Remote

✦ Sitewide commands, such as Check Links Sitewide and Find And Replace Entire Site

✦ Synchronize

✦ Asset panel contents

✦ Template and library updating

Cloaking and uncloaking site folders is a breeze:

1. In the Site panel, select the desired site from the drop-down list box.

   Note that this site must be cloaking-enabled, which is the default site setting. If, however, you should need to cloaking-enable a site, select it in the Site panel and choose Site ➪ Cloaking ➪ Enable Cloaking.

2. Select the folder(s) you want to cloak or uncloak.

3. From the Site panel menu, choose Site ➪ Cloaking ➪ Cloak or Site ➪ Cloaking ➪ Uncloak. Alternatively, you can right-click (Control+click) a selected folder and use the context menu.

   A red, diagonal line across the selected folders appears or disappears to show that they are cloaked or uncloaked, as shown in Figure 5-9.

Uncloaking folders (and files)

Dreamweaver enables you to easily uncloak folders (and the files they contain) in a site. Just perform the following steps:

1. In the Site panel, select the desired site from the list box.

   Again, this site must be cloaking-enabled.

2. Select the desired site folder.

3. To uncloak only the selected folder (and the files it contains), choose Site ➪ Cloaking ➪ Uncloak from the Site panel menu or the context menu that appears when you right-click (Control+click) the selected folder.

   To uncloak all site folders (and files), choose Site ➪ Cloaking ➪ Uncloak All from the Site panel menu or the pop-up context menu.

   The red, diagonal lines across all specified folder and file icons disappear, indicating that they are uncloaked.

Caution

When you uncloak an entire site, you cannot undo it! If you want to recloak folders, you'll have to do so manually.

Figure 5-9: You can easily cloak or uncloak your site folders.

Managing Site Info

You can change any of the information associated with your local site roots by selecting Site ➪ Edit Sites from the Site panel or main Dreamweaver menu. Choose the site you want to modify from the Edit Sites dialog box, and click the Edit button; you'll see the corresponding information for you to edit.

After your participation in a project has ended, you can remove the site from your list. In the Edit Sites dialog box, choose the site you want to remove, and click the Remove button. Note that this action removes the site only from Dreamweaver's internal site list; it *does not* actually delete any files or folders from your hard drive.

Tip   Before you remove a site, make sure you jot down the site user name and password for reference in case you need to resurrect the site someday.

With the local site root folder established, Dreamweaver can properly manage links regardless of which address format is used. The various address formats are explained in the following section.

Building Placeholder Pages

One technique you might find helpful—and especially so with the use of *document-relative addressing* in Dreamweaver Web projects—is what I call *placeholder pages*. These placeholder pages can fill the need to include links as you create each Web page, in as effortless a manner as possible.

Suppose, for example, you've just finished laying out most of the text and graphics for your home page and you want to put in some navigation buttons. You drop in your button images and align them just so. All that's missing are the links. If you're using document-relative addressing, the best way to assign a link would be to click the Browse for File button in the Property inspector and select your file. But what do you do if you haven't created any other pages yet and there aren't any files to select? That's when you can put placeholder pages to work.

After you've designed the basics of your site and created your local site root, as described previously in this chapter, start with a blank Dreamweaver page. Type a single identifying word on the page and save it in the local site root. Repeat this step for all the Web pages in your plan. When it comes time to make your links, all you have to do is point and click to the appropriate placeholder page. This arrangement also gives you an immediate framework for link testing. When it comes time to work on the next page, just open up the correct placeholder page and start to work.

Another style of working involves using the Site panel as your base of operations, rather than the Document window. It's very easy in Dreamweaver to choose File ➪ New File from the Site panel menu several times and create the basic files of your site. You can even create a file and immediately link to it by choosing Site ➪ Link to New File from the Site map. A dialog box opens, which enables you to specify the filename, the title of the new document, and the text for the link. Moreover, you can create any needed subfolders, such as ones for images or other media, by selecting File ➪ New Folder.

Creating and Saving New Pages

You've considered message, audience, and budget issues. You've chosen a design. You've set up your site and its address. All the preliminary planning is completed, and now you're ready to really rev up Dreamweaver and begin creating pages. This section covers the basic mechanics of opening and saving Web pages in development.

Starting Dreamweaver

Start Dreamweaver as you would any other program. Double-click the Dreamweaver program icon, or single-click if you are using Internet Explorer's Desktop Integration feature in Windows. After the splash screen, Dreamweaver opens with a new blank page. This page is created from the `Default.html` file found in Dreamweaver's Configuration/DocumentTypes/ NewDocuments folder. Of course, it's likely that you'll want to replace the original `Default.html` file with one of your own—perhaps with your copyright information. All of your blank pages will then be created from a template that you've created.

 Note

As mentioned in Chapter 2, you can run Dreamweaver MX in two workspace modes: the "classic" Dreamweaver 4 mode or the new Dreamweaver MX mode. In Dreamweaver 4 mode, each document resides in its own window, and panels reside in floating windows. In Dreamweaver MX mode—which is supported by Windows only—all Document windows and panels reside in a single application window. The screen shots in this chapter are of Dreamweaver running in its new MX mode.

If you do decide to create your own Default template, it's probably a good idea to rename the Dreamweaver Default template — as `Original-Default.html` or something similar — prior to creating your new, personalized Default template.

Opening existing files

To open an existing file that belongs to a site you've defined in Dreamweaver, select the site in the Site panel, and double-click the file icon.

To open an existing file that does not belong to a site defined in Dreamweaver — or that was created in a different program — choose File ➪ Open or Ctrl+O (Command+O), and choose the file from the File Open dialog box.

You can enable/disable Dreamweaver from automatically repairing HTML syntax errors in your files when it opens them. Choose Edit ➪ Preferences to open the Preferences dialog box, select the Code Rewriting category, and check/uncheck the desired options: Fix Invalidly Nested and Unclosed Tags, Rename Form Items when Pasting, Remove Extra Closing Tags, and so on. To have Dreamweaver report its syntax repairs, select the Warn When Fixing or Removing Tags option.

To add an entry, place your cursor at the end of the line above where you want your new file format to be placed, and press Enter (Return). Type in your file extension(s) in capital letters followed by a colon and then the text description. Save the `Extensions.txt` file and restart Dreamweaver to see your modifications.

Opening a new file

You can work on as many Dreamweaver files as your system memory can sustain. When you choose File ➪ New or the keyboard shortcut, Ctrl+N (Command+N), and choose a file type from the New Document dialog box, Dreamweaver opens a new blank file of your specified type. (For more on this, see the section "Creating New Documents" later in this chapter.)

If you are using the Windows MX flavor of Dreamweaver and are working with maximized documents, you can easily switch among open files by clicking their respective tabs (at the bottom of the Document window) or by using the Window menu.

Each time you open a new file, Dreamweaver temporarily names the file `Untitled-n`, where *n* is the next number in sequence. This naming convention prevents you from accidentally overwriting a new file opened in the same session.

Using the New Document dialog box to create new documents of all types (HTML, JavaScript, ASP, ColdFusion, and so on.) is discussed in detail later in this chapter, in the section "Creating New Documents."

Saving your file

Saving your work is very important in any computer-related task, and Dreamweaver is no exception. To initially save the current file, choose File ➪ Save or the keyboard shortcut, Ctrl+S (Command+S). The Save dialog box opens; you can enter a filename and, if desired, a different path.

Opening Other Types of Files

Dreamweaver defaults to searching for HTML files with an extension of .htm, .html, or .xhtml. To look for other types of files, select the Files of Type arrow button. Dreamweaver allows several other file types, including server-side includes (.shtml, .shtm, .stm, or .ssi), Active server pages (.asp), and ColdFusion (.cfm , .cfml, or .cfc). If you need to load a valid HTML file with a different extension, select the All Files option.

If you are working consistently with a different file format, you can add your own extensions and file types to Dreamweaver's Open dialog box. In the Configuration folder, there is an editable text file called `Extensions.txt`. Open this file in Dreamweaver or in your favorite text editor to make any additions. The syntax must follow the format of the standard `Extensions.txt` file:

```
HTM,HTML,XHTML,SHTM,SHTML,HTA,HTC,STM,SSI,JS,AS,XML,XSL,XSD,⊃
DTD,XSLT,LBI,DWT,ASP,ASPX,ASCX,ASMX,CONFIG,CS,CSS,CFM,CFML,⊃
CFC,TLD,TXT,PHP,PHP3,PHP4,LASSO,JSP,VB,VTM,VTML,INC,JAVA,⊃
EDML,WML:All Documents
HTM,HTML,XHTML,HTA,HTC:HTML Documents
SHTM,SHTML,STM,SSI:Server-Side Includes
JS:JavaScript Documents
XML,DTD,XSD,XSL,XSLT:XML Files
LBI:Library Files
DWT:Template Files
CSS:Style Sheets
ASP:Active Server Pages
ASPX,ASCX,ASMX,CS,VB,CONFIG:Active Server Plus Pages
CFM,CFML,CFC:ColdFusion Templates
AS:ActionScript Files
TXT:Text Files
PHP,PHP3,PHP4:PHP Files
LASSO:Lasso Files
JSP,JST:Java Server Pages
JSF:Fireworks Script
TLD:Tag Library Descriptor Files
JAVA:Java Files
WML:WML Files
EDML:EDML Files
```

By default, all HTML files are saved with an .htm filename extension for Windows, and an .html extension for Macintosh. Different file formats are saved with different extensions; XML documents, for example, are stored with an .xml extension. To save your file with another extension, such as .shtml or .xhtml, change the Save as Type option to the specific file type and then enter your full filename, *with* the extension.

Caution   Although it may seem kind of backward in this day and age of long filenames, it's still a good idea to choose all-lowercase names for your files without spaces or punctuation other than an underscore or hyphen. Otherwise, not all servers will read the filename correctly, and you'll have problems linking your pages.

Closing the file

When you're done working on a file, you can close it by choosing File ➪ Close or the keyboard shortcut, Ctrl+W (Command+W). If you've made any changes to your file since last saving it, Dreamweaver prompts you to save it. Click Yes to save the file or No to close it without saving your changes.

Note   You can easily tell whether a file has been altered since the last save by looking at the title bar. Dreamweaver places an asterisk after the filename in the title bar for modified files. Dreamweaver is even smart enough to properly remove the asterisk should you reverse your changes with the Undo command or the History panel.

Quitting the program

Once you're done for the day — or, more often, the late, late night — you can close Dreamweaver by choosing File ➪ Exit (File ➪ Quit) or the standard keyboard shortcut, Ctrl+Q (Command+Q).

Creating New Documents

Dreamweaver MX provides two methods for creating new documents:

✦ You can use the New Document dialog box to create a new document of a type that you select from a comprehensive list within the following categories: Basic Page, Dynamic Page, Template Page, Other, CSS Style Sheets, Framesets, and Page Designs. If you work with multiple document types, this is the way to go.

✦ You can create a new document of a default type that you've specified in the Preferences dialog box. If you work mostly with one document type — HTML, ColdFusion, or ASP, for example — this method can prove very convenient.

Using the New Document dialog box

To create a new document using the New Document dialog box:

1. Choose File ➪ New to open the New Document dialog box, shown in Figure 5-10.

2. In the Category list of the General panel, select the category of document that you want to create: Basic Page, Dynamic Page, Template Page, Other, etc.

3. In the Document Type list, select the specific type of document you want to create: HTML, ColdFusion, JavaScript, etc.

4. If desired, select the Make Document XHTML Compliant option. Note that this setting is *sticky;* once you set it, Dreamweaver will remember your setting each time you use the New Document dialog box to create a file of this type.

5. Click Create to create a new, blank document of the selected category/type.

If you want to create a new document based on a custom template, use the Templates — rather than the General — panel of the New Document dialog box. For more information on creating/using templates, see Chapter 28.

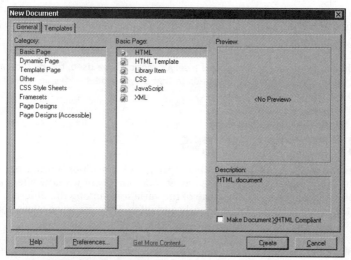

Figure 5-10: Choose the type of new file you want to start with through the New Document dialog box.

Creating a new default document

If you often create one type of document—HTML or ColdFusion files, for example—you can take advantage of Dreamweaver's default document feature to save yourself some document creation time and trouble. By using the techniques described in this section, you can open a new document of your default type (HTML, ColdFusion, and so on) with one quick keyboard shortcut—in other words, without having to work your way through the powerful, but clunky, New Document dialog box. It's a must for the Dreamweaver power user!

Use the following steps to create a new default document:

1. Choose Edit ⇨ Preferences to open the Preferences dialog box, and select New Document to view the New Document panel.

   If your desired document type is not already defined as the Default Document Type, do so now.

   Note the Show New Document Dialog on Control+N (Command+N) option. Turn this option off if you want Ctrl+N (Command+N) to create a new default document without showing the New Document dialog box; turn it on if you want Ctrl+N (Command+N) to show the New Document dialog box.

Tip   If you are a Windows user, no matter what Show New Document Dialog on Control+N setting you choose, Ctrl+Shift+N always creates a new default document *without* showing the New Document dialog box.

   If desired, select the Make Document XHTML Compliant option. As mentioned earlier, be aware that this setting is sticky; once you set it, Dreamweaver will remember your setting each time you use the New Document dialog box to create a file of this type.

   When you're done, click OK to close the Preferences dialog box.

2. After you perform the preceding step, you're done. To create a new default document, simply choose Ctrl+Shift+N (Windows only). If you turned off the Show New Document Dialog on Control+N option, you can also choose Ctrl+N (Command+N).

Note   If, when defining your site, you specified a server model to be used, the new default document will be the file type that corresponds to that server model — despite the Preferences dialog box setting you have chosen.

Previewing Your Web Pages

When using Dreamweaver or any other Web authoring tool, it's important to frequently check your progress in one or more browsers. Dreamweaver's Document window offers a near-browser view of your Web page, but because of the variations among the different browsers, it's imperative that you preview your page early and often. Dreamweaver offers you easy access to a maximum of 20 browsers — and they're just a function key away.

Note   Don't confuse Dreamweaver's View Live Data mode with the Preview in Browser feature. With View Live Data, Dreamweaver can only show you an approximation of how your page will look on the Web, and not all aspects — such as links and rollovers — are active. You need to preview and test your page in a variety of browsers to truly see how your page looks and behaves on the Web.

You add a browser to your preview list by selecting File ➪ Preview in Browser ➪ Edit Browser List or by choosing the Preview in Browser category from the Preferences dialog box. Both actions open the Preview in Browser Preferences category. The steps for editing your browser list are described in detail in Chapter 4. Here's a brief recap:

1. Select File ➪ Preview in Browser ➪ Edit Browser List to open the Preview in Browser Preferences category.

2. To add a browser (up to 20), click the Add (+) button and fill out the following fields in the Add Browser dialog box (see Figure 5-11):

   • **Application:** Type in the path to the browser program or click the Browse button to locate the browser executable (.exe) file.

   • **Name:** When you choose the browser application, Dreamweaver automatically provides a name for the browser. You can accept this name, or change it by typing a new name in the Name field.

   • **Primary Browser/Secondary Browser:** If desired, select one of these checkboxes to designate the current browser as such.

   • **Preview Using Temporary File:** When this option is on, Dreamweaver creates and submits a temporary copy of the current file to the previewing browser. You can see this by looking in the browser's Location field; the file will begin with TMP, as in TMP3roxnugqf6.htm. When the option is off, Dreamweaver submits the actual file to the browser.

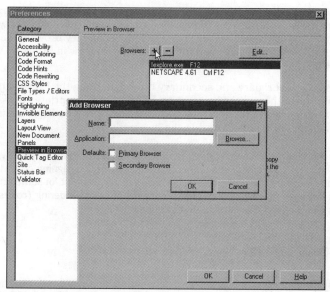

Figure 5-11: In the Preview in Browser Preferences category, you can add, modify, and delete preview browsers.

3. After you've added a browser to your list, you can easily edit or delete it. Reopen the Preview in Browser Preferences category and highlight the browser you want to modify or delete.

4. To alter your selection, click the Edit button. To delete your selection, click the Remove (–) button.

5. After you've completed your modifications, click OK to close the dialog box.

Once you've added one or more browsers to your list, you can preview the current page in these browsers. Select File ➪ Preview in Browser ➪ *BrowserName*, where *BrowserName* indicates the particular program. Dreamweaver saves the page to a temporary file, starts the browser, and loads the page.

In order to view any changes you've made to your Web page under construction, you must select the Preview in Browser menu option again (or press one of the function keys for primary/secondary browser previewing, described in the following paragraph). Clicking the Refresh/Reload button in your browser will not load in any modifications. The temporary preview files are deleted when you quit Dreamweaver.

Tip

Dreamweaver saves preview files with a filename like the following: TMP5c34jymi4q.asp; a unique name is generated with each preview to ensure that the browser does not load the page from the cache. If Dreamweaver unexpectedly quits, these TMP files are not deleted. Feel free to delete any such TMP files you find in your site; or use them as backups to restore unsaved work should a crash occur.

You can also use keyboard shortcuts to preview two different browsers by pressing a function key. Press F12 to preview the current Dreamweaver page in your primary browser, and Ctrl+F12 (Command+F12) to preview the same page in your secondary browser. These are the primary and secondary browser settings you establish in the Preview in Browser Preferences panel, explained in Chapter 4.

You can easily reassign your primary and secondary browsers. Go to the Preview in Browser Preferences category, select the desired browser, and select the appropriate checkbox to designate the browser as primary or secondary. In the list of browsers, you'll see the indicator of F12 or Ctrl+F12 (Command+F12) appear next to the browser's name.

Tip   In addition to checking your Web page output on a variety of browsers on your system, it's also a good idea to preview the page on other platforms. If you're designing on a Macintosh, try to view your pages on a Windows system, and vice versa. Watch out for some not-so-subtle differences between the two environments, in terms of color rendering (colors in Macs tend to be brighter than in PCs) and screen resolution.

Putting Your Pages Online

The final phase of setting up your Dreamweaver site is publishing your pages to the Web. When to begin this publishing process is up to you. Some Web designers wait until everything is absolutely perfect on the local development site and then upload everything at once. Others like to establish an early connection to the remote site and extend the transfer of files over a longer period of time.

I fall into the latter camp. When I start transferring files at the beginning of the process, I find that I catch my mistakes earlier and avoid having to effect massive changes to the site after everything is up. For example, in developing one large site, I started out using mixed-case filenames, as in ELFhome.html. After publishing some early drafts of a few Web pages, however, I discovered that the host had switched servers; on the new server, filenames had to be entirely lowercase. Had I waited until the last moment to upload everything, I would have been faced with an unexpected and laborious search-and-replace job.

Once you've established your local site root — and you've included your remote site's FTP information in the setup — the actual publishing of your files to the Web is a very straightforward process. To transfer your local Web pages to an online site, follow these steps:

1. Choose Window ⇨ Site or F8 to open the Site panel, and select the desired site from the Site drop-down list.

2. In the Site panel, click the Connect button. (You may need to connect to the Internet first.) Dreamweaver displays a message box showing the progress of the connection.

3. If you didn't enter a password in the Remote Info category when you defined the site, or if you entered a password but didn't opt to save it, Dreamweaver asks you to type in your password.

   Once the connection is complete, the directory listing of the remote site appears in the Site panel.

4. Click the Expand/Collapse button to expand the Site panel into its two-pane view: Remote pane on the left, Local pane on the right.

   In the Local pane (green icons), select the folder(s) and file(s) you want to upload — or, to upload the entire site, select the site folder (at the top of the list) — and then click the Put File(s) button, as shown in Figure 5-12.

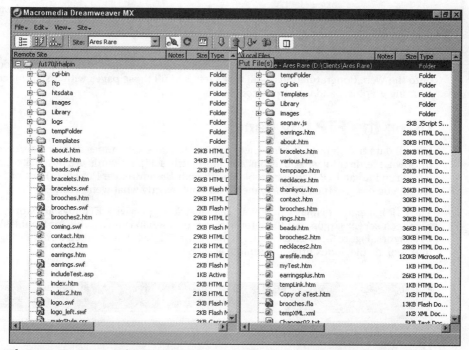

Figure 5-12: You use the Put File(s) button in the Site panel to transfer files, folders, and entire sites.

5. If Dreamweaver asks if you would like to move the dependent files as well, select Yes to transfer all embedded graphics and other objects, or No if you'd prefer to move these yourself. You can also select the Don't Ask Me Again checkbox to make transfers of dependent files automatic in the future. Dreamweaver displays the progress of the file transfer.

6. After each file has successfully transferred, Dreamweaver places a checkmark next to its icon — provided that File Check In/Out is enabled in the site's Remote Info category.

7. When you've finished transferring your files, click the Disconnect button.

Note   Dreamweaver MX provides an FTP Log panel that displays all of your FTP file transfer activity (Puts, Gets, and so on). This panel is particularly useful for troubleshooting FTP transfer errors. For more information, see the next section, "Using the FTP Log panel."

Remember that the only files you have to highlight for transfer to the remote site are the HTML files. As noted previously, Dreamweaver automatically transfers any dependent files (if you allow it), which means that you'll never forget to move a GIF again! (Nor will you ever move an unnecessary file, such as an earlier version of an image, by mistake.) Moreover, Dreamweaver automatically creates any subfolders necessary to maintain the site's integrity. These two features combined will save you substantial time and worry.

Caution   Be aware that Dreamweaver does not always know to include files that are used within scripts; you might need to upload these files manually.

Now you have made your site a reality, from the planning stages to the local site root and onto the Web. Congratulations — all that's left is to fill those pages with insightful content, amazing graphics, and wondrous code. Let's get to it!

Using the FTP Log panel

Like all data transfers on the Internet, FTP file transfers sometimes go awry: servers are busy or down, file/directory permissions are improperly set, passwords are misspelled, and so on. If you run into an FTP transfer problem with your Dreamweaver Put File(s) or Get File(s) command, you can use the FTP Log panel to find out exactly what went wrong.

The FTP Log panel displays all of your FTP file-transfer activity. FTP logs are wordy and full of high-tech server jargon, but the information they contain is invaluable for troubleshooting FTP errors. Figure 5-13, for example, displays the FTP log that resulted from Putting (uploading) a single file, index.htm, to a remote server.

```
▾ Results                                                                          ≣,
  Search  Validation  Target Browser Check  Link Checker  Site Reports  FTP Log  Server Debug
FTP Command:
-rw-r--r--  1 rhalpin user     1107 May 28 12:08 mainStyle.css
-rw-r--r--  1 rhalpin user      648 Jun  2 21:03 myTest.htm
-rw-r--r--  1 rhalpin user       17 Dec 17 13:57 myinc.inc
-rw-r--r--  1 rhalpin user    27697 Jun  6 20:08 necklaces.htm
-rw-r--r--  1 rhalpin user     1624 May 28 12:09 necklaces.swf
-rw-r--r--  1 rhalpin user    26607 Jun  2 20:50 necklaces2.htm
-rw-r--r--  1 rhalpin user    29596 Jun  6 20:08 rings.htm
-rw-r--r--  1 rhalpin user     1310 Jan 28 15:48 rings.swf
-rw-r--r--  1 rhalpin user     1115 Jun  2 21:04 seqnav.js
drwxr-xr-x  2 rhalpin user     1024 May 15 21:01 tempFolder
-rw-r--r--  1 rhalpin user    27662 Jun  6 20:08 temppage.htm
-rw-r--r--  1 rhalpin user      497 Feb  3 13:08 testMail.htm
-rw-r--r--  1 rhalpin user    19173 Jan 28 13:54 test_adv_mailer.asp
-rw-r--r--  1 rhalpin user    13537 Jan 28 13:55 test_asp_components.asp
-rw-r--r--  1 rhalpin user    25830 Jun  6 20:08 thankyou.htm
-rw-r--r--  1 rhalpin user    27490 Jun  6 20:08 various.htm
-rw-r--r--  1 rhalpin user     1587 Jan 28 15:50 various.swf
226 Transfer complete.
```

Figure 5-13: The FTP Log generated when the index.htm file is uploaded to a remote server.

To display the FTP Log panel, choose the FTP Log button (the Site panel must be expanded in the Dreamweaver MX workspace to do so) or use the keyboard shortcut Ctrl+Shift+F12 (Command+Shift+F12).

Summary

In this chapter, you learned some options for planning your Web site and what you need to do in Dreamweaver to initialize the site. This planning and initialization process is not a detailed one, but taking preliminary steps can greatly smooth your development path down the road.

✦ Put as much time into planning your site as possible. The more clearly conceived the site, the cleaner the execution.

✦ Set up your local site root in Dreamweaver right away. The local site root is essential for Dreamweaver to properly publish your files to the remote site later.

✦ If you are creating a Web application, choose one server model per site and set it when you define your site. This step is needed so that Dreamweaver knows the type of server code to write.

✦ Preview early, often, and with various browsers. Dreamweaver gives you quick function-key access to a primary (F12) and secondary (Ctrl+F12/Command+F12) browser. Check your pages frequently in these browsers, and then spend some time checking your pages against other available browsers and browser versions.

✦ Establish an early connection to the Web and use it frequently. You can begin publishing your local site through Dreamweaver's Site window almost immediately.

In the next chapter, you learn how to use Dreamweaver to begin coding your Web pages.

✦   ✦   ✦

Web Design and Layout

Accessing the Code Directly

As far as most designers are concerned, in a perfect world, you could lay out a complex Web site with a visual authoring tool and never have to see the HTML and other code, much less modify it. Dreamweaver takes you a long way toward this goal — in fact, you can create many types of Web pages using only Dreamweaver's Design view. As your pages become more complex, however, you will probably need to tweak your code in one way or another.

Programmers, on the other hand, are happiest working directly with the code. To accomplish their goals efficiently, coders need a responsive, flexible editor capable of handling a wide range of computer languages. Just how much assistance is required is a matter of personal taste: Some code writers want all the help they can get, with features such as syntax coloring, code completion, and Code Hints, among others, whereas other programmers just want their editor to stay out of their way.

Dreamweaver tries to give coders the best of both worlds by providing a full-featured editor with numerous options. In addition to the features mentioned in the preceding paragraph, Dreamweaver includes full tag libraries in numerous languages: HTML, CFML, ASP.NET, JSP, and PHP, to name a few. Both hand-coders and visual designers can enjoy the benefits of Dreamweaver tools such as the Snippets panel, for adding chunks of code via drag-and-drop, and the Tag Inspector, for displaying all the attributes of a chosen tag — and making them editable as well. This chapter covers all of these features and more.

While the Internet is made up of a plethora of technologies, HTML is still at the heart of a Web page. This chapter gives you a basic understanding of how HTML works and provides you with the specific building blocks you need to begin creating Web pages. This chapter also gives you your first look at a Dreamweaver innovation: Code view, for altering the code side-by-side with the visual environment. The other Dreamweaver-specific material in this chapter — which primarily describes how Dreamweaver sets and modifies a page's properties — is suitable for even the most accomplished Web designers. Armed with these fundamentals, you are ready to begin your exploration of Web page creation.

The Structure of a Web Page

The simplest explanation of how HTML works derives from the full expansion of its acronym: Hypertext Markup Language. *Hypertext* refers to one of the World Wide Web's main properties — the capability to jump from one page to another, no matter where the pages are located on the Web. *Markup Language* means that a Web page is actually a heavily annotated text file. The basic building blocks of HTML, such as <strong> and <p>, are known as *markup elements,* or *tags.* The terms *element* and *tag* are used interchangeably.

An HTML page, then, is a set of instructions (the tags) suggesting to your browser how to display the enclosed text and images. The browser knows what kind of page it is handling based on the tag that opens the page, <html>, and the tag that closes the page, </html>. The great majority of HTML tags come in such pairs, in which the closing tag always has a forward slash before the keyword. Two examples of tag pairs are: <p>. . .</p> and <title>. . .</title>. A few important tags are represented by a single element: the image tag <img>, for example.

The HTML page is divided into two primary sections: the <head> and the <body>. Information relating to the entire document goes in the <head> section: the title, description, keywords, and any language subroutines that may be called from within the <body>. The content of the Web page is found in the <body> section. All the text, graphics, embedded animations, Java applets, and other elements of the page are found between the opening <body> and the closing </body> tags.

When you start a new document in Dreamweaver, the basic format is already laid out for you. Listing 6-1 shows the code from a Dreamweaver blank Web page.

Listing 6-1: **The HTML for a New Dreamweaver Page**

```
<!DOCTYPE HTML PUBLIC "-//W3C//DTD HTML 4.01 Transitional//EN">
<html>
<head>
<title>Untitled Document</title>
<meta http-equiv="Content-Type" content="text/html; charset=iso-8859-1">
</head>

<body>

</body>
</html>
```

We'll cover the opening <!DOCTYPE> tag a little later in this chapter in "Doctype and Doctype Switching". First you should notice how the <head>. . .</head> pair is separate from the <body>. . .</body> pair, and that both are contained within the <html>. . .</html> tags.

Note also that the <meta> tag has two additional elements:

```
http-equiv="Content-Type"
```

and

```
content="text/html; charset=iso-8859-1"
```

These types of elements are known as *attributes*. Attributes modify the basic tag and can either be equal to a value or stand alone. We'll cover the specifics of the `<meta>` tag later in this chapter, for now you should just focus on the syntax. Attributes are made up of name/value pairs where the attribute is set to be equal to some value, typically in quotes. Not every tag has attributes, but when they do, the attributes are specific.

One last note about an HTML page: You are free to use carriage returns, spaces, and tabs as needed to make your code more readable. The interpreting browser ignores all but the included tags and text to create your page. Some minor, browser-specific differences in interpretation of these elements are pointed out throughout the book, but generally, you can indent or space your code as you desire.

Cross-Reference   The style in which Dreamweaver inserts code is completely customizable. See Chapter 4 for details on changing your code preferences and Chapter 33 to see how you can adjust your tags more specifically with the Tag Library Editor.

Expanding into XHTML

The latest version of HTML is known as XHTML, short for eXtensible HTML. XHTML is based on XML and, as such, has a more rigid syntax than HTML. For example, tags that do not enclose content — the so-called *empty tags* — are written differently. In HTML, a line-break tag is

```
<br>
```

whereas in XHTML, the line-break tag is

```
<br />
```

Note the additional space and the closing slash. Other differences include an opening XML declaration as well as a specific `doctype` tag placed before the opening `<html>` tag. All tags must be in lowercase, and all attribute values must appear in quotes, (but not necessarily lowercase) as follows:

```
<table align="RIGHT">
```

Dreamweaver makes it easy to code in XHTML, and even to convert existing pages from HTML to XHTML. To work in XHTML from the ground up, select the Make Document XHTML Compliant option on the New Document category of Preferences (available when you choose Edit ➪ Preferences). Selecting this option will automatically select an identical option on the New Document dialog box (File ➪ New) — which, if necessary, you can disable on a case-by-case basis. Once a document has been set as an XHTML file, all the tags are written in the proper style.

To switch an HTML page to an XHTML one, choose File ➪ Convert ➪ XHTML. The conversion is automatically applied to the current document; there is no standard method to convert an entire site.

Since Dreamweaver has taken the pain out of using XHTML, the question is, should you code in XHTML or HTML? As in most situations, it depends. Many larger companies that work extensively in XML require well-formed XHTML pages. As the latest version of the Web's core language — and recommended by the W3C — you'll be perfectly poised for the future. One aspect of the future is the proliferation of Internet devices other than the computer: PDAs, cell phones, and set-top boxes, among others. XHTML is far more portable to these types of devices than HTML.

However, you should be aware that not all browsers render XHTML pages exactly the same as they do HTML pages. The problems stem largely from older browsers (version 4 and earlier for both Internet Explorer and Netscape). If the audience for your site is heavily dependent on older browsers, you should probably stick with HTML for the time being; on the other hand, if the site's audience is fairly up-to-date and forward-looking, code in XHTML.

doctype and doctype Switching

The very first element of an HTML page — even before the <html> tag — is, increasingly, a doctype declaration. As the name implies, a doctype declaration specifies the language or, more specifically, the DTD (Document Type Definition) in use for the file that follows. To validate their page, many authors include doctype statements like the following:

```
<!DOCTYPE HTML PUBLIC "-//W3C//DTD HTML 4.01 Transitional//EN">
```

This doctype is inserted by default when Dreamweaver creates a new static HTML page.

Note   The latest — in fact, the last — version of HTML recommended by the W3C is version 4.01. After this version, the W3C recommended the switch to XHTML.

Recent browser versions have begun inspecting the doctype element in order to determine how the page should be rendered. Engaging in a practice known as *doctype switching*, these browsers (Internet Explorer 5 on the Macintosh, Internet Explorer 6, and Netscape 6) work in two modes: strict and regular. When in strict mode, a page must be well-formed and validate without error to be rendered properly. Strict rendering is more consistent across browsers. The regular mode is far looser and more forgiving in how the page is coded; however, your page is more likely to be rendered differently in the varying browser versions.

You can ensure that your pages are rendered in the regular mode in a number of ways:

✦ Do not include a doctype declaration at all.

✦ Use a doctype declaration that specifies an HTML version earlier than 4.0.

✦ Use a doctype declaration that declares a transitional DTD of HTML 4.01, but does not include a URL to the DTD.

To trigger a browser's strict rendering mode:

✦ Use a doctype declaration for XML or XHTML.

✦ Use a doctype declaration that declares a strict DTD of HTML 4.01.

✦ Use a doctype declaration that declares a transitional DTD of HTML 4.01 that includes a URL to the DTD.

When including a URL to the DTD, the doctype looks as follows:

```
<!DOCTYPE HTML PUBLIC "-//W3C//DTD HTML 4.01 Transitional//EN"
"http://www.w3.org/TR/html4/loose.dtd">
```

You have several alternatives in Dreamweaver for including whichever doctype you choose. Hand-coding is a sure but tedious method; the doctype statement is somewhat cumbersome and certainly not easy to remember precisely. You could also alter the standard HTML page by changing the Default.html file found in your Configuration\DocumentTypes\NewDocuments folder.

For more details on altering the default page template, see Chapter 28.

Another approach would be to create a custom snippet that would enable you to drag the desired code right onto the page on a case-by-case basis. Use of the Snippets panel is covered later in this chapter in the "Adding Code through the Snippets panel" section.

Which approach you take — strict or regular — depends, as with HTML and XHTML, on your audience. If a significant amount of your site's audience uses older browsers, stay with a regular doctype. If the statistics for your site indicate that a high percentage of visitors are using more current browsers, go with a strict doctype. Of course, some designers may be mandated by their client or manager to use a specific doctype.

Defining <head> Elements

Information pertaining to the Web page overall is contained in the <head> section of an HTML page. Browsers read the <head> to determine how to render the page — for example, is the page to be displayed using the Western, the Chinese, or some other character set? Search engine spiders also read this section to quickly glean a summary of the page.

When you begin inserting JavaScript (or code from another scripting language such as VBScript) into your Web page, all the subroutines and document-wide declarations go into the <head> area. Dreamweaver uses this format by default when you insert a JavaScript behavior.

Dreamweaver enables you to insert, view, and modify <head> content without opening an HTML editor. Dreamweaver's View Head Content capability enables you to work with <meta> tags and other <head> HTML code as you do with the regular content in the visual editor.

Establishing page properties

When you first start Dreamweaver, your default Web page is untitled, with no background image, and only a plain, white background. You can change any of these properties and more through Dreamweaver's Page Properties dialog box.

Attributes entered through the Page Properties dialog box are written into the <body> tag. An increasing number of Web designers prefer to control these attributes through a Cascading Style Sheet (CSS). For more information on CSS, see Chapter 20.

You can also change the document title in Dreamweaver's Document toolbar. Just enter the information in the Title field and press Enter (Return) to confirm the modification. You'll see the new title appear in the program's title bar and whenever you preview the page in a browser.

As usual, Dreamweaver gives you more than one method for accessing the Page Properties dialog box. You can select Modify ➪ Page Properties, or you can use the keyboard shortcut Ctrl+J (Command+J).

Here's another way to open the Page Properties dialog box: Right-click (Control+click) any open area in the Document window — that is, any part of the screen not occupied by an image, table, or other object (text outside of tables is okay to click, however). From the bottom of the context menu, select Page Properties.

The Page Properties dialog box, shown in Figure 6-1, gives you easy control over your HTML page's overall look and feel.

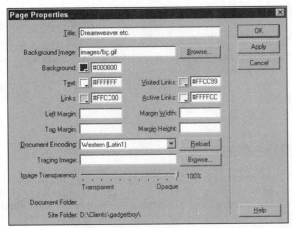

Figure 6-1: Change your Web page's overall appearance through the Page Properties dialog box.

 Technically, some of the values you assign through the Page Properties dialog box are applied to the <body> tag. Because they affect the overall appearance of a page, however, they are covered in this <head> section.

The key areas of the Page Properties dialog box are as follows:

Page Property	Description
Title	The title of your Web page. The name you enter here appears in the browser's title bar when your page is viewed. Search engine spiders also read the title as one of the important indexing clues.
Background Image	The filename of the graphic you want in the page background. Either type in the path directly or pick a file by clicking the Browse (Choose) button. You can embed the graphic of your choice in the background of your page; if the image is smaller than your content requires, the browser tiles the image to fill out the page. Specifying a background image overrides any selection in the Background color field.
Background	Click this color swatch to change the background color of the Web page. Select one of the browser-safe colors from the drop-down list, or enter its name or hexadecimal representation (for example, "#FFFFFF") directly into the text box.
Text	Click this color swatch to control the color of default text.
Links	Click this color swatch to modify the color of any text designated as a link, or the border around an image link.

Page Property	Description
Visited Links	Click this color swatch to select the color that linked text changes to after a visitor to your Web page has selected that link and then returned to your page.
Active Links	Click this color swatch to choose the color to which linked text changes briefly when a user selects the link.
Left Margin, Top Margin, Margin Width, Margin Height	Enter values here to change the default margin settings used by browsers. The Left Margin and Top Margin settings are used by Microsoft, whereas Margin Width and Margin Height are used by Netscape.
Document Encoding	The character set in which you want your Web page to be displayed. Choose one from the drop-down list. The default is Western (Latin 1).
Tracing Image	Selects an image to use as a layout guide.
Image Transparency	Sets the degree of transparency for the tracing image.

The Page Properties dialog box also displays the document folder if the page has been saved, and the current site root folder if one has been selected.

Cross-Reference The Tracing Image option is a powerful feature for quickly building a Web page based on design comps. For details about this feature and how to use it, see Chapter 21.

Choosing a page palette

Getting the right text and link colors to match your background color has been largely a trial-and-error process. Generally, you'd set the background color, add a contrasting text color, and then add some variations of different colors for the three different link colors — all the while clicking the Apply button and checking your results until you found a satisfactory combination. This is a time-intensive chore, to say the least.

However, Dreamweaver ships with a command that enables you to quickly pick an entire palette for your page in one fell swoop. The Set Color Scheme Command dialog box, shown in Figure 6-2, features palette combinations from noted Web designers Lynda Weinman and Bruce Heavin. The command colors available are all Web-safe — which means that they will appear the same in the major browsers on all Macintosh and Windows systems without dithering.

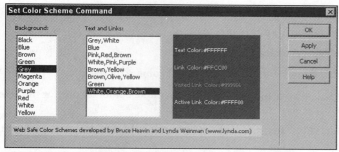

Figure 6-2: Get a Web-safe page palette with one click by using the Set Color Scheme Command dialog box.

Choosing Colors from an Onscreen Image

One of the features found throughout Dreamweaver, the Eyedropper tool, is especially useful in the Page Properties options. The Eyedropper tool appears whenever you open any of Dreamweaver's color swatches, such as those attached to the Background, Text, and Links colors. You can not only pick a color from the Web-safe palette that appears, but also use the Eyedropper to select any color on any page — including system colors such as those found in dialog boxes and menu strips.

To use the Eyedropper tool to choose a color for the background (or any of the other options) from an onscreen image, follow these steps:

1. Insert your image on the page and, using the vertical scroll bar, position the Document window so that the image and the Page Properties dialog box can be viewed simultaneously.

   If your image is too big to fit both it and the Page Properties dialog box on the same screen, temporarily resize your image by dragging its sizing handles. You can restore the original image size when you're done by selecting the Refresh button on the Image Property inspector.

2. Open the Page Properties dialog box by choosing Modify ➪ Page Properties or using the keyboard shortcut, Ctrl+J (Command+J).

3. Drag the Page Properties dialog box to a place where the image can be seen.

4. Select the Background color swatch (or whichever one you wish to change).

   The Dreamweaver color picker opens, and the pointer becomes an eyedropper.

5. Move the Eyedropper tool over the image until you find the correct color. (On Windows, you must hold the mouse button down as you drag the Eyedropper off the Dreamweaver dialog box to the image.) As you move the Eyedropper over an image, its colors are reflected in the color well and its hex value is shown on the color picker. Click once when you've found the appropriate color.

   The color picker closes.

6. Repeat Steps 4 and 5 to grab other colors from the screen for other color swatches. Click OK when you've finished modifying the page properties.

You don't have to keep the image on your page to get its color. Just insert it temporarily and then delete it after you've used the Eyedropper to grab the shade you want.

To use the Set Color Scheme Command dialog box, follow these steps:

1. Choose Commands ➪ Set Color Scheme.

   The Set Color Scheme Command dialog box opens.

2. Select the background color from the Background column on the left.

   The Text and Links column is updated to show available combinations for the selected background color.

3. Select a color set from the Text and Links column to see various combinations in the Preview pane.

The color names — such as White, Pink, Brown — refer to the Text, Link, and Visited Link colors, generally. If only one color name is offered, the entire color scheme uses shades of that color. Note that the background color changes slightly for various color combinations to work better with the foreground color choices.

4. Click Apply to see the effect on your current page. Click OK when you finish.

To learn more about commands in general — including how to build your own — check out Chapter 33.

Understanding <meta> and other <head> tags

Summary information about the content of a page — and a lot more — is conveyed through <meta> tags used within the <head> section. The <meta> tag can be read by the server to create a header file, which makes it easier for indexing software used by search engines to catalog sites. Numerous different types of <meta> tags exist, and you can insert them in your document just like other objects.

One <meta> tag is included by default in every Dreamweaver page. The Document Encoding option of the Page Properties dialog box determines the character set used by the current Web page and is displayed in the <head> section as follows:

```
<meta http-equiv="Content-Type" content="text/html; charset=iso-8859-1">
```

The preceding <meta> tag tells the browser that this page is, in fact, an HTML page and that the page should be rendered using the specified character set (the charset attribute). The key attribute here is http-equiv, which is responsible for generating a server response header.

Once you've determined your <meta> tags for a Web site, the same basic <meta> information can go on every Web page. Dreamweaver gives you a way to avoid having to insert the same lines repeatedly: templates. Once you've set up the <head> elements the way you'd like them, choose File ➪ Save As Template. If you want to add <meta> or any other <head> tags to an existing template, you can edit the template and then update the affected pages. For more information about templates, turn to Chapter 28.

In Dreamweaver, you can insert a <meta> tag or any other tag using the <head> tag objects, which you access via the Head category in the Insert bar or the Insert ➪ Head Tags menu option. The <head> tag objects are described in Table 6-1 and subsequent subsections.

Table 6-1: Head Tag Objects

Object	Description
Meta	Inserts information that describes or affects the entire document
Keywords	Includes a series of words used by some search engines to index the current Web page and/or site
Description	Includes a text description of the current Web page and/or site
Refresh	Reloads the current document or loads a new URL within a specified number of seconds
Base	Establishes a reference for all other URLs in the current Web page
Link	Inserts a link to an external document, such as a style sheet

Inserting tags with the Meta object

The Meta object is used to insert tags that provide information for the Web server, through the HTTP-equiv attribute, and other overall data that you want to include in your Web page but not make visible to the casual browser. Some Web pages, for example, have built-in expiration dates after which the content is to be considered outmoded. In Dreamweaver, you can use the Meta object to insert a wide range of descriptive data.

You can access the Meta object in the Head category of the Insert bar or via the Insert menu by choosing Insert ➪ Head Tags ➪ Meta. Like all the Head objects, you don't have to have the Head Content visible to insert the Meta object; although you do have to choose View ➪ Head Content if you wish to edit the object. To insert a Meta object, follow these steps:

1. Select Insert ➪ Head Tags ➪ Meta or select the Meta object from the Head category of the Insert bar. Your current cursor position is irrelevant.

   The Meta dialog box opens, as shown in Figure 6-3.

Meta icon

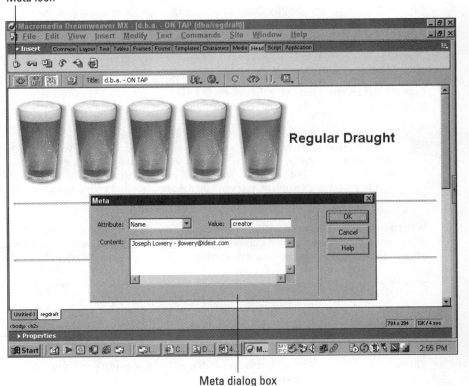

Meta dialog box

Figure 6-3: The Meta object enables you to enter a full range of <meta> tags in the <head> section of your Web page.

Built-in Meta Commands

Although Dreamweaver presents six different Head objects, `<meta>` tags form the basis of four of them: Meta, Keywords, Description, and Refresh. By specifying different `name` attributes, the purpose of the `<meta>` tags changes. For example, a Keywords object uses the following format:

```
<meta name="keywords" content="dreamweaver, web, authoring,
HTML, DHTML, CSS, Macromedia">
```

whereas a Description object inserts this type of code:

```
<meta name="description" content="This site is devoted to
extensions made possible by Macromedia's Dreamweaver, the
premier Web authoring tool.">
```

It is possible to create all your `<meta>` tags with the Meta object by specifying the `name` attribute and giving it the pertinent value, but it's easier to just use the standard Dreamweaver Head objects.

2. Choose the desired attribute: `Name` or an HTTP equivalent from the Attribute list box. Press Tab.

3. Enter the value for the selected attribute in the Value text box. Press Tab.

4. Enter the value for the content attribute in the Content text box.

5. Click OK when you're done.

You can add as many Meta objects as you need to by repeating Steps 1 through 4. To edit an existing Meta object, you must first choose View ➪ Head Content to reveal the `<head>` code, indicated by the various icons. Select the Meta icon and make your changes in the Property inspector.

Aiding search engines with the Keywords and Description objects

Let's take a closer look at the tags that convey indexing and descriptive information to some search engine spiders. These chores are handled by the Keywords and Description objects. As noted in the sidebar, "Built-in Meta Commands," the Keywords and Description objects output specialized `<meta>` tags.

Both objects are straightforward to use. Choose Insert ➪ Head Tags ➪ Keywords or Insert ➪ Head Tags ➪ Description. You can also choose the corresponding objects from the Head category of the Insert bar. Once selected, these objects open similar dialog boxes with a single entry area, a large text box, as shown in Figure 6-4. Enter the values — whether keywords or a description — in the text box and click OK when you're done. You can edit the Keywords and Description objects, like the Meta object, by selecting their icons in the Head area of the Document window, revealed by choosing View ➪ Head Contents.

Caution   Although you can enter paragraph returns in your Keywords and Description objects, there's no reason to. Browsers ignore all such formatting when processing your code.

Keywords icon

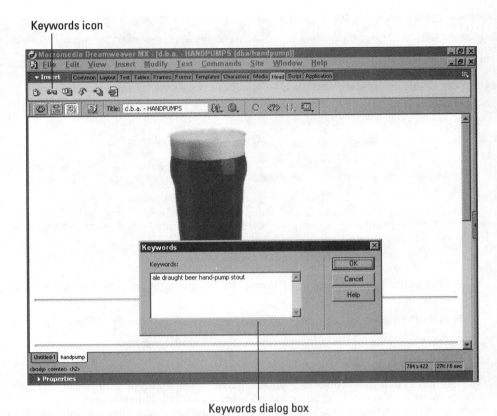

Keywords dialog box

Figure 6-4: Entering information through the Keywords object helps search engines correctly index your Web page.

What you place in the Keywords and Description objects can have a big impact on your Web page's accessibility. If, for example, you want to categorize your Web page as an homage to the music of the early seventies, you could enter the following in the Content area of the Keywords object:

```
music, 70s, 70's, eagles, ronstadt, bee gees, pop, rock
```

In the preceding case, the content list is composed of words or phrases, separated by commas. Use sentences in the Description object, as follows:

```
The definitive look back to the power pop rock stylings of early 1970s
music, with special sections devoted to the Eagles, Linda Ronstadt, and
the Bee Gees.
```

Keep in mind that the content in the Description should complement and extend both the Keywords and the Web page title. You have more room in both the Description and Keywords objects — actually, an unlimited amount — than in the page title, which should be on the short side in order to fit into the browser's title bar.

Caution   When using ⟨meta⟩ tags with the Keywords or Description objects, don't stuff the ⟨meta⟩ tags repeatedly with the same word. The search engines are engineered to reject multiple instances of the same words, and your description will not get the attention it deserves.

Refreshing the page and redirecting users

The Refresh object forces a browser to reload the current page or to load a new page after a user-set interval. The Web page visitor usually controls refreshing a page; if, for some reason, the display has become garbled, the user can choose Reload or Refresh from the menu to redraw the screen. Impatient Web surfer that I am, I often stop a page from loading to see what text links are available and then — if I don't see what I need — hit Reload to bring in the full page. The code inserted by the Refresh object tells the server, not the browser, to reload the page. This can be a powerful tool but leads to trouble if used improperly.

To insert a Refresh object, follow these steps:

1. Choose Insert ⇨ Head Tags ⇨ Refresh or select the Insert Refresh object from the Head category of the Insert bar.

    The Refresh dialog box, shown in Figure 6-5, opens.

Refresh icon

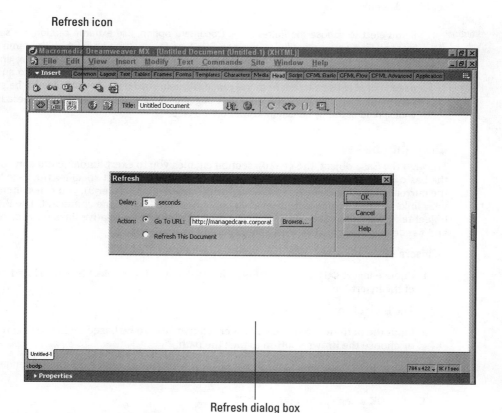

Refresh dialog box

Figure 6-5: Use the Refresh object to redirect visitors from an outdated page.

2. Enter the number of seconds you want to wait before the Refresh command takes effect in the Delay text box.

The Delay value is calculated from the time the page finishes loading.

3. Select the desired Action:

   • Go to URL

   • Refresh This Document

4. If you selected Go to URL, enter a path to another page in the text box or select the Browse button to select a file.

5. Click OK when you're done.

The Refresh object is most often used to redirect a visitor to another Web page. The Web is a fluid place, and sites often move from one address to another. Typically, a page at the old address contains the Refresh code that automatically takes the user to the new address. It's good practice to include a link to your new URL on the "change-of-address" page because not all browsers support the Refresh option. One other tip: Keep the number of seconds to a minimum — there's no point in waiting for something to happen automatically when you could click a link.

Caution   If you elect to choose the Refresh This Document option, use extreme caution, for several reasons. First, you can easily set up an endless loop for your visitors in which the same page is constantly being refreshed. If you are working with a page that updates often, enter a longer Refresh value, such as 300 or 500. You should be sure to include a link to another page to enable users to exit from the continually refreshed page. You should also be aware that many search engines will not index pages using the <meta> refresh tag because of widespread abuse by certain industries on the Web.

Changing bases

Through the Base object, the <head> section enables you to exert fundamental control over the basic HTML element: the link. The code inserted by this object specifies the base URL for the current page. If you use relative addressing (covered in Chapter 9), you can switch all your links to another directory — even another Web site — with one command. The Base object takes two attributes: Href, which redirects all the other relative links on your page; and target, which specifies where the links will be rendered.

To insert a Base object in your page, follow these steps:

1. Choose Insert ➪ Head Tags ➪ Refresh or select the Base object from the Head category of the Insert bar.

   The Base dialog box opens.

2. Input the path that you want all other relative links to be based on in the Href text box or choose the Browse button to pick the path.

3. If desired, enter a default target for all links without a specific target to be rendered in the Target text box.

4. Click OK when you're done.

How does a `<base>` tag affect your page? Suppose you define one link as follows:

```
images/backgnd.gif
```

Normally, the browser looks in the same folder as the current page for a subfolder named images. A different sequence occurs, however, if you set the `<base>` tag to another URL in the following way:

```
<base href="http://www.testsite.com/client-demo01/">
```

With this `<base>` tag, when the same `images/backgnd.gif` link is activated, the browser looks for its file in the following location:

```
http://www.testsite.com/client-demo01/images/backgnd.gif
```

Caution   Because of the all-or-nothing capability of `<base>` tags, many Webmasters use them cautiously, if at all.

Linking to other files

The Link object indicates a relationship between the current page and another page or file. Although many other intended uses exist, the `<link>` tag is most commonly used to apply an external Cascading Style Sheet (CSS) to the current page. This code is entered automatically in Dreamweaver when you create a new linked style sheet (as described in Chapter 20), or you can add the attributes yourself with the Link object. The `<link>` tag is also used to include TrueDoc dynamic fonts.

Tip   One other popular use of the `<link>` tag is to create *favicons*. A favicon is a small icon that appears in the Favorites menu of Internet Explorer browsers when you mark a site as a Favorite or bookmarked. To have a favicon appear when a page is bookmarked, create a favicon using one of the tools listed at `www.favicon.com` and upload that image file to your site. Then put a tag like this on your page:

```
<LINK REL="SHORTCUT ICON" HREF="/images/fav.ico">.
```

where fav.ico is the name of the icon file, here stored in the images folder at the root of the site.

To insert a Link object, first choose Insert ➪ Head Tags ➪ Link or select the Insert Link object from the Head category of the Insert bar. This action opens the Link dialog box, shown in Figure 6-6.

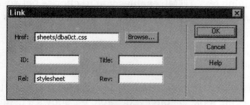

Figure 6-6: The Link object is primarily used to include external style sheets.

Next, enter the necessary attributes:

Attribute	Description
Href	The path to the file being linked. Use the Browse button to open the Select File dialog box.
ID	The ID attribute can be used by scripts to identify this particular object and affect it if need be.
Title	The Title attribute is displayed as a ToolTip by Internet Explorer browsers.
Rel	A keyword that describes the relationship of the linked document to the current page. For example, an external style sheet uses the keyword stylesheet.
Rev	Rev, like Rel, also describes a relationship but in the reverse. For example, if home.html contained a link tag with a Rel attribute set to intro.html, intro.html could contain a link tag with a Rev attribute set to home.html.

Note Aside from the style sheet use, there's little browser support for the other link functions. However, the World Wide Web Consortium (W3C) supports an initiative to use the <link> tag to address other media, such as speech synthesis and Braille devices, and it's entirely possible that the Link object will be used for this purpose in the future.

Adding to the <body>

The content of a Web page — the text, images, links, and plugins — is all contained in the <body> section of an HTML document. The great majority of <body> tags can be inserted through Dreamweaver's visual layout interface.

To use the <body> tags efficiently, you need to understand the distinction between logical styles and physical styles used in HTML. An underlying philosophy of HTML is to keep the Web as universally accessible as possible. Web content is intended to be platform- and resolution-independent, but the content itself can be styled by its intent as well. This philosophy is supported by the existence of logical <body> tags (such as <code> and <cite>), with which a block of text can be rendered according to its meaning, and physical style tags for directly italicizing or underlining text. HTML enables you to choose between logical styles, which are relative to the text, or physical styles, which can be regarded as absolute.

Logical styles

Logical styles are contextual, rather than explicit. Choose a logical style when you want to ensure that the meaning, rather than a specific look, is conveyed. Table 6-2 shows a listing of logical style tags and their most common usage. Tags not supported through Dreamweaver's visual interface are noted.

Table 6-2: HTML Logical Style Tags

Tag	Usage
`<big>`	Increases the size of the selected text relative to the surrounding text. Not currently supported by Dreamweaver
`<cite>`	Citations, titles, and references; usually shown in italic
`<code>`	Code; for showing programming code, usually displayed in a monospaced font
`<dfn>`	Defining instance; used to mark the introduction of a new term
`<em>`	Emphasis; usually depicted as underlined or italicized text
`<kbd>`	Keyboard; used to render text to be entered exactly
`<s>`	Strikethrough text; used for showing text that has been deleted
`<samp>`	Sample; a sequence of literal characters
`<small>`	Decreases the size of the selected text relative to the surrounding text; not currently supported by Dreamweaver.
`<strong>`	Strong emphasis; usually rendered as bold text
`<sub>`	Subscript; the text is shown slightly lowered beneath the baseline.
`<sup>`	Superscript; the text is shown slightly raised above the baseline.
`<tt>`	Teletype; displayed with a monospaced font such as Courier
`<var>`	Variable; used to distinguish variables from other programming code

Logical styles are becoming increasingly important now that more browsers accept Cascading Style Sheets. Style sheets make it possible to combine the best elements of both logical and physical styles. With CSS, you can easily make the text within your `<code>` tags blue, and the variables, denoted with the `<var>` tag, green.

Tip   By default, Dreamweaver is now set to use logical styles `<strong>` and `<em>` whenever you select the Bold and Italic buttons on the Property inspector, respectively. Choose Edit ➪ Preferences and, in the General category of the Preferences dialog box, deselect the Use `<strong>` and `<em>` in place of `<b>` and `<i>` option if you'd prefer not to use the logical styles.

Physical styles

HTML picked up the use of physical styles from modern typography and word processing programs. Use a physical style when you want something to be absolutely bold, italic, or underlined (or, as we say in HTML, `<b>`, `<i>`, and `<u>`, respectively). You can apply the bold and the italic tags to selected text through the Property inspector or by selecting Text ➪ Style; the underline style is available only through the Text menu.

With HTML version 3.2, a fourth physical style tag was added: `<font>`. Most browsers recognize the size attribute, which enables you to make the selected text larger or smaller, relatively or directly. To change a font size absolutely, select your text and then select Text ➪ Size; Dreamweaver inserts the following tag, where *n* is a number from 1 to 7:

```
<font size=n>
```

To make text larger than the default text, select Text ⇨ Size Increase and then choose the value you want. Dreamweaver inserts the following tag:

```
<font size=+n>
```

The plus sign (+) indicates the relative nature of the font. Make text smaller than the default text by selecting Text ⇨ Size Decrease; Dreamweaver inserts this tag:

```
<font size=-n>
```

You can also expressly change the type of font used and its color through the `face` and `color` attributes. Because you can't be sure what fonts will be on a user's system, common practice and good form dictate that you should list alternatives for a selected font. For instance, rather than just specifying Palatino—a sans serif font common on PCs but relatively unknown on the Mac—you could insert a tag such as the following:

```
<font face=" Palatino, Times New Roman, Times, sans-serif">
```

 Caution   In the preceding case, if the browser doesn't find the first font, it looks for the second one (and so forth, as specified). Dreamweaver handles the `font face` attribute through its Font List dialog box, which is explained fully in Chapter 7.

Working with Code View and Code Inspector

Although Dreamweaver offers many options for using the visual interface of the Document window, sometimes you just have to tweak the code by hand. Dreamweaver's acceptance by professional coders is due in large part to the easy access of the underlying code. Dreamweaver includes several methods for directly viewing, inputting, and modifying code for your Web page. For large-scale additions and changes, you might consider using an external HTML editor such as BBEdit or Homesite, but for many situations, the built-in Code view and Code inspector are perfectly suited and much faster to work with.

Code view is one of the coolest tools in Dreamweaver's code-savvy toolbox. You can either view your code full-screen in the Document window, split-screen with Design view, or in a separate panel, the Code inspector. The underlying engine for all Code views is the same—and, for Dreamweaver, the code editor has had significant enhancements made to the feature set and performance.

You can use either of the following methods to display the full-screen Code view:

✦ Select View ⇨ Code.

✦ Choose the Show Code View button from the toolbar. Code view is displayed, as shown in Figure 6-7.

You can access the split-screen Code and Design view with any of the following methods:

✦ Choose View ⇨ Code and Design.

✦ Select the Show Code and Design Views button on the toolbar.

✦ Press Ctrl+` (Command+`) when in Design view and the Code inspector is closed. The ` character is the grave accent paired with the tilde (~) on keyboards.

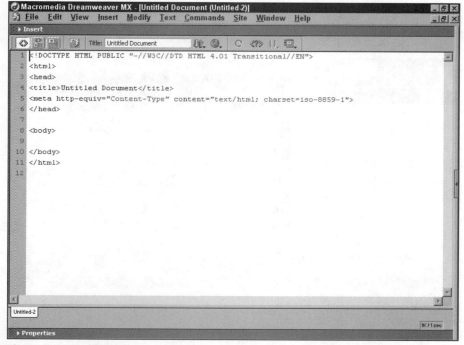

Figure 6-7: Code view.

To change the relative size of the Code and Design views, drag the splitter bar up or down. In the split-screen Code and Design view, Code view is shown on top of the Design view. You can reverse that order by choosing View ➪ Design View on Top or selecting Design View on Top from the View Options button on the toolbar.

You have several ways to open the Code inspector:

✦ Choose Window ➪ Code Inspector.

✦ Select the Show Code Inspector button in the Launcher.

✦ Use the keyboard shortcut F10.

Once opened, the Code inspector (see Figure 6-8) behaves like any other floating panel in Dreamweaver: The window can be resized, moved, or hidden, and the inspector can be docked above or below the Document window or dragged out onto its own panel. When the Code inspector is opened initially, it is automatically selected. If you click in the Document window with the Code inspector open, the inspector dims but still reflects changes made in the document.

In all Code views, Dreamweaver does not update the Design view of the document immediately — whereas changes in Design view are instantly reflected in any open Code view. This delay is enforced to enable the code to be completed before being applied. To apply modifications made in the code, switch to Design view; if Design view is open, click anywhere in it to give it focus. Should Dreamweaver detect any invalid HTML, such as an improperly closed tag, the offending code is flagged with a yellow highlight in both Design and Code views. Select the marked tag to see an explanation and suggestions for correcting the problem in the Property inspector.

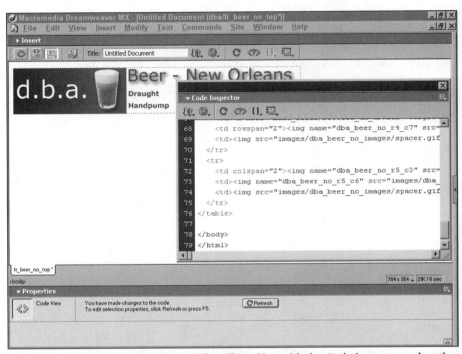

Figure 6-8: To update Design view while still working with the Code inspector, select the handy Refresh button — either on the toolbar or the Property inspector — or choose F5.

You can also apply code changes to Design view by saving the document or by choosing the Refresh button on the toolbar or the Property inspector. The Refresh button becomes active only when modifications are made in any Code view. You also have a keyboard and menu alternative: pressing F5 has the same effect as choosing View ➪ Refresh Design View.

Generally, the Code view and Code inspector act like a regular text editor. Simply click anywhere in the inspector to add or modify code. Double-click a word to select it. Select an entire line by moving your pointer to the left edge of the code — where the pointer becomes a right-pointing arrow — and clicking once. Multiple lines can be selected in this same fashion by dragging the right-pointing arrow. Once a section of code is selected, you can drag and drop it into a new location; pressing the Ctrl (Option) key while dragging makes a copy of the selection. Moving from word to word is accomplished by pressing Ctrl (Command) in combination with any of the arrow keys.

Enabling Code view options

Some special features in Dreamweaver's code editor simplify the task of writing HTML and other types of code. When in any Code view, some of these features can be toggled on and off by choosing the command either from the View ➪ Code View Options list or under the View Options button on the Document toolbar:

✦ **Word Wrap:** Wraps lines within the boundaries of the Code view window or Code inspector to eliminate the need for horizontal scrolling.

✦ **Line Numbers:** Displays a number for every line in the code; this feature is extremely helpful when used in combination with the JavaScript Debugger, which reports the line number of an error in the code.

✦ **Highlight Invalid HTML:** Toggles the highlighting of invalid tags in Code view when Design view is refreshed. Invalid tags are always highlighted in the Design view.

✦ **Syntax Coloring:** Syntax coloring makes code easier to read. Basic tags and keywords are shown in one color, with text in another color. Three different types of code are given different colors: Reserved Keywords, Other Keywords, and Strings. These colors are set in the Code Color category of Preferences. You can also set a color for an individual tag to further distinguish it if you like.

✦ **Auto Indent:** Auto Indent is another feature intended to improve code readability. With Auto Indent enabled, pressing Enter (Return) at the end of a line causes the new line to start at the same indentation as the preceding line. Press Backspace (Delete) to move the indented line closer to the left margin. The number of characters for each indentation is set in the Code Format category of Preferences.

You can also easily change the indentation — in or out — for selected blocks of code. To further indent a block of code, select it and then choose Tab. To decrease the level of indentation for a selected code block, choose Shift+Tab. Alternatively, you can select Edit ⇨ Indent Code or use the keyboard shortcut Ctrl+> (Command+>) to indent a code block, and Edit ⇨ Outdent Code or the keyboard shortcut Ctrl+< (Command+<) to outdent it.

As a further aid to help you find your way through a maze of code, Dreamweaver includes the Balance Braces command. JavaScript is notorious for using parentheses, brackets, and curly braces to structure its code — and it's easy to lose sight of where one enclosing brace begins and its closing mate ends. Dreamweaver highlights the content found within the closest pair of braces to the cursor when you select Edit ⇨ Balance Braces or use the keyboard shortcut Ctrl+' (Command+'). If you select the command again, the selection expands to the set of surrounding braces. When the selection is not enclosed by parentheses, brackets, or curly braces, Dreamweaver sounds an alert.

Although most Web designers prone to using the code editor in Dreamweaver prefer to manually enter their code, the power of the Insert bar is still at your disposal for rapid code development. Any element available from the Insert bar can be inserted directly into Code view or the inspector. To use the Insert bar, you must first position your cursor where you would like the code for the object to appear. Then select the element or drag and drop the element from the Insert bar to Code view or the inspector.

Keep in mind that Dreamweaver's code editor is highly customizable. You can change the way the lines wrap, by using indents for certain tag pairs; you can even control the amount of indentation. All the options are outlined for you in Chapter 4.

Printing code

Although you may spend the vast majority of your time writing, modifying, and debugging your code onscreen, there are times when you need to see it in hard copy.

Dreamweaver now offers the option of printing out your code. Choose File ⇨ Print Code to open the standard operating system Print dialog box. You have the option to print all of the code or a selection; you cannot, however, print individual pages of your code. Press the keyboard shortcut, Ctrl+P (Command+P) to send your code directly to the printer. Although Dreamweaver does not print the syntax coloring, you can print line numbers just by enabling them in Code view options.

Enhancing Code Authoring Productivity

One of the reasons why the Web grew so quickly is that the basic tool for creating Web pages was ubiquitous: Any text editor would do. That's still true, but just as you can cut down any tree with a hand saw, it doesn't make it the right tool—the most efficient tool—for the job. Dreamweaver includes numerous features and options that make it a world-class code editor and not just for HTML. The Tag Library feature makes Dreamweaver a terrific code-editing environment for almost any Web language, including XHTML, XML, ColdFusion, ASP, ASP.NET, JSP, and PHP. Moreover, the database structure underlying the tag libraries means that the libraries can be expanded or modified at any time. New tags, attributes, and even entire languages can be added by hand or imported in a number of methods, including from a DTD schema.

Dreamweaver's tag libraries offer numerous benefits that greatly enhance the coding experience. Chief among these benefits are Code Hints and Tag Completion.

Code Hints and Tag Completion

Writing code is an exact art. If you enter `<blickquote>` instead of `<blockquote>`, neither Dreamweaver nor the browser will render the tag properly. Perhaps an even bigger problem than misspelling tags and attributes is remembering them all. As more and more developers of static Web pages go dynamic, many are finding the sheer amount of information needed to be quite daunting. Don't worry, hand-coders, Dreamweaver's Code Hints feature will help you avoid those misspellings and prompt your memory—and make you more efficient in the process.

New Feature

The Code Hints tool is a valuable aid to all Web designers, even beginners. It's a quick way to develop a tag as you type it by displaying a pop-up list of tags (as shown in Figure 6-9), attributes and, in some cases, even values for each tag. Best of all, Code Hints work the way you want to work. If you're a touch-typist, your hands never have to leave the keyboard to accept a particular tag or attribute. If you prefer to use the mouse, you can easily double-click to select your entry. If you like, Dreamweaver will even complete your code with an ending tag.

The Code Hints that appear are stored in Dreamweaver's Tag Library database and can be modified by choosing Edit ➪ Tag Libraries. Code Hints are available for Web languages HTML (including XHTML), CFML, ASP.NET, JSP, JRun Custom Library, ASP, PHP, and WML, as well as Dreamweaver template tags and Sitespring Project Site tags.

Cross-Reference

Code Hints are enabled by default. To disable them or to control the speed with which the pop-up list appears, choose Edit ➪ Preferences and select the Code Hints category. See Chapter 4 for a detailed explanation of all the options.

When Code Hints is turned on, follow these steps to use this helpful feature:

1. In Code view, enter the opening tag bracket, `<`.

   The Code Hint pop-up list instantly shows all the tags for the current page's document type.

2. To move down the list, type the first letter of the tag.

   With each letter that you type, Dreamweaver hones in on the indicated tag.

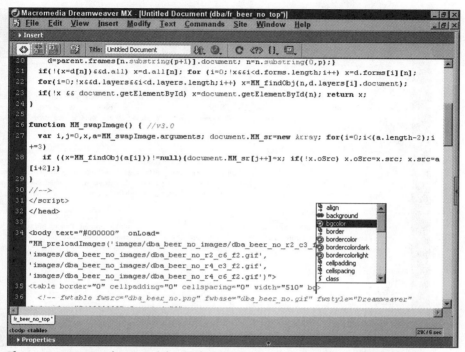

Figure 6-9: Master the use of the Code Hints feature to give your code writing a major productivity boost.

3. When the proper tag is highlighted, press Enter (Return) and the code is inserted.

   Alternatively, you can scroll down the list and double-click the desired tag to insert it.

4. To add attributes to the tag, enter a space.

   The attribute list for the current tag is displayed.

5. As with the tag, type until the desired attribute is highlighted in the list and then press Enter (Return).

   Attributes are, for the most part, followed by an equal sign and a pair of quotes for the value. The cursor is positioned in-between the quotes.

6. Enter the desired value for the attribute.

7. If the attribute can accept only a certain range of values, such as the `align` attribute, the accepted values also appear in the Code Hints pop-up list.

   If you choose one of the specified values, the cursor moves to the end of the name-value pair after the closing quote.

8. Enter a space to continue adding attributes or enter the closing tag bracket, `>`.

9. If the Tag Completion feature is enabled, the closing tag is automatically inserted, as shown on line 77 in Figure 6-10.

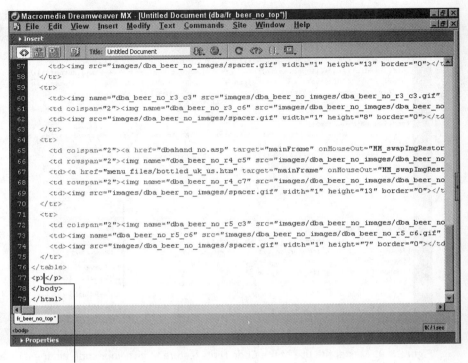

Code completed for <p> tag

Figure 6-10: You'll never forget to end a tag again with Dreamweaver's Tag Completion feature.

In addition to straight text, Dreamweaver offers several types of attribute values, each with its own special type of drop-down list:

✦ **Color:** When a color-related attribute is entered, Dreamweaver displays a color palette and eyedropper cursor for sampling the color. When a color is picked, its corresponding hexadecimal value is entered into the code.

✦ **Font:** For attributes requiring the name of a font, such as the `<font>` tag's `face` attribute, Dreamweaver displays the current font list of font families (such as Arial, Helvetica, sans-serif), as well as an option to edit that list.

✦ **Style:** Enter the class attribute in almost any tag, and you'll see a complete list of available CSS styles defined for the current page. Other CSS controls, such as Edit Style Sheet and Attach Style Sheet, are also available.

✦ **File:** Should an attribute require a filename, Dreamweaver opens the standard Select File dialog box to enable you to easily locate a file or choose a data source.

Code Hints aren't just for entering new tags; you can take advantage of their prompting when modifying existing code as well. To add an attribute, place your cursor just before the closing bracket and press the spacebar to trigger the Code Hints pop-up menu. To change an entered value, delete both the value and the surrounding quotes; the pop-up options will appear after the opening quote is entered.

Inserting code with the Tag Chooser

If you'd rather point and click than type, Dreamweaver has you covered.

New Feature

With the Dreamweaver Tag Chooser, you have access to all the standard tags in HTML/XHTML, CFML, ASP.NET, JSP, JRun Custom Library, ASP, PHP, and WML, and the Macromedia-specific tags for Dreamweaver templates and Sitespring Project Sites.

Open the Tag Chooser in one of several ways:

✦ Select Insert ➪ Tag.

✦ Right-click (Control+click) in Code view and choose Insert Tag from the context menu.

✦ Choose the keyboard shortcut, Ctrl+E (Command+E).

✦ Position your cursor where you'd like the tag to appear — in either Code or Design view — and select Tag Chooser from the Insert bar.

✦ Drag the Tag Chooser button from the Insert bar into its desired place in either Code or Design view.

The tags are grouped under their respective languages. Selecting any of the languages from the list on the left displays all the available tags on the right. Most of the languages have a plus sign which, when selected, expands the chosen language and displays various functional groupings of tags, such as Page Composition, Lists, and Tables, as shown in the background of Figure 6-11. Under HTML Tags, you can expand the tag groupings further to see, in some cases, tags separated into additional categories such as General, Browser-specific, and Deprecated.

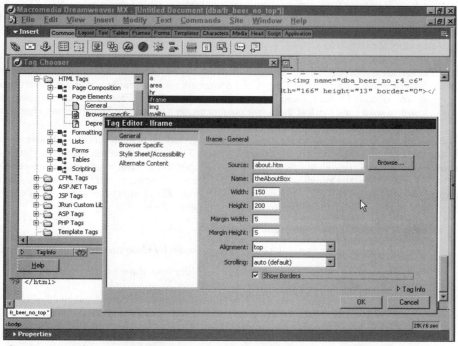

Figure 6-11: When you select your page element from the Tag Chooser (shown in the background), you have a wealth of options in the Tag Editor (foreground).

If you're confused about what a specific tag is for or how it's used, select the Tag Info button. The bottom half of the dialog box converts to a context-sensitive reference panel. Exactly what information is available depends on the tag itself. For most HTML tags, you'll find a description, examples, and in which browsers the tag is recognized. Much of the information available is also available in the Reference panel (covered later in this chapter); however, not all tags are covered.

When you've chosen a tag and either double-clicked it or selected Insert, the Tag Editor opens. Each tag has its own user interface with full accessibility and CSS options. As shown in Figure 6-11, selecting a category from the list on the left displays the available options on the right.

Note   Custom tags or attributes entered into the Tag Library are not displayed in the Tag Chooser.

After entering all the desired parameters in the Tag Editor, selecting OK inserts the code into the page with the cursor in-between the opening and closing tags (or after the tag if it is empty). The Tag Chooser uses a nonmodal window and remains open until Close is selected.

Caution   Because the Tag Chooser is nonmodal, you may not realize that you have already inserted the desired tag, and select Insert again. Dreamweaver does not prevent you from entering multiple versions of the same tag.

Adding Code through the Snippets Panel

You can save portions of HTML code for easy recall in other files, using the valuable Snippets feature. It's a lot easier than copying and pasting blocks of code from various files. Tag snippets range from a single tag, such as an HTML comment, to a full navigation layout. Commonly used JavaScript and other language functions and methods are also good candidates to be turned into a snippet for later use.

New Feature   Dreamweaver provides a notable assortment of snippets, but the most important aspect of this feature is that it's extensible. Coders and noncoders alike can easily add any commonly used section of code for later re-use. Snippets work in one of two different ways: A snippet either inserts a solid code block at the cursor point or wraps a selection with before and after code.

The Snippets panel is found under the Code panel group; to open it directly, choose Window ⇨ Snippets or use the keyboard shortcut, Shift+F9. The Snippets panel, shown in Figure 6-12, shows a preview of the selected snippet. If the snippet itself is not rendered onscreen, like a JavaScript function, the preview shows the code itself; otherwise, you'll see exactly what the code will look like on the page, minus any CSS stylings. Rearrange your snippets by dragging them within the panel, from folder to folder, if you like.

To insert a snippet, follow these steps:

1. Display the Snippets panel if it's not already open by choosing Window ⇨ Snippets.

2. Find the desired snippet by expanding the folder and, if necessary, subfolders.

3. To insert a snippet as a block of code:

    a. Position the cursor where you'd like the code to appear.

    b. Double-click the snippet (or snippet icon) or select the snippet and choose Insert.

Alternatively, you can drag the snippet into position in either Code view or Design view.

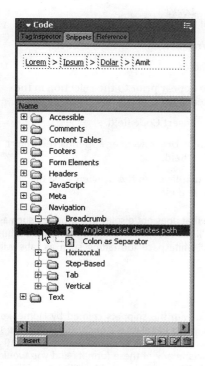

Figure 6-12: Use the handy Snippets panel to quickly re-use portions of your code.

4. To wrap a snippet around some existing code or page elements:

   a. Select the code or elements.

   b. Double-click the snippet or select the snippet and choose Insert.

   Again, you can drag the snippet onto the selected code.

Tip   You can quickly hide a section of a page by selecting it and then choosing the Comment, Multi-line snippet from the Comments category of the Snippets panel.

While Dreamweaver's standard code snippets are handy, the real value of the Snippets panel is not realized until you begin adding your own. To help you manage your snippets, Dreamweaver enables you to create new folders, rename existing ones, or delete ones no longer needed. All of this functionality is available through the options menu on the Snippets panel as well as through the context menu. Snippets, as well as folders, can be renamed, deleted, edited and, of course, created.

Tip   Before you begin to create your own code snippet, select it first. The Snippets dialog box is modal, and you cannot access other Dreamweaver windows while it is open. The selected code is copied to the Insert Before text field.

To save code as a snippet, follow these steps:

1. Select the New Snippets button from the bottom of the Snippets panel.

2. Enter a name to be displayed in the Snippets panel in the Name field.

3. If you like, you can enter a brief description of the snippet in the Description field.

4. Choose the type of Snippet you're creating: Wrap Selection or Insert Block.

   The dialog box changes depending on your choice.

5. If you chose Wrap Selection, enter the code to appear prior to the selection in the Insert Before field, and the code to appear after in the Insert After field.

6. If you chose Insert Block, enter the code in the Insert Code field.

   If you switch from Wrap Selection to Insert Block, Dreamweaver appends the Insert Before field with the contents of the Insert After field.

7. Choose how you would like the snippet to be displayed in the preview area of the Snippets panel, rendered as in Design view or as code.

Caution

If you choose the Design preview option for code that does not display in a browser, such as a JavaScript function, it won't be as readable. You'll still see the code in the preview area, but it will not appear in a monospace font, and all whitespace formatting such as tabs will appear to be lost.

8. Click OK when you're done.

Tip

Snippets in Dreamweaver MX are not compatible with the snippets created by HomeSite, ColdFusion Studio, or using Massimo Foti's TMT Snippets Panel extension for Dreamweaver 4. Massimo has, however, developed a converter that is available at www.DreamweaverFAQ. com/Snippets/. If you have a number of snippets in any of these formats and you would like to use them in Dreamweaver MX, be sure to pick up this invaluable utility. Speaking of invaluable, you'll find over 200 snippets ready for download at the DreamweaverFAQ site.

Using the Reference Panel

Pop quiz: What value of a form tag's `enctype` attribute should you use if the user is submitting a file?

   A. `application/x-www-form-urlencoded`

   B. `multipart/form-data`

   C. `multipart/data-form`

Unless you've recently had to include such a form in a Web page, you probably had to pull down that well-worn HTML reference book you keep handy and look up the answer. All code for the Web — including HTML, JavaScript, and Cascading Style Sheets (CSS) — must be precisely written or it will, at best, be ignored; at worst, an error will be generated whenever the user views the page. Even the savviest of Web designers can't remember the syntax of every tag, attribute, and value in HTML or every function in JavaScript or every style rule in CSS. A good reference is a necessity in Web design. (By the way, the answer to the pop quiz is B.)

Macromedia has lightened the load on your bookshelf considerably with the addition of the Reference panel, shown in Figure 6-13. With the Reference panel, you can quickly look up any HTML tag and its attributes, as well as JavaScript objects and CSS style rules. Dynamic site builders can rely on references for CFML, ASP, and JSP. In addition, the panel contains detailed information on Sitespring's Project Site tags, as well as a complete reference on

Web-related accessibility issues from UsableNet. Not only does the Reference panel offer the proper syntax for any code in question, in most situations it also displays the level of browser support available. Moreover, you don't have to dig through the tag lists to find the information you need—just highlight the tag or object in question and press the keyboard shortcut, Shift+F1.

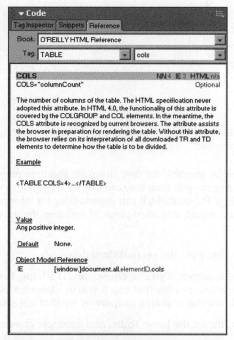

Figure 6-13: To quickly look up a tag, select it in the Tag Selector or in Code view and then choose Shift+F1 to open the Reference panel.

You have four different ways to open the Reference panel:

✦ Choose Window ➪ Reference.

✦ Select the Reference button on the toolbar.

✦ Use the Shift+F1 keyboard shortcut.

Tip   To find reference details for the attributes of an HTML tag, a JavaScript object, or a CSS style rule included on a Web page, open Code view and select the code in question prior to choosing Shift+F1 or selecting the Reference button from the toolbar.

To look for information about code not included in the page, follow these steps:

1. Display the Reference panel by choosing Window ➪ Reference or using the keyboard shortcut Shift+F1.

2. Select the required guide from the Book drop-down list. The standard options are as follows:

- Macromedia CFML Reference
- O'Reilly CSS Reference
- O'Reilly HTML Reference
- O'Reilly JavaScript Reference
- Sitespring Project Site Tag Reference
- UsableNet Accessibility Reference
- Wrox ASP 3.0 Reference
- Wrox JSP Reference

3. Choose the primary topic from the Style/Tag/Object drop-down list. The list heading changes depending on which Book is selected.

Tip   Windows users can move quickly to a topic by selecting the drop-down list and then pressing the key for the first letter of the term being sought. Then they can use the down arrow to move through items that start with that letter. For example, if you were looking for information about the JavaScript regular expressions object, you could press "r" and then the down arrow to reach RegExp.

4. If desired, you can select a secondary topic from the second drop-down list.

The second list is context-sensitive. For example, if you've chosen an HTML tag, the secondary list displays all the available attributes for that tag. If you've chosen a JavaScript object, the secondary list shows the available properties for that object.

The information shown depends, naturally, on the book, topic, and subtopic chosen.

The Reference panel's context menu enables you to switch between three different font sizes: small, medium, and large. This capability is especially useful when working at resolutions higher than 800 × 600. You'll also find an option to connect directly to O'Reilly Books Online.

Modifying Code with the Tag Inspector

Since Dreamweaver's beginning, one of my favorite features has been the Tag Selector. I really appreciated the precision it brought to the entire selection process. However, the Tag Selector is not without its drawbacks. The feature's main deficiency is key to its design—the Tag Selector only displays the tags enclosing the current position of the cursor. As pages have become increasingly complex, it's not always easy to see where you are on the page with the Tag Selector. To give developers a better handle on the overall structure of a page—without sacrificing any attention to detail—Dreamweaver has introduced the Tag Inspector.

New Feature   The Tag Inspector actually has a three-fold function. First, the panel displays an overview of the page in a collapsible tree structure. You can expand the page elements to drill down as far as necessary or collapse them to get an overall sense of the page. Second, it's a navigation aid. Use the Tag Inspector to quickly select any element anywhere on the page. Finally—and I saved the best for last—the Tag Inspector is like a Property inspector on steroids. Select any tag, and all the possible attributes for that tag are displayed—and ready for editing—in the panel's lower portion. Not only does the Tag Selector make it extremely easy to check a tag's attributes at a glance, but it also puts all of an element's properties right at your fingertips.

Like the Snippets panel, the Tag Inspector is found under the Code panel group. To directly open the Tag Inspector, choose Window ➪ Tag Inspector. You can select tags in several ways:

✦ Locate the tag in the tree view of the Tag Inspector.

✦ Highlight the tag in Code view or in the Code inspector.

✦ Choose the tag in the Tag Selector, shown in Figure 6-14.

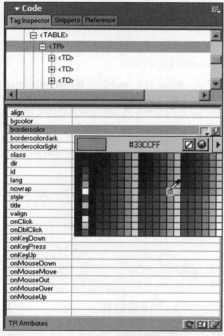

Figure 6-14: Use the Tag Inspector to quickly modify any or all attributes of any tag on the page.

Once a tag is selected, enter or change values for attributes in the Tag Inspector's list view. Values may be entered directly as text or, in some cases, with the aid of a Dreamweaver drop-down list or two. For example, the bgcolor attribute for the <td> tag offers a color picker as well as a connection to dynamic data. Other helpers include a drop-down list of preset values and a point-to-file icon.

Tip Unlike the Tag Chooser, the Tag Inspector does work with custom tags and attributes entered through the Tag Library Editor.

Rapid Tag Modification with the Quick Tag Editor

I tend to build Web pages in two phases: Generally, I first lay out my text and images to create the overall design, and then I add details and make alterations to get the page just right. The second phase of Web page design often requires that I make a small adjustment to the HTML code, typically through the Property inspector, but occasionally I need to go right to the source—code, that is.

Dreamweaver offers a feature for making minor but essential alterations to the code: the Quick Tag Editor. The Quick Tag Editor is a small pop-up window that appears in the Document window and enables you to edit an existing tag, add a new tag, or wrap the current selection in a tag. One other feature makes the Quick Tag Editor even quicker to use: A handy list of tags or attributes appears to cut down on your typing.

To call up the Quick Tag Editor, use any of the following methods:

✦ Choose Modify ➪ Quick Tag Editor.

✦ Press the keyboard shortcut Ctrl+T (Command+T).

✦ Select the Quick Tag Editor icon on the Property inspector.

The Quick Tag Editor has three modes: Insert HTML, Wrap Tag, and Edit HTML. Although you can get to all three modes from any situation, which mode appears initially depends on the current selection. The Quick Tag Editor's window (see Figure 6-15) appears above the current selection when you use either the menu or keyboard method of opening it, or next to the Property inspector when you select the icon. In either case, you can move the Quick Tag Editor window to a new location onscreen by dragging its title bar. (See the "Working with the Hint List" sidebar later in this chapter for details about this feature.)

Tip   Regardless of which mode the Quick Tag Editor opens in, you can toggle to the other modes by pressing the keyboard shortcut Ctrl+T (Command+T).

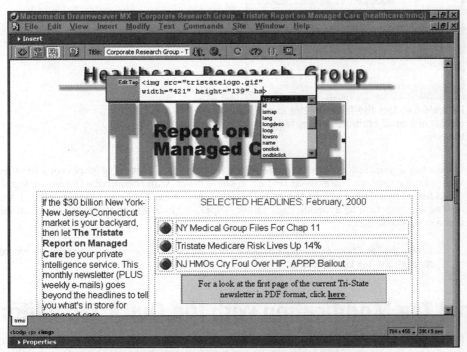

Figure 6-15: The Quick Tag Editor is great for quickly tweaking your code.

Insert HTML mode

The Insert HTML mode of the Quick Tag Editor is used for adding new tags and code at the current cursor position; it is the initial mode when nothing is selected. The Insert HTML mode starts with a pair of angle brackets enclosing a blinking cursor. You can enter any desired tag—whether standard HTML or custom XML—and any attribute or content within the new tag. When you're done, just press Enter (Return) to confirm your addition.

To add new tags to your page using the Quick Tag Editor Insert HTML mode, follow these steps:

1. Position your cursor where you would like the new code to be inserted.

2. Choose Modify ➪ Quick Tag Editor or use the keyboard shortcut, Ctrl+T (Command+T), to open the Quick Tag Editor.

   The Quick Tag Editor opens in Insert HTML mode, as shown in Figure 6-16.

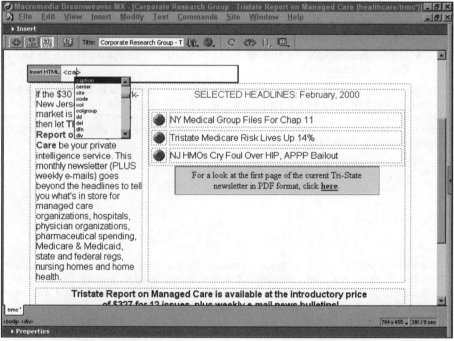

Figure 6-16: Use the Quick Tag Editor's Insert HTML mode to add tags not available through Dreamweaver's visual interface.

3. Enter your HTML or XML code.

Tip

Use the right arrow key to move quickly past the closing angle bracket and add text after your tag.

4. If you pause while typing, the hint list appears, selecting the first tag that matches what you've typed so far. Use the arrow keys to select another tag in the list and press Enter (Return) to select a tag.

Working with the Hint List

The Quick Tag Editor has a rather nifty feature referred to as the *hint list*. To make it even quicker to use the Quick Tag Editor, a list of tags pops up when you pause in your typing. When you're entering attributes within a tag, a list of appropriate parameters pops up instead of tags. These lists are tied to what, if anything, you've already typed. Suppose, for instance, you've begun to enter **blockquote** and have only gotten as far typing **b** and **l**. When the hint list appears, it scrolls to "blink" — the first tag in the list starting with those two letters. If you continue typing **o**, "blockquote" is selected. All you have to do to insert it into your code is press Enter (Return).

Following are a few other hint list hints:

✦ Scroll to a tag by using the up or down arrow keys.

✦ Double-clicking the selected hint list item also inserts it into the code.

✦ Once the hint list is open, press Esc if you decide not to enter the selected tag or attribute.

✦ If an attribute has a set series of values that can be applied (for example, the `<div>` tag's `align` attribute can only be set to left, right, or center), those values are accessible via the hint list.

✦ Control how quickly the hint list appears — or even if it appears at all — by altering the Quick Tag Editor preferences.

The tags and attributes that appear in the hint list are contained in the TagAttributeList.text file found in the Dreamweaver Configuration folder. The list is in a format known as Data Type Declaration (DTD), in which each tag is listed as a separate element and any corresponding attributes are displayed under each of those elements. Here, for example, is the DTD listing for the background sound tag, `<bgsound>`:

```
<!ELEMENT BGSOUND Name="Background sound" >
<!ATTLIST BGSOUND
     Balance
     Loop
     Src
     Volume
>
```

As with almost all other Dreamweaver aspects, the TagAttribute.txt list can be modified to include any special tags (and their attributes) that you might need to include on a regular basis. Just relaunch Dreamweaver after making your changes in a standard text editor and your modifications will be included the next time you use the Quick Tag Editor.

  5. Press Enter (Return) when you're done.

The Quick Tag Editor is fairly intelligent and tries to help you write valid HTML. If, for example, you leave off a closing tag, such as `</b>`, the Quick Tag Editor automatically adds it for you.

Wrap Tag mode

Part of the power and flexibility of HTML is the capability to wrap one tag around one or more other tags and content. To make a phrase appear bold and italic, the code is written as follows:

```
<b><i>On Sale Now!</i></b>
```

Note how the inner `<i>. . .</i>` tag pair is enclosed by the `<b>. . .</b>` pair. The Wrap Tag mode of the Quick Tag Editor surrounds any selection with your entered tag in one easy operation.

The Wrap Tag mode appears initially when you have selected just text (with no surrounding tags) or an incomplete tag (the opening tag and contents but no closing tag). The Wrap Tag mode is visually similar to the Insert HTML mode, as can be seen in Figure 6-17. However, rather than just include exactly what you've entered into the Quick Tag Editor, Wrap Tag mode also inserts a closing tag that corresponds to your entry. For example, suppose you want to apply a tag not available as an object: the subscript, or `<sub>`, tag. After highlighting the text you want to mark up as subscript (a "2" in the formula H_2O, for example), you open the Quick Tag Editor and enter **sub**. The resulting code looks like the following:

```
H<sub>2</sub>0
```

Caution   You can enter only one tag in Wrap Tag mode; if more than one tag is entered, Dreamweaver displays an alert informing you that the tag you've entered appears to be invalid HTML. The Quick Tag Editor is then closed, and the selection is cleared.

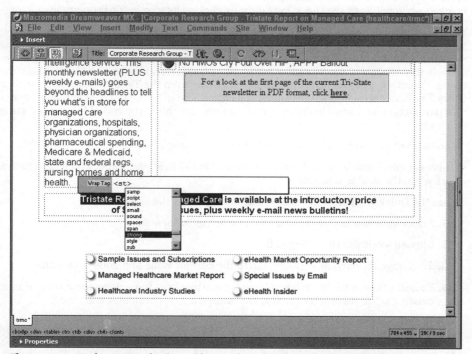

Figure 6-17: Enclose any selection with a tag by using the Quick Tag Editor's Wrap Tag mode.

To wrap a tag with the Quick Tag Editor, follow these steps:

1. Select the text or tags you want to enclose in another tag.

2. Choose Modify ➪ Quick Tag Editor or use the keyboard shortcut, Ctrl+T (Command+T), to open the Quick Tag Editor.

3. If you select a complete tag, the Quick Tag Editor opens in Edit Tag mode; press the keyboard shortcut, Ctrl+T (Command+T), to toggle to Wrap Tag mode.

4. Enter the desired tag.

5. If you pause while typing, the hint list appears, selecting the first tag that matches what you've typed so far. Use the arrow keys to select another tag in the list and press Enter (Return) to select a tag from the hint list.

6. Press Enter (Return) to confirm your tag.

   The Quick Tag Editor closes and Dreamweaver adds your tag before your selection, with a corresponding closing tag after it.

Edit Tag mode

If a complete tag—either a single tag, such as <img>, or a tag pair, such as <h1>. . .</h1>—is selected, the Quick Tag Editor opens in Edit Tag mode. Unlike the other two modes in which you are presented with just open and closing angle brackets and a flashing cursor, the Edit Tag mode displays the entire selected tag with all the attributes, if any. The Edit Tag mode is always invoked when you start the Quick Tag Editor by clicking its icon in the Property inspector.

The Edit Tag mode has many uses. It's excellent for adding a parameter not found on Dreamweaver's Property inspector. For example, when building a form some text fields have pre-existing text in them—which you want to clear when the user clicks into the field. To achieve this effect you need to add a minor bit of JavaScript, a perfect use for the Edit Tag mode. Therefore, you can just select the <input> tag from the Tag Selector and then click the Quick Tag Editor icon to open the Quick Tag Editor. The <input> tag appears with your current parameters, as shown in Figure 6-18. Once opened, tab to the end of the tag and enter this code:

```
onFocus="if(this.value=='Email Required')this.value='';"
```

In this example, Email Required is the visible text in the field, the value, which automatically clears when the field is selected.

To use the Quick Tag Editor in Insert HTML mode, follow these steps:

1. Select an entire tag by clicking its name in the Tag Selector.

2. Choose Modify ➪ Quick Tag Editor.

3. To change an existing attribute, tab to the current value and enter a new one.

4. To add a new attribute, tab and/or use the arrow keys to position the cursor after an existing attribute or after the tag, and enter the new parameter and value.

Tip   If you don't close the quotation marks for a parameter's value, Dreamweaver does it for you.

5. If you pause briefly while entering a new attribute, the hint list appears with attributes appropriate for the current tag. If you select an attribute from the hint list, press Enter (Return) to accept the parameter.

6. When you're done editing the tag, press Enter (Return).

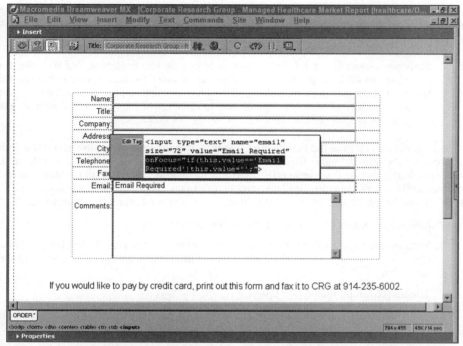

Figure 6-18: In Edit Tag mode, the Quick Tag Editor shows the entire tag, with attributes and their values.

In addition to this capability to edit complete tags, Dreamweaver has a couple of navigational commands to help select just the right tag. The Select Parent Tag command — keyboard shortcut Ctrl+[(Command+[) — highlights the tag immediately surrounding the present tag. Going the other direction, Select Child Tag — keyboard shortcut Ctrl+] (Command+]) — chooses the next tag, if any, contained within the current tag. Both commands are available under the Edit menu. Exercising these commands is equivalent to selecting the next tag in the Tag Selector to the left (parent) or right (child).

Caution   Although it works well in Design view, unfortunately the Select Child command does not function in Code view.

Adding Java Applets

Java is a platform-independent programming language developed by Sun Microsystems. Although Java can also be used to write entire applications, its most frequent role is on the Web in the form of an applet. An *applet* is a self-contained program that can be run within a Web page.

Java is a compiled programming language similar to C++. Once a Java applet is compiled, it is saved as a class file. Web browsers call Java applets through, aptly enough, the `<applet>` tag. When you insert an applet, you refer to the primary class file much as you call a graphic file for an image tag.

Each Java applet has its own unique set of parameters — and Dreamweaver enables you to enter as many as necessary in the same manner as plugins and ActiveX controls. In fact, the Applet object works almost identically to the Plugin and ActiveX objects.

Caution   Keep two caveats in mind if you're planning to include Java applets in your Web site. First, most (but not all) browsers support some version of Java — the newest release has the most features but the least support. Second, all the browsers that support Java enable the user to disable it because of security issues. Be sure to use the Alt property to designate an alternative image or some text for display by browsers that do not support Java.

A Java applet can be inserted in a Web page with a bare minimum of parameters: the code source and the dimensions of the object. Java applets derive much of their power from their configurability, and most of these little programs have numerous custom parameters. As with plugins and ActiveX controls, Dreamweaver enables you to specify the basic attributes through the Property inspector, and the custom ones via the Parameters dialog box.

To include a Java applet in your Web page, follow these steps:

1. Position the cursor where you want the applet to originate and choose Insert ➪ Media ➪ Applet. You can also select the Insert Applet button from the Special category of the Insert bar.

   The Insert Applet dialog box opens.

2. From the Select File dialog box, enter the path to your class file in the File Name text box or select the Browse (Choose) button to locate the file.

   An Applet object placeholder appears in the Document window. In the Applet Property inspector (see Figure 6-19), the selected source file appears in the Code text box, and the folder appears in the Base text box.

Note   The path to your Java class files cannot be expressed absolutely; it must be given as an address relative to the Web page that is calling it.

3. Enter the height and width of the Applet object in the H and W text boxes, respectively. You can also resize the Applet object by clicking and dragging any of its three sizing handles.

4. You can enter any of the usual basic attributes, such as a name for the object, as well as values for Align, V and/or H Space in the appropriate text boxes in the Property inspector.

5. If desired, enter the online directory where the applet code can be found in the Base text box. If none is specified, the document's URL is assumed to be this attribute, known as the *codebase*.

6. To display an alternative image if the Java applet is unable to run (typically because the user's browser does not support Java or the user has disabled Java), enter the path to the image in the Alt field. You can use the folder icon to locate the image as well.

   Text may also serve as the alternative content if you don't want to use an image. Any text entered into the Alt field is displayed in the browser as a ToolTip.

7. To enter any custom attributes, select the Parameters button to open the Parameters dialog box.

8. Select the Add (+) button and enter the first parameter. Press Tab to move to the Value column.

Applet placeholder

Applet icon

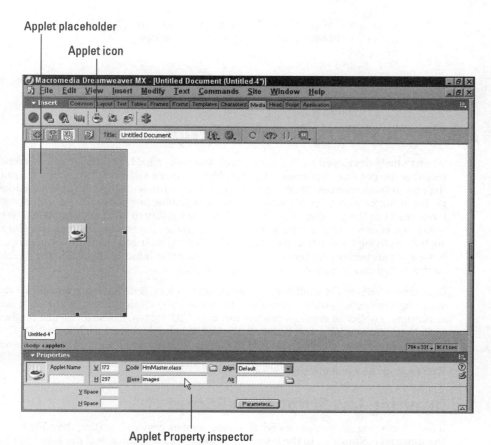

Applet Property inspector

Figure 6-19: Use the Insert Applet button to insert a Java Applet object and display the Applet Property inspector.

9. Enter the value for the parameter, if any. Press Tab.

10. Continue entering desired parameters in the left column, with their values in the right. Click OK when you're finished.

Tip

Because of the importance of displaying alternative content for users not running Java, Dreamweaver provides a method for displaying something for everyone. To display an image, enter the URL to a graphics file in the Alt text box. To display text as well as an image, you have to do a little hand-coding. First select a graphics file to insert in the Alt text box and then open Code view. In the `<img>` tag found between the `<applet>` tags, add an `alt="your_message"` attribute by hand (where the text you want to display is the value for the `alt` attribute). Now your Java applet displays an image for browsers that are graphics-enabled but not Java-enabled, and text for text-only browsers such as Lynx. In this sample code, I've bolded the additional `alt` attribute.

```
<applet code="animate.class" width=100 ⊃
height=100>
<param name=img1 value="/images/1.jpg">
<param name=img2 value="/images/2.jpg">
```

```
<img src="animation.gif" alt="Animate for ⊋
Life!" width=100 height=100>
</applet>
```

Some Java class files have additional graphics files. In most cases, you need to store both the class files and the graphics files in the same folder.

Adding JavaScript and VBScript

When initially developed by Netscape, JavaScript was called LiveScript. This browser-oriented language did not gain importance until Sun Microsystems joined the development team and the product was renamed JavaScript. Although the rechristening was a stroke of marketing genius, it has caused endless confusion among beginning programmers — JavaScript and Java have almost nothing in common outside of their capability to be incorporated in a Web page. JavaScript is used primarily to add functionality on the client-side of the browser (for tasks such as verifying form data and adding interactivity to interface elements) or to script Netscape's servers on the server-side. Java, on the other hand, is an application development language that can be used for a wide variety of tasks.

Conversely, VBScript is a full-featured Microsoft product. Both VBScript and JavaScript are scripting languages — which means you can write the code in any text editor and compile it at runtime. JavaScript enjoys more support than VBScript — JavaScript can be rendered by both Netscape and Microsoft browsers (as well as other browsers such as WebTV, Opera, and Sun's HotJava), whereas VBScript is read only by Internet Explorer on Windows systems — but both languages have their fans. In Dreamweaver, both types of code are inserted in the Web page in the same manner.

Inserting JavaScript and VBScript

If only mastering JavaScript or VBScript itself were as easy as inserting the code in Dreamweaver! Simply go to the Insert bar's Invisibles pane and select the Insert Script button, or choose Insert ⇨ Invisible Tags ⇨ Script from the menus and enter your code in the small Insert Script window. After you click OK, a Script icon appears in place of your script.

Of course, JavaScript or VBScript instruction is beyond the scope of this book, but every working Web designer must have an understanding of what these languages can do. Both languages refer to and, to varying degrees, manipulate the information on a Web page. Over time, you can expect significant growth in the capabilities of the JavaScript and VBScript disciplines.

Cross-Reference   Dreamweaver, through the application of its behaviors, goes a long way toward making JavaScript useful for nonprogrammers. To learn more about behaviors, see Chapter 23.

Use the Script Property inspector (see Figure 6-20) to select an external file for your JavaScript or VBScript code. You can also set the language type by opening the Language drop-down list from the Script window and choosing either JavaScript or VBScript. Because different features are available in the various releases of JavaScript, you can also specify JavaScript 1.1 or JavaScript 1.2. If you need to choose a specific version of JavaScript, you must do it when you initially insert the script — you cannot change the setting from the Script Property inspector. Naturally, you could also make the adjustment in Code view.

Script icon

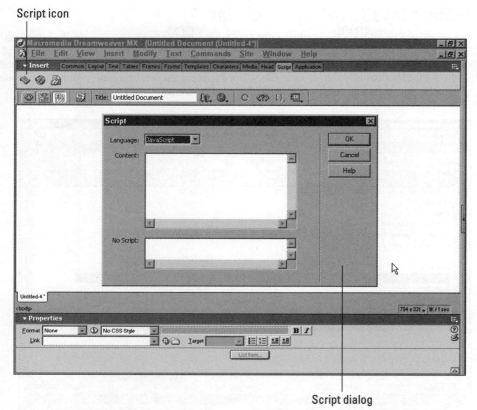

Script dialog

Figure 6-20: The generous Script window provides plenty of room for modifying your JavaScript or VBScript.

When you choose JavaScript or VBScript as your Language type, Dreamweaver writes the code accordingly. Both languages use the `<script>` tag pair, and each is specified in the `language` attribute, as follows:

```
<script language="JavaScript">alert("Look Out!")</script>
```

With Dreamweaver, you are not restricted to inserting code in just the `<body>` section of your Web page. Many JavaScript and VBScript functions must be located in the `<head>` section. To insert this type of script, first select View ➪ Head Content or, from the Options menu of the toolbar, choose Head Content. Next, select the now visible `<head>` window and choose Insert ➪ Invisible Tags ➪ Script, or click the Insert Script object. Enter your script as described earlier in this section and then select the main Document window, or choose View ➪ Head Content again to deselect it.

You can also indicate whether your script is based on the client-side or server-side by choosing the Type option from the Property inspector. If you choose server-side, your script is enclosed in `<server>`. . .`</server>` tags and is interpreted by the Web server hosting the page.

Editing JavaScript and VBScript

Dreamweaver provides a large editing window for modifying your script code. To open this Script Properties window, select the placeholder icon for the script you want to modify and then choose the Edit button on the Script Property inspector. You have the same functionality in the Script Properties window as in the Script Property inspector; namely, you can choose your language or link to an external script file (see Figure 6-21).

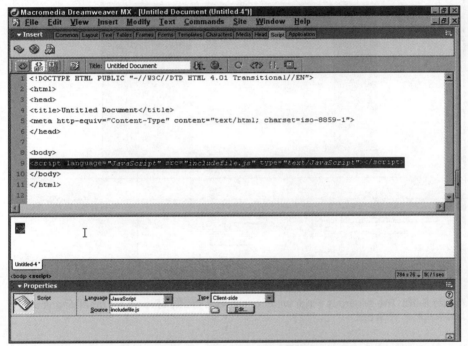

```
1  <!DOCTYPE HTML PUBLIC "-//W3C//DTD HTML 4.01 Transitional//EN">
2  <html>
3  <head>
4  <title>Untitled Document</title>
5  <meta http-equiv="Content-Type" content="text/html; charset=iso-8859-1">
6  </head>
7
8  <body>
9  <script language="JavaScript" src="includefile.js" type="text/JavaScript"></script>
10 </body>
11 </html>
12
```

Figure 6-21: Insert either JavaScript or VBScript through the Insert bar's Script object, available in the Invisibles category.

 Tip Some older browsers "break" when loading a JavaScript Web page and display the code written between the `<script>. . .</script>` tag pair. Although Dreamweaver doesn't do it by default, you can use a trick to prevent this anomaly. In Code view or the Code inspector, insert the opening comment tag (`<!--`) right after the opening `<script>` tag. Then insert the closing comment tag (`-->`), preceded by two forward slashes, right before the closing `</script>`. An example follows:

```
<script language="Javascript">
<!--
[JavaScript code goes here]
//-->
</script>
```

The comment tags effectively tell the older browser to ignore the enclosed content. The two forward slashes in front of the closing comment tag are JavaScript's comment indicator, which tells it to ignore the rest of the line.

Validating Your Page

Syntax — the rules governing the formation of statements in a programming language — is important regardless of which language your pages employ. Earlier browsers tended to be more relaxed about following the syntactical rules of HTML, but as standardization becomes increasingly important, browsers — and businesses — are following suit. Certain languages, such as XML, require the code to be proper or it just won't work. To ensure that a page is correctly written, the page should be validated. The Web offers numerous validation services — most notably the one run by the W3C at `http://validator.w3.org/` — but you don't need to leave Dreamweaver to validate your pages ever again.

New Feature

With Dreamweaver's Validation feature you can check a single page or an entire site. Once checked, the resulting errors and warnings, if any, can be stored in an XML file for future output. Any error can be double-clicked to go right to the offending element for immediate correction.

As with other Dreamweaver-style reports, the Validation feature resides in the Results panel, as shown in Figure 6-22. To display the Validation panel, choose Windows ➪ Results ➪ Validation or use the keyboard shortcut, Ctrl+Shift+F7 (Command+Shift+F7). Controls for the Validation panel are found along the left, and the panel is divided into three sections: File, which lists the file being referenced; Line, which lists the line number on which the error can be found; and Description, which contains a brief overview of the problem.

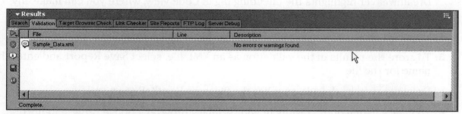

Figure 6-22: You can easily validate your pages from within Dreamweaver using the Validation feature.

Selecting the Validate button — the triangle in the left margin of the Validation tab shown in Figure 6-22 — unveils a menu of options:

✦ **Validate Current Document:** Checks the onscreen document against the validation preferences

✦ **Validate Current Document as XML:** Used for checking both XML and XHTML documents for the proper syntax

✦ **Validate Entire Site:** Runs through the entire current site, checking for validation errors

✦ **Validate Selected Files:** Checks files selected in the Site panel

Note

If no files are selected in the Site panel and Validate Selected Files is chosen, the entire site is validated. To halt a site validation in process, choose the Stop button on the Validation panel.

✦ **Settings:** Displays the Validation category in Preferences

Cross-Reference

Part of the power of Dreamweaver's Validation feature comes from its extensive options. To get a full overview of all your options, see Chapter 4.

To validate a page, follow these steps:

1. Make sure the Validation options are set as you want them in Preferences. If not, select the Validate button and choose Settings.

   When you select some languages, the Validator automatically selects other, related languages. For example, when you select HTML 4.0, the Validator automatically selects HTML 3.2 and HTML 2.0, because the definition for HTML 4.0 includes the definitions of HTML 3.2 and 2.0.

Caution

If you validate CFML (ColdFusion) and HTML in the same document, the Validator won't be able to assess the number sign (#) correctly. Why not? Because, in CFML, # is an error and ## is correct; in HTML, the converse is true: ## is an error and # is correct.

2. Select Validate and choose Validate Current Document.

   Dreamweaver's validation engine goes through the entire page and displays any errors, warnings, and other messages in the Validation panel.

3. To correct an error, double-click the entry.

   Dreamweaver highlights the offending tag in Code view, where you can make any modifications necessary.

4. Select More Info to see additional details, if available, about the current error.

5. To store the results of the validation as an XML file, select Save Report and enter the name for the file.

   Dreamweaver, by default, supplies the filename ResultsReport.xml.

6. To view a listing of the results in your primary browser, choose Browse Report.

Tip

Use Browse Report and then print the file from your browser as a quick way to get a hard copy of the validation results.

Inserting Symbols and Special Characters

When working with Dreamweaver, you're usually entering text directly from your keyboard, one keystroke at a time, with each keystroke representing a letter, number, or other keyboard character. Some situations, however, require special letters that have diacritics or common symbols, such as the copyright symbol, which are outside of the regular, standard character set represented on your keyboard. HTML enables you to insert a full range of such character entities through two systems. The more familiar special characters have been assigned a mnemonic code name to make them easy to remember; these are called *named characters*. Less typical characters must be inserted by entering a numeric code; these are known as *decimal characters*. For the sake of completeness, named characters also have a corresponding decimal character code.

Both named and decimal character codes begin with an ampersand (&) symbol and end with a semicolon (;). For example, the HTML code for an ampersand symbol follows:

```
&amp;
```

Its decimal character equivalent follows:

&

Caution

If, during the browser-testing phase of creating your Web page, you suddenly see an HTML code onscreen rather than a symbol, double-check your HTML. The code could be just a typo; you may have left off the closing semicolon, for instance. If the code is correct and you're using a named character, however, switch to its decimal equivalent. Some of the earlier browser versions are not perfect in rendering named characters.

Named characters

HTML coding conventions require that certain characters, including the angle brackets that surround tags, be entered as character entities. Table 6-3 lists the most common named characters.

Table 6-3: Common Named Characters

Named Entity	Symbol	Description
&lt;	<	A left angle bracket or the less-than symbol
&gt;	>	A right angle bracket or the greater-than symbol
&amp;	&	An ampersand
&quot;	"	A double quotation mark
	°	A non-breaking space
&copy;	©	A copyright symbol
&reg;	®	A registered mark
&trade;	™	A trademark symbol, which cannot be previewed in Dreamweaver but is supported in Internet Explorer

Tip

Those characters that you can type directly into Dreamweaver's Document window, including the brackets and the ampersand, are automatically translated into the correct named characters in HTML. Try this when in split-screen Code and Design view. You can also enter a non-breaking space in Dreamweaver by typing Ctrl+Shift+spacebar (Command+Shift+spacebar) or by choosing the Non-breaking Space object.

Decimal characters and UTF-8 encoding

To enter almost any character that has a diacritic — such as á, ñ, or â — in Dreamweaver, you must explicitly enter the corresponding decimal character into your HTML page. As mentioned in the preceding section, decimal characters take the form of &#number;, where the number can range from 00 to 255. Not all numbers have matching symbols; the sequence from 14 through 31 is currently unused, and the upper range (127 through 159), only partially supported by Internet Explorer and Netscape Navigator, is now deemed invalid by the W3C. In addition, not all fonts have characters for every entity.

New Feature Dreamweaver now uses UTF-8 encoding for characters higher than 127. UTF-8 is an ASCII compatible version of Unicode character set; Unicode provides a unique number for every character in every language, however the raw Unicode number is rendered in 16-bit words, unreadable by browsers — a problem solved by UTF-8.

UTF-8 also uses numbers, but does away with the upper limit of 255. For example, the UTF-8 encoding for the trademark symbol is ™ whereas the no-longer-used number entity was ™. Fortunately, you don't have to remember complex codes — all you have to do is use the Character objects.

Using the Character objects

Not only is it difficult to remember the various name or number codes for the specific character entities you need, it's also time-consuming to enter the code by hand. The Dreamweaver engineers recognized this problem and created a series of Character objects, which have their own category on the Insert bar.

Ease of use is the guiding principal for the new Character objects. Eleven of the most commonly used symbols, such as © and ™, are instantly available as separate objects. Inserting the single Character objects is a straightforward point-and-click affair. Either drag the desired symbol to a place in the Document window or position your cursor and select the object.

The individual Character objects are described in Table 6-4.

Table 6-4: Character Objects

Icon	Name	HTML Code Inserted
BR⏎	Line-break	` `
⬇	Non-breaking space	` `
"	Left Quote	`&#8220;`
"	Right Quote	`&#8221;`
—	Em-Dash	`&#8212;`
£	Pound	`&pound;`
€	Euro	`&#8364;`

Icon	Name	HTML Code Inserted
 ¥	Yen	`&yen;`
 ©	Copyright	`&copy;`
 ®	Registered Trademark	`&reg;`
 ™	Trademark	`&#8482;`

Note

You may notice that the Character objects insert a mix of named and number character entities. Not all browsers recognize the easier-to-identify named entities, so for the widest compatibility, Dreamweaver uses the number codes for a few objects.

The final object in the Characters category is used for inserting these or any other character entity. The Insert Other Character object displays a large table with symbols for 99 different characters, as shown in Figure 6-23. Simply select the desired symbol, and Dreamweaver inserts the appropriate HTML code at the current cursor position. By the way, the very first character—which appears to be blank—actually inserts the code for a non-breaking space, also accessible via a keyboard shortcut, Ctrl+Shift+spacebar (Command+Shift+spacebar). The non-breaking space is also available in the Characters category of the Insert bar.

Note

Keep in mind that the user's browser must support the character entity for it to be visible to the user; again testing is essential. In the case of the Euro symbol, for example, that support is still not widespread. In some instances, where the appearance of a particular character is critical, a graphic may be a better option than a UTF-8 entity.

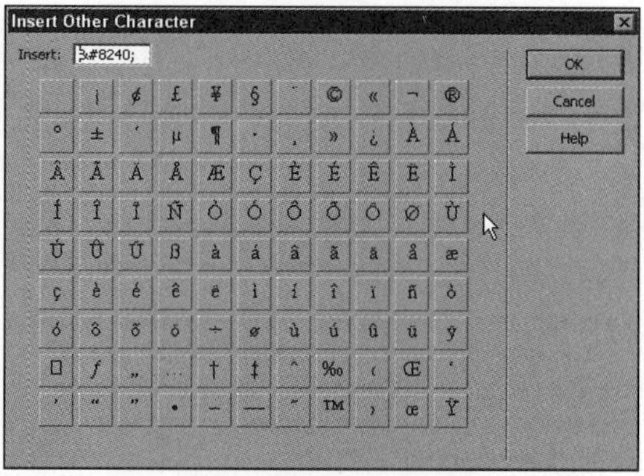

Figure 6-23: Use the Insert Other Character object to insert the character entity code for any of 99 different symbols.

Summary

Creating Web pages with Dreamweaver is a special blend of using visual layout tools and HTML coding. Regardless, you need to understand the basics of HTML so that you have the knowledge and the tools to modify your code when necessary. This chapter covered the following key areas:

✦ An HTML page is divided into two main sections: the <head> and the <body>. Information pertaining to the entire page is kept in the <head> section; all the actual content of the Web page goes in the <body> section.

✦ You can change the color and background of your entire page, as well as set its title, through the Page Properties dialog box.

✦ Use <meta> tags to summarize your Web page so that search engines can properly catalog it. In Dreamweaver, you can use the View Head Contents feature to easily alter these and other <head> tags.

✦ When possible, use logical style tags, such as <strong> and <cite>, rather than hard-coding your page with physical style tags. Style sheets bring a great deal of control and flexibility to logical style tags.

✦ Java applets can be inserted as Applet objects in a Dreamweaver Web page. Java source files, called *classes*, can be linked to the Applet object through the Property inspector.

✦ Dreamweaver offers a simple method for including both JavaScript and VBScript code in the <body> section of your HTML page. Script functions that need to be inserted in the <head> section can now be added by selecting View ➪ Head Content.

✦ Special extended characters such as symbols and accented letters require the use of HTML character entities, which can either be named (as in ") or in decimal format (as in ").

In the next chapter, you learn how to insert and format text in Dreamweaver.

✦   ✦   ✦

Working with Text

If content is king on the Web, then certainly style is queen; together they rule hand in hand. Entering, editing, and formatting text on a Web page is a major part of a Webmaster's job. Dreamweaver gives you the tools to make the task as clear-cut as possible. From headlines to comments, this chapter covers the essentials of working with basic text; inserting and formatting dynamic data is covered in Chapter 16.

At first, Web designers didn't have many options for manipulating text. However, now the majority of browsers understand a number of text-related commands, and the designer can specify the font as well as its color and size. Dreamweaver includes a range of text-manipulation tools. All these topics are covered in this chapter, along with an important discussion of how to manipulate whitespace on the Web page.

Starting with Headings

Text in HTML is primarily composed of headings and paragraphs. Headings separate and introduce major sections of the document, just as a newspaper uses headlines to announce a story and sub-heads to highlight essential details. HTML has six levels of headings; the syntax for the heading tags is <hn>, where n is a number from 1 to 6. The largest heading is <h1>, and the smallest is <h6>.

Note   Although Dreamweaver is capable of outputting several different types of Web pages — ASP, ColdFusion, JSP, etc. — after the page has been executed on the application server, straight HTML is returned to the visitor's browser. Therefore, although you'll find numerous references to HTML pages throughout this chapter, understand that, even though the pages may be stored as ASP pages or other types, HTML is the result.

Remember that HTML headings are not linked to any specific point size, unlike type produced in a page layout or word processing program. Headings in a Web document are sized relative to one another, and their final, exact size depends on the browser used. The sample headlines in Figure 7-1 depict the basic headings as rendered through Dreamweaver and as compared to the default paragraph font size. As you can see, some headings are rendered in type smaller than that used for the default paragraph. Headings are usually displayed with a boldface attribute.

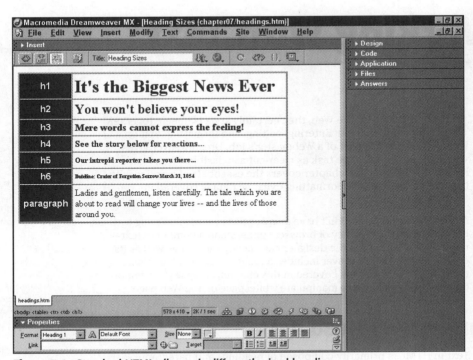

Figure 7-1: Standard HTML allows six differently sized headings.

Several methods set text as a particular heading size in Dreamweaver. In all cases, you first need to select the text you want to affect. If you are styling a single line or paragraph as a heading, just position the cursor anywhere in the paragraph to select it. If you want to convert more than one paragraph, click and drag out your selection.

Tip   You can't mix heading levels in a single paragraph. That is, you can't have a word with an <h1> heading in the same line with a word styled with an <h4> heading. Furthermore, headings belong to a group of HTML text tags called *block elements*. All block elements are rendered with a paragraph return both above and below, which isolates ("blocks") the text. To work around both of these restrictions, use Cascading Style Sheets, described in Chapter 20, to achieve the effect of varying sizes for words within the same line or for lines of different sizes close to one another.

After the text for the heading is selected, choose your heading level in one of the following ways:

✦ Choose Text ➪ Paragraph Format and then one of the Headings 1 through 6 from the submenu.

✦ Choose the Heading 1, Heading 2, or Heading 3 button from the Text category of the Insert bar.

✦ Make your selection from the Text Property inspector. (If it's not already open, display the Text Property inspector by selecting Window ➪ Properties.) In the Text Property inspector, open the Format drop-down list (see Figure 7-2) and choose one of the six headings.

Tip   You can also use keyboard shortcuts for assigning headings. Headings 1 through 6 correspond to Ctrl+1 through Ctrl+6 (Command+1 through Command+6). The Paragraph option is rendered with Ctrl+Shift+P (Command+Shift+P); remove all formatting with Ctrl+0 (Command+0).

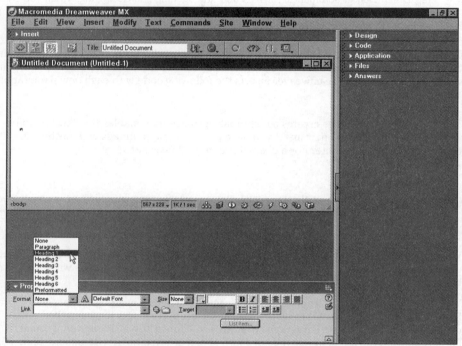

Figure 7-2: You can convert any paragraph or line into a heading through the Format options in the Text Property inspector.

Headings are often used in a hierarchical fashion, largest to smallest — but you don't have to do it that way. You can have an ⟨h3⟩ line followed by an ⟨h1⟩ paragraph, if that's what your design needs.

Caution   Be careful when using the smallest headings, ⟨h4⟩ – ⟨h6⟩; they are likely to be difficult to read on any resolution higher than 800 × 600.

Working with Paragraphs

Usually the bulk of text on any Web page is composed of paragraphs. Paragraphs in HTML are denoted by the ⟨p⟩ and ⟨/p⟩ pair of tags. When your Web page is processed, the browser formats everything between those two tags as one paragraph and renders it to fit the user's screen, word wrapping as needed at the margins. Any additional line breaks and unnecessary whitespace (beyond one space between words and between sentences) in the HTML code are ignored.

Tip

In the earliest versions of HTML, paragraphs used just the opening `<p>` tag. Browsers rendered everything after a `<p>` tag as one paragraph, until they reached another `<p>` tag. As of HTML 3.2, however, an optional closing `</p>` tag was added. Because so many Web pages have been created with just the opening paragraph tag, most browsers still recognize the single-tag format, even though the latest versions of the HTML standard require the closing tag. Dreamweaver automatically inserts both the opening and closing tags when you create a paragraph. To be on the safe side in terms of future compatibility, enclose your paragraphs within both opening and closing tags when you do any hand-coding.

Dreamweaver starts a new paragraph every time you press Enter (Return) when composing text in the Document window. If you have the Code view or the Code inspector open when you work, you can see that Dreamweaver inserts the following code with each new paragraph:

```
<p> </p>
```

The code between the tags creates a non-breaking space that enables the new line to be visible. You won't see the new line if you have just the paragraph tags with nothing in between (neither a character nor a character entity, such as ` `):

```
<p></p>
```

Caution

Some browsers, such as Netscape Navigator 4.x, totally ignore empty `<p></p>` tags. If you are hand-coding an empty paragraph, be sure to include a non-breaking space within the paragraph.

When you continue typing, Dreamweaver replaces the non-breaking space with your input, unless you press Enter (Return) again. Figure 7-3 illustrates two paragraphs with text followed by paragraphs with the non-breaking space still in place.

You can easily change text from most other formats, such as a heading, to paragraph format. First, select the text you want to alter. Then, in the Property inspector, open the Format drop-down list and choose Paragraph. You can also choose Text ➪ Paragraph Format ➪ Paragraph from the menu or use the keyboard shortcut Ctrl+Shift+P (Command+Shift+P).

All paragraphs are initially rendered on the page in the default font at the default size. The user can designate these defaults through the browser preferences, although most people don't bother to alter them. If you want to change the font name or the font size for selected paragraphs explicitly, use the techniques described in the upcoming section "Modifying Text Format" or using Cascading Style Sheets, described in Chapter 20.

Tip

Remember that you can always use the Tag Selector on the status bar to select and highlight any tag surrounding your current cursor position. This method makes it easy to see exactly what a particular tag is affecting.

Editing paragraphs

By and large, the editing features of Dreamweaver are similar to other modern word processing programs — with one or two Web-oriented twists. Like other programs, Dreamweaver has Cut, Copy, and Paste options, as well as Undo and Redo commands.

The "twists" come from the relationship between the Design and Code views of the Document window, which give Dreamweaver special functionality for copying and pasting text and code. You'll learn how that works in the following sections.

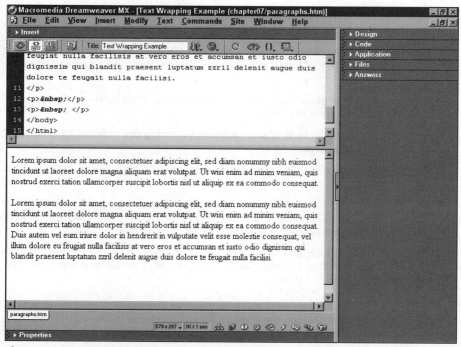

Figure 7-3: Dreamweaver automatically wraps any text inserted into the Document window. If you press Enter (Return) without entering text, Dreamweaver enters paragraph tags surrounding a non-breaking space.

Inserting text

You've already seen how you can position the cursor on the page and directly enter text. In this sense, Dreamweaver acts like a word processing program, rather than a page layout program. On a blank page, the cursor starts at the top-left corner of the page. Words automatically wrap to the next line when the text exceeds the right margin. Press Enter (Return) to end the current paragraph and start the next one.

New Feature

In previous versions of Dreamweaver, if you create a paragraph formatted as a heading and then press Enter (Return), the new paragraph is also formatted as a heading. Now you can control this behavior. If you select Edit ➪ Preferences and then select the Switch to Plain Paragraph After Heading option, pressing Enter (Return) after a heading creates a plain paragraph. By default, this option is enabled.

Cutting, copying, and pasting

Text can be moved from one place to another — or from one Web document to another — using the standard cut-and-paste techniques. No surprises here: Before cutting or copying anything, you must select it. Select by clicking the mouse at the beginning of the text you want to cut or copy, drag the highlight to the end of your selection, and then release the mouse button.

Here are some other selection methods:

✦ Double-click a word to select it.

✦ Move the pointer to the left margin of the text until the pointer changes to a right-facing arrow. Click once to highlight a single line. Click and drag down the margin to select a group of lines.

✦ Position the cursor at the beginning of your selection. Hold down the Shift key and then click once at the end of the selection.

✦ Select everything in the body of your document by using Edit ➪ Select All or the keyboard shortcut Ctrl+A (Command+A).

✦ Use the Tag Selector in the status bar to select text or other objects contained within specific tags.

✦ You can also select text by holding down the Shift key and using the right or left arrow key to select one character at a time. If you hold down Ctrl+Shift (Command+Shift), click the right or left arrow key to select one word at a time.

✦ Hold down the Shift key and then press the up or down arrow key to select a line at a time. Pressing Ctrl+Shift (Command+Shift) as you press the up or down arrow key selects a paragraph at a time.

New Feature Dreamweaver now provides quick access to the most common editing commands, such as Cut, Copy, and Paste, through the Standard toolbar. To enable the toolbar, choose View ➪ Toolbars ➪ Standard.

When you want to move a block of text, first select it and then use Edit ➪ Cut, the Cut button on the Standard toolbar or the keyboard shortcut Ctrl+X (Command+X). This sequence places the text on your system's clipboard. To paste the text, move the pointer to the new location and click once to place the cursor; then select Edit ➪ Paste or the keyboard shortcut Ctrl+V (Command+V). The text is copied from the clipboard to its new location. You can continue pasting this same text from the clipboard until another block of text is copied or cut.

To copy text, the procedure is much the same. Select the text using one of the preceding methods and then use Edit ➪ Copy, the Copy button on the Standard toolbar, or Ctrl+C (Command+C). The selected text is copied to the clipboard, and the original text is left in place. You then position the cursor in a new location and select Edit ➪ Paste (or use the keyboard shortcut).

Using drag-and-drop

The other, quicker method for moving or copying text is the drag-and-drop technique. After you've selected your text, release the mouse button and move the cursor over the highlighted area. The cursor changes from an I-beam to an arrow. To move the text, click the selected area with the arrow cursor and drag your mouse to a new location. The arrow cursor now has a box attached to it, indicating that it is carrying something. As you move your cursor, a bar (the insertion point) moves with you, indicating where the text will be positioned. Release the mouse button to drop the text.

You can duplicate text in the same manner by holding down the Ctrl (Option) key as you drag and drop your selected text. When copying this way, the box attached to the cursor is marked with a plus sign (on Macintosh computers, the box is the same size as the text selection, and no plus sign appears).

Inserting Text from Other Text Applications

The Paste command can also insert text from another program into Dreamweaver. If you cut or copy text from a file in any other program—whether it is a word processor, spreadsheet, or database program—Dreamweaver inserts it at the cursor position. The results of this Paste operation vary, however.

Dreamweaver can paste only plain, unformatted text—any bold, italic, or other styling in the original document is not retained in Dreamweaver. Paragraph breaks, however, are retained and reproduced in two different ways. A single paragraph return becomes a line-break (a <br> tag) in Dreamweaver, whereas text separated by two returns is formatted into two HTML paragraphs, using the <p>...</p> tag pair.

If you need to import a great deal of text and want to retain as much formatting as possible, you can use another text application, such as Microsoft Word, to save your text as an HTML file. Then open that file in Dreamweaver with the Import ➪ Word HTML command.

To completely remove text, select it and then choose Edit ➪ Clear or press Delete. The only way to recover deleted text is to use the Undo feature described later in this section.

Copying and pasting code

As mentioned earlier in this chapter, Dreamweaver includes a couple of "twists" to the standard Cut, Copy, and Paste operations. Dreamweaver's Design and Code views enable you to copy and paste both text and code.

Put simply, to copy only text from Dreamweaver to another application, use the Edit ➪ Copy command in Design view; to copy both text and code, use the Edit ➪ Copy command in Code view. Dreamweaver also supplies two commands, available only in Design view, that allow you to copy and paste HTML code without switching to Code view. These commands are Edit ➪ Copy HTML and Edit ➪ Paste HTML. To understand how copying and pasting in the two views interact, examine how they are used. Table 7-1 explains the variations.

Note

Dreamweaver, by default, uses the <strong> tag to indicate a bolded entry as the <b> tag is deprecated. In the following example, I use the <b> tag for illustration purposes.

Table 7-1: Results of Copy/Paste from Design and Code Views

Selected Text	Copy From	Paste To	Result
Example Text	Design view using Edit ➪ Copy	Other program	Example Text
Example Text	Design view using Edit ➪ Copy	Code view	<b>Example Text</b>
Example Text	Design view using Edit ➪ Copy	Design view	**Example Text**
Example Text	Design view using Edit ➪ Copy HTML	Other program	<b>Example Text</b>
Example Text	Design view using Edit ➪ Copy HTML	Code view	<b>Example Text</b>
Example Text	Design view using Edit ➪ Copy HTML	Design view	<b>Example Text</b>

Continued

Table 7-1: *(continued)*

Selected Text	Copy From	Paste To	Result
<b>Example Text</b>	Code view or other program	Code view	<b>Example Text</b>
<b>Example Text</b>	Code view or other program	Design view using Edit ⇨ Paste	<b>Example Text</b>
<b>Example Text</b>	Code view or other program	Design view using Edit ⇨ Paste HTML	**Example Text**

Notice that in the second-to-last row of Table 7-1, if you copy formatted text such as the bold-face Example Text sample from Code view and insert it in the Design view, you get the following HTML code:

```
&lt;b&gt;Example Text&lt;/b&gt;
```

You may recognize < as the code for the less-than symbol (<) and > as the code for the greater-than symbol (>). These symbols are used to represent tags such as <b> and </b> to prevent a browser from interpreting them as tag delimiters.

So what possible real-life uses could there be for Dreamweaver's implementation of the regular Copy/Paste commands in the different views? These options are a major benefit for programmers, teachers, and writers who constantly have to communicate in both HTML code and regular text. If an instructor is attempting to demonstrate a coding technique on a Web page, for example, she can just copy the code in the Code view and Paste it into the Design view — instantly transforming the code into something readable online.

Undo, Redo, and the History panel

The Undo command has to be one of the greatest inventions of the 20th century. Make a mistake? Undo! Want to experiment with two different options? Undo! Change your mind again? Redo! The Undo command reverses your last action, whether you changed a link, added a graphic, or deleted the entire page. The Redo command enables you to reverse your Undo actions.

To use the Undo command, choose Edit ⇨ Undo, select Undo from the Standard toolbar, or press the keyboard shortcut Ctrl+Z (Command+Z); any of these commands undoes a single action at a time. Dreamweaver displays all your previous actions on the History panel, so you can easily see what steps you took. Choose Windows ⇨ Others ⇨ History to view the History panel. To undo multiple actions, drag the slider in the History panel to the last action you want to keep, or just click in the slider track at that action.

Dreamweaver's implementation of the Undo command enables you to back up as many steps as set in Maximum Number of History Steps, found in the General category of Preferences. The History steps can even undo actions that took place before a document was saved. Note that the History panel has additional features besides multiple applications of undo.

The complement to the Undo command is the Redo command. To reverse an Undo command, choose Edit ⇨ Redo, click the Redo button on the Standard toolbar, or press Ctrl+Y (Command+Y). To reverse several Undo commands, drag the slider in the History panel back over the grayed-out steps; alternately, click once in the slider track at the last of the steps you'd like to redo.

Tip   The best use I've found for the Redo command is in concert with Undo. When I'm trying to decide between two alternatives, such as two different images, I'll replace one choice with another and then use the Undo/Redo combination to go back and forth between them. Because Dreamweaver replaces any selected object with the current object from the clipboard — even if one is a block of text and the other is a layer — you can easily view two separate options with this trick. The History panel enables you to apply this procedure to any number of steps.

A variation of the Redo command is the Repeat command. When your last action was the Undo command, the Edit menu shows the Redo command. But if the last action you performed was not Undo, the Edit menu shows the Repeat command, which allows you to repeat your last action. You can use the same button on the Standard toolbar to Repeat and Redo. In addition, the Repeat command has the same keyboard shortcut as Redo: Ctrl+Y (Command+Y). One example of when the Repeat command is useful is when you need to create several links to the same location. To do this, create the first link, and then select the next text you want to link and use the Repeat command to add the link.

On the CD-ROM   Although the History panel enables you to replay any series of selected steps at the click of a button, you have to click that button every time you want to replay the steps. I developed a custom extension called Repeat History with which you can repeat selected steps any number of times. You'll find Repeat History in the Additional Extensions folder on the CD-ROM.

Checking Your Spelling

A typo can make a significant impression, and not the one you are seeking to make. Not many things are more embarrassing than showing a new Web site to a client and having that client point out a spelling error. Dreamweaver includes an easy-to-use Spell Checker to avoid such awkward moments. Make it a practice to spell check every Web page before it's posted online.

You start the process by choosing Text ➪ Check Spelling or press the keyboard shortcut Shift+F7. This sequence opens the Check Spelling dialog box, as seen in Figure 7-4.

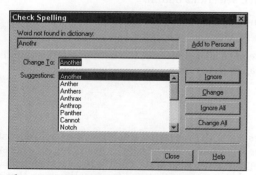

Figure 7-4: Dreamweaver's Spell Checker double-checks your spelling and can find the typos on any Web page.

Spell-Checking in Non-English Languages

A variety of language dictionaries are built into Dreamweaver, so you can check spelling in a number of languages. Dreamweaver can check spelling in the following languages: Danish, Dutch, English (American), English (British), English (Canadian), Finnish, French, German, Italian, Norwegian, Portuguese (Brazilian), Portuguese (Iberian), Spanish, and Swedish.

Open Preferences (Edit ⇨ Preferences) and, in the General category, expand the Spelling Dictionary list. Choose the new language from the drop-down list, and you're ready to spell correctly in another tongue.

After you've opened the Check Spelling dialog box, Dreamweaver begins searching your text for errors. Unless you have selected a portion of your document, Dreamweaver checks the full document, regardless of where your cursor is placed. When text is selected, Dreamweaver checks the selection first and then asks if you'd like to do the entire document.

Dreamweaver checks your Web page text against two dictionaries: a standard dictionary for your chosen language and a personal dictionary to which you can add words. If the Spell Checker finds any text that is not in either of the program's dictionaries, the text is highlighted in the Document window and appears in the "Word not found in dictionary" field of the dialog box. A list of suggested corrections appears in the Suggestions list box, with the topmost one highlighted and also displayed in the Change To box. If Dreamweaver cannot find any suggestions, the Change To box is left blank. At this point, you have the following options:

✦ **Add to Personal:** Select this button to include the word in your personal dictionary and prevent Dreamweaver from tagging it as an error in the future.

✦ **Ignore:** Select this button when you want Dreamweaver to leave the currently highlighted word alone and continue searching the text.

✦ **Change:** If you see the correct replacement among the list of suggestions, highlight it and select the Change button. If no suggestion is appropriate, type the correct word into the Change To text box and then select this button.

✦ **Ignore All:** Select this button when you want Dreamweaver to disregard all occurrences of this word in the current document.

✦ **Change All:** Select this button to replace all instances of the current word within the document with the word in the Change To text box.

Using Find and Replace

Dreamweaver's Find and Replace features are both timesaving and lifesaving (well, almost). You can use Find and Replace to cut your input time substantially by searching for abbreviations and expanding them to their full state. You can also find a client's incorrectly spelled name and replace it with the correctly spelled version—that's a lifesaver! However, that's just the tip of the iceberg when it comes to what Find and Replace can really do. The Find and Replace engine should be considered a key power tool for any Web developer. Not only can you search multiple files, you can also easily check the code separately from the content.

Here's a short list of what the Find and Replace feature makes possible:

✦ Search the Document window to find any type of text.

✦ Search the underlying HTML to find tags, attributes, or text enclosed within tags.

✦ Look for text within specific tags with specific attributes—or look for text that's outside of a specific tag with specific attributes.

✦ Find and replace patterns of text, using wildcard characters called *regular expressions*.

✦ Apply any of the preceding Find and Replace operations to the current document, the current site, any folder, or any group of selected files.

The basic command, Find and Replace, is found with its companion, Find Next (Find Again, on the Macintosh), under the Edit menu. You can use both commands in either Dreamweaver's Design or Code view. On Windows systems, if you are using the Dreamweaver 4 workspace, the Find and Replace command is also available from the Edit menu in the Site panel. Although invoked by a single command, the Find feature can be used independently or in conjunction with Replace.

Find and Replace operations can be applied to one or a series of documents. In addition to searching the current document, you can also apply Find and Replace to all the files in a folder or an entire site. Furthermore, individual files selected in the Site panel are also searchable.

Finding on the visual page

The most basic method of using Find and Replace takes place in the Document window. Whenever you need to search for any text that can be seen by the public on your Web page—whether it's to correct spelling or change a name—Dreamweaver makes it fast and simple.

Tip   The Find and Replace dialog box, unlike most of Dreamweaver's dialog boxes, is actually a *nonmodal window*. This technical term just means that you can easily move back and forth between your Document window and the Find and Replace dialog box without having to close the dialog box first, as you do with the other Dreamweaver dialog boxes.

To find some text on your Web page, follow these steps:

1. From the Document window, choose Edit ⇨ Find and Replace or use the keyboard shortcut Ctrl+F (Command+F). If the Search panel is open, you can also click the Find and Replace button (the small green triangle) on the panel.

2. In the Find and Replace dialog box, shown in Figure 7-5, make sure that Text is the selected Search For option.

3. In the text box next to the Search For option, type the word or phrase you're looking for.

Tip   If you select your text *before* launching the Find dialog box, it automatically appears in the Search For text box.

Search For options list   Search For text box

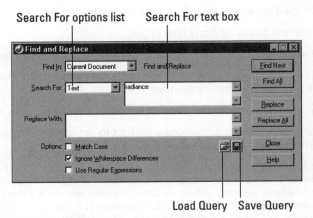

Load Query   Save Query

Figure 7-5: The Find and Replace dialog box.

4. Select the appropriate search options, if any:

   • If you want to find an exact replica of the word as you entered it, select the Match Case checkbox; otherwise, Dreamweaver searches for all variations of your text, regardless of case.

   • To force Dreamweaver to disregard any whitespace variations, such as additional spaces, hard spaces, or tabs, select the Ignore Whitespace Differences option. For most situations, it's a good idea to leave this default option enabled.

   • Selecting Use Regular Expressions enables you to work with Dreamweaver's wild-card characters (discussed later in this section). Use Regular Expressions and Ignore Whitespace Differences are mutually exclusive options.

5. Click the Find Next button to begin the search from the cursor's current position.

   • If Dreamweaver finds the desired text, it highlights the text in the Document window.

   • If Dreamweaver doesn't find the text in the remaining portion of the document, it automatically continues the search from the beginning of the document until the entire document has been checked.

   • If Dreamweaver doesn't locate the search term, it displays a message saying the term was not found.

6. If you want to look for the next occurrence of your selected text, click the Find Next button again.

7. You can enter other text to search or exit the Find dialog box by clicking the Close button.

The text you enter in the Find and Replace dialog box is kept in memory until it's replaced by your next use of the Find feature. After you have executed the Find command once, you can continue to search for your text without redisplaying the Find and Replace dialog box, by selecting Edit ➪ Find Next (Find Again), or by using the keyboard shortcut F3 (Command+G). If Dreamweaver finds your text, it is highlighted just as it is when the Find and Replace dialog box is open. However, the Edit ➪ Find Next (Find Again) command will search indefinitely through your document; no message displays after you have searched the entire file. The

Find Next (Find Again) command gives you a quick way to search through a long document—especially when you put the F3 (Command+G) key to work.

Instead of locating one instance of your text at a time, you can also look for all occurrences of your text at once. To do this, open and set up the Find and Replace dialog as previously described, but choose Find All instead of Find Next. When you choose Find All, Dreamweaver closes the Find and Replace dialog box and opens the Search panel. The Search panel displays each found occurrence on a separate line, as shown in Figure 7-6. A message at the bottom of the Search panel also tells you how many occurrences of your selection, if any, were found. If you wish to search for a different term, click the Find and Replace button (the small green triangle) in the Search panel to reopen the Find and Replace dialog box.

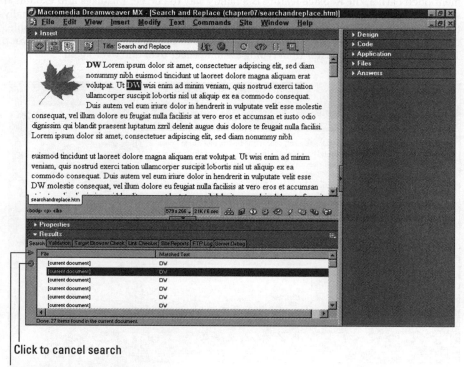

Click to cancel search

Click to reopen Find and Replace box

Figure 7-6: The Search panel displays results of a Find All command.

Tip   To quickly move from one found selection to another in the Document window, double-click an entry in the Search panel. Dreamweaver highlights the selection, scrolling the Document window, if necessary. Note, however, that the results listed in the Search panel may take you to the wrong location if you add or remove content in the document after you perform the search.

If you perform two Find All operations in a row, the Search panel automatically clears the results of the first search and replaces them with the results of the new search. To manually clear the Search panel, right-click (Control+click) and then choose Clear Results.

Caution   If you edit the document after performing a Find All, the results of the search may no longer be valid. In this situation, double-clicking an item in the Search panel may no longer take you to the correct place in the document. If you have added or removed text in the document after performing a Find All, perform the search again by clicking the Find and Replace button (the small green triangle) in the Search panel to reopen the Find and Replace dialog box. If no text is selected in the Document window before you open the Find and Replace dialog box, the search parameters should automatically be set up; you only need to click Find All again.

When you add the Replace command to a Find operation, you can search your text for a word or phrase and, if it's found, replace it with another word or phrase of your choice. As mentioned earlier, the Replace feature is a handy way to correct mistakes and expand abbreviations. Figure 7-7 shows an example of the latter operation. This example intentionally uses the abbreviation DW throughout the input text of a Web page article. Then the example uses the Replace All function to expand all the DWs to Dreamweaver — in one fell swoop. This technique is much faster than typing *Dreamweaver* over and over again.

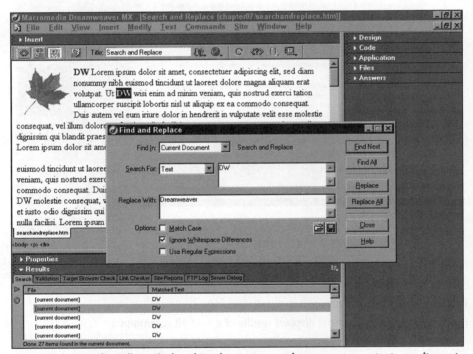

Figure 7-7: Use the Edit ⇨ Find and Replace command to correct your text, one item at a time or all at once.

When you replace text in the Document window, it is replaced regardless of its formatting. For example, suppose you had the following paragraph:

Mary's accusation reminded Jon of studying synchrones in high school. *Synchrones*, he recalled, were graphs in which the lines constantly approached zero, but never made it. "Yeah," he thought, "That's me, all right. I'm one big **synchrone**."

Upon discovering that "synchrone" should actually be "asymptote," you could use the Find and Replace feature to replace all the plain, italic, and bold versions of the *synchrone* text simultaneously.

Tip It's possible to alter formatting as well—to change all the formatting to just bold, for example—but for that you need to perform your Find and Replace operations on the underlying code, as discussed in the following section.

Follow these steps to use Dreamweaver's Replace feature in the Document window:

1. Choose Edit ⇨ Find and Replace or use the keyboard shortcut Ctrl+F (Command+F).

2. In the Find and Replace dialog box, make sure that Text is the selected Search For option and then, in the text box next to the Search For option, type the word or phrase you're looking for. You can also copy and paste text from the Document window into the Search For box.

3. In the Replace With text box, type the substitute text.

Tip Need more room for your Find or Replace entries? The Find and Replace dialog box can now be widened by dragging the border as you would a window; Macintosh users should drag the lower-right corner as usual. Note, however, that the Find and Replace dialog box can only be widened; it can't be made taller.

4. Click the Find Next button. Dreamweaver begins searching from the current cursor position. If Dreamweaver finds the text, it is highlighted.

5. To replace the highlighted occurrence of the text, select the Replace button. Dreamweaver replaces the found text with the substitute text and then automatically searches for the next occurrence.

6. If you want to replace all instances of the Search For text, select the Replace All button.

When Dreamweaver has found all the occurrences of your Search For text, it displays a message telling how many replacement operations were made.

Caution The Search panel applies to Find operations, but not to Replace operations. When you select Replace All, Dreamweaver does not update the Search panel to list items that have been replaced. Further, if you select Find All and then perform a Replace All, the previous results in the Search panel may no longer correctly reflect the location of the text you just replaced, and changed items in the Search panel are not flagged.

Tip To rerun individual Find and Replace operations, highlight the appropriate step in the History panel (choose Window ⇨ Others ⇨ History) and choose the Replay button. You cannot, however, use the History panel to repeat a Find All operation.

Searching the code

The power curve ramps up significantly when you start to explore Dreamweaver's Find and Replace capabilities for HTML code. Should your client decide that he wants the company's name to appear in blue, bold, 18-point type throughout the 300-page site, you can accommodate him with a few keystrokes—instead of hours of mind-numbing grunt work.

Storing and Retrieving Queries

Dreamweaver enables you to develop extremely complex search queries. Rather than forcing you to repeatedly reenter Find and Replace queries, Dreamweaver enables you to save and load them when needed. Dreamweaver saves the queries with a .dwr file extension.

To save a query, select the Diskette icon on the Find and Replace dialog box. The standard Save Query (Save Query to file) dialog box appears for you to enter a filename; the appropriate file extension is appended automatically. To load a previously saved query, select the Folder icon on the Find and Replace dialog box to open the Load Query dialog box. Although only queries with a .dwr extension are being saved in the current version, you can still load both .dwq and .dwr files saved from previous Dreamweaver versions.

Although saving and opening queries is an obvious advantage when working with complex wild-card operations, you can also make it work for you in an everyday situation. If, for example, you have a set series of acronyms or abbreviations that you must convert repeatedly, you can save your simple text queries and use them as needed without having to remember all the details.

You can perform three different types of searches that use the HTML in your Web page:

✦ You can search for text anywhere in the HTML code. With this capability, you can look for text within alt or any other attribute—and change it.

✦ You can search for text relative to specific tags. Sometimes you need to change just the text contained within the ⟨b⟩ tag and leave all other matching text alone.

✦ You can search for specific HTML tags and/or their attributes. Dreamweaver's Find and Replace feature gives you the capability to insert, delete, or modify tags and attributes.

Looking for text in the code

Text that appears onscreen is often replicated in various sections of your off-screen HTML code. It's not uncommon, for example, to use the alt attribute in an ⟨img⟩ tag that repeats the caption under the picture. What happens if you replace the wording using the Find and Replace dialog box with the Search For field set to Text? You're still left with the task of tracking down the alt attribute and making that change as well. Dreamweaver enables you to act on both content and programming text in one operation—a major savings in time and effort, not to mention aggravation.

To find and replace text in both the content and the code, follow these steps:

1. Choose Edit ➪ Find and Replace to open the Find and Replace dialog box.

2. Select the parameters of your search from the Find In option: Current Document, Entire Current Local Site, Selected Files in Site, or Folder. If you choose Selected Files in Site, select the files of interest in the Site panel.

3. From the Search For drop-down list, select the Source Code option.

4. Enter the text you're searching for in the text box next to the Search For option.

5. If you are replacing, enter the new text in the Replace With text box.

6. Select any options desired: Match Case, Ignore Whitespace Differences, or Use Regular Expressions.

7. Choose your Find/Replace option: Find Next, Find All, Replace, or Replace All.

If you are in Design view, the Code inspector opens.

8. If Dreamweaver hasn't automatically closed the Find and Replace dialog box (it closes automatically for the Find All and Replace All commands), select Close when you are finished.

Caution As with all Find and Replace operations — especially those in which you decide to Replace All — you need to exercise extreme caution when replacing text throughout your code. If you're unsure about what's going to be affected, choose Find All first and, with Code view or inspector open, step through all the selections to be positive no unwanted surprises occur. Should you replace some code in error, you can always undo the operation — but only if the document is open. Replacing text or code in a closed file — as is done when the operation is performed on a folder, the current site, or selected files in the Site panel — is not undoable. Therefore, it is wise to back up your site before performing a Replace All operation.

Using advanced text options in Find and Replace

In Find and Replace operations, the global Replace All isn't appropriate for every situation; sometimes you need a more precise approach. Dreamweaver enables you to fine-tune your searches to pinpoint accuracy. You can look for text within particular tags — and even within particular tags with specific attributes. Moreover, you can find (and replace) text that is outside of particular tags with specific attributes.

Dreamweaver assists you by providing a drop-down list of standard tags. The tags shown depend on the type of document you are viewing, as determined by the filename extension of the open file. For example, although most document types see HTML tags, a document with the .cfm extension would also see ColdFusion tags. You can also search for your own custom tags. In addition, you don't have to try to remember which attributes go with which tag; Dreamweaver supplies you with a context-sensitive list of attributes that changes according to the tag selected.

In addition to using the tag's attributes as a search filter, Dreamweaver can also search within the tag for text or another tag. Most HTML tags are so-called *container tags* that consist of an opening tag and a closing tag, such as `<em>` and `</em>`. You can set up a filter to look for text surrounded by a specific tag pair — or text outside of a specific set of tags. For example, if you are searching for the word *big*

```
The big, red boat was a <em>big</em> waste of money.
```

you can build a Find and Replace operation that changes one instance of the word (big, red) but not the other (`<em>big</em>`) — or vice versa.

To look for text in or out of specific tags and attributes, follow these steps:

1. Choose Edit ➪ Find and Replace to open the Find and Replace dialog box.

2. Select the parameters of your search from the Find In option: Current Document, Current Site, Folder, or Selected Files in Site.

3. From the Search For drop-down list, select the Text (Advanced) option. The Add (+) and Remove (–) tag options are made available, as shown in Figure 7-8.

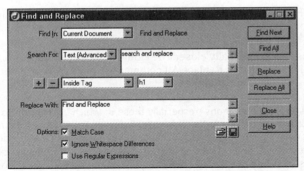

Figure 7-8: The advanced text features of Find and Replace enable you to manipulate text and code simultaneously.

4. Enter the text you're searching for in the text box next to the Search For drop-down list.

5. Select either Inside Tag or Not Inside Tag from the drop-down list. Remember that Inside Tag refers to text that is enclosed within a beginning and ending tag pair, such as `<h2></h2>`.

6. Select the tag to include or exclude from the adjacent drop-down list or type your own tag.

7. To add a further restriction on the search, click the Add (+) button .

   Another line of search options is added to the dialog box.

8. Select the additional search filter. The available options are listed in Table 7-2.

Table 7-2: Search Filters

Filter	Description
With Attribute	Enables you to select any attribute from the adjacent drop-down list. You can set this attribute to be equal to, less than, greater than, or not equal to any given value by choosing from the available drop-down lists.
Without Attribute	Finds text within a particular tag that does not include a specific attribute. Choose the attribute from the adjacent drop-down list.
Containing	Searches the tag for either specified text or another user-selectable tag found within the initial tag pair.
Not Containing	Searches the tag for either text or a tag not found within the initial tag pair.
Inside Tag	Enables you to look for text that is within two (or more) sets of specific tags.
Not Inside Tag	Enables you to look for text that is in one tag, but not in another tag, or vice versa.

9. To continue adding filter conditions, select the Add (+) button and repeat Step 8.

10. To remove a filter condition, select the Remove (–) button.

11. If you are replacing text, enter the new text in the Replace With text box.

12. Select any options desired: Match Case, Ignore Whitespace Differences, or Use Regular Expressions.

13. Choose your Find/Replace option: Find Next, Find All, Replace, or Replace All.

Tip

You can continue to add conditions by clicking the Add (+) button. In fact, I was able to add so many conditions, the Find/Replace dialog box began to disappear off the screen (although I wouldn't recommend this in practice). To quickly erase all conditions, change the Search For option to Text or Source Code and then change it back to Text (Advanced).

Replacing HTML tags and attributes

Let's say a new edict has come down from the HTML gurus of your company: No longer is the `<b>` tag to be used to indicate emphasis; from now on; use only the `<strong>` tag. Oh, and by the way, change all the existing pages — all 3,000+ Web and intranet pages — so that they're compliant. Dreamweaver makes short work out of nightmare situations such as this by giving you the power to search and replace HTML tags and their attributes.

But Dreamweaver doesn't stop there. Not only can you replace one tag with another, you can also perform the following:

✦ Change or delete the tag (with or without its contents).

✦ Set an attribute in the tag to another value.

✦ Remove any or all attributes.

✦ Add text and/or code before or after the starting or the ending tag.

To alter your code using Dreamweaver's Find and Replace feature, follow these steps:

1. As with other Find and Replace operations, choose Edit ⇨ Find and Replace to open the dialog box.

2. Select the parameters of your search from the Find In drop-down list: Current Document, Entire Current Local Site, Folder, or Selected Files in Site.

3. From the Search For drop-down list, select the Specific Tag option.

   The dialog box changes to include the tag functions.

4. Select the desired tag from the option list next to the Search For drop-down list.

Tip

You can either scroll down the list box to find the tag or you can type the first letter of the tag in the box. Dreamweaver scrolls to the group of tags that begin with that letter when the list is visible (Windows only). To scroll further in the list, type the second and subsequent letters, or use the down or up arrow keys.

5. If desired, limit the search by specifying an attribute and value, or with other conditions, as discussed in detail in the previous section.

Note   If you want to search for just a tag, select the Remove (–) button to eliminate the additional condition.

6. Make a selection from the Action list, shown in Figure 7-9. The options are listed in Table 7-3.

Table 7-3: Action List Options

Action	Description
Replace Tag & Contents	Substitutes the selected tag and all included content with a text string; the text string can include HTML code
Replace Contents Only	Changes the content between the specified tag to a given text string, which can also include HTML code
Remove Tag & Contents	Deletes the tag and all contents
Strip Tag	Removes the tag but leaves the previously enclosed content
Change Tag	Substitutes one tag for another
Set Attribute	Sets an existing attribute to a new value or inserts a new attribute set to a specific value
Remove Attribute	Deletes a specified attribute
Add Before Start Tag	Inserts a text string (with or without HTML) before the opening tag
Add After End Tag	Inserts a text string (with or without HTML) after the ending tag
Add After Start Tag	Inserts a text string (with or without HTML) after the opening tag
Add Before End Tag	Inserts a text string (with or without HTML) before the end tag

Note   Not all the options listed in the preceding list are available for all tags. Some so-called empty tags, such as <img>, consist of a single tag, not tag pairs. Empty tags have only the Replace Tag and Remove Tag options (instead of Replace Tag & Contents, Replace Contents Only, and Remove Tag & Contents) and the Add Before and Add After options (instead of Add Before Start Tag, Add After Start Tag, Add Before End Tag, and Add After End Tag).

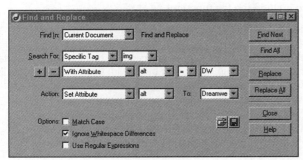

Figure 7-9: The Action list enables you to replace tags or modify them by setting the existing attributes or adding new ones.

7. Select any options desired: Match Case, Ignore Whitespace Differences, or Use Regular Expressions.

8. Choose your Find/Replace option: Find Next, Find All, Replace, or Replace All.

Tip

You don't have to apply a single action to all the instances Dreamweaver locates if you choose Find All. In the Search panel, select a single item and then choose Replace. Dreamweaver makes the revision and places a green dot next to the item so you can tell it has been altered. If you want, you can then select another item from the list, choose a different action, and select Replace.

Concentrating your search with regular expressions

As powerful as all the other Find and Replace features are, they are boosted to a higher level of flexibility with the addition of regular expressions. I've referred to regular expressions as being similar to wildcards in other programs, but their capabilities are actually far more extensive.

Regular expressions are best described as a *text pattern matching system*. If you can identify any pattern in your text, you can manipulate it with regular expressions. What kind of pattern? Imagine you have a spreadsheet-like table with lots of numbers, showing both dollars and cents, mixed with explanatory text. With regular expressions, you can match the pattern formed by the dollar sign and the decimal point and reformat the entire table, turning all the figures deep blue with a new font — all in one Find and Replace operation.

Note

If you're into Unix, you recognize regular expressions as being very close to the grep utility — *grep*, by the way, stands for Get Regular Expressions and Print. The Find and Replace feature in BBEdit, available only on a Macintosh, also features grep-like syntax.

You can apply regular expressions to any of the types of Find and Replace operations previously discussed by just clicking the Use Regular Expressions checkbox. Note that when you select Use Regular Expressions, the Ignore Whitespace Differences option is deselected. This is because the two options are mutually exclusive.

The most basic regular expression is the text itself. If you enable the feature and then enter **th** in the Search For text box, Dreamweaver locates every example of "th" in the text and/or source. Although this capability by itself has little use beyond what you can also achieve with standard Find and Replace operations, it's important to remember this functionality as you begin to build your patterns.

Caution

When entering text in the Search For field of the Find and Replace dialog box, do not include any extra spaces after your search string. Dreamweaver will interpret the spaces as part of your search string, and the search will only find your text when it is followed by a space.

Wildcard characters

Initially, it's helpful to be able to use what are traditionally known as *wildcards* — characters that match different types of characters. The wildcards in regular expressions represent single characters and are described in Table 7-4. In other words, no single regular expression represents all the characters, as the asterisk does when used in PC file searches (such as *.*). However, such a condition can be represented with a slightly more complex regular expression (described later in this section).

Table 7-4: Regular Expression Wildcard Characters

Character	Matches	Example
.	Any single character, including letters, numbers, spaces, punctuation, control characters (like line feed) etc.	**w.c** matches **wac**ky and "Ho**w c**ould you?" but not watch
\w	Any single alphanumeric character, including the underscore	**w\wc** matches **wac**ky and **W3C** but not "How could you?"
\W	Any single non-alphanumeric character	**jboy\Widest.com** matches **jboy@idest.com**
\d	Any single numeric character 0–9	**y\dk** matches **Y2K**
\D	Any single nonnumeric character	**\D2\D** matches **Y2K** and **H2O**
\s	Any single whitespace character, including space, non-breaking space, tab, form feed, or line feed	**\smedia** matches "the **media**" but not Macromedia
\S	Any single non-whitespace character	**\Smedia** matches Macr**omedia** but not "the media"
\t	A tab character	Matches any single tab character in the HTML source
\f	Form feed	Matches any single form-feed character in the HTML source.
		A form-feed is a control character used to force a page break when printing. Although unlikely, it is possible for this character to appear in your HTML document if you converted a print document to HTML. Most browsers ignore the form feed character, but you might wish to search for and remove the form feed using the \f regular expression. A form feed is more likely to occur in a text document.
\n	Line feed	Matches any single line-feed character in the HTML source
\r	Carriage return	Matches any single carriage-return character in the HTML source

Tip   The backslash character (\) is used to escape special characters so that they can be included in a search. For example, if you want to look for an asterisk, you need to specify it as follows: *. Likewise, when trying to find the backslash character, precede it with another backslash character: \\.

Matching character positions and repeating characters

With regular expressions, not only can you match the type of character, you can also match its position in the text. This feature enables you to perform operations on characters at the beginning, end, or middle of the word or line. Regular expressions also enable you to find instances in which a character is repeated an unspecified number of times or a specific number of times. Combined, these features broaden the scope of the patterns that can be found. Table 7-5 details the options available for matching by text placement and character repetition.

Table 7-5: Regular Expression Character Positions and Repeating Characters

Character	Matches	Example
^	If searching text in the current document, this only finds the search string if it immediately follows the cursor; if searching source code or searching text in multiple documents, this regular expression only finds the search string if it is at the beginning of the document	If searching text in the current document, **^l** matches the first l in Ca**l**l me Ishmael." only if the cursor is positioned after the "a" in the word "Call." Clicking Find Next would find the second l in "Call," but clicking next again would not find the l in Ishmael, since the character immediately following the cursor is not an l. If searching source code, **^<** matches the opening < in the HTML <!DOCTYPE . . . > statement, assuming the < is the first character in the document.
$	End of a document	**d$** matches the final "d" in "Be afraid. Be very afrai**d**" if that is the last character in the document.
\b	A word boundary, such as a space or carriage return	**\btext** matches **text**book but not SimpleText
\B	A nonword boundary inside a word	**\Btext** matches Simple**Text** but not textbook
*	The preceding character zero or more times	**b*c** matches **BB**C and "the **c**old" In the first example, both **B**s and the **C** match because the expression **b*c** causes Dreamweaver to look for any number of **b**'s followed by a **c**. In the second example, only the **c** matches because **b*** means to search for zero or more instances of the **b**.
+	The preceding character one or more times	**b+c** matches **BB**C but not cold
?	The preceding character zero or one time	**ac?e** matches **ace** and **aerie** but not axiomatic
{n}	Exactly *n* instances of the preceding character	**e{2}** matches r**ee**d and each pair of two e's in "Ai**ee**eeeee!"; but nothing in Dreamweaver

Continued

Table 7-5: *(continued)*

Character	Matches	Example
{n,m}	A minimum of *n* and a maximum of *m* instances of the preceding character	**C{2,4}** matches #**CC**00FF and #**CCCC**00, but not the full string #**CCCCCC**
		If you searched with the regular expression **C{2,4}**, it would first locate the first four C's in the string #**CCCC**CC. If you clicked Find Next, the search would locate the last two C's in the string, since the search is looking for two, three, or four C's in a row.

Matching character ranges

Beyond single characters, or repetitions of single characters, regular expressions incorporate the capability of finding or excluding ranges of characters. This feature is particularly useful when you're working with groups of names or titles. Ranges are specified in set brackets. A match is made when any one of the characters within the set brackets, not necessarily all the characters, is found. Descriptions of how to match character ranges with regular expressions can be found in Table 7-6.

Table 7-6: Regular Expression Character Ranges

Character	Matches	Example
[abc]	Any one of the characters a, b, or c	**[lmrt]** matches the individual l and m's in **l**e**mm**ings, and the r and t in **r**oad**t**rip
[^abc]	Any character except a, b, or c	**[^etc]** matches each character in **GIFs,** but not etc in the phrase "**GIFs** etc."
[a-z]	Any character in the range from a to z	**[l-p]** matches l and o in **lo**wery, and m, n, o, and p in **pointm**an
x|y	Either x or y	**boy|girl** matches both **boy** and **girl**

Using grouping with regular expressions

All the regular expressions described previously relate to finding a certain string of text within your documents. But after you've located a particular string using regular expressions, how can you use that particular string in the Replace With field? For example, the following list of names:

✦ John Jacob Jingleheimer Schmidt

✦ James T. Kirk

✦ Cara Fishman

can be rearranged so that the last name is first, separated by a comma, like this:

✦ Schmidt, John Jacob Jingleheimer

✦ Kirk, James T.

✦ Fishman, Cara

Dreamweaver enables replacement of regular expressions through grouping expressions. Grouping is perhaps the single most powerful concept in regular expressions. With it, any matched text pattern is easily manipulated. To group a text pattern, enclose it in parentheses in the Find text field. Regular expressions can manage up to nine grouped patterns. In the Replace text field, each grouped pattern is designated by a dollar sign ($) in front of a number (1–9) that indicates the position of the group. For example, enter **$3** in the Replace With box to represent the third grouped pattern in the Find box.

Caution

Remember that the dollar sign is also used after a character or pattern to indicate the last character in a line in a Find expression.

Table 7-7 shows how regular expressions use grouping.

Table 7-7: Regular Expressions Grouping

Character	Matches	Example
(p) (entered in the Find In box)	Any pattern p	**(\b\w*)\.(\w*\b)** matches two patterns, the first before a period and the second, after; such as in a filename with an extension. The backslash before the period escapes it so that it is not interpreted as a regular expression.
$1, $2 . . . $9 (entered in the Replace With box)	The *n*th pattern noted with parentheses	If the Search For field contains the pattern **(\b\w*)\.(\w*\b)** and the Replace With field contains the pattern **$1's extension is ".$2"**, Chapter09.txt would be replaced with **Chapter09's extension is ".txt"**

Controlling Whitespace

Whitespace refers to any portion of the page that doesn't contain text, images, or other objects. It includes the space between words and the space above and below paragraphs. This section introduces ways to adjust paragraph margins and the spacing between paragraphs.

Indenting text

In Dreamweaver, you cannot indent text as you do with a word processor. Tabs normally have no effect in HTML. One method to indent a paragraph's first line uses non-breaking spaces, which can be inserted with the keyboard shortcut Ctrl+Shift+spacebar (Command+Shift+spacebar). Non-breaking spaces are an essential part of any Web designer's palette because they provide single-character spacing—often necessary to nudge an image or other object into alignment. You've already seen the code for a non-breaking space— —that Dreamweaver inserts between the <p>...</p> tag pair to make the line visible.

You can optionally configure Dreamweaver to insert non-breaking spaces in situations where it would normally ignore the spaces that you type. For example, whenever you type more than one space in a row, or when you enter a space at the beginning of a paragraph, HTML, and therefore Dreamweaver, ignores the space. However, if you choose Edit ⇨ Preferences and select the Allow Multiple Consecutive Spaces option in the General category, Dreamweaver will insert non-breaking spaces automatically as you type. If you find yourself inserting non-breaking spaces frequently, enabling this option speeds up your work. Use care when enabling this feature, though. If you are used to having extra spaces ignored, you may inadvertently add undesired spaces within your text.

Tip   If you normally create paper documentation, you may be used to adding two spaces between sentences. For online documentation, use only a single space after a period. Adding two spaces not only goes against the norm, it's more work, and can increase your file size by inserting all those extra non-breaking spaces!

Dreamweaver offers other methods for inserting a non-breaking space. You can enter its character code— —directly into the HTML code or you can use the Non-Breaking Space button in the Characters category of the Insert bar. You can also style your text as preformatted; this technique is discussed later in this chapter.

Tip   Cascading Style Sheets offer another method for indenting the first line of a paragraph. You can set an existing HTML tag, such as <p>, to any indent amount using the Text Indent option found on the Block panel of the Style Sheet dialog box. Be aware, however, that style sheets are only partially implemented in browsers. A full discussion of text indent and other style sheet controls is covered in Chapter 20.

Working with preformatted text

Browsers ignore formatting niceties considered irrelevant to page content: tabs, extra line feeds, indents, and added whitespace. You can force browsers to read all the text, including whitespace, exactly as you have entered it by applying the preformatted tag pair, <pre>...</pre>. This tag pair directs the browser to keep any additional whitespace encountered within the text. By default, the <pre>...</pre> tag pair also renders its content with a monospace font such as Courier. For these reasons, the <pre>...</pre> tag pair was used to lay out text in columns in the early days of HTML, before tables were widely available.

You can apply the preformatted tag through the Property inspector, the Insert bar, or the menus. Regardless of the technique for inserting preformatted text, it is easiest to work in Code and Design views, applying changes in Code view and seeing the result in Design view. Select the text, or position the cursor where you want the preformatted text to begin; then use one of these methods to insert the <pre>...</pre> tags:

✦ In the Property inspector, open the Format list box and choose Preformatted.

✦ On the Insert bar, choose the Text category and then click the Preformatted Text button.

✦ Choose Text ⇨ Paragraph Format ⇨ Preformatted Text.

✦ Choose Insert ⇨ Text Objects ⇨ Preformatted Text.

The <pre> tag is a block element format, like the paragraph or the headings tags, rather than a style. This designation as a block element format has two important implications. First, you can't apply the <pre>...</pre> tag pair to part of a line; when you use this tag pair, the entire paragraph is altered. Second, you can apply styles to preformatted text — this enables you to increase the size or alter the font, but at the same time maintain the whitespace feature made possible with the <pre> tag. All text in Figure 7-10 uses the <pre> tag; the column on the left is the standard output with a monospace font; the column on the right uses a different font in a larger size.

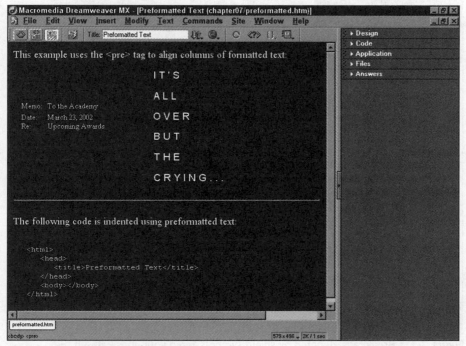

Figure 7-10: Preformatted text gives you full control over the line breaks, tabs, and other whitespace in your Web page.

The <br> tag

Just like headings, the paragraph tag falls into the class of HTML objects called *block elements*. As such, any text marked with the <p>...</p> tag pair is always rendered with an extra line above and below the text. To have a series of blank lines appear one after the other, use the break tag <br>.

Note   In XHTML documents, the break tag is coded as <br />. Dreamweaver inserts the correct tag based on the document type.

Break tags are used within block elements, such as headings and paragraphs, to provide a line break where the <br> is inserted. Dreamweaver provides two ways to insert a <br> tag: Choose the Line Break button from the Characters category of the Insert bar, or use the keyboard shortcut Shift+Enter (Shift+Return).

Figure 7-11 demonstrates the effect of the <br> tag. The menu items in Column A on the left are the result of using the <br> tag within a paragraph. In Column B on the right, paragraph tags alone are used. The <h1> heading is also split at the top with a break tag to avoid the insertion of an unwanted line.

Line Break
button

Line Break
symbol

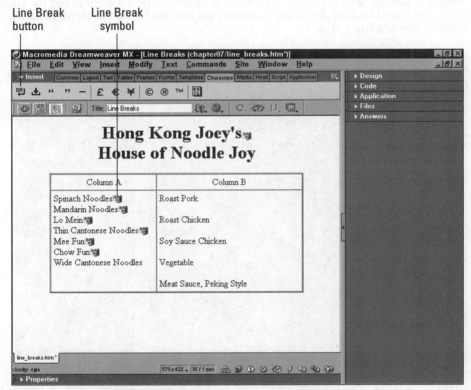

Figure 7-11: Break tags, denoted by shield symbols, wrap your lines without the additional line spacing created by <p> tags.

You can enable Dreamweaver to mark <br> tags with a symbol: a gold shield with the letters BR and the standard Enter/Return symbol. To make the break symbol visible, you must first choose Edit ➪ Preferences and select the Line Breaks checkbox in the Invisible Elements category. Then show invisible elements by choosing View ➪ Visual Aids ➪ Invisible Elements.

Other whitespace tags

If you can't get the alignment effect you want through the regular text options available in Dreamweaver, two other tags can affect whitespace: <nobr> and <wbr>. Although a tad on the obscure side, these tags can be just the ticket in certain circumstances. Let's see how they work.

Overcoming Line-Spacing Difficulties

Line spacing is a major issue and a common problem for Web designers. A design often calls for lines to be tightly spaced, but also to be of various sizes. If you use the break tag to separate your lines, you get the tight spacing required, but you won't be able to make each line a different heading size. As far as HTML and your browser are concerned, the text is still one block element, no matter how many line breaks are inserted. If, on the other hand, you make each line a separate paragraph or heading, the line spacing will be unattractively "open."

You can use one of several workarounds for this problem. First, if you're using line breaks, you can alter the size of each line by selecting it and choosing a different font size, either from the Property inspector or the Text ⇨ Size menu.

A second option renders all the text as a graphics object and inserts it as an image. This gives you total control over the font's appearance and line spacing, at the cost of added download time.

For a third possible solution, look at the section on preformatted text in this chapter. Because you can apply styles to a preformatted text block (which can include line breaks and extra whitespace), you can alter the size, color, and font of each line, if necessary.

Ultimately, the best solution is to use Cascading Style Sheets (CSS). The majority of browsers now in use support line spacing through CSS; however, if 3.0 browser compatibility is a site requirement, you'll have to use one of the other methods outlined here.

The <nobr> tag

Most of the time, you want the user's browser to handle word-wrapping chores automatically. Occasionally, however, you may need to make sure that a particular string of text is rendered in one piece. For these situations, you can use the no break tag <nobr>. Any text that appears between the opening and closing tag pair — <nobr>...</nobr> — is displayed in one continuous line. If the line of text is wider than the current browser window, a horizontal scroll bar automatically appears along the bottom of the browser.

The <nobr> tag is not defined in any version of the HTML specification, but it is supported through the Netscape and Microsoft browsers. The <nobr>...</nobr> tag pair must be entered by hand into your HTML code. Use the <nobr> tag under very special circumstances.

The <wbr> tag

The companion to the <nobr> tag is the word break tag <wbr>. Similar to a soft hyphen in a word processing program, the <wbr> tag tells the browser where to break a word, if necessary. When used within <nobr> tags, <wbr> is the equivalent of telling a browser, "Keep all this text in one line, but if you have to break it, break it here." The <wbr> tag has no corresponding closing tag. The following example breaks before the word *this* if the browser window is sized such that the line must wrap.

```
<nobr>In some circles, <wbr>this could be considered a lot of text.</nobr>
```

Like the <nobr> tag, <wbr> is not defined in the HTML specification, but it is supported by Netscape and Microsoft browsers. The tag must be entered by hand via the Quick Tag Editor, Code view, the Code inspector, or your external editor.

Importing Word HTML

Microsoft Word has offered an option to save its documents as HTML since the release of Word 97. Unfortunately, Microsoft's version of HTML output is, at best, highly idiosyncratic. Although you could always open a Word HTML file in Dreamweaver, if you ever had to modify the page—which you almost always do—it took so long to find your way through the convoluted code that you were almost better off building the page from scratch. Fortunately, that's no longer the case with Dreamweaver.

Tip   Another reason to import an HTML file exported from Word, rather than just directly opening and editing it in Dreamweaver, is file size. Results vary, but importing a Word HTML document can reduce its size by half, or even more.

The capability to import Word HTML is a key workflow enhancement for Dreamweaver. Dreamweaver can successfully import and automatically clean up files from Microsoft Word 97, Word 98, Word 2000, or Word 2002. The cleanup takes place automatically upon import, but you can also finely tune the modifications that Dreamweaver makes to the file. Moreover, you can even apply the current Code Format profile from Preferences so that the HTML is styled to look like native Dreamweaver code.

Naturally, before you can import a Word HTML file, you must create one. To export a document in HTML format in Word 97/98, you choose File ➪ Save as HTML; in Word 2000/2002, the command has changed to File ➪ Save as Web Page. Although the wording change may seem to be a move toward less jargon, it's significant what Word actually exports. Starting with Word 2000 (and all the Office 2000 products), Microsoft heartily embraced the XML standard and uses a combination of standard HTML and custom XML code throughout its exported Web pages. For example, here's the opening tag from a Word 2000 document, saved as a Web page:

```
<html xmlns:o="urn:schemas-microsoft-com:office:office"
xmlns:w="urn:schemas-microsoft-com:office:word"
xmlns:dt="uuid:C2F41010-65B3-11d1-A29F-00AA00C14882"
xmlns="http://www.w3.org/TR/REC-html40">
```

Dreamweaver alters the preceding code to

```
<html>
```

If you accept the defaults, importing a Word HTML file is a two-step affair:

1. Choose File ➪ Import ➪ Word HTML. When the Select Word HTML File to Import dialog box opens, navigate and select the file that you exported from Word.

   Dreamweaver imports the file and opens the Clean Up Word HTML dialog box. Dreamweaver detects whether the HTML file was exported from Word 97/98 or 2000/2002 and changes the interface options accordingly.

Caution   If Dreamweaver can't determine what version of Word generated the file, an alert appears. Although Dreamweaver will still try to clean up the code, it may not function correctly. The same alert appears if you inadvertently select a standard non-HTML Word document.

2. Select options as desired and click OK to confirm the import operation. Dreamweaver cleans up the code according to the options you've selected; for large documents, you may have to wait a noticeable amount of time for this operation to complete. If the Show Log on Completion option is selected, Dreamweaver informs you of the modifications made.

For most purposes, accepting the defaults is the best way to quickly bring in your Word HTML files. However, because Web designers have a wide range of code requirements, Dreamweaver provides a full set of options for tailoring the Word-to-Dreamweaver transformation to your liking. Two different sets of options exist: one for documents saved from Word 97/98 and one for those saved from Word 2000/2002. The different sets of options can be seen on the Detailed tab of the Import Word HTML dialog box; the Basic tab is the same for both file types. Table 7-8 details the Basic tab options, the Word 97/98 options, and the Word 2000/2002 options.

Table 7-8: Import Word HTML Options

Option	Description
Basic	
Remove all Word specific markup	Deletes all Word-specific tags, including Word XML, conditional tags, empty paragraphs, and margins in `<style>` tags
Clean up CSS	Deletes Word-specific CSS code, including inline CSS styles where styles are nested, Microsoft Office (mso) designated styles, non-CSS style declarations, CSS style attributes from tables, and orphaned (unused) style definitions
Clean up <font> tags	Deletes `<font>` tags that set the default body text to an absolute font size
Fix invalidly nested tags	Deletes tags surrounding paragraph and block-level tags
Set background color	Adds a background color to the page. Word normally doesn't supply one. The default added color is white (#ffffff). Colors can be entered as hexadecimal triplets with a leading hash mark or as a valid color name, such as `red`.
	Dreamweaver sets the background color by adding the `bgcolor` attribute to the `<body>` tag. If you do not have to support older browsers, you may instead wish to assign a background color using Cascading Style Sheets, described in Chapter 20.
Apply source formatting	Formats the imported code according to the guidelines of the current Code Format profile set in Preferences
Show log on completion	Displays a dialog box that lists all alterations when the process is complete
Detailed Options for Word 97/98	
Remove Word specific markup	Enables the general clean-up of Word-inserted tags
Word meta and link tags from <head>	Specifically enables Dreamweaver to remove Word-specific `<meta>` and `<link>` tags from the `<head>` section of a document
Clean up <font> tags	Enables the general clean-up of `<font>` tags

Continued

Table 7-8: *(continued)*

Option	Description
Convert size [7-1] to	Specifies which tag, if any, is substituted for a `<font size=n>` tag. Options are
	* `<h1>` through `<h6>`
	* `<font size=1>` through `<font size=7>`
	* Default size
	* Don't change

Detailed Options for Word 2000/2002

Option	Description
Remove Word specific markup	Enables the general clean-up of Word-inserted tags.
XML from <html> tag	Deletes the Word-generated XML from the `<html>` tag
Word meta and link tags from <head>	Specifically enables Dreamweaver to remove Word-specific `<meta>` and `<link>` tags from the `<head>` section of a document
Word XML markup	Enables the general clean-up of Word-inserted XML tags
<![if...]><![endif]> conditional tags and their contents	Removes all conditional statements
Remove empty paragraphs and margins from styles	Deletes `<p>` tags without a closing `</p>`, empty `<p></p>` pairs, and styles tags including margin attributes — for example, `style='margin-top:0in'`
Clean up CSS	Enables the general clean-up of Word-inserted CSS tags
Remove inline CSS styles when possible	Deletes redundant information in nested styles
Remove any style attribute that starts with "mso"	Eliminates Microsoft Office (mso) specific attributes
Remove any non-CSS style declaration	Deletes nonstandard style declarations
Remove all CSS styles from table rows and cells	Eliminates style information from `<table>`, `<tr>`, and `<td>` tags
Remove all unused style definitions	Deletes any declared styles that are not referenced in the page

You don't have to remember to run the Import Word HTML command to take advantage of Dreamweaver's clean-up features. If you've already opened a document saved as Word HTML, choose Commands ➪ Clean Up Word HTML to gain access to the exact same dialog box for the existing page.

Styling Your Text

Initially, the Internet was intended to make scientific data widely accessible. Soon it became apparent that even raw data could benefit from being styled contextually, without detracting from the Internet's openness and universality. Over the short history of HTML, text styles have become increasingly important, and the W3C has sought to keep a balance between substance and style.

Dreamweaver enables the Web designer to apply the most popular HTML styles directly through the program's menus and Property inspector. Less prevalent styles can be inserted through the integrated text editors or by hand. All the styling techniques covered in this section can be applied to dynamically inserted text.

Depicting various styles

HTML contains two types of style tags that are philosophically different from each other: logical tags and physical tags. The physical tags describe what text looks like; these include tags for bold, italic, and underlined text. HTML's logical styles denote what the text represents (such as code, a citation, or something typed from the keyboard) rather than what the text will actually look like. The eventual displayed appearance of logical styles is up to the viewer's browser.

Logical styles can be described as structural. They are useful when you are working with documents from different sources — reports from different research laboratories around the country, for instance — and you want a certain conformity of style. If you are trying to achieve a particular look using logical styles, you should consider using the Cascading Style Sheets feature instead of, or in addition to, logical styles. You can apply logical style tags and then use Cascading Style Sheets to define how that style will look when viewed in a browser.

Cross-Reference

The styles that can be applied through regular HTML are just the tip of the iceberg compared to the possibilities available using Cascading Style Sheets. For details about using this feature, see Chapter 20.

Whereas logical styles are utilitarian; physical styles such as boldface and italic are decorative or presentational. With the advent of Cascading Style Sheets, use of the physical style tags is no longer the preferred method of styling text. However, physical tags are still supported and are still very widely used. Even with Cascading Style Sheets, both physical and logical styles have their uses in material published on today's Web. In Dreamweaver, logical and physical style tags can be accessed by choosing Text ⇨ Style and selecting from the available style name options. A checkmark appears next to the selected tags. Style tags can be nested (put inside one another), and you can mix logical and physical tags within a word, line, or document. You can have a bold, strikethrough, variable style; or you can have an underlined cited style. (Both variable and cite are particular logical styles covered later in this section.)

Note

You can also add the most commonly used styles: bold, italic, strong and emphasis by clicking the appropriate button in the Text category of the Insert bar.

Figure 7-12 compares how styles are rendered in Dreamweaver, Internet Explorer 6.0, and Netscape Communicator 6.2. Although the various renderings are mostly the same, notice the difference between how the Keyboard style is rendered in Dreamweaver (far left) and in either browser. The various styles may be rendered differently in other browsers and other browser versions.

Two of the physical style tags — bold and italic — are controlled by a preferences setting. Although you can use the <b> and <i> tags to style text, it is considered better practice to use the equivalent logical tags, <strong> and <em>. Dreamweaver allows you to specify which tags to use via the "Use <strong> and <em> in place of <b> and <i>" option in the General category of Preferences. If this option is checked (the default), <strong> and <em> tags are used to code bold or italic text, respectively; if the option is clear, <b> and <i> tags are used.

To actually apply bold or italic formatting using either the logical or physical tags, select the text and then click the Bold or Italic button on the Text Property inspector, or use the keyboard shortcuts (Ctrl+B or Command+B, and Ctrl+I or Command+I, respectively). Buttons for bold, italic, strong, and emphasis are also available in the Text category of the Insert bar. If the General Preference setting discussed above is set, then the Bold button on the Insert bar does the same thing as the Strong button, and the Italic button inserts the same code as the Emphasis button.

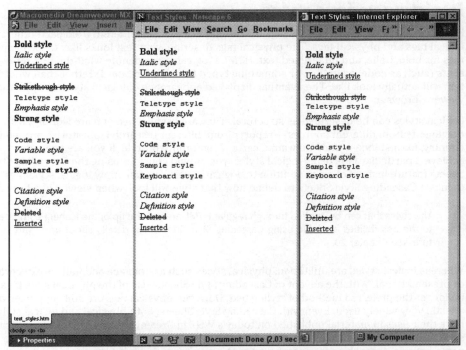

Figure 7-12: In this comparison chart, the various renderings of style tags are from Dreamweaver, Netscape Communicator 6.2, and Internet Explorer 6.0 (from left to right, respectively).

Caution One physical style, the underline tag, <u>, is available only through the Text ⇨ Style menu. Use this tag with caution. By default, browsers use underlining to designate links; if you style text with an underline, users will expect that text to link somewhere. It's good practice to restrict use of underlining to hotspots, and to avoid underlining as a way to highlight text, even for headings.

Both physical and logical style tags are described in Table 7-9.

Table 7-9: Text Style Tags

Style	Tag	Description
Bold	`<b>`	Text is rendered with a bold style.
Italic	`<i>`	Text is rendered with an italic style.
Underline	`<u>`	Text is rendered underlined.
Strikethrough	`<s>`	Used primarily in edited documents to depict edited text. Usually rendered with a line through the text.
Teletype	`<tt>`	Used to represent an old-style typewriter. Rendered in a monospace font such as Courier.
Emphasis	`<em>`	Used to accentuate certain words relative to the surrounding text. Most often rendered in italic.
Strong	`<strong>`	Used to strongly accentuate certain words relative to the surrounding text. Most often rendered in boldface.
Code	`<code>`	Used to depict programming code, usually in a monospace font.
Sample	`<samp>`	Used to display characters in a literal sequence, usually in a monospace font.
Variable	`<var>`	Used to mark variables in programming code. Most often displayed in italics.
Keyboard	`<kbd>`	Used to indicate what should be user input. Often shown in a monospace font, sometimes in boldface.
Citation	`<cite>`	Used to mark citations, references, and titles. Most often displayed in italic.
Definition	`<dfn>`	Used to denote the first, defining instance of a term. Usually displayed in italic.
Deleted	`<del>`	Used to denote deleted text, to aid in document authoring and editing. You can often find these tags in documents imported from Word HTML files that used the Track Changes feature. Although not fully supported in some browser versions, this style is typically depicted as a line through the text.
Inserted	`<ins>`	Used to denote inserted text. Like the Deleted style, this is used during the authoring process to keep track of changes. You can often find these tags in documents imported from Word HTML files that used the Track Changes feature. The style is usually depicted as underlined text.

Using the `<address>` tag

Currently, Dreamweaver does not support one useful style tag: the `<address>` tag. Rendered as italic text by browsers, the `<address>`...`</address>` tag pair often marks the signature and e-mail address of a Web page's creator.

Note   An easy way to do this in Dreamweaver is to use the Quick Tag Editor. Select your text and then press Ctrl+T (Command+T) to automatically enter Wrap Tag mode. If Tag Hints is enabled, all you have to do is start typing **address,** and press Enter (Return) twice to accept the hint and confirm the tag. In Code view and the Code inspector, the `<address>...</address>` tag pair is also available as a Code Hint.

If you're applying the `<address>` tag to multiple lines, use `<br>` tags to form line breaks. The following example shows the proper use of the `<address>` tags:

```
<address><p>The President<br>
1600 Pennsylvania Avenue<br>
Washington, DC 20001</p></address>
```

This preceding code is shown on a Web browser as follows:

> *The President*
>
> *1600 Pennsylvania Avenue*
>
> *Washington, DC 20001*

Tip   To remove a standard style, highlight the styled text, choose Text ⇨ Style, and select the name of the style you want to remove. The checkmark disappears from the style name. To remove a nonstandard tag such as `<address>`, choose the tag in the Tag Selector and right-click (Control+click) to open the context menu, and select Remove Tag.

Adding abbreviations and acronyms

Two other tags worth noting designate abbreviations, `<abbr>...</abbr>`, and acronyms, `<acronym>...</acronym>`. The abbreviation or acronym is enclosed within the tag pair. Both tags include a `title` attribute, which is used to specify the full text of the abbreviation or acronym. The following code shows examples of both tags:

```
<abbr title="Incorporated">Inc.</abbr>
<acronym title="Object-oriented Programming">OOP</acronym>
```

The `<abbr>` and `<acronym>` tags are relatively new, and are not yet widely used. These tags are not intended to actually change the visual style of the text in a browser, but instead allow programs that process the document to clearly identify acronyms and abbreviations. For example, in the future, words marked as abbreviations could allow non-visual browsers to read the expanded word, rather than sounding out the abbreviation. If designated as an abbreviation, the letters *PA* could be read as *Pennsylvania* rather than as the word *pa*. In the future, this tag could also be used to provide alternate text for search engines, spell checkers, and translation programs.

In Dreamweaver, you can insert acronyms or abbreviations by clicking the Acronym or Abbreviation button on the Text category of the Insert bar. You can also choose the appropriate command from the Insert ⇨ Text Objects menu. These commands open a dialog box where you can enter the expanded text for the acronym or abbreviation.

Using HTML Styles

In the world of Web design, consistency is a good thing. A site in which headings, subheads, and body text are consistent from page to page is far easier for the visitor to grasp quickly than one in which each page has its own style. Although the best approach for a consistently designed site may be the use of Cascading Style Sheets (CSS), that approach requires 4.0 and later browsers, and some clients are not willing to disregard potential Web visitors using older software.

In terms of Web design best practices, using CSS is a much-preferred way to style your text. To learn more about CSS, see Chapter 20.

To bridge the gap between old and new — and to make it easier to repeatedly apply the same set of tags — Dreamweaver uses HTML Styles. HTML Styles are similar to CSS in that you define a custom style for text and give it any attributes you want: font name, size, color, format, and so on. You can apply that style to either a selection or an entire block of text. The primary difference is that with HTML Styles, Dreamweaver adds the necessary standard HTML tags, instead of CSS style declarations, to re-create your style. In other words, if you always set your legal disclaimers in Verdana at a –1 size in a deep red color, you can define your "legal" style once and repeatedly apply it with one step, anywhere on the site.

HTML Styles, however, are not a replacement for CSS styles, and you should keep in mind some important differences:

✦ Modifying an HTML Style definition affects only subsequent applications of the style. When a CSS style is altered, the change is immediately seen wherever the style has been applied on the current page as well as in all future applications.

✦ HTML Styles use standard text tags and cannot, therefore, create some of the special effects possible in CSS. For example, you cannot create a HTML Style that eliminates the underline from a link or changes the leading of a paragraph.

✦ Although defined HTML Styles are accessible from anywhere within a site, they are applied on a document-by-document basis, whereas with CSS, an external style sheet can be defined and linked to pages anywhere on your site.

✦ HTML Styles tend to add more code to your page than Cascading Style Sheets, increasing file size. This is particularly true if you repeatedly apply the same style many times within your document.

Even with these differences, however, HTML Styles facilitate the designer's workflow and are extremely easy to use.

In the remainder of this section, when I refer to a style or styles, I'm referring to HTML Styles. CSS style references are designated as such.

Defining HTML styles

Before applying HTML styles to your text, you have to define the styles. Dreamweaver gives you a number of methods to define a style:

✦ **Style by Example:** Create a new style from formatted text onscreen.

✦ **Build a New Style:** Select all the desired attributes for your selection or paragraph style and try it out right away on selected text.

✦ **Modify an Existing Style:** Edit another custom style to your liking. You can even duplicate the style first, so both old and new versions are available.

All style definitions are managed in the Define HTML Style dialog box, shown in Figure 7-13. How the dialog box is opened depends on which method you're using to create or modify your style.

✦ To create a style by example, select tags you want to include in the style from the Document window or the Tag Selector and then choose the New Style button from the HTML Styles panel. This opens the Define HTML Style dialog box with some settings preset to match the text selected in the Document window. Note, however, that some of the preset selections may not be immediately obvious; click the Other button to see additional settings.

✦ To create a style from the ground up, position the cursor in an unstyled paragraph and choose the New Style button on the HTML Styles panel.

✦ To create a new style built on an existing one, select the style and then, from the context-sensitive menu of the HTML Styles panel, select Duplicate.

✦ To modify an existing style, double-click its name in the HTML Styles panel list.

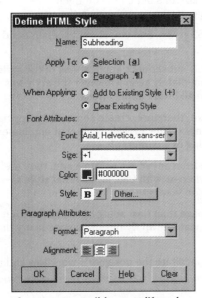

Figure 7-13: Build or modify styles in the Define HTML Style dialog box.

To define an HTML Style, follow these steps:

1. Open the Define HTML Style dialog box using one of the previously described methods.

2. Enter a unique name for your style, if creating a new one.

3. Choose whether your style is to apply to a selection or a paragraph.

4. Select whether your style will add to the existing style or clear the existing style.

5. Choose the desired font attributes:

   • Font

   • Size

   • Color

- Style: Bold, Italic, or Bold-Italic

- Other . . . (Additional Optional Styles): Underline, Strikethrough, Teletype, Emphasis, Strong, Code, Variable, Sample, Keyboard, Citation, Definition, Deleted, Inserted

6. If defining a paragraph style, select from the following attribute options:

- Format: None, Paragraph, Heading 1 through Heading 6, or Preformatted

- Alignment: Right, Center, Left.

7. Click OK when you're done.

Tip   To start over at any time, select the Clear button.

Applying HTML styles

The HTML Styles panel is the tool you'll use when working with HTML styles. The HTML Styles panel, shown in Figure 7-14, displays all currently available styles, and enables you to apply or remove style formatting, define new styles, edit existing styles, or remove styles from the panel.

Selection style

Paragraph style

Add-on style

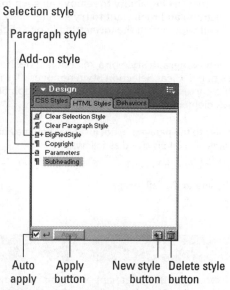

Auto   Apply   New style Delete style
apply   button   button   button

Figure 7-14: Manage your standard formatting through the HTML Styles panel.

HTML Styles are divided into two distinct types: paragraph styles and selection styles. A paragraph style affects an entire block element, whether it is a single heading, a paragraph, or another block element such as a block quote. Paragraph styles are designated with a ¶ symbol in the HTML Styles panel. A paragraph style is applied to the entire current block element, whether the cursor has selected the text or is just within the block. A selection style, on the other hand, applies formatting only to selected text. Selection styles are marked in the HTML Styles panel with an underlined, lowercased *a*, like this: <u>a</u>.

It's possible for both paragraph and selection styles to either add the new formatting to the existing style or clear the existing style before adding the new formatting. The default behavior is for existing formatting to be removed; if the style is to be added, a small plus sign (+) is shown in front of the style name.

To apply an HTML Style, follow these steps:

1. Open the HTML Styles panel by selecting Window ➪ HTML Styles or by pressing the keyboard shortcut, Ctrl+F11 (Command+F11).

2. To apply a style to the currently selected text, choose any designated (<u>a</u>) HTML Style.

Tip   It's easiest to always have the Auto Apply option selected so that your choices are applied immediately; if this option is not selected, click the Apply button.

3. To apply a style to the current block element, choose any so-designated (¶) HTML Style.

Removing HTML styles

As useful as applying new HTML Styles is, I find that the capability to remove all such formatting is even more beneficial. I often style a paragraph and then want to try a completely different approach—with the HTML Styles panel, I can wipe out all the formatting in one click and start fresh.

As with applying styles, you can remove either a paragraph style or a selection style. Both are available as the first items in the HTML Styles panel. Clear Selection Style removes all <font> and other text formatting tags surrounding the current selection, and Clear Paragraph Style eliminates all such tags from the current block element.

Caution   Removing a paragraph style removes all styles to the paragraph, not just ones you may have added via the HTML Styles panel. For example, if a line is styled as follows:

```
<h1><font color="#FFFF00">Welcome</font></h1>
```

selecting Clear Paragraph Style converts the line to the following:

```
<p>Welcome</p>
```

Moving HTML Styles from Site to Site

Custom HTML styles are available from any page in your site. But what happens if you start a new site? Do you have to re-create your custom styles again? No: You can easily transfer styles you've created for one site to another just by copying the right file.

The information describing the custom HTML styles is stored in each site's Library folder in a file named styles.xml. To transfer the HTML styles, just copy the styles.xml file from one site's Library folder to the Library folder for another site. Library folders are created within a site when they are first needed, so if you've just defined your site, the Library folder may not yet exist. You can, however, safely create it within the local site root and copy your styles.xml file into the folder.

The Clear Selection Style command does not require that the formatting tags be adjacent to the selection. If you select some text in the middle of a paragraph styled in a particular color and font, choosing Clear Selection Style inserts appropriate tags before and after the selection so that the selection has no style whatsoever The surrounding text, however, remains styled. A before and after view of the process is shown in Figure 7-15.

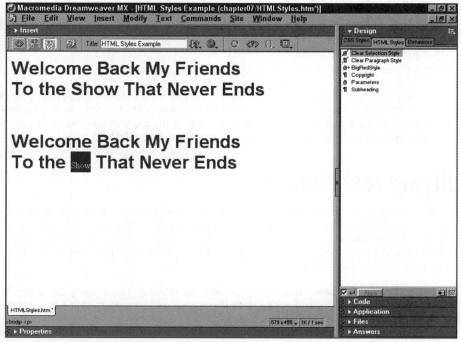

Figure 7-15: You can remove all styling from a bit of text and keep the surrounding styling with the Clear Selection Style command.

If you no longer wish to have a defined style displayed in the HTML Styles panel, select that style and choose the Delete Style button. Alternatively, select the style and choose Delete from the context-sensitive menu on the panel.

Changing default styles

If you find yourself using the same HTML Styles in all or most of your work—and don't want to keep copying the styles.xml file from site to site as described in the sidebar "Moving HTML Styles from Site to Site"—you can define default styles with which Dreamweaver opens. The default styles must be contained in a file named defaultStyles.xml, which must be saved in the Configuration folder. The file is a series of XML tags that look like the following:

```
<mm:style name="Bold" type="char" apply="add" bold />
<mm:style name="Caption" format="p" align="center" apply="replace" ⊃
font="Arial, Helvetica, sans-serif" size="2" color="#808080" bold italic />
```

Although you could write-in the style by hand, following the given format, there's an easier way:

1. Create the styles within a site that you want to add to the Dreamweaver default HTML Styles.

2. Copy the styles.xml file from your site's Library folder to the Dreamweaver Configuration folder.

3. Rename the copied file as defaultStyles.xml.

4. Launch Dreamweaver again.

Your new styles will be available with every new site.

Tip   To add more default styles, use a text editor to cut and paste style definitions from your site-specific styles.xml file to defaultStyles.xml. When copying, notice that the name of the style is the first attribute of the XML tag. Be sure to get all of the tag, including the closing />. You must restart Dreamweaver for the new default styles to be available.

Modifying Text Format

As a Web designer, you easily spend at least as much time adjusting your text as you do getting it into your Web pages. Luckily, Dreamweaver puts most of the tools you need for this task right at your fingertips. All the text-formatting options are available through the Text Property inspector. Instead of hand-coding `<font>`, `<blockquote>`, and alignment tags, just select your text and click a button.

Note   In HTML text formatting today, programmers are moving toward using Cascading Style Sheets and away from hard-coding text with `<font>` and other tags. Both 4.0+ versions of the major Web browsers support Cascading Style Sheets to some extent, and Internet Explorer has had some support since version 3.0. To support the widest range of browser versions, Web designers continue to use the character-specific tags, sometimes in combination with Cascading Style Sheets. Even with Cascading Style Sheets gaining widespread acceptance, you'll probably still need to apply tags on the "local level" occasionally.

Adjusting font size

The six HTML heading types enable you to assign relative sizes to a line or to an entire paragraph. In addition, HTML gives you a finer degree of control through the `size` attribute of the font tag. In contrast to publishing environments, both traditional and desktop, font size is not specified in HTML with points. Rather, the `<font>` tag enables you to choose one of seven different explicit sizes that the browser can render (absolute sizing), or you can select one relative to the page's basic font. Figure 7-16 shows the default absolute and relative sizes, compared to a more page designer–friendly point chart (accomplished with Dreamweaver's Cascading Style Sheets features).

Which way should you go—absolute or relative? Some designers think that relative sizing gives them more options. As you can see by the chart in Figure 7-16, browsers are limited to displaying seven different sizes no matter what—unless you're using Cascading Style Sheets. Relative sizing does give you additional flexibility, though, because you can resize all the fonts in an entire Web page with one command. Absolute sizes, however, are more straightforward to use and can be coded in Dreamweaver without any additional HTML programming. Once again, it's the designer's choice.

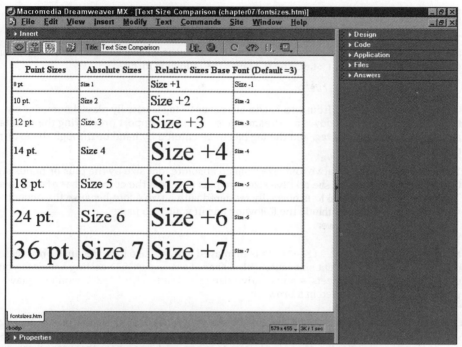

Figure 7-16: This chart shows the relationships between the various font sizes in an HTML browser as compared to "real-world" point sizes.

Absolute size

You can assign an absolute font size through either the Property inspector or the menus. In both cases, you choose a value, 1 (smallest) through 7 (largest), to which you want to resize your text; you might note that this order is the reverse of the heading sizes, which range from H1 to H6, largest to smallest.

To use the Property inspector to pick an absolute font size, follow these steps:

1. Select your text.

2. In the Property inspector, open the Size drop-down list of options. If the Size drop-down list is not visible on the Text Property inspector, click the Toggle CSS/HTML Mode icon, located to the right of the Format drop-down list.

3. Choose a value from 1 to 7.

To pick an absolute font size from the menu, follow these steps:

1. Select your text.

2. Choose Text ➪ Size and pick a value from 1 to 7, or Default (which is 3).

Note   You can also click the Font Tag Editor button in the Text category of the Insert bar to adjust font size, color, and so on.

Relative size

To what exactly are relative font sizes relative? The default font size, of course. The advantage of relative font sizes is that you can alter a Web page's default font size with one command, the `<basefont>` tag. The tag takes the following form:

```
<basefont size="value">
```

where value is a number from 1 to 7. The `<basefont>` tag is usually placed immediately following the opening `<body>` tag. Dreamweaver does not support previewing the results of altering the `<basefont>` tag, and the tag has to be entered by hand or through the external editor.

You can distinguish a relative font size from an absolute font size by the plus or minus sign that precedes the value. The relative sizes are plus or minus the current `<basefont>` size. Thus, a `<font size= "+1">` is normally rendered with a size 4 font because the default `<basefont>` is 3. If you include the following line in your Web page

```
<basefont size="5">
```

text marked with a `<font size="+1">` is displayed with a size 6 font. Because browsers display only seven different size fonts with a `<basefont size="5">` setting — unless you're using Cascading Style Sheets — any relative size over `<font size="+2">` won't display differently when previewed in a browser.

Caution If you change the basefont value, some browsers will not correctly handle relative font sizes for text within tables. In this case, you should use absolute sizes. Also, Dreamweaver itself does not recognize the `<basefont>` tag; so to accurately see a page that uses relative sizes and the `<basefont>` tag, view it in a browser.

Relative font sizes can also be selected from either the Property inspector or the menus. To use the Property inspector to pick a relative font size, follow these steps:

1. Select your text or position the cursor where you want the new text size to begin.

2. In the Property inspector, open the Size drop-down list of options. If the Size drop-down list is not visible on the Text Property inspector, click the Toggle CSS/HTML Mode icon, located to the right of the Format drop-down list.

3. To increase the size of your text, choose a value from +1 through +7. To decrease the size of your text, choose a value from –1 to –7.

To pick a relative font size from the menus, follow these steps:

1. Select your text or position the cursor where you want the new text size to begin.

2. To increase the size of your text, choose Text ➪ Size Change and pick a value from +1 to +4. To decrease the size of your text, choose Text ➪ Size Change and pick a value from –1 to –3. Note that the full range of relative sizes (+1 to +7 and –1 to –7) is not available through the Size Change menu because Dreamweaver assumes the base font value is 3.

Adding font color

Unless you assign a color to text on your Web page, the browser uses its own default, typically black. To change the font color for the entire page, choose Modify ➪ Page Properties and select a new color from the Text Color swatch.

Dreamweaver's Color Pickers

Dreamweaver includes a color picker for selecting colors for all manner of HTML elements: text, table cells, and page background. Dreamweaver's color picker — in keeping with the Macromedia common user interface — offers a number of palettes from the context menu to choose your colors: Color Cubes, Continuous Tone, Windows OS, Mac OS, and Grayscale. The most common choices for Web designers are Color Cubes and Continuous Tone, both of which display the 216 Web-safe colors common to the Macintosh and Windows palettes.

After you've opened the text color picker by selecting the color box on the Property inspector, the cursor changes shape into an eyedropper. This eyedropper can sample colors from any of the displayed swatches or from any color onscreen. Simply click the color box and drag the eyedropper over any graphic to choose a color.

If you choose a color outside of the "safe" range, you have no assurances of how the color is rendered on a viewer's browser. Some systems select the closest color in RGB values; some use dithering (positioning two or more colors next to each other to simulate another color) to try to overcome the limitations of the current screen color depth. Therefore, be forewarned: If possible, stick with the browser-safe colors, especially when coloring text. Select the Snap to Web Safe option in the color picker's context menu to automatically convert the colors you choose to the closest browser-safe color.

Mac Users: The system color picker is brought up by clicking the System Color Picker button on the Dreamweaver color picker. The system color picker for Macintosh is far more elaborate than the one available for Windows. The Mac version has several color schemes to use: CMYK (for print-related colors), RGB (for screen-based colors), HTML (for Web-based colors) and Crayon (for kid-like colors). The CMYK, HTML, and RGB systems offer you color swatches and three or four sliders with text entry boxes; and they accept percentage values for RGB and CMYK, and hex values for HTML. Depending on your OS version, one or more of the color systems also have a Snap-to-Web color option for matching your chosen color to the closest browser-safe color. The Hue, Saturation, and Value (or Lightness) sliders also have color wheels.

You can also apply color to individual headings, words, or paragraphs that you have selected in Dreamweaver. The `<font>` tag goes to work again when you add color to selected elements of the page — this time, with the `color` attribute set to a particular value.

HTML color is expressed in either a hexadecimal color number or a color name. Dreamweaver understands both color names and hexadecimal color numbers. The hexadecimal color number is based on the color's red-green-blue value and is written as follows:

```
#FFFFFF
```

The preceding represents the color white. You can also use standard color names instead of the hexadecimal color numbers. A sample color code line follows:

```
I'm <font color="green">GREEN</font> with envy.
```

Again, you have several ways to add color to your text in Dreamweaver. Click the color box in the Property inspector to display the color picker, displaying a limited palette of colors. Clicking the System Color Picker button in the color picker enables you to choose from a full-spectrum Color dialog box.

Tip

If you want to apply the same color that you've already used elsewhere in your site to your text, you can display the Color category on the Assets panel (choose Window ➪ Assets). Just select the text in the Document window, select the color swatch in the Assets panel, and click the Apply button in the Assets panel.

If you approach your coloring task via the menus, the Text ➪ Color command takes you immediately to the Color dialog box. To use the Property inspector to color a range of text, follow these steps:

1. Select the text you want to color or position the cursor where you want the new text color to begin.

2. From the Property inspector, you can

   • Type a hexadecimal color number directly into the Text Color text box

   • Type a color name directly into the Text Color text box

   • Select the color box to open the color picker

Note

If the Color box and Color text box are not visible on the Text Property inspector, click the Toggle CSS/HTML Mode icon, located to the right of the Format drop-down list.

3. If you chose to type a color name or number directly into the Text Color text box, press Tab or click the Document window to see the color applied.

4. If you clicked the color box, select your color from the palette of colors available. As you move your pointer over the color swatches, Dreamweaver displays the color and the color's hexadecimal number above.

5. For a wider color selection, open the Color dialog box by selecting the System Color Picker icon in the upper-right corner of the color picker.

To access the full-spectrum color picker in Windows, follow these steps:

1. Select your text or position your cursor where you want the new text color to begin.

2. Choose Text ➪ Color to open the Color dialog box, shown in Figure 7-17.

3. Select one of the 48 preset standard colors from the color swatches on the left of the Color dialog box, or use either of the following methods:

   • Select a color by moving the Hue/Saturation pointer and the Luminance pointer.

   • Enter decimal values directly into either the Red, Green, and Blue boxes or the Hue, Saturation, and Luminance boxes.

4. If you create a custom color, you can add it to your palette by selecting Add to Custom Colors. You can add up to 16 custom colors.

5. Click OK when you are finished.

Caution

When you add a custom color to your palette in Windows, the new color swatch goes into the currently selected swatch or, if no swatch is selected, the next available swatch. Make sure you have selected an empty or replaceable swatch before selecting the Add to Custom Color button. To clear the custom colors, first set the palette to white by bringing the Luminance slider all the way to the top. Then, select the Add to Custom Color button until all the color swatch text boxes are empty.

Luminance pointer

Hue Saturation pointer

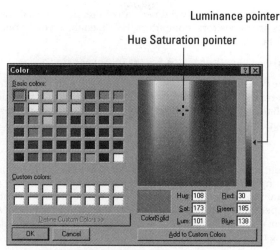

Figure 7-17: Use the Color dialog box in Windows to choose a color for your font outside of the browser-safe palette.

To access the full-spectrum color picker in Macintosh systems, follow these steps:

1. Select the text or position your cursor where you want the new text color to begin.

2. Choose Text ➪ Color to open the Color dialog box.

3. In the Macintosh color picker, the list of available pickers is displayed in the left pane, and each particular interface is shown in the right pane. Choose the desired color picker icon from the left pane and create the color desired in the right pane.

   The number and type of color pickers vary from system to system, depending on the version of the operating system and whether you've added any third-party color pickers.

4. When you've found the desired color, click OK.

Assigning a specific font

Along with size and color, you can also specify the typeface in which you want particular text to be rendered. Because of HTML's unique way of handling fonts, Dreamweaver uses a special method for choosing font names for a range of selected text. Before you learn how to change a typeface in Dreamweaver, you should more fully examine how fonts in HTML work.

About HTML fonts

Page layout designers can incorporate as many different fonts as available to their own systems. Web layout designers, on the other hand, can use only those fonts on their viewers' systems. If you designate a paragraph to be in Bodoni Bold Condensed, for instance, and put it on the Web, the paragraph is displayed with that font only if that exact font is on the user's system. Otherwise, the browser uses the default system font, which is often Times or Times New Roman.

Fonts are specified with the `<font>` tag, aided by the `face` attribute. Because a designer can never be certain of which fonts are on visitors' computers, HTML enables you to offer a number of options to the browser, as follows:

```
<font face="Arial, Helvetica, sans-serif">Swiss Maid Foundry</font>
```

The browser encountering the preceding tag first looks for the Arial font to render the enclosed text. If Arial isn't there, the browser looks for the next font in the list, which in this case is Helvetica. If it fails to find any of the specified fonts listed, the browser uses whichever font has been assigned to the category for the font — sans-serif in this case.

Selecting a font

The process for assigning a font name to a range of text is similar to that of assigning a font size or color. Instead of selecting one font name, however, you're usually selecting one font series. That series could contain three or more fonts, as previously explained. Font series are chosen from the Property inspector or through a menu item. Dreamweaver enables you to assign any font on your system — or even any font you can name — to a font series, as covered in the section "Editing the Font List," later in this chapter.

Font Categories

The W3C and some Web browsers recognize five main categories of fonts. Although serif and sans serif are most commonly used, the most recent versions of Internet Explorer and Netscape Navigator support all five generic font categories. In some browsers, the user can control which fonts display for each category.

The generic font categories, illustrated in the following figure, include the following:

✦ **Serif:** These fonts are distinguished by serifs, small cross strokes that appear at the ends of the main strokes of each character. Serif fonts tend to be slightly easier to read on paper, and more difficult when viewed on a screen; you may wish to limit use of serif fonts to headings or small blocks of text, unless your document is meant to be printed. Examples of serif fonts include Times New Roman, MS Georgia, and Garamond.

✦ **Sans-serif:** These fonts are "without serifs," meaning that the letters do not have finishing strokes at the tops and bottoms. Sans-serif fonts are easier to read on a screen, and are a good choice for large blocks of text within a Web page. Sans-serif fonts found on many computers include Arial, Helvetica, and Verdana.

✦ **Monospace:** The distinguishing characteristic of monospace fonts is that all their characters are the same width. These fonts are typically used to depict code samples or in other circumstances that require characters to be precisely aligned. Commonly used monospace fonts include Courier and Courier New.

✦ **Fantasy:** The characters in these fonts are highly decorative, but still represent letters and numbers (as opposed to pictures or symbols). Similar to Cursive fonts, you may not want to use these for large blocks of text, but rather to lend emphasis or to set the tone for a page. Examples of Fantasy fonts include Curlz MT, Critter, and Jokerman.

✦ **Cursive:** These fonts simulate writing in long hand, with strokes joining adjacent letters in a word. Because they can be difficult to read onscreen, you should avoid using large blocks of cursive text. These fonts are more appropriate for page banners or headings, to provide an elegant tone for a Web page. Examples of cursive fonts are Zapf-Chancery and Lucida Handwriting.

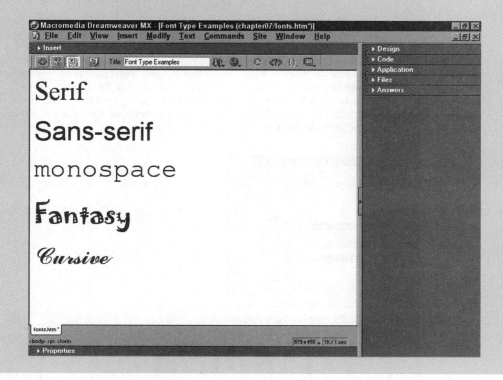

To assign a specific font series to your text, follow these steps:

1. Select the text or position your cursor where you want the new text font to begin.

2. From the Property inspector, open the drop-down list of font names. If the Font drop-down list is not visible on the Text Property inspector, click the Toggle CSS/HTML Mode icon, located to the right of the Format drop-down list. You can also display the list of fonts by choosing Text ➪ Font from the menu bar.

3. Select a font from the Font List. To return to the system font, choose Default Font from the list.

It's also possible to enter the font name or font series directly in the Property inspector's Font drop-down list box.

Tip   Font peculiarities are one of the main reasons to always test your Web pages on several plat-forms. Macintosh and Windows have different names for the same basic fonts (Arial in Windows is almost identical to Helvetica in Macintosh, for instance), and even the standard font sizes vary between the platforms. On the plus side, standard Microsoft fonts (Arial and Verdana, for example) are more common on the Macintosh since Mac OS 8.1, but differences still exist. Overall, PC fonts are larger than fonts on a Macintosh. Be sure to check out your page on as many systems as possible before finalizing your design.

Editing the Font List

With the Edit Font List dialog box, Dreamweaver gives you a point-and-click interface for building your font lists. After the Edit Font List dialog box is open, you can delete an existing font series, add a new one, or change the order of the list so your favorite ones are on top. Figure 7-18 shows the sections of the Edit Font List dialog box: the current Font List, the Available Fonts on your system, and the Chosen Fonts. The Chosen Fonts are the individual fonts that you've selected to be incorporated into a font series.

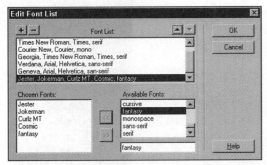

Figure 7-18: Dreamweaver's Edit Font List dialog box gives you considerable control over the fonts that you can add to your Web page.

Let's step through the process of constructing a new font series and adding it to the font list:

1. To open the Edit Font List dialog box, either expand the Font drop-down list in the Property inspector and choose Edit Font List, or select Text ⇨ Font ⇨ Edit Font List.

2. If the Chosen Fonts box is not empty, clear the Chosen Fonts box by selecting the Add (+) button at the top of the dialog box. You can also scroll down to the bottom of the current Font List and select "(Add fonts in list below)."

3. Select a font from the Available Fonts list. The font categories, such as sans-serif and cursive, appear at the end of the available fonts list.

4. Click the << button to transfer the selected font to the Chosen Fonts list.

5. To remove a font you no longer want or have chosen in error, highlight it in the Chosen Fonts list and select the >> button.

6. Repeat Steps 3 through 5 until the Chosen Fonts list contains the alternative fonts desired.

7. If you want to add another, separate font series, repeat Steps 2 through 6.

8. Click OK when you are finished adding fonts.

To change the order in which font series are listed in the Font List, follow these steps:

1. In the Edit Font List dialog box, select the font series that you want to move.

2. If you want to move the series higher up the list, select the up arrow button at the top right of the Font List. If you want to move the series lower down the list, select the down arrow button.

To remove a font series from the current Font List, highlight it and select the Remove (–) button at the top-left of the list.

Remember that you need to have the fonts on your system to make them a part of your font list. To add a font unavailable on your computer, type the name of the font into the text box below the Available Fonts list and press Enter (Return).

Aligning text

You can easily align text in Dreamweaver, just as you can in a traditional word processing program. HTML supports the alignment of text to the left or right margin, or in the center of the browser window. Another option, called Justify, causes text to be flush against both left and right margins, creating a block-like appearance. The Justify value is supported in browsers 4.0 and later on Windows platforms; Internet Explorer 4.0 running on a Mac does not support the Justify value.

Like a word processing program, Dreamweaver aligns text one paragraph at a time. You can't left-align one word, center the next, and then right-align the third word in the same paragraph.

To align text, use one of several methods: a menu command, the Property inspector, or a keyboard shortcut. To use the menus, choose Text ➪ Align and then pick the alignment you prefer (Left, Right, Center, or Justify). Figure 7-19 illustrates the Text Property inspector's Alignment buttons. If the Alignment buttons are not visible on the Text Property inspector, click the Toggle CSS/HTML Mode icon, located to the right of the Format drop-down list.

The keyboard shortcuts are as follows:

✦ **Left:** Ctrl+Alt+Shift+L (Command+Option+Shift+L)

✦ **Center:** Ctrl+Alt+Shift+C (Command+Option+Shift+C)

✦ **Right:** Ctrl+Alt+Shift+R (Command+Option+Shift+R)

✦ **Justify:** Ctrl+Alt+Shift+J (Command+Option+Shift+J)

Note   Another way to align text is through the Cascading Style Sheets. Any style can be set to align your text, and this is the preferred method if you do not have to support older browsers.

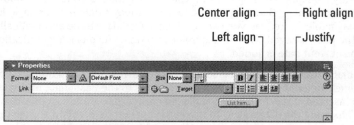

Figure 7-19: The Text Property inspector includes buttons to left align, center, right align, and justify your text.

Traditional HTML alignment options are limited. For a finer degree of control, be sure to investigate precise positioning with layers in Chapter 21.

Indenting entire paragraphs

HTML offers a tag that enables you to indent whole paragraphs, such as inset quotations or name-and-address blocks. Not too surprisingly, the tag used is called the `<blockquote>` tag. Dreamweaver gives you instant access to the `<blockquote>` tag through the Indent and Outdent buttons located on the Text Property inspector, as shown in Figure 7-20.

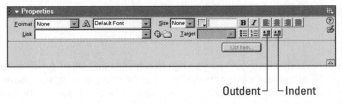

Outdent⏌ ⎿Indent

Figure 7-20: Indent paragraphs and blocks of text with the Indent and the Outdent buttons.

To indent one or more paragraphs, select them and click the Indent button in the Property inspector. Paragraphs can be indented multiple times; each time you click the Indent button, another `<blockquote>`...`</blockquote>` tag pair is added. Note that you can't control how much space a single `<blockquote>` indents a paragraph—that characteristic is determined by the browser.

You also have the option of indenting your paragraphs through the menus by choosing Text ➪ Indent. You can also add the `<blockquote>` tag by choosing the Blockquote button in the Text category of the Insert bar.

If you find that you have over-indented, use the Outdent button, also located on the Property inspector. The Outdent button has no effect if your text is already at the left edge. Alternatively, you can choose Text ➪ Outdent.

Tip   You can tell how many `<blockquote>` tags are being used to create a particular look by placing your cursor in the text and looking at the Tag Selector.

Incorporating Dates

With the Web constantly changing, keeping track of when information is updated is important. Dreamweaver includes a command that enables you to insert today's date in your page, in almost any format imaginable. Moreover, you can set the inserted date to be automatically updated every time the page is saved. This means that every time you make a modification to a page and save it, the current date is added.

The Insert Date command uses your system clock to get the current date. In addition, you can elect to add a day name (for example, Thursday), and the time to the basic date information. After the date text is inserted, it can be formatted like any other text—adding color or a specific font type or changing the date's size. To insert the current date, follow these steps:

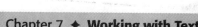
1. Choose Insert ⇨ Date or select the Date button from the Common category of the Insert bar. The Insert Date dialog box, shown in Figure 7-21, is displayed.

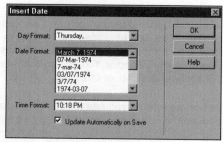

Figure 7-21: Keep track of when a file is updated by using the Date command.

2. If desired, select a Day Format to include in the date from the drop-down list. The options are as follows:

[No Day]	Thu
Thursday,	thu,
Thursday	thu
Thu,	

3. Select the desired date format from the drop-down list. The example formats are as follows:

March 7, 1974	7/03/74
07-Mar-1974	07.03.1974
7-mar-74	07.03.74
03/07/1974	7-03-1974
3/7/74	7 March, 1974
1974-03-07	74-03-07
7/3/74	

Tip If you are creating Web pages for the global market, consider using the format designated by the 1974-03-07 example. This year-month-day format is an ISO (International Organization for Standardization) standard and is computer-sortable.

4. Select the desired time format, if any, from the drop-down list. The example formats are as follows:

[No Time]

10:18 PM

22:18

5. If you want the date modified to include the current date every time the file is saved, select the Update Automatically on Save option.

6. Click OK when you're done.

Tip It's easy to format an inserted date when the Update Automatically on Save option is *not* selected — it's just plain text, and the formatting can be added easily through the Text Property inspector. However, if the date is to be automatically updated, it's inserted as a special Macromedia data type with its own Property inspector. You can style it, however, by selecting options from the Text menu or applying an HTML or CSS style.

If your date object includes the Automatic Update option, you can modify the format. Select the date and, in the Property inspector, choose the Edit Date Format button. The Edit Date Format dialog box opens, which is nearly identical to the Insert Date dialog box, except the Update Automatically on Save option is not available.

Commenting Your Code

How will you know when to begin inserting comments into your HTML code? The first time you go back to an earlier Web page, look at the code, and say, "What on earth was I thinking?" You should plan ahead and develop the habit of commenting your code now.

Browsers run fine without your comments, but for any continued development — of the Web page or of yourself as a Webmaster — commenting your code is extremely beneficial. Sometimes, as in a corporate setting, Web pages are co-developed by teams of designers and programmers. In this situation, commenting your code may not just be a good idea; it may be required. An HTML comment looks like the following:

```
<!-- Created by Hummer Associates, Inc. -->
```

You're not restricted to any particular line length or number of lines for comments. The text included between the opening of the comment, `<!--`, and the closing, `-->`, can span regular paragraphs or HTML code. In fact, one of the most common uses for comments during the testing and debugging phase of page design is to "comment out" sections of code as a means of tracking down an elusive bug.

To insert a comment in Dreamweaver, first place your cursor in either the Document window or the Code inspector, where you want the comment to appear. Then select the Comment button from the Common category of the Insert bar. This sequence opens the Comment dialog box, where you can type the desired text; click OK when you've finished. Figure 7-22 shows a completed comment in Design and Code views, with the corresponding Property inspector open.

By default, Dreamweaver inserts a Comment symbol in the Document window. You can hide the Comment symbol by choosing Edit ➪ Preferences and then deselecting the Comments checkbox in the Invisible Elements category. You can also hide any displayed Invisibles by selecting View ➪ Visual Aids ➪ Invisible Elements or using the keyboard shortcut, Ctrl+Shift+I (Command+Shift+I).

You can also add a comment using the Snippets panel. To use this method, select Window ➪ Snippets to open the panel and then expand the Comments folder. In the Document window, position the cursor where you want the comment to go. then In the Snippets panel, double-click the type of comment you want to add or select the comment, and click the Insert button. If you are working in Code view, type your comment between the inserted tags. If you are working in Design view, select the Comment symbol; then, in the Comment Property inspector, replace any default text that Dreamweaver may have added with your comment.

Comment symbol   Comment Property inspector   Insert Comment button   Comment in HTML code

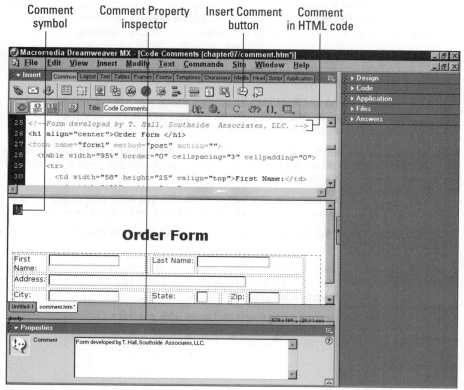

Figure 7-22: Comments are extremely useful for inserting into the code information not visible on the rendered Web page.

Tip   The Snippets panel is really good for commenting out a section of code or text already on the page. With your code or text selected, choose the desired comment style and drop it right on your selection. Presto, chango — instant comments!

When you need to edit a comment, double-click the Comment symbol to display the current comment in the Property inspector. A comment can be moved or duplicated by selecting its symbol and then using the Cut, Copy, and Paste commands under the Edit menu. You can also right-click (Control+click) the Comment symbol to display the context menu. Finally, you can click and drag Comment symbols to move the corresponding comment to a new location.

Summary

Learning to manipulate text is an essential design skill for creating Web pages. Dreamweaver gives you all the tools you need to insert and modify the full range of HTML text quickly and easily.

✦ HTML headings are available in six different sizes: `<h1>` through `<h6>`. Headings are used primarily as headlines and subheads to separate divisions of the Web page.

✦ Blocks of text are formatted with the paragraph tag <p>. Each paragraph is separated from the other paragraphs by a line of whitespace above and below. Use the line break tag, <br>, to make lines appear directly above or below one another.

✦ Dreamweaver offers a full complement of text-editing tools — everything from Cut and Paste to Find and Replace. Dreamweaver's separate Design and Code views make short work of switching between text and code.

✦ Dreamweaver's Find and Replace feature goes a long way toward automating your work on the current page as well as throughout the Web site. Both content and code can be searched in a basic or very advanced fashion.

✦ Where possible, text in HTML is formatted according to its meaning. Dreamweaver applies the styles selected through the Text ⇨ Style menu. For most styles, the browser determines what the user views.

✦ You can format Web page text much as you can text in a word processing program. Within certain limitations, you can select a font's size and color, as well as the font face.

✦ Dreamweaver's HTML Styles feature enables you to consistently and quickly format your text.

✦ HTML comments are a useful (and often requisite) vehicle, which remains unseen by the casual viewer, for embedding information into a Web page. Comments can annotate program code or insert copyright information.

In the next chapter, you learn how to insert and work with graphics.

✦   ✦   ✦

Inserting Images

The Internet started as a text-based medium primarily used for sharing data among research scientists and among U.S. military commanders. Today, the Web is as visually appealing as any mass medium. Dreamweaver's power becomes even more apparent as you use its visual layout tools to incorporate background and foreground images into your Web page designs.

Completely baffled by all the various image formats out there? This chapter opens with an overview of the key Web-oriented graphics formats, including PNG. This chapter also covers techniques for incorporating both background and foreground images — and modifying them using the methods available in Dreamweaver. You will also learn about animation graphics and how you can use them in your Web pages, as well as techniques for creating rollover buttons and navigation bars.

Web Graphic Formats

If you've worked in the computer graphics field, you know that virtually every platform — as well as every paint and graphics program — has its own proprietary file format for images. One of the critical factors driving the Web's rapid, expansive growth is the use of cross-platform graphics. Regardless of the system you use to create your images, these versatile files ensure that the graphics can be viewed by all platforms.

The trade-off for universal acceptance of image files is a restricted field: just two file formats, with a possible third coming into view. Currently, only GIF and JPEG formats are fully supported by browsers. A third alternative, the PNG graphics format, is experiencing a limited, but growing acceptance.

You need to understand the uses and limitations of these formats in order to apply them successfully in Dreamweaver. Let's look at the fundamentals.

GIF

The Graphics Interchange Format (GIF) was developed by CompuServe in the late 1980s to address the problem of cross-platform compatibility. With GIF viewers available for every system from PC and Macintosh to Amiga and NeXT, the GIF format became a natural choice for an inline (adjacent to text) image graphic. GIFs are bitmapped images, which means that each pixel is given or mapped to a specific color. You can have up to 256 colors for a GIF graphic. These images are generally used for line drawings, images of text, logos, or cartoons — anything that doesn't require thousands of colors for a smooth color blend, such as a photograph. With a proper graphics tool like Macromedia Fireworks, you can reduce the number of colors in a GIF image to a minimum, thereby compressing the file and reducing download time.

The GIF format has two varieties: "regular" (technically, GIF87a) and an enhanced version known as GIF89a. This improved GIF file brings three important attributes to the format. First, GIF89a supports transparency, whereby one or more colors can be set to automatically match the background color of the page containing the image. This property is necessary for creating nonrectangular-appearing images. Whenever you see a round or irregularly shaped logo or illustration on the Web, a rectangular frame is displayed as the image is loading — this is the actual size and shape of the graphic. The colors surrounding the irregularly shaped central image are set to transparent in a graphics-editing program (such as Macromedia Fireworks or Adobe Photoshop) before the image is saved in GIF89a format.

Note   Most of the latest versions of the popular graphic tools default to using GIF89a, so unless you're working with older, legacy images, you're not too likely to encounter the less flexible GIF87a format.

Although the outer area of a graphic seems to disappear with GIF89a, you won't be able to overlap your Web images using this format without using layers. Figure 8-1 demonstrates this situation. In this figure, the same image is presented twice — one lacks transparency, and one has transparency applied. The image on the left is saved as a standard GIF without transparency, and you can plainly see the shape of the full image. The image on the right was saved with the white background color made transparent, so the central figure seems to float on the background.

Figure 8-1: The same image, saved without GIF transparency (left) and with GIF transparency (right).

The second valuable attribute contributed by GIF89a format is *interlacing*. One of the most common complaints about graphics on the Web is lengthy download times. Interlacing won't speed up your GIF downloads, but it gives your Web page visitors something to view other than a blank screen. A graphic saved with the interlacing feature turned on gives the appearance of "developing," like an instant picture, as the file is downloading. Use of this design option is up to you and your clients. Some folks swear by it; others can't abide it.

Animation is the final advantage offered by the GIF89a format. Certain software programs enable you to group your GIF files together into one large page-flipping file. With this capability, you can bring simple animation to your page without additional plugins or helper applications. Unfortunately, the trade-off is that the files get very big, very fast. For more information about animated GIFs in Dreamweaver, see the section "Applying Simple Web Animation," later in this chapter.

JPEG

The JPEG format was developed by the Joint Photographic Experts Group specifically to handle photographic images. JPEGs offer millions of colors at 24 bits of color information available per pixel, as opposed to the GIF format's 256 colors and 8 bits. To make JPEGs usable, the large amount of color information must be compressed, which is accomplished by removing what the compression algorithm considers redundant information.

Note   JPEG files can be named with a file extension of .jpg, .jpeg, or .jpe. However, the most commonly used extension is .jpg.

The more compressed your JPEG file, the more degraded the image. When you first save a JPEG image, your graphics program asks you for the desired level of compression. As an example, consider the three images shown in Figure 8-2. Here, you can compare the effects of JPEG compression ratios and resulting file sizes to the original image itself; note, however, that results will vary depending on the image. As you can probably tell, JPEG does an excellent job of compression, with even the highest degree of compression having only minimal visible impact. Keep in mind that every graphic has its own reaction to compression.

JPEG - No compression - 26K   JPEG - 50% Compression - 6K   JPEG - 90% Compression - 2K

Figure 8-2: JPEG compression can save your Web visitors substantial download time, with little loss of image quality.

Tip   With the JPEG image-compression algorithm, the initial elements removed from a compressed image are the least noticeable. Subtle variations in brightness and hue are the first to disappear. When possible, preview your image in your graphics program while adjusting the compression level to observe the changes. With additional compression, the image grows darker and less varied in its color range.

If you use Fireworks as your graphics editor, you can optimize image file size without leaving Dreamweaver. See Chapter 24 to learn more.

With JPEGs, what is compressed for storage must be uncompressed for viewing. When a JPEG picture on your Web page is accessed by a visitor's browser, the image must first be downloaded to the browser and then uncompressed before it can be viewed. This dual process adds additional time to the Web-browsing process, but it is time well spent for photographic images.

JPEGs, unlike GIFs, have neither transparency nor animation features. A newer strand of JPEG called Progressive JPEG gives you the interlacing option of the GIF format, however. Although not all browsers support the interlacing feature of Progressive JPEG, they render the image regardless.

PNG

The latest entry into the Web graphics arena is the Portable Network Graphics format, or PNG. Combining the best of both worlds, PNG has lossless compression, like GIF, and is capable of rendering millions of colors, like JPEG. Moreover, PNG offers an interlacing scheme that appears much more quickly than either GIF or JPEG, as well as superior transparency support.

One valuable aspect of the PNG format enables the display of PNG pictures to appear more uniform across various computer platforms. Generally, graphics made on a PC look brighter on a Macintosh, and Mac-made images seem darker on a PC. PNG includes gamma correction capabilities that alter the image depending on the computer used by the viewer.

Before the 4.0 versions, the various browsers supported PNG only through plugins. After PNG was endorsed as a new Web graphics format by the W3C, both 4.0 versions of Netscape and Microsoft browsers added native, inline support of the new format for Windows. On Macs, PNG format is supported in Internet Explorer 5.0 and up; Netscape browsers still require the plugin. Perhaps most important, however, Dreamweaver was among the first Web authoring tools to offer native PNG support. Inserted PNG images are previewed in the Document window just like GIFs and JPEGs. Browser support for all PNG features is currently not widespread enough to warrant a total switch to the PNG format (image transparency is not fully supported in Internet Explorer for Windows, for example), but its growing acceptance certainly bears watching.

Tip   If you're excited about the potential of PNG, check out Macromedia's Fireworks, the first Web graphics tool to use PNG as its native format. Fireworks takes full advantage of PNG's alpha transparency features and enhanced palette.

Excellent resources for more information about the PNG format are the PNG home page at `www.libpng.org/pub/png/` and the W3C's PNG page at `www.w3.org/Graphics/PNG`.

Using Inline Images

An inline image can appear directly next to text — literally in the same line. The capability to render inline images is one of the major innovations in the evolution of the World Wide Web. This section covers all the basics of inserting inline images and modifying their attributes using Dreamweaver.

Inserting images

Dreamweaver can open and preview any graphic in a GIF, JPEG, or PNG format. With Dreamweaver, you have many options for placing a graphic on your Web page.

     ✦ Position your cursor in the document, and from the Common category of the Insert bar, select the Image button.

✦ Position your cursor in the document, and from the menu bar, choose Insert ⇨ Image.

✦ Position your cursor in the document, and from the keyboard, press Ctrl+Alt+I (Command+Option+I).

✦ Drag the Image button from the Insert bar onto your page.

✦ Drag an icon from your file manager (Explorer or Finder) or from the Site panel onto your page.

✦ Drag a thumbnail or filename from the Image category of the Assets panel onto your page. This capability is covered in detail in a subsequent section, "Dragging images from the Assets panel."

For all methods except those using the Assets panel or the file manager, Dreamweaver opens the Select Image Source dialog box (shown in Figure 8-3) and asks you for the path or address to your image file. Remember that in HTML, all graphics are stored in separate files linked from your Web page.

Note   Dreamweaver's Select Image Source dialog box includes two main options at the top: Select File Name from File System or from Data Sources. This chapter covers inserting static images from the file system. For information about including dynamic images from data sources, see Chapter 16.

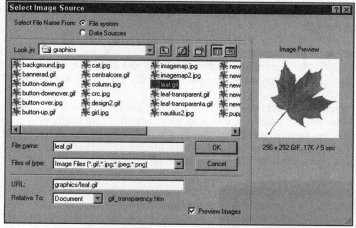

Figure 8-3: In the Select Image Source dialog box, you can keep track of your image's location relative to your current Web page.

Note   When you insert an image, you may also see the Image Tag Accessibility Attributes dialog box, depending on your preference settings. See the section, "Adding image descriptions," for more information about this dialog box.

Whether you are choosing from the file system or a data source, the image's address can be a filename; a directory path and filename on your system; a directory path and filename on your remote system; or a full URL to a graphic on a completely separate Web server. The file doesn't need to be immediately available in order for the code to be inserted into your HTML.

From the Select Image Source dialog box, you can browse to your image folder and preview images before you load them. If you are using Mac OSX, the image preview is automatically enabled. To enable this feature on Mac OS9, click the Show Preview button; on Windows, select the Preview Images option. In the lower portion of the dialog box, the URL text box displays the format of the address Dreamweaver inserts into your code. Below the URL text box is the Relative To list box. Here, you can choose to declare an image relative to the document you're working on (the default) or relative to the site root. (After you've saved your document, you can see its name displayed beside the Relative To list box.)

> **Cross-Reference** To take full advantage of Dreamweaver's site management features, you must open a site, establish a local site root, and save the current Web page before beginning to insert images. For more information about how to begin a Dreamweaver project, see Chapter 5.

Relative to Document

Once you've saved your Web page and chosen Relative to Document, Dreamweaver displays the address in the URL text box. If the image is located in a folder on the same level as, or within, your current site root folder, the address is formatted with just a path and filename. For instance, if you're inserting a graphic from the subfolder named images, Dreamweaver inserts an address like the following:

```
images/logo.jpg
```

If you try to insert an image currently stored outside of the local site root folder, Dreamweaver automatically copies the image file to your Default Images Folder, specified when you first created the site.

> **Tip** To change the setting for your Default Images Folder, select Site ➪ Edit Sites, and in the Edit Sites dialog box, select the current site and click Edit. In the Local Info category of the Advanced tab of the Site Definition dialog box, you can specify the Default Images Folder.

If your site does not include a Default Images Folder, you can see the prompt window shown in Figure 8-4, asking if you want to copy this image to your local site root folder. If you answer Yes, Dreamweaver gives you an opportunity to specify where the image should be saved within the local site. Whenever possible, keep all of your images within the local site root folder so that Dreamweaver can handle site management efficiently.

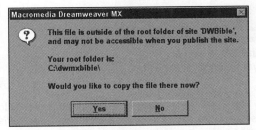

Figure 8-4: Dreamweaver reminds you to keep all your graphics within the local site root folder for easy site management.

If you attempt to drag an out-of-site image file from the Site panel or from your file manager, and you select No to the prompt asking to copy the file to your site, the file is not inserted. If you attempt to insert the file using the Select Image Source dialog box and answer No, the file is inserted with the src attribute pointing to the path of the file. In this case, Dreamweaver appends a prefix that tells the browser to look on your local system for the file. For instance, the file listing would look like the following in Windows:

```
file:///C|/Dreamweaver/images/logo.jpg
```

whereas on the Macintosh, the same file is listed as follows:

```
file:///Macintosh HD/Dreamweaver/images/logo.jpg
```

Caution   If you upload Web pages with this file:///C| (file:///Macintosh HD) prefix in place, the links to your images will be broken. It is easy to miss this error during your testing. Because your local browser can find the referenced image on your system, even when you are browsing the remote site, the Web page appears perfect. However, anyone else browsing your Web site only sees placeholders for broken links. To avoid this error, always save your images within your local site.

Dreamweaver also appends the file:///C| prefix (or file:///Macintosh HD in Macintosh) if you haven't yet saved the document in which you are inserting the image. However, when you save the document, Dreamweaver automatically updates the image addresses to be document-relative.

Relative to Site Root

If you select Site Root in the Relative To field of the Select Image Source dialog box, and you are within your site root folder, Dreamweaver appends a leading forward slash to the directory in the path. The addition of this slash enables the browser to correctly read the address. Thus, the same logo.jpg file appears in both the URL text box and the HTML code as follows:

```
/images/logo.jpg
```

When you use site root–relative addressing and you select a file outside of the site root, the image file will automatically be copied to your Default Images Folder, if one exists. If your site does not have a Default Images Folder, you get the same reminder from Dreamweaver about copying the file into your local site root folder — just as with document-relative addressing.

Cross-Reference   For more details about using dynamic sources for your images, see Chapter 16.

Dragging images from the Assets panel

Web designers often work from a collection of images, much as a painter uses a palette of colors. Re-using images builds consistency in the site, making it easier for a visitor to navigate through it. However, trying to remember the differences between two versions of a logo — one named logo03.gif and another named logo03b.gif — used to require inserting them both to find the desired image. Dreamweaver eliminates the visual guesswork and simplifies the re-use of graphics with the Assets panel.

The Images category is key to the Assets panel. Not only does the Assets panel list all the GIF, JPEG, and PNG files found in your site — whether or not they are embedded in a Web page — selecting any graphic from the list instantly displays a thumbnail. Previewing the images makes it easy to select the proper one. Moreover, once you've found the correct image, all you need to do is drag it from the Assets panel onto the page.

Before you can use graphics from the Assets panel, you must inventory the site by choosing the Refresh Site List button, as shown in Figure 8-5. When you click the Refresh button (or

Making Images Dynamic

Once you're familiar with creating data source connections and establishing recordsets in Dreamweaver, you can display images dynamically. Dreamweaver doesn't actually insert images from a database, but rather inserts the path and filenames of the images—right into the `src` attribute of the `<img>` tag.

The data contained in the field can consist of either just a filename, like `logo.gif`, or a path and filename, like `/images/logo.gif`. Under most circumstances, it's better to have just the filename; this structure provides the most flexibility, as the path to the file can be prepended by Dreamweaver.

Follow these steps to include an image dynamically:

1. Choose Edit ⇨ Preferences; in the Accessibility category, clear the Images check box.

   Caution: Dreamweaver does not correctly insert the code for a dynamic image if this Accessibility option is enabled.

2. Make sure you have defined a recordset with at least one field consisting of paths to graphics.

3. Position your cursor where you want your dynamic image to appear.

4. From the Common category of the Insert bar, select Image.

   Alternatively, you can drag the Image button to the proper place on the page. In either case, the Select Image Source dialog box appears.

5. Navigate to any folder within your Local Root directory.

   Dreamweaver mishandles the insertion of the image from a data source if the dialog attempts to reference an image outside the site.

6. From the Select Image Source dialog box, Windows users should choose the Select File Name From Data Sources option at the top of the page. Macintosh users should select the Data Source button found just above the URL field.

7. If necessary, expand the data source to locate and select the desired image field.

   Dreamweaver places the code for inserting the dynamic image into the URL field.

8. If your image data (the paths to the images) contains spaces, tildes, or other nonstandard characters, the data must be encoded in order to be read properly by the server. From the Format list, select one of the following:

   Encode – Server.HTMLEncode (ASP JavaScript or Visual Basic)

   Encode – HTMLEncodedFormat (ASP C#)

   Encode – URLEncoded Format (ColdFusion)

   Encode – Response.EncodeURL (JSP)

9. If your data is stored as filenames only, enter any required path in the URL field before the existing code.

   The path information may be document-relative, site-root–relative, or absolute.

10. Click OK when you're done.

choose Refresh Site List from the context menu on the Assets panel), Dreamweaver examines the current site and creates a list of the graphics, including their sizes, file types, and full paths. To see an image, just click its name, and a thumbnail appears in the preview area of the panel.

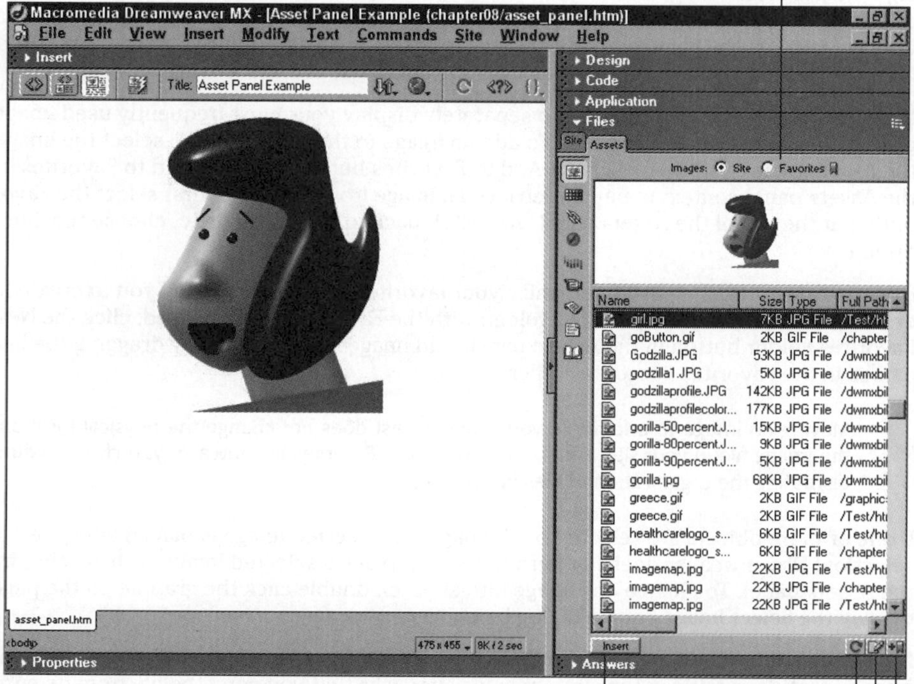

Click to view Favorites list

Click to insert image   Refresh Site List

Edit

Add to Favorites

Figure 8-5: Re-use any graphic in your site or from your Favorites collection by dragging it from the Assets panel.

Tip

To increase the size of the thumbnail, make the preview area larger by dragging open the border between the preview and list areas and/or the size of the entire panel. Dreamweaver increases the size of the thumbnail while maintaining the width:height ratio, so if you just move the border or resize the panel a little bit, you may not see a significant change. Thumbnails are never displayed larger than their actual size.

You can insert an image from the Assets panel onto your Web page in two ways:

✦ Drag the image or the file listing onto the page.

✦ Place your cursor where you'd like the image to appear. Select the desired image in the Assets panel, and then click the Insert button.

Caution   Do not double-click the image or listing in the Assets panel to insert it onto the page; double-clicking invokes the designated graphics editor, be it Macromedia Fireworks, Adobe Photoshop, or another program, and opens that graphic for editing. From the Document window, Ctrl+double-clicking (Command+double-clicking) accomplishes the same thing.

The Dreamweaver Assets panel is designed to help you work efficiently with sites that contain many images. For example, in large sites, it's often difficult to scroll through all the names looking for a particular image. To aid your search, Dreamweaver enables you to sort the Images category by any of the columns displayed in the Assets panel: Name, Size, Type, or Full Path. Clicking once on the column heading sorts the assets in an ascending order by that criterion; click the column again to sort by that same criterion, but in a descending order.

You can also use the Favorites list to separately display your most frequently used images, giving you quicker access to them. To add an image to the Favorites list, select the image in the Assets panel, and then click the Add to Favorites button or select Add to Favorites from the Assets panel context menu. To retrieve an image from Favorites, first select the Favorites option at the top of the Assets panel. To switch back to the current site, choose the Site option.

Dreamweaver makes it easy to organize your favorite images by enabling you to create folders in the Favorites list. To create a folder, with the Favorites list displayed, click the New Favorites Folder button in the Assets panel. Add images to the folder by dragging the image names in the Favorites list to the folder.

Note   Moving an image to a folder in your Favorites list does not change the physical location of the image file in your site. You can organize your Favorites list however you choose without disrupting the organization of files in your site.

If one or more objects are selected on the page, the inserted image is placed after the selection; Dreamweaver does not permit you to replace a selected image with another from the Assets panel. To change one image into another, double-click the graphic on the page to display the Select Image Source dialog box.

Note one final point about adding images from the Assets panel: If you reference a graphic from a location outside of the site, Dreamweaver asks that you copy the file from its current location. You must select the Refresh Site Files button to display this new image in the Assets panel.

Tip   When you select the Refresh button, Dreamweaver adds new images (and other assets) to the cache of current assets. If you add assets from outside of Dreamweaver — using, for example, a file manager — you might need to completely reload the Assets panel by Ctrl+clicking (Command+clicking) the Refresh button, or by selecting Recreate Site List from the Assets panel context menu.

Modifying images

When you insert an image in Dreamweaver, the image tag, <img>, is inserted into your HTML code. The <img> tag takes several attributes; the most commonly used can be entered through the Property inspector. Code for a basic image looks like the following:

```
<img src="images/myimage.gif" width="172" height="180">
```

Dreamweaver centralizes all of its image functions in the Property inspector. The Image Property inspector, shown in Figure 8-6, displays a small thumbnail of the image as well as its file size. Dreamweaver automatically inserts the image filename in the Src text box (as the src attribute). To replace a currently selected image with another, click the folder icon next to the Src text box, or double-click the image itself. This sequence opens the Select Image Source dialog box. When you've selected the desired file, Dreamweaver automatically refreshes the page and corrects the code.

Figure 8-6: The Image Property inspector gives you total control over the HTML code for every image.

With the Image Property inspector open when you insert your image, you can begin to modify the image attributes immediately.

Editing images

Dreamweaver is a terrific Web authoring tool, but it's not a graphics editor. After inserting an image into your Web page, you often find that the picture needs to be altered in some way. Perhaps you need to crop part of the image or make the background transparent. Dreamweaver enables you to specify your primary graphics editor for each type of graphic in the File Types/Editors category of Preferences.

Once you've picked an image editor, clicking the Edit button in the Property inspector opens the application with the current image. After you've made the modifications, just save the file in your image editor and switch back to Dreamweaver. The new, modified graphic has already been included in the Web page. If you change the image size, you may need to click the Reset Size button on the Image Property inspector to see your changes.

If you are using Macromedia Fireworks as your image editor, here is some good news: Dreamweaver and Fireworks are closely integrated, enabling you to modify and optimize images with ease. Find out more in Chapter 24.

Adjusting height and width

The width and height attributes are important because browsers build Web pages faster when they know the size and shape of the included images. Dreamweaver reads these attributes when the image is first loaded. The width and height values are initially expressed in pixels and are automatically inserted as attributes in the HTML code.

Browsers can dynamically resize an image if its height and width on the page are different from the original image's dimensions. For example, you can load your primary logo on the home page and then use a smaller version of it on subsequent pages by inserting the same image with reduced height and width values. Because you're only loading the image once and the browser is resizing it, download time for your Web page can be significantly reduced.

Resizing an image just means changing its appearance onscreen; the file size stays exactly the same. To reduce a file size for an image, you need to scale it down in a graphics program such as Fireworks.

To resize an image in Dreamweaver, select the image and type the desired number of pixels in the Property inspector H (height) and W (width) fields. With Dreamweaver, you can also visually resize your graphics by using the click-and-drag method. A selected image has three sizing handles located on the right, bottom, and lower-right corners of its bounding box. Click any of these handles and drag it out to a new location—when you release the mouse, Dreamweaver resizes the image. To maintain the current height/width aspect ratio, hold down the Shift key after dragging the corner sizing handle.

If you alter either the height or the width of an image, Dreamweaver displays the Property inspector values in bold in their respective fields. You can restore an image's default measurements by clicking the H or the W independently—or you can choose the Reset Size button to restore both values.

If you elect to enable your viewer's browser to resize your image on the fly using the height/width values you specify, keep in mind that the browser is not a graphics-editing program and that its resizing algorithms are not sophisticated. View your resized images through several browsers to ensure acceptable results.

Using margins

You can offset images with surrounding whitespace by using the margin attributes. The amount of whitespace around your image can be designated both vertically and horizontally through the vspace and hspace attributes, respectively. These margin values are entered, in pixels, into the V Space and H Space text boxes in the Image Property inspector.

The V Space value adds the same amount of whitespace along the top and bottom of your image; the H Space value increases the whitespace along the left and right sides of the image. These values must be positive; HTML doesn't allow images to overlap text or other images (outside of layers). Unlike in page layout, "negative whitespace" does not exist.

The hspace and vspace attributes are deprecated in HTML 4.0. This means that, although the attributes are currently still supported, there is another, preferred method to achieve the same effect in newer browsers. In this case, the margins can also be implemented using Cascading Style Sheets, described in Chapter 20.

Naming your image

When you first insert a graphic into the page, the Image Property inspector displays a blank text box next to the thumbnail and file size. Fill in this box with a unique name for the image, to be used in JavaScript and other applications.

Adding image descriptions

It's easy for Web designers to get caught up in the visual design of their Web pages; after all, designers can devote hours to creating a single graphic, or to perfectly positioning a graphic on the page relative to other information. Remember, however, that graphics aren't the most effective communication method in every circumstance. Luckily, the <img> tag includes two attributes that enable you to describe your image using plain text: the alt attribute and the longdesc attribute.

The alt attribute gives you a way to include a short description of a graphic. The alt attribute is used in many ways:

✦ As a page is loading over the Web, the image is first displayed as an empty rectangle if the <img> tag contains width and height information. Some browsers display the alt description in this rectangle while the image is loading, offering the waiting user a preview of the forthcoming image.

✦ In many browsers, the alt text displays as a ToolTip when the user's pointer passes over the graphic.

✦ A real benefit of alt text is providing input for browsers not displaying graphics. Remember that text-only browsers are still in use, and some users, interested only in content, turn off the graphics to speed up the text display.

✦ The W3C is working toward standards for browsers for the visually impaired, and the alt text can be used to describe the image.

For all these reasons, it's good coding practice to associate an alt description with all of your graphics. In Dreamweaver, you can enter this alternative text in the Alt text box of the Image Property inspector.

Tip   If the <img> tag does not contain an alt attribute, some screen readers read the filename when they encounter the image, which slows down how quickly visually impaired users can get to the real information on your page. For images that are purely visual and don't contribute to the meaning of your content, such as bullets or spacer images, include a blank alt attribute. To do this, open the Image Property inspector and select <empty> from the Alt drop-down list.

Currently, the alt attribute is the most valuable tool you have for providing a textual description of your images. However, some images are just too complicated to describe in a few words, and are too important to gloss over. For these situations, the latest HTML specification includes the longdesc attribute. Although none of the major browsers currently support this attribute, Dreamweaver is anticipating the future by enabling you to specify a longdesc for your images.

In Dreamweaver, choose Edit Preferences, and in the Accessibility category, select the Images option. When you add a new image to your page, the Image Tag Accessibility Attributes dialog box appears, as shown in Figure 8-7. In the Long Description text box, click the folder icon to navigate to an HTML file that contains a textual description of the image.

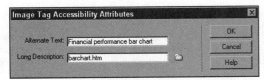

Figure 8-7: The Image Tag Accessibility Attributes dialog box appears when you have selected the Images option in the Accessibility Preferences.

Caution   The Image Tag Accessibility Attributes dialog box is not displayed if you add a new image by dragging it from the Site panel. It does, however, appear if you drag the image from the Assets panel, or use the Insert bar or Insert menu to add the image.

Bordering a graphic

When you're working with thumbnails (small versions of images) on your Web page, you may need a quick way to distinguish one from another. The border attribute enables you to place a one-color rectangular border around any graphic. To turn on the border, enter the desired width of the border, measured in pixels, in the Border text box located on the lower half of the Image Property inspector. Entering a value of zero explicitly turns off the border.

Note   A preferred method to add a border to an image is to use Cascading Style Sheets, described in Chapter 20. Note, however, that Cascading Style Sheets are not supported in older browsers.

One of the most frequent cries for help among beginning Web designers results from the sudden appearance of a bright blue border around an image. Whenever you assign a link to an image, HTML automatically places a border around that image; the color is determined by the Page Properties Link color, where the default is bright blue. Dreamweaver intelligently assigns a zero to the border attribute whenever you enter a URL in the Link text box. If you've already declared a border value and enter a link, Dreamweaver won't zero-out the border. You can, of course, override the no-border option by entering a value in the Border text box.

Specifying a lowsrc

Another option for loading Web page images, the lowsrc attribute, displays a smaller version of a large graphics file while the larger file is loading. The lowsrc file can be a grayscale version of the original, or a version that is physically smaller or reduced in color or resolution. This option is designed to significantly reduce the file size for quick loading.

Select your lowsrc file by choosing the file icon next to the Low Src text box in the Image Property inspector. The same criteria that apply to inserting your original image also apply to the lowsrc picture.

Tip   One handy lowsrc technique first proportionally scales down a large file in a graphics-processing program. This file becomes your lowsrc file. Because browsers use the final image's height and width information for both the lowsrc and the final image, your visitors immediately see a "blocky" version of your graphic, which is replaced by the final version when the picture is fully loaded.

Working with alignment options

Just like text, images can be aligned to the left, right, or center. In fact, images have much more flexibility than text in terms of alignment. In addition to the same horizontal alignment options, you can align your images vertically in nine different ways. You can even turn a picture into a floating image type, enabling text to wrap around it.

Horizontal alignment

When you change the horizontal alignment of a line—from left to center or from center to right—the entire paragraph moves. Any inline images that are part of that paragraph also move. Likewise, selecting one of a series of inline images in a row and realigning it horizontally causes all the images in the row to shift.

In Dreamweaver, the horizontal alignment of an inline image is changed in exactly the same way you realign text, with the alignment buttons found on the Image Property inspector. As with text, buttons exist for left, center, and right. Although these are very conveniently placed on the Image Property inspector, the alignment attribute is actually written to the `<p>` or other block element enclosing the image.

Note The `align` attribute, whether attached to a `<p>` tag for horizontal alignment, or to an `<img>` tag for vertical alignment (as described in the following section), is deprecated in HTML 4.0. Instead of aligning images using the `align` attribute, you can use Cascading Style Sheets, described in Chapter 20.

Vertical alignment

Because you can place text next to an image—and images vary so greatly in size—HTML includes a variety of options for specifying just how image and text line up. As you can see from the chart shown in Figure 8-8, a wide range of possibilities is available.

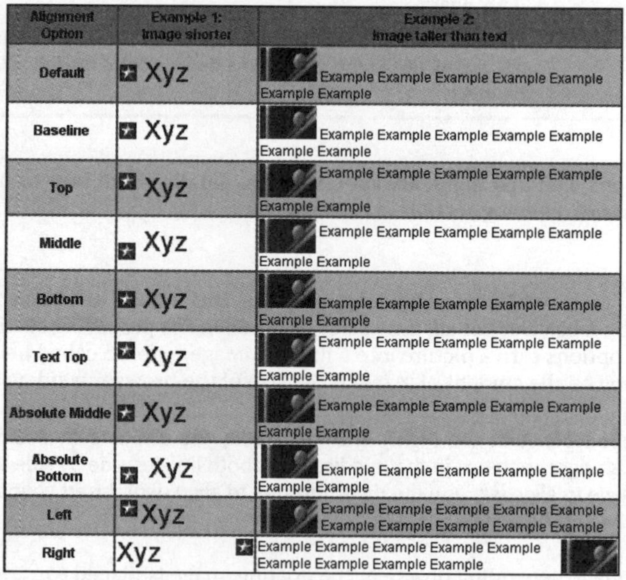

Alignment Option	Example 1: Image shorter	Example 2: Image taller than text
Default	Xyz	Example Example Example Example Example Example Example
Baseline	Xyz	Example Example Example Example Example Example Example
Top	Xyz	Example Example Example Example Example Example Example
Middle	Xyz	Example Example Example Example Example Example Example
Bottom	Xyz	Example Example Example Example Example Example Example
Text Top	Xyz	Example Example Example Example Example Example Example
Absolute Middle	Xyz	Example Example Example Example Example Example Example
Absolute Bottom	Xyz	Example Example Example Example Example Example Example
Left	Xyz	Example Example Example Example Example Example Example Example Example
Right	Xyz	Example Example Example Example Example Example Example Example Example

Figure 8-8: You can align text and images in one of nine different ways.

To change the vertical alignment of any graphic in Dreamweaver, open the Align drop-down list in the Image Property inspector and choose one of the options. Dreamweaver writes your choice into the `align` attribute of the `<img>` tag. The various vertical alignment options are listed in the following table, and you can see examples of each type of alignment in Figure 8-8.

Vertical Alignment Option	Result
Browser Default	No alignment attribute is included in the `<img>` tag. Most browsers use the baseline as the alignment default.
Baseline	The bottom of the image is aligned with the baseline of the surrounding text.
Top	The top of the image is aligned with the top of the tallest object in the current line.
Middle	The middle of the image is aligned with the baseline of the current line.
Bottom	The bottom of the image is aligned with the baseline of the surrounding text.
Text Top	The top of the image is aligned with the tallest letter or object in the current line.
Absolute Middle	The middle of the image is aligned with the middle of the tallest text or object in the current line.
Absolute Bottom	The bottom of the image is aligned with the descenders (as in y, g, p, and so forth) that fall below the current baseline.
Left	The image is aligned to the left edge of the browser or table cell, and all text in the current line flows around the right side of the image.
Right	The image is aligned to the right edge of the browser or table cell, and all text in the current line flows around the left side of the image.

The final two alignment options, Left and Right, are special cases; details about how to use their features are covered in the following section.

Wrapping text

Long a popular design option in conventional publishing, wrapping text around an image on a Web page is also supported by most, but not all, browsers. As noted in the preceding section, the Left and Right alignment options turn a picture into a floating image type, so called because the image can move depending on the amount of text and the size of the browser window.

 Tip Using both floating image types (Left and Right) in combination, you can actually position images flush-left and flush-right, with text in the middle. Insert both images side by side and then set the leftmost image to align left, and the rightmost one to align right. Insert your text immediately following the second image.

Your text wraps around the image depending on where the floating image is placed (or anchored). If you enable the Anchor Points for Aligned Elements option in the Invisible Elements category of Preferences, Dreamweaver inserts a Floating Image Anchor symbol to mark the floating image's place. Note, however, that the image itself may overlap the anchor, thus hiding the anchor from view. Figure 8-9 shows two examples of text wrapping: a left-aligned image with text flowing to the right, and a right-aligned image with text flowing to the left.

Floating Image anchor

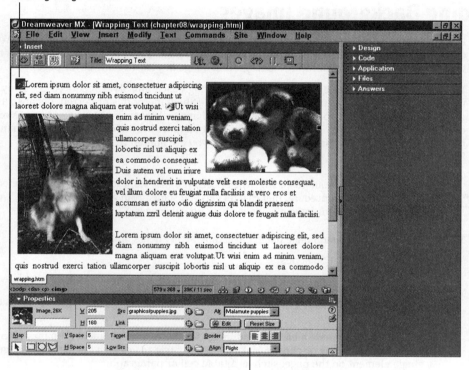

Set image alignment

Figure 8-9: Aligning an image left or right enables text to wrap around your images.

The Floating Image Anchor is not just a static symbol. You can click and drag the anchor to a new location and cause the paragraph to wrap in a different fashion. Be careful, however; if you delete the anchor, you also delete the image it represents.

You can also wrap a portion of the text around your left- or right-aligned picture and then force the remaining text to appear below the floating image. However, the HTML necessary to do this task cannot currently be inserted by Dreamweaver in Design view. You have to force an opening to appear by inserting a break tag, with a special `clear` attribute, where you want the text to break. This special `<br>` tag has three forms:

- ✦ `<br clear=left>`: Causes the line to break, and the following text moves down vertically until no floating images are on the left

- ✦ `<br clear=right>`: Causes the line to break, and the following text moves down vertically until no floating images are on the right

- ✦ `<br clear=all>`: Moves the text following the image down until no floating images are on either the left or the right

A quick way to add the `clear` attribute is to position your cursor where you want the text to break, and press Shift+Enter. Then, in Code view, right-click on the `<br>` tag and select Edit Tag `<br>` from the context menu. In the resulting Tag Editor dialog box, select the appropriate Clear option, and click OK.

Adding Background Images

In this chapter, you've learned about working with the surface graphics on a Web page. You can also have an image in the background of an HTML page. This section covers some of the basic techniques for incorporating a background image in your Dreamweaver page.

You add an image to your background either by using Cascading Style Sheets (CSS), or by modifying the Page Properties. The Cascading Style Sheet method is preferred, because it gives you additional control over your background image. However, older browser versions do not support Cascading Style Sheets; if you must support browser versions earlier than Internet Explorer 4.0 and Netscape Navigator 4.0, you are limited to changing the Page Properties.

If you aren't familiar with Cascading Style Sheets, you may want to read Chapter 20 before trying the following procedure. That chapter gets you started with general CSS concepts and outlines specific options for implementing background images.

To implement a background image using Cascading Style Sheets, follow these steps:

1. Choose Window ➪ CSS Styles.

2. On the CSS Styles panel, click Edit Styles and then click the New CSS Style button.

3. In the New Style dialog box, choose Redefine HTML Tag, and in the Tag drop-down list, select Body.

   These selections create a background image for the entire document. You may also choose a different tag or choose Make a Custom Style to assign a background image to a single element on the page, such as a table cell or paragraph.

4. Specify whether you wish to save the style definition in an external style sheet or in the current document, and then click OK.

5. In the CSS Style Definition dialog box, select the Background category.

6. In the Background Image field, type the path and filename for the image file, or click Browse (Choose) to navigate to the file.

7. Designate other background options as desired, and then click OK.

To specify a background image using the Page Properties, choose Modify ➪ Page Properties or select Page Properties from the shortcut menu that pops up when you right-click (Control+click) in any open area on the Web page. In the Page Properties dialog box, select a graphic by choosing the Browse (Choose) button next to the Background Image text box. You can use any file format supported by Dreamweaver — GIF, JPEG, or PNG.

Note two key differences between background images and the foreground inline images discussed in the preceding sections of this chapter. First and most obvious, all other text and graphics on the Web page are superimposed over your chosen background image. This capability can bring extra depth and texture to your work; unfortunately, you have to make sure the foreground text and images work well with the background.

Basically, you want to ascertain that enough contrast exists between foreground and background. You can set the default text and the various link colors using Cascading Style Sheets, described in Chapter 20, or through the Page Properties dialog box, shown in Figure 8-10. When trying out a new background pattern, you should set up some dummy text and links. Then use the Apply button on the Page Properties dialog box to test different color combinations.

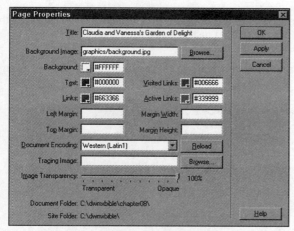

Figure 8-10: If you're using a background image, be sure to check the default colors for text and links to make sure enough contrast exists between background and foreground.

The second distinguishing feature of background images is that the viewing browser completely fills either the browser window or the area behind the content of your Web page; whichever is larger. Therefore, suppose you have created a splash page with only a 200 × 200 foreground logo, and you've incorporated an amazing 1,024 × 768 background that took you weeks to compose. No one can see the fruits of your labor in the background — unless they resize their browser window to 1,024 × 768. On the other hand, if your background image is smaller than either the browser window or what the Web page content needs to display, the browser and Dreamweaver repeat (or tile) your image to make up the difference.

If you implement the background image using Page Properties, the image will always tile both horizontally and vertically, filling the page as just described. But if you implement your background image using Cascading Style Sheets, you can control whether the image tiles horizontally, vertically, in both directions, or not at all.

Tip   With Cascading Style Sheets, you can not only attach a background image to a page, but also to an individual element on a page, such as a single paragraph. Cascading Style Sheets also allow you to designate whether the background image should scroll with the foreground text, or if it should remain stationary while the foreground text scrolls over the background. These options are not available with the Page Properties method.

Tiling Images

Web designers use the tiling property of background images to create a variety of effects with very low file-size overhead. The columns typically found on one side of Web pages are a good example of tiling. Columns are popular because they enable the designer to place navigational buttons in a visual context. An easy way to create a column that runs the full length of your Web page is to use a long, narrow background image.

In the following figure, the background image is 45 pixels high, 800 pixels wide, and only 6K in size. When the browser window is set at 640 × 480 or 800 × 600, the image is tiled down the page to create the vertical column effect. You could just as easily create an image 1,000 pixels high by 40 pixels wide to create a horizontal column.

If you are using Cascading Style Sheets to implement your background image, you can control whether the image tiles horizontally, vertically, in both directions, or not at all.

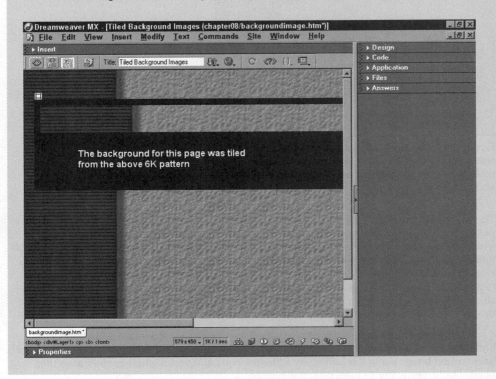

Dividing the Web Page with Horizontal Rules

HTML includes a standard horizontal line that can divide your Web page into specific sections. The horizontal rule tag, <hr>, is a good tool for adding a little diversion to your page without adding download time. You can control the width (either absolutely or relative to the browser window), the height, the alignment, and the shading property of the rule. These horizontal rules appear on a line by themselves; you cannot place text or images on the same line as a horizontal rule.

To insert a horizontal rule in your Web page in Dreamweaver, follow these steps:

1. Place your cursor where you want the horizontal rule to appear.

2. From the Common category of the Insert bar, select the Horizontal Rule button or choose the Insert ⇨ Horizontal Rule command.

   Dreamweaver inserts the horizontal rule; and the Property inspector, if visible, shows the attributes that you can change for a horizontal rule (see Figure 8-11).

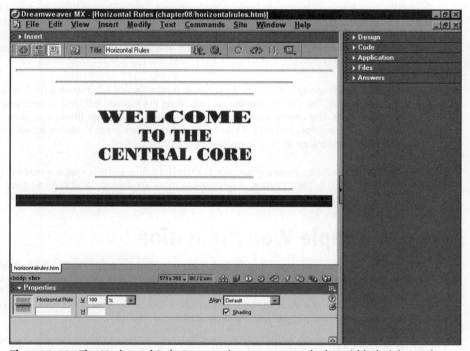

Figure 8-11: The Horizontal Rule Property inspector controls the width, height, and alignment for these HTML lines.

3. To change the width of the line, enter a value in the Property inspector width (W) text box. You can insert either an absolute width in pixels or a relative value as a percentage of the screen:

   • To set a horizontal rule to an exact width, enter the measurement in pixels in the width (W) text box and press the Tab key. If it is not already showing, select Pixels in the drop-down list.

   • To set a horizontal rule to a width relative to the browser window, enter the percentage amount in the width (W) text box and press the Tab key. Then select the percent sign (%) in the drop-down list.

4. To change the height of the horizontal rule, type a pixel measurement in the height (H) text box.

5. To change the alignment from the default (centered), open the Align drop-down list and choose another alignment.

6. To disable the default "embossed" look for the rule, clear the Shading checkbox.

7. If you intend to reference your horizontal rule in JavaScript or in another application, you can give it a unique name. Type it into the unlabeled text box located directly to the left of the H text box.

Note The HTML 4.0 standard lists the `align`, `noshade`, `width`, and `size` attributes of the `<hr>` tag as deprecated. However, current browsers still support these attributes.

To modify any inserted horizontal rule, simply click it. (If the Property inspector is not already open, you have to double-click the rule.) As a general practice, size your horizontal rules using the percentage option if you are using them to separate items on a full screen. If you are using the horizontal rules to divide items in a specifically sized table column or cell, use the pixel method.

Tip The Shading property of the horizontal rule is most effective when your page background is a shade of gray. The default shading is black along the top and left, and white along the bottom and right. The center line is generally transparent (although Internet Explorer enables you to assign a color attribute). If you use a different background color or image, be sure to check the appearance of your horizontal rules in that context.

Many designers prefer to create elaborate horizontal rules; in fact, custom rules are an active area of clip art design. These types of horizontal rules are regular graphics and are inserted and modified as such.

Applying Simple Web Animation

Why include a section on animation in a chapter on inline images? On the Web, animations are, for the most part, inline images that move. Outside of the possibilities offered by Dynamic HTML (covered in Part IV), Web animations typically either are animated GIF files or are created with a program such as Flash that requires a plugin. This section takes a brief look at the capabilities and uses of GIF animations.

A GIF animation is a series of still GIF images flipped rapidly to create the illusion of motion. Because animation-creation programs compress all the frames of your animation into one file, a GIF animation is placed on a Web page in the same manner as a still graphic.

In Dreamweaver, click the Image button in the Insert bar or choose Insert ➪ Image and then select the file. Dreamweaver shows the first frame of your animation in the Document window. To play the animation, preview your Web page in a browser.

As you can imagine, GIF animations can quickly grow to be very large. The key to controlling file size is to think small: Keep your images as small as possible with a low bit-depth (number of colors) and use as few frames as possible.

To create your animation, use any graphics program to produce the separate frames. One excellent technique uses an image-processing program such as Adobe Photoshop and progressively applies a filter to the same image over a series of frames. Figure 8-12 shows the individual frames created with Photoshop's Lighting Effects filter. When animated, a spotlight appears to move across the word.

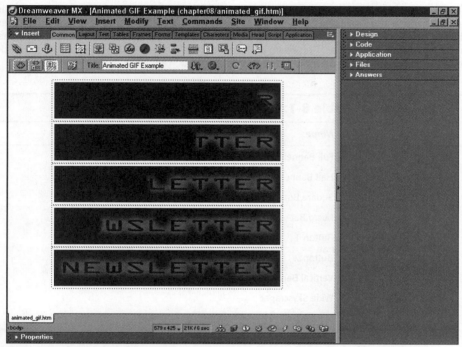

Figure 8-12: The five images shown are frames of an animated GIF image that are compressed into one file using an image-editing program.

You need an animation program to compress the separate frames and build your animated GIF file. Many commercial programs, including Macromedia's Fireworks, can handle GIF animation. QuickTime Pro can turn individual files or any other kind of movie into an animated GIF, too. Most animation programs enable you to control numerous aspects of the animation: the number of times an animation loops, the delay between frames, and how transparency is handled within each frame.

Tip   If you want to use an advanced animation tool but still have full backward compatibility, check out Flash, from Macromedia. Flash is best known for outputting small vector-based animations that require a plugin to view, but it can also save animations as GIFs or AVIs. See Chapter 25 for more information.

Dreamweaver Technique: Including Banner Ads

Banner ads have become an essential aspect of the World Wide Web; in order for the Web to remain, for the most part, freely accessible, advertising is needed to support the costs. Banner ads have evolved into the de facto standard. Although numerous variations exist, a banner ad is typically an animated GIF of a particular width and height, and within a specified file size.

The Standards and Practices Committee of the Interactive Advertising Bureau (IAB) established a series of standard sizes for banner ads. Although no law dictates that these guidelines have to be followed, the vast majority of commercial sites adhere to the suggested dimensions. The most common banner sizes (in pixels) and their official names are listed in Table 8-1; additional banner guidelines are available at the IAB Web site (www.iab.net).

Table 8-1: IAB Advertising Banner Sizes

Dimensions	Name
468 × 60	Full Banner
234 × 60	Half Banner
125 × 125	Square Button
88 × 31	Micro Bar
120 × 90	Button 1
120 × 60	Button 2
120 × 240	Vertical Banner
160 × 600	Wide Skyscraper
120 × 600	Skyscraper

Acceptable file size for a banner ad is not as clearly specified, but it's just as important. The last thing a hosting site wants is for a large, too-heavy banner to slow down the loading of its page. Most commercial sites have an established maximum file size for any given banner ad size. Generally, banner ads are around 10KB, and no more than 12KB. The lighter your banner ad, the faster it loads and — as a direct result — the more likely Web page visitors stick around to see it.

Note   Major sites often have additional criteria for using rich media in banner ads, such as Flash animations or JavaScript. These may include file size, length of animation, behavior when the ad is clicked, and so on.

Inserting a banner ad on a Web page is very straightforward. As with any other GIF file, animated or not, all you have to do is insert the image and assign the link. As any advertiser can tell you, the link is as important as the image itself, and you should take special care to ensure that it is correct when inserted. Advertising links are often quite complex because they not only link to a specific page, but may also carry information about the referring site. Several companies monitor how many times an ad is selected — the *clickthru rate* — and often a CGI program is used to communicate with these companies and handle the link. Here's a sample URL from CNet's News.com site:

```
http://home.cnet.com/cgi-acc/clickthru.acc?↩
clickid=00001e145ea7d80f00000000&adt=003:10:100&edt=cnet&cat=1:1002:&site=CN
```

Obviously, copying and pasting such URLs is highly preferable to entering them by hand.

Advertisements often come from an outside source, so a Web page designer may have to allow space for the ad without incorporating the actual ad. Some Web designers create a plain rectangular image of the appropriate size to serve as a placeholder, until the actual image is ready. In Dreamweaver, placeholder ads can easily be maintained as Library items and placed as needed from the Assets panel, as shown in Figure 8-13.

 Cross-Reference   See Chapter 29 for information on creating and using Dreamweaver Library items.

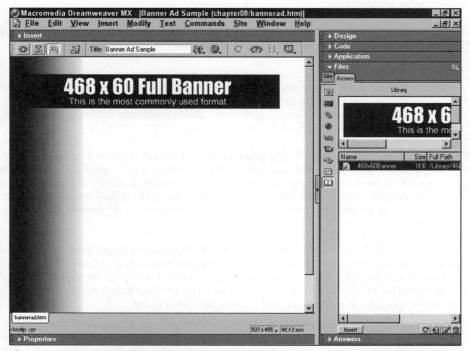

Figure 8-13: Use the Library to store standard banner ad images for use as placeholders.

If you'd prefer not to use placeholder graphics as described above, you can instead insert a plain `<img>` tag—with no `src` parameter. When an `<img>` tag without a `src` attribute is in the code, Dreamweaver displays a plain rectangle that can be resized to the proper banner ad dimensions in the Property inspector.

New Feature   You can insert a placeholder image by clicking the Image Placeholder button on the Insert bar, or by choosing Insert ➪ Image Placeholder. In the resulting Image Placeholder dialog box, you can enter an image name, dimensions, color, and alternate text. When the real graphics file is ready, use the Src text box on the Property inspector to specify the new file. The image name and alternate text will remain unchanged when you assign the new file, but the dimensions will automatically change to match those of the actual image.

Inserting Rollover Images

Rollovers are among the most popular of all Web page effects. A *rollover* (also known as a *mouseover*) occurs when the user's pointer passes over an image and the image changes in some way. It may appear to glow or change color and/or shape; when the pointer moves away from the graphic, the image returns to its original form. The rollover indicates interactivity, and attempts to engage the user with a little bit of flair.

Rollovers are usually accomplished with a combination of HTML and JavaScript. Dreamweaver was among the first Web authoring tools to automate the production of rollovers through its Swap Image and Swap Image Restore behaviors. Later versions of Dreamweaver make rollovers even easier with the Rollover Image object. With the Rollover Image object, if you can pick two images, you can make a rollover.

Cross-Reference   If you use Fireworks as your image-editing tool, refer to Chapter 24 to learn another method for creating rollover images.

Technically speaking, a rollover is accomplished by manipulating an `<img>` tag's `src` attribute. Recall that the `src` attribute is responsible for providing the actual filename of the graphic to be displayed; it is, quite literally, the source of the image. A rollover changes the value of `src` from one image file to another. Swapping the `src` value is analogous to having a picture within a frame and changing the picture while keeping the frame.

Caution   The picture frame analogy is appropriate on one other level: It serves as a reminder of the size barrier inherent in rollovers. A rollover changes only one property of an `<img>` tag, the source — it cannot change any other property, such as height or width. For this reason, both your original image and the image that is displayed during the rollover should be the same size. If they are not, the alternate image is resized to match the dimensions of the original image.

Dreamweaver's Rollover Image object automatically changes the image back to its original source when the user moves the pointer off the image. Optionally, you can elect to preload the images with the selection of a checkbox. Preloading is a Web page technique that reads the intended file or files into the browser's memory before they are displayed. With preloading, the images appear on demand, without any download delay.

Rollovers are typically used for buttons that, when clicked, open another Web page. In fact, JavaScript requires that an image include a link before it can detect when a user's pointer moves over it. Dreamweaver automatically includes the minimum link necessary: the # link. Although JavaScript recognizes this symbol as indicating a link, no action is taken if the image is clicked by the user; the #, by itself, is an empty link. You can supply whatever link you want in the Rollover Image object.

Tip   Some browsers link to the top of the page when they encounter a # link. If you wish to create a rollover image that doesn't link anywhere, change the # to the following:

```
javascript:;
```

You can change this directly in Code view, or in the Link field of the Property inspector for the button.

To include a Rollover Image object in your Web page, follow these steps:

1. Place your cursor where you want the rollover image to appear and choose Insert ➪ Rollover Image, or select Rollover Image from the Common category of the Insert bar. You can also drag the Rollover Image button to any existing location on the Web page.

   Dreamweaver opens the Insert Rollover Image dialog box shown in Figure 8-14.

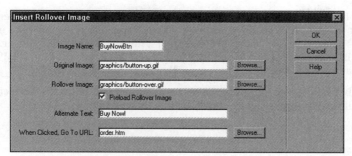

Figure 8-14: The Rollover Image object makes rollover graphics quick and easy.

2. If desired, you can enter a unique name for the image in the Image Name text box, or you can use the name automatically generated by Dreamweaver.

3. In the Original Image text box, enter the path and name of the graphic you want displayed when the user's mouse is not over the graphic. You can also choose the Browse (Choose) button to select the file. Press Tab when you're done.

4. In the Rollover Image text box, enter the path and name of the graphic file you want displayed when the user's pointer is over the image. You can also choose the Browse (Choose) button to select the file.

5. In the Alternate Text field, type a brief description of the graphic button.

6. If desired, specify a link for the image by entering it in the When Clicked, Go To URL text box or by clicking the Browse (Choose) button to select the file.

7. To enable images to load only when they are required, deselect the Preload Images option. Generally, it is best to leave this option selected (the default) so that no delay occurs in the rollover appearing.

8. Click OK when you're finished.

Tip Keep in mind that the Rollover Image object inserts both the original image and its alternate, whereas the Swap Image technique is applied to an existing image in the Web page. If you prefer to use the Rollover Image object rather than the Swap Image behavior, nothing prevents you from deleting an existing image from the Web page and inserting it again through the Rollover Image object. Just make sure that you note the path and name of the image before you delete it, so you can find it again.

Adding a Navigation Bar

Rollovers are nice effects, but a single button does not constitute a navigation system for a Web site. Typically, several buttons with a similar look and feel are placed next to one another to form a *navigation bar*. To make touring a site as intuitive as possible, the same navigation bar should appear on each page. You can achieve this effect by placing a copy of the navigation bar on each page, or by creating a frameset with one frame containing the navigation bar. Consistency of design and repetitive use of the navigation bar simplifies getting around a site — even for a first-time user.

Some designers build their navigation bars in a separate graphics program and then import them into Dreamweaver. Macromedia Fireworks, with its capability to export both images and code, makes this a strong option. Other Web designers, however, prefer to build separate rollover images in a graphics program and then assemble all the pieces at the HTML layout stage. Dreamweaver automates such a process with its Navigation Bar object.

The Navigation Bar object incorporates rollovers—and more. A Navigation Bar element can use up to four different images, each reflecting a different user action:

✦ **Up:** The user's pointer is away from the image.

✦ **Over:** The pointer is over the image.

✦ **Down:** The user has clicked the image.

✦ **Over While Down:** The user's pointer is over the image after it has been clicked.

One key difference separates a fully functioning navigation bar from a group of unrelated rollovers. When the Down state is available, if the user clicks one of the buttons, any other Down button is changed to the Up state. The effect is like a series of mutually exclusive radio buttons: You can show only one selected in a group. The Down state is often used to indicate the current selection.

Tip Although you can use the Navigation Bar object on any type of Web design, it works best in a frameset context, with one frame for navigation and one for content. If you insert a navigation bar with Up, Over, Down, and Over While Down states for each button in the navigation frame, you can target the content frame and gain the full effect of the mutually exclusive Down states.

Before you can use Dreamweaver's Navigation Bar object, you have to create a series of images for each button—one for each state you plan to use, as demonstrated in Figure 8-15. It's completely up to the designer how the buttons appear, but it's important that a consistent look and feel be applied for all the buttons in a navigation bar. For example, if the "over" state for Button A reveals a green glow, rolling over Buttons B, C, and D should cause the same glow.

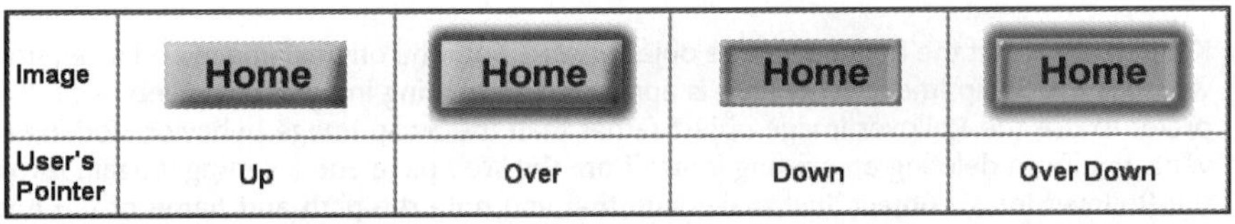

Image	Home	Home	Home	Home
User's Pointer	Up	Over	Down	Over Down

Figure 8-15: Before you invoke the Navigation Bar object, create a series of buttons, using a separate image for each state to be used.

To insert a navigation bar, follow these steps:

1. From the Insert bar, select the Navigation Bar button.

   The Insert Navigation Bar dialog box appears, as shown in Figure 8-16.

2. Enter a unique name for the first button in the Element Name field and press Tab.

Caution Be sure to use Tab rather than Enter (Return) when moving from field to field. When Enter (Return) is pressed, Dreamweaver attempts to build the navigation bar. If you have not completed the initial two steps (providing an Element Name and a source for the Up Image), an alert is displayed; otherwise, the navigation bar is built.

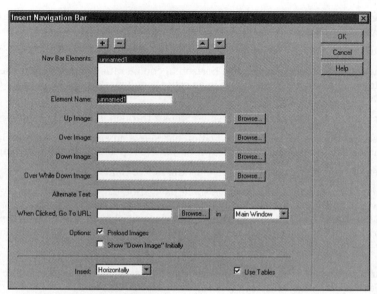

Figure 8-16: Add elements one at a time in the Insert Navigation Bar dialog box.

3. In the Up Image field, enter a path and filename or browse to a graphic file to use.

4. Select files for each of the remaining states: Over, Down, and Over While Down.

   If you don't want to use all four states, just specify the same image more than once. For example, if you don't want a separate Over While Down state, use the same image for Down and Over While Down.

5. If desired, enter a brief description of the button in the Alternative Text field.

6. Enter a URL or browse to a file in the When Clicked, Go To URL field.

Tip

If you do not enter a URL, Dreamweaver will insert a hash mark (#) in the generated code to create a "null link" for the button. Although the hash mark is supposed to cause a jump to nowhere when the button is clicked, the hash mark actually causes some browsers to jump to the top of the page. Although this is unusual in a navigation bar, if you wish to create a button that doesn't link anywhere, consider entering `javascript:;` in the Go To URL field to create a null link that won't cause browsers to jump to the top of the page.

7. If you're using a frameset, select a target for the URL from the drop-down list.

8. Enable or disable the Preload Images option as desired.

   For a multistate button to be effective, the reaction has to be immediate, and the images must be preloaded. It is highly recommended that you enable the Preload Images option.

9. If you want the current button to display the Down state first, select the Show "Down Image" Initially option.

   When this option is chosen, an asterisk appears next to the current button in the Nav Bar Elements list. Generally, you don't want more than one Down state showing at a time.

10. To set the orientation of the navigation bar, select either Horizontally or Vertically from the Insert drop-down list.

11. If you want to contain your images in a table, keep the Use Table option selected.

    If you decide not to use tables in a horizontal configuration, images are presented side by side; when you don't use tables in a vertical configuration, Dreamweaver inserts a line break (`<br>` tag) between each element.

12. Select the Add (plus) button and repeat Steps 2 through 9 to add the next element.

13. To reorder the elements in the navigation bar, select an element in the Nav Bar Elements list and use the Up and Down buttons to reposition it in the Elements list.

14. To remove an element, select it and click the Delete (minus) button.

Each page can have only one Dreamweaver-built navigation bar. If you try to insert a second, Dreamweaver asks if you'd like to modify the existing series. Clicking OK opens the Modify Navigation Bar dialog box, which is identical to the Insert Navigation Bar dialog box, except you can no longer change the orientation or table settings. You can also alter the inserted navigation bar by choosing Modify ➪ Navigation Bar.

Cross-Reference

If you're looking for even more control over your navigation bar, Dreamweaver also includes the Set Nav Bar Image behavior, which is fully covered in Chapter 23.

Summary

In this chapter, you learned how to include both foreground and background images in Dreamweaver. Understanding how images are handled in HTML is an absolute necessity for the Web designer. Some of the key points of this chapter are as follows:

✦ Web pages are restricted to using specific graphic formats. Virtually all browsers support GIF and JPEG files. PNG is also gaining acceptance. Dreamweaver can preview all three image types.

✦ Images are inserted in the foreground in Dreamweaver through the Image button on the Insert bar or from the Assets panel. Once the graphic is inserted, almost all modifications can be handled through the Property inspector.

✦ You can use HTML's background image function to lay a full-frame image or a tiled series of the same image underneath your text and graphics. Tiled images can be employed to create columns and other designs with small files.

✦ The simplest HTML graphic is the built-in horizontal rule. Useful for dividing your Web page into separate sections, you can size the horizontal rule either absolutely or relatively.

✦ Animated images can be inserted alongside, and in the same manner as, still graphics. The individual frames of a GIF animation must be created in a graphics program and then combined in an animation program.

✦ With the Rollover Image object, you can easily insert simple rollovers that use two different images. To build a rollover that uses more than two images, you have to use the Swap Image behavior.

✦ You can add a series of interrelated buttons — complete with four-state rollovers — by using the Navigation Bar object.

In the next chapter, you learn how to use hyperlinks in Dreamweaver.

✦   ✦   ✦

Establishing Web Links

Links *are* the Web. Everything else about the medium can be replicated in another form, but without links, there would be no World Wide Web. As your Web design work becomes more sophisticated, you'll find additional uses for links: sending mail, connecting to an FTP site — even downloading software.

In this chapter, you learn how Dreamweaver helps you manage various types of links, set anchors within documents to get smooth and accurate navigation, and establish targets for your links. This chapter begins with an overview of Internet addresses, called URLs, to give you the full picture of the possibilities.

Understanding URLs

URL stands for Uniform Resource Locator. An awkward phrase, it is one that, nonetheless, describes itself well — the URL's function is to provide a standard method for finding anything on the Internet. From Web pages to newsgroups to the smallest graphic on the most esoteric of pages, everything can be referenced through the URL mechanism.

For Web pages, a typical URL can have up to six different parts. Each part is separated by some combination of a slash, colon, and hashmark delimiter. When entered as an attribute's value, the entire URL is generally enclosed within quotes to ensure that the address is read as one unit. A generic URL using all the parts looks like the following:

```
scheme://server:port/path/file#anchor
```

Here's an example that uses every section:

```
http://www.idest.com:80/Dreamweaver/index.htm#bible
```

In order of appearance in the body of an Internet address, left to right, the parts denote the following:

- ✦ `http:` — The URL scheme used to access the resource. A scheme is an agreed-upon mechanism for communication, typically between a client and a server. The scheme to reference Web servers uses the HyperText Transfer Protocol (HTTP). Other schemes and their related protocols are discussed later in this section.

✦ www.idest.com — The name of the server providing the resource. The server can be either a domain name (with or without the "www" prefix) or an Internet Protocol (IP) address, such as 199.227.52.143.

✦ :80 — The port number to be used on the server. Most URLs do not include a port number, which is analogous to a telephone extension number on the server, because most servers use the defaults.

✦ /Dreamweaver — The directory path to the resource. Depending on where the resource (for example, the Web page) is located on the server, the following paths can be specified: no path (indicating that the resource is in the public root of the server), a single folder name, or a number of folders and subfolders.

✦ /index.htm — The filename of the resource. If the filename is omitted, the Web browser looks for a default page, often named index.html or index.htm. The browser reacts differently depending on the type of file. For example, GIFs and JPEGs are displayed by themselves; executable files and archives (Zip, StuffIt, and so on) are downloaded.

✦ #bible — The named anchor in the HTML document. This part is another optional section. The named anchor enables the Web designer to send the viewer to a particular section of an HTML page.

Although http is one of the most prevalent communication schemes used on the Internet, other schemes are also available. Whereas HTTP is used for accessing Web pages, the other schemes are used for such things as transferring files between servers and clients, or for sending e-mail. Table 9-1 describes the most common schemes used in URLs.

Table 9-1: Common URL Schemes and Associated Protocols

Scheme Syntax	Protocol	Usage
ftp://	File Transfer Protocol (FTP)	Links to an FTP server that is typically used for uploading and downloading files. The server may be accessed anonymously, or it may require a user name and password.
http://	HyperText Transfer Protocol (HTTP)	Used for connecting to a document available on a World Wide Web server
javascript:	JavaScript	Although it is not part of a true URL, some browsers support a scheme of javascript:, indicating the browser should execute JavaScript code. This provides an easy way to execute JavaScript code when a user clicks on a link.
mailto:	Simple Mail Transfer Protocol (SMTP)	Opens an e-mail form with the recipient's address already filled in. These links are useful when embedded in your Web pages to provide visitors with an easy feedback method.
news://	Network News Transfer Protocol (NNTP)	Connects to the specified Usenet newsgroup. Newsgroups are public, theme-oriented message boards on which anyone can post or reply to a message.
telnet://	TELNET	Enables users to log on directly to remote host computers and interact directly with the operating system software

Part of the richness of today's Web browsers stems from their capability to connect with all the preceding (and additional) services.

Tip

The `mailto:` scheme enables you not only to open up a preaddressed e-mail form, but also, with a little extra work, to specify the topic. For example, if I want to include a link to my e-mail address with the subject heading "Book Feedback," I can insert a link such as the following:

```
mailto:jlowery@idest.com?subject=Book%20Feedback
```

The question mark acts as a delimiter that enables a variable and a value to be passed to the browser; the `%20` is the decimal representation for a space that must be read by various servers. When you're trying to encourage feedback from your Web page visitors, every little bit helps.

Surfing the Web with Hypertext

Often, you assign a link to a word or phrase on your page, an image such as a navigational button, or a section of graphic for an image map (a large graphic in which various parts are links). To test the link, you preview the page in a browser; links are not active in Dreamweaver's Document window.

Designate links in HTML through the anchor tag pair: `<a>` and `</a>`. The anchor tag generally takes one main attribute—the hypertext reference, which is written as follows:

```
href="link name"
```

When you create a link, the anchor pair surrounds the text or object that is being linked. For example, if you link the phrase "Back to Home Page," it may look like the following:

```
<a href="index.html">Back to Home Page</a>
```

When you attach a link to an image, logo.gif, your code looks as follows:

```
<a href="home.html"><img src="images/logo.gif"></a>
```

Creating a basic link in Dreamweaver is easy. Simply follow these steps:

1. Select the text, image, or object you want to establish as a link.

2. In the Property inspector, enter the URL in the Link text box as shown in Figure 9-1. You can use one of the following methods to do so:

   - Type the URL directly into the Link text box.

   - Select the Folder icon to the right of the Link text box to open the Select File dialog box, where you can browse for the file.

   - Select the Point-to-File icon and drag your mouse to an existing page in the Site panel or anchor on the current page. This feature is explained later in this section.

You can also create a link by dragging a URL from the Assets panel onto a text or image selection. This procedure is covered more fully later in this chapter.

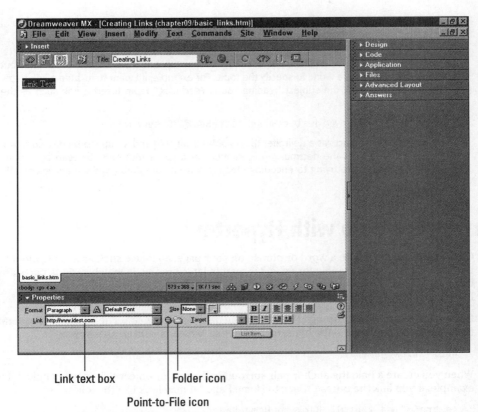

Link text box   Folder icon

Point-to-File icon

Figure 9-1: You can enter your link directly into the Link text box, select the Folder icon
to browse for a file, or point to the file directly with the Point-to-File icon.

Finally, you can create a link using the Insert menu or Insert bar. Without first selecting any
text, choose Insert ✦ Hyperlink, or in the Common category of the Insert bar, click the
Hyperlink button. This action opens the Hyperlink dialog box, where you can specify the
hotspot text, the URL for the link, and a link target (described later). This method also allows
you to specify the following:

✦ **Tab index:** A number specifying the order in which a user can tab through the page.
   Links with lower numbers will be tabbed to first, and links with no tab index defined
   will appear last in the tab order.

✦ **Title field:** A description of the link. In Netscape 6.0 and Internet Explorer 6.0, this text
   appears as a ToolTip when the user holds the cursor over the link.

✦ **Access key:** A single letter that serves as the keyboard equivalent for the hyperlink.
   Access keys work only in the most recent browser versions, and do not work consistently. Pressing the Alt (Option) key plus the access key may just select the link, or it
   may actually execute the link.

Note

If you don't see the Hyperlink dialog box when you insert a hyperlink, choose Edit ✦
Preferences and in the Common category, select the Show Dialog when Inserting Objects
option.

Regardless of how you create a link in Dreamweaver, a few restrictions exist for specifying URLs. Dreamweaver does not support any letters from the extended character set (also known as High ASCII), such as ¡, à, or ñ. Complete URLs must have fewer than a total of 255 characters. You should be cautious about using spaces in pathnames and, therefore, in URLs. Although most browsers can interpret the address, spaces are changed to a %20 symbol for proper UNIX usage. This change can make your URLs difficult to read.

Note   Whitespace in your HTML code usually doesn't have an adverse effect on what is displayed in a browser. However, Netscape browsers are sensitive to whitespace when assigning a link to an image. If you isolate your image tag from the anchor tags like this

```
<a href="index.htm">
<img src="images/Austria.gif" width="34" height="24">
</a>
```

some Netscape browser versions attach a small blue underscore—a tail, really—to your image. Because Dreamweaver automatically codes the anchor tag properly, without any additional whitespace, this odd case applies only to hand-coded or previously coded HTML.

Text links are most often rendered with a blue color and underlined. Depending on the background color for your page, you may wish to change the color of text links to improve readability. You can specify the document link color by choosing Modify ⇨ Page Properties and selecting the Links color box. In Page Properties, you can also alter the color to which the links change after being selected (the Visited Links color), and the color flashed when the link is clicked (the Active Links color).

Cross-Reference   If your target audience will be using newer browsers (Internet Explorer 4.0 and above, or Netscape Navigator 4.0 and above), you can also change link colors using Cascading Style Sheets. Using style sheets is actually the preferred method of specifying the color in newer browsers. Chapter 20 explains how to change link colors with style sheets.

Tip   Want to add a little variety to your text links? You can actually change the color of the link on an individual basis. To do this, you have to enter the link in the Property inspector before you apply the color. Be sure to exercise a little discretion though—using too many colors may distract or confuse your Web page visitors.

Links without Underlines

To remove the underlined aspect of a link, you can use one of two methods. The classic method—which works for all graphics-capable browsers—uses an image, rather than text, as the link. You must make sure the `border` attribute of your image is set to 0 because a linked image usually displays a blue border if a `border` attribute exists. Dreamweaver adds `border="0"` to all image links, as a default.

The second, newer method uses Cascading Style Sheets. Although this is an excellent one-stop solution for 4.0 and later browsers, the links still appear with underlines on earlier browser versions. Refer to the Dreamweaver Technique for eliminating the underlines in links in Chapter 20.

Inserting URLs from the Assets panel

Internet addresses get more complicated every day. Trying to remember them all correctly and avoid typos can make the Web designer's job unnecessarily difficult. Dreamweaver makes this task easier with the URLs category in the Assets panel. Using the Assets panel, you can drag-and-drop the trickiest URLs with ease.

The Assets panel lists URLs that are already referenced somewhere within your site. If you want to link to the same URL again, just drag it from the Assets panel.

Tip   To avoid rework, after you have typed a URL for a link in a document, test that link in a browser to be sure it's correct. Then when you assign the same URL to other links using the Assets panel, you can be confident that the link will work as expected.

The Assets panel lists only full Internet addresses — whether to files (such as `http://www.idest.com/UltraDev/`) or to e-mail addresses (such as `mailto:jlowery@idest.com`). Document- or site-relative links are not listed as Assets. To assign a link to a document- or site-relative page, use one of the other linking methods discussed in this chapter, such as pointing to a file.

To assign a URL from the Assets panel, follow these steps:

1. If it's not already visible, select Window ➪ Assets or click the Assets icon on the Launcher bar to display the Assets panel.

2. Select the URLs icon on the side of the Assets panel to show that category, as shown in Figure 9-2.

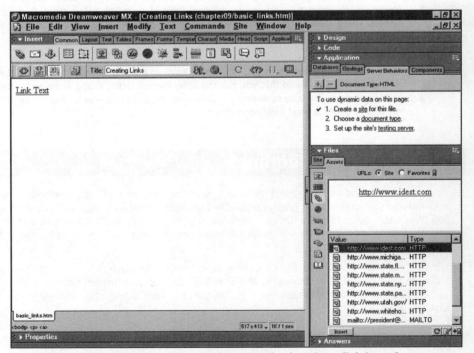

Figure 9-2: Banish typos from your absolute URLs by dragging a link from the Assets panel to any selected text or graphic.

3. If necessary, select the Refresh Site List button on the Assets panel to list the most current links found in the site.

Note   As with other Assets panel categories, you need to select the Refresh Site List button to make available all the possible URLs in a site. Alternatively, you could choose Refresh Site List from the context menu on the panel. Either action causes Dreamweaver to scan all the Web pages within the site and extract all the complete Internet addresses found.

4. In the Document window, select the text or image you want the link assigned to.

5. Drag the desired link from the Assets panel onto the selected text or image; alternatively, highlight the link in the panel and then click the Apply button.

If you don't select text or an image before dragging the URL from the Assets panel, a link will still be created in your document. In this situation, Dreamweaver uses the URL name as the hotspot.

You'll notice that the Edit button on the Assets panel is unavailable for the URLs category. Links cannot be edited; they can only be applied as shown in the preview area.

Pointing to a file

Dreamweaver provides an alternative method of identifying a link — pointing to it. By using the Point-to-File icon on the Property inspector, you can quickly fill in the Link text box by dragging your mouse to any existing named anchor or file visible in the Dreamweaver environment. With the Point-to-File feature, you can avoid browsing through folder after folder as you search for a file you can clearly see onscreen.

You can point to another open document, to a document in another frame in the same window, or to any named anchor visible on the screen. If your desired link is a named anchor located further down the page, Dreamweaver automatically scrolls to find it. You can even point to a named anchor in another document, and Dreamweaver enters the full syntax correctly. Named anchors are covered in detail later in this chapter.

Perhaps one of the slickest ways to apply the Point-to-File feature is to use it in tandem with the Site panel. The Site panel lists all the existing files in any given Web site, and when both it and the Document window are onscreen, you can quickly point to any file.

Pointing to a file uses what could be called a "drag-and-release" mouse technique, as opposed to the more ordinary point-and-click or drag-and-drop method. To select a new link using the Point-to-File icon, follow these steps:

1. Select the text or the graphic that you'd like to make into a link.

2. In the Property inspector, click and hold the Point-to-File icon located to the right of the Link text box.

3. Holding down the mouse button, drag the mouse until it is over an existing link or named anchor in the Document window or a file in the Site panel.

   As you drag the mouse, a line extends from the Point-to-File icon, and the reminder "Drag to a file to make a link" appears in the Link text box.

4. When you locate the file you want to link to, release the mouse button. The filename with the accompanying path information is written into the Link text box as shown in Figure 9-3.

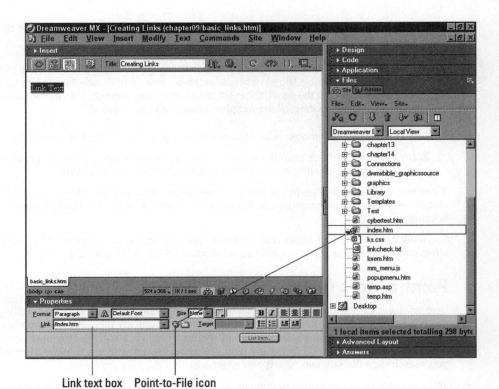

Link text box   Point-to-File icon

Figure 9-3: The Point-to-File icon enables you to quickly insert a link to any onscreen file.

Addressing types

Three types of URLs are used as links: absolute addresses, document-relative addresses, and site-root–relative addresses. Let's briefly look at these address types.

✦ Absolute addresses require the full URL, as follows:

```
http://www.macromedia.com/software/Dreamweaver/
```

This type of address is most often used for referencing links on another Web server.

✦ Document-relative addresses know the scheme, server, and path aspects of the URL. You need to include additional path information only if the link is outside of the current Web page's folder. Links in the current document's folder can be addressed with their filenames only. To reference an item in a subfolder, just name the folder, enter a forward slash, and then enter the item's filename, as follows:

```
images/background.gif
```

✦ Site-root–relative addresses are indicated with a leading forward slash:

```
/navigation/upndown.html
```

The preceding address links to a file named upndown.html stored in the navigation directory at the current site root. Dreamweaver translates site-relative links to document-relative links when the Preview in Browser feature is used.

Checking links

A Webmaster must often perform the tedious but necessary task of verifying the links on all the Web pages in a site. Because of the Web's fluid nature, links can work one day and break the next. Dreamweaver includes powerful link-checking and link-updating capabilities.

Dreamweaver can generate reports for broken links, external links (links to files outside your site) and to orphaned files (files in your site with no links to them). You can check links for an open document, for all documents in a site, or for selected documents in the Site panel.

To check links in the current document, choose File ➪ Check Page ➪ Check Links, or press Shift+F8. To generate the link report for the entire site, open the Site panel (Window ➪ Site), and from the Site menu on the Site panel, choose Check Links Sitewide. To report on links for certain files, select the files or folders in the Site panel, right-click (control-click) and then choose Check Links ➪ Selected Files/Folders. If the Link Checker panel is open, you can also click the Check Links button and then select the scope of your check: current document, entire site, or selected files in the site.

Tip   To stop an in-progress link check, click the Cancel button in the Link Checker panel.

All of these methods open the Link Checker panel, displaying the results of the link check. In the Show drop-down list at the top of the Link Checker panel, select the report you wish to see: Broken links, External links, or Orphaned Files. The Orphaned Files report is only available if you check the entire site. Note that the broken links report verifies not only clickable hotspots to other HTML files, but also checks references to graphics and other external files.

You can save the link report by clicking the Save Report button on the Link Checker panel, or by right-clicking (control-clicking) in the panel and choosing Save Results from the pop-up menu. To clear the Link Checker panel, right-click (control-click) in the Link Checker panel and then choose Clear Results.

Double-clicking on an entry in the Link Checker panel opens the document where the error occurred, with the broken link selected. You can quickly correct the link using the Property inspector or by choosing Modify ➪ Change Link. To remove the link but leave the hotspot text, clear the Link field in the Property inspector, or choose Modify ➪ Remove Link. If the same URL is referenced in more than one place in your site, you can change all occurrences of it at once. To do this, in the Site panel, choose Site ➪ Change Link Sitewide, and enter the URL to be changed, and the new URL before clicking OK.

Adding an E-Mail Link

E-mail links are very common on the Web. When a user clicks an e-mail link, it displays a window for sending a new e-mail message (rather than opening a new Web page like a regular link). The message window is already preaddressed to the recipient, making it convenient to use. All the user has to do is add a subject, enter a message, and select Send.

Dreamweaver includes an object that streamlines the process of adding e-mail links. Just enter the text of the line and the e-mail address, and the link is ready. E-mail links, like other links, do not work in Dreamweaver when clicked. They must be previewed in a browser.

To enter an e-mail link, follow these steps:

1. Position your cursor where you want the e-mail link to appear.

2. From the Common category on the Insert bar, select the Email Link button.

   The Email Link dialog box, shown in Figure 9-4, appears.

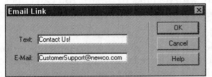

Figure 9-4: The Email Link dialog box helps you create links that make it simple for your Web page visitors to send e-mail messages.

3. In the Email Link dialog box, enter the visible text for the link in the Text field.

4. Enter the e-mail address in the E-Mail field.

Caution   The e-mail address must be in the format `name@company.com`. Dreamweaver does not check to make sure you've entered the proper format.

5. Click OK when you're done.

Note   If you already have the text for the e-mail link in the document, you can also use the Property inspector to insert an e-mail link. Just highlight the text and in the Link field of the Property inspector, enter the URL in the following format:

   `mailto:name@company.com`

   Make sure that the URL is a valid e-mail address with the @ sign properly placed.

E-mail Warnings

Here's a bit of the frustration that Web designers sometimes face: On some browsers, notably Internet Explorer, the user may see a dialog box when the e-mail link is first selected. The dialog box informs her that she is about to send an e-mail message over the Internet. The user has the option not to see these warnings, but there's no way for the Web designer to prevent them from appearing when using an e-mail link. However, another method of collecting data from a user — HTML forms — doesn't require the user to have e-mail software installed on her computer, and allow the user to send information to the server without receiving the warning message. Chapter 11 explains how to create HTML forms.

Navigating with Anchors

Whenever you normally link to an HTML page, through absolute or relative addressing, the browser displays the page from the top. Your Web visitors must scroll to any information rendered below the current screen. One HTML technique, however, links to a specific point anywhere on your page regardless of the display window's contents. This technique uses *named anchors*. A named anchor is simply an HTML anchor tag pair (`<a></a>`) that includes a `name` attribute. The named anchor serves as a target for links, allowing links to the middle of a page, or wherever the named anchor is located within the document.

Using named anchors is a two-step process. First, you place a named anchor somewhere on your Web page. This placement is coded in HTML as an anchor tag using the `name` attribute, with nothing between the opening and closing tags. In HTML, named anchors look like the following:

```
<a name="bible"></a>
```

The second step includes a link to that named anchor from somewhere else on your Web page. If used, a named anchor is referenced in the final portion of an Internet address, designated by the hash mark (#), as follows:

```
<a href="http://www.idest.com/Dreamweaver/index.htm#bible>
```

You can include any number of named anchors on a page and any number of links to named anchors on the current page or different pages. Named anchors are commonly used with a table of contents or index.

To insert a named anchor, follow these steps:

1. Place the cursor where you want the named anchor to appear.

2. Choose Insert ➪ Named Anchor. You can also select the Named Anchor button from the Common category of the Insert bar, or use the key shortcut Ctrl+Alt+A (Command+Option+A).

3. The Named Anchor dialog box opens. Type the anchor name into the text box.

Named anchors are case-sensitive and must be unique within the page.

When you click OK, Dreamweaver places a named anchor symbol in the current cursor location and opens the Named Anchor Property inspector (shown in Figure 9-5).

In Design view, named anchors are represented by a small book icon in the page. If you can't see the named anchor symbol, choose View ➪ Visual Aids ➪ Invisible Elements; if the symbol is still not visible, update your Preference settings for the Invisible Elements category.

4. To change an anchor's name, click the named anchor symbol within the page and alter the text in the Property inspector.

As with other invisible symbols, the named anchor symbol can be cut and pasted or moved using the drag-and-drop method.

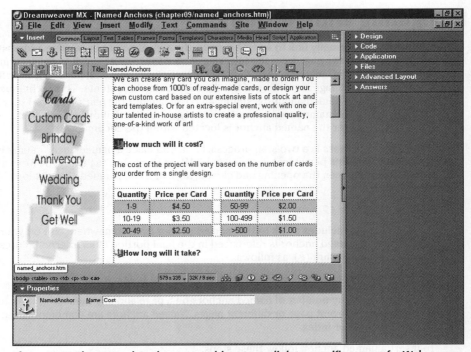

Figure 9-5: The Named Anchor tag enables you to link to specific areas of a Web page.

Moving within the same document

One of the major advantages of using named anchors is the almost instantaneous response viewers receive when they link to named anchors from the same page. The browser just scrolls to the particular place in the document because the entire page is already loaded. For long text documents, this capability is an invaluable timesaver.

After you have placed a named anchor in your document, you can link to the anchor. You can create more than one named anchor in your document before adding links to the anchors. Follow these steps to create a link to a named anchor in the same document:

1. Select the text or image that you want to designate as a link.

2. In the Link text box of the Property inspector, type a hash mark (#) followed by the exact anchor name:

   #start

   Remember that anchor names are case-sensitive and must be unique in each document.

Tip　You should place the named anchor one line above the heading or image to which you want to link the viewer. Browsers tend to be quite literal. If you place the named anchor on the same line, the browser renders it up against the top of the window. Placing your named anchor up one line gives your topic a bit of breathing room in the display.

In Dreamweaver, you can also use the Point-to-File icon to choose a named anchor link. If your named anchor is in the same document, just drag the Point-to-File icon to the named anchor symbol. When you release the mouse, the address for the named anchor is inserted into the Link text box. If the named anchor is on the same page, but off screen, Dreamweaver automatically scrolls the Document window as you drag toward the edge. In Windows, the closer you move to the edge, the faster Dreamweaver scrolls. Dreamweaver even returns the screen to your original location, with the new link at the top of the screen, after you release the mouse button.

In long documents with a table of contents or index linking to a number of named anchors, it's common practice — and a good idea — to place a link back to the top of the page after every screen or every topic. This technique enables your users to return to the menu quickly and pick another topic without having to manually scroll all the way back.

Using named anchors in a different page

If your table of contents is on a separate page from the topics of your site, you can use named anchors to send the viewer anywhere on a new page. The technique is the same as already explained for placing named anchors, but with one minor difference when it comes to linking. Instead of placing a hash mark and name to denote the named anchor, you must first include the URL of the linked page.

Suppose you want to call the disclaimer section of a legal page from your table of contents. You could insert something like the following in the Link text box of the Property inspector:

```
legal.htm#disclaimer
```

This link, when activated, first loads the referenced Web page (legal.htm) and then goes directly to the named anchor place (#disclaimer). Figure 9-6 shows how you enter this in the Property inspector. Keep in mind that you can use any form of addressing prior to the hash mark and named anchor.

Figure 9-6: You can link to any part of a separate Web page using named anchors.

Creating Null Links

One of the more obscure uses for named anchors comes into play when you are trying to use Dreamweaver's JavaScript Behavior feature. Because JavaScript needs to work with a particular type of tag to perform onMouseOver and other events, a useful trick is to create a null link — a link that doesn't actually link to anywhere.

You can create a null link by marking some text or an image with a link to #nowhere. You can use any name for the nonexistent named anchor. In fact, you don't even have to use a name — you can just use a hash mark by itself (#).

Note one problem, however: Netscape browsers have a tendency to send the page to the top if a link of this type is used. Many programmers have begun to substitute a JavaScript function instead, such as javascript:;. Dreamweaver itself now uses javascript:; instead of # when a new behavior is attached to an image.

Targeting Your Links

Thus far, all the links discussed in this chapter have had a similar effect: They open another Web page or section in your browser's window. What if you want to force the browser to open another window and load that new URL in the new window? HTML enables you to specify the target for your links.

Cross-Reference Targets are most often used in conjunction with frames—that is, you can make a link in one frame open a file in another. For more information about this technique, see Chapter 14.

Targets have uses outside of displaying a page in a certain frame. Let's take a look at one of the HTML predefined targets useful in a situation where you want to load another URL into a new window.

To specify a new browser window as the target for a link, follow these steps:

1. Select the text or image you want to designate as your new link.

2. In the Property inspector, enter the URL into the Link text box.

   After you've entered a link, the target option becomes active.

3. In the Target drop-down list, select _blank. You can also type it in the list box.

   Dreamweaver inserts a _blank option in the Target list box, as shown in Figure 9-7. Now, when your link is activated, the browser spawns a new window and loads the referenced link into it. The user has both windows available.

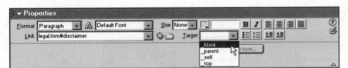

Figure 9-7: With the Target attribute, you can force a user's browser to open a separate window to display a specific link.

The _blank target is most often used when the originating Web page is acting as a jump station and has numerous links available. By keeping the original Web page open, the user can view another site without losing the origin point. You can even use a _blank target with links to named anchors in the same document.

Note Three other system-wide targets exist: _top, _parent, and _self. Both _top and _parent are primarily used with framesets: The _top target replaces the outermost frameset, and _parent replaces the frameset containing the current page. These two have the same effect, except in the case of nested framesets. The _self target is the default behavior, and only the current page is replaced.

Caution Some versions of key online services, such as America Online and WebTV, don't enable their built-in browsers to open new windows. Every link that is accessed is displayed in the same browser window.

Summary

Whether they are links for Web site navigation or jumps to other related sites, hypertext links are an essential part of any Web page. Dreamweaver gives you full control over your inserted anchors.

✦ Through a unique URL, you can access virtually any Web page, graphic, or other item available on the Internet.

✦ The HyperText Transfer Protocol (HTTP) is one of the most common methods of Internet connection, but Web pages can link to other formats, including FTP, e-mail, and newsgroups.

✦ Any of the three basic address formats — absolute, document-relative, or site-root–relative — can be inserted in the Link text box of Dreamweaver's Property inspector to create a link.

✦ Dreamweaver has several quick linking capabilities in the Assets panel and Point-to-File feature.

✦ Named anchors give you the power to jump to specific parts of any Web page, whether the page is the current one or one that is located on another server.

✦ With the `_blank target` attribute, you can force a link to open in a new browser window, leaving your original window available to the user.

In the next chapter, you learn how to work with tables in Dreamweaver.

✦   ✦   ✦

Setting Up Tables

Tables bring structure to a Web page, and they are especially important when displaying data for Web applications. Whether it is used to align numbers in a spreadsheet or arrange columns of information on a page, an HTML table brings a bit of order to otherwise free-flowing content. Initially, tables were implemented to present raw data in a more readable format. It wasn't long before Web designers adopted tables as the most capable tool to control page layout.

Dreamweaver's implementation of tables reflects this trend in Web page design. Drag-and-drop table sizing, easy organization of rows and columns, and instant table reformatting all help get the job done in the shortest time possible. Table editing features enable you to select and modify anything in a table—from a single cell to multiple columns. Moreover, using Dreamweaver's commands, you can sort static table data in a variety of ways or completely reformat it.

This chapter covers everything you need to know to get started creating HTML tables in Dreamweaver. You can also dynamically add data to tables from an external data source using server-side processing. Using dynamic data is covered in Chapter 16.

Dreamweaver includes a feature that takes table layout to the next level of ease of use and power. With the Layout view, designers can draw out individual cells with a stroke of the mouse, and Dreamweaver will automatically create a borderless, content-ready table. You can even add nested tables to maintain design integrity. While you still need to know the basics of table functionality to get the most out of this tool, Layout view offers you a technique for visually structuring your Web page.

Although Dynamic HTML gives Web designers another route to precise layout control, many Web designers use a combination of tools to get desired effects and maintain wide browser compatibility. In other words, HTML tables are going to be around for a long time.

HTML Table Fundamentals

A table is basically a grid that expands as you add text or images. Tables consist of three main components: rows, columns, and cells. *Rows* extend across a table from left to right, and *columns* extend up and down. A *cell* is the area within the intersection of a row and a column; it's where you enter your information. Cells expand to fit whatever they hold. If you have enabled the table border, your browser shows the outline of the table and all its cells.

In HTML, the structure and all the data of a table are contained between the table tag pair, `<table>` and `</table>`. The `<table>` tag can take numerous attributes, determining a table's width (which can be given in absolute measurement or as a percentage of the screen) as well as the border, alignment on the page, and background color. You can also control the size of the spacing between cells and the amount of padding within cells.

Note You can insert a `<table>. . .</table>` pair directly in your code by choosing Insert ➪ Table Objects ➪ Table or by clicking the Table Tag button in the Tables category of the Insert bar. This must be done in Code view, where you can see the exact location of your cursor before inserting the tag pair.

HTML uses a strict hierarchy when describing a table. You can see this clearly in Listing 10-1, which shows the HTML generated from a simple table in Dreamweaver.

Listing 10-1: Code for an HTML table

```
<table border="1" width="75%">
  <tr>
    <td> </td>
    <td> </td>
    <td> </td>
  </tr>
  <tr>
    <td> </td>
    <td> </td>
    <td> </td>
  </tr>
  <tr>
    <td> </td>
    <td> </td>
    <td> </td>
  </tr>
</table>
```

Note The   in the table code is HTML for a non-breaking space. Dreamweaver inserts this code in each empty table cell because some browsers collapse the cell without it. Enter any text or image in the cell, and Dreamweaver automatically removes the   code.

Rows

After the opening `<table>` tag comes the first row tag `<tr>. . . </tr>` pair. Within the current row, you can specify attributes for horizontal alignment or vertical alignment. In addition, browsers recognize row color as an added option.

If you are working directly in Code view, you can insert a `<tr>. . .</tr>` pair by choosing Insert ➪ Table Objects ➪ TR or by choosing the Table Row button in the Tables category of the Insert bar. See "Inserting rows and columns," later in this chapter, for methods of inserting rows in Design view.

Cells

Cells are marked in HTML with the `<td>. . .</td>` tag pair. No specific code exists for a column; rather, the number of columns is determined by the maximum number of cells within a single table row. For example, in Listing 10-1, notice the three sets of `<td>` tags between each `<tr>` pair. This means the table has three columns.

A cell can span more than one row or column—in these cases, you see a `rowspan=value` or `colspan=value` attribute in the `<td>` tag, as illustrated in Listing 10-2. This code is also for a table with three rows and three columns, but the second cell in the first row spans two columns.

Listing 10-2: HTML table with column spanning

```
<table width="75%"  border="0">
  <tr>
    <td> </td>
    <td colspan="2"> </td>
  </tr>
  <tr>
    <td> </td>
    <td> </td>
    <td> </td>
  </tr>
  <tr>
    <td> </td>
    <td> </td>
    <td> </td>
  </tr>
</table>
```

Cells can also be given horizontal or vertical alignment attributes; these attributes override any similar attributes specified by the table row. When you give a cell a particular width, all the cells in that column are affected. Width can be specified in either an absolute pixel measurement or as a percentage of the overall table.

In Code view, you can insert a `<td>. . .</td>` pair to define a single table cell by choosing Insert ⇨ Table Objects ⇨ TD or by choosing the Table Data button in the Tables category of the Insert bar.

Column and row headings

HTML uses a special type of cell called a *table header* for column and row headings. Information in these cells is marked with a `<th>` tag and is generally rendered in boldface, centered within the cell.

To insert a `<th>. . .</th>` pair for a table heading cell, choose Insert ⇨ Table Objects ⇨ TH or click the Table Heading button in the Tables category of the Insert bar. See the section "Setting cell, column, and row properties," later in this chapter, for another way to designate table header cells.

Tip

After the initial `<table>` tag, you can place an optional caption for the table. In Dreamweaver, you can enter the `<caption>` tag in the Code view or Code inspector by choosing Insert ⇨Table Objects ⇨ Caption. From Code view, you can also choose the Table Caption button from the Tables category of the Insert bar.

The following example shows how the tag works:

```
<caption valign="bottom">Table of Periodic Elements</caption>
```

Inserting Tables in Dreamweaver

You can control almost all of a table's HTML features through Dreamweaver's point-and-click interface. To insert a table in the current cursor position, use one of the following methods:

✦ Select the Insert Table button on the Insert bar.

✦ Choose Insert ⇨ Table from the menus.

✦ Use the keyboard shortcut: Ctrl+Alt+T (Command+Option+T).

Depending on your preference settings, any of these methods will either immediately insert a table into your page or open the Insert Table dialog box. See "Setting Table Preferences" in this chapter for more about this preference setting. The Insert Table dialog box, shown in Figure 10-1, contains the following values when it is first displayed:

Attribute	Default	Description
Rows	3	The number of horizontal rows
Columns	3	The number of vertical columns
Width	75 percent	Sets the preset width of the table. This can be specified as a percentage of the containing element (screen, layer, or another table) or an absolute pixel size.
Border	1 pixel	The width of the border around each cell and the entire table
Cell Padding	0	The space between a cell's border and its contents, measured in pixels. A value of 0 indicates no margin space within the cell.
Cell Spacing	0	The number of pixels between each cell. A value of 0 indicates no space between cells.

Note

Depending on your Preference settings, you may also see the Accessibility Settings for Tables dialog box when you insert a table. Refer to the section "Setting Table Preferences," later in this chapter, for more information.

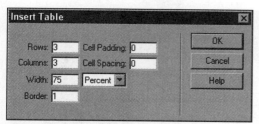

Figure 10-1: The Insert Table dialog box starts out with a default table of three columns and three rows; you can adjust it as needed.

If you aren't sure of the number of rows and/or columns you need, put in your best guess — you can add or delete rows or columns as necessary.

The default table is sized to take up 75 percent of the browser window. You can alter this percentage by changing the value in the Width text box. The table maintains this proportion as you add text or images, except in the following situations:

◆ When an image is larger than the specified percentage

◆ When the `nowrap` attribute is used for the cell or table row and there is too much text to fit

In either case, the percentage set for the table is ignored, and the cell and table expand to accommodate the text or image. (For further information on the `nowrap` attribute, see the section "Cell Wrap," later in this chapter.)

Note The Insert Table dialog box uses what are called *sticky* settings, displaying your previously used settings the next time you open the dialog box. This handy feature enables you to set the border width to 0, for example, and forget about resetting it each time.

If you prefer to enter the table width as an absolute pixel value, as opposed to the relative percentage, type the number of pixels in the Width text box and select Pixels in the drop-down list of width options.

Figure 10-2 shows three tables: At the top is the default table, with the width set to 75 percent. The middle table, set to 100 percent, will take up the full width of the browser window. The third table is fixed at 300 pixels — approximately half of a 640 × 480 window.

Tip You don't have to declare a width for your table at all. If you delete the value in the Width text box of the Insert Table dialog box, your table starts out as small as possible and only expands to accommodate inserted text or images. However, this can make it difficult to position your cursor inside a cell to enter content. You can always delete any set size — pixel or percentage — later.

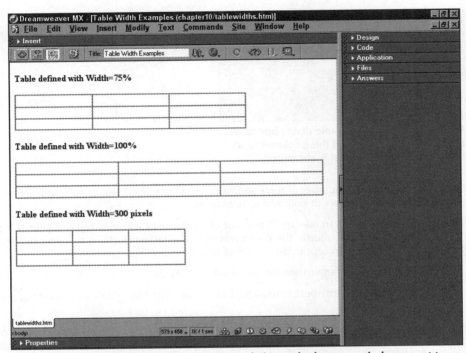

Figure 10-2: The width of a table can be set relative to the browser window or set to an absolute width in pixels.

Setting Table Preferences

Several preferences directly affect tables. Two can be set by choosing Edit ➪ Preferences and looking in the General category; another can be found in the Accessibility category.

The first pertinent option is the Show Dialog When Inserting Objects checkbox. If this option is turned off, Dreamweaver inserts a default table (3 rows by 3 columns at 75 percent width of the screen with a 1-pixel border), without displaying a dialog box and asking for your input. If you have previously inserted tables using the Insert Table dialog box, and then turn off this Preferences option, any subsequent table will have the same characteristics as the last table you inserted. Should you wish to change these values, you can adjust them from the Table Property inspector once the table has been inserted.

The second notable preference in the General category is labeled Faster Table Editing (Deferred Update). Because tables expand and contract dynamically depending on their contents, Dreamweaver gives you the option of turning off the continual updating. (Depending on the speed of your system, the updating can slow down your table input.) If the Faster Table Editing option is enabled, the table is updated whenever you click outside of it or press the keyboard shortcut, Ctrl+space (Command+space).

Note　If you enable Faster Table Editing and begin typing in one cell of your table, notice that the text wraps within the cell, and the table expands vertically. However, when you click outside of the table or press Ctrl+space (Command+space), the table cells adjust horizontally as well, completing the redrawing of the table.

Whether or not you should leave the Faster Table Editing option on depends on your system and the complexity of your tables. Nested tables tend to update more slowly, and you may need to take advantage of the Faster Table Editing option if tables aren't getting redrawn quickly enough. You might try turning off Faster Table Editing until it seems that you need it.

The Accessibility category in the Preferences dialog box contains another setting that affects tables. If you select the Tables option in the Accessibility category, the Accessibility Options for Tables dialog box appears when you insert a new table, as shown in Figure 10-3.

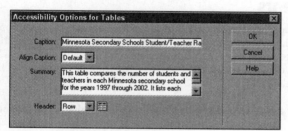

Figure 10-3: With the Tables accessibility option selected, the Accessibility Options for Tables dialog box appears when you insert a new table.

The table attributes that you can set with the accessibility option include the following:

✦ **Caption** and **Align Caption:** A table caption is just a brief description of the table. By setting the Align Caption option, you can specify whether the table caption appears at the top, bottom, left or right of the table. Choosing default does not add an align attribute to the `<caption>` tag, and instead uses the browser's default alignment. Note that the align attribute on the `<caption>` tag is deprecated in HTML 4.0. This means that, although the attribute is currently still supported, there is another, preferred method to achieve the same effect in newer browsers. In this case, the alignment can also be achieved using Cascading Style Sheets, described in Chapter 20.

✦ **Summary:** Entering text in this box adds the summary attribute to your `<table>` tag. The summary should be a verbal description of the table layout, so that people who are having the page read to them (for example, through a nonvisual browser) can understand the layout of the table information when it is read to them. For example, your summary could say "This table compares the number of students and teachers in each Minnesota secondary school for the years 1997 through 2002. It lists each school in the Minnesota, grouped by school district. For each of the years 1997 through 2002, there are columns for the number of students and number of teachers in each school." This is particularly important for complex tables. The text you enter for the summary is not displayed in visual browsers.

✦ **Header:** You can choose to add a header row, column, or both, to your table using the Header control. In addition to simply creating the heading cells with `<th>` tags instead of the usual `<td>`, this adds the scope attribute to the cell. The scope attribute helps nonvisual browsers interpret and present the structure of the table, by indicating whether the cell is a column heading or a row heading. In visual browsers, text in header rows or columns is typically displayed as bold and centered.

Modifying Tables

Most modifications to tables start in the Property inspector. Dreamweaver helps you manage the basic table parameters — width, border, and alignment — and provides attributes for other useful but more arcane features of a table, such as converting table width from pixels to percentage of the screen, and vice versa.

Selecting table elements

As with text or images, the first step in altering a table (or any of its elements) is selection. Dreamweaver simplifies the selection process, making it easy to change both the properties and the contents of entire tables, selected rows or columns, and even non-adjacent cells. You can change the font size and color of a row with a click or two of the mouse — instead of highlighting and modifying each individual cell.

Note   All of the following discussions about table selections pertain only to Standard view; they are not applicable in Layout view.

In Dreamweaver, you can select the following elements of a table:

✦ The entire table

✦ A single row

✦ Multiple rows, either adjacent or separate

✦ A single column

✦ Multiple columns, either adjacent or separate

✦ A single cell

✦ Multiple cells, either adjacent or separate

Once a table element is selected, you can modify its properties.

Selecting an entire table

Several methods are available for selecting the entire table, whether you're a menu- or mouse-oriented designer. To select the table via a menu, do one of the following:

✦ With the cursor positioned in the tables, choose Modify ➪ Table ➪ Select Table.

✦ With any table row already selected, choose Edit ➪ Select Parent Tag or use the keyboard shortcut, Ctrl+[(Command+[).

✦ Right-click (Control+click) inside a table to display the context menu and choose Table ➪ Select Table.

To select an entire table with the mouse, use one of the following techniques:

✦ Click the bottom or right border of the table. You can also click anywhere along the table border when the pointer becomes a four-sided arrow.

✦ Select the <table> tag in the Tag Selector.

✦ Click immediately to one side of the table and drag the mouse over the table.

However you select the table, the selected table is surrounded by a black border, with sizing handles on the right, bottom, and bottom-right corner (as shown in Figure 10-4), just like a selected graphic.

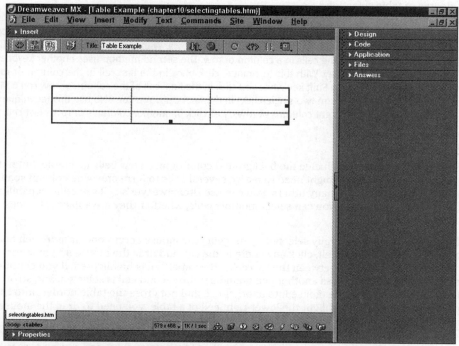

Figure 10-4: A selected table can be identified by the black border outlining the table and the three sizing handles.

Selecting a row or column

Altering rows or columns of table text without Dreamweaver is a major time-consuming chore. Each cell has to be individually selected, and the changes applied. Dreamweaver has an intuitive method for selecting single or multiple columns and rows, comparable — and in some ways, superior — to major word processing programs.

As with entire tables, you have several methods for selecting columns or rows. None of the techniques, however, use the menus; row and column selections are handled primarily with the mouse. In fact, you can select an entire row or column with one click.

The one-click method for selecting a single column or row requires that you position your pointer directly above the column or to the left of the row you want to choose, similar to how you would select a row or column in a Microsoft Word table. Move the pointer slowly toward the table — when the pointer becomes a single arrow, with the arrowhead pointing down for columns and to the right for rows, click the mouse. All the cells in the selected column or row are bounded with a black border. Any changes now made in the Property inspector, such as a change in font size or color, affect the selected column or row.

You can select multiple, contiguous columns or rows by dragging the single arrow pointer across several columns or rows. To select a number of columns or rows that are not next to one another, use the Ctrl (Command) key. Press the Ctrl (Command) key while selecting each individual column, using the one-click method. (Not even Word 2000 can handle this complex a degree of table selection.)

Tip   If you have trouble positioning the mouse so that the single-arrow pointer appears, you can use two other methods for selecting columns or rows. With the first method, you can click and drag across all the cells in a column or row. The second method uses another keyboard modifier, the Shift key. With this technique, click once in the first cell of the column or row. Then, hold down the Shift key while you click in the final cell of the column or row (on a Mac OSX, you must perform two single-clicks in the final cell). You can also use this technique to select multiple adjacent columns or rows; just click in another column's or row's last cell.

Selecting cells

Sometimes you need to change the background color of just a few cells in a table, but not the entire row — or you might need to merge several cells to form one wide column span. In these situations, and many others, you can use Dreamweaver's cell selection capabilities. Like columns and rows, you can select multiple cells, whether they are adjacent to one another or not.

Individual cells are generally selected by dragging the mouse across one or more cell boundaries. To select a single cell, click anywhere in the cell and drag the mouse into another cell. As you pass the border between the two cells, the initial cell is highlighted. If you continue dragging the mouse across another cell boundary, the second cell is selected, and so on. Note that you have to drag the mouse into another cell and not cross the table border onto the page; for example, to highlight the lower-right cell of a table, you need to drag the mouse up or to the left.

Tip   You can also select a single cell by pressing the Ctrl (Command) key and clicking once in the cell, or you can select the rightmost `<td>` tag in the Tag Selector.

Extended cell selection in Dreamweaver is handled identically to extended text selection in most word processing programs. To select adjacent cells, click in the first desired cell, press and hold the Shift key, and click in the final desired cell. Dreamweaver selects everything in a rectangular area, using the first cell as the upper-left corner of the rectangle and the last cell as the lower-right corner. You could, for instance, select an entire table by clicking in the upper-left cell and then Shift+clicking the lower-right cell.

Just as the Shift key is used to make adjacent cell selections, the Ctrl (Command) key is used for all non-adjacent cell selections. You can highlight any number of individual cells — whether or not they are next to one another — by pressing the Ctrl (Command) key while you click in the cell.

Tip   If you Ctrl+click (Command+click) a cell that is already selected, that cell is deselected — regardless of the method you used to select the cell initially.

Editing a table's contents

Before you learn how to change a table's attributes, let's look at basic editing techniques. Editing table text in Dreamweaver is slightly different from editing text outside of tables. When you begin to enter text into a table cell, the table borders expand to accommodate your new data, assuming no width has been set. The other cells appear to shrink, but they, too, expand once you start typing in text or inserting an image. Unless a cell's width is specified, the cell currently being edited expands or contracts, and the other cells are forced to adjust their width. Figure 10-5 shows the same table (with one row and three columns) in three different states. In the top table, only the first cell contains text; notice how the other cells have contracted. In the middle table, text has been entered into the second cell as well, and you can see how the first cell is now smaller. Finally, in the bottom table, all three cells contain text, and the other two cells have adjusted their width to compensate for the expanding third cell.

The expandability of table cells is very significant when inserting information from a data source because the data is often of varying length. See Chapter 18 for details about how to use Dreamweaver's Live Data view to check your layout.

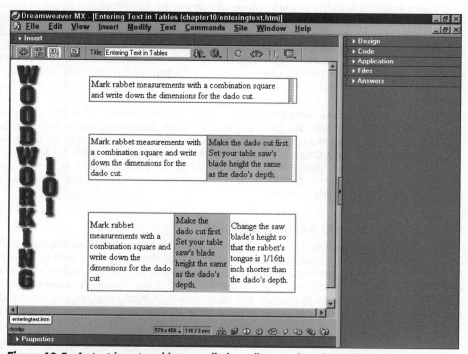

Figure 10-5: As text is entered into a cell, the cell expands; other cells contract, even if they already contain text.

If you look closely at the bottom table in Figure 10-5, you can also see that the text doesn't line up vertically. That's because the default vertical alignment in Dreamweaver, as in most browsers, provides for entries to be positioned in the middle of the cell. (Later in this section, you learn how to adjust the vertical alignment.)

Moving through a table

When you've finished entering your text in the first cell, you can move to the next cell in the row by pressing the Tab key. When you reach the end of a row, pressing Tab takes your cursor to the first cell of the next row. To go backward, cell to cell, press Shift+Tab.

Tip   Pressing Tab has a special function when you're in the last cell of a table — it adds a new row, with the same column configuration as the current one.

The Home and End keys take you to the beginning and end, respectively, of the cursor's current line. If a cell's contents are large enough for the text to wrap in the cell, move to the top of the current cell by pressing Ctrl+Home (Command+Home). To get to the bottom of the current cell in such a circumstance, press Ctrl+End (Command+End).

When you're at the beginning or end of the contents in a cell, you can also use the arrow keys to navigate from cell to cell. Use the left and right arrows to move from cell to cell in a row, and the up and down arrows to move down a column. When you come to the end of a row or column, the arrow keys move to the first cell in the next row or column. If you're moving left to right horizontally, the cursor goes from the end of one row to the beginning of the next row — and vice versa if you move from right to left. When moving from top to bottom vertically, the cursor goes from the end of one column to the start of the next, and vice versa when moving bottom to top.

Tip   To enter a table without using the mouse, position the cursor directly before the table, press Shift+right arrow to select the table, and then press the down arrow key to move into the first cell. To move out of a table without using the mouse, move the cursor to the first or last cell in the table, press Ctrl+A (Control+A) to select the cell, and then press the left arrow if the cursor is in the first table cell, or the right arrow if the cursor is in the last cell. Alternatively, press Ctrl+A (Control+A) twice to select the entire table and then use either the left or right arrow to exit the table.

Cutting, copying, and pasting in tables

In the early days of Web design (about five years ago), woe if you should accidentally leave out a cell of information. It was often almost faster to redo the entire table than to make room by meticulously cutting and pasting everything, one cell at a time. Dreamweaver ends that painstaking work forever with its advanced cutting and pasting features. You can copy a range of cells from one table to another and maintain all the attributes (such as color and alignment as well as the content — text or images), or you can copy just the contents and ignore the attributes.

Dreamweaver has one basic restriction to table cut-and-paste operations: Your selected cells must form a rectangle. In other words, although you can select non-adjacent cells, columns, or rows and modify their properties, you can't cut or copy them. Should you try, you get a message from Dreamweaver like the one shown in Figure 10-6; the table above the notification in this figure illustrates an incorrect cell selection.

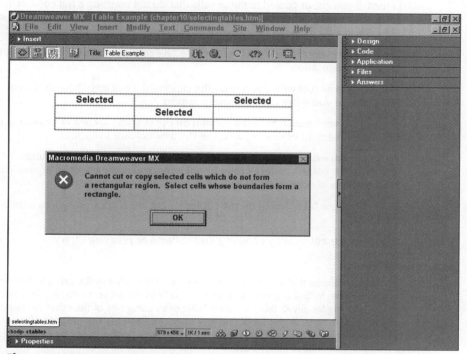

Figure 10-6: Dreamweaver enables you to cut or copy selected cells only when they form a rectangle, unlike the cells in the table depicted here.

Copying attributes and contents

When you copy or cut a cell using the regular commands, Dreamweaver automatically copies everything—content, formatting, and cell format—in the selected cell. Then, pasting the cell reproduces it—however, you can get different results depending on where the cell (or column or row) is pasted. To cut or copy both the contents and the attributes of any cell, row, or column, follow these steps:

1. Select the cells you wish to cut or copy.

   Remember that in order to cut or copy a range of cells in Dreamweaver, they must form a solid rectangular region.

2. To copy cells, choose Edit ➪ Copy or use the keyboard shortcut, Ctrl+C (Command+C).

3. To cut cells, choose Edit ➪ Cut or use the keyboard shortcut, Ctrl+X (Command+X).

   If you cut an individual cell, the contents are removed, but the cell remains. If, however, you cut an entire row or column, the cells are removed.

4. Position your cursor to paste the cells in the desired location:

- To replace a cell with a cell on the clipboard, click anywhere in the cell to be replaced. If you cut or copied multiple cells that do not make up a full column or row, click in the upper-left corner of the cells you wish to replace. For example, a range of 6 cells in a 2 × 3 configuration replaces the same configuration when pasted.

   Dreamweaver alerts you if you try to paste one configuration of cells into a different cell configuration.

- To insert a new row with the row on the clipboard, click anywhere in the row below where you'd like the new row to appear.

- To insert a new column with the column on the clipboard, click anywhere in the column to the right of where you'd like the new column to appear.

- To replace an existing row or column in a table, select the row or column. If you've cut or copied multiple rows or columns, you must select an equivalent configuration of cells to replace.

- To insert a new table based on the copied or cut cells, click anywhere outside of the table.

5. Paste the copied or cut cells by choosing Edit ➪ Paste or pressing Ctrl+V (Command+V).

Tip   To move a row or column that you've cut from the interior of a table to the exterior (the right or bottom), you have to first expand the number of cells in the table. To do this, first select the table by choosing Modify ➪ Table ➪ Select Table or by using one of the other techniques previously described. Next, in the Table Property inspector, increase the number of rows or columns by altering the values in the Rows or Cols text boxes. Finally, select the newly added rows or columns and choose Edit ➪ Paste.

Copying contents only

You often need to move data from one cell to another, while keeping the destination cell's attributes, such as its background color or border, intact. For this, use Dreamweaver's facility for copying just the contents of a cell.

To copy only the contents, you select a cell and copy as previously described; then, instead of choosing Edit ➪ Paste, choose Edit ➪ Paste HTML or use the keyboard shortcut, Ctrl+Shift+V (Command+Shift+V). Unlike the copying of both contents and attributes described in the previous section, content-only copying has a couple of limitations:

- ✦ You can copy the contents only one cell at a time. You can't paste contents only across multiple cells.

- ✦ You can't replace the entire contents of one cell with another and maintain all the text attributes (font, color, and size) of the destination cell. If you select all the text to be replaced, Dreamweaver also selects the <font> tag that holds the attributes, and replaces those as well. The workaround is to select and copy the source text as usual, and then select all but one letter or word in the destination cell, paste the contents, and delete the extra text.

Working with table properties

The <table> tag has a large number of attributes, and most of them can be modified through Dreamweaver's Property inspector. As with all objects, you must select the table before it can be altered. Choose Modify ➪ Table ➪ Select Table or use one of the other selection techniques previously described.

Once you've selected the table, if the Property inspector is open, it presents the table properties, as shown in Figure 10-7. Otherwise, you can open the Table Property inspector by choosing Window ➪ Properties.

Figure 10-7: The expanded Table Property inspector gives you control over all the table-wide attributes.

Setting alignment

Aligning a table in Dreamweaver goes beyond the expected left, right, and center options — you can also make a table into a free-floating object around which text can wrap to the left or right.

With HTML, you can align a table using two different methods, each of which gives you a different effect. Using the text alignment method (Text ➪ Align) results in the conventional positioning (left, right, and center); using the Table Property inspector method enables you to wrap text around your re-aligned table. Figure 10-8 illustrates some of the different results you get from aligning your table with the two methods.

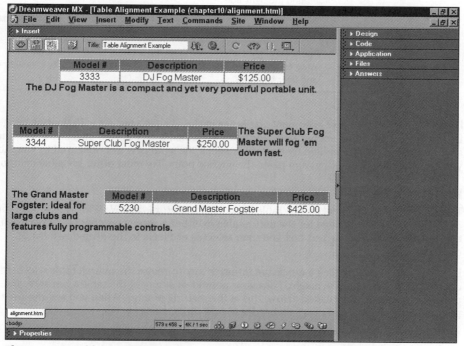

Figure 10-8: Tables can be centered, as well as aligned left or right — with or without text wrapping.

To align your table without text wrapping, follow these steps:

1. Select your table using one of the methods described earlier.

2. In the Property inspector, make sure the Align option is set to Default.

3. Choose Text ⇨ Align and then choose one of the following options: Left, Center, or Right.

   Typically, Dreamweaver surrounds your table code with a division tag pair, `<div>`. . .`</div>`, with an `align` attribute set to your chosen value. If you choose center alignment, your table may instead be surrounded by `<center>`. . .`</center>` tags, depending on the options you have set in the Code Format category of Preferences.

To align your table with text wrapping, making your table into a floating object, follow these steps:

1. Select the table.

2. In the Table Property inspector, open the Align drop-down list and choose one of the following options:

Alignment Option	Result
Default	No alignment is specified. The table aligns to the browser's default, usually left, with no text wrapping.
Left	Aligns the table to the left side of the browser window and wraps text around the right side
Right	Aligns the table to the right side of the browser window and wraps text around the left side
Center	The table aligns with the center of the browser window. Text does not wrap around either side. **Note:** This alignment option works only with 4.0 and later browsers.

Dreamweaver codes these alignment attributes in the `<table>` tag. As with floating images, Dreamweaver places an anchor point for floating elements on the Web page. However, the anchor symbol is often hidden by the table itself. If the symbol is not obscured by the table, you can drag-and-drop or cut-and-paste the anchor point like most other Invisible symbols.

Resizing a table

The primary sizing control on the Table Property inspector is the W (Width) text box. You can enter a new width value for the entire table in either a screen percentage or pixels. Just enter your value in the W text box and then select % or Pixels in the drop-down list of options.

Dreamweaver also provides a quick and intuitive way to resize the overall table width, the column widths, or the row height. Pass your pointer over any of the table's borders, and the pointer becomes a two-headed arrow; this is the resizing pointer. When you see the resizing pointer, you can click and drag any border to new dimensions.

Centering a Table in CSS

The align attribute in the `<table>` tag is deprecated in HTML 4.0, which means a newer, preferred method of achieving the same effect is now available. In this case, Cascading Style Sheets, covered in Chapter 20, provide the preferred method of setting an object's alignment. To center a table using CSS, you'll need two CSS rules: one for the table itself and one for a `<div>` surrounding the table. If, for example, the `class` of the `div` was `centerDiv`, the CSS rules would look like this:

```
.centerDiv {
    text-align: center;
}
.centerDiv table {
    margin-right: auto;
    margin-left: auto;
    text-align: left;
}
```

Without the text-align: left attribute in the .centerDiv table rule, the text in the table would be centered. This approach works in all current browsers, in both strict and regular modes. (To find out more about strict and regular modes, see Chapter 6.)

Unfortunately, if you must support older browser versions, you can't use Cascading Style Sheets. For compatibility, newer browsers tend to continue supporting deprecated tags and attributes.

As noted earlier, tables are initially sized according to their contents. Once you move a table border in Dreamweaver, however, the new sizes are written directly into the HTML code, and the column width or row height is adjusted — unless the contents cannot fit. If, for example, an inserted image is 115 pixels wide and the cell has a width of only 90 pixels, the cell expands to fit the image. The same is true if you try to fit an extremely long, unbroken text string, such as a complex URL, in a cell that's too narrow to hold it.

Dreamweaver enables you to set the height of a table using the H (Height) text box in much the same way as the Width box. However, the height of a table — whether in pixels or a percentage — is maintained only as long as the contents do not require a larger size. A table's width, though, takes precedence over its height, and a table expands vertically before it expands horizontally.

Note   The height attribute for the `<table>` tag has been deprecated by the W3C, and its further use is discouraged. Although rendered in Dreamweaver, the attribute no longer functions properly in certain browsers, such as Netscape 6.x.

Changes to the width of a cell or column are shown in the `<td>` tags, as are changes to a row's height and width, using the `width` and `height` attributes, respectively. You can see these changes by selecting the table, cell, column, or row affected and looking at the W (Width) and H (Height) text box values.

Note   You can also set the height and width using Cascading Style Sheets, described in Chapter 20. If you don't have to support older browsers, using styles is the preferred method of designating these attributes.

For an overall view of what happens when you resize a cell, row, or column, it's best to look at the HTML. Here's the HTML for an empty table, resized:

```
<table border="1" width="70%">
  <tr>
    <td width="21%"> </td>
    <td width="34%"> </td>
    <td width="45%"> </td>
  </tr>
  <tr>
    <td width="21%" height="42"> </td>
    <td width="34%"> </td>
    <td width="45%"> </td>
  </tr>
  <tr>
    <td width="21%" height="42"> </td>
    <td width="34%"> </td>
    <td width="45%"> </td>
  </tr>
</table>
```

Notice how the width for both the cells and the entire table are expressed as percentages. If the table width were initially set at a pixel value, the cell widths would have been, too. The row height values, on the other hand, are shown as an absolute measurement in pixels.

You can switch from percentages to pixels in all the table measurements, and even clear all the values at once — with the click of a button. Several measurement controls appear in the lower-left portion of the expanded Table Property inspector, as shown in Figure 10-9.

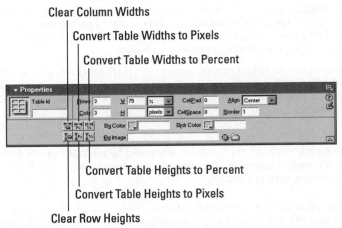

Clear Column Widths

Convert Table Widths to Pixels

Convert Table Widths to Percent

Convert Table Heights to Percent

Convert Table Heights to Pixels

Clear Row Heights

Figure 10-9: You can make table-wide changes with the control buttons in the Table Property inspector.

The measurement controls are as follows:

Measurement Control Button	Description
Clear Column Widths	Deletes all the width attributes found in the <td> tags
Convert Table Widths to Pixels	Translates the current width of all cells and the entire table from percentages to pixels
Convert Table Widths to Percent	Translates the current width of all cells and the entire table from pixels to percentages
Clear Row Heights	Erases all the height attributes in the current table
Convert Table Heights to Pixels	Translates the current height of all cells and the entire table from percentages to pixels
Convert Table Heights to Percent	Translates the current height of all cells and the entire table from pixels to percentages

Note Selecting Clear Row Heights doesn't affect the table height value.

If you clear both row heights and column widths, the table goes back to its "grow as needed" format and, if empty, shrinks to its smallest possible size.

Caution When converting width percentages to pixels, and vice versa, keep in mind that the percentages are relative to the size of the browser window—and in the development phase that browser window is Dreamweaver. Use the Window Size option on the status bar to expand Dreamweaver's Document window to the size you expect to be seen in various browser settings.

Note, however, that row height is a percentage of the table's height, not the window's height.

Inserting rows and columns

You can change the number of rows and columns in a table at any time. Dreamweaver provides a variety of methods for adding and removing rows and columns.

You have several options for adding a single row:

✦ Position the cursor in the last cell of the last row and press Tab to add a new row below the present one.

✦ Choose Modify ➪ Table ➪ Insert Row to insert a new row above the current row.

✦ Right-click (Control+click) in the table to open the context menu and select Table ➪ Insert Row. Rows added in this way are inserted above the current row.

You have two ways to add a new column to your table:

✦ Choose Modify ➪ Table ➪ Insert Column to insert a new column to the left of the current column.

✦ Right-click (Control+click) to open the context menu and select Table ➪ Insert Column from the context menu. The column is inserted to the left of the current column.

You can add multiple rows and columns in either of the following ways:

✦ Increase the number of rows indicated in the Rows text box of the Table Property inspector. All new rows added in this manner appear below the last table row. Similarly, you can increase the number of columns indicated in the Cols text box of the Table Property inspector. Columns added in this way appear to the right of the last column.

✦ Use the Insert Rows or Columns dialog box.

The Insert Rows or Columns feature enables you to include any number of rows or columns anywhere relative to your current cursor position.

To add multiple columns using the Insert Rows or Columns dialog box, follow these steps:

1. Position the cursor anywhere in the row or column next to where the new row or column will be inserted.

2. Open the Insert Rows or Columns dialog box (shown in Figure 10-10) by selecting Modify ⇨ Table ⇨ Insert Rows or Columns or by choosing Table ⇨ Insert Rows or Columns from the context menu.

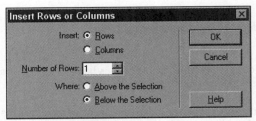

Figure 10-10: Use the Insert Rows or Columns feature to add several columns or rows simultaneously.

3. Select either Rows or Columns.

4. Enter the number of rows or columns you wish to insert — you can either type in a value or use the arrows to increase or decrease the number.

5. Select where you want the rows or columns to be inserted.

   • If you have selected the Rows option, you can insert the rows either above or below the selection (the current row).

   • If you have selected the Columns options, you can insert the columns either before or after the current column.

6. Click OK when you're finished.

Deleting rows and columns

The easiest way to delete a row or column is to select the row or column and then press the Delete key. When you want to delete a column or row, you can also use either the context menu or the Table Property inspector. On the context menu, you can remove the current column or row by choosing Delete Column or Delete Row, respectively. Using the Table Property inspector, you can delete multiple columns and rows by reducing the numbers in the Cols or Rows text boxes. Columns are deleted from the right side of the table, and rows are removed from the bottom.

Caution Exercise extreme caution when deleting columns or rows. Dreamweaver does not ask for confirmation, and removes these columns and/or rows whether or not they contain data.

Setting table borders and backgrounds

Borders are the solid outlines of the table itself. A border's width is measured in pixels; the default width is 1 pixel. You can alter this width in the Border field of the Table Property inspector.

You can make the border invisible by specifying a border of 0 width. You can still resize your table by clicking and dragging the borders, even when the border is set to 0. When the View ➪ Visual Aids ➪ Table Borders option is selected, Dreamweaver displays a thin dashed line to represent the border; this line is not visible when the page is viewed in a browser.

When the border is visible, you can also see each cell outlined. The width of the outline around the cells stays constant, regardless of the border's width. However, you can control the amount of space between each cell with the CellSpace value in the Table Property inspector, covered in the section "Working with cell spacing and cell padding," later in this chapter.

To change the width of a border in Dreamweaver, select your table and enter a new value in the Border text box. With a wider border, you can see the default shading: The top and left sides are a light shade, and the bottom and right sides are darker. This gives the table border a pseudo-3D appearance. Figure 10-11 shows single-cell tables with borders of various widths.

In Dreamweaver, you can directly assign colors to the border. To choose a color for the border, select the Brdr color box or enter a color name or hexadecimal color value in the adjacent text box.

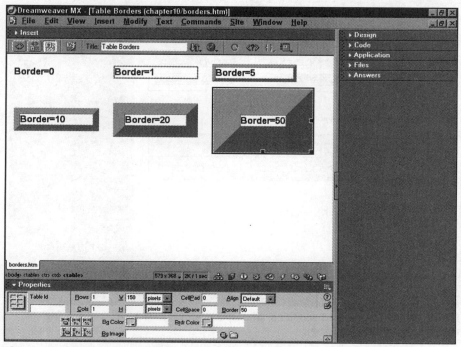

Figure 10-11: Changing the width of the border can give your table a 3D look.

In addition to colored borders, a table can also have a colored background. (By default, the table is initially transparent.) Choose the background color in the Table Property inspector by selecting a color in the Bg color box or entering a color name or hexadecimal color value in the adjacent text box. As you learn later in this chapter, in "Setting cell, column, and row properties," you can also assign background colors to rows, columns, and individual cells — if used, these specific colors override the background color of the entire table.

Working with cell spacing and cell padding

HTML gives you two methods to add whitespace in tables. Cell spacing controls the width between each cell, and cell padding controls the margins within each cell. You can set these values independently through the Table Property inspector.

Tip   If no cell spacing or padding value is indicated in the Table Property inspector, most browsers use a default value of 2 pixels for cell spacing and 1 pixel for cell padding. If your Web page design calls for a close arrangement of cells, explicitly change either (or both) the CellSpace or CellPad values to 1 or 0.

To change the amount of whitespace between each cell in a table, enter a new value in the CellSpace text box of the Table Property inspector. If you want to adjust the amount of whitespace between the borders of the cell and the actual cell data, alter the value in the CellPad text box of the Table Property inspector. Figure 10-12 shows an example of tables with wide (10 pixels) cell spacing and cell padding values.

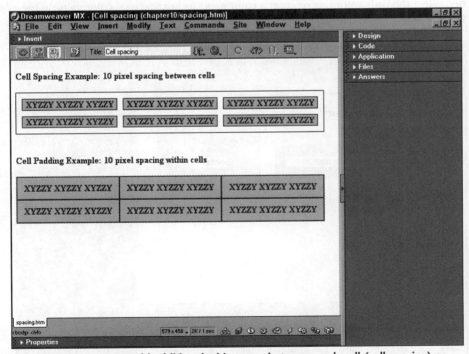

Figure 10-12: You can add additional whitespace between each cell (cell spacing) or within each cell (cell padding).

Merging and splitting cells

You have seen how cells in HTML tables can extend across (span) multiple columns or rows. By default, a cell spans one column or one row. Increasing a cell's span enables you to group any number of topics under one heading. You are effectively merging one cell with another to create a larger cell. Likewise, a cell can be split into multiple rows or columns.

Dreamweaver enables you to combine and divide cells in two different ways. If you're more comfortable with the concept of merging and splitting cells, you can use two handy buttons on the Property inspector. If, on the other hand, you prefer the older method of increasing and decreasing row or column span, you can still access these commands through the main menu and the context menus.

To combine two or more cells, first select the cells you want to merge. Then, from the Property inspector, select the Merge Cells button or press the keyboard shortcut, M. If the Merge button is not available, multiple cells have not been selected.

To divide a cell, follow these steps:

1. Position your cursor in the cell to be split.

2. From the Property inspector, select the Split Cell button or press the keyboard shortcut, Ctrl+Alt+S (Command+Option+S). The Split Cell dialog box (shown in Figure 10-13) appears.

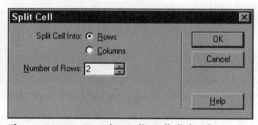

Figure 10-13: Use the Split Cell dialog box to divide cells horizontally or vertically.

3. Select either the Rows or Columns option to indicate whether the cell will be split horizontally or vertically.

4. Enter the number of rows or columns in the text box or use the arrows to change the value.

5. Select OK when you're done.

You can achieve the same effect by using the menus. To do so, first position the cursor in the cell to be affected and then choose one of the following commands from the Modify ➪ Table menu:

Command	Description
Increase Row Span	Joins the current cell with the cell below it
Increase Column Span	Joins the current cell with the cell immediately to its right
Decrease Row Span	Separates two or more previously spanned cells from the bottom cell
Decrease Column Span	Separates two or more previously spanned cells from the right edge

Existing text or images are put in the same cell if the cells containing them are joined to span rows or columns. Figure 10-14 shows a table containing both row and column spanning.

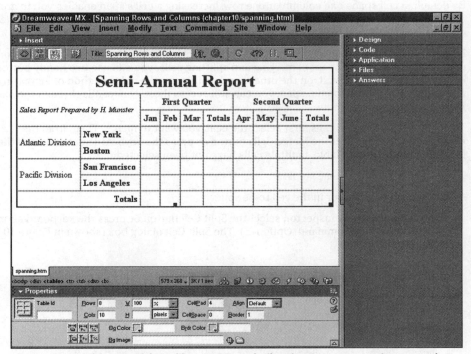

Figure 10-14: This spreadsheet-like report was built using Dreamweaver's row- and column-spanning features.

Tip   Show restraint when splitting and merging cells, or your table will be difficult to maintain. When you need to build a complex table such as the one in Figure 10-14, it's best to map out your table before you begin constructing it, and complete it prior to entering your data.

Setting cell, column, and row properties

In addition to the overall table controls, Dreamweaver helps you set numerous properties for individual cells one at a time, by the column or by the row. When attributes overlap or conflict, such as different background colors for a cell in the same row and column, the more specific target has precedence. The hierarchy, from most general to most specific, is as follows: tables, rows, columns, and cells.

You can call up the specific Property inspector by selecting the cell, row, or column you want to modify. The Cell, Row, and Column Property inspectors each affect similar attributes. The following sections explain how the attributes work, both in general and — if any differences exist — specifically (in regard to the cell, column, or row).

Horizontal alignment

You can set the Horizontal Alignment attribute, align, to specify the default alignment, or Left, Right, or Center alignment, for the contents of a cell, column, or row. This attribute can be overridden by setting the alignment for the individual line or image. Generally, left is the default horizontal alignment for cells.

Vertical alignment

The HTML valign attribute specifies whether the cell's contents are vertically aligned to the cell's top, middle, or bottom, or along the baseline. Typically, browsers align cells vertically in the middle by default. Select the Vertical Alignment option arrow in the Cell, Column, or Row Properties inspector to specify a different alignment.

Top, middle, and bottom vertical alignments work pretty much as you would expect. A baseline vertical alignment displays text near the top of the cell and positions the text — regardless of font size — so that the baselines of all the text in the affected row, column, or cell are the same. Figure 10-15 illustrates how images and text of various sizes are displayed under the various vertical alignment options.

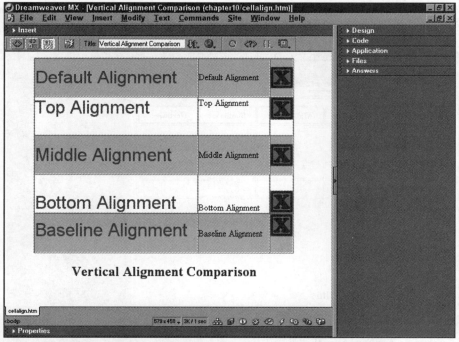

Figure 10-15: You can vertically align text and images in several arrangements in a table cell, row, or column.

Cell wrap

Normal behavior for any cell is to automatically wrap text or a series of images within the cell's borders. You can turn off this automatic feature by selecting the No Wrap option in the Property inspector for the cell, column, or row.

You might use this option, for example, if you need three images to appear side by side in one cell. In analyzing the results, however, you might find that on some lower-resolution browsers, the last image wraps to the next line.

Note   Another, preferred method of preventing the contents of a cell from wrapping is to use Cascading Style Sheets to define a style with the `white-space` attribute set to `nowrap`. However, Cascading Style Sheets are not supported in older browsers. To learn how to define and apply styles, see Chapter 20.

Table header cells

Quite often in tables, a column or row functions as the heading for that section of the table, labeling all the information in that particular section. Dreamweaver has an option for designating these cells: the Header option. Table header cells are usually rendered in boldface and centered in each cell. Figure 10-16 shows an example of a table in which both the first row and first column are marked as table header cells.

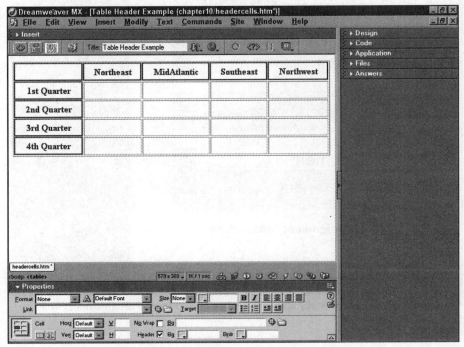

Figure 10-16: Table header cells are a good way to note a category's label—for a row, column, or both.

Cell width and height

The gridlike structure of a table makes it impossible to resize only one cell in a multicolumn table. Therefore, the only way you can enter exact values for a cell's width is through the Width text box available in the Column Properties inspector. You can enter values in pixels or as a percentage of the table. The default enables cells to automatically resize with no restrictions outside of the overall dimensions of the table.

Similarly, whenever you change a cell's height, the entire row is altered. If you drag the row to a new height, the value is written into the H (Height) text box for all cells in the row. On the other hand, if you specify a single cell's height, the row resizes, but you can see the value only in the cell you've changed. If different cells in the same row are assigned different heights, the row is sized to the tallest height.

Color elements

Just as you can specify color backgrounds and borders for the overall table, you can do the same for columns, rows, or individual cells. Corresponding color swatches and text boxes are available in the Property inspector for the following:

✦ **Bg (Background Color):** Specifies the color for the selected cell, row, or column. Selecting the color box opens the standard color picker.

✦ **Brdr (Border Color):** Controls the color of the single-pixel border surrounding each cell.

As with all Dreamweaver color pickers, you can use the Eyedropper tool to select a color from the Web-safe palette or from any item on a page. You can also select the Default color button to delete any previously selected color. Finally, choose the System Color Picker button to open the Color dialog box and select any available color.

Working with Table Formats

Tables keep data organized and generally make it easier to find information quickly. Large tables with many rows, however, tend to become difficult to read unless they are formatted with alternating rows of color or some other device. Formatting a large table is often an afterthought as well as a time-consuming affair. Unless, of course, you're using Dreamweaver's Format Table command.

The Format Table command enables you to choose from a variety of preset formats that you can further customize. This versatile command can style the top row, alternating rows in the body of the table, the left column, and the border. It's best to completely build the structure of your table — although you don't have to fill it with data — before formatting it; otherwise, you might have to reformat it when new rows or columns are added. To apply one of the preset table formats, follow these steps:

1. Position the cursor anywhere within the table to be formatted.

2. Choose Commands ➪ Format Table. The Format Table dialog box (shown in Figure 10-17) opens.

3. Select any of the options from the scrolling list box on the left side of the Format Table dialog box.

   As you select an option, a representation of the table appears to the right, and the attribute values used are displayed below.

4. When you've found a table format that's appropriate, select OK to close the dialog box, and the format is applied.

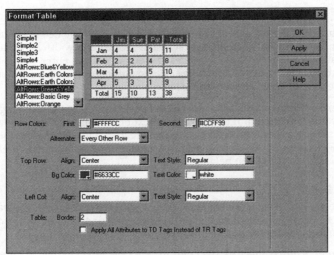

Figure 10-17: Select any one of the preset formats from the Format Table dialog box or customize your own.

The preset formats are divided into three groups: Simple, AltRows, and DblRows. The Simple formats maintain the same background color for all rows in the body of the table but change the top row and the left column. The AltRows formats alternate the background color of each row in the body of the table; you have eight different color combinations from which to choose. The final category, DblRows, alternates the background color of every two rows in the body of the table.

Although 17 different formats may seem like a lot of options, it's actually just the jumping-off place for what's possible with the Format Table command. After selecting a preset format, you can further customize any of the variables applied to create that format. Moreover, you don't have to apply the changes to your selected table to see the effect — you can preview the results directly in the Table Format dialog box. Following are the variable attributes in the Table Format dialog box:

Attribute	Description
Row Colors: First	Enters a color (in color name or hexadecimal format) for the background of the first row in the body of a table. The row colors do not affect the top row of a table unless no top row color is defined.
Row Colors: Second	Enters a color (in color name or hexadecimal format) for the background of the second row in the body of a table. The row colors do not affect the top row of a table.
Row Colors: Alternate	Establishes the pattern for using the specified row colors. Options are <do not alternate>, Every Other Row, Every Two Rows, Every Three Rows, and Every Four Rows.
Top Row: Align	Sets the alignment of the text in the top row of the table to left, right, or center

Attribute	Description
Top Row: Text Style	Sets the style of the text in the top row of the table to Regular, Bold, Italic, or Bold Italic
Top Row: Bg Color	Sets the background color of the top row of the selected table. Use either color names or hexadecimal values. If not specified, the first row color will be used.
Top Row: Text Color	Sets the color of the text in the top row of the selected table. Use either color names or hexadecimal values.
Left Col: Align	Sets the alignment of the text in the left column of the table to Left, Right, or Center
Left Col: Text Style	Sets the style of the text in the left column of the table to Regular, Bold, Italic, or Bold Italic
Border	Determines the width of the table's border, in pixels
Options: Apply All Attributes to TD Tags Instead of TR Tags	Specifies attribute changes at the cell level, <td>, rather than the default, the row level, <tr>

The final option in the Format Table dialog box, Apply All Attributes to TD Tags Instead of TR Tags, should be used in only two situations: One, the selected table is nested inside of another table and you want to override the outer table's <tr> format; or two, you anticipate moving cells from one table to another and want to maintain the formatting. Generally, the code produced by selecting this option is bulkier, and it could affect a page's overall download size if the table is sufficiently large.

Caution   Currently, you can't save your custom format without editing the tableFormats.js JavaScript file in the Commands folder. Otherwise, you need to reenter the selections each time you apply them.

Sorting Tables

Have you ever painstakingly built a table, alphabetizing every last entry by last name and first name, only to have the client call with a list of 13 additional names? "Oh, and could you sort them by zip code instead of last name?" Dreamweaver contains a Table Sort command designed to make short work of such requests. All you need to do is select your table, and you're ready to do a two-level-deep sort, either alphabetically or numerically.

The Sort Table command can rearrange a table of any size; more important, it's HTML savvy, and gives you the option of keeping the formatting of your table rows. This capability enables you to maintain a table with alternating row colors and still sort the data—something not even the most powerful word processors can handle. The Sort Table command is useful for generating different views of the same data, without having to use a database. The Sort Table command is straightforward to use; just follow these steps:

1. Position the cursor inside the table.

2. Choose Commands ➪ Sort Table. The Sort Table dialog box (shown in Figure 10-18) opens.

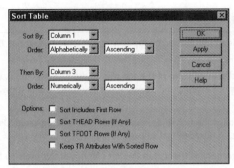

Figure 10-18: Sort your tables numerically or alphabetically with the Sort Table command.

3. Choose the primary sort column from the Sort By option list.

   Dreamweaver automatically lists the number of columns in the selected table in the option list.

4. Set the type of the primary sort by choosing either Alphabetically or Numerically from the first Order option list.

5. Choose the direction of the sort by selecting either Ascending or Descending from the second Order option list.

6. If you wish to add a second level of sorting, repeat Steps 3 through 5 in the Then By section.

7. If your selected table does not include a header row, select the Sort Includes First Row option.

8. If your selected table includes one or more rows coded within `<thead>. . .</thead>` or `<tfoot>. . .</tfoot>` tags, and you wish those rows to be included in the sort, select the appropriate option.

Note   The `<thead>` and `<tfoot>` HTML tags designate one or more table rows as forming a table heading or footer. The footer displays at the bottom of the table, and is typically used to duplicate the heading for long tables. These tags are not supported on all browsers.

9. If you have formatted your table with alternating row colors, choose the Keep TR Attributes With Sorted Row option.

10. Click OK when you're finished.

Tip   As with any sorting program, if you leave blank cells in the column on which you're basing the sort, those rows appear as a group on top of the table for an ascending sort and at the end for a descending sort. Make sure that all the cells in your sort criteria column are filled correctly.

Importing Tabular Data

In the computer age, there's nothing much more frustrating than having information in a digital format and still having to enter it manually—either typing it in or cutting and pasting—to get it on the Web. This frustration is multiplied when it comes to table data, whether created in a spreadsheet or database program. You have to transfer numerous small pieces of data, and it all has to be properly related and positioned.

Dreamweaver's Import Table Data command goes a long way toward alleviating the tedium—not to mention the frustration—of dealing with tabular information. The Import Table Data command reads any delimited text file and inserts the information in a series of rows and columns. You can even set most characteristics for the table to be created, including the width, cell padding, cell spacing, and border.

Quite often, the first step in the process of importing table data into Dreamweaver is exporting it from another program. Most spreadsheet and database programs have some capability to output information in a text file. Each bit of data (whether it's from a cell of a spreadsheet or a field of a database) is separated—or *delimited*—from every other bit of data by a special character, typically a tab or comma. In Dreamweaver, you can use the Import Table Data dialog box to choose which delimiter is used, ensuring a clean transfer with no loss of data.

Tip
Although you have many types of delimiters to choose from, you might want to default to exporting tab-delimited files. With a tab-delimited file, you usually don't have to worry if any of your data contains the delimiter—which would throw off the import. However, testing has shown that Dreamweaver correctly handles comma-delimited files with and without quotes, so you can also use that format safely.

To import a tabular data file, follow these steps:

1. Be sure the data you wish to import has been saved or exported in the proper format: a delimited text file.

2. Open the Import Tabular Data dialog box, shown in Figure 10-19, in one of the following ways:

   - Choose File ➪ Import ➪ Tabular Data.

   - Choose Insert ➪ Table Objects ➪ Import Tabular Data.

   - Choose the Tabular Data button from the Common category of the Insert bar.

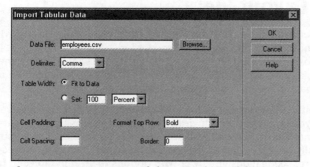

Figure 10-19: Any external data saved in a delimited text file can be brought into Dreamweaver with the Import Tabular Data command.

3. Select the Data File Browse (Choose) button to find the desired file.

4. Choose the delimiter used to separate the fields or cells of data from the Delimiter option list. The options are Tab, Comma, Semicolon, Colon, and Other.

Tip

If you select a file with a .csv extension, the comma delimiter is automatically chosen, although you can change the option if necessary. CSV is short for Comma Separated Values.

5. If you choose Other from the Delimiter list, a blank field appears to the right of the list. Enter the special character, such as the pipe (|), used as the delimiter in the exported file.

Now that the imported file characteristics are set, you can predefine the table into which the information will be imported, if desired.

6. If you want to set a particular table width, enter a value in the Set field and choose either Pixels or Percent from the option list. If you want the imported file to determine the size of the table, keep the Fit to Data option selected.

7. Enter any Cell Padding or Cell Spacing values desired, in their respective fields.

As with standard tables, if you don't enter a value, most browsers will interpret Cell Padding as 2 pixels and Cell Spacing as 1 pixel.

8. If you'd like to style the first row, choose Bold, Italic, or Bold Italic from the Format Top Row option list.

This option is typically used when the imported file contains a header row.

9. Set the Border field to the desired width, if any. If you don't want a border displayed at all, set the Border field to 0.

10. Click OK when you're done.

Although the Import Table Data option is under the File menu, it doesn't open a new file—the new table is created at the current cursor position.

Caution

If your data is imported incorrectly, double-check the delimiter used (by opening the file in a text editor). If Dreamweaver is expecting a comma delimiter and your file uses tabs, data is not formatted properly.

Designing with Layout View

At the beginning of this chapter, it was pointed out that some Web designers regard tables as one of their primary layout tools. This is because, except for CSS layers, tables are the only way you can even get close to positioning your page elements the way you want them to appear. Granted, it takes a lot of work to do this with raw tables, but designers are a persistent group—and now that persistence has paid off in a big way.

Structuring your page with tables just got a whole lot easier, thanks to Dreamweaver's Layout view. When you're in Layout view, you simply draw out separate areas to hold your content and Dreamweaver automatically converts these areas to cells and tables. The layout cells are very pliable and can easily be moved about the page, resized, and reshaped. Moreover, Layout view gives you professional design power with options to stretch tables to fit the browser window and to size columns precisely.

Although they share the same underlying HTML structure, tables and cells created in Layout view differ from those created in Standard view in several ways:

✦ Borders are set to 0, thus, turned off.

✦ Cell padding and cell spacing are also set to 0 to enable content to appear directly side-by-side.

✦ Layout tables optionally include an extra row, whose columns hold a 1-pixel-high, transparent GIF image called a *spacer*.

✦ Columns in a layout table are either set to a fixed pixel width or designed to automatically stretch to the full width of the page.

In addition to these physical differences, Layout view has a different look as well. Each layout table is marked with a tab, and the column width is identified at the top of each column (as shown in Figure 10-20).

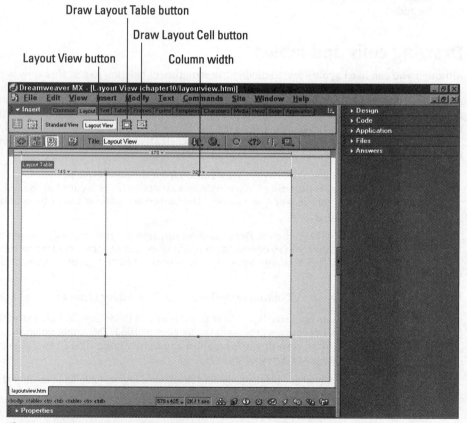

Figure 10-20: In Layout view, tables and columns are immediately identifiable and extremely flexible.

Dreamweaver puts the access to Layout view on the Insert bar. In the Dreamweaver MX and HomeSite/Coder Style workspaces, the buttons for switching between Standard and Layout views are in the Layout category. In the Dreamweaver 4 workspace, the buttons are located at the bottom of the Insert bar, regardless of which category is selected. To switch modes, click the Layout View button; to return to the traditional mode, select the Standard View button. If the Insert bar is not open, you can also switch to Layout view by choosing View ⇨ Table View ⇨ Layout View or by using the keyboard shortcut, Ctrl+F6 (Command+F6). To switch to Standard view, you can also choose View ⇨ Table View ⇨ Standard View or use the keyboard shortcut Shift+Ctrl+F6 (Shift+Command+F6).

Note   Don't fret about your existing pages: They'll show up just fine in Layout view. In fact, looking at a well-designed legacy page in Layout view is very helpful for understanding the layout of professionally designed pages by clearly showing table structure and nested tables.

One caveat applies when changing from Standard to Layout view, however: standard table cells without content — those that are either totally empty or contain only a non-breaking space — must be explicitly created in Layout view before text, graphics, or other content can be added.

Drawing cells and tables

Although you can use Layout view to modify the structure of existing pages, this view is best when designing Web pages from the ground up. The Draw Layout Cell and Draw Table commands enable you to quickly lay out the basic structure of your page by defining the key document areas. For example, with just four mouse moves in Layout view, you can design a page with sections for a logo, a navigation bar, a copyright notice, and a primary content area. Then you'd be ready to fill out the design with graphics, text, and other assets. Here's how it works:

1. On a blank page, choose the Layout View button from the Insert bar. In the Dreamweaver MX and HomeSite/Coder Style workspaces, this is located in the Layout category; in the Dreamweaver 4 workspace, the button is visible at the bottom of the Insert bar for all categories.

   When you first enter Layout view, Dreamweaver displays a Help screen to explain how the feature works. After you're comfortable working in Layout view, feel free to select the Don't Show Me This Message Again option to prevent further appearances of the dialog box.

2. Select the Draw Layout Cell button in the Insert bar. The cursor changes to a plus sign.

   Although it may seem backwards, it's best to initially use Draw Layout Cell, rather than Draw Layout Table. Dreamweaver automatically creates the HTML table necessary to hold any cells you draw, resulting in less tables and tighter code. The Draw Table command is best used to make a nested table.

3. Move your cursor anywhere on the page and drag out a layout cell. The result is shown in Figure 10-21.

   Dreamweaver creates a table around the cell; the cell is drawn in the current background color with the surrounding table shown in an alternate color. The outline of a layout cell is highlighted in red when the mouse moves over it and turns blue when selected; likewise, a Layout table's outline is green. All of these colors can be user-defined in Preferences.

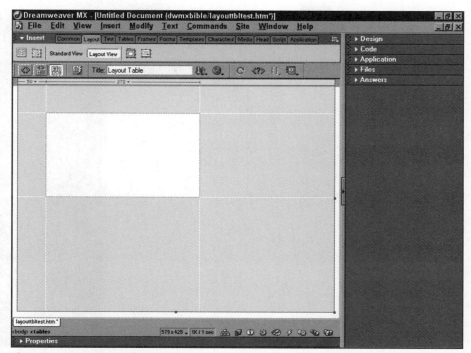

Figure 10-21: Use the Draw Layout Cell command to define the basic page structure in Layout view.

Tip

If you're within 8 pixels of the edge of the Document window or another layout cell, the border of the new layout cell snaps to that edge. Press the Alt (Option) key while drawing a layout cell to temporarily disable snapping.

4. Repeat Step 3 until your layout is complete.

Dreamweaver drops out of Draw Layout Cell mode after your first cell is created; to create several layout cells in a row, press Ctrl (Command) while dragging.

Note that when you draw the first cell, the cell is drawn in the current background color with the surrounding table shown in an alternate color. The cells in the alternate color represent areas of the page where you can draw more cells, but these do not necessarily represent part of the actual table structure. Think of these cells as a Layout view visual aid, which suggests where additional cells may be added. If you switch to Standard view, you will see that the table in Figure 10-21 actually consists of four cells, not the nine shown in Layout view. Figure 10-22 shows the same table in Standard view.

As indicated earlier, the Draw Table command is best suited for creating nested tables. Just as it sounds, a table is nested when it is placed within an existing table. Nested tables are useful when a design requires that a number of elements — for example, a picture and a related caption — remain stationary in relation to one another while text on the page flows according to the size of the browser window.

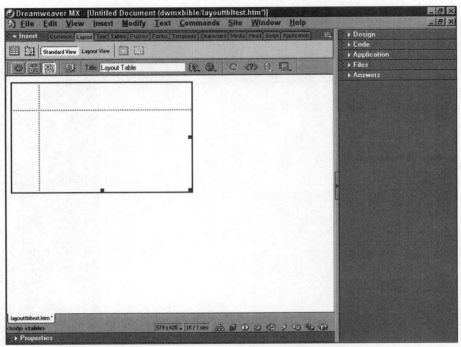

Figure 10-22: Standard view shows only the actually defined table cells.

Tip Although the tabs designating a layout table are very handy, at a certain stage of your design, you may want to turn them off. To hide them, choose View ➪ Table View ➪ Show Layout Table Tabs to disable the option. Select the command again to bring them back into view.

To create a nested table in Layout view, follow these steps:

1. Choose the Layout View button from the Insert bar.

2. Select the Draw Layout Table button, also from the Insert bar.

3. When the cursor is over an area of the table unoccupied by a layout cell, the cursor changes to a plus sign, and a layout table can be dragged out. When not over a valid area, the cursor is shown as a slashed circle—the universal sign for "not allowed."

The new layout table is inserted as shown in Figure 10-23.

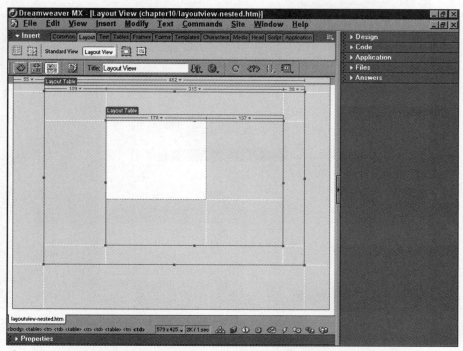

Figure 10-23: Nested tables are easily added with the Draw Layout Table command.

4. To divide the nested layout table into multiple areas, choose the Draw Layout Cell button to drag out new cells.

5. As with the Draw Layout Cell command, the Draw Layout Table command defaults to dragging one table at a time. To draw several tables in a row, select Ctrl (Command) while dragging out a layout table.

Note

To convert a nested table to rows and columns in the outer table, click a column heading in the nested table and then select Remove Nesting from the drop-down list, as shown in Figure 10-24.

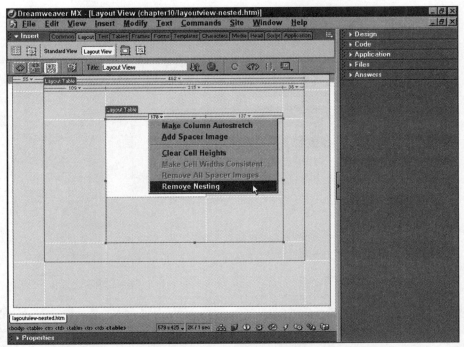

Figure 10-24: Choose the Remove Nesting command to integrate a nested table into the parent table.

Although Layout view is an excellent method for quickly structuring a page, you should be aware of some limitations:

✦ Layout tables and cells can only be drawn in the area of the Document window that does not have any code associated with it. In other words, you need to draw layout cells and tables below the apparent end of the document. The result is that the new table code is placed right before the closing body tag.

✦ Two objects are disabled while in Layout view: the standard Table object and the Layer object. To add either of these objects to the page, you need to return to Standard view.

✦ Layout cells and tables cannot be copied, cut, or pasted. These operations are available from the Standard view, however.

It's worthwhile to note that Layout view works exceedingly well with Dreamweaver's Grid feature. With the grid showing (View ⇨ Grid ⇨ Show Grid) and Snap to Grid enabled (View ⇨ Grid ⇨ Snap to Grid), precisely laying out cells and tables is quite literally a snap. With Dreamweaver's Layout view, complex but useful designs, like the one shown in Figure 10-25, are within reach.

Caution   Under certain circumstances, Dreamweaver mistakenly creates empty table cells — cells without a non-breaking space — which can break a table's structure in certain browsers. This occurs most frequently when the table is resized by dragging the border of a layout table. You can avoid this problem by resizing the table via the Property inspector. If you do encounter any empty cells, be sure to enter a non-breaking space in the `<td>` tag by hand in the code or explicitly draw out a cell in Layout view.

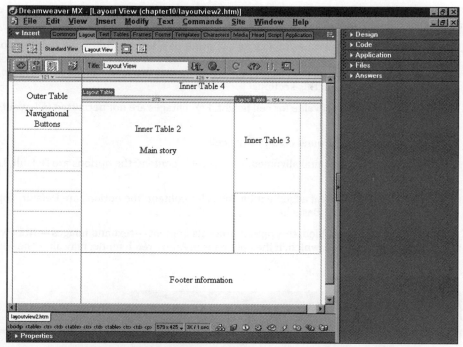

Figure 10-25: Nested tables — created in Dreamweaver's Layout view — offer the Web designer tighter command of Web page elements.

Modifying layouts

Layout view not only facilitates creating the initial design for a page, it also makes the inevitable modifications more straightforward. You can position cells within a layout table much like layers on a page. Cells, however, unlike layers, cannot overlap. Resizing layout cells and tables is also simpler. Unlike the Standard view, in which any table or cell border is draggable, in Layout view, cells and tables have sizing handles — much like a selected image.

Changing layout cell properties

In order to easily manipulate layout and cells, the cells have to be easily selectable. Dreamweaver handles that chore with colorful flair. Pass your cursor over any layout cell; when you pass the border of a cell, it changes from blue to red. Click once on the red highlighting, and the cell is selected. A selected cell is notable by the eight sizing handles placed on its perimeter. Once a cell is selected, the Property inspector displays its available attributes.

Tip   To select a cell without moving the cursor over the border, Ctrl+click (Command+click) anywhere in the cell.

The Layout Cell Property inspector (shown in Figure 10-26) offers the following key attributes:

✦ **Width:** Enter a pixel value for a Fixed cell width or select the Autostretch option to allow the cell to grow as needed. The width of each cell is shown on top of each column in Layout view. The column width property is an important one and is explained in greater detail later in this section.

✦ **Height:** Enter a pixel value for cell height. Percentages are not permitted in Layout view.

✦ **Bg:** Choose a background color for the cell.

✦ **Horz:** Select a horizontal alignment for the cell's content; the options are Default, Left, Center, and Right.

✦ **Vert:** Choose a vertical alignment for the cell's content; the options are Default, Top, Middle, Bottom, and Baseline.

✦ **No Wrap:** When enabled, this option prevents content — text and images — from wrapping to the next line, which, if the column is in Autostretch mode, may alter the width of the cell.

Figure 10-26: Although similar to the standard Cell Property inspector, the Layout Cell Property inspector offers a different set of options.

 Note   Not all the attributes of a table cell are available through the Layout Cell Property inspector. To add a background image, specify a border color, designate the cell as a header cell, or split the cell, you need to switch to Standard view.

To reshape or resize a layout cell, drag any one of the sizing handles on the border of the cell into the unused area of a table. Likewise, you can drag a cell into any open table area — that is, any area of the table unoccupied by another cell — by holding down the Ctrl key (Command key) as you click and drag.

 Tip   To maintain the width-height ratio of a cell, press Shift while resizing.

Changing layout table properties

Tables may be similarly selected and resized. Layout tables are selected by clicking the title bar marking the table, or by Ctrl+clicking (Command+clicking) inside an open area within the table or on the table border. If the layout table is nested within another table, it can even be dragged to a new location within the outer table. Non-nested tables cannot be dragged to a new location on the page, however.

Once a layout table is selected, the attributes in the Property inspector become available, as shown in Figure 10-27. These attributes include the following:

✦ **Width:** Enter a pixel value for a Fixed table width or select the Autostretch option to allow the table to grow as needed.

✦ **Height:** Enter a pixel value for table height. Percentages are not permitted in Layout view.

✦ **Bg:** Choose a background color for the table.

✦ **CellPad:** This controls the amount of space between the content and the cell border throughout the table. The default value is 0.

✦ **CellSpace:** This controls the amount of space between cells throughout the table. The default value is 0.

✦ **Clear Row Heights:** This button removes any set height values for all rows, and reduces the table to existing content.

Caution When used with nested tables, Dreamweaver doesn't redraw the cell border to match the table border; to correct this, drag the bottom cell border to match that of the table.

✦ **Make Cell Widths Consistent:** This button changes the width of all cells to the size of their respective content. If a cell is stretched beyond its original fixed size by an image or some text, the column header of the layout cell shows the fixed size next to the actual size in parentheses. Choosing Make Cell Widths Consistent adjusts the fixed size to match the actual size.

✦ **Remove All Spacers:** Choosing this button deletes all single-pixel images used, to ensure browser compatibility for layout tables and their corresponding rows. Spacers are discussed in the section "Altering column widths," later in this chapter.

✦ **Remove Nesting:** This button converts a nested table to rows and cells of the outer table. This feature is available only in Layout view, and it provides a quick way of removing nested tables from a page.

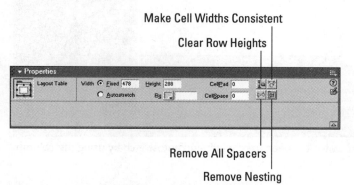

Make Cell Widths Consistent

Clear Row Heights

Remove All Spacers

Remove Nesting

Figure 10-27: The Layout Table Property inspector includes important options for converting nested tables and sizing cells to fit existing content.

Altering column widths

The table elements in Layout view borrow a couple of pages from the professional Web designer's manual. For example, any column can easily be converted from a fixed width to a flexible width — in Dreamweaver this is known as *autostretch*. When a table uses the autostretch option, one column has a flexible width, and all other columns are of fixed width.

You can alter the width of a fixed-width column in a number of ways:

✦ Visually select the cell and then drag a sizing handle to a new position.

✦ For pixel-precise width, use the Layout Cell Property inspector and enter the desired size in the Width field. If the cell is currently in Autostretch mode, select the Fixed Width option to enable the value field.

✦ To convert an Autostretch column to its current onscreen pixel width, choose Make Column Fixed Width from the column header menu, as shown in Figure 10-28.

✦ Insert content wider than the set width and then choose Make Column Width Consistent from the Layout Table Property inspector.

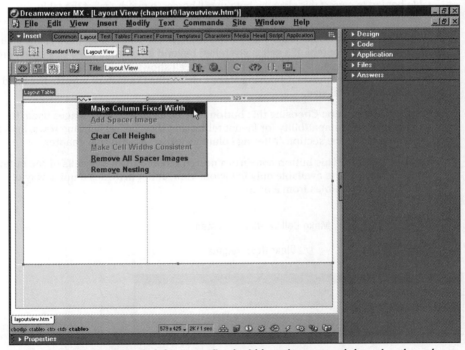

Figure 10-28: You can switch between fixed width and autostretch by using the column header menu.

To make a fixed-width column automatically stretch, choose Make Column Autostretch from the column header menu. Only one column can be made to autostretch. When you set a column to autostretch, Dreamweaver automatically converts any previously defined autostretch column to have a fixed width.

When the autostretch option is chosen for a layout table, Dreamweaver inserts a spacer (a single-pixel, transparent GIF) in a new row along the bottom of the table. The spacer is sized to match the width of each of the fixed-width columns. Only the autostretch column does not have a spacer image.

If you've ever painstakingly created a complex table only to find that it looks great in one browser but collapses into an unidentifiable mess in another, you're going to love spacers. Spacer images have long been used by Web site designers as a method of ensuring a table's stability. Because no browser will collapse a column smaller than the size of the largest image it contains, spacers retain a table's design under any circumstances.

Dreamweaver gives you several options when working with spacers:

✦ You can have Dreamweaver create a spacer for you.

✦ You can use an existing image as a spacer.

✦ You can opt to never include spacers.

The first time autostretch is applied as an option in a table, Dreamweaver displays the Choose Spacer Image dialog box (see Figure 10-29), which enables you to create or locate a spacer image. If you choose to create a new spacer, you are then asked to select a location in the current site in which to store it. Generally, you would save such a file in an images, assets, or media folder.

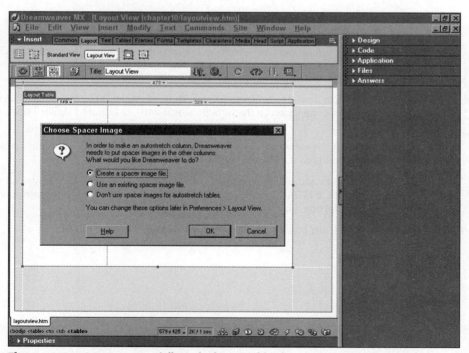

Figure 10-29: Spacers essentially make layout tables browser-proof; you can either let Dreamweaver create one for you or use an existing image.

This image is then automatically inserted whenever an autostretch table or cell is created. One circumstance for using an existing image rather than a new one is if you work with sliced tables from Fireworks. Fireworks creates a single-pixel GIF image titled shim.gif. The choice of a spacer image is a site-wide preference that can be viewed or changed by selecting the Layout View category of Preferences. Although it is not recommended practice, you can disable spacers in the Layout View category.

Summary

Tables are extremely powerful Web page design tools. Dreamweaver enables you to modify both the appearance and the structure of your HTML tables through a combination of Property inspectors, dialog boxes, and click-and-drag mouse movements. Mastering tables is an essential task for any modern Web designer and worth the somewhat challenging learning curve. The key elements to keep in mind are as follows:

✦ An HTML table consists of a series of rows and columns presented in a gridlike arrangement. Tables can be sized absolutely, in pixels, or relative to the width of the browser's window, as a percentage.

✦ Dreamweaver inserts a table whose dimensions can be altered through the Insert bar or the Insert ➪ Table menu. Once in the page, the table needs to be selected before any of its properties can be modified through the Table Property inspector.

✦ Table editing is greatly simplified in Dreamweaver. You can select multiple cells, columns, or rows — and modify all their contents in one fell swoop.

✦ You can assign certain properties — such as background color, border color, and alignment — for a table's columns, rows, or cells through their respective Property inspectors. The properties of a cell override those set for its column or row.

✦ Dreamweaver brings power to table-building with the Format Table and Sort Table commands, as well as a connection to the outside world with its Import Tabular Data option.

✦ Dreamweaver's Layout view enables you to quickly prepare the basic structure of a page by drawing out layout cells and tables.

✦ Putting a table within another table — also known as *nesting tables* — is a powerful (and legal) design option in HTML. Nested tables are easily accomplished in Dreamweaver's Layout view by inserting a layout table.

In the next chapter, you learn how to create and use forms in your Web pages.

✦   ✦   ✦

Interactive Forms

A form, in the everyday world as well as on the Web, is a type of structured communication. When you apply for a driver's license, you're not told to randomly write down personal information; you're asked to fill out a form that asks for specific information, one piece at a time, in a specific manner. Web-based forms are just as precise, if not more so.

Dreamweaver has a robust and superior implementation of HTML forms — from the dedicated Forms category in the Insert bar to various form-specific Property inspectors. In addition to their importance as a communication tool between the browsing public and Web server applications, forms are an integral part of building some of Dreamweaver's own objects. Forms also serve as a major tool for Web developers because they can be altered on the fly; it's possible, for example, for a selection in one drop-down list to determine the contents of another. The dynamic aspects of forms are covered in Chapter 19.

In this chapter, you learn how forms are structured and then created within Dreamweaver. Each form object is explored in detail — text fields, radio buttons, checkboxes, menus, list boxes, command buttons, hidden fields, and password fields.

How HTML Forms Work

Forms have a special function in HTML: They support interaction. Virtually all HTML elements apart from forms are concerned with layout and presentation — delivering the content to the user, if you will. Forms, on the other hand, enable the user to not just passively read information on the screen, but also to send information back. Without forms, the Web would be a one-way street.

Forms have numerous uses on the Web, such as for surveys, electronic commerce, guest books, polls, and even real-time custom graphics creation. For such feedback to be possible, forms require an additional component beyond what is seen onscreen so that each form can complete its function. Every form needs some type of connection to a Web server, whether it is through one of the Dreamweaver server models or a common gateway interface (CGI) script.

Forms, like HTML tables, can be thought of as self-contained units within a Web page. All the elements of a form are contained within the form tag pair <form> and </form>. Unlike tables, you cannot nest forms, although there's nothing to stop you from having multiple forms on a page.

The most commonly used attributes of the `<form>` tag include the following:

✦ The `method` attribute tells the browser and the Web server how to present the form contents to the application that will process the form. The two possible `method` values are `get` and `post`. The `get` method passes the attached information with a URL; it is less frequently used these days because it places limitations on the amount and format of data that can be passed to the application. The `post` method allows the application program to receive the information as standard input and imposes no limits on the passed data.

✦ The `action` attribute determines what should be done with the form content. Most commonly, `action` is set to a URL for running a specific Web application or for sending e-mail.

Typical HTML for a `<form>` tag looks something like the following:

```
<form method="post" action="http://www.idest.com/_cgi-bin/mailcall.pl">
```

Note   The .pl extension in the preceding example form tag stands for *Perl* — a scripting language often used to create CGI programs. Perl can be edited in any regular text editor.

Within each form is a series of input controls — text fields, radio buttons, check boxes, and so on. Each type handles a particular sort of input; in fact, the main tag for these elements is the `<input>` tag. With one exception, the `<textarea>` tag, all form input types are implemented by specifying the `type` attribute. The text box tag, for example, is written as follows:

```
<input type="text" name="lastname">
```

All form input tags must have a `name` attribute, which identifies the control. In the example above, the `name` is assigned a value of `"lastname"`. Information input by the user in a control, such as a text field, is sent to the server along with the `value` of that control's `name` attribute. Thus, if I were to fill out a form with a text box asking for my last name, such as the one produced by the foregoing tag, part of the message sent to the server would include the following string:

```
lastname=Lowery
```

Browsers send all the information from a form in one long text string to whatever program or address is specified in the `action` attribute. It's up to the program or the recipient of the form message to parse the string. For instance, if I were to fill out a small form with my name, e-mail address, and a short comment such as "Good work!", the server would send a text string similar to the following:

```
lastname=Lowery&address=jlowery@idest.com&comment=Good+work%21
```

As you can see, the various fields are separated by ampersands (&), and the individual words within the responses are separated by plus signs. Most non-alphanumeric characters — such as the exclamation mark in the example — are represented by their hexadecimal values. Decoding this text string is called *parsing* the response.

Tip   To ease maintenance of your code, choose a name that is descriptive, but that is not a reserved word. For example, it is better to name a text field "lastname" than "name."

Inserting a Form in Dreamweaver

A form is inserted just like any other object in Dreamweaver. Place the cursor where you want your form to start and then either select the Form button from the Forms category of the Insert bar or choose Insert ➪ Form from the menu. Dreamweaver inserts a red, dashed outline stretching across the Document window to indicate the form.

Tip If you can't see the outline of the form, choose View ➪ Visual Aids ➪ Invisible Elements. If you still can't see the form, choose Edit ➪ Preferences and select the Form Delimiter option in the Invisible Elements category. Clear the option if you don't want to see the form outline.

If you have the Property inspector open, the Form Property inspector appears when you insert a form. As you can see from Figure 11-1, you can specify several values regarding forms: In addition to the Action and the Method, which correspond to the attributes previously discussed, you can also specify a Form Name, Enctype value, and Target.

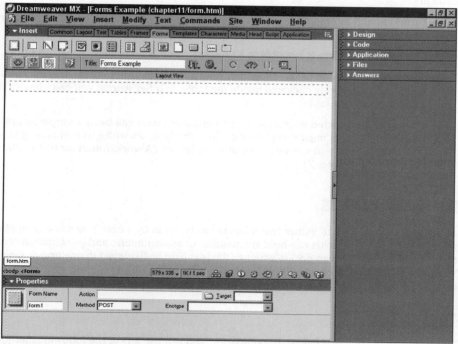

Figure 11-1: Inserting a form creates a dashed, red outline of the form and displays the Form Property inspector, if available.

Because of the interactive nature of forms, Web programmers often use them to gather information from the user. To do this, programmers must specify a form name, which enables them to reference a form using JavaScript or other languages.

In the Action text box, you can directly enter a URL or mailto address, or you can select the Folder icon and browse for a file.

Note   Sending your form data via a mailto address is not without its problems. Some browsers, most notably Internet Explorer, are set to initially warn the user whenever a form button using mailto is selected. While many users let the mail go through, they do have the option to stop it from being sent.

The method defaults to `post`, the most commonly used option. You can also choose `get` or `default`, which leaves the method up to the browser. In most cases, you should leave the method set to `post`.

`Enctype` stands for encoding type; this value tells the server in what format the data is being sent. For more information, refer to the sidebar titled "Declaring the Encoding Type (Enctype)" in this chapter. Finally, the Target field tells the server the frame or window to use when displaying a response to the form. If you don't specify a target, any response will display in the current frame or window.

Forms cannot be placed inline with any other element such as text or graphics. Keep in mind the following additional considerations when it comes to mixing forms and other Web page elements:

✦ Forms expand as objects are inserted into them; you can't resize a form by dragging its boundaries.

✦ The outline of a form is invisible in a browser; there is no border to turn on or off.

✦ Forms and tables can be used together only if the form either completely encloses the table or is completely enclosed inside the table. In other words, you can't have a form spanning part of a table.

✦ Forms can be inserted within layers, and multiple forms can be in multiple layers. However, the layer must completely enclose the form. As with forms spanning tables, you can't have a form spanning two or more layers. (A workaround for this limitation is discussed in Chapter 21.)

Using Text Fields

Anytime you use a form to gather text information typed in by a user, you use a form object called a *text field*. Text fields can hold any number of alphanumeric and punctuation characters. The Web designer can decide whether the text field is displayed in one line or several. When the HTML is written, a multiple-line text field uses a `<textarea>` tag, and a single-line text field is coded with `<input type="text">`.

Text fields

To insert a single-line text field in Dreamweaver, you can use any of the following methods:

✦ From the Forms category of the Insert bar, select the Text Field button to place a text field at your current cursor position.

✦ Choose Insert ➪ Form Objects ➪ Text Field from the menu, which inserts a text field at the current cursor position.

✦ Drag the Text Field button from the Insert bar to any existing location in the Document window and release the mouse button to position the text field.

Declaring the Encoding Type (Enctype)

The `<form>` attribute `enctype` is helpful in formatting material returned via a form. It specifies how the information is being sent, so the server software will know how to interpret the input.

By default, `enctype` is set to `application/x-www-form-urlencoded`, which is responsible for encoding the form response with ampersands between entries, equal signs linking form element names to their values, spaces as plus signs, and all non-alphanumeric characters in hexadecimal format, such as `%3F` (a question mark).

A second `enctype` value, `text/plain`, is useful for e-mail replies. Instead of one long string, your form data is transmitted in a more readable format, with each form element and its value on a separate line, as shown in the following example:

```
fname=Joseph
lname=Lowery
email=jlowery@idest.com
comment=Please send me the information on your new products!
```

Another `enctype` value, `multipart/form-data`, is used only when a file is being uploaded as part of the form. There's a further restriction: The method must be set to `post` instead of `get`.

Dreamweaver includes an Enctype list box on the Form Property inspector so you can easily specify the encoding type. You can choose a value from the drop-down list, or manually enter a value in the Enctype list box.

Note   You can use any of these methods to insert text fields in either Design view or Code view. When you insert a text field or most other form controls in Code view, the Tag Editor for the `<input>` tag opens automatically, allowing you to specify any attributes for the tag.

When you insert a text field, the Property inspector, when displayed, shows you the attributes that can be changed (see Figure 11-2). The size of a text field is measured by the number of characters it can display at one time. You can change the length of a text field by inserting a value in the Char Width text box. By default, Dreamweaver inserts a text field approximately 20 characters wide. The *approximately* is important here because the *final* size of the text field is ultimately controlled by the browser used to view the page. Unless you limit the number of possible characters by entering a value in the Max Chars text box, the user can enter as many characters as desired, but not all the characters will necessarily be visible at one time; the text scrolls horizontally in the box as the user types.

Note   The value in Char Width determines the visible width of the field, whereas the value in Max Chars actually determines the number of characters that can be entered.

The Init Value text box on the Text Field Property inspector is used to insert a default text string. The user can overwrite this value, if desired.

Text Field

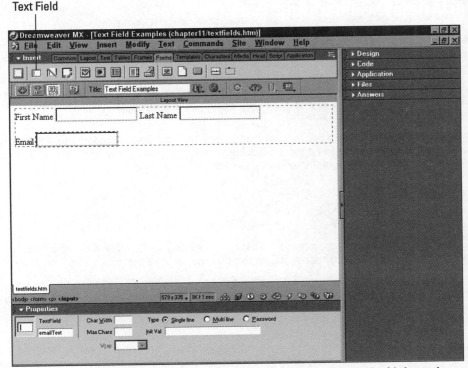

Figure 11-2: The text field of a form enables the user to type any required information.

Password fields

Normally, any text entered into text fields is displayed as you expect — programmers refer to this process as *echoing*. You can turn off the echoing by selecting the Password option in the Text Field Property inspector. When a text field is designated as a password field, all text entered by the user shows up as asterisks or dots.

Use the password field when you want to protect the user's input from prying eyes (as your PIN number is hidden when you enter it at an ATM, for instance). The information entered in a password field is not encrypted or scrambled in any way, and when sent to the Web application, it is received as regular text.

Only single-line text fields can be set as password fields. You cannot make a multiline `<textarea>` tag act as a password field without employing JavaScript or some other programming language.

Cross-Reference

Making sure that your user fills out the form properly is called *validating* the input. Dreamweaver includes a standard form validation behavior, covered in Chapter 23.

Multiline text areas

When you want to give your users a generous amount of room to write, you can expand not just the width of the text area, but also its height. Dreamweaver gives you the following options for creating a multiline text area:

✦ Insert a single-line text field on the page and convert the field to have multiple lines using the Text Field Property inspector. To use this method, insert a single-line text field on the page as previously described; and in the Text Field Property inspector, choose the Multiline option.

✦ Directly insert the Textarea form element using the Insert bar or Insert menu. To do this, position your cursor where you want to insert the text area, and choose Insert ➪ Form Objects ➪ Textarea or click the Textarea button in the Forms category of the Insert bar.

The initially created text area is approximately 18 characters wide and 3 lines high, with horizontal and vertical scroll bars. Figure 11-3 shows a typical multiline text field embedded in a form.

You control the width of a multiline text area by entering a value in the Char Width text box of the Text Field Property inspector, just as you do for single-line text fields. The height of the text area is set equal to the value in the Num Lines text box. As with the default single-line text field, the user can enter any amount of text desired. Unlike the single-line text field, which can restrict the number of characters that can be input through the Max Chars text box, you cannot restrict the number of characters the user enters into a multiline text area.

Neat Forms

Text field width is measured in a monospaced character width. Because regular fonts are not monospaced, however, lining up text fields and other form objects can be problematic at best. The two general workarounds are preformatted text and tables.

Switching the labels on the form to preformatted text enables you to insert any amount of whitespace to properly space (or *kern*) your text and other input fields. Previously, Web designers were stuck with the default preformatted text format—the rather plain-looking Courier monospaced font. Now, however, newer browsers (3.0 and later) can read the face attribute. Therefore, you can combine a regular font with the preformatted text option and get the best of both worlds. For example, the following code was used to create the first line of the preformatted form in the figure that follows:

```
<pre><font face="Times New Roman, Times, serif">  First Name:
</font><input name="textfield" type="text" size="20">  <font face="Times
New Roman, Times, serif">Last Name: </font> <input name="textfield2"
type="text" size="24">
```

Going the preformatted text route requires you to insert a lot of spaces. Therefore, when you are working on a larger, complex form, using tables is probably a better way to go. Besides the speed of layout, the other advantage that tables offer is the capability to right-align text labels next to your text fields. The top form in the following sidebar figure uses preformatted text to get differently sized form fields to line up properly, while the bottom form in the figure uses a table.

Continued

Continued

Combining differently sized text fields on a single row—for example, when you're asking for a city, state, and zip code combination—can make the task of lining up your form even more difficult. Most often, you'll spend a fair amount of time in a trial-and-error effort to make the text fields match. Be sure to check your results in the various browsers as you build your form.

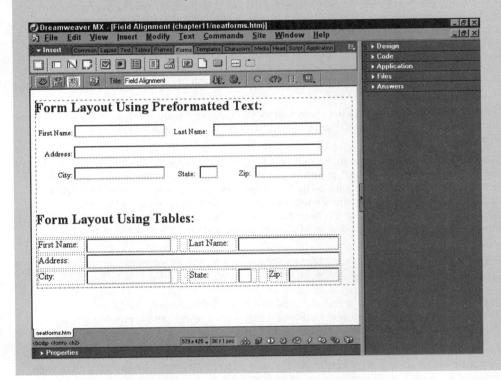

When you place a multiline text field on a form, you can specify how text entered into that field should wrap. You indicate this using the Wrap field in the Property inspector. You may select one of the following options:

> ✦ **Default:** With this option, the scrolling characteristics of the multiline text field are determined by the browser. Browsers and browser versions vary in their default handling of wrapping.

> ✦ **Off:** With this option, text entered into a multiline text field does not wrap when it reaches the right edge of the text area; rather, it keeps scrolling until the user presses Enter (Return).

✦ **Virtual:** This option wraps text on the screen when it reaches the right edge of the text area, but not when the response is submitted to the server; the text is sent as one long string without hard carriage returns.

✦ **Physical:** This option wraps text on the screen and converts the soft returns on the screen to hard returns when the data is submitted to the server.

The `wrap` attribute is not supported consistently between browsers or even between different versions of the same browser. For example, Netscape 6.0 ignores any value of the `wrap` attribute, and simply never wraps text, while Netscape Navigator 4.61 does respect the wrapping options.

Another option when creating multiline text fields is to preload the text area with any default text you like. Enter this text in the Init Val text box of the Text Field Property inspector. When Dreamweaver writes the HTML code, this text is not entered as a value, as for the single-line text field, but rather goes in between the `<textarea>. . .</textarea>` tag pair.

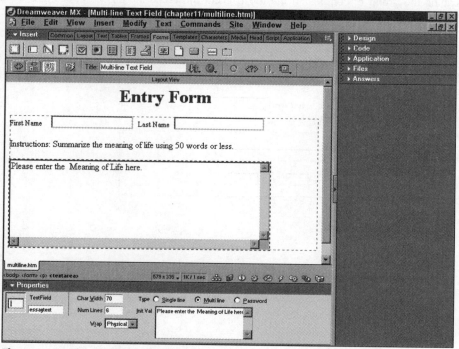

Figure 11-3: The Multiline option of the Text Field Property inspector opens up a text area for more user information.

Grouping Form Controls

In desktop applications, you may be used to seeing related controls grouped together, with a thin border around them. You can achieve a similar effect in your HTML forms by enclosing the related form elements within the `<fieldset>`. . .`</fieldset>` tag pair, as shown in the following code:

```
<fieldset>
  <legend>Address</legend>
    <label>Street <input type="text" name="street" ></label>
    <label>City <input type="text" name="city" ></label>
    <label>State <input type="text" name="state" ></label>
    <label>Zip <input type="text" name="zip"></label>
</fieldset>
```

In this example, the `<fieldset>` tags group the text fields, and the `<legend>` tag creates a label describing the group of controls. In the most recent browsers, the legend appears as a label above the control group, as shown in the following figure.

In Dreamweaver's Code view, you can add the `<fieldset>` and `<legend>` tags by selecting a set of existing controls that you'd like to group, and then choosing the Fieldset button in the Forms category of the Insert bar. If you are in Design view when you select the Fieldset button, Dreamweaver will automatically switch to the split view and make Code view active. However, it is best to apply the `<fieldset>` tag in Code view, so you can be sure you have correctly selected all the HTML tags to be grouped.

Note that the `<fieldset>` tag is not supported in all browsers, and when viewed within Dreamweaver, although the legend is visible, no line is displayed around the form elements.

Providing Checkboxes and Radio Buttons

When you want your Web page user to choose between a specific set of options in your form, you can use either checkboxes or radio buttons. Checkboxes enable you to offer a series of options from which the user can pick as many as desired. Radio buttons, on the other hand, restrict your user to only one selection from a number of options.

Tip

You can achieve the same functionality as checkboxes and radio buttons with a different look by using drop-down lists and menu boxes. These methods for presenting options to the user are described shortly.

Checkboxes

Checkboxes are often used in a "Select All That Apply" type of section, when you want to enable the user to choose as many of the listed options as desired. You insert a checkbox in much the same way you do a text field: Select or drag the Check Box object from the Insert bar or choose Insert ➪ Form Objects ➪ Check Box.

Like other form objects, checkboxes can be given a unique name in the CheckBox Property inspector (see Figure 11-4). If you don't provide a name, Dreamweaver inserts a generic one, such as checkbox4.

In the Checked Value text box, fill in the information you want passed to a program when the user selects the checkbox. By default, a checkbox starts out unchecked, but you can change that by changing the Initial State option to Checked.

Radio buttons

Radio buttons on a form provide a set of options from which the user can choose only one. If a user changes his or her mind after choosing one radio button, selecting another one automatically deselects the first choice. Dreamweaver gives you the following options for inserting radio buttons:

✦ To insert radio buttons one at a time, choose or drag Radio Button from the Forms category of the Insert bar, or choose Insert ➪ Form Objects ➪ Radio Button.

✦ To insert several related radio buttons at one time, choose or drag the Radio Group button from the Forms category of the Insert bar, or choose Insert ➪ Form Objects ➪ Radio Group.

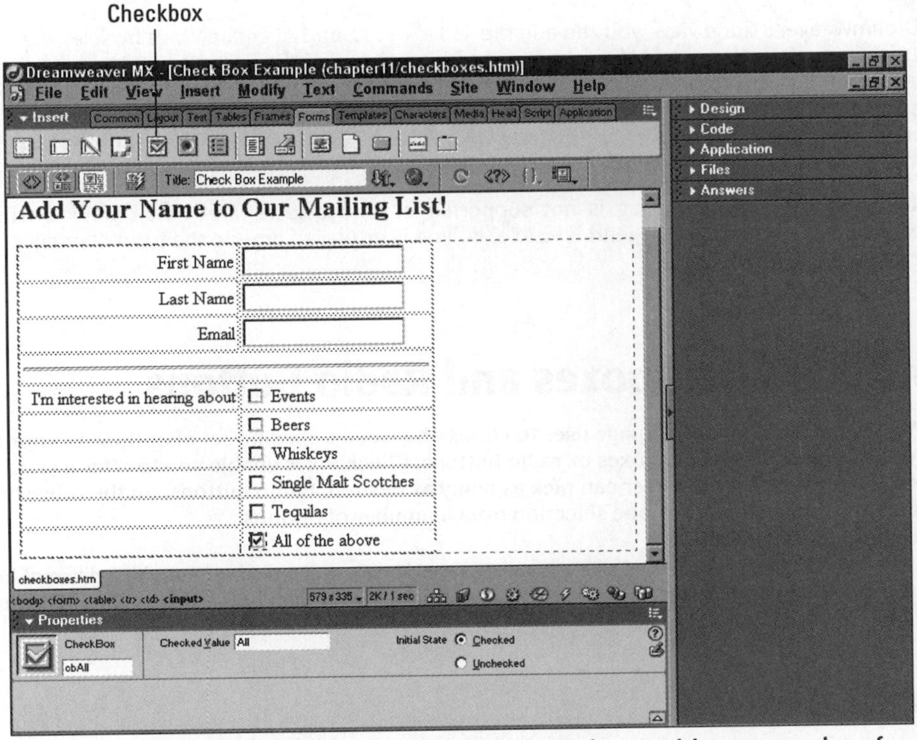

Checkbox

Figure 11-4: Checkboxes are one way of offering the Web page visitor any number of options to choose.

Unlike checkboxes and text fields, each radio button in the set does not have a unique name—instead, each group of radio buttons does. Giving the entire set of radio buttons the same name enables browsers to assign one value to the radio button set. That value is determined by the contents of the Checked Value text box in the Property inspector. Figure 11-5 shows two different sets of radio buttons. The figure shows the Property inspector for one of the radio buttons in the osRadio group, on the right. In this example, each button in the group is assigned the name osRadio.

To designate the default selection for each radio button group, you select the particular radio button and make the Initial State option Checked instead of Unchecked. In the form shown in Figure 11-5, the default selection for the osRadio group is Macintosh.

Tip

Because you must give all radio buttons in the same set the same name, you can speed up your work a bit by creating one button, copying it, and then pasting the others. Don't forget to change the Checked Value for each button, though.

Radio Button

Radio Group

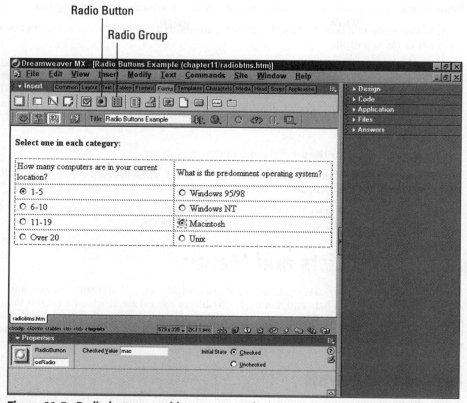

Figure 11-5: Radio buttons enable a user to make just one selection from a group of options.

You can create an entire set of radio buttons at one time using the Radio Group command. When you choose the Radio Group button from the Forms category of the Insert bar, or choose Insert ➪ Form Objects ➪ Radio Group, the Radio Group dialog box appears, as shown in Figure 11-6. This dialog box not only lets you define multiple radio buttons at once, it automatically formats them either in a table or using line breaks, at your discretion.

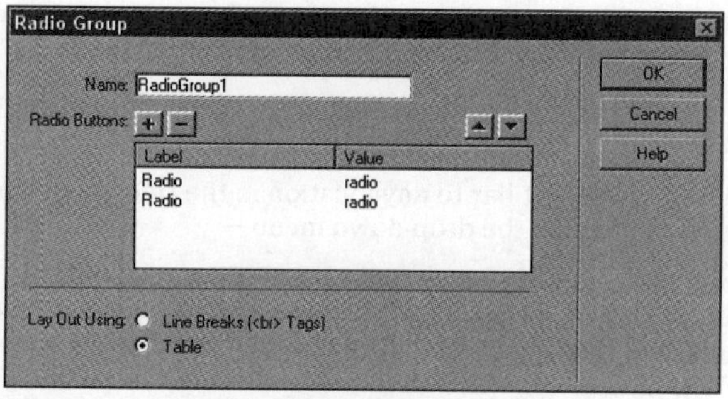

Figure 11-6: Use the Radio Group dialog box to create an entire set of radio buttons at one time.

Follow these steps to set up your radio button group in the Radio Group dialog box:

1. In the Name text box, replace the default name with a meaningful name for your new set of radio buttons.

2. Each entry in the list represents a separate radio button in the group; the dialog box opens with two filler buttons as an example. Click on the first entry in the Label list, and replace the word Radio with the label for the first button in your group. Press Tab to move to the Value column, and replace the default with the appropriate value for your button; this is the data that will be sent to the server when the radio button is selected.

   Repeat this step for the second radio button in your set.

3. If you have more than two radio buttons in your set, click the Add (+) button to add another item to the list, and fill out the appropriate values, as explained in Step 2.

4. Specify whether you want your radio buttons inserted on separate lines using the <br> tag, or automatically formatted in a table. Then click OK.

Creating Form Lists and Menus

Another way to offer your user options, in a more compact form than radio buttons and checkboxes, is with form lists and menus. Both objects can create single-line entries in your form that expand or scroll to reveal all the available options. You can also determine how deep you want the scrolling list to be; that is, how many options you want displayed at one time.

Drop-down menus

A drop-down menu should be familiar to everyday users of computers: The menu is initially displayed as a single-line text box with an arrow button at the right end; when the button is clicked, the other options are revealed in a list or menu. (Whether the list "pops up" or "drops down" depends on its position on the screen at the time it is selected. Normally, the list drops down, unless it is close to the bottom of the screen.) After the user selects one of the listed options and the mouse is released, the list closes, and the selected value remains displayed in the text box.

Insert a drop-down menu in Dreamweaver as you would any other form object, with one of the following actions:

✦ From the Forms category of the Insert bar, select the List/Menu button to place a drop-down menu at the current cursor position.

✦ Choose Insert ➪ Form Objects ➪ List/Menu from the menu to insert a drop-down menu at the current cursor position.

✦ Drag the List/Menu button from the Insert bar to any location in the Document window and release the mouse button to position the drop-down menu.

With the List/Menu object inserted, make sure the Menu option (not the List option) is selected in the Property inspector, as shown in Figure 11-7. You can also name the drop-down menu by typing a name in the Name text box; if you don't, Dreamweaver supplies a generic "select" name.

List/Menu

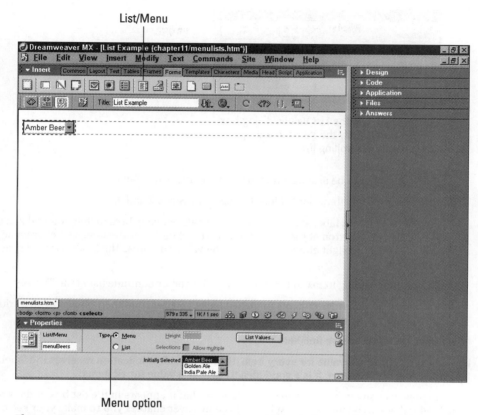

Menu option

Figure 11-7: Create a drop-down menu by inserting a List/Menu object and then selecting the Menu option in the List/Menu Property inspector.

Menu values

The HTML code for a drop-down menu uses the `<select>. . .</select>` tag pair surrounding a number of `<option>. . .</option>` tag pairs. Dreamweaver gives you a straightforward user interface for entering labels and values for the options on your menu. The menu item's label is what is displayed on the drop-down list; its value is what is sent to the server-side processor when this particular option is selected.

To enter the labels and values for a drop-down menu — or for a scrolling list — follow these steps:

1. Select the menu for which you want to enter values.

2. From the List/Menu Property inspector, select the List Values button. The List Values dialog box appears (see Figure 11-8).

3. In the Item Label column, enter the label for the first item. Press the Tab key to move to the Value column.

Figure 11-8: Use the List Values dialog box to enter and modify the items in a drop-down menu or scrolling list.

4. Enter the value to be associated with this item. Press the Tab key.

5. Continue entering items and values by repeating Steps 3 and 4.

6. To delete an item's label and value in the List Values dialog box, highlight it and select the Remove (–) button at the top of the list. To delete either the item's label or value, but not both, highlight either the label or the value and press the Delete or backspace key.

7. To continue adding items, select the Add (+) button or continue using the Tab key.

8. To rearrange the order of items in the list, select an item and then press the up or down arrow key to reposition it.

9. Click OK when you've finished.

If you haven't entered a value for every item, the server-side application receives the label instead. Generally, however, it is a good idea to specify a value for all items.

You can preselect any item in a drop-down menu so that it appears in the list box initially and is highlighted when the full list is displayed. Dreamweaver enables you to make your selection from the Initially Selected menu in the Property inspector. The Initially Selected menu is empty until you enter items through the List Values dialog box. You can preselect only one item for a drop-down menu.

Tip   To clear the selection in the Initially Selected list, hold down the Ctrl (Command) key as you click the highlighted item.

Scrolling lists

A scrolling list differs from a drop-down menu in three respects. First, and most obviously, the scrolling list field has up and down arrow buttons, rather than an option arrow button; and the user can scroll the list, showing as little as one item at a time, instead of the entire list. Second, you can control the height of the scrolling list, enabling it to display more than one item — or all available items — simultaneously. Third, you can enable the user to select more than one item at a time, as with checkboxes.

A scrolling list is inserted in the same manner as a drop-down menu — through the Insert bar or the Insert ➪ Form Objects menu. Once the object is inserted, select the List option in the List/Menu Property inspector.

You enter items for your scrolling list just as you do with a drop-down menu, by starting with the List Values button in the Property inspector and filling in the List Values dialog box. Figure 11-9 shows a sample list box, as it appears in the Document window.

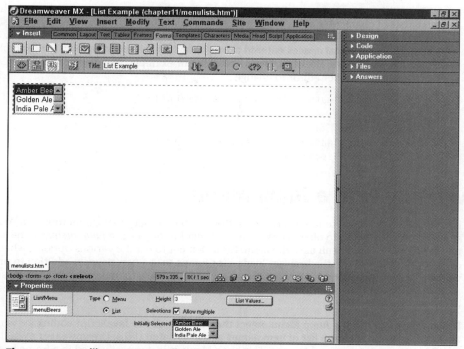

Figure 11-9: Unlike menus, scrolling lists can show more than one item on the screen at a time.

By default, the Selections checkbox for Allow Multiple is cleared in the List/Menu Property inspector. When you enable multiple selections (by selecting the Allow Multiple checkbox), the user can select more than one item in the list by using two keyboard modifiers, the Shift and Ctrl (Command) keys:

✦ To select several adjacent items in the list, the user must click the first item in the list, press the Shift key, and select the last item in the list.

✦ To select several nonadjacent items, the user must hold down the Ctrl (Command) key while selecting the items.

Other than the highlighted text, no acknowledgment (such as a checkmark) appears in the list. As with drop-down menus, the Web designer can preselect options by highlighting them in the Initially Selected menu. Use the same techniques with the Shift and Ctrl keys as a user would.

Keep in mind several factors as you are working with scrolling lists:

✦ If you disable the Allow Multiple Selections box and set a Height value of 1 or clear the Height field entirely, the list appears as a drop-down menu.

✦ With Allow Multiple Selections enabled, if you do not set a Height value at all, the number of items that appear onscreen is left up to the browser. Internet Explorer, by default, shows four items at a time; and Netscape Navigator displays all the items in your list. In the Dreamweaver Document window, only one item is displayed. To exercise control over your scrolling list, it is best to insert a Height value.

✦ The widths of both the scrolling list and the drop-down menu are determined by the number of characters in the longest label. To widen the List/Menu object, you must directly enter additional spaces ( ) in the HTML code; Dreamweaver does not recognize additional spaces entered through the List Values dialog box. For example, to expand the Favorite Beer List/Menu object in our example, you'd need to use the Code inspector or another editor to change

```
<option value="oatmeal">Oatmeal Stout</option>
```

to the following:

```
<option value="oatmeal">Oatmeal Stout ⤺
   </option>
```

Navigating with a Jump Menu

It's not always practical to use a series of buttons as the primary navigation tool on a Web site. For sites that want to offer access to a great number of pages, a *jump menu* can be a better way to go. A jump menu uses the menu form element to list the various options; when one of the options is chosen, the browser loads — or jumps to — a new page. In addition to providing a single mechanism for navigation, a jump menu is easy to update because it doesn't require laying out the page again. Because they are JavaScript-driven, jump menus can even be updated dynamically.

Dreamweaver includes a Jump Menu object that handles all the JavaScript coding for you — all you have to provide is a list of item names and associated URLs. Dreamweaver even drops in a Go button for you, if you choose. The Jump Menu object is easily used in a frame-based layout for targeting specific frames. Once inserted, you can modify the Jump Menu object like any other list object, through the List/Menu Property inspector. To insert a jump menu, follow these steps:

1. Position your cursor in the current form, if one exists, where you'd like the jump menu to appear.

   If you haven't already inserted a form, don't worry. Dreamweaver automatically inserts one for you.

2. From the Forms category of the Insert bar, choose the Jump Menu button.

   The Insert Jump Menu dialog box, shown in Figure 11-10, is displayed.

3. In the Insert Jump Menu dialog box, enter the label for the first item in the Text field.

   When you confirm your entry by tabbing out of the field, Dreamweaver updates the Menu Items list.

4. Enter the path and filename of the page you want opened for the current item in the When Selected, Go To URL field; alternatively, you can select the Browse (Choose) button to select your file.

5. To add additional jump menu items, select the Add (+) button and repeat Steps 3 and 4.

6. You can adjust the positioning of the items in the jump menu by selecting an item in the Menu Items list and using the up and down arrows to move it higher or lower.

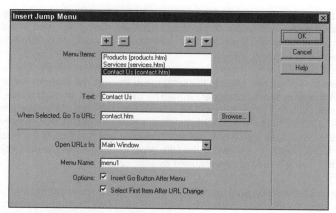

Figure 11-10: Consolidate your Web site navigation through a jump menu.

7. Pick the destination target for the page from the Open URLs In list.

Unless you're working in a frameset, you have only one option — Main Window. When a Jump Menu object is added in a frameset, Dreamweaver displays all frame names, as well as Main Window, as options.

8. If desired, enter a unique name for the jump menu in the Menu Name field.

9. To add a button that activates the jump menu choice, select the Insert Go Button After Menu option.

10. To reset the menu selection to the top item after every jump, choose the Select First Item After URL Change.

11. Click OK when you're done.

Dreamweaver inserts the new jump menu with the appropriate linking code.

On the CD-ROM

Macromedia's Jump Menu object opens the selected URL in the current page or in one of the frames in a frameset. To open a Web page in a new window, you'll need to use another extension, Jump Menu Fever! by Drew McLellan. This object is located in the Additional Extensions folder on the CD-ROM. To open a new window with Jump Menu Fever!, choose _Blank from the list of available targets.

Modifying a jump menu

Once you've inserted your Jump Menu object, you can modify it in one of two ways: through the standard List/Menu Property inspector or through the Jump Menu behavior. Whereas the List Property inspector uses a List Value dialog box, editing the Jump Menu behavior opens a dialog box similar to the one used to insert the Jump Menu object.

To alter the items in an existing jump menu via the List/Menu Property inspector, select the jump menu and click the List Values button. In the List Values dialog box, you see the jump menu labels on the left and the URLs on the right. You can add, move, or delete items as you would with any other list.

Caution   Note one caveat for adding new URLs to the jump menu through the Property inspector: Any filenames with spaces or special characters should be URL-encoded. In other words, if one of your filenames is about us.htm, it should be entered using the hexadecimal equivalent for a space (%20): about%20us.htm. Also, if you enter a filename or URL that contains special characters in the List Values dialog box, the resulting code will translate the special characters into their HTML codes, thus breaking the URL. Most notably, an ampersand (&) entered in the List Values dialog box would be encoded as &.

If you'd prefer to work in the same environment as you did when creating the Jump Menu object, go the Behaviors panel route. Select the jump menu. Then, from the Behaviors panel, double-click the Jump Menu action. The Jump Menu dialog box opens — it is identical to the Insert Jump Menu dialog box except that the Go button option is not available.

Activating Go buttons

The Dreamweaver jump menu is activated immediately whenever a user makes a selection from the list. So why would you want a Go button? The Go button, as implemented in Dreamweaver, is useful for selecting the first item in a jump menu list. To ensure that the Go button is the sole means for activating a jump selection, you need to remove an attached behavior. Select the jump menu item and then open the Behaviors panel. From the Behaviors panel, delete the Jump Menu event.

Tip   Some Web designers prefer to use a non-URL option for the first item, such as Please Select A Department. When entering such a non-URL option, set the Go to URL (or the value in the List Value Properties) to javascript:; to create a null link.

Wrapping Graphics Around a Jump Menu

Jump menus are useful in many circumstances, but as a raw form element, they often stick out of a Web page design like a sore thumb. Some designers solve this dilemma by including their jump menu within a specially constructed graphic. The easiest way to create such a graphic is to use a program such as Fireworks, which enables a single image to be sliced into separate parts. The slices are then exported to an HTML file and reassembled in a table.

When you create your graphic, you need to leave room for the jump menu to be inserted in Dreamweaver. Reserving space for a jump menu usually entails designating one slice as a non-graphic or text-only slice in your graphics program. Once you bring the HTML into Dreamweaver, insert the Jump Menu object in the empty table cell.

Here are a few pointers for wrapping a graphic around a jump menu:

✦ Use a flat color — not a gradient — as the background for the menu.

✦ Work with Web-safe colors in the graphics program; they're far easier to match in Dreamweaver.

✦ Set the background color of the graphic to be the background color of the cell of the table holding your jump menu.

✦ Make sure you leave enough height in your graphic to accommodate the jump menu in all browsers. Netscape displays a standard list/menu form element approximately 24 pixels high on a PC; try leaving about 30 pixels in your graphic.

✦ Form elements are drawn by the user's operating system and are vastly different on each platform. Test your designs extensively.

✦ Integrate your Go button, if you're using one, right in the graphic. Be sure to set it as its own slice, so that it comes in as a separate image and can be activated with a Jump Menu Go behavior. In the following figure, a graphical Go button appears to the right of the jump menu.

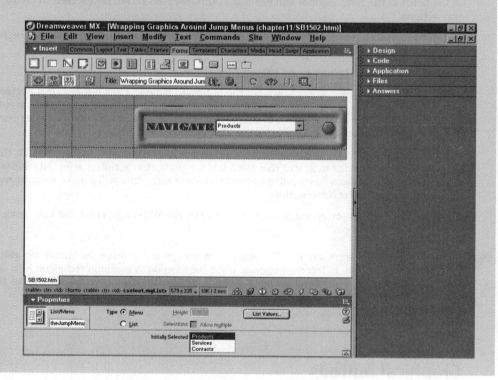

The generic Go button is a nice convenience, but it's a little, well, generic. To switch from a standard Go button to a graphical Go button of your choosing, follow these steps:

1. Insert the image that you want to use as your new Go button next to the jump menu.

2. With the new graphic selected, open the Behaviors panel.

3. Select Jump Menu Go from the Add Event drop-down list.

   Dreamweaver displays a dialog box showing all available jump menus.

4. Choose the name of the current jump menu from the Jump Menu Go dialog box list and click OK when you're done.

5. If necessary, delete the Dreamweaver-inserted Go button.

Activating Your Form with Buttons

Buttons are essential to HTML forms. You can place all the form objects you want on a page, but until your user presses that Submit button, there's no interaction between the client and the server. HTML provides three basic types of buttons: Submit, Reset, and Command.

Submit, Reset, and Command buttons

A Submit button sends the form to the specified action (generally the URL of a server-side program or a mailto address) using the noted method (generally post). A Reset button clears all the fields in the form. Submit and Reset are both reserved HTML terms used to invoke specific actions.

A Command button permits the execution of functions defined by the Web designer, as programmed in JavaScript or other languages.

To insert a button in Dreamweaver, follow these steps:

1. Position the cursor where you want the button to appear. Then either select Button in the Forms category of the Insert bar, or choose Insert ➪ Form Objects ➪ Button from the menu. Alternatively, you can simply drag the Button control from the Insert bar and drop it into place on an existing form.

2. In the Button Property inspector, choose the button Action type. In Figure 11-11, the Property inspector indicates that the Submit form button action is selected (this is the default). To make a Reset button, select the Reset form option. To make a Command button, select the None option.

3. To rename a button as you want it to appear on the Web page, enter the new name in the Label text box.

Tip   When working with Command buttons, it's not enough to just insert the button and give it a name. You have to link the button to a specific function. A common technique is to use JavaScript's onClick event to call a function detailed in the <script> section of the document:

```
<input type="BUTTON" name="submit2" value="yes" ⤸
onClick="doFunction()">
```

Graphical buttons

HTML doesn't limit you to the browser-style default buttons. You can also use an image as a Submit, Reset, or Command button. Dreamweaver has the capability to add an image field just like other form elements: Place the cursor in the desired position and choose Insert ➪ Form Objects ➪ Image Field, or select the Image Field button from the Forms category of the Insert bar. You can use multiple image fields in a form to give users a graphical option, as shown in Figure 11-12.

When the user clicks the picture that you've designated as an image field for a Submit button, the form is submitted. Any other functionality, such as resetting the fields, must be coded in JavaScript or another language and triggered by attaching an onClick event to the button. This can be handled through the Dreamweaver behaviors, covered in Chapter 23, or by hand-coding the script and adding code for the onClick event to the button.

Button

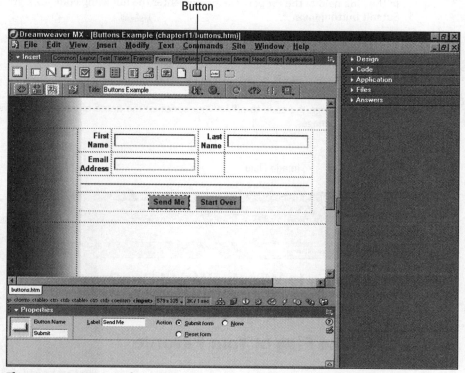

Figure 11-11: You can choose an action and a label for a button through the Button Property inspector.

In fact, when the user clicks a graphical button, not only does it submit your form, it passes along the x, y coordinates of the image. The x coordinate is submitted using the name of the field with an .x attached; likewise, the y coordinate is submitted with the name of the field with a .y attached. Although this latter feature isn't often used, it's always good to know all the capabilities of your HTML tools.

Another technique is involved if you want to include more graphical buttons than a single Submit button on your form. As only one image field can be used as a Submit button, a standard image is inserted, and JavaScript handles the programming chores required for submitting or resetting the form. An advantage to this technique is that the image can even be set up as a rollover, meaning that the image changes as the user moves the mouse over the button.

To use an image for a Submit or Reset button, follow these steps:

1. Choose Insert ➪ Image or select the Image button from the Common category of the Insert bar.

2. In the Insert Image dialog box, enter the path to your image or select the folder icon to locate the file. The image can be in GIF, JPEG, or PNG format.

3. Give the image a name and, if desired, alternative text using the appropriate text boxes in the Property inspector.

4. In the Link field of the Property inspector, enter the following code for a graphical Submit button:

```
javascript:document.form1.submit()
```

Similarly, enter this code for a Reset button:

```
javascript:document.form1.reset()
```

Note   Be sure to change the code to reflect your specifics: the name of your form as well as the name of your images.

Image Field

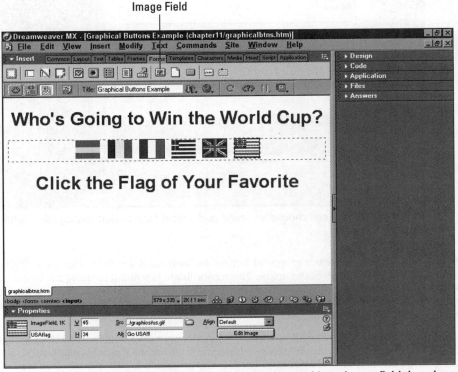

Figure 11-12: Each flag in this page is more than an image; it's an image field that also acts as a Submit button.

Using the Hidden Field and the File Field

You should also be aware of two other special-purpose form fields. The *hidden field* and the *file field* are supported by all major browsers. The hidden field is extremely useful for passing variables to your Web application programs, and the file field enables users to attach a file to the form being submitted.

The hidden input type

When passing information from a form to a CGI program, the programmer often needs to send data that should not be made visible to the user. The data could be a variable needed by the CGI program to set information on the recipient of the form, or it could be a URL to which the server program will redirect the user after the form is submitted. To send this sort of information unseen by the form user, you can use a hidden form object.

The hidden field is inserted in a form much like the other form elements. To insert a hidden field, place your cursor in the desired position and choose Insert ➪ Form Objects ➪ Hidden Field or choose the Hidden Field button from the Forms category of the Insert bar.

The hidden object is another input type, just like the text, radio button, and checkbox types. A hidden variable looks like the following in HTML:

```
<input type="hidden" name="recipient" value="jlowery@idest.com">
```

As you would expect, this tag has no representation when it's viewed through a browser. However, Dreamweaver does display a Hidden Form Element symbol in the Document window. You can turn off the display of this symbol by deselecting the Hidden Form Field option from the Invisible Elements category of Preferences.

The file input type

Much more rarely used is the file input type, which enables any stored computer file to be attached to the form and sent with the other data. Used primarily to enable the easy sharing of data, the file input type has been largely supplanted by modern e-mail methods, which also enable files to be attached to messages.

The file field is inserted in a form much like the other form elements. To insert a file field, place your cursor in the desired position and choose Insert ➪ Form Objects ➪ File Field or choose the File Field button from the Forms category of the Insert bar. Dreamweaver automatically inserts what appears to be a text box with a Browse (Choose) button. In a browser, the user's selection of the Browse (Choose) button displays a standard Open File dialog box from which a file can be selected to go with the form.

Improving Accessibility

You can do several things to make your HTML forms more accessible to people with visual impairments, who may be using a nonvisual browser. Many of these options are also useful for users accessing the page visually.

New Feature Dreamweaver makes it easy for Web page authors to improve the accessibility of their Web forms by setting an option in the Accessibility category of the Preferences dialog box.

To turn on the accessibility controls for forms, choose Edit ➪ Preferences and then, in the Accessibility category, select the Form Objects option. With this option enabled, every time you insert a form object, the Input Tag Accessibility Attributes dialog box, shown in Figure 11-13, is displayed.

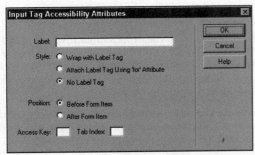

Figure 11-13: The Input Tag Accessibility Attributes dialog box is displayed only when you have enabled the Forms Accessibility Preference option.

Note The Input Tag Accessibility Attributes dialog box does not appear when you insert Jump Menus or Radio Groups. However, it does appear when you insert individual radio buttons.

In the Input Tag Accessibility Attributes dialog box, the Label field associates a textual label with the form object you are inserting. It does this by inserting `<label>. . .</label>` tags in your form. The label will be visible in the browser window. By using the `<label>` tag, you can explicitly associate the text with a particular control. You have two options for achieving this association:

✦ Choose the Wrap with Label Tag option, which encloses the form element within the `<label>. . .</label>` pair. This construct is shown in the following example:

```
<label>First Name
   <input type="text" name="mytextfield">
</label>
```

✦ Choose the Attach Label Tag Using 'for' Attribute option, which adds an attribute to the `<label>` tag that matches the id attribute of the form element. You would choose this option, for example, when you use a table to align form elements, and the label and control appear in separate table cells. The following example illustrates the use of the for attribute:

```
<label for="mytextfield">First Name</label>
   <input type="text" name="textfield2" id="mytextfield">
```

Note You can also insert a `<label>. . .</label>` pair by choosing the Label button from the Forms category of the Insert bar. This button is best used in Code view.

Although you may visually achieve the same effect by simply typing the text in the Document window, a nonvisual browser cannot associate plain text with any particular object. This effect is also what happens if you choose the No Label Tag option.

The final option you have when inserting a label is whether it should appear before or after the form element you are inserting.

In the AccessKey field of the Input Tag Accessibility Attributes dialog box, type a single letter that will serve as a shortcut to the form element. When users press the shortcut key for a given control, focus goes to that form element. Depending on their browser and operating system, users may have to hold down an additional key, such as Ctrl, Alt, or Command, for the shortcut to work.

The final control in the Input Tag Accessibility Attributes dialog box is the Tab Index. This control adds the `tabindex` attribute to the `<input>` HTML tag. In this field, type a positive, nonzero number indicating the order in which the control should receive focus when the user is tabbing through the form. Lower numbers receive focus first in the tabbing order; if items have the same number, the form element that appears first in the page receives focus first. Form elements with a `tabindex` of zero or with no `tabindex` specified appear last in the tab order.

Summary

HTML forms provide a basic line of communication from Web page visitor to Web site applications. With Dreamweaver, you can enter and modify most varieties of form inputs, including text fields and checkboxes.

✦ For the most part, a complete form requires two working parts: the form object inserted in your Web page and a CGI program stored on your Web server.

✦ To avoid using a server-side script, you can use a mailto address, rather than a URL pointing to a program in a form's `action` attribute. However, you still have to parse the form reply to convert it to a usable format.

✦ The basic types of form input are text fields, text areas, radio buttons, checkboxes, drop-down menus, and scrolling lists.

✦ Dreamweaver includes a Jump Menu object, which uses a drop-down list as a navigational system.

✦ After a user completes a form, it has to be sent to the server-side application, usually through a Submit button on the form. Dreamweaver also supports Reset and user-definable Command buttons.

In the next chapter, you learn how to use Dreamweaver to create bulleted and numbered lists.

✦　　✦　　✦

Creating Lists

Lists serve several different functions in all publications, including Web pages. A bulleted list can itemize a topic's points or catalog the properties of an object. A numbered list is helpful for giving step-by-step instructions. From a page designer's point of view, a list can break up the page and simultaneously draw the viewer's eye to key details.

Lists are an important alternative to the basic textual tools of paragraphs and headings. In this chapter, you study Dreamweaver's tools for designing and working with each of the three basic types of lists available in HTML:

◆ Unordered lists

◆ Ordered lists

◆ Definition lists

The various list types can also be combined to create outlines. Dreamweaver supplies a straightforward method for building these nested lists.

Creating Unordered (Bulleted) Lists

What word processing programs and layout artists refer to as *bulleted lists* are known in HTML as *unordered lists*. An unordered list is used when the sequence of the listed items is unimportant, as in a recipe's list of ingredients. Each unordered list item is set off by a leading character, and the remainder of the line is indented. By default, the leading character is the bullet, a small, filled-in circle; however, you can create a custom bullet through Cascading Style Sheets.

You can either create the unordered list from scratch or convert existing text into the bulleted format. To begin an unordered list from scratch, position the cursor where you want to start the list. Then click the Unordered List button, supplied conveniently on the Text Property inspector or use the Text ⇨ List ⇨ Unordered List command. You can also click the Unordered list button in the Text category of the Insert bar. Figure 12-1 shows an unordered list and the associated Text Property inspector.

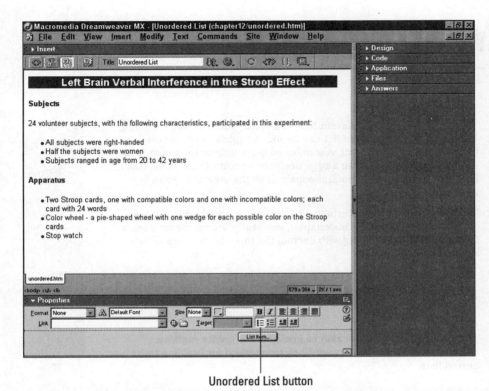

Unordered List button

Figure 12-1: An itemized list that doesn't need to be in any specific order is perfect for formatting as an unordered list.

If you are changing existing text into a list, select the paragraphs first and then use the menu command or the Unordered List button on the Property inspector or Insert bar.

Dreamweaver creates one list item for every paragraph. As you can see from Figure 12-1, list items are generally rendered closer together than regular paragraphs. A list, unlike block elements such as paragraphs or headings, is not formatted with additional space above and below each line.

Caution   In terms of lists in Dreamweaver, the word *paragraph* is used literally to mean any text designated with a paragraph tag. Certainly you can apply a heading format to an HTML list, but you probably won't like the results: The heading format reinserts that additional space below and above each list item — the ones generally not used by the list format. If you want your list items to appear larger, change the font size through Cascading Style Sheets, the Property inspector, or with Text ➪ Size Change.

Editing unordered lists

After a series of paragraphs is formatted as an unordered list, you can easily add additional bulleted items. The basic editing techniques are the same for all types of lists:

✦ To continue adding items at the end of a list, simply press Enter (Return) to create each new list item. Another bullet is inserted, as long as the last item is not empty.

✦ To insert an item within an unordered list, place your cursor at the end of the item above the desired position for the added item and press Enter (Return).

✦ List items can be copied or cut and pasted in a different place on the list. When selecting a list item, use the Tag Selector in the status bar to be sure you select the tags enclosing the list item, and not just the list item text. Position your cursor at the start of the list item that will follow the pasted entry, and choose Edit ➪ Paste.

✦ To end a bulleted list, you can press Enter (Return) twice or deselect the Unordered List button on the Text Property inspector.

List tags

You may occasionally need to tweak your list code by hand. Two HTML tags are used in creating an unordered list. The first is the outer tag, which defines the type of list; the second is the item delimiter. Unordered lists are designated with the ⟨ul⟩...⟨/ul⟩ tag pair, and the delimiter is the ⟨li⟩...⟨/li⟩ pair. The unordered list code in the Code inspector looks like the following:

```
<ul>
  <li>All subjects were right-handed</li>
  <li>Half the subjects were women</li>
  <li>Subjects ranged in age from 20 to 42 years</li>
</ul>
```

Tip   If you are working in Code view, you can click the List Item button in the Text category of the Insert bar to insert a ⟨li⟩...⟨/li⟩ pair. Insert the tags ⟨ul⟩...⟨/ul⟩ by clicking the Unordered List button on the Insert bar.

If a list item is too long to fit in a single line, the browser indents the line when it wraps. By inserting a line break code, you can emulate this behavior even when you're working with lines that aren't long enough to need wrapping. To insert a line break, choose the Line Break button from the Characters category of the Insert bar, or select Insert ➪ Special Characters ➪ Line Break. Alternatively, use the key combination Shift+Enter (Shift+Return), or just type ⟨br⟩ in your code. Figure 12-2 shows examples of both approaches: the long paragraph that wraps naturally and the inserted line breaks to force the wrapping.

Note   If you are creating an XHTML document, instead of typing ⟨br⟩, you must type ⟨br /⟩. When you press Shift+Enter (Shift+Return), Dreamweaver automatically determines the correct format to use for the break tag based on the DOCTYPE statement, visible at the top of the document in Code view.

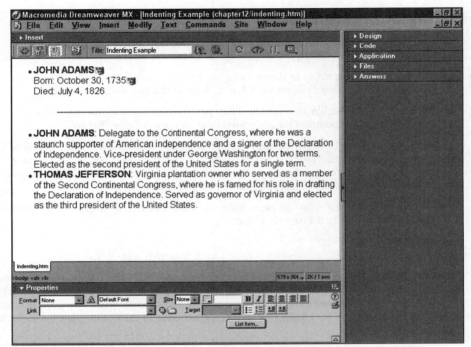

Figure 12-2: A list is indented if the text wraps around the screen or if you insert a line break.

Using other bullet symbols

Most browsers depict the default bullet as a small filled-in circle. In HTML, you can use any of three strategies to change the shape of your bullets. Dreamweaver supports all of these strategies. Your choices are

    ✦ Add an attribute to the `<ul>` or `<li>` tag to specify one of several other bullet shapes.

    ✦ Simulate an unordered list by using an image of the bullet.

    ✦ Use Cascading Style Sheets to define a new bullet shape.

In HTML, the `<ul>` and <li> tags can include a `type` attribute that defines the shape of the bullet. Although the `type` attribute doesn't include a wide range of different bullet symbols, you have a few options. Most browsers recognize three bullet styles: bullet (the default), circle, and square. You can apply the style to the entire unordered list or to one list item at a time.

Caution   In the HTML 4.0 specification, the `type` attribute is deprecated. This means that although still supported by current browsers, the attribute has been replaced by a newer or more desirable method of achieving the same thing. In this case, the `type` attribute has been replaced by newer Cascading Style Sheet attributes. Because the `type` attribute is deprecated, it may not be supported at all in future versions of HTML. On a practical level, though, major browsers tend to continue supporting deprecated tags and elements so that older Web pages continue to display correctly. According to the HTML specification, if a browser stops supporting the attribute, the browser should simply ignore the attribute when encountered in a page.

Dreamweaver gives you access to the `type` attribute in Code view. To change the bullet style for the entire unordered list, follow these steps:

1. In Code view, right-click (Control+click) on the `<ul>` tag for your list and then choose Edit Tag `<ul>` from the context menu.

2. In the Tag Editor dialog box that appears, select one of the following from the Type drop-down list:

   • **[Default]:** No style is listed, and the browser applies its default, usually a solid circle

   • **Disc:** A solid circle

   • **Circle:** An open circle

   • **Square:** A solid square on Windows; an open square for Macs

3. Click OK.

The previous steps change the bullet style for all items within the list. You can also change the bullet style for just one item in a list, although it would be unusual to do so. Just follow these steps:

1. In Code view, right-click (Control-click) on the `<li>` tag for the list item you wish to change, and then choose Edit Tag <li> from the context menu.

2. In the Tag Editor dialog box that appears, make sure the Unordered List option is selected. This setting ensures that the correct list of options appears in the Type drop-down list.

3. In the Type drop-down list, select one of the bullet options (described in the preceding steps).

Note Dreamweaver also allows you to change the `type` attribute for one list item or for an entire list by using the List Properties dialog box. To access this dialog box, click any single item in your list, and on the Properties inspector, click the List Item button. You can change the shape of the bullet for the entire list by selecting an option in the Style list; you change the bullet for just the selected item using the New Style list. Note, however, that not all shapes are available in the List Properties dialog box; for example, the Circle option is not included.

A second method of changing the bullet symbol involves the time-tested solution of substituting a graphic for the bullet. Just as it does with graphical horizontal rules, the Web offers a substantial clip art collection of bullets. Using this method, you don't format your list as an unordered list at all; instead, you format your text in plain paragraphs or tables and then insert a graphic for each bullet.

Tip The quickest method to add graphical bullets is the drag-and-drop copy technique: Hold down the Ctrl (Command) key and then click and drag the bullet graphic—this sequence places a copy of the bullet wherever you release the mouse. See "Dreamweaver Technique: Building Graphical Bullets," later in this chapter, for more details.

The newer technique for installing bullet styles uses style sheets. Cascading Style Sheets (CSS) can switch a list or list item's bullet style to the same shapes that the `<ul>` and `<li>` `type` attribute can; but with a style sheet, you can perform one additional task. You can assign the bullet style type to a specific file—in other words, you can customize your bullet image. The drawback to using this technique is that the list aspect of style sheets is currently supported only by Internet Explorer versions 4.0 and later and Netscape versions 6.0 and later.

CSS is an extension to HTML that enables Web developers to separately assign style information to particular HTML page elements. For example, you can use CSS to change the spacing, bullet style, and even the font and text color for any list items. Cascading Style Sheets are covered in depth in Chapter 20.

Here is a brief version of the steps for using a style sheet to assign a new bullet symbol:

1. Choose Window ➪ CSS Styles.

2. In the CSS Styles panel, select the New CSS Style button.

3. In the New CSS Style dialog box, choose the Redefine HTML Tag radio button.

4. From the option list, choose the ul tag.

5. Select a Define In option to determine whether the style definition will be saved in the current document or a separate style sheet file. Refer to Chapter 20 for more information about making this decision.

6. Click OK.

7. In the CCS Style Definition dialog box that appears, choose List in the Category list (see Figure 12-3).

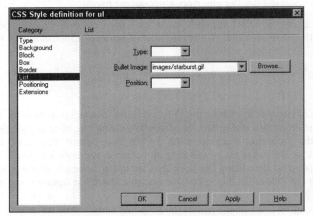

Figure 12-3: You can use Cascading Style Sheets to specify a bullet image for your Web page.

8. Find your graphics file by clicking the Browse (Choose) button next to the Bullet Image text box. Click OK when you're done.

Mastering Ordered (Numbered) Lists

Unlike a bulleted list, in which sequence is not vital, order is important in the ordered, or numbered, list. The major advantage of an ordered list is the automatic generation of list item numbers and automatic renumbering when you're editing. If you've ever had to renumber a legal document because paragraph 14.b became paragraph 2a, you recognize the timesaving benefits of this feature.

Ordered lists offer a slightly wider variety of built-in styles than unordered lists, but you cannot customize the leading character further. For instance, you cannot surround a character with parentheses or offset it with a dash. Once again, the browser is the final arbiter of how your list is viewed.

Many of the same techniques used with unordered lists work with ordered lists. To start a new numbered list in Dreamweaver, place your cursor where you want the new list to begin. Then, in the Text Property inspector, select the Ordered List button or choose Text ➪ List ➪ Ordered List. You can also choose the Ordered List button in the Text category of the Insert bar.

As with unordered lists, you can also convert existing paragraphs into a numbered list. First, select your text; and then select either the Ordered List button on the Property inspector or the Text ➪ List ➪ Ordered List command.

As shown in Figure 12-4, the default numbering system is Arabic numerals: 1, 2, 3, and so forth. In a following section, you learn how to alter this default to use other numbering formats, or to create an alphabetic list.

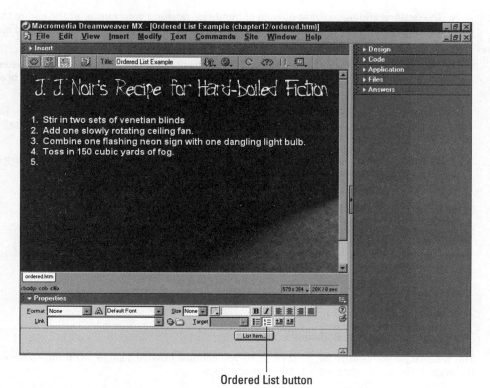

Ordered List button

Figure 12-4: Ordered lists are used on this page to create a numbered sequence.

Editing ordered lists

The HTML code for an ordered list is <ol>. Both <ol> and <ul> use the list item tag, <li>, to mark individual entries, and Dreamweaver handles the formatting identically:

```
<ol>
  <li>Stir in two sets of Venetian blinds.</li>
  <li>Add one slowly rotating ceiling fan.</li>
  <li>Combine one flashing neon sign with one dangling light bulb.</li>
  <li>Toss in 150 cubic yards of fog.</li>
  <li></li>
</ol>
```

The empty list item pair, <li>...</li>, is displayed on the page as the next number in sequence.

Modifications to an ordered list are handled in the same manner as for an unordered list. The results are far more dramatic, however.

✦ To continue adding to the sequence of numbers, position your cursor at the end of the last item and press Enter (Return). The next number in sequence is generated, and any styles in use (such as font size or name) are carried over.

✦ To insert a new item within the list, put your cursor at the end of the item above where the new item will be positioned, and press Enter (Return). Dreamweaver inserts a new number in sequence and automatically renumbers the following numbers.

✦ To rearrange a numbered list, highlight the entire list item you want to move. Using the drag-and-drop method, release the mouse when your cursor is at the front of the item below the new location for the moved item.

✦ To end an item in a numbered list, press Enter (Return) twice, or press Enter (Return) and deselect the Ordered List button on the Text Property inspector.

Using other numbering styles

You can apply these different numbering styles to your numbered lists:

✦ **Arabic Numerals:** 1, 2, 3, and so forth (this is the default style)

✦ **Roman Small:** i, ii, iii, and so forth

✦ **Roman Large:** I, II, III, and so forth

✦ **Alphabet Small:** a, b, c, and so forth

✦ **Alphabet Large:** A, B, C, and so forth

You can restyle your entire list all at once, or you can just change a single list item. To change the style of the entire ordered list, follow these steps:

1. Position your cursor anywhere in an existing list.

2. If necessary, click the expander arrow on the Text Property inspector to display the additional options. Select the List Item button.

The List Properties dialog box opens with Numbered List showing as the List Type, as shown in Figure 12-5.

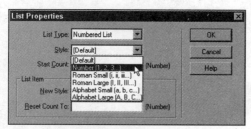

Figure 12-5: Use the List Properties dialog box to alter the numbering style in an ordered list.

3. Open the drop-down list of Style options, and choose any of the numbering types.

4. Click OK.

Caution

If the List Item button is inactive in your Text Property inspector, make sure that you have only one list item selected. Selecting more than one list item deactivates the List Item button.

As with unordered lists, when you modify the style of one ordered list item, all the other items in the same list adopt that style. To alter the style of a single item, follow these steps:

1. Select the item you wish to change.

2. In the expanded portion of the Text Property inspector, select the List Item button.

3. From the List Item section of the List Properties dialog box, open the New Style list of options.

4. Select one of the numbering options.

Although you can't automatically generate an outline with a different numbering system for each level, you can simulate this kind of outline with nested lists. See "Using Nested Lists" later in this chapter.

Making Definition Lists

A definition list is another type of list in HTML. Unlike ordered and unordered lists, definition lists don't use leading characters such as bullets or numbers in the list items. Definition lists are commonly used in glossaries or other types of documents in which you have a list of terms followed by their descriptions or explanations.

Browsers generally render a definition list with the definition term flush left and the definition data indented, as shown in Figure 12-6. As you can see, no additional styling is added. You can, however, format either the item or the definition with the Text ➪ Style options or by using Cascading Style Sheets.

Definition term

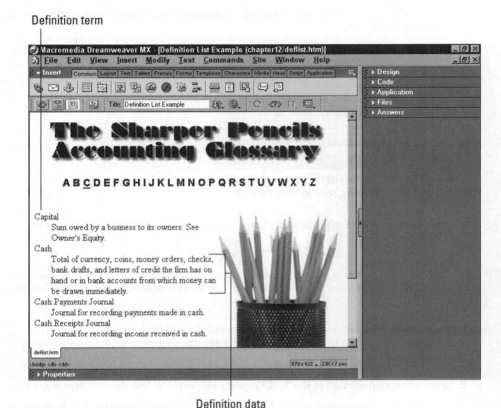

Definition data

Figure 12-6: Definition lists are ideal for glossaries or other situations in which you have a list of terms followed by their definitions.

To begin your definition list in Dreamweaver, follow these steps:

1. Choose Text ➪ List ➪ Definition List or click the Definition List button in the Text category of the Insert bar.

2. Type in the definition term and press Enter (Return) when you are finished. Dreamweaver indents the line.

3. Type in the definition data and press Enter (Return) when you are finished.

4. Repeat Steps 2 and 3 until you have finished your definition list.

5. Press Enter (Return) twice to stop entering definition list items.

Tip

If you have an extended definition, you may want to format it in more than one paragraph. Because definition lists are formatted with the terms and their definition data in alternating sequence, you have to use the line break tag,
 (or <br /> for XHTML documents), to create blank space under the definition if you want to separate it into paragraphs. Press Shift+Enter (Shift+Return) or select the Line Break button from the Insert bar to enter one or two <br> tags to separate paragraphs with one or two additional lines.

When you insert a definition list, Dreamweaver denotes it in code using the `<dl>...</dl>` tag pair. Definition terms are marked with a `<dt>` tag, and definition data uses the `<dd>` tag. A complete definition list looks like the following in HTML:

```
<dl>
  <dt>Capital</dt>
  <dd>Sum owed by a business to its owners. See Owner's Equity.</dd>
  <dt>Cash</dt>
  <dd>Total of currency, coins, money orders, checks, bank
    drafts, and letters of credit the firm has on hand or in bank
    accounts from which money can be drawn immediately.</dd>
  <dt>Cash Payments Journal</dt>
  <dd>Journal for recording payments made in cash.</dd>
</dl>
```

Tip

You can vary the structure of a definition list from the standard definition term followed by the definition data format, but you have to code this variation by hand. For instance, if you want a series of consecutive terms with no definition in between, you need to insert the `<dt>...</dt>` pairs directly in Code view or in the Code inspector. To facilitate the insertion of these tags, you can click the Definition Term and Definition Description buttons in the Text category of the Insert bar to insert the appropriate tags in Code view.

Using Nested Lists

You can combine, or nest, lists in almost any fashion. For instance, you can mix an ordered and unordered list to create a numbered list with bulleted points. You can have one numbered list inside of another numbered list. You can also start with one numbering style such as Roman Large, switch to another style such as Alphabet Small, and return to Roman Large to continue the sequence (like an outline).

Dreamweaver offers an easy route for making nested lists. The Indent button in the Text Property inspector — when used within a list — automatically creates a nested list. As an example, the ordered list in Figure 12-7 has a couple of bulleted points (or unordered list items) inserted within it. Notice how the new items are indented one level.

Follow these steps to create a nested list in Dreamweaver:

1. Select the text in an existing list that you want to indent and reformat with a different style.

2. In the Text Property inspector, choose the Indent button. You can also select the Text ➪ Indent command. Dreamweaver indents the selected text and creates a separate list in the HTML code with the original list's properties.

Note

Nested unordered lists exhibit a cool feature in most browsers — they automatically change the list style for each level. In many browsers, the outermost level is displayed with a bullet, the second level with a circle, and the third level with a square. This feature provides automatic outlining from an unexpected source! For ordered lists, the style of indented items does not change automatically.

3. Go to the List Properties dialog box and select another list type or style, as described in preceding sections.

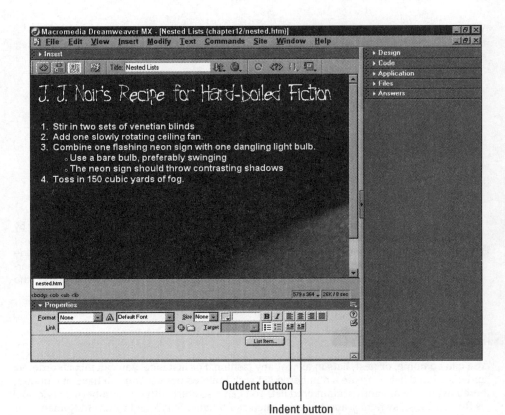

Outdent button

Indent button

Figure 12-7: Dreamweaver automatically generates the code necessary to build nested lists when you use the Indent button on the Text Property inspector.

Caution   You can unnest your list and reverse the effects of the Indent button by selecting the Outdent button in the Text Property inspector or by choosing Text ➪ Outdent. Be careful, however, when selecting your text for this operation. When you use the mouse to perform a click-and-drag selection, Dreamweaver tends to grab the closing list item tag above your intended selection. A better way to highlight the text in this case is to use the Tag Selector on the status bar. Place the cursor in the indented list you want to outdent and choose the innermost <ol> or <ul> tag from the Tag Selector.

To examine the origins of the term *nested list*, look at the code created by Dreamweaver for the following list type:

```
<ol>
  <li>Stir in two sets of Venetian blinds.</li>
  <li>Add one slowly rotating ceiling fan.</li>
  <li>Combine one flashing neon sign with one dangling light bulb.
    <ul>
      <li>Use a bare bulb, preferably swinging.</li>
      <li>The neon sign should throw contrasting shadows.</li>
    </ul>
```

```
    </li>
    <li>Toss in 150 cubic yards of fog.</li>
</ol>
```

Notice how the unordered tag pair, `<ul>...</ul>`, is completely contained between the ordered list items.

Caution   If you don't indent your list items before you change the list format, Dreamweaver breaks the current list into three separate lists: one for the original list above the selected text, another for the selected text itself, and a third list for the items following the selected text. If you don't want this arrangement, use the Tag Selector to select the entire list you want to indent, and then choose the Indent button in the Text Property inspector. Dreamweaver will nest the list as described previously.

Accessing Special List Types

Dreamweaver gives you access to a couple of special-use list types: *menu lists* and *directory lists*. When the tags for these lists — `<menu>` and `<dir>`, respectively — were included in the HTML 2.0 specification, they were intended to offer several ways to present lists of short items. Unfortunately, browsers tend to render both tags in the same manner: as an unordered list. You can use Cascading Style Sheets to restyle these built-in tags for use in 4.0 and later browsers.

Note   Both the `<menu>` and `<dir>` tags are deprecated in HTML 4.0. Since most browsers format these lists like unordered lists, you should typically just use ordered lists instead of either of these list types. Ordered lists are supported in both older browsers and will continue to be supported in the future.

Menu lists

A menu list generally comprises single items, with each item on its own individual line. To apply a menu list style, follow these steps:

1. In an existing list, select one item.

2. In the expanded Text Property inspector, select the List Item button.

3. In the List Properties dialog box, open the List Type drop-down list and choose Menu List, as shown in Figure 12-8.

4. Click OK.

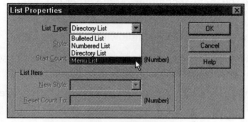

Figure 12-8: Making a menu list.

Directory lists

The directory list was originally intended to provide Web designers with an easy way to create multiple-column lists of short items. Unfortunately, the most current browsers present the directory list's items in one long list, rather than in columns.

The directory list format is applied in the same way as the menu list, and here as well, most browsers render the format as an unordered list with bullets. To create a directory list, follow these steps:

1. In the current list, select one item.

2. In the expanded Text Property inspector, select the List Item button.

3. In the List Properties dialog box, open the List Type list (refer to Figure 12-8) and choose Directory List.

4. Click OK.

Dreamweaver Technique: Building Graphical Bullets

HTML unordered lists are functional and often useful, but they're not particularly decorative. If you are a Web designer, you might very well want to spice up your bulleted list of items with graphics. Although the CSS technique described earlier offers the possibility of selecting an image to use as the bullet, this solution is not available to older Netscape browsers or 3.0 versions of Internet Explorer. Moreover, you don't have much control over the vertical placement of the bullet, so the image often appears higher than desired.

Tip   The following technique is intended for designers working just with Dreamweaver and any graphics editor. However, if you have Fireworks 3 or later, you can automate the process of replacing an unordered list with graphical bullets. The Convert Bullets to Images command (originally developed by the author as BulletBuilder) converts list items to paragraph lines and places a custom bullet — available in 10 different shapes and any Fireworks style — before the line. You'll find this extension on the Macromedia Exchange.

Substituting a graphical bullet for the HTML versions is practical and often desirable. Because a small, single image is used repeatedly, the impact on a Web page's size is negligible, and the image downloads quickly. You can include graphical bullets in two basic ways: inline and tables. Inline graphical bullets put the bullet image right next to the text, whereas the table technique keeps all the bullets in one column and the bullet items in another. Which technique you use depends on the length of the bulleted item. If your bulleted items are short enough so that they won't wrap, use the inline technique; on the other hand, if the text is wrapping from one line to the next, use the table technique.

To use graphic images as bullets in an inline technique, follow these steps:

1. Create your image in a graphics editor, such as Fireworks, and save the file so that it is accessible to your local site.

2. If necessary, convert your unordered list to standard paragraph format by selecting the entire list and deselecting the Bullet button on the Property inspector.

3. Choose Image from the Insert bar and place the bullet graphic before the first line item.

4. Select the correct vertical alignment for the image from the Align list on the image Property inspector.

   Although your alignment choice may vary according to the height of your text and your image, Absolute Middle works in many situations.

5. In the Image Property inspector, select <empty> from the Alt drop-down list.

Tip

Normally, you should not specify alternate text for a bullet image. Adding alternate text to a bullet typically does not enhance the understanding of your page for either those using visual or non-visual browsers.

However, you should not just leave the Property inspector Alt field blank. If you do, some screen readers read the filename when they encounter the image, which slows down how quickly people using non-visual browsers can get to the real information on your page. Explicitly selecting <empty> in the Property inspector Alt field includes a blank alt attribute, which causes screen readers to ignore the bullet image.

6. If necessary, add a non-breaking space or two between the image and the list item by pressing Ctrl+Shift+spacebar (Command+Shift+spacebar).

7. Select the image and any added non-breaking spaces.

8. Ctrl+drag (Option+drag) the selection to copy it to the beginning of the next line item, as shown in Figure 12-9.

9. Repeat Step 8 for each line item.

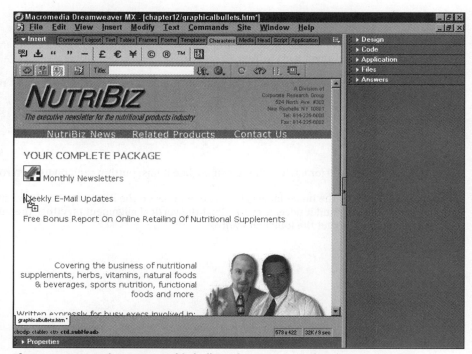

Figure 12-9: Copying your graphic bullets after you've set the alignment and alternate text saves you many steps later.

Cross-Reference The following technique requires a basic understanding of tables in HTML in general and Dreamweaver in particular. If you're not familiar with inserting and formatting tables, you may want to look at Chapter 10 before proceeding.

If your text lines are too long, they wrap at the browser window and—here's the unsightly part—under the graphical bullet. To avoid this wrapping problem, use the table technique, detailed in the following steps:

1. Create your bullet in your favorite graphics program.

2. If necessary, convert your unordered list to standard paragraph format by selecting the entire list and deselecting the Bullet button on the Property inspector.

3. Position your cursor above the first line item and choose the Insert Table button from the Insert bar.

4. In the Insert Table dialog box, set the Columns value to 2, and the Rows value to the number of line items you have. Turn off the borders by setting Border value to 0. Click OK when you're done.

   The table is inserted in the Document window.

5. Select the first column of the table by dragging down its length.

6. In the Property inspector, set the Horiz (horizontal alignment) value to Right, and the Vert (vertical alignment) to Top.

7. Select the second column by dragging down its length.

8. In the Property inspector, set the Horiz (horizontal alignment) value to Left and the Vert (vertical alignment) to Top.

9. Select the Image button and place your bullet image in the first column, first row.

10. Select the first line item and drag it into the second column, first row.

11. Copy the bullet image from the first cell and paste it into the first column for every remaining row.

12. Repeat Step 10 for each of the remaining line items, putting each on its own row.

When you're done, the bullet images line up evenly, as do the line items, as shown in Figure 12-10. You may find it necessary to adjust the vertical alignment on either the bullet or line item column to get the look you want.

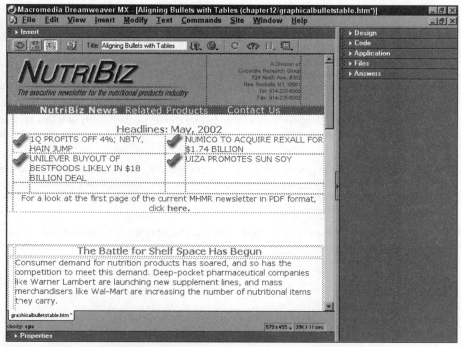

Figure 12-10: Placing bullet items in a table enables you to keep equal spacing with longer, wrapping lines.

Summary

Lists are extremely useful to the Web site designer from the perspectives of both content and layout. Dreamweaver offers point-and-click control over the full range of list capabilities.

✦ The primary list types in HTML are unordered, ordered, and definition lists.

✦ Use unordered lists when you want to itemize your text in no particular order. Dreamweaver can apply any of the built-in styles to unordered lists, or you can customize your own list style through Cascading Style Sheets.

✦ An ordered list is a numbered list. Items are automatically numbered when added, and the entire list is renumbered when items are rearranged or deleted. Dreamweaver gives you access to different styles of numbering—including regular Arabic, Roman numerals, and upper- or lower-case letters.

✦ Definition lists are designed to display glossaries and other documents in which terms are followed by definitions. A definition list is generally rendered without leading characters such as bullets or numbers; instead, the list terms are displayed flush left, and the definitions are indented.

✦ Dreamweaver gives you the power to nest your lists at the touch of a button — the Indent button on the Text Property inspector. Nested lists enable you to show different outline levels and to mix ordered and unordered lists.

✦ Menu and directory lists are also supported by Dreamweaver. Both of these special lists are rendered in a similar fashion, but they can be adapted through style sheets for extensive use.

✦ It's easy to substitute graphic images for standard bullets in Dreamweaver. One method of doing this uses Cascading Style Sheets. You can also simply insert a bullet image in the page like any other image. Two different techniques are used — inline and table — depending on the length of the line item.

In the next chapter, you learn how to create and use image maps in Dreamweaver.

✦   ✦   ✦

Making Client-Side Image Maps

By their very nature, HTML images are rectangular. Although you can make portions of a rectangular graphic transparent, giving the impression of an irregularly shaped picture, the image itself — and thus its clickable region — is still a rectangle. For more complex images in which shapes overlap and you want several separate areas of a picture (not just the overall graphic) to be hyperlinked, you need an image map.

Dreamweaver puts its image map tools front and center so you can draw and manage your hotspots right on your graphics in the Document window. The onscreen image map tools make it much easier to manipulate your hotspots, but there's another major advantage: Behaviors can easily be attached to hotspots.

This chapter introduces you to Dreamweaver's hotspot tools and also covers more advanced techniques for creating server-side and rollover image maps.

Client-Side Image Maps

For an almost literal example of an image map, visualize a map of the United States being used on a Web page. Suppose you want to be able to click each state and link to a different page in your site. How would you proceed? With the exception of Colorado and Wyoming, all the states have highly irregular shapes, so you can't use the typical side-by-side arrangement of rectangular images. You need to be able to specify a region on the graphic, to which you could then assign a link. This is exactly how an image map performs.

Two different kinds of image maps exist: client-side and server-side. With a server-side image map, all the map data is kept in a file on the server. When the user clicks a particular spot on the image, often referred to as a *hotspot*, the server compares the coordinates of the clicked spot with its image map data. If the coordinates match, the server loads the corresponding link. The key advantage to a server-side image map is that it works with any image-capable browser. The disadvantages are that it consumes more of the server's processing resources and tends to be slower than the client-side version.

With client-side image maps, on the other hand, all the data that is downloaded to the browser is kept in the Web page. The comparison process is the same, but it requires a browser that is image map savvy. Originally, only server-side image maps were possible. It wasn't until Netscape Navigator 2.0 was released that the client-side version was even an option. Microsoft began supporting client-side image maps in Internet Explorer 3.0. The vast majority of image maps used on the Web today are client-side, and server-side image maps should only be considered for special purposes.

In HTML, a client-side image map has two parts. In the <img> tag, Dreamweaver includes a usemap="mapname" attribute. The map name value refers to the second part of the image map's HTML, the <map> tag. One of the first steps in creating an image map is to give it a unique name. Dreamweaver stores all your mapping data under this map name. Here's an example of the code for an image map with three hotspots:

```
<img src="images/imagemap.jpg" width="640" height="480" 
usemap="#navbar">
<map name="navbar">
  <area shape="poly" coords="166,131,165,131,160,143,164,179, 
127,180,143,200,156,203,118,229,119,236,158,229,177,217,199, 
238,212,247,220,242,196,203,232,190,241,189,241,182,223,177, 
185,182,175,134,166,132" href="/starpro.html"
alt="High Risk Funds">
  <area shape="circle" coords="312,202,56" href="/nestegg.html" 
alt="Mutual Funds">
  <area shape="rect" coords="389,138,497,244" href="/prodfunds.html" 
alt="Money Markets">
</map>
```

Dreamweaver directly supports client-side image maps. After you've inserted an image into your Web page, it can be an image map. Select any image and open the expanded version of the Property inspector. The image map tools are in the lower-left corner, as shown in Figure 13-1.

Creating Image Hotspots

Image maps are created with tools similar to those you find in any drawing program. After you've selected your graphic, you can click a tool to describe a rectangle, oval, or polygon shape.

You can make an image map from any graphic format supported by Dreamweaver: GIF, JPEG, or PNG. Follow these steps to create hotspots on an image in Dreamweaver:

1. Select your image and, if necessary, open the Image Property inspector to full height by clicking the expander arrow.

2. Enter a unique name for your image map in the Map text box. It's generally a good practice to use a meaningful name, such as navMap, rather than something generic like Map1.

Map drawing tools

Pointer Hotspot tool

Map Name field

Figure 13-1: From the Image Property inspector, select the image map tools to draw hotspots directly on graphics within Dreamweaver.

3. Choose the appropriate drawing tool to outline your hotspot: Rectangle, Circle, or Polygon. Outline one hotspot, as described in the section "Using the drawing tools," later in this chapter.

When you complete the hotspot, Dreamweaver displays the Hotspot Property inspector, shown in Figure 13-2.

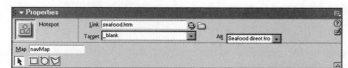

Figure 13-2: Enter image map attributes through the Hotspot Property inspector.

4. Enter the URL for this image map in the Link text box, or click the Folder icon and browse for the file.

Tip

If you don't want the hotspot to open a page, you can create a null link by entering a hash mark (#) or javascript:; (preferred) in the Link text box. You might do this, for example, if you wanted to attach a JavaScript behavior to the hotspot. Refer to the sidebar "Attaching Behaviors to Image Maps" in this chapter for more about behaviors.

5. If desired, enter a frame name or other target in the Target text box.

Cross-Reference

A target can refer to a specific section of a frameset or to a new browser window. For more information about using targets in frames, see Chapter 14. To learn more about targeting a new browser window, see the section "Targeting Your Links" in Chapter 9.

6. In the Alt text box, you can enter text you want to appear as a ToolTip that appears when the user's mouse moves over the area.

In Windows, the information taken from the Alt text box appears as a ToolTip only in Microsoft browsers. Another attribute, title, is used in Netscape browsers. Dreamweaver automatically adds the alt attribute, but you must manually add the title attribute to achieve cross-browser compatibility.

7. Repeat Steps 3 through 6 to add additional hotspots to the graphic.

Using the drawing tools

You'll find the hotspot drawing tools to be straightforward and easy to use. Each one produces a series of coordinates that are incorporated into the HTML code. In the following steps, you use the hotspot drawing tools to outline a rectangular hotspot:

1. Click on the image in the Document window, and select the Rectangular Hotspot tool from the Image Property inspector.

2. Click one corner of the area you want to map and drag toward the opposite corner to draw a rectangle. To draw a square, hold down the Shift key as you click and drag.

3. Release the mouse button. Dreamweaver shades the defined area.

4. Fill in the Link, Target, and Alt text boxes in the Property inspector.

Follow these steps to use the Oval Hotspot tool in the Image Map Editor:

1. Select the Oval Hotspot tool from the Image Property inspector.

Caution

Although the tool is named *Oval*, you are actually limited to drawing circles with it.

2. Click anywhere on the perimeter of the area you want to define and drag out the circle until it reaches the correct size.

3. Release the mouse button. Dreamweaver shades the defined area.

4. As before, complete the Link, Target, and Alt text boxes.

To define an irregularly shaped hotspot, use the polygon drawing tool. Follow these steps:

1. Select the Polygon Hotspot tool from the Property inspector.

2. Click the first point for your hotspot object.

3. Release the mouse button and move the mouse to the next point.

4. Continue outlining the object by clicking and moving the mouse.

5. For the last point in the shape, double-click the mouse to close the area.

6. Fill in the Link, Target, and Alt text boxes.

You can use the drawing tools in any combination. In Figure 13-3, all three drawing tools have been used to create three different hotspots on a single image map. The star-shaped image is currently selected, as indicated by the control points visible on that hotspot. The other defined areas (the circular and rectangular objects) are shown with light blue overlays around them.

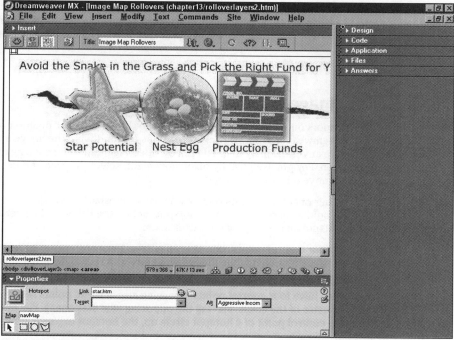

Figure 13-3: The image map drawing tools enable you to define both regular and irregularly shaped areas.

Tip

After you've created your hotspots, you may want to view your page without the highlighted areas. To turn off the overlays, choose View ⇨ Visual Aids ⇨ Image Maps to disable the option; if the toolbar is visible, you can also choose the View Options button and then select Visual Aids ⇨ Image Maps.

Setting the Default URL

What happens when Web site visitors pass their pointers over parts of your image that are not the primary hotspots? Prior to the fourth generation of browsers, a default URL property was supported to handle this issue. Now, however, the necessary code, `<area shape="default" href="url">`, is ignored by Internet Explorer 4 and later, although it remains supported by Netscape.

One workaround to this drawback is to completely cover the graphic with an area, using the Rectangular Hotspot tool, and then assign the desired default URL. If you add the overall rectangle hotspot after other hotspots have been created, be sure to send the full-graphic rectangle behind the other hotspots using the Modify ➪ Arrange ➪ Send to Back command. Where hotspots overlap, browsers detect only the uppermost hotspot.

Note that just assigning a link to the image itself, such as by entering a URL in the Link field of the Image Property inspector, will not work; you must define a separate rectangular hotspot as described above.

Alternatively, open the Code view and locate the `<map>` tag. Next, place the following code: `<area shape="default" href="url">` — where URL is replaced by a relative or absolute Web address — just above the closing `</map>` tag. Remember, however, that this solution only works in Netscape browsers.

Modifying an image map

When you draw the hotspots on your image map, you may not initially size or position them exactly as you'd like. Dreamweaver gives you several options for modifying the image maps you create. You can move any previously defined area by selecting it and then clicking and dragging to a new location. For precise pixel-by-pixel movement, select the area and use your keyboard arrow keys to move it in any direction.

Each hotspot has a number of control points that can be used to resize or reshape it. To move any of the control points, select the Pointer Hotspot tool on the Property inspector. The different types of hotspots have varying characteristics:

✦ The rectangle has four control points, one at each corner. Drag any corner to resize or reshape the rectangle. Press Shift while dragging to convert a rectangle into a square or to resize an existing square.

✦ Circle hotspots also have four control points. Dragging any of these points increases or decreases the diameter of the circle, leaving the opposing side stationary. For example, if you drag the top control point of a hotspot circle up, the hotspot expands upward from the bottom.

✦ Each point in a polygon hotspot is a control point that can be dragged into a new position to reshape the hotspot.

Hotspots can also be aligned with other hotspots or resized to match. To align two image maps, select both hotspots by holding down the Shift key as you click each image; then use one of the following alignment commands found under the Modify ➪ Align menu:

✦ **Align Left:** Aligns selected hotspots to the leftmost edge of the selection

✦ **Align Right:** Aligns selected hotspots to the rightmost edge of the selection

✦ **Align Top:** Aligns selected hotspots to the topmost edge of the selection

✦ **Align Bottom:** Aligns selected hotspots to the bottommost edge of the selection

✦ **Make Same Width:** Converts all selected hotspots to the width of the last selected hotspot. Polygon hotspots cannot be resized using this command, although rectangular or oval hotspots can be changed to match the polygon width if a polygon hotspot is selected last.

✦ **Make Same Height:** Converts all selected hotspots to the height of the last selected hotspot. As with the Make Same Width command, polygon hotspots cannot be resized using this command. Again, rectangular or oval hotspots can be changed to match the polygon height if a polygon hotspot is selected last.

Caution Although Dreamweaver lists keyboard shortcuts for all the alignment options under Modify ⇨ Align, these apply only to layers. You must use the menus (either the Modify menu or the context menu) to align hotspots.

Should your hotspots overlap, you can change the depth of any hotspot so that the desired hotspot is on top and has the focus in a particular area. Select the hotspot and then choose one of these commands, found under the Modify ⇨ Arrange menu:

✦ **Bring to Front:** Brings the selected hotspot in front of all other overlapping hotspots

✦ **Send to Back:** Sends the selected hotspot behind all other overlapping hotspots

Of course, Dreamweaver also enables you to delete any existing area. Simply select the area and press the Delete or Backspace key.

Converting Client-Side Maps to Server-Side Maps

Although most Web browsers support client-side image maps, some sites still rely on server-side image maps. You can take a client-side image map generated by Dreamweaver and convert it to a server-side image map; you can even include pointers for both maps in the same Web page to accommodate older browsers as well as the newer ones. Such a conversion does require, however, that you use a text editor to modify and save the file. You also need to add one more attribute, `ismap`, to the `<img>` tag; this attribute tells the server that the image referenced in the `src` attribute is a map.

Note If you are concerned about making your Web site accessible to people with disabilities, use client-side image maps instead of server-side image maps. Server-side image maps may not be usable to people using voice-controlled browsers, or who otherwise do not have access to a mouse.

Adapting the server script

Let's examine the differences between a client-side image map and a server-side image map from the same graphic. The HTML for a client-side image map looks like the following:

```
<map name="navbar">
  <area shape="rect" coords="1,1,30,33" href="home.html" alt="Home Page">
  <area shape="circle" coords="65,64,62" href="contacts.html" ⊃
alt="Information">
  <area shape="default" href="index.html">
</map>
```

The same definitions for a server-side image map are laid out as follows:

```
rect home.html 1,1 30,33
circle contacts.html 65,64 62
default index.html
```

As you can see, the server-side image map file is much more compact. Notice that all the `alt="string"` code is thrown out because ToolTips can be shown only through client-side image maps.

A server expects the information in the following form:

```
shape URL coordinates
```

Therefore, you need to remove the `<area>` tag and its delimiters, as well as the phrases `shape=`, `coords=`, and `href=`. You then reverse the order of the URL and the coordinates.

The last step in this phase of adapting the server-side script is to format the coordinates correctly. The format depends on the shape being defined:

✦ For rectangles, group the *x, y* coordinates into comma-separated pairs with a single space in between each pair.

✦ For circles, separate the center point coordinates from the diameter with a space.

✦ For polygons, group the *x, y* coordinates into comma-separated pairs with a single space in between each pair — just like rectangles.

Your new map file should be stored on your server, probably in a subfolder of the cgi-bin directory.

Caution

Not all servers expect server-side image maps in the same format. The format offered here conforms to the NCSA HPPD standard. If you're unsure of the required format or of where to put your maps on your server, check with your server administrator before creating a server-side image map.

Including the map link

The second phase of converting a client-side map to a server-side one involves making the connection between the Web page and the map file. A client-side image map link directly calls the URL associated with it. In contrast, all references from a server-side link call the map file — which in turn calls the specified URL.

You add the connection to a server-side map as you would add any link to a graphic. You can, of course, do this directly in Dreamweaver. Simply select your graphic and, in the Image Property inspector, insert the map file URL in the Link text box. Be sure the image's border property is set to zero to avoid the link outline.

The final addition to your script is the `ismap` attribute. Place the `ismap` attribute in the `<img>` tag of the graphic being used for the image map, as follows:

```
<img href="images/biglogo.gif" width="200" height="350" ismap>
```

As noted earlier, it is entirely possible to use client-side and server-side image maps together. The easiest way to do it is to keep the image map data as written by Dreamweaver and add the `ismap` attribute. The HTML example shown in the previous section, "Client-Side Image Maps," would then read as follows:

```
<a href="http://www.idest.com/cgi-bin/maps/imap.txt">
<img src="images/imagemap.jpg" width="640" height="480" ⤶
usemap="#navbar" ismap></a/>
```

Attaching Behaviors to Image Maps

A hotspot is basically an interactive trigger. Although hotspots are used most frequently to open new Web pages, they can also be used to trigger other events, such as swapping an image on the page, showing or hiding a layer, or even opening another smaller browser window. In Dreamweaver, you accomplish these things by assigning behaviors to linked text or images. With its upfront image maps, Dreamweaver makes it straightforward to assign behaviors to hotspots as well.

To attach a behavior to a hotspot, first select the hotspot and then choose the Add (+) button in the Behaviors panel. Select your behavior from the list, and enter its parameters. After you've confirmed your options, you may find it necessary to change the event from its default, which is often onMouseDown or onMouseOver. To do so, select the down triangle between the event and the action in the Behaviors panel and choose a new event from the list.

Here's a cool and useful feature: If you copy an image with defined hotspots and behaviors, all the associated behaviors are copied as well as the image map.

Dreamweaver Technique: Building an Image Map Rollover

One of the most popular Web page techniques today is known as a *rollover*. A rollover occurs when a user's mouse moves over a button or graphic in the page and the button or graphic changes in some way. You learned how to create these graphic rollovers in Chapter 8. In this section, you'll try out one method for applying the same technique to an image map.

Cross-Reference

The following method uses advanced techniques involving JavaScript behaviors and layers. If you're unfamiliar with these concepts, you might want to examine Chapters 21 and 23 before proceeding.

Before you get underway, keep in mind that this technique — because it uses layers — works only with 4.0 browsers and later.

Step 1: Create two images

As with behavior-based button rollovers, you use two images to represent the "off" and "over" states of the graphic. However, because you are using image maps here, rather than separate graphics, you only need a total of two images (versus two for every button). In this example, three buttons are "carved" from one graphic; but there could very easily have been eight or a dozen separate buttons, which would have required 16 or 24 separate images. All you need are two image maps.

After building your first image, bring it into your favorite image-processing program and make the alterations necessary to create the second image. Figure 13-4 shows examples of the two images you need, inserted into Dreamweaver. As you can see, all that was necessary to make the "over" image was to add a glow effect to each of the three hotspots.

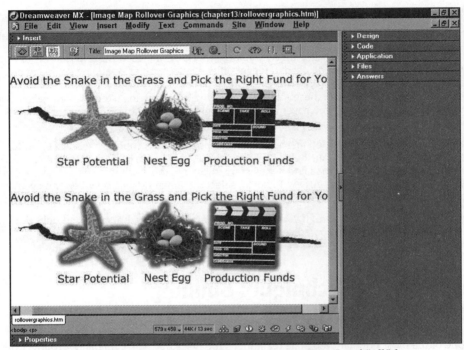

Figure 13-4: You need two separate images, representing "over" and "off," for a rollover image map.

Tip   One of the methods used in this technique involves clipping a region of an image. Presently, layers support only rectangular clipping. Keep this in mind as you build your primary image, and avoid placing hotspots too close together.

Step 2: Set up the layers

This technique takes advantage of three different layer properties: absolute positioning, visibility, and clipping. The idea is to display just a portion of a hidden layer during an onMouseOver event. To perform this function without rewriting the code, a layer for each of the hotspots is necessary. Each layer will later be clipped to show just that hotspot. The beauty of this technique is that although it uses multiple layers, only two images are required, as the single "over" image is used for each rollover.

To get started, you just need two layers — one for each of the images. Follow these steps to establish the initial layers:

1. Choose Insert ⇨ Layer or select the Draw Layer button on the Insert bar to create the layer that will hold the image displayed when the mouse is over the graphic. I gave my layer the name overLayer.

   If you use the menu option instead of drawing out the layer, it is created at a standard size, and you won't have to spend as much time adjusting the layer sizes later.

2. Making sure the cursor is in the layer, choose Insert ⇨ Image or select the Image button on the Insert bar. Load your "over" graphic. If the layer is smaller than the image, the layer automatically expands.

3. Create a second layer that will hold the image displayed when the mouse is off the image; I named my example offLayer.

4. Insert the "off" graphic in the new layer.

5. If necessary, open the Layers panel by choosing Window ⇨ Others ⇨ Layers or pressing F2, and make sure of the following:

   • Both layers must have unique names. In this example, you use offLayer and overLayer.

   • The offLayer must be visible.

   • The overLayer must be hidden.

   • The overLayer must be exactly on top of the offLayer, so that when you make a portion of the overLayer visible, it obscures the offLayer. For precise positioning of each layer, set the left and top attributes using the layer Property inspector.

Figure 13-5 shows how the screen looks with both layers in place and the visibility properties set correctly.

Invisible Layer icon

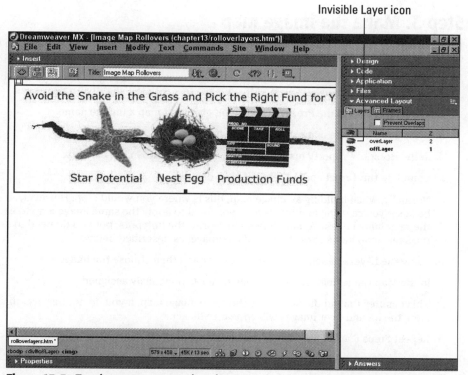

Figure 13-5: Two image maps are placed on top of each other in layers, and the top layer is hidden.

Aligning Layers

In Dreamweaver you can use layer alignment commands to easily line up the two layers. The commands are covered in detail in Chapter 21, but here are the steps briefly. Select both layers by clicking each layer name in the Layers panel while pressing the Shift key. Choose two of the Modify ⇨ Align options—Align Left and Align Top, for example—so that the layers are in the same position. The layer alignment commands all work the same; all layers are aligned to the edge of the last layer selected. If the layers are different shapes, you can make them the same size by choosing Modify ⇨ Align ⇨ Make Same Width and/or Modify ⇨ Align ⇨ Make Same Height.

After you've created your initial layers, you need to create a layer for each remaining hotspot. I name these layers sequentially, such as overLayer2 and overLayer3, and then insert the "over" graphic in each of these layers. Finally, all the overLayers should be in the same position as, but on top of, the offLayer and hidden layer. Basically you have a stack of identical overLayers on top of the offLayer.

Tip If you have many hotspots, you may want to name the overLayers something more recognizable. For example, with my three shapes, I could name the layers overLayer_star, overLayer_nest, and overLayer_clapboard. You need to be able to match the layers to the hotspot as part of the technique. A proper naming scheme can smooth your workflow.

Step 3: Make the image map

The first part of this step is to make the actual image map that will eventually be used to activate the onMouseOver and onMouseOut events. Follow these steps to complete this task:

1. Select the image in one of the layers. You can use either image (the "over" or the "off") to draw the image map. I selected the overLayer, with the slightly fuzzier edges.

2. In the Map field of the Property inspector, give your map a unique name.

3. Draw out the image maps using the drawing tools.

4. In the Hotspot Property inspector, give each area a URL in the Link box.

5. Complete the Target and Alt text boxes, if desired.

   Normally, when building an image map, this is where you would stop. However, because you're using multiple layers, you need to apply the same image map to each of the remaining layers. You don't need to redraw the hotspots, but you do need to assign the same map name to each copy of the image, as described below.

6. Using the Layers panel, select the next layer and then choose the image.

7. In the Map Name field, enter the same name as previously assigned.

   This ensures that all the layers use the same image map; if you do not perform this step, the off and over images will appear to flicker.

8. Repeat Steps 6 and 7 for each of the remaining layers.

Step 4: Attach the behaviors

Dreamweaver includes a JavaScript behavior called Show/Hide Layers that does exactly what you need for this technique. Follow these steps to assign the Show/Hide Layers behavior to the layers:

1. Be sure the offLayer (the layer holding the basic, unchanged image) is visible and that all the overLayers are hidden. You can select the visibility options in the Layers panel to open and close the "eyes" of the respective layers.

2. Select the first hotspot of the image in the offLayer.

3. Open the Behaviors panel by clicking the Show Behavior button in the Launcher, or by selecting Window ➪ Behaviors.

4. In the Behaviors panel, click the Add (+) button and then click Show Events For ➪ 4.0 and Later Browsers, if it's not already selected.

5. Still in the Behaviors panel, select the Add (+) button again and choose Show-Hide Layers from the drop-down menu.

Note

If the appropriate command is not enabled in the drop-down menu, make sure the hotspot is selected in the Document window.

6. When the Show-Hide Layers dialog box opens, Dreamweaver searches for all the layers in your document. After they are displayed, select overLayer and click the Show button (see Figure 13-6). Click OK when you've finished.

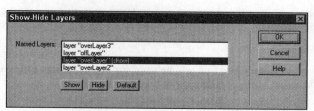

Figure 13-6: Highlight overLayer and then click the Show button to ensure that the Show-Hide Layers behavior makes the appropriate layer visible.

7. The item listed in the Events column should be onMouseOver. If it isn't, select the item and click the down arrow between the Event and Action lists. Choose onMouseOver from the Add Event drop-down list.

So far, you've assigned one behavior to make overLayer visible when the pointer is over the image. Now you have to assign another behavior to hide overLayer when the pointer moves away from the image.

8. Click the Add (+) button and again select Show-Hide Layers from the option list.

9. Now select overLayer again and click the Hide button. Click OK when you're finished.

10. Finally, change the event to onMouseOut for this new behavior, following the same procedure described in Step 7.

You now have two behaviors assigned to one image. You need to repeat the attachment of the behaviors to each of the additional hotspots in your graphic. However, instead of showing and hiding overLayer, each hotspot has its own overLayer to show and hide. For example, after I've selected my second hotspot, I show and hide overLayer02, and so on.

Step 5: Add the clipping

If you test the image map rollover at this stage, you'll see the entire over graphic for every hotspot. To achieve the rollover effect, each of the overLayers must be clipped. All that is left to do now is assign the clipping values.

The clipping property of a layer essentially crops the visible portion of that layer. Four values are used to define the clipped section: Left, Top, Right, and Bottom. These values are pixel measurements relative to the upper-left corner of the layer. Although you could bring your image into an image editor to find the measurements, you can, with a slight bit of trickiness, also get the measurements right from Dreamweaver.

To get the relative pixel values within a layer, I use another temporary layer drawn over my clipped area. I can shape this temporary layer to the exact size of the clip and then note the layer's coordinates and dimensions. Because one layer can nest inside another, I can find the relative positioning—the Left and Top values—very easily. Finding the Right and Bottom values then requires only a minor calculation.

To add the clipping values to your overLayers, follow these steps:

1. From the Layers panel, select the first of the overLayers.

2. Click the graphic in the overLayer.

3. Press the left-arrow key once to move your cursor in front of the image but within the layer.

4. Choose Insert ➪ Layer.

   This new layer is a temporary one that will be used for measurement purposes only and then deleted.

5. Drag the temporary layer into position for the first area to be clipped.

6. Use the resizing handles to reshape the temporary layer until it frames the area you want to clip, as shown in Figure 13-7.

7. In the Property inspector, note the values for Left, Top, Width, and Height (L, T, W, and H, respectively) of the temporary layer.

8. From the Layers panel, select the overLayer.

9. In the Clip section of the Property inspector, enter the Left and Top values as noted from the temporary layers.

Caution   You must include the letters *px*, for pixels, after your clip value, without a space in between. For example, 20px. If you just enter the number, the clipping may not be displayed properly in either Netscape Navigator or Internet Explorer.

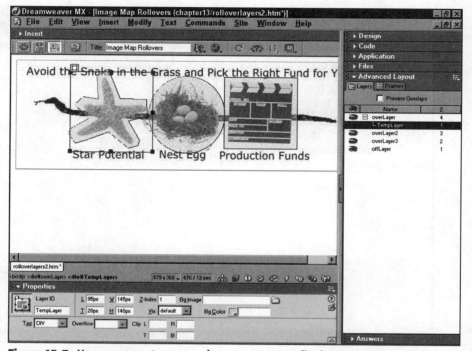

Figure 13-7: You can use a temporary layer to get exact clipping measurements.

10. For the Clip Right (R) value, enter the sum of the temporary layer's Left and Width values.

11. For the Clip Bottom (B) value, enter the sum of the temporary layer's Top and Height values.

    For example, the example temporary layer's initial values were as follows: Left, 95; Top, 20; Width, 145; and Height, 140. This translates into the following clip values: Left, 95px; Top, 20px; Right, 240px (Left + Width); and Bottom, 160px (Top + Height).

    After you've entered the last clipping value (and pressed Tab or Enter/Return to confirm), Dreamweaver displays just the clipped area.

12. Repeat this procedure (Steps 1 through 11) for each of the remaining overLayers, until all have clip values.

13. Delete the temporary layer when you are done.

After you've implemented these changes, test your object. You should see the type of reaction demonstrated in Figure 13-8.

Note   When you preview your work in a browser, make sure that visibility is set correctly for each layer.

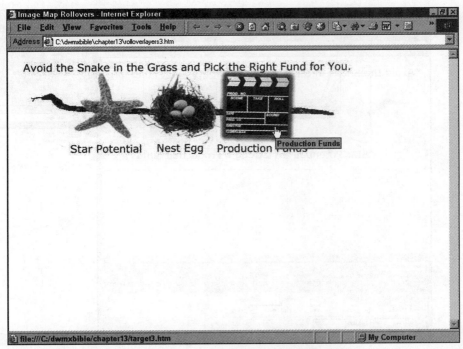

Figure 13-8: The completed image map rollover technique in action.

Summary

Image maps provide a necessary capability in Web page design. Without them, you wouldn't be able to link irregularly shaped graphics or to group links all in one image. Dreamweaver's built-in Image Map Editor gives you all the tools you need to create simple, effective client-side image maps.

✦ Image maps enable you to define separate areas of one graphic and link them to different URLs. Image maps come in two varieties: client-side and server-side. Dreamweaver creates client-side image maps through its Image Map Editor.

✦ Dreamweaver offers three basic drawing tools for creating rectangular, circular, and irregularly shaped image maps, selectable from the Image Property inspector.

✦ If your Web site uses server-side image maps, you can make them by modifying and converting Dreamweaver-generated client-side image maps.

✦ It's possible to create the effect of a graphic rollover, common on Web pages, using client-side image maps. This chapter's Dreamweaver technique shows you how.

In the next chapter, you learn about frames in Dreamweaver.

✦   ✦   ✦

Using Frames and Framesets

The first time I fully appreciated the power of frames, I was visiting a site that displayed examples of what the Webmaster considered "bad" Web pages. The site was essentially a jump-station with a series of links. The author used a frameset with three frames: one that ran all the way across the top of the page, displaying a logo and other basic information; one narrow panel on the left with a scrolling set of links to the sites themselves; and the main viewing area, which took up two-thirds of the center screen. Selecting any of the links caused the site to appear in the main viewing frame.

I was astounded when I finally realized that each frame was truly an independent Web page and that you didn't have to use only Web pages on your own site — you could link to any page on the Internet. That was when I also realized the amount of work involved in establishing a frame Web site: Every page displayed on that site used multiple HTML pages.

Caution

Although the technology allows you to include any page on the Web within your own frameset, Internet etiquette and, in some cases copyright law, dictate that you obtain permission to display another site's pages within your own site, and that you clearly credit work that is not your own.

Dreamweaver takes the head-pounding complexity out of coding and managing frames with a point-and-click interface. You get easy access to the commands for modifying the properties of the overall frame structure, as well as each individual frame. This chapter gives you an overview of frames, as well as all the specifics you need for inserting and modifying frames and framesets. Special attention is given to defining the unique look of frames through borders, scroll bars, and margins.

Frames and Framesets: The Basics

It's best to think of frames in two major parts: the frameset and the frames. The frameset is the HTML document that defines the framing structure — the number of individual frames that make up a page, their initial size, and the shared attributes among all the frames. A frameset by itself is never displayed. Frames, on the other hand, are complete HTML documents that can be viewed and edited separately or together in the organization described by the frameset.

A frameset takes the place of the `<body>` tags in an HTML document, where the content of a Web page is found. Here's what the HTML for a basic frameset looks like:

```
<frameset rows="50%,50%">
  <frame src="top.html">
  <frame src="bottom.html">
</frameset>
```

Notice that the content of a `<frameset>` tag consists entirely of `<frame>` tags, each one referring to a different Web page. The only other element that can be used inside a `<frameset>` tag is another `<frameset>` tag.

In Dreamweaver's Code view, you can directly add a `<frameset>`. . .`</frameset>` tag pair by clicking the Frameset button in the Frames category of the Insert bar. Add a `<frame>` tag in Code view by clicking the Frame button in the Insert bar. Of course, Dreamweaver gives you other ways to create framesets in Design view; see the section "Creating a Frameset and Frames" for more information.

Columns and rows

Framesets, much like tables, are made up of columns and rows. The columns and rows attributes (`cols` and `rows`) are lists of comma-separated values. The number of values indicates the number of either columns or rows, and the values themselves establish the size of the columns or rows. Thus, a `<frameset>` tag that looks like this:

```
<frameset cols="67,355,68">
```

denotes three columns of widths 67, 355, and 68, respectively. And this frameset tag:

```
<frameset cols="270,232" rows="384,400">
```

declares that two columns exist, with the specified widths (270 and 232); and two rows exist, with the specified heights (384 and 400).

Sizing frames

Column widths and row heights can be set as absolute measurements in pixels, or expressed as a percentage of the entire screen. HTML frames also support an attribute that assigns the size relative to the other columns or rows. In other words, the relative attribute (designated with an asterisk) assigns the balance of the remaining available screen space to a column or row. For example, the following frameset:

```
<frameset cols="80,*">
```

sets up two frames, one 80 pixels wide and the other as large as the browser window allows. This ensures that the first column will always be a constant size — making it perfect for a set of navigational buttons — while the second is as wide as possible.

The relative attribute can also be used proportionally. When preceded by an integer, as in n*, this attribute specifies that the frame is allocated n times the space it would have received otherwise. Therefore, frameset code like this:

```
<frameset rows="4*,*">
```

ensures that one row is proportionately four times the size of the other.

Creating a Frameset and Frames

Dreamweaver offers you two strategies for creating a frameset. You can explicitly create a frameset file and add content to each of the frames, or you can start with existing content and create a frameset around it. You can achieve the same results using either method. Within Dreamweaver, you can create a frameset in any of the following ways:

✦ Create a new, empty frameset using the File ➪ New command, and then add content to the frames.

✦ Start with an existing document, and use drag-and-drop to draw frames around the document.

✦ Start with an existing document and apply one of several common frameset layouts to it, using menu commands or the Insert bar.

Creating a new frameset file

Most of the framesets in use on the Web today use two or three frames, albeit in different configurations. For example, a common setup is to have one narrow frame spanning the top of the page to hold a banner and some site navigation; a lower-left frame to hold a table of contents or additional navigation; and a large lower-right frame to hold the content of the site (see Figure 14-1).

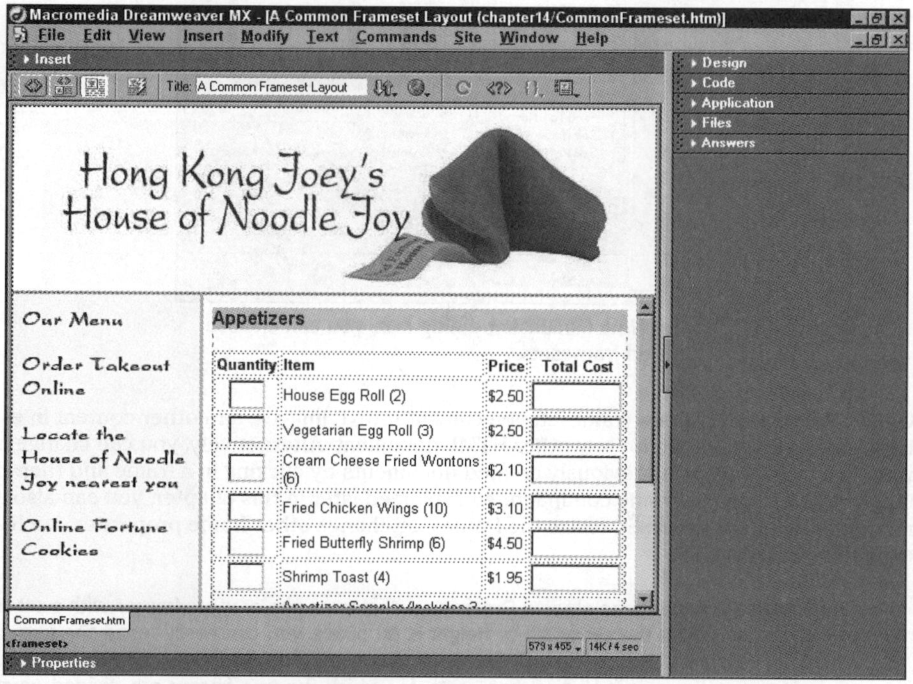

Figure 14-1: The most common designs using framesets call for only two or three frames.

New Feature

Dreamweaver gives you quick access to a full array of the most common setups when you create a frameset document from scratch using the File ➪ New command. Of course, you can customize any of these initial frameset setups by resizing the frames or adding new frames, as described in the sections "Working with the Frameset Property Inspector" and "Adding More Frames," later in this chapter.

To explicitly create a new frameset file, follow these steps:

1. Choose File ➪ New or press Ctrl+N (Command+N).

2. In the New Document dialog box, choose the Framesets category. A list of possible framesets appears, as shown in Figure 14-2.

3. Select the desired entry from the Framesets list. Selecting an entry displays a description of that frameset.

4. Click Create to create the frameset and display it in the Document window.

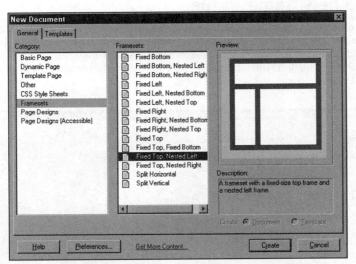

Figure 14-2: In the New Document dialog box, you can choose from many preformed framesets.

Once you've created a new frameset, you can enter text, images, and other content in each of the frames, as you would for any other HTML document. Alternatively, you can change individual frames to contain previously created documents by clicking in a frame and then choosing the File ➪ Open in Frame command. As explained later in this chapter, you can also add more frames to the frameset, resize the frames, or change other frame properties, such as the capability to scroll.

Note

For almost all of the frame objects, Dreamweaver creates one or more frames with a set size. Although by default the set width or height is 80 pixels, you can easily resize the frame by dragging the frame border. The only framesets that do not have at least one set frame are the Split Horizontal and Split Vertical framesets, for which the two frames are divided equally. Dreamweaver also sets the Scroll option to No for frames with absolute sizes.

Creating a frameset visually

Another way of creating a frameset is to start with an existing document and use the mouse to drag-and-drop the frame borders into position. To create a frameset visually, using the mouse, follow these steps:

1. If necessary, switch to Design view by clicking the Show Design View button on the Document toolbar, or by choosing View ⇨ Design. (You can also work in Design and Code view, but these steps do not apply to Code view.)

2. Turn on the frame borders in Design view by selecting View ⇨ Visual Aids ⇨ Frame Borders.

   A 3-pixel-wide inner border appears along the edges of your Design view. These borders indicate the boundaries of your frames so you edit them easily; these borders do not appear when the frameset is viewed in a browser window. See "Working with the Frameset Property Inspector," later in this chapter, to learn how to make the borders visible in a browser.

3. Position the cursor over any of the frame borders.

   If your pointer is over a frame border, the pointer changes into a two-headed arrow when over an edge; it changes into a four-headed arrow (or a drag-hand on the Mac) when over a corner.

4. Drag the frame border into the Document window. Figure 14-3 shows a four-frame frameset.

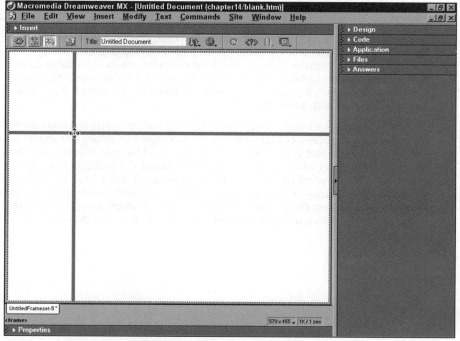

Figure 14-3: After you've enabled the frame borders, you can drag out your frameset structure with the mouse.

Dreamweaver initially assigns a temporary filename and an absolute pixel value to your HTML frameset code. Both can be modified later if you wish.

Tip   With the other methods of frameset creation, you can initially create a frameset with only two or three frames. Although you can further split these into additional frames, the fastest way to create a frameset with four frames is by Alt+dragging (Option+dragging) the corner of the frame border.

When the frameset is selected, Dreamweaver displays a black, dotted line along all the frame borders and within every frame. You can easily reposition any frameset border by clicking and dragging it. If you just want to move the border, make sure you don't press the Alt (Option) key while dragging the border; this action creates additional frames.

Note   Another method of creating a frameset by splitting the page into frames uses the menus. Open a document that you want to appear in one of the frames. Then choose Modify ⇨ Frameset and, from the submenu, select the direction in which you would like to split the frame: left, right, up, or down. Left or right splits the frame in half vertically; up or down splits it horizontally in half. The direction indicates where the content will go; for example, the Split Frame ⇨ Left command splits the page into "columns" and places the existing document into the left frame.

Quickly creating framesets with frame objects

Dragging out your frameset in Dreamweaver is a clear-cut method of setting up the various frames. However, despite its ease, it can still be a bit of a chore to create even simple framesets by clicking and dragging. To hasten the development workflow, Dreamweaver uses frame objects, which can build a frameset with a single click.

As previously mentioned, most of the Web sites using frames follow a simple, general pattern. Dreamweaver includes frame objects for the most common frameset configurations. The frame objects are available through the Insert ⇨ Frames menu commands and through the Frames category of the Insert bar, shown in Figure 14-4. Choose one of the basic designs, and you're ready to tweak the frame sizes and begin filling in the content. It's a great combination: ease of use mixed with design flexibility.

The frame objects are roughly organized from simplest framesets to most complex. On the Insert bar, you might notice that each of the icons shows an example frameset with one blue section. The placement of the color is significant. The blue indicates in which frame the current page will appear when the frameset is constructed. For example, if you begin to construct your main content page, and then decide to turn it into a frameset with separate navigation strip frames to the left and beneath it, you would choose the Left and Nested Bottom Frame button. Figure 14-5 provides a before-and-after example, first with the pre-frame content and then the same content after a Left and Nested Bottom Frame object has been applied.

Frame tags (available only in Code view)

Common frameset configurations

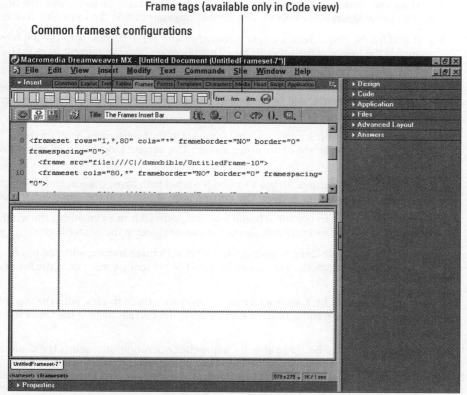

Figure 14-4: The Frames category of the Insert bar holds the most commonly used frameset configurations.

The different framesets available from the Frames category of the Insert bar, and the Insert ⇨ Frames menu commands are as follows:

✦ **Left:** Inserts a blank frame to the left of the current page.

✦ **Right:** Inserts a blank frame to the right of the current page.

✦ **Top:** Inserts a blank frame above the current page.

✦ **Bottom:** Inserts a blank frame below the current page.

✦ **Bottom and Nested Left:** Makes a nested frameset with three frames; the bottom frame spans the width of the other frames. The current page is placed in the upper-right frame.

✦ **Bottom and Nested Right:** Makes a nested frameset with three frames, with the bottom frame spanning the other frames. The current page appears in the upper-left frame.

✦ **Left and Nested Top:** Creates a nested frameset with three frames, with the left frame spanning the height of the other frames. Dreamweaver puts the current page in the lower-right frame.

✦ **Left and Nested Bottom:** Opens a nested frameset with three frames. The left frame spans the other frames, and Dreamweaver places the current page in the upper-right frame.

✦ **Right and Nested Top:** Inserts a nested frameset with three frames, with the right frame spanning the height of the other frames. The current page is placed in the lower-left frame.

✦ **Right and Nested Bottom:** Makes a nested frameset with three frames, with the right frame spanning the other frames. The current page is placed in the upper-left frame.

✦ **Top and Bottom:** Inserts a three-frame frameset, with all frames spanning the width of the entire window. Dreamweaver places the current page in the center frame.

✦ **Top and Nested Left:** Creates a nested frameset with three frames, with the upper frame spanning the width of the other frames. The current page is put in the lower-right frame.

✦ **Top and Nested Right:** Inserts a nested frameset with three frames, with the top frame spanning the other frames. Dreamweaver inserts the current page in the lower-left frame.

Using the frame object can be, quite literally, a one-click operation. Just select the desired frameset from the Frames category of the Insert bar or the Insert ➪ Frames menu, and Dreamweaver automatically turns on Frame Borders, if necessary, and creates and names the required frames. For all frame objects, the existing page is moved to a frame in which the scrolling option is set at Default, and the size is relative to the rest of the frameset. In other words, the existing page can be scrolled, and it expands to fill the content.

Tip   Because Dreamweaver automatically puts the existing document in an expandable frame with scroll bars, it's most efficient to apply a frame object to an existing page only if that page is intended to be the primary content frame. Otherwise, it's better to select the frame object while a blank page is open and then use the File ➪ Open in Frame command to load any existing pages into the individual frames.

Adding More Frames

Regardless of how you create your initial frameset, you're not at all limited to your initial frame choices. In addition to being able to move frame borders visually, you can also set the size through the Frameset Property inspector, as described in the next section. Furthermore, you can continue to split either the entire frame or each column or row as needed — using either menu commands or the mouse. When you divide a column or row into one or more frames, you are actually nesting one frameset inside another.

Tip

Once you've created the basic frame structure, you can select View ➪ Visual Aids ➪ Frame Borders again (it's a toggle) to turn the borders off and create a more accurate preview of your page.

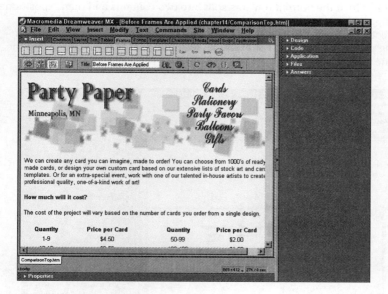

Left and Nested Bottom button

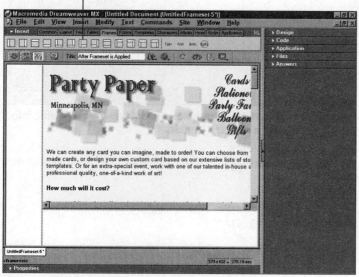

Figure 14-5: *Top:* Before. *Bottom:* After. Existing content is incorporated into a new frameset when a frame object is chosen.

Using the menus

To split an existing frame using the menus, position the cursor in the frame you want to alter and choose Modify ➪ Frameset ➪ Split Frame Left, Right, Up, or Down. Figure 14-6 shows a two-row frameset in which the bottom row was split into two columns and then repositioned. The Frameset Property inspector indicates that the inner frameset (2 columns, 1 row) is selected. The direction in the command (Left, Right, Up, or Down) indicates the frame in which the existing page will be placed. For example, selecting Split Frame Right places the current page in the right frame.

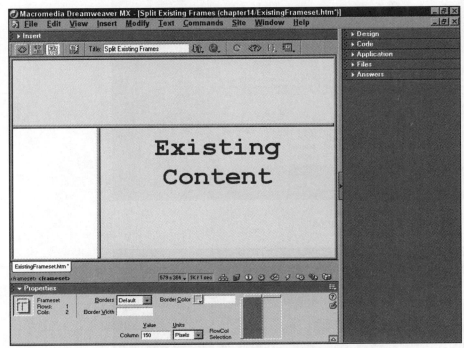

Figure 14-6: Use the Modify ➪ Frameset menu command to split an existing frame into additional columns or rows and create a nested frameset.

You can clearly see the "nested" nature of the code in the following HTML fragment describing the frameset in Figure 14-6:

```
<frameset rows="80,*">
  <frame src="ExistingTop.htm" name="topFrame">
  <frameset rows="*" cols="130,614">
    <frame src="UntitledFrame-12">
    <frame src="ExistingLower.htm" name="mainFrame">
  </frameset>
</frameset>
```

Using the mouse

Notice that when you use the menus to split a frame, only the currently selected frame is split. When you need to create additional columns or rows that span the entire Web page, use the mouse method instead. Select the specific frameset to which you want to add rows or columns, and then Alt+drag (Option+drag) any of the frame's borders that span the entire page, such as one of the outer borders. Figure 14-7 shows a new row added along the bottom of our previous frame structure.

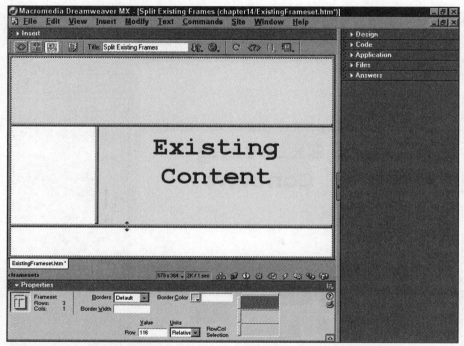

Figure 14-7: An additional frame row was added using the Alt+drag (Option+drag) method.

Selecting, Saving, and Closing Framesets

Once you've initially created your frameset in Dreamweaver, you should know some other basics before modifying the frameset or individual frames. For example, it may not be obvious how to select framesets or individual frames at first, but it's easy once you know how. Before changing your framesets, you'll also want to know how to save your changes and close the frameset files.

Selecting framesets and frames

To change or view the properties of a frameset or a specific frame, you first have to select the frameset or frame. You can select either the frameset itself or one of the frames within it from Design view or from the Frame panel.

The Frame panel shows an accurate representation of all the frames in your Web page. Open the Frame panel by choosing Window ➪ Others ➪ Frames. As you can see on the right in Figure 14-8, the Frame panel displays the names, if assigned, of the individual frames, and (no name) if not. Nested framesets are shown with a heavier border.

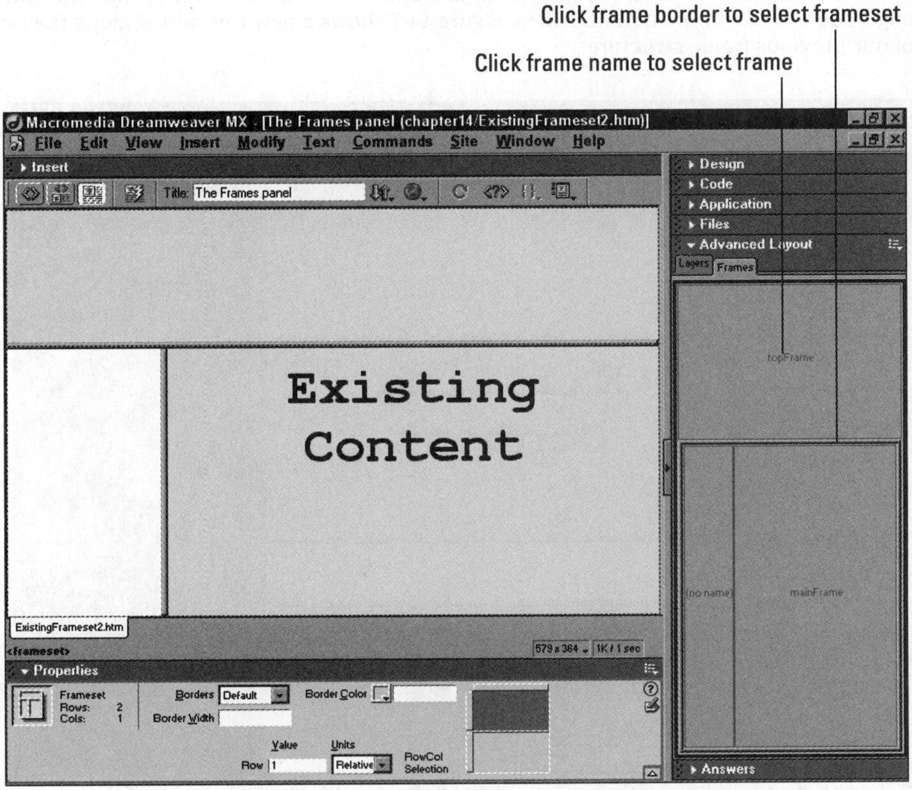

Click frame border to select frameset

Click frame name to select frame

Figure 14-8: Use the Frame panel to visually select a frame to modify.

To select a frameset, click on an outside border of the frameset in the Frame panel. You can also select a frameset by clicking on any border of the frameset in Design view. If you can't see the frame borders, choose View ➪ Invisible Elements ➪ Frame Borders.

To select a specific frame, click inside the represented image of the frame in the Frame panel. For more complex Web pages, you can resize the Frame panel to get a better sense of the page layout. You can also select a frame by pressing Alt (Option+Shift) and clicking in the desired frame in the Document window.

Tip   When you are working with multiple framesets, use the Tag Selector together with the Frame panel to identify the correct nested frameset. Selecting a frameset in the Tag Selector causes it to be identified in the Frame panel with a heavy black border.

Once a frame is selected, you can move from one frame to another within the same frameset by pressing Alt (Command) and then using the right and left arrow keys. You can move from a nested frameset to its "parent" by using the keyboard shortcut Alt+up arrow (Command+up arrow). Likewise, you can move from a parent frameset to its "child" by pressing Alt+down arrow (Command+down arrow).

Saving framesets and frames

Remember that when you're working with frames, you're working with multiple HTML files. You must be careful to save not only all the individual frames that make up your Web page, but also the frameset itself.

Dreamweaver makes it easy to save framesets and included frames by providing several special commands. To save a frameset, select the frameset as previously described and choose File ➪ Save Frameset to open the standard Save File dialog box. You can also save a copy of the current frameset by choosing File ➪ Save Frameset As and then specifying a filename and location for the new copy.

You can save a single frame by clicking in the frame and then choosing File ➪ Save Frame. Make a copy of a document within a frame by choosing File ➪ Save Frame As and then entering a filename and location.

Although you can separately save each frame in the frameset, saving each frame can be a chore unless you choose File ➪ Save All. The first time this command is invoked, Dreamweaver cycles through each of the open frames and displays the Save File dialog box. Each subsequent time you choose File ➪ Save All, Dreamweaver automatically saves every updated file in the frameset.

Tip   As you are saving all the files in the frameset for the first time, you will see a separate Save As dialog box for each previously unsaved file. You can tell which file you are currently saving by looking in Design view—a dotted, black line borders the frame currently being saved.

Closing framesets

There's no real trick to closing a Dreamweaver frameset: Just choose File ➪ Close, as you would for any other file. If you have made changes to any of the frames or the frameset itself since the last time you've saved, Dreamweaver will ask if you want to save your changes before it closes the files. When you are asked to save a file, in Design view, a dotted black border appears around the frame or frameset that needs to be saved.

Working with the Frameset Property Inspector

The Frameset Property inspector manages elements, such as the borders, that are common to all the frames within a frameset. It also offers more precise sizing control over individual rows and columns than you can achieve visually by dragging the borders. To access the Frameset Property inspector, choose Window ➪ Properties, if the Property inspector is not already open, and then select any of the frame borders in Design view.

Tip

When a browser visits a Web page that uses frames, it displays the title found in the frameset HTML document for the entire frame. The easiest way to set that title is to select the frameset and then enter the name directly in the Title field of the Document toolbar, if visible. You can also set the title by selecting the frameset and then choosing Modify ⇨ Page Properties. In the Page Properties dialog box, enter your choice of title in the Title text box, as you would for any other Web page. All the other options in the Page Properties dialog box — including background color and text color — apply to the `<noframes>` content, covered in the section "Handling Frameless Browsers," later in this chapter.

Resizing frames in a frameset

With HTML, when you want to specify the size of a frame, you work with the row or column in which the frame resides. Dreamweaver gives you two ways to alter a frame's size: by dragging the border or, for more precision, by specifying a value in the Property inspector.

As shown in Figure 14-9, Dreamweaver's Frameset Property inspector contains a Row/Column selector to display the structure of the selected frameset. For each frameset, you select the tab along the top or left side of the Row/Column selector to choose the column or row you want to modify.

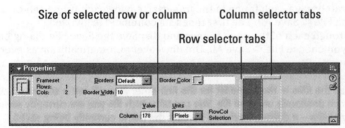

Figure 14-9: In the Frameset Property inspector, you use the Row/Column selector tabs to choose which frame you are going to resize.

Tip

The Row/Column selector shows only the rows and columns for one frameset at a time. Therefore, if your design uses nested framesets, you won't see an exact duplicate of your entire Web page in the Row/Column selector.

Whether you need to modify just a row, a column, or both a row and a column depends on the location of the frame:

✦ If your frame spans the width of an entire page, like the top or bottom row shown in Figure 14-7, select the corresponding tab on the left side of the Row/Column selector.

✦ If your frame spans the height of an entire page, select the equivalent tab along the top of the Row/Column selector.

✦ If your frame does not span either the entire height or width, like the middle row in Figure 14-7, you need to select both its column and its row and modify the size of each in turn.

Once you have selected the row or column, follow these steps to specify its size:

1. To specify the size in pixels, enter a number in the Property inspector's Value text box and select Pixels as the Units option.

2. To specify the size as a percentage of the screen, enter a number from 1 to 100 in the Value text box and select Percent as the Units option.

3. To specify a size relative to the other columns or rows, first select Relative as the Units option. Now you have two options:

   • To set the size to occupy the remainder of the screen, delete any number that may be entered in the Value text box; optionally, you can enter 1.

   • To scale the frame relative to the other rows or columns, type the scale factor in the Value text box. For example, if you want the frame to be twice the size of another relative frame, put a 2 in the Value text box.

Tip The Relative size operator is generally used to indicate that you want the current frame to take up the balance of the frameset column or row. This operator makes it easy to specify a size without having to calculate pixel widths and ensures that the frame has the largest possible size.

Manipulating frameset borders

By default, Dreamweaver sets up your framesets so that all the frames have borders that are invisible when viewed in a browser. You can, however, set borders to be visible, alter the border color, or change the border width. All of the border controls are handled through the Frameset Property inspector.

Tip Dreamweaver also provides border controls for individual frames. Just as table cell settings override options set for the entire table, the individual frame options override those determined for the entire frameset, as described in the section "Working with the Frame Property inspector," later in this chapter. Use the frameset border controls when you want to make a global change to the borders, such as turning them all off.

If you are working with nested framesets, it's important that you select the outermost frameset before you begin making any modifications to the borders. You can tell that you've selected the outermost frameset by looking at the Dreamweaver Tag Selector; it shows only one <frameset> in bold. If you select an inner nested frameset, you see more than one <frameset> in the Tag Selector.

Enabling borders

When a frameset is first created, Dreamweaver sets borders to be invisible in all browsers. You can expressly turn the frameset borders on or off through the Property inspector.

Unfortunately, different browsers control frame borders differently. Some browsers base the presence of borders on the value in the Borders drop-down list, while others use the Border width text box. To enable borders for all browsers, enter a nonzero number in the Border Width text box; and in the Borders drop-down list of options, choose Yes.

The opposite is also true; if you want borders to be invisible for all browsers, set the Borders drop-down list to No, and specify 0 for the Border Width. If you turn off the borders for your frameset, you can still work in Dreamweaver with View ➪ Frame Borders enabled, which gives you quick access to modifying the frameset. The borders are not displayed, however, when your Web page is previewed in a browser.

Border color options

To change the frameset border color, select the Border Color text box and then enter either a color name or a hexadecimal color value. You can also select the color box and choose a new border color from the color picker. Clicking the small painter's palette in the upper-right corner of the color picker opens the Color dialog box, just as for other color pickers in Dreamweaver.

 Caution   If you have nested framesets on your Web page, make sure you've selected the correct frameset before you make any modifications through the Property inspector.

Modifying a Frame

What makes the whole concept of a Web page frameset work so well is the flexibility of each frame:

✦ You can design your page so that some frames are fixed in size while others are expandable.

✦ You can attach scroll bars to some frames and not others.

✦ Any frame can have its own background image, and yet all frames can appear as one seamless picture.

✦ Borders can be enabled—and colored—for one set of frames but left off for another set.

Dreamweaver uses a Frame Property inspector to specify most of a frame's attributes. Others are handled through devices already familiar to you, such as the Page Properties dialog box.

Page properties

Each frame is its own HTML document, and as such, each frame can have independent page properties. To alter the page properties of a frame, position the cursor in the frame and then choose Modify ➪ Page Properties. You can also use the keyboard shortcut, Ctrl+J (Command+J). Alternatively, you can select Page Properties from the context menu by right-clicking (Control+clicking) any open space on the frame's page.

From the Page Properties dialog box, you can assign a title, although it is not visible to the user unless the frame is viewed as a separate page. If you plan to use the individual frames as separate pages in your `<noframes>` content (see "Handling Frameless Browsers," at the end of this chapter), it's good practice to title every page.

You can also assign a background and the various link colors to the nonframe content by selecting the desired color box or entering a color name into the appropriate text box. However, the HTML attributes inserted by these options are deprecated; you may wish to instead use Cascading Style Sheets, discussed in Chapter 20, to control these page properties.

Working with the Frame Property inspector

Using the Frame Property inspector, you can assign names to each of your frames, specify what document should display within each frame, add or remove scroll bars, specify whether the user can resize the frame, and more. To view the Property inspector for a frame, you must first select the frame by using the Frame panel or by holding down the Alt (Option+Shift) key as you click within the frame.

Joining Background Images in Frames

One popular technique inserts background images into separate frames so that they blend into a seamless, single image. This takes careful planning and coordination between the designer of the graphic and the author of the Web page.

To accomplish this image consolidation operation, you must first "slice" the image in an image-processing program, such as Macromedia Fireworks or Adobe Photoshop. Then save each part as a separate graphic, making sure that no border is around these image sections — each cut-up piece becomes the background image for a particular frame. Next, set the background image of each frame to the matching graphic. Be sure to turn off the borders for the frameset and set the border width to zero.

It is important to correctly size each piece to ensure that no gaps appear in your joined background. A good technique is to use absolute pixel measurements for images that fill the frame; and where the background images tile, set the frame spacing to Relative. In the following figure, the corner frame has the same measurement as the background image (155 ×160 pixels), and all the other frames are set to Relative.

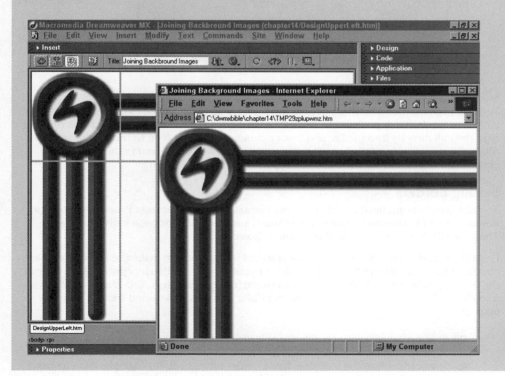

Naming your frames

Naming each frame is essential to getting the most power from a frame-structured Web page. The frame's name is used to make the content inserted from a hyperlink appear in that particular frame. For more information about targeting a link, see the section "Targeting Frame Content," later in this chapter.

Frame names must follow specific guidelines, as explained in the following steps:

1. Select the frame you want to name. You can use either the Frame panel or Alt+click (Option+Shift+click) inside the frame.

2. If necessary, open the Property inspector by choosing Window ⇨ Properties.

3. In the Frame Property inspector, shown in Figure 14-10, add the frame's name in the text box under the Frame Name label. Frame names have the following restrictions:

   • You must use one word, with no spaces.

   • You may not use special characters such as quotation marks, question marks, and hyphens. You may use the underscore character.

   • You may not use certain reserved frame names: _blank, _parent, _self, and _top.

Figure 14-10: The Frame Property inspector enables you to name your frame and control all of a frame's attributes.

Opening a Web page into a frame

You don't have to build all Web pages in frames from scratch. You can load an existing Web page into any frame. If you've selected a frame and the Frame Property inspector is open, just type the link directly into the Src text box or choose the Folder icon to browse for your file. Alternatively, you can position your cursor in a frame (without selecting the frame) and choose File ⇨ Open in Frame.

Setting borders

You can generally set most border options adequately in the Frameset Property inspector; however, you can override some of the options, such as color, for each individual frame. These possibilities have practical limitations, however.

From the Frame Property inspector for a selected frame, you can make the borders visible by choosing Yes in the Borders drop-down list, or make them invisible by choosing No. Leaving the Borders option at Default gives control to the frameset settings. You can also change a frame's border color by choosing the Border Color swatch in a selected frame's Property inspector.

Caution Different browser versions on different operating systems treat the border settings for individual frames differently. To complicate the situation, sometimes the settings on the overall frameset control how the individual frame border settings act. For example, if the frameset border is set to Default, and the individual frame Border is set to No, the border still appears in Internet Explorer 6.0 running on Windows—but as flat, rather than three-dimensional. If you elect to set the border property for an individual frame, be sure to test on as many browsers and platforms as possible.

Additional limitations come into play when you try to implement one of your border modifications. Because frames share common borders, it is difficult to isolate an individual frame and have the change affect just the selected frame. As an example, Figure 14-11 shows a frameset in which the borders are set to No for all frames except the one on the lower right. Notice how the left border of the lower-right frame extends to the top, including the left border of the upper-right frame. You have two possible workarounds for this problem. First, you can design your frames so that their borders do not touch, as in a multirow frameset. Second, you can create a background image for a frame that includes a border design.

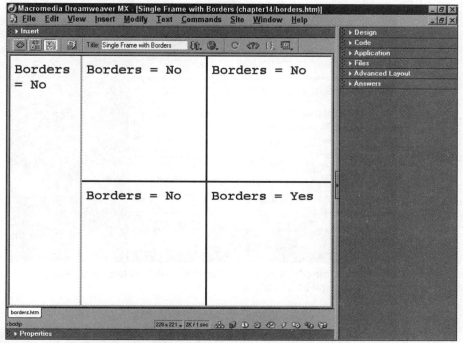

Figure 14-11: If you want to use isolated frame borders, you have to carefully plan your Web page frameset to avoid overlapping borders.

Adding scroll bars

One of the features that has given frames the wide use they enjoy of late is the capability to enable or disable scroll bars for each frame. Scroll bars are used when the browser window is too small to display all the information in the Web page frame. The browser window's size is completely controlled by the user, so the Web designer must apply the various scroll bar options on a frame-by-frame basis, depending on the look desired and the frame's content.

Four options are available from the Scroll drop-down list on the Frame Property inspector:

✦ **Default:** Leaves the use of scroll bars up to the browser.

✦ **Yes:** Forces scroll bars to appear regardless of the amount of content.

✦ **No:** Disables scroll bars.

✦ **Auto:** Turns scroll bars on if the content of the frame extends horizontally or vertically beyond what the browser window can display.

Figure 14-12 uses automatic scroll bars in the lower-right frame; you can see one on the far right.

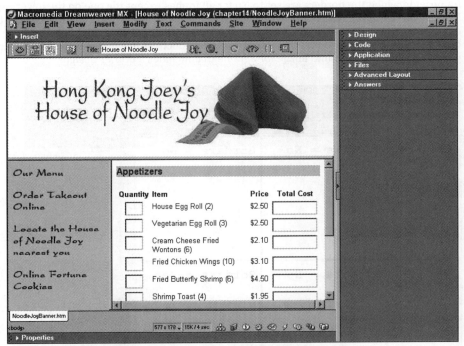

Figure 14-12: The top frame of this Web page has the scroll bars turned off, and the bottom-right frame has scroll bars enabled.

Resizing

Unless otherwise specified, frames are resizable by the user; that is, a visitor to your Web site can widen, narrow, lengthen, or shorten a frame by dragging the border to a new position. You can disable this resizing capability, however, on a frame-by-frame basis. In the Frame Property inspector, select the No Resize option to turn off the resizing feature.

Tip   Although it might be tempting to select No Resize for every frame, it's best to enable resizing, except in frames that require a set size to maintain their functionality (for instance, frames containing navigational controls).

When you first create a frameset using the Frames category on the Insert Bar, the Insert ⇨ Frames menu, or by selecting an item in the Framesets category when you choose File ⇨ New, the frame designated as containing the body of the page will be resizable, and all other frames will be fixed. Frames adding by Alt+dragging (Option+dragging) the frame borders with the mouse, or by choosing the Modify ⇨ Frameset menu commands will be resizable by default.

Setting margins

Just as you can pad table cells with additional space to separate text and graphics, you can offset content in frames. Dreamweaver enables you to control the left/right margins and the top/bottom margins independently. If no margin values are specified, about 6 pixels of space are between the content and the left or right frame borders, and about 15 pixels of space are between the content and the top or bottom frame borders.

To alter the left and right margins, change the value in the Frame Property inspector's Margin Width text box; to change the top and bottom margins, enter a new value in the Margin Height text box. If you don't see the Margin Width and Height text boxes, select the expander arrow in the lower-right corner of the Property inspector.

Caution Dreamweaver currently inserts only the `marginwidth` and `marginheight` attributes when you enter values in the Margin Width and Margin Height text boxes, respectively. The values are not fully recognized by Netscape 3.x and earlier browsers. To ensure full compatibility, enter the attributes `topmargin=value` and `leftmargin=value` directly to the HTML code as follows:

```
<frame src="navigation.htm" marginwidth="10" marginheight="10"
topmargin="10" leftmargin="10">
```

Although Dreamweaver includes fields to input the Left Margin, Top Margin, Margin Height, and Margin Width values in the Page Properties dialog box, if applied to a frameset, these values are written into the No Frames Content page.

Modifying content

You can update a frame's content in any way you see fit. Sometimes, it's necessary to keep an eye on how altering a single frame's content affects the entire frameset. Other times, it is easier — and faster — to work on each frame individually and later load them into the frameset to see the final result.

With Dreamweaver's multiple document structure, you can have it both ways. Work on the individual frame files in one or more Document windows and the frameset in yet another. If you use File ➪ Save All to save your changes in an individual frame document, switching back to the frameset window will automatically show your changed frames.

Caution To preview changes made to a Web page using frames, you must first save the changed files.

Deleting frames

As you're building your Web page frameset, you inevitably try a frame design that does not work. How do you delete a frame once you've created it? Click the frame border and drag it into the border of the enclosing, or parent, frame. When no parent frame is present, drag the frame border to the edge of the page. If the frame being deleted contains any unsaved content, Dreamweaver asks if you'd like to save the file before closing it.

Tip Because the enclosing frameset and each individual frame are all discrete HTML pages, each keeps track of its own edits and other changes. Therefore, each has its own undo memory. If you are in a particular frame and try to undo a frameset alteration, such as adding a new frame to the set, it won't work. To reverse an edit to the frameset, you have to select the frameset and then choose Edit ➪ Undo, or use one of the keyboard shortcuts (Ctrl+Z or Command+Z). To reverse the creation of a frameset, you must select Undo twice.

Targeting Frame Content

One of the major uses of frames is for navigational control. One frame acts as the navigation center, offering links to various Web pages in a site. When the user selects one of the links, the Web page appears in another frame on the page; and that frame, if necessary, can scroll independently of the navigation frame. This technique keeps the navigation links always visible and accessible.

When you assign a link to appear in a particular frame of your Web page, you are said to be assigning a *target* for the link. You can target specific frames in your Web page, and you can target structural parts of a frameset. In Dreamweaver, targets for typical text or image links are assigned through the Text and Image Property inspectors. You will also encounter frame target options elsewhere in the Dreamweaver interface, such as when you create a navigation bar (see Chapter 8) or when you use behaviors that create links, such as the Jump Menu behavior (see Chapter 23).

Targeting sections of your frameset

In the section "Naming your frames," you learned that certain names are reserved. The following four special names are reserved by HTML for the parts of a frameset that are used in targeting: _blank, _parent, _self, and _top. With them, you can cause content from a link to overwrite the current frame or to appear in an entirely new browser window.

To target a link to a section of your frameset, follow these steps:

1. Select the text or image you want to use as your link.

2. In the Text (or Image) Property inspector, enter the URL and/or named anchor in the Link text box. Alternatively, you can select the Folder icon to browse for the file.

3. Select the Target text box. You may need to expand the Property inspector to see the Target text box.

4. Select one of the following reserved target names from the list of Target options (see Figure 14-13) or type an entry into the text box:

   • _blank: Opens the link into a new browser window and keeps the current window available.

   • _parent: Opens the link into the parent frameset of the current frame, if any.

   • _self: Opens the link into the current frame, replacing its contents (the default).

   • _top: Opens the link into the outermost frameset of the current Web page, replacing all frames.

Figure 14-13: Choose your frame target from the Property inspector's Target list.

The generic nature of these reserved target names enables you to use them repeatedly on different Web pages, without having to code a particular reference each time.

Caution A phenomenon known as *recursive frames* can be dangerous to your site setup. Let's say you have a frameset named index_frame.html. If you include in any frame on your current page a link to index_frame.html and leave the target empty or set the target as _self, when the user selects that link, the entire frameset loads into the current frame — including another link to index_frame.html. Browsers can handle about three or four iterations of this recursion before they crash. To avoid the problem, set your frameset target to _top.

Targeting specific frames in your frameset

Recall the importance of naming each frame in your frameset. Once you have entered a name in the Name text box of the Frame Property inspector, Dreamweaver dynamically updates the Target list to include that name. This feature enables you to target specific frames in your frameset in the same manner that you target the reserved names noted previously.

Although you can always type the frame name directly in the Target text box, the drop-down list comes in handy for this task. Not only can you avoid keeping track of the various frame names in your Web page, but typing errors as well. Targets are case-sensitive, and names must match exactly or the browser won't be able to find the target.

Updating two or more frames at once

Sooner or later, most Web designers using frames need to update more than one frame with a single click. The problem is, you can't group two or more URLs together in an anchor tag. Here is an easy-to-implement solution, thanks to Dreamweaver's behaviors.

Cross-Reference If you're not familiar with Dreamweaver's JavaScript behaviors, you might want to look at Chapter 23 before continuing.

To update more than one frame target from a single link, follow these steps:

1. Select your link text or image in the frame.

2. If you selected text for your hotspot, type javascript:; in the Link field of the Text Property inspector.

   The behavior cannot be attached directly to the text; instead, it must be associated with an anchor or an image. Typing javascript:; in the Link field creates the necessary anchor tag.

Tip If one of the multiple links targets the frame that contains the hotspot, you can enter the path to the file that will load in that frame, instead of typing javascript:; in the Link field.

3. Open the Behavior panel from the Launcher or by choosing Window ➪ Behaviors.

4. Click the Add (+) button at the top of the Behavior panel, and in the drop-down menu, choose Show Events For ➪ 4.0 and Later Browsers.

5. Select the Add (+) button again to display the list of available behaviors and then choose Go To URL.

6. Dreamweaver displays the Go To URL dialog box (see Figure 14-14) and scans your document for all named frames. Select a target frame from the list of windows or frames.

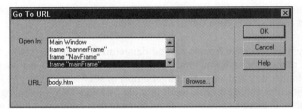

Figure 14-14: You can cause two or more frames to update from a single link by using Dreamweaver's Go To URL behavior.

Caution   You won't be able to use this behavior until you name your frames as detailed in the section "Naming your frames," earlier in this chapter.

7. Enter a URL or choose the Browse (Choose) button to select one.

   Dreamweaver places an asterisk after the targeted frame to indicate that a URL has been selected for it.

8. Repeat Steps 6 and 7 for any additional frames you want to target.

9. Click OK when you're finished.

10. If onClick is not already listed in the Events column of the Behavior panel, click the arrow button next to the event and choose (onClick) from the event list.

Now, whenever you click your one link, the browser opens the URLs in the targeted frames in the order specified.

Handling Frameless Browsers

Not all of today's browsers support frames. Netscape began supporting frames in Navigator version 2.0; Microsoft didn't start until IE version 3.0 — and a few of the earlier versions for both browsers are still in use, particularly among AOL users. Nor do some less prevalent browsers support frames. HTML has a built-in mechanism for working with browsers that are not frame-enabled: the ⟨noframes⟩. . .⟨/noframes⟩ tag pair.

When you begin to construct any frameset, Dreamweaver automatically inserts a ⟨noframes⟩ area just below the closing ⟨/frameset⟩ tag. If a browser is not frames-capable, it ignores the frameset and frame information and renders what is found in the ⟨noframes⟩ section.

Note   If you are manually coding a frameset, in Code view, you can insert the ⟨noframes⟩. . . ⟨/noframes⟩ tag pair by clicking the No Frames button in the Frames category of the Insert bar.

What should you put into the ⟨noframes⟩ section? To ensure the widest possible audience, Webmasters typically insert links to a nonframe version of the site. The links can be as obvious or as discreet as you care to make them. Perhaps a more vital reason to use the ⟨noframes⟩ content is that most of the search engine indexing systems (called *spiders*) don't work with frames. If your frameset is index.html and you want the spider to find the rest of your site, your ⟨noframes⟩ content must include descriptive text as well as navigational links to other pages in your site. Many Webmasters also include links to current versions of Communicator or Internet Explorer, to encourage their nonframe-capable visitors to upgrade.

Dreamweaver includes a facility for easily adding and modifying the <noframes> content. Choose Modify ➪ Frameset ➪ Edit NoFrames Content to open the NoFrames Content window. As you can see in Figure 14-15, this window is identical to the regular Dreamweaver Document window, with the exception of the text "NoFrames Content" in a label at the top of the editing area. In this window, you have access to all the same objects and panels that you normally do. When you have finished editing your <noframes> content, Choose Modify ➪ Frameset ➪ Edit NoFrames Content again to deselect the option and return to the frameset.

Label indicates NoFrames content is displayed

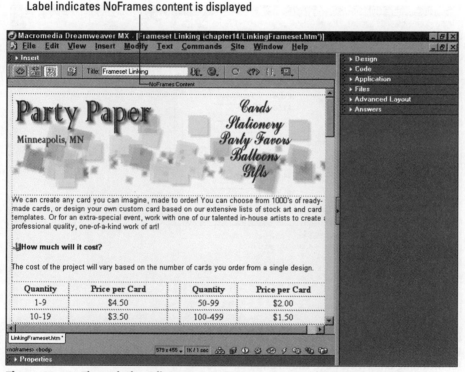

Figure 14-15: Through the Edit NoFrames Content command, Dreamweaver enables you to specify what's seen by visitors whose browsers are not frame-capable.

Keep the following pointers in mind when working in the NoFrames Content window:

✦ The page properties of the <noframes> content are the same as the page properties of the frameset. You can select the frameset and then choose Modify ➪ Page Properties to open the Page Properties dialog box. While in the NoFrames Content window, you can also right-click (Control+click) in any open space to access the Page Properties command.

✦ Dreamweaver disables the File ➪ Open commands when the NoFrames Content window is onscreen. To move existing content into the <noframes> section, use Dreamweaver's Copy and Paste features.

✦ The <noframes> section is located in the frameset page, which is the primary page examined by search engine spiders. It's a good idea to enter <meta> tag information detailing the site in the frameset page. While you're in the NoFrames Content window, you can insert the <meta> tags using the Head category of the Insert bar.

Investigating Iframes

Iframes (short for inline frames) are an HTML 4.0 specification worth noting. An iframe is used to include one HTML document inside another — without building a frameset. What makes iframes visually arresting and extremely useful is their ability to display scroll bars automatically, as shown in Figure 14-16. Iframes are supported only by Internet Explorer 4 and later and Netscape 6; other browsers do not support iframes at this time.

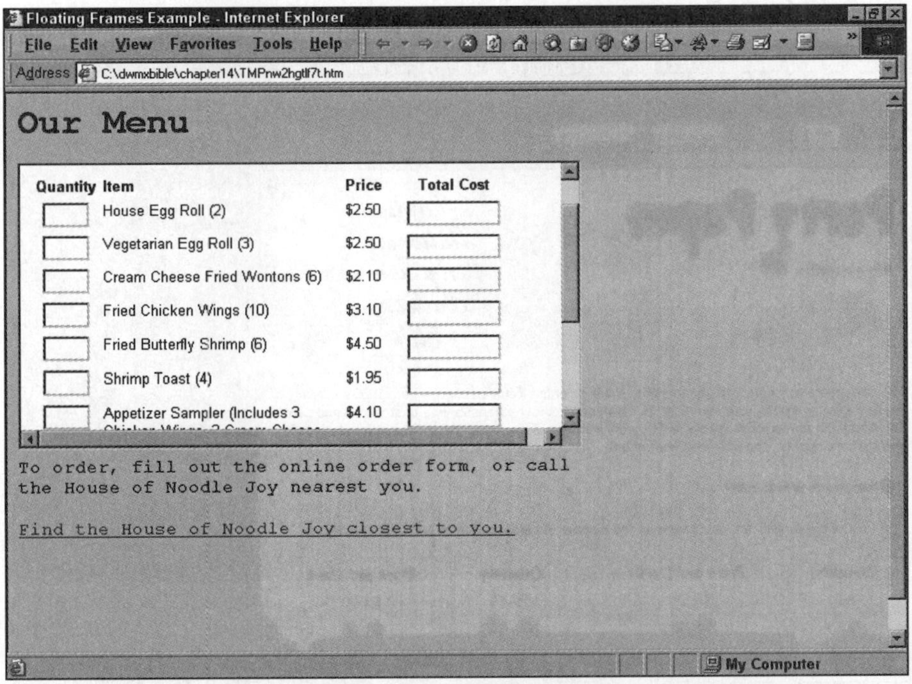

Figure 14-16: The iframe — also known as an inline frame — is a cutting-edge technique for including one HTML page within another.

The iframe tag uses the src attribute to specify which HTML file is to be included. Any content — whether text, images, or whatever — found between the opening and closing iframe tags is displayed only if the browser does *not* support iframes. In other words, it's the no-iframe content. Here's an iframe code example:

```
<iframe src="/includes/salespromo.htm" name="promoFrame"
style="position:absolute; width:200px; height:300px; top:139px;
left:530px">Iframes are not supported by this browser.</iframe>
```

If you're familiar with Cascading Style Sheet layers, you'll notice that the style attribute is identical in iframes. This has an interesting effect in Dreamweaver: iframe code with the style attribute set to position:absolute is displayed like a layer, with the "no-iframe content" visible, as shown in Figure 14-17. This makes positioning and resizing the iframe very straightforward. To see the actual iframe content, you need to preview the page in a compatible browser.

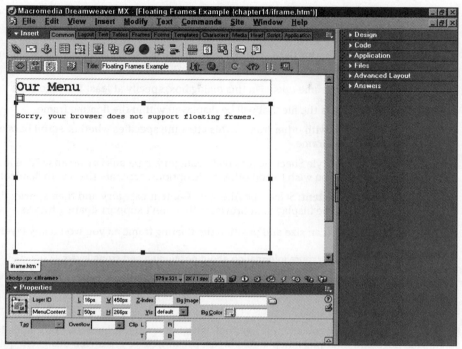

Figure 14-17: When you view an iframe tag in Dreamweaver, it appears like a layer, showing the no-iframe content.

Caution

Specifying `position:absolute` in the `style` attribute enables you to exactly position your floating frame on the page. However, if you specify `position:absolute` and your other content is not contained within layers, your floating frame may overlap the other content on your page. For this reason, it is best to use floating frames in combination with layers.

You can also specify a style of `position:relative`. In this case, browsers will display the floating frame on the page relative to the other page content, even if that content is not contained within layers. Note, however, that Design view does not always correctly display floating frames that are positioned relatively, and sometimes the floating frame will overlap existing content, making it difficult to edit. Again, it is best to lay out your content using layers, and specify `position:absolute` for your `<iframe>` if you are using floating frames.

In Dreamweaver, iframes are referred to as *floating frames*. Now, Dreamweaver facilitates the inclusion of iframes in your documents with the Floating Frame button in the Frames category of the Insert bar.

To insert a floating frame in your document, follow these steps:

1. If you are working in Design view, switch to Code view by choosing View ⇨ Code.

2. Position the cursor after the `<body>` tag in your document.

3. Insert the `<iframe>` tag by choosing the Floating Frame button on the Frames category of the Insert bar, or choose Insert ⇨ Frames ⇨ Floating Frame.

Note You cannot access the floating frame command while you are in Design view. If you are in Code and Design view, the cursor must be in the Code window for the command to be available.

4. Specify the attributes for the `<iframe>` tag. To do this, right-click (Ctrl+click) on the tag and choose Edit Tag <iframe> from the drop-down list.

5. The Tag Editor for Iframe opens. In this dialog box, specify at least the following:

   • **Source:** This is the file that will be displayed within the floating frame.

   • **Scrolling:** As with other frames, this attribute specifies whether scroll bars will appear in the frame.

   • **Style:** In the Style Sheet/Accessibility category, type `position:absolute` in the Style box. If you wish to add other style options, separate them with semicolons.

   • **Alternate Content:** Select the Alternate Content category and then specify the text that will be displayed in browsers that don't support floating frames.

6. In Design view, you can size and position the floating frame as you would any layer.

Cross-Reference Refer to Chapter 21 for more information about positioning and sizing layers.

Summary

Frames are a significant Webmaster design tool. With frames and framesets, you can divide a single Web page into multiple, independent areas. Dreamweaver gives Web designers quick and easy access to frame design through its drag-and-drop interface.

✦ A framed Web page consists of a separate HTML document for each frame and one additional file that describes the frame structure, called the *frameset*.

✦ A frameset comprises columns and rows, which can be sized absolutely in pixels, as a percentage of the browser window, or relative to the other columns or rows.

✦ Dreamweaver enables you to reposition frame borders by dragging them to a new location. You can also add new frames by Alt+clicking (Option+clicking) as you drag any existing frame border.

✦ Framesets can be nested to create more complex column and row arrangements. Selecting the frame border displays the Frameset Property inspector.

✦ Select any individual frame through the Frame panel or by Alt+clicking (Option+Shift+clicking) within any frame. Once the frame is selected, the Frame Property inspector can be displayed.

✦ Make your links appear in a specific frame by assigning targets to the links. Dreamweaver supports both structured and named targets. You can update two or more frames with one link by using the Dreamweaver Go To URL behavior.

✦ You should include information and/or links for browsers that are not frame-capable, through Dreamweaver's Edit NoFrames Content feature.

✦ Floating frames, a newer feature defined in HTML 4.0, can be implemented in Dreamweaver by initially hand-editing the `<iframe>` tag in Code view. After inserting the tag, the floating frame can be sized and positioned in Design view.

In the next chapter, you'll begin working with active content by learning the basics of establishing database connections and building recordsets.

✦   ✦   ✦

Incorporating Dynamic Data

Establishing Connections and Recordsets

Although Dreamweaver may be used to build any sort of Web application, the program's primary use is to present and manage dynamically accessed data. In other words, most designers use Dreamweaver to display and alter information from a database on the Web. But in order for that information to be addressed, two conditions must be met. First, a connection must be established between the Web page and the desired data source. Second, a selection of records from that data source must be defined.

Dreamweaver is adept at handling both requirements. You may connect to virtually any data source — databases, spreadsheets, and even standard text files — in a number of different ways. Dreamweaver offers a variety of connection types, ranging from the simplest (DSN, short for Data Source Name), with the highest overhead, to the most direct, but less straightforward, OLE DB. This chapter explains how the connections are made in Dreamweaver and why some are more robust than others.

After you have established a connection and your Web page is ready to communicate with your data source, the recordset must be specified. You can think of a *recordset* as the key topic of conversation in a dialogue between a Web application and a data source. A recordset is the result of a query made to the database based on your specifications. For most basic recordsets, Dreamweaver provides a point-and-click interface. More advanced recordsets that make extensive use of Structured Query Language (SQL) may also be constructed within Dreamweaver. Both methods are detailed in this chapter; beginners unfamiliar with database concepts should be sure to read the section on database basics that follows.

Data Source Basics

Data sources store information systematically. Here, the key word is *systematically*. Many other technologies, both low-end and high-end, store information — a shelf of books, a shoebox full of receipts, even a collection of Web pages — but few store the information in such a way that retrieval is structured and uniform. Naturally, the precise nature of the structure varies from one type of database to another, but fundamentally, they are all the same.

Note The term *data source* is a more generic name for databases. In this book, the two terms are used interchangeably.

There are basically two different types of data sources: system-based or file-based. File-based data sources store their data in physical files; Access, Excel, and dBase are all examples of file-based data sources. System-based data sources work with data stored in their own dedicated server where the database system resides; MS SQL Server 7, Oracle, PostgreSQL, and MySQL are system-based. Both types of data sources are structured fundamentally the same.

A database is made up of a series of *records*. Each record can be thought of as a snapshot of a particular set of details. These details are known as *fields*, and each field contains the pertinent information or data. A single database record can be made up of any number of fields of varying types — some fields hold only numbers or only dates, whereas others are open-ended and can hold any type of information. A series of database records, all with the same fields, is commonly referred to as a *table* — a simple table is also known as a *flat-file database*. As with a word processing or HTML table, a database table has rows and columns. Each column represents a field, and each row represents a record. For example, the following table that I call `BookTitles` describes a series of books.

Title	Author	Pages	Published
JavaScript Bible	Danny Goodman	1,015	1998
HTML Manual of Style	Larry Aronson and Joseph Lowery	385	1997
Netrepreneur	Joseph Lowery	424	1998

The first row in the table contains the field names: Title, Author, Pages, and Published. Each subsequent row contains a complete record. As presented here, this table is in no particular order; however, one of the reasons why databases are so powerful is their sorting capability. If I were to sort the `BookTitles` table by page count, listing the books with the fewest pages first, it would look like the following table.

Title	Author	Pages	Published
HTML Manual of Style	Larry Aronson and Joseph Lowery	385	1997
Netrepreneur	Joseph Lowery	424	1998
JavaScript Bible	Danny Goodman	1,015	1998

To simplify data manipulation, many databases require that a table have an *index field* in which each entry is unique. In the preceding table, the Title field could serve as an index field because each title is unique. Not all tables can use a regular field as an index, however, as there may be duplicate titles or names. For example, you may not be able to use a CustomerName field as an index because you may have more than one John Smith in your database. If that's the case, you need to create a separate ID field using an AutoNumber type if you're working in Microsoft Access. If you're working in SQL Server, you need to create an integer field and mark it as an Identity type. Either method guarantees a unique ID for each record by assigning an incrementing number to each entry in the database.

Index fields, also referred to as *key fields,* become an absolute necessity when two or more tables — or flat-file databases — are combined to create a *relational database*. As the name implies, a relational database presents information that is related. For example, suppose that I created another table called BookSales to accompany the previous book database example.

Region	Sales	Title
East	10,000	*JavaScript Bible*
South	20,500	*JavaScript Bible*
West	42,000	*JavaScript Bible*
North	25,000	*JavaScript Bible*
East	15,000	*Netrepreneur*
South	12,000	*Netrepreneur*
West	8,000	*Netrepreneur*
North	21,000	*Netrepreneur*
East	8,330	*HTML Manual of Style*
South	6,500	*HTML Manual of Style*
West	8,000	*HTML Manual of Style*
North	7,400	*HTML Manual of Style*

To get a list of authors sorted according to sales figures, you have to combine the two databases. A field common to both tables is used to create the juncture, or *join;* here, the common field is the index field Title. Although flat-file databases can be used in many situations, most industrial-strength applications use relational databases to access information.

In addition to changing the sort order of a table, database information can also be selectively retrieved by using a *filter*. A filter is often represented by a WHERE statement, as in "Show me the books where regional sales were over 10,000 but under 20,000." Applying this filter to the BookSales table would result in the following table.

Region	Sales	Title
East	10,000	*JavaScript Bible*
East	15,000	*Netrepreneur*
South	12,000	*Netrepreneur*

The common language understood by many Web-available databases is SQL, which stands for *Structured Query Language*. A SQL statement tells the database precisely what information you're looking for and in what form you want it. Although SQL statements can become quite complex, a relatively simple SQL statement has just four parts, as follows:

✦ SELECT: Picks the fields to display

✦ FROM: Chooses the tables from which to gather the information

✦ WHERE: Describes the filter criteria and/or the joins

✦ ORDER: Specifies the sorting criteria

A sample SQL statement translation of our "Show me the books where regional sales were over 10,000 but under 20,000" example would look like the following:

```
SELECT Title
FROM BookSales
WHERE (Sales > 10000) AND (Sales < 20000)
ORDER by Sales
```

Joins between two or more tables are depicted in SQL with an equal sign and are considered part of the filter in the WHERE statement. To show the sales by author's name, I'd have to revise my SQL statement to read as follows:

```
SELECT Title, Author
FROM BookTitles, BookSales
WHERE BookTitles = BookSales AND ((Sales > 10000) AND (Sales < 20000))
ORDER by Author
```

Tip   The quick way to display all the fields in a table is to use a SQL statement with a wildcard, like this:

```
SELECT * FROM Booktitles
```

The asterisk indicates that you want to choose every field. From a server resources standpoint, however, this is an inefficient way to retrieve all records. If possible, select all your fields individually. Using the asterisk forces the database to determine what all the field names are, instead of being told exactly what to retrieve.

Understanding How Active Content Pages Work

The journey for a static Web page from user to server is straightforward, even for the most complex, graphics-laden and JavaScript-laden page. The user clicks a link that sends a signal to the server to send that page. An active content page — with full database connectivity — travels a much different route, however.

An active content page is a blend of traditional HTML and a database server language, such as Active Server Pages (ASP) or ColdFusion Markup Language (CFML). When a user accesses an active content page, the requested page is passed through the database server where the code is processed, and a new HTML page is generated. This page is then returned to the regular Web server and sent on to the user. Figure 15-1 illustrates this process.

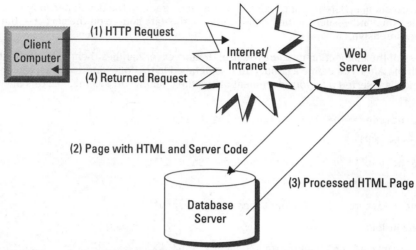

Figure 15-1: An active content page is processed by a database server prior to being sent to the user.

Active content servers can connect to more than databases, however. Other possibilities include the following:

✦ **Directory servers:** Directory servers control the permissions for large corporations and determine who is granted access to what group of files. With a directory server, two people — with different clearances — could see two different pages when clicking the same link.

✦ **Mail servers:** E-mail communication can be fully automated through a mail server. Responses to forms are categorized and forwarded to the proper parties, mass mailings can go out at the click of a button, and messages can be automatically incorporated into Web pages.

✦ **File servers:** By and large, HTML by itself has no file manipulation capabilities. However, with a file server, files can be uploaded, copied, renamed, moved, deleted, and more.

The primary HTML vehicle for interfacing with a database server is the form.

Opening a Connection to a Data Source

If you're a Star Trek fan (of any generation), you're likely to remember the phrase "Open a channel, Lieutenant." With these words, the commander was asking to establish a communication link between the Enterprise and whatever alien vessel was hovering nearby. Not only are the technical lines of communication enabled, but any necessary translation services are also put into play. When you connect to a data source in Dreamweaver, you're opening a channel between your Web pages and a designated data source. (Notice that I'm referring to lowercase data, not Data, the android; I'll save that extended metaphor for another time.)

As noted earlier, you have numerous ways to connect to a data source. The simplest, DSN, requires some administrative setup, and has a negative impact on server performance.

Alternatives, such as DSN-less and OLE DB connections, require the developer to have more information on hand — such as the exact location of the data source on the server — but are less server-intensive.

Regardless of the connection method you use, Dreamweaver handles them in basically the same fashion. After you define a connection, as detailed in the following sections, a server-side include is inserted into your document above the opening <html> tag, like this one for ASP:

```
<!--#include file="Connections/connDBA.asp" -->
```

or this one for .NET:

```
<!--#include file ="Connections/connDBA.aspx">
```

or this one for ColdFusion:

```
<cfinclude template="Connections/connDBA.cfm">
```

or this one in JSP:

```
<%@ include file="Connections/connDBA.jsp" %>
```

or this one in PHP:

```
<?php require_once('Connections/connDBA.php'); ?>
```

In each case, Dreamweaver creates a folder called Connections at the site root for the server-side include files. The same file is referenced on every page that uses the defined data source connection. By using a server-side include, Dreamweaver provides a one-step method for updating all the pages using the same connection in the site. To define, edit, and manage your connections, open the Databases panel in the Application panel group, as shown in Figure 15-2.

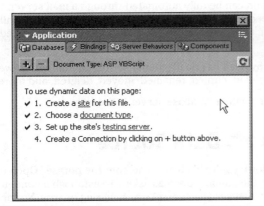

Figure 15-2: Data source connections are managed on a site-by-site basis through the Databases panel.

New Feature   The Databases panel is new to Dreamweaver MX, and provides a one-stop shop for all your connection needs. You can add and remove connections, as well as ensure that your site definition is correct so that you can start adding connections.

The first thing you'll see in your Databases panel is a short checklist of what you need to do before you can start adding connections. You must meet three criteria before you can start working:

1. You must have a site defined.

2. You must have a default dynamic document type defined for your site.

3. You must set up the site's Testing Server.

Some server languages may have additional requirements. Each criterion contains a link that opens the appropriate dialog box for changing these settings. After all the criteria have checkmarks next to them, you're ready to start adding connections. After you create your first connection, you have access to all the database information in the panel, as shown in Figure 15-3.

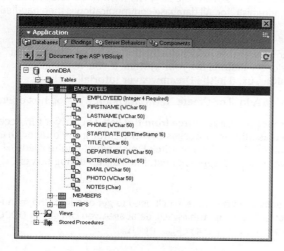

Figure 15-3: Connecting to a database gives you access to all the tables, views, and stored procedures for that database.

After you define your connections, you must upload the files in the Connection folder in order for them to work on your remote server. If you upload a file containing a connection and opt to Include Dependent Files, the connection files are uploaded automatically.

Using Data Source Names (DSN)

Data sources, like graphic files, come in different formats. Databases developed in Access are different from those developed in Oracle or FoxPro. To enable applications to access a variety of data sources, the Open Database Connectivity (ODBC) standard was developed. ODBC is a type of universal translator, which, with a specific driver for a particular database type, enables Web (and other) applications to read from and write to databases. Windows systems include drivers for data sources created in Microsoft Access, SQL Server, dBase, Oracle, FoxPro, Excel, and Paradox. There's even a driver for reading straight text files, which usually contain comma-separated values. Macintosh users should connect to the ODBC driver on their Testing Server.

To simplify the process of connecting via ODBC, the Data Source Names protocol was established. Just as a domain name, such as www.idest.com, is an alias for an Internet Protocol number (for example, 64.70.242.110), a DSN is an alias for the actual location of a data source. Locally, on Windows systems, DSNs are managed through the ODBC Data Source Administrator. Remotely, DSNs are set up by system administrators on the Testing Server.

Even if you ultimately decide to use a more efficient method of connecting to your data source, DSNs are very useful during the development phase. Every server model except for PHP and .NET supports DSNs. To set a local DSN on a Windows system, follow these steps:

1. For Windows 95, 98, or ME systems, from the Control Panel folder, select ODBC Data Source (32 bit); Windows NT users should choose ODBC. Windows 2000 users should select Data Sources (ODBC) from the Administrative Tools folder. The ODBC Data Source Administrator opens.

Note If you're working with a Macintosh and want to use an ODBC DSN connection — or just prefer to work with the actual data on the server — the DSN will have to be established on your Testing Server by the system administrator. All database communication is then handled online.

2. From the ODBC Data Source Administrator, select the System DSN tab. The System DSN tab lists all the DSNs previously defined for your system. If you've installed Dreamweaver, you'll see GlobalCar, used in the Dreamweaver tutorial, in the list.

3. From the System DSN tab, choose Add. The Create New Data Source dialog box opens.

4. Choose the appropriate driver for your data source from the list. The driver for Access databases, for example, is listed as Microsoft Access Driver (*.mdb); the one for Oracle databases is shown as Microsoft ODBC for Oracle. Click Finish when you're ready. A setup dialog box for the driver selected appears next. Each setup dialog box is somewhat different.

Tip If you don't see a driver for your database listed here, you'll need to get one from the manufacturer or database sponsor. If you are working with MySQL databases, you can get an ODBC driver from www.mysql.com/downloads/api-myodbc.html.

5. In the setup dialog box, enter the desired Data Source Name and select the data source. Following are examples of the most commonly used data sources:

   • For Access databases, choose Select to locate the database (see Figure 15-4). If a user name and password are required, select Advanced to enter that information.

   • For Excel spreadsheets, choose Select Workbook to locate the proper file. Select Options to limit the number of rows accessed.

   • For SQL Server, select a name from the Server drop-down list. Choose (local) if your system also acts as the SQL Server. Choose Finish when you are done.

   • For MySQL databases, enter the MySQL host name or IP address and the full path to the MySQL database. A user name and password, if necessary, may be entered on the same screen. The MySQL ODBC driver also offers a wide range of options that you may enable.

6. When you've closed the setup dialog box, choose OK to close the ODBC Data Source Administrator.

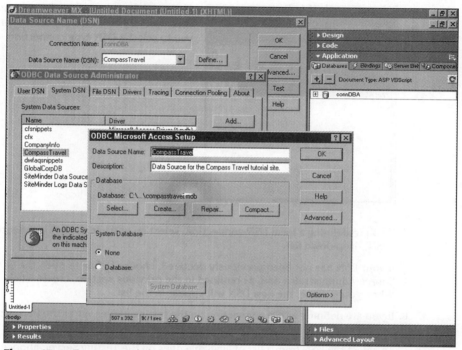

Figure 15-4: To use an existing Access database, choose the Select button from the ODBC Microsoft Access Setup dialog box.

After you've created a DSN for your data source, you're ready to create an ODBC DSN connection in Dreamweaver. Although the basic procedure is the same for all five server models, the specific steps are different enough to warrant the individual descriptions presented in the following sections.

ASP

A DSN connection is often an ASP developer's first choice for rapid development because of its easy setup. To establish a DSN connection in Dreamweaver, follow these steps:

1. Choose Window ➪ Databases to display the Databases panel, as shown in Figure 15-5.

2. Click the Add (+) button and, from the drop-down list, select Data Source Name (DSN). The Data Source Name (DSN) dialog box is displayed.

3. If you're creating a connection on a Testing Server, choose the Dreamweaver Should Connect Using DSN On Testing Server option; otherwise, choose the Using Local DSN option. These two options are not available on the Mac, you must always use the Testing Server.

4. Enter a label for your new connection in the Connection Name field. It's a good habit to identify your connections with the prefix conn; for example, you might label your connection connDBA.

Figure 15-5: A drop-down list appears when you click the Add (+) button, enabling you to select a DSN-type connection.

5. If you're defining a local DSN connection, select an entry from the Data Source Name (DSN) drop-down list.

   If your DSN has not been previously declared, choose Define to open the ODBC Data Source Administrator and, as outlined in the previous section, create a new DSN. When you're done, the new DSN will appear in the list.

6. If you are defining a DSN connection on the testing server, enter the DSN name in the field.

   To select the DSN from a list of available ones on the Testing Server, choose the DSN button. Dreamweaver will attempt to connect to the Testing Server and retrieve a list of assigned DSNs. Select one from this list, if desired.

Caution   If your host has not set up his or her security properly, you may see DSNs other than those for your site. Alert your ISP to this security problem, as it indicates that your data is accessible by others. A Tech Note on the Dreamweaver support site (www.macromedia.com/go/ 14961) describes steps to take to remedy this problem, which has been reported only on IIS 4.0 and 5.0 servers.

7. If necessary, enter a user name and password in the appropriate fields.

8. Certain databases, such as those from Oracle, enable you to restrict the number of database items available from a connection. To limit the available tables, choose Advanced and enter the desired Schema and/or Catalog.

9. To ensure that your connection is properly set up, choose Test from the Data Source Name (DSN) dialog box. If the connection is established, Dreamweaver tells you the connection was successful.

10. Click OK when you're done to close the Data Source Name (DSN) dialog box. The new connection is listed in the Connections dialog box.

11. Click Done to close the Connections dialog box.

ColdFusion

ColdFusion seamlessly integrates with the ODBC Data Source Administrator to use the DSNs already established on the system. Furthermore, new DSNs may be set up from within the ColdFusion Administrator. This compatibility makes establishing standard DSN connections very straightforward in Dreamweaver.

Note There is, however, a limitation in Dreamweaver when it comes to DSN connections in ColdFusion. Dreamweaver only supports the use of stored procedures, a type of encapsulated SQL statement, for SQL Server 7.0 databases with the standard DSN connection. To use stored procedures with databases other than SQL Server 7.0, you must connect via a JDBC (Java Database Connectivity) driver available through the Data Source Name – Advanced option, covered later in this section. The JDBC driver also enables Macintosh users to connect to a local database without going through ColdFusion. (Currently, ColdFusion Server is not available for the Macintosh.)

You can enter new DSNs for ColdFusion either through the ODBC Data Source Administrator as detailed previously, or you can use the ColdFusion Administrator. To make a standard DSN connection for ColdFusion server models, follow these steps:

1. Choose Window ➪ Databases to display the Databases panel.

2. Click the Modify Data Sources button (see Figure 15-6) to open the CF Data Source Administrator (see Figure 15-7). The Modify Data Sources button takes you to the ColdFusion Administrator home page.

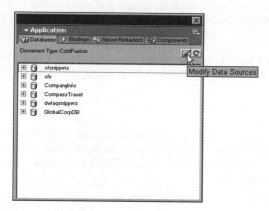

Figure 15-6: The standard Data Source Name dialog box is used for most cases when establishing a DSN connection in ColdFusion.

3. From the ColdFusion Administrator home page, choose ODBC under the Data Sources category.

4. On the ODBC Data Sources page, select the proper driver from the drop-down list and then choose Add (refer to Figure 15-7).

5. On the Create ODBC Data Source page, first enter a new name for your DSN in the Data Source Name field. Enter the path to the database in the Database File or System Database field; alternatively, you can select the appropriate Browser Server button to locate the file. If needed, enter a user name and password.

6. When you're finished, select Create. ColdFusion will create and verify the DSN, displaying it in the ODBC Data Sources page.

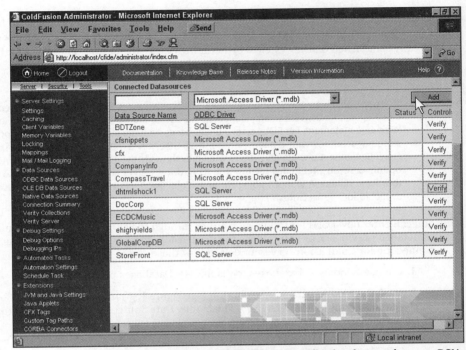

Figure 15-7: The ColdFusion Administrator includes an application for creating new DSNs.

New Feature   All ColdFusion data sources are now created using the ColdFusion Administrator, which removes the burden from Dreamweaver and makes it much easier to ensure that your connections will work correctly.

JSP

As you would expect, JavaServer Pages use the Java Database Connectivity (JDBC) standard. Dreamweaver includes six different drivers, along with an option for installing a custom driver, in its JDBC implementation. The six drivers included for the JDBC connection are as follows (see Table 15-1 for the syntax of each driver):

✦ IBM DB 2 App Driver, for use with local DB2 applications

✦ IBM DB 2 Net Driver

✦ MySQL Driver

✦ Oracle Thin Driver

✦ Inet Driver for SQL Server

✦ Sun JDBC-ODBC Driver

Table 15-1: JDBC Driver Parameters

Sun JDBC-ODBC Bridge

Supports	Any ODBC driver, such as the one for Microsoft Access
Driver Field Parameters	sun.jdbc.odbc.JdbcOdbcDriver
URL Field Parameters	jdbc:odbc:your_DSN
URL Field Example	jdbc:odbc:dbaEvents

I-net JDBC Driver

Supports	SQL Server databases
Driver Field Parameters	com.inet.tds.TdsDriver
URL Field Parameters	jdbc:inetdae:server_name:database_port?database=databasename
URL Field Example	jdbc:inetdae:euripedes:1343?database=dbaEvents.mdb

Oracle Thin JDBC Driver

Supports	Oracle databases
Driver Field Parameters	oracle.jdbc.driver.OracleDriver
URL Field Parameters	jdbc:oracle:thin:@server_name:database_port:SID (SID is the Oracle database system identifier)
URL Field Example	jdbc:oracle:thin@euripedes:1343:dbaEvents

Many more drivers are available: A list of well over 100 can be found on the Sun Web site at java.sun.com/products/jdbc/drivers. Since the emergence of JDBC, four different types of JDBC drivers have been developed. Type 1 is the earliest prototype and the least robust; the Sun JDBC-ODBC Driver is a Type 1 driver. Type 4 drivers are native Java applications and offer the best connectivity. Whenever possible, it's best to use a Type 4 driver.

The Data Source Name is really an ODBC protocol; outside of the JDBC drivers intended to interface with ODBC, other drivers do not use DSNs. However, the process is much the same — all you need to do is supply the proper parameters identifying the data source. To establish a connection in JSP, follow these steps:

1. Choose Window ⇨ Databases to display the Databases panel.

2. Click the Add (+) button and, from the drop-down list, select one of the drivers. The connection dialog box for the chosen driver is displayed. Figure 15-8 shows the dialog box for the MySQL driver.

3. If you're creating a connection on a Testing Server, choose the Using Driver On Testing Server option; otherwise, choose the Using Driver On This Machine option.

4. Enter a label for your new connection in the Connection Name field.

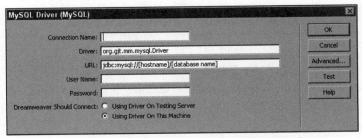

Figure 15-8: Each of the standard drivers for JSP connections uses placeholders in brackets to indicate parameters to be completed.

5. Verify that the information in the Driver field is correct. If you are defining a Custom JDBC connection, enter in the field the driver name as specified by the manufacturer.

   All standard Dreamweaver JSP drivers display the required syntax in the URL field; user-supplied parameters are surrounded with brackets.

6. If you are using a standard Dreamweaver JSP driver, replace the bracketed parameters with the information for your connection. For example, the supplied MySQL driver URL is `jdbc:mysql://[hostname]/[database name]`. If I were using a database named dbaEvents on a server named euripedes, my completed URL would be `jdbc:mysql://euripedes/dbaEvents`.

7. If you are defining a custom JDBC connection, enter the full URL as required by the driver.

8. If necessary, enter a user name and password in the appropriate fields.

9. To limit the available tables, choose Advanced and enter the desired Schema and/or Catalog. Not all databases support the capability to limit tables.

10. To ensure that your connection is properly set up, choose Test. If the connection is established, Dreamweaver tells you the connection was successful.

11. Click OK when you're done to close the dialog box. The new connection is listed in the Connections dialog box.

12. Click Done to close the Connections dialog box.

ASP.NET and PHP

ASP.NET and PHP don't support DSN connections. ASP.NET supports only OLE DB connections, and Dreamweaver's PHP server model supports only MySQL connections through its own ODBC drivers. See the "DSN-less connections for ASP" section for more information about making connections with these two server models.

Specifying connection strings

Although a DSN connection may be the easiest to set up, it's not the most robust type of connection. In Dreamweaver, you can explicitly state the details implied by a DSN connection by specifying a connection string. The connection string states the name of the driver, the path to the data source, and any additional information needed, such as user name and password—all in one long string of text. Two types of connection strings are used in Dreamweaver: DSN-less connections and OLE DB connections.

DSN-less connections for ASP

One real-world problem faced by ASP developers wishing to use the Data Source Name protocol is the inability to get system administrators to assign DSNs. Some hosting companies limit the number of DSNs per site or charge a fee for each one. Often, it's difficult to get a hosting company to respond in a timely fashion. ASP developers can bypass all these potential headaches in Dreamweaver by using a DSN-less connection.

A DSN-less connection uses the same driver as a DSN connection but without relying on a Data Source Name being defined. The syntax of a DSN-less connection varies for each type of database, but basically has five parts:

✦ **Provider:** The underlying mechanism that connects the ODBC driver to the application. For ODBC drivers, the provider is MSDASQL; because the provider is always the same for ODBC, the entry is optional in a connection string and understood if omitted.

✦ **Driver:** The proper name of the driver as listed in the ODBC Data Source Administrator.

✦ **Path to data source:** Typically, this is a full path to a database called the DBQ; however, with some data sources, such as Oracle and SQL Server, this parameter appears in two parts, listing both the server and the database name.

✦ **User name:** The user name, if any, required for access to the data source. This element is often abbreviated UID in a connection string.

✦ **Password:** The password, if any, required for access to the data source. This element is often abbreviated PWD in a connection string.

For example, a DSN-less connection string to an Access database named dbaEvents.mdb could read like the following:

```
Provider=MSDASQL;Driver={Microsoft Access Driver ⤶
(*.mdb)};DBQ=c:\clients\dba\data\dbaEvents.mdb;UID=jlowery;PWD=hoosier7;
```

If the same data source were in SQL Server format (on a server named euripedes), the DSN-less connection string would look like the following:

```
Provider=MSDASQL;Driver={SQL Server};
Server=euripedes;Database=dbaEvents.mdb;
UID=jlowery;PWD=hoosier7;
```

To enter a DSN-less connection in Dreamweaver, follow these steps:

1. Choose Window ➪ Databases to display the Databases panel.

2. Click the Add (+) button and choose Custom Connection String from the drop-down list. The Custom Connection String dialog box is displayed (see Figure 15-9).

3. Enter a label for your new connection in the Connection Name field.

4. Enter the complete connection string in the Connection String field.

   It's often easier to type your connection string into a text editor first — making sure that your syntax and parameters are correct — and then cut and paste it into the dialog box field.

5. If you're creating a connection on a Testing Server, choose the Using Driver On Testing Server option; otherwise, choose the Using Driver On This Machine option.

Figure 15-9: For a DSN-less connection, all your data source connectivity information — the driver, the path to the database, and even the user name and password — is entered in one long text string.

6. Certain databases, such as those from Oracle, enable you to restrict the number of database items available from a connection. To limit the available tables, choose Advanced and enter the desired Schema and/or Catalog.

7. To make sure your connection is properly set up, choose Test from the Custom Connection String dialog box. If the connection is established, Dreamweaver tells you the connection was successful.

8. Click OK to close the Custom Connection String dialog box. The new connection is now listed in the Databases panel.

OLE DB

Although DSN-less connections don't require an actual Data Source Name to be registered, they still rely on the same ODBC drivers. ODBC itself is a type of translator that relies on an OLE (Object Linking and Embedding) DB provider to make the connection. The most efficient way to connect to a data source is to use an OLE DB provider directly. Dreamweaver enables direct OLE DB connections through the Custom Connection String option.

OLE DB connection strings are similar to DSN-less connections except that only the provider parameter and not the driver parameter is included. Here, for example, is an OLE DB connection string to an Access database:

```
Provider=Microsoft.Jet.OLE DB.4.0;
Data Source=d:\clients\dba\data\dbaEvents.mdb;
```

Different data sources require different providers. SQL Server uses SQLOLE DB, for example, whereas Oracle needs OraOLE DB. Follow these steps to create an OLE DB connection string:

1. Choose Window ➪ Databases to display the Databases panel.

2. Click the Add (+) button and select Custom Connection String from the drop-down list. The Custom Connection String dialog box is displayed.

3. Enter a label for your new connection in the Connection Name field.

4. Enter the complete connection string in the Connection String field.

5. If you're creating a connection on a Testing Server, choose the Using Driver On Testing Server option; otherwise, choose the Using Driver On This Machine option. This option is not available on the Mac.

6. To limit the available tables, choose Advanced and enter the desired Schema and/or Catalog.

7. To ensure that your connection is properly set up, choose Test from the Custom Connection String dialog box. If the connection is established, Dreamweaver tells you the connection was successful.

8. Click OK when you're done to close the Custom Connection String dialog box. The new connection is listed in the Connections dialog box.

Tip

Create a blank .NET document and use the OLE DB Connection builders to create your DSN-less strings; then copy and paste the strings into your ASP connection dialog box.

Finding the Path with Server.MapPath

Right up there with the importance of getting your ASP hosting company to set up a DSN quickly is getting the company to tell you exactly where your virtual site is set up on its server — information that you need if you're going to successfully use a DSN-less connection. Luckily, ASP includes a server-side command that you can use to find the path to your data source. The `Server.MapPath()` command returns the full path of the server when given the relative path to your data source.

For example, let's say I have a site called `myway.com`. Within my site, I have a database, thehighway.mdb, located in the data folder off my site root. On my system, the relative path to the database is `\myway\data\thehighway.mdb`. When I issue the following command on my host's server:

```
Server.MapPath("\myway\data\thehighway.mdb")
```

I'll get back the full path, which might be something like the following:

```
E:\HTDOCS\jlowery\myway\data\thehighway.mdb
```

The `Server.MapPath()` function can be used in an ASP page or within the Custom Connection String dialog box to find the location of a file. To use an ASP page, use code similar to the following:

```
<%@ LANGUAGE="VBSCRIPT" %>
<%
Dim ThatPath
ThatPath = Server.MapPath("\myway\data\thehighway.mdb")
Response.Write "Path to database: " & ThatPath
%>
```

After saving the ASP page and uploading it to your server, execute the page by typing in its URL. The full path to your data source will appear in the browser.

While this is adequate, your pages could break if your site is moved on the server or to another server altogether. A better method is to include the `Server.MapPath()` function as part of the custom connection string. Here's an example of such a string:

```
"Driver={Microsoft Access Driver (*.mdb)};DBQ=" &
Server.MapPath("\myway\data\thehighway.mdb")
```

Note the use of quotes and the ampersand before the `Server.MapPath()` function. Essentially, you are concatenating two text strings to make one long one.

The `Server.MapPath()` function may only be used when the Using Driver on Testing Server option in the Custom Connection String dialog box is selected.

ASP.NET and OLE DB connections

The Dreamweaver engineers have outdone themselves when it comes to creating new connections in .NET. The connection dialog box may not be much to look at, but the Build and Template buttons on the right-hand side will make creating your connections a breeze.

New Feature   The new Build and Template buttons in the .NET OLE DB Connection dialog boxes are a boon for developers tired of manually entering long DSN-less connections.

To create a new OLE DB connection, follow these steps:

1. Choose Window ➪ Databases to display the Databases panel.

2. Click the Add (+) button and choose OLE DB Connection from the drop-down list. The OLE DB Connection dialog box is displayed, as shown in Figure 15-10.

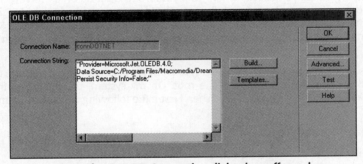

Figure 15-10: The OLE DB Connection dialog box offers a large space for you to manually type a connection string.

3. Enter a label for your new connection in the Connection Name field.

4. Enter the complete connection string in the Connection String field.

To avoid manually typing in a connection, click the Build button to the right of the Connection String field, and the Data Link Properties dialog box is displayed, as shown in Figure 15-11. Make sure that each tab is completed correctly to create your connection string. The Build button isn't available on Macs.

Alternatively, you can click the Templates button in the OLE DB Connection dialog box to get a list of predefined connection string templates. Choose a template and click OK to add the connection string to the OLE DB Connection dialog box. The variables will be surrounded with [and]. Just replace the brackets and variables and click OK.

5. To ensure that your connection is properly set up, choose Test from the OLE DB Connection dialog box. Dreamweaver will prompt you whether or not the test is successful.

6. Click OK when you're done to close the OLE DB Connection dialog box. The new connection is listed in the Connections dialog box.

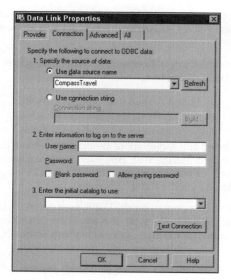

Figure 15-11: The Data Link Properties dialog box provides a quick way to create complicated connection strings.

PHP

This release of Dreamweaver's PHP model supports MySQL connections only. To set up your MySQL connections, follow these steps:

1. Choose Window ➪ Databases to display the Databases panel.

2. Click the Add (+) button and choose MySQL Connection from the drop-down list. The MySQL Connection dialog box is displayed, as shown in Figure 15-12.

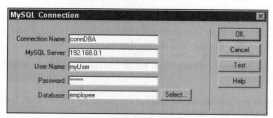

Figure 15-12: Just complete a few form items to set up your MySQL connections in PHP.

3. Enter a label for your new connection in the Connection Name field.

4. Enter the IP or domain address of your MySQL server in the MySQL Server field.

5. Enter your database user name in the User Name field.

6. Enter your database password in the Password field.

7. Enter the database name in the Database field, or click Select to get a list of all the databases to which you have access.

8. To ensure that your connection is properly set up, choose Test from the Custom Connection String dialog box. Dreamweaver will prompt you to let you know whether the test failed or succeeded.

9. Click OK when you're done to close the Custom Connection String dialog box. The new connection is listed in the Connections dialog box.

Managing Connections

In general, you create connections as needed and forget about them. All you have to do is include them in a page, and Dreamweaver handles the rest. However, there are occasions when existing connections must be altered, or outdated connections should be removed. All management of connections is handled inside the Databases panel.

To change the parameters of an existing connection, open the Databases panel, right-click (Control+click) on the connection, and select Edit. The type of connection determines which dialog box is then opened; a DSN connection, for example, opens the Data Source Name (DSN) dialog box.

Although you may alter any of the existing parameters during an editing session, you cannot switch from a DSN-type connection to a DSN-less type connection via the Edit option. Moreover, Dreamweaver will not allow you to rename an existing connection. To convert a connection from DSN to a DSN-less or OLE DB type connection, follow these steps:

1. Create a new connection of the desired type using one of the procedures described previously. This is a temporary connection that will be removed in the final step.

2. Right-click (Control+click) the old DSN connection from the Databases panel, and choose Delete Connection. It's a good idea to jot down the name of the original connection before deleting it; you use the same name later in this procedure.

3. Dreamweaver warns you that this action cannot be undone. Choose OK to proceed.

4. Right-click (Control+click) the new connection and choose Duplicate Connection. Depending on the type of connection being duplicated, either the Data Source Name or the Custom Connection String dialog box is displayed.

5. In the dialog box for the duplicated connection, enter the name of the original connection. Click OK when you're done.

6. In the Connections dialog box, delete the second, temporary connection by right-clicking (Control+clicking) and choosing Delete Connection.

Although the preceding procedure is somewhat convoluted, after you've completed it, you have effectively upgraded your connection from a DSN to an OLE DB type connection. The next time you put any of your Web pages on the remote server, be sure to include the dependent files for that page. Alternatively, you could put the file found in the Connections folder of the site on the server directly.

Extracting Recordsets

Establishing a connection with a data source is not enough to begin working with that data — you must explicitly state what part of the data you want, whether it's all of it or just one record. This defined collection of data is called a *recordset*.

Within the code, a query written in SQL is used to define a recordset. Dreamweaver provides two methods of building recordsets:

✦ The simple Recordset dialog box, which uses a subset of SQL to enable point-and-click recordset building

✦ The advanced Recordset dialog box, which exposes the SQL format and enables you to write your SQL statement directly

After you define a recordset, Dreamweaver displays the available columns in the Bindings panel for use in Web applications, as well as a few generic data items such as first record and last record. The columns may then be placed on the page wherever needed, much like an image from the Assets panel.

Building simple recordsets

Many recordsets are straightforward and can be expressed in a simple sentence:

"Show me all the salesmen in the Eastern region."

"Tell me which beers are currently on tap."

"Give me a list of all the CDs in my collection by Elvis Costello."

Dreamweaver provides a point-and-click interface for creating simple recordsets, one that does not require the developer to know or write SQL, as shown in Figure 15-13. You can think of working with the simple Recordset dialog box as drilling down to the required information. You start by selecting a previously defined connection. Within that connection, there may be many tables of data — in the simple Recordset dialog box, you may work with only one table. Once the table is selected, you choose which columns you need. You may use all of the columns, some of them, or just one. Because servers maintain a recordset in memory during its use, it's always best to select only the data you need. Next, you filter the selected columns to a particular set of data. If you leave the filter wide open, all the records will be available. In the simple recordset, you may use one column as a filter; in the previous examples, the filters would be something like "Region = Eastern"; "On Tap = Yes"; and "Artist = Elvis Costello." Finally, once you have defined a recordset, it may be sorted by one field in either an ascending or descending order.

Maintaining Design and Runtime Connections

The initial release of UltraDev enabled developers to set up two different connections — one for design time and one for runtime — with the same connection name. Dreamweaver no longer has this explicit capability, but with a little care it's possible, for example, to use a DSN connection locally and an OLE DB connection remotely.

The first step is to create the connection you'd like to use on the server and then put it on the site in the Connections folder. Next, create a local connection of a different type, named the same as the remote connection. Because Dreamweaver uses a server-side include referencing only the name of the file, your different connections will be the same on both locations.

Caution: The one caveat is that when uploading your local files to your remote site, you must not use Dreamweaver's Put Dependent Files option. If you do, Dreamweaver overwrites the remote connection file with the local one.

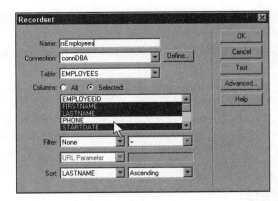

Figure 15-13: Although it is limited in power, the Recordset dialog box enables developers to construct a recordset without knowing SQL.

To create a simple recordset, follow these steps:

1. From either the Bindings panel or the Server Behaviors panel, click the Add (+) button and choose Recordset (Query) from the drop-down list.

   If neither panel is visible, select one of their icons from the Launcher on the status bar to bring the panel to the front.

2. In the Recordset dialog box, enter an identifying label for your recordset in the Name field.

   It's good practice to prefix your recordset name with rs — as in rsDBA. This prefix quickly identifies the recordset in the code.

3. Select a connection from the drop-down list of that name.

4. If the desired connection has not been declared, choose Define to open the Connections dialog box. After a connection has been selected, the available tables are shown.

5. Select a table to work with from the Tables drop-down list. The chosen table's fields are displayed in the Columns list.

6. By default, all of the columns are included in the recordset. To specify certain columns, choose the Selected option and then choose any desired field. Shift+click to select contiguous columns, and Ctrl+click (Command+click) to select columns not next to one another.

7. By default, all of the records in the selected columns will be available. To limit the recordset further, use the four Filter drop-down lists as follows:

   • Choose the field you want to base your filter on from the first drop-down list. This list changes dynamically according to which table you've selected.

   • From the second drop-down list, choose the expression you want to compare with the data from the selected column in the first drop-down list. Available expressions are =, >, <, >=, <=, <>, begins with, ends with, and contains. Most of these are obvious except for <>, which means "not equal to".

- Choose the type of value to compare to the selected field from the third drop-down list. Available types are as follows: URL Parameter, Form Variable, Cookie, Session Variable, Application Variable, or Entered Value. (These types are explained in the following bullet list.)

- Enter the value to compare to the selected field in the fourth input field. Values entered are not case-sensitive.

8. To sort the data, select a column from the first drop-down list under Sort, and then choose either Ascending or Descending from the second list.

9. At any time, you can see what results will be returned for the recordset by choosing Test.

Tip

To see how your simple recordset translates into SQL, choose the Advanced button. You can return to the original dialog box by selecting Simple on the advanced Recordset dialog box.

10. Click OK when you're done.

Perhaps the most challenging aspect to building a recordset is selecting the proper filter. Many Web applications rely on the filter mechanism of recordset queries to display the proper data. The following section describes how each of the different filter types is used:

✦ **URL Parameter:** URL parameters are arguments added onto the address of a page, typically by a form using the GET method. For example, the URL http://www.idest. com/mail_list.asp?email=jblow@anyhoo.com indicates that the e-mail field would be set to jblow@anyhoo.com. URL parameters are encoded so that no spaces or high ASCII characters are transmitted directly.

✦ **Form Variable:** Form variables are passed by forms using the Post method. Let's say, for example, a form is submitted in which there is a text field named emailText. Using the Form Variable type, you could derive a recordset based on the domain of the e-mail address submitted.

✦ **Cookie:** A cookie is a small text file placed on the client's machine, and it may be read or written to by a Web application. Cookies are often used for authentication. Once a user has been verified, the stored cookie value may be examined to permit — or deny — entrance to particular sections of the Web site.

✦ **Session Variable:** A session variable is similar to a cookie, but it is maintained on the server side. Session variables are often used to track a visitor's progress through the site.

✦ **Application Variable:** Application variables are maintained throughout the life of an application. Page counters are good examples of application variables. The life of an application lasts from the time the Web site starts (because the server was turned on or the site started) to the time the Web site stops (a server reboot or shutting down the site service).

✦ **Entered Value:** The entered value is an absolute value to which the selected field is compared. If, for example, I wanted to display only the DVDs in my database whose title started with the letter D, I would choose begins with as an operator, and D as my entered value.

Writing advanced SQL statements

The simple Recordset dialog box is perfectly suited for building recordsets derived from one table and determined by one parameter. Many Web applications, however, require data to be supplied from multiple, related tables based on numerous factors. The SQL language is flexible enough to handle the most complex query — and Dreamweaver provides the advanced Recordset dialog box for this very purpose. To get a better idea of what is meant by the phrase "advanced recordset," compare the following SQL for the plain language query "Show me all the salesmen in the Eastern region"

```
SELECT salesmen FROM employees WHERE region = "east"
```

to the SQL necessary for the query "Show me all the salesmen booking over $200,000 in sales in the Eastern and Southern regions"

```
SELECT salesmen FROM employees WHERE sales > 200000 AND ⮌
((region = "east") OR (region = "south"))
```

In Dreamweaver, the rule of thumb is as follows: Whenever any portion of your SQL query uses more than one component, you must use the advanced Recordset dialog box. The advanced Recordset dialog box, shown in Figure 15-14, is comprised of four main areas:

✦ The topmost section includes fields for entering the recordset's name and data source connection.

✦ The SQL section is comprised of a large text area. In whatever manner the query is entered into this area — directly, via copy and paste, or using the Database Items section — the SQL section contains the code that is executed to create the recordset.

Tip   To write advanced SQL queries, you can create your queries using the Query Builder in Microsoft Access or the View Builder in Microsoft SQL. Then you can copy and paste the generated SQL directly into the SQL window in Dreamweaver.

✦ The third area is used for defining variables to be included in the SQL query; variables defined here must be entered into the SQL area manually.

✦ The area marked Database Items contains an expandable tree of all the data items available through the currently selected connection, including all tables (and their associated columns), views (also known as *queries* in Access), and stored procedures. Next to the tree is a button for three of the major clauses of a SQL statement: SELECT, WHERE, and ORDER BY.

To create an advanced recordset, follow these steps:

1. From either the Bindings or the Server Behaviors panel, click the Add (+) button and choose Recordset (Query) from the drop-down list.

2. If the simple Recordset dialog box is displayed, choose Advanced. Dreamweaver displays the last type of Recordset dialog box accessed, so the next time you create a recordset, the advanced Recordset dialog box will be displayed.

3. In the advanced Recordset dialog box, enter an identifying label for your recordset in the Name field.

4. Select a connection from the drop-down list of that name.

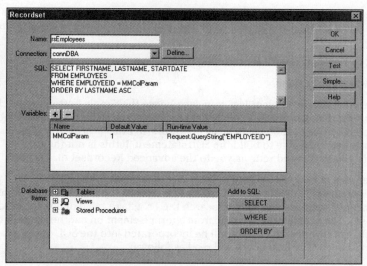

Figure 15-14: To work with more than one table or to filter against more than one field, use Dreamweaver's advanced Recordset dialog box.

5. If the desired connection has not been declared, choose Define to open the Connections dialog box. After a connection has been selected, the available tables are shown in the Database Items tree. With the connection selected, you may proceed either by entering your SQL query by hand or by using the Database Items tree.

6. To create your SQL statement manually, enter it directly into the SQL text area.

Tip

If you're using Microsoft Access for your database, you can create your query using the Access Query Builder, copy the code, switch to SQL View, and paste the code directly into the SQL text area. This is a fast way to create complex join statements and can save a lot of trouble-shooting time.

7. Select from the following to use the Database Items point-and-click method:

• For the Select clause of the SQL query, expand the Tables section of the tree to pick the desired table and, under that table, the desired column. With the column selected, choose Select.

You can only add one column at a time; repeat the preceding step to include additional columns.

• For the WHERE clause of the SQL query, choose the desired column and the Where button. Complete the clause by entering an operator (such as =, <, >, or LIKE) and a comparative value. The value may be a constant or a variable defined in the Variables area.

• For the ORDER BY clause of the SQL query, choose the desired column and select the Order By button. Add the keyword ASC for an ascending sort; add DESC for a descending sort.

8. To include a variable in the SQL statement, choose the Add button in the Variables section. Enter a name for the variable and its default and runtime values in the appropriate columns.

9. Choose Test to see what results are returned by your SQL query.

10. Choose OK when you're done.

After you complete your advanced recordset, you can choose the Simple button to switch to the simple Recordset dialog box *only* if the defined recordset references one table that is filtered and ordered by one column using basic operators. In other words, the simple Recordset dialog box has to be able to build the SQL statement. If this is not the case, Dreamweaver alerts you to this and returns you to the advanced Recordset dialog box.

To give you a better idea of how the advanced Recordset dialog box is used, let's look at a step-by-step procedure used to create the SQL query that returns the results of a user-run search. For this example, suppose you want to search the TripName table of dbadata.mdb (an Access database). The search criteria come from a form element on another page, a text field named searchText; the search criteria will be incorporated into the SQL query as a variable named varSearch. The final query will read as follows:

```
SELECT TRIPNAME
FROM TRIPS
WHERE TRIPNAME LIKE '%varsearch%'
ORDER BY TRIPNAME
```

Here's one approach to building this SQL query in the advanced Recordset dialog box:

1. First, open the advanced Recordset dialog box by clicking the Add (+) button on the Bindings panel and choosing Recordset (Query) from the drop-down list.

2. After choosing the appropriate connection, connDBA, begin building the SQL query.

3. In the Database Items section, expand the Tables tree and then select TRIPS. Finally, select TRIPNAME as the column under TRIPS.

4. With TRIPNAME highlighted, click Select.

   Dreamweaver puts the initial part of the query, SELECT TRIPNAME FROM TRIPS, in the SQL field.

5. While TRIPNAME is still selected, click Where. Dreamweaver adds the Where clause. The SQL query now reads as follows: SELECT TRIPNAME FROM TRIPS WHERE TRIPNAME.

6. With DEPARTUREDATE selected, click ORDER BY.

   After Dreamweaver adds the Order By clause, the SQL query reads as follows: SELECT TRIPNAME FROM TRIPS WHERE TRIPNAME ORDER BY DEPARTUREDATE. You've now done as much as you can with the Database Items section, and it's time to add the variables and keywords.

7. Under the Variables section, select the Add button and enter the following values (shown in parentheses):

   • **Name** (varSearch): This is the name that will appear in the SQL query.

   • **Default Value** (%): The percent sign acts as a wildcard character for most databases. The default value is inserted into the variable if no other value is entered. With a wildcard character as my default value, if the search is submitted with no criteria, all of the draught beers in the database will be returned.

• **Run-time Value** (`Request("searchText")`): The runtime value is the value submitted to the application server and returns with whatever was entered in the form from the input field named `searchText`.

Now that the variable is set up, you're ready to enter it into the SQL query.

8. In the SQL text field, add the phrase `LIKE '%varSearch%'` to the `WHERE TRIPNAME` clause, as shown in Figure 15-15. The `LIKE` operator compares two text fields; and the variable is put in quotes with wildcard characters, the percent sign, on either side. This use of wildcards ensures that the entire data string will be compared against the search criteria. Without these wildcards, only exact matches would return results.

Note   Keywords in SQL, such as `SELECT`, `FROM`, and `LIKE`, are often uppercased to distinguish them from field names and other code; however, it is not required.

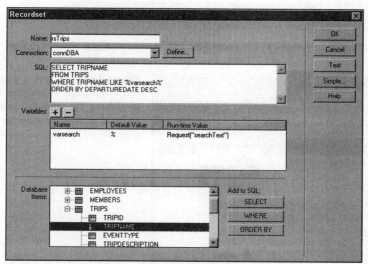

Figure 15-15: The LIKE operator, not available in the simple Recordset dialog box, is essential for constructing database searches.

9. The final step is to add the keyword ASC after the ORDER BY TRIPNAME clause. This specifies that my results will be sorted alphabetically, A-Z.

An alternative approach to the method just described would be to work out the SQL in advance and enter it directly into the SQL area without using the Database Items area at all. The only other element that would need to be included is the variable. Which approach should you use? If you need to include complicated field names, I recommend using the point-and-click method to avoid typos. This method is also useful when you are using columns from different tables that have the same name; in this situation, Dreamweaver prepends the table name followed by a period, as follows: `TRIPS.TRIPNAME`.

Working with recordsets

Recordsets need to be modified from time to time. To alter an existing recordset, double-click its name in the Bindings panel. The Recordset dialog box will reopen with the existing values. Which Recordset dialog box opens — simple or advanced — depends on two things: whether the recordset can be displayed only in the advanced dialog box and which dialog box was open last. If, for example, you are working with a simple recordset but had the advanced Recordset dialog box open last, the advanced Recordset dialog box will open.

Caution   When you're editing the recordset, be sure you're double-clicking its name, rather than the plus or minus sign or the symbol in front of the name. Double-clicking the symbols only expands and collapses the recordset tree.

It's not unusual for the same recordsets to be used on different pages — and it's even more likely that similar recordsets will be. Dreamweaver allows you to copy a recordset from one page to another. While this is good for the occasional times you need to use the same recordset on multiple pages, it's great for the frequent times when recordsets are only slightly different. To copy a recordset from one page to another, follow these steps:

1. In the Bindings panel, select the recordset you'd like to copy.

2. Right click (Control+click) the recordset and choose Copy, as shown in Figure 15-16.

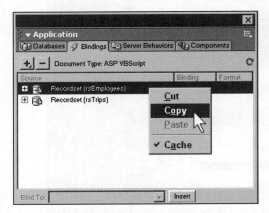

Figure 15-16: Copying a recordset from one page to another and then modifying the copy is a quick way to build similar recordsets.

3. Open the page to which you want to copy the recordset.

4. From the context menu of the Bindings panel, choose Paste. Alternatively, you can also choose Edit ➪ Paste or use the keyboard shortcut, Ctrl+V (Command+V). However, you may only use the Copy command from the context menu of the Bindings panel.

Deleting a recordset from a page is very straightforward. Simply select the recordset from the Bindings panel and choose the Remove (–) button.

Summary

Although some Web applications don't use a data source, the vast majority do. Dreamweaver enables you to connect to any data source for which you have a driver through a variety of methods, ranging from simplest to most robust. With a connection established, setting up a recordset is the essential next step. Only after a recordset has been created can you place data on a Dreamweaver page. Mastering these two conditions gives your Dreamweaver Web applications the access they require and the data they need. As you are laying the foundation for your Dreamweaver pages, keep the following points in mind:

✦ A Dreamweaver connection—once defined—is available sitewide. Dreamweaver uses one server-side include per page for each connection, but the connection file itself only needs to be uploaded to the site once.

✦ Although DSN connections are the most straightforward, they also carry the greatest overhead. Whenever possible, use OLE DB connections for the runtime connection.

✦ ASP developers may use the `Server.MapPath()` function to determine the physical location of their database on a remote system. Dreamweaver allows `Server.MapPath()` to be used in a custom connection string as well.

✦ Dreamweaver offers two entirely different interfaces for creating recordsets. The simple Recordset dialog box can create recordsets relying on a single table and a single criterion, whereas the advanced Recordset dialog box offers unlimited options, permitting you to write your own SQL query.

✦ Recordsets may be copied from one page to another. Once copied, you can modify the recordset to receive a different set of data with a minimum of effort.

In the next chapter, you'll learn how basic text is inserted, edited, and styled in Dreamweaver.

✦　　✦　　✦

Making Data Dynamic

◆ ◆ ◆ ◆

In This Chapter

Integrating text
from a data source

Formatting dynamic text

Inserting graphics
dynamically

Working with
Flash dynamically

◆ ◆ ◆ ◆

By the time an active Web page is seen in a visitor's browser, the data should blend seamlessly into the rest of the page. Like a well-crafted form letter, the reader shouldn't be able to tell where the basic structure starts and the dynamically generated data begins. Much of the work in Dreamweaver consists of properly placing and formatting your data into a page layout.

You're not limited to dynamically integrating basic text into your Web applications with Dreamweaver. After text is included, you can format its look and feel on both the client and the server sides. Additionally, you can include images, form elements like checkboxes and drop-down lists, and even multimedia such as Flash movies on the fly. Finally, Dreamweaver permits almost any HTML attribute to be dynamically altered. This chapter explores all the fundamentals necessary for integrating dynamic data into your Web page.

Working with Dynamic Text

The Bindings panel is the key tool for accessing dynamic text. With a recordset expanded, any or all of the available fields within it are ready to be placed on the page. Moreover, after a field is inserted into the page and selected, the Bindings panel reflects its current data format.

 Cross-Reference Before you begin including dynamic data in your pages, you need to set them with a data source connection and a recordset, so be sure you're familiar with the techniques described in Chapter 15 before proceeding.

Inserting dynamic text

After you have a recordset or other data source declared, adding dynamic text is as simple as dragging a field name onto the page. After the field is inserted, by default Dreamweaver displays it with the syntax {`recordset_name.field_name`}. For example, the column named RETURNDATE located in a recordset named rsTrips would be displayed as {`rsTrips.RETURNDATE`}. If the View ⇨ Visual Aids ⇨ Invisible Elements option is enabled, the inserted data is highlighted as shown in Figure 16-1, according to the color selected in Preferences.

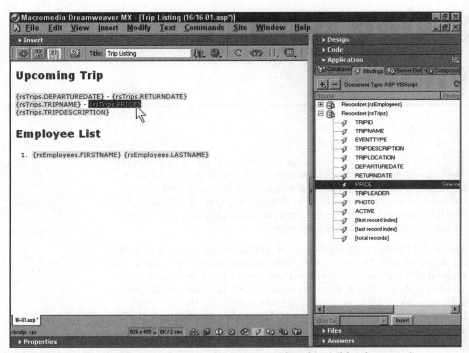

Figure 16-1: Placeholders for dynamic data are considered invisible elements in Dreamweaver and highlighted accordingly.

Dynamic pages are a combination of standard HTML and dynamic elements. It's possible to build the page in any order: You can insert your dynamic elements first, followed by HTML objects; or you can take the reverse approach and build the HTML page before adding your data. Many designers, whether they're working by themselves or on a team, find the latter method more productive. One common technique is to use static placeholders to mark where the dynamic data should go, as shown in Figure 16-2.

Perhaps the quickest way to bring dynamic data onto the page is to use the drag-and-drop capability, as detailed in the following steps:

1. In the Document window, select the static placeholder text that will be replaced by the dynamic data.

2. From the Bindings panel, expand your recordset or other data source until the desired field or dynamic element is displayed.

3. Drag the dynamic data from the Bindings panel and drop it on the selected text.

   If you are not using placeholder text, you can drop the dynamic data wherever you'd like it to appear.

In some situations, for example when a table has many dynamic data fields, the Insert method is easier than the drag-and-drop technique. For those cases, first select the placeholder text — or position your cursor if there are no placeholders. Then highlight the desired dynamic data and choose Insert from the bottom of the Bindings panel.

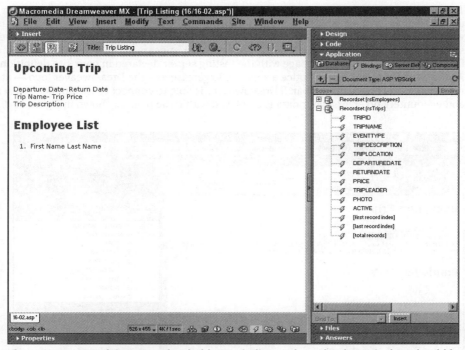

Figure 16-2: Use plain HTML placeholders to indicate where the dynamic data should be dropped from the Bindings panel.

Tip

Occasionally the dot notation syntax leads to extremely long names, which can make the layout process more difficult. You can switch from using the curly braces and full data name to just using the curly braces — and back again — by choosing the desired option from the Show Dynamic Text As drop-down list found under the Invisible Elements category of Preferences.

Viewing dynamic data

There are three basic ways to see your page with the data extracted from the data source and fully integrated into the HTML:

✦ Upload the page to your remote testing server and view it through a Web browser.

✦ Use Dreamweaver's Preview in Browser feature to test your page on the testing server. Dreamweaver takes care of uploading the files for you.

✦ Switch to Live Data view within Dreamweaver.

The final method is, by far, the handiest to use during the design process, although the other two methods are important and should be included in a regular routine of Web application development. Live Data view has one key advantage over the other methods: You can continue to work on your page with the data in place. This facility is a major boon to application productivity.

To quickly see your data within the page choose View ⇨ Live Data. Alternatively, you can use the keyboard shortcut, Ctrl+Shift+R (Command+Shift+R) or, if the Document toolbar is visible, select Show Live Data View. However you choose to enter into Live Data view, you'll see the same actions take place. The Live Data toolbar appears in the Document window as Dreamweaver processes your page with the testing server declared in your site definition. As the page processes, you'll notice a spinning lowercase *d* — the Dreamweaver logo — at the right end of the Live Data toolbar. If Dreamweaver is able to connect to the application server and encounters no errors, your data is displayed within the page as shown in Figure 16-3.

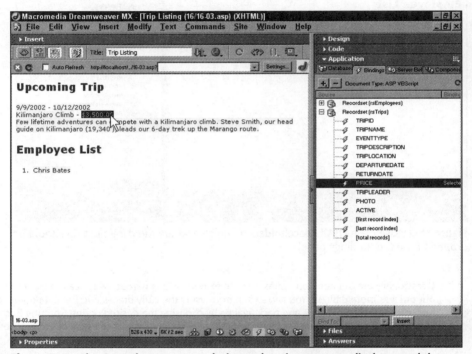

Figure 16-3: Live Data view uses your designated testing server to display actual data from your data source during design time.

Within Live Data view, you can use Dreamweaver as you would normally. If the Auto Refresh option, found on the Live Data toolbar, is enabled, any new dynamic data added to the page from the Bindings panel is automatically converted from a placeholder to the recordset data. Without any additional server behaviors — most notably Repeat Region — all data displayed is from the first record of the chosen recordset.

Cross-Reference   Live Data view has many more features than are noted here — all of which are covered in Chapter 18.

Formatting Dynamic Data

After a field has been incorporated into a page, the field acts just like any other text within a tag. Dynamic text may be stylized with either HTML tags—such as ⟨h2⟩, ⟨b⟩, or ⟨font⟩—or with Cascading Style Sheet classes. The easiest method is simply to replace the static placeholder text, styled as your layout demands, with the dynamic text. The tags and CSS classes surrounding any dynamic text can be altered at any time.

Tip   It's also possible to include HTML tags in the stored data. When the data is included in the page, the browser interprets the HTML normally. For example, you can have a memo field in an Access database (for data containing more than 255 characters) with italic tags (⟨i⟩) surrounding key phrases. This is perfectly acceptable to Access—which sees the tags as just text—and perfectly acceptable to Dreamweaver.

Data formatting

Dreamweaver not only supports client-side formatting of your dynamic data—with HTML tags and CSS classes—it also offers a wide range of server-side formats, plus it gives you the ability to create your own. Information is stored in databases according to a particular type; some fields may be designated as text, whereas others may be numbers and still others fall under the date/time category. The same data type within a specific category may be formatted in numerous ways.

Dates are a good example of why data formatting is important. In the United States, dates are typically presented in a month-day-year format, such as March 31, 2002. In much of the rest of the world, however, dates are presented in a day-month-year format, as in 31 March 2002. By default, servers are generally set to display dates appropriate to their regions. The same holds true for currency: U.S. currency figures are presented with a dollar sign, whereas U.K. currency is shown as euros or English pounds.

When initially inserted onto the page from the Bindings panel, dynamic data does not have a specific format applied. Data from currency and time/date use the default formats for their data types. Different formats are chosen from the Bindings panel, as outlined in the following steps:

1. Select the dynamic data that you want to format from the Document window. The corresponding field in the Bindings panel is highlighted.

2. From the Bindings panel, select the down arrow under the Format column to reveal the Format List, as shown in Figure 16-4.

Tip   The Bindings panel is usually pretty narrow. The Format column may be hidden off the right side of the screen. Use the scrollbar to move to the right, resize the Source column to make it narrower or simply make the Bindings panel wider to get access to the right-hand columns.

3. From the Format List, select the appropriate category for your data.

4. If more than one format is available, choose a specific format from the category's submenu.

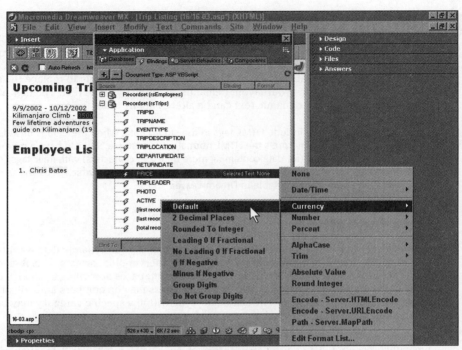

Figure 16-4: The Format List, which is different for each server model, lets you specify your data's format according to its type.

To see the newly applied format, choose View ➪ Live Data or select the Live Data button from the Document toolbar.

Tip If you're already in Live Data view, enable the Auto Refresh option when applying new formats. Dreamweaver will reprocess the page and display your new formats automatically.

Each of Dreamweaver's five server models offers slightly different data formats through the Bindings panel. You'll find complete lists of all the standard data formats, with relevant examples, in Tables 16-1 (ASP), 16-2 (ColdFusion), 16-3 (JSP), 16-4 (.NET) and 16-5 (PHP).

Table 16-1: ASP Data Formats

Format	Option	Example
Date/Time	General Format	3/31/2001
	Long Format	Saturday, March 31, 2001
	Short Format	3/31/2001
	Weekday, Month Date, Year	Saturday, March 31, 2001
	Date Month Year	31 March 2001
	Month Date, Year	March 31, 2001
	YY-M-DD	01-3-31
	YY-MM-DD	01-03-31
	DD-MM-YYYY	31-03-2001
	M/D/YY	3/31/01
	DD/MM/YY	31/03/01
	YY/MM/DD	01/03/31
	Long Time Format	9:15:00 PM
	Short Time Format	21:15
	h:MM:SS AM/PM	9:15:00 PM
	HH:MM:SS	21:15:00
	hh:MM:SS a.m./p.m.	09:15:00 p.m.
	HH:MM	21:15
Currency	Default	$2,300.99
	2 Decimal Places	$23.99
	Rounded to Integer	$23.51 = $24
	Leading 0 If Fractional	$0.99
	No Leading 0 If Fractional	$.99
	( ) If Negative	($23.99)
	Minus If Negative	-$23.99
	Group Digits	$2,300.99
	Do Not Group Digits	$2300.99
Number	Default	2,300
	2 Decimal Places	23.00
	Rounded to Integer	23.51 = 24
	Leading 0 If Fractional	0.99
	No Leading 0 If Fractional	.99
	( ) If Negative	(23)
	Minus If Negative	-23
	Group Digits	2,300
	Do Not Group Digits	2300

Continued

Table 16-1: *(continued)*

Format	Option	Example
Percent	Default	2,300%
	2 Decimal Places	23.00%
	Rounded to Integer	23.51% = 24%
	Leading 0 If Fractional	0.99%
	No Leading 0 If Fractional	.99%
	( ) If Negative	(23%)
	Minus If Negative	-23%
	Group Digits	2,300%
	Do Not Group Digits	2300%
AlphaCase	Upper	Mixed Case = MIXED CASE
	Lower	Mixed Case = mixed case
Trim	Left	" Widgets " = "Widgets "
	Right	" Widgets " = " Widgets"
	Both	" Widgets " = "Widgets"
Absolute Value	N/A	+23 or -23 = 23
Round Integer	N/A	23.51 = 24
Encode — Server. HTMLEncode	N/A	I'm bold = I'm <b>bold</b>
Encode — Server. URLEncode	N/A	www.idest.com/Party Time = www.idest.com/Party%20Time
Path — Server.MapPath	N/A	Server.MapPath(/myDocs) = D:/HTDOCS/lowery/myDocs

Table 16-2: ColdFusion Data Formats

Format	Option	Example
Date/Time	General Date Format	31-Mar-01
	Weekday, Month Date, Year	Saturday, March 31, 2001
	Date Month Year	31 March 2001
	Month Date, Year	March 31, 2001
	DD-MM-YY	31-03-01
	YY-M-DD	01-3-31
	YY-MM-DD	01-03-31
	DD-MM-YYYY	31-03-2001
	M/D/YY	3/31/01
	DD/MM/YY	31/03/01
	YY/MM/DD	01/03/31
	General Time Format	9:15 PM
	h:MM:SS AM/PM	9:15:00 PM
	HH:MM:SS	21:15:00
	hh:MM:SS A/P	09:15:00 P
	HH:MM	21:15
Currency	General Format	2,300.99
	Dollar Format	$2,300.99
	Local Format	$2,300.99
	International Format	USD2,300.00
Number	Default	2,300.99
	2 Decimal Places	23.99
	Rounded to Integer	23.51 = $24
	() If Negative	(23.99)
	Minus If Negative	-23.99
	Do Not Group Digits	2300.99
AlphaCase	Upper	Mixed Case = MIXED CASE
	Lower	Mixed Case = mixed case
Trim	Left	" Widgets " = "Widgets "
	Right	" Widgets " = " Widgets"
	Both	" Widgets " = "Widgets"
	StripCR	"TheEnd" = "The End"

Continued

Table 16-2: *(continued)*

Format	Option	Example
Math	Abs	Returns the absolute value
	Atn	Returns the arctangent
	Ceiling	Returns the next highest integer
	Cos	Returns the cosine
	DecrementValue	Lowers the number by 1
	Exp	Returns the exponent
	Fix	Rounds the number toward zero
	IncrementValue	Increases the number by 1
	Int	Returns an integer
	Log	Returns the natural logarithm
	Log10	Returns the logarithm to base 10
	Randomize	Seeds the random number generator
	Round	Rounds to the closest integer
	Sgn	Returns 1 for positive numbers, -1 for negative numbers
	Sin	Returns the sine
	Sqr	Returns the square root
	Tan	Returns the tangent
Encode — URLEncoded Format	N/A	www.idest.com/Party Time = www.idest.com/Party%20Time
Encode — PreserveSingleQuotes	N/A	'The Answer' = 'The Answer'
String — Reverse	N/A	'The Answer' = 'rewsnA ehT'

Table 16-3: JSP Data Formats

Format	Option	Example
Date/Time	General Format	31-Mar-01
	Long Format	Saturday, March 31, 2001
	Short Format	3/31/01
	Weekday, Month Date, Year	Saturday, March 31, 2001
	Date Month Year	31 March 2001
	Month Date, Year	March 31, 2001
	YY-M-DD	01-3-31
	YY-MM-DD	01-03-31
	M/D/YY	3/31/01
	DD/MM/YY	31/03/01

Format	Option	Example
Currency	Default	$2,300.99
	2 Decimal Places	$23.99
	Rounded to Integer	$23.51 = $24
	() If Negative	($23.99)
	Minus If Negative	-$23.99
	Group Digits	$2,300.99
	Do Not Group Digits	$2300.99
Percent	Default	2,300%
	2 Decimal Places	23.00%
	Rounded to Integer	23.51% = 24%
	() If Negative	(23%)
	Minus If Negative	-23%
	Group Digits	2,300%
	Do Not Group Digits	2300%
Number	Default	2,300.99
	2 Decimal Places	23.99
	Rounded to Integer	23.51 = $24
	() If Negative	(23.99)
	Minus If Negative	-23.99
	Group Digits	2,300.99
	Do Not Group Digits	2300.99
AlphaCase	Upper	Mixed Case = MIXED CASE
	Lower	Mixed Case = mixed case
Trim - Both	N/A	" Widgets " = "Widgets"
Math	Absolute Value (Double)	Returns a double precision number
	Absolute Value (Float)	Returns a floating point number
	Absolute Value (Integer)	Returns an integer
	Absolute Value (Long)	Retuns a long integer
	Round Integer (Double)	Rounds to the nearest double precision integer
	Round Integer (Float)	Rounds to the nearest floating point integer
Encode – Response. EncodeURL	N/A	www.idest.com/Party Time = www.idest.com/Party%20Time
Path – GetRealPath	N/A	GetRealPath('/myDocs') = D:/HTDOCS/lowery/myDocs

Table 16-4: .NET Data Formats

Format	Option	Example
Date/Time	17-01-2001 Monday, January 17, 2001 January 17 January, 2001 2:35 PM 2:35:18 PM	17-01-2001 Monday, January 17, 2001 January 17 January, 2001 2:35 PM 2:35:18 PM
Currency	Default	$2,300.99
Percent	Default Round	2,300% 23.51% = 24%
Number	Default Round	2,300.99 23.51 = 24
AlphaCase	Upper Lower	Mixed Case = MIXED CASE Mixed Case = mixed case
Trim	Left Right Both	" Widgets " = "Widgets " " Widgets " = " Widgets" " Widgets " = "Widgets"
Encode — HTMLEncodedFormat	N/A	I'm bold = I'm <b>bold</b>
Encode — URLEncodedFormat	N/A	www.idest.com/Party Time = www.idest.com/Party%20Time
Map — Server.MapPath	N/A	Server.MapPath(/myDocs) = D:/HTDOCS/lowery/myDocs

Table 16-5: PHP Data Formats

Format	Option	Example
AlphaCase	Lower	My Widgets = my widgets
	Upper	My Widgets = MY WIDGETS
	First Letter Upper	My Widgets = My widgets
	Capitalize	My Widgets = My Widgets
Trim	Left	" Widgets " = "Widgets "
	Right	" Widgets " = " Widgets"
	Both	" Widgets " = "Widgets"
Encode	HTML Encode	I'm bold =I'm <b>bold</b>
	URL Encode	www.idest.com/Party Time = www.idest.com/Party+Time
	Raw URL Encode	www.idest.com/Party Time = ww.idest.com/Party%20Time
	URL Decode	www.idest.com/Party+Time = www.idest.com/Party Time
	Raw URL Decode	www.idest.com/Party%20Time = www.idest.com/Party Time

Editing and creating new data formats

Although Dreamweaver includes a wide variety of format selections, there are times when only a custom format will do. In Dreamweaver, you may edit existing currency, number, or percent formats, or you may create your own version of any of these types from scratch. After a new format has been defined — or an old one has been altered — that format is available for any sites using the same server model under which it was created. To edit or create a new data format, follow these steps:

1. Select the inserted dynamic data in the Document window that requires the custom format. The corresponding field is highlighted in the Bindings panel.

2. From the Bindings panel, select the down arrow in the Format column and choose Edit Format List from the drop-down menu. The Edit Format List dialog, shown in Figure 16-5, is displayed.

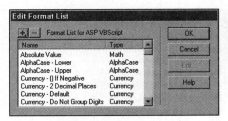

Figure 16-5: Only currency, number, and percent format types may be edited or created through the Edit Format List dialog box.

3. To alter an existing currency, number, or percent format, select the format and choose Edit. If you prefer to create an entirely new format, choose Add and from the pop-up list, select Number, Currency, or Percent. The appropriate dialog box opens, depending on the format type selected. If you attempt to edit a format other than the three types allowed, Dreamweaver notes that this format has no parameters to customize.

It's not possible to edit any of the built-in formats or add additional formats in the .NET server model without manually editing the format configuration files in the Dreamweaver Configuration folder.

Although each of the dialog boxes offers different options, they work exactly the same. You can also choose Get More Formats from the drop-down list to go directly to the Macromedia Exchange.

4. In the Number, Currency, or Percent dialog box, design your format by adjusting the four available drop-down lists:

   • **# Digits after Decimal Point:** Choose a value from 0 to 20

   • **Leading Zero** (if Fraction): Select Yes, No, or Default for locale

   • **Negative:** Select Parentheses, Minus sign, or Default for locale

   • **Group Digits:** Select Yes, No, or Default for locale

5. Select OK when you're done to close the specific format dialog box.

6. Give the format a name to be displayed in the Format column in the Bindings panel.

7. To edit or create another format, repeat Steps 3 through 6.

8. To delete a format, select it from the list, and choose Remove.

9. Click OK when you're done.

After you've finished editing the Format List, Dreamweaver applies your newly created format to the selected dynamic data. Use the Live Data view to preview your new format.

There is a known problem with Windows 98 and the Edit Format List option. After applying an edited format (not a new one) to the dynamic data, Dreamweaver correctly identifies the format name in the Bindings panel. However, if you deselect the dynamic data and then re-select it, the Bindings panel Format column indicates that None is applied. Although the name is not shown, the code has not changed, and the data will render appropriately. To avoid this issue, create a new format with the desired options.

Additional Time/Date Formatting

The Edit Format List option works well for currency, number, and percent formats, but it does not permit new time and/or date formats. I recently built a site where the client wanted the time to be shown in a particular way, as, for example, 9PM. The closest format in Dreamweaver would display that time as 9:00:00 PM. To show the time as desired, I needed to add some hand-coding.

This site uses an ASP server model with VBScript as its scripting language. My first task was to show only the hour portion of time. VBScript has a function that does exactly this, aptly named Hour(). When applied to my dynamic data code, it looks like this:

```
<%=Hour(rsEvents.Fields.Item("showTime").Value) %>
```

Unfortunately, the Hour() function returns values according to a 24-hour clock (also known as military time), so 9PM becomes 21. The second, and related problem, is that the Hour() function only returns a number and does not include an AM or PM designation. To solve these problems, I wrote a small ASP routine that incorporated the Dreamweaver generated code:

```
<%
Dim myTime, myShift
myShift = "AM"
myTime = Hour(rsEvents.Fields.Item("showTime").Value)
If (myTime > 12) Then
    myTime = myTime-12
    myShift = "PM"
End If
Response.write myTime & myShift
%>
```

This routine works well for my site, but would have to be modified to handle 12 Noon and 12 Midnight circumstances. In addition to the Hour() function, VBScript has similar functions to extract other time elements: Minute() and Second(). For dates, use the comparable Month(), Day(), and Year() functions. All these functions return number values, which you can convert to names by further use of the MonthName() function. The Weekday() and WeekdayName() functions are used together to display either full or abbreviated day names. For example, if I wanted the date as Sunday, February 11 — without the year imposed by Dreamweaver's standard formats, I would use code like this:

```
<%= WeekdayName(Weekday((rsEvents.Fields.Item("showDate").Value)))
& ", "
MonthName(Month((rsEvents.Fields.Item("showDate").Value)))
& " "
Day((rsEvents.Fields.Item("showDate").Value))
%>
```

ColdFusion developers have a much easier way of manipulating times and dates with the TimeFormat() and DateFormat() functions. For example, here's the ColdFusion code for displaying a date in my example format (such as Sunday, February 11):

```
#DateFormat("#rsEvents.showDate#", "dddd, mmmm d")#
```

Making Images Dynamic

The Web is both a textual and visual medium. You've seen how Dreamweaver replaces static text with dynamic text from a database. But how does it handle images? Dreamweaver dynamically inserts images by using the path to the image rather than the image itself. Proper database setup is critical for Dreamweaver to correctly deliver dynamic images. For example, a product database might have the following records:

SKU#	Name	Cost	Image
10101	Widget-O-Wonder	$99.99	/images/products/w_wonder.gif
10102	WidgetMatic	$49.99	/images/products/w_matic.gif
10103	Widget-Ultimo	$999.99	/images/products/w_ultimo.gif

In this example, Dreamweaver extracts the data from the Image field and plugs that data into an attribute of the `<img>` tag, `src`. Because site-root–relative links are used in the data source, the images may be inserted dynamically from any page in the site. If your dynamic images are located on a remote server, a full URL—with the `http://` prefix—should be entered in a text field in the data source.

Caution   Some databases, including Microsoft Access, allow fields to be set up as hyperlink types. Although it may seem logical, fields containing paths to images should not be a hyperlink type, but rather a text type. Hyperlink type fields are for use only inside Access applications and should never be used for live sites. Hyperlink type images already include the HTML code for a link. That won't work in Dreamweaver.

It is also possible to use document-relative pathnames in image fields of the database. However, you have to be careful which pages the dynamic images are inserted into; the pages must be stored in the proper location, relative to the path of the images.

Perhaps the best course of action is to store just the filenames of the images themselves in the data source. When the dynamic image is inserted into Dreamweaver, additional path information may be added as needed. For example, suppose the image field contained only filenames with no path information, like w_wonder.gif in a field name images of a recordset rsProducts. Here's an example of how that code would be generated by Dreamweaver for ASP:

```
<%=(rsProducts.Fields.Item("images").Value)%>
```

In Dreamweaver, you can preface that code—either when it is inserted or through the Property inspector—with any necessary path information. If my document is at the site root and the images are stored in the /images/products folder, I adjust the code like this:

```
images/products/<%=(rsProducts.Fields.Item("images").Value)%>
```

After your data source is correctly set up for images, inserting them in Dreamweaver is very straightforward, as shown in the following steps:

1. Make sure you define a recordset with at least one field consisting of paths to graphics.

2. Position your cursor where you want your dynamic image to appear.

3. From the Common category of the Insert bar, select Insert Image.

   Alternatively, you can drag the Insert Image button to the proper place on the page. In either case, the Select Image Source dialog box appears.

4. From the Select Image Source dialog, Windows users should choose the Select File Name From Data Sources option at the top of the page. Macintosh users should select the Data Source button found just above the URL field.

5. If necessary, expand the data source to locate and select the desired image field, as shown in Figure 16-6. Dreamweaver places the code for inserting the dynamic image into the URL field.

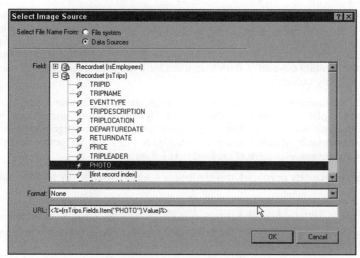

Figure 16-6: When inserting a dynamic image, you only need to specify the data source and field. Dreamweaver automatically inserts the image with the correct dimensions.

6. If your image data (the paths to the images) contains spaces, tildes, or other nonstandard characters, the data must be encoded properly to be read by the server. From the Format List, select Encode — Server.HTMLEncode (ASP); Encode — HTMLEncodedFormat (.NET); Encode — URLEncoded Format (ColdFusion), or Encode — Response.EncodeURL (JSP).

7. If your data is stored as filenames only, enter any required path in the URL field before the existing code. The path information may be document-relative, site-root–relative, or absolute.

8. Click OK when you're done.

You can get a quick view of your work by choosing View ➪ Live Data or selecting the Live Data button from the Document toolbar. The placeholder icon for the dynamic image will initially appear in its default size of 32 × 32 pixels, but will expand to full size after Live Data is enabled or the page is viewed through the testing server.

If you use static graphic placeholders in your design, you can use an alternative technique. From the Bindings panel, drag the field containing the image names onto the static graphic. If your data is just filenames without path information, you'll have to add the required path to the beginning of the src attribute in the Property inspector or Tag inspector

Note   Some databases support storing the actual images as a Binary Large Object (BLOB). The BLOB protocol is not supported directly in Dreamweaver.

Altering attributes dynamically

Just as you can assign a dynamic value to the <img> tag's src attribute, you can assign any data source–derived value to any other attribute by *binding* or attaching the field to the attribute. Attributes are generally assigned dynamic values through the Bindings panel or the Property inspector. Once assigned, the Bindings panel displays which attribute is attached to which field in the Binding column. A data field used for dynamic images, for instance, shows img.src in its Binding column.

I recently used Dreamweaver to create a content-management system for a client. The page uses a standard template with areas for the heading, bylines, content, and images, served dynamically according to the topic. The images each have a specific alignment — some are set to the browser default, whereas others are aligned left or right. To handle this properly, a separate field for image alignment is created in the data source.

With the database properly prepared, the attributes are set dynamically by following these steps:

1. Select the placeholder for the dynamic image, already inserted on the page.

2. From the Bindings panel, select the field that contains the data for the attribute you'd like to dynamically generate.

3. At the bottom of the Bindings panel, choose the desired attribute from the Bind To list, or click the down arrow in the Binding column as shown in Figure 16-7.

   The Bind To list changes according to the object selected. To change the alignment on an <img> tag, choose img.align from the list.

4. Select Bind. The selected attribute is displayed in the Binding column of the chosen field.

To get an idea of what's possible, select a dynamic image and then look at the list in the Binding column. The <img> tag offers 21 different attributes that may be dynamically generated — everything from the heavily recommended alt parameter to the special case vrml attribute.

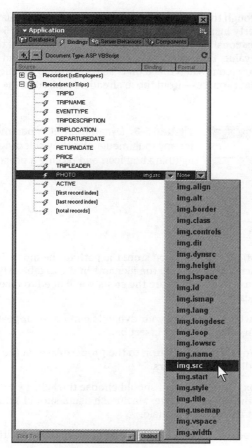

Figure 16-7: Change more than just the image dynamically by using the Bind To feature to link any tag attribute to a data source.

Integrating Flash and Other Dynamic Media

Just as text and images may be inserted into documents on-the-fly, all manner of multimedia—including Flash and files requiring ActiveX controls or applets—may also be dynamically incorporated. The core technique of attaching a data source is the same for multimedia files as it is for images; when you insert a multimedia object, choose the desired data source from Dreamweaver's dialog box. The linking code will automatically be written into the proper parameter for the object.

Most multimedia objects are inserted into HTML by using an <object> tag, an <embed> tag, or a combination of the two; Java applets use the <applet> tag. Dreamweaver handles the basic file assignments for specific programs with its own icon in the Insert bar. Examples are Flash, Director, and Generator. If, however, you examine the code, you'll see that even these objects use the <param> tag, short for *parameter*, to declare the source of the media file. ActiveX and applet files rely on <param> tags to specify needed attributes. Dreamweaver allows you to choose either static or dynamic values for any <param> tag.

The <param> values are entered through the Parameters dialog box, which is displayed when the Parameters button on the Property inspector is selected. As shown in Figure 16-8, the Dreamweaver Parameters dialog box consists of two columns, one for the name of the parameter and one for the corresponding value. Entries in either column may be assigned dynamic content by selecting the lightning bolt icon. When this icon is selected, the Dynamic Data dialog box opens and an appropriate data source—from those already declared in the Bindings panel—may be assigned.

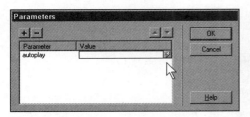

Figure 16-8: Dynamically alter parameters for any multimedia object by selecting the lightning bolt icon and picking a proper data source.

If you're dynamically switching Flash movies, how you store the path to the movie is critical. As with images, perhaps the best tactic is to use only the filename in the database field and supply additional path information as needed. Here are the steps you'll need to take to display different Flash movies, dynamically:

1. With your cursor positioned where you'd like your dynamic content to appear, click Insert Flash from the Common category of the Insert bar.

   Alternatively, you can drag the Insert Flash button to the proper place on the page. In either case, the Select File dialog box appears.

2. From the Select File dialog box, Windows users should choose the Select File Name From Data Sources option at the top of the page. Macintosh users should select the Data Source button found just above the URL field.

3. If necessary, expand the data source to locate and select the desired field with the Flash movie filenames.

4. If your Flash data (the paths to the movies) contains spaces, tildes, or other nonstandard characters, the data must be encoded to be read properly by the server. From the Format List, select Encode—Server.HTMLEncode (ASP); Encode—HTMLEncodedFormat (.NET); Encode—URLEncoded Format (ColdFusion), or Encode—Response.EncodeURL (JSP).

5. If your data is stored as filenames only, enter any required path in the URL field before the existing code.

6. You can also link any Flash attributes to a dynamic source by choosing the Parameters button. After the Parameters dialog box is open, enter a dynamic value by selecting the lightning bolt symbol under the Name or Value column and choosing an appropriate data source from the Dynamic Data dialog box.

7. Click OK when you're finished.

Cross-Reference

For more details on integrating Flash movies in your Web pages, see Chapter 25.

Summary

Incorporating dynamic data into your standard Web pages is a core technology for data-driven Web applications, along with establishing a data source connection and defining a recordset. After you have these three components in place, you can begin combining HTML pages with text, images, and even multimedia data. Dreamweaver combines sophisticated connectivity with drag-and-drop simplicity for quick insertion of dynamic content. Keep the following items in mind as you begin to integrate data-driven and static content:

✦ The Bindings panel displays fields available for inserting into a Web document, much like the Assets panel, which shows available images and other elements. Like the Assets panel, data is inserted from the Bindings panel through a drag-and-drop procedure. For complex layouts, you can position your cursor precisely and choose the Insert button instead of dragging-and-dropping the dynamic fields.

✦ Dynamic text accepts two types of formatting: client-side and server-side. Client-side formatting is another term for standard HTML and CSS formatting; dynamic text may be styled with the same tags and attributes as regular text. The final look for these tags and attributes is interpreted by the browser. Server-side formatting, on the other hand, reshapes the data from the data source before it passes it on to the browser.

✦ If you encounter trouble inserting dynamic images into your Web applications, chances are you're not doing anything wrong in Dreamweaver, but rather the error may lie in your database setup. It's key to store the path and/or filename of the images in the data source as a text field rather than as a hyperlink.

✦ Dreamweaver does not support loading images as binary images from data sources, otherwise known as Binary Large Objects (BLOBs).

✦ Flash movies — in fact, any multimedia file — may be dynamically inserted into a Dreamweaver page. Again, storing just the filename or, at most, the filename and path in the database field is the best approach.

✦ Any attribute, whether to a multimedia object or regular image, may be dynamically derived. The Parameters dialog offers options for inputting either dynamic or static attributes and values on multimedia objects, and the Bindings panel allows you to bind dynamic data to attributes.

In the next chapter, you'll see how to begin building Web applications in Dreamweaver.

✦　　✦　　✦

Managing Data

◆ ◆ ◆ ◆

In This Chapter

Repeating data
on a page

Selectively showing
and hiding areas

Moving from record
group to record group

Using Application
Objects for instant
recordset navigation

Dreamweaver
Technique: Using
Flash Buttons to
navigate recordsets

◆ ◆ ◆ ◆

With the power to access the data of the world—or, at the very least, your part of it—comes great responsibility. As a Web page designer, you need to determine how best to present that information. Not only does this mean the surrounding look-and-feel, but also how the data itself is structured. How many records should you show at once? One? Ten? All of them? How should the user navigate from one group of records to another? What should the user see when there are no more records to display? Obviously, there are no definitive answers to these questions; each response must take into account the intent of the page, the type of data involved, and the audience for that data. Obviously, this chapter can't give you precise solutions for every Web application, but it does give you the tools to devise your own resolutions.

The Web is almost by definition a hotbed of constantly changing technologies. It can be frustrating when a new technology such as Dreamweaver's Flash Buttons is introduced and provisions are not made to use it to its fullest. For instance, there hasn't been an easy way to use Flash Buttons to navigate recordsets—at least, not until now. The final section in this chapter describes a technique for combining the functionality of Dreamweaver's Recordset Navigation Bar with the coolness of animated (and possibly sound-enabled) Flash Buttons.

Displaying Data Conditionally

What makes a Web page into a Web application? Arguably, connectivity to a data source by itself does not make a Web application—after all, you're merely setting up the possibility for data integration, not actually utilizing it. Some would say that it is the power to programmatically control the display of the data that is at the heart of an application. Dreamweaver handles this conditional display of data primarily through its Server Behaviors panel. You can, for example, opt to display the data—or any other page element—only if certain conditions, such as an empty recordset, are met. Before we look at the options for showing and hiding data conditionally, let's examine what is perhaps the most commonly used Dreamweaver server behavior: Repeat Region.

Repeating data

After establishing a data source connection and defining a recordset, Dreamweaver displays all the available fields in the Bindings panel. Regardless of how many records are contained within the declared recordset, you'll see only the one record when you drag one or more fields onto your page and preview the file. In order to see multiple records from the same recordset on a single page, you can apply the Repeat Region server behavior.

The Repeat Region server behavior is very straightforward to use, and extremely flexible. After selecting the dynamic data and any surrounding code you'd like to repeat, you specify the number of repetitions—there is also an option to display all the records in the recordset. The key phrase in the previous sentence is "and any surrounding code." If you select only the dynamic data itself, the record data will be repeated one after another. You have to include some HTML element to enable the repeated data to appear separately. Some of the most commonly used separation elements and their HTML tags are as follows:

✦ Line break: `<br>`

✦ Paragraph: `<p>` . . . `</p>`

✦ Table row: `<tr>` . . . `</tr>`

✦ Table data: `<td>` . . . `</td>`

✦ Unordered or ordered list item: `<li>` . . . `</li>`

Note that in all cases except that of the line break tag, for the Repeat Region to work you must select both the opening and the closing tags that surround the dynamic data, as shown in Figure 17-1. The surest way to do this is to place your cursor on the dynamic data and choose the surrounding element from the tag selector.

To implement a Repeat Region, follow these steps:

1. Select the dynamic data and surrounding code that you would like to repeat.

2. From the Server Behaviors panel, choose Add, and select Repeat Region from the list. The Repeat Region dialog box, shown in Figure 17-2, appears.

3. From the Repeat Region dialog box, choose the recordset you want to work with from the Recordset list.

4. If you want to display a subset of the recordset, enter the number of records you would like to display in the Show Records field.

5. If you want every record in the recordset to be displayed, choose the Show All Records option.

6. Click OK when you're done.

Tip   To test your implementation, make sure that the View ➪ Visual Aids ➪ Invisible Elements option is enabled. Then choose the Live Data button from the Document toolbar. Dreamweaver displays each repeated selection with a highlight.

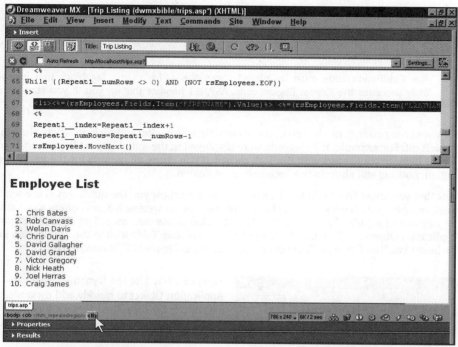

Figure 17-1: To automatically number your data, apply a Repeat Region to the `<li>` tag within an ordered (or numbered) list.

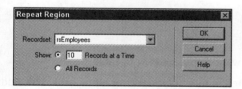

Figure 17-2: With the Repeat Region server behavior, you can show some or all of the records in the chosen recordset.

Although all of the repeated elements are displayed on the screen, only the initial element within a Repeat Region can be altered. If you change the initial element's formatting, you need to select the Refresh button from the Live Data toolbar to apply those changes to the other elements; this holds true even if you have Auto Refresh enabled.

Multiple Repeat Region server behaviors may coexist on the same page, extracting data from either the same recordset or a different one. However, if you use the same recordset again, you need to reset it so that Dreamweaver is extracting from the beginning. To do this, locate the second Repeat Region server behavior in the code by selecting its entry from the Server Behaviors panel and opening the Code view. Above the first line of server code, add the code appropriate to your server model (substitute the name of your recordset for `rsMine`):

```
ASP              <% rsMine.MoveFirst() %>
ColdFusion       <cfset rsMine_Index = 1>
JSP              <% rsMine.first() %>
PHP              <? mysql_data_seek($rsMine, 0) ?>
```

Note   The ColdFusion code must be placed above the `<cfscript>` tag block that immediately precedes the Repeat Region code. ASP.NET handles this for you. If you start a new `<asp:repeater>`, it will start from the beginning again.

If the resetting code is not inserted, the second Repeat Region will pick up where the first one left off. For example, if 10 records were displayed in the initial Repeat Region, the second Repeat Region would start with the 11th record. If you chose all records for the first Repeat Region, nothing will show in the second Repeat Region.

Now that you know how to do this by hand, it's time to show you the quick way (I know it's cruel, but everyone has to learn the hard way first). Dreamweaver MX now offers a fast and simple way to add a table of records with a repeat region in one easy step. Just choose Insert ⇨ Application Objects ⇨ Dynamic Table or click the Dynamic Table icon in the Application tag of the Insert bar. The Dynamic Table dialog box, shown in Figure 17-3, is now active.

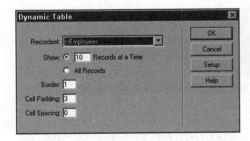

Figured 17-3: Use the Dynamic Table Application Object to quickly add dynamic lists of tabular data. You can save lots of time by skipping the tedious task of adding all your dynamic text manually.

This dialog box has just a few options:

✦ **Recordset:** Choose the recordset you want displayed in your table.

✦ **Show:** Choose whether to show a limited number of records or all records. This adds a regular Repeat Region to your field, just as you did earlier in this section.

✦ **Table attributes:** Choose your table border, cell padding, and cell spacing.

You can also click the Setup button if you don't currently have a recordset on your page, or your page can't currently accept dynamic data. This button enables you to quickly access the Recordset dialog box without ever leaving the Dynamic Table dialog box. After you click OK, your table will contain the field names in the first row, the data items in the second row, and a Repeat Region wrapped around the second row, as shown in Figure 17-4.

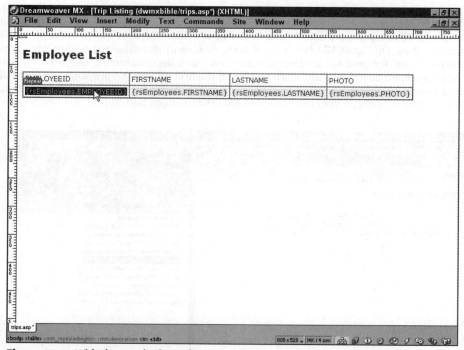

Figure 17-4: With the results from the Dynamic Table Application Object, all you need to change is basic table formatting and your table headings, and you're done.

Showing and hiding page elements

In the rush to push a site live, designers often pay too little attention to the user experience. When you are designing static Web pages, it's especially easy to lose sight of the importance of the user interface. However, with dynamic pages — where user interaction often determines what's on the page — an intuitive, reactive design helps to focus the audience on the content, rather than the engine driving the content.

The six Show Region server behaviors are as follows:

✦ Show Region If Recordset Is Empty

✦ Show Region If Recordset Is Not Empty

✦ Show Region If First Record

✦ Show Region If Not First Record

✦ Show Region If Last Record

✦ Show Region If Not Last Record

Tip Don't let the terminology throw you: Although they are all called Show Region server behaviors, you can easily use them to hide an area as well.

Dreamweaver's ability to conditionally hide or reveal areas of the page is extremely helpful for smoothing the user experience. For example, suppose you have a Web application that shows all 23 items in a particular recordset, five at a time with next and previous links, like the one shown in Figure 17-5. The record navigation controls enable the user to page through the recordset, forward and backward. When they reach the final record, the Next and Last buttons should be hidden, and when they're on the first record, the previous and first buttons should be hidden. I've used the Show Region If Not Last Record to hide the next button and the Show Region If Not First Record to hide the previous button.

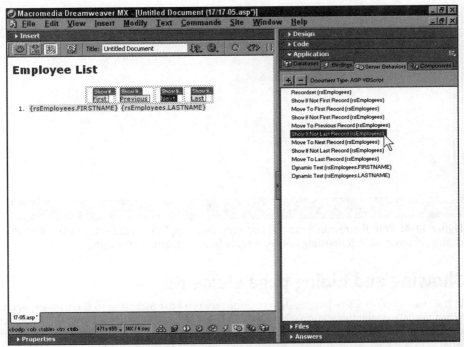

Figure 17-5: Use Dreamweaver's Show Region server behavior to display or hide navigation buttons depending on the dynamic data shown.

To apply a Show Region server behavior, follow these steps:

1. Select the page area you would like to conditionally show.

2. From the Server Behaviors panel, choose Add and select one of the server behaviors from the Show Record submenu. The dialog box for the specific Show Record server behavior you chose is displayed, like the one shown in Figure 17-6. The dialog boxes for all the Show Record server behaviors are identical.

3. From the Recordset list, select the recordset on which to base the Show Record condition.

4. Click OK when you're done.

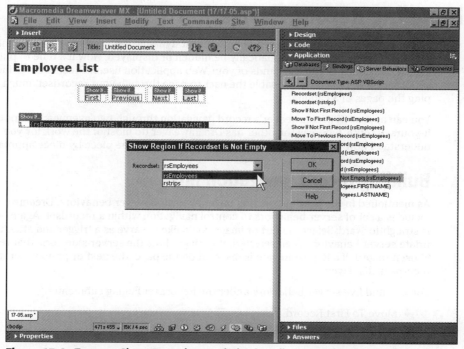

Figure 17-6: To use a Show Record server behavior, all you need to do is choose a recordset.

Typically, the Show Region server behaviors are used in pairs. Apply a Show Region If Not First Record server behavior to a Previous Record link — this will hide the link when the user is on the first record. Similarly, apply a Show Region If Not Last Record server behavior to the Next Record link, which will cause the link to disappear when the last record is called.

Only the first two Show Region server behaviors — Show Region If Recordset Is Empty and Show Region If Recordset Is Not Empty — may be applied to a page without any preconditions. The other four Show Region server behaviors require that one other type of server behavior be present on the page: the Recordset Paging server behavior. The Recordset Paging server behaviors act like VCR controls, adding a link that, when selected, displays the first, last, next, or previous set of records. The Recordset Paging server behaviors are covered in more detail in the following section.

Caution   When adding any of the Show Region server behaviors to a table with a Repeat Region server behavior, you need to apply the Show Region server behavior to the repeated region separately. If, for example, your table has a header row and a repeating row, you would apply the Show Region server behavior twice: once to the header row and once to the row containing the Repeat Region server behavior. Tables without a Repeat Region may be conditionally shown with one Show Region server behavior.

Handling Record Navigation

So far in this chapter, you've seen how to repeat dynamic data and how to make that data and other page elements programmatically be hidden or displayed. Now it's time to put some real interactive controls into the hands of your Web application users. Dreamweaver includes a set of server behaviors that enable the user to page through your recordset, much like flipping the pages of a catalog.

You can approach Dreamweaver's record navigation through two avenues: One option is a do-it-yourself route, whereas the other has Dreamweaver do most of the work for you. To better understand how record navigation works, you'll examine the piece-by-piece approach first.

Building record navigation links

As mentioned in the previous section on Show Region server behaviors, Dreamweaver also includes a set of server behaviors to control navigation within a recordset. Again, application is straightforward: Select the text or image you'd like to serve as a trigger and attach the appropriate server behavior. When selected, the trigger fires the server-side code that retrieves the chosen record. If a Repeat Region is inserted on the page, the next or previous group of records is displayed.

You can find five server behaviors under the Recordset Paging submenu:

- ✦ Move To First Record
- ✦ Move To Previous Record
- ✦ Move To Next Record
- ✦ Move To Last Record
- ✦ Move To Specific Record

Note   The final Recordset Paging server behavior, Move To Specific Record, is most often used in conjunction with a search routine or a master-detail application.

As noted, you can use either text or images as your controls. Navigation links, such as those shown in Figure 17-7, may even include rollovers or other client-side behaviors. You can even use Flash Buttons to trigger recordset navigation; see "Dreamweaver Technique: Using Flash Buttons for Recordset Navigation," later in this chapter, for a detailed explanation of how it's done.

Tip   You don't need to add an initial or placeholder link to your image or text. When the Recordset Paging server behavior is applied, the link will be written for you.

To create recordset navigation links, follow these steps:

1. Select the text or image to which you'd like to attach the server behavior.

2. From the Server Behaviors panel, select Add, and choose the desired behavior from the Recordset Paging submenu. The appropriate Recordset Paging dialog box appears. If you've made a selection, it's highlighted in the Link list; otherwise, a new text link is created, as shown in Figure 17-8.

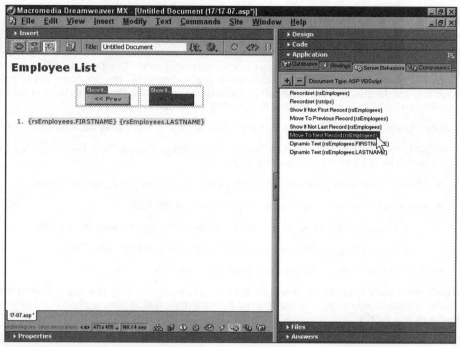

Figure 17-7: You can use images—with or without rollovers—to navigate through a recordset with Dreamweaver's Recordset Paging server behaviors.

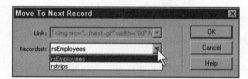

Figure 17-8: The Recordset Paging server behaviors identify your selected target, whether it is an image or text.

3. Make sure that the link selected is the desired one in the Link list.

4. Choose the recordset you want to work with from the Recordset drop-down list.

5. Click OK when you're done.

6. Repeat Steps 1 through 5 to add more recordset navigation elements.

Note   Record navigation is done within a particular recordset; you can't link from one recordset to another using the Dreamweaver server behaviors or Application Objects.

After you've added your navigation controls, you may want to take the next step toward a more complete user interface by adding Show Region server behaviors to ensure that the controls are displayed only when they serve a purpose. For example, if you have a navigation element that moves to the last record of a recordset, you probably want to attach a Show If Not Last Record server behavior to the trigger.

Using Application Objects for record navigation

Although the process for setting up a single navigation control is fairly simple, you'd have to perform that process four times (as well as attach four additional server behaviors) to accomplish what the Recordset Navigation Bar does in one operation. The Recordset Navigation Bar is one of Dreamweaver's Application Objects — one that can take the drudgery out of a repetitious implementation. All the Application Objects are accessible through either the Insert ➪ Application Objects menu or the Application tab in the Insert bar.

The Recordset Navigation Bar Application Object serves the following multiple purposes:

✦ Adds four links to the page in a borderless, single row table: First, Previous, Next, and Last. The links may be either text or graphics.

✦ Attaches the appropriate Recordset Paging server behavior to the four links.

✦ Inserts a Show Region server behavior to each of the links:

• Show If Not First Record is added to the First and Previous record links.

• Show If Not Last Record is added to the Next and Last record links.

✦ Centers the table on the page and sets the width to 50%.

What's even more impressive about this list of functions is that they are implemented with a single command, which, in turn, references a very simple dialog box, as shown in Figure 17-9. Here's how it works:

1. Choose Insert ➪ Application Objects ➪ Recordset Navigation Bar or choose Insert Recordset Navigation Bar from the Application category of the Insert bar. The Recordset Navigation Bar dialog box is displayed.

2. Select the data you want to control from the Recordset list.

3. To create a series of text links, choose the Display Using Text option.

4. To use graphics to trigger the navigation, choose the Display Using Images option.

You must save your page if you select the Display Using Images option. Dreamweaver copies images from the Shared/Dreamweaver/Images folder when you choose this option, and the page into which they are being inserted must be saved in order to store them in the site properly. The images are stored in the same folder as the page containing them.

Figure 17-9: The Recordset Navigation Bar dialog box offers a choice between text links or graphics.

After the Recordset Navigation Bar has been inserted, you can adjust the text or images in any way you see fit. The text may be styled or modified, and you can even swap out the images — by changing the src attribute — for another graphic.

Tracking record status

Another Application Object inserts the text and all the server behaviors necessary to display the records currently being viewed. By default, the syntax used by the Recordset Navigation Status Application Object is as follows:

```
Records First_Record_Shown to Last_Record_Shown of Total_Records
```

This syntax works perfectly for Web applications that use a Repeat Region server behavior to show multiple records. When viewed through the browser, the Recordset Navigation Status output looks like the following:

```
Records 5 to 10 of 37.
```

If you're displaying one record at a time, you can adjust the Application Object code inserted to something similar to the following:

```
Record First_Record_Shown of Total_Records
```

Like the Recordset Navigation Bar, this Application Object works with only one recordset at a time; applying the Recordset Navigation Status Application Object works similarly, as shown in the following steps:

1. Choose Insert ➪ Application Objects ➪ Recordset Navigation or click the Recordset Navigation Status icon on the Application category of the Insert bar. The Recordset Navigation Status dialog box is displayed, as shown in Figure 17-10.

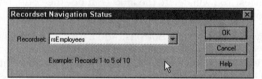

Figure 17-10: The Recordset Navigation Status Application Object inserts three different server behaviors in one operation.

2. Select the data you want to control from the Recordset list.

3. Click OK when you're done.

Dreamweaver Technique: Using Flash Buttons for Recordset Navigation

Flash Buttons are an excellent Dreamweaver tool for adding lively navigation aids to your Web page, but they're intended for page-to-page linking, not recordset navigation. However, with a little additional work, you can adapt standard or custom Flash Buttons to control Dreamweaver's Recordset Paging server behaviors.

Flash Buttons are actually Macromedia Generator Templates, which when processed by Dreamweaver become Flash movies. As a Generator Template, the link information is compiled into the Flash movie and is not accessible for server-side processing—a necessity for moving from one record to another. Enabling Flash Buttons to control recordset navigation requires four main components:

✦ Server-side code for moving from record to record

✦ A JavaScript call from the Flash Button

✦ A JavaScript function in the <head> of the document

✦ A hidden field variable in a form

The first requirement is actually the easiest, as the necessary server-side code is provided by Dreamweaver.

Step 1: Prepare the page

Before you can begin the specific steps for converting the Flash Buttons for your use, some preliminary work needs to be in place. First, make sure that you have added your recordset and any necessary fields. You can always add more fields from the Bindings panel later, but it's good to have one or two in the page to test the navigation buttons.

Next, add the server-side code. You can accomplish this in one of two ways: Either enter some text and attach a Recordset Paging server behavior to it, or use Dreamweaver's Recordset Navigation Bar from the Insert ➪ Application Object menu. To save time — and because you'll likely be adding multiple controls — choose the Application Object route by selecting Insert ➪ Application Object ➪ Recordset Navigation Bar. If you follow this path, choose the Display Using Text option, rather than images. You will delete the links (but not the code) later; and when you do, you'll have extraneous files in your local site if you opt for graphics now.

One final bit of prep work before you add the Flash Buttons: Add a form to your page if one is not already present. If you like, give it a unique name; one convention you might try is to identify the forms on your pages with the name theForm. The form may enclose the other elements, as shown in Figure 17-11, or be separate.

Step 2: Add the Flash Buttons

Now you're ready to insert your Flash Buttons. Note one small difference between the regular Flash Buttons and the ones used in the Dreamweaver technique. In your version, you call a JavaScript function, rather than link to another page.

If you're not familiar with Flash Buttons, be sure to look over Chapter 25 to understand their basic usage and learn how you can create your own custom Flash Buttons with Flash MX.

To insert your modified Flash Button, follow these steps:

If you're already familiar with Flash Buttons, skip to Step 7.

1. Make sure that the current document has been saved.

   If you're working on a new document, Dreamweaver requires that you save it before adding a Flash Button.

2. Choose Insert ➪ Interactive Images ➪ Flash Button. The Insert Flash Button dialog box, shown in Figure 17-12, is displayed.

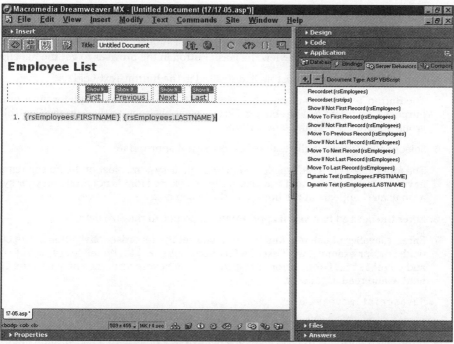

Figure 17-11: To prepare for the Flash Recordset Navigation buttons, add a form and Dreamweaver's standard Recordset Navigation Bar.

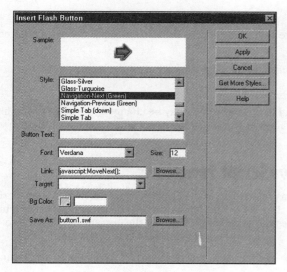

Figure 17-12: Instead of a relative URL, put a call to a JavaScript function in the Link field of your Flash Button.

3. Select a button type from the Style list.

   The previews shown in the Sample area are live demonstrations and will play as designed when moused-over and/or clicked. Note, however, one exception: No sounds are played in preview; you have to preview the Flash Button in the browser to get the full effect.

4. If appropriate, enter the custom text desired in the Button Text field.

   The Button Text field is physically limited to 50 characters, although for most practical purposes, your text will be shorter. Certain symbols, such as those in the Control group, ignore the text and font settings.

5. Select a typeface from the Font drop-down list if appropriate.

   The fonts listed are TrueType fonts found on your system. Most of the button templates have a preselected font and text size. If the preselected font is not found on your system, a small alert appears at the bottom of the dialog box.

6. Enter the desired font size if appropriate, in points, in the Size field.

7. Enter a JavaScript call to a function that will set the recordset navigation in the Link field. For our example, we'll use the functions `moveNext()`, `movePrev()`, `moveFirst()`, and `moveLast()`. For a button that moves to the next record, the entry into the Link field would read as follows:

   ```
   javascript:moveNext();
   ```

8. Leave the Target field blank.

9. If the Flash Button is to be placed on a page or in a table with a background color other than white, select the Bg Color swatch to choose an appropriate background. Alternatively, enter the hexadecimal color number or standard color name directly into the Bg Color text field.

10. Enter a path and filename for the Flash Button file. If you like, you can use the suggested default name in the site root, or select the Browse button to choose a different location.

11. Choose Apply to insert the button at the cursor location on the page.

12. Click OK when you're done.

The JavaScript function names listed in the steps here may be changed to whatever you like. However, be sure to use the same names as the actual functions when you insert them in your code, as described in the next step.

Step 3: Include the JavaScript functions

Now it's time to include the functions referenced in the Flash Button Link field. As JavaScript functions go, these are as simple as they get — with just one line of code each. When executed, each of the JavaScript functions does the same thing: They set the current URL to a value specified in a hidden form variable. You'll set the form variables in the next step.

Although there are four variations — one for each type of recordset navigation — the basic function looks like the following:

```
function moveNext() {
    document.location.href=document.theForm.nextHidden.value
}
```

The function name—here, moveNext()—is arbitrary, but note that it matches the function name specified in the Flash Button setup. The reference to the hidden form variable is also specific to our code—again, you can name the variables whatever you like; just ensure that the names match the code in the function.

Our code uses the following four functions:

```
function moveNext() {
    document.location.href=document.theForm.nextHidden.value
}

function movePrev() {
    document.location.href=document.theForm.prevHidden.value
}

function moveFirst() {
    document.location.href=document.theForm.firstHidden.value
}

function moveLast() {
    document.location.href=document.theForm.lastHidden.value
}
```

If you're totally unfamiliar with writing JavaScript, you can use Dreamweaver's Script object to insert the code. However, make sure that the code goes in the <head> section of the document. Use the following steps to accomplish that:

1. Choose View ➪ Head Content or use the keyboard shortcut, Ctrl+Shift+W (Command+Shift+W), to expose the <head> region in Dreamweaver's Document window.

2. Select Insert ➪ Script Objects ➪ Script. Alternatively, you could select the Script icon from the Script tab of the Insert bar. The Script dialog box, shown in Figure 17-13, is displayed.

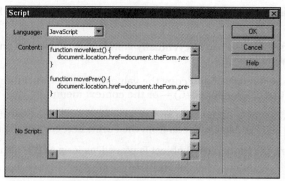

Figure 17-13: If you are new to JavaScript, use Dreamweaver's Script object for inserting code.

3. Select JavaScript from the Language list.

4. Enter the desired functions into the Content text area. You can enter as many of the functions as you'd like, or all of them.

5. Click OK when you're done.

If you're more familiar with JavaScript, you can enter the functions directly through Dreamweaver's Code view. The functions may be inserted into an existing `<script>` . . . `</script>` tag pair or you can create your own. Now you're ready to add the final piece of the basic puzzle: the hidden variables.

Step 4: Insert the hidden variables

So far, everything you've done could also be done in a static Web page, but it's time to add the server-side component. Whenever a Recordset Paging server behavior is applied, whether manually or automatically by inserting a Application Object, Dreamweaver writes a bit of server-side code in the `href` attribute of the `<a>` tag surrounding the trigger element. It is this code that you must make accessible in order for the Flash Button to work properly as a recordset navigation tool.

The server-side code varies from server model to server model, but in essence it's quite similar. Here, for example, is the code inserted when a Move To Next Record server behavior is applied:

```
ASP -- <%=MM_moveNext%>
ColdFusion -- <cfoutput>#MM_moveNext#</cfoutput>
JSP - <%=MM_moveNext%>
.NET - <%# Request.ServerVariables("SCRIPT_NAME") %>?rs_currentPage=<%#
rs.CurrentPage + 1 %>
```

To keep this code accessible for server-side processing — and viable for the JavaScript function to use — it must be embedded in a hidden variable form element. After the code is transferred, the temporary recordset navigation elements previously inserted can be deleted. Here's how to accomplish this task, step by step:

1. Select the text link that matches the recordset navigation intended for your Flash Button.

   You can start anywhere because you're eventually going to add Flash Buttons for all your recordset navigation moves.

2. From the Property inspector, select and copy the value of the `href` attribute using the keyboard shortcut — Ctrl+C (Command+C) — or the context menu.

3. Position your cursor anywhere in the form and choose Insert ⇨ Form Objects ⇨ Hidden Field or select the Hidden Field icon from the Forms category of the Insert bar.

   It doesn't matter where the Hidden Field object is placed, as long as it's within the `<form>` tag.

4. In the Hidden Field Property inspector, change the name from the default hiddenField to a unique name. This name must be the same as the one used in the JavaScript function.

You might want to create a name for form elements by first describing what the element relates to, followed by the type of form element. For example, the four hidden fields used in recordset navigation are called firstHidden, lastHidden, nextHidden, and prevHidden.

5. In the Value field of the Property inspector, paste in the copied code as shown in Figure 17-14.

Figure 17-14: The Hidden Field form element acts as a conduit to the JavaScript function, passing the processed server-side value, which, in turn, is called by the Flash Button.

6. Repeat Steps 1 through 5 for every Flash Button recordset control intended for the page.

7. After you've added all the hidden fields needed, you're free to delete the temporary recordset navigation text links.

Dreamweaver alerts you that not all of the server behaviors have been deleted; you can safely ignore this warning. The part left behind is exactly what you'll use.

Your Flash Button is now recordset navigation ready. Test your page by using Dreamweaver's Preview in Browser feature.

Tip Remember: If the folder for your testing server is on a different machine or in a different location from your local site root, you'll need to transfer all the dependent files — including the SWF files used by the Flash Buttons — before the Flash Buttons will work correctly.

To make your Flash Button interface as intuitive as possible, add Show Region server behaviors to the various buttons, as detailed in the "Showing and hiding page elements" section earlier in this chapter (and shown in Figure 17-15).

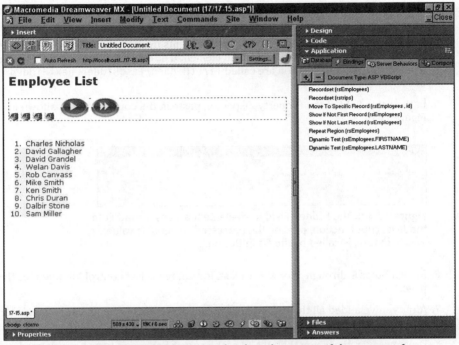

Figure 17-15: The Flash Buttons appear only when they are useful, courtesy of Dreamweaver's Show Region server behaviors.

Summary

In order to be part of an effective Web application, dynamic data can't just be displayed; it has to be designed. Dreamweaver, through a variety of server behaviors, gives you the power to selectively repeat page elements as well as show them programmatically. Data design is an important aspect of integrating the server side with the client side. As you look for ways to manage the data in your Web applications more effectively, remember the following points:

✦ With the aid of the Repeat Region server behavior, Dreamweaver can help you to show as much of the data on a single page as you desire. Repeat Region server behaviors are usually applied to table rows, but they may also be used with line-breaks or paragraphs, `<br>` and `<p>` tags, respectively.

✦ It's often necessary to show data only if a certain condition is met. Dreamweaver handles these operations through a variety of Show Region server behaviors. With these tools, you can also selectively display any element — text, graphic, or dynamic data — on the current page.

✦ Once you have the capability to display a portion of your data, you need to be able to navigate the recordset. Dreamweaver's Recordset Paging server behaviors can show the next or previous record (or group of records, if the Repeat Region server behavior is used), as well as quickly navigate to the first or last record of your data.

✦ Recordset navigation can be integrated in several ways: You can add each building block (the graphics or the text, the server behaviors, and so on) by itself, or you can accomplish the same task in one operation by using a Dreamweaver Application Object. Depending on the Web application, you might find it quicker to insert and modify the Recordset Navigation Bar Application Object, rather than build your own step-by-step.

✦ You can convert Flash Buttons to act as recordset navigation aids. The step-by-step Dreamweaver Technique details the necessary modifications.

In the next chapter, you'll learn how you can use Dreamweaver's Live Data view to enhance your workflow and test your application under a variety of circumstances.

✦　　✦　　✦

Working with Live Data

When I first started with print and design layout, I would drive all over the city to finish a job. After receiving the client's go-ahead, I had to pick my type from a phototypesetter, and my images from a stat house. Then, back at my studio, I'd cut and paste — and I mean literally with scissors and glue — the text and images into place, hoping against hope that I had specified the type and image sizes correctly. If not, it was back in the car for another trip or two around town. Ah, the good old days.

Now, designers (especially those who design for the Web) have the luxury of developing their creations right in their own studio. Until Dreamweaver, however, the development of a Web application often undertook a faster, albeit parallel, course to my inner-city travels. After a basic page was designed, complete with server-side code, the document had to be uploaded to a testing server and then viewed in a browser over the Internet. If — make that *when* — changes were needed, the pages were revamped back in the studio. Because the designer was not able to lay out the page with the actual data in place, modifications were a trial-and-error process that often required many, many trips to the server and back.

Dreamweaver's Live Data view eliminates the tedium and the lengthy time required for the upload-preview-modify-upload cycle. With Live Data view, developers work with the layout while the actual data is live on the page. If a table width needs to be adjusted because one of the records appearing in it is too long, you can make the change immediately with no guesswork. Live Data view processes the page on the chosen server model and, because the page may require variables, such as search criteria, in order to run properly, the Live Data feature enables you to set such values as needed. Although a preliminary discussion of Live Data is covered in Chapter 16, this chapter covers all the necessary details for using both basic and advanced Live Data capabilities.

While Live Data is a terrific timesaving feature, you can't rely on it totally for testing your Web application. You still need to preview the page in various browsers to ensure cross-browser compatibility. The final section of this chapter is dedicated to Dreamweaver's Preview in Browser feature and its relationship to your testing server.

Viewing Live Data

Once your site is properly set up, entering Live Data view is just a click away. Select the Show Live Data View button on the toolbar to refresh Dreamweaver's Document window and to replace all of the dynamic data placeholders with information from the declared data source If the Invisible Elements option is enabled, the newly visible Live Data is highlighted in whatever color is specified in Preferences.

In order to get the most out of Live Data view — and to avoid any problems that might be encountered — it's best to have a firm grasp of how Dreamweaver is able to present your data, live.

How Live Data works

In the right-hand corner of the Live Data toolbar, you may notice an animation of a spinning Dreamweaver logo before the page is refreshed. When the animation stops, Dreamweaver has all the information needed to present the completed page. Here is what's really happening behind that spinning lower-case *d*:

1. The developer inserts dynamic data elements into a standard HTML page. The dynamic data is represented by placeholders that combine the recordset and field names in a set of curly braces, like {rsEvents.eventTime}.

2. When the Live Data view is enabled, Dreamweaver creates a hidden, temporary copy of the current page.

3. The temporary page is then stored in the folder designated in the Testing Server category of the Site Definition dialog box.

4. Dreamweaver instructs the defined testing server to execute the server-side code within the page, and passes along any variables that may have been specified. The URL prefix designated in the Site Definition Testing Server category is used to invoke the page.

5. When the code is executed, Dreamweaver reads the resulting HTML code.

6. Finally, Dreamweaver uses its translator capability to substitute the dynamic data placeholders shown in the original document with the data generated. The temporary document is deleted from the server.

If all goes well, a page with dynamic data placeholders, as shown in Figure 18-1 is replaced with the Live Data view, as shown in Figure 18-2.

If Dreamweaver encounters an error, a message is displayed that explains where the process failed and suggests some possible remedies.

Setting up for Live Data

As noted in the summary of how Live Data works, several values found in the Testing Server category of the Site Definition are key to this feature's operation. Live Data must know the location of the site root for the temporary page and how that location may be reached with an HTTP request. If either of these values is not found, the attempt to switch to Live Data view is aborted, and an error message appears.

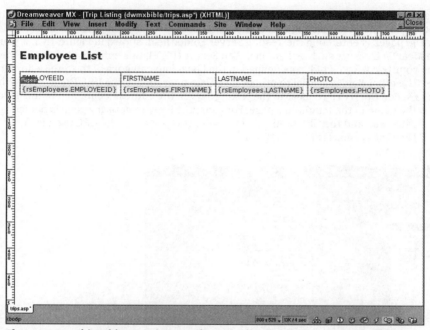

Figure 18-1: This table contains two dynamic data fields, surrounded by a Repeat Region server behavior.

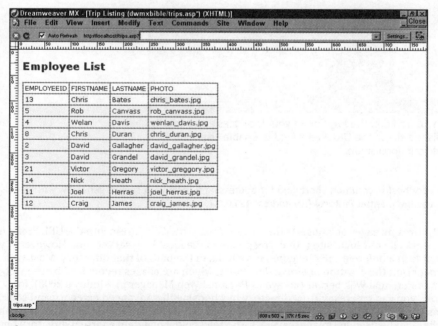

Figure 18-2: After Live Data view is enabled, the full number of records allowed by the Repeat Region is displayed and includes an accurate representation of the data.

There are two different methods for accessing the testing server: locally, through a network or remotely via FTP. If the testing server is to be accessed locally, the location of the folder storing the pages is entered in the Testing Server Folder field, shown in Figure 18-3. If you're using a local Web server such as Personal Web Server (PWS), this entry is likely to be the same as your Local Root Folder, as defined in the Local Info category of the Site Definition dialog box. The other field essential to proper Live Data operation is the URL Prefix field. When Live Data sends the HTTP request to the testing server, the address contained in this field prefaces the name of the temporary page. For example, if my temporary page is named `TMPGX123455.asp` and the URL prefix is `http://localhost/dba`, the URL used is `http://localhost/dba/TMPGX123455.asp`.

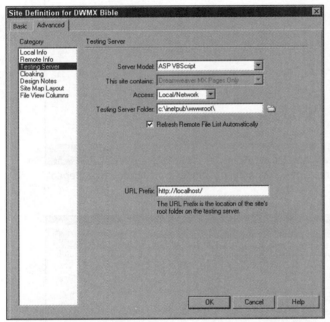

Figure 18-3: Enter the location of your local files and a locally established site in the URL Prefix field to enable Live Data view to find your application.

Tip   Localhost is common shorthand for addressing a local Web server; generally, you can also use the Internet Protocol (IP) address 127.0.0.1.

Initially, Dreamweaver only inserts the `http://localhost/` address into the URL Prefix field, which works if your local site root corresponds to the local Web server root. However, if your site root is in a different directory, you have to fill in the path of that directory. Most Web servers permit the creation of *virtual directories*, which are aliases recognized by the Web server. In Personal Web Server (known as Personal Web Manager in Windows 2000), for example, you can create a virtual directory by choosing the Advanced category and selecting Add, as shown in Figure 18-4. Once you've located the desired directory and given it an alias, that alias can be used in Dreamweaver's URL Prefix field. I maintain a virtual directory on my system, for example, called dba for one of my clients. For this site, the complete URL prefix is `http://localhost/dba`.

Note   ColdFusion MX developers with a local testing server need to specify their port number. By default, ColdFusion MX uses 8500 which would result in a URL Prefix of `http://localhost:8500/`.

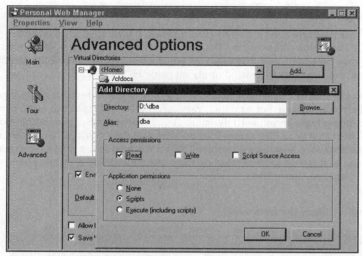

Figure 18-4: Personal Web Server uses virtual directories to enable Web folders to be stored in various locations on a local system.

If you're connecting to a remote testing server, choose the FTP from the Access list on the Testing Server category of the Site Definition dialog box. When FTP is selected, Dreamweaver displays the same information entered under the FTP heading in the Remote Info category. Additionally, Dreamweaver combines the entries under FTP Host and Host Directory in the URL prefix with an initial `http://`. For example, if your entry under FTP Host is `www.drinkgoodstuff.com` and Host Directory is blank, the URL prefix will read `http://www.drinkgoodstuff.com/`.

Caution   You may have to edit your URL prefix if your FTP host uses an `ftp` prefix. If my host directory were `ftp.drinkgoodstuff.com`, Dreamweaver would create the URL prefix entry `http://ftp.drinkgoodstuff.com`, an unworkable URL. Here, the `ftp` would need to be changed to `www`.

Entering and exiting Live Data view

Dreamweaver provides three different methods for invoking Live Data view; use the technique that best suits your work style:

✦ Choose View ➪ Live Data from the main menu.

✦ Use the keyboard shortcut, Ctrl+Shift+R (Command+Shift+R).

✦ Click the Show Live Data View button on the toolbar.

Once in Live Data view, executing any of these three actions again returns you to Standard view, where dynamic data placeholders are shown.

Tip

If, for any reason, you need to interrupt the Live Data connection process, select the Stop button on the Live Data toolbar. The Stop button remains active only while Dreamweaver is transitioning into Live Data view.

Making changes in Live Data

If a feature in a software program can be said to have a raison d'etre, then modifying the layout must surely be the raison d'etre of Live Data. When in Live Data view, new elements — dynamic or static — may be added, and existing ones adjusted or removed entirely. Anything, including the dynamic data, may be formatted or styled using HTML or CSS.

Live Data view solves the thorny challenges of layout in a table without resorting to a time-consuming trial-and-error approach. For example, varying lengths of data in the same column often complicate designing table layout with dynamic data. If, for example, your sample data includes a last name field that is 12 characters long and the real data contains a hyphenated name that is 25 characters long, you have a problem. When working in Live Data view, you can see the entire page as it would be generated on the server, including dynamic elements and repeating table rows (see Figure 18-5).

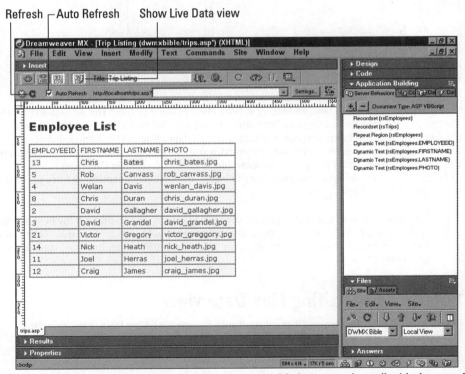

Figure 18-5: Use Live Data view to make sure your table layout works well with the actual data that will appear on the page.

The Live Data toolbar includes a Refresh button that, when selected, resends your application to the server for processing, and then redisplays the page in the Document window. The Refresh option is valuable in the following circumstances:

✦ Information from the data source is reassessed. This feature enables you to make changes in the database and then see those changes incorporated into your page.

✦ Server formatting changes are applied to dynamic data. If you don't refresh after altering the current format of the inserted data, the modified element reverts to being displayed as a dynamic data placeholder.

✦ HTML formatting applied to dynamic data is also applied to Live Data displayed through a Repeat Region server behavior. Without refreshing, only the initial data is shown correctly formatted.

Repeat Region server behaviors enable multiple records from the same recordset to be incorporated into a page. For details on how to insert and manage a Repeat Region, see Chapter 17.

Two refresh-oriented captions are found on the Live Data toolbar: the Refresh Live Data button and the Auto Refresh option. When Auto Refresh is enabled, server formatting changes are automatically applied. However, to display HTML formatting on Repeat Region data or to see changes made to a data source, you must select the Refresh Live Data button.

Live Data Settings

While the capability to work with data from the current recordset is impressive, it's really only half the story of Live Data view. Many Web applications depend on variables used when the page is processed by the testing server. Users may intentionally submit these variables when they fill out a form. Conversely, users may submit variables unintentionally — without express knowledge — when they navigate from a particular page. Session or application variables, from authentication routines or simple counters, may also be integrated into a page. Dreamweaver permits developers to interactively alter all such variables and, thus, preview the resulting Web page. This facility not only enables the Dreamweaver designer to work with a wide range of real-life conditions, it also facilitates testing of the application under a variety of circumstances. Dreamweaver offers two avenues of approach to variable handling: through the query string field and the Settings dialog box.

Getting the query string

Remember the first time you noticed that the link you clicked was carrying quite a bit of additional baggage? Where you might have selected a link that took you to a specific product page with a URL like `http://www.web-shorts.com/products/widgets.htm`, the link in the Location field of your browser looked more like the following:

```
http://www.web-shorts.com/products/products.asp?prod=
widget&sessionID=2343215&login=no&visited=gadgets%20%r%20us
```

The text following the question mark is called a *query string,* or the URL parameters. Query strings are a tool used by Web applications to pass information from one page to the next. Frequently, you'll see a query string after submitting a form. Forms using the `Get` method pass their variables by appending a question mark and the form information to the URL of the requested page. The form information is in a series of name/value pairs; and each name/value pair is linked by an equals sign, as follows:

```
Firstname=Joseph
```

Query strings may include any number of name/value pairs, separated by an ampersand. Thus, for a form that passes the data entered into a first name field and a last name field, the query string may look like the following:

```
?firstname=Joseph&lastname=Lowery
```

Note that neither single nor double quotes are used, because they are in HTML attributes. Quotes and other characters — including spaces, apostrophes, and tildes — are represented by hexadecimal values so that they are properly understood by servers. Such strings are said to be *URL encoded,* and they are designated by an initial percent sign, followed by the ASCII value of the character in hexadecimal. Some commonly used encoding values are as follows:

✦ **Space:** %20

✦ **Apostrophe** (or single quote): %27

✦ **Double quote:** %22

✦ **Tilde:** %7E

✦ **Less than** (<): %3C

✦ **Greater than** (>): %3E

The query string field appears in the Live Data toolbar by default, prefaced by the URL path used by Live Data plus a question mark. The URL path, question mark, and the text entered into the field comprise the complete URL submitted to the testing server when Live Data is invoked or refreshed.

Note   Depending on the length of the pathname, some elements, such as folders, may be represented by an ellipsis (three dots) so that Dreamweaver may display the filename and question mark.

Consider an example that uses the query string. Suppose you've developed a page for an organization that displays events of different types. The type of event shown depends on the link selected by the user; the links are identical except for the query string portion. For events of type 1, the link reads events.asp?type=1, whereas for events of type 2, the link is events.asp?type=2. The recordset on the events.asp page uses a filter that sets the EventType field equal to the URL parameter called type.

Note   Although the query string field is present by default, you can disable it by switching the Method option in the Live Data Settings dialog box from Get to Post. To re-enable the query string field, choose View ➪ Live Data Settings and select Get as the Method option.

After entering Live Data view by any of the methods described previously, you can switch back and forth between the two sets of returned data by changing the value in the query string name=value pair. In this instance, the two accepted values — as defined in the data source — are 1 for Event Type 1 and 2 for Event Type 2. After changing the value and pressing Enter (Return), the Live Data is refreshed, as shown in Figure 18-6.

Caution   If you encounter a Live Data error indicating that the page cannot be displayed because the current record could not be found, you're probably including values in the query string that do not match any records in a recordset on the page. You have a couple of options for proceeding. Press the Esc key to dismiss the error dialog box and enter a new value in the query string field. (Don't click the Close button on the dialog box, or Live Data view and the Live Data toolbar will close.) Alternatively, you can enter a name value/pair through the Live Data Settings dialog box as outlined in the following section.

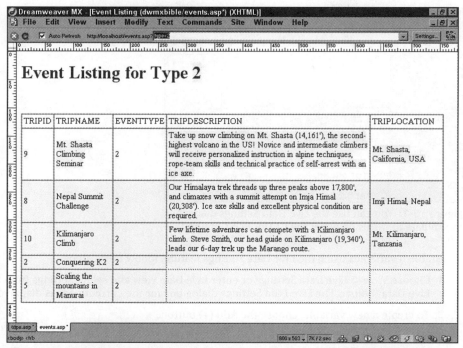

Figure 18-6: You may use the query string field of the Live Data toolbar to test different scenarios for your Web application.

Posting responses with Live Data settings

Although the query string is handy for changing one or two simple variables, the more complex the variables, the less convenient it becomes. Dreamweaver offers another route to controlling Live Data variables: Live Data settings. The Live Data Settings dialog box, shown in Figure 18-7, offers several important advantages over the query string:

✦ The name/value pairs are easier to enter and maintain in a straightforward two-column table.

✦ URL encoding is handled automatically by Dreamweaver; with query strings, you have to enter any necessary URL encoding manually.

✦ Variables may be sent to the application by either the Get or Post method. The query string uses only the Get method.

✦ Additional initializing code may be applied to the page. This feature allows different session or environmental variables in the page to be tested, as if the server had set the values.

✦ Variable settings may be optionally stored. If this option is selected, Dreamweaver uses its Design Notes facility to maintain the variables.

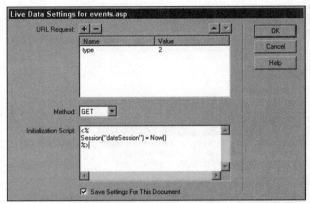

Figure 18-7: You can use the Live Data Settings dialog box to simulate forms using either the GET or POST method.

To establish variables using the Live Data Settings feature, follow these steps:

1. Choose View ⇨ Live Data Settings or enter Live Data view and select Settings from the Live Data toolbar. The Live Data Settings dialog box for the current page is displayed.

2. To create a new variable, choose the Add (+) button.

3. In the Name column, enter the name of the variable.

4. In the corresponding field under the Value column, enter a value for the variable.

5. Repeat Steps 2 through 4 to add additional variables.

6. To delete a name/value pair, select it and then choose the Remove button.

7. You can adjust the sequence in which the variables are presented to the page by using the Up and Down buttons to move name/value pairs higher or lower in the list.

8. By default, Dreamweaver sends variables to a page using the Get method, which appends URL-encoded name/value pairs in a query string. To simulate a form passing variables in an encapsulated, hidden manner, choose Post from the Method list.

Tip   If you choose the Get method, enter the variables and their values without encoding them for the URL. Dreamweaver will translate any necessary characters into their hexadecimal equivalents when the Live Data page is processed.

9. To establish a particular server environment, enter any code necessary in the Initialization Script text area. This code is specific to each server model and must be completely self-contained within any required tags or delimiters.

10. To store your variable settings, select the Save Settings For This Document option. Dreamweaver requires that Design Notes be enabled in order to save the Live Data settings. If Design Notes is disabled when you select this option, you'll be given an opportunity to enable it.

Previewing in the Browser

Live Data saves a tremendous amount of time in the early design phase. However, when it comes time to test your application in various browsers — a necessary step for virtually all Web developers — there is no substitute for previewing in the browser. Dreamweaver does a decent job of approximating a browser-eye view of your page; however, with so many variations between the major browsers — not to mention the versions within each major browser — you must test your page in as many browsers as possible. Dreamweaver's Preview in Browser feature enables you to specify up to 13 different browsers in Preferences. Once defined, you may test your page by selecting File ➪ Preview in Browser ➪ *Browser Name* at any point. If the toolbar is available, you may also choose a browser under the Preview/Debug in Browser option.

Previewing in the browser was a major Dreamweaver 4 enhancement that, in Dreamweaver MX, carries one additional responsibility. In order to view Web applications properly, Dreamweaver must process the pages with a testing server. To use this facility, you must satisfy two requirements:

✦ Specify the route to the testing server, either via a local (or networked) folder or through FTP in the Testing Server category of the Site Definition dialog box.

✦ Transfer any dependent or related files to the testing server. Although you don't have to include dependent files such as graphics on the current page, you do need to transfer server-side includes, such as the connection script. Related files are other pages referenced in the Web application; Dreamweaver only uploads a copy of the current page during the Preview in Browser operation.

Once the testing server is properly set up (as described in Chapter 5), you can quickly transfer any necessary files in the Site window. From the Site window toolbar, select the Testing Server button; the files on the testing server are displayed in the remote pane of the Site window, as shown in Figure 18-8. Transfer files from the local site by dragging them from the local pane to the testing server pane or by selecting the files and then choosing the Put or Check In button.

Tip

When you begin to test a new page, let Dreamweaver transfer the dependent files for you. Simply transfer a saved copy of the current page to the testing server and okay the request to transfer the dependent files as well. Make sure you select the Dependent Files: Prompt on Put/Check In option, found in the Site category of Preferences, to take advantage of this feature.

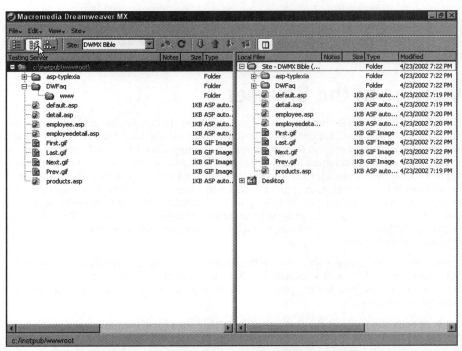

Figure 18-8: The Dreamweaver Site window enables you to connect to the testing server as well as the remote server.

Using the Server Debug Panel with ColdFusion MX

Macromedia tightens their Dreamweaver and ColdFusion integration with every product release. Dreamweaver MX is no exception. The new Server Debug panel offers you an integrated view of all errors and server variables on your ColdFusion pages. The Server Debug view also gives you the capability to browse your site inside the Dreamweaver interface, testing values as you go. The Server Debug options are displayed for any ColdFusion page but only work for ColdFusion MX on Windows.

New Feature

Use the new Server Debug view to see all the errors and server variables for your ColdFusion MX pages.

To enable debugging directly inside Dreamweaver, follow these simple steps:

1. Enable server debugging by choosing Debugging Settings in the left-hand pane of the ColdFusion MX Administrator (see Figure 18-9). The Debugging Options page will open in the right-hand pane.

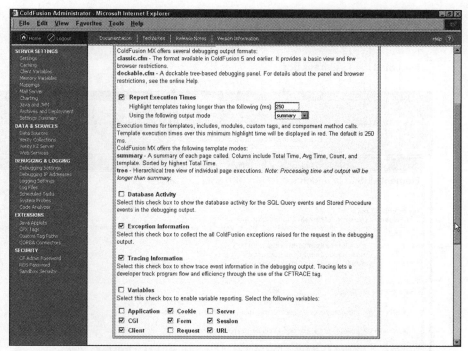

Figure 18-9: Enable the server debugging options in ColdFusion MX before using the Server Debug panel in Dreamweaver.

2. Click the Server Debug icon in the Standard Toolbar. After you click the Server Debug icon an additional toolbar will show directly above your document window.

- **Backward:** Emulates the browser Back button and takes you to the previous page in your history.

- **Forward:** Emulates the browser Forward button and takes you to the next page in your history.

- **Stop:** Emulates the browser Stop button and stops the current page from processing.

- **Refresh:** Emulates the browser Refresh button and reloads the current page.

- **Server Debug:** Toggles server debugging on and off.

- **Address Bar:** Passes querystring values to your page and also enables you to see where you are in your site.

When you preview Live Data, you can see all the CF MX Server Debug output, and you can browse through your pages just like you would in a regular Web browser (see Figure 18-10).

3. Open the Server Debug panel by choosing Window ➪ Results ➪ Server Debug or pressing Ctrl+Shift+F5. The Server Debug panel should now be shown below the Property inspector (see Figure 18-11).

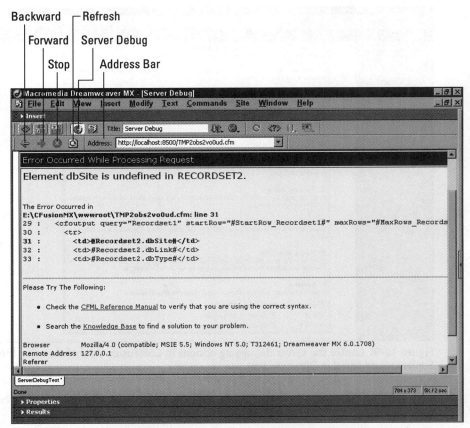

Figure 18-10: The Server Debug view gives you additional options on the toolbar for browsing your ColdFusion MX documents.

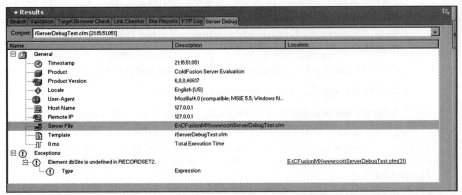

Figure 18-11: The Server Debug panel gives you a quick overview of all the returned variables from the ColdFusion MX server.

After you open the Server Debug panel, you can see all your variables, as well as any errors. Any exceptions will provide a link to the page that is throwing the error. If that error was contained inside a <CFINCLUDE>, the URL for the page is a clickable link next to the error.

Tip   If you right-click inside the Server Debug panel, you can choose Select All and copy the contents of the panel by choosing Copy from the context menu. You can then paste it inside a new document — in Dreamweaver or another text editor — for future reference or to send to another ColdFusion developer for further debugging.

Summary

Sometimes, when a brand-new idea appears in a software program, it's hard to separate the merely glitzy from the truly grand. As implemented in Dreamweaver, Live Data view proves to be bottom-line functional and, thus, more than a flash in the pan — although I have to admit, it's pretty darn cool as well. To make the most of Live Data view, remember the following points:

✦ Live Data view depends on proper setup of the testing server in order to run smoothly. If any of the information entered into the Testing Server category of the Site Definition dialog box is incomplete or incorrect, Dreamweaver won't be able to process your Web application successfully and display the results.

✦ Select the Auto Refresh option on the Live Data toolbar to take advantage of Dreamweaver's capability to reformat dynamic data when the server formatting has changed.

✦ The query string field and the Settings button in the Live Data toolbar both offer developers a way to test their Web application with different variables. Use the query string field to emulate the passing of URL parameters, and the Settings dialog box for Post-enabled forms.

✦ To try different server environments, enter the appropriate code in the Initialization Script field of the Settings dialog box. This facility enables you to test different application variables, session variables, and other variables easily.

✦ Be sure to use Dreamweaver's Preview in Browser feature to give your Web application a real-world tryout before going live. To test your page, transfer dependent and related files using the Site window from the local site to the testing server pane.

✦ User Dreamweaver's tight ColdFusion MX integration and the Server Debug panel to quickly debug your ColdFusion applications.

In the next chapter, you'll learn how to implement the use of cookies and other variables in your Dreamweaver Web application.

✦   ✦   ✦

Crafting Multiple-Page Applications

In a Web site composed of static HTML pages, each page generally stands on its own and is developed individually. On a dynamic Web site, however, applications often require multiple pages to be effective. A prime example is the master-detail Web application where a search box on one page leads to a master list of results on a second page, each of which, in turn, is linked to a third dynamically generated detail page. To execute the application, variables and other information must be passed from one page to the next. The active Web site developer has a variety of tools capable of handling this task: forms, cookies, and session variables to name a few. All these methods for creating multiple-page Web applications are available in Dreamweaver and are covered in this chapter. You'll also look at a one-step procedure for developing a master-detail Web application.

Additionally, this chapter covers the use of form elements, such as text fields, checkboxes, and drop-down lists for dynamic data display. Form elements are extremely useful to the Web application developer. For example, form objects can be updated on-the-fly; making a choice in one drop-down list may determine which options are available in another list. Moreover, form elements are inherently interactive. For example, a checked checkbox, which indicates a `true` value for a record in a database, may be cleared by the user; when that record is submitted, the cleared checkbox will change the field value to `false`. Finally, this chapter describes how to put this new knowledge to work creating a search field.

Using the URL to Pass Parameters

In a static Web site, links are used to navigate from one page to another. In a dynamic site, links can have an additional function: passing parameters to an application server so that it can determine the dynamic content on the linked page. The added parameters are known as a *query string* and follow the standard URL after a question mark, like this:

```
dvd_details.asp?movie=Bedazzled
```

Every parameter is composed of a name/value pair separated by an equals sign. If more than one parameter is sent, each pair is separated by an ampersand, as in the following example:

```
dvd_details.asp?movie=Bedazzled&genre=western
```

Notice that unlike with HTML or other languages, quotation marks are not used to set off the values. Quotation marks and other non-alphanumeric characters including spaces, single quotes, and tildes must be translated into encoded characters so that the server may interpret them correctly. Spaces, for instance, are rendered as a %20, as shown here:

```
dvd_details.asp?movie=Bedazzled&genre=western&star=Clint%20Eastwood
```

Dreamweaver provides all the tools necessary for constructing query strings within its point-and-click interface. However, if you understand the required syntax, you can quickly test your page using the URL field found on the Live Data toolbar.

Sending parameters

With a master-detail Web application, typically only a single parameter is used. The parameter uniquely identifies the record selected on the master page and is appended to the link for the detail page. For example, suppose the detail page is dbadetails.asp, the identifying variable is called tripid, and the specific item is Conquering K2. The full link, with the query string, would read:

```
dbadetails.asp?tripid=Conquering%20K2
```

Note   Master pages are one of two types: Either the master list is defined by the designer or by search criteria submitted by the user. The examples in this section are designer-based and rely on a specific recordset being declared. Details on how to create a search field are covered later in this chapter in the "Dreamweaver Technique: Building a Search Engine" section.

To create the proper code within Dreamweaver, apply a Go To Detail Page server behavior to the linking text, image, or dynamic data. Master pages also include a Repeat Region server behavior; the Go To Detail Page server behavior is attached to the text or graphic within the region, as shown in Figure 19-1.

To attach a Go To Detail Page server behavior, follow these steps:

1. Select the page element—text, graphic, or dynamic data—you'd like to use as the link to the detail page.

2. From the Server Behaviors panel, choose Add (+) and then select Go To Detail Page from the drop-down list. The Go To Detail Page dialog box, shown in Figure 19-2, is displayed. (This option is not available for ColdFusion or PHP.)

3. Make sure that the page element selected is represented in the Link field. If no selection is made, Dreamweaver creates a new Detail text link.

4. Enter the path to the detail page in the Detail Page field or use Browse to locate the file in the Select File dialog box.

Tip   It's a good idea to prototype all the pages in your application before you begin adding content, especially server-side code. Existing pages are easy to link to through a Select File dialog box, and doing so reduces the chance of typographical errors.

5. Enter the variable name you'd like to be sent in the Pass URL Parameter field. You can use a name of your own choosing or the name of the field in the database; whichever name you decide upon, make a note of it somewhere because you'll need to reference it when the detail page itself is constructed.

6. From the Recordset list, select the recordset that contains the URL parameter.

7. From the Column list, choose the field that the URL parameter's value is related to.

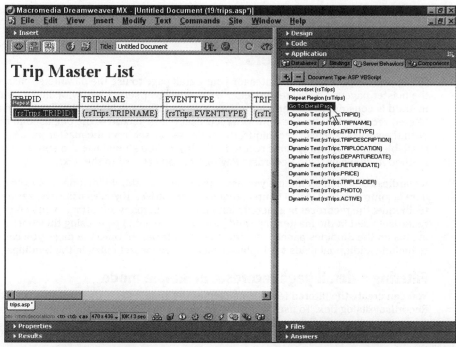

Figure 19-1: The Go To Detail Page server behavior within the Repeat Region connects the master page to the proper detail page.

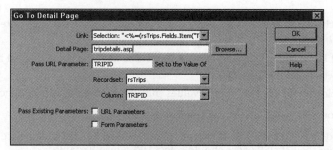

Figure 19-2: Specify the linking parameter sent from the master page in the Go To Detail Page server behavior.

8. Unless you have pre-existing URL or form parameters to send to the detail page, leave the Pass Existing Parameters options unchecked.

Caution Make sure that you leave the Pass Existing Parameters options unselected especially if you are linking back to your master page from the detail page. Otherwise, the parameters will begin to accumulate, and your linking URL will look like this nonfunctioning example:

```
detailpage.cfm?id=23&id=36
```

9. Click OK when you're done.

Now that the link is passing parameters successfully, it's time to make sure that the detail page is set up for receiving them properly.

Receiving parameters

Dreamweaver provides two routes for your detail page to use the parameter passed to it by the master page: a filtered recordset or a Dreamweaver server behavior. In general, the first method is considered less processor-intensive and thus the better choice of the two. The filtered recordset technique returns a recordset of one record—the one used in the detail. With the server behavior technique, the entire recordset from the master page is made available, and only the specific record is displayed. You should use the entire recordset method if you want to do Recordset Paging from one record to the next.

Regardless of which technique you use, the detail page should include whatever dynamic data is appropriate. This, of course, requires a recordset. If you're using the server behavior technique, the recordset is generally left unfiltered; in many situations, you can copy the recordset used in the master page and paste it in the detail page using the context-sensitive menus on the Bindings panel. After the recordset is pasted onto the page, you can modify it to include additional fields by double-clicking the recordset entry in the Bindings panel.

Filtering a detail page recordset in Simple mode

You can create the filtered recordset in either the simple Recordset or the advanced Recordset dialog box. To use the simple Recordset dialog, follow these steps:

See Chapter 15 for more on the simple and advanced Recordset dialog boxes.

1. From the Bindings panel, select the Add (+) button and then choose Recordset from the list.

2. After you've chosen the name, connection, and table, select the fields required by your details page from the Columns list.

3. From the first Filter list, select the field that coincides with the value passed by the URL parameter as shown in Figure 19-3.

   Again, this field should contain unique values that can be used to identify each record.

4. From the second Filter list, select the equals operator (=).

5. From the third Filter list, ASP, .NET, PHP and ColdFusion users should choose URL Parameter from the list; JSP users should select URL/Form Variable.

6. In the fourth Filter field, enter the variable name passed by the master page in the Go To Detail Page server behavior.

   Avoid names with spaces or other special characters; these names must be URL encoded and may be difficult to manage.

7. Click OK when you're done.

You can preview the results of your detail page in Live Data view, but make sure you set up the Live Data settings option first. Choose View ➪ Live Data Settings to begin. When the Live Data Settings dialog box is open, enter the URL parameter name in the Name column and the value you'd like to test in the Value column. Make sure the Method option is set to Get and click OK. Your preview should now include the specified record just as if it had been chosen by the user.

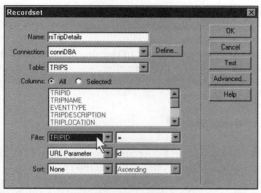

Figure 19-3: Setting a filter in the simple Recordset dialog box requires completing four fields under the Filter heading.

Tip   After entering Live Data view, you can test a variety of different records without reopening the Live Data Settings dialog. In the URL Parameter field found on the Live Data toolbar, change the URL parameter's current value and press Enter (Return). If you enter a value not found in the data source, Dreamweaver will display an error indicating the page cannot be displayed.

To test your master-detail application, save both pages and then begin by previewing the master page in the browser. When you select the link to the detail page, you should see your chosen record.

Filtering a detail page recordset in Advanced mode

Sometimes you need to define a more complex recordset than is possible in the simple Recordset dialog box. You can effectively add the same filter-by-URL-parameter argument for such recordsets in the advanced Recordset dialog box by altering the SQL statement. Filtering in a SQL statement is handled by the WHERE clause.

To create a detail page filter, you declare a variable and add a WHERE clause referencing that variable. The runtime value portion of the variable is different for each server model. Assume you want to declare a variable called theBrand, and the field is named Brand. In the Variables section of the Advanced Recordset dialog box, select the Add (+) button and then enter the following values, according to your server model:

Server Model	Name	Default Value	Runtime Value
ASP and .NET	theBrand	%	Request.QueryString("Brand")
ColdFusion	theBrand	%	#URL.Brand#
JSP	theBrand	%	request.getParameter ("Brand")
PHP	TheBrand	%	<?php echo $HTTP_GET_VARS ['Brand']; ?>

In this example, the WHERE clause would read:

    WHERE Brand = 'theBrand'

If you have already created a URL parameter filtered recordset in the simple Recordset dialog box and then switch to the Advanced mode, you notice that Dreamweaver uses the variable name MMColParam. You can continue to use this variable name or change it to something more meaningful if you prefer.

Using a server behavior to filter a recordset

As noted earlier, the other method for connecting a master page with a detail page involves using a Dreamweaver server behavior. The Move To Specific Record server behavior is applied on the detail page itself and may be attached at any time. Unlike the filtered recordset approach, which uses a single record in the recordset, Move To Specific Record requires a recordset that includes all the possible records and their data. This gives you the ability to move through the recordset using the Recordset Paging Server Behaviors. The record specified by the URL parameter, as interpreted by the server behavior, is extracted from the overall recordset and its data displayed. To use the Move To Specific Record server behavior to create a detail page, follow these steps:

1. Establish a recordset that contains all the possible records that could be requested by the master page.

2. From the Server Behaviors panel, choose Move To Specific Record from the Move To Record submenu. The Move To Specific Record dialog box is displayed as shown in Figure 19-4.

3. Select the desired recordset from the list labeled Move To Record In.

4. Choose the field referenced in the URL parameter from the Where Column field.

5. Enter the variable in the URL parameter in the Matches URL Parameter field.

6. Click OK when you're done.

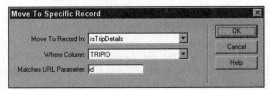

Figure 19-4: An alternative method for creating a detail page uses the Move To Specific Record server behavior.

Caution Although Dreamweaver provides this method for creating a detail page — and I've covered it here for the sake of completeness — it's really not recommended. Because this technique relies on the use of a full recordset, it is far more resource-intensive than the filtered recordset method. However, this is method is required if you are going to use Recordset Paging.

Automating master-detail page production

Although Dreamweaver has made crafting master-detail Web applications by hand extremely accessible, it can be a tedious series of steps, especially if you have to produce a number of applications for a site. To ease the tedium — and enhance your production efforts — Dreamweaver includes the Master Detail Page Set Application Object that, after a single dialog box is completed, creates all the elements for a linked master-detail Web application.

The master page elements are inserted in the current document, which must contain a recordset. The inserted elements and code, shown in Figure 19-5, are as follows:

✦ A two-row table with a column for each field

✦ A header row comprised of all the field names selected in the dialog

✦ Dynamic text for all selected fields, placed into the second row

✦ A Repeat Region server behavior surrounding the second row

✦ A Go To Detail Page server behavior linking to the newly created detail page

✦ Recordset Navigation Bar with text links and appropriate Show Region server behaviors in place

✦ Recordset Status Bar showing the current record count

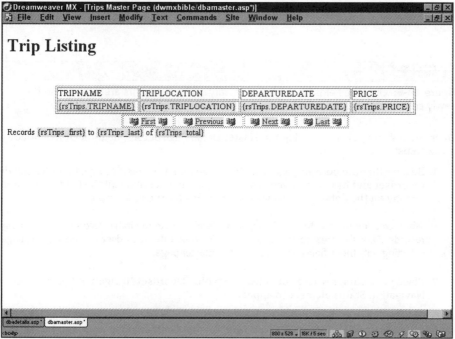

Figure 19-5: The Master Detail Page Set Application Object adds all the designated fields and the required server behaviors to the current page.

The detail page is created when the Master Detail Page Set Object is executed. As shown in Figure 19-6, the detail page is blank except for a two-column table, which contains a row for each field. The first column displays all the field names in the designated order, and the second column holds Dynamic Text elements, one for each of the fields.

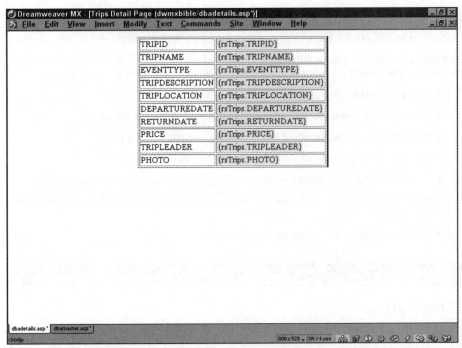

Figure 19-6: Only the fields, data, and necessary server behaviors are included in the newly created detail page.

To create a Web application using the Master Detail Page Set Application Object, follow these steps:

1. Be sure that the current page, which will become the master page, includes the desired recordset and has been saved. The recordset must contain all the fields you want to display on the detail page, as well as the fields for the master page.

Tip

When creating the master-detail pages I generally create my initial recordset and choose all records. After I've created my page set, I trim down the recordset on the master page by selecting only those fields necessary for the master page.

2. Place your cursor where you'd like the table, Recordset Navigation Bar, and Recordset Navigation Status element to appear.

3. Choose Insert ➪ Application Object ➪ Master Page Detail Set. You can also drag the Insert Master Detail Page Set icon from the Application category of the Insert bar to the desired location on the page. The Insert Master Detail Page Set dialog box is shown in Figure 19-7. (Note that this option is not available in PHP.)

4. Select the recordset you'd like to use from the Recordset list.

5. In the Master Page Fields area, choose any fields you do not want to appear on the master and click the Remove (–) button.

   Dreamweaver, by default, includes all the available fields in a selected recordset. If there are any fields not in the current recordset that you'd like to include, you must select Cancel and modify the recordset.

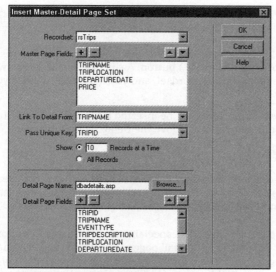

Figure 19-7: Select the fields and their relative positions to lay out the columns for both the master and detail pages.

6. If you change your mind after you have removed a field from the list of fields that will be inserted into the master page, select the Add (+) button and reinsert the field.

7. Alter the positioning of the fields in the master page table by selecting the field and using the up and down arrows above the Master Page Fields area.

   The master page table is horizontal with the topmost fields in the Master Page Fields area appearing on the left and the bottommost fields on the right. Selecting the up arrow moves a field to the left, whereas selecting the down arrow moves it to the right.

8. Choose a field from the Link To Detail From list that will serve as a link to the detail page. Only the fields remaining in the Master Page Fields area are available in the Link to Detail From list.

9. From the Pass Unique Key list, select the field that identifies each record for use in the URL parameter.

   Although the field in the Link To Detail From list and the one in the Pass Unique Key list could be the same, they don't have to be. You could, for example, use an employee's last name as the link and the employee ID number — not displayed in the master page fields — as the unique key. The Pass Unique Key list includes all the fields in the chosen recordset whether they are displayed on screen or not.

10. Select the number of records you'd like displayed in the Repeat Region. Choose All to display every record in the recordset.

    Now that the master page portion of your application is defined, you define the elements for the detail page.

11. Enter the path to the detail page in the Detail Page Name field or select Browse to locate the file, if it exists.

Note The master and detail pages must be in the same folder for the Master Detail Page Set Application Object to function properly.

12. From the Detail Page Fields area, select any fields that you do not want to display on the detail page and choose the Remove (–) button. Again, by default, Dreamweaver displays all the available fields in the recordset, and you must delete those you don't want to have shown.

13. To change the order in which the fields will be inserted into the detail page table, select the field and use the up or down buttons above the Detail Page Fields area.

14. Click OK when you're done.

Note After the Application Object has finished inserting master page elements and creating the detail page, be sure to save the master page. Dreamweaver will save the detail page automatically, but it does not save the master page as part of the creation process.

The Master Detail Page Set Application Object — especially the detail page — works well with Dreamweaver templates. After the master and detail pages are created, you can apply any Dreamweaver template to integrate the results into your site. To prepare the template, just make sure that there is at least one editable region for all the visual elements inserted into the master and detail pages. I say that the Server-Object–generated detail page is especially well suited to template use because the created page contains only the table and its dynamic elements. After applying such a template, as shown in Figure 19-8, you may still need to tweak the design further by altering the table properties.

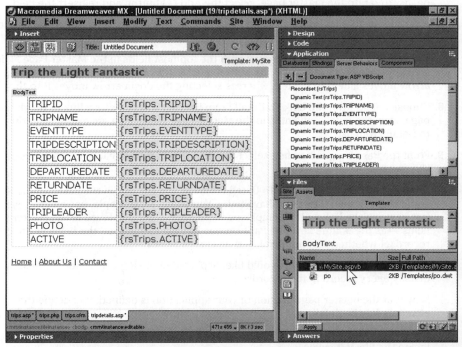

Figure 19-8: Drag a template from the Assets panel onto a detail page to quickly change the look-and-feel of a generated document.

Cross-Reference   To find out more about Dreamweaver templates, see Chapter 28.

Getting Values from a Form

Next to clicking on links, a user's prime interaction with a Web page is through the form. Forms are used in almost every Web application in one form (minor pun intended) or another. A Web page that is gathering information from a user always contains a form, and uses a variety of elements, such as text fields, checkboxes, radio buttons, and drop-down lists. Although forms are important to Web applications, not every page containing a form needs to be executed by an application server. You can, however, pass information from a form to a dynamic page.

In the earlier discussions of master-detail Web applications, the master page was always generated by the developer's recordset selection without any user input. This section will examine how user-driven master pages can be developed in Dreamweaver. Here are the four key elements:

✦ A static HTML page containing a form (Although it's possible to use a dynamic page, none of what this page accomplishes requires server-side code.)

✦ One or more uniquely named form elements (The naming of the form element is vital to getting the correct value into the application.)

✦ A link from the static page to the dynamic page inserted as a relative or an absolute URL in the action parameter of the form

✦ A filter on the recordset of the dynamic page that reads the value passed from the form

Passing single values from a form

The recordset filter, if it relates to a single form element, may be set in the simple Recordset dialog box. More sophisticated filters, which depend on values received from multiple form elements, must be created in the advanced Recordset dialog box. To set up a form to send user selections to a master page or other Web application, follow these steps:

1. Create a static HTML page (File ⇨ New) and choose Insert ⇨ Form or drag an Insert Form icon onto the page from the Forms tab of the Insert bar.

2. Add the desired input form elements into the form by selecting them from the Insert ⇨ Form Objects submenu or from the Insert bar.

3. Be sure to name each form element appropriately and uniquely. You'll need to recall this name when you're building your application page.

Tip   It's best to adopt a naming strategy that you can use over and over again. My preference is to name each form element with two parts: context and type. The first part of the name describes its context or how it is used on the page; the second part indicates what kind of form element is named. For example, a text field that holds the last name of a visitor would be called lastnameText; whereas a drop-down list that lists office locations would be locationsList. After a while, your naming convention becomes second nature to you, and you can easily remember what each form element has been named.

4. Select the ‹form› tag on the Tag Selector and, in the Action field of the Property inspector, enter the path to the dynamic page containing the application. Alternatively, you can click the folder icon to locate the file.

5. Also in the Property inspector, set the Method property of the form to Post.

When you're passing variables and values via the URL query-string technique, described previously in "Using the URL to Pass Parameters," use the Get method. To pass the values of the form without exposing them in the URL, use Post.

Note   When you're deciding whether to use POST or GET to pass your parameters, you need to decide whether you'll need to easily pass those variables to other pages. If you do need to continue using the parameters, GET is an easier method to use when passing variables. If you're only going to use them for this single page, use POST to keep the query string clean.

6. Save your page.

Now you're ready to implement the receiving portion of your form-value passing application.

1. Create a new dynamic page for your master page application.

2. Insert a recordset by choosing the Add (+) button from the Bindings panel and selecting Recordset from the list.

3. In the simple Recordset dialog box, choose your recordset name, connection, table, and columns.

4. In the Filter area, from the first Filter list, select the field that matches the value passed by the form element. For example, if you are filtering a recordset based on the location specified in a form's drop-down list, you would choose the field — called location, perhaps — which would contain that specified value.

5. From the second Filter list, select the equals operator (=).

6. From the third Filter list, ASP and ColdFusion users should choose Form Variable from the list; JSP users should select URL/Form Variable.

7. In the fourth Filter field, enter the name of the form element. In our example, the form element would be named locationList.

8. Click OK when you're done.

9. Apply the Master-Detail Page Application object to create the master page.

Test your application by saving the master page and previewing the initial page with the form. You can also use View ➪ Live Data Settings to try different values for your form variable; be sure to change the Method to Post in the Live Data Settings dialog box.

Passing multiple values from a form

For more complex recordsets, you'll have to write the SQL statement in Dreamweaver's advanced Recordset dialog box. The same technique described earlier in the "Filtering a detail page recordset in Advanced mode" section applies here. Declare a variable that uses one of the following runtime values:

Server Model	Name	Default Value	Runtime Value
ASP and .NET	theVariable	%	Request.Form("Fieldname")
ColdFusion	theVariable	%	#Form.Fieldname#
JSP	theVariable	%	request.getParameter ("Fieldname")
PHP	TheVariable	%	<?php echo $HTTP_POST_VARS ['Fieldname']; ?>

The WHERE clause of the SQL sets the fieldname to the variable, as in this example:

```
WHERE dbadata.Location = 'theLocation'
```

Multiple form variables can also be set up in the advanced Recordset dialog box. Let's presume that you want your master page to display a list of employees in a particular department at a specific office. The form might include a drop-down list that displays a number of departments as well as a radio button group for the different offices. If theDept were the variable for the department form list value and theLocation for the office radio button value, the SQL statement would look like this:

```
SELECT * FROM Employees WHERE Department = 'theDept' ⊃
AND Location = 'theLocation'
```

Passing form and URL values to a related page

Master-detail Web applications aren't the only applications that can benefit from information entered on a form. Other applications sometimes offer a link to a related page — like a special note pertinent only to a user-specified selection. To implement such pages, the application page needs the same form information passed to the master page. Dreamweaver includes a Go To Related Page server behavior that delivers the form values to the linked page; the Go To Related Page server behavior can also pass URL values by themselves or in conjunction with values from forms.

As with other server behaviors in the Go To category, Go To Related Page may be applied to text, image, or dynamic page element. In a master page with a Repeat Region, you can attach the Go To Related Page to an element within the repeating region and have it be available for every entry. To attach a Go To Related Page server behavior, follow these steps:

1. On a page that has had form or URL values passed to it, select the page element — text, image, or dynamic data — you'd like to use as the trigger for your behavior.

2. From the Server Behaviors panel, choose the Add (+) button and then select Go To Related Page from the list. The Go To Related Page server behavior dialog box appears, as shown in Figure 19-9.

3. In the dialog box, verify that the text or code for the selected element displayed in the Link field is correct.

4. Enter the path to the target page in the Related Page field or choose Browse to locate an existing dynamic page.

5. If you want to carry over values received from a query string, select the URL Parameters option.

6. If you want to pass values received from a form, select the Form Parameters option.

7. Click OK when you're done.

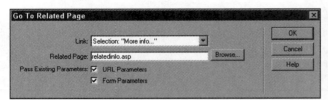

Figure 19-9: The Go To Related Page server behavior can convey form values, URL values, or both to another dynamic page.

The Go To Related Page server behavior may also be used to carry results of a form within a series of pages. In other words, if your first Go To Related Page server behavior passed the form or URL values from the master page to the first related page, you could include another Go To Related Page server behavior linked to a second related page.

Caution You cannot use the Go To Related Page server behavior to link to a dynamic page that uses the Move To Specific Record server behavior. The Move To Specific Record server behavior overwrites the form or URL values passed by the Go To Related Page server behavior with its own. Instead of a Move To Specific Record server behavior on the target page, create a recordset filtered from the passed form/URL values.

Dreamweaver Technique: Building a Search Engine

One of the most common uses of passing form values to create a master page is the search engine. The user interface for the search engine may contain most of the available form objects: text field, checkbox, radio button, or list. After you've passed the entered form values to the master page application, the key is in filtering the recordset. To create a search application for a single criterion, follow these steps:

1. Create a form on your search page. The search fields do not have to be on a dynamic page.

2. Select the form and in the Property inspector, set the Action attribute to the URL of the master page.

3. From the Method list, choose Post.

4. Add any desired form elements, such as text fields, radio buttons or drop-down lists, and a Submit button. Be sure to name each element uniquely.

5. On the master page, choose Recordset from the Bindings panel to create a recordset for the results of the search.

6. Choose the recordset name, connection, table, and columns.

7. In the Filter area, set the four fields as described in the "Passing single values from a form" section found earlier in this chapter and as shown in Figure 19-10.

Tip   If you're using a text field in your form, you'll get the widest number of results by using the Contains operator rather than the equals sign. To replicate the Contains operator in SQL statement, use the `LIKE` keyword or—if you're data source does not support that keyword—use the equals operator and place wildcard characters on either side of the variable, as in this SQL clause: `WHERE Lastname = '%lastnameText%'`.

8. Optionally, you can arrange your results by choosing a field and either Ascending or Descending from the Sort area.

9. Click OK when you're done.

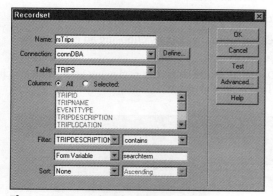

Figure 19-10: Using the Contains operator in conjunction with the Form Variable assures you of the widest range of results.

The search may be based on more than one criterion. Multiple criteria require the use of the advanced Recordset dialog box. In the advanced Recordset dialog box, create a variable for every form element used in the search and then concatenate those variables in the `WHERE` clause of the SQL statement, as in this example:

```
WHERE Department = 'theDept' AND Lastname = '%theLastname%'
```

Establishing Dynamic Form Elements

Forms and form elements play a much larger role in Web applications than just filtering recordsets. Forms are also necessary for inserting new records in a data source as well as for updating existing records. Dreamweaver lets you convert standard form elements into dynamic ones so that they can reflect and modify a record's data.

Although the general conversion from a static to a dynamic form element is handled in the same fashion for all elements—apply a Dynamic Form Elements server behavior to an existing form element—almost every element has different dialog boxes with varying parameters.

Text fields

Text fields are extremely flexible and essential for inputting freeform text into data sources. To create a dynamic text field, follow these steps:

1. Insert a text field into a form on a page with a recordset or other data source.

   It's a good idea to name the text field and form at this point. Although you can always change the names later, I find that naming the elements early avoids problems later.

2. Select the text field.

3. From the Server Behaviors panel, choose Dynamic Form Elements ➪ Dynamic Text Field.

4. In the Dynamic Text Field dialog box that appears (Figure 19-11), verify that the correct form element was chosen in the Text Field list. If necessary, choose a different text field.

5. Select the Set Value To lightning bolt icon to display the available data sources.

6. Choose a field from the Dynamic Data dialog box.

7. If desired, you can apply a server format to the data by choosing an entry in the Format list.

8. Click OK to close the Dynamic Data dialog box and, after reviewing your choices, click OK again to close the Dynamic Text Field dialog box.

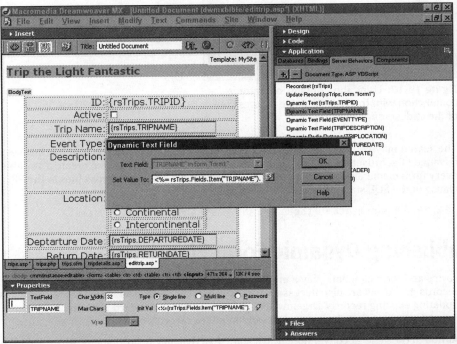

Figure 19-11: Use a dynamically linked text field to display data in an editable format.

The dynamic data is inserted into what is called the *initial value* of the form field. You can see the data of the current recordset by selecting View ➪ Live Data. It's likely that you'll need to adjust the width of the text field to accommodate your dynamic data. You may adjust the width — and all the other standard parameters of a text field — through the Property inspector.

Tip If the use of Cascading Style Sheets is an option on your Web application, it's often far better to create a custom class for the text field to control the width. Not only is the measurement standard more precise in CSS than in standard HTML, but it can be updated for all applicable text fields in one operation rather than in a tag-by-tag fashion.

After you become familiar with Dreamweaver's workings, you can use the Bindings panel to skip most of the previous steps. To use the Bindings panel, follow these steps:

1. Insert a text field into a form on a page with a recordset or other data source.

2. Select the text field.

3. Open the Bindings panel and select the dynamic data to bind to your text field.

4. Click Bind at the bottom of the Bindings panel.

Checkboxes

When you attach a checkbox to dynamic data, the checked and unchecked state reflects the true or false state of a Yes/No (also known as a Boolean) type of database field. Not only is this visual method easily understood at a glance, checkboxes are also extremely easy to update. To convert a static checkbox to a dynamic one, follow these steps:

1. Select a checkbox in a form on a page with a recordset.

2. From the Server Behaviors panel, choose Dynamic Form Elements ⇨ Dynamic CheckBox. The Dynamic CheckBox dialog box appears, as shown in Figure 19-12.

Tip Click the Dynamic button in the Property inspector to go straight to the Dynamic CheckBox dialog box.

3. Verify that your selected checkbox is correctly named in the CheckBox list.

4. Select the Check If lightning bolt icon to display the available data sources.

5. Choose a field from the Dynamic Data dialog box.

6. If desired, you can apply a server format to the data by choosing an entry in the Format list. Click OK when you're done to close the Dynamic Data dialog box.

7. Enter the value expected for a selected checkbox in the Equal To field.

   This value is data-source dependent. For many data sources, 1 is used to represent true; for others, a -1 is used. When working with Yes/No fields from Access databases, enter **True**; be sure to capitalize the word as "true" will not work properly.

8. Select OK when you're done.

Tip Although checkboxes are used most typically to show the state of Yes/No data fields, they can also be tied to text data fields and selected if the field is equal to a given value. When applying the Dynamic CheckBox server behavior, choose the text field and enter the exact text string in the Equal To field.

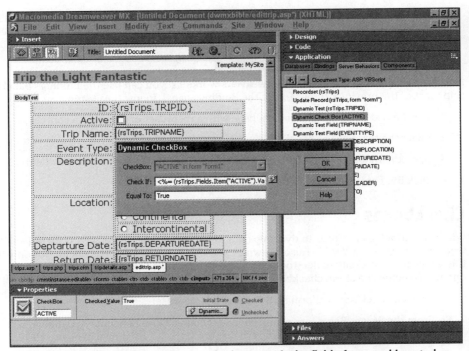

Figure 19-12: Checkboxes can depict whether a particular field of a record is noted as True in the data source.

Radio buttons

Radio buttons provide a good way to represent a field that has a limited number of options. Suppose your data source includes an event type field and there are three possible choices: Local (loc), Continental (con) and Intercontinental (int). To illustrate which type of event your trip was, your Web application might display a series of three radio buttons next to each entry, one for each type. If the radio buttons are dynamically tied to the Event Type field, they show the correct type for each trip. Like checkboxes, radio buttons are very easy to modify—one click and you're done. To link radio buttons to dynamic data, follow these steps:

1. Select a group of radio buttons on a dynamic page with an available data source.

2. From the Server Behaviors panel, choose Dynamic Form Elements ⇨ Dynamic Radio Buttons. The Dynamic Radio Buttons dialog box appears, as shown in Figure 19-13.

3. Verify that your selected form element is displayed in the Radio Button Group list.

4. In the Radio Button Values area, choose the first entry shown and, if necessary, change the Value field to reflect the expected data.

5. Repeat Step 4 for every radio button in the group.

6. Select the Select Value Equal To lightning bolt icon to display the available data sources.

7. Choose a field from the Dynamic Data dialog box. Be sure to select a data source field with values parallel to those entered in the radio button group.

8. If desired, you can apply a server format to the data by choosing an entry in the Format list. Click OK when you're done to close the Dynamic Data dialog box.

9. When you're done, click OK to close the Dynamic Radio Buttons dialog box.

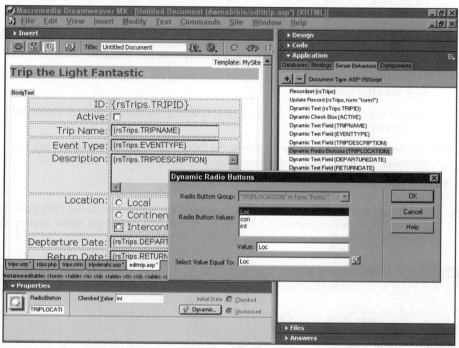

Figure 19-13: Radio buttons can reflect a limited number of choices within a data source field.

List/Menus

Typographical errors are the bane of data entry. Regardless of how careful users are, whenever an exact phrase of any length must be entered, typos are inevitable. The list/menu form element provides a good alternative to a text field when a limited set of responses is needed. An eCommerce site, for instance, might use a list/menu form element (also called a drop-down list or select list) to allow the user to navigate from one product line to another. With Dreamweaver, the drop-down list may be filled — or *populated* — with dynamic data, so that the navigation tool can keep track with the products entered in the data source.

A drop-down list is composed of two parts: the label and the value. The *label* is what users see when they select the list; the *value* is what is submitted by the user when a particular list choice is made. In many situations, both the label and the value may be the same; in these cases, you can use the same data source field for both. Otherwise, you need to have data source fields available — this is how the product navigation example works. One data source field contains an entry for every product line (the label), and another field contains a URL to that product line's page on the Web site (the value). To link a drop-down list to dynamic data, follow these steps:

1. Insert a list/menu form element on a dynamic page with a recordset.

2. If you have more than one list/menu on the page, select the one you want to convert.

3. From the Server Behaviors panel, choose Dynamic Form Elements ⇨ Dynamic List/Menu. The Dynamic List/Menu dialog box, shown in Figure 19-14 is displayed.

4. In the Static Options box, add any nondynamic items you want to the top of your list menu. This could be something as simple as a label for the list menu or as complicated as a full URL with query strings for search pages.

5. Choose the recordset you want to work with from the Options From Recordset list.

6. Verify that the desired drop-down list is displayed in the Menu list.

7. Choose the field from your data source containing the items you want submitted by the user from the Values list.

8. Choose the field from your data source containing the items you want displayed to the user from the Labels list.

9. To preselect an item, enter its value in the Select Value Equal To field, or use the lightning bolt icon to choose a value from the established data sources.

10. Click OK when you're done.

New Feature You should also notice the new Dynamic button on the Property inspector. Click the button to open the corresponding dialog box. This is another quick way to get to the options without going through the Server Behaviors panel.

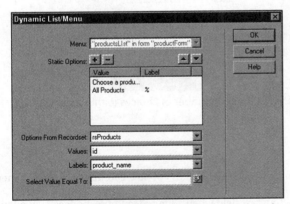

Figure 19-14: Lists give the user a distinct series of items from which to choose.

Managing Data Sources Online

Data source connectivity is a two-way street. Not only can data be extracted and displayed over the Web, but Web applications can also manage records found in data sources. With the power to add, modify, and remove data comes a terrific opportunity. From a Web application-builder's perspective, I find that almost half of my client work is concerned with data source management.

As with the common master-detail application, Dreamweaver offers both a manual and an automatic method of performing the most common management tasks. There are Application Objects for both inserting and updating records. Both methods are detailed in the following sections.

Inserting data

To insert records into a data source, you need the following:

✦ An active page

✦ A form placed on the page

✦ One form element per data source field

✦ A Submit button

✦ An Insert Record server behavior

Notice that no recordset or other data source is necessary, nor are there are any special requirements for the form itself — you don't even have to specify an action or a method. The Insert Record server behavior handles most of the coding chores.

The form elements are typically arranged in a table with labels for each field as shown in Figure 19-15. Naturally you can format the table however you'd like; I generally prefer a two-column table with the labels in the first column, right-aligned, and the form elements in the second column, left-aligned. It's best to name the form elements so that you can identify them easily and ensure that each element is unique. A reset button is optional — but recommended if the form has many fields.

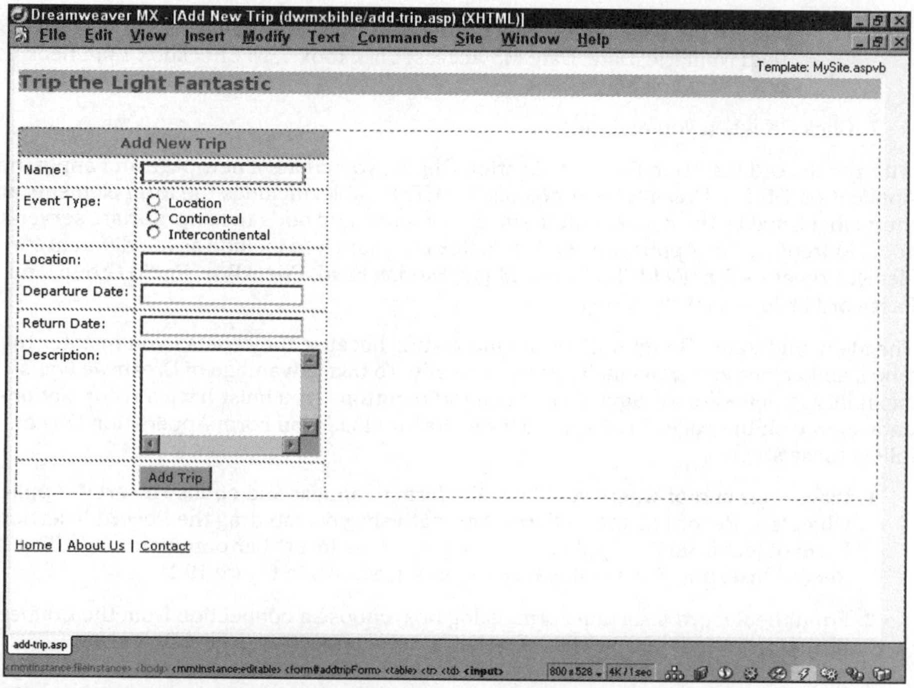

Figure 19-15: You don't need to define a recordset for an insert record page.

Tip   You can save a step in the Insert Record server behavior setup by naming your form elements the same as their relevant data source fields. Dreamweaver automatically assigns the form elements to any data fields with matching names. Unfortunately, this process could expose the field names in your database and give hackers more information about your database than you'd like them to know.

After you've constructed your table inside the form and placed the form elements, you're ready to add the Insert Record server behavior by following these steps:

1. From the Server Behaviors panel, choose Insert Record. The Insert Record dialog box appears.

2. From the Insert Record dialog box, choose a connection from the Connection drop-down list. If you need to establish a new connection, select Define.

3. Select the data table you want to use from the Insert Into Table list.

4. Enter the path to the destination page in the After Inserting, Go To field; or choose the Browse button to locate the file.

   It's important that you select a confirmation or other page to go to after the form is submitted. If you don't, there is no feedback to the user, and no change is apparent.

5. Select the name of the form to be used from the Get Values From list. If there is only one form on the page, the form will be preselected.

6. For each object listed in the Form Elements area

   • Select the data source field that the value of the form object is to be inserted into from the Column list.

   • Choose the data source type for the data from the Submit As list. The options are Text; Numeric; Date; Date MS Access; Checkbox Y, N; Checkbox 1,0; Check -1,0; and Checkbox MS Access.

7. Click OK when you're done.

With the Record Insertion Form Application Object, you create a new page and apply the Application Object. Dreamweaver creates the HTML table, includes the form elements and their labels, makes the connection to the data source, and adds the appropriate server-side code. Moreover, this Application Object is flexible enough to include seven different form element types — Text Field, Text Area, Menu, Hidden Field, CheckBox, Radio Group, and Password Field — as well as Text.

The Menu and Radio Group options are interesting because they enable you to enter the labels and values either manually or dynamically. To take advantage of Dreamweaver's capability to generate dynamic menus and radio buttons, you must have a recordset or other data source on the page. To insert the Insert Record Insertion Form Application Object, follow these steps:

1. Place your cursor where you'd like the form to appear and choose Insert ⇨ Application Objects ⇨ Record Insertion Form. Alternatively, you can drag the Record Insertion Form object from the Application category of the Insert bar onto your page. The Record Insertion Form dialog box appears as shown in Figure 19-16.

2. From the Record Insertion Form dialog box, choose a connection from the Connection drop-down list. If you need to establish a new connection, select Define.

3. Select the data table you want to use from the Insert Into Table list.

4. Enter the path to the destination page in the After Inserting, Go To field or choose the Browse button to locate the file.

   At this point, Dreamweaver has added an entry in the Form Fields area for every field in the data source.

5. Delete any unwanted fields by selecting their entries in the Form Fields area and choosing the Remove (–) button.

   It's best to remove any fields that use auto-incrementing numbers. Such fields are commonly used to generate unique identification numbers for each record and are automatically incremented when a new record is added

6. Select the first entry in the Form Fields area.

7. If desired, modify the text in the Label field to a more descriptive term than the name of the data source column automatically supplied by Dreamweaver.

8. Choose the desired form element type from the Display As list. By default, Dreamweaver uses Text Field.

   If you choose either Menu or Radio Group, select the Properties button that appears to further define the form element. With text fields, text areas, and text you may set an initial value in the Default Value field. For checkboxes, select whether the element should be Checked or Unchecked.

9. Choose the data format from the Submit As list.

10. Click OK when you're done.

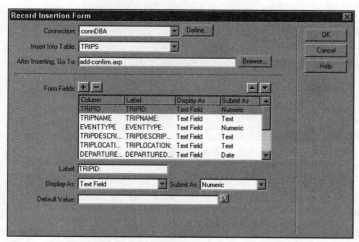

Figure 19-16: The Record Insertion Form Application Object automatically creates a label and form element for every field in the selected data table.

Updating data

In the day-to-day operations of most Web sites, you'll be updating records more often than inserting new records. The process in Dreamweaver for creating an update records page is similar to the one for the insert records application with one important difference — you must have a recordset defined. Detail pages are good candidates to transform into update applications. They already have the features necessary for an update application; namely, they have a recordset or other method for specifying a single record, and they are often generated from master-type pages. The major difference is that an update records application also requires specific server-side code — which is supplied in Dreamweaver by the Update Record server behavior.

As with the insert record application, you can choose to either create all the components of an update record page yourself or use the Application Object to build them for you. To prepare the page for adding the Update Record server behavior, make sure you include a form element for every data field you wish to update as well as a Submit button. Neither the action nor method attributes of the form need to be set — the Update Record server behavior handles that chore. To insert an Update Record server behavior, follow these steps:

1. From the Server Behaviors panel, choose Update Record. The Update Record dialog box appears, as shown in Figure 19-17.

2. From the Update Record dialog box, choose a connection from the Connection drop-down list. If you need to establish a new connection, select Define.

3. Select the data table you want to use from the Table to Update list.

4. Choose the data source on which to base your update from the Select Record From list.

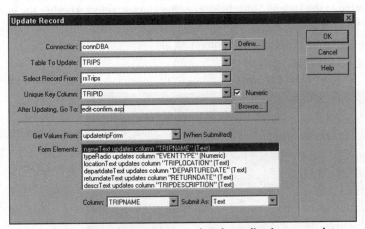

Figure 19-17: With an Update Record Web application, your data source can be modified remotely.

5. Select the key field from the Unique Key Column list. Dreamweaver attempts to detect whether the field is a number type and, if so, it selects the Numeric option.

6. Enter the path to the destination page in the After Updating, Go To field; or choose the Browse button to locate the file.

7. Select the name of the form to be used from the Get Values From list. If there is only one form on the page, the form will be preselected.

8. For each object listed in the Form Elements area

   - Select the data source field that the value of the form object is to be inserted into from the Column list.

   - Choose the data source type for the data from the Submit As list. The options are Text; Numeric; Date; Date MS Access; Checkbox Y, N; Checkbox 1,0; Check -1,0; and Checkbox MS Access.

9. Click OK when you're done.

If you'd prefer Dreamweaver to set up the form elements for you, use the Record Update Form Application Object. Before you can insert this Application Object, you must define a recordset or other data source from which to extract the data. The advantage is sheer speed. Instead of manually creating the form, let Dreamweaver do the grunt work for you. To create an update record application using the Application Object, follow these steps:

1. Place your cursor where you'd like the form to appear and choose Insert ➪ Application Objects ➪ Record Update Form. Alternatively, you can drag the Insert Record Update Form object from the Live category of the Insert bar onto your page. The Insert Record Update Form dialog box is displayed.

2. From the Insert Record Update Form dialog box, choose a connection from the Connection drop-down list. If you need to establish a new connection, select Define.

3. Select the data table you want to modify from the Table to Update list.

4. Choose the data source to base your update on from the Select Record From list.

5. Select the key field from the Unique Key Column list. Dreamweaver attempts to detect whether the field is a number type and, if so, selects the Numeric option.

6. Enter the path to the destination page in the After Updating, Go To field; or choose the Browse button to locate the file. At this point, Dreamweaver has added an entry in the Form Fields area for every field in the data source.

7. Delete any unwanted field by selecting its entry in the Form Fields area and choosing the Remove (–) button.

8. Select the first entry in the Form Fields area.

9. If desired, modify the text in the Label field to a more descriptive term than the name of the data source column automatically supplied by Dreamweaver.

10. Choose the desired form element type from the Display As list. By default, Dreamweaver uses Text Field.

Tip For fields that you want to display, but that you don't want users to alter—such as a unique key field—choose Text.

If you choose either Menu or Radio Group, select the Properties button that appears to further define the form element. With text fields, text areas, and text you may set an initial value in the Default Value field. For checkboxes, select whether the element should be Checked or Unchecked.

11. Choose the data format from the Submit As list.

12. Click OK when you're done.

When completed, Dreamweaver inserts a borderless two-column table with the requested form elements and labels, similar to the one shown in Figure 19-18. As with other Application Objects, you can easily apply a template and include the generated elements in an editable region.

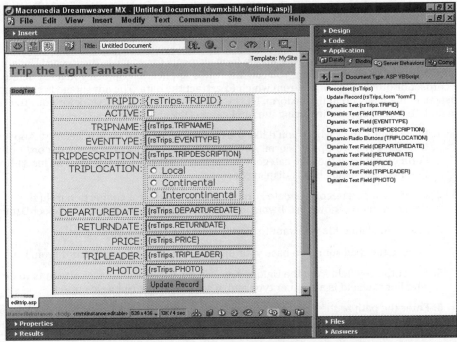

Figure 19-18: The Record Update Form Application Object creates all the elements and code necessary for modifying data source records online.

Deleting data

Eliminating outdated or otherwise unneeded records is a key task in properly maintaining a data source. The Delete Record server behavior greatly simplifies the chore. All that the Delete Record server behavior requires is a recordset and a form with a Submit button.

Tip   Although it's not mandatory, it's good practice to provide enough detail—displayed in a read-only format—so that the user can be sure he is removing the correct record. A confirmation message with something akin to "Are you sure you want to do this?" on the Submit button is nice also.

To attach a Delete Record server behavior to a form, follow these steps:

1. Make sure that a form exists on a dynamic page that includes at least one recordset.

2. From the Server Behaviors panel, choose Delete Record. The Delete Record dialog box is displayed, as shown in Figure 19-19.

3. From the Delete Record dialog box, choose the Connection from the drop-down list. If you need to establish a new connection, select Define.

4. Select the data table you want to modify from the Delete From Table list.

5. Choose the data source to base your update on from the Select Record From list.

6. Select the key field from the Unique Key Column list. Dreamweaver attempts to detect whether the field is a number type and, if so, selects the Numeric option.

7. Enter the path to the destination page in the After Deleting, Go To field; or choose the Browse button to locate the file.

8. Choose the form that contains the delete Submit button.

The Delete Record server behavior is executed when the Submit button in the form is selected by the user. It's a good idea to confirm the deletion with your user on the destination page.

Caution   There's a known problem with JSP pages that use Dreamweaver's Delete Record server behavior when they run on Apache's Jakarta Tomcat application server. The problem arises from the use of a redirect page. As a workaround, place all dynamic data on the delete page within a Show Region If Recordset is Not Empty server behavior. By doing so, you'll allow Jakarta to link properly to the redirect page without generating an error.

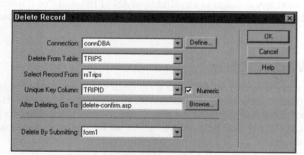

Figure 19-19: Maintain an up-to-date data source with the Delete Record server behavior.

Inserting Variables

Variables are essential to any programming; and various variables are available depending on the server model. Although all setting of variables in Dreamweaver must be done by hand or using a custom server behavior, Dreamweaver provides a method for reading or displaying almost every kind of variable.

All variables are made available through the Add list of the Bindings panel. After a variable has been added as a data source, it can be dragged and dropped anywhere on the page or included via the Insert button. Which variables are available depends upon the server model. The vast majority of dialog boxes for variables are single entry fields, requesting the name of the specific variable, like the one shown in Figure 19-20.

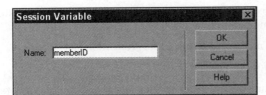

Figure 19-20: After you establish a variable, it is made available for use in the Bindings panel.

Application and session variables

Both application and session variables are used throughout Web applications. An *application* variable is one that continues to exist as long as the application is active; in this situation, the application is the Web site itself. Application variables are available to all users of a site. A hit counter often uses an application variable to track the number of visitors to a site.

Although all users can see the results of a calculation involving application variables, *session* variables are user-specific. A session starts when a user first visits a site and ends shortly after the user leaves. Session variables are often used for user authentication and to maintain information about users as they travel through the site; shopping carts often employ session variables. Both application and session variables are available in ASP, PHP, and ColdFusion; in JSP only session variables may be inserted through the Bindings panel; .NET doesn't allow any declared variables.

Request and other variables

Each of the server models, with the exception of .NET, has a range of variables available aside from application and server variables. All of them are accessible through the Add (+) button of the Bindings panel and all, except for ASP Request variables, use a one-field dialog box for the name of the variable. In the case of the ASP Request variables, all five types of variables are available through a drop-down list on the Request Variable dialog box. After you've chosen your variable, enter the desired name in the Name field. Here's a breakdown of the available variables for each of the Dreamweaver server models:

Server Model	Variables
ASP	Request, Cookie, QueryString, Form, ServerVariables, ClientCertificate
ColdFusion	Form, URL, Cookie, Client, Application, Cookie, CGI, Local Variable
JSP	Request Variables
PHP	Form, URL, Cookie, Environmental

Connecting to the Customer

Fundamentally, there are two types of customers: new customers and returning customers. The goal of almost every enterprise is to turn the former into the latter. To that end, e-commerce sites try to make the customer experience as pleasant as possible. What makes for an enjoyable customer visit? Volumes have been written on that subject, so we'll concentrate here on one facet: the customer's account.

Early on in the history of Web stores, it wasn't uncommon to require returning customers to re-enter all of their pertinent billing and shipping information. The eCommerce sites had no way of tracking all that data. Now, the vast majority of online stores — particularly the successful ones — offer a way for customers to open an account to store their basic information. Just as important, customers can easily identify themselves on their return, thus accessing their account information and enabling it to be applied to a new order. You may also want to restrict certain areas of your site to registered users or those who have paid for a subscription to your site. Many levels of sophistication are feasible here, but what's required at the most fundamental level is a way to identify returning customers and a way to add new ones.

Logging in existing customers

The most common way to identify returning customers is to allow them to log in. A login page can be as simple as a three-element form: two text fields — one for the user name and one for the password — and a Submit button. The form connects to a data source containing a list of users and their passwords, among other information, and verifies that the submitted user name corresponds with the submitted password. Dreamweaver accomplishes this task with the appropriately named Log In User server behavior.

The Log In User server behavior redirects authorized users to one page and unauthorized users to another. In addition, a session variable containing the user name is created. This session variable can then be employed on other pages as required.

To apply the Log In User server behavior, make sure your page has, at a minimum, a form with text fields for the user name and password, and a Submit button. You're now ready to follow these steps:

1. From the Server Behaviors panel, select the Add (+) button and choose User Authentication ⇨ Log In User. The Log In User dialog box is displayed, as shown in Figure 19-21.

2. If there is more than one form on the page, select the form containing the user name and password fields from the Get Input From Form list.

3. Select the form element used to gather the user name from the Username Field list.

4. Select the form element used to gather the password from the Password Field list.

5. Choose a connection to the data source containing the table of registered users from the Validate Using Connection list.

6. Select the table of registered users from the Table list.

7. Choose the field containing the user name from the Username Column list.

8. Choose the field containing the password from the Password Column list.

9. Enter the path to the page for the authorized user in the If Log In Succeeds, Go To field.

10. If you want the user to proceed to the previously selected link, rather than the page entered in Step 9, select the Go To Previous URL option.

11. Enter the path to the page for the unauthorized user in the If Log In Fails, Go To field.

12. If access levels should be evaluated as part of the authentication, choose from the following:

    • Select the Restrict Access Based On Username, Password, and Access Level option.

    • Choose the datasource field containing the access-level data from the Get Level From list.

13. Click OK when you're done.

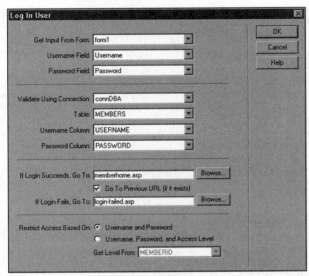

Figure 19-21: The Log In User server behavior can be used to gather information about a returning customer.

Restricting access

Now that you've got your users added and logging in, you need to protect those pages that require authorized access. These could be their user profile information or perhaps information they've paid a subscription to access. Dreamweaver provides two different types of access restriction. The first method just determines if a user is logged in or not. The second includes restriction based on access levels defined in your database.

To restrict access based on whether a user has logged in or not, follow these steps:

1. Open a dynamic page to restrict access to.

2. In the Server Behaviors panel, choose the Add (+) button and select User Authentication ⇨ Restrict Access To Page.

    The Restrict Access To Page dialog box, shown in Figure 19-22, is displayed.

3. Choose the Username and Password radio button to restrict access to those users already logged in.

4. In the If Access Denied, Go To box, browse to the URL you want to send users to if they're not authorized to view the page. This page should have a sentence or two telling users why they're at this page, as well as a form for them to log in.

To restrict pages based on access level, add a login page as shown in Figure 19-21. This is handy if you want to have one login for both your administrators and your regular customers. One access level may be able to change user details, while another can only view those details. In Step 12 of creating the login form in the previous section, choose the Restrict Access based on Username, Password and Access Level option, and choose the field from your table that contains the access levels, as shown in Figure 19-23.

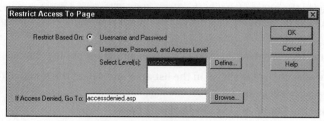

Figure 19-22: Dreamweaver's Restrict Access To Page server behaviors allow you to restrict access to sensitive parts of your site.

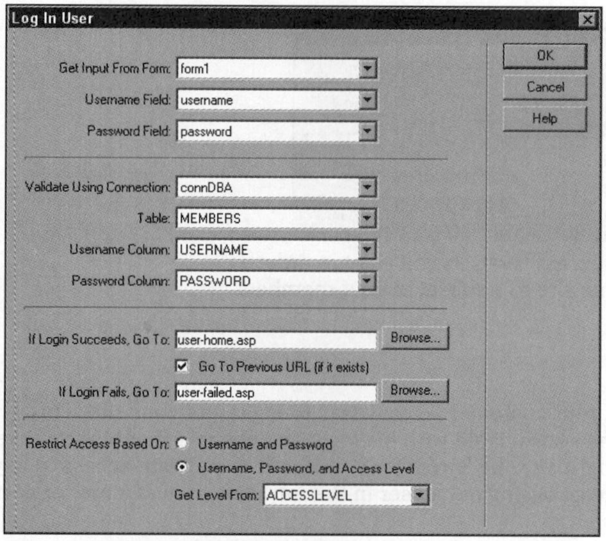

Figure 19-23: Restrict access-by-access level to provide more granular control over your site.

To restrict access based on access levels, follow these steps:

1. Open a dynamic page to which you want access restricted.

2. In the Server Behaviors panel, choose the Add (+) button and select User Authentication ⇨ Restrict Access To Page.

   The Restrict Access To Page dialog box, shown in Figure 19-24, is displayed.

3. Choose the Username, Password and Access Level radio button.

4. Choose one or more groups from the Select Level(s) area.

5. To add new groups to the Select Level(s) list:

   • Choose Define and the Define Access Levels dialog opens.

   • Enter the name for the access level in the Name field. The name must match a value stored in your data source in whichever column is designated for the group access levels.

   • To add additional levels, select the Add (+) button and enter another name.

   • To delete any levels, choose the level in the list area and select the Remove (–) button.

   • Click OK to close the Define Access Levels dialog box.

6. Enter the path to the file to which you redirect unauthorized users in the If Access Denied, Go To field. Alternatively, select the Browse button to locate the file.

7. Click OK when you're done.

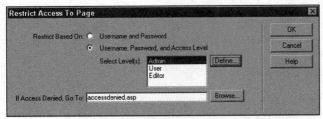

Figure 19-24: Define as many access levels as you want in order to restrict certain sections of your site to a subset of your members.

Log out users

It's always a good idea to give your customer an easy way to log out of your site. This destroys all the session variables associated with his login and ensures that his coworkers can't jump on his computer (right after he leaves for some coffee) and gain access to any information they shouldn't have. Logging out a user in Dreamweaver is just a matter of one simple server behavior.

To use the Log Out User server behavior, follow these steps:

1. To apply the server behavior to a specific link on the page, select that link.

2. From the Server Behaviors panel, select the Add (+) button and then choose User Authentication ⇨ Log Out User.

   The Log Out User dialog box is displayed as shown in Figure 19-25.

3. To trigger the server behavior with a link, choose the Log Out When Link Clicked option and make sure your selected link is chosen in the list.

   If no link was preselected, Dreamweaver offers to apply the server behavior to a new link, Log Out.

4. To automatically log out users when the current page is viewed, select Log Out When Page Loads option.

5. If you're using a link as a trigger, enter the path to the destination page in the When Done, Go To field. Alternatively, select the Browse button to locate the file.

Caution Do not use the When Done, Go To option if you are automatically logging out a user when the page loads. If you do, the user will never see the current page.

6. Click OK when you're done.

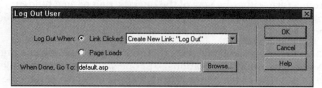

Figure 19-25: You can log a user out automatically by choosing the Log Out When Page Loads option on an order confirmation page.

Adding new customers

An application that adds new customers is essentially the same as an insert record application, with one additional function. If you've ever tried to get a user name on America Online that even remotely resembles your own name, chances are you've encountered the function I'm talking about—just ask bobsmith01234x. For a user name to be useful, it must be unique; therefore, the Web application must check a submitted user name for uniqueness. Dreamweaver's Check New Username server behavior does just this.

Before you can apply the Check New Username server behavior, however, you must create a page with the proper form elements for all the data necessary. Moreover, a Dreamweaver Insert Record server behavior (see Figure 19-15 earlier in this chapter) is needed. As the name implies, the Insert Record server behavior creates a new record and adds it to the specified datasource.

The one difference between a standard Insert Record server behavior and the one used in this circumstance is that you leave the destination page field (After Inserting, Go To) blank. Leaving this field empty enables the Check New Username server behavior to control the redirection.

The Check New Username server behavior verifies that the requested user name is not already in the datasource and redirects the user if it is. To add a Check New Username server behavior to your page, follow these steps:

1. From the Server Behaviors panel, select the Add (+) button and choose User Authentication ⇨ Check New Username. The Check New Username dialog box is displayed.

2. Select the form element that contains the requested user name from the Username list. If a form element is called `username`, Dreamweaver automatically selects that entry.

3. Enter the path to the file you want a user to see if her requested name is already stored in the datasource in the If Already Exists, Go To field; or select Browse to locate the file.

4. Click OK when you're finished.

Summary

Although there are numerous Web applications that use only a single dynamic page, the possibilities rise far more than exponentially with multiple-page applications. It's key for every Web developer to master the various methods for passing information from one page to another. When building your first multiple-page Web applications, keep these points in mind:

✦ Dreamweaver can send and receive parameters from one page to another by appending them in an encoded fashion to the linked URL. The additional text is known as a query string.

✦ You can send values from a form either by way of the query string or, in a hidden manner, in a separate object seen only by the server. The first technique uses the Get method and the second, Post.

✦ Dreamweaver includes several Application Objects that reduce the building of common dynamic components — or even whole applications — to one step. Application Objects may be combined with Dreamweaver templates for rapid application development.

✦ To craft applications that update records in a data source, you must know how to tie the various form elements to dynamic data. In Dreamweaver, the basic procedure is to include a standard form element and then choose the appropriate server behavior from the Dynamic Elements submenu of the Server Behaviors panel.

✦ Many Web applications are not concerned with publicly viewed sites on the Web, but rather with administrative-oriented pages designed to manage data sources remotely. Dreamweaver includes a full complement of tools for inserting new records, updating existing ones, and deleting data that is no longer required.

✦ After you've declared a variable in Dreamweaver, it is available for display through the Bindings panel. Each of the server models has its own set of variables.

✦ Dreamweaver allows you to create a user authentication system quickly to protect valuable customer information or paid subscription sites. You can even set different access levels for administrators and regular customers.

In the next chapter, you'll learn how to integrate graphics created in Fireworks into your Dreamweaver application.

✦   ✦   ✦

Dynamic HTML and Dreamweaver

Building Style Sheet Web Pages

All publications, whether on paper or the Web, need a balance of style and content to be effective. Style without content is all flash with no real information. Content with no style is flat and uninteresting, thus losing the substance. Traditionally, HTML has tied style to content wherever possible, preferring logical tags such as <strong> to indicate emphasis to physical tags such as <b> for bold. But although this emphasis on the logical worked for many single documents, its imprecision made achieving style consistency across a broad range of Web pages unrealistic, if not impossible.

The Cascading Style Sheets specification has changed this situation—and much more. As support for Cascading Style Sheets (CSS) grows, more Web designers can alter font faces, type size, spacing, and many other page elements with a single command—and have the effect ripple not only throughout the page, but also throughout a Web site. Moreover, an enhancement of CSS initially called CSS-P (for positioning) is the foundation for what has become commonly known as *layers*.

Dreamweaver was one of the first Web authoring tools to make the application of Cascading Style Sheets user-friendly. Through Dreamweaver's intuitive interface, the Web designer can access over 70 different CSS settings, affecting everything from type specs to multimedia-like transitions. Dreamweaver enables you to work the way you want: Create your complete style sheet first and then link it when you're ready, or make up your styles one-by-one as you build your Web page.

In this chapter, you find out how CSS works and why you need it. A Dreamweaver Technique for removing underlines from links walks you through a typical style sheet session. With that experience under your belt, you're ready for the later sections with detailed information on the current CSS commands—and how to apply those commands to your Web page and site. Also, the section on defining styles helps you understand what's what in the Style Definition dialog box. Finally, you learn how you can create external style sheets to establish—and maintain—the look and feel of an entire Web site with a single document.

Understanding Cascading Style Sheets

The Cascading Style Sheets system significantly increases the design capabilities for a Web site. If you are a designer used to working with desktop publishing tools, you will recognize many familiar features in CSS, including the following:

✦ Commands for specifying and applying font characteristics

✦ Traditional layout measurement systems and terminology

✦ Pinpoint precision for page layout

Cascading Style Sheets are able to apply many features with a simple syntax that is easy to understand. If you're familiar with the concept of using styles in a word processing program, you'll have no trouble grasping style sheets.

Here's how the process works: CSS instructions are given in rules; a style sheet is a collection of these rules. A rule is a statement made up of an HTML or custom style, called a *selector*, and its defined properties, referred to as a *declaration*. For example, a CSS rule that makes the contents of all <h1> tags (the selector) red (#FF0000 in hexadecimal) in color (the declaration) looks like the following:

```
h1 {
    color: #FF0000;
}
```

In the following sections, you see the various characteristics of CSS — grouping, inheritance, and cascading — working together to give style sheets their flexibility and power.

Grouping properties

A Web designer often needs to change several style properties at once. CSS allows you to group declarations by separating them with semicolons. For example:

```
h1 {
   color:#FF0000;
   font-family:Arial,Helvetica,sans-serif;
   font-size:18pt;
}
```

The Dreamweaver interface provides a wide range of options for styles. Should you ever need to look at the code, you'll find that Dreamweaver groups your selections exactly as shown in the preceding example. You can group selectors as well as declarations. Separate grouped selectors with commas rather than semicolons. For example:

```
h1, h2, p, em {
   color:green;
   text-align:left;
}
```

Inheritance of properties

CSS rules can also be applied to more than one tag through inheritance. The HTML tags enclosed within the CSS selector can inherit most, but not all, CSS declarations. Suppose you set all <p> tags to the color red. Any tags included within a <p>...</p> tag pair then inherit that property and are also colored red.

Inheritance is also at work within HTML tags that involve a parent-child relationship, such as a list. Whether numbered (ordered, <ol>) or bulleted (unordered, <ul>), a list comprises any number of list items, designated by <li> tags. Each list item is considered a child of the parent tag, <ol> or <ul>. Look at the following example:

```
ol {
  color:#FF0000;
}
ul {
  color:#0000FF;
}
```

With the preceding example, all ordered list items appear in red (#FF0000); all unordered list items appear in blue (#0000FF). One major benefit to this parent-child relationship is that you can change the font for an entire page with one CSS rule. The following statement accomplishes this change:

```
body {
    font-family: Verdana, Arial, Helvetica, sans-serif;
}
```

The change is possible in the previous example because the <body> tag is considered the parent of every HTML element on a page.

Tip

There's one exception to the preceding rule: tables. Netscape browsers (through version 4.75) treat tables differently than the rest of the HTML <body> when it comes to style sheets. To change the font of a table, you'd have to specify something like the following:

```
td {
    font-family: Verdana, Arial, Helvetica, sans-serif;
}
```

Because every cell in a table uses the <td> tag, this style sheet declaration affects the entire table.

Cascading characteristics

The term *cascading* describes the capability of a local style to override a general style. Think of a stream flowing down a mountain; each ledge encountered by the stream has the potential to change its direction. The last ledge determines the final direction of the stream. In the same manner, one CSS rule applying generally to a block of text can be overridden by another rule applied to a more specific part of the same text.

For example, let's say you've defined, using style sheets, all normal paragraphs — <p> tags — as a particular font in a standard color, but you mark one section of the text using a little-used tag such as <samp>. If you make a CSS rule altering both the font and color of the <samp> tag, the section takes on the characteristics of that rule.

The cascading aspect of style sheets also works on a larger scale. One of the key features of CSS is the capability to define external style sheets that can be linked to individual Web pages, acting on their overall look and feel. Indeed, you can use the cascading behavior to fine-tune the overall Web-site style based on a particular page or range of pages. Your company may, for instance, define an external style sheet for the entire company intranet; each division could then build upon that overall model for its individual Web pages. For example, suppose that the company style sheet dictates that all <h2> headings are in Arial and black. One department could output its Web pages with <h2> tags in Arial, but colored red rather than black, whereas another department could make them blue.

Defining new classes for extended design control

Redefining existing HTML tags is a step in the right direction toward consistent design, but the real power of CSS comes into play when you define custom tags. In CSS-speak, a custom tag is called a *class*, and the selector name always begins with a period. Here's a simple example: To style all copyright notices at the bottom of all pages of a Web site to display in 8-point Helvetica all caps, you could define a tag like this:

```
.cnote {
  font-family:Helvetica, sans-serif;
  font-size:8pt;
  font-transform:uppercase
}
```

If you define this style in an external style sheet and apply it to all 999 pages of your Web site, you have to alter only one line of code (instead of all 999 pages) when the edict comes down from management to make all the copyright notices a touch larger. After a new class has been defined, you can apply it to any range of text, from one word to an entire page.

How styles are applied

CSS applies style formatting to your page in one of three ways:

✦ Via an external, linked style sheet

✦ Via an internal style sheet

✦ Via embedded style rules

External style sheets

An external style sheet is a file containing the CSS rules; it links one or more Web pages. One benefit of linking to an external style sheet is that you can customize and change the appearance of a Web site quickly and easily from one file.

Two different methods exist for working with an external style sheet: the link method and the import method. Dreamweaver initially defaults to the link method, but you can also choose import if you prefer.

For the link method, a line of code is added outside of the <style> tags, as follows:

```
<link href="mainstyle.css" rel="stylesheet" type="text/css">
```

The import method writes code within the style tags, as follows:

```
<style type="text/css">
<!--
@import url("newstyles.css");
-->
</style>
```

Between the link and the import methods, the link method is better supported among browsers, including Netscape 4.x. Because of Netscape 4.x's lack of standards support in CSS and other issues, however, the link method isn't necessarily your best choice.

Tip You can take advantage of Netscape 4.x's lack of support for the `import` method to offset its rather quirky support of CSS in general. Create two style sheets: one to handle Netscape 4.x issues and one for newer browsers, such as Internet Explorer 4.x and up and Netscape 6.x. Use the `link` technique to bring in the NS4.x-based style sheet and `import` for the second style sheet. By writing the code in the following sequence, the second style sheet overrides the same selector rules in the first style sheet and is ignored by Netscape 4.x:

```
<link href="mainstyleNS.css" rel="stylesheet"⏎
type="text/css">
<style type="text/css">
<!--
@import url("mainstyles.css");
-->
</style>
```

Internal style sheets

An internal style sheet is a list of all the CSS styles for a page.

Dreamweaver inserts all the style sheets at the top of a Web page within a `<style>...</style>` tag pair. Placing style sheets within the header tags has become a convention that many designers use, although you can also apply a style sheet anywhere on a page.

The `<style>` tag for a Cascading Style Sheet identifies the type attribute as `text/css`. A sample internal style sheet looks like the following:

```
<style type="text/css">
<!--
p {
  font-family: "Arial, Helvetica, sans-serif";
  color: #000000;
}
.cnote {
  font: 8pt "Arial, Helvetica, sans-serif";
  text-transform: uppercase;
}
h1 {
  font: bold 18pt Arial, Helvetica, sans-serif;
  color: #FF0000;
}
-->
</style>
```

The HTML comment tags `<!--` and `-->` prevent older browsers that can't read style sheets from displaying the CSS rules.

Embedded style rules

The final method of applying a style inserts it within HTML tags using the `style` attribute — a technique known as *inline styles*. This method is the most "local" of all the techniques; that is, it is closest to the tag it is affecting and, therefore, has the ultimate control — because of the cascading nature of style sheets as previously discussed.

Caution As my mother used to say, "Just because you can do something, doesn't mean you should." Generally, inline styles are not used because they exert such a high level of control, and modifying the style must be done on an item-by-item basis, which defeats much of the purpose of CSS.

When you create a layer within Dreamweaver, you notice that the positioning attribute is a Cascading Style Sheet embedded within a `<div>` tag like the following:

```
<div id="Layer1" style="position:absolute; visibility:inherit; left:314px;
top:62px; width:194px; height:128px; z-index:1">
</div>
```

For all its apparent complexity, the Cascading Style Sheets system becomes straightforward in Dreamweaver. You often won't have to write a single line of code. But even if you don't have to write code, you should understand the CSS fundamentals of grouping, inheritance, and cascading.

Creating and Applying a Style Sheet in Dreamweaver

Dreamweaver uses three primary tools to implement Cascading Style Sheets: the CSS Styles panel, the Edit Style Sheet dialog box, and the Style Definition dialog box. The CSS Styles panel itself has two modes: Apply Styles and Edit Styles. The Apply Styles mode is used to apply styles created in the Edit Style Sheet dialog box and specified with the Style Definition dialog box. The Edit Styles mode is used to view all the styles available and to provide a direct link to modifying any given style. With these three interfaces, you can accomplish the following:

✦ Link or import all your styles from an external style sheet

✦ Create new selectors and specify their rules

✦ Apply styles to selected text or to a particular tag surrounding that text

✦ Modify any styles you created

Caution The fourth-generation browsers (and above) support many of the attributes from the first draft of the Cascading Style Sheets standard. Unfortunately, neither Netscape Navigator 4.0 nor Microsoft Internet Explorer 4.0 fully supports CSS Level 1. Of the earlier browsers, only Internet Explorer 3.0 supports a limited set of the CSS Level 1 features: font attributes, indents, and color. However, this support is rendered differently in Internet Explorer 3.0 and 4.0. Netscape Navigator 3.0 does not support any of the features of CSS Level 1. On the brighter side, Netscape Navigator 6.2 shows an almost complete compliance of CSS 1 and quite a lot of CSS 2. The current version of Internet Explorer (6.0) is almost as complete.

Dreamweaver Technique: Eliminating underlines from links

Because Dreamweaver's interface for CSS has so many controls, initially creating and applying a style can be a little confusing. Before delving into the details of the various panels, dialog boxes, and floating windows, let's quickly step through a typical style sheet session. The goal is to give you an understanding of how all the pieces fit together.

Note Don't panic if you encounter unfamiliar elements of Dreamweaver's interface in this introductory technique. You'll see them at work again and again as you work through the chapter.

Disabling the underline for the anchor tag, <a>, which is normally associated with hyperlinked text, is one modification commonly included in style sheets.

Caution Be careful when using this technique. Underlined text is a standard method of indicating a hyperlink on the Web, and some clients or users may find your pages not as intuitive if the underline indicator is no longer visible.

To accomplish this task, follow these steps:

1. Open the CSS Styles panel by choosing Windows ⇨ CSS Styles or selecting the Show CSS Styles button from the Launcher.

   The CSS Styles panel, shown in Figure 20-1, can be in either Apply Styles or Edit Styles mode.

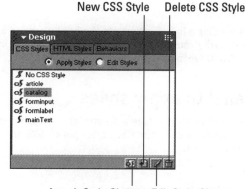

New CSS Style   Delete CSS Style

Attach Style Sheet   Edit Style Sheet

Figure 20-1: The Dreamweaver CSS Styles panel helps you apply consistent styles to a Web page.

2. In the CSS Styles panel, select the New CSS Style button. This action opens the New CSS Style dialog box.

3. In the New CSS Style dialog box, select Redefine HTML Tag and then choose the anchor tag, a, from the drop-down list. Finally, select Define In This Document Only to create an internal CSS style sheet. Click OK, and the CSS Style Definition dialog box opens.

Tip You can also select the Use CSS Selector option and choose a:link from the drop-down list. You can even employ the a:hover style, which enables text to change color or style on rollover. You must, however, define the four CSS Selector styles in a particular order for them to work correctly. Start by defining the a:link class and then proceed to define a:visited, a:hover, and a:active, in that order. Note that you can preview only the a:link altered styles in Dreamweaver; to see the other styles you need to preview your page in a browser.

4. In the Style Definition window, make sure that the correct category is displayed by selecting Type from the list of categories.

5. In the Decoration section of the Type category, select the None option. You can also make any other modifications to the anchor tag style, such as color or font size. Click OK when you're done.

> **Tip** Many designers, myself included, like to make the link apparent by styling it bold and in a different color.

The Style Definition window closes, and any style changes instantly take effect on your page. If you have any previously defined links, the underline disappears from them.

Now, when viewed through a browser any links that you insert on your page still function as links — the user's pointer still changes into a pointing hand, and the links are active — but no underline appears.

One variation on this technique is to make the underline appear only when the mouse rolls over the link. To accomplish this variation, define a CSS style for the a:hover selector and set the Decoration to Underline.

> **Tip** This technique works for any text used as a link. To eliminate the border around an image designated as a link, the image's border must be set to zero in the Property inspector. Dreamweaver handles this automatically when a graphic is made into a link.

Using the CSS Styles panel to apply styles

The CSS Styles panel is a flexible and easy-to-use interface with straightforward command buttons listing all available style items. You can open the CSS Styles panel, like all Dreamweaver's primary panels, in several ways:

✦ Choose Windows ➪ CSS Styles.

✦ Select the Show CSS Styles button from the Launcher.

✦ Press Shift+F11.

The CSS Styles panel is divided into two modes, Apply Styles and Edit Styles. Switch between the two modes by selecting the desired radio button choice. In Apply Styles mode, the main part of the CSS Styles panel is the list of defined custom styles or classes. Every custom tag you create is listed alphabetically in this window. After you've chosen the portion of your HTML document that you're styling, you can choose one of the custom styles listed here by simply selecting it.

At the bottom of the CSS Styles panel are four buttons. The first of these, Attach Style Sheet, is a new addition in Dreamweaver MX and is used for quickly linking the current Web page to an existing style sheet. Clicking the second — the New Style button — begins the process of defining a new CSS style, either in an external or internal style sheet.

The functionality of the third button, Edit Style Sheet, is only available in the Edit Styles mode and depends on what is selected in the CSS panel. With the current document name or that of an external style sheet selected, the Edit Style Sheet button opens the multifaceted Edit Style Sheet dialog box, in which you can create a new style, link a style sheet, edit or remove an existing style, or duplicate a style that you can then alter. You get a close look at this tool in the upcoming section, "Editing and managing style sheets."

If an individual style rule is selected when the Edit Style Sheet button is chosen, the CSS Style Definition dialog box is displayed. This dialog contains numerous categories for setting or modifying all of the desired CSS properties and is covered in depth in the "Styles and Their Attributes" later in this chapter.

The final button is for deleting styles after they are defined.

Applying styles through the Property inspector

In addition to applying CSS styles via the CSS Styles panel, Dreamweaver also allows you to apply any defined style directly through the Property inspector. The immediate availability of CSS styles is a major boon to productivity and is extremely helpful for designers working in a site fully committed to using Cascading Style Sheets.

New Feature Just to the right of the Format drop-down list on the Property inspector you'll find the CSS/HTML toggle. When in HTML mode, the toggle is an uppercase A; click the A once to switch to CSS mode, and the toggle becomes the CSS icon. The Property inspector changes in other ways as well. In CSS mode, the font list displays defined custom styles as well as offering options to add a new style, edit an existing one, or attach an external style sheet. Unneeded elements—the font size list, font color swatch, and alignment buttons—are replaced with a description of the current style, if any. You can also use the Property inspector options menu to switch between HTML and CSS modes.

To apply a style from the Property inspector, simply select the page element desired and select the style from the drop-down list to the right of the CSS symbol as shown in Figure 20-2.

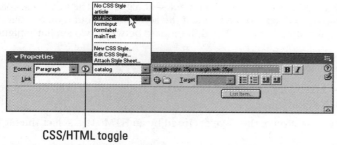

CSS/HTML toggle

Figure 20-2: In Dreamweaver MX, you can apply CSS styles right from the Property inspector.

Attaching an external style sheet

As CSS-enabled browsers begin to predominate, more Web designers are encountering clients with existing external style sheets. To apply the site's design specifications to a new page, all the designer need do is connect the current page to the CSS document. Dreamweaver MX provides a streamlined method for doing just that.

The Attach Style Sheet button, found on the CSS Styles panel, is a straightforward solution for linking external style sheets to the current document. When Attach Style Sheet is selected, the Link External Style Sheet dialog box, shown in Figure 20-3, appears. Here, you can choose between the two previously discussed methods for attaching an external style sheet: link or import.

Figure 20-3: Use the Link method for style sheets readable by older browsers like Netscape 4.x.

After you've made your choice, select Browse to locate a previously existing style sheet. When selected, a standard Select File dialog box appears with the *.css filter set. Simply locate the desired style sheet and select it: Dreamweaver inserts the necessary code into the `<head>` of your document. If any HTML tags — such as `<p>` or any of the heading tags — on your page are defined in the style sheet, you'll see an immediate change in your document.

Tip   If you don't have an external style sheet and want to create one, just enter the path and file-name in the text field, making sure to use the .css extension.

Applying, changing, and removing a style

As noted above, any HTML tags redefined as CSS styles in an attached style sheet will automatically be applied to your document. However, any custom CSS style must be applied on a case-by-case basis. Most Web designers use a combination of HTML and custom CSS styles. Only custom CSS styles appear in the CSS Styles panel when in Apply Styles mode.

Dreamweaver enables you to tell where a custom style is from — whether it's from a linked external style sheet or included in the current document — at a glance. The CSS Styles panel displays a small chain-link symbol next to the listing if the style can be found on a separate style sheet. In larger sites, it's often important to differentiate between two similarly named custom styles.

To apply an existing custom style, follow these steps:

1. Choose Windows ➪ CSS Styles or select the Show CSS Styles button from the Launcher to open the CSS Styles panel.

2. To apply the style to a section of the page enclosed by an HTML tag, select the tag from the Tag Selector.

   To apply the style to a section that is not enclosed by a single HTML tag, use your mouse to select that section in the Document window.

3. Select the desired custom style from the CSS Styles panel.

   Dreamweaver applies the custom style either by setting the `class` attribute of the selected tag to the custom style or, if just text (and not an enclosing tag) is selected, by placing a `<span>` tag that wraps around the selection.

Dreamweaver offers another way of applying a style to your pages via the menus:

1. Highlight the text to which you're applying the style, either by using the Tag Selector or by using the mouse.

2. Select Text ➪ CSS Styles ➪ Your Style. Alternatively, you can choose the style from the Property inspector's drop-down list when in CSS mode.

   The same dynamic CSS Style list is maintained in the context menu, accessible through a right-click (Ctrl-click) on the selected text.

Changing styles

In prior versions of Dreamweaver, multiple <span> tags were a common phenomenon as designers tried different styles without properly selecting the <span> tag. It was not unusual to see this type of code:

```
<span class="head1"><span class="head2"><span class="head3">News of ⊃
the Moment</span></span></span>
```

In situations like these, the CSS style in the span tag closest to the text, in this example head3, is rendered. The other span tags are just so much cluttered code. Dreamweaver now strives to prevent nested <span> tags, automatically.

Changing from applied custom style to another is extremely straightforward in Dreamweaver. No longer do you have to be sure to select the enclosing tag—whether it's a <span> or other tag—to replace the style. In fact, you don't have to select anything: Just place your cursor anywhere within the styled text and select a different custom style from the CSS Styles panel. Dreamweaver changes the old style to the new without adding additional <span> tags.

But what if you want to apply a new style to a text range within an existing <span> tag? Again, Dreamweaver's default is to avoid nested span tags. Here's how it works. Suppose you're working with the following code:

```
<span class="bodyCopy">Developing strategies to survive requires
industry insight and forward thinking in this competitive
marketplace.</span>
```

If you apply a custom style called *hype* to the phrases "industry insight" and "forward thinking" by first selecting those phrases and then choosing hype from the CSS Styles panel, the code will look like this:

```
<span class="bodyCopy">Developing strategies to survive requires
</span><span class="hype">industry insight</span> and <span
class="hype">forward thinking</span><span class="bodyCopy"> in this
competitive marketplace.</span>
```

Dreamweaver wraps each phrase in a distinct <span> tag so that nesting is entirely avoided. This behavior allows the style of each phrase to be altered more easily.

Tip   If you positively, absolutely would prefer to nest your <span> tags, you can do so by Shift-clicking on the desired style in the CSS Styles panel.

If your cursor is positioned within a tag without an existing style, you can still quickly apply the custom CSS style. Dreamweaver now automatically applies the chosen style to the surrounding tag.

Removing applied styles

Getting rid of an applied style also gets a whole lot simpler in Dreamweaver MX. Now, just position your cursor anywhere in the stylized text and select No CSS Style from the CSS Styles panel. Dreamweaver removes the class attribute if the style was attached to a tag other than <span>, and surrounding <span> tags are completely deleted. If the Property inspector is in CSS mode, you can also select No CSS Style from the drop-down list.

Note   Be sure your cursor is *positioned within* styled text and *not selecting any*. Selecting No CSS Style from either the CSS Styles panel or the Property inspector when just text—no tags—is highlighted, has no effect.

One final way to remove a style is through the Tag Selector — just right-click (Control-click) any styled tag on the Tag Selector and choose Set Class ⇨ None.

Defining new styles

Selecting the New CSS Style button in the CSS Styles panel brings up a new dialog box (see Figure 20-4) where you specify the type of style you're defining. You can opt to create the new styles in an external style sheet or in the current document. After you've chosen the type of style desired, select the Define In This Document Only option to create an internal style sheet. Any style sheets already linked to (or imported into) the current document appear in the drop-down list along with the New Style Sheet File option. If you choose Define In New Style Sheet File, a standard file dialog box opens for you to name and in which to store your new CSS file.

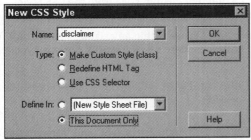

Figure 20-4: The first step in defining a new style is to select a style type and enter a name for the style, if it's a custom one.

The following sections explain the three style types in depth:

✦ Make Custom Style (class)

✦ Redefine HTML Tag

✦ Use CSS Selector

Make Custom Style (class)

Making a custom style is the most flexible way to define a style on a page. The first step in creating a custom style is to give it a name; this name is used in the class attribute. The name for your class must start with a period and must be alphanumeric without punctuation or special characters. If you do not begin the name of your custom style with a period, Dreamweaver inserts one for you. Following are typical names you can use:

```
.master
.pagetitle
.bodytext
```

Caution   Although you can use names such as body, title, or any other HTML tag, this approach is not a good idea. Dreamweaver warns you of the conflict if you try this method. You should also be aware that class names are case sensitive.

Redefine HTML Tag

The second radio button in the New Style dialog box is Redefine HTML Tag. This type of style is an excellent tool for making quick, global changes to existing Web pages. Essentially, the Redefine HTML Tag style enables you to modify the features of your existing HTML tags. When you select this option, the drop-down list displays over 90 HTML tags in alphabetical order. Select a tag from the drop-down list and click OK.

Use CSS Selector

When you use the third style type, Use CSS Selector, you define *pseudo-classes* and *pseudo-elements*. A pseudo-class represents dynamic states of a tag that may change under user action or over time. Several standard pseudo-classes associated with the <a> tag are used to style hypertext links. When you choose Use CSS Selector, the drop-down list box contains four customization options, which can all be categorized as pseudo-classes:

✦ a:link: Customizes the style of a link that has not been visited recently

✦ a:visited: Customizes the style of a link to a page that has been recently visited

✦ a:hover: Customizes the style of a link while the user's mouse is over it

Note The a:hover pseudo-class is a CSS Level 2 specification and is not supported by Netscape 4.x. Furthermore, a:active links will always be colored red, regardless of the CSS specifications.

✦ a:active: Customizes the style of a link when it is selected by the user

Tip Dreamweaver does not preview pseudo-class styles (except for a:link), although they can be previewed through a supported browser.

A pseudo-element, on the other hand, enables control over contextually defined page elements: for example, p:first-letter would style the first letter in every paragraph tag, enabling a drop-cap design. Because of their specific nature, Dreamweaver does not display any pseudo-elements in the Use CSS Selector list. You can, however, enter your own.

Note Dreamweaver does not currently render any pseudo-elements, including :first-letter, :first-line, :before and :after in the Design view. Preview your page in a compatible browser, such as Netscape 6.x or Internet Explorer 5.5 or higher.

Descendant, ID, and other advanced selectors

Dreamweaver also allows you to enter some of the more advanced additions to the CSS selector palette through the Use CSS Selector field.

New Feature One such selector is the *descendant* selector. Descendant selectors are contextual selectors as they specify one tag within another. A descendant selector would permit you to style paragraphs within a table differently than paragraphs outside of a table. Similarly, text that is nested within two blockquotes (giving the appearance of being indented two levels) can be given a different color, font, and so on than text in a single blockquote.

For example, to style text within nested blockquotes, enter the following in the Use CSS Selector field of the New Style dialog box:

```
blockquote blockquote
```

In essence, you are creating a custom style for a set of HTML tags used in your document. This type of CSS selector acts like an HTML tag that has a CSS style applied to it; that is, all page elements fitting the criteria are automatically styled. You can also combine custom styles with redefined HTML styles in a descendant selector.

Another advanced selector commonly used by designers is the id selector. Any page element can be assigned a unique identifier with the id attribute, like this:

```
<div id="footer">
```

An id selector is identified by a pound sign followed by the id attribute value, like this: #footer. The id selector can also be entered directly into the Use CSS Selector field.

Other advanced selectors that can be entered in the Use CSS Selector field include:

✦ **Child:** Selects an element that is a direct child of another element. For example, in a div tag with nested div elements, div > p selects the paragraphs in the outermost div tag only.

✦ **Adjacent-sibling:** Selects an element that immediately follows another. For example, in an unordered list with two list items, li + li selects the second list item, but not the first.

✦ **Universal:** Selects any element. This selector may be used to skip one or more "generations" of tags. Use body * p to select paragraphs contained within div elements that are children of the body tag, for example.

✦ **Attribute selectors:** Selects tags with specified attributes. You can select tags if they either contain the attribute (p[align]) or if they contain an attribute set to a specific value (p[align="left"]).

Best of all, these selectors are rendered correctly in Dreamweaver's Design view. As of this writing, only the most CSS-compliant browsers, such as Netscape 6.2, properly renders these selectors; but CSS support is gaining ground in each new browser release.

Note Dreamweaver warns you if you enter what it considers an invalid selector type; however, you are given the option to use the selector if you choose.

Editing and managing style sheets

Style sheets, like most elements of a Web page, are almost never set in stone. Designers need to be able to modify style rules — whether they're from an internal or an external style sheet — at a moment's notice. Through the CSS panel's Edit Styles mode, Dreamweaver provides near-immediate access.

New Feature When in Edit Styles mode, the CSS panel displays all the styles attached to the current page. Presented in a collapsible outline (Figure 20-5), Dreamweaver shows the internal styles first, if any, followed by the external styles. The style list is more than just a pretty display — it's a direct pipeline to editing each style. Double-click any style, and the CSS Style Definition dialog box with the current style's settings is displayed. You can also select any style and choose the Edit Style Sheet button to achieve the same effect. To delete a style, select the style and choose the Delete CSS Style button.

Figure 20-5: Both internal and external styles are shown in the CSS panel's Edit Styles mode.

If you'd prefer a more centralized dialog box for your style sheet management chores, the Edit Style Sheet dialog box is available. To open this dialog box, select a style sheet—not a specific style—in the CSS Styles panel and choose the Edit Style Sheet button. You can also choose Edit Style Sheet from the drop-down list on the Property inspector when in CSS mode. The Edit Style Sheet dialog box, shown in Figure 20-6, displays all your current styles— including HTML tags and custom styles—and provides various controls to link a style sheet and edit, create, duplicate, or remove a style.

Figure 20-6: The Edit Style Sheet dialog box lists and defines any given style, in addition to presenting several command buttons for creating and managing styles.

Tip To start editing one of your styles immediately, double-click the style in the list window of the Edit Style Sheet dialog box. This sequence takes you to the CSS Style Definition dialog box, in which you redefine your selected style.

Use the five command buttons along the right side of the Edit Style Sheet dialog box to create new external sheets or manage your existing style sheets:

✦ **Link:** Enables you to create an external style sheet, or link to (or import) an existing external style sheet

✦ **New:** Begins the creation of a new style by first opening the New CSS Style dialog box, described in the following section

✦ **Edit:** Modifies any existing style

✦ **Duplicate:** Makes a copy of the selected style as a basis for creating a new style

✦ **Remove:** Deletes an existing style

External style sheets are displayed in the Edit Style Sheet dialog box with a (link) or (import) following the filename. You can double-click the file listing to open a new Edit Style Sheet dialog box for your external style sheet file. The defined styles within the style sheet then appear in the CSS Styles panel.

Tip

Style sheets can also be edited by hand or in another CSS editor, such as the Windows-only program, TopStyle. To open the file for editing in Dreamweaver, double-click any CSS file in the Site panel. To use another CSS editor, set the .css file type to the desired editor in the File Types/Editors category of Preferences. Next, right-click (Control+click) the CSS file in the Site panel and choose Edit With *Editor Name*. If you'd like to be able to double-click the filename and launch the external editor, you'll need to remove .css from the file extension listed in the Open in Code View option, also found in the File Types / Editors category of Preferences.

There is one final technique for accessing the external CSS editor. With your editor defined in Preferences, choose Use External Editor from the options menu of the CSS Styles panel. Double-clicking a style in the CSS Styles panel when in Edit Styles mode launches the desired editor instead of using Dreamweaver's internal editor.

If you've already defined styles in the current document and you want to convert them to an external style sheet, Dreamweaver has you covered. Just choose File ⇨ Export ⇨ Export CSS Styles and enter a filename in the Export Styles as CSS File dialog box. Follow the directions in this section for linking this newly created file to your other Web pages as a style sheet.

Styles and Their Attributes

After you've selected a type and name for a new style or chosen to edit an existing style, the CSS Style Definition dialog box opens. A Category list from which you select a style category (just as you select a category of preferences in Dreamweaver's Preferences dialog box) is located on the left side of this dialog box.

Dreamweaver offers you eight categories of CSS Level 1 styles to help you define your style sheet:

✦ Type

✦ Background

✦ Block

✦ Box

✦ Border

✦ List

✦ Positioning

✦ Extensions

You can define styles from one or all categories. The following sections describe each style category and its available settings.

Note   All the CSS rendering has been vastly improved in Dreamweaver MX, not all possible CSS attributes are viewable in the Design view.

Type options

The Type category specifies the appearance and layout of the typeface for the page in the browser window. The Type category, shown in Figure 20-7, is one of the most widely used and supported categories — it can be rendered in Internet Explorer 3.0 and above and Navigator 4.0 and above. Table 20-1 explains the settings available in this category.

Table 20-1: CSS Type Attributes

Type Setting	Description
Font	Specifies the font or a collection of fonts, known as a *font family*. You can edit the font list by selecting Edit Font List from the drop-down list. (This sequence opens the Edit Font List dialog box, as described in Chapter 7.)
Size	Selects a size for the selected font. If you enter a value, you can then select the measurement system in the adjacent text box (the default is pixels). The relative sizes, such as small, medium, and large, are set relative to the parent element. Values may be selected from the drop-down list or entered by hand.
Style	Specifies a normal, oblique, or italic attribute for the font. An oblique font may have been generated in the browser by electronically slanting a normal font.
Line Height	Sets the line height of the line (known as *leading* in traditional layout). Typically, line height is a point or two more than the font size, although you can set the line height to be the same as or smaller than the font size, for an overlapping effect.
Decoration	Changes the decoration for text. Options include underline, overline, strike-through, blink, and none. The blink decoration is displayed only in Netscape 4.x and earlier browsers.
Weight	Sets the boldness of the text. You can use the relative settings (light, bold, bolder, and boldest) or apply a numeric value. Normal is around 400; bold is 700.
Variant	Switches between normal and small caps. Small caps is a font style that displays text as uppercase, but the capital letters are a slightly larger size.
Case	Forces a browser to render the text as uppercase, lowercase, or capitalized.
Color	Sets a color for the selected font. Enter a color name or select the color swatch to choose a browser-safe color from the color picker.

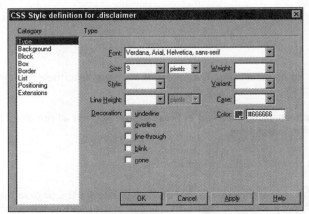

Figure 20-7: The Type settings category includes some of the best supported CSS attributes.

Background options

Since Netscape Navigator 2.0, Web designers have been able to use background images and color. Thanks to CSS Background attributes, designers can now use background images and color with increased control. Whereas traditional HTML background images are restricted to a single image for the entire browser window, CSS backgrounds can be specified for a single paragraph or any other CSS selector. (To set a background for the entire page, apply the style to the <body> tag.) Moreover, instead of an image automatically tiling to fill the browser window, CSS backgrounds can be made to tile horizontally, vertically, or not at all (see Figure 20-8). You can even position the image relative to the selected element.

The latest versions of both primary browsers support the CSS Background attributes shown in Figure 20-9 and listed in Table 20-2.

Table 20-2: CSS Background Attributes

Background Setting	Description
Background Color	Sets the background color for a particular style. Note that this setting enables you to set background colors for individual paragraphs or other elements.
Background Image	Specifies a background image.
Repeat	Determines the tiling options for a graphic:
	no repeat displays the image in the upper-left corner of the applied style.
	repeat tiles the background image horizontally and vertically across the applied style.
	repeat-x tiles the background image horizontally across the applied style.
	repeat-y tiles the background image vertically down the applied style.

Background Setting	Description
Attachment	Determines whether the background image remains fixed in its original position or scrolls with the page. This setting is useful for positioned elements. If you use the overflow attribute, you often want the background image to scroll in order to maintain layout control.
Horizontal Position	Controls the positioning of the background image in relation to the style sheet elements (text or graphics) along the horizontal axis.
Vertical Position	Controls the positioning of the background image in relation to the style sheet elements (text or graphics) along the vertical axis.

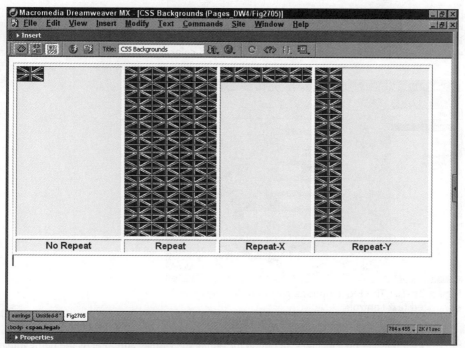

Figure 20-8: You can achieve a number of different tiling effects by using the Repeat attribute of the CSS Backgrounds category.

Block options

One of the most common formatting effects in traditional publishing, long absent from Web publishing, is justified text — text that appears as a solid block. Justified text is possible with the Text Align attribute, one of the seven options available in the CSS Block category, as shown in Figure 20-10. Indented paragraphs are also a possibility.

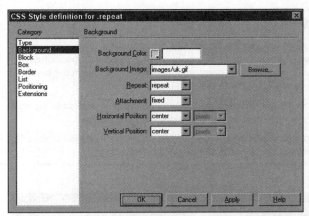

Figure 20-9: The CSS Background options enable a much wider range of control over background images and color.

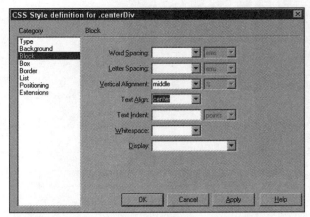

Figure 20-10: The Block options give the Web designer enhanced text control.

New Feature

Dreamweaver now includes an option for setting the Display attribute. As the name implies, the Display attribute determines how an element should be presented. Display accepts a wide-range of values — 18 in all — but only a few are currently supported by even the latest browsers. That said, the supported values — block, inline and, curiously enough, none — are very important indeed. Setting a Display attribute to none effectively hides the element to which the CSS attribute is applied; setting the same attribute to block or inline, reveals the element. Many collapsible/expandable lists depend on the Display attribute to achieve their effects.

Table 20-3: CSS Block Attributes

Block Setting	Description
Word Spacing	Defines the spacing between words. You can increase or decrease the spacing with positive and negative values, set in *ems* by default (in CSS, one *em* is equal to the height of a given font); with a 12 pt font, to increase the spacing between words to 24 pt, set the Word Spacing value to 2ems.
Letter Spacing	Defines the spacing between the letters of a word. You can increase or decrease the spacing with positive and negative values, set in ems by default.
Vertical Alignment	Sets the vertical alignment of the style. Choose from baseline, sub, super, top, text-top, middle, bottom, or text-bottom, or add your own value.
Text Align	Sets text alignment (left, right, center, and justified).
Text Indent	Indents the first line of text on a style by the amount specified.
Whitespace	Controls display of spaces and tabs. The normal option causes all whitespace to collapse. The pre option behaves similarly to the <pre> tag; all whitespace is preserved. The nowrap option enables text to wrap if a tag is detected.
Display	Determines how a tag is represented. Possible values include none, inline, block, list-item, run-in, compact, marker, table, inline-table, table-row-group, table-header-group, table-footer-group, table-row, table-column-group, table-column, table-cell, and table-caption.

Box options

The Box attribute defines the placement and settings for elements (primarily images) on a page. Many of the controls (shown in Figure 20-11) emulate spacing behavior similar to that found in <table> attributes. If you are already comfortable using HTML tables with cell padding, border colors, and width/height controls, you can quickly learn how to use these Box features, which are described in Table 20-4.

Tip

To have the same padding or margins all around a box area, check the Same for All option. This option allows you to set one value — Top — to use for all four sides.

Table 20-4: CSS Box Attributes

Box Setting	Description
Width	Sets the width of the element.
Height	Defines the height of the element.
Float	Places the element at the left or right page margin. Any text that encounters the element wraps around it.
Clear	Sets the side on which layers cannot be displayed next to the element. If a layer is encountered, the element with the Clear attribute places itself beneath the layer.

Continued

Table 20-4: *(continued)*

Box Setting	Description
Margin	Defines the amount of space between the borders of the element and other elements in the page.
Padding	Sets the amount of space between the element and the border or margin, if no border is specified. You can control the padding for the left, right, top, and bottom independently.

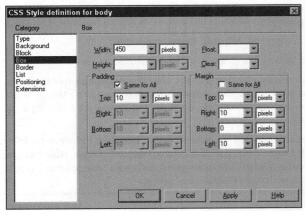

Figure 20-11: The CSS Box attributes define the placement of HTML elements on the Web page.

Border options

With Cascading Style Sheets, you can specify many parameters for borders surrounding text, images, and other elements such as Java applets. In addition to specifying separate colors for any of the four box sides, you can also choose the width of each side's border, as shown in the CSS Border panel (see Figure 20-12). You can use eight different types of border lines, including solid, dashed, inset, and ridge. As with the Padding and Margin attributes in the Box category, Dreamweaver includes a Same for All option under the Style, Width, and Color attributes to save you the work of having to enter the same value for all four sides. Table 20-5 lists the Border options.

Table 20-5: CSS Border Attributes

Border Setting	Description
Style	Sets the style of the border. You can use any of the following as a border: dotted, dashed, solid, double, groove, ridge, inset, and outset.
Width	Determines the width of the border on each side. Choose thin, medium, thick or enter a number to set a width.
Color	Sets the color of the border on each side.

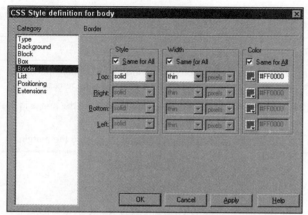

Figure 20-12: Borders are useful when you need to highlight a section of text or a graphic.

Tip

CSS Border attributes are especially useful for highlighting paragraphs of text with a surrounding box. Use the Box panel's Padding attributes to inset the text from the border.

List options

CSS gives you greater control over bulleted points. With Cascading Style Sheets, you can now display a specific bulleted point based on a graphic image, or you can choose from the standard built-in bullets, including disc, circle, and square. The CSS List category also enables you to specify the type of ordered list, including decimal, Roman numerals, or A-B-C order. Figure 20-13 shows and Table 20-6 describes the settings for lists.

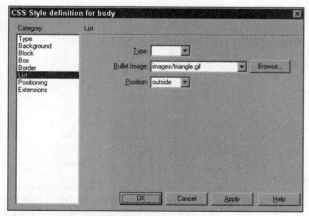

Figure 20-13: Specify a graphic to use as a bullet through the CSS List category.

Table 20-6: List Category for Styles

List Setting	Description
Type	Selects a built-in bullet type. The options include disc, circle, square, decimal, lowercase Roman, uppercase Roman, lowercase alpha, and uppercase alpha.
Bullet Image	Sets an image to be used as a custom bullet. Enter the path to the image in the text box.
Position	Determines if the list item wraps to an indent (the default) or to the margin.

Positioning options

For many designers, positioning has increased creativity in page layout design. With positioning, you have exact control over where an element is placed on a page. The positioning attributes are often applied to div tags to create page layouts without resorting to tables. Figure 20-14 shows the various attributes that provide this pinpoint control of your page elements. The options are described in Table 20-7.

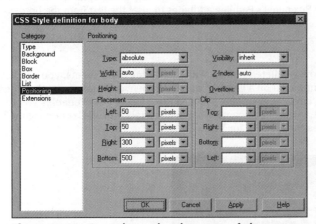

Figure 20-14: Control over the placement of elements on a page frees the Web designer from the restrictions imposed with HTML tables and other old-style formats.

Table 20-7: CSS Positioning Attributes

Positioning Setting	Description
Type	Determines whether an element can be positioned absolutely or relatively on a page. The third option, static, does not enable positioning and renders elements as they would be positioned with regular HTML.
Width	Sets the width of the element.
Height	Sets the height of the element.

Positioning Setting	Description
Visibility	Determines whether the element is visible, hidden, or inherits the property from its parent.
Z-Index	Sets the apparent depth of a positioned element. Higher values are closer to the top.
Overflow	Specifies how the element is displayed when it's larger than the dimensions of the element. Options include the following: clip, where the element is partially hidden; none, where the element is displayed and the dimensions are disregarded; and Scroll, which inserts scroll bars to display the overflowing portion of the element.
Placement	Sets the styled element's placement and dimensions with the left and top attributes and the width and height attributes respectively.
Clip	Sets the visible portion of the element through the top, right, bottom, and left attributes.

Cross-Reference

Dreamweaver layers are built upon the foundation of CSS positioning. For a complete explanation of layers and their attributes, see Chapter 21.

Extensions options

The specifications for Cascading Style Sheets are rapidly evolving, and Dreamweaver has grouped some cutting-edge features in the Extensions category. As of this writing, most of the Extensions attributes (see Table 20-8) are supported by Internet Explorer 4.0 and above, whereas only the Cursor extension is supported in Netscape Navigator 6.x. The Extensions settings shown in Figure 20-15 affect three different areas: page breaks for printing, the user's cursor, and special effects called *filters*.

Table 20-8: CSS Extensions Attributes

Extensions Setting	Description
Pagebreak	Inserts a point on a page where a printer sees a page break. Currently supported only by Internet Explorer, versions 5.0 and higher.
Cursor	Defines the type of cursor that appears when the user moves the cursor over an element. Currently supported by Internet Explorer, versions 4.0 and higher as well as Netscape 6.
Filter	Filters enable you to customize the look and transition of an element without having to use graphic or animation files. Currently supported only by Internet Explorer 4.0 and above.

Note

One of the problems with the Web's never-ending evolution of page design is evident when you begin to print the page. The Pagebreak attribute alleviates this problem by enabling the designer to designate a style that forces a page break when printing; the break can occur either before or after the element is attached to the style. This attribute is especially important for print media styles.

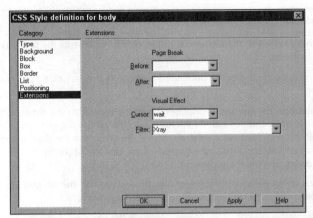

Figure 20-15: The CSS Extensions panel enables some terrific effects, which, unfortunately, are not well supported across the board.

The Filter attribute offers 16 different special effects that can be applied to an element. Many of these effects, such as Wave and Xray, are quite stunning. Several effects involve transitions, as well. Table 20-9 details all these effects.

Table 20-9: CSS Filters

Filter	Syntax	Description
Alpha	alpha(Opacity=*opacity*, FinishOpacity=*finishopacity*, Style=*style*, StartX=*startX*, StartY=*startY*, FinishX=*finishX*, FinishY=*finishY*) *Opacity* is a value from 0 to 100, where 0 is transparent and 100 is fully opaque. *StartX*, *StartY*, *FinishX*, and *FinishY* are pixel values indicating where the effect should start and end. *Style* can be 0 (uniform), 1 (linear), 2 (radial), or 3 (rectangular).	Sets the opacity of a specified gradient region. This can have the effect of creating a burst of light in an image.
BlendTrans*	blendTrans (duration=*duration*) *Duration* is a time value for the length of the transition, in the format of *seconds.milliseconds*.	Causes an image to fade in or out over a specified time.

Filter	Syntax	Description
Blur	blur (Add=*add*, Direction=*direction*, Strength=*strength*)	Emulates motion blur for images.
	Add is any integer other than 0.	
	Direction is any value from 0 to 315 in increments of 45.	
	Strength is any positive integer representing the number of pixels affected.	
Chroma	chroma (Color= *color*)	Makes a specific color in an image transparent.
	Color must be given in hexadecimal form, for example, #rrggbb.	
DropShadow	dropshadow (Color=*color*, OffX=*offX*, OffY=*offY*, Positive=*positive*)	Creates a drop shadow of the applied element, either image or text, in the specified color.
	Color is a hexadecimal triplet.	
	OffX and *OffY* are pixel offsets for the shadow.	
	Positive is a Boolean switch; use 1 to create shadow for nontransparent pixels and 0 to create shadow for transparent pixels.	
FlipH	FlipH	Flips an image or text horizontally.
FlipV	FlipV	Flips an image or text vertically.
Glow	Glow (Color=*color*, Strength=*strength*)	
	Adds radiance to an image in the specified color.	
	Color is a hexadecimal triplet.	
	Strength is a value from 0 to 100.	
Gray	Gray	Converts an image in grayscale.
Invert	Invert	Reverses the hue, saturation, and luminance of an image.
Light*	Light	Creates the illusion that an object is illuminated by one or more light sources.
Mask	Mask(Color=*color*)	Sets all the transparent pixels to the specified color and converts the nontransparent pixels to the background color.
	Color is a hexadecimal triplet.	

Continued

Table 20-9: *(continued)*

Filter	Syntax	Description
RevealTrans*	RevealTrans(duration=*duration*, transition=*style*) *Duration* is a time value that the transition takes, in the format of *seconds.milliseconds*. *Style* is one of 23 different transitions.	Reveals an image using a specified type of transition over a set period of time.
Shadow	Shadow(Color=*color*, Direction=*direction*) *Color* is a hexadecimal triplet. *Direction* is any value from 0 to 315 in increments of 45.	Creates a gradient shadow in the specified color and direction for images or text.
Wave	Wave(Add=*add*, Freq=*freq*, LightStrength=*lightstrength*, Phase=*phase*, Strength=*strength*) *Add* is a Boolean value, where 1 adds the original object to the filtered object and 0 does not. *Freq* is an integer specifying the number of waves. *LightStrength* is a percentage value. *Phase* specifies the angular offset of the wave, in percentage (for example, 0% or 100% = 360 degrees, 25% = 90 degrees). *Strength* is an integer value specifying the intensity of the wave effect.	Adds sine wave distortion to the selected image or text.
Xray	Xray	Converts an image to inverse grayscale for an X-rayed appearance.

* These three transitions require extensive documentation beyond the scope of this book.

Design Time Style Sheets

Cascading Style Sheets give the designer an awesome flexibility with respect to the overall look and feel of a site. In fact, it's entirely possible for sites to be designed with multiple style sheets, each one applicable according to a particular condition. With a little JavaScript or server-side coding, different style sheets can be applied according to which browser is being used, the platform employed, even the screen resolution at work. How does Dreamweaver know which style sheet to use? With the design time style sheets feature, of course.

The design time style sheets feature enables you to show a specific style sheet while hiding others as you work. One key use of this command is to utilize a style sheet that is linked from your page dynamically at runtime. Your style sheets, in other words, do not have to be specifically attached to your page for you to be able to use them.

To set up design time style sheets, follow these steps:

1. From the CSS panel options menu choose Design Time Style Sheets. Alternatively, select Text ➪ CSS Styles ➪ Design Time Style Sheets.

   Whichever method you choose, the Design Time Style Sheets dialog box, shown in Figure 20-16, is displayed.

2. To show a specific style sheet, select the Add (+) button above the Show Only at Design Time list area and select an external style sheet from the Select File dialog box.

3. To hide a specific style sheet, select the Add (+) button above the Hide at Design Time list area and select an external style sheet from the Select File dialog box.

4. To delete a listed style sheet from either list, select the entry and then choose the Remove (() button above the list.

The Design Time Style Sheets information is stored in a Design Note; make sure that you do not unwittingly delete any such Design Note file.

5. Click OK when you're done.

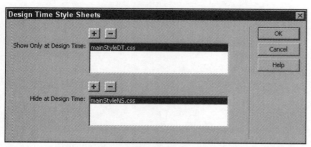

Figure 20-16: Use the Design Time Style Sheets feature to display a variety of style sheets while you're creating the page.

Summary

In this chapter, you discovered how you can easily and effectively add and modify Cascading Style Sheets. You can now accomplish all of the following:

✦ Update and change styles easily with the CSS Styles panel

✦ Easily apply generated styles to an element on a page

✦ Apply a consistent look and feel with linked style sheets

✦ Position fonts and elements, such as images, with pinpoint accuracy

✦ Exercise control over the layout, size, and display of fonts on a page

✦ Define external style sheets to control the look and feel of an entire site

✦ Set up style sheets so that they're visible only at design time

In the next chapter, you learn how to position elements on a page in Dreamweaver using layers.

✦   ✦   ✦

Working with Layers

♦ ♦ ♦ ♦

In This Chapter

Understanding
how layers work
in Dreamweaver

Modifying layers:
Resizing, moving,
and altering
properties

Using forms
in layers

Making
interactive layers
with Dreamweaver
behaviors

♦ ♦ ♦ ♦

For many years, page designers have taken for granted the capability to place text and graphics anywhere on a printed page—even enabling graphics, type, and other elements to "bleed" off a page. This flexibility in design has eluded Web designers until recently. Lack of absolute control over layout has been a high price to pay for the universality of HTML, which makes any Web page viewable by any system, regardless of the computer or the screen resolution.

Lately, however, the integration of positioned layers within the Cascading Style Sheets specification has brought true absolute positioning to the Web. Page designers with a yen for more control will welcome the precision offered with Cascading Style Sheets-Positioning (CSS-P).

Dreamweaver's implementation of layers turns the promise of CSS-P into an intuitive, designer-friendly, layout-compatible reality. As the name implies, layers offer more than pixel-perfect positioning. You can stack one layer on another, hide some layers while showing others, move a layer across the screen, and even move several layers around the screen simultaneously. Layers add an entirely new dimension to the Web designer's palette. Dreamweaver enables you to create page layouts using layers and then convert those layers to tables that are viewable by earlier browsers.

This chapter explores every aspect of how layers work in HTML—except for animation with timelines, which is covered in Chapter 22. With the fundamentals under your belt, you learn how to create, modify, populate, and activate layers on your Web page.

Layers 101

When the World Wide Web first made its debut in 1989, few people were concerned about the aesthetic layout of a page. In fact, because the Web was a descendant of Standard Generalized Markup Language (SGML)—a multiplatform text document and information markup specification—layout was trivialized. Content and the capability to use hypertext to jump from one page to another were emphasized. After the first graphical Web browser software (Mosaic) was released, it quickly became clear that a page's graphics and layout could enhance a Web site's accessibility and marketability. Content was still king, but design was moving up quickly.

The first attempt at Web page layout was the server-side image map. This item was typically a large graphic (usually too hefty to be downloaded comfortably) with hotspots. Clicking a hotspot sent a message

Positioning Measurement

The positioning of layers is determined by aligning elements on an x-axis and a y-axis. In CSS, the x-axis (defined as "Left" in CSS syntax) begins at the left side of the page, and the y-axis (defined as "Top" in CSS syntax) is measured from the top of the page down. As with many of the other CSS features, you have your choice of measurement systems for Left and Top positioning. All measurements are given in Dreamweaver as a number followed by the abbreviation of the measurement system (without any intervening spaces). The measurement system options are as follows:

Unit	Abbreviation	Measurement
Pixels	Px	Relative to the screen
Points	pt	1 pt = 1/72 in
Inches	in	1 in = 2.54 cm
Centimeters	cm	1 cm = 0.3937 in
Millimeters	mm	1 mm = 0.03937 in
Picas	pc	1 pc = 12 pt
EMS	Em	The height of the element's font
Percentage	%	Relative to the browser window

If you don't define a unit of measurement for layer positioning, Dreamweaver defaults to pixels. If you edit out the unit of measurement, the Web browser defaults to pixels.

to the server, which returned a link to the browser. The download time for these files was horrendous, and the performance varied from acceptable to awful, depending on the server's load.

The widespread adoption of tables, released with HTML 2.0 and enhanced with HTML 3.2, radically changed layout control. Designers gained the capability to align objects and text — but a lot of graphical eye candy was still left to graphic files strategically located within the tables. The harder designers worked at precisely laying out their Web pages, the more they had to resort to workarounds such as nested tables and 1-pixel-wide GIFs used as spacers. To relieve the woes of Web designers everywhere, the W3C included a feature within the new Cascading Style Sheets specifications that allows for absolute positioning of an element upon a page. Absolute positioning enables an element, such as an image or block of text, to be placed anywhere on the Web page. Both Microsoft Internet Explorer 4.0 and Netscape Navigator 4.0 (and later) support layers under the Cascading Style Sheets-Positioning specification.

The addition of the third dimension, depth, truly turned the positioning specs into layers. Now objects can be positioned side by side, and they have a *z-index* property as well. The z-index gets its name from the practice in geometry of describing three-dimensional space with *x*, *y*, and *z* coordinates; z-index is also called the *stacking order* because objects can be stacked upon one another.

A single layer in HTML looks like the following:

```
<div id="Layer1" style="position:absolute; visibility:inherit; ⊃
width:200px; height:115px; z-index:1"></div>
```

Positioned layers are most commonly placed within the `<div>` tag. Another popular location is the `<span>` tag. These tags were chosen because they are seldom used in the HTML 3.2 specification (Dreamweaver supports both tags). Both Microsoft and Netscape encourage users to employ either of these tags, because the two primary browsers are designed to credit full CSS-P features to either the `<div>` or `<span>` tag.

Note Netscape has developed two additional proprietary tags for using layers in its 4.x browser: `<layer>` and `<ilayer>`. The primary difference between the two tags has to do with positioning: The `<layer>` tag is used for absolute positioning, and the `<ilayer>` tag for relative positioning. Unfortunately, layers created by the `<div>` tag and the `<layer>` tag have different feature sets. These tags are no longer supported in Navigator 6.0; instead, Netscape's latest browser fully supports the CSS standard tags, `<div>` and `<span>`.

Creating Layers with Dreamweaver

Dreamweaver enables you to create layers creatively and precisely. You can drag out a layer, placing and sizing it by eye, or choose to do it by the numbers — it's up to you. Moreover, you can combine the methods, quickly eyeballing and roughing out a layer layout and then aligning the edges precisely. For Web design that approaches conventional page layout, Dreamweaver even includes rulers and a grid to which you can snap your layers. Creating layers in Dreamweaver can be handled in one of three ways:

✦ You can drag out a layer after selecting the Draw Layer button from the Insert bar.

✦ You can add a layer in a predetermined size by choosing Insert ➪ Layer.

✦ You can create a layer with mathematical precision through the CSS Styles panel.

The first two methods are quite intuitive and are explained in the following section. The CSS Styles panel method is examined later, in the section "Embedding a layer with style sheets."

Inserting a layer object

When you want to draw out your layer quickly, use the object approach. If you come from a traditional page-designer background and are accustomed to using a program such as QuarkXPress or PageMaker, you're already familiar with drawing out frames or text boxes with the click-and-drag technique. Dreamweaver uses the same method for placing and sizing new layer objects. To draw out a layer as an object, follow these steps:

1. From the Common category of the Insert bar, select the Draw Layer button. Your pointer becomes a crosshairs cursor. (If you decide not to draw out a layer, you can press Shift+Esc at this point or just click once without dragging to abort the process.)

2. Click anywhere in your document to position the layer and drag out a rectangle. Release the mouse button when you have an approximate size and shape with which you're satisfied (see Figure 21-1).

Layer icon   Drag Layer button

Selected layer   Layer Property inspector

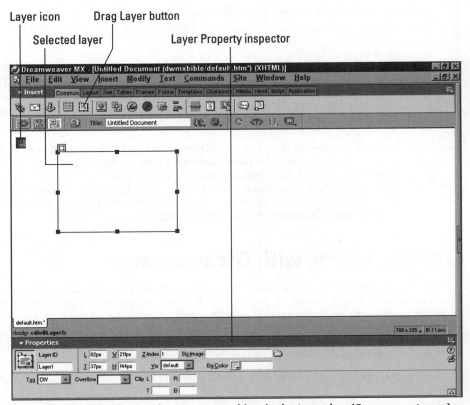

Figure 21-1: After selecting the Drag Layer object in the Insert bar (Common category), the pointer becomes crosshairs when you are working on the page. Click and drag to create the layer.

After you've dragged out your layer, notice several changes to the screen. First, the layer now has a small box on the outside of the upper-left corner. This box, shown in Figure 21-2, is the Selector handle, which you can use to move an existing layer around the Web page. When you click the selection handle, eight resize handles appear around the perimeter of the layer.

Selection handle

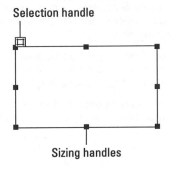

Sizing handles

Figure 21-2: Once a layer is created, you can move it by dragging the selection handle and size it with the resize handles.

Another subtle but important addition to the screen is the Layer icon. Like the other Invisibles icons, the Layer icon can be cut, copied, pasted, and repositioned. When you move the Layer icon, however, its corresponding layer does not move—you are actually only moving the code for the layer to a different place in the HTML source. Generally, the location of the actual layer code in the HTML is immaterial—however, you may want to locate your layer source in a specific area to be backwardly compatible with 3.0 browsers. Dragging and positioning Layer icons one after another is a quick way to achieve this task.

Using the Insert ➪ Layer command

The second method to create a layer is through the menus. Instead of selecting an object from the Insert bar, choose Insert ➪ Layer. Unlike the click-and-drag method, inserting a layer through the menu automatically creates a layer in the upper-left corner; the default size is 200 pixels wide and 115 pixels high.

Although the layer is by default positioned in the upper-left corner of the Document window, it does not have any coordinates listed in the Property inspector. The position coordinates are added when you drag the layer into a new position. If you repeatedly add new layers through the menus without moving them to new positions, each layer stacks directly on top of the previous one, with no offset.

Caution

It's important to assign a specific position (left and top) to every layer. Otherwise, the browser displays all layers directly on top of one another. To give a layer measurements, after you've inserted it through the menu, be sure to drag the layer, even slightly, or manually type in coordinates in the Property inspector.

Setting default characteristics of a layer

You can designate the default size—as well as other features—of the inserted layer with Insert ➪ Layer. Choose Edit ➪ Preferences or use the keyboard shortcut Ctrl+U (Command+U) to open the Preferences dialog box. Select the Layers category. The Layers Preferences category (see Figure 21-3) helps you to set the layer attributes described in Table 21-1.

Table 21-1: Layers Preferences

Layer Preference	Description
Tag	Sets the HTML code to use when creating layers. The options are `<div>` (the default) and `<span>`.
Visibility	Determines the initial state of visibility for a layer. The options are default, inherit, visible, and hidden.
Width	Sets the width of the layer in the measurement system of your choice. The default is 200 pixels.
Height	Sets the height of the layer in the measurement system of your choice. The default is 115 pixels.
Background Color	Sets a color for the layer background. Select the color from the color palette of Web-safe colors.

Continued

Table 21-1: *(continued)*

Layer Preference	Description
Background Image	Sets an image for the layer background. In the text box, enter the path to the graphics file or click the Browse (Choose) button to locate the file.
Nesting Option	If you want to nest layers when one layer is placed in the other automatically, check the Nest When Created Within a Layer checkbox.
Netscape 4 Compatibility	Select this option to add code for a workaround to a known problem in Navigator 4.x browsers, which causes layers to lose their positioning coordinates when the user resizes the browser window.

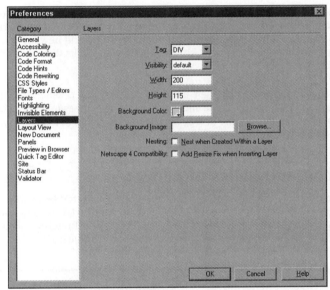

Figure 21-3: If you're building layers to a certain specification, use the Layers Preferences category to designate your options.

Embedding a layer with style sheets

In addition to laying out your layer by eye, or inserting a default layer with Insert ➪ Layer, you can also specify your layers precisely through style sheets. Although this method is not as intuitive as either of the preceding methods, creating layers through style sheets has notable advantages:

✦ You can enter precise dimensions and other positioning attributes.

✦ The placement and shape of a layer can be combined with other style factors such as font family, font size, color, and line spacing.

✦ Layer styles can be saved in an external style sheet, which enables you to control similar elements on every Web page in a site from one source.

Cross-Reference If you haven't yet read Chapter 20, which covers style sheets, you may want to look it over before continuing here.

To create a layer with style sheets, follow these steps:

1. Choose Window ⇨ CSS Styles or select the Show CSS Styles button from the Launcher. This selection opens the CSS Styles panel.

Tip If you haven't enabled the launcher, choose Edit ⇨ Preferences and click the Panels category. Check the Show icons in Panels and Launcher box.

2. From the CSS Styles panel, select the New Style button. This selection opens the New Style dialog box.

3. From the New Style dialog box, set the Type option to Make Custom Style (class). Enter a name for your new style and then choose Define In This Document Only. Click OK.

4. Next up is the CSS Style Definition dialog box. Select the Positioning category.

5. From the Positioning category (see Figure 21-4), enter desired values for the following attributes: Type, Visibility, Z-Index, Overflow, Placement (Left, Top, Width, and Height), and Clip settings (Top, Right, Bottom, Left). Overflow and Clip settings are optional.

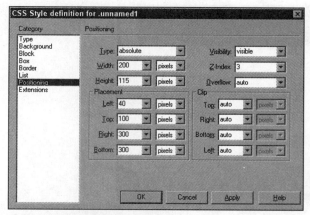

Figure 21-4: Use the Positioning category of the CSS Style Definition dialog box to set layer attributes in an internal or external style sheet.

The Type attribute offers three options: Absolute, Relative, and Static. Although you are familiar with the first two options, the third option, Static, is probably new to you. Use Static when you don't want to add content to a layer, but you still want to specify a rectangular block. Static `<div>` types ignore the Left and Top attributes.

6. If appropriate, select other categories and enter any additional style sheet attributes desired. Click OK when you're done.

7. Select the layer you want to apply the style to, and click the style name in the CSS Styles panel.

Tip   You can also create styles using the ID of the layer, which negates the need to apply styles directly to the layer. As an example, if your layer's name is `MyLayer`, you can create a custom style named `#MyLayer`. The # selector looks for any element with the `MyLayer` ID and applies the appropriate style. You should also remove any inline styles (those applied with the `style` attribute) from the layer.

Keep in mind that layers are part of the overall Cascading Style Sheets specification and can benefit from all of the features of style sheets. You may decide that a specific area of text — a header, for instance — must always be rendered in a bold, red, 18-point Arial font with a green background, and that it should always be placed 35 pixels from the left margin and 25 pixels from the top of the page. You can place the style sheet within a CSS file, link your Web pages to this file, and receive a result similar to what's shown (in black and white) in Figure 21-5. Within one component — the Cascading Style Sheet file — you can contain all of your positioning features for a page's headers, titles, and other text, graphics, or objects. This capability gives you the benefit of controlling the position and look of every page linked to one style sheet.

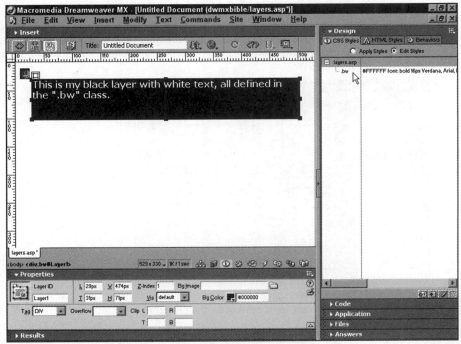

Figure 21-5: You can apply the layer style to any element on any Web page linked to the style sheet.

Note   After applying a style to a layer, the style attributes will show in the Property inspector when the layer is selected. If there isn't a style attribute already applied to the layer tag, changing the values using the Property inspector will change the style declaration in the style sheet. If you do have a style tag in the layer and use the Property inspector to define attributes that conflict with the style sheet, the attributes assigned directly to the layer will be displayed in the Property inspector.

Choosing relative instead of absolute positioning

In most cases, absolute positioning uses the top-left corner of the web page for positioning. The browser may also use the position at which the <body> tag begins as the point of origin for positioning the layers. You can also specify measurements relative to objects. Dreamweaver offers two methods to accomplish relative positioning.

Using the relative attribute

In the first method, you select Relative as the Type attribute in the Style Sheet Positioning category. Relative positioning does not force a fixed position; instead, the positioning is guided by the HTML tags around it. For example, you may place a list of some items within a table and set the positioning relative to the table. You can see the effect of this sequence in Figure 21-6.

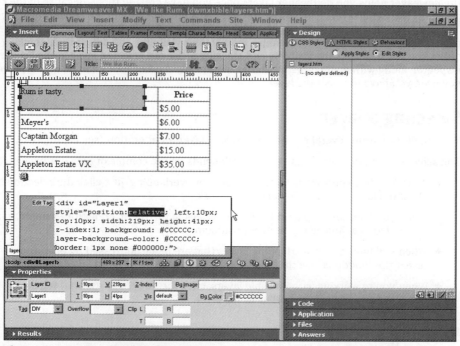

Figure 21-6: Layer1 is positioned relative to the bottom of the table, but Dreamweaver draws the layer as if it were using absolute positioning.

Note   Dreamweaver doesn't preview relative positioning unless you're working with a nested layer or haven't set any top or left attributes, so you should check your placement by previewing the page in a browser.

Relative attributes can be useful, particularly if you want to place the positioned objects within free-flowing HTML. Free-flowing HTML repositions itself based on the size of the browser. When you're using this technique, remember to place your relative layers within absolutely positioned layers. Otherwise, when the end user resizes the browser, the relative layers position themselves relative to the browser and not to the absolutely positioned layers. This situation can produce messy results — use relative positioning with caution when mixed with absolute layers.

Using nested layers

The second technique for positioning layers relatively uses nested layers. Once you nest one layer inside another, the inner layer uses the upper-left corner of the outer layer as its orientation point. For more details about nesting layers, refer to the section "Nesting with the Layers panel," later in this chapter.

Modifying a Layer

Dreamweaver helps you deftly alter layers once you have created them. Because of the complexity of managing layers, Dreamweaver offers an additional tool to the usual Property inspector: the Layers panel. This tool enables you to select any of the layers on the current page quickly, change layer relationships, modify their visibility, and adjust their stacking order. You can also alter the visibility and stacking order of a selected layer in the Property inspector, along with many other attributes. Before any modifications can be accomplished, however, you have to select the layer.

Selecting a layer

You can choose from several methods to select a layer for alteration (see Figure 21-7).

The selection method you choose generally depends on the complexity of your page layout:

✦ When you have only a few layers that are not overlapping, just click the selection handle of the layer with which you want to work.

✦ When you have layers placed in specific places in the HTML code (for example, a layer embedded in a table using relative positioning), choose the Layer icon.

✦ When you have many overlapping layers that are being addressed by one or more JavaScript functions, use the Layers panel to choose the desired layer by name.

✦ When you're working with invisible layers, click the <div> (or <span>) tag in the Tag Selector to reveal the outline of the layer.

Resizing a layer

To resize a layer, position the pointer over one of the eight resize handles surrounding the selected layer. When over the handles, the pointer changes shape to a two- or four-headed arrow. Now click and drag the layer to a new size and shape.

You can also use the arrow keys to resize your layer with more precision. The following keyboard shortcuts change the width and height dimensions while the layer remains anchored by the upper-left corner:

✦ When the layer is selected, press Ctrl+arrow (Command+arrow) to expand or contract the layer by 1 pixel.

✦ Press Ctrl+Shift+arrow (Command+Shift+arrow) to increase or decrease the selected layer by 10 pixels.

Tag Selector   Layers panel

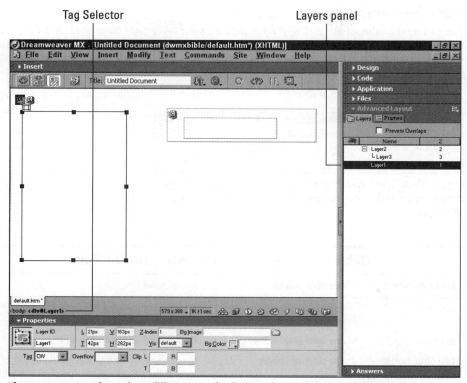

Figure 21-7: You have four different methods for selecting a layer to modify.

Tip

You can quickly preview the position of a layer on a Web page without leaving Dreamweaver. Deselecting the View ➪ Visual Aids ➪ Layer Borders option leaves the layer outline displayed only when the layer is selected; otherwise, it is not shown.

Moving a layer

The easiest way to reposition a layer is to drag the selection handle. If you don't see the handle on a layer, click anywhere in the layer. You can drag the layer anywhere on the screen—or off the bottom or right side of the screen. To move the layer off the left side or top of the screen, enter a negative value in the left and top (L and T) text boxes of the Layer Property inspector.

Tip

To hide the layer completely, match the negative value with the width or height of the layer. For example, if your layer is 220 pixels wide and you want to position it offscreen to the left (so that the layer can slide onto the page at the click of a mouse), set the Left position at –220 pixels.

As with resizing layers, you can also use the arrow keys to move the layer more precisely:

✦ Press any arrow key to move the selected layer 1 pixel in any direction.

✦ Use Shift+arrow to move the selected layer by 10 pixels.

Using the Layer Property inspector

You can modify almost all the CSS-P attributes for your layer right from the Layer Property inspector (shown in Figure 21-8). Certain attributes, such as width, height, and background image and color are self-explanatory or recognizable from other objects. Other layers-only attributes such as visibility and inheritance require further explanation. Table 21-2 describes all the Layer properties, and the following sections discuss the features unique to layers.

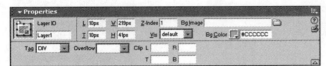

Figure 21-8: The Layer Property inspector makes it easy to move, resize, hide, and manipulate all of the visual elements of a layer.

Table 21-2: Layer Property Inspector Options

Layer Attribute	Possible Values	Description
BgColor	Any hexadecimal or valid color name	Background color for the layer
BgImage	Any valid graphic file	Background image for the layer
Clip (Top, Bottom, Left, Right)	Any positive integer	Measurements for the displayable region of the layer. If the values are not specified, the entire layer is visible.
H (Height)	Any integer measurement in pixels, centimeters, millimeters, inches, points, percentage, ems, or picas	Vertical measurement of the layer
L (Left)	Any integer measurement in pixels, centimeters, millimeters, inches, points, percentage, ems, or picas	Distance measured from the origin point on the left
Name	Any unique name without spaces or special characters	Labels the layer so that it can be addressed by style sheets or JavaScript functions
Overflow	visible, scroll, hidden, or auto	Determines how text or images larger than the layer should be handled
T (Top)	Any integer measurement in pixels, centimeters, millimeters, inches, points, percentage, ems, or picas	The distance measured from the origin point on the top
Tag	span or div	Type of HTML tag to use for the layer
Vis (Visibility)	default, inherit, visible, or hidden	Determines whether a layer is displayed. If visibility is set to inherit, the layer takes on the characteristic of the parent layer.

Layer Attribute	Possible Values	Description
W (Width)	Any integer measurement in pixels, centimeters, millimeters, inches, points, percentage, ems, or picas	The horizontal measurement of the layer
Z-Index	Any integer	Stacking order of the layer relative to other layers on the Web page. Higher numbers are closer to the top.

Name

Names are important when working with layers. To refer to them properly for both CSS and JavaScript purposes, each layer must have a unique ID attribute: unique among the layers and unique among every other object on the Web page. Dreamweaver automatically names each layer as it is created in sequence: Layer1, Layer2, and so forth. You can enter a name that is easier for you to remember by replacing the provided name in the text box on the far left of the Property inspector.

Caution Netscape Navigator 4.x is strict about its use of the ID attribute. You must ensure that you call the layer with an alphanumeric name that does not use spacing or special characters such as the underscore or percentage sign. Moreover, make sure your layer name begins with a letter and not a number—in other words, layer9 works, but 9layer can cause problems.

Tag attribute

The Tag drop-down list contains the HTML tags that can be associated with the layer. By default, the positioned layer has <div> as the tag, but you can also choose <span>. As previously noted, the <div> and <span> tags are endorsed by the World Wide Web Consortium group as part of its CSS standards.

<div> versus <span>

As a general rule, the <span> and <div> tags can be used interchangeably. The major difference between <div> and <span> is that the <div> tag is a BLOCK LEVEL element, and the <span> tag is INLINE.

With the <div> tag, when positioning relatively (the elements are in the normal flow of the document) a <div> will always cause the next element to appear on a new line. Block level elements (like <h1> and <p>, two other block level elements) will always create a new line unless the display property is set to inline using CSS.

The reverse is true of <span>s. The <span> tag is an inline element and will display just like an image or link, without altering the text around it.

Generally <div>s should be used for block level elements that require positioning, and <span>s are more commonly used to apply inline formatting over positioning.

If you're trying to manipulate layers via JavaScript, you should also note that Netscape 4 will not allow scripting of spans. For this point alone, if you wish to keep Netscape support it is advisable to use <div>s over <span>s for positioned elements.

Visibility

Visibility (Vis in the Property inspector) defines whether or not you can see a layer on a Web page. Four values are available:

✦ **Default:** Enables the browser to set the visibility attribute. Most browsers use the inherit value as their default.

✦ **Inherit:** Sets the visibility to the same value as that of the parent layer, which enables a series of layers to be hidden or made visible by changing only one layer.

✦ **Visible:** Causes the layer and all of its contents to be displayed.

✦ **Hidden:** Makes the current layer and all of its contents invisible.

Remember the following when you're specifying visibility:

✦ Whether or not you can see a layer, remember that the layer still occupies space on the page and demands some of the page loading time. Hiding a layer does not affect the layout of the page, and invisible graphics take just as long to download as visible graphics.

✦ When you are defining the visibility of a positioned object or layer, you should not use default as the visibility value. A designer does not necessarily know whether the site's end user has set the default visibility to visible or hidden. Designing an effective Web page can be difficult without this knowledge. The common browser default is for visibility to be inherited, if not specifically shown or hidden.

Overflow

Normally, a layer expands to fit the text or graphics inserted into it. You can, however, restrict the size of a layer by changing the height and width values in the Property inspector. What happens when you define a layer to be too small for an image, or when an amount of text depends on the setting of the layer's overflow attribute? CSS layers (the <div> and <span> tags) support four different overflow settings:

✦ **Visible (Default):** All of the overflowing text or image is displayed, and the height and width settings established for the layer are ignored.

✦ **Hidden:** The portion of the text or graphic that overflows the dimensions is not visible.

✦ **Scroll:** Horizontal and vertical scroll bars are added to the layer regardless of the content size or amount, and regardless of the layer's measurements.

✦ **Auto:** When the content of the layer exceeds the width and/or height values, horizontal and vertical scroll bars appear.

Currently, support for the overflow attribute is spotty at best. Dreamweaver doesn't display the result in the Document window; it must be previewed in a browser to be seen. Navigator offers limited support: Only the attribute's hidden value works correctly, and even then, just for text. Only Internet Explorer 4.0 or later and Netscape 6 render the overflow attribute correctly, as shown in Figure 21-9.

Clipping

If you're familiar with the process of cropping an image, you'll quickly grasp the concept of clipping layers. Just as desktop publishing software hides but doesn't delete the portion of the picture outside of the crop marks, layers can mask the area outside the clipping region defined by the Left, Top, Right, and Bottom values in the Clip section of the Layer Property inspector.

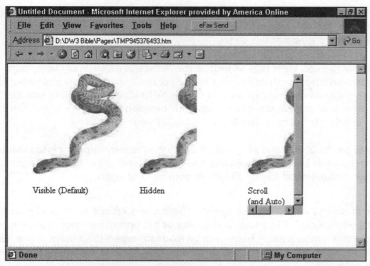

Figure 21-9: When your contents are larger than the dimensions of your layer, you can regulate the results with the overflow attribute.

All clipping values are measured from the upper-left corner of the layer. You can use any CSS standard measurement system: pixels (the default), inches, centimeters, millimeters, ems, or picas.

The current implementation of CSS supports only rectangular clipping. When you look at the code for a clipped layer, you see the values you inserted in the Layer Property inspector in parentheses following the `clip` attribute, with the `rect` (for rectangular) keyword, as follows:

```
<div id="Layer1" style="position:absolute; left:54px; top:24px; ⊃
width:400px; height:115px; z-index:1; visibility:inherit; ⊃
clip:rect(10px 100px 100px 10px)">
```

Generally, you specify values for all four criteria: Left, Top, Right, and Bottom. You can also leave the Left and Top values empty or use the keyword `auto`—which causes the Left and Top values to be set at the origin point: 0,0. If you leave any of the clipping values blank, the blank attributes will be set to auto.

Cross-Reference
Clipping is a powerful function that you can employ in interesting ways. This property is the basis for the image map rollover technique discussed in Chapter 13.

Z-index

One of a layer's most powerful features is its capability to appear above or below other layers. You can change this order, known as the *z-index*, dynamically. Whenever a new layer is added, Dreamweaver automatically increments the z-index—layers with higher z-index values are positioned above layers with lower z-index values. The z-index can be adjusted manually in either the Layer Property inspector or the Layers panel. The z-index must be an integer, either negative or positive.

Tip   Although some Web designers use high values for the z-index, such as 3,000, the z-index is completely relative. The only reason to increase a z-index to an extremely high number is to ensure that a particular layer remains on top.

The z-index is valid for the CSS layer tags as well as the Netscape proprietary layer tags. Netscape also has two additional attributes that can affect the apparent depth of either the `<layer>`- or `<ilayer>`-based content: `above` and `below`. With above and below, you can specify which existing layer is to appear directly on top of or beneath the current layer. You can set only one of the depth attributes, either the `z-index`, or `above` or `below`.

Note   The only way to get the `above` and `below` attributes in the Property inspector is to manually create a `<layer>` or `<ilayer>`. Considering the `<layer>` and `<ilayer>` are proprietary Netscape 4 tags, I recommend staying away from both types of layers.

Caution   Certain types of objects—including Java applets, Plugins, and ActiveX controls—ignore the z-index setting when included in a layer and appear as the uppermost layer. However, certain ActiveX controls—most notably Flash—can be made to respect the z-index. If you need HTML content on top of active content, you can always hide the layer containing the ActiveX control when necessary.

When you designate the layer's tag attribute to be either `<layer>` or `<ilayer>`, the Property inspector displays an additional field: the A/B attribute for setting the above or below value, as shown in Figure 21-10. Choose either attribute from the A/B drop-down list and then select the layer from the adjacent list. The layer you choose must be set up in the code before the current layer. You can achieve this condition in the Document window by moving the icon for the current layer to a position after the other layers. Although you must use either `<layer>` or `<ilayer>` to specify the above or below attribute, the layer specified can be either a CSS or Netscape type.

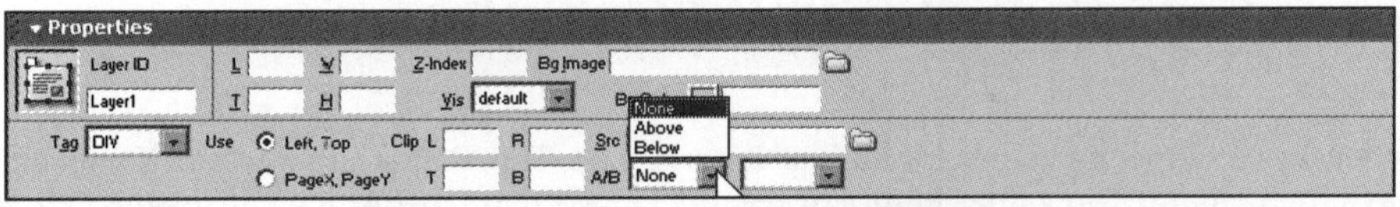

Figure 21-10: Choosing the Netscape-specific tags <layer> or <ilayer> from the Property inspector causes several new options to appear, including the A/B switch for the above/below depth position.

A Visual Clipping Technique

In Dreamweaver, you cannot draw the clipping region visually—the values have to be explicitly input in the Clip section of the Layer Property inspector. That said, a trick using a second temporary layer can make it easier to position your clipping. Follow these steps to get accurate clipping values:

1. Insert your original layer and image.

2. Nest a second, temporary layer inside the first, original layer (select the Draw Layer button in the Insert bar and draw out the second layer inside the first).

If you have your Layer Preferences set so that a layer does not automatically nest when created inside another layer, press the Alt (Option) key while you draw your layer, to override the preference.

3. Position the second layer over the area you want to clip. Use the layer's sizing handles to alter the size and shape, if necessary.

4. Note the position and dimensions of the second layer (the Left, Top, Width, and Height values).

5. Delete the second layer.

6. In the Property inspector for the original layer, enter the Clip values as follows:

   • **L:** Enter the Left value for the second layer.

   • **T:** Enter the Top value for the second layer.

   • **R:** Add the second layer's Left value to its Width value.

   • **B:** Add the second layer's Top value to its Height value.

Dreamweaver displays the clipped layer after you enter the final value. The following figure shows the original layer and the temporary layer on the left, and the final clipped version of the original layer on the right.

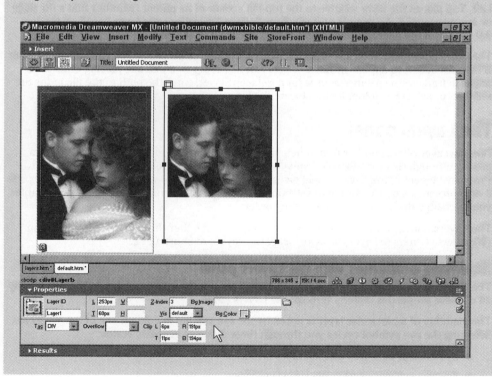

Caution   Working with the above and below attributes can be confusing. Notice that they determine which layer is to appear on top of or underneath the current layer, and not which layer the present layer is above or below.

Background image or color

Inserting a background image or color with the Layer Property inspector works in a similar manner to changing the background image or color for a table (as explained in Chapter 10). To insert an image, enter the path to the file in the Bg Image text box or select the folder icon to locate the image file on your system or network. If the layer is larger than the image, the image is tiled, just as it would be in the background of a Web page or table.

To give a layer a background color, enter the color name (either in its hexadecimal or nominal form) in the Bg Color text box. You can also select the color box to pick your color from the color palette.

Additional Netscape properties

In addition to the above and below values for the z-index attribute, two other Netscape variations must be noted for the sake of completeness. Both appear as options in the Property inspector when either `<layer>` or `<ilayer>` is selected as the layer tag.

When either `<layer>` or `<ilayer>` is selected, the Page X, Page Y option becomes available as a radio button in the Property inspector, in addition to Left, Top. With Netscape layers, Left, Top places the layer relative to the top-left corner of its parent (whether that's the page or another layer if the layer is nested). Page X, Page Y positions the layer based on the top-left corner of the page, regardless of whether the layer is nested.

The other additional Netscape layer attribute is the source property. You can specify another HTML document to appear within a `<layer>` or `<ilayer>` — much like placing other Web pages in frames. To specify a source for a Netscape layer, enter the path to the file in the Src text box or select the folder icon to locate the file.

The Layers panel

Dreamweaver offers another tool to help manage the layers in your Web page: the Layers panel. Although this tool doesn't display as many properties about each element as the Property inspector, the Layers panel gives you a good overview of all the layers on your page. It also provides a quick method of selecting a layer — even when it's offscreen — and enables you to change the z-index and the nesting order.

The Layers panel, shown in Figure 21-11, can be opened either through the Window menu (Window ➪ Others ➪ Layer) or by pressing the keyboard shortcut F2.

Modifying properties with the Layers panel

The Layers panel lists the visibility, name, and z-index settings for each layer. You can modify all of these properties directly through the Layers panel.

The visibility of a particular layer is noted by the eye symbol in column one of the inspector. Selecting the eye symbol cycles you through three different visibility states:

✦ **Eye closed:** Indicates that the layer is hidden

✦ **Eye open:** Indicates that the layer is visible

✦ **No eye:** Indicates that the visibility attribute is set to the default (which, for both Navigator and Internet Explorer, means `inherit`)

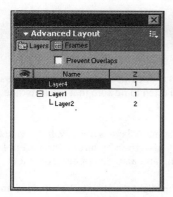

Figure 21-11: Use the Layers panel to quickly select — or alter the visibility or relationships of — all the layers on your page.

 Tip To change all of your layers to a single state simultaneously, select the eye symbol in the column header. Unlike the individual eyes in front of each layer name, the overall eye toggles between open and shut.

You can also change a layer's name (in the second column of the Layers panel). Just double-click the current layer name in the inspector; the name is highlighted. Type in the new name and press Enter (Return) to complete the change.

You can alter the z-index (stacking order) in the third column in the same manner. Double-click the z-index value; and then type in the new value and press Enter (Return). You can enter any positive or negative integer. If you're working with the Netscape proprietary layer tags, you can also alter the above or below values previously set for the z-index through the Property inspector. Use A for above and B for below.

 Tip To change a layer's z-index interactively, you can drag one layer above or below another in the Layers panel. This action causes all the other layers' z-index values to change accordingly.

Nesting with the Layers panel

Another task managed by the Layers panel is nesting or unnesting layers. This process is also referred to as *creating parent-child layers*. To nest one layer inside another through the Layers panel, follow these steps:

1. Choose Window ⇨ Others ⇨ Layers or press F2 to open the Layers panel.

2. Press the Ctrl (Command) key, click the name of the layer to be nested (the child), and drag it on top of the other layer (the parent).

3. When you see a rectangle around the parent layer's name, release the mouse.

   The child layer is indented underneath the parent layer, and the parent layer has a minus sign (a down-pointing triangle on the Mac) attached to the front of its name.

4. To hide the child layer from view, select the minus sign (a down-pointing triangle on the Mac) in front of the parent layer's name. Once the child layer is hidden, the minus sign turns into a plus sign (a right-pointing triangle on the Mac).

5. To reveal the child layer, select the plus sign (a right-pointing triangle on the Mac).

6. To undo a nested layer, select the child layer and drag it to a new position in the Layers panel.

Caution   When it comes to nested layers, Netscape Navigator 4.0 does not "play well with others." When you do decide to use nested layers, test early and often to be sure that pre-Netscape 6 browsers are behaving.

You can use the nesting features of the Layers panel to hide many layers quickly. If the visibility of all child layers is set to the default — with no eye displayed — then by hiding the parent layer, you cause all the child layers to inherit that visibility setting and also disappear from view.

Tip   You can also delete a layer from the Layers panel. Just highlight the layer to be removed and press the Delete key. Dreamweaver also enables you to delete nested layers as a group by selecting the parent layer and pressing Delete. If you want to remove a parent layer but keep all children, the Tag Selector can be used. Select the parent tag, then right-click (Control+ click on Mac) and then choose remove tag.

Aligning layers with the ruler and grid

With the capability to position layers anywhere on a page comes additional responsibility and potential problems. In anything that involves animation, correct alignment of moving parts is crucial. As you begin to set up your layers, their exact placement and alignment become critical. Dreamweaver includes two tools to simplify layered Web page design: the ruler and the grid.

Rulers and grids are familiar concepts in traditional desktop publishing. Dreamweaver's ruler shows the x-axis and y-axis in pixels, inches, or centimeters along the outer edge of the Document window. The grid crisscrosses the page with lines to support a visual guideline when you're placing objects. You can even enable a snap-to-grid feature to ensure easy, absolute alignment.

Using the ruler

With traditional Web design, "eyeballing it" was the only option available for Web page layout. The absolute positioning capability of layers remedied this deficiency. Now online designers have a more precise and familiar system of alignment: the ruler. Dreamweaver's ruler can be displayed in several different measurement units and with your choice of origin point.

To toggle the ruler in Dreamweaver, choose View ➪ Rulers ➪ Show or use the keyboard shortcut Ctrl+Alt+R (Command+Option+R). Horizontal and vertical rulers appear along the top and the left sides of the Document window, as shown in Figure 21-12. As you move the pointer, a light-gray line indicates the position on both rulers.

By default, the ruler uses pixels as its measurement system. You can change the default by selecting View ➪ Rulers and choosing either inches or centimeters.

Dreamweaver also enables you to move the ruler origin to a new position. Normally, the upper-left corner of the page acts as the origin point for the ruler. On some occasions, it's helpful to start the measurement at a different location — at the bottom-right edge of an advertisement, for example. To move the origin point, select the intersection of the horizontal and vertical rulers and drag the crosshairs to a new location. When you release the mouse button, both rulers are adjusted to show negative values above and to the right of the new origin point. To return the origin point to its default setting, choose View ➪ Rulers ➪ Reset Origin, or you can simply double-click the intersection of the rulers.

Figure 21-12: Use the horizontal and vertical rulers to assist your layer placement and overall Web page layout.

Tip

You can access a ruler context menu by right-clicking (Control+clicking) the ruler itself. The context menu enables you to change the system of measurement, reset the origin point, or hide the rulers.

Aligning objects with the grid

Rulers are generally good for positioning single objects, but a grid is extremely helpful when aligning one object to another. With Dreamweaver's grid facility, you can align elements visually or snap them to the grid. You can set many of the grid's other features, including grid spacing, color, and type.

To turn on the grid, choose View ➪ Grid ➪ Show or press Ctrl+Alt+G (Command+Option+G). By default, the grid is displayed with tan lines set at 50-pixel increments.

The snap-to-grid feature is enabled by choosing View ➪ Grid ➪ Snap To or with the keyboard shortcut Ctrl+Alt+Shift+G (Command+Option+Shift+G). When activated, snap-to-grid causes the upper-left corner of a layer to be placed at the nearest grid intersection when the layer is moved.

Like most of Dreamweaver's tools, you can customize the grid. To alter the grid settings, choose View ➪ Grid ➪ Settings. In the Grid Settings dialog box, shown in Figure 21-13, you can change any of the following settings (just click OK when you're done):

Grid Setting	Description
Color	Change the default color (light blue) by selecting the color box (which brings up color palette) or by typing a new value in the text box.
Show Grid	Show or hide the grid with this checkbox toggle.
Snap to Grid	Toggle the checkbox to enable or disable the snap-to-grid feature.
Spacing	Adjust the distance between grid points by entering a numeric value in the text box.
Spacing Unit of Measure	Select pixels, inches, or centimeters from the Spacing drop-down list.
Display	Choose either solid lines or dots for the gridlines.

Figure 21-13: Dreamweaver's grid feature is extremely handy for aligning a series of objects.

Adding elements to a layer

Once you have created and initially positioned your layers, you can begin to fill them with content. Inserting objects in a layer is just like inserting objects in a Web page. The same insertion methods are available to you:

✦ Position the cursor inside a layer, choose Insert in the menu bar, and select an object to insert.

✦ With the cursor inside a layer, select any object from the Insert bar. Note that you cannot select the Draw Layer object.

✦ Drag an object from the Insert bar and drop it inside the layer.

A known problem exists with Netscape Navigator 4.*x* browsers and nested layers — and layers in general — using the `<div>` tag. Whenever the browser window is resized, the layers lose their left and top position and are displayed along the left edge of the browser window or parent layer. Dreamweaver includes the capability to insert code that serves as a workaround for this problem. With this code in place, if the browser is resized, the page reloads, repositioning the layers. If you want the code to be automatically inserted the first time you add a layer to your page, select the Add Resize Fix When Inserting Layers option found on the Layers category of Preferences. You can also insert it on a case-by-case basis by choosing Commands ⇨ Add/Remove Netscape Resize Fix. As the name implies, this command also deletes the Netscape Resize Fix code.

Forms and layers

When you're mixing forms and layers, follow only one rule: Always put the form completely inside the layer. If you place the layer within the form, all form elements after the layer tags are ignored. With the form completely enclosed in the layer, the form can safely be positioned anywhere on the page and all form elements still remain completely active.

Although this rule means that you can't split one form onto separate layers, you can set up multiple forms on multiple layers — and still have them all communicate to one final CGI or other program. This technique uses JavaScript to send the user-input values in the separate forms to hidden fields in the form with the Submit button. Suppose, for example, that you have three separate forms gathering information in three separate layers on a Web page. Call them formA, formB, and formC on layer1, layer2, and layer3, respectively. When the Submit button in formC on layer3 is selected, a JavaScript function is first called by means of an `onClick` event in the button's `<input>` tag. The function, in part, looks like the following:

```
function gatherData() {
  document.formC.hidden1.value = document.formA.text1.value
  document.formC.hidden2.value = document.formB.text2.value
}
```

Notice how every value from the various forms is sent to a hidden field in formC, the form with the Submit button. Now, when the form is submitted, all the hidden information gathered from the various forms is submitted along with formC's own information.

Note

The code for this separate-forms approach, as shown in the preceding listing, works in Internet Explorer. Netscape 4.*x*, however, uses a different syntax to address forms in layers. To work properly in Netscape 4.*x*, the code must look like the following:

```
document.layers["layer3"].document.formC.⊃
hidden1.value=document.layers["layer1"].⊃
document.formA.text1.value
```

To make the code cross-browser compatible, you can use an initialization function that allows for the differences, or you can build it into the `onClick` function. (For more information about building cross browser–compatible code, see Chapter 30.)

Creating Your Page Design with Layers

While the advantage to designing with layers is the greater flexibility it affords, one of the greatest disadvantages of using layers is that they are viewable in only the most recent generation of browsers. Dreamweaver enables you to get the best of both worlds by making it possible for you to use layers to design complex page layouts, and then to transform those layers into tables that can be viewed in earlier browsers. Designing this way has some limitations — you can't, for example, actually layer items on top of one another. Nevertheless, Dreamweaver's capability to convert layers to tables (and tables to layers) enables you to create complex layouts with ease.

Using the Tracing Image

Page-layout artists are often confronted with Web-page designs that have been mocked up in a graphics program. Dreamweaver's Tracing Image function enables you to use such images to guide the precise placement of graphics, text, tables, and forms in your Web page, enabling you to match the original design as closely as possible.

In order to use a Tracing Image, the graphic must be saved in either JPG, GIF, or PNG format. Once the Tracing Image has been placed in your page, it is viewable only in Dreamweaver — it will never appear in a browser. A placed Tracing Image hides any background color or background graphic in your Web page. Preview your page in a browser, or hide the tracing image, to view your page without the Tracing Image.

Caution   If you're concerned about your page validating, be sure to remove the Tracing Image after you've completed the page. The Tracing Image uses a `tracingsrc` attribute inside the `<body>` tag, which doesn't validate.

Adding the Tracing Image to your page

To add a Tracing Image to your Dreamweaver page, select View ➪ Tracing Image ➪ Load. This brings up a Select Image Source dialog box that enables you to select the graphic you would like to use as a Tracing Image. Clicking Select brings up the Page Properties dialog box, shown in Figure 21-14, in which you may specify the opacity of the Tracing Image, from Transparent (0%) to Opaque (100%). You can change the Tracing Image or its transparency at any point by selecting Modify ➪ Page Properties to bring up the Page Properties dialog box. You can toggle between hiding and showing the Tracing Image by selecting View ➪ Tracing Image ➪ Show. You can also enter the Tracing Image directly in the Page Properties dialog box by entering its path in the Tracing Image text box or by selecting the Browse (Choose) button to locate the image.

Note   Even though the Browse dialog for the Tracing Image allows you to choose from a data source, the image will not be displayed on the page.

Moving the Tracing Image

The Tracing Image cannot be selected and moved the same way as other objects on your page. Instead, you must move the Tracing Image using menu commands. You have several options for adjusting the Tracing Image's position to better fit your design. First, you can align the Tracing Image with any object on your page by first selecting the object and then choosing View ➪ Tracing Image ➪ Align with Selection. This lines up the upper-left corner of the Tracing Image with the upper-left corner of the bounding box of the object you've selected.

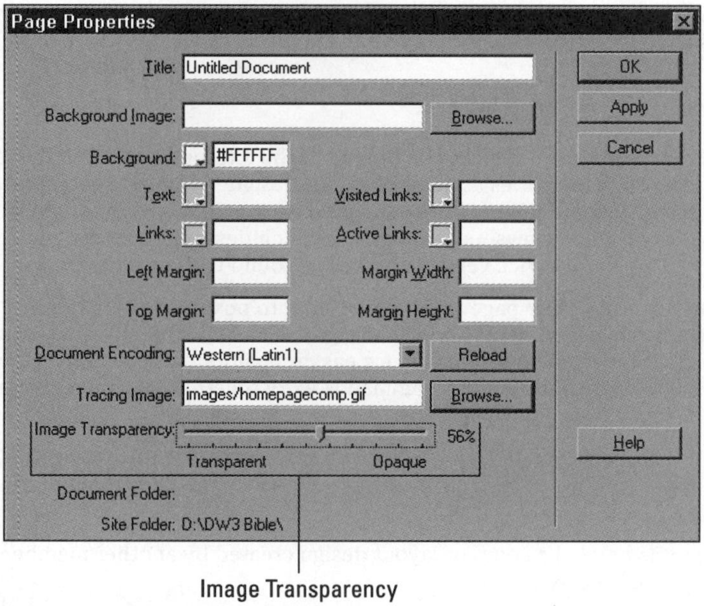

Image Transparency

Figure 21-14: Setting the transparency of the Tracing Image to a setting such as 56 percent can help you differentiate between it and the content layers you are positioning.

To precisely or visually move the Tracing Image to a specific location, select View ➪ Tracing Image ➪ Adjust Position. Enter the *x* and *y* coordinates into their respective boxes in the Adjust Tracing Image Position dialog box, shown in Figure 21-15. For more hands-on positioning, use the arrow keys to nudge the tracing layer up, down, left, or right, one pixel at a time. Holding down the Shift key while pressing the arrow keys moves the Tracing Image in 5-pixel increments. Finally, you can return the Tracing Image to its default location of 9 pixels down from the top and 11 pixels in from the left by selecting View ➪ Tracing Image ➪ Reset Position.

Figure 21-15: Use the Adjust Tracing Image Position dialog box to precisely place your graphic template.

Preventing overlaps

In order to place layers on your page that can later be converted to a table, the layers must not overlap. Before you begin drawing out your layers, open the Layers panel — either by selecting Windows ➪ Others ➪ Layers or by pressing F2 — and put a checkmark in the

Prevent Overlap box at the top of the Layers panel. You can also select Modify ➪ Arrange ➪ Prevent Layer Overlaps to toggle overlap protection on and off.

Designing precision layouts

As noted earlier, layers brought pixel-perfect positioning to the Internet. Now, Web designers can enjoy some of the layout capabilities assumed by print designers. Unfortunately, you need a 4.0 browser or later to view any page created with layers, and a portion of the Web audience is still using 3.0 or older browsers. Dreamweaver includes a feature that enables you to convert layers to tables, and vice versa as part of its round-trip repertoire.

Web designers can freely design their page and then lock it into position for posting. Moreover, if the design needs adjustment—and all designs need adjustment—the posted page can be temporarily converted back to layers for easy repositioning. The Convert Tables to Layers and Convert Layers to Tables menu commands work together magnificently and greatly enhance the designer's workflow.

The two commands are described in detail in the following sections, but the following steps outline a typical Dreamweaver layout session, enabling you to see how they function together:

1. The Web designer is handed a comp or layout design created by another member of the company or a third-party designer.

2. After creating the graphic and type elements, the Web designer is ready to compose the page in Dreamweaver.

3. Ideally, the comp is converted to an electronic graphic format and brought into Dreamweaver as a Tracing Image.

4. If at all possible, it's best for conversion purposes not to overlap any layers, so the Web designer enables the Prevent Overlap option.

5. Each element is placed in a separate layer and placed in position, following the Tracing Image, if any.

6. With one command (Convert Layers to Tables), the layout is restructured from appearing in layers to being in tables for backward browser compatibility.

7. After the client has viewed the page—and specified the inevitable changes—the page is converted from tables to layers. Again, in Dreamweaver MX, you can accomplish this with one command (Convert Tables to Layers), and it takes just seconds to complete.

8. The trip from tables to layers and back again is made as many times as necessary to get the layout pixel-perfect.

Convert Tables to Layers and Convert Layers to Tables is a one-two combination that cuts layout time tremendously and frees the designer to create visually instead of programmatically.

Converting content to layers

With Dreamweaver, you can take any page and enclose all the contents in layers for easy design layout with drag-and-drop ease. Convert Tables to Layers is very flexible and enables you to convert pages previously constructed with tables (either partially or totally), or ones that already have layers in place. You can even quickly convert an all-text page into a layer.

Tip   One valuable use for this command is to better prepare a page to use another Dreamweaver feature: File ➪ Convert to 3.0 Browser Compatible. Although it isn't necessary to have every page element in a layer to use this feature, if you use the Convert Tables to Layers command first, you get better results.

Caution   The Convert to 3.0 Browser Compatible command cannot be undone. Make sure you save a copy of the page before running the conversion in case you need to go back and make a change.

With the page open in Dreamweaver, select Modify ➪ Convert ➪ Tables to Layers to view the command's dialog box, shown in Figure 21-16.

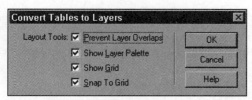

Figure 21-16: Choose the appropriate Layout Tools options to help you reposition your content using layers.

By default, each of the following Layout Tools options is enabled:

✦ **Prevent Layer Overlaps:** Turn this option on if you plan to convert the layers back to a table.

✦ **Show Layers Panel:** This option automatically opens the Layers panel for you, with each layer given a default name by Dreamweaver.

✦ **Show Grid:** This option reveals the grid overlay that can help with precision layout.

✦ **Snap to Grid:** With this turned on, layers snap to the nearest gridlines as they are moved onscreen.

You can uncheck any of these options before you convert the page.

Tip   Turn off Show Grid and Snap to Grid if you are laying out objects on top of a Tracing Image, as they may interfere with the absolute positions that you are trying to achieve.

Converting layers to tables

To convert a Web page that has been designed with layers into a table for viewing in older browsers, simply select Modify ➪ Convert ➪ Layers to Tables. This opens the Convert Layers to Table dialog box, shown in Figure 21-17, with the following options:

✦ **Most Accurate:** This creates as complex a table as is necessary to guarantee that the elements on your Web page appear in the exact locations that you've specified. This is the default setting.

✦ **Smallest:** This option collapses empty cells less than *n* pixels wide: Selecting this option simplifies your table layouts by joining cells that are less wide than the number of pixels that you specify. This may result in a table that takes less time to load; however, it also means that the elements on your page may not appear in the precise locations where you've placed them.

✦ **Use Transparent GIFs:** When you select this option, Dreamweaver adds a single row at the bottom with transparent GIFs to keep the table dimensions correct. If you make later edits to the table cell sizes, be sure to either remove the bottom row of the table, or change the size of the transparent GIFs. When Dreamweaver creates the table layout, it places the file transparent.gif in the same folder as your Web page. Make sure you include this file when you upload your page to your server in order for it to be displayed correctly.

✦ **Center on Page:** Selecting this option puts `<div align=center>` tags around your table so that it is displayed in the middle of a browser window. Deselecting this option omits these tags so that the table starts from its default position in the upper-left corner of a browser.

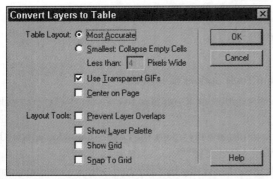

Figure 21-17: Select the necessary Layout Tools options to help reposition your content as a table.

Once you have converted your layout into a table, as shown in Figure 21-18, you should preview it in your browser. If you aren't happy with the way your layout looks, or if you want to make further modifications, you can convert the table back into layers. Select Modify ➪ Convert ➪ Convert Tables to Layers as described previously, selecting the layers to drag and drop the contents into new positions. Finally, transform your layout back into a table and preview it again.

Tip   It's worth pointing out that the two Modify ➪ Convert commands can be easily reversed by choosing Edit ➪ Undo, whereas the corresponding File ➪ Convert commands cannot.

Figure 21-18: You can easily transform layers into a table, using the default settings.

Activating Layers with Behaviors

While absolute positioning is a major reason to use layers, you may have other motives for using this capability. All the properties of a layer — the coordinates, size and shape, depth, visibility, and clipping — can be altered dynamically and interactively. Normally, dynamically resetting a layer's properties entails some fairly daunting JavaScript programming. Now, with one of Dreamweaver's hallmarks — those illustrious behaviors — activating layers is possible for nonprogrammers as well.

Cross-Reference   If you want to learn more about behaviors, Chapter 23 describes Dreamweaver's rich behaviors feature.

Behaviors consist of two parts: the event and the action. In Dreamweaver, three standard actions are designed specifically for working with layers:

✦ **Drag Layer:** Enables the user to move the layer and get a response to that movement.

✦ **Set Text of Layer:** Enables the interactive alteration of the content of any layer to include any HTML, not just text.

✦ **Show-Hide Layers:** Controls the visibility of layers, either interactively or through some preprogrammed action on the page.

You can find detailed information about these actions in their respective sections in Chapter 23. The following sections outline how to use these behaviors to activate your layers.

Drag Layer

For the Web designer, positioning a layer is easy: Click the selection handle and drag the layer to a new location. For the readers of your pages, moving a layer is next to impossible — unless you incorporate the Drag Layer action into the page's design.

With the Drag Layer action, you can set up interactive pages in which the user can rearrange elements of the design to achieve an effect or make a selection. Drag Layer includes an option that enables your application to execute a JavaScript command if the user drops the layer on a specific target. In the example shown in Figure 21-19, each pair of shoes is in its own layer. When the user drops a pair in the bag, a one-line JavaScript command opens the desired catalog page and order form.

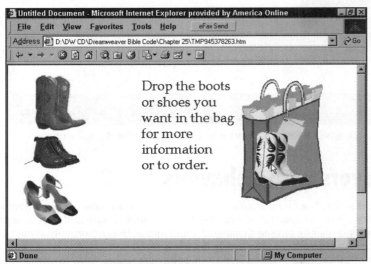

Figure 21-19: On this interactive page, visitors can drop merchandise into the shopping bag; this feature is made possible with the Drag Layer action.

After you've created all your layers, you're ready to attach the behavior. Because Drag Layer initializes the script to make the interaction possible, you should always associate this behavior with the <body> tag and the onLoad event. Follow these steps to use the Drag Layer action, and to designate the settings for the drag operation:

1. Choose the <body> tag from the Tag Selector in the status bar.

2. Choose Window ➪ Behaviors or select the Show Behaviors button from the Launcher. The Behaviors panel opens.

3. In the Behaviors panel, make sure that 4.0 and Later Browsers is displayed in the browser list.

4. Click the Add (+) button and choose Drag Layer from the Add Action drop-down list.

5. In the Drag Layer dialog box, select the layer you want to make available for dragging.

6. To limit the movement of the dragged layer, select Constrained from the Movement drop-down list. Enter the coordinates needed to specify the direction to which you want to limit the movement in the Up, Down, Left, and/or Right text boxes.

7. To establish a location for a target, enter coordinates in the Drop Target: Left and Top text boxes. You can fill these text boxes with the selected layer's present location by clicking the Get Current Position button.

8. You can also set a snap-to area around the target's coordinates. When released in the target's location, the dragged layer snaps to this area. Enter a pixel value in the Snap if Within text box.

9. Click the Advanced tab.

10. Designate the drag handle:

   • To enable the entire layer to act as a drag handle, select Entire Layer from the drop-down menu.

   • If you want to limit the area to be used as a drag handle, select Area within Layer from the drop-down menu. Enter the Left and Top coordinates as well as the Width and Height dimensions in the appropriate text boxes.

11. If you want to keep the layer in its current depth and not bring it to the front, deselect the checkbox for While Dragging: Bring Layer to the Front. To change the stacking order of the layer when it is released after dragging, select either Leave on Top or Restore z-index from the drop-down list.

12. To execute a JavaScript command when the layer is dropped on the target, enter the code in the Call JavaScript text box. If you want the script to execute every time the layer is dropped, enter the code in the When Dropped: Call JavaScript text box. If the code should execute only when the layer is dropped on the target, make sure there's a check in the Only if Snapped checkbox.

13. To change the event that triggers the action (the default is `onLoad`), select an event from the drop-down list in the Events column.

Targeted JavaScript Commands

You can enter the following simple yet useful JavaScript commands in the Snap JavaScript text box of the Drag Layer dialog box:

✦ To display a brief message to the user after the layer is dropped, use the `alert()` function:

```
alert("You hit the target")
```

✦ To send the user to another Web page when the layer is dropped in the right location, use the JavaScript location object:

```
location = "http://www.yourdomain.com/yourpage.html"
```

The location object can also be used with relative URLs.

Set Text of Layer

You've seen how layers can dynamically move, and change their visibility and their depth—but did you know that you can also change a layer's *content* dynamically? With Dreamweaver, you can do it easily. A standard behavior, Set Text of Layer, enables you to swap the entire contents of one layer for whatever you'd like. You're not limited to exchanging just text either. Anything you can put into HTML, you can swap—which is pretty much everything!

This behavior is extremely useful for putting up context-sensitive help and other information. Rather than construct a series of layers that you show and hide, a single layer is used, and just the contents change. To use Set Text of Layer, follow these steps:

1. Insert and name your layers as desired.

2. Select the graphic, button, or text link you'd like to act as the trigger for changing the content of the layer.

3. Choose Window ⇨ Behaviors or select the Show Behaviors button from the Launcher to open the Behaviors panel.

4. Choose Set Text ⇨ Set Text of Layer from the (Add)+ drop-down list.

   The Set Text of Layer dialog box (shown in Figure 21-20) shows a list of the available layers in the current Web page and provides a space for the new content.

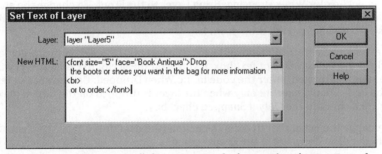

Figure 21-20: Swap out all the contents of a layer using the Set Text of Layer behavior.

5. Select the layer you want to alter from the Layer drop-down list.

6. Enter the text or code in the New HTML text area.

   You can enter either plain text, which is rendered in the default paragraph style, or any amount of HTML code, including <img>, <table>, or other tags.

Tip   If you're entering a large amount of HTML, don't bother doing so by hand—Dreamweaver can do it for you. On a blank page, create your HTML content and then select and copy it. Then, in the Set Text of Layer dialog box, paste the code using Ctrl+V (Command+V).

7. Click OK when you're done.

If you want several layers to change when a single event is triggered, just add more Set Text of Layer behaviors to the same object.

Note   You may need to change the behavior event from its default; to do so, select the down arrow in between the Event and Action columns on the Behaviors panel and choose a new event from the list.

Show-Hide Layers

The capability to implement interactive control of a layer's visibility offers tremendous potential to the Web designer. The Show-Hide Layers action makes this implementation straightforward and simple to set up. With the Show-Hide Layers action, you can simultaneously show one or more layers while hiding as many other layers as necessary. Create your layers and give them a unique name before invoking the Show-Hide Layers action. To use Show-Hide Layers, follow these steps:

1. Select an image, link, or other HTML tag to which to attach the behavior.

2. Choose Window ⇨ Behaviors or select the Show Behaviors button from the Launcher to open the Behaviors panel.

3. Choose Show-Hide Layers from the Add (+) drop-down list. The Show-Hide Layers Dialog (see Figure 21-21) shows a list of the available layers in the open Web page.

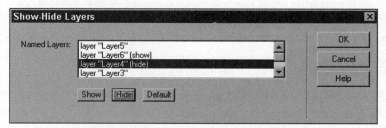

Figure 21-21: With the Show-Hide Layers behavior attached, you can easily program the visibility of all the layers in your Web page.

4. To cause a hidden layer to be revealed when this event is fired, select the layer from the list and choose the Show button.

5. To hide a visible layer when this event is fired, select its name from the list and select the Hide button.

6. To restore a layer's default visibility value when this event is fired, select the layer and choose the Default button.

7. Click OK when you are done.

8. If the default event is not suitable, use the drop-down list in the Events column to select a different one.

Dreamweaver Technique: Creating a Loading Layer

As Web creations become more complex, most designers want their layers to zip onscreen and offscreen or appear and disappear as quickly as possible for the page's viewer. A layer can act only when it has finished loading its content — the text and images. Rather than have the user see each layer loading in, some designers use a loading layer to mask the process until everything is downloaded and ready to go.

A loading layer is fairly easy to create. Dreamweaver supplies all the JavaScript necessary in one behavior, Show-Hide Layers. Keep in mind that because this technique uses layers, it's good only for 4.0 browsers and later. Use the following steps to create a loading layer:

1. Create all of your layers with the contents in place and the visibility property set as default.

2. Create the loading layer. (Choose Insert ➪ Layer or select the Draw Layer button from the Insert bar.)

3. Enter and position whatever contents you want displayed in the loading layer while all the other layers are loading.

4. Open the Layers panel (F2).

5. Turn off the visibility for all layers except the loading layer. In essence, you're hiding every other layer.

6. Select the <body> tag from the Tag Selector.

7. Choose Window ➪ Behaviors or select Show Behaviors from the Launcher to open the Behaviors panel.

8. Select the Add (+) action button and choose Show-Hide Layers from the drop-down list.

9. In the Show-Hide Layers dialog box, select the loading layer and then click the Hide button.

10. Select all the other layers and set them to Show. Click OK when you are done.

11. Leave onLoad (the default) as the event to trigger this action.

Now, when you test your Web page, you should see only your loading layer until everything else is loaded. Then the loading layer disappears, and all the other layers are made visible.

Summary

Layers are effective placement tools for developing the layout of a page. Anyone used to designing with desktop publishing tools can quickly learn to work with layers effectively.

✦ Layers are visible only on fourth-generation and later browsers.

✦ Layers can be used to place HTML content anywhere on a Web page.

✦ You can stack layers on top of one another. This depth control is referred to as the *stacking order* or the *z-index*.

✦ Dreamweaver can convert layers to tables for viewing in earlier browsers, and back again for straightforward repositioning.

✦ Layers can be constructed so that the end user can display or hide them interactively, or alter their position, size, and depth dynamically.

✦ Dreamweaver provides rulers and grids to help with layer placement and alignment.

✦ Layers can easily be activated by using Dreamweaver's built-in JavaScript behaviors.

In the next chapter, you learn how to develop timelines, which enable layers and their contents to move around the Web page.

✦　　✦　　✦

Working with Timelines

Motion implies time. A static object, such as an ordinary HTML Web page, can exist either in a single moment or over a period of time. Conversely, moving objects (such as Dynamic HTML layers flying across the screen) need a few seconds to complete their path. All of Dreamweaver's Dynamic HTML animation effects use the Timeline feature to manage this conjunction of movement and time.

Timelines can do much more than move a layer across a Web page, however. A timeline can coordinate an entire presentation: starting the background music, scrolling the opening rolling credits, and cueing the voice-over narration on top of a slideshow. These actions are all possible with Dreamweaver because, in addition to controlling a layer's position, timelines can also trigger any of Dreamweaver's JavaScript behaviors on a specific frame.

This chapter explores the full and varied world of timelines. After an introductory section brings you up to speed on the underlying concepts of timelines, you learn how to insert and modify timelines to achieve cutting-edge effects. A Dreamweaver Technique shows you, step by step, how to create a multiscreen slideshow complete with fly-in and fly-out graphics. From complex multilayer animations to slideshow presentations, you can do it all with Dreamweaver timelines.

Note   Because timelines are so intricately intertwined with layers and behaviors, you need to have a good grasp of these concepts. If you're not familiar with the topics of layers and behaviors, be sure to read Chapters 21 and 23.

Into the Fourth Dimension with Timelines

Web designers in the early days had little control over the interaction between their Web pages and the fourth dimension (time). Only animated GIFs, Java, or animation programs such as Macromedia's Flash could create the illusion of motion events. Unfortunately, all of these technologies have some limitations.

The general problem with animated GIF images is file size. An animated GIF starts out as an image for every frame. Therefore, if you incorporate a 3-second, 15-frames-per-second animation, you are asking the user to download the compressed equivalent of 45 separate images. Although an animated GIF is an indexed color file with a limited 256 colors and uses the format's built-in compression, the GIF file is still a relatively large graphic file. Moreover, for all their apparent animated qualities, GIFs enable no true interaction other than as links to other URLs. Animations created with Dynamic HTML and Dreamweaver's timelines, on the other hand, do not significantly increase the overall size of the Web page and are completely interactive.

DHTML is not the only low-bandwidth approach to animations with interactive content for the Web. You can create animations, complete with user-driven interactions, using Java — provided, of course, that you're a Java programmer. Certainly, Java development tools are making the language easier to use, but you still must deal with the rather long load time of any Java applet and the increasing variety of Java versions. As another option, Macromedia Director movies can be compressed or "shocked" to provide animation and interactivity in your pages. Like Java, the Director approach requires a bit of a learning curve. Shockwave movies can also have long load times and require the user to have a plugin application.

Macromedia's Flash might be the best alternative to DHTML and animated GIFs, though Flash has its own set of caveats to keep in mind. On the plus side, Flash files are small and can be streamed through their own player. This arrangement is tempting, and if you just want animation on a page, Flash is probably a superior choice to any of the approaches previously described. On the minus side, Flash is limited to its own proprietary features and functions, and every user must have the Flash Plugin or ActiveX control installed — although the pervasiveness of the Flash player is rapidly making this point moot. However, you cannot layer Flash animation on top of other layers on a page. Moreover, once you, or another designer, have created a Flash animation, the animation must be edited with the same animation package.

Timeline capabilities

Dreamweaver timelines are implemented in HTML code. For the movement of one layer straight across a Web page, Dreamweaver generates about 70 lines of code devoted to initializing and playing the timeline. But just what is a timeline? A timeline is composed of a series of frames. A frame is a snapshot of what the Web page — more specifically, the objects on the timeline — look like at a particular moment. You probably know that a movie is made up of a series of still pictures; when viewed quickly, the pictures create the illusion of movement. Each individual picture is a frame; movies show 24 frames per second, and video uses about 30 frames per second. Web animation, on the other hand, generally displays about 15 frames per second (fps). Not surprisingly, Dreamweaver's timeline is similar to the one used in Macromedia's timeline-based, multimedia authoring tool and animation package, Director.

If you have to draw each frame of a 30-second animation, even at 15 fps you won't have time for other work. Dreamweaver uses the concept of *keyframes* to make a simple layer movement workable. Each keyframe contains a change in the timeline object's properties, such as position. For example, suppose you want your layer to start at the upper-left (represented by the coordinates 0,0) and travel to the lower-right (at 750,550). To accomplish this task, you need only specify the layer's position for the two keyframes — the start and the finish — and Dreamweaver generates all the frames in between.

Timelines have three primary roles:

✦ A timeline can alter a layer's position, dimensions, visibility, and depth.

✦ Timelines can change the source for any image on a Web page and cause another graphic of the same height and width to appear in the same location.

✦ Any of Dreamweaver's JavaScript behaviors can be triggered on any frame of a timeline.

A few ground rules

Keep the following basic guidelines in mind when you're using timelines in the Web pages you create with Dreamweaver:

✦ Timelines require a 4.0 or later browser.

✦ For a timeline to be able to animate an object, such as text, the object must be within a layer. If you try to create a timeline with an element that is not in a layer, Dreamweaver warns you and prevents you from adding the object to the timeline.

✦ Events don't have to start at the beginning of a timeline. If you want to have an action begin 5 seconds after a page has loaded, you can set the behavior on frame 60 of the timeline, with a frame rate of 15 frames per second.

✦ The selected frame rate is a "best-case scenario" because the actual frame rate depends on the user's system. A slower system or one that is simultaneously running numerous other programs can easily degrade the frame rate.

✦ You can include multiple animations on one timeline. The only restriction is that you can't have two animations affecting the same layer at the same time. Dreamweaver prevents you from making this error.

✦ You can have multiple timelines that animate different layers simultaneously or the same layer at different times. Although you can set two or more timelines to animate the same layer at the same time, the results are difficult to predict and generally unintended.

Tip   If you move a timeline's JavaScript code from its file of origin into an external JS file, serious timeline execution problems can occur in some browsers. For this reason, I heartily recommend leaving all your timeline code in its original file.

Creating Animations with Timelines

Dreamweaver provides an excellent tool for managing timelines — the Timelines panel. Open this tool by choosing Window ➪ Others ➪ Timelines or using the keyboard shortcut Alt+F9 (Option+F9).

The Timelines panel uses VCR-style controls combined with a playback head, which is a visual representation showing which frame is the current one. As shown in Figure 22-1, the Timelines panel gives you full control over any of the timeline functions.

Animation channels

Behavior channels

Playback head   Timeline   Frames

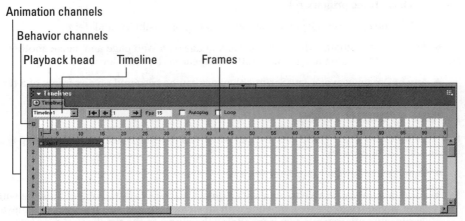

Figure 22-1: Dreamweaver's Timelines panel enables you to quickly and easily master animation control.

The Timelines panel has four major areas:

✦ **Timeline controls:** Includes the Timeline drop-down list for selecting the current timeline; the Rewind, Back, and Play buttons; the Fps (frame rate) text box; and the Autoplay and Loop checkboxes

✦ **Behavior channel:** Shows the placement of any behaviors attached to specific frames of the timeline

✦ **Frames:** Displays the frame numbers for all timelines and the playback head showing the current frame number

✦ **Animation channels:** Represents the animations for any included layers and images

Adding Layers to the Timelines Panel

As with many of Dreamweaver's functions, you can add a layer or an image to the Timelines panel in more than one way. You can insert a layer into a timeline through the menus (Modify ➪ Timeline ➪ Add Object to Timeline), you can drag-and-drop an object into a timeline, or you can use the keyboard shortcut, Ctrl+Alt+Shift+T (Command+Option+Shift+T). When you add an object to a timeline, Dreamweaver inserts an animation bar of 15 frames in length, labeled with the object's name. The animation bar shows the duration (the number of frames) of the timeline's effect on the object. An animation bar is initially created with two keyframes: the start and the end. To add a layer or image to the Timelines panel through the menus, follow these steps:

1. Choose Window ➪ Others ➪ Timelines or use the keyboard shortcut, Alt+F9 (Option+F9), to open the Timelines panel.

2. In the Document window, select the layer or image you want to add to the timeline.

   Bear in mind that you can use timelines to move a layer around the browser window, but not to move an image (unless it is contained in a layer). The only thing timelines can do with respect to an image is to change its source, causing another graphic of the same height and width to appear in the same location.

3. Choose Modify ➪ Timeline ➪ Add Object to Timeline. An animation bar appears in the first frame of the timeline, as shown in Figure 22-2.

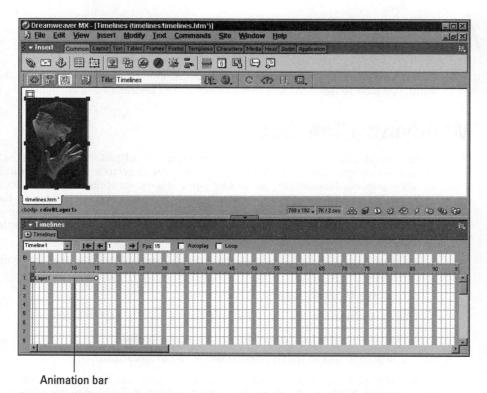

Animation bar

Figure 22-2: The default animation bar is set at 15 frames but can easily be modified.

4. To add another object, repeat Steps 2 and 3. As previously noted, you can add as many objects to a timeline as you desire. Each additional animation bar is inserted beneath the preceding bar.

Tip

The first time you add an image or layer to the Timelines panel, Dreamweaver displays an alert message that details the limitations of timelines. If you don't want to see this alert, turn it off by checking the Don't Show Me This Message Again checkbox.

You have a little more flexibility when you add an object by dragging it into the timeline. Instead of the animation bar always beginning at frame 1, you can drop the object in to begin on any frame. This approach is useful, especially if you are putting more than one object into the same animation channel. To place an object in a timeline with the drag-and-drop method, follow these steps:

1. Open the Timelines panel by choosing Window ➪ Others ➪ Timelines or using the keyboard shortcut Alt+F9 (Option+F9).

2. In the Document window, select the object — layer or image — that you want to add to the timeline and drag it to the Timelines panel. As soon as the object is over the Timelines panel, a 15-frame animation bar appears.

3. Holding the mouse button down, position the animation bar so that the animation begins in the desired frame. Release the mouse button to drop the object into the timeline.

Note Your placement does not have to be exact; you can modify it later.

Placing a layer or image on a timeline is just the first step. To begin using your timeline in depth, you have to make changes to the object for the keyframes and customize the timeline.

Modifying a Timeline

When you add an object — either an image or a layer — to a timeline, notice that the animation bar has an open circle at its beginning and end. An open circle marks a keyframe. As previously explained, the designer specifies a change in the state of the timeline object in a keyframe. For example, when you first insert a layer, the two generated keyframes have identical properties — the layer's position, size, visibility, and depth are unchanged. For any animation to occur, you have to change one of the layer's properties for one of the keyframes. For example, to move a layer quickly across the screen, follow these steps:

1. Create a layer. If you like, add an image or a background color so that the layer is more noticeable.

2. Open the Timelines panel.

3. Drag the layer into the Timelines panel and release the mouse button.

4. Select the ending keyframe of the layer's animation bar.

The playback head (red rectangle) moves to the new frame.

5. In the Document window, grab the layer's selection handle and drag the layer to a new location. A thin line connects the starting position of the layer to the ending position, as shown in Figure 22-3. This line is the *animation path*.

6. To preview your animation, first click the Rewind button in the Timelines panel and then click and hold down the Play button.

If you want to change the beginning position of your layer's animation path, select the starting keyframe and then move the layer in the Document window. To alter the final position of the layer's animation path, select the ending keyframe and then move the layer.

Tip For more precise control of your layer's position in a timeline, select a keyframe and then, in the layer's Property inspector, change the Left and/or Top values. You can also select the layer and use the arrow keys to move it.

Altering the animation bars

A Web designer can easily stretch or alter the range of frames occupied by a layer or image in an animation bar. You can make an animation longer or smoother, or have it start at an entirely different time. You can also move the layer to a different animation channel so it runs before or after another animation.

Rewind button   Play button   Animation path

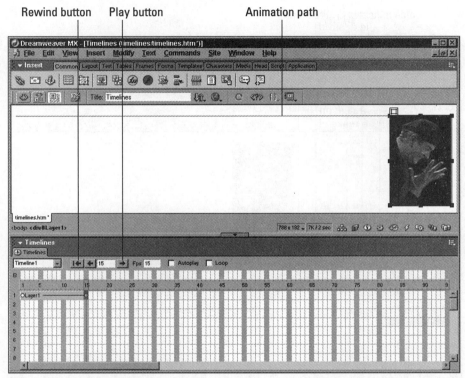

Figure 22-3: When you move a layer on a timeline, Dreamweaver displays an animation path.

Use the mouse to drag an animation bar around the timeline. Click any part of the bar except the keyframe indicators and move it as needed. To change the length of an animation, select the first or final keyframe and drag it forward or backward to a new frame.

Use either of the following techniques to remove (delete) an animation bar:

✦ Select the animation bar by clicking anywhere on it, and choose Modify ➪ Timeline ➪ Remove Object.

✦ Right-click (Control+click) the animation bar and choose Remove Object from the context menu.

Using the Timeline controls

As you probably noticed if you worked through the example in the preceding section, you don't have to use a browser to preview a timeline. The Timeline controls shown in Figure 22-4 enable you to fine-tune your animations before you view them through a browser.

Tip

If you're using the Timelines panel controls to play a timeline animation that moves down below the visible portion of the Document window, you can press F4 to hide the Timelines panel (and all other Dreamweaver panels) to maximize screen space. To redisplay your panels, press F4 again.

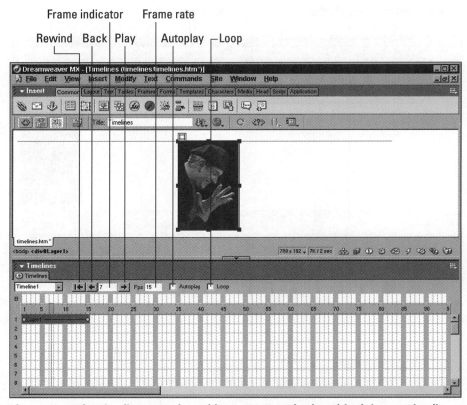

Figure 22-4: The Timeline controls enable you to move back and forth in your timeline, easily and precisely.

At the top-left corner is the Timeline drop-down list, which is used to indicate the current timeline. By default, every new timeline is given the name Timeline*n*, where *n* indicates how many timelines have been created. You can rename the timeline by selecting it and typing in the new name. As you accumulate and use more timelines, you should give them descriptive, recognizable names.

Caution   A timeline name must have an alphanumeric, one-word name that begins with a letter.

The next three buttons in the control bar enable you to move through the frames of a time-line. From left to right:

✦ **Rewind:** Moves the playback head to the first frame of the timeline.

✦ **Back:** Moves the playback head to the previous frame of the timeline. You can hold down the Back button to play the timeline in reverse. This behavior loops: When the first frame is reached, the playback head automatically moves to the last frame of the timeline and continues playing it.

✦ **Play:** Moves the playback head to the next frame; hold down the Play button to play the timeline normally. As with the Back button, this behavior loops: When the last frame is reached, the playback head moves to the first frame of the current timeline and continues.

The field between the Back and Play buttons is the Frame Indicator text box. To jump to any specific frame, enter the frame number in this box.

The next item in the control bar is the Fps (frames per second) text box. To change the frame rate, enter a new value in the Fps text box and press Tab or Enter (Return). The frame rate you set is an ideal number that a user's browser attempts to reach. The default rate of 15 frames per second is a good balance for both Macintosh and Windows systems.

Tip

Because browsers play every frame regardless of the frame rate setting, increasing the frame rate does not necessarily make your animations smoother. A better way to create smooth animations is to drag the end keyframe farther out, which increases the number of frames used by your animation.

The next two checkboxes, Autoplay and Loop, affect how the animation is played.

Autoplay

If you enable the Autoplay option, the timeline begins playing as soon as the Web page is fully downloaded. Dreamweaver alerts you to this arrangement by telling you that the Play Timeline action is attached to an onLoad event. Autoplay is achieved by inserting code that looks similar to the following into the <body> tag:

```
<body bgcolor="#FFFFFF" onload="MM_timelinePlay('Timeline1')">
```

Caution

If you don't use the Autoplay feature, you must attach the Play Timeline action to another event and tag, such as onClick and a button graphic. Otherwise, the timeline will not play. Note that if your Show Events For option is set to 3.0 and Later Browsers, the only available event is onMouseOver. To make onClick and other events available, change the Show Events For to 4.0 and Later Browsers by choosing Add (+) from the Behaviors panel, then selecting Show Events For ➪ 4.0 and Later Browsers.

Looping

Mark the Loop checkbox if you want an animation to repeat once it has reached the final frame. When Loop is enabled, the default causes the layer to replay itself an infinite numbers of times; however, you can change this setting.

When you first enable the Loop checkbox, Dreamweaver alerts you that it is placing a Go To Timeline Frame action after the last frame of your timeline. To set the number of repetitions for a looping timeline, follow these steps:

1. In the Timelines panel, check the Loop checkbox.

2. Dreamweaver displays an alert informing you that the Go To Timeline Frame action is being added one frame past your current final frame. To disable these alerts, select the Don't Show Me This Message Again option.

3. In the Behaviors channel (the Timeline channel marked with a B, as shown in Figure 22-1), double-click the behavior you just added.

Note   When you first add a behavior to a timeline, Dreamweaver presents a dialog box reminding you how to perform this action. Select the Don't Show Me This Message Again option when you've mastered the technique.

The Behaviors panel opens, with an `onFrame` event in the Events column and a Go To Timeline Frame action in the Actions pane.

4. Double-click the `onFrame` event. The Go To Timeline Frame dialog box opens (see Figure 22-5).

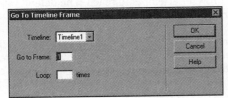

Figure 22-5: Selecting the Loop option on the Timelines panel adds a Go To Timeline Frame action, which you can customize.

5. Enter a positive number in the Loop text box to set the number of times you want your timeline to repeat. To keep the animation repeating continuously, leave the Loop text box blank.

6. Click OK when you are finished.

Tip   Your animations don't have to loop back to the beginning each time. By entering a different frame number in the Go to Frame text box of the Go To Timeline Frame dialog box, you can repeat just a segment of the animation.

Adding keyframes

Animating a timeline can go far beyond moving your layer from point A to point B. Layers (and the content within them) can dip, swirl, zigzag, and generally move in any fashion — all made possible by keyframes in which you have entered some change for the object. Dreamweaver calculates all the differences between each keyframe, whether the change is in a layer's position or size. Each timeline starts with two keyframes: the beginning and the end; you have to add other keyframes before you can insert the desired changes.

You can add a keyframe to a timeline in two different ways. The first method uses the Add Keyframe command, and the second method uses the mouse to click a keyframe into place.

Note   Do not confuse the Add Keyframe command with the Add Frame command, both of which are found in the Modify ➪ Timeline menu. The former adds a keyframe to the timeline; the latter adds a normal frame to the timeline.

Adding keyframes with the Add Keyframe command

To add a keyframe with the Add Keyframe command, follow these steps:

1. In the Timelines panel, select the animation bar for the object with which you are working.

2. Select the frame in which you want to add a keyframe.

3. Add your keyframe by any of the following methods:

   • Choose Modify ➪ Timeline ➪ Add Keyframe.

   • Press the F6 key.

   • Right-click (Control+click) the frame in the animation bar and, from the context menu, choose Add Keyframe.

   A new keyframe is added on the selected frame, signified by the open circle in the animation bar.

While your new keyframe is selected, you can alter the layer's position, size, visibility, or depth. For example, if your animation involves moving a layer across the screen, you can drag the layer to a new position while the new keyframe is selected. The animation path is redrawn to incorporate this new position, as illustrated in Figure 22-6.

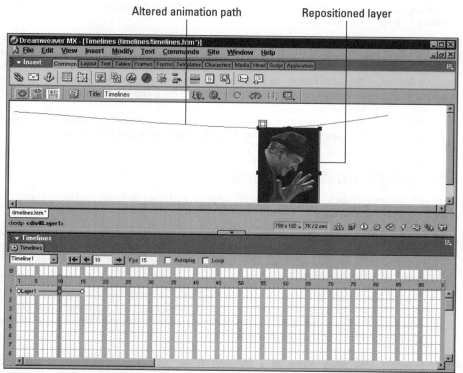

Figure 22-6: Repositioning a layer while a keyframe is selected can redirect your animation path.

Adding a keyframe with the mouse

The second method for adding a keyframe is quicker. To add a keyframe using the mouse, simply hold down the Ctrl (Command) key. Click anywhere in the animation bar to add a keyframe. Your cursor turns into a small open circle when it is over the Timeline window to show that it is ready to add a new keyframe.

What if you want to move the keyframe? Simply click and drag the keyframe to a new frame, sliding it along the animation bar in the Timelines panel.

Tip If, after plotting out an elaborate animation with a layer, you discover that you need to shift the entire animation—for example, 6 pixels to the right—you don't have to redo all your work. Just select the animation bar in the Timelines panel and then, in the Document window, move the layer in question. Dreamweaver shifts the entire animation to your new location.

Removing timeline elements

To remove an element from the Timelines panel:

1. Select the element that you want to remove.

2. Choose Modify ➪ Timeline ➪ Remove *Element*, where *Element* is the element you want to remove.

For example, to remove a keyframe, you would select the keyframe and then choose Modify ➪ Timeline ➪ Remove Keyframe.

The context menu in the Timelines panel also contains all the removal commands. Right-click (Control+click) the Timelines panel element you want to remove and, in the context menu (see Figure 22-7), choose the desired removal command: Remove Keyframe, Remove Object, Remove Behavior, Remove Frame, or Remove Timeline. Alternatively, right-click (Control+click) the element and simply choose Delete from the context menu.

Tip To copy or move an entire timeline to another document, select the timeline and use the handy Cut, Copy, and Paste commands from the Timelines panel context menu.

Changing animation speed

You can alter your Dynamic HTML animation speed with two different methods that can be used separately or together:

✦ Drag out the final keyframe in the animation bar to cover additional frames, or drag it back to cover fewer frames. Any keyframes within the animation bar are kept proportional to their original settings. This method works well in conjunction with altering the speed of an individual animation bar.

✦ Change the frames per second value in the Fps text box of the Timelines panel. Increasing the number of frames per second accelerates the animation, and vice versa. Adjusting the Fps value affects every layer contained within the timeline; you cannot use this method for individual layers.

Caution Browsers play every frame of a Dynamic HTML animation, regardless of the system resources. Some systems, therefore, play the same animation faster or slower than others. Don't assume every system has the same timing.

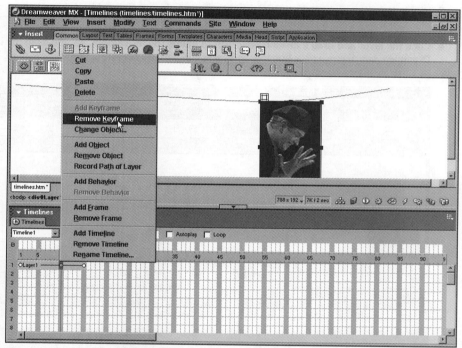

Figure 22-7: The Timelines panel context menu is extremely handy for quick editing.

Recording a layer's path

Plotting keyframes and repositioning your layers works well when you need to follow a pixel-precise path, but it can be extremely tedious when you're trying to move a layer more freely on the screen. Luckily, Dreamweaver provides you with an easier method for defining a layer's movement path. You can simply drag your layer around the screen to create a path, and refine the path or its timing afterward.

The Record Path of Layer command automatically creates the necessary series of keyframes, calculated from your dragging of the layer. To fine-tune your work, you can select any of these keyframes and reposition the layer or even delete it entirely. This feature is a definite time-saver for DHTML animationists.

Keep in mind that a timeline represents not only positions but also positions over time and, therefore, movement. The Record Path of Layer command is very smart when it comes to time; the slower you drag the layer, the more keyframes are plotted. You can vary the positioning of the keyframes by changing the tempo of your dragging. Moreover, the duration of the recorded timeline reflects the length of time spent dragging the layer. To record a layer's path, perform the following steps:

1. In the Document window, select the layer you are going to move.

Caution

Make sure that you've selected the layer itself and not its contents. If you've correctly selected the layer, it has eight selection boxes around it.

2. Drag the layer to the location in the document where you want it to be at the start of the movement.

3. Right-click (Control+click) the selected layer and choose Record Path from the context menu. If it's not already open, the Timelines panel appears.

4. Click the layer and drag it around onscreen to define the movement. As you drag the layer, Dreamweaver draws a gray line that indicates the path it is creating (see Figure 22-8).

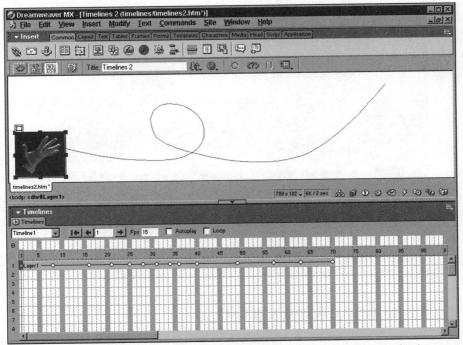

Figure 22-8: To record a layer's path, Select Modify ➪ Timeline ➪ Record Path of Layer and then drag your layer in the Document window.

Each gray dot represents a keyframe. The slower you draw, the closer the keyframes are placed; moving quickly across the Document window causes Dreamweaver to space out the keyframes.

5. Release the mouse to end the recording.

Dreamweaver displays an alert reminding you of the capabilities of the Timelines panel. Select the Don't Show Me This Message Again option to prevent this dialog box from reappearing.

After you've finished recording a layer's movement, you see a new animation bar in the Timelines panel, representing the motion you just recorded. The duration of the new timeline matches the duration of your dragging of the layer. The keyframes that define your layer's movement (as described in the preceding paragraphs) are inserted in this animation bar. You can use any of the procedures previously described in this chapter to modify the timeline or its keyframes. If you select the same layer at the end of the generated timeline and perform the Record Path operation again, another animation bar is added at the end of the current timeline.

Caution   Any new paths recorded with the same layer are added after the last animation bar. You can't select a keyframe in the middle of a path and then record a path from that point; the starting keyframe of the newly recorded path corresponds to the position of the layer in the last keyframe.

Triggering Behaviors in Timelines

Adding a behavior to a timeline is similar to adding a behavior to any object on a Web page. Because timelines are written in JavaScript, they behave exactly the same as any object enhanced with JavaScript.

Use the Behaviors channel section of the Timelines panel to work with behaviors in timelines. You can attach a behavior to a timeline in four ways:

✦ Select the frame in which you wish to have the behavior and then right-click (Control+click). Select Add Behavior from the context menu.

✦ Select the frame in which you want to activate the behavior and choose Modify ⇨ Timeline ⇨ Add Behavior to Timeline.

✦ Open the Behaviors panel and click the frame you wish to modify in the Behaviors channel.

✦ Double-click the frame for which you want to add a behavior in the Behaviors channel.

When you attach a behavior to a frame, you can see in the Behaviors panel that the event inserted in the Events column is related to a frame number — for example, onFrame20. Each frame can trigger multiple actions.

Cross-Reference   For more specifics about Dreamweaver behaviors, see Chapters 23 and 35.

Behaviors are essential to timelines. Without behaviors, you cannot play or stop your timeline-based animations. Even when you select the Autoplay or Loop options in the Timelines panel, you are enabling a behavior. The three behaviors always deployed for timelines are Play Timeline, Stop Timeline, and Go to Timeline Frame.

If you are not using the Autoplay feature for your timeline, you must explicitly attach a Play Timeline behavior to an interactive or other event on your Web page. For example, a timeline is typically set to start playing once a specific picture has loaded, or once the user has entered a value in a form's text box, or — more frequently — once the user selects a Play button. You could use the Stop Timeline behavior to pause an animation temporarily.

To use the Play Timeline or Stop Timeline behavior, follow these steps:

1. In the Document window, select a tag, link, or image that you want to trigger the event.

2. Choose Window ⇨ Behaviors or select the Show Behavior button from the Launcher to open the Behaviors panel.

3. In the Behaviors panel, click the Add (+) button, and from the drop-down list, choose either of the following methods:

   • Timeline ⇨ Play Timeline to start a timeline

   • Timeline ⇨ Stop Timeline to end a timeline

4. In the Play Timeline or Stop Timeline dialog box (see Figure 22-9), choose the timeline that you want to play (or stop) from the appropriate Timeline drop-down list.

Figure 22-9: You can use the Stop Timeline behavior to stop all timelines or a specific timeline.

5. Click OK when you are finished.

6. Select an event to trigger the behavior from the drop-down list in the Events column in the Behaviors panel.

As mentioned earlier, if your Show Events For option is set to 3.0 and Later Browsers, the only available event is onMouseOver. To make onClick and other events available, change the Show Events For to 4.0 and Later Browsers by choosing Add (+) from the Behaviors panel, then selecting Show Events For ➪ 4.0 and Later Browsers.

When you select the option to loop your timeline, Dreamweaver automatically inserts a Go to Timeline Frame behavior—with the first frame set as the target. You can display any frame on your timeline by inserting the Go to Timeline Frame behavior manually. To use the Go to Timeline Frame behavior, follow these steps:

1. In the Document window, select a tag, link, or image that you want to trigger the event.

2. Choose Window ➪ Behaviors or select the Show Behavior button from the Launcher to open the Behaviors panel.

3. In the Behaviors panel, select the Add (+) button and choose Timeline ➪ Go to Timeline Frame from the drop-down list.

4. In the Timeline field of the Go To Timeline Frame dialog box, choose the timeline you want to affect.

5. Enter the desired frame number in the Go to Frame text box.

6. If you'd like the timeline to loop a set number of times, enter a value in the Loop text box. Click OK when you are finished.

Remember that if you don't enter a value, the timeline loops endlessly.

Depending on the type of effect desired, you may want to use two of the timeline behaviors together. To ensure that your timeline always starts from the same point, first attach a Go to Timeline Frame behavior to the event and then attach the Play Timeline behavior to the same event.

Dreamweaver Technique: Creating a Multiscreen Slideshow

Moving layers around the screen is pretty cool, but you've probably already figured out that you can do a lot more with timelines. One of the possibilities is a graphics slideshow displaying a rotating series of pictures. To demonstrate the range of potential available to timelines, the following sample project shows you how to construct a slideshow with more than one screen, complete with moving layers and triggered behaviors.

This technique has four steps:

1. **Prepare the graphic elements.** The process is easier if you have most (if not all) of your images for the slideshow — as well as the control interface — ready to go.

2. **Create the slideshow timeline.** In this project, one timeline is devoted to rotating images on four different "screens."

3. **Create the moving layers timeline.** The slideshow begins and ends with a bit of flair, as the screens fly in and fly out.

4. **Add the behaviors.** The slideshow includes controls for playing, pausing, restarting, and ending the slideshow, which then takes the user to another Web page.

This technique is intended to act as a basis for your own creations, not as an end in itself. You can add many variations and refinements; for example, you can preload images, make rollover buttons, and add music to the background. What follows is a fundamental structure focused on the use of timelines, which you can extend with additional objects as needed.

Note   The result of this Dreamweaver Technique can be viewed only by 4.0 browsers or later.

Step 1: Preparing the graphic elements

Using a timeline for a slideshow presentation has only one restriction, but it is significant: All the graphics in one "screen" must have the same dimensions. The timeline doesn't actually change the image tag; it only changes the file source for the tag. Thus, the Height and Width values of the last image inserted override all the values for the foregoing graphics.

Luckily, all major image-processing software can resize and extend the canvas of a picture with little effort. When creating a slideshow, you may find it useful to do all of the resizing work at one time. Load in your images with the greatest width and height — they may or may not be the same picture — and use these measurements as your common denominators for all graphics.

Create your interface buttons early, rather than later. Experience shows that the more design elements you prepare ahead of time, the less adjusting you have to do later. Also, activating a timeline with a behavior is a straightforward process, and a finished interface enables you to incorporate the buttons quickly.

Finally, you should create and place the layers you want to use. The sample Web page in this technique is comprised of four screens, all of the same dimensions. The four different layers are uniquely named, but they are all the same size.

Tip

If you are making multiple versions of the same layer, consider changing the default layer size to fit your design. Choose Edit ➪ Preferences; then, in the Layers panel, set your desired Width and Height values. All the layers incorporated in the Web page with the Insert ➪ Layer command will now automatically size to these default settings.

To recap, use the following steps to prepare your graphics:

1. Create the images to be used as slides. Remember to make all the slides for a given slideshow screen the same height and width.

2. Prepare and place your interface buttons.

3. Create the number of layers that you need for the different screens in the slideshow.

4. Position your layers so that each can hold a different slide. The example has four layers, centered on the screen in two rows.

5. Insert your opening slides into each of the layers.

Note

Your opening slide doesn't have to be a graphic image. You could also use a solid-colored GIF or a slide with text.

Try to work backward from a final design whenever layer positioning is involved. At this stage, all of the elements are in their final placement, ready for the slideshow to begin (see Figure 22-10). Next, you can activate the slideshow.

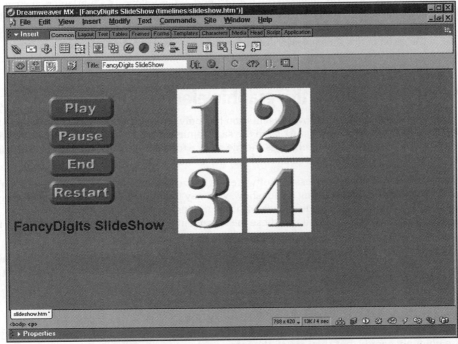

Figure 22-10: Before activating any layers or setting up the slideshow, design the layout.

Step 2: Creating the slideshow timeline

For all the attention that timelines and layers receive, you may be surprised that one of the best features of Dreamweaver timelines has nothing to do with layers. You can use timelines to change images anywhere on your Web page — whether or not they are in layers. As explained in Step 1, the timeline doesn't actually replace one `<img>` tag with another, but rather alters an image by swapping its `src` attribute value. The `src` attribute changes — just as changes in a layer's position, shape, or depth — must happen at a keyframe.

In planning your slideshow, you need to decide how often a new slide appears, because you must set keyframes at each of these points. If you are changing your slides every few seconds, you can change the frame rate to 1 fps. This setting helps you easily keep track of how many seconds occur between each slide change (and because no animation is involved with this timeline, a rapid frame rate is irrelevant). Note, however, that on the timeline involving moving layers described previously in this chapter, the frame rate should be maintained at around 15 fps. Each timeline can have its own frame rate.

The only other choices involve the Autoplay and Loop options. As with frame rate, you can set each timeline to its own options without interfering with another timeline. This example has the slideshow loop, but does not start automatically. Use the Play button to enable the user to start the show. First, however, let's add the images to the slides. To put images into a slideshow on a timeline, follow these steps:

1. Choose Window ➪ Others ➪ Timelines to open the Timelines panel.

2. If desired, rename Timeline1 by selecting the name and typing your own unique name.

3. Select one image from those onscreen in the positioned layers and drag the graphic to the Timelines panel.

Be sure to grab the image, not the layer.

4. Release the animation bar at the beginning of the timeline.

5. Repeat Step 3 and Step 4 for each image until all images are represented on the timeline.

6. Change the frame rate by entering a new value in the Fps text box. This example changes the frame rate to 1.

7. Select the Loop and/or Autoplay option, if desired.

8. On one of the animation bars representing images, select the frame for a keyframe.

9. Choose Modify ➪ Timeline ➪Add Keyframe, or right-click (Control+click) the frame on the timeline and choose Add Keyframe from the context menu.

10. With the keyframe selected, in the Image Property inspector, select the Src folder to locate the graphic file for the next slide image.

11. Repeat Step 9 and Step 10 until every animation bar has keyframes for every slide change, and each keyframe has a new or different image assigned.

In this slideshow example, the slide changes are staggered: slideshow 1 changes slides every two seconds, slideshow 2 and 3 change slides every four seconds, and slideshow 4 changes slides every eight seconds. You can see this in Figure 22-11 by looking at the keyframe placement (the white circles).

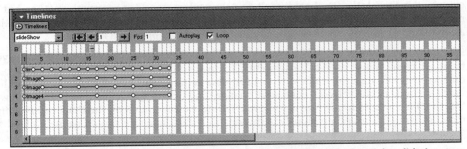

Figure 22-11: Each keyframe on each animation bar signals a change of the slide image.

Tip

To preview your slide changes, you don't have to go outside of Dreamweaver. Just click and hold down the Play button on the Timelines panel.

Step 3: Creating the moving layers timeline

At this stage, the slideshow is functional but a little dull. To add a bit of showmanship, you can "fly in" the layers from different areas of the Web page to their final destination. This task is easy—and to complete the effect, the layers "fly out" when the user is ready to leave.

You can achieve these fly-in/fly-out effects in several ways. You can put the opening fly-in on one timeline and the ending fly-out on another. A more concise method combines the fly-in and fly-out for each layer on one timeline—separating them with a Stop Timeline behavior. After the fly-in portion happens when the page has loaded (because the example selects the Autoplay option for this timeline), the fly-out section does not begin to play until signaled to continue with the Play Timeline behavior. To create the moving layers' opening and closing for the slideshow, follow these steps:

1. Choose Modify ➪ Timeline ➪ Add Timeline, or right-click (Control+click) the Timelines panel and choose Add Timeline from the context menu.

2. Rename your new timeline if desired.

3. Select any one of the layers surrounding your images and drag it onto the Timelines panel.

Caution

This time, make sure you move the layers—not the images.

4. To set the amount of time for the fly-in section to span, drag the final keyframe of the animation bar to a new frame. The example sets the end at 30 frames, which at 15 fps lasts 2 seconds.

5. From the Document window, select the same layer again and drag it to the Timelines panel. Place it directly after the first animation bar. This animation bar becomes the fly-out portion.

6. Drag the final keyframe to extend the time, if desired.

7. At this point, all four keyframes — two for each animation bar — have exactly the same information. Now change the positions for two keyframes to enable the layer to move. Select the first keyframe in the opening animation bar.

8. Reposition the layer so that it is offscreen. Although you can complete this task manually to the right or bottom of the screen by dragging the layer to a new location, you can also use the Layer Property inspector to input new values directly for the Left and Top attributes.

Tip   Use negative Top or Left values to move a layer offscreen above or to the left of the browser window.

9. From the Timelines panel, select the last keyframe of the closing animation bar.

10. Reposition the layer offscreen. If you want the layer to return in the same manner as it arrived, enter the same values for the Left and Top attributes as in the first keyframe of the opening animation bar.

11. Repeat Steps 3 through 10 for every layer.

12. Finally, select the Autoplay checkbox so that this timeline begins playing automatically when the Web page is loaded.

Now, when you preview this timeline, the layers fly in and immediately fly out again. Figure 22-12 shows the layers in the example toward the end of their initial fly-in animation. In the final phase of the technique, you add behaviors to put the action under user control.

Figure 22-12: You can use two animation bars side by side to achieve a back-and-forth effect.

Step 4: Adding the behaviors

Although it may be fun to watch an unexpected effect take place, giving the user control over aspects of a presentation is much more involving—for the designer as well as the user. The example is ready to incorporate the user-interaction aspect by attaching Dreamweaver behaviors to the user interface and to the Behaviors channel of the Timelines panel.

Two timeline behaviors have already been attached to the example. When the Loop option is selected in Step 2 for the slideshow timeline, Dreamweaver automatically includes a Go to Timeline Frame behavior after the final frame; this sends the timeline back to the first frame. In the moving layers timeline, enabling the Autostart option causes Dreamweaver to attach a Play Timeline behavior to the onLoad event of the Web page's <body> tag. To complete the project, you need to add five behaviors.

First, you need a behavior to stop the moving layers from proceeding after the fly-in portion of the animation:

1. From the Timelines panel, double-click the final frame of the first animation bar in the Behaviors channel.

2. In the Behaviors panel, select Timeline ⇨ Stop Timeline from the Add (+) button drop-down list.

3. From the Stop Timeline dialog box, select the timeline that contains the moving layers.

4. Click OK. An onFrame event is set for the Stop Timeline action by default.

Second, you need a behavior to enable the user to begin playing the slideshow:

1. In the Document window, select the Play button.

2. In the Behaviors panel, select the Timeline ⇨ Play Timeline action from the Add (+) button drop-down list.

3. In the Play Timeline dialog box, choose the timeline representing the slideshow.

4. Click OK. Use the drop-down arrow in the Events column to select an onMouseDown event to trigger the action.

The next behavior enables the user to stop the slideshow temporarily:

1. In the Document window, select the Pause button.

2. In the Behaviors panel, select the Timeline ⇨ Stop Timeline action.

3. Choose the layer representing the slideshow in the Stop Timeline dialog box.

4. Click OK. Use the Events column drop-down arrow to select an onMouseDown event to trigger the action.

To enable the user to begin the slideshow from the beginning, follow these steps:

1. In the Document window, select the Restart button.

2. In the Behaviors panel, select the Timeline ⇨ Go to Timeline Frame action.

3. In the Go to Timeline Frame dialog box, choose the layer representing the slideshow.

4. Enter a 1 in the Go to Frame text box.

5. Click OK. Use the Events column arrow to select an onMouseDown event to trigger the action.

6. With the Restart button still selected, add the Timeline ➪ Play Timeline action.

7. In the Play Timeline dialog box, choose the layer representing the slideshow.

8. Click OK. Use the Events arrow to select an onMouseDown event to trigger the action.

To end the presentation and move the user on to the next Web page, follow these steps:

1. In the Document window, select the End button.

2. In the Behaviors panel, select the Timeline ➪ Play Timeline action.

3. Choose the timeline representing the moving layers in the Play Timeline dialog box and click OK. The timeline begins playing where it last stopped — just before the layers are about to fly out. Use the Events arrow to select an onMouseDown event to trigger the action.

4. With the End button still selected, add the Go to URL action.

5. In the Go to URL dialog box, enter the path to the new page in the URL text box or select the Browse (Choose) button to locate the file. Click OK when you are finished.

The project is complete and ready to test. Feel free to experiment, trying out different timings to achieve different effects.

 You can test the final working version by using your browser to view the Multiscreen Slideshow Demo in the Examples folder of the CD-ROM that accompanies this book.

Summary

Timelines are effective tools for developing pages in which events need to be triggered at specific points in time.

✦ Timelines can affect particular attributes of layers and images, or they can start any Dreamweaver behavior.

✦ Use the Timelines panel to set an animation to play automatically, to have it loop indefinitely, and to change the frames-per-second display rate of the timeline.

✦ You must use one of the timeline behaviors to activate your timeline if you don't use the Autoplay feature.

In the next chapter, you learn how to use Dreamweaver behaviors to enhance the interactivity of your sites.

✦   ✦   ✦

Using Behaviors

Behaviors are truly the power tools of Dreamweaver. With Dreamweaver behaviors, any Web designer can make layers appear and disappear, execute any number of rollovers, or control a Shockwave movie — all without knowing even a snippet of JavaScript. In the hands of an accomplished JavaScript programmer, Dreamweaver behaviors can be customized or created from scratch to automate the most difficult Web effect.

Creating behaviors is one of the more challenging Dreamweaver features to master; we'll tackle it in Chapter 35. Implementing these gems, however, is a piece of cake. This chapter examines the concepts behind behaviors and the reality of using them. It details the use of all the behaviors included with Dreamweaver, as well as some from notable third-party sources. This chapter also contains tips on managing your ever-increasing library of behaviors.

Here's a guarantee for you: After you get the hang of using Dreamweaver behaviors, your Web pages will never be the same.

Understanding Behaviors, Events, and Actions

A *behavior*, in Macromedia parlance, is the combination of an event and an action. In the electronic age, one pushes a button (the event), and something (the action) occurs — such as changing the channel on the TV. In Dreamweaver, events can be something as interactive as a user's click of a link or as automatic as the loading of a Web page. Behaviors are said to be *attached* to a specific element on your page, whether it's a text link, an image, or even the <body> tag.

Dreamweaver has simplified the process of working with behaviors by including default events in every object on the Web page. Instead of having to think about both *how* you want to do something and *what* you want to do, you only have to focus on the *what* — the action.

To understand conceptually how behaviors are structured, examine the four essential steps for adding a behavior to your Web page:

1. **Pick a tag.** All behaviors are connected to a specific HTML element (tag). You can attach a behavior to everything from the <body>, to an <a> tag, to the <textarea> of a form, and so on. If a certain behavior is unavailable, it's because the necessary element isn't present on the page.

2. **Choose your target browser.** Different browsers — and the various browser versions — support different events. Dreamweaver enables you to choose either a specific browser, such as Internet Explorer 6, or a browser range, such as version 4 and higher browsers.

3. **Select an action.** Dreamweaver enables only those actions available to the specific elements on your page. You can't, for instance, choose the Show-Hide Layer action until you insert one or more layers. Behaviors guide you to the workable options.

4. **Enter the parameters.** Behaviors get their power from their flexibility. Each action comes with its own dialog box that contains parameters you can use to customize the JavaScript code output. Depending on the action, you can choose source files, set attributes, and enable/disable features. The parameter dialog box can even dynamically update to reflect your current Web page.

Dreamweaver MX comes with 27 cross-browser–compatible actions, and both Macromedia and third-party developers have made many additional actions available, with even more in the works. Behaviors greatly extend the range of possibilities for the modern Web designer — with no requirement to learn JavaScript programming. All you need to know about attaching behaviors is presented in the following section.

Cross-Reference

Dreamweaver supports two main types of behaviors: client-side and server-side. Client-side behaviors, consisting of JavaScript and HTML, are the focus of this chapter. Server-side behaviors are covered in Chapter 36.

Attaching a Behavior

When you see the code generated by Dreamweaver, you understand why setting up a behavior is also referred to as *attaching* a behavior. As previously noted, Dreamweaver needs a specific HTML tag to assign the behavior (Step 1). The anchor tag `<a>` is often used because, in JavaScript, links can respond to several different events, including `onClick`. Here's an example:

```
<a href="#" onClick="MM_popupMsg('Thanks for coming!')">Exit Here</a>
```

You're not restricted to one event per tag or even one action per event. Multiple events can be associated with a tag to handle various user actions. For example, you may have an image that does all the following things:

✦ Highlights when the user's pointer moves over the image

✦ Reveals a hidden layer in another area of the page when the user clicks the mouse button on the image

✦ Makes a sound when the user releases the mouse button on the image

✦ Starts a Flash movie when the user's pointer moves away from the image

Likewise, a single event can trigger several actions. Updating multiple frames through a single link used to be difficult — but no more. Dreamweaver makes it easy by enabling you to attach several Go to URL actions to the same event, `onClick`. In addition, you are not restricted to attaching multiple instances of the same action to a single event. For example, in a site that uses a lot of multimedia, you can tie all the following actions to a single `onClick` event:

✦ Begin playing an audio file (with the Play Sound action)

✦ Move a layer across the screen (with the Play Timeline action)

✦ Display a second graphic in place of the first (with the Swap Image action)

✦ Show the copyright information for the audio piece in the status bar (with the Set Text of Status Bar action)

You can even determine the order of execution for the actions connected to a single event.

With Dreamweaver behaviors, hours of complex JavaScript coding are reduced to a handful of mouse clicks and a minimum of data entry. All behavior assigning and modification are handled through the Behaviors panel.

Using the Behaviors panel

The Behaviors panel provides two columns (see Figure 23-1) that neatly sum up the behaviors concept in general: events and actions. After attaching a behavior, the triggering event (`onClick`, `onMouseOver`, and so on) is shown on the left, and its associated action — what exactly is triggered — is on the right. A down arrow between the event and action, when clicked, displays other available events for the current browser model. Double-click the action to open its parameter dialog box, where you can modify the action's attributes.

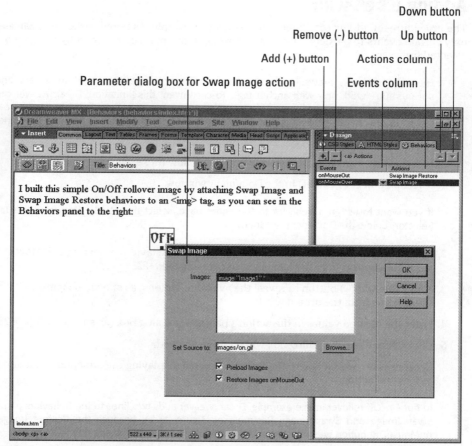

Figure 23-1: You can handle everything about a behavior through the Behaviors panel.

As usual in Dreamweaver, you have your choice of methods for opening the Behaviors panel:

+ Choose Window ➪ Behaviors.

+ Select the Show Behaviors button from the Launcher.

+ Use the keyboard shortcut Shift+F3 (an on/off toggle).

Tip   The Behaviors panel can be closed by toggling it off with Shift+F3 or hidden along with all the other panels by pressing F4.

After you have attached a behavior to a tag and closed the associated action's parameter dialog box, Dreamweaver writes the necessary HTML and JavaScript code into your document. Because it contains functions that must be callable from anywhere in the document, the bulk of the JavaScript code is placed in the <head> section of the page; the code that links selected tags to these functions is written in the <body> section. A few actions, including Play Sound, place HTML code at the bottom of the <body>, but most of the code—there can be a lot of code to handle all the cross-browser contingencies—is placed between <script>...</script> tags in the <head>.

Adding a behavior

The procedure for adding (or attaching) a behavior is simple. As noted earlier, you can assign only certain events to particular tags, and those options are further limited by the type of selected browser.

Note   Even in the latest browsers, key events such as onMouseDown, onMouseOver, and onMouseOut work only with anchor tags. To circumvent this limitation, Dreamweaver can enclose an element, such as <img>, with an anchor tag that links to nowhere— src="javascript:;". Events that use the anchor tag in this fashion appear in parentheses in the drop-down list of events.

To add a behavior to an element in your Web page, follow these steps:

1. Select an object (element) in the Document window.

Tip   If you want to assign a behavior to the entire page, select the <body> tag from the Tag Selector (below the Document window).

2. Open the Behaviors panel by choosing Window ➪ Behaviors, selecting the Show Behaviors button from the Launcher, or pressing Shift+F3.

3. Select the Add (+) button to reveal the available options, as shown in Figure 23-2. Choose one from the drop-down list.

4. Enter the desired values in the action's parameter dialog box (as shown in Figure 23-2).

5. Click OK to close the dialog box when you're finished.

    Dreamweaver adds a line to the Behaviors panel displaying the attached event and its associated action.

Note   In our On/Off rollover image example, Dreamweaver adds two lines to the Behaviors panel, Swap Image and Swap Image Restore (see Figure 23-2), because the Restore Images onMouseOut option was selected in the Swap Image parameter dialog box.

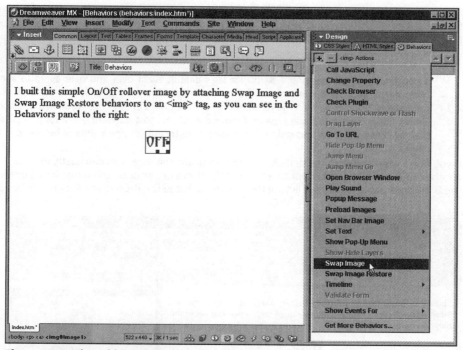

Figure 23-2: The Add (+) drop-down list changes according to what's on the current page and which tag is selected.

A trigger — whether it's an image or a text link — may have multiple behaviors attached to it. One graphical navigation element can, for instance, perform a Swap Image when the user's mouse moves over it, a Swap Image Restore when the mouse moves away, and, when clicked, show another Web page in an additional, smaller window with the Open Browser Window behavior.

Tip   Dreamweaver includes a Get More Behaviors menu option at the bottom of the Add (+) drop-down list. To use this feature, connect to the Internet and then choose Get More Behaviors in Dreamweaver. You will be whisked away to the Dreamweaver Exchange, a service from Macromedia with a huge selection of extensions of all flavors, including behaviors.

Managing events

Every time Dreamweaver attaches a behavior to a tag, it also inserts an event for you. The default event that is chosen is based on two criteria: the browser type and the selected tag. The different browsers in use have widely different capabilities, notably when it comes to understanding the various event handlers and associated tags.

For every browser and browser combination in the Show Events For submenu of the Add (+) drop-down list, Dreamweaver has a corresponding file in the Configuration\Behaviors\Events folder. Each of the tags listed in each file, such as IE 4.0.htm, has at least one event associated with it. The entries look like this:

```
<INPUT TYPE="Text" onBlur="*" onChange="" onFocus="" onSelect="">
```

The default event for each tag is marked with an asterisk; in the previous example, `onBlur` is the default event. After you've selected an action and completed its parameter dialog box, the default event appears in the Events column of the Behaviors panel alongside the action in the Actions column.

Tip   If you find yourself changing a particular tag's default event over and over again to some other event, you might want to modify the appropriate Event file to pick your alternative as the default. To do this, open the relevant browser file found in the Configuration\Behaviors\Events folder, switch to Code view and move the asterisk to a different event for that particular tag. Resave the file and restart Dreamweaver to try out your new default behavior.

If you don't want to select the default event in a certain instance, you can easily choose another. Choose a different event by selecting the down arrow next to the displayed event in the Behaviors panel and then clicking the desired event in the drop-down list (see Figure 23-3).

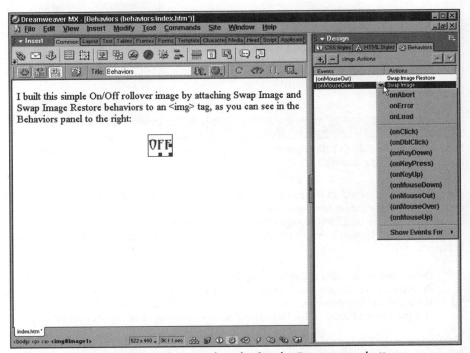

Figure 23-3: You can change the event by selecting the Events arrow button.

The browser model selected determines which events are available. By default, 4.0 and Later Browsers is chosen. To change browser models, choose Show Events For from the Events list and then select one of the following:

✦ 3.0 and Later Browsers

✦ 4.0 and Later Browsers

✦ IE 3.0

✦ IE 4.0

✦ IE 5.0

✦ IE 5.5

✦ IE 6.0

✦ Netscape 3.0

✦ Netscape 4.0

✦ Netscape 6.0

Dreamweaver's Configuration\Behaviors\Events folder contains HTML files corresponding to these 10 browser models offered in the Show Events For submenu. You can open these files in Dreamweaver, but Macromedia asks that you not edit them — with one exception. Each file contains the list of tags that have supported *event handlers* (the JavaScript term for events) in that browser. The older the browser, the fewer event handlers are included — unfortunately, this also means that if you want to reach the broadest Internet audience, your event options are limited. In the broadest category, 3.0 and Later Browsers, only 13 different tags can receive any sort of event handler. This is one of the reasons why, for example, Internet Explorer 3 can't handle rollovers: The browser doesn't understand what an `onMouseOut` event is, and so the image can't revert to its original state.

Listing 23-1 shows the event-handler definitions for the 3.0 and Later Browsers category:

Listing 23-1: **The Event File for 3.0 and Later Browsers**

```
<A onMouseOver="*">
<AREA onClick="" onMouseOut="" onMouseOver="*">
<BODY onLoad="*" onUnload="">
<FORM onReset="" onSubmit="*">
<FRAMESET onLoad="*" onUnload="">
<INPUT TYPE="Button" onClick="*">
<INPUT TYPE="Checkbox" onClick="*">
<INPUT TYPE="Radio" onClick="*">
<INPUT TYPE="Reset" onClick="*">
<INPUT TYPE="Submit" onClick="*">
<INPUT TYPE="Text" onBlur="*" onChange="" onFocus="" onSelect="">
<SELECT onBlur="" onChange="*" onFocus="">
<TEXTAREA onBlur="" onChange="*" onFocus="" onSelect="">
```

By contrast, the Event file for Internet Explorer 6.0 shows support for every tag under the HTML sun — 94 in all — with almost every tag able to handle any type of event.

Tip   Although any HTML tag could potentially be used to attach a behavior, the most commonly used by far are the `<body>` tag (for entire-page events such as `onLoad`), the `<img>` tag (used as a button), and the link tag, `<a>`.

To find the default event for a tag, simply select the tag in a document, use Add Actions to attach any valid action to it, and see what event appears alongside the action in the Behaviors panel. To find the default event for a tag as used by a particular browser, specify the browser in the Show Events For submenu of the Add (+) drop-down list, and then proceed as above.

Standard actions

As of this writing, 27 standard actions ship with Dreamweaver MX. Each action operates independently and differently from the others, although many share common functions. Each action is associated with a different parameter dialog box to enable easy attribute entry.

The following sections describe each of the standard actions: what the action does, what requirements must be met for it to be activated, what options are available, and most important of all, how to use it. Each action is written to work with all browser versions 4 and above; however, some actions do not work as designed in the older browsers. The charts, included with every action, show the action's compatibility with older browsers. (The information in these charts was adapted from the Dreamweaver Help pages and is used with permission.)

Note   The following descriptions assume that you understand the basics of assigning behaviors and that you know how to open the Behaviors panel.

Call JavaScript

With Call JavaScript, you can execute any JavaScript function — standard or custom — with a single mouse click or other event. As your JavaScript savvy grows, you'll find yourself using this behavior again and again.

Call JavaScript is straightforward to use; simply type in the JavaScript code or the name of the function you want to trigger into the dialog box. If, for example, you want to get some input from a visitor, you can use JavaScript's built-in `prompt()` method like this:

```
result = prompt('Whom shall I say is calling?','')
```

When this code is triggered, a small dialog box appears with your query (here, `'Whom shall I say is calling?'`) and a blank space for an input string. The second argument in the `prompt()` method enables you to include a default answer — to leave it blank, just use an empty string (`' '`, two single quotes with nothing in between), as shown in the preceding code snippet.

Note   You can use either single or double quotes in your Call JavaScript behavior; Dreamweaver automatically adjusts for whichever you choose. However, I find it easier to use single quotes because Dreamweaver translates double quotes into character entities; that is, " becomes `&quot;`.

Naturally, you can use Call JavaScript to handle more complex chores as well. To call a specific custom function that is already in the `<head>` section of your page, just enter its name — along with any necessary arguments — in the Call JavaScript dialog box, shown in Figure 23-4.

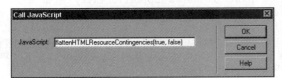

Figure 23-4: Trigger any JavaScript function by attaching a Call JavaScript behavior to an image or text.

To use the Call JavaScript behavior, follow these steps:

1. Select the object to trigger the action.

2. From the Behaviors panel, select the Add (+) button and then choose Call JavaScript.

3. In the Call JavaScript dialog box, enter your code in the JavaScript text box.

4. Click OK when you're done.

Note

In the following charts that detail action behaviors for both newer and older browsers, the phrase "Fails without error" means that the action won't work in the older browser, but neither will it generate an error message for the user to see. When the table indicates "error," it means that the action won't work and *will* generate a visible error message.

Here's the browser compatibility chart for the Call JavaScript behavior:

Call JavaScript	Netscape 3.0	Internet Explorer 3.0x	Internet Explorer 3.01
Macintosh	Okay	Fails without error	
Windows	Okay		Okay

Change Property

The Change Property action enables you to dynamically alter a property of one of the following tags:

✦ <div>

✦ <form>

✦ <img>

✦ <layer>

✦ <select>

✦ <span>

✦ <textarea>

You can also alter the following <input> types:

✦ checkbox

✦ password

✦ radio

✦ text

The tags, as well as the browser being targeted, determine exactly which properties can be altered. For example, the <div> tag and Internet Explorer 4.0 combination enable you to change virtually every style sheet option on-the-fly. The Change Property dialog box (see Figure 23-5) offers a list of the selected tags in the current page.

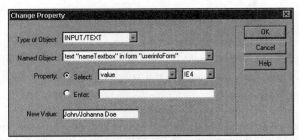

Figure 23-5: The Change Property dialog box enables you to alter attributes of certain tags dynamically.

Caution   It's important that you name the objects you want to alter so that Dreamweaver can properly identify them. Remember to use unique names that begin with a letter and contain no spaces or special characters.

This behavior is especially useful for changing the properties of forms and form elements. Be sure to name the form if you want to use Change Property in this manner. To use the Change Property action, follow these steps:

1. Select the object to trigger the action.

2. From the Behaviors panel, select the Add (+) button and then choose Change Property.

3. In the Change Property dialog box, choose the type of object whose property you want to change — FORM, DIV, INPUT/TEXT, and so on — from the Type of Object drop-down list.

4. In the Named Object drop-down list, choose the name of the object whose property you want to change.

5. Click the Select radio button. Select the target browser in the small list box on the far right and then choose the property to change. If you don't find the property in the drop-down list box, you can type it yourself into the Enter text box.

Note   Many properties in the various browsers are read-only and cannot be dynamically altered. Those properties listed in the option list are always dynamic.

6. In the New Value text box, type the property's new value to be inserted when the event is fired.

7. Click OK when you're done.

Here's the browser compatibility chart for the Change Property behavior:

Change Property	*Netscape 3.x*	*Internet Explorer 3.0*	*Internet Explorer 3.01*
Macintosh	Okay	Fails without error	
Windows	Okay		Okay

Check Browser

Some Web sites are increasingly split into multilevel versions of themselves to gracefully handle the variety of browsers in operation. The Check Browser action acts as a type of browser "router" capable of sending browsers to appropriate URLs, or just letting them stay on the current page. The Check Browser action is generally assigned to the <body> tag and uses the onLoad event. If used in this fashion, it's a good idea to keep the basic page accessible to all browsers, even those with JavaScript disabled.

The Check Browser parameter dialog box (see Figure 23-6) is quite flexible and enables you to specify decimal version numbers for the two main browsers. For instance, you may want to let all users of Navigator 4.04 or later stay on the current page and send everyone else to an alternative URL. The URLs can be either relative, such as dreamweaver/index.htm, or absolute, such as http://www.idest.com/dreamweaver/index.htm.

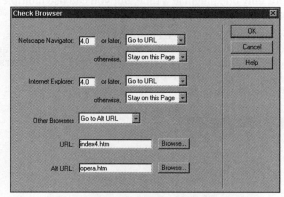

Figure 23-6: The Check Browser action is a great tool for segregating old and new browsers.

To use the Check Browser action, follow these steps:

1. Select the object to trigger the action.

2. From the Behaviors panel, select the Add (+) button and then choose Check Browser.

3. Use the Check Browser parameter fields to specify the Netscape Navigator and Internet Explorer versions and whether you want the browser to stay on the current page, go to another URL, or proceed to a third alternative URL.

Note   With both major browsers, you can specify the URL that the lower version numbers should visit.

4. Set the same options for all other browsers, such as Opera.

5. Enter the URL and alternate URL options in their respective text boxes; or select the Browse (Choose) button to locate the files.

6. Click OK when you're done.

Cross-Reference   The Check Browser action works well with another Dreamweaver feature: Convert to 3.0 Compatible. Learn all about this capability in Chapter 30.

Here's the browser compatibility chart for the Check Browser behavior:

Check Browser	Netscape 3.x	Internet Explorer 3.0	Internet Explorer 3.01
Macintosh	Okay	Fails without error	
Windows	Okay		Okay

Check Plugin

If certain pages on your Web site require the use of one or more plugins, you can use the Check Plugin action to see if a visitor has the necessary plugin installed. After Check Plugin has examined this, it can route users with the appropriate plugin to one URL and users without it to another URL. You can look for only one plugin at a time, but you can use multiple instances of the Check Plugin action, if needed.

By default, the parameter dialog box for Check Plugin (see Figure 23-7) offers five plugins: Flash, Shockwave, LiveAudio, QuickTime, and Windows Media Player. You can check for any other plugin by entering its name in the Enter text box. Use the name exactly as it appears in bold (without the version number) in Netscape's About Plug-ins area; for example: `QuickTime Plug-in` **or** `Shockwave Flash`.

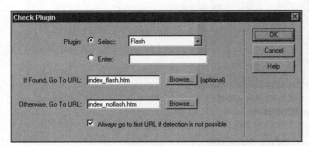

Figure 23-7: Running a media-intensive site? Use the Check Plugin action to divert visitors without plugins to alternative pages.

One very unfortunate hitch: Internet Explorer is pretty much crippled with respect to cross-browser plugin detection. In Windows, Internet Explorer can only detect Flash and Shockwave plugins. And on Macintosh platforms, Internet Explorer cannot detect any plugins at all. The best way to handle both browsers is to use both ActiveX controls and plugins.

Tip If you use a particular plugin regularly, you may also want to modify the Check Plugin.js file found in your Actions folder. Add your new plugin to the `PLUGIN_NAMES` array (this holds "nice" plugin names as they appear in the parameter dialog box) and `PLUGIN_VALUES` array (this holds "internal" plugin names, as they appear in Netscape's About Plug-ins) in the `initGlobals()` function.

Another method for determining whether a plugin or other player is available is to use the Check MIME action included in the Additional Extensions\Joseph Lowery\Behaviors folder on the CD-ROM that accompanies this book. This action works in the same way as the Check Plugin action, except you enter the MIME type.

To use the Check Plugin action, follow these steps:

1. Select the object to trigger the action.

2. From the Behaviors panel, select the Add (+) button and then choose Check Browser.

3. Select a plugin from the drop-down list or, alternatively, type another plugin name in the Enter text box.

The names presented in the drop-down list are abbreviated — more recognizable names and not the formal names inserted into the code. For example, when you select Shockwave, Shockwave for Director is actually input into the code. On the other hand, any plugin name you enter manually into the Enter field is inserted verbatim.

4. If you want to send users who are confirmed to have the plugin to a different page, enter that URL (absolute or relative) in the If Found, Go To URL text box or use the Browse (Choose) button to locate the file. If you want these users to stay on the current page, leave the text box empty.

5. In the Otherwise, Go To URL text box, enter the URL for users who do not have the required plugin.

6. Should the plugin detection fail — which, as explained above, will happen regularly for Internet Explorer, whether or not the plugin is actually present — you can keep the user on the initial page by enabling the "Always go to first URL if detection is not possible" option. Otherwise, if the detection fails, for any reason, the users are sent to the URL listed in the Otherwise field.

7. Click OK when you're done.

Here's the browser compatibility chart for the Check Plugin behavior:

Check Browser	*Netscape 3.x*	*Internet Explorer 3.0*	*Internet Explorer 3.01*
Macintosh	Okay	Fails without error	
Windows	Okay		Okay

Control Shockwave or Flash

The Control Shockwave or Flash action enables you to command your Shockwave and Flash movies through external controls. With Control Shockwave or Flash, you can build your own interface for your Shockwave or Flash movie. This action can be used in conjunction with the autostart=true attribute (entered through the Property inspector's parameter dialog box for the Shockwave or Flash file) to enable a replaying of the movie.

You must have a Shockwave or Flash movie inserted in your Web page for the Control Shockwave or Flash action to be available. The parameter dialog box for this action (see Figure 23-8) lists by name all the Shockwave or Flash movies that are found in either an `<embed>` or `<object>` tag. You can set the action to control the movie in one of four ways: Play, Stop, Rewind, or Go to Frame. You can choose only one option each time you attach an action to an event. If you choose the last option, you need to specify the frame number in the text box. Note that specifying a Go to Frame number does not start the movie there; you need to attach a second Control Shockwave or Flash action to the same event to play the file.

Figure 23-8: Build your own interface and then control a Shockwave and Flash movie externally with the Control Shockwave or Flash action.

Tip   Be sure to name your Shockwave or Flash movie. Otherwise, the Control Shockwave or Flash action lists both unnamed `<embed>` and unnamed `<object>` for each file, and you cannot write to both tags as you can with a named movie.

To use the Control Shockwave or Flash action, follow these steps:

1. Select the object to trigger the action.

2. From the Behaviors panel, select the Add (+) button and then choose Control Shockwave or Flash.

3. In the Control Shockwave or Flash dialog box, select a movie from the Movie drop-down list.

4. Select a control by choosing its button:

   • **Play:** Begins playing the movie at the current frame location.

   • **Stop:** Stops playing the movie.

   • **Rewind:** Returns the movie to its first frame.

   • **Go to Frame:** Displays a specific frame in the movie. If you choose this option, you must enter a frame number in the text box.

5. Select OK when you're done.

Here's the browser compatibility chart for the Control Shockwave or Flash behavior:

Control Shockwave or Flash	Netscape 3.x	Internet Explorer 3.0	Internet Explorer 3.01
Macintosh	Okay	Fails without error	
Windows	Okay		Fails without error

Drag Layer

The Drag Layer action provides some spectacular — and interactive — effects with little effort on the part of the designer. Drag Layer enables your Web page visitors to move layers — and all that they contain — around the screen with the drag-and-drop technique. With the Drag Layer action, you can easily set up the following capabilities for the user:

✦ Enable layers to be dragged anywhere on the screen

✦ Restrict the dragging to a particular direction or combination of directions — a horizontal sliding layer can be restricted to left and right movement, for instance

✦ Limit the drag handle to a portion of the layer such as the upper bar or enable the whole layer to be used

✦ Provide an alternative clipping method by enabling only a portion of the layer to be dragged

✦ Enable changing of the layers' stacking order while dragging or on mouse release

✦ Set a snap-to target area on your Web page for layers that the user releases within a defined radius

✦ Program a JavaScript command to be executed when the snap-to target is hit or every time the layer is released

Cross-Reference

Layers are one of the more powerful features of Dreamweaver. To get the most out of the layer-oriented behaviors, familiarize yourself with layers by examining Chapter 21.

One or more layers must reside in your Web page before the Drag Layer action becomes available for selection from the Add (+) drop-down list. You must attach the action to the <body> — you can, however, attach separate Drag Layer behaviors to different layers to get different layer-dragging effects.

Drag Layer's parameter dialog box (see Figure 23-9) includes a Get Current Position button that puts the left and top coordinates of the selected layer into the Drop Target Left/Top boxes. If you plan on using targeting, make sure to place your layer at the target location *before* attaching the behavior.

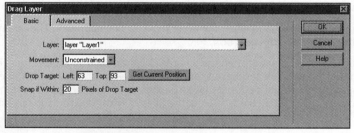

Figure 23-9: With the Drag Layer action, you can set up your layers to be repositioned by the user.

To use the Drag Layer action, follow these steps:

1. Make sure you have one or more layers on your page; then select the <body> tag.

2. From the Behaviors panel, select the Add (+) button and choose Drag Layer.

3. If the Basic tab of the parameter dialog box is not selected, select it now.

4. In the Layer drop-down list, select the layer you want to make draggable.

5. To limit the movement of the layer, change the Movement option from Unconstrained to Constrained. Text boxes for Up, Down, Left, and Right appear. Enter pixel values in the text boxes to control the range of motion:

   • To constrain movement vertically, enter positive numbers in the Up and Down text boxes and zeros in the Left and Right text boxes.

   • To constrain movement horizontally, enter positive numbers in the Left and Right text boxes and zeros in the Up and Down text boxes.

   • To enable movement in a rectangular region, enter positive values in all four text boxes.

6. To establish a location for a target for the dragged layer, enter coordinates in the Drop Target: Left and Top text boxes. Select the Get Current Position button to fill these text boxes with the layer's current location.

7. To set a snap-to area around the target coordinates where the layer falls if released in the target location, enter a pixel value in the Snap if Within text box.

8. For additional options, select the Advanced tab of the parameter dialog box.

9. If you want the whole layer to act as a drag handle, select Entire Layer from the Drag Handle drop-down list.

   If, instead, you want to limit the area to be used as a drag handle, select Area Within Layer from the Drag Handle drop-down list. L(eft), T(op), W(idth), and H(eight) text boxes appear. In the appropriate boxes, enter the left and top coordinates of the drag handle in pixels, as well as the dimensions for the width and height.

10. To control the positioning of the dragged layer, set the following While Dragging options:

    • To keep the layer in its current depth (that is, it avoid bringing it the front when it is dragged), deselect the checkbox for While Dragging: Bring Layer to the Front.

    • To change the stacking order of the layer when it is released, select the checkbox and then choose either Leave on Top or Restore z-index from the drop-down list.

11. To execute a JavaScript command while the layer is being dragged, enter the command or function in the Call JavaScript text box.

12. To execute a JavaScript command when the layer is dropped on the target, enter the code in the When Dropped: Call JavaScript text box. If you want the JavaScript to execute only when the layer is snapped to its target, select the Only if Snapped option. This option requires that a value be entered in the Snap if Within text box in the Basic tab.

13. Click OK when you're done.

> **Note**
>
> If you — or someone on your team — has the requisite JavaScript programming skills, you can gather information output from the Drag Layer behavior to enhance your pages. Dreamweaver declares three variables for each draggable layer: MM_UPDOWN (the *y* coordinate), MM_LEFTRIGHT (the *x* coordinate), and MM_SNAPPED (true, if the layer has reached the specified target). Before you can get any of these properties, you must get an object reference for the proper layer. Another function, MM_findObj(*layername*), handles this chore.

Here's the browser compatibility chart for the Drag Layer behavior:

Drag Layer	Netscape 3.x	Internet Explorer 3.0	Internet Explorer 3.01
Macintosh	Fails without error	Fails without error	
Windows	Fails without error		Fails without error

Go to URL

Dreamweaver brings the same power of links — with a lot more flexibility — to any event with the Go to URL action. One of the trickier tasks in using frames on a Web page is updating two or more frames simultaneously with a single button click. The Go to URL action handily streamlines this process for the Web designer. Go to URL can also be used as a preload router that sends the user to another Web page after the onLoad event has finished the Go To URL dialog box (see Figure 23-10) displays any existing frames in the current page or frameset. To load multiple URLs at the same time: Select the first frame from the Open In list, and enter the desired page or location in the URL text box; then select the second frame from the list and enter its URL; and so on. If you select a frame to which a URL is already assigned, that address appears in the URL text box.

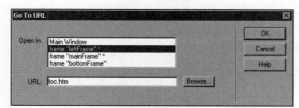

Figure 23-10: Update two or more frames at the same time with the Go to URL action. To use the Go to URL action, follow these steps:

1. Select the object to trigger the action.

2. From the Behaviors panel, select the Add (+) button and then choose Go to URL.

3. From the Go To URL dialog box, select the target for your link from the list in the Open In window.

4. Enter the path of the file to open in the URL text box or click the Browse (Choose) button to locate a file. An asterisk appears next to the frame name to indicate that a URL has been chosen.

5. To select another target to load a different URL, repeat Steps 3 and 4.

6. Click OK when you're done.

Here's the browser compatibility chart for the Go to URL behavior:

Go to URL	Netscape 3.x	Internet Explorer 3.0	Internet Explorer 3.01
Macintosh	Okay	Fails without error	
Windows	Okay		Okay

Show Pop-Up Menu and Hide Pop-Up Menu

New to the built-in Dreamweaver MX behavior set is the powerful Show Pop-Up Menu/Hide Pop-Up Menu duo. With the greatest of ease, you can use these behaviors to create a DHTML-style pop-up menu. A user mouses over a navigational link and, lo and behold, down pops a lovely menu with a set of context-sensitive sublinks. When the user mouses away, the pop-up menu disappears.

To use the Show Pop-Up Menu and Hide Pop-Up Menu actions to create a pop-up menu, perform these steps:

1. Select the object to trigger the action.

2. From the Behaviors panel, select the Add (+) button and then choose Show Pop-Up Menu, as shown in Figure 23-11.

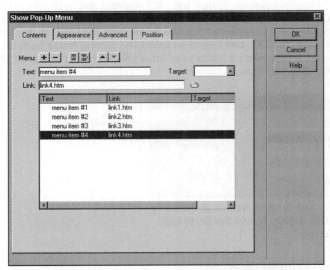

Figure 23-11: You can easily create a sophisticated DHTML-style pop-up menu using the Show Pop-Up Menu behavior.

3. The Show Pop-Up Menu dialog box that appears comprises four tabs: Contents, Appearance, Advanced, and Position.

4. Use the Contents tab to set the name (Text field), structure (Outdent/Indent Item and Move Item Up/Down buttons), URL (Link field), and target (_blank, _parent, _top, or _self) of the items to appear in the pop-up menu.

5. Use the Appearance tab to set the orientation of the pop-up menu (Vertical or Horizontal), various properties of the menu items' font, and the items' Up State and Over State colors.

6. Use the Advanced tab to set various properties of the menu cells, including size, spacing, color, text indent, border width, and delay before the menu appears after the trigger object is moused over.

7. Use the Position tab to set where the menu appears relative to the trigger object.

8. Click OK when you're done. After you've successfully attached a Show Pop-Up Menu action to an object, Dreamweaver automatically attaches a Hide Pop-Up Menu item to it.

Here's the browser compatibility chart for the Show Pop-up Menu behavior:

Go to URL	Netscape 3.x	Internet Explorer 3.0	Internet Explorer 3.01
Macintosh	Fails without error	Fails without error	
Windows	Fails without error		Fails without error

Jump Menu and Jump Menu Go

Although most behaviors insert original code to activate an element of the Web page, several behaviors are included to edit code inserted by a Dreamweaver object. The Jump Menu and Jump Menu Go behaviors both require a previously inserted Jump Menu object before they become active. The Jump Menu behavior is used to edit an existing Jump Menu object, while the Jump Menu Go behavior adds a graphic image as a "Go" button.

To find out more about the Jump Menu object, see Chapter 11.

To use the Jump Menu behavior to edit an existing Jump Menu object, follow these steps:

1. Select the Jump Menu object previously inserted into the page.

2. In the Behaviors panel, double-click the listed Jump Menu behavior.

3. Make your modifications in the Jump Menu dialog box, as shown in Figure 23-12.

   You can alter the existing menu item names or their associated URLs, add new menu items, or reorder the list through the Jump Menu dialog box.

4. Select OK when you're done.

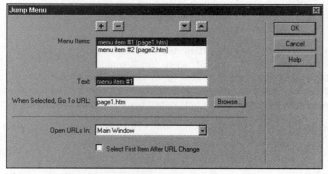

Figure 23-12: The Jump Menu behavior is used to modify a previously inserted Jump Menu object.

To add a button to activate the Jump Menu object, follow these steps:

1. Select the image or form button you'd like to make into a Go button.

   A Jump Menu object must be on the current page for the Jump Menu Go behavior to be available.

2. From the Behaviors panel, select Jump Menu Go from the Add (+) drop-down list.

   The Jump Menu Go dialog box, shown in Figure 23-13, is displayed.

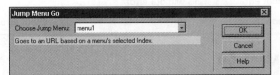

Figure 23-13: Add a graphic or standard button as a Go button with the Jump Menu Go behavior.

3. Select the name of the Jump Menu object you want to activate from the option list.

4. Click OK when you're done.

Here's the browser compatibility chart for both Jump Menu behaviors:

Jump Menu	Netscape 3.x	Internet Explorer 3.0	Internet Explorer 3.01
Macintosh	Okay	Fails without error	
Windows	Okay		Fails without error

Open Browser Window

Want to display your latest design in a borderless, nonresizable browser window that's exactly the size of your image? With the Open Browser Window action, you can open a new browser window and specify its exact size and attributes. You can even set it up to receive JavaScript events.

You can also open a new browser window with a regular link by specifying `target="_blank"`, but you can't control any of the window's attributes with that method. You do get this control with the parameter dialog box of the Open Browser Window action (see Figure 23-14); here you can set the window width and height, and select whether to display the Navigation Toolbar, Location Toolbar, Status Bar, Menu Bar, Scrollbars as Needed, and/or Resize Handles. You can also name your new window, a necessary step for advanced JavaScript control.

You have to explicitly select any of the attributes that you want to appear in your new window. Your new browser window contains only the attributes you've checked, plus basic window elements such as a title bar and a Close button. To use the Open Browser Window action, follow these steps:

1. Select the object to trigger the action.

2. From the Behaviors panel, select the Add (+) button and then choose Open Browser Window.

3. In the URL to Display text box, enter the address of the Web page you want to display in the new window. You can also select the Browse (Choose) button to locate the file.

4. To specify the window's size, enter the width and height values in the appropriate text boxes.

   You must enter *both* a width and height measurement, or the new browser window opens to its default size.

5. Check the appropriate Attributes checkboxes to show the desired window features.

6. If you plan on using JavaScript to address or control the window, type a unique name in the Window Name text box. This name cannot contain spaces or special characters. Dreamweaver alerts you if the name you've entered is unacceptable.

7. Click OK when you're done.

Figure 23-14: Use the Open Browser Window action to program a pop-up advertisement or remote control.

Here's the browser compatibility chart for the Open Browser Window behavior:

Open Browser Window	*Netscape 3.x*	*Internet Explorer 3.0*	*Internet Explorer 3.01*
Macintosh	Okay	Fails without error	
Windows	Okay		Okay

Play Sound

The Play Sound action is used to add external controls to an audio file that normally uses the Netscape LiveAudio plugin or the Windows Media Player. Supported audio file types include WAV, MID, AU, and AIFF files. The Play Sound action — which is generally used to add invisible background music to a page — inserts an `<embed>` tag with the following attributes:

✦ `loop=false`

✦ `autostart=false`

✦ `mastersound`

✦ `hidden=true`

✦ `width=0`

✦ `height=0`

Instead of automatically detecting which sound files have been inserted in the current Web page, Play Sound looks for the sound file to be inserted through the action's dialog box (see Figure 23-15).

Figure 23-15: Give your Web page background music and control it with the Play Sound action.

 Note   Dreamweaver can detect if a visitor's browser has the Windows Media Player installed and, if so, issue the appropriate commands.

To use the Play Sound action, follow these steps:

1. Select the object to trigger the action.

2. From the Behaviors panel, select the Add (+) button and then choose Play Sound.

3. To play a sound, enter the path to the audio file in the Play Sound text box or select the Browse (Choose) button to locate the file.

4. Select OK when you're done.

Here's the browser compatibility chart for the Play Sound behavior:

Play Sound	*Netscape 3.x*	*Internet Explorer 3.0*	*Internet Explorer 3.01*
Macintosh	Okay	Fails without error	
Windows	Okay		Fails without error

Popup Message

You can send a quick message to your users with the Popup Message behavior. When triggered, this action opens a JavaScript alert box that displays your specified message. You enter your message in the Message text box on the action's parameter dialog box (see Figure 23-16).

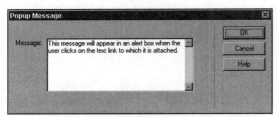

Figure 23-16: Send a message to your users with the Popup Message action.

To use the Popup Message action, follow these steps:

1. Select the object to trigger the action.

2. From the Behaviors panel, select the Add (+) button and then choose Popup Message.

3. Enter your text in the Message text box.

4. Click OK when you're done.

Tip　You can include JavaScript functions or references in your text messages by surrounding the JavaScript with curly braces. For example, today's date could be incorporated in a message like this:

Welcome to our site on {new Date()}!

You could also pull data from a form into your alert-box message, as in this example:

Thanks for filling out our survey, {document.surveyForm.firstname.value}.

If you need to display a curly brace in a message, you must precede it with a backslash character, as in \{ or \}.

Here's the browser compatibility chart for the Popup Message behavior:

Popup Message	Netscape 3.x	Internet Explorer 3.0	Internet Explorer 3.01
Macintosh	Okay	Fails without error	
Windows	Okay		Okay

Preload Images

Designs commonly require a particular image or several images to be displayed immediately when called by an action or a timeline. Because of the nature of HTML, all graphics are separate files that are normally downloaded when needed. To get the snappy response required for certain designs, graphics need to be preloaded or cached so that they will be available. The Preload Images action performs this important service. You designate the images you want to cache for later use through the Preload Images parameter dialog box (see Figure 23-17).

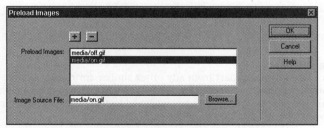

Figure 23-17: Media-rich Web sites respond much faster when images have been cached with the Preload Images action.

Note You don't need to use the Preload Images action if you're creating rollovers. Both the Rollover object and the Swap Image action enable you to preload images from their dialog boxes.

To use the Preload Images action, follow these steps:

1. Select the object to trigger the action.

2. From the Behaviors panel, select the Add (+) button and then Preload Images.

3. In the Preload Images parameter dialog box, enter the path to the image file in the Image Source File text box, or select the Browse (Choose) button to locate the file.

4. To add another file, click the Add (+) button and repeat Step 2.

Caution After you've specified your first file to be preloaded, be sure to click the Add (+) button for each successive file you want to add to the list. Otherwise, the highlighted file is replaced by the next entry.

5. To remove a file from the Preload Images list, select it and then click the Remove (–) button.

6. Click OK when you're done.

Here's the browser compatibility chart for the Preload Images behavior:

Preload Images	*Netscape 3.x*	*Internet Explorer 3.0*	*Internet Explorer 3.01*
Macintosh	Okay	Fails without error	
Windows	Okay		Fails without error

Set Nav Bar Image

The Set Nav Bar Image action, like the Jump Menu actions, enables you to edit an existing Dreamweaver object, the Navigation Bar object. This object, inserted from the Common panel of the Insert bar, consists of a series of user-specified images acting as a group of navigational buttons. The Set Nav Bar Image action enables you to modify the current Navigation Bar object by adding, reordering, or deleting images as buttons, as well as by setting up advanced rollover techniques. In fact, the Set Nav Bar Image action can be thought of as a super-duper Swap Image behavior.

Cross-Reference To refresh your memory about the capabilities of the Navigation Bar object, see Chapter 8.

The main aspect that sets a navigation bar apart from any other similar series of rollover images is that the navigation bar elements relate to one another. When you select one element of a navigation bar, by default, all the other elements are swapped to their up state. The Set Nav Bar Image action enables you to modify that default behavior to a rollover in another area or any other image swap desired. You can also use Set Nav Bar Image to include another image button in the navigation bar. To modify an existing Navigation Bar object, follow these steps:

1. Choose any image in the Navigation Bar object.

2. From the Behaviors panel, double-click any of the Set Nav Bar Image actions displayed for the image.

The same Set Nav Bar Image dialog box (Figure 23-18) opens regardless of whether you select an action associated with the onClick, onMouseOver, or onMouseOut event.

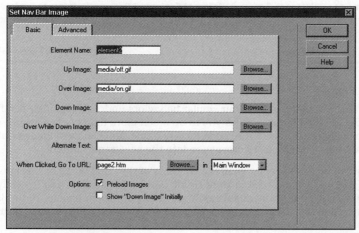

Figure 23-18: Modify an existing Navigation Bar object through the Set Nav Bar Image action.

3. Make any desired edits — changing the Up, Over, Down, or Over While Down state images or their respective URLs or targets — from the Basic column of the dialog box.

4. To change any other images that interact with the current image, select the Advanced tab.

5. In the Advanced category, choose which state you want to trigger any changes from the drop-down list:

   • Over Image or Over While Down Image

   • Down Image

6. Select the image you wish to change from the Also Set Image list.

   Dreamweaver lists all the named images on the current page, not just those in the navigation bar.

7. Select the path of the new image to be displayed in the To Image File text field.

   An asterisk appears after the current image in the list box, signifying that a swap image has been chosen.

8. If you choose Over Image or Over While Down Image as the triggering event, an optional field, If Down, To Image File enables you to specify another graphic to swap for the image of the down state image as well.

9. To alter other images with the same triggering event, repeat Steps 6 through 8.

Note Only one Navigation Bar object can exist on a page.

Here's the browser compatibility chart for the Set Nav Bar Image behavior:

Set Nav Bar Image	Netscape 3.x	Internet Explorer 3.0	Internet Explorer 3.01
Macintosh	Okay	Fails without error	
Windows	Okay		Fails without error

Set Text of Frame

Dreamweaver has grouped together four similar behaviors under the Set Text heading. The first of these, Set Text of Frame, enables you to do much more than change a word or two—you can dynamically rewrite the entire code for any frame. You can even incorporate JavaScript functions or interactive information into the new frame content.

The Set Text of Frame action replaces all the contents of the <body> tag of a frame. Dreamweaver supplies a handy Get Current HTML button that enables you to easily keep everything you want to retain and change only a heading or other element. Naturally, you must be within a frameset to use this behavior, and the frames must be named correctly—that is, uniquely without special characters or spaces.

To change the content of a frame dynamically, follow these steps:

1. Select the triggering object.

2. From the Behaviors panel, select the Add (+) button and then choose Set Text ➪ Set Text of Frame.

   The Set Text of Frame dialog box opens as shown in Figure 23-19.

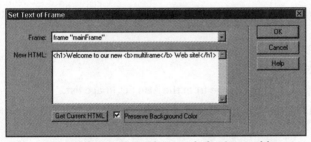

Figure 23-19: The Set Text of Frame behavior enables you to interactively update the contents of any frame in the current frameset.

3. Choose the frame you wish to alter from the Frame drop-down list.

4. Enter the code for the changing frame in the New HTML text area.

   Keep in mind that you're changing not just a word or phrase, but all the HTML contained in the <body> section of the frame.

Tip   With all four Set Text behaviors, you can include JavaScript code by enclosing it in curly braces: {...}.

5. If you want to keep the majority of the code, select the Get Current HTML button and change only those portions necessary.

6. To maintain the frames `<body>` attributes, such as the background and text colors, select the Preserve Background Color option.

   If this option is not selected, the frames background and text colors are replaced by the default values (a white background and black text).

7. Click OK when you're done.

Here's the browser compatibility chart for the Set Text of Frame behavior:

Set Text of Frame	Netscape 3.x	Internet Explorer 3.0	Internet Explorer 3.01
Macintosh	Okay	Fails without error	
Windows	Okay		Okay

Set Text of Layer

The Set Text of Layer behavior is similar to the previously described Set Text of Frame behavior in that it replaces the entire HTML contents of the target. The major difference, of course, is that with one behavior, you're replacing the code of a layer; with the other behavior, you're replacing the code of the frame's `<body>`.

Tip Unlike Set Text of Frame, Set Text of Layer provides no button for getting the current HTML. Here's a workaround. Before invoking the behavior, select and copy all the elements inside the layer. Because Dreamweaver copies tags as well as text in the Document window, you can just paste the clipboard into the New HTML text area. Be careful not to select the layer tag, `<div>`, or the layer's contents — if you do, you are pasting a layer in a layer.

To set the text of a layer dynamically, follow these steps:

1. Make sure that the layer you want to change has been created and named properly.

2. Select the object to trigger the action.

3. From the Behaviors panel, select the Add (+) button and then choose Set Text ➪ Set Text of Layer from the option list.

   The Set Text of Layer dialog box opens, as shown in Figure 23-20.

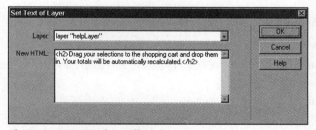

Figure 23-20: Replace all of the HTML in a layer with the Set Text of Layer behavior.

4. Select the layer to modify from the Layer drop-down list.

5. Enter the replacement code in the New HTML text area.

6. Click OK when you're done.

Here's the browser compatibility chart for the Set Text of Layer behavior:

Set Text of Layer	Netscape 3.x	Internet Explorer 3.0	Internet Explorer 3.01
Macintosh	Fails without error	Fails without error	
Windows	Fails without error		Fails without error

Set Text of Status Bar

Use the Set Text of Status Bar action to display a text message in the browser's status bar based on a user's action, such as moving the pointer over an image. The message stays displayed in the status bar until another message replaces it. System messages, such as URLs, tend to be temporary and visible only when the user's mouse is over a link.

The only limit to the length of the message is the size of the browser's status bar; you should test your message in various browsers to make sure that it is completely visible.

Tip   To display a message only when a user's pointer is over an image or link, use one Set Text of Status Bar action, attached to an `onMouseOver` event, with your desired status-bar message. Use another Set Text of Status Bar action, attached to an `onMouseOut` event, that has a null string (" ") as the text.

All text is entered in the Set Text of Status Bar parameter dialog box (see Figure 23-21) in the Message text box.

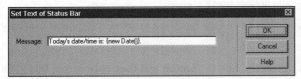

Figure 23-21: Use the Set Text of Status Bar action to guide your users with instructions in the browser window's status bar.

To use the Set Text of Status Bar action, follow these steps:

1. Select the object to trigger the action.

2. From the Behaviors panel, select the Add (+) button and then choose Set Text of Status Bar.

3. Enter your text in the Message text box.

4. Click OK when you're done.

Here's the browser compatibility chart for the Set Text of Status Bar behavior:

Set Text of Status Bar	Netscape 3.x	Internet Explorer 3.0	Internet Explorer 3.01
Macintosh	Okay	Fails without error	
Windows	Okay		Okay

Set Text of Text Field

The final Set Text behavior enables you to update any text or textarea field, dynamically. A text field must be present on the page for the behavior to be available. To change the displayed text of a text or textarea field, follow these steps:

1. From the Behaviors panel, select the Add (+) button and then choose Set Text ➪ Set Text of Text Field from the Add Action list. The Set Text of the Text Field dialog box is displayed, as shown in Figure 23-22.

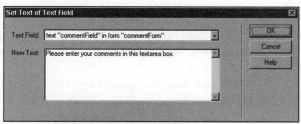

Figure 23-22: Dynamically update text/textarea form elements with the Set Text of Text Field behavior.

2. Choose the desired text field from the drop-down list.

3. Enter the new text and/or JavaScript in the New Text area.

4. Click OK when you're done.

Here's the browser compatibility chart for the Set Text of Text Field behavior:

Set Text of Text Field	Netscape 3.x	Internet Explorer 3.0	Internet Explorer 3.01
Macintosh	Okay	Fails without error	
Windows	Okay		Okay

Show-Hide Layers

One of the key features of Dynamic HTML layers is their capability to appear and disappear on command. The Show-Hide Layers action gives you easy control over the visibility attribute for all layers in the current Web page. In addition to explicitly showing or hiding layers, this action can also restore layers to the default visibility setting.

The Show-Hide Layers action typically reveals one layer while concealing another; however, you are not restricted to hiding or showing just one layer at a time. The action's parameter dialog box (see Figure 23-23) shows you a list of all the layers in the current Web page from which you can choose as many as you want to show or hide.

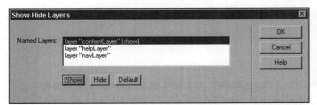

Figure 23-23: The Show-Hide Layers action can make any number of hidden layers visible, hide any number of visible layers, or both.

To use the Show-Hide Layers action, follow these steps:

1. Select the object to trigger the action.

2. From the Behaviors panel, select the Add (+) button and then choose Show-Hide Layer. The Show-Hide Layers parameter dialog box displays a list of the available layers in the current Web page.

3. To show a hidden layer, select the layer from the Named Layers list and then click the Show button.

4. To hide a shown layer, select its name from the list, and click the Hide button.

5. To restore a layer's default visibility value, select the layer and then click the Default button.

Here's the browser compatibility chart for the Show-Hide Layers behavior:

Show-Hide Layers	*Netscape 3.x*	*Internet Explorer 3.0*	*Internet Explorer 3.01*
Macintosh	Fails without error	Fails without error	
Windows	Fails without error		Fails without error

Swap Image and Swap Image Restore

Button rollovers are one of the most commonly used techniques in Web design today. In a typical button rollover, a user's pointer moves over one image, and the graphic appears to change in some way, seeming to glow or change color. Actually, the onMouseOver event triggers the almost instantaneous swapping of one image for another. Dreamweaver automates this difficult coding task with the Swap Image action and its companion, the Swap Image Restore action.

In recognition of how rollovers most commonly work in the real world, Dreamweaver makes it possible to combine Swap Image and Swap Image Restore in one easy operation — as well as to preload all the images. Moreover, you can use a link in one frame to trigger a rollover in another frame without having to tweak the code as you did in earlier Dreamweaver versions.

When the parameters form for the Swap Image action opens, it automatically loads all the images it finds in the current Web page (see Figure 23-24). You select the image you want to change—which could be the same image to which you are attaching the behavior—and specify the image file you want to replace the rolled-over image. You can swap more than one image with each Swap Image action. For example, if you want an entire submenu to change when a user rolls over a particular option, you can use a single Swap Image action to switch all the submenu button images.

Figure 23-24: The Swap Image action is used primarily for handling button rollovers.

If you choose not to enable the Restore Images onMouseOut option, which changes the image back to the original, you need to attach the Swap Image Restore action to another event. The Swap Image Restore action can be used only after a Swap Image action. No parameter dialog box exists for the Swap Image Restore action—just a dialog box confirming your selection.

Caution   If the swapped-in image has different dimensions than the image it replaces, the swapped-in image is resized to the height and width of the first image.

To use the Swap Image action, follow these steps:

1. Select the object to trigger the action.

2. From the Behaviors panel, select the Add (+) button and then choose Swap Image.

3. In the Swap Image parameter dialog box, choose an available image from the Named Images list of graphics on the current page.

4. In the Set Source To text box, enter the path to the image that you want to swap in. You can also select the Browse (Choose) button to locate the file. An asterisk appears at the end of the selected image name to indicate an alternate image has been selected.

5. To swap additional images using the same event, repeat Steps 3 and 4.

6. To preload all images involved in the Swap Image action when the page loads, make sure the Preload Images option is checked.

7. To cause the selected images to revert to their original source when the user mouses away from the selected object, make sure that the Restore Images onMouseOut option is selected.

8. Click OK when you're done.

Here's the browser compatibility chart for the Swap Image and Swap Image Restore behaviors:

Swap Image and Swap Image Restore	Netscape 3.x	Internet Explorer 3.0	Internet Explorer 3.01
Macintosh	Okay	Fails without error	
Windows	Okay		Fails without error

Timelines: Play Timeline, Stop Timeline, and Go to Timeline Frame

Any Dynamic HTML animation in Dreamweaver happens with timelines, but a timeline can't do anything without the actions written to control it. The three actions in the timeline set — Play Timeline, Stop Timeline, and Go to Timeline Frame — are all you need to set your Web page in motion.

Before the Timeline actions become available, at least one timeline must be on the current page. All three of these related actions are located in the Timeline submenu. Generally, when you are establishing controls for playing a timeline, you first attach the Go to Timeline Frame action to an event and then attach the Play Timeline action to the same event. By setting a specific frame before you enable the timeline to start, you ensure that the timeline always begins at the same point.

Cross-Reference For more detailed information on using timelines, see Chapter 22.

The Play Timeline and Stop Timeline actions have only one element on their parameter dialog box: a drop-down list box offering all timelines in the current page.

The Go to Timeline Frame action's parameter dialog box (see Figure 23-25), aside from enabling you to pick a timeline and enter a specific go-to frame, also gives you the option to loop the timeline a set number of times.

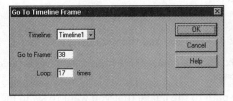

Figure 23-25: The Go To Timeline Frame parameter dialog box enables you to choose a go-to frame and designate the number of loops for the timeline.

Tip If you want the timeline to loop an infinite number of times, leave the Loop text box empty and turn on the Loop option in the Timelines panel.

To use the Go to Timeline Frame action, follow these steps:

1. Select the object to trigger the action.

2. From the Behaviors panel, select the Add (+) button and then choose Timeline ⇨ Go to Timeline Frame.

3. In the Go To Timeline Frame parameter dialog box, choose the timeline for which you want to set the start frame.

4. Enter the frame number in the Go to Frame text box.

5. If you want the timeline to loop a set number of times, enter a value in the Loop text box.

6. Click OK when you're done.

To use the Play Timeline action, follow these steps:

1. Select an object to trigger the action and then choose Timeline ⇨ Play Timeline from the Add (+) drop-down list in the Behaviors panel.

2. In the Play Timeline parameter dialog box, choose the timeline that you want to play. Click OK when you're done.

To use the Stop Timeline action, follow these steps:

1. Select an object to trigger the action and then choose Timeline ⇨ Stop Timeline from the Add (+) drop-down list in the Behaviors panel.

2. In the Stop Timeline parameter dialog box, choose the timeline that you want to stop. Click OK when you're done.

Note You can also choose All Timelines to stop every timeline on the current Web page from playing.

Here's the browser compatibility chart for the Timeline behaviors:

Timelines: Play Timeline, Stop Timeline, and Go to Timeline Frame	Netscape 3.x	Internet Explorer 3.0	Internet Explorer 3.01
Macintosh	Image source animation and invoking behaviors work, but layer animation fails without error	Fails without error	
Windows	Image source animation and invoking behaviors work, but layer animation fails without error		Fails without error

Validate Form

When you set up a form for user input, each field is established with a purpose. The name field, the e-mail address field, and the zip code field all have their own requirements for input. Unless you are using a CGI program specifically designed to check the user's input, form fields usually accept input of any type. Even if the CGI program can handle it, this server-side method ties up server time and is relatively slow. The Dreamweaver Validate Form action checks any text field's input and returns the form to the user if any of the entries are unacceptable. You can also use this action to designate any text field as a required field.

Validate Form can be used to check either single or multiple text fields in a form. Attaching a Validate Form action to a single text box alerts the user to any errors as this field is being filled out. To check multiple form fields, the Validate Form action must be attached to the form's <form> tag.

The Validate Form dialog box (see Figure 23-26) enables you to designate any text field as required, and you can evaluate its contents. You can require the input of a text field to be a number, an e-mail address (for instance, `jdoe@anywhere.com`), or a number within a range. The number range you specify can include positive whole numbers, negative numbers, or decimals.

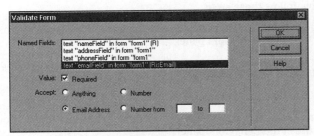

Figure 23-26: The Validate Form action checks your form's entries client-side, without CGI programming.

To use the Validate Form action, follow these steps:

1. Select the form object to trigger the action: a single text field or the `<form>` tag (use the Tag Selector) for multiple text fields.

2. From the Behaviors panel, select the Add (+) button and then choose Validate Form.

3. If validating an entire form, select a text field from the Named Fields list.

   If validating a single field, the selected form object is chosen for you and appears in the Named Fields list.

4. To make the field required, select the Value: Required checkbox.

5. To set the kind of input expected, choose from one of the following Accept options:

   - **Anything:** Accepts any input.

   - **Number:** Enables any sort of numeric input. You cannot mix text and numbers, however, as in a telephone number such as (212) 555-1212.

   - **Email Address:** Looks for an e-mail address with the @ sign. (Note that this is not a foolproof e-mail address check, as it will validate illegal addresses such as human@somewhere, @somewhere.com, human@somewhere.overtherainbow, etc.)

   - **Number from:** Enables you to enter two numbers, one in each text box, to define the number range.

6. Click OK when you're done.

Here's the browser compatibility chart for the Validate Form behavior:

Validate Form	*Netscape 3.x*	*Internet Explorer 3.0*	*Internet Explorer 3.01*
Macintosh	Okay	Fails without error	
Windows	Okay		Okay

Installing, Managing, and Modifying Behaviors

The standard behaviors that come with Dreamweaver are indeed impressive, but they're really just the beginning. Because existing behaviors can be modified and new ones created from scratch, you can continue to add behaviors as you need them.

To install a new Dreamweaver behavior:

1. Locate the behavior, which must be packaged as an MXP extension file; for example: alignLayer.mxp, cleanupPage.mxp, and so on.

The CD-ROM that comes with this book contains several useful MXP behavior extension files.

In addition, you can find a large selection of MXP extension files on the Dreamweaver Exchange site, which you can reach by choosing Help ⇨ Dreamweaver Exchange.

2. To install the extension in Dreamweaver, either double-click the MXP extension file, or choose Help ⇨ Manage Extensions to open the Extension Manager (as shown in Figure 23-27), and choose File ⇨ Install Extension to select the file. Note that some extensions remain inaccessible until you've quit and restarted Dreamweaver; in most cases, you will be prompted to do so.

Depending on your browser, you might be given the choice of installing a Dreamweaver Exchange extension file directly from the Exchange site or to save it first to disk and install it from there. If you choose to install the extension file directly from the Exchange site, the Extension Manager will handle the installation automatically. If you choose to save the extension file to disk, a good place to save it is the Downloaded Extensions folder within your Dreamweaver MX folder.

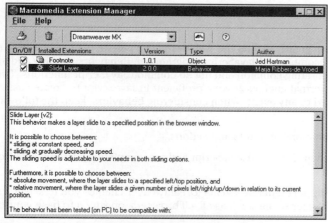

Figure 23-27: You use the Extension Manager to install and remove MXP extension files from Dreamweaver.

Altering the parameters of a behavior

You can alter any of the attributes for your inserted behaviors at any time. To modify a behavior you have already attached, follow these steps:

1. Open the Behaviors panel.

2. Select the object in the Document window or the tag in the Tag Selector to which your behavior is attached.

3. Double-click the action that you want to alter. The appropriate dialog box opens, with the previously selected parameters.

4. Make any modifications to the existing settings for the action.

5. Click OK when you are finished.

Sequencing behaviors

When you have more than one action attached to a particular event, the order of the actions is often important. For example, you should generally implement the Go to Timeline Frame action ahead of the Play Timeline action to make sure the timeline is playing from the correct frame. To specify the sequence in which Dreamweaver triggers the actions, reposition them as necessary in the Actions column. To do this, simply select an action and then use the up and down arrow buttons (as shown in Figure 23-1) to reposition it in the list.

Deleting behaviors

To remove a behavior from a list of behaviors attached to a particular event, simply highlight the behavior and click the Remove (–) button.

Summary

Dreamweaver behaviors can greatly extend the Web designer's palette of possibilities — even if the Web designer is an accomplished JavaScript programmer. Behaviors simplify and automate the process of incorporating common and not so common JavaScript functions. The versatility of the behavior format enables anyone proficient in JavaScript to create custom actions that can be attached to any event. When considering behaviors, keep the following points in mind:

✦ Behaviors are combinations of events and actions.

✦ Behaviors are written in HTML and JavaScript and are completely customizable from within Dreamweaver.

✦ Different browsers support different events. Dreamweaver enables you to select a specific browser or a browser range, such as all 4.0 browsers, on which to base your event choice.

✦ Dreamweaver includes 27 standard actions. Some actions are not available unless a particular object is included on the current page.

In the next chapter, you learn how to integrate Fireworks MX with Dreamweaver MX — an unbeatable combo!

✦   ✦   ✦

Adding Multimedia Elements

Fireworks Integration

Imagine demonstrating a newly completed Web site to a client who *didn't* ask for an image to be a little bigger, or the text on a button to be reworded, or the colors for the background to be revised. In the real world, Web sites — particularly the images — are constantly being tweaked and modified. This fact of Web life explains why Fireworks, Macromedia's premier Web graphics tool, is so popular. One of Fireworks' main claims to fame is that everything is editable all the time. If that were all that Fireworks did, the program would have already earned a place on every Web designer's shelf just for its sheer expediency. Fireworks is far more capable a tool, however, and that power can be tapped directly from within Dreamweaver.

Macromedia's Dreamweaver MX and Fireworks MX are tightly integrated products. You can optimize your images — reduce the file size, crop the graphic, make colors transparent — within Dreamweaver using the Fireworks interface. Moreover, you can edit your image in any fashion in Fireworks and, with one click of the Done button, automatically export the graphic with its updated settings. Perhaps most important of all, Dreamweaver can control Fireworks — creating graphics on-the-fly — and then insert the results in Dreamweaver.

A key Fireworks feature is the capability to output HTML and JavaScript for easy creation of rollovers, sliced images, and image maps with behaviors. With Fireworks, you can specify Dreamweaver-style code, so that all your Web pages are consistent. After Fireworks generates the HTML, Dreamweaver's Insert Fireworks HTML object makes code insertion effortless. Dreamweaver recognizes images — whether whole or sliced — as coming from Fireworks, and displays a special Property inspector.

Web pages and Web graphics are closely tied to each other. With the tight integration between Dreamweaver MX and Fireworks MX, the Web designer's world is moving toward a single design environment.

Easy Graphics Modification

It's not uncommon for graphics to need some alteration before they fully integrate into a Web design. In fact, I'd say it's far more the rule than the exception. The traditional workflow generally goes like this:

1. Create the image in one or more graphics-editing programs.

2. Place the new graphic on a Web page via your Web-authoring tool.

3. Note where the problems lie—perhaps the image is too big or too small, maybe the drop shadow doesn't blend into the background properly, or maybe the whole image needs to be flipped.

4. Reopen the graphics program, make the modifications, and save the file again.

5. Return to the Web page layout to view the results.

6. Repeat Steps 3 through 5 *ad infinitum* until you get it right.

Although you're still using two different programs, integrating Dreamweaver and Fireworks enables you to open a Fireworks window from within the Dreamweaver screen. You can make your alterations with the Web page visible in the background. I've found that this small advantage cuts my trial-and-error to a bare minimum and streamlines my workflow.

If you're not familiar with Fireworks, you're missing an extremely powerful graphics program made for the Web. Fireworks combines the best of both vector and bitmap technologies and was one of the first graphics programs to use PNG as its native format. Exceptional export capabilities are available in Fireworks with which images can be optimized for file size, color, and scale. Moreover, Fireworks is terrific at generating GIF animations, rollovers, image maps, and sliced images.

With Dreamweaver MX and Fireworks MX, you have two ways to alter your inserted graphics: the Optimize Image in Fireworks command, and the Edit button in the Image Property inspector.

Note   The full integration described in this chapter requires that Fireworks MX be installed *after* Dreamweaver MX. Certain features, such as the Optimize Image in Fireworks command, work with Fireworks 2 and later; but any others requiring direct communication between the two programs work only with Fireworks MX.

Optimizing an image in Fireworks

Although you can design the most beautiful, compelling image possible in your graphics program, if it's intended for the Internet, you need to view it in a Web page. Not only must the graphic work in the context of the entire page, but you also have to take the file size of the Web graphic into account. All these factors mean that most, if not all, images need to undergo some degree of modification once they're included in a Web page. Dreamweaver's Optimize Image in Fireworks command facilitates this modification by opening the Export module of Fireworks right from within Dreamweaver, as shown in Figure 24-1.

The Export module consists of three tabbed panels: Options, File, and Animation. Although a complete description of all its features is beyond the scope of this book, here's a breakdown of the major uses of each area:

✦ **Options:** The Options panel is primarily used to try different export options and preview them. You can switch file formats from GIF to JPEG (or animated GIF or PNG) as well as alter the palette, color depth, loss (quality), and dithering. Transparency for GIF and PNG images is set in the Options panel. Fireworks also has an Optimize to Size wizard that enables you to target a particular file size for your graphic.

✦ **File:** An image's dimensions are defined in the File panel. Images can be rescaled by a selected percentage or pixel size. Moreover, you can crop your image either numerically (by defining the export area) or visually (with the Cropping tool).

✦ **Animation:** Frame-by-frame control for animated GIFs is available on the Animation panel. Each frame's delay (how long it is onscreen) can be defined independently, and the entire animation can be set to either play once or loop a user-determined number of times.

Note

If you crop or rescale an inserted image in Fireworks, you need to update its height and width in Dreamweaver. The easiest way to accomplish this is to select the Reset Size button in the image's Property inspector.

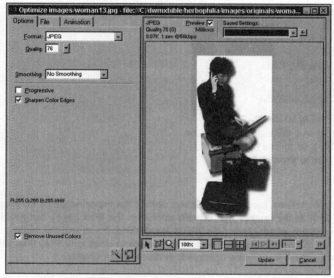

Figure 24-1: With Fireworks MX installed, you can optimize your images from within Dreamweaver.

Fireworks saves its source files in an expanded PNG format to maintain full editability of the images. Graphics for the Web must be exported from Fireworks in GIF, JPEG, or standard PNG format. Dreamweaver's Optimize Image in Fireworks command can modify either the source file or the exported file. In most situations, better results are achieved from using the source file, especially when optimizing includes rescaling or resampling. Some situations, however, require that you leave the source file as is and modify only the exported files. Suppose, for example, that one source file is used to generate several different export files, each with different backgrounds (or *canvases*, as they are called in Fireworks). In that case, you'd be better off modifying the specific exported file, rather than the general source image.

Dreamweaver enables you to choose which type of image you'd like to modify. When you first execute the Optimize Image in Fireworks or the Edit Image command, a Find Source dialog box (see Figure 24-2) appears. If you want to locate and use the source file, choose Yes; to use the exported image that is inserted in Dreamweaver, select No. If you opt for the source file — and the image was created in Fireworks MX — Dreamweaver reads the Design Note associated with the image to find the location of the source file and open it. If the image was created with an earlier version of Fireworks or the image has been moved, Dreamweaver asks you to locate the file with a standard Open File dialog box. By setting the Fireworks Source Files option, you can always open the same type of file: source or exported. Should you change your mind about how you'd like to work, open Fireworks and select Edit ➪ Preferences; then choose the desired option from the Launch and Edit panel.

Note There's one case when Fireworks does not follow your Launch and Edit preferences: If the image chosen is a sliced image, Fireworks always optimizes the exported file rather than the source, regardless of your settings.

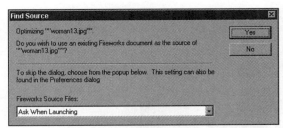

Figure 24-2: Set the Find Source dialog box to use the source graphics image (PNG), or to use the exported image (GIF, JPEG, or PNG), or to prompt for each optimization.

Tip Due to server capacity limitations, most Web designers upload the exported GIF/JPEG image files to their server (such as the images that actually appear in the Web page), but not the source PNG image files from which these GIFs/JPEGs are derived. If you use this approach, you can take advantage of Dreamweaver MX's Cloaking feature to cloak your PNG files, thus automatically preventing them from being uploaded, as discussed in Chapter 5.

To use the Optimize Image in Fireworks command, follow these steps:

1. Select the image you'd like to modify in Dreamweaver.

Note The current page must have been saved at least once before the Optimize Image in Fireworks command can be run. The current state of the page doesn't have to have been saved, but a valid file must exist for the command to work properly. If you haven't saved the file, Dreamweaver alerts you to this fact when you call the command.

2. Choose Commands ➪ Optimize Image in Fireworks.

Tip You can also invoke the Optimize Image in Fireworks command from the context menu — just right-click (Control+click) on the image and then choose Optimize in Fireworks.

3. If your Fireworks Preferences are set to ask whether a source file should be used in editing, and if you have not yet specified this source file, the Find Source dialog box opens. Choose Yes to use the PNG format source file; choose No to work with the exported file. The Optimize Images dialog box appears.

4. Make whatever modifications are desired from the Options, File, or Animation tabs of the Optimize Images dialog box.

5. When you're finished, select the Update button.

Note   If you're working with a Fireworks source file, the changes are saved to both your source file and exported file; otherwise, only the exported file is altered.

Editing an image in Fireworks

Optimizing an image is great when all you need to do is tweak the file size or rescale the image. Other images require more detailed modification — such as when a client requests that the wording or order of a series of navigational buttons be changed. Dreamweaver enables you to specify Fireworks as your graphics editor; and if you've done so, you can take advantage of Fireworks' capability to keep every element of your graphic always editable. Believe me, this is a major advantage.

In Dreamweaver, external editors can be set for any file format; you can even assign more than one editor to a file type. When installing the Dreamweaver/Fireworks Studio, Fireworks is preset as the primary external editor for GIF, JPEG, and PNG files. If Fireworks is installed outside of the Studio setup, the external editor assignment is handled through Dreamweaver Preferences. To assign Fireworks to an existing file type, follow these steps:

1. Choose Edit ➪ Preferences to open the Preferences dialog box.

2. Select the File Types / Editors category.

3. Select the file type (GIF, JPEG, or PNG) from the Extensions list as shown in Figure 24-3.

4. Choose the Add (+) button above the Editors list. The Select External Editor dialog box opens.

5. Locate the editor application and click Open when you're ready.

6. Click the Make Primary button while your desired editor is highlighted in the Editors list.

Exploring Fireworks Source and Export Files

The separate source file is an important concept in Fireworks, and its use is strongly advised. Generally, when working in Fireworks, you have a minimum of two files for every image output to the Web: your source file and your exported Web image. Whenever you make major alterations, it's best to make them to the source file and then update the export files. Not only is this an easier method of working, you also get a better image.

Source files are always Fireworks-style PNG files. Fireworks-style PNG files differ slightly from regular PNG format because they include additional information, such as paths and effects used that can be read only by Fireworks. The exported file is usually in GIF or JPEG format, although it could be in standard PNG format. Many Web designers keep their source files in a separate folder from their exported Web images so the two don't get confused. This source-and-export file combination also prevents you from inadvertently re-editing a lossy compressed file such as a JPEG image and reapplying the compression (thus exacerbating the lossiness).

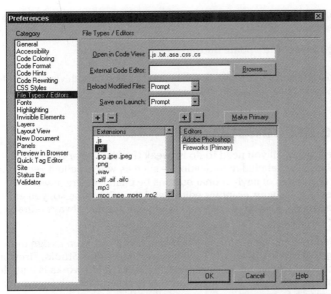

Figure 24-3: Define Fireworks as your external editor for GIF, JPEG, and PNG files to enable the back-and-forth interaction between Dreamweaver and Fireworks.

Now, whenever you want to edit a graphic, select the image and click the Edit button in the Property inspector. (You can also right-click [Control+click] the image and select Edit with Fireworks to start editing it.) Fireworks starts up, if it's not already open. As with the Optimize Image in Fireworks command, if the inserted image is a GIF or a JPEG and not a PNG, Fireworks asks if you'd like to work with a separate source file, if that option in Fireworks Preferences is set. If so, Fireworks automatically loads the source file.

When the image opens in Fireworks, the graphics window indicates that the image is being edited from Dreamweaver in Fireworks, as shown in Figure 24-4. In the same title bar, a Done button is available for completing the operation after you've made your alterations to your file in Fireworks. Alternatively, you can choose File ➪ Update or use the keyboard shortcut Ctrl+S (Command+S). If you're working with a Fireworks source file (PNG), both the source file and the exported file are updated and saved.

Replacing an image placeholder using Fireworks

As discussed in Chapter 8, when designing a page, you can defer the task of inserting final artwork by using image placeholders instead of actual images; then, at the appropriate time, you can replace these image placeholders with the actual images. Working this way can facilitate smooth, trouble-free interaction between your Web site design and graphics departments.

You can easily use Fireworks to replace your Dreamweaver image placeholders; such as to create the actual images. Here's how:

1. In Dreamweaver, open the page that contains the image placeholder you want to replace.

2. Select the image placeholder and click the Property inspector Create button. Or simply Ctrl-double-click (Command-double-click) the image placeholder.

   Fireworks launches and creates a new, blank PNG file whose canvas size is set to the width/height of the placeholder image, as shown in Figure 24-5.

3. In Fireworks, create the desired image.

4. When you are finished, click Done.

   Fireworks first prompts you to save the image as a PNG (source) file. It then prompts you to export the file in a suitable Web format, GIF or JPEG. Dreamweaver automatically replaces the selected image placeholder with this exported image.

After you've used this procedure to replace a Dreamweaver image placeholder, you can easily edit the image in Fireworks by using the techniques described in the previous section of this chapter (the Property inspector Edit button and the Edit with Fireworks command).

Figure 24-4: Fireworks graphically depicts the source of the current image being edited.

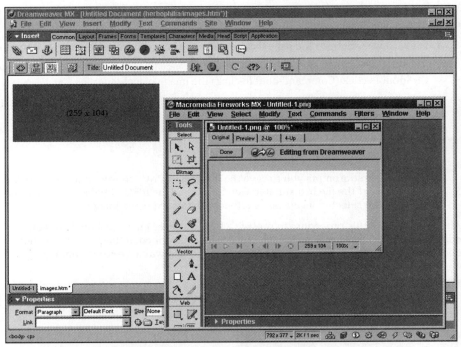

Figure 24-5: You can easily use Fireworks to replace your Dreamweaver image placeholders with actual images.

Inserting Rollovers

The rollover is a fairly common, but effective Web technique to indicate interactivity. Named after the user action of rolling the mouse pointer over the graphic, this technique uses from two to four different images per button. With Fireworks, you can both create the graphics and output the necessary HTML and JavaScript code from the same program. Moreover, Fireworks adds some sophisticated twists to the standard "on/off" rollovers to enable you to easily enhance your Web page.

Rollovers created in Fireworks can be inserted into Dreamweaver through several methods. First, you can use Fireworks to build the images, and then you just export them and attach the behaviors in Dreamweaver. This technique works well for graphics going into layers or images with other attached behaviors. The second method of integrating Fireworks-created rollovers involves transferring the actual code generated by Fireworks into Dreamweaver — a procedure that can be handled with one command: Insert Fireworks HTML.

Using Dreamweaver's behaviors

With its full-spectrum editability, Fireworks excels at building consistent rollover graphics simply. The different possible states of an image in a rollover — up, over, down, and over while down — are handled in Fireworks as separate frames. As with an animated GIF, each frame has the same dimensions, but the content is slightly altered to indicate the separate user actions. For example, Figure 24-6 shows the different frame states of a rollover button, side-by-side.

Image	button	button	button	button
Viewer's pointer	up	over	down	over while down
Fireworks frame	1	2	3	4

Figure 24-6: A Fireworks-created rollover can be made of four separate frames.

Note

Many Web designers use just the initial two states—up and over—in their rollover buttons. The third state, down, takes place when the user clicks the button, and it is useful if you want to indicate that moment to the user. The down state also indicates which button has been selected (which is "down") when a new page appears, but the same navigation bar is used, notably with frames. The fourth state, over while down, is called when the previously selected button is rolled over by the user's pointer.

To create a rollover by attaching Dreamweaver behaviors to Fireworks-created graphics, follow these steps:

1. Create your graphics in Fireworks, using a different frame for each rollover state.

Caution

You cannot use Fireworks' Edit ➪ Insert ➪ New Button command to build your button for this technique because the separate states are not stored as frames.

2. In Fireworks, choose File ➪ Export. The Export dialog box opens (see Figure 24-7).

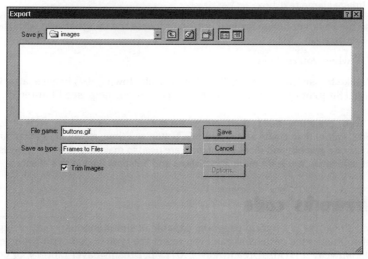

Figure 24-7: From Fireworks, you can export each frame as a separate file to be used in Dreamweaver rollovers.

3. Type a new name in the File Name text box, if desired.

   In this operation, the File Name is used as a base name by Fireworks to identify multiple images exported from a single file. When exporting frames, the default settings append _f*n*, where *n* is the number of the frame. Frame numbers 1–9 are listed with a leading zero (for example, MainButton_f01).

4. In the Save As Type list box, select Frames to Files.

5. If desired, select the Trim Images option.

   When Trim Images is on, Fireworks automatically crops the exported images to fit the objects on each frame. This procedure makes for smaller, more flexible image files.

I recommend that, in most situations, you opt to trim your images when exporting frames as files. But here's an exception to watch out for: If a button in one frame has a drop shadow, its trimmed size will be slightly larger than the non-drop–shadow buttons; swapping it will force it to fit the smaller button's image space, which will cause a jagged, amateurish swap display.

6. Select the Save button to store your frames as separate files.

You can attach the rollover behaviors to your images in several ways in Dreamweaver. The following technique uses Dreamweaver's Rollover object.

7. From the Common category of the Insert bar, choose the Rollover Image object.

8. In the Insert Rollover Image dialog box, choose the Original Image Browse button to locate the image stored with the first frame designation, _f01.

9. If desired, give your image a unique name different from the one automatically assigned in the Image Name text box.

10. Choose the Rollover Image Browse button to locate the image stored with the second frame designation, _f02.

11. Click OK when you're done.

12. If you'd like to use the down (_f03) and over while down (_f04) images, attach additional Swap Image behaviors to the image files; for help, see Chapter 23.

Many Web designers build their entire navigation bar—complete with rollovers—in Fireworks. Rather than create and export one button at a time, all the navigation buttons are created as one graphic, and slices or hotspots are used to make the different objects or areas interact differently. You learn more about slices and hotspots later in this chapter.

Using Fireworks' code

In some ways, Fireworks is a hybrid program, capable of simultaneously outputting terrific graphics and sophisticated code. You can even select the type of code you want generated in Fireworks: Dreamweaver HTML, Dreamweaver XHTML, Dreamweaver Library, or code compatible with other programs such as GoLive and FrontPage. You'll also find a more general Generic code option. All these options can be chosen during the Export procedure.

For rollovers, Fireworks generally outputs to two different sections of the HTML document, the <head> and the <body>; only the FrontPage style keeps all the code together. The <head> section contains the JavaScript code for activating the rollovers and preloading the images; <body> contains the HTML references to the images themselves, their links, and the event triggers (onClick or onMouseOver) used.

The general procedure is to first create your graphics in Fireworks and then export them, simultaneously generating a page of code. Now, the just-generated Fireworks HTML page can be incorporated in Dreamweaver. Dreamweaver includes two slick methods for including your Fireworks-output code and images. The Insert Fireworks HTML object places the code — and the linked images — right at your current cursor position. You also have the option to export your Fireworks HTML directly to the clipboard and paste it, verbatim, into Dreamweaver.

Caution

If you paste the Fireworks rollover code manually into a Dreamweaver HTML document, take care to merge the existing <head> and <body> code with the Fireworks rollover code. And remember: An HTML document can only have one <head> and one <body> tag!

Just as an image requires a link to create a rollover in Dreamweaver, a Fireworks image needs to be designated as either a *slice* or a *hotspot*. The Fireworks program describes slices and hotspots as being part of the graphic's Web layer. The Web layer can be hidden or locked, but not deleted. Figure 24-8 shows the same button with both a slice and a hotspot attached.

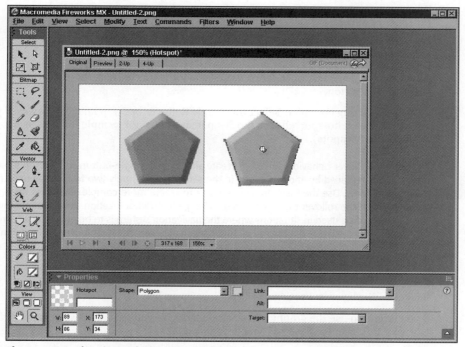

Figure 24-8: The Fireworks image on the left uses a slice object, whereas the image on the right uses a polygon hotspot.

Slices are rectangular areas that permit different parts of the same graphic to be saved as separate formats — the entire graphic is formatted as an HTML table. Each slice can also be given its own URL and have one or more behaviors attached to it.

A Fireworks *hotspot* is an area defined for an image map. Hotspots can be rectangular, elliptical, or polygonal — just like those created by Dreamweaver with the Image Map tools. Because Fireworks is an object-oriented graphics program, any selected image (or part of an image) can be automatically converted to a hotspot. Like slices, hotspots can have both URLs and behaviors assigned to them.

Note   In addition to the technique outlined in the text that follows, you can also use Fireworks' Button Editor (available by choosing Insert ⇨ New Button) to create your rollover images and behaviors.

To include Fireworks-generated code in your Dreamweaver document, follow these steps in Fireworks:

1. Create your graphics in Fireworks, placing the image for each interactive rollover state — up, over, down (optional), and over while down (optional) — in its own frame.

2. With the object in its first frame selected, create your desired hotspot(s) or slice(s).

    To do so automatically, choose Edit ⇨ Insert ⇨ Hotspot or Edit ⇨ Insert ⇨ Slice. To do so manually, use the Hotspot or Slice tools in the Fireworks toolbox.

3. Where appropriate, use the Fireworks' Property inspector to assign URLs to your hotspots or slices.

4. Click the target symbol displayed in the center of the hotspot or slice to display a menu of available behaviors.

    Alternatively, you could open Fireworks' Behavior inspector and choose the Add Behavior (+) button.

5. If you are working on a slice, select the Simple Rollover or Swap Image behavior. If you are working on a hotspot, choose the Swap Image behavior (Simple Rollover is not available for hotspots).

Tip   The Simple Rollover behavior is used to create single- or multiple-button rollovers in which one image is replaced by another image in the same location; only two frames are used for a Simple Rollover. Use the Swap Image behavior to create more complex rollovers, such as those in which the rollover triggers an image change in another location. A third alternative, Nav Bar, should be used in situations where the navigation system is to be placed in a frameset; the Nav Bar behavior can display all four states (up, over, down, and over while down).

6. Export the object by choosing File ⇨ Export to open the Export dialog box.

7. Enter a name in the File Name text box and make sure that the choice HTML and Images is displayed in the Save As Type drop-down list.

    If you intend to use the graphics in several places on your site, choose Dreamweaver Library (.lbi) from the Save As Type drop-down list.

8. To change the type of HTML/XHTML code generated, choose the Options button and make a selection from the Style drop-down list.

    Dreamweaver HTML code is the default style; other options include GoLive, FrontPage, and Generic HTML and XHTML.

9. Choose the location in which to store your HTML code by navigating to the desired folder. Note that Dreamweaver Library code must be saved in a site's Library folder.

   If you prefer to not save your HTML, choose Copy to Clipboard from the HTML drop-down list.

10. To save your graphics in a separate folder, select the Put Images in Subfolder option.

Caution

Fireworks defaults to placing the graphics in a subfolder called Images, even if one does not exist. To specify a different folder, choose the Browse button.

11. Click Save when you're done.

When Fireworks completes the exporting, you have one HTML file (unless you've chosen the Copy to Clipboard option) and multiple image files, one for each slice and frame. Now you're ready to integrate these images and code into your Dreamweaver page. Which method you use depends on the HTML style you selected when the graphics were exported from Fireworks:

✦ If you chose Dreamweaver HTML, use the Insert Fireworks HTML object.

✦ If you chose Dreamweaver Library, open the Library palette in Dreamweaver and insert the corresponding Library item.

✦ If you chose Copy to Clipboard, position your cursor where you'd like the graphics to appear and select Edit ➪ Paste or Ctrl+V (Command+V).

Both the Library and Clipboard methods are one-step, self-explanatory techniques — and the Insert Fireworks HTML is only a bit more complex. To insert the Fireworks code and images into your Dreamweaver page using the Insert Fireworks HTML object, follow these steps:

1. Make sure that you've exported your graphics and HTML from Fireworks with the Dreamweaver HTML style selected.

2. Select the Fireworks HTML object from the Common panel of the Insert bar or choose Insert ➪ Interactive Media ➪ Fireworks HTML. The Insert Fireworks HTML dialog box, shown in Figure 24-9, appears.

Figure 24-9: Import Fireworks code directly into Dreamweaver with the Insert Fireworks HTML object.

3. If you want to delete the Fireworks-generated HTML file after the code is inserted, select the Delete File After Insertion option. This can help keep your site folder tidy.

4. Enter the path to the Fireworks HTML file or select the Browse button to locate the file.

5. Click OK when you're done. Dreamweaver inserts the Fireworks HTML and graphics at the current cursor location.

Note

If you're a hands-on Web designer, you can also use the Code inspector to copy and paste the JavaScript and HTML code. If you do, you can find helpful comments in the Fireworks-generated HTML file such as "Begin copying here" and "Stop copying here."

All the methods for inserting Fireworks HTML work with images with either hotspots or sliced objects (or both), with or without behaviors attached.

Modifying sliced images

Placing sliced images on your Web page couldn't be simpler — thanks to the Insert Fireworks HTML command. However, like standard non-sliced graphics, sliced images often need to be modified. One technique that many designers use is to create a framing graphic that contains HTML text; in Fireworks, a sliced area designated as a text slice can hold any HTML content. Often, text has to be modified. If it is in a framing graphic, the image may need to be changed so that the table cells remain the same size as in the original design. This prevents the separate slices from becoming apparent.

In Dreamweaver, sliced images from Fireworks are recognized as a Fireworks Table and may be modified through a dedicated Property inspector, as shown in Figure 24-10. The Fireworks Table Property inspector displays the PNG source file and an Edit button for sending the entire table back to Fireworks for alterations. As with non-sliced graphics, select Done from the document title bar in Fireworks when your modifications are complete to update the source and exported files. The newly exported images are then reloaded into Dreamweaver.

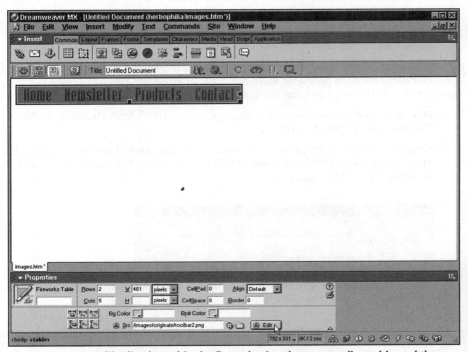

Figure 24-10: Modify sliced graphics by first selecting the surrounding table and then choosing Edit from the Fireworks Table Property inspector.

Caution

Although Fireworks attempts to honor any changes you may have made to the HTML table in Dreamweaver, certain changes may cause Fireworks to modify your Dreamweaver table code. If, for example, you add or remove cells from the table in Dreamweaver, when you go to edit the table in Fireworks, Fireworks displays an alert that it will replace the table in Dreamweaver. To avoid the risk of having your original table modified in an undesired way by Fireworks, simply click Done right away (before making any changes) in Fireworks when you get such an alert, to leave the original table as-is in Dreamweaver. At this point, make a backup of the entire current page, then go ahead and try out your Fireworks table edit.

Editing Fireworks-Created Pop-Up Menus

As discussed in Chapter 23, you can use the Dreamweaver Show Pop-Up Menu and Hide Pop-Up Menu behaviors to create a pop-up menu that is activated by mousing over an entire image or an image hotspot/slice. You can create the same type of pop-up menu in Fireworks. Conveniently, if you are working in Dreamweaver and encounter a Fireworks-created pop-up menu that you need to edit, you can do so right within Dreamweaver, as follows:

1. In Dreamweaver, select the image, hotspot, or slice with which the pop-up menu is associated.

2. In the Behaviors panel, double-click the Show Pop-Up Menu behavior to open the Show Pop-Up Menu dialog box.

3. Make your desired changes to the pop-up menu, as shown in Figure 24-11.

4. When you are finished, click OK.

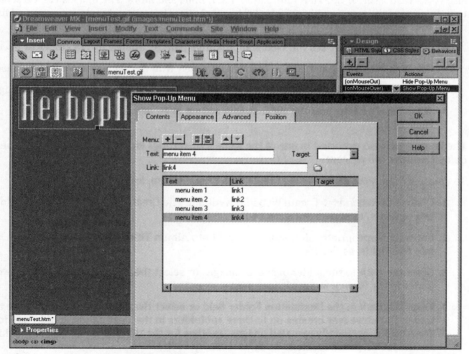

Figure 24-11: You can easily edit pop-up menus created in Dreamweaver or in Fireworks.

Controlling Fireworks with Dreamweaver

Dreamweaver and Fireworks integration extends deeper than just the simplified insertion of code and graphics. Dreamweaver can communicate directly with Fireworks, driving it to execute commands and return custom-generated graphics. This facility enables Web designers to build their Web page images based on the existing content. This interprogram communication promises to streamline the work of the Webmaster like never before—and that promise is already beginning to be fulfilled with existing Dreamweaver commands.

Web photo album

Online catalogs and other sites often depend on imagery to sell their products. Full-scale product shots can be large and time-consuming to download, so it's not uncommon for Web designers to display a thumbnail of the images instead. If the viewer wants to see more detail, clicking the thumbnail loads the full-size image. Although it's not difficult to save a scaled-down version of an image in a graphics program and link the two in a Web layout program, creating page after page of such images is an overwhelming chore. The Dreamweaver/Fireworks interoperability offers a way to automate this tedious task.

The Dreamweaver Create Web Photo Album command examines any user-specified folder of images and then uses Fireworks to scale the graphics to a set size. When the scaling is completed, the thumbnail graphics are brought into a Dreamweaver table, complete with links to a series of pages with the full-size images. Create Web Photo Album is an excellent example of the potential that Dreamweaver and Fireworks intercommunication offers.

The Create Web Photo Album command works with a folder of images in any format that Fireworks reads: GIF, JPEG, TIFF, Photoshop, PICT, BMP, and more. The images can be scaled to fit in a range of sizes, from 36×36 to 200×200 pixels. These thumbnails are exported in one of four formats:

✦ **GIF WebSnap 128:** Uses the WebSnap Adaptive palette, limited to 128 colors or fewer.

✦ **GIF WebSnap 256:** Same as the preceding format, with as many as 256 colors available.

✦ **JPEG Better Quality:** Sets the JPEG quality setting at 80 percent, with no smoothing.

✦ **JPEG Smaller File:** Sets the JPEG quality setting at 60 percent, with a smoothing value of 2.

The images are also exported in one of the same four settings at a user-selected scale; the default scale is 100 percent.

To create a thumbnail gallery using Create Web Photo Album, follow these steps:

1. Choose Commands ⇨ Create Web Photo Album. The Create Web Photo Album dialog box appears, as shown in Figure 24-12.

2. Enter the appropriate information in the Photo Album Title, Subheading Info, and Other Info text fields, as desired.

3. Enter the path to the folder of source images or select the Browse button to locate the folder in the Source Images Folder field.

4. Enter the path in the Destination Folder field or select the Browse button to locate the folder. Dreamweaver creates up to three subfolders in the Destination Folder: one for the original, optionally rescaled images; another for the thumbnail images; and a third for the HTML pages created.

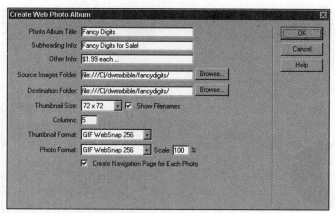

Figure 24-12: Use the Create Web Photo Album command to create a thumbnail gallery page, linked to full-size originals.

5. Select the desired thumbnail size from the drop-down list with the following options: 36 × 36, 72 × 72, 100 × 100, 144 × 144, and 200 × 200.

6. Select the Show Filenames option if you want the filename to appear below the image.

7. Choose the number of columns for the table.

8. Select the export settings for the thumbnail images from the Thumbnail Format option list.

9. Select the export settings for the linked large-sized images from the Photo Format option list.

10. Choose the size of the linked large-sized images in the Scale field. If you don't want to rescale the images, leave the setting at its default value of 100%.

11. Select the Create Navigation Page for Each Photo option, if desired. Each photo's navigation page includes links to the Next and Previous images as well as the Home (main thumbnail) page, as shown in Figure 24-13.

12. Click OK when you're done.

If not open, Fireworks starts and begins processing the images. When all the images are created and exported, Fireworks returns control to Dreamweaver. Dreamweaver then creates a single HTML page with the title, subheading, and other information at the top, followed by a borderless table. As shown in Figure 24-14, each image is rescaled proportionately to fit within the limits set in the dialog box.

Building Dreamweaver/Fireworks extensions

To make communication between Dreamweaver and Fireworks viable, two conditions had to be met. First, Fireworks had to be scriptable. Second, a link between the two programs needed to be forged. The Dreamweaver/Fireworks combination meets both criteria — and then some.

Figure 24-13: You can add simple, clear navigation options to your Web Photo Album.

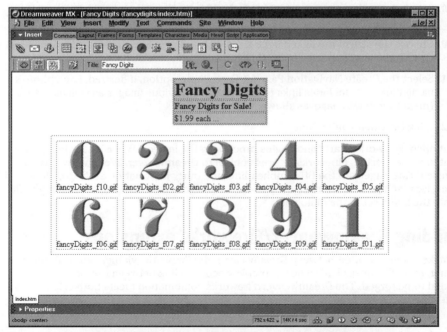

Figure 24-14: Here is the thumbnail gallery that Dreamweaver (with Fireworks' help) automatically created from the dialog box settings in Figure 24-12.

Custom Graphic Makers: Converting Text and Bullets to Images

Excited by the potential of Dreamweaver and Fireworks communication, I built two custom extensions, originally called StyleBuilder and BulletBuilder. Macromedia took these extensions, enhanced them, and then released them as two-thirds of the InstaGraphics Extensions. StyleBuilder — now called Convert Text to Image — enables you to convert any standard text in your Dreamweaver Web page to a graphic. The command converts all text in a standard HTML tag (such as <h1> or <b>), any custom XML tag, or any selection. The graphics are based on Fireworks styles displayed in a small swatch in the Convert Text to Image dialog box; you can specify a font on your system as well as a text size to be used. Fireworks styles can be updated at any time, and the swatch set re-created on-the-fly in Fireworks.

Convert Bullets to Images (BulletBuilder) is similar, but instead of changing text to graphics, this command converts the bullets of an unordered list to different graphic shapes. Choose from ten different shapes including diamonds, stars, starbursts, and four different triangles. The chosen shape is rendered in any available Fireworks style at a user-selected size. You have the option to convert the current bulleted list or all such lists on the page.

Both commands can be found online at the Dreamweaver Exchange as part of the InstaGraphics Extensions — be sure to get the Dreamweaver MX compatible version!

As with Dreamweaver, almost every operation is under command control in Fireworks. This is most apparent when using either program's History palette. If your action appears as a repeatable item in the History palette, a corresponding JavaScript function controls it. Fireworks' wealth of JavaScript functions also serves to expose its control to Dreamweaver — and the first condition for interoperability is handled. To create a strong link between programs, Dreamweaver engineers expanded on the Fireworks API used in the Optimize Image in Fireworks command, where Dreamweaver actually launches a streamlined version of Fireworks. This operation is controlled by a C-level extension called FWLaunch. Here's a step-by-step description of how Dreamweaver typically is used to communicate with Fireworks:

1. The user selects a command in Dreamweaver.

2. Dreamweaver opens a dialog box.

3. After the user has filled in the dialog box and clicked OK, the command begins to execute.

4. All user-supplied parameters are read and used to create a JavaScript scriptlet or function, which serves as instructions for Fireworks.

5. If used, the scriptlet is stored on the disk.

6. Fireworks is launched with a command to run the Dreamweaver-created scriptlet or function.

7. Fireworks processes the scriptlet or function while Dreamweaver tracks its progress via a cookie on the user's machine.

8. After Fireworks has finished, a positive result is returned.

   The Fireworks API includes several error codes if problems, such as a full disk, are encountered.

9. While tracking the Fireworks progress, Dreamweaver sees the positive result and integrates the graphics by rewriting the DOM of the current page.

10. The dialog box is closed, and the current page is refreshed to correctly present the finished product.

To successfully control Fireworks, you need a complete understanding of the Fireworks DOM and its extension capabilities. Macromedia provides documentation for extending Fireworks from its support site: www.macromedia.com/support/fireworks.

Tip   I've also found the History panel in Fireworks to be useful — especially the Copy Command to Clipboard function. To see the underlying JavaScript used to create an object in Fireworks, first make the object. Then highlight the History panel steps and select the Copy to Clipboard button. Paste the clipboard contents in a text editor to see the exact steps Fireworks used; you can then begin to generalize the statements with variables and other functions.

On the Dreamweaver side, seven useful methods are in the FWLaunch C Library, detailed in Table 24-1.

Table 24-1: FWLaunch Methods

Method	Returns	Use
bringDWToFront()	N/A	Brings the Dreamweaver window in front of any other application running
bringFWToFront()	N/A	Brings the Fireworks window in front of any other application running

Method	Returns	Use
execJsInFireworks (javascriptOrFileURL)	Result from running the scriptlet in Fireworks. If the operation fails, it returns an error code: 1: The argument proves invalid 2: File I/O error 3: Improper version of Dreamweaver 4: Improper version of Fireworks 5: User canceled operation	Executes the supplied JavaScript function or scriptlet
mayLaunchFireworks()	Boolean	Determines if Fireworks may be launched
optimizeInFireworks (fileURL, docURL, {targetWidth}, {targetHeight})	Result from running the scriptlet in Fireworks. If the operation fails, it returns an error code: 1: The argument proves invalid 2: File I/O error 3: Improper version of Dreamweaver 4: Improper version of Fireworks 5: User canceled operation	Performs an Optimize in Fireworks operation, opening the Fireworks Export Preview dialog box
validateFireworks (versionNumber)	Boolean	Determines if the user has a specific version of Fireworks

Summary

Creating Web pages is almost never done with a single application: In addition to a Web layout program, you need a program capable of outputting Web graphics — and Fireworks is a world-class Web graphics generator and optimizer. Macromedia has integrated several functions with Dreamweaver and Fireworks to streamline production and simplify modification. Following are some of the key features:

✦ You can update images placed in Dreamweaver with Fireworks in two ways: optimize or edit. With the Optimize Image in Fireworks command, just the Export Preview portion of Fireworks opens; with the Edit Image command, the full version of Fireworks is run.

✦ Graphics and HTML exported from Fireworks can be incorporated into a Dreamweaver page in numerous ways: as a Library item; as an HTML file (complete with behavior code); or as an item pasted from the clipboard.

✦ New interapplication communication between Dreamweaver and Fireworks makes commands such as Create Web Photo Album possible.

✦ Dreamweaver includes a special C-level extension called FWLaunch, which provides the primary link to Fireworks.

In the next chapter, you learn how to incorporate Flash, Shockwave, and Generator movies into your Dreamweaver Web pages.

✦   ✦   ✦

Inserting Flash and Shockwave Elements

Animated splash screens, sound-enabled banners, button bars with special fonts, and other exciting Web elements are often built with Macromedia's Flash. Flash combines vector graphics and streaming audio into great-looking, very low–bandwidth files that can be viewed in a browser using the Flash Player Plugin. Flash's vector graphics have also turned out to be just the thing for Web-based cartoons. Beginning with version 4, Flash gained its own scripting language, ActionScript, and added MP3 compression to its streaming audio. With a huge base of installed players — as of this writing, well over 90 percent of browsers can view basic Flash content — Flash is an excellent way to liven up a Web page.

But Flash is not Macromedia's only solution for building interactive presentations for the Web. To many Web designers, Shockwave has represented the state of the art in Web interactivity since Macromedia first created the format in 1995. With Shockwave, multimedia files created in Macromedia's flagship authoring package, Director, can be compiled to run in a browser window. This functionality gives Web designers the capability to build just about anything — including interactive Web interfaces with buttons that look indented when pushed, arcade-style games, multimedia Web front-ends, and complete Web sites built entirely in Director — bringing a CD-ROM look-and-feel to the Web. Today, Shockwave continues to be an important force on the Web, as the enormous success of Macromedia's Shockwave.com amply demonstrates.

The final component in Macromedia's vector-graphic toolbox is a server-side technology called Generator. Generator works with templates built in Flash to display customized graphics, built on-demand. In its initial release, Generator was available only to designers working on big-budget, high-end sites and did not gain a sizeable foothold in the market. However, Macromedia has recently changed its pricing policy on Generator, making the technology much more accessible to developers.

As you might expect, Macromedia makes it easy to incorporate Shockwave, Flash, and Generator files into your Dreamweaver projects. All these formats have special objects that provide control over nearly all their parameters through the Property inspector — and each format is cross-browser compatible by default. Using

Dreamweaver's Flash Button and Flash Text tools, it's delightfully easy to incorporate customized, well-crafted Flash elements in your Web page without knowing a bit of Flash.

To take full advantage of the enhanced graphics potential of Flash and Shockwave's multimedia capabilities, you need to understand the differences between Director and Flash, as well as the various parameters available to each format. In addition to covering this material, this chapter also shows you how to use independent controls — both inline and with frames — for your Shockwave and Flash movies.

Director and Flash: What's the Difference?

Director (the program you use to make Shockwave movies) and Flash share many features: interactivity, streaming audio, support for both bitmaps and vector graphics, and "shocked fonts." Both can save their movies in formats suitable for viewing on the Web. So how do you choose which program to use? Each has its own special functions, and each excels at producing particular types of effects. Director is more full-featured, with a complete programming language called Lingo that enables incredible interactivity. And Director movies can include Flash animations. Director also has a much steeper learning curve than does Flash. Flash is terrific for short, low-bandwidth animations with or without a synchronized audio track; however, the interactive capabilities in Flash are limited compared to Director.

Director is really a multimedia production program used for combining various elements: backgrounds, foreground elements called *sprites*, and various media such as digital audio and video (see Figure 25-1). With Director's Lingo programming language, you can build extraordinarily elaborate demos and games with Internet-specific commands. When you need to include a high degree of interactivity, build your movie with Shockwave.

One of the primary differences between Director and Flash is the supported graphic formats. Director is generally better for bitmap graphics, in which each pixel is mapped to a specific color; both GIF and JPEG formats use bitmap graphics. Flash, on the other hand, uses primarily vector graphics, which are drawing elements described mathematically. Because vector graphics use a description of a drawing — a blue circle with a radius of 2.5 centimeters, for instance — rather than a bitmap, the resulting files are much smaller. A fairly complex animation produced with Flash might be only 10K or 20K, whereas a comparable digital video clip could easily be 10 times that size.

Aside from file size, the other feature that distinguishes vector graphics from bitmap graphics is the smoothness of the line. When viewed with sufficient magnification, bitmap graphics always display telltale "stair-steps" or "jaggies," especially around curves. Vector graphics, on the other hand, are much smoother. In fact, Flash takes special advantage of this characteristic and enables users to zoom into any movie — an important effect that saves a lot of bandwidth when used correctly.

However, these differences were significantly blurred with the release of Director 7, which incorporates its own native vector graphics and introduces the capability to include Flash movies within Director movies. In Director 8.5 — aka Director 8.5 Shockwave Studio — 3D-graphics creation is heavily supported. Flash 4 blurred the line the other way by incorporating streaming MP3-encoded audio and QuickTime integration, both things that were traditionally the province of Director. In Flash 5, Flash's scripting capabilities have been significantly beefed up with the expansion of ActionScript into a JavaScript-based programming language. And Flash MX, its most recent incarnation, contains many exciting new features, such as support for incorporating video in Flash movies, enhanced graphic design tools, a customizable ActionScript editor, and much more.

Figure 25-1: Director works mainly with bitmaps and video and enables "multimedia programming" using Lingo.

Flash animations can be used as special effects, cartoons, and navigation bars within (or without) frames (see Figure 25-2). Although Flash isn't the best choice for games and other complex interactive elements, you can use Flash to animate your navigation system — complete with sound effects for button-pushing feedback.

If Flash is a power tool, Director is a bulldozer. Director has been significantly expanded to handle a wide variety of file types — such as QuickTime, MP3, RealAudio, and RealVideo — with advanced streaming capabilities. Supporting multimedia interactivity is Director's own programming language, Lingo, which has also been enhanced. Furthermore, Director now includes multiplayer support for network game play and chat rooms, XML parsing, embedded compressed fonts, up to 1,000 sprite channels, and a potential frame rate of 999 frames per second (one heckuva fast-forward . . .). Luckily, Dreamweaver enables you to pack all that power into a Web page with its Shockwave object.

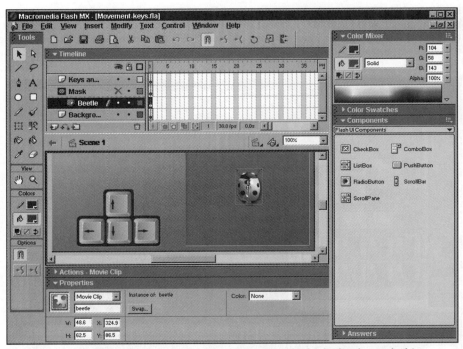

Figure 25-2: Flash movies range from a more cartoon-like look, thanks to Flash's lightweight vector graphics, to full-motion video.

Including Flash and Shockwave Movies in Dreamweaver Projects

Dreamweaver makes it easy to bring Shockwave and Flash files into your Web pages. The Insert bar provides an object for each type of movie, both located in the Media category.

Because Shockwave and Flash objects insert both an ActiveX control and a plugin, Dreamweaver enables you to play the movie in the Document window. When not playing, it displays a plugin placeholder icon (see Figure 25-3).

Before you can successfully include a Shockwave file, you need to know one small bit of information — the dimensions of your movie. Dreamweaver automatically reads the dimensions of your Flash file when you insert the Flash movie object. Unfortunately, if you're incorporating a Shockwave movie, you still need to enter the dimensions in the Shockwave Property inspector.

To find the width and height of a Shockwave movie, load it in Director and then choose Modify ➪ Movie ➪ Properties to open the movie's Property inspector. You'll find the dimensions therein.

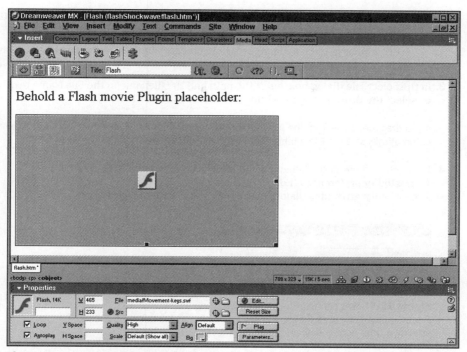

Figure 25-3: Dreamweaver includes many interface elements for working with Shockwave and Flash.

 Note

It is essential to know the movie's height and width before you can include it successfully in Dreamweaver-built Web pages. During the development phase of a Dreamweaver project, I often include the movie dimensions in a filename, as an instant reminder to take care of this detail. For example, if I'm working with two different Shockwave movies, I can give them names such as navbar125x241.dcr and navbar400x50.dcr. (The .dcr extension is automatically appended by Director when you save a movie as a Shockwave file.) Because I consistently put width before height in the filename, this trick saves me the time it takes to reopen Director, load the movie, and choose Modify ⇨ Movie to check the measurements in the Movie Properties dialog box. The alternative to keeping track of the Director movie's dimensions is to choose File ⇨ Save as Shockwave Movie in Director. Doing this creates an HTML file with all the necessary parameters (including width and height), which can be inserted into Dreamweaver. You'll find a detailed description of this process later in this chapter.

To include either a Shockwave or Flash file in your Web page, follow these steps:

1. Position the cursor in the Document window where you'd like the movie to appear.

2. Insert the movie using any of the following methods:

   • Choose Insert ⇨ Media ⇨ Shockwave or Insert ⇨ Media ⇨ Flash from the main Dreamweaver menu.

- In the Media category of the Insert bar, select the Shockwave or Flash Button.

- Drag the movie object from the Assets panel to the Document window. Remember to choose the appropriate category in the Assets panel: Shockwave or Flash.

3. In the Select File dialog box, enter the path and the filename in the File Name text box or select the Browse (Choose) button to locate the file. Click OK.

Note   If you drag the movie from the Assets panel, this step is not applicable because Dreamweaver automatically sets the File attribute to that of your movie file.

4. If you clicked OK in the Select File dialog box, and if Media is selected in your Accessibility preferences (Edit ⇨ Preferences ⇨ Accessibility), the Object Tag Accessibility Attributes dialog box appears, as shown in Figure 25-4:

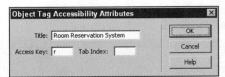

Figure 25-4: You can use the Object Tag Accessibility Attributes dialog box to specify a title, access key, and tab index for your inserted media objects.

In the Title field, enter a title for your media object.

In the Access Key field, enter a one-letter access key for your object. To select the object in the browser, you would press Alt (Command) + access key; for example: Alt+G (Command+G).

Note   Entering an Access Key value only places the accesskey attribute in the <object> tag; it's up to the browser to properly interpret what action, if any, should be taken when the access key combination is pressed.

In the Tab Index field, enter a number for the tab index of your object. By entering a number, you can specify the order in which users tab through objects and links on your page. Pressing Tab successively jumps from the object or link whose tab index is set to 1, to the object or link whose tab index is set to 2, and so on. For this to work correctly, you must specify the tabindex attribute for all of the page's objects and links.

5. Dreamweaver inserts a small plugin placeholder in the current cursor position, and the Property inspector displays the appropriate information for Shockwave or Flash.

If you inserted a Shockwave movie, make sure to enter the correct width and height dimensions in the Property inspector. Dreamweaver supplies this information automatically for Flash files.

6. Preview the Flash or Shockwave movie in the Document window by selecting the Play button in the Property inspector. You can also choose View ⇨ Plugins ⇨ Play.

7. End the preview of your file by selecting the Stop button in the Property inspector or selecting View ⇨ Plugins ⇨ Stop.

Generating HTML within Director

In Director, you can generate a file with all the appropriate HTML code at the same time that you save your Shockwave movie with just the selection of a checkbox. When you choose File ➪ Save as Shockwave Movie in Director, the dialog box contains a Generate HTML option. Selecting this option causes Director to save an HTML file with the same name as your Shockwave movie but with an appropriate file extension (.html for Macintosh and .htm for Windows). You can easily copy and paste this HTML code directly into Dreamweaver.

When you open the Director-generated HTML file, you see the name of your file and the Shockwave placeholder, correctly sized and ready to preview. To move this object into another Web page in progress, just select the Shockwave object and choose Edit ➪ Copy. Then switch to your other page and choose Edit ➪ Paste. Naturally, you can also use the keyboard shortcuts or, if both pages are accessible, just drag and drop the object from one page to another.

Tip   If you have more than one Flash or Shockwave movie on your page, you can control them all by choosing View ➪ Plugins ➪ Play All, and View ➪ Plugins ➪ Stop All. If your files appear in different pages in a frameset, you have to repeat the Play All command for each page.

Shockwave and Flash have some different features in the Dreamweaver Property inspector. These differences are covered separately in the following sections.

Specifying Shockwave Properties

After you've inserted your Shockwave file, you're ready to begin entering the specific parameters in the Property inspector. The Property inspector takes care of all but one Shockwave attribute, the `palette` parameter. Some of the information, including the ActiveX Class ID, is automatically set in the Property inspector when you insert the movie.

On the CD-ROM   In the Additional Extensions\Joseph Lowery\Commands folder on the CD-ROM, you can find a custom command called Insert Shockwave HTML that automates the process of inserting a Shockwave movie and its Director-generated HTML. If you'd prefer a version developed by Macromedia that does the same job, visit the Dreamweaver Exchange to download the Insert Shockwave extension. To access the Dreamweaver Exchange, choose Help ➪ Dreamweaver Exchange from within Dreamweaver or go to www.macromedia.com/exchange/dreamweaver.

To set or modify the parameters for a Shockwave file, follow these steps:

1. Select the Shockwave placeholder icon.

2. In the Shockwave Property inspector, enter the width and height values in the W and H text boxes, respectively, as shown in Figure 25-5. Alternately, you can click and drag any of the three resizing handles on the placeholder icon.

Tip   Pressing the Shift key while dragging the corner resizing handle maintains the current aspect ratio.

3. Set and modify other Shockwave movie attributes as needed; see Table 25-1 for a list.

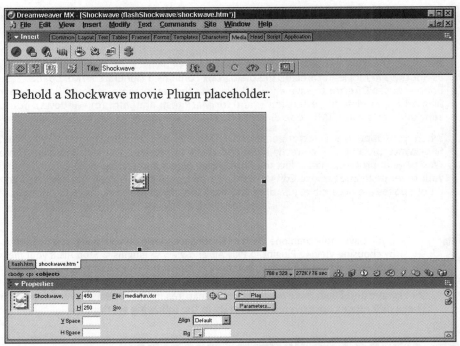

Figure 25-5: Modify parameters for a Shockwave property through the Shockwave Property inspector.

Table 25-1: Property Inspector Options for Shockwave Objects

Shockwave Property	Description
Align	Choose an option to alter the alignment of the movie. In addition to the browser default, your options include Baseline, Top, Middle, Bottom, Texttop, Absolute Middle, Absolute Bottom, Left, and Right.
Bg	Use this option to specify a background color for the movie area. Note that this color also appears while the movie is loading and after it is done playing.
V Space	To increase the amount of space between other elements on the page and the top and bottom of the movie Plugin, enter a pixel value in the V (Vertical) Space text box. Again, the default is zero.
H Space	You can increase the space to the left and right of the movie by entering a value in the H (Horizontal) Space text box. The default is zero.
Name	If desired, you can enter a unique name in this unlabeled field on the far left of the Property inspector. The name is used by JavaScript and other languages to identify the movie.

Additional parameters for Shockwave

As with other Plugins, you can pass other attributes to the Shockwave movie via the Parameters dialog box — available by clicking the Parameters button on the Property inspector. Use Tab or the Add (+) button to insert additional parameters. Enter the attributes in the left column and their respective values in the right. To remove an attribute, highlight it and select the Remove (–) button.

Automatic settings for Shockwave files

When you insert a Shockwave or Flash file, Dreamweaver writes a number of parameters that are constant and necessary. In the `<object>` portion of the code, Dreamweaver includes the ActiveX Class ID number as well as the `codebase` URL; the former calls the specific ActiveX control, and the latter enables users who don't have the control installed to receive it automatically. Likewise, in the `<embed>` section, Dreamweaver fills in the `pluginspage` attribute, designating the location where Navigator users can find the necessary plugin. Make sure you don't accidentally remove any of this information — however, if you should, all you have to do is delete and reinsert the object.

Only one other general attribute is usually assigned to a Shockwave file, the `palette` parameter. If you want to deploy this attribute, you'll have to add it by hand in Code view. `palette` takes a value of either background or foreground:

✦ If `palette` is set to background, the movie's color scheme does not override that of the system; this is the default.

✦ When `palette` is set to foreground, the colors of the selected movie are applied to the user's system, which includes the desktop and scroll bars.

Note that `palette` is not supported by Internet Explorer.

Caution

Web designers should take care when specifying the `palette=foreground` parameter. This effect is likely to prove startling to the user; moreover, if your color scheme is sufficiently different, the change may render the user's system unusable. If you do use the `palette` parameter, be sure to include a Director command to restore the original system color scheme in the final frame of the movie.

Designating Flash Attributes

Flash movies require the same basic parameters as their Shockwave counterparts — and Flash movies have a few additional optional ones as well. As it does for Shockwave files, Dreamweaver sets almost all the attributes for Flash movies through the Property inspector. The major difference is that several more parameters are available.

To set or modify the attributes for a Flash file, follow these steps:

1. After your Flash movie has been inserted in the Document window, make sure that it is selected. Dreamweaver automatically inserts the correct dimensions for your Flash movie.

2. Set any attributes in the Property inspector as needed for your Flash movie. (Refer to the previous descriptions of these attributes in the section "Specifying Shockwave Properties.") In addition, you can also set the parameters described in Table 25-2.

Table 25-2: Additional Property Inspector Options for Flash Objects

Flash Parameter	Possible Values	Description
Autoplay	Checked (default)	Enables the Flash movie to begin playing as soon as possible.
Loop	Checked (default)	If Loop is checked, the movie plays continuously; otherwise, it plays once.
Quality		Controls anti-aliasing during playback.
	High (default)	Anti-aliasing is turned on. This can slow the playback frame rate considerably on slower computers.
	Low	No anti-aliasing is used; this setting is best for animations that must be played quickly.
	Auto High	The animation begins in High (with anti-aliasing) and switches to Low if the host computer is too slow.
	Auto Low	Starts the animation in Low (no anti-aliasing) and then switches to High if the host machine is fast enough.
Src		Src specifies the .fla Flash source file. To edit a .swf Flash movie file, you must modify the movie's .fla source file.
Scale		Scale determines how the movie fits into the dimensions as specified in the Width and Height text boxes.
	Show All (default)	Displays the entire movie in the given dimensions while maintaining the file's original aspect ratio. Some of the background may be visible with this setting.
	Exact Fit	Scales the movie precisely into the dimensions without regard for the aspect ratio. It is possible that the image could be distorted with this setting.
	No Border	Fits the movie into the given dimensions so that no borders are showing and maintains the original aspect ratio. Some of the movie may be cut off with this setting.

Setting the scale in Flash movies

Be careful with your setting for the Scale parameter to avoid unexpected results. If you have to size a Flash movie out of its aspect ratio, the Flash Player needs to know what to do with any extra room it has to fill. Figure 25-6 demonstrates the different results that the Scale attribute can provide. Only the figure in the lower right is at its proper dimensions. The gray box is the actual size of the authoring canvas.

Tip

Dreamweaver makes it easy to rescale a Flash movie. First, from the Property inspector, enter the precise width and height of your file in the W and H text boxes. Then, while holding down the Shift key, click and drag the corner resizing handle of the Flash placeholder icon to the new size for the movie. By Shift+dragging, you retain the aspect ratio set in the Property inspector, which enables you to quickly enlarge or reduce your movie without distortion.

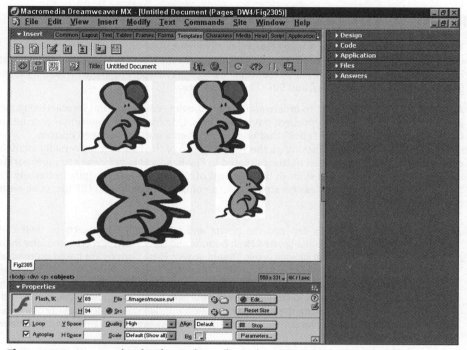

Figure 25-6: Your setting for the Scale attribute determines how your movie is resized within the plugin width and height measurements.

Additional parameters for Flash

Flash has two additional attributes that can be entered through the Parameters dialog box (click the Parameters button on the Property inspector): salign and swliveconnect. The salign attribute determines how the movie aligns itself to the surrounding frame when the Scale attribute is set to Show All. In addition, salign determines which portion of the image is cut off when the Scale attribute is set to No Border. The alignment can be set to L (left), R (right), T (top), or B (bottom). You can also use these values in combination. For example, if you set salign to RB, the movie aligns with the right-bottom edge or the lower-right corner of the frame.

The swliveconnect attribute comes into play when you're using FSCommands or JavaScript in your Flash movies. FSCommands are interactive commands, such as Go to URL, issued from inside the Flash movie. The Netscape browser initializes Java when first called — and if your Flash movie uses FSCommands or JavaScript, it uses Java to communicate with the Netscape Plugin interface, LiveConnect. Because not all Flash movies need the LiveConnect connection, you can prevent Java from being initialized by entering the swliveconnect attribute in the Parameters dialog box and setting its value to false. When the swliveconnect=false parameter is found by the browser, the Java is not initialized as part of the loading process — and your movie loads more quickly.

Creating Flash Buttons and Crafting Templates

The original argument against using Flash was: "Not everyone has the Flash plugin, so not everyone can see Flash movies." Nowadays, this argument is more or less moot with Flash Plugin market penetration at 98+ percent (for Flash 2 players), 97+ percent (Flash 3 players), 96+ percent (Flash 4 players), and 90+ (Flash 5 players).

Although Flash is often used to create standalone movies, cartoons, and interactive games, it is also capable of making excellent navigation aids. One feature of traditional user interfaces—audio feedback, the "click" that one hears when a button has been chosen onscreen—has been long missing on the Web because of the lack of a universally available sound engine. With navigation buttons created in Flash, sound is very easy to incorporate, as are animation effects and smooth blends. Best of all, these effects require extremely low bandwidth and often weigh less on a page than a comparable animated GIF file, even without the sound.

New Feature   Dreamweaver designers can add the power and beauty of Flash objects to their Web-page–design palette. Both animated Flash buttons and static Flash Text (covered later in this chapter) may be created directly within Dreamweaver. Flash buttons are based on template designs created in Flash and customized in Dreamweaver. This separation of design and implementation enables Flash graphic designers to create the overall look for a navigational button or button series, and Dreamweaver layout artists can incorporate this look into the proper page design, adding the appropriate button text, links, and background color where needed. Flash buttons, like any Flash movie, may be previewed in Dreamweaver and resized as needed.

Dreamweaver comes with 44 different Flash Button templates, with additional styles available at the Macromedia Exchange. The buttons are primarily intended to be used as links to other Web pages, although some are designed as VCR-like player controls. To insert a Flash button, follow these steps:

1. Make sure that the current document has been previously saved.

   If you're working on a new document, Dreamweaver requires that you save it before adding a Flash button.

2. Choose the Flash Button object from the Media category of the Insert bar or select Insert ➪ Interactive Images ➪ Flash Button. The Insert Flash Button dialog box, shown in Figure 25-7, is displayed.

3. Select a button type from the Style list.

   The previews shown in the Sample area are live demonstrations and will play as designed when moused-over and/or clicked. There is, however, one exception: No sound is heard in preview; you have to preview the Flash button in the browser to get the full effect.

4. Enter your desired button text label in the Button Text field. If you leave this field blank, the button will have no label.

   The Button Text field is physically limited to 50 characters, although for most practical purposes, your text will be shorter. Certain symbols, such as those in the Control group, ignore the text and font settings.

5. Select a typeface from the Font drop-down list.

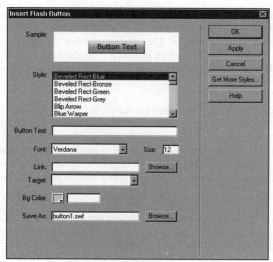

Figure 25-7: Choose Apply to test typeface and text-size variations when creating your Flash button.

The fonts listed are TrueType fonts found on your system. Most of the button templates have a preselected font and text size. If the preselected font is not found on your system, a small alert appears at the bottom of the dialog box.

6. Enter the desired font size, in points, in the Size field.

7. If the button is to link to another page, enter the absolute or document-relative URL in the Link field. Alternatively, you can choose the Browse button to locate the file.

   Flash movies don't handle site-root–relative links correctly, so your link needs to be either absolute, such as `www.idest.com/dreamweaver/`, or document-relative. Use document-relative links only if the Flash button is to be stored in the same folder as the page referenced.

8. If you are working in a frame-based site or you want the link to open in another page, select an option from the Target drop-down list.

   The standard system targets — _blank, _self, _parent, and _top — are always available. Additional frame names appear if the Flash button is inserted in an existing frameset.

9. If the Flash button is to be placed on a page or in a table with a background color other than white, select the Bg Color swatch to choose an appropriate background. Alternatively, the hexadecimal color number or standard color name may be entered directly into the Bg Color text field.

10. In the Save As text box, enter a path and filename for the Flash button file. If you like, you can use the suggested default name in the site root or select the Browse button to choose a different location.

11. Choose Apply to insert the button in the cursor location on the page.

12. Click OK when you're done.

Tip   If you'd like to see what other styles are available, open the Insert Flash Button dialog box and choose Get More Styles. Your primary browser will launch and go to the Dreamweaver Exchange, where you can search for new styles. After you've installed the additional extensions using the Extension Manager, you'll need to relaunch Dreamweaver to see the new styles. Note that selecting Get More Styles immediately closes the dialog box without creating a button.

After your Flash button is inserted, it can be modified on the page. Select the Flash Button object to activate the Flash Button Property inspector that, along with the standard Flash Property inspector, offers two new useful custom controls: Edit and Reset Size. Selecting Edit reopens the Insert Flash Button dialog box and enables you to modify any of the settings. Use Reset Size if you have altered the dimensions of the Flash button — by dragging one of the sizing handles or entering new values in the Width and/or Height fields — and want to return to the original size.

Tip   If you've moved an existing Flash button to a frame-based design, select the button and choose Edit from the Property inspector. Under Target, you'll find names for all the frames in your new frameset to make it easy to position your content.

Creating your own Flash Button templates

The Flash button samples that ship with Dreamweaver are nice, but to be truly useful, you — or someone on your team — must be able to create your own templates that fit the design of your site. The Flash Button templates you see previewed in Dreamweaver are actually Generator templates, created in Flash.

Note   Generator is only available in Flash 5 and has been discontinued in Flash MX. Thus, Flash MX may not be used to create custom templates.

To create the Generator templates, you'll need Flash 5 and the free Generator authoring extensions from Macromedia. The authoring extensions are included in Flash or can be downloaded from the Macromedia site at `www.macromedia.com/software/generator/download/extensions.html`.

The next step is to create a button in Flash. As with other Flash buttons, your graphic should be converted to a button-type symbol, and it may use all four keyframes: Up, Over, Down, and Hit. After you've built the button, follow these steps to add the Generator functionality:

1. In Flash, choose Window ➪ Generator Objects.

2. From the Generator Objects panel, drag the Insert Text object over the previously built button.

   Position the Insert Text object so that its center is located where you'd like your button text to appear.

3. When the Insert Text object is in place and selected, the Generator Insert Text panel, displaying the appropriate properties, appears. Double-click the Insert Text object to bring the panel to the front if necessary.

   Within the panel, set several parameters to placeholder values so that the Insert Flash Button dialog box in Dreamweaver can function properly. In each case, enter the value in the right column.

4. Enter the following values in the Generator Insert Text panel:

- **Text:** Enter {Button Text}
- **Font:** Enter {Button Font}
- **Font Size:** Enter {Button Size}
- **Alignment:** Enter left, right, center, or justified
- **Vertical Alignment:** Enter top, center, or bottom
- **URL:** Enter {Button URL}
- **Window:** Enter {Button Target}

5. Shrink the movie to the size of your button by dragging the button to the upper-left corner of the stage and choosing Modify ➪ Movie. In the Movie Properties dialog box, select the Match Contents option.

6. Save the movie as a .fla file so that you may adjust it later.

7. Choose File ➪ Export Movie and select Generator Template as the file type. Save the template in the Dreamweaver/Configuration/Flash Objects/Flash Buttons folder.

Now your Flash button is almost ready to use. If you like, you can choose the Flash Button object in Dreamweaver and see your button; however, no sample text is displayed. There's one last procedure that's required if you want to preview your Flash button with sample text. Interestingly enough, you use the Flash Button object to create the preview:

1. Open Dreamweaver and save a blank page.

2. Choose the Flash Button object.

3. Select your newly inserted button from the Style list. New buttons are found at the end of the list.

4. Enter desired default values in the Text, Font, and Size fields. These values are preset whenever this particular Flash button is chosen.

5. In the Save As field, store the file under the same name as your style in the Dreamweaver/Configuration/Flash Objects/Flash Buttons Preview folder.

6. Click OK when you're done.

The next time you access the Flash Button object, your custom template will display a full preview with text.

Working with Flash Text

The addition of Flash Text to Dreamweaver goes a long way toward solving one of the Web designer's most perplexing problems: how to achieve good-looking text that uses nonstandard fonts. HTML enables you to specify the use of a nonstandard font in a Web page, but this font appears in a user's browser only if the user happens to have that particular font installed on his or her system. For this reason, few designers stray outside tried-and-true options, such as Arial, Helvetica, and Times New Roman, for the majority of their content. This use of limited fonts is especially grating to print designers coming to the Web who rely on typography as a primary design tool. The advent of Dynamic HTML promised to bring a wider selection of typefaces with so-called *dynamic font technology,* but lack of built-in cross-browser support for any one system dashed those hopes.

The Flash Text feature enables the designer to use any TrueType font to create low-weight, jaggies-free headings, right from within Dreamweaver itself. The ubiquitous nature of the Flash Player ensures cross-browser support without resorting to GIF images, which are often not as crisp as required. Moreover, with Flash Text, you can easily declare a second color for automatically enabled rollovers — you don't even have to attach a Dreamweaver behavior.

The Flash Text feature is especially useful for creating headings in a corporate-approved typeface. Because it doesn't involve downloading a font resource, as dynamic font technologies do, there is no concern about the misuse of copyrighted fonts. The only downside to Flash Text over a dynamic font technology is that unlike dynamically created fonts, Flash Text cannot be searched on a page. To overcome this limitation, Web designers can include key phrases in <meta> tags.

To use the Flash Text object, follow these steps:

1. Make sure your page has been saved before proceeding.

2. Choose Flash Text from the Media category of the Insert bar or select Insert ➪ Interactive Images ➪ Flash Text. The Insert Flash Text dialog box appears, as shown in Figure 25-8.

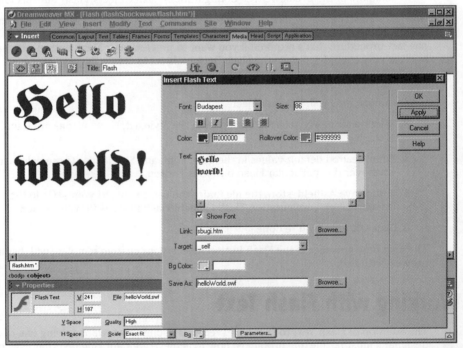

Figure 25-8: Use the Flash Text object to create headlines with a nonstandard or custom font.

3. Select the desired typeface from the Font drop-down list.

4. Enter the font size desired in the Size field.

5. Choose Bold and/or Italic styles for your text.

6. Select the alignment on the page: left, center, or right.

7. Select a basic color from the color swatch or enter a hexadecimal value or valid color name in the Color field.

8. If desired, choose a secondary color for the text to change to when the user moves his or her mouse over the Flash Text from the Rollover Color swatch.

9. Enter the desired text in the Text field.

   Other than practical considerations, there's no real limit to the amount of text that can be entered, and line returns are acceptable.

10. If you want to see the text in the default font in the Text field — rather than your selected font — disable the Show Font option.

11. If desired, enter an absolute or document-relative URL in the Link field.

    As with Flash buttons, site-relative links are not available in Flash Text objects.

12. If you're working in a frame-based site or want the link to open in a new browser window, choose the appropriate Target from the drop-down list.

13. Optionally, choose a background color from the Bg Color swatch.

14. Enter a path and filename to store the object in the Save As field. Alternatively, select the Browse button to locate a folder.

    If you're using document-relative links in the Flash Text object, be sure to store the object in the same folder as the current document.

15. Click Apply to preview what your button will look like in your document and then click OK when you're done.

Caution When you are editing a Flash Text button, clicking Apply overwrites the existing button file and replaces it with your new, edited version. Alas, there is no undo for the Apply command . . . so think twice before clicking that Apply button!

As with Flash buttons, you can resize a Flash Text object by dragging the resizing handles; press the Shift key while dragging to constrain the dimensions to their initial width and height ratio. Click Reset Size on the Property inspector to restore the original dimensions. To edit a Flash Text object, choose Edit from the Property inspector or simply double-click the object to open its Insert Flash Text dialog box.

When you create a Flash Text object, Dreamweaver makes a GIF representation that can be displayed during layout — you may notice some roughness in the lines, especially if you resize the object. You can, at any time, select Play from the Flash Text Property inspector (or choose Preview in Browser) to see the true Flash object with its smooth vector shape.

Configuring MIME Types

As with any plugin, your Web server has to have the correct MIME types set before Shockwave files can be properly served to your users. If your Web page plays Shockwave and Flash movies locally, but not remotely, chances are good that the correct MIME types need to be added. The system administrator generally handles configuring MIME types.

The system administrator needs to know the following information to be able to correctly configure the MIME types:

✦ **Shockwave:** application/x-director (.dcr, .dir, .dxr)

✦ **Flash:** application/x-shockwave-flash (.swf)

Both Shockwave and Flash are popular plugins, and it's likely that the Web server is already configured to recognize the appropriate file types.

Tip   Movies made by an earlier version of Flash, called FutureSplash, can also be played by the Flash Plugin — but only if the correct MIME type is added: application/futuresplash, with the file extension .spl.

Managing Links in Flash Movies with Dreamweaver

Many Web sites rely heavily on Flash movies, substituting movies for entire pages that would otherwise be created with HTML. Others take advantage of Flash's interactivity in their main navigation buttons. Adding links to buttons in Flash is easy, but embedding multiple URLs into multiple SWF files can make modifying a site's structure a nightmare, forcing you to re-create every SWF file in your site. Luckily, Dreamweaver comes to the rescue with link management features that are SWF-savvy.

Dreamweaver extends its link management capabilities to include the links contained in Flash SWF movies. Edit links within an SWF file manually in the Site Map, or move SWF files in the Site Files view and let Dreamweaver clean up behind you.

Within the Site panel, you can drag SWF files to new folders just as you would an HTML file. Unless your Update Links when Moving Files preference is set to Never, Dreamweaver will either modify the links in the SWF file accordingly or prompt you for permission to do so.

Caution   Be careful with the type of links you use — Flash (or, more accurately, browser playback of Flash) can't handle every type. Absolute URLs are very common in Flash movies because they can be used in every situation. Document-relative links may be used successfully in all cases if the Web page and the Flash file are stored in the same folder. Site-root–relative links, such as /products/widgets.htm, should not be used in Flash movies.

To modify the links in an SWF file manually, follow these steps:

1. Display the Site Map of your desired site by pressing F8 to open the Site panel, selecting the site from the drop-down list, choosing the Expand/Collapse button to display the expanded Site panel, and clicking the Site Map button.

2. Choose View ➪ Show Dependent Files to include dependent files such as Flash movies in the Site Map.

3. Locate the SWF file that you want to modify. If it contains any links, a plus sign is shown next to its icon. Click the plus sign to expand a branch of links from the SWF file, as shown in Figure 25-9.

4. To change a link, select it and choose Site ➪ Change Link, press Ctrl+L (Command+L), or right-click (Control+click) the link and choose Change Link from the shortcut menu. Dreamweaver displays a Select HTML File dialog box.

5. Select a new file by navigating to an HTML file or entering a URL. Click OK when you're done.

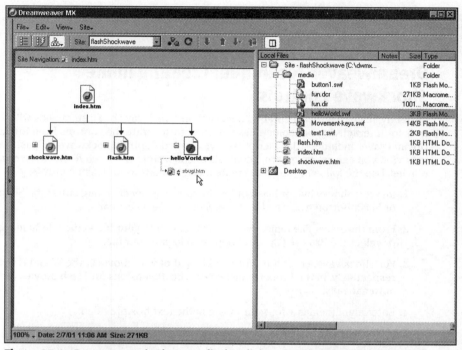

Figure 25-9: Dreamweaver's Site Map displays links contained in Flash SWF movies.

Note If your preferences call for Dreamweaver to prompt you before updating links, Dreamweaver will ask you to confirm that you want the link changed.

The link in your SWF file is changed.

Caution Dreamweaver changes links within SWF files, but the links in the original Flash document that you edit in Flash itself will remain unchanged. Make sure you update your Flash document before exporting a revised SWF file.

Providing User Interaction with Shockwave Movies

What happens after you've installed your Shockwave or Flash files? Many movies are set to play automatically or upon some action from the user, such as a mouse click of a particular hotspot within the page. But what if you want the user to be able to start or stop a movie in one part of the page, using controls in another part? How can controls in one frame affect a movie in a different frame?

Dreamweaver includes a Control Shockwave or Flash behavior that makes inline controls — controls on the same Web page as the movie — very easy to set up. However, establishing frame-to-frame control is slightly more complex in Dreamweaver and requires a minor modification to the program-generated code.

Cross-Reference Both of the following step-by-step Techniques rely on Dreamweaver behaviors. If you're unfamiliar with using behaviors, you should review Chapter 23 before proceeding.

Dreamweaver Technique: Creating inline Shockwave controls

Certainly, it's perfectly acceptable to make your Shockwave or Flash movies with built-in controls for interactivity, but sometimes you want to separate the controls from the movie. Dreamweaver includes a JavaScript behavior called Control Shockwave or Flash. With this behavior, you can set up external controls to start, stop, and rewind Shockwave and Flash movies. Use the following steps to create inline Shockwave or Flash controls:

1. Insert a Shockwave or Flash object in your page by choosing either the Shockwave or Flash Button from the Media category of the Insert bar.

2. From the Select File dialog box, enter the path to your file in the File Name text box or select the Browse (Choose) button to locate your file.

3. For Shockwave, enter the width and height of your movie in the W and H text boxes, respectively, in the Property inspector. The dimensions for Flash movies are entered automatically.

4. Enter a unique name for your movie in the text box provided.

5. If you are inserting a Flash movie, deselect the Autoplay and Loop options.

6. To insert the first control, position the cursor where you'd like the control to appear on the page.

7. Type the text or insert the image that will function as your control. Select this text or image.

8. In the Link box of the Property inspector, enter `javascript:;` to create an empty target.

9. Open the Behaviors panel by selecting the Show Behaviors button from the Launcher or by pressing Shift+F3.

10. If necessary, change the selected browser to 4.0 and Later Browsers by clicking the Add Action (+) button and selecting Show Events For ➪ 4.0 and Later Browsers.

11. Use the Add Action (+) button to choose the Control Shockwave or Flash action.

12. In the Control Shockwave or Flash dialog box (see Figure 25-10), select the movie you want to affect from the Movie drop-down list.

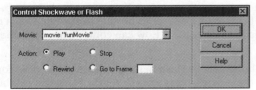

Figure 25-10: In the Control Shockwave or Flash dialog box, you assign a control action to an image button or text link.

13. Now select the desired action for your control. Choose from the four options: Play, Stop, Rewind, and Go to Frame. If you choose the Go to Frame option, enter a frame number in the text box.

14. Click OK to close the Control Shockwave or Flash dialog box.

15. Repeat Steps 6 through 14 for each movie control you'd like to add. Figure 25-11 shows a sample Web page with Play, Stop, and Rewind text controls.

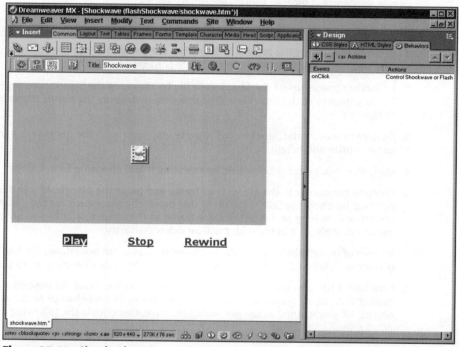

Figure 25-11: Simple Play, Stop, and Rewind controls were added to this page in just a few minutes using the Control Shockwave or Flash behavior.

Dreamweaver Technique: Playing Shockwave movies in frames

Framesets and frames are great for Web sites in which you want your navigation and other controls kept in one frame, and you also want the freedom to vary the content in another frame. It's entirely possible to set up your movie's playback buttons in one frame and the Shockwave movie in another. The method and the tools used are similar to those used in the preceding Dreamweaver Technique for adding same-page controls to a Shockwave movie. For this Technique using frames, some HTML hand-coding is necessary, but it is relatively minor — only one additional line per control!

As you saw in the previous section, Dreamweaver's Control Shockwave or Flash behavior lists all the Shockwave and Flash movies in the page and enables you to choose the one you want to affect (refer back to Figure 25-9). Unfortunately, the behavior looks on only one page, not through an entire frameset. However, with a little sleight-of-hand and a bit of JavaScript, you can get the effect you want.

> **Note**   Before you begin applying this Technique, you should construct (and save) your frameset and individual frames. Be sure to give each frame a unique name, because you have to provide the names in order to address the correct frames.

Use the following steps to place Shockwave controls in frames, as shown in Figure 25-12:

1. In one frame, insert the images or links that are going to act as the Shockwave controls. (For this demonstration, the control frame is named `frControl`.)

2. In another frame, insert the Shockwave file by choosing the Shockwave object from the Media category of the Insert bar. (For this demonstration, the movie frame is named `frMovie`.)

3. Be sure to modify the Shockwave Property inspector with the necessary parameters: name, width, and height.

4. Copy the Shockwave placeholder by selecting it and choosing Edit ➪ Copy.

5. Position the cursor in the `frControl` frame and paste the placeholder in a temporary position by choosing Edit ➪ Paste. At this point, the placement for the placeholder is not critical, as long as it is in the same frame as the images or links you are going to use as controls. The placeholder will be deleted shortly.

   Instead of using the Copy and Paste commands, you can hold down the Ctrl (Command) key and click and drag the placeholder to its new temporary position.

6. Now select the first image or link you want to use as a control. As described in the preceding Technique, attach the Control Shockwave or Flash behavior to the selected object. As you learned in the preceding exercise, this entails the following actions:

   • With the image or link selected, open the Behaviors panel.

   • Add the Control Shockwave or Flash action.

   • In the Control Shockwave or Flash dialog box, specify the movie and select the required action (Play, Rewind, Stop, or Go to Frame).

7. The major work is finished now. All you still need to do is add a little HTML. Switch to Code view, open the Code inspector, or use your favorite external editor to edit the file.

8. Locate the image or link controls in the code. Each JavaScript routine is called from within an `<a>` tag and reads something like the following, where `fMovie` is the name of the Flash movie:

```
<a href="javascript:;"
    onClick="MM_controlShockwave('document.fMovie',⤸
'document.fMovie','Play')">
```

9. Wherever you see the JavaScript reference to document, change it to

```
parent.frameName.document
```

where *frameName* is the unique name you gave to the frame in which your movie appears. In our example, frameName is frMovie, so after the replacement is made, the tag reads as follows:

```
<a href="javascript:;"
onClick="MM_controlShockwave('parent.frMovie.document.
fMovie','document.fMovie','Play')">
```

By making this substitution, you've pointed the JavaScript function first to the "parent" of the current document — and the parent of a frame is the entire frameset. Now that we're looking at the entire frameset, the next word (which is the unique frame name) points the JavaScript function directly to the desired frame within the frameset.

Tip   If you have a number of controls, you might want to use Dreamweaver's Find and Replace features to ensure that you've updated all the code.

10. Finally, delete the temporary Shockwave movie that was inserted into the frame containing the controls.

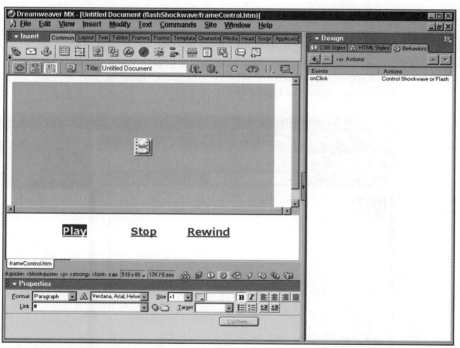

Figure 25-12: The same setup as in the previous figure, but with the controls and movie in separate frames.

Test the frameset by pressing F12 (primary browser) or Shift+F12 (secondary browser). If you haven't changed the Property inspector's default Tag attribute (the default is Object and Embed), the Shockwave movie should work in both Netscape and Internet Explorer.

Dreamweaver Technique: Triggering behaviors from Flash movies

Flash includes several of its own behaviors for creating interactivity, but Flash behaviors don't use JavaScript as Dreamweaver behaviors do. A Flash-heavy project might benefit from Dreamweaver's Open Browser Window or Popup Message behaviors as much as the next site. The Technique in this section shows you how to trigger Dreamweaver behaviors from buttons in a Flash movie.

What Flash buttons do is specified in the Flash authoring environment, not in Dreamweaver. Dreamweaver can attach behaviors to HTML elements such as anchor tags and body tags, but not to plugins. The solution lies in creating dummy "buttons" in Dreamweaver and copying the JavaScript code from those links into the actions attached to Flash buttons, within Flash itself.

Note

The following Technique can be used for any Dreamweaver behavior. The JavaScript Integration Kit for Flash 5 (JIK) extension, covered later in this chapter, has several built-in functions, including Open Browser Window and Swap Image. Use the following procedure if you don't want to use the JIK extension or you need to incorporate a behavior not included in that extension.

To trigger Dreamweaver behaviors from Flash buttons, follow these steps:

1. Create a new Dreamweaver document or open an existing one.

2. Create a null link that represents a button in your Flash movie. If you want a Flash button to open a new browser window, attach the Open Browser Window behavior to your null link, as shown in Figure 25-13.

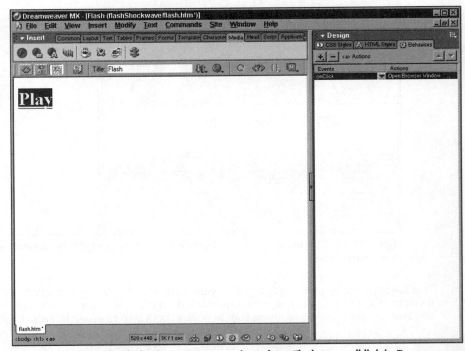

Figure 25-13: Attach a behavior you want to trigger from Flash to a null link in Dreamweaver.

3. Place your cursor within the null link and choose the `<a>` tag from the Tag Selector in Dreamweaver's status bar to completely select the link.

4. Choose View ➪ Code and Design to display page code and design together. Note that the null link is selected in both the Code and Design portions of the Document window and looks something like the following:

```
<a href="javascript:;"
   onClick="MM_openBrWindow('index.htm','newWindow',
   'status=yes,scrollbars=yes,width=200,height=300')">
Play</a>
```

5. Select everything between the "..." quotes in the `onClick` attribute — including the parentheses (as shown in Figure 25-14) — and copy it to the clipboard. This is the actual JavaScript that you want the Flash button to execute.

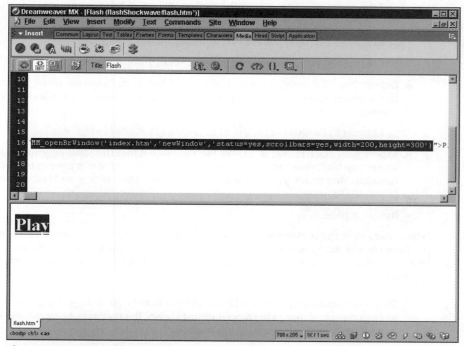

Figure 25-14: Select the JavaScript that the Flash button should execute from within the `onClick` attribute of your anchor tag.

6. In Flash, select the button to which you want to add the Dreamweaver behavior and then open the Actions panel, as shown in Figure 25-15.

7. Click the Add Action (+) button and choose Actions ➪ Browser/Network ➪ getURL to add a getURL behavior to your Flash button. In the URL text box, enter the following:

```
javascript:
```

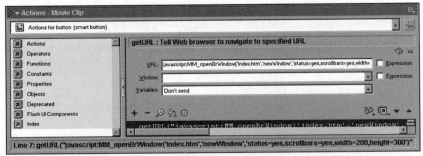

Figure 25-15: Add your JavaScript code to a Flash button Get URL behavior in the Object Actions tab of the Instance Properties dialog box in Flash.

and then paste the contents of the clipboard — your JavaScript code — so that you have something that looks like the following (refer to Figure 25-15):

```
javascript:MM_openBrWindow('myBuddy.htm','','↩
scrollbars=yes','width=250,height=200')
```

8. Repeat Steps 2 through 7 for each additional button or behavior you'd like to use. Note that multiple function calls in a javascript: statement must be separated by semi-colons:

```
javascript:funcCall1(arglist); funcCall2(arglist); etc.
```

9. Export your Flash movie as an SWF file and place it into the same page in Dreamweaver where you built your null links. Note that the <head> tag of this page contains JavaScript functions that match your null links and the JavaScript inside your Flash movie.

10. Delete your null links — but not the JavaScript functions in the <head> tag — and publish your page.

When users click the buttons in your Flash movie, `javascript: URL` sends the commands to the browser, executing the JavaScript functions in your Web page. Flash buttons open new browser windows, pop-up messages, and so on. This works in Netscape and in Internet Explorer.

Tip   Shockwave authors can also use JavaScript URLs from Lingo to trigger Dreamweaver behaviors in a manner similar to the procedure just shown. The JavaScript-savvy can also reference its own JavaScript functions using this method.

Dreamweaver Technique: Using the JavaScript Integration Kit for Flash

With an eye toward smoothing the integration between Flash and Dreamweaver, Macromedia released the JavaScript Integration Kit for Flash (JIK). The JIK is a suite of commands and behaviors installable in Dreamweaver — versions 3 and later — via the Extension Manager. You can download the current version from the Macromedia Exchange; choose Commands ⇨ Get More Commands to go directly online. The JavaScript Integration Kit for Flash consists of four main components:

✦ **Macromedia Flash Player Controls:** Enable the designer to include interactive control over Flash movies in a Web page. New Dreamweaver behaviors assign play, stop, rewind, fast-forward, pan, and zoom actions to any graphic element. In addition, an HTML drop-down menu can be turned into a Flash movie selector.

✦ **Advanced Form Validations:** Ensures that your visitors are entering the proper type of information in your Flash form. You can apply any of 18 client-side form validations — everything from a required, non-blank to an International Phone Validation.

✦ **Browser Scripts for Flash:** Embeds up to 10 different JavaScript functions in the Dreamweaver page, callable from any Flash 5 movie. With these functions, your Flash movie can control form elements such as text fields and select lists, open remote browser windows, set cookies, and swap images on the Web page.

✦ **Flash Dispatcher Behavior:** Detects the visitor's Flash Player version and redirects to a suitable Web page.

The beauty of the JIK is that its various components can be mixed and matched to achieve a wide range of effects and control. The resulting Web page offers a greater degree of interactivity for the visitor as well as for the Flash designer.

Macromedia Flash Player Controls

One method of engaging your Web page visitors is to give them more control over their viewing experiences. Rather than just displaying a movie from beginning to end, allow the viewer to pause, rewind, and play the animation at will. Flash's vector-based nature even enables the user to zoom in and out, without loss of image clarity. Although all this functionality is available through Flash ActionScript, not all designs require the controls to be maintained within a Flash movie. The Flash Player Controls allow all the common VCR-like functionality — and then some — to be assigned to HTML elements such as images or hotspots.

When the JavaScript Integration Kit is installed, 10 different behaviors are grouped under the MM Flash Player Controls:

✦ Fast Forward Flash

✦ Go To Flash Frame

✦ Go To Flash Frame Based on Cookie

✦ Load Flash Movie

✦ Pan Flash

✦ Play Flash

✦ Rewind Flash

✦ Set Flash by List

✦ Stop Flash

✦ Zoom Flash

As with any other Dreamweaver behavior, the Player Controls must be assigned to a target: a text link, an image map hotspot, or a graphic with a link attached. Typically, such a graphic button would use the null link `javascript:;` to act as a trigger but not actually open a URL.

You must have at least one Flash movie in the page before the Flash Player Controls become available, as shown in Figure 25-16. Once activated, the user interfaces for the Flash Player Controls vary according to their function, as detailed below. With the Play, Stop, Rewind Flash behaviors, you just pick the Flash movie you want to control from the drop-down list. All the other behaviors also include this option, so you can affect any movie on the page.

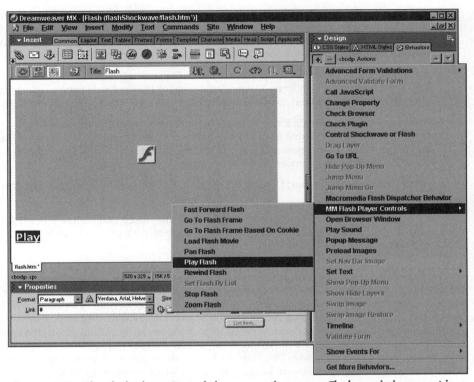

Figure 25-16: The Flash Player Controls become active once a Flash movie is present in the current Dreamweaver document.

To use the Flash Player Controls, follow these steps:

1. Insert at least one Flash movie by choosing it from the Assets panel or selecting the Flash object.

2. Enter a unique name in the name field of the Flash Property inspector (the blank field in the upper left of the inspector) for each movie.

3. Select the text link, hotspot, or image to trigger the behavior.

   If you'd like to apply the Set Flash By List behavior, select a form list object. Note that this behavior is dimmed in Figure 25-16, because a form list object is not selected.

4. Choose Window ➪ Behaviors or click the Show Behaviors button in the Launcher to open the Behaviors panel.

5. Choose the Add Action (+) button from the Behaviors panel and select the desired behavior under the MM Flash Player Controls heading.

   The chosen behavior's dialog box appears, similar to the one shown for Pan Flash in Figure 25-17.

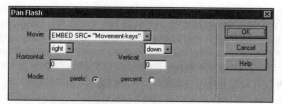

Figure 25-17: With the Pan Flash behavior, your viewer can move around a Flash movie in any direction. As shown, this behavior pans in a diagonal direction, down and to the right, every time it is triggered.

6. Select the parameters for your behavior.

- For the Play Flash, Rewind Flash, and Stop Flash behaviors, select the desired animation to affect from the Movie drop-down list.

- For the Fast Forward Flash behavior, select the desired animation to affect from the Movie drop-down list. In the first blank field, enter the desired value you want the movie to advance by. Select either Frames or Percent from the drop-down list. For example, to advance the movie by 5 percent each time the behavior is called, enter **5** in the first field and choose Percent from the list.

- For the Go To Flash Frame behavior, select the desired animation to affect from the Movie drop-down list and then enter the frame number to move to in the Go To Frame field.

- For the Go To Flash Frame Based on Cookie behavior, select the desired animation to affect from the Movie drop-down list, enter the name of the cookie to read in the Cookie Name field, enter the value to look for in the Cookie Value field, and then enter the frame number to advance to when the cookie name and value are read in the Go To Frame field.

- For the Load Flash Movie behavior, select the desired animation you want to replace from the Replace Movie drop-down list. Enter the filename for the movie to load in the With Movie field or locate the movie by selecting the Browse button. Input the level to load the movie into in the Level field.

  To replace an existing movie with the loaded movie, enter a level number that is currently occupied by another movie. To replace the original movie and unload every level, choose 0 for the level. To begin playing the movie immediately, set the Play option to Yes; otherwise, set Play to No.

Caution   As Dreamweaver warns you, the Load Flash Movie behavior is not supported for Netscape browsers.

- For the Pan Flash behavior, select the desired animation to affect from the Movie drop-down list. Choose the Horizontal and/or Vertical direction — up, down, right, or left — to pan to from the drop-down lists, and then select the degree of the pan by entering a value in the fields below each direction. You can pan diagonally by entering nonzero values for both the Horizontal and Vertical direction. Choose whether you'd like the pan values to operate in either Pixel or Percent mode.

- For the Set Flash by List behavior, select the desired animation to affect from the Movie drop-down list. Choose the list object from the Select Box drop-down list, and input the level to load the movie into in the Level field. To replace an existing movie with the loaded movie, enter a level number that is currently occupied by another movie. To replace the original movie and unload every level, choose 0 for the level.

  To begin playing the movie immediately, set the Play option to Yes; otherwise, set Play to No. In order for the Set Flash by List behavior to work properly, you'll also need to set the values of each of the list items to a relative or absolute file URL pointing to an .swf file. Click the Parameters button on the List/Menu Property inspector to enter new labels and their corresponding values.

Caution   As Dreamweaver warns you, the Set Flash By List behavior is not supported for Netscape browsers.

- For the Zoom Flash behavior, select the desired animation to affect from the Movie drop-down list. Enter the value desired in the Zoom field. To zoom in, enter a number greater than 100; to zoom out, enter a number below 100. To reset the movie to the original zoom level, enter **0**.

7. After you've chosen all the desired parameters from the dialog box, select OK to close it. The Behaviors panel displays the event and action for the behavior just applied.

8. By default, onClick is the selected event. To change the triggering event to onMouseOver or onMouseOut, select the down arrow between the event and the action and choose the desired event from the list.

Advanced form validations

HTML forms can be tricky: The more you use forms to gather information from your visitors, the greater the possibility for user error. If, for example, your online form includes two fields for a telephone number — one for the United States and one for international visitors — you'll want to ensure that the proper data is entered in the correct field. To ensure that a user enters the type of information that you're expecting in your Flash form, the information needs to be validated. The JavaScript Integration Kit includes methods for validating 18 different types of data.

For the advanced form validations to work, you must work with both your Flash movie and the Dreamweaver page in which the movie is embedded. Here's an overview of the process:

On the Dreamweaver side:

✦ Create a form with hidden fields — one for each of the Flash fields you want to validate.

✦ Attach the Advanced Validate Form behavior to the form itself.

✦ Add one of the Browser Scripts for Flash functions, FDK_setFormText, to the page.

✦ Attach the desired validation behavior to the <body> tag of the current document.

On the Flash side:

✦ Make sure every form field has a unique variable name assigned to it.

✦ Add a getURL action to the on (press) event of the Submit button, calling the FDK_setFormText function inserted into the Dreamweaver page.

✦ Add another getURL action to the on (release) event of the Submit button, which invokes the FDK_Validate function — which was put on the Dreamweaver document by the Advanced Validate Form behavior.

Keep track of the names of the Hidden field inputs inserted in Dreamweaver, as well as the name of the form itself; they both are referenced when the functions are added in Flash.

Now that you have an overview, go through the process in a little more detail. Again, start with the Dreamweaver page:

1. Choose Insert ➪ Form to add a form to your document.

   In Dreamweaver, the form is automatically named (form*n*).

2. Within the form, add a Hidden form field for every Flash field you'd like to validate. Give each Hidden field a unique name and leave the Value field blank.

3. Select the ⟨form⟩ tag in the Tag Selector and, from the Behaviors panel, choose the Advanced Validate Form behavior. The Advanced Validate Form dialog box appears, as shown in Figure 25-18.

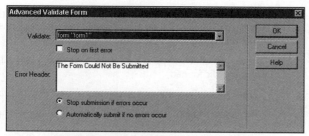

Figure 25-18: The Advanced Validate Form behavior controls how validations overall are applied.

4. In the Advanced Validate Form dialog box:

   • Select the form containing the Hidden elements you want to use from the Validate drop-down list.

   • To stop validating when an incorrect entry is encountered, check the Stop on First Error option.

   • Enter any desired message in the Error Header text area. The Error Header information is displayed in addition to any validation-specific error messages.

   • If your behavior is assigned to an onSubmit event (the default), choose the Stop Submission If Errors Occur option; otherwise, select the Automatically Submit If No Errors Occur option.

   • Select OK to close the dialog box when you're done.

5. Choose Commands ➪ Browser Scripts for Flash.

   The Browser Scripts for Flash command, discussed in more detail later in this section, embeds functions in the Dreamweaver page for communicating with Flash.

6. When the Browser Scripts for Flash dialog box opens, select the FDK_setFormText option; close the dialog box when you're done.

   The final preparation in Dreamweaver is to add the individual validation behaviors required.

7. Select the `<body>` tag from the Tag Selector and choose the Add Action (+) button in the Behaviors panel. From the drop-down list, select the desired validation behavior from the Advanced Form Validations category.

Most of the Advanced Form Validations behaviors have similar dialog boxes in which you can choose the particular form element (the Hidden field relating to the Flash form field) affected, make the field required, and set the error message. The differences between the various behaviors are detailed in Table 25-3.

Repeat Step 7 for every validation you'd like to apply in the form.

Table 25-3: Advanced Form Validation Behaviors

Behavior	Description
Alphanumeric Validation	Displays an error if non-alphanumeric characters are entered.
Credit Card Validation	Removes any spaces or hyphens and then displays an error message if the card number is not valid; this behavior does not authorize credit card purchases.
Date Validation	Optionally allows dates in the future, past, or in a particular range and specific format.
E-mail Validation	Ensures that the entry contains an ampersand (&) and a period (.).
Entry Length Validation	Accepts a defined number range of characters — for example, from 5 to 10.
Floating Point Validation	Displays an error if a non-number is entered; floating-point numbers can contain decimals.
Integer Validation	Displays the message if a non-number or a number with decimals is entered; you can also set an acceptable number range.
International Phone Validation	Removes parentheses, spaces, and hyphens and then ensures that at least six digits are entered.
Like Entry Validation	Checks one form field entry against another; this is typically used for password verification.
Mask Validation	Enables the designer to require a specific pattern of text, and/or numbers to be entered. Use A to indicate a letter, # for numbers, and ? if the entry can be either a letter or a number. For example, the mask A###?? requires a letter followed by three numbers, followed by two other alphanumeric characters.
Nonblank Validation	Displays a message if the field is left empty.
Radio Button Validation	Ensures that at least one option in a specified radio button group is selected. *Note:* This behavior is used only with HTML form elements.
Selection Made in List Validation	Displays an error if the user does not make a selection from a specific drop-down list. *Note:* This behavior is used only with HTML form elements.
Social Security Validation	Removes any hyphens, checks for a proper length, and then reformats the number into a 3-2-4 configuration, as in 123-45-6789.

Behavior	Description
Time Validation	Displays an error if a valid time with minutes within a certain range is not entered. Military time and most variations of A.M. and P.M. are accepted.
URL Validation	Looks for valid URL protocols and displays an error message if one is not found at the start of the entry. Accepted URLs include the following: `ftp://`, `http://`, `javascript:`, `file://`, `gopher://`, `https://`, `mailto:`, `rlogin://`, `shttp://`, `snews://`, `telnet://`, `tn3270://`, and `swais://`.
US Phone Validation	Verifies that the entered information is either 7 or 10 digits after removing any parentheses and hyphens.
US Zip Code Validation	Requires the entry to be either 5 or 9 digits.

Now that the Dreamweaver page is prepped, you're ready to prepare the Flash movie:

1. In Flash, add the required form fields as text input fields.

2. In the Text Options panel, enter a unique name in the Variable field.

3. Make sure your form has a graphic that acts as a Submit button.

4. Select the Submit button graphic and open the Object Actions panel.

5. Add an `on (press)` event and attach a `getURL` function to the event.

6. In the `getURL` function, call the `FDK_setFormText` function that was embedded into the Dreamweaver page. The `FDK_setForm Text` function takes three arguments: the name of the form, the name of the field to be validated, and the variable name assigned to the corresponding field in Flash.

   For example, say the form is named `theForm`, and you've created a field for gathering an e-mail address and given it a name in Dreamweaver such as `emailHidden`. In Flash, the variable assigned to the corresponding text field might be called `emailField`. In this case, the `getURL` function would read as follows:

   ```
   getURL("javascript:FDK_setFormText('theForm','emailHidden','"↻
   add emailField add "')";)
   ```

   Note the addition of the word `add` on either side of the variable name. This syntax is required for the parameters to be passed correctly.

7. Continue adding as many `FDK_setFormText` functions as you have fields to validate to the same `getURL` action. Separate each function with a semicolon.

   After you've entered all the required `FDK_setFormText` functions, you'll need to add one last event and function.

8. In the Object Actions panel for the Submit button graphic, add an `on (release)` event and attach a `getURL` action to it.

9. In the `getURL` action, insert the `FDK_Validate` function. This function takes four arguments, which correspond to the options available in Dreamweaver's Advanced Form Validations dialog box: `FormName`, `stopOnFailure`, `AutoSubmit`, and `ErrorHeader`. Both `stopOnFailure` and `AutoSubmit` are Booleans and accept either `true` or `false`.

As an example, suppose the form is again called theForm. Also suppose that you'd like the form to stop processing when an error is encountered. You also want it to be automatically submitted. Your general error message reads, "Attention!! I found an error on the form!" In this case, the getURL function would look like the following:

```
getURL("javascript:FDK_Validate('theForm',true,true,'Attention!!↵
I found an error on the form!\\n\\n');");
```

The \n\n (escaped as \\n\\n) after the function call acts as a hard return in the alert box to separate the generic message header from the specific validation error.

The final step is to cross the bridge again from Flash to Dreamweaver, bringing your exported Flash movie into the Dreamweaver page. Be sure to give it a unique name in the Property inspector.

Browser Scripts for Flash

With the JavaScript Integration Kit, integration is a two-way street: Not only is it easier to control Flash movies, the Flash movies can also affect the HTML page. The JIK includes one overall command called Browser Scripts for Flash, which offers five different types of control:

✦ Setting a form element's value

✦ Opening a remote browser window

✦ Setting a cookie

✦ Setting list menu items

✦ Swapping images for rollovers

Implementing these functions in Dreamweaver is simplicity itself: Just choose Commands ➪ Browser Scripts for Flash and check off the desired options, as shown in Figure 25-19. The various functions are grouped into five different categories. If you open a page with these functions already in place, you'll find the option already selected; deselecting the checkbox removes the function from the page when the dialog box is closed.

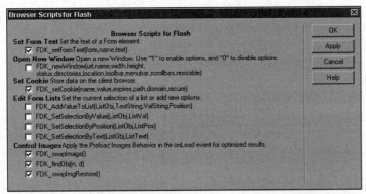

Figure 25-19: The Browser Scripts for Flash dialog box enables you to easily insert or remove functions that you can call from Flash.

Like the form validations, using the Browser Scripts is a two-program process. After you've installed them in Dreamweaver, you call the function in a Flash action. Each of the functions takes its own series of parameters; and, typically, each one is invoked using an action such as getURL. The functions and their arguments are explained in Table 25-4.

Table 25-4: Browser Scripts for Flash Functions

Function	Arguments	Description
FDK_setFormText	formName elementName variableName	Sets the value of a form element.
FDK_newWindow	URL windowName width height status directories location toolbar menubar scrollbars resizable	Opens a remote browser window. The width and height values are entered in pixels; for all other parameters (except URL and windowName), enter a **0** to disallow the element, and a **1** to include it.
FDK_setCookie	cookieName cookieValue expiresWhen path domain secureBoolean	Sets a cookie from within a Flash movie and can be used in conjunction with the Go To Flash Frame Based on Cookie behavior.
FDK_swapImage	imageName [blank] replacementPath 1	Performs an image swap in the HTML document. The second parameter is intentionally left blank.
FDK_swapImgRestore	n/a	Restores a previously executed image swap. For complex pages using multiple image swaps, it's best to explicitly swap the image from its replacement to its original source, rather than use the FDK_SwapImgRestore behavior.
FDK_findObj	n/a	Used in conjunction with the FDK_SwapImage behavior.
FDK_AddValueToList	ListObj TextString ValString Position	Inserts a new value into a form list element.

Continued

Table 25-4: *(continued)*

Function	Arguments	Description
FDK_SetSelectionByValue	ListObj ListValue	Determines the selection of a list item with a given value.
FDK_SetSelectionByPosition	ListObj ListPos	Determines the selection of a list item in a particular list position.
FDK_SetSelectionByText	ListObj ListText	Determines the selection of a list item with a given label.

Flash Dispatcher behavior

The final component of the JavaScript Integration Kit, the Flash Dispatcher behavior, is designed to smooth visitor access to your Web-based Flash content. The Flash Dispatcher checks to see if the visitor to your site already has the Flash Player and, if so, what version. If the proper version — or no player at all — is found, this behavior gives you several options. The visitor's browser can be redirected to a Flash-less page or to a site for downloading an appropriate version if an automatically downloaded version is not possible.

To apply this behavior, select the <body> tag from the Tag Selector and, from the Behaviors panel, choose Macromedia Flash Dispatcher Behavior. In the dialog box (see Figure 25-20), you have the following options:

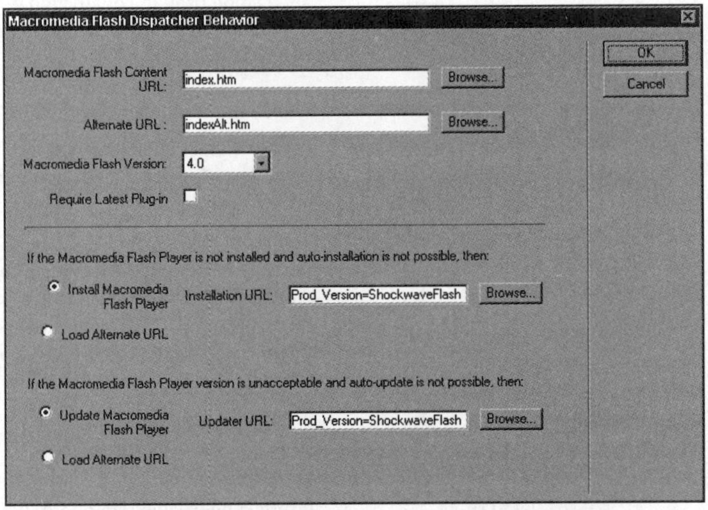

Figure 25-20: Make sure that only visitors with the proper Flash Player can see your movies with the Flash Dispatcher Behavior.

✦ **Macromedia Flash Content URL:** Enter or locate the path to the page containing the Flash movie.

✦ **Alternate URL:** Enter or locate the path to a Web page the visitor should go to if the proper Flash Player is not found.

✦ **Macromedia Flash Version:** Choose the lowest permissible version from 2.0, 3.0, 4.0, or 5.0.

✦ **Require Latest Plugin:** Select this option to require the latest version of the Flash Player.

✦ **Player Not Installed Options:** Any visitors who do not have the Flash Player installed are sent to a selectable download page or are directed to use the alternate URL.

✦ **Player Unacceptable Version:** Any visitors who do not have the required version of the Flash Player installed are sent to a selectable upgrade page or are directed to use the alternate URL.

The Flash Content URL can be the same page that the behavior is applied to or, in the case of what is referred to as a *gateway script*, another page.

Editing Flash Movies from within Dreamweaver

I'd like to close this chapter with a lovely new Dreamweaver MX feature: Flash Edit. Yes, that's right: You can now edit your Flash movies from within Dreamweaver (provided, of course, that you have Flash MX installed on your system). Dreamweaver doesn't do the actual movie editing work, of course. Here's how it works:

New Feature

When you click on the Flash Edit button, Dreamweaver launches Flash; you edit your movie in Flash, save your update, exit Flash, and end up back in Dreamweaver. It makes for a seamless Dreamweaver/Flash collaboration.

To edit a Flash movie from Dreamweaver:

1. In Dreamweaver, open the document that contains the Flash movie.

2. Do one of the following to begin editing your movie in Flash:

   • Select the Flash movie placeholder, and in the Flash Property inspector, click the Edit button.

   • Ctrl+double-click (Command+double-click) the Flash movie placeholder.

   • Right-click (Control+click) the movie placeholder, and choose Edit With Flash from the shortcut menu.

3. Dreamweaver launches Flash and automatically opens the selected movie's source FLA file or prompts you to open it manually. (To enable Flash to open the the FLA file automatically, you must assign it to the Flash object's Src field in Dreamweaver.)

4. In Flash, make the desired changes to your movie. The Flash Document window indicates that you are editing a movie from Dreamweaver, as shown in Figure 25-21.

5. When you are finished editing in Flash, click the Done button.

   Flash saves your changes to the source FLA file, updates the SWF file, and then whisks you back to Dreamweaver.

Caution

Whenever you edit a Flash movie from within Dreamweaver, a new iteration of Flash starts — even if Flash is already running. Unfortunately there is no known workaround for this known bug.

Done button

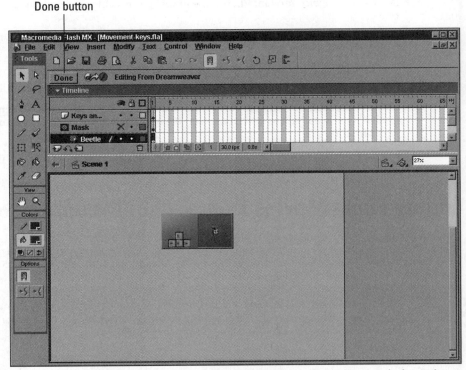

Figure 25-21: Using Dreamweaver's Flash Edit button, you can edit your Flash movies without having to exit/restart the Dreamweaver program.

Summary

Together, the interactive power of Shockwave and the speedy glitz of Flash can enliven Web content like nothing else. Dreamweaver is extremely well suited for integrating and displaying Shockwave and Flash movies. Here are some key pointers to keep in mind:

✦ Saving your Director movies as Shockwave movies enables them to be played on the Web with the help of a plugin or ActiveX control.

✦ Flash movies are a way to enhance your Web pages with vector animations, interactivity, and streaming audio. Flash movies require the Flash Player Plugin or ActiveX control.

✦ Dreamweaver has built-in objects for both Director and Flash movies. All the important parameters are accessible directly through the Property inspector.

✦ You need only three parameters to incorporate a Shockwave movie: the file's location, height, and width. Dreamweaver automatically imports a Flash movie's dimensions. You can get the exact measurements of a Shockwave movie from within Director.

✦ Dreamweaver comes with a JavaScript behavior for controlling Shockwave and Flash movies. This Control Shockwave or Flash behavior can be used as-is for adding external controls to the same Web page, or — with a minor modification — for adding the controls to another frame in the same frameset.

✦ Dreamweaver behaviors can be triggered from a Shockwave or Flash movie.

✦ The JavaScript Integration Kit for Flash is a powerful set of extensions that enables Flash movies to control Dreamweaver behaviors and HTML elements to activate Flash movies.

✦ You can launch Flash to edit Flash movies right from within Dreamweaver.

In the next chapter, you will learn how to add video to your Web pages.

✦   ✦   ✦

Adding Video to Your Web Page

I n a world accustomed to being entertained by moving images
50 feet high, it's hard to understand why people are thrilled to see
a grainy, jerky, quarter-screen-size video on a Web page. And in truth,
it's the promise of video on the Web, not the current state of it that
has folks excited. Many of the industry's major players, including
Microsoft and Apple, are spending big bucks to bring that promise
a little closer to reality.

QuickTime and RealVideo are the most popular formats on the Web,
and both are cross-platform. Video can be downloaded to the user
and then automatically played with a helper application, or it can be
streamed to the user so that it plays while it's downloading.

This chapter describes the many different methods for incorporating
video — whether you're downloading an MPEG file or streaming a
RealVideo movie — into your Web pages through Dreamweaver.

Video on the Web

It may be hard for folks not involved in the technology of computers
and the Internet to understand why the high-tech Web doesn't always
include something as "low-tech" as video. After all, television has been
around forever, right? The difficulties arise from the fundamental difference between the two media: Television and radio signals are analog, and computers are pure digital. Sure, you can convert an analog
signal to a digital one — but that's just the beginning of the solution.

The amount of information stored on a regular (analog) VHS cassette
is truly remarkable. Moving that amount of information about in the
ones and zeros of the digital world is a formidable task. For example,
storing the digital video stream from any digital video camcorder
uses up storage space at the rate of about 1 gigabyte every 5 minutes,
and that video is already compressed. Large file sizes also translate
into enormous bandwidth problems when you are transmitting video
over the Web.

To resolve this issue of mega-sized files, industry professionals and
manufacturers have developed various strategies, or *architectures*, for
the creation, storage, and playback of digital media. Each architecture has a different file format, and thus each requires the user to
have a playback system — whether a plug-in, ActiveX control, or Java
applet — capable of handling that particular format.

In an effort to keep file sizes as small as possible, Web videos are often presented in very small dimensions. It's not uncommon to display a video at a puny 180 by 120 pixels. Furthermore, you'll notice a major difference between conventional and Web-based video in terms of quality. Television video displays at roughly 30 frames per second, and film at 24 frames per second; but the best Web video rarely gets above 15 frames per second — virtually guaranteeing choppy motion in scenes with any action in them. Lossy compression also leads to *artifacting* — visible flaws introduced by the compression itself.

Given all the restrictions that video suffers on the Web, why use it at all? Simply because nothing else like it exists, and when you need video, you have to use video. Take heart, though. Advances are occurring at a rapid rate, both in the development of new video architectures and codecs (a codec is a compression algorithm) and in new, higher-speed Internet delivery systems, such as cable modems and DSL telephone lines. What you learn in this chapter enables you to include video in your Dreamweaver-built Web pages today and gives you a good foundation for accommodating future enhancements.

The Streaming Media Big Three

Technologies — and the companies that create them — come and go on the Internet. Over the past few years, quite a few different streaming media solutions have presented themselves and then faded away, leaving us with the current "Big Three": RealMedia, QuickTime, and Windows Media. These three technologies together represent almost the entire streaming media market, and the vast majority of Internet users have at least one of the corresponding players; many have two or even all three.

RealMedia

RealNetworks released the first streaming media system — RealAudio — in 1995. Over the years, RealAudio has evolved into RealMedia and now supports video, images, text, Flash movies, and standard audio types such as AIFF and MP3. All these media types can be combined into a single presentation using Synchronized Multimedia Integration Language (SMIL). The three primary software components of RealMedia are as follows:

✦ **RealOne Player:** This is the newest client software for viewing RealMedia content. RealOne Player is free and offers a full set of basic RealMedia viewing features. RealOne Player Plus is a subscription service that costs about $10/month and offers advanced viewing features along with 24/7 exclusive access to CNN.com, ABCNEWS.com, E!, FOXSports.com, and more. The RealOne Players are available at www.real.com/player. The RealOne Player interface is shown in Figure 26-1.

Note At the time this book was being written, both RealOne Players were available only for Windows 98, 2000, ME, NT and XP, although, presumably, the RealNetworks engineers were hard at work on Macintosh and Unix versions. If the RealOne Players are not yet available for your platform when you read this, you can always turn to RealOne's predecessors, the cross-platform RealPlayers, which are available from www.download.com.

✦ **RealSystem Producer:** This encoding software converts most types of audio and video (MPEG, QuickTime, and so forth) files to RealMedia (.rm) files. You can get RealSystem Producer Basic for free or the full-featured RealSystem Producer Plus for around $200. Read all about it at www.realnetworks.com/products/producer.

Figure 26-1: RealOne Player's interface enables the user to forego a Web browser completely when browsing for streaming media.

✦ **RealSystem Server:** This server software serves up RealMedia over Real-Time Streaming Protocol (RTSP). RealSystem Server Basic, which is free, is limited to 25 concurrent users. To support more users, you need to move up to a commercial product: RealSystem Server Plus (60 users) or RealSystem Server Professional (100–2,000 users). For more information, go to www.realnetworks.com/products/basicserverplus.

Note You can still offer RealMedia to your users over the Web's regular HTTP without any special server software. HTTP streaming is, however, far more limited than RTSP streaming.

RealNetworks has led the way in cross-platform authoring and playback. Versions of RealPlayer are available for Windows, Macintosh, Unix, Linux, and OS/2. (Hopefully, when you read this, the same will be true for RealOne Players.) Versions of RealProducer are available for almost as many platforms. WebTV even plays RealAudio 3.0. By contrast, QuickTime is limited to Windows and Macintosh, and Microsoft's streaming video solution is basically Windows-only.

RealNetworks has also led the way in terms of users; for years it was the only option for large-scale streaming media sites. Even now, when it faces the stiffest competition it's ever had, its market share is very high. RealPlayer is included with major browsers, as well as with Windows and Red Hat Linux.

Tip See www.real.com for examples of RealMedia content.

QuickTime

What "QuickTime" refers to is widely misunderstood. Some people confuse the video format QuickTime Video with QuickTime itself, but QuickTime Video is just one of the things a QuickTime movie might contain. Sometimes the high-profile QuickTime Player is confused with QuickTime, but it is just one dependent application.

The best way to explain QuickTime is to say that it's a multimedia operating system, enabling applications such as CD-ROM titles to run on top of it and use the features it provides. These features include support for audio, video, images, 3D objects, MIDI music (including a software wavetable synthesizer), streaming video, Flash movies, and MP3 audio. After you have QuickTime 4+ installed on your computer, Macromedia Director can access digital video, Flash can export complete QuickTime presentations, and otherwise pedestrian applications can play synthesized music.

With the inclusion of streaming video in QuickTime, Apple dressed up the QuickTime MoviePlayer with an eye-catching brushed aluminum look and changed its name to QuickTime Player. Apple positioned itself as a competitor to RealNetworks in the Web broadcasting field and now has almost *35 percent* of the streaming market. QuickTime movies have a .mov filename extension.

Like RealMedia, QuickTime streaming has three main software components:

✦ **QuickTime and QuickTime Player:** All the viewing goodness of QuickTime and QuickTime Player (see Figure 26-2) is free and available for Macintosh and Windows at `www.apple.com/quicktime`. QuickTime is also included with all Macintosh computers, and installed on Windows by CD-ROM titles. Just as with RealOne and RealPlayer, users can spend more time in QuickTime Player and less in a browser because of the favorites storage and Flash navigation elements in many streaming presentations.

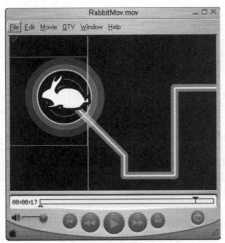

Figure 26-2: The QuickTime player offers a slick interface with retractable controls.

✦ **QuickTime Pro and QuickTime Player Pro:** For about $30, Apple sells you a key code that unlocks the content creation features of QuickTime and turns it into QuickTime Pro, enabling QuickTime-dependent applications to create a vast range of QuickTime content. QuickTime Player becomes QuickTime Player Pro: a great piece of software that provides easy content conversion and cut-and-paste video compositing, although the interface is Spartan and sometimes hides functionality. Apple has a directory of third-party QuickTime authoring resources at `http://developer.apple.com/quicktime/`.

✦ **QuickTime Streaming Server:** QuickTime Streaming Server delivers video over the Web using the standard RTSP, just like RealPlayer. Apple released QuickTime Streaming Server as open source software, and it is available completely free — no per stream charge, either — for Mac OS X, Linux, Solaris, and Windows NT/2000. See `www.apple.com/quicktime/servers`.

Tip   Examples of QuickTime streaming content can be found on the QuickTime home page at `www.apple.com/quicktime`.

Windows Media

Microsoft has released a succession of media technologies over the years in an effort to gain some sort of foothold in content creation and delivery. The history of Microsoft multimedia is an incredible story of acquisitions, rebranding, orphaned technologies, and outright copying of everybody else.

With Windows Media, however, Microsoft has gone all out, providing a solid — if unexciting — solution with lots of partners. Still, Windows Media's greatest asset is its automatic inclusion with every Windows PC, virtually guaranteeing it a huge installed base as time goes on. Windows Media files have filename extensions of .asf or .asx. The software involved in Windows Media includes the following:

✦ **Windows Media Player:** The supercharged Windows Media Player (see Figure 26-3) received a complete face-lift when it evolved from version 6 to version 7 — and with the new changeable skins feature, it's quite the literal face-lift. In addition to Web streaming, the Windows Media Player accesses many other media types, including audio CDs, Internet radio, and portable devices. It supports many file extensions, including .asf, .asx, .avi, .mpg, .mpeg, .mp3, .qt, .aif, .mov, and .au. The Windows Media Player home page is at `www.microsoft.com/windows/mediaplayer`.

Figure 26-3: The Windows Media Player offers instant access to many media types as well as switchable skins (shown here is the sexy "Raptor" skin).

✦ **Content creation and server software:** A directory of tools for working with Windows Media can be found at www.microsoft.com/windows/windowsmedia. Most are from Microsoft themselves, and all are Windows-only.

Tip The Windows Media home page is located at www.windowsmedia.com and includes sample content.

Working with Video Clips

If you have short video clips you'd like to put on the Web, you may not need the industrial strength — or the hassle and expense — of a streaming media solution. Short video clips can be included in a Web page just by linking to them or embedding them.

Depending on the viewer's software setup, video clips either download completely and then start playing right away; or start playing as soon as enough of the video has arrived to make uninterrupted playback possible, as shown in Figure 26-4.

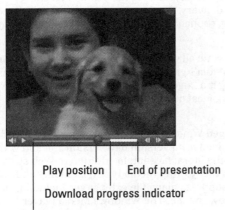

Play position   End of presentation

Download progress indicator

Beginning of presentation

Figure 26-4: QuickTime Player starts playing video clips when it has downloaded enough to ensure that playback is uninterrupted.

Video clips come in a few common formats, described in Table 26-1. In addition to the video format itself, what *codec* (en**co**der/**dec**oder) a particular video clip uses is also important. A codec provides video compression, and it is required for decompression at playback time. Many codecs are included with Windows and with QuickTime, so codecs are not usually a problem, unless you're authoring for platforms other than Windows and Macintosh.

Caution One codec to watch out for if you're making cross-platform movies is the Intel Indeo Video codec, sometimes used for Video for Windows (AVI) files. The Indeo codec for Macintosh is not included with QuickTime and must be installed manually by Macintosh users.

Table 26-1: Video Clip File Formats

Video Format	Typical File Name Extension	Description
MPEG	.mpg, .mpeg, .mpe	The MPEG video format is the work of the Motion Picture Experts Group. Windows computers usually play MPEG video clips with Windows Media Player or another, older Microsoft player. Macintosh systems play MPEG clips with QuickTime.
QuickTime	.mov	QuickTime movies can contain a multitude of media types and usually require QuickTime for playback.
QuickTime Video	.mov	A QuickTime movie that contains plain video only and can be played by almost any video player on a machine that doesn't have QuickTime installed, as long as the right codec is available.
Video for Windows (AVI)	.avi	The popular (but now officially unsupported) format used by Microsoft's Video for Windows (also known as ActiveMovie or NetShow). As with QuickTime Video, clips can be played in almost any player, as long as the right codec is installed.

MPEG, QuickTime Video, or AVI clips are good candidates for linking or embedding because there are a wide variety of players on multiple platforms that can play them. QuickTime movies are best aimed squarely at the QuickTime Player because of the multiple media types that they contain.

Linking to video

To keep 21st-century TV/movie-addicted users interested in your site, you might want to spice things up by including a (low-bandwidth!) video or two. To add a video clip to your Dreamweaver Web page, follow these steps:

1. Select the text, image, or dynamic element that you want to serve as the link to the video file.

Tip

If you use an image as a link, you might want to use a frame from the video clip in order to provide a preview.

2. In the Property inspector, enter the name of the video file in the Link text box or select the Folder icon to browse for the file.

   To choose a dynamic source, choose the Select File Name From Data Sources option in the Select File dialog box. Be sure your selected data source contains either relative or absolute links to a video file.

3. Because video files can be quite large, it's also good practice to note the file size next to the link name or enter it in the Alt text box, as shown in Figure 26-5.

Figure 26-5: You can insert any video file for user download by creating a link to it, as if it were a simple Web page.

Embedding video

You can gain more control over the way your video clip plays by embedding it in the Web page with the `<embed>` tag. Modifying the attributes of the `<embed>` tag enables you to modify how the video is presented. Video clips inserted this way play back in whatever players are available, just as linked video clips do.

New Feature The Assets panel includes a Movies category that holds QuickTime movies, MPEG videos, and Windows Media file types. As with all the other Assets panel categories, you must select the Refresh Site List button (the curved arrow at the bottom of the Assets panel) to initially populate the panel with all the movies in the current site. The preview pane includes a Play button for displaying the movies before they are inserted in the page.

To embed a simple video clip in a Web page, follow these steps:

1. Choose Insert ⇨ Media ⇨ Plugin, or select the Plugin object from the Media category of the Insert bar, or drag the file from the Movie category of the Assets panel to your Web page.

2. If you inserted a Plugin object, select the video file in the Select File dialog box.

   Movies dragged onto the page from the Assets panel already include the source path. The Plugin placeholder is displayed as a 32 × 32 icon.

3. In the Plugin Property inspector, enter the dimensions of your video clip in the width and height boxes, marked W and H, respectively. Or size the Plugin object directly by dragging one of its selection handles.

Playing Videos within Dreamweaver

Dreamweaver can access and use Netscape plugins to display video right in the Document window at design-time. These plugins can be installed in Netscape's Plugins folder, in Internet Explorer's Plugins folder, or in Dreamweaver's own Plugins folder. Dreamweaver checks all three every time it starts up. Installing the correct plugins into Netscape and enabling Dreamweaver to use them from there can make maintaining your plugins easier, because many come with browser-specific installation programs that are hard to adapt to Dreamweaver.

Whenever a file is embedded for playback via a plugin, a green Play button appears in the Property inspector. To play a particular video in Dreamweaver's Document window, all you have to do is select the Plugin placeholder and click the Play button. The video begins playing, and the green Play button becomes a red Stop button, as shown in Figure 26-6. To stop playback — surprise! — just click the Stop button.

Tip How can playing a video during the design phase be useful? I've used this capability to sample the background color of the page from the background of a video's title or ending frame so that the video clip fits seamlessly into the page.

Figure 26-6: Playing video within Dreamweaver is as simple as having the right plugin installed and clicking Play.

You can also use the menus and the corresponding keyboard shortcuts to control the digital video in the Document window: View ➪ Plugins ➪ Play or Ctrl+Alt+P (Command+Option+P), and View ➪ Plugins ➪ Stop or Ctrl+Alt+X (Command+Option+X). If you have multiple videos inserted on the page, you can play them all by choosing View ➪ Plugins ➪ Play All or by using the keyboard shortcut Ctrl+Alt+Shift+P (Command+Option+Shift+P), and stop them with View ➪ Plugins ➪ Stop All or Ctrl+Alt+Shift+X (Command+Option+Shift+X).

Caution Unsupported plugins are listed in the UnsupportedPlugins.txt file in Dreamweaver's Configuration/Plugins folder. The one plugin identified by Macromedia as not working with Dreamweaver is the Video for Windows Plugin on Windows. If you're relying on this plugin for video playback, you still have to preview your video files through a browser.

Inserting QuickTime Movies

The HTML command for incorporating a QuickTime movie (or any other medium that requires a plugin) is the `<embed>` tag. Because so many different types of plugins exist, Dreamweaver uses a generic Plugin inspector that enables an unlimited number of parameters to be specified. If you regularly work with QuickTime movies, using a custom QuickTime Dreamweaver object such as the one shown in Figure 26-7 can streamline the process. Although you still need to add some parameters by hand, having easy access to the most common ones can be a real time-saver.

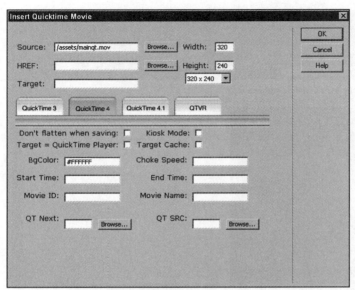

Figure 26-7: Add a third-party QuickTime object to Dreamweaver to simplify embedding QuickTime movies.

Only three `<embed>` tag parameters are absolutely required for a QuickTime movie: the source of the file, the movie's width, and the movie's height. The QuickTime Plugin, however, also offers an amazing array of additional `<embed>` tag attributes to enable you to fine-tune the way content is presented.

Note   The QuickTime Plugin is used by both Netscape and Internet Explorer on both Windows and Macintosh to enable the browser to interface with QuickTime.

To insert a QuickTime movie in your Web page, follow these steps:

1. Choose Insert ⇨ Media ⇨ Plugin, or select the Plugin object from the Media category of the Insert bar, or drag the movie file from the Movie category of the Assets panel to your Web page.

2. If you inserted a Plugin object, select the QuickTime movie file in the Select File dialog box. If you dragged the movie file from the Assets panel, the Plugin's Src attribute is automatically set to the QuickTime movie file pathname.

Tip   If you're working on a Macintosh and your QuickTime movie doesn't have a filename extension, add **.mov** to the end of its name before embedding it or placing it on the Web.

3. In the Plugin Property inspector (shown in Figure 26-8), enter the dimensions of your QuickTime movie in the width (W) and height (H) boxes, or size the Plugin object directly by dragging one of its selection handles.

Width box

Height box | Plugin Src text box

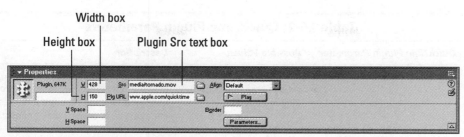

Figure 26-8: When inserting a QuickTime movie, specify the properties and values in the Plugin Property inspector.

Tip

If you don't know the dimensions of your QuickTime movie, open it in the QuickTime Player, choose Movie ➪ Get Movie Properties, and select Size from the options list on the right of the dialog box that appears.

4. In the Plg URL text box, enter `http://www.apple.com/quicktime`. This is the Web address to which users who don't have QuickTime are directed by their browser.

5. Select the Parameters button to open the Parameters dialog box (see Figure 26-9), where you can enter additional `<embed>` tag attributes: the name in the left column and the value in the right column. Use Tab to move between the columns. Table 26-2 lists the most commonly used `<embed>` tag parameters for QuickTime movies. Use this list to add any parameters that you may require and click OK when you're done.

Note

Any of the parameters or their values may be linked to a data source by selecting the lightning-bolt icon and choosing an appropriate field from the Dynamic Data dialog box.

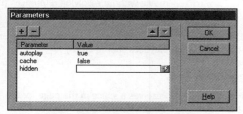

Figure 26-9: Use the Parameters dialog box to enter attributes for any plug-in. Dynamic values may be entered by selecting the lightning-bolt icon and choosing a field from a defined recordset.

Tip

Dreamweaver's Plugin Property inspector enables you to enter several additional attributes generally used with other objects, such as images. These include Align (alignment), V Space (vertical space), H Space (horizontal space), and Border (border). You can also enter a name in the Plugin text box if you plan to refer to your QuickTime movie in JavaScript or another programming language.

Table 26-2: QuickTime Plugin Parameters

QuickTime Plugin Parameter	Possible Values	Description
Autoplay	true or false; default set by user in QuickTime Plug-in Settings	When set to false, a movie won't play until the user clicks Play in the controller. Otherwise, it starts playing as soon as enough data is downloaded to ensure uninterrupted playback.
Bgcolor	RGB colors in hexadecimal, such as "#FFFFFF"; or valid HTML color names, such as "red"	Specifies the color of the space set aside by the width and height attributes but not taken up by the QuickTime movie. Add a border to a QuickTime movie by setting the appropriate bgcolor and increasing the width and height attributes by a few pixels.
Cache	true or false; default set by user in QuickTime Plug-in Settings	Specifies whether the browser should store the movie in its cache for later retrieval. Doesn't work in IE.
Controller	true (default for most movies) or false (default for QuickTime VR, Flash, and image files)	Displays the controller panel attached to the bottom of the movie
Dontflattenwhensaving	(does not take a value)	When included, using the Save As QuickTime option on the QuickTime Plugin's controller menu saves the movie without resolving references (not self-contained).
endtime	30-frame SMPTE time-code — hours:minutes: seconds:frames (30ths of a second)	Indicates the point in the movie where playback should stop
Height	A value in pixels; usually the height of the movie	Reserves a space in the page for the QuickTime movie
Hidden	(does not take a value)	Tells the QuickTime Plugin not to show the movie. Audio is played, however.
Href	URL	A link to go to when the movie is clicked. You can supply either an absolute or a relative URL. QuickTime movies replace the current movie in-place; Web pages open in the browser.
kioskmode	true or false (default)	Eliminates the QuickTime Plugin's controller menu when set to true
loop	true, false (default), or palindrome	Causes the movie to loop continuously when set to true. The palindrome value causes the QuickTime Player to play alternately forward and backward.

QuickTime Plugin Parameter	Possible Values	Description
Movieid	a number	A number identifying the movie so that another wired sprite movie can control it
Moviename	a name	A name identifying the movie so that another wired sprite movie can control it
Playeveryframe	true or false (default)	When set to true, forces the movie to play every frame, even if it must do so at a slower rate than real time. Disables audio and QuickTime Music tracks.
Pluginspage	www.apple.com/ quicktime	Where users who don't have QuickTime should be sent to get it
Qtnext*n*	URL	Specifies a movie as being *n* in a sequence of movies. The movie specified in the src attribute is movie 0 (zero).
Qtnext	goto*n*	Tells the QuickTime Plugin to open movie *n* in an already specified sequence of movies
Qtsrc	URL	Tells the QuickTime Plugin to open this URL instead of the one specified by the src attribute. This is a way to open files that don't have a .mov filename extension — such as MP3 files — with the QuickTime Plugin, regardless of how the user's system is set up. Use a dummy movie in the src attribute.
qtsrcchokespeed	movie-rate, or a number in bytes per second	Downloads the movie specified in the qtsrc attribute in chunks; movie-rate indicates to use the movie's data rate.
scale	tofit, aspect, or a number (default is 1)	Resizes the QuickTime Player movie. By setting scale to fit, you can scale the movie to the dimensions of the embedded box as specified by the height and width values. Setting scale to aspect resizes the movie to either the height or the width while maintaining the proper aspect ratio of the movie. Set to a number, the size of the movie is multiplied by that number.
starttime	30-frame SMPTE time-code — hours:minutes: seconds:frames (30ths of a second)	Indicates the point in the movie where playback should start

Continued

Table 26-2: *(continued)*

QuickTime Plugin Parameter	Possible Values	Description
`Target`	name of a valid frame or window (_self, _parent, _top, _blank, or an explicit frame/window name) or QuickTimePlayer	Enables the link specified in the `href` attribute to be targeted to a specific frame or window. The value QuickTimePlayer causes the movie specified in the `href` attribute to be opened in the QuickTime Player.
`Targetcache`	true or false (default)	Same as the `cache` attribute but for the movie called by a poster movie using the `href` attribute
`Volume`	0 to 100 (default)	Controls the volume of the audio track(s). 0 is softest; 100 is loudest.
`Width`	A value in pixels; usually the width of the movie	Reserves a space in the page for the QuickTime movie

QuickTime versions

Before inserting a QuickTime movie into a Web page, it's helpful to know what version of QuickTime your movie requires. Because QuickTime movies can contain a variety of track types, each containing a different type of medium, some movies may play back with QuickTime 3, whereas others require QuickTime 4 or higher.

You can identify the different tracks in a QuickTime movie by opening it in QuickTime Player and choosing Movie ➪ Get Movie Properties. In the QuickTime dialog box that appears, the options list on the left details the various tracks, as shown in Figure 26-10. If your movie has Flash or MP3 audio tracks, it requires QuickTime 4 or higher for playback. It's a good idea to note this somewhere in your Web page and offer users a link to `http://www.apple.com/quicktime` so that they can upgrade if necessary.

Figure 26-10: In addition to the streaming video track, this QuickTime movie has a Flash track that provides the opening titles and closing credits.

Playing QuickTime VR

QuickTime VR (QTVR) enables the user to "look around" in a virtual space created from a panoramic image or to rotate an object around its center point in three dimensions ("object movies"). The QuickTime VR author can also designate certain areas in the movie as hotspots that, when selected by the user, activate a link to another page or another movie. Although purists argue that QTVR is not really virtual reality, the technology is a low-bandwidth, quick-and-dirty virtual reality that makes sense on today's Web. QTVR is commonly used to show homes, cars, and other products to potential buyers.

When you view a QuickTime VR movie, the QuickTime Player provides Zoom buttons (– and +), (see Figure 26-11) and a custom mouse pointer pans the image left and right.

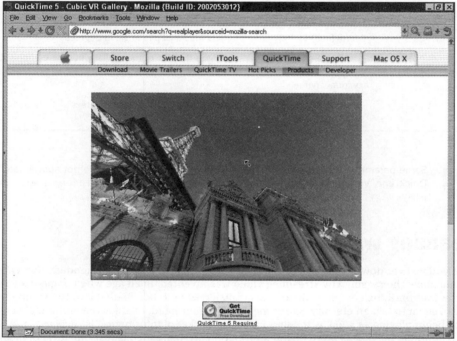

Figure 26-11: QuickTime VR's panoramic views enable the user to look around in a panoramic picture by moving the cursor right, left, up, and down.

QuickTime VR <embed> tag attributes are entered in the same manner as other QuickTime Plugin attributes: Click the Parameters button in the Plugin Property inspector to open the Parameters dialog box and enter attributes and values. As with a regular QuickTime Player movie, the only required parameters for a QTVR movie are the source file, movie width, and movie height.

Table 26-3 lists the QuickTime Plugin <embed> tag attributes that work with QuickTime VR only.

Table 26-3: Additional Parameters for QuickTime VR Movies

QuickTime VR Parameter	Possible Values	Description
Correction	none or full (default)	Applies the correction filter
Fov	0 (default) to 360	Specifies the initial field-of-view angle, in degrees
Hotspot*n*	URL	Defines the URL for any designated hotspot. Replace *n* with the identification number given the hotspot during QTVR authoring.
Node	A number less than or equal to the number of nodes in the movie	Specifies which node of a multinode movie is opened first
pan	0 (default) to 360	Sets the initial pan angle in degrees
target{n}	_self, _parent, _top, _blank, a frame or window name	Targets the URL of the similarly numbered hotspot at a specific frame or window
tilt	−42.5 to 42.5 (0 is the default)	Sets the initial tilt angle in degrees

Caution   Some parameters, meaningful to regular QuickTime Player movies, are not appropriate for QuickTime VR movies. These include autoplay, controller, hidden, href, loop, playeveryframe, target, and volume.

Streaming with RealMedia

If you've ever downloaded a few minutes of digital video over a slow modem connection, you know the reason why streaming video was invented. In an age when immediacy rules, the wait until the complete video file is transferred and then loaded into the video player can seem to last an eternity. *Streaming*, on the other hand, enables the multimedia content to begin playing as soon as the first complete packet of information is received, and then to continue playing as more digital information arrives. Video is just one form of media to get the streaming treatment: You can also stream audio, animation, text, and other formats.

Using a Poster Movie

One of the nicest features of the QuickTime Plugin is the capability to have one movie replace itself with another. This enables you to place very lightweight (small file size), single-image "poster movies" into your Web pages instead of the full clips, so that the rest of the elements in your page load quickly. When the user clicks a poster movie, it replaces itself with your full movie, which begins downloading or streaming immediately. A poster movie can be a preview of the full movie that replaces it or a generic QuickTime image, as shown in the following figure.

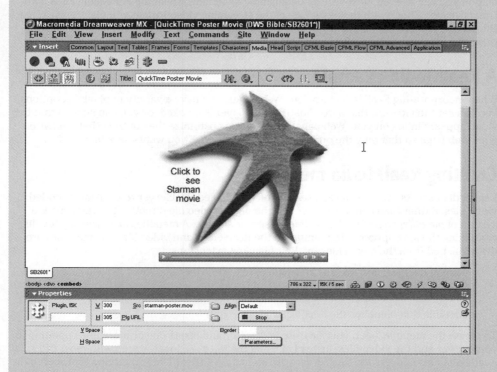

Creating a poster movie requires QuickTime Pro. Simply open your movie in QuickTime Player Pro, move to the frame you'd like to use as a preview, choose File ➪ Export, and select Movie to Picture from the Export options list and Photo-JPEG from the Use options list. This exports the current frame as a QuickTime Image using JPEG compression. Choose File ➪ New Player to create a new untitled movie, and then select File ➪ Import to import your picture into this new movie. Save your work as a self-contained movie. A good idea for a filename might be the name of your full movie with "poster" prefixed.

Embed your poster movie in your Web page as described previously in this chapter and use the Plugin Property inspector's Parameters button to add the `href` attribute with the value set to the URL of your full movie, so that the `<embed>` tag looks like the following:

```
<embed src="my_poster_movie.mov" width="360" height="180"
    href="my_full_movie.mov">
</embed>
```

You can also make multiple-frame poster movies if you like. As long as you keep the file size low, your pages will seem to load more quickly, and you'll provide your users more control over the way they experience them.

Regardless of which streaming video protocol you use, the procedure for incorporating the file on your Web page is basically the same, although the details (such as filename extensions) differ. In order to demonstrate the general technique and still offer some specific information you can use, the next section details how to include streaming RealMedia clips with Dreamweaver. Check with the developer of the streaming video format you plan to use to get the precise installation details. Typically, a great deal of information is available for free on the developers' Web sites.

A RealMedia example

When incorporating RealMedia into your Web pages, you have a variety of playback options. You can set the video so that a free-floating RealPlayer is invoked, or you can specify that the video appears inline on your Web page. You can also customize the controls that appear on your Web page so that only the ones you want — at the size you want — are included.

Creating RealMedia metafiles

RealMedia uses its own specialized server software called RealServer to transmit encoded video files. Rather than call this server and the digital video file directly, RealMedia uses a system of *metafiles* to link to the RealMedia server and file. A metafile is an ordinary text file containing the appropriate URL pointing to the RealServer and video file. The metafiles are distinguished from the media files by their filename extensions:

✦ RealMedia files: .rm, .ra, .rp, .rt, .swf

✦ Metafile that launches the independent RealPlayer: .ram

✦ Metafile that launches the RealPlayer Plugin: .rpm

To create the metafile, open your favorite text editor and insert one or more lines pointing to your server and the video files. Instead of using the `http://` locator seen with most URLs, RealMedia files address the RealServer with an `rtsp://` (Real-Time Streaming Protocol) indicator. The contents of the file should take the following form:

```
rtsp://hostname/path/file
```

where *hostname* is the domain name of the server on which the RealMedia files are stored, *path* is the path to the file, and *file* is the name of the RealMedia file. For example, to display a training video, the metafile contents might look like the following:

```
rtsp://www.trainers.com/videos/training01.rm
```

You can include multiple video clips by putting each one on its own line, separated by a single return. RealMedia plays each clip in succession, and the user can skip from one clip to another.

Inserting RealMedia in your Web page

After you've created both the encoded RealMedia file and the metafiles, you're ready to insert them into your Web page. You have two basic techniques for including RealMedia, either as a link or using the `<embed>` tag.

Using a link

Generally, if you want to invoke the free-floating RealPlayer, you use a link; the `href` attribute is set to an address for a metafile, as follows:

```
<a href="videos/howto01.ram">Demonstration</a>
```

When the link is selected, it calls the metafile that, in turn, calls the video file on the RealServer. As the file begins to download to the user's system, the RealPlayer program is invoked and starts to display the video as soon as possible through the independent video window, as shown in Figure 26-12. The link can be inserted in Dreamweaver through either the Text or Image Property inspector.

Figure 26-12: You can set up your RealMedia clip so that it plays in its own RealPlayer window. This is the RealOne Player's "compact" view (compare with Figure 26-1).

Using <embed>

If, on the other hand, you'd like to make the video appear inline with the Web page's text or graphics, you use Dreamweaver's Plugin object to insert an `<embed>` tag. Position the pointer where you want the RealMedia to be displayed, and either choose Insert ⇨ Media ⇨ Plugin, or select the Plugin object from the Media category of the Insert bar. In the Select File dialog box that appears, select the video's metafile.

HTTP Streaming

To gain the maximum throughput of your RealVideo files, it's best to use the RealServer software. However, some Web site clients must economize and can't afford the specialized server. Not widely known is the fact that you can use a regular World Wide Web server to stream RealVideo and other RealMedia files over HTTP.

Two prerequisites exist for HTTP streaming: Your system administrator must first correctly configure the MIME types, and you must provide multiple files to match the right user-selectable modem speeds. The proper MIME types are as follows:

✦ audio/x-pn-RealAudio (for .ra, .rm, or .ram files)

✦ audio/x-pn-RealAudio-plugin (for .rpm files)

✦ video/x-pn-RealVideo (for .ra, .rm, or .ram files)

✦ video/x-pn-RealVideo-plugin (for .rpm files)

RealServer automatically selects the right file for the user's modem connection. If you are using HTTP streaming capabilities, you should offer multiple files to accommodate the various Internet connection rates, such as 28.8K, 56K, and higher (for cable and DSL).

Besides a reduction in download speed, the other disadvantage to using HTTP streaming instead of RealServer streaming is the reduced number of simultaneous users who can be served. RealServer can handle hundreds of connections at the same time; HTTP streaming is far more limited.

When the Plugin object representing the RealMedia clip is selected, you can enter values for the <embed> tag in the Property inspector. The only attributes required for a RealMedia clip, as with the QuickTime Player object, are the file source and the width and height of the movie. Similarly, as you can with QuickTime Player, you can control your RealMedia movie with a healthy number of attributes. Enter attributes by selecting the Parameters button on the Plugin Property inspector and entering attributes and their values in the Parameters dialog box (shown earlier in Figure 26-9). RealMedia parameters are listed in Table 26-4.

Table 26-4: Parameters for RealMedia Movies

RealMedia G2 Parameter	Possible Values	Description
Autostart	true or false (default)	Tells RealPlayer to start playing as soon as content is available
Console	*name*, _master, _unique	Determines the console name for each control in a Web page that has multiple controls. Force controls on a page to refer to the same file by giving them all the same *name*. A value of _master links to all controls on a page, whereas _unique connects to no other instances.

RealMedia G2 Parameter	Possible Values	Description
Controls	all (default), controlpanel, imagewindow, infovolumepanel, infopanel, playbutton, positionslider, positionfield, statuspanel, statusbar, stopbutton, statusfield, volumeslider	Enables the placement of individual control panel elements in the Web page. You can use multiple controls in one attribute or multiple <embed> tags to build a custom RealMedia interface.
nolabels	true or false (default)	Suppresses the Title, Author, and Copyright labels in the Status panel. If you set nolabels to true, the actual data is still visible.

Summary

Digital video on the Web is in its infancy. Bandwidth is still too restricted to enable full-screen, full-motion movies, no matter what the format. However, you can include download-able as well as streaming video content through Dreamweaver's Plugin object and Plugin Property inspector.

✦ Even with compression, digital video has steep storage and download requirements.

✦ You can include a digital video movie to be downloaded in your Web page by linking to it as if it were a Web page.

✦ Use Dreamweaver's Plugin object when you want your video to be presented inline on your Web page. The Plugin Property inspector then enables you to alter the video's parameters for any video architecture.

✦ QuickTime is a cross-platform, multimedia architecture that offers much more than just video. QuickTime movies can include QuickTime VR, MIDI music, 3D objects, Flash movies, and more.

✦ To enable your visitors to view your digital video clips as soon as possible, use a streaming video technology such as RealMedia, QuickTime, or Windows Media. Streaming video files can be displayed in a separate player or embedded in the Web page.

In the next chapter, you learn how Dreamweaver helps you incorporate sound and music into your Web pages.

✦   ✦   ✦

Using Audio on Your Web Page

Web sites tend to be divided into two categories: those totally without sound, and those that use a lot of it — there's not much middle ground. Many music and entertainment sites rely heavily on both streaming audio and downloadable audio files, such as MP3.

In this chapter, you learn how to use audio in the Web pages you design with Dreamweaver. You look at traditional digital audio formats such as AIFF and WAV, and how you can turn these into files suitable for publishing on the Web, in formats such as MP3 and RealAudio. You also look at music formats, such as standard MIDI files and QuickTime Music.

Lest you forget that you're Dreamweaving here, you look at some Dreamweaver extensions you can use to get audio-enabled sites up and running in no time. But before you leap into those deep waters, it'd be a good idea to get an overview of digital audio and its place on the Web.

 Cross-Reference Because the primary technologies for distributing streaming audio are also the primary technologies for streaming video, you may find it helpful to familiarize yourself with the Big Three streaming media technologies — RealMedia, QuickTime, and Windows Media — introduced in Chapter 26.

Digital Audio Fundamentals

Digital audio files are digitized representations of sound waves. Although not as heavy as digital video, digital audio files — even those that have been compressed — are still a strain for today's Web. As usual, minimizing file sizes wherever possible makes for a better experience for users of your Web site.

File formats

Many different formats for digital audio files are in use today across the various computer platforms. The most common formats are described in Table 27-1 and can be identified by their unique filename extensions and/or by their icons on Macintosh systems.

Table 27-1: Web Digital Audio File Formats

Audio Format	Typical File Name Extension	Description
AU	.au, .snd	Very common on the early Unix-dominated Web. Uncompressed and no longer suitable for Web use.
AIFF	.aif, .aiff	The Audio Interchange File Format was developed by Apple. Uncompressed versions can be played in most browsers, but avoid using AIFF on the Web if possible.
Flash	.swf	Not just an animation format, Flash streams PCM- or MP3-compressed audio at various bit rates.
MP3	.mp3, .mp2	The MPEG Audio Layer 3 format features high-quality digital audio files with excellent compression. MP3 has become the standard for downloadable music. It plays in QuickTime Player 4+, RealPlayer G2 6+, Windows Media Player 5.2+, and a whole range of standalone players that work as browser helper applications.
QuickTime	.mov	A QuickTime movie with a soundtrack only
RealAudio	.ra or .ram	The audio component of RealNetworks' RealMedia. Lots of players. Good quality at low bit rates, but not as good as MP3.
Rich Music Format	.rmf	Beatnik's hybrid audio/music format. Samples are either PCM or MP3 compressed.
Shockwave Audio	.swa	The audio component of Shockwave, they're low bit-rate MP3 files with a different file header. They stream over HTTP, and any MP3 player can play them locally.
WAV	.wav	Co-developed by Microsoft and IBM, this is the default audio format for Windows. Uncompressed versions play in browsers, but avoid using them on the Web whenever possible because of their large file sizes.
Windows Media	.asf, asx, .wma, .wmv	Microsoft's streaming media solution

Which audio format should you choose? That depends on a combination of factors, including your target audience, available bandwidth, and the purpose of the audio's content.

Although most browsers can play standard digital audio files, such as AIFF and WAV, the sheer uncompressed bulk of these files renders them unsuitable for the Internet, especially now that so many highly compressed formats exist. In the early days of the Web, with slower computers and less advanced compression technologies, these uncompressed audio files were the only game in town. But today, fast computers are capable of easily decoding MP3 and RealAudio, and free players for those formats are common.

A live Internet broadcast dictates a streaming solution such as RealAudio, QuickTime, or Windows Media. If you're offering complete songs for download, you may not have to look any further than MP3. It's not uncommon to offer a sound file in multiple formats. Although many users have more than one player, offering your audio in a few formats gives you a better chance of reaching everybody.

Cross-Reference   For more on RealAudio, QuickTime, and Windows Media, refer to Chapter 26.

Converting one audio file format to another typically involves opening the source file in an audio editor that can read that format and exporting it in another format. If you lack a professional audio editor such as SoundForge or Peak, a simple alternative is to use QuickTime Pro; it reads and writes a lot of formats. You can also easily cut and paste sections of files — to remove or add a few seconds of silence, for example.

Making audio files lighter

As well as categorizing audio by file format, you can also think of audio on the Web as being in one of two categories: uncompressed and compressed. AIFF and WAV audio files come in compressed and uncompressed formats, but only the uncompressed versions play in Web browsers. If you can't compress an audio file in some way, the only way to reduce its file size is to reduce its quality in one of three ways:

✦ **Convert a stereo file into a mono file:** A stereo file has two audio channels, whereas a mono file has only one. Converting a stereo file to mono halves its file size.

✦ **Lower the bit depth:** from 16-bit to 8-bit, for example. A lower bit depth reduces the accuracy and cleanness of the stored audio waveforms.

✦ **Lower the sample rate:** from 44 kHz to 22 kHz, for example. This lowers the range of audio frequencies in the recording, chopping off the "high end" or treble frequencies.

You can make the preceding conversions by opening the audio file in an application such as Sonic Foundry Sound Forge and changing the desired parameters, as shown in Figure 27-1.

Network-ready audio file types that were specifically created for the Internet, such as MP3 and RealAudio, are compressed through encoding. Rather than arbitrarily lower the quality of the file to make it lighter, you pick a target bit rate, as shown in Figure 27-2, and the encoding software produces the best quality file it can at that bit rate. If you've ever exported a JPEG graphic from an image editor and specified a target file size, the principle is the same.

When working with a compressed audio format, you ideally start with the best "master copy" that you have in an uncompressed format, such as AIFF or WAV, and then encode that audio file as MP3 or RealAudio. If you want your audio to move quickly, even over dial-up connections, choose a low bit rate such as 24 Kbps, but be aware that the sound quality will be less than ideal.

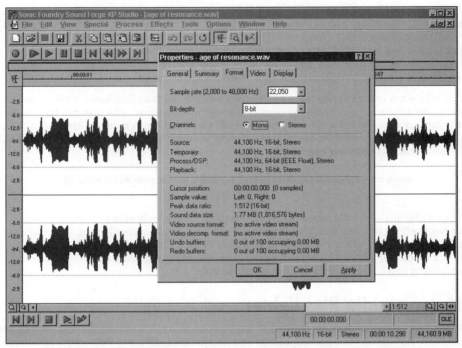

Figure 27-1: Changing a WAV file's sample rate, bit-depth, and channels settings in Sound Forge from 44,100, 16-bit, stereo to 22,050, 8-bit, mono will produce a much smaller file with significantly degraded sound quality.

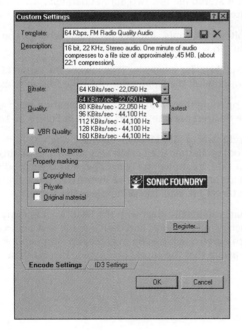

Figure 27-2: Choosing a 32K bits-per-second (32 Kbps) rate when converting a WAV file to an MP3 file in Sound Forge.

Caution Always keep a master copy of your audio file when you're encoding. Encoding a file is often a "lossy" compression; in other words, information/quality is lost in order to create smaller files. Although you can convert an MP3 back to an AIFF, it will not be the same quality as the original AIFF from which the MP3 was made. The process is similar to converting a TIFF to a JPEG, rather than zipping and unzipping the TIFF files.

Music Files

In the nineteenth century, before the technology to electronically record audio existed, a musical performance could be "recorded" by making a series of stipples on a cylinder. The performance could then be played "live" for the listener through a music box. Later, player pianos used rolls of paper with appropriate holes punched in them to cause the piano keys to mimic the performances of far away or long-dead musicians. In the early 1980s, electronic musical instrument manufacturers created Musical Instrument Digital Interface (MIDI) to enable the keys of one electronic keyboard to trigger the sounds in another. It wasn't long before somebody realized that the MIDI information being output by all electronic keyboards could be recorded, thus turning any electronic instrument into a modern-day music box or player piano.

The key to using music files on the Web is their very small file size. A music file is the ultimate in compressed sound: The musical instruments aren't even included! For example, a three-minute, full-fidelity, 128 bps stereo MP3 file would weigh in at just under 3MB. A QuickTime movie that only contains a music track could give you ten minutes of music for 60k and have similar fidelity, although you're limited to the sounds contained in the QuickTime synthesizer, of course.

Today, music files appear on the Web in one of three ways:

✦ **QuickTime Music:** MIDI information is stored as a music track within a QuickTime movie, and it is played back through the QuickTime software synthesizer (or through a hardware synthesizer such as a sound card if the user has configured QuickTime to use one). The QuickTime synthesizer sounds have often been criticized for being a little bland. Music tracks can coexist with all other kinds of QuickTime media in one movie, so they make excellent soundtracks for digital video tracks. QuickTime movies have a filename extension of .mov.

✦ **Rich Music Format:** Beatnik's hybrid audio/music format. MIDI information is played through the Beatnik player's software synthesizer, which contains generally excellent and often original sounds. Moreover, additional instrument sounds can be included in an RMF by adding digital audio samples with the Beatnik Editor. RMF files are unique among music file formats in that users cannot get the raw MIDI data out of them. Some content authors see this is as an advantage. RMF files have an .rmf filename extension.

✦ **Standard MIDI files:** This is the "raw data" of MIDI music files. The biggest drawback to these is that the Web author cannot know what kind of synthesizer the user will use to play back a MIDI file. On older Windows machines, this synthesizer may not even include actual instrument sounds, but instead use FM synthesis to come up with very poor approximations. Standard MIDI files have a filename extension of .mid, .midi, or .smf.

Occasionally, you may want to render a music file as a digital audio file in order to play it in a situation where a synthesizer is unavailable. Doing this the hard way involves playing the file through a synthesizer and recording the output to a digital audio file. You have an easier way, however, if you have QuickTime Player Pro. Open your QuickTime Music or import your Standard MIDI file into QuickTime Player Pro and then choose File ➪ Export and specify Music to AIFF. QuickTime Player Pro creates a digital audio file of its "performance" of the music using the QuickTime software synthesizer. You can also convert a QuickTime Music track back into a Standard MIDI file. Choose Music to Standard MIDI when you export.

Caution   RMF files are designed to disallow this conversion. Always keep the original Standard MIDI file when you create an RMF.

MP3 Mini-Primer

The MP3 audio format has quite simply taken the Web—and the world—by storm. Whereas other downloadable music formats come with caveats such as ownership by one company or built-in limitations on how users can use the files they purchase, MP3 just did the work and got the job done. MP3 software players are common. A number of manufacturers offer MP3 hardware for a variety of uses, including home, car, and personal stereos.

Tip   MP3.com remains the one-stop place for information about MP3. Visit www.mp3.com.

Generally, the MP3 "scene" shows interest in new and/or unusual artists, offers a selection of dynamic, full-featured players (see Figure 27-3), and maintains an attitude of music appreciation. Conversely, non-MP3 downloadable music has generally featured bland players, corporate music, proprietary technologies, and an unhealthy fascination with watermarking and controlling content. It's not hard to see why the market chose MP3.

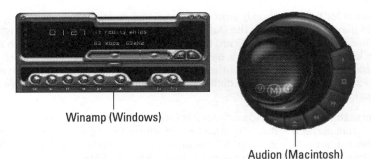

Winamp (Windows)

Audion (Macintosh)

Figure 27-3: Many standalone MP3 players, such as Winamp and Audion, feature sexy looks that can be changed by applying new "skins."

Player support

Table 27-2 lists common MP3 player software—including old friends such as RealPlayer that now handle MP3—and the URLs where they can be found. Many of these applications offer to set themselves up as browser helper applications. You might feature some of these links at the bottom of pages with MP3 content, so users who are new to MP3 can get a leg up.

Table 27-2: Common MP3 Players

Player Software	URL
Audion (Mac only)	`www.panic.com/audion`
iTunes (Mac only)	`www.apple.com/itunes`
QuickTime Player	`www.apple.com/quicktime`
RealJukebox	`www.real.com/jukeboxplus`
RealOne Player	`www.real.com/realone`
Winamp (Windows only)	`www.winamp.com`
Windows Media Player	`www.microsoft.com/windows/windowsmedia/en/download`

Note
Providing users with a link to MP3.com (`www.mp3.com`) is another way to offer them a great selection of players.

Encoding MP3

The most common MP3 files are downloadable music files. These files aim for "CD quality" and so are recorded with a bit rate of 128 Kbps. This works out to a little less than 1 megabyte per minute for a stereo, 44.1 kHz file, which is too heavy to move quickly on today's Web. You can encode an MP3 using a variety of bit rates, though. Lower bit rates mean lower quality, but even at 16 Kbps, speech sounds pretty good, and the 60k per minute bulk of a mono file will be music to your ears.

Caution
Beware of MP3 encoders that sacrifice quality for speed. Many encoders simply eliminate the upper audio frequency range so that they can encode the rest in record time. Although this might be fine if you're encoding your CD collection into a massive jukebox on your computer, it is less than ideal for content creators who want the best-quality encoded files. One source for more information is `www.mp3-converter.com/encoders/mp3_encoder_reviews.htm`.

Linking to Audio Files

The simplest way to add sound to a Web page is to create a link to an audio file by specifying the filepath in the Link text box of the Text or Image Property inspector. When the user clicks that link, the sound file downloads, and whatever program has been designated to handle that type of file opens in a separate window. An exception to this is the QuickTime Plugin. Instead of opening linked audio files in the QuickTime Player, it opens them within the browser window as if they were a new Web page. To get back to your Web page, the user clicks the browser's Back button.

To create a link to an audio file in Dreamweaver, follow these steps:

1. Select the text or image that you want to serve as the link to the audio file.

2. In the Property inspector, enter the name of the audio file in the Link text box, or select the Folder icon to browse for the file.

   To link to a dynamic source, choose Select File Name from Data Sources and select an appropriate field from the available recordset(s).

3. Because audio files can be large, it's good practice to note the file size next to the link name, as shown in Figure 27-4, or to enter it in the Alt text box for your image.

When you use the link technique for incorporating sound, you have no control over the position or appearance of the player. However, you can control these factors and more by embedding your audio.

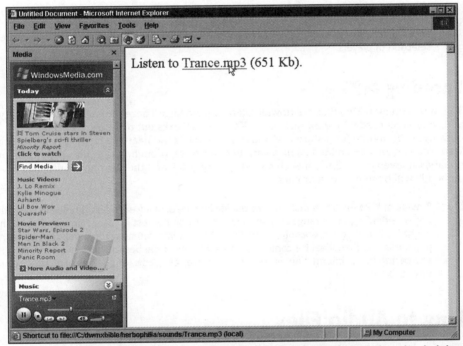

Figure 27-4: When the Trance.mp3 link was clicked, Internet Explorer 6 downloaded the Trance.mp3 file and then opened/played it in the browser's built-in MP3 player (lower left).

Embedding Sounds and Music

Embedding a sound file truly integrates the audio into your Web page. Embedding the sound file also gives you a much greater degree of control over the presentation of the audio player itself, including the following:

✦ The clip's play volume

✦ Which part, if any, of the player's controls is visible

✦ The starting and ending points of the music clip

As with any other embedded object, you can present the visual display inline with other text elements — aligned to the top, middle, or bottom of the text, or blocked left or right to enable text to flow around it. Dreamweaver controls all these parameters through two different objects: the Plugin object and the ActiveX object. Each type of object calls a specific type of player. For example, the default Plugin object calls the LiveAudio Plugin in a Netscape browser and the Windows Media Player control in Internet Explorer. Calling the Windows Media Player as an ActiveX object explicitly enables you to modify a great number of parameters for Internet Explorer — which are completely ignored by Navigator. You learn all of your embedding options, including techniques for cross-browser audio, in the next few sections.

Note   Unfortunately, the Assets panel does not include a Sound or Audio button. To insert audio elements, you must use the Plugin button in the Media category of the Insert bar.

As with video, Dreamweaver uses the generic Plugin object to embed audio in your Web page. The object requires only three parameters: the source of the audio file and the width and height of the object. To embed an audio file in your Web page, follow these steps in Dreamweaver:

1. Position the cursor where you want the control panel for the audio file to appear.

2. Insert the Plugin object by choosing Insert ⇨ Media ⇨ Plugin or by clicking the Plugin button from the Media category of the Insert bar.

3. In the Select File dialog box that appears, choose your audio file.

4. Use *either* of these two techniques to size the Plugin placeholder:

   • Click the resizing handles on the Plugin placeholder and drag it out to a new size.

   • Enter the desired values in the W (Width) and the H (Height) text boxes of the Property inspector.

   For a default audio plugin, use a width of 144 pixels and a height of 60 pixels. These dimensions are slightly larger than necessary for Internet Explorer's audio controls, but they fit Navigator's controls perfectly, as shown in Figure 27-5, and the control panel does not appear to be "clipped" when viewed through any browser.

When the Plugin object is inserted, Dreamweaver displays the generic Plugin placeholder.

Playing background music

Background music, played while the user is viewing online material, is one of the Web's hidden treasures. When used tastefully, background music can enhance the overall impact of the page. Conversely, when abused, it can drive users away in droves.

Making a regular embedded sound into a background sound is as simple as adding a few parameters to the embed tag: hidden tells the browser not to display any controls, autostart tells it to start playback automatically, and loop tells it to play the audio continuously. Although you can add these attributes to the embed tag manually in the HTML Code window, it's easier to add them using the Property inspector. Follow these steps to embed background music in a Web page:

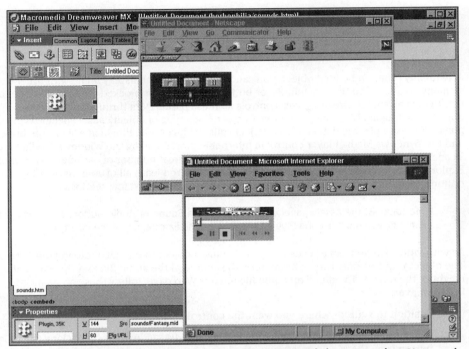

Figure 27-5: Internet Explorer's Windows Media Player needs less space than Netscape's LiveAudio player, so it fills the rest with a crushed version of its logo.

1. Position the cursor near the top of your Web page. Choose Insert ⇨ Media ⇨ Plugin or click the Plugin button from the Media category of the Insert bar.

2. Choose your audio file in the Select File dialog box.

3. In the Property inspector, enter **2** in both the H (Height) and W (Width) text boxes.

Note Entering a width and height attribute is necessary for compatibility with older browsers.

4. If your Property inspector is not already expanded, expand it now (by clicking the arrow icon in the lower-right corner of the inspector). Click the Parameters button to open the Parameters dialog box.

5. In the Parameters dialog box, select the Add (+) button and enter `hidden` in the Parameter column. Click in the Parameter column and type in the first parameter. Use Tab to move to the Value column and enter `true`, as shown in Figure 27-6. Use Tab again to move to the next parameter.

   • Use Shift+Tab if you need to move backwards through the list.

   • To delete a parameter/value pair, highlight it and select the Remove (–) button at the top of the Parameters column.

- To add a new parameter, select the Add (+) button to move to the first blank line, and use Tab to move to the next parameter.

- To move a parameter from one position in the list to another, highlight it and select the up or down arrow buttons at the top of the Parameters column.

6. Enter `autostart` as the next parameter and give it the value `true`.

7. To make the audio clip repeat, enter `loop` as the next parameter; and in the Value column, enter the number of times you want the sound to repeat. To make the audio repeat indefinitely, enter `true` as the value.

8. Click OK to finish.

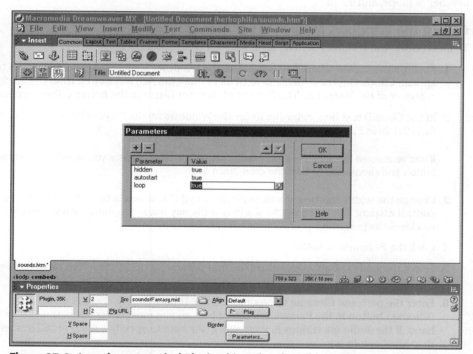

Figure 27-6: Inserting a 2x2 pixel Plugin object (barely visible, in the upper-left corner) that plays Fantasy.mid as background music.

Targeting Specific Plugins

You can exercise a much finer degree of control over the audio in your pages by calling specific plugins. The trade-off, unfortunately, is that by designating a plugin, you reduce the size of your potential audience. Some plugins are specific to a browser or browser version. Moreover, plugins that aren't distributed with the major browsers face an uphill battle in terms of market penetration. If you use a plugin, you can always expect some users to be resistant to downloading the necessary software. Before you incorporate any plugin, you must weigh these issues against your overall design plan.

Tip A great number of audio plugins are available and offer a broad variety of functionality and features. A good place to see a list of those available is the Plugin Plaza (`http://browserwatch.internet.com/plug-in.html`). In addition to offering complete descriptions, this site also has links directly to the download areas.

Windows Media Player audio

The Windows Media Player is Internet Explorer's default multimedia player. You can use it to play the standard audio formats, including MP3, WAV, AIFF, AU, or MIDI files. Calling Windows Media Player directly as an ActiveX control, however, gives you far more flexibility over the player's appearance and functionality: its width, height, control panel display, loudness, number of loops, and so on.

Calling the Windows Media Player ActiveX control

To incorporate the Windows Media Player ActiveX control, follow these steps:

1. Position the cursor where you would like the Windows Media Player control panel to appear. Choose Insert ➪ Media ➪ ActiveX or click the ActiveX button from the Media category of the Insert bar. The Property inspector displays the ActiveX object options.

2. In the ClassID text box, enter the ID for the Windows Media Player control: `CLSID:22d6f312-b0f6-11d0-94ab-0080c74c7e95`.

Tip   If you've entered this long Windows Media Player class ID previously, you can click the arrow button and choose the ID from the drop-down list.

3. Change the width and height values in the W and H text boxes to match the desired control display. The Windows Media Player display resizes to match your dimensions as closely as possible.

4. Click the Parameters button.

5. Select the Add (+) button and enter the first parameter: `FileName`. Use Tab to move to the Value column.

6. Enter the path and filename for your audio file. Unfortunately, there is no Browse (Choose) button in the Parameters dialog box, so you must enter the pathname by hand. If the audio file resides in your site, make sure to specify a relative URL rather than an absolute one.

7. Continue entering the desired parameters and values for your audio file, as shown in Figure 27-7.

8. Click OK when you're finished.

The Windows Media Player ActiveX control has many parameters to choose from — 34, to be exact. Explaining all of these parameters is beyond the scope of this book, but Table 27-3 describes the key parameters that parallel the LiveAudio attributes.

Note   As with plugins, all of the parameters and/or values of an ActiveX control may be linked to a dynamic source. From the Parameters dialog box, select the lightning-bolt icon in either the Parameter or Value column to expose the available recordset fields.

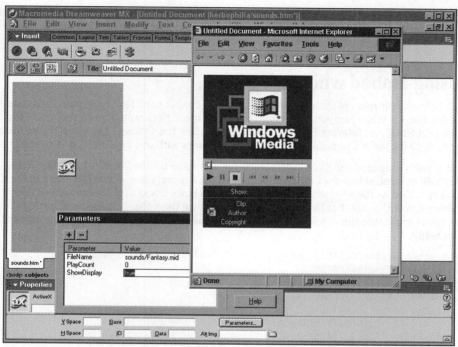

Figure 27-7: Inserting a Windows Media Player ActiveX control object into a Web page.

Table 27-3: Windows Media Player Parameters

WMP Parameter	Possible Values	Description
AutoStart	true (default) or false	Determines if the sound begins playing when the download is complete
FileName	Any valid sound-file URL	Specifies the sound file to be played
PlayCount	Any integer	Sets the number of times the file should repeat. If the value is 0, the sound loops continuously. The default is 1.
SelectionStart	Number of seconds	Determines the beginning point for the audio clip, relative to the start of the file
SelectionEnd	Number of seconds	Determines the ending point for the audio clip, relative to the start of the file
ShowControls	true (default) or false	Shows the control panel if set to true
ShowDisplay	true or false (default)	Shows the display panel if set to true
Volume	Any integer, from 0 (loudest, default) to 10,000 (softest)	Sets the loudness of the audio

Caution   Windows Media Player's default volume setting is 0, but this is the highest setting, not the lowest setting. Specifying a higher number for the volume parameter lowers the volume of the sound.

Using Embed with ActiveX

All ActiveX controls are included in HTML's <object>...</object> tag pair. Dreamweaver codes this for you when you insert any ActiveX control. Netscape doesn't recognize the <object> tag, and Internet Explorer doesn't recognize the <embed> tag when it's within an <object> tag, so it's possible to target both browsers with one <object> and <embed> pair.

After you've entered the FileName parameter and value for the Windows Media Player ActiveX control, select the Embed checkbox in the Property inspector. The same name that you specified as the FileName now appears in the Embed text box. Dreamweaver takes advantage of the fact that Netscape doesn't recognize the <object> tag by inserting the <embed> tag inside the <object>...</object> tag pair. The resulting HTML looks like the following:

```
<object classid="CLSID:22d6f312-b0f6-11d0-94ab-0080c74c7e95"
 width="193" height="270">
  <param name="FileName" value="sounds/Fantasy.mid">
  <param name="PlayCount" value="0">
  <param name="ShowDisplay" value="true">
  <embed src="sounds/Fantasy.mid" width="193" height="270"
   filename="sounds/Fantasy.mid" playcount="0" showdisplay="true">
  </embed>
</object>
```

Note that Dreamweaver picks up the attributes and parameters from the ActiveX control to use in the <embed> tag. You often have to adjust these, especially the width and height values, which differ markedly for Internet Explorer and Netscape audio player displays.

Using Netscape's LiveAudio Plugin

LiveAudio is Netscape 4.x's default audio player and is used when you do basic embedding of an audio file, as well as when you attach a sound file to a URL. Both of these methods of incorporating audio, however, barely scratch the surface of what LiveAudio is capable of doing. LiveAudio uses up to 13 different parameters to shape its appearance and functionality in the Web page, and it also accepts a full range of JavaScript commands.

Note   The LiveAudio plugin is not installed by default with Netscape 6.x. In fact, at the time this is being written, Netscape 6.x has no default audio plugin. (Netscape recommends downloading/installing the Winamp plugin for audio playback.) Therefore, this section pertains to Netscape 4.x browsers.

To take advantage of LiveAudio's full capabilities, you must enter the audio file's parameters and values through Dreamweaver's Property inspector. Follow these steps to specify the parameters for your Plugin object:

1. Insert the Plugin object — either by choosing Insert ⇨ Media ⇨ Plugin or by dragging the Plugin object from the Media category of the Insert bar to a place on your Web page.

2. In the Select File dialog box, choose your audio file.

3. From the expanded Property inspector, select Parameters to open the Parameter dialog box.

4. Click in the Parameter column and type in the first parameter. Use Tab to move to the Value column and enter the desired value. Use Tab again to move to the next parameter, then the next value, and so on.

   For most plugins, including LiveAudio, the order of the parameters is irrelevant.

5. Repeat Step 4 until all parameters are entered, as shown in Figure 27-8.

6. Click OK when you're done.

The parameters for LiveAudio affect either the look of the player or the qualities of the sound. The main parameter for altering the player's appearance is `controls`. Depending on the value used, you can display the default control panel, a smaller version, or individual controls.

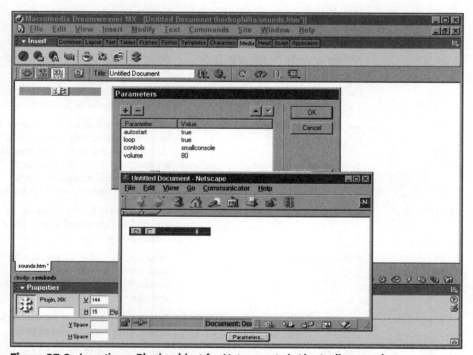

Figure 27-8: Inserting a Plugin object for Netscape 4.x's LiveAudio console.

You can embed individual controls anywhere on your Web page. To link the various controls, you use the `mastersound` keyword in each `<embed>` statement and set the `name` parameter to one unique value for all files. Finally, set the source in one `<embed>` tag to the actual sound file and set the other sources in the other files to a dummy file called a *stub* file, such as this one:

```
<embed src="bgMusic.mid" name="background" mastersound
 moreParameters...></embed>
...
<embed src="dummy.mid" name="background" mastersound
 moreParameters...></embed>
```

```
...
<embed src="dummy.mid" name="background" mastersound
moreParameters...></embed>
```

Table 27-4 describes all the parameters available for LiveAudio, except those set by Dreamweaver's Property inspector (source, height, width, and alignment).

Table 27-4: LiveAudio Parameters

Parameter	Acceptable Values	Description
autostart	true or false (default)	If autostart is set to true, the audio file begins playing as soon as the download is completed.
controls	console (default), smallconsole, playbutton, pausebutton, stopbutton, or volumelever	Sets the sound control to appear
endtime	minutes:seconds; for example, 00:00	Determines the point in the sound clip at which the audio stops playing
hidden	true	Expressly hides all the audio controls; sound plays in the background
loop	true, false, or an integer	Setting loop to true forces the sound file to repeat continuously until the Stop button is selected or the user goes to another page. To set the number of times the sound repeats, set loop equal to an integer. The default is false.
mastersound	none	Enables several <embed> tags to be grouped and controlled as one. Used in conjunction with the name attribute.
name	a unique name	Links various <embed> tags in a file to control them as one. Used in conjunction with the <mastersound> attribute.
starttime	minutes:seconds; for example, 00:00	Determines the point in the sound clip at which the audio begins playing
volume	1 to 100	Sets the volume of the audio clip on a scale from 1 to 100 percent

Installing Streaming Audio

Although audio files are not nearly as large as video files, downloading them can take a long time. Audio-on-demand — or *streaming audio* — is an alternative to such lengthy downloads.

Cross-Reference

Streaming audio files have a lot in common with streaming video files, as covered in Chapter 26.

For streaming audio, you have the same Big Three choices as with streaming video—RealMedia, QuickTime, and Windows Media—plus Shockwave streaming audio and Flash movies.

Cross-Reference   Shockwave and Flash are covered in Chapter 25.

Working with floating or embedded RealAudio players

Before including a link to a RealAudio file, you first must make a basic choice: Is the player going to be free-floating or will it be embedded in the page? It's purely a design decision, but the coding necessary is completely different. To insert a RealAudio streaming audio file with a free-floating player, shown in Figure 27-9, follow these steps:

1. Select the link or image that you want to use to begin the RealAudio file.

2. In the Property inspector, enter the path to the RealAudio metafile in the Link text box or use the Browse For File button to locate the file. Make sure that the metafile has a .ram or .rpm extension.

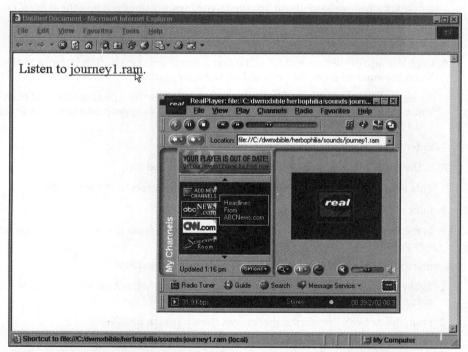

Figure 27-9: This is a free-floating RealPlayer player, opened by clicking on the journey1.ram link.

An embedded player is best inserted using Dreamweaver's ActiveX object—the embedded player consists of multiple ActiveX objects, one for the player control (or controls) and one for audio file itself. The separation of content and player makes it easy to link the content to a data source while maintaining the same control panel.

Note   ActiveX objects can only be displayed/played in Internet Explorer; Netscape does not support ActiveX.

If desired, your design may include a single control panel or a series of controls — play, stop, fast-forward, rewind, and so on — all affecting your audio. The two key RealAudio parameters are `controls` and `console`. The `controls` parameter sets the type of control being inserted; the `console` parameter indicates which embedded audio file is being played.

To embed a RealAudio file with separate controls, you must follow a two-phase procedure. First, embed the actual audio file or, if the source is dynamic, a link to a data source:

1. Choose Insert ⇨ Media ⇨ ActiveX or select the ActiveX object from the Media category of the Insert bar. Dreamweaver inserts an ActiveX placeholder.

2. From the ActiveX Property inspector, set the ClassID to RealPlayer.

3. Change the Width and Height values in the W and H text boxes to 0 for audio-only playback.

4. If you know the `codebase` URL, enter it in the Base text box.

   The `codebase` property is an Internet location from which the ActiveX control can be automatically downloaded and installed if the browser does not find the control on the user's system. The codebase values are provided by the ActiveX control creator.

5. Click the Parameters button to display the Parameters dialog box.

6. Click the Add (+) button and enter the first parameter: `src`. Use Tab to move to the Value column and enter the path and filename for your file.

   To serve different audio files from a data source, select the lightning-bolt icon from the Value column. In the Dynamic Data dialog box, select an appropriate field containing URLs of RealMedia files.

7. Enter the next parameter, `console`, in the left column.

8. In the Value column, enter a unique name for the sound file.

   This unique console name will be used to link the controls to the audio file.

9. Click OK when you're finished.

10. In the Property inspector, select the Embed option to make the audio cross-browser compatible.

Now you're ready to add the controls that enable user interactivity:

1. Again, choose Insert ⇨ Media ⇨ ActiveX or select the ActiveX object from the Media category of the Insert bar.

2. From the ActiveX Property inspector, set the ClassID to RealPlayer.

3. Change the Width and Height values to the size desired for the type of controls selected. Some common dimensions are as follows:

   - **All:** Width: 375, Height: 100
   - **ControlPanel:** Width: 350, Height: 36
   - **PlayButton:** Width: 44, Height: 26
   - **PlayOnlyButton:** Width: 26, Height: 26 (These dimensions apply to all individual controls, such as PauseButton and FFCtrl.)

4. Select Parameters in the Property inspector.

5. In the Parameters dialog box, enter `controls` in the first column; and enter the name of the control (that is, `controlpanel`, `playbutton`, `pausebutton`, and so on) in the second column.

6. Add a second parameter, `console`. The value of console should be the same as entered for the audio file in Step 8 of the previous series of steps.

7. Click OK to close the Parameters dialog box.

8. Select Embed on the Property inspector to ensure cross-browser compatibility, as shown in Figure 27-10.

Repeat these steps to add additional individual controls. When you're done, test your Web page by previewing it in a browser.

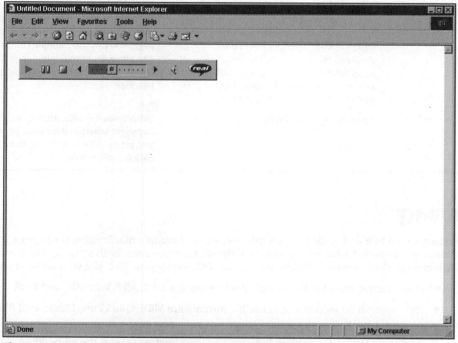

Figure 27-10: This is an embedded RealPlayer control panel.

Accessing RealAudio parameters

For a streaming audio file, only the source file and the dimensions are really required, but it probably comes as no surprise to you that a great number of attributes are available. You can add any of the attributes found in Table 27-5 through the Parameters button of the selected RealAudio file's Property inspector.

Table 27-5: RealAudio Parameters

RealPlayer Attribute	Possible Values	Description
autostart	true (default) or false	Enables the RealAudio clip to start playing as soon as content is available
console	_master or _unique	Determines the console name for each control in a Web page that uses multiple controls. To force controls on a page to refer to the same file, use the same console=name attribute. The console name _master links to all controls on a page; _unique connects to no other instances.
controls	all, controlpanel, infovolumepanel, infopanel, statuspanel, statusbar, playbutton, playonlybutton, pausebutton, ffctrl, rwctrl, stopbutton, mutectrl, mutevolumectrl, volumeslider, positionslider, positionfield, or statusfield	Enables the placement of individual control panel elements in the Web page. You can use multiple controls in one attribute, or multiple <embed> tags to build a custom RealAudio interface.
nolabels	true or false (default)	Suppresses the Title, Author, and Copyright labels in the Status panel. If you set nolabels to true, the actual data are still visible.

Summary

Adding sound to a Web page brings it into the realm of multimedia. Dreamweaver gives you numerous methods to handle the various different audio formats, both static and streaming. With custom Dreamweaver objects and actions, enhancing your Web site with audio is a snap.

✦ The common downloadable audio file formats are MP3, AIFF, WAV, AU, and RMF.

✦ The common downloadable music file formats are MIDI, QuickTime Music, and RMF.

✦ You can either link to a sound or embed it in your Web page. With standard audio, the linking technique calls an independent, free-floating player; the embedding technique incorporates the player into the design of the page. Hiding the player creates background music or sound.

✦ Third-party plugins offer far greater control over the appearance and functionality of the sound than relying on a browser's default plugin; to use a third-party plugin, however, your user must download it.

✦ Streaming audio provides almost instant access to large audio files, and RealAudio is one of the leaders in player deployment.

In the next chapter, you learn how to use Dreamweaver templates to enhance your Web-page creation skills.

✦   ✦   ✦

Enhancing Web Site Management and Workflow in Dreamweaver

Using Dreamweaver Templates

Let's face it: Web design is a combination of glory and grunt work. Creating the initial design for a Web site can be fun and exciting, but when you have to implement your wonderful new design on 200 or more pages, the excitement fades as you try to figure out the quickest way to finish the work. Enter templates. Using templates properly can be a tremendous time-saver. Moreover, a template ensures that your Web site has a consistent look and feel, which, in turn, generally means that it's easier for users to navigate.

In Dreamweaver, new documents can be produced from a standard design saved as a template, as in a word processing program. Furthermore, you can alter a template and update all the files that were created from it earlier; this capability extends the power of the repeating element Libraries to overall page design. Templates also form the bridge to one of the hottest technologies shaping the Web — Extensible Markup Language (XML).

Dreamweaver makes it easy to access all kinds of templates — everything from your own creations to the default blank page. This chapter demonstrates the mechanism behind Dreamweaver templates and shows you strategies for getting the most out of them.

Understanding Templates

Templates exist in many forms. Furniture makers use master patterns as templates to create the same basic design repeatedly, using new wood stains or upholstery to differentiate the final product. A stencil, in which the inside of a letter, word, or design is cut out, is a type of template as well. With computers, templates form the basic document into which specific details are added to create new, distinct documents.

Dreamweaver templates, in terms of functionality, are a combination of traditional templates and updateable Library elements. After a new page is created from a template, the document remains attached to the original template unless specifically separated or detached. The new document maintains a connection to previous pages in a site, if the original template is altered, all the documents created from it can be automatically updated. This relationship is also true of Dreamweaver's repeating element Libraries. In fact, templates can include Library elements.

Library items work hand-in-hand with templates. See Chapter 29 for a detailed discussion of Library items.

When a template is first created, the entire page is locked; locked sections of a template cannot be changed in a document derived from that template. A key process in defining a template is to designate certain areas as a type of region that can be changed in some way in a template-derived document. Dreamweaver supports four different regions in a template:

- ✦ **Editable regions:** The area, such as all the code, within an editable region may be altered. Thus in a page where all the navigation code is locked, the content area may be designated as an editable region.

- ✦ **Editable attributes:** Within a locked tag, specific attributes may be made editable. You could, for example, unlock the border attribute for a table while keeping the cell padding and cell spacing secure.

- ✦ **Optional regions:** Content within an optional region may or may not be displayed, depending on certain conditions set by the template designer.

- ✦ **Repeating regions:** Certain areas in an otherwise locked object (typically a table), may be repeated as many times as needed in a template-derived document. Repeating regions are great for controlling the overall look and feel of a table although allowing the number of detail rows to vary.

All the various region types require template markup within the document. You can also combine certain template regions — you could, for example, make some of the content within a repeating region editable and keep some of it locked.

Naturally, templates can be altered to mark additional editable areas or to relock editable areas. Moreover, you can detach a document created from a template at any time and edit anything in the document. You cannot, however, reattach the document to the template without losing (or seriously misplacing) inserted content. On the other hand, a document based on one template can be changed to a completely different look but with the same content, if another template with identical regions is applied.

Let's look at some templates for the Web site of a fictional travel company called Compass. The pages in the Destinations section are designed so that all the sample pages for the different trips are basically the same — only the destination title, description, and Flash movie vary. The layout, background, and navigation controls are identical on every page. One basic template page (shown in Figure 28-1) is created, and all the final pages are created from the template. Notice the highlighting surrounding certain areas in the template. In a template, the specified regions are highlighted, and the locked areas are not. A tab further identifies each region to make it easier to add the right content in the right area.

Templates category

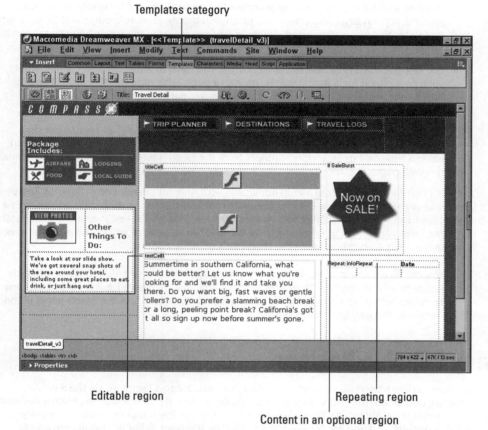

Editable region

Repeating region

Content in an optional region

Figure 28-1: In a template, designated regions are clearly marked and distinguished from the rest of the page, which is locked and cannot be changed.

Creating Your Own Templates

You can use any design that you like for your own template. Perhaps the best course to take is to finalize a single page that has all the elements that you want to include in your template. Then, convert that document to a template and proceed to mark all the changeable areas—whether text or image—as a type of region. Before saving your file as a template, consider the following points when designing your basic page:

✦ **Use placeholders where you can:** Whether it's dummy text or a temporary graphic, placeholders give shape to your page. They also make it easier to remember which elements to include. If you are using an image placeholder, set a temporary height and width through the Property inspector or by dragging the image placeholder's sizing handles; of course, you can also just insert a sample graphic.

✦ **Finalize and incorporate as much content as possible in the template:** If you find yourself repeatedly adding the same information or objects to a page, add them to your template. The more structured elements you can include, the faster your pages can be produced.

✦ **Use sample objects on the template:** Often, you have to enter the same basic object, such as a plugin for a digital movie, on every page, with only the filename changing. Enter your repeating object (with as many preset parameters as possible) on your template page. That way, you only have to select a new filename for each page.

✦ **Include your ‹meta› information:** Search engines rely on ‹meta› tags to get the overview of a page and then scan the balance of the page to get the details. You can enter a Keyword or Description object from the Head panel of the Insert bar so that all the Web pages in your site have the same basic information for cataloging.

You can create a template from a Web document with one command: File ➪ Save As Template. Dreamweaver stores all templates in a Templates folder created for each defined site with a special file extension (.dwt). After you've created your page and saved it as a template, notice that Dreamweaver inserts ‹‹Template›› in the title bar to remind you of the page's status. Now you're ready to begin defining the template's editable regions.

Note   You can also create a template from an entirely blank page if you like. To do so, open the Assets panel and select the Templates category. From the Templates category, select the New Template button. You can find more information about how to use the Assets panel of the Templates category later in this chapter.

Using Editable Regions

As noted earlier, when you convert an existing document into a template via the Save As Template command, the entire document is initially locked. If you attempt to create a document from a template at this stage, Dreamweaver alerts you that the template doesn't have any editable regions, and you cannot change anything on the page. Editable regions are a key element in templates.

Marking existing content as editable

Editable regions can either surround existing content or stand alone without any content. As noted earlier, in both cases you must give the region a unique name. Dreamweaver uses the unique name to identify the editable region when entering new content, applying the template, and exporting or importing XML.

Note   As noted, each editable region must have a unique name, but the name need only be different from any other editable region on the same page. The same name could be used for objects, JavaScript functions, or editable regions on a different template.

To mark an existing area as an editable region, follow these steps:

1. Select the text, object, or area on the page that you want to convert to an editable region.

Tip

The general rule of thumb with editable regions is that you need to select a complete tag pair, such as `<table>...</table>`. This strategy has several implications. For instance, although you can mark an entire table, one or more contiguous rows, or a single cell as editable, you can't select multiple cells, separated rows, or a column to be so marked; attempting to do so will mark a multiple row region. You have to select each cell individually (`<td>...</td>`). In addition, you can select the content of a layer to be editable and keep the layer itself locked (so that its position and other properties cannot be altered). However, if you select the layer to be editable, you can't lock the content.

2. Choose Insert ➪ Template Objects ➪ Editable Region.

You can also use the keyboard shortcut Ctrl+Alt+V (Command+Option+V), or right-click (Control+click) the selection and choose Templates ➪ New Editable Region from the context menu. Whichever method you choose, Dreamweaver displays the New Editable Region dialog box shown in Figure 28-2.

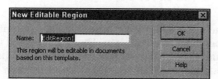

Figure 28-2: The descriptive name you enter for a new editable region must be unique.

New Feature

Now editable template regions — as well as the other region types — are just a mouse click away. From the Insert bar, choose the Template category and click once on the Editable Region icon. You can also drag the icon over the selected text. Either action brings up the New Editable Region dialog box.

3. Enter a unique name for the selected area. Click OK if you're done, or click Cancel to abort the operation.

Caution

Although you can use spaces in editable region names, some characters are not permitted. The illegal characters are the ampersand (&), double quote ("), single quote ('), and left and right angle brackets (< and >).

Dreamweaver outlines the selection with the color picked in Preferences on the Highlighting panel, shown if View ➪ Visual Aids ➪ Invisible Elements is enabled. The name for your newly designated region is displayed on a tab marking the area; the region is also listed in the Modify ➪ Templates submenu. If still selected, the region name has a checkmark next to it in the Templates submenu. You can jump to any other editable region by selecting its name from this dynamic list.

Tip

Make sure you apply any formatting to your text — either by using HTML codes or by using CSS styles — before you select it to be an editable region. Generally, you want to keep the defined look of the content while altering just the text, so make sure that only the text is within the editable region and exclude the formatting tags. It's often helpful to have both the Code and Design views open for this detailed work.

Inserting a new editable region

Sometimes it's helpful to create a new editable region in which no content currently exists. In these situations, the editable region name doubles as a label identifying the type of content expected, such as CatalogPrice. Dreamweaver always highlights the entry in the template in a small tab above the region. To insert a new editable region, follow these steps:

1. Place your cursor anywhere on the template page without selecting any item in particular.

2. Choose Insert ⇨ Template Objects ⇨ Editable Region. Alternately, select the Editable Region icon from the Templates category of the Insert bar.

3. Enter a unique name for the new region. Click OK when you're done, or select Cancel to abort the operation.

Dreamweaver inserts the new region name in the document, marks it with a named tab, and adds the name to the dynamic region list (which you can display by choosing Modify ⇨ Templates).

Two editable regions, one for the Web page's title and one for other <head> content, are automatically created when you save a document as a template. The title is stored in a special editable region called doctitle, and the <head> content region is named head. To change the title (which initially takes the same title as the template), enter the new text in the Title field of the toolbar. You can also use the keyboard shortcut Ctrl+J (Command+J) to open the Page Properties dialog box. Finally, you can select View ⇨ Head Elements and choose the Title icon — with the visible region outline — to enter the new text in the Property inspector.

Creating Links in Templates

A common problem that designers encounter with Dreamweaver templates centers on links. People often add links to their templates and discover that these links do not work when new pages are derived from the templates. The main cause of this error stems from linking to a non-existent page or element by hand — that is, typing in the link, rather than using the Select File dialog box to choose it. Designers tend to set the links according to their final site structures without taking into account how templates are stored in Dreamweaver.

For example, when creating a template, suppose you have links to three pages — products.htm, services.htm, and about.htm — all in the root of your site. Both products.htm and services.htm have been created, so you select the Folder icon in the Property inspector and select those files. Dreamweaver inserts those links as follows: ../products.htm and ../services.htm. The ../ indicates the directory above the current directory — which makes sense only when you remember that all templates are stored in a subfolder of the site root called Templates. These links are correctly resolved when a document is derived from this template to reflect the stored location of the new file.

Let's assume that the third file, about.htm, has not yet been created, and so that link is entered by hand. The common mistake is entering the pathname as it should be when it's used: about.htm. However, because the page is saved in the Templates folder, Dreamweaver converts that link to /Templates/about.htm for any page derived from the template — and the link will fail. This type of error also applies to dependent files, such as graphics or other media.

The best solution is to always use the Folder or the Point-to-File icon to link to an existing file when building your templates. If the file does not exist, and if you don't want to create a placeholder page for it, link to another existing file in the same folder and modify the link manually.

The head editable region may not appear very useful during the template creation phase, but when you begin creating documents based on a template it really shines. New <meta> tags, CSS style links and rules, and behavior-added JavaScript all take advantage of the head editable region.

Locking an editable region

Inevitably, you'll mark as editable a region that you'd prefer to keep locked. Similarly, you may discover that every page constructed to date has required inputting the same content, so it should be entered on the template and locked. In either event, converting an editable region to a locked one is a simple operation. To lock an editable region, follow these steps:

1. Place your cursor in the editable region you want to lock.

2. Choose Modify ➪ Templates ➪ Remove Template Markup. The same menu selection is available from the context menu.

If you are removing a newly inserted editable region that only contains the region name — which happens when an empty editable region is added — the content is not removed and must be deleted by hand on the template. Otherwise, it appears as part of the document created from a template and won't be accessible.

Adding Content to Template Documents

Constructing a template is only half the job — using it to create new pages is the other half. Because your basic layout is complete and you're only dropping in new images and entering new text, pages based on templates take a fraction of the time needed to create regular Web pages. Dreamweaver makes it easy to enter new content as well — you can even move from one template region to the next, much like filling out a form (which, of course, is exactly what you're doing). To create a new document based on a template, follow these steps:

1. In the Template category of the Assets panel, select the desired template and then choose the New from Template option from the panel's context menu. Alternatively, choose File ➪ New; then from the New Document/New from Template dialog box (the title of the dialog changes according to which tab is chosen) select the Templates category and choose the site and desired template as shown in Figure 28-3.

2. If you want to maintain a connection between the template-derived document and the template, leave the Update Page When Template Changes option selected. To detach the template from the newly created document and make the entire page editable, deselect the option.

3. Click OK when you're done.

When your new page opens, the editable regions are again highlighted, as shown in Figure 28-4; furthermore, the cursor is only active when it is over an unlocked region. If you have the Code view open, you will also see that the locked region is highlighted in a different color — by default, gray. Document highlighting makes it easy to differentiate the two types of regions.

A document created from a template is known as an *instance* of that template.

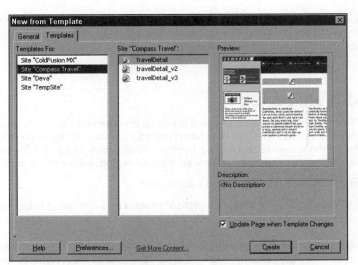

Figure 28-3: A list of all the templates by site is accessible by selecting File ➪ New.

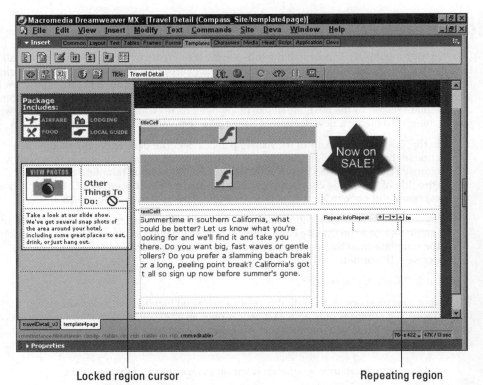

Locked region cursor   Repeating region

Figure 28-4: In a document based on a template, the template regions are clearly marked, as are the locked portions in the Code view.

Generally, it is easiest to select the editable region name or placeholder first and then enter the new content. Selecting the editable regions can be handled in several ways:

✦ Highlight the region name or placeholder with the mouse.

✦ Position your cursor inside any editable region and then select the `<mmtinstance:editable>` tag in the Tag Selector.

✦ Choose Modify ➪ Templates and then select the name of your editable region from the dynamic list.

Note   If all your editable regions are separate cells in a table, you can tab forward and Shift+Tab backward through the cells. With each press of the Tab key, all the content in the cell is selected, whether it is an editable region name or a placeholder.

Naturally, you should save your document to retain all the new content that's been added.

Tip   Behaviors can be added without any additional coding or work-arounds to links within editable regions. You cannot, however, add a behavior to text or an image in a locked region.

Making Attributes Editable

Now that you understand the basics of template design and implementation, you can proceed to some of the more advanced features. Editable regions can encompass any portion of the page, from a single tag up to the entire `<body>`. But what if you want to make just a portion of a tag — an attribute — editable and keep the rest of the tag locked? I once worked on a site where the client wanted to tie the background color of a table's header row to a graphic on the page. Every couple of weeks, I would get an e-mail asking for help to fix the page — broken while trying to change the one attribute, `bgcolor`. It was a frustrating situation for both the client and myself.

New Feature   Dreamweaver now gives you control over your editable areas right down to the attribute level. Not only can an attribute be made editable, but you can restrict its type and even provide default values. All the editable attributes on a page are displayed within a single dialog box, centralizing updates. The various types of attributes — text, number, URL, color, Boolean — each have a specific interface for choosing a value. A color type attribute, for example, uses a Dreamweaver-style color picker.

To make an attribute editable, follow these steps:

1. With the template open for editing, select the tag or object that contains the attribute you want to make editable.

Note   Your selection should be outside of an editable region. If you try to change the attribute of a tag within an editable region, Dreamweaver reminds you that this tag is already fully editable.

2. Choose Modify ➪ Templates ➪ Make Attribute Editable to display the Editable Tag Attributes dialog box as shown in Figure 28-5.

3. Select the desired attribute from the Attribute drop-down list.

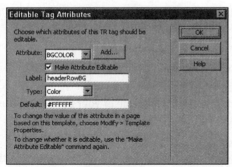

Figure 28-5: With the Editable Tag Attributes dialog box, you can extend access to any attribute — even a custom one — of any tag in a locked area.

Tip   For quicker editing, make sure your selected tag already contains the attribute you'd like to make editable. The Attribute drop-down list shows all the parameters within a selected tag, whether they have values or not.

4. If the attribute you want is not available from the drop-down list, choose Add and enter the attribute in the pop-up dialog box.

   After you've confirmed your entry in the pop-up dialog box by clicking OK, your attribute appears in the Attribute drop-down list. New entries are always uppercased in the list, but do not appear uppercased in the code if specified otherwise in the Tag Library Editor.

5. Select the Make Attribute Editable option.

   The Make Attribute Editable option may seem redundant in this dialog box, but it allows you to make a number of attributes editable in the same tag while leaving others locked.

6. Enter a unique name for the tag's editable attribute in the Label field.

   The Label is used to identify this specific editable attribute and is displayed in the Template Properties dialog box when the attribute is modified. Pick a name that identifies both the tag and the attribute, like logoTableBgColor for the bgcolor attribute of a table containing the logo.

7. Select a Type from the drop-down list. Here are the five options:

   • **Text:** Select this type for attributes requiring a text-based value, such as the `<img>` tag's `alt` attribute.

   • **URL:** Choose this type when the attribute value points to a file or requires an Internet address, such as the `href` attribute of the `<a>` tag. Designating an attribute as a URL type allows Dreamweaver to update the link if the file is moved or renamed.

   • **Color:** Use the Color type for those attributes specifying a color value, such as the `<tr>` tag's `bgcolor` attribute. The major benefit for identifying color-related attributes as such is the color picker made available in the Template Properties dialog box.

- **True/False:** Select this type if the attribute is a Boolean, meaning it accepts value only of true or false — for example, the `<embed>` tag's `hidden` attribute.

- **Number:** Choose the Number type when an attribute requires a numeric value, such as the `<img>` tag's `height` and `width` attribute.

Caution If you need to enter a percentage, like 50%, or other value that contains both numbers and other characters, select the Text type for your editable attribute. While you might think the Number type is more logical, Dreamweaver will generate errors when the template is saved.

8. Enter the desired initial value for the attribute in the Default field.

    If the attribute is already found in the selected tag, the current value is displayed in the Default field. For new attributes, the Default field is initially blank.

9. Click OK when you're done.

Editable attributes are noted in the code by surrounding the values with double @ signs, like this:

```
<img src="@@(monthlyImageSrc)@@" width="100" height="50"
align="@@(monthlyImageAlign)@@">
```

In this example, the `<img>` tag has two editable attributes, `src` and `align`, which are set to variable values: `@@(monthlyImageSrc)@@` and `@@(monthlyImageAlign)@@`, respectively.

Tip You can apply the same editable attribute to different tags. For example, you might want different cells of various tables on the page to share the same bgcolor. Although you can repeat the Make Attribute Editable command for every variable, you might find it more efficient to simply copy and paste the variable value.

On closer examination of your template file, you might notice two Macromedia comments inserted in the `<head>` section:

```
<!-- TemplateParam name="monthlyImageSrc" type="URL" value="../images/admin.gif" -->
<!-- TemplateParam name="monthlyImageAlign" type="text" value="left" -->
```

These `TemplateParam` tags are used by Dreamweaver to identify the editable attributes and provide their types and default values.

Caution The default values set in Editable attributes are not rendered when viewing the template in the Design view, only in the template-derived document. This is a known bug in Dreamweaver.

Setting Editable Attributes

After you've inserted your editable attributes in the template, Dreamweaver provides a straightforward user interface for editing them in template-derived documents. Whether you choose File ➪ New or select the template in the Assets panel to create your new document, you'll find a new command available under the Modify menu: Template Properties.

The Template Properties dialog box, shown in Figure 28-6, lists all the editable attributes found on a single page. Selecting each property brings up the editing options for that particular attribute type (text, number, color, URL, and true/false) and the current associated value. After modifying any or all the template properties, Dreamweaver refreshes the page and displays the attributes with their new values.

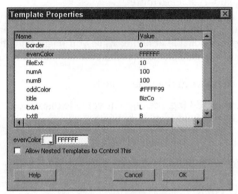

Figure 28-6: How you specify the value for an editable attribute in the Template Properties dialog box depends on the type of attribute. A color attribute type, for example, uses Dreamweaver's standard color picker.

With each of the Template Properties types, you have the option to allow the nested template to control the attribute. Select this option if you intend to save the current document as a template — thus creating a nested template — and if you want documents based on that nested template to set the attribute value. You can also choose this option when editing a nested template. Nested templates are covered in depth later in this chapter.

To set the editable attributes on a template-based document, follow these steps:

1. Choose Modify ➪ Template Properties.

   The Template Properties dialog box is displayed.

2. Select the attribute to specify its value.

3. If you want to allow the attribute to be modified in a document based on a nested template, choose the Allow Nested Templates to Control This option.

   If the option is selected, the phrase `pass through` in parentheses replaces the attribute value editing options.

4. Enter the new value for the attribute. Depending on the type of attribute selected, the value is entered differently:

   • For Text, Number, and URL type attributes, enter the new value in the text field next to the editable attribute name.

   • For Color type attributes, select the color picker to sample the desired color from the color palette or any area on the screen. You can also enter the hexadecimal color value or color name directly in the associated text field.

   • For True/False type attributes, select the Show Attribute Name option to set the value to true and deselect it to set the value to false.

5. To set the value of any other editable attribute on the page, choose the attribute from the list and repeat Steps 3 and 4.

6. Click OK when you're done.

Enabling Repeating Regions

Data-driven pages handle repeating regions elegantly. A single row of a table is bound to data, and the application server returns as many requested rows as are available. However, not all pages are data-driven — and not all areas of a page that repeat can be bound to a data source. Dreamweaver provides solutions for both the server-side — the Repeat Region server behavior — and the client-side — the template-based Repeating Region feature.

New Feature

A repeating region is, like an editable region, applied to a template and may surround any tag-complete (containing both a beginning tag and an ending tag) area on a page. Typically repeating regions wrap around the same type of areas as their server behavior cousins, such as table rows. However, unlike the Repeat Region server behavior, template repeating regions are expanded and manipulated manually in a template-based document. One other important aspect of repeating regions to keep in mind: They aren't automatically editable — you have to include an editable region within a repeating region to make it so. The ability to lock specific portions of repeating regions makes this an extremely powerful feature.

To insert a repeating region, follow these steps:

1. Select the portion of the page that you want to repeat.

   As noted earlier, a repeating region cannot overlap a tag pair. If you attempt to do this, Dreamweaver automatically extends the selection so that the entire tag is included.

2. Choose Insert ⇨ Template Objects ⇨ Repeating Region or, from the Templates category of the Insert bar, select the Repeating Region icon as seen in Figure 28-7

3. Enter a unique name in the New Repeating Region dialog box, and click OK.

   Dreamweaver automatically provides a name, but, as always, it's best if you supply a meaningful name yourself.

As mentioned earlier, repeating regions are not, by default, editable. To make a repeating region editable, select the content within the repeating region — not the repeating region itself — and then create an editable region by either selecting the Editable Region icon from the Insert bar or choosing Insert ⇨ Template Objects ⇨ Editable Region. You'll need to give the editable region a unique name as usual.

Caution

You may notice that the repeating and editable regions tabs overlap, making it difficult to see the repeating region name. I've found it handy to use fairly long names for the repeating region, like dataRowRepeating, and relatively short names for the editable region, such as dataRow, to enable me to see portions of both tabs. Also, you might notice although all template regions use the same color established in Preferences, the highlight for a repeating region is significantly lighter than that for editable regions. This color variation makes it much easier to identify the different types of regions.

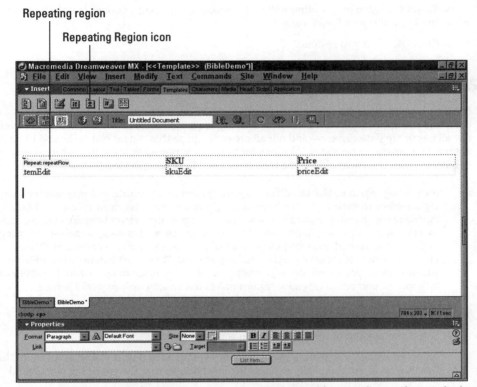

Figure 28-7: Repeating regions are marked in templates with an outline and named tab, just like editable and optional regions.

Modifying a repeating region

The power of repeating regions isn't apparent until you open a template-based document containing one. With Invisible Elements enabled, you notice a series of buttons above each repeating region, as shown in Figure 28-8. With these controls, new entries — identical to the content contained within the repeating region — are added, deleted, or moved from one position to another. You can even copy and paste content within a repeating region.

To modify a repeating region in a template-based document, follow these steps:

1. Make sure View ➪ Visual Aids ➪ Invisible Elements is enabled.

2. Locate the four buttons above the repeating region:

   • To add a new entry, select the Add (+) button. New entries are inserted below the current cursor selection. New entries are selected once created.

   • To delete an existing entry, position your cursor in the entry and choose the Remove (–) button.

   • To move an entry down, place your cursor in the entry and choose the Down button.

   • To move an entry up, place your cursor in the entry and choose the Up button.

3. To copy and paste an entry:

- Position your cursor in the entry.

- Choose Edit ⇨ Repeating Entries ⇨ Copy Repeated Entry.

- Select Edit ⇨ Paste or Edit ⇨ Repeating Entries ⇨ Paste Repeated Entry.

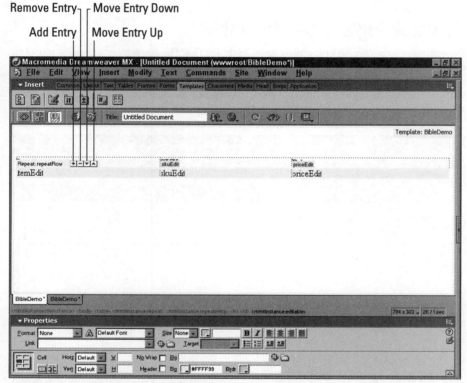

Figure 28-8: Entries can not only be added and removed in a repeating region; they can also be re-ordered.

If you prefer to work with Invisible Elements off, Dreamweaver provides corresponding menu options under both the main and context menus. In fact, the menu options are, in some ways, more powerful and can be immediate time-savers. Look in the main menu under Modify ⇨ Templates ⇨ Repeating Entries or, in the context menu under Templates, for these commands:

✦ New Entry Before Selection

✦ New Entry After Selection

✦ New Entry At End

✦ New Entry At Beginning

✦ Cut Repeating Entry

✦ Copy Repeating Entry

✦ Delete Repeating Entry

✦ Move Entry Up

✦ Move Entry Down

✦ Move Entry to Beginning

✦ Move Entry to End

Constructing a Repeating Table

Repeating regions are so commonly used in tables that Dreamweaver provides a tool to create both a table and a repeating region at the same time. The Repeating Table object opens the standard table dialog box with the added capability to define which rows are within a repeating region. When inserted, the repeating region is all set up — and even includes a separate editable region in each cell as shown in Figure 28-9.

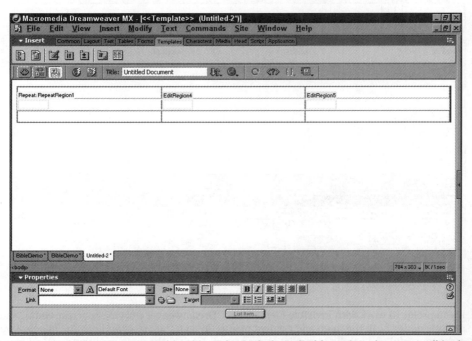

Figure 28-9: The Repeating Table object also includes editable regions for every cell in the repeating region rows. The label for the repeating region obscures the label for the editable region in the first cell.

To insert a Repeating Table, follow these steps:

1. In your template open for editing, position your cursor where you'd like the table to appear and choose Insert ➪ Template Objects ➪ Repeating Table. Alternatively, you can drag the Repeating Table icon from the Templates category of the Insert bar.

   The Repeating Table dialog box, shown in Figure 28-10, is displayed.

2. Enter the values desired for the table attributes: Rows, Columns, Cell Padding, Cell Spacing, Width and Border.

Cross-Reference

If you're not familiar with setting up a table, see Chapter 10.

3. Determine which rows of the table are to be repeated by entering the number of the first row in the Starting Row field and number of the last row in the Ending Row field.

   For example, if you want only the second row of the table to repeat, your values are Starting Row: 2 and Ending Row: 2. However, if you wanted three rows to repeat starting with row 2, the values are Starting Row: 2 and Ending Row: 5.

4. Enter a unique name for the repeating region in the Region Name field or leave the Dreamweaver supplied default name.

5. Click OK when you're done.

After the table is created, you'll notice that every cell in the designated repeating region is editable. Dreamweaver automatically inserts a separate editable region and names them incrementally EditRegion1, EditRegion2, and so on. By defining each cell as editable, rather than the entire row, Dreamweaver gives you the option to retain the editability on a cell-by-cell basis. If the cell should not be editable, position your cursor anywhere in the cell and choose Modify ➪ Templates ➪ Remove Template Markup.

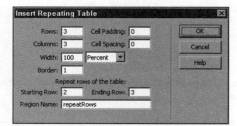

Figure 28-10: With the Repeating Table feature, you can define multiple rows to repeat.

Establishing Optional Regions

One of my clients quite regularly wants to feature one of his products over the others, so we developed a special logo for exactly that purpose. Whenever a product was to be highlighted, I modified the page to include the special logo rather than the standard one. Typically this would take up to a half-hour every time the change was made. Not only did I have to find the catalog page with the to-be-featured item and replace the logo — something else I had to hunt for — I also had to find the previously featured item page and revert the special logo placed there to the standard one. Not difficult work, but certainly tedious.

New Feature

Dreamweaver's Optional Region feature is intended to reduce, if not eliminate, such tiresome chores. Content placed on a template within an optional region is conditionally shown or not shown on the template-derived page. In the just-described situation, this feature enables me to put both logos in the same template each in its own optional region. By default, the main logo would be shown, but if I decide not to show it, the special logo would be shown in its place. Optional regions are extremely powerful.

Optional regions work somewhat like a cross between repeating region and editable attributes. Like repeating regions, optional regions can surround any portion of a page; also, they are also not editable by default, although it's possible to create an editable optional region. After an optional region has been placed on the template page — as with editable attributes — the Template Properties dialog box is used to set the condition that displays or hides the content on a template-derived page.

The conditions that control an optional region range from a basic true-false or Boolean statement to more complex evaluated expressions. Reflecting this, the New Optional Region dialog box contains two tabs, Basic and Advanced. Under the Basic tab, you simply enter the name for the optional region and indicate whether to display the region by default or not. The Advanced tab, shown in Figure 28-11, allows you the opportunity to set the condition dependent on another existing template parameter or enter a template expression.

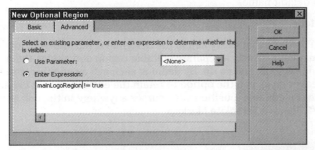

Figure 28-11: Optional regions may be controlled by the state of another parameter directly or by the evaluation of a template expression.

Note The Basic and Advanced tabs are mutually exclusive. The tab showing when OK is selected determines which template parameter is used.

Now, look at an example to see how both the Basic and Advanced approaches work together. Take the situation, described at the beginning of this section, which required the use of a special logo every so often. To accomplish this, I create one optional region using the Basic tab of the New Optional Region dialog box. In this region, I just enter a name, mainLogoRegion, and enable the Show By Default option. In this region, I place my standard logo. The Basic tab creates a template parameter with code like this in the `<head>`:

```
<!-- TemplateParam name="mainLogoRegion" type="boolean" value="true" -->
```

Next, I create a second optional region and, this time, select the Advanced tab of the New Optional Region dialog box. I want this region to be displayed only when the other region is not. To achieve this effect, I select the Enter Expression option and enter the following in the text area:

```
mainLogoRegion != true
```

With optional regions, the name is the same as the condition, so translated into English, this expression would read, "Show this region if mainLogoRegion is not shown." As shown in Figure 28-12, Dreamweaver uses the condition as the name of the optional region, and this name is represented in the tab above the optional regions.

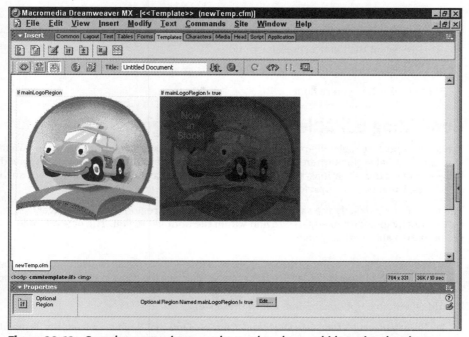

Figure 28-12: Complex expressions may be used to show or hide optional regions.

Dreamweaver template expressions support a subset of JavaScript operators, so I could have also written this expression like this:

```
!mainLogoRegion
```

In a different situation, I might want to tie a number of noncontiguous optional regions together so that if the main region shows, the others would as well. You achieve this by setting Use Parameter to the name of the main region. You'll find a more detailed discussion of template expressions a little later in this chapter.

To insert an optional region, follow these steps:

1. Choose Insert ⇨ Template Objects ⇨ Optional Region or, from the Templates category of the Insert bar, select the Optional Region icon.

2. If you want to create a template parameter, from the Basic tab

   • Enter a unique name for the optional region in the Name field.

   • Choose the Show By Default option if you want to make the region initially viewable.

3. If you want to link this optional region to the state of another optional region, from the Advanced tab

   • Select the Use Parameter option.

   • Choose an existing optional region from the drop-down list.

4. If you want to control the optional region display with a template parameter, from the Advanced tab

   - Select the Enter Expression option.

   - Enter the desired expression in the text area.

5. Click OK when you're done.

Combining editable and optional regions

Similar to repeating regions, optional regions by themselves are not editable. There are many uses for optional regions where the designed content is either displayed or not displayed. However, in certain situations, the optional content needs to be editable as well. For such situations, Dreamweaver provides the Editable Optional Region object.

The procedure is exactly the same as inserting an optional region—Dreamweaver automatically includes an editable region within the optional region. The new editable region is also automatically named.

Tip   You can change the name of the automatically added editable region by selecting the template region tab or its tag in the Tag Selector and then changing the name in the Property inspector.

To add an editable optional region, follow these steps:

1. Choose Insert ➪ Template Objects ➪ Editable Optional Region or, from the Templates category of the Insert bar, select the Editable Optional Region icon.

2. Follow the procedure outlined for inserting an optional region.

3. Click OK when you're done.

Of course, if you ever decide to add an editable region to an optional region containing locked content, you can always do so when editing the template.

Setting optional region properties

Although you set up an area of the page to be optionally displayed in the template, you actually choose the display option—whether to show or hide the region—in the document created from the template. As with editable attributes, the Template Properties dialog box handles control of the optional regions. Unlike editable attributes, optional regions only use true/false values setting whether a selected region is either shown (true) or not shown (false).

Instead of the template parameter statement found in templates, Dreamweaver inserts instance parameters into the `<head>` section of the template-derived document, like this one:

```
<!-- InstanceParam name="mainLogoRegion" type="boolean" value="true" -->
```

To set the parameters of an optional region in a template-based document, follow these steps:

1. Choose Modify ➪ Template Properties.

   The Template Properties dialog box is displayed.

2. Select the optional region you want to affect.

3. If you want to allow the optional region to be modified in a document based on a nested template, choose the Allow Nested Templates to Control This option.

   If the option is selected, the phrase `pass through` in parentheses replaces the Show Attribute Name options and appears in the list.

4. Otherwise, select the Show *Attribute Name* option to set the value to true and deselect it to set the value to false.

5. To set the value of any other optional regions on the page, choose the entry from the list and repeat Steps 2 through 4.

6. Click OK when you're done.

Evaluating template expressions

So far in this chapter, you've seen a little of what template expressions can do. With optional regions, template expressions are either set explicitly or evaluated to true or false. Template expressions can also be used throughout the template to great effect. Here is a short list of what's possible with template expressions:

✦ Alternate the background color of a row contained in a repeating region.

✦ Automatically number each row in a repeating region.

✦ List the total number of rows in a repeating region.

✦ Show an optional region if a certain number of rows are used, or another region if that number of rows is exceeded.

✦ Create sequential navigation links, allowing users to page to the next — or previous — document in a series.

✦ Compute values displayed in a table, displaying items such as basic cost, tax, shipping, and total.

✦ Display particular content depending on the position of the row — first, second, second-to-last, or last, for example — in the repeating region.

There are two types of template expressions: template expression statements and inline template expressions. Template expression statements take the form of a specialized HTML comment, like this:

```
<!-- TemplateExpr expr="fileExt" -->
```

Template expression statements are coded by hand. Inline template expressions are surrounded by parentheses and double-@ signs, like this:

```
@@(fileExt)@@
```

Inline template expressions can only be entered by hand but are very flexible. You can insert an inline template expression as an attribute into any of Dreamweaver's text field interfaces, such as the Link field of the text Property inspector or the Bg (Background Color) field of the row Property inspector. Template expressions not entered as attributes appear as an Invisible Element with a double-@ sign symbol as shown in Figure 28-13. Template expression statements appear with a script icon.

 Caution   While you can enter an inline template expression without a problem in the Code view, you cannot enter one on the page in Design view.

Template expression statement

Inline template expression

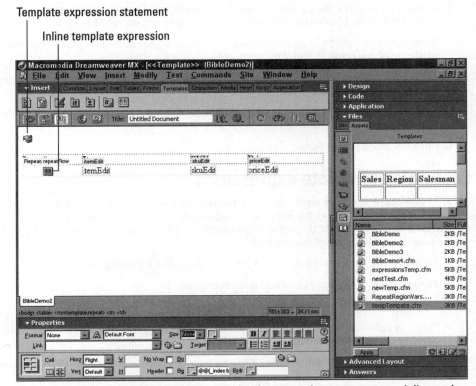

Figure 28-13: Template expressions can either be entered as statements or inline code.

Template expression language and object model

Template expressions are written in their own language, which uses a subset of JavaScript operators and its own object model. The syntax of template expressions closely resembles that of JavaScript, and both use a similar dot notation to refer to the properties of a specific object. Similar to JavaScript, Dreamweaver template expressions also have their own object model, although the object model for template expressions is much more limited in scope.

The elements supported by Dreamweaver template expressions are detailed in Table 28-1.

Table 28-1: Template Expression Features and Operators

Literals	Syntax	Example
Numeric Literal	Double-quoted numbers	"123"
String Literal	Double-quoted string	"Chapter"
Boolean Literals	true/false	true
String Concatenation	string1 + string2	"Number of rows: " + _numRows

Literals	Syntax	Example
Ternary Operators		
Conditional	condition ? resultA : resultB	(_index & 1) ? #FFFFFF : #CCCCCC
Logical Operators		
Logical NOT	!operand	!mainLogoRegion
Logical AND	operand1 && operand2	
Logical OR	operand1 || operand2	
Arithmetic Operators		
Addition	operand1 + operand2	_numRows + 1
Subtraction	operand1 – operand2	_index – 1
Multiplication	operand1 * operand2	basePrice * taxBase
Division	operand1 / operand2	numSold / quantityShown
Modulo	operand1 % operand2	_index % 2
Comparison Operators		
Less Than	operand1 < operand2	inStock < numSold
Greater Than	operand1 > operand2	numSold > numShipped
Less Than or Equal	operand1 <= operand2	_index <= _numRows
Greater Than or Equal	operand1 >=operand2	_numRows >= pageLimit
Equal	operand1 == operand2	_index == 10
Not Equal	operand1 != operand2	_numRows != 1
Bitwise Operators		
Bitwise NOT	~operand	~4
Bitwise AND	operand1 & operand2	_index & 1
Bitwise OR	operand1 | operand2	4 | 8
Bitwise XOR	operand1 ^ operand2	2 ^ 4
Bitwise Signed Right Shift	operand1 >> n	8 >> 1
Bitwise Left Shift	operand << n	1 << 0

The template expressions document model is made up of two primary objects: document and repeat. The document object contains all the template variables found on the page. For example, if you create an optional region with the name altImageRegion, you can refer to it in a document expression with the following statement:

```
<!-- TemplateBeginIf cond="_document.altImageRegion" -->
```

However, the _document prefix is implicit, and the same statement can be written like this:

```
<!-- TemplateBeginIf cond="altImageRegion" -->
```

As you may suspect, the _repeat object refers to a repeating region. The _repeat object has a number of very useful properties as shown in Table 28-2.

Table 28-2: _repeat Object Properties

Property	Description
_index	Returns the index number of the current entry. The _index property is zero-based, so for the first entry of a repeating region, _index equals zero.
_numRows	Returns the total number of entries in a repeating region.
_isFirst	Returns true if the current entry is the first entry of a repeating region, false otherwise.
_isLast	Returns true if the current entry is the last entry of a repeating region, false otherwise.
_prevRecord	Returns the _repeat object for the entry before the current entry. For example, if _index = 2, then _prevRecord._index = 1. If _prevRecord is used in the first entry, an error occurs.
_nextRecord	Returns the _repeat object for the entry after the current entry. For example, if _index = 2, then _nextRecord._index = 3.
_parent	Returns the _repeat object for a repeating region enclosing the current repeating region. For example, use _parent._numRows to find the total number of rows of the outer repeating region.

The _repeat object is also implicit, and it is not necessary to reference it specifically in a template expression.

Multiple-If template expressions

Certain template expressions cannot be handled by referencing a single condition — "If A is true, show B" does not cover every possible circumstance. What if you wanted to test against multiple conditions and provide multiple results? Can Dreamweaver handle something like "If A is true, show B; but if C is true, show D — and if neither of them are true, show E."? With the help of multiple-if expressions, you bet it can.

With a multiple-if template expression, you can test for any number of conditions and act accordingly. Multiple-if expressions use two different template expressions: one to close the entire expression and another one for each separate case. Here is an example:

```
<!-- TemplateBeginMultipleIf -->
<!-- checks value of template parameter SKU and shows the desired image-->
  <!-- TemplateBeginIfClause cond = "SKU == 101">
    <img src = "/images/ring101.gif" width="125" height="125">
  <!-- TemplateEndIfClause-->

  <!-- TemplateBeginIfClause cond = "SKU == 102">
   <img src = "/images/bracelet102.gif" width="125" height="125">
```

```
<!-- TemplateEndIfClause-->

<!-- TemplateBeginIfClause cond = "SKU == 103">
 <img src = "/images/necklace103.gif" width="125" height="125">
<!-- TemplateEndIfClause-->

//default display if none of the other conditions are met
<!-- TemplateBeginIfClause cond = "SKU != 103">
 <img src = "/images/spacer.gif" width="125" height="125">
<!-- TemplateEndIfClause-->
<!-- TemplateEndMultipleIf -->
```

In this code, if none of the conditions are met, a blank spacer image is displayed. As with other template expressions, multiple-if expressions must be coded by hand.

Dreamweaver Technique: Template Expression examples

Template expressions obviously have a great deal of power built-in, but how do you put it to use? Let's look at some specific examples to help you get a better understanding of template expressions in general, as well to give you some useful tools.

Alternating row background colors

With a data-filled table of any significant size, alternating background colors for each row greatly increases the readability of the data. Template expressions provide a technique for specifying the two background colors — and automatically applying the right color whenever a new row is added in a repeating region. The key to this technique is the conditional operator.

The conditional operator has three parts: the condition and the two results. If the condition is evaluated as true, the first result is applied; if not, the second. In this case, the condition that is examined involves the _index property, which returns the position of the current row. By combining the _index property with the bitwise AND operator, &, like this

```
_index & 1
```

true is returned every other row, starting with the second row. The full template expression specifies the two colors as hexadecimal values; the second value specified (here, a light yellow) is returned in the first row and the first value (white) in the following row, and so on:

```
@@((_index & 1) ? '#FFFFFF' : '#FFFF99')@@
```

This template expression is entered as the bgcolor attribute for the table row containing your data in a template's repeating region. Note the use of the single quotes around the color values; quotes are needed in the conditional operator syntax, and single quotes are used here because Dreamweaver encloses the entire attribute value with double quotes.

Here's the code for the entire table in the template document, with the tag containing the alternating row background color in bold:

```
<table width="100%" border="0" cellspacing="0" cellpadding="0">
  <tr>
    <th>Item</th>
    <th>SKU</th>
    <th>Price</th>
  </tr>
  <!-- TemplateBeginRepeat name="repeatRow" -->
 <tr bgcolor="@@((_index & 1) ? '#FFFFFF' : '#FFFF99')@@">
```

```
    <td><!-- TemplateBeginEditable name="itemEdit" -->itemEdit<!--
TemplateEndEditable ---></td>
    <td><!-- TemplateBeginEditable name="skuEdit" -->skuEdit<!--
TemplateEndEditable --></td>
    <td><!-- TemplateBeginEditable name="priceEdit" -->priceEdit<!--
TemplateEndEditable -->
    </td>
  </tr>
  <!-- TemplateEndRepeat -->
</table>
```

You won't see any changes in the template itself—for the full effect, you have to open up a document based on the template and added a few rows. As you can see in Figure 28-14, whenever another entry is added to the repeating region in the template-based document, the alternating color is automatically applied.

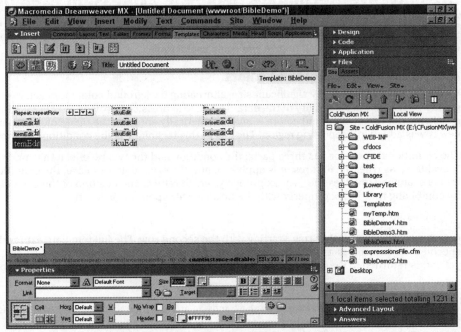

Figure 28-14: Using a conditional operator for the bgcolor attribute automatically generates alternating row colors in a repeating region.

Tip   As written, the code in this technique alternates color every row. To alternate the color every two rows, change the value in the condition from 1 to 2 so that the template expression reads:

```
@@((_index & 2) ? '#FFFFFF' : '#FFFF99')@@
```

Automatic row numbering

In a template with a repeating region, you often want the flexibility of adding as many rows as required and adding a reference number to each row. The _index property of the template object model provides an easy way to number rows automatically. The only trick to this technique is to remember that _index is a zero-based property and you'll need to add a 1 to have the correct row number displayed.

Here's the template expression by itself:

```
@@(_index + 1)@@
```

This code should be entered directly in Code view within the repeating region. You can combine this with any other text, such as a following period or color or styles. Here's an example, bolded, in a right-aligned table cell with several non-breaking spaces trailing to create a decimal-align look:

```
<td align="right">@@(_index + 1)@@     </td>
```

The right-align and non-breaking space combination keep numbering in line when over 10 entries are involved, as shown in Figure 28-15.

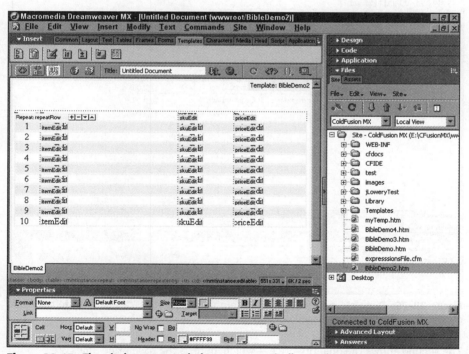

Figure 28-15: The _index property helps to automatically number rows in a repeating region.

Computing values in a table

After a value has been entered for a template expression variable, it can be used in calculations and can also be used as a deciding factor in a multiple-if statement. For example, each page of a template shows a catalog item and all the relevant information. Included in that relevant information is the price—an element that may fluctuate far more than the description or picture of the item. Should the client want to offer a special discount for higher quantities, template expressions can automatically calculate the new price as well as the savings.

In this example, I've set up one template parameter, priceVar, and given it a default value of 100:

```
<!-- TemplateParam name="priceVar" type="number" value="100" -->
```

This code goes in the non-editable portion of the template's `<head>`. The example application, shown in Figure 28-16, uses three different template expressions. The first, @@priceVar@@, displays the parameter set with the Template Properties dialog box.

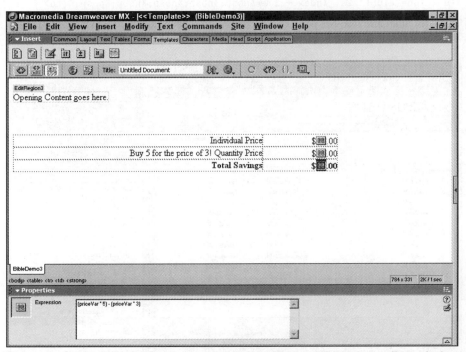

Figure 28-16: Template expressions, set in Template Properties, can be used to calculate other values in a template-based document.

The second shows the quantity price—which, here, is the base price times 3:

```
@@(priceVar * 3)@@
```

The third expression displays the savings a buyer could receive by buying in quantity. In this example formula, the price times 3 is subtracted from the price times 5:

```
@@((priceVar * 5) - (priceVar * 3))@@
```

Again, you can add whatever text or styles are necessary. Here, a dollar sign is placed in front of every expression that is followed by a decimal point and two zeroes as you can see in Listing 28-1.

Listing 28-1: **Template Expressions Computing Example**

```
<table width="100%"  border="0" cellspacing="0" cellpadding="0">
  <tr>
    <td width="77%" align="right">Individual Price</td>
    <td width="23%" align="right">$@@(priceVar)@@.00</td>
  </tr>
  <tr>
    <td align="right">Buy 5 for the price of 3! Quantity Price</td>
    <td align="right">$@@(priceVar * 3)@@.00</td-
  </tr>
  <tr>
    <td align="right"><strong>Total Savings</strong></td>
    <td align="right"><strong>$@@((priceVar * 5) - ⤵
(priceVar * 3))@@.00</strong></td>
  </tr>
</table>
```

Now the calculations on this template are ready to be used by any product in the catalog, at any price point, offering the same deal.

Sequential navigation links

Although much of the Web is based on the principal that you can link to any page from any other page, there are certain situations — such as help or instructional applications — where sequential navigation is needed. Numerous help applications use some form of Previous and Next buttons, for example. If these files are named sequentially — such as docFile10, docFile11, docFile12, and so on — template expressions may be used to automatically code the links to the prior and subsequent pages.

Rely on template expressions for the capability to handle string concatenation to create these auto-updating links. The first task is to set up a template parameter to be used as the number of the current file in the series. If, for example, you're creating docFile5.htm from your template, the template parameter will be set to 5. To accomplish this task, use Dreamweaver's editable attribute facility to create the template parameter. This example assumes that you are editing a template with Previous and Next buttons already in place.

1. Select the `<a>` tag surrounding the Previous button from the Tag Selector.

2. Choose Modify ➪ Templates ➪ Make Attribute Editable.

3. In the Editable Tag Attributes dialog box, select Add (+) and then enter a dummy attribute name such as **baseLink**.

   Choose an attribute name that will be ignored by browsers rather than a real attribute.

4. Make sure that Make Attribute Editable is selected.

5. Choose Number as the Type of attribute from the drop-down list.

6. Enter a default number.

   This number will be set for every file created, so the default value is merely a placeholder.

Now you can use the template parameter set up in a template expression.

1. Choose the Previous button or link on the template page.

2. In the Property inspector, enter code similar to the following in the Link field:

   ```
   @@('cFile' + (baseLink - 1) + '.htm')@@
   ```

   In this example, the sequential files are all within the same folder and named docFile1.htm, docFile2.htm, and so on. My template parameter, defined in the previous step, is called **baseLink**.

3. Next, choose the Next button to perform a similar operation.

4. In the Link field, enter code like this:

   ```
   @@('docFile' + (baseLink + 1) + '.htm')@@
   ```

   Here, instead of subtracting a number from the base value, as was done for the Previous button link, one is added.

After the template is saved, create a file based on the template. Now we're ready to specify the template parameter.

1. Begin by choosing Modify ⇨ Template Properties and selecting the editable attribute establishing in the template.

2. Enter the number value corresponding to the filename of the current sequentially name page. For example, if the file is named docFile5.htm, enter **5**.

3. Click OK when done.

When you preview your page, you'll notice that the Previous and Next buttons now link the proper pages in the sequence as shown in Figure 28-17.

Tip   You can also use optional regions to hide the Previous button when the template-based page is the first in the series and the Next button when a page is the last in the series. It's all in the power of template expressions.

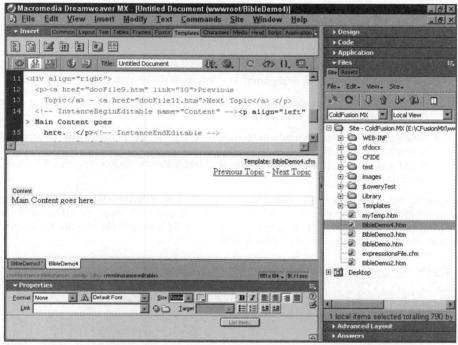

Figure 28-17: Although it looks like a standard link, this code was generated by the Dreamweaver during the design-time construction of this template-based document.

Nesting Templates

The simple template with its combination of locked and editable regions truly reflects the reality of many Web pages where the overall structure is constant and the details of the content vary. Often, however, a single locked area is too rigid to really be useful in a complex site. Suppose for a moment you're working on a site for a magazine publisher with multiple brands. The client wants a general look and feel for the entire site with separate navigation and content for each magazine. One way to achieve this effect is to use multiple templates — one set for each magazine, all incorporating the parent-company style. The problem here is that to affect changes on the highest level; all the templates need to be changed. Another way — a better way — is to use nested templates.

New Feature

Nested templates allow template-based documents to have numerous tiers of locked regions. With nested templates, the magazine publisher in our example could make a change to just the master template and the modifications would ripple through all the other magazine-specific templates and on down to their related pages. Best of all, there's no real limit on nesting templates: Your template-based files can be as deeply nested as you need them to be.

Here's an overview of how nested templates work:

✦ A new page based on the master template is created and saved as a template; this new document is the nested template.

✦ Within the editable areas originally setup in the master template, new editable areas are placed. All areas not designated as editable in the nested template are locked.

✦ A new document is created, based on the nested template. The only editable areas are those inserted in the nested template.

✦ When modifications are made to the nested template, the changes are reflected in the pages based on that template. When modifications are made to the master template, the changes are applied to both the nested template and to documents based on the nested template.

Dreamweaver employs a color-coding system to help you differentiate editable regions inserted in the master template from those added in the nested template. Although it's not obvious in the black-and-white Figure 28-18, master template editable regions are shown in orange, whereas nested template editable regions are blue.

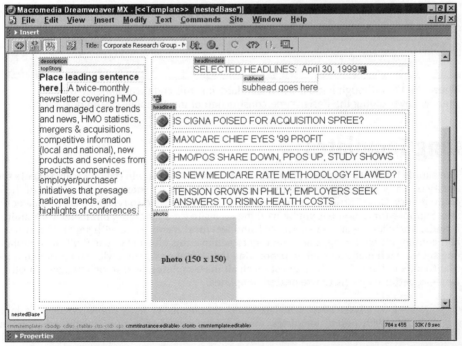

Figure 28-18: The master template editable region — the outer region here — is highlighted with an orange outline while the nested template editable region, the inner region, is blue.

To create a nested template, follow these steps:

1. Create a master root-level template by choosing File ➪ Save As Template for an existing page or selecting New Template from the Template category of the Assets panel for new documents.

   The master template contains all the elements — navigation, logos, footers, and so on — common to all template-based pages in the site.

2. Insert editable regions wherever variable content is desired in the master template and save the template when you're ready.

3. Create a new document based on the master template by:

   - Choosing File ➪ New to open the New Document dialog box
   - Selecting the Templates category
   - Making sure the current site is selected in the Templates For list
   - Selecting the desired master template from the Template list
   - Choosing Create

4. Save the newly created document as a template.

   By saving a template-derived document as a template, a nested template is created.

5. In the nested template, make any changes needed within the editable regions.

   These changes will be locked in any document based on the nested template.

6. Add any desired template regions (editable, repeating, or optional) within the existing editable regions from the master template.

   When the first editable region is inserted in the nested template, the editable regions from the master template turn orange to differentiate them from the new regions.

7. After you've finished adding the desired template regions to the nested template, save the file.

Now, when creating documents based on the nested template, you are still able to modify content within an editable region — but only those editable regions added in the nested template.

Working with Templates in the Assets Panel

As a site grows, so does the number of templates it employs. Overall management of your templates is conducted through the Templates category of the Assets panel. You can open the Templates category by choosing Windows ➪ Templates. The Templates category, shown in Figure 28-19, displays a list of the current site's available templates in the lower pane and a preview of the selected template in the upper pane.

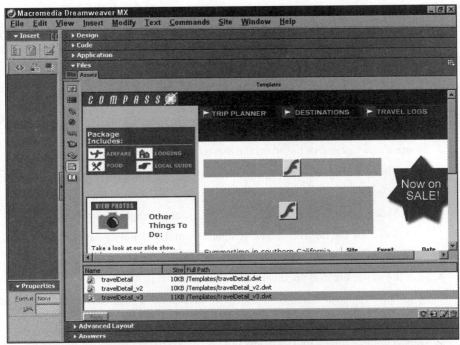

Figure 28-19: Use the Templates category of the Assets panel to preview, delete, open, create, or apply your current site's templates.

The Templates category has five buttons along the bottom.

✦ **Apply:** Creates a document derived from the currently selected template if the current document is blank; if the current document is based on a template, this option changes the locked regions of the document to match the selected template.

✦ **Refresh Site List:** Displays the list of all templates currently in the site

✦ **New Template:** Creates a new blank template

✦ **Edit:** Loads the selected template for modification

✦ **Delete:** Removes the selected template

The Assets panel's context menu offers all these options and more, as explained in Table 28-3.

Table 28-3: Template Category Context Menu

Command	Description
Refresh Site List	Displays the list of all templates currently in the site cache.
Recreate Site List	Reloads the template site list into the cache.
New Template	Starts a new blank template.
Edit	Opens the selected template for modifying.

Command	Description
Apply	Creates a document derived from the currently selected template if the current document is blank. If the current document is based on a template, this option changes the locked regions of the document to match the selected template. The same effects can also be achieved by dragging the template from the Assets panel to the current document.
Rename	Renames the selected template.
Delete	Removes the selected template.
Update Current Page	Applies any changes made in the template to the current page, if the current page is derived from a template.
Update Site	Applies any changes made in any templates to all template-based documents in the site.
Copy to Site	Copies the highlighted template, but none of the dependent files, to the selected site.
Locate in Site	Opens the Site panel and highlights the selected template.

Creating a blank template

Not all templates are created from existing documents. Some Web designers prefer to create their templates from scratch. To create a blank template, follow these steps:

1. Open the Templates category of the Assets panel by selecting its symbol or by choosing Window ➪ Templates.

2. From the Templates category, select New Template. A new, untitled template is created.

3. Enter a title for your new template and press Enter (Return).

4. While the new template is selected, press the Edit button. The blank template opens in a new Dreamweaver window.

5. Insert your page elements.

6. Mark any elements or areas as editable regions using one of the methods previously described.

7. Save your template.

Deleting and opening templates

As with any set of files, there comes a time to clean house and remove files that are no longer in use. To remove a template, first open the Templates category of the Assets panel. Next, select the file you want to remove and choose the Delete button.

Caution

Be forewarned: Dreamweaver does not alert you if files exist that were created from the template that you're about to delete. Deleting the template, in effect, "orphans" those documents, and they can no longer be updated via a template.

You can edit a template—to change the locked or editable regions—in several ways. To use the first method, choose File ➪ Open and, in the Select File dialog box, change the Files of Type to Template Files (*.dwt) on Window systems, or choose Template Files from the Show drop-down list on Macintosh systems. Then, locate the Templates folder in your defined site to select the template to open.

The second method of opening a template for modification uses the Templates category of the Assets panel. Select a template to modify and choose the Edit button. You can also double-click your template to open it for editing. Finally, if you're working in the Site panel, open a template by selecting the Templates folder for your site and open any of the files found there.

Tip   After you've made your modifications to the template, you don't have to use the Save As Template command to store the file—you can use the regular File ➪ Save command or the keyboard shortcut Ctrl+S (Command+S). Likewise, if you want to save your template under a new name, use the Save As command.

Applying templates

Dreamweaver makes it easy to try a variety of different looks for your document while maintaining the same content. After you've created a document from a template, you can apply any other template to it. The only requirement is that the two templates have editable regions with the same names. When might this feature come in handy? In one scenario, you might develop a number of possible Web site designs for a client and create templates for each different approach, which are then applied to the identical content. Or, in an ongoing site, you could completely change the look of a catalog seasonally but retain all the content. Figure 28-20 shows two radically different schemes for a Web site with the same content.

To apply a template to a document, follow these steps:

1. Open the Templates category of the Assets panel.

2. Make sure the Web page to which you want to apply the style is the active document.

3. From the Templates category, select the template you want to use and click the Apply button.

Tip   You can also drag onto the current page the template you'd like to apply or choose Modify ➪ Templates ➪ Apply Template to Page from the menus.

4. If content exists without a matching editable region, Dreamweaver displays the Choose Editable Region for Orphaned Content dialog box. To receive the content, select one of the listed editable regions from the template being applied and then click OK.

The new template is applied to the document, and all the new locked areas replace all the old locked areas.

Mapping inconsistent template regions

When Dreamweaver applies a template to a page, it attempts to map the regions on the two pages to one another. If there is a one-to-one correspondence between the page's regions—for every editable region in the template, there is an editable region with the same name on the page—everything goes smoothly, and the template is applied without incident. If, however, the region names do not match — the template's main content area is called theContent whereas the pages' main content area is called mainContent, for example — Dreamweaver gives you the opportunity to place the content properly with the Inconsistent Region Names dialog box, shown in Figure 28-21.

New Feature

The Inconsistent Region Names dialog box appears automatically when Dreamweaver finds regions that do not match in a template and the document to which the template is being applied. You can map the content in the document to any region in the template or discard the content. However, you cannot ignore the unmapped content; Dreamweaver will not proceed with the template application until all inconsistently named regions are addressed in some fashion.

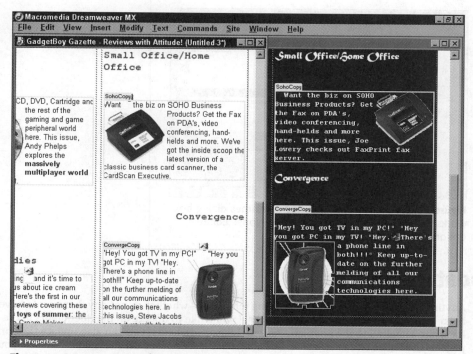

Figure 28-20: You can apply a template to a document created from another template to achieve different designs with identical content.

To handle inconsistently named regions, follow these steps:

1. When the Inconsistent Region Names dialog box appears, select the first unresolved region.

2. From the Move Content To New Region drop-down list, select the region you want to assign to the unmapped region.

3. If there is no region suitable and you want to discard the content, choose Nowhere from the list.

4. To use the same choice for all regions displayed, choose the Use For All option.

5. To map another region, select its name from the list and repeat Steps 2 through 4.

6. Click OK when you're done.

You'll always find certain regions, such as `doctitle` and `head`, listed in the Move Content To New Region list. In general, you would not want to move any body area content into these regions.

Tip   The region names must match precisely—including the case of the two names—or the Inconsistent Region Names dialog box appears.

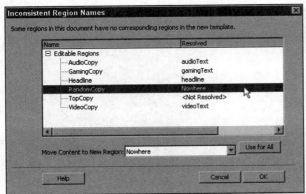

Figure 28-21: The Inconsistent Region Names dialog box works with the full range of template regions: editable, optional and repeating.

Updating Templates

Anytime you save a change to an existing template—whether or not any documents have been created from it—Dreamweaver asks if you'd like to update all the documents in the local site attached to the template. As with Library elements, you can also update the current page or the entire site at any time. Updating documents based on a template can save you an enormous amount of time—especially when numerous changes are involved.

Caution   The template structure changed significantly in Dreamweaver MX when compared to earlier versions of the program. When you open a template created in a previous version in Dreamweaver MX, the template structure is updated. After being updated, the template cannot be modified in any version except Dreamweaver MX.

To update a single page, open the page and choose Modify ➪ Templates ➪ Update Current Page or select the same command from the context menu of the Assets panel. Either way, the update is instantly applied.

To update a series of pages or an entire site, follow these steps:

1. Choose Modify ➪ Templates ➪ Update Pages. The Update Pages dialog box, shown in Figure 28-22, appears.

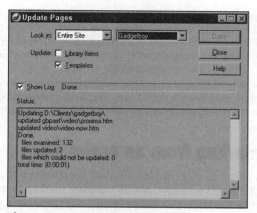

Figure 28-22: Any changes made to a template can be applied automatically to the template's associated files by using the Update Pages command.

2. To update all the documents using all the templates for an entire site, choose Entire Site from the Look In option; then select the name of the site from the accompanying drop-down list.

3. To update pages using a particular template, choose Files That Use from the Look In option and then select the name of the template.

4. To view a report of the progress of the update, make sure that the Show Log option is enabled.

5. Click Start to begin the update process.

The log window displays a list of the files examined and updated, the total number of files that could not be updated, and the elapsed time.

Removing Template Markup

Mistakes are made, clients change their minds, bosses change directions — for whatever reason, you'll find that you need to remove template markup from time to time. Luckily, Dreamweaver has made it as easy to delete the template indicators as it is to insert them. With a little know-how, you can remove template markup from an editable attribute for an entire site.

Deleting template markup individually

Quite often I find I need to convert an editable region to a locked area. You can accomplish this change in one of two ways — you can delete the surrounding template tags in the code or you can use a Dreamweaver command, Remove Template Markup. Personally, I find the command approach to be much faster and more efficient. Individual template markup can only be removed from the template itself.

To remove any surrounding template code via the command, place your cursor within the template region and choose Modify ➪ Templates ➪ Remove Template Markup. Alternatively, right-click (Control+click) and choose Templates ➪ Remove Template Markup.

The Remove Template Markup command works only on the template markup immediately enclosing the cursor position. If, for example, you need to remove an editable optional region and convert the content to being locked, you'll need to issue the Remove Template Markup command twice: once to remove the editable region and again to remove the optional region.

Caution   Using the Remove Template Markup command to remove an optional region will not delete the corresponding TemplateParam statement in the `<head>` tag. If no other optional region uses the same TemplateParam statement, you'll need to remove the code manually.

Removing template markup from an entire page

Template-derived documents don't need to stay template-derived documents forever. All you need do is to detach the document from its template, and all template markup in the page is removed. To detach a document from the template choose Modify ➪ Templates ➪ Detach from Template.

Note   If, for any reason, you need to remove all the markup from a template itself, the fastest way is to create a document from that template and then issue the Detach from Template command.

Exporting a site without template markup

Not all sites are template-based. Dreamweaver gives you the power to strip all the template markup from template-based documents in an entire site. This command is particularly useful when migrating previously template-based documents to a site that does not use templates. Just to hedge your bets, Dreamweaver will optionally export the data from your template-based documents into XML files so that, if necessary, the data can be applied to a new template.

New Feature   The Export without Markup command handles more than just the templates, however. An entire copy of your site is copied to a new folder, sans template markup. Even the Template folder itself, with all the site's templates in tact is copied. Best of all, this is not necessarily a one-time feature. If repeated, you have the option to extract only the modified files.

To export a site without template markup, follow these steps:

1. Choose Modify ➪ Templates ➪ Export without Markup.

   The Export Site Without Template Markup dialog box, shown in Figure 28-23, appears.

Figure 28-23: The Export without Markup command duplicates your entire site in another folder while simultaneously removing all markup from template-derived files.

2. Enter the path to the folder to hold the exported site or select the Browse button to locate the folder.

   Because the entire site is exported, the folder you choose may not be contained in the current site.

3. If you want to maintain the data from the template-based documents, choose the Keep Template Data Files option.

Dreamweaver stores the data in a standard XML file format. For more about Dreamweaver's XML export features, see Chapter 32.

4. If you have previously exported the site with this command and want to update your export, choose the Extract Only Changed Files option.

5. Click OK when you're done.

After the operation is completed, you'll probably want to define a new site to manage the exported files — Dreamweaver does not do this task for you automatically.

Changing the Default Document

Each time you open a new document in Dreamweaver, a blank page is created. The code that makes up that blank page depends on which document type you choose — HTML, XML, ColdFusion, and ASP.NET, among others. The default documents on which the new pages are based are all stored in the Configuration\DocumentTypes\NewDocuments folder. A selected default page works in a similar fashion to the templates in that you can create new documents from it, but no editable or locked regions exist — everything in the page can always be altered. For example, the basic HTML document is a bare-bones structure with only a few properties specified — a document type and a character set:

```
<!DOCTYPE HTML PUBLIC "-//W3C//DTD HTML 4.01 Transitional//EN">
<HTML>
<HEAD>
<TITLE>Untitled Document</TITLE>
<meta http-equiv="Content-Type" content="text/html; charset=">
</HEAD>

<BODY>

</BODY>

   </HTML>
```

Naturally, you can change any of these elements — and add many, many more — after you've opened a page. But what if you want to have a <meta> tag with creator information in every page that comes out of your Web design company? You can do it in Dreamweaver manually, but it's a bother; and chances are good that you'll forget. Luckily, Dreamweaver provides a more efficient solution.

In keeping with its overall design philosophy of extensibility, Dreamweaver enables you to modify the default file as you would any other file. Just choose File ➪ Open and select the appropriate file from the Configuration\DocumentTypes\NewDocuments folder. After you have made your changes, save the file as you would normally. Now, to test your modifications, choose File ➪ New and select your document type. Your modifications appear in your new document.

Summary

Much of a Web designer's responsibility is related to document production, and Dreamweaver offers a comprehensive template solution to reduce the workload. When planning your strategy for building an entire Web site, remember that templates provide multiple advantages:

✦ Templates can be created from any Web page.

✦ Dreamweaver templates combine locked and editable regions. Editable regions must be defined individually.

✦ After a template is declared, new documents can be created from it.

✦ With Dreamweaver's repeating regions, you can add or remove data from tables without altering the table structure.

✦ Show or hide content with each new template-derived document with Dreamweaver optional regions.

✦ Nested templates may be used to structurally organize locked and editable content.

✦ If a template is altered, pages built from that template can be automatically updated.

✦ The default template that Dreamweaver uses can be modified so that every time you select File ➪ New and choose a file type, a new version of your customized template is created.

In the next chapter, you learn how to streamline production and site maintenance with repeating page elements from the Dreamweaver Library.

✦   ✦   ✦

Using the Repeating Elements Library

One of the challenges of designing a Web site is ensuring that buttons, copyright notices, and other cross-site features always remain consistent. Fortunately, Dreamweaver offers a useful feature called *Library items* that helps you insert repeating elements, such as a navigation bar or a company logo, into every Web page you create. With one command, you can update and maintain Library items efficiently and productively.

In this chapter, you examine the nature and the importance of repeating elements and learn how to effectively use the Dreamweaver Library feature for all your sites.

Dreamweaver Library Items

Library items within Dreamweaver are another means for you, as a designer, to maintain consistency throughout your site. Imagine that you have on every page a navigation bar that contains links to all the other pages on your site. It's highly likely that you'll eventually (and probably more than once) need to make changes to the navigation bar. In a traditional Web development environment, you must modify every single page. This creates numerous opportunities for making mistakes, missing pages, and adding code in the wrong place. Moreover, the whole process is tedious — ask anyone who has had to modify the copyright notice at the bottom of every Web page for a site with over 200 pages.

One traditional method of updating repeating elements is to use *server-side includes*. A server-side include causes the server to place a component, such as a copyright notice, in a specified area of a Web page when it's sent to the user. This arrangement, however, increases the strain on your already overworked Web server, and many hosting computers do not permit server-side includes for this reason. To add to the designer's frustrations, you can't lay out a Web page in a WYSIWYG (What You See Is What You Get) format and simultaneously see the server-side scripts (unless you're using a Dreamweaver translator). Therefore, you either take the time to calculate that a server-side script will take up a specific amount of space on the Web page, or you cross your fingers and guess.

In Dreamweaver, there is a better way. You can use an important innovation called the *Library*. The Library is designed to make repetitive updating quick, easy, and as error-free as possible. The Library's key features include the following:

✦ Any item — whether text or graphic — that goes into the body of your Web page can be designated as a Library item.

✦ Once created, Library items can be placed instantly in any Web page in your site, without your having to retype, reinsert, or reformat text and graphics.

✦ Library items can be altered at any time. After the editing is complete, Dreamweaver gives you the option to update the Web site immediately or postpone the update until later.

✦ If you are making a number of alterations to your Library items, you can wait until you're finished with all the updates and then make the changes across the board in one operation.

✦ You can update one page at a time, or you can update the entire site all at once.

✦ A Library item can be converted back to a regular non-Library element of a Web page at any time.

✦ Library items can be copied from one site to another.

✦ Library items can combine Dreamweaver behaviors — and their underlying JavaScript code — with onscreen elements, so you don't have to rebuild the same navigation bar every time, reapplying the behaviors repeatedly.

Using the Library Assets Panel

Dreamweaver's Library control center is located on the Assets panel in the Library category. There you find the tools for creating, modifying, updating, and managing your Library items. Shown in Figure 29-1, the Library category is as flexible and easy to use as all Dreamweaver's primary panels, with straightforward command buttons, a listing of all available Library items, and a handy Preview area.

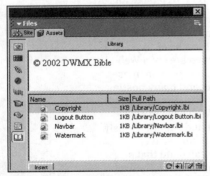

Figure 29-1: With the Dreamweaver Library feature, you can easily add and modify consistent objects on an entire Web site.

To access the Library items:

✦ Choose Window ⇨ Assets.

✦ Select the Library symbol on the Assets panel.

Caution

To use Library items, you must first create a site root folder for Dreamweaver, as explained in Chapter 5. A separate Library folder is automatically created to hold the individual Library items and is used by Dreamweaver during the updating process.

Ideally, you save the most time by creating all your Library items before you begin constructing your Web pages, but most Web designers don't work that way. Feel free to include, modify, and update your Library items as often as necessary as your Web site evolves — that's part of the power and flexibility you gain through Dreamweaver's Library.

Adding a Library item

Before you can insert or update a Library item, that item must be designated as a Library item within the Web page. To add an item to your site's Library, follow these steps:

1. Select any part of the Web page that you want to make into a Library item.

2. Open the Library category of the Assets panel.

3. From the Library category (see Figure 29-1), select the New Library Item button.

   The selected page element is displayed in the preview area of the Library category. In the Site list — the Library item list — a new entry is highlighted with the default name "Untitled."

Note

If the text you've selected has been styled by a CSS rule, Dreamweaver warns you that the appearance may be different because the style rule is not included in the Library item. To ensure that the appearance is the same, include the Library item only on those pages with the appropriate CSS styles.

4. Enter a unique name for your new Library item and press Enter (Return).

   The Library item list is re-sorted alphabetically, if necessary, and the new item is included.

When a portion of your Web page has been designated as a Library item, yellow highlighting is displayed over the entire item within the Document window. The highlighting helps you to quickly recognize what is a Library item and what is not. If you find the yellow highlighting distracting, you can disable it. Go to Edit ⇨ Preferences and, from the Highlighting panel of the Preferences dialog box, deselect Show check box for Library Items. Alternately, deselecting View ⇨ Visual Aids ⇨ Invisible Elements hides Library Item highlighting, along with any other invisible items on your page.

Caution

At this writing, Dreamweaver can include Library items only in the <body> section of an HTML document. You cannot, for instance, create a series of <meta> tags for your pages that must go in the <head> section.

Drag-and-Drop Creation of Library Items

A second option for creating Library items is the drag-and-drop method. Simply select an object or several objects on a page and drag them to the Library category (either the preview area or the Site list pane); release the mouse button to drop them in.

You can drag any object into the Library panel: text, tables, images, Java applets, plugins, and/or ActiveX controls. Essentially, anything in the Document window that can be HTML code can be dragged to the Library. Similarly, as you might suspect, the reverse is true: Library items can be placed in your Web page by dragging them from the Library category and dropping them anywhere in the Document window.

Moving Library items to a new site

Although Library items are specific to each site, they can be used in more than one site. When you make your first Library item, Dreamweaver creates a folder called Library in the local root folder for the current site. To move the Library item to a new site, use the following steps:

1. Open the Library category from the Assets panel.

2. Right-click (Control+click) the Library item you want to move.

3. Choose Copy to Site context menu from the context menu and then choose the site you want to copy the Library item to.

Caution   Be sure to also move any dependent files or other assets such as images and media files associated with Library items. The Copy to Site function does not move dependent files.

Inserting a Library item in your Web page

When you create a Web site, you always need to incorporate certain features, including a standard set of link buttons along the top, a consistent banner on various pages, and a copyright notice along the bottom. Adding these items to a page with the Library items can be as easy as dragging and dropping them.

You must first create a Web site and then designate Library items (as explained in the preceding section). After these items exist, you can add the items to any page created within your site. To add Library items to a document, use the following steps:

1. Position the cursor where you want the Library item to appear.

2. From the Library category, select the item you want to use.

3. Select the Insert button. The highlighted Library item appears on the Web page.

Tip   As noted earlier, you can also use the drag-and-drop method to place Library items in the Document window.

When you add a Library item to a page, you notice a number of immediate changes. As mentioned, the added Library item is highlighted. If you click anywhere on the item, the entire Library item is selected.

It's important to understand that Dreamweaver treats the entire Library item entry as an external object being linked to the current page. You cannot modify Library items directly on a page. For information about editing Library entries, see the section "Editing a Library Item," later in this chapter.

While the Library item is highlighted, notice that the Property inspector also changes. Instead of displaying the properties for the HTML object that is selected, the item is identified as a Library item, as shown in Figure 29-2.

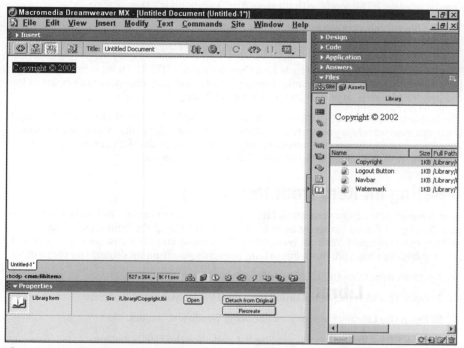

Figure 29-2: The Library Item Property inspector identifies the source file for any selected Library entry. You can also see evidence of Library items in the HTML for the current page. Open the Code inspector, and you see that several lines of code have been added. The following code example indicates one Library item:

```
<!-- #BeginLibraryItem "/Library/Copyright.lbi" --><span
class="fineprint">Copyright &copy; 2002</span><!-- #EndLibraryItem -->
```

In this case, the Library item happens to be a phrase: "Copyright © 2002." (The character entity © is used to represent the c-in-a-circle copyright mark in HTML.) In addition to the span wrapping the copyright, notice the text before and after the HTML code. These are commands within the comments that tell Dreamweaver it is looking at a Library item. One line marks the beginning of the Library item:

```
<!-- #BeginLibraryItem "/Library/Copyright.lbi" -->
```

and another marks the end:

```
<!-- #EndLibraryItem -->
```

Two items are of interest here. First, notice how the Library demarcation surrounds not just the text ("Copyright © 2000"), but all its formatting attributes as well. Library items can do far more than just cut and paste raw text. The second thing to note is that the Library markers are placed discretely within HTML comments. Web browsers ignore the Library markers and render the code in between them.

The value in the opening Library code, `"/Library/Copyright.lbi"`, is the source file for the Library entry. This file is located in the Library folder, inside of the current site root folder. Library source (.lbi) files can be opened with a text editor or in Dreamweaver; they consist of plain HTML code without the `<html>` and `<body>` tags.

The .lbi file for our title example contains the following:

```
<span class="fineprint">Copyright &copy; 2000</span>
```

The power of repeating elements is that they are simply HTML. There is no need to learn proprietary languages to customize Library items. Anything, except for information found in the header of a Web page, can be included in a Library file.

The importance of the `<!-- #BeginLibraryItem>` and `<!-- #EndLibraryItem>` tags becomes evident when you start to update Library items for a site. You examine how Dreamweaver can be used to automatically update your entire Web site in the section "Updating Your Web Sites with Libraries," later in this chapter.

Deleting an item from the Library

Removing an entry from your site's Library is a two-step process. First, you must delete the item from the Library category. Second, if you want to keep the item on your page, you must make it editable again. Without completing the second step, Dreamweaver maintains the Library highlighting and, more important, prevents you from modifying the element.

To delete an item from the Library, follow these steps:

1. Open the Web page containing the Library item you want to delete.

2. Open the Library category by choosing Window ⇨ Assets.

3. Select the Library item in the Site list and click the Delete button.

4. Dreamweaver asks if you are sure you want to delete the item. Select Yes, and the entry is removed from the Library item list. (Or select No to cancel.)

5. In the Document window, select the element you are removing from the Library.

6. In the Property inspector, click Detach from Original.

7. As shown in Figure 29-3, Dreamweaver warns you that if you proceed, the item cannot be automatically updated (as a Library element). Select OK to proceed. The yellow Library highlighting vanishes, and the element can now be modified individually. Check the "Don't warn me again" box to disable any future warnings about detaching Library items.

Note   Should you unintentionally delete a Library item in the Library category, you can restore it if you still have the entry included in a Web page. Select the element within the page and, in the Property inspector, choose the Recreate button. Dreamweaver restores the item to the Library item list, with the original Library name.

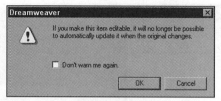

Figure 29-3: When making an item editable from the Library, Dreamweaver alerts you that, if you proceed, you won't be able to update the item automatically using the Library function.

Renaming a Library item

It's easy to rename a Library item, both in the Assets panel and across your site. Dreamweaver automatically updates the name for any embedded Library item. To give an existing Library entry a new name, open the Library category and click the name of the item twice, slowly — do not double-click. Alternatively, you can choose Rename from the context menu of the Assets panel. The name is highlighted, and a small box appears around it. Enter the new name and press Enter (Return).

Dreamweaver then displays the Update Files dialog box with a list of files in which the renamed Library item is contained. Select Update to rename the Library item across the site. If you select Don't Update, the Library item will be renamed only in the Library category. Furthermore, your embedded Library items will be orphaned — that is, no master Library item will be associated with them, and they will not be updateable.

Editing a Library Item

Rarely do you create a Library item that is perfect from the beginning and never needs to be changed. Whether it is due to site redesign or the addition of new sections to a site, you'll find yourself going back to Library items and modifying them, sometimes repeatedly. You can use the full power of Dreamweaver's design capabilities to alter your Library items, within the restraints of Library items in general. In other words, you can modify an image, reformat a body of text, or add new material to a boilerplate paragraph, and resulting changes are reflected across your Web site. However, you cannot add anything to a Library item that is not contained in the HTML <body> tags.

To modify Library items, Dreamweaver uses a special editing window identifiable by the double-angle brackets surrounding the phrase "Library Item" in the title bar. You access this editing window through the Library category or the Property inspector. Follow these steps to modify an existing Library item:

1. In the Library category, select the item you wish to modify from the list of available entries.

2. Click the Open Library Item button. The Library editing window opens with the selected entry, as shown in Figure 29-4.

3. Make any necessary modifications to the Library entry.

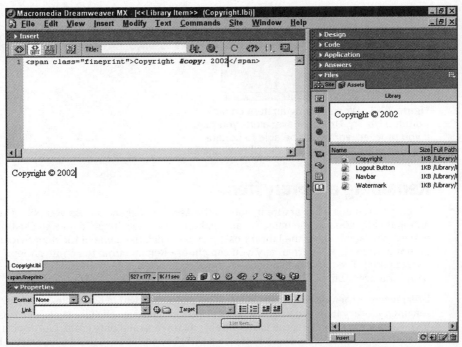

Figure 29-4: Use the Library editing window to modify existing Library items.

4. When you are finished with your changes, choose File ➪ Save or press Ctrl+S (Command+S).

5. Dreamweaver notes that your Library item has been modified, and it then asks if you would like to update all the Web pages in your site that contain the item. Select Yes to update all the Library items, including the one just modified, or select No to postpone the update. (See the next section, "Updating Your Web Sites with Libraries," for a more in-depth explanation of the updating process.)

6. Close the editing window by clicking the Close button or choosing File ➪ Close.

After you've completed the editing operation and closed the editing window, you can open any Web page containing the modified Library item to view the changes.

New Feature

Dreamweaver now allows you to use native Dreamweaver behaviors inside Library items. That means you can place a navigation bar, a link for a pop-up window, or any other Dreamweaver behavior inside your Library item. When the Library item is added to the page, the accompanying JavaScript is also added.

Caution

You cannot use some features to their fullest when editing Library items. These include custom JavaScript and styles. Each of these modifications requires a function or link to be placed in the <head> tags of a page — a task that the Dreamweaver Library function cannot handle for styles and custom JavaScript.

Updating Your Web Sites with Libraries

The effectiveness of the Dreamweaver Library feature becomes more significant when it comes time to update an entire multipage site. Dreamweaver offers two opportunities for you to update your site:

✦ Immediately after modifying a Library item, as explained in the preceding steps for editing a Library item

✦ At a time of your choosing, through the Modify ➪ Library command

An immediate update to every page on your site can be accomplished when you edit a Library item. After you save the alterations, Dreamweaver asks if you'd like to apply the update to Web pages in your site. If you click Yes, Dreamweaver not only applies the current modification to all pages in the site, but it also applies any other alterations that you have made previously in this Library.

The second way to modify a Library item is by using the Modify ➪ Library command; when you use this method, you can choose to update the current page or the entire site.

To update just the current page, choose Modify ➪ Library ➪ Update Current Page. Dreamweaver quickly checks to see what Library items you are managing on the current page and then compares them to the site's Library items. If any differences exist, Dreamweaver modifies the page accordingly.

To update an entire Web site, follow these steps:

1. Choose Modify ➪ Library ➪ Update Pages. The Update Pages dialog box opens (see Figure 29-5).

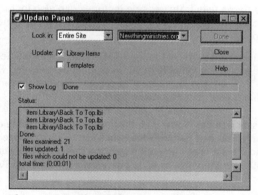

Figure 29-5: The Update Pages dialog box enables you to apply any changes to your Library items across an entire site and informs you of the progress.

2. If you want Dreamweaver to update all the Library items in all the Web pages in your site, select Entire Site from the Look In drop-down list and choose the name of your site in the drop-down list on the right. You can also have Dreamweaver update only the pages in your site that contain a specific Library item. Select the Files That Use option from the Look In drop-down list and then select the Library item that you would like to have updated across your site from the drop-down list on the right.

3. If you want to see the results from the update process, leave the Show Log checkbox selected. (Turning off the Show Log option reduces the size of the Site Update dialog box.)

4. Choose the Start button. Dreamweaver processes the entire site for Library updates. Any Library items contained are modified to reflect the changes.

Note   Although Dreamweaver does modify Library items on currently open pages during an Update Site operation, you have to save the pages to accept the changes.

The Update Pages log displays any errors encountered in the update operation. A log containing the notation

```
item Library\Untitled2.lbi -- not updated, library item not found
```

indicates that one Web page contains a reference to a Library item that has been removed. Although this is not a critical error, you might want to use Dreamweaver's Find and Replace feature to search your Web site for the code and remove it.

Note   When updating Library items, every page is physically changed with the necessary Library item code. This means that every that contains a Library item must be uploaded to the server.

Applying Server-Side Includes

In some ways, the server-side include (SSI) is the predecessor of the Dreamweaver Library item. The difference is that with Library items, Dreamweaver updates the Web pages at design time; whereas with server-side includes, the server handles the updating at runtime (when the files are actually served to the user). Server-side includes can also include server variables, such as the current date and time (both locally and Greenwich mean time) or the date the current file was last saved.

Because server-side includes are integrated in the standard HTML code, a special file extension identifies pages using them. Any page with server-side includes is most often saved with either the .shtml or .shtm extension on *NIX servers and .asp or .aspx on Windows servers. When a server encounters such a file, the file is read and processed by the server.

Caution   Not all servers support server-side includes. Some Web-hosting companies disable the function because of potential security risks and performance issues. Each .shtml page requires additional processing time, and if a site uses many SSI pages, the server can slow down significantly. Be sure to check with your Web host as to its policy before including SSIs in your Web pages.

Server-side includes are often used to insert header or footer items into the <body> of an HTML page. Typically, the server-side include itself is just a file with HTML. To insert a file, use SSI code like the following:

```
<!-- #include file="footer.html" -->
```

Note how the HTML comment structure is used to wrap around the SSI directive. This ensures that browsers ignore the code, but servers do not. The file attribute defines the pathname of the file to be included, relative to the current page. To include a file relative to the current site root, use the virtual attribute, as follows:

```
<!-- #include virtual="/main/images/spaceman.jpg" -->
```

As evident in this example, you can use SSIs to include more than just HTML files — you can also include graphics.

With Dreamweaver's translator mechanism, server-side includes can be visible in the Document window during the design process. In Dreamweaver, server-side include translation is now automatic.

One of the major benefits of SSIs is that information can be inserted from the server itself, such as the current file size or time. One tag, `<!-- #echo -->`, is used to define a custom variable that is returned when the SSI is called, as well as numerous *environmental variables*. An environmental variable is information available to the server, such as the date a file was last modified or its URL.

Table 29-1 details the possible server tags and their attributes.

Table 29-1: Server-Side Include Variables

Tag	Attribute	Description
`<!-- #config -->`	`errmsg`, `sizefmt`, or `timefmt`	Used to customize error messages, file size, or time and date displays
`<!-- #echo -->`	`var` or environmental variables such as `last_modified`, `document_name`, `document_url`, `date_local`, or `date_gmt`	Returns the specified variable
`<!-- #exec -->`	`cmd` or `cgi`	Executes a system command or CGI program
`<!-- #flastmod -->`	`file` or `virtual`	Displays the last modified date of a file other than the current one
`<!-- #fsize -->`	`file` or `virtual`	Displays the size of a file other than the current one
`<!-- #include -->`	`file` or `virtual`	Inserts the contents of the specified file into the current one

Adding server-side includes

Dreamweaver has made inserting a server-side include in your Web page very straightforward. You can use a Dreamweaver object to easily select and bring in the files to be included. Any other type of SSI, such as declaring a variable, must be entered in by hand, but you can use the Comment object to do so without opening the Code View.

To use server-side includes to incorporate a file, follow these steps:

1. In the Document window, place your cursor at the location where you would like to add the server-side include.

2. Select Insert ➪ Script Objects ➪ Server-Side Include or choose Include from the ASP category (or other supported language) of the Insert bar.

The standard Select File dialog box appears.

3. In the Select File dialog box, type in the URL of the HTML page you would like to include in the File Name text box or use the Browse (Choose) button to locate the file. Click OK when you're done.

Dreamweaver displays the contents of the HTML file at the desired location in your page. Should the Property inspector be available, the SSI Property inspector is displayed (see Figure 29-6).

4. In the Property inspector, if the server-side include calls a file-relative document path, select the Type File option. Alternatively, if the SSI calls a site-root–relative file, choose the Type Virtual option.

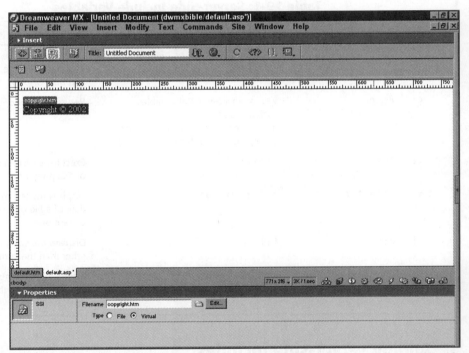

Figure 29-6: The selected text is actually a server-side include automatically translated by Dreamweaver, as evident from the SSI Property inspector.

Editing server-side includes

As is the case with Library items, you cannot directly edit files that have been inserted into a Web page using server-side includes. In fact, should you try, the entire text block highlights as one. The text for a server-side–included file is not editable through Dreamweaver's Code view, although the SSI code is.

To edit the contents of the server-side–included file, follow these steps:

1. Select the server-side include in the Document window.

2. Select the Edit button from the SSI Property inspector.

   The file opens in a new Dreamweaver window for editing.

3. When you've finished altering the file, select File ➪ Save or use the keyboard shortcut, Ctrl+S (Command+S).

4. Close the file editing window by choosing File ➪ Close.

Dreamweaver automatically reflects the changes in your currently open document.

Unlike editing Library items, Dreamweaver does not ask if any other linked files should be updated because all blending of regular HTML and SSIs happens at runtime or when the file is open in Dreamweaver and the SSI translator is engaged.

Summary

In this chapter, you learned how you can easily and effectively create Library items that can be repeated throughout an entire site to help maintain consistency.

✦ Library items can consist of any text, object, or HTML code contained in the <body> of a Web page.

✦ The quickest method to create a Library item is to drag the code from the Dreamweaver Document window into the Library category's list area.

✦ Editing Library items is also easy: Just click the Edit button in the Assets panel or choose Open from the Property inspector, and you can swiftly make all your changes in a separate Dreamweaver Library Item window.

✦ The Modify ➪ Library ➪ Update Pages command enables easy maintenance of your Web site.

✦ Server-side includes enable files to be inserted into the final HTML at runtime by the server. Dreamweaver's translation feature enables you to preview these effects.

In the next chapter, you learn how to ensure cross-browser compatibility with Dreamweaver.

✦   ✦   ✦

Maximizing Browser Targeting

Each new release of a browser is a double-edged sword. On the one hand, an exciting array of new features becomes possible. On the other, Web designers have to cope with yet another browser-compatibility issue. In today's market, you find all the following in use:

- ✦ A rapidly increasing number of 6.x browsers that, although fairly standards-compliant, are still different from one another in implementation

- ✦ Browsers for different platforms that interpret code differently—even though the browsers are the same version number and from the same company

- ✦ A host of fourth-generation browsers (and higher), varying widely in their capabilities

- ✦ A decreasing number of 3.x/4.x browsers, which are limited in some basic functionality (The exception here is Netscape 4.x, which maintains a small but significant cadre of loyal users.)

- ✦ A miniscule contingent of 2.x browsers in the machines of determined users who have never (and may never) upgrade

- ✦ A diverse assortment of browsers outside the mainstream, including Opera, WebTV, and Navigator for Linux

- ✦ Various versions of America Online browsers, which range from being completely proprietary to being a blend of current and special technologies. (As a specific example, AOL 5.0is not the same as Internet Explorer 5.0, although it is based on it.)

Browser compatibility is one of a Web designer's primary concerns (not to mention the source of major headaches); and many strategies are evolving to deal with this matter. Dreamweaver is in the forefront of cross-browser Web page design, both in terms of the type of code it routinely outputs and in its specialty functions. This chapter examines the browser-targeting techniques available in Dreamweaver. From multibrowser code to conversion innovations to browser-validation capabilities, Dreamweaver helps you get your Web pages out with the most features to the widest audience.

Converting Pages in Dreamweaver

DHTML's gifts of layers and Cascading Style Sheets are extremely tempting to use because of their enhanced typographic control and absolute-positioning capabilities. Many Web designers, however, have resisted using these features because only fourth-generation (and higher) browsers can view them. Although Dreamweaver can't change the capabilities of 3.0 browsers, it can make it easy for you to create alternative content for them.

Dreamweaver makes it possible to convert Web pages designed with layers and CSS into pages that can be rendered by 3.0 browsers. Moreover, if you want to upgrade your site from nested tables to layers, you don't have to do it by hand. Dreamweaver also includes a command to convert tables to layers, preserving their location but enabling greater design flexibility and dynamic control. A Webmaster's life just got a tad easier.

Cross-Reference   To learn how to use Dreamweaver's Layers to Tables roundtrip features, see Chapter 21.

Making 3.0-compatible pages

It's a slight misstatement to say that Dreamweaver converts 4.0 feature-laden pages into pages that can be read by 3.0 browsers. Actually, Dreamweaver creates a new 3.0-compatible page based on the 4.0 page—and does it in almost no time at all. After you've converted your page, you can use Dreamweaver's Check Browser behavior to route users to the appropriate pages, based on their browser versions.

Preparing your page for conversion

When Dreamweaver makes a new 3.0-compatible page, layers are converted to nested tables, and Cascading Style Sheet references are converted to inline character styles. You have the option to convert either or both features. To accomplish the conversion of your 4.0 Web page, your document must meet the following conditions:

✦ **All content must be in layers:** Because Dreamweaver converts layers to tables, it must start with everything absolutely positioned.

✦ **Layers must not overlap:** During the conversion process, Dreamweaver warns you when it finds overlapping layers and even tells you which ones they are.

A feature in Dreamweaver prevents you from encountering the problem of overlapping layers in the design stage. Enable the option by choosing Modify ➪ Arrange ➪ Prevent Layer Overlaps or turning on the Prevent Overlaps option in the Layers panel. Although this can't separate layers that are currently overlapping—you have to do that by hand—it does stop you from accidentally laying one layer on top of another, and it makes 3.0 conversion a breeze.

✦ **Nesting layers are not allowed:** When one layer is inside another, the inner layer is placed relative to the outer layer. Dreamweaver cannot convert relatively positioned layers.

✦ **The `<ilayer>` tag cannot be used:** Because the `<ilayer>` tag is based on relative positioning, Dreamweaver cannot convert it. Use `<layer>`, `<div>`, or `<span>` instead.

Some Web pages you might like to convert—or devolve—from 4.0 to 3.0 applicability have content both in and out of layers. And, as noted, Dreamweaver needs to have all the Web page elements in a layer before proceeding with conversion. Previously, it was necessary to cut elements outside of a layer and paste them in to prepare the page for conversion. Dreamweaver does it for you — just choose Modify ➪ Convert ➪ Tables to Layers. In the Convert Tables to Layers dialog box that appears, be sure to choose the Prevent Layer Overlaps option to avoid that problem. Click OK, and Dreamweaver places everything in a layer, automatically — without generating a new page.

For more information about using the Convert Tables to Layers feature, see Chapter 21.

Running the conversion

After your page is prepped, generating a 3.0-compatible Web page from a 4.0 version is straightforward. You have only a few options — whether to convert layers, CSS styles, or both — and once you make your choice and click OK, the rest of the process is almost instantaneous. To create a 3.0-compatible version of a properly prepped Web page with 4.0 or later features, follow these steps:

1. Choose File ➪ Convert ➪ 3.0 Browser Compatible. The Convert to 3.0 Browser Compatible dialog box opens, as shown in Figure 30-1.

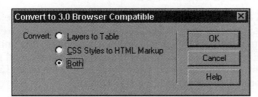

Figure 30-1: Begin to build your cross browser-compatible site with Dreamweaver's Convert to 3.0 Browser Compatible feature.

2. From the Convert to 3.0 Browser Compatible dialog box, select your options:

   • If you are converting layers to tables only, choose the Layers to Table option.

   • If you are converting Cascading Style Sheet styles to HTML tags only, choose the CSS Styles to HTML Markup option.

   • If you are making both of these conversions, select the Both option.

3. Click OK, and Dreamweaver starts the conversion. A message box informs you if a problem is encountered, such as a nested layer or overlapping layers. If the Web page has overlapping layers, the Overlapping Layers Detected dialog box (shown in Figure 30-2) tells you which layers are overlapping. Dreamweaver cannot proceed until all conflicts are resolved. If no problems occur, Dreamweaver creates the page in a new window.

The CSS-to-HTML conversion disregards any CSS feature, such as line spacing, that is not implemented in regular HTML. In addition, the exact point size that can be specified in CSS is roughly translated to the relative size equivalents in HTML. Any font over 36 points is set to the largest HTML size, which is 7.

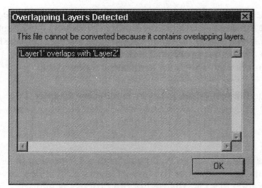

Figure 30-2: On a page with multiple layers, Dreamweaver spots the "illegal" overlapping ones when you try to convert the page to tables.

Evolving 3.0 pages to 4.0 standards

Web sites are constantly upgraded and modified. You'll eventually need to enhance a more traditional site with new features, such as layers. Some of the older 3.0-oriented sites used elaborately nested tables on their pages to create a semblance of absolute positioning; normally, upgrading these Web pages takes hours and hours of tedious cutting and pasting. Dreamweaver can bring these older pages up to speed with the Convert Tables to Layers command, which you reach via Modify ➪ Convert ➪ Tables to Layers.

The Convert Tables to Layers command can also be used to convert a page created by another Web authoring program (NetObjects Fusion, for example) that uses nested tables for positioning. After tables have been transformed into layers, the layout of the entire page is much easier to modify. It's even possible to make the switch from 3.0 to 4.0 capabilities, modify your page, and then, with the Convert Layers to Tables command, re-create your 3.0-compliant page.

The name of the Convert Tables to Layers command is a little misleading. After you issue this command, *every* HTML element in the new page—not just the tables—is placed in a layer. Moreover, every cell with content in every table is converted into its own layer. In other words, if you are working with a 3×3 table in which one cell is left empty, Dreamweaver creates eight different layers for just the table.

Note   If you want to convert a 3.0-compatible page to a page with layers, but the page has no tables, Dreamweaver places all the content in one layer, as if the <body> tag were one big single-cell table.

To convert a 3.0-browser–compatible Web page with (or without) tables to a 4.0-browser–compatible Web page with layers, choose Modify ➪ Convert ➪ Tables to Layers. If you need to return to a table-based layout, choose Modify ➪ Convert ➪ Layers to Tables.

Ensuring Browser Compatibility

As more browsers and browser versions become available, a Web designer has two basic options to stay on the road to compatibility: *internal* and *external*.

✦ The **internal** method uses scripts on the same Web page; the scripts deliver the proper code depending on the browser detected. Many of Dreamweaver's own behavior functions manage the browser issue internally.

✦ The **external** approach examines each visitor's browser right off the bat and reroutes the user to the most appropriate Web page.

Both methods have their pluses and minuses, and each is better suited to particular situations. For example, it is impractical to use the external method of creating multiple versions of the same Web pages when you are working with a large site. Suddenly, you've gone from managing 300 pages of information to 900 or 1,200. Of course, you don't have to duplicate every page — but because of the open nature of the Web, where any page can be bookmarked and entered directly, you have to plan carefully and provide routing routines at the key locations. Conversely, sometimes you have no choice but to use multiple versions, especially if a page employs many browser-specific features.

The internal and external strategies are not mutually exclusive. Several sites today are routing 3.0 browsers to one page and using internal coding methods to differentiate between the various 4.0 browser versions on another page. This section examines techniques for implementing browser compatibility from both the internal and external perspective.

Internal coding for cross-browser compatibility

Imagine the shouts of joy when the Web development community learned that the 4.0 versions of Navigator and Internet Explorer both supported Cascading Style Sheet layers! Now imagine the grumbling when it became apparent that each browser uses a different JavaScript syntax for calling them. You get the picture: It all boils down to differences in each browser's Document Object Model (DOM).

Note   Navigator 6.0 incorporates the W3C standard for layers, which is also largely supported by Internet Explorer 4.0 and later. Although this standard will eventually simplify compatibility issues for Web designers, Navigator 4.x browsers will remain in use for some time, and the code for handling layers in those browsers must be taken into consideration.

Calling layers

When referring to a layer, Navigator 4.x uses the following syntax:

```
document.layers["layerName"]
```

whereas Internet Explorer uses this syntax:

```
document.all["layerName"]
```

The trick to internal code-switching is to assign the variations — the document.layers from Navigator and the document.all from Internet Explorer — to the same variable, depending on which browser is being used. Here's a sample function that does just that:

```
function init() {
  if (navigator.appName == "Netscape") {
    var layerRef = "document.layers";
  }
  else {
    var layerRef = "document.all";
  }
}
```

In this function, if the visitor is using a Netscape 4.x browser, the variable `layerRef` is assigned the value `document.layers`; otherwise, `layerRef` is set to `document.all`.

Calling properties

If you're trying to assign or read a layer property, one variable is only half the battle. Another difference exists in the way properties are called. With Navigator, it's done like this:

```
document.layers["layerName"].top
```

and with Internet Explorer, it's as follows:

```
document.all["layerName"].style.top
```

Internet Explorer inserts an extra hierarchical division, `style` that Navigator doesn't use. The solution is another variable, `styleRef`, which for Internet Explorer is set as follows:

```
var styleRef = "style";
```

The Navigator `styleRef` is actually set to a *null string*, or nothing. You can combine the two variables into one initialization function, which is best called from an `onLoad` event in the `<body>` tag:

```
function init() {
  if (navigator.appName == "Netscape") {
    var layerRef = "document.layers";
    var styleRef = "";
  }
  else {
    var layerRef = "document.all";
    var styleRef = "style";
  }
}
```

After these differences are accommodated, the variables are ready to be used in a script. To do this, you can use JavaScript's built-in `eval()` function to combine the variables and the object references. Here's an example that sets a new variable, `varLeft`, to the `left` value of the layer named `myLayer`:

```
varLeft = eval(layerRef + '["myLayer"]' + styleRef + '.left');
```

Luckily, the variations between the Navigator and Internet Explorer DOM are consistent enough that a JavaScript function can assign the proper values with a minimum of effort.

Calling objects within layers

There's one other main area in which the two DOMs diverge. When you are attempting to address almost any entity inside a layer, Navigator uses an additional hierarchical layer to reference the object. Thus, a named image in a named layer in Navigator is referenced as follows:

```
document.layers["layerName"].document.imageName
```

whereas the same object in Internet Explorer is called like this:

```
document.imageName
```

Macromedia gets around this problem by using the `dwscripts.findDOMObject()` function, which you can examine in the Configuration\Shared\Common\Scripts\dwscripts.js file.

Designing Web pages for backward compatibility

The previous section describes a technique for handling the differences between 4.0 and later browsers, but how do you handle the much larger gap between third- and fourth-generation browsers? When this gap becomes a canyon, with DHTML-intensive pages on one side and incompatible browsers on the other, the ultimate solution is to use *redirection* to send a particular browser to an appropriate page. However, browsers can coexist in plenty of cases — with a little planning and a little help from Dreamweaver.

When designing backwardly compatible Web pages, browsers generally offer one major advantage: ignorance. If a browser doesn't recognize a tag or attribute, it just ignores it and renders the rest of the page. Because many of the newer features are built on new tags, or on tags such as `<div>` that previously were infrequently used, your Web pages can gracefully devolve from 4.0 to 3.0 behavior, without causing errors or grossly misrendering the page.

Take layers, for instance. One advantage offered by this DHTML feature is the capability to make something interactively appear and disappear. Although that's not possible in 3.0 browsers (without extensive image-swapping), it is possible to display the same material and even enable some degree of navigation. The key is proper placement of the layer code — not the layer itself. Browsers basically read and render the code for a Web page from top to bottom. You can, for example, make several layers appear one after another in a 3.0 browser, even if they are stacked on top of one another in a 4.0 browser. All you have to do is make sure that the HTML code of the layers appears in the document sequentially. You can see this effect in Figure 30-3: The three layers are overlapped, but their HTML code is sequential:

```
<div id="Layer1" style="position:absolute; left:150px; top:110; ↵
width:200; height:170; z-index:3">
  Layer1 code ...
</div>
<div id="Layer2" style="position:absolute; left:150px; top:80; ↵
width:200; height:200; z-index:2">
  Layer2 code ...
</div>
<div id="Layer3" style="position:absolute; left:150px; top:50px; ↵
width:200; height:230; z-index:1">
  Layer3 code ...
</div>
```

The navigational links in the upper-left have two roles: They are linked to the named anchor next to the layer's code and, through the Behaviors panel, are set to show and hide the appropriate layers when selected (using the `onClick` event).

Because the HTML code for the three layers is situated sequentially, browsers that do not understand the `style` attribute in the `<div>` tags — which create the layers — simply render the information contained within all three tags, one after the other.

Note   Although it may seem obvious, don't forget to preview your pages in a 3.0 browser to see the results of these positioning techniques.

The Dreamweaver Technique in the upcoming section is based on methods used by George Olsen, Design Director of 2-Lane Media and on an article by Trevor Lohrbeer in the Dynamic HTML Zone.

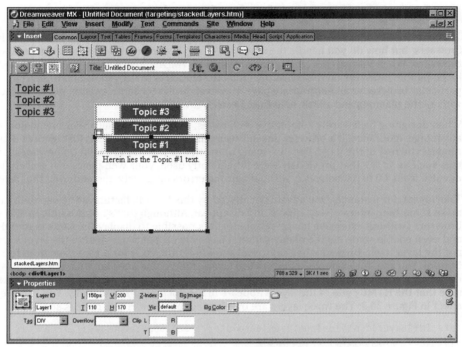

Figure 30-3: Careful placement of the code for layers can be an effective tool for backward compatibility.

Tip   It's even possible to animate your layers for the benefit of Dynamic HTML-enabled browsers and, at the same time, enable 3.0 browsers to just show the static images. The key is to make sure that your animations begin and end in the same location.

Dreamweaver Technique: Browser checking

Because of the major differences between third- and fourth-generation (and beyond) browsers, it is an increasingly popular practice to create a Web page geared to each browser and then use a *gateway script* to direct users to the proper page. A gateway script uses JavaScript to determine a visitor's browser version and route the page accordingly. Dreamweaver includes the Check Browser behavior (see Chapter 23), which makes this process relatively effortless.

For maximum efficiency, the best strategy is to use three pages: one page for 4.0 and later browsers, one page for 3.0 browsers, and a blank page that serves as your home page. Then, the Check Browser action can be assigned to the onLoad event of the blank page and can execute immediately.

The other alternative is to use only two pages, one for 3.0 browsers and the other for 4.0 browsers. All browsers initially load the 4.0 page. Within this page, you use the Check Browser action to detect 3.0 browsers and then send them off to the 3.0 page. 4.0 browsers simply stay on the initial page.

Tip

The disadvantage to the latter, two-page approach is that some of your visitors will have to wait for the loading of the initial (4.0) page, only to be whisked off to the other (3.0) page and wait for loading all over again. To get around this, you can put your browser detection and redirection code in the ⟨head⟩ of the page, rather than in an onLoad event handler; this causes the browser to run the code right away, without having to wait for the page to fully load.

On the CD-ROM

Other variations besides those encountered in different browser versions may cause you to redirect a visitor to a different Web page. Screen resolution, color depth, MIME types — each has myriad possibilities. Using different behaviors, you can detect the differences and direct your users accordingly. You can find a number of these redirection helpers on the Additional Extensions section of CD-ROM that accompanies this book in the various Behavior folders under each author's name.

The following technique takes you through the conversion of a layers-based page to a 3.0-compatible page, the creation of a new gateway page, and the incorporation of a Check Browser action that automatically directs users to the appropriate page based on their browser types:

1. In Dreamweaver, construct the fourth-generation browser version of your Web page — the one that uses layers and Cascading Style Sheets — first.

Note

Ensure that no layers overlap and that the Web page otherwise meets the criteria noted in the section "Preparing your page for conversion," earlier in this chapter.

2. Choose File ⇨ Convert ⇨ 3.0 Browser Compatible. Save the new version of the page, created by Dreamweaver, with a name similar to the original (4.0) page but with a different prefix or suffix. For example, you might call the page intended for 4.0 browsers index4.htm and the 3.0 version index3.htm.

3. Use File ⇨ New to open the New Document dialog box and create a new HTML page. (If your default document type is set to HTML, you can simply press Ctrl+Shift+N [Command+Shift+N] to create a new HTML page.) This new page will serve as the gateway for the other two pages (index3.htm and index4.htm).

4. By default, Dreamweaver creates new pages with a blank ⟨body⟩ tag, which causes them to have a white background. To make the gateway page as unobtrusive as possible, it's best to use the same background color as your target pages. Use CSS to do this, as discussed in Chapter 20.

5. In your blank gateway page, choose Window ⇨ Behaviors to open the Behaviors panel.

6. From the Tag Selector in the status bar of the Document window, select the ⟨body⟩ tag.

7. In the Behaviors panel, select the Add (+) button and choose the Check Browser action from the drop-down list.

8. In the Check Browser parameter form:

   • Enter the URL for your 4.0 browser page in the URL text box or select the Browse (Choose) button to locate the file.

   • Enter the URL for your 3.0 browser page in the Alt URL text box or select the Browse (Choose) button to locate the file.

Click OK when you are done. If you haven't changed any of the other Check Browser default settings, all Netscape and IE 4.0 browsers go to the address in the URL text box, and all 3.0 versions are directed to the address in the Alt URL text box (see Figure 30-4).

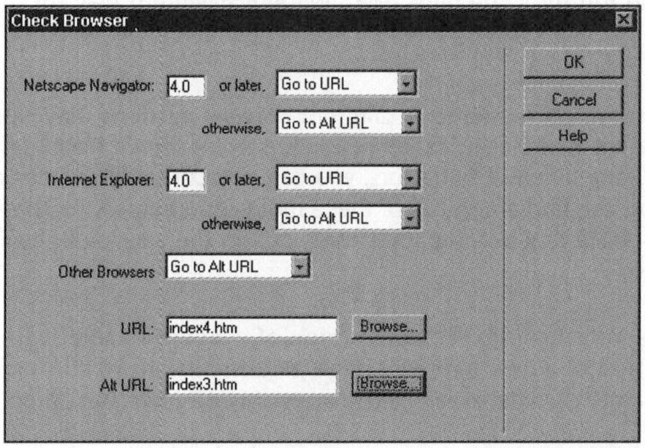

Figure 30-4: You can forego the pains of manual JavaScript coding when you use the Check Browser behavior to build a gateway script.

9. Save your gateway page. If this page is to serve as the gateway for the home page(s) for your domain, save it as index.htm or whatever name your server uses for default documents.

   The gateway can now be preliminarily tested. However, because any Web page can be an entry point to a site—for example, a user could open index4.htm directly—you also have to add the Check Browser action to each of the version-specific pages.

10. Reopen the 4.0 browser page. If necessary, open the Behaviors panel by choosing Window ⇨ Behaviors or selecting the Show Behaviors button from the Launcher.

11. Repeat Steps 6 and 7 to get to the Check Browser parameter form.

12. Enter the URL for your 3.0 browser page in the Alt URL text box, or select the Browse (Choose) button to locate the file.

13. In the drop-down lists for both Netscape and Internet Explorer 4.0 or later, choose the Stay on This Page option.

14. Select OK when you are finished and save the file.

15. Repeat Steps 10 through 14 for your 3.0 browser page. But this time, in the Check Browser parameter form, enter the URL for the 4.0 browser page in the Alt URL text box, and choose Stay on This Page in both Otherwise drop-down lists.

Now visitors can come in through the front door of your home page or through any side door and be served the correct page. Generally, not all the pages in your site will use the high-end features available to the 4.0 browsers, so you have to create gateways only for those pages that do. If you plan your site with this strategy in mind—and avoid putting a moving layer on every page as a logo, for instance—you can manage your site more effectively.

Testing Your Page with a Targeted Browser

Testing is an absolute must when building a Web site. It's critical that you view your pages on as many browsers/versions and platforms as possible. Variations in color, gamma, page offset, and capabilities must be observed before they can be adjusted.

A more basic, preliminary type of testing can also be done right from within Dreamweaver: code testing. Browsers usually ignore tags and attributes they do not understand. However, sometimes these tags can produce unexpected and undesirable results, such as exposing code to the viewer.

Dreamweaver's Browser Targeting feature (File ➪ Check Page ➪ Check Target Browsers) enables you to check a Web page—or an entire Web site—against any number of browser profiles. Currently, Dreamweaver comes with profiles for the following browsers:

✦ Internet Explorer 2.0

✦ Internet Explorer 3.0

✦ Internet Explorer 4.0

✦ Internet Explorer 5.0

✦ Internet Explorer 5.5

✦ Internet Explorer 6.0

✦ Navigator 2.0

✦ Navigator 3.0

✦ Navigator 4.0

✦ Navigator 6.0

✦ Opera 2.1

✦ Opera 3.0

✦ Opera 3.5

✦ Opera 4.0

✦ Opera 5.0

✦ Opera 6.0

You can choose to check your page or site against a single browser profile, all of them, or anything in between. Though not a substitute for real-world testing, Browser Targeting gives you an overview of potential errors and problematic code.

Testing browser compatibility for a Web page

To check a single Web page against specific browser targets, follow these steps:

 Caution
With Browser Targeting, Dreamweaver checks the saved version of a Web page. Therefore, if you've made any modifications to your current page, save it *before* beginning the following process.

1. Choose File ➪ Check Page ➪ Check Target Browsers. The Check Target Browsers dialog box opens as shown in Figure 30-5.

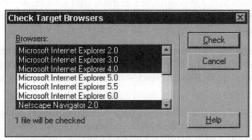

Figure 30-5: Select the browsers for which you'd like to check your current page code.

2. Select the browsers for which you want the current page to be checked. The usual selection techniques apply: To choose various browsers, press Ctrl (Command) while selecting. To specify a contiguous range of browsers, select the first one, press Shift, and then select the last one.

3. After you've chosen the target browsers, click the Check button. Dreamweaver does its checking and lists the results in the Target Browser Check panel (one of the many panels in the Results panel group), as shown in Figure 30-6. This is a very handy debugging tool. For each error found, the filename, line number, and a short description are listed. Double-clicking on an item in the list displays the offending code in Code view, all highlighted and ready to be debugged.

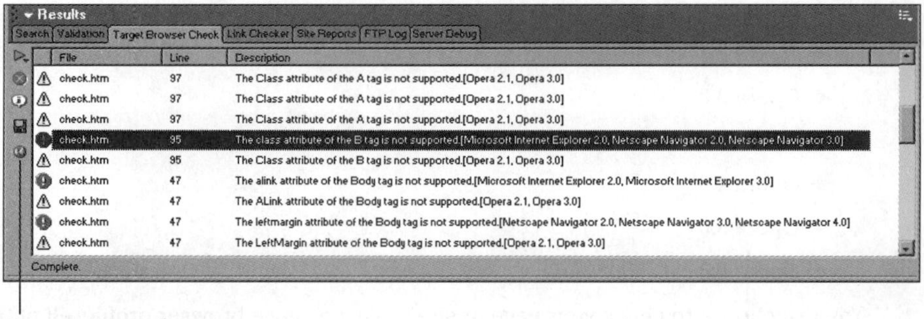

Browse Report button

Figure 30-6: The Target Browser Check panel displays a summary of all the errors it finds for the current file.

4. But wait, there's more! In the Target Browser Check panel, click the Browse Report button to display a lovely report of these results in your primary browser (see Figure 30-7).

5. Dreamweaver stores the check results temporarily and deletes them afterwards. To keep a hardcopy record, print the Target Browser Check page (Figure 30-7). To keep a digital record, click the Save Report button in the Target Browser Check panel to generate an XML report file.

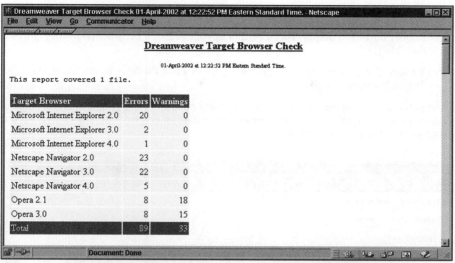

Figure 30-7: The Browse Report button inspires Dreamweaver to display a lovely summary of all the errors it found in the current page.

The Dreamweaver Target Browser Check report offers both a summary and a detail section. The summary, shown in Figure 30-7, lists the browser(s) being tested and any errors or warnings. Totals for each category are listed beneath the columns.

The detail section of the browser check report, shown in Figure 30-8, lists the following:

✦ Each offending tag or attribute

✦ The browsers that do not support the tag or attribute

✦ An example HTML line

✦ Additional line numbers indicating where the error occurred

Testing browser compatibility for an entire site

With Dreamweaver, you can check browser compatibility for an entire Web site as easily as you can check a single page. Dreamweaver checks all the HTML files in a given folder, whether or not they are actually used in the site. To check an entire site against specific browser targets, follow these steps:

1. Open the Site panel (by choosing Window ➪ Site, pressing F8, or selecting the Show Site button from the Launcher).

2. Select the desired site from the drop-down Site list. If you want to check only certain folders or files in the site, select them. If you want to check the entire site, make sure that the site root folder icon is selected in the Site panel.

3. Choose File ➪ Check Page ➪ Check Target Browsers from the main Dreamweaver menu. The Check Target Browsers dialog box opens (refer to Figure 30-5). Below the list of browsers is a statement of how many files are to be checked.

4. Select the browsers against which you want these files checked.

5. When you're ready, select the Check button. Dreamweaver does its checking, and lists the results in the Target Browser Check panel (refer to Figure 30-6). Click the Browse Report button to display these results in your primary browser (refer to Figures 30-7 and 30-8).

   To save the results, print the browser page or click the Save Report button (in the Target Browser Check panel).

When you're checking multiple files, the summary section of the Target Browser Check report gives you a list of the files containing errors as well as an error count. For clarity, each file's errors are grouped together in the report.

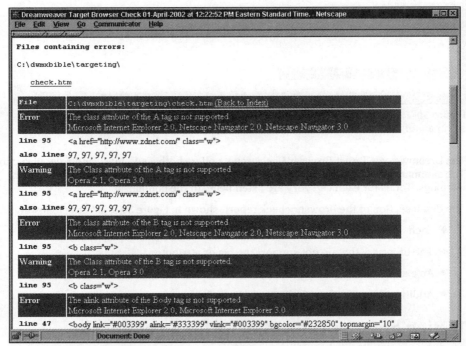

Figure 30-8: You can find detailed information on the lower half of the Dreamweaver Target Browser Check report.

Using the results of the browser check

How you handle the flagged errors in Dreamweaver's Target Browser Check report is entirely dependent on the design goals you have established for your site. If your mission is to be totally accessible to every browser on the market, you need to look at your page and/or site with the earliest browsers and pay special attention to those areas of possible trouble noted by the report. On the other hand, if your standards are a little more relaxed, you can probably ignore the 2.0 and 3.0 browser warnings and concentrate on those appearing in the NS4.x and IE 5 and higher categories.

Note   Many code items flagged as errors aren't, *per se*, incorrect — they're just not supported in the targeted browser. For example, checking a page with rollovers against Internet Explorer 3 displays an error stating "The onMouseOut attribute of the Hyperlink Anchor tag is not supported." If you load this page in Internet Explorer 3, the rollover won't work, but Explorer will fail gracefully, without displaying an error message box.

Customizing a Browser Profile

For Dreamweaver's Browser Targeting feature to be effective, you must have access to profiles for all the browsers you need to check. You can create custom browser profiles to cover any new browser versions or browsers as they become available. The browser profile file is a text file and can be created or altered in any text editor.

This section describes the required structure and format for a browser profile file and the steps for building one based on an existing file.

Understanding the browser profile structure

In order for Dreamweaver to properly process an HTML file using any browser profile, the profile must follow a precise format. Here's an excerpt from the Internet Explorer 6.0 browser profile:

```
<!ELEMENT Fieldset >
<!ATTLIST Fieldset
      Align ( left | center | right )    !Warning !msg="The reference of Internet
Explorer 4.0 lists the <ALIGN> attribute as valid. However, it only appears to
have some effect on the FIELDSET itself, not on the contents of the FIELDSET as
documented."
      Class
      Dir
      ID
      Lang
      Language
[...]
>
```

As you can see, the HTML tag is listed in a very specific syntax. Here's how the syntax is formed:

```
<!ELEMENT htmlTag >
<!ATTLIST htmlTag
unsupportedAttribute1 !Error !msg="The unsupportedAttribute1 of the ⊃
htmlTag is not supported. Try using thisAttribute for a similar effect."
supportedAttribute1
supportedAttribute2 ( validValue1 | validValue2 | validValue3 )
unsupportedAttribute2 !Error !htmlmsg="<b>Don't ever use this ⊃
unsupportedAttribute2 of the  htmlTag !!</b>"
>
```

The variables in the syntax are as follows:

✦ htmlTag: The tag as it appears in an HTML document; in our example this is the fieldset **tag**.

✦ `unsupportedAttribute`: Indicates invalid attributes so that a custom error message can be offered. Otherwise, all attributes not specifically listed are assumed to be unsupported. In our example, use of the `Align` attribute will trigger a warning.

✦ `supportedAttribute`: A valid attribute; all valid attributes must be listed. Only attributes listed without an `!Error` designation are supported. `Class`, `Dir`, `ID` and `Lang` are all supported attributes in our example.

✦ `validValue`: A value, like `left`, `right` and `center`, supported by the attribute.

Several other not-so-obvious rules must be followed in order for Dreamweaver to correctly read the profile:

✦ The name of the profile must appear as the first line of the file, followed by a single carriage return. This is the profile name that appears in the Check Target Browser(s) dialog box and in the report.

✦ The key phrase `PROFILE_TYPE=BROWSER_PROFILE` must appear as the second line.

✦ In every `<!ELEMENT` line, a single blank space must appear before the closing angle bracket (`>`).

✦ In the attribute sections, a blank space must appear after every opening parenthesis (`(`), before every closing parenthesis (`)`), and before *and* after each pipe character (`|`) .

✦ An exclamation point (`!`) must appear, without an intervening space, before every instance of the words `ELEMENT`, `ATTLIST`, `Error`, `msg`, and `htmlmsg`, as follows:

`!ELEMENT`, `!ATTLIST`, `!Error`, `!msg`, `!htmlmsg`.

✦ You can only use plain text in `!msg` messages, but an `!htmlmsg` message can use any valid HTML, including links.

✦ Don't use HTML comment tags, `<!-- -->`, because they interfere with the regular Dreamweaver processing of the file.

Creating a browser profile

As you can see, Dreamweaver browser profiles have a specific structure. Consequently, it's far easier to modify an existing profile than to write one from scratch. To create a browser profile:

1. Find an existing profile that is similar to the one you are creating. Open this profile in a text editor. Rename the profile file, if necessary, so that you don't accidentally overwrite the existing profile.

2. Add any tags and attributes that are supported in the target browser but not in the existing profile.

3. Remove any tags or attributes not supported by your target browser. Alternatively, you can add an `!Error` message after any attribute to flag it for Dreamweaver's Target Browser Check operation.

For example, the code fragment illustrated in Listing 30-1 contains a portion of the browser profile I created for WebTV. Note the custom error messages after the `<applet>` tag and the `rel` attribute of the `<a>` tag.

Listing 30-1: **Excerpt from Browser Profile File for WebTV**

```
WebTV 1.0
PROFILE_TYPE=BROWSER_PROFILE
-- Copyright 1997 Macromedia, Inc. All rights reserved.

<!ELEMENT A Name="Hyperlink Anchor" >
<!ATTLIST A
        Class           !Error
        HREF
        ID
        Name
        OnClick
        OnMouseOut
        OnMouseOver
        Rel             !Warning !msg "The rel attribute has been ⤶
modified by WebTV."
        Style           !Error
        Selected        !Error
        Target          !Error
>

<!ELEMENT Address >
<!ATTLIST Address
        Class           !Error
        ID              !Error
        Style           !Error
>

<!ELEMENT APPLET Name="Java Applet" > !Error !msg "WebTV does not ⤶
support Java Applets."
<!ATTLIST APPLET
        Align ( top | middle | bottom | left | right | absmiddle | ⤶
absbottom | baseline | texttop )
        Alt
        Archive         !Error
        Code
        Codebase
        Height
        HSpace
        Name
        VSpace
        Width
        Class
        ID
        Style
>

<!ELEMENT AREA Name="Client-side image map area" >
<!ATTLIST AREA
```

Continued

Listing 30-1: *(continued)*

```
        Alt             !Error
        Class           !Error
        Coords
        HREF
        ID
        Name
        NoHREF
        NoTab
        OnMouseOut
        OnMouseOver
        Shape
        Style           !Error
        Target
>

<!ELEMENT AUDIOSCOPE Name="Audioscope" >
<!ATTLIST AUDIOSCOPE
        Align
        Border
        Gain
        Height
        LeftColor
        LeftOffset
        MaxLevel
        RightColor
        RightOffset
        Width
>

<!ELEMENT B Name="Bold" >
<!ATTLIST B
        Class           !Error
        ID              !Error
        Style           !Error
>

<!ELEMENT Base >
<!ATTLIST Base
        HREF
        Target
>

<!ELEMENT BaseFont >
<!ATTLIST BaseFont
        Size
>
<!ELEMENT BGSOUND Name="Background sound" >
<!ATTLIST BGSOUND
        Loop
```

```
        Src
>

<!ELEMENT Big >
<!ATTLIST Big
        Class
        ID
        Style
>

<!ELEMENT Blackface >

<!ELEMENT Blink !Error >

<!ELEMENT Blockquote >

<!ELEMENT Body >
<!ATTLIST Body
        ALink               !Error
        Background
        BGColor
        BGProperties
        Credits
        LeftMargin
        Link
        Logo
        OnBlur              !Error
        OnFocus             !Error
        OnLoad
        OnUnload
        Style               !Error
        Text
        VLink
>

<!ELEMENT BQ Name="Block Quote" >

<!ELEMENT BR Name="Line break" >
<!ATTLIST BR
        Clear ( left | right | all )
>
```

Validating Your Code

Most browsers are very forgiving. They can take a document riddled with HTML infractions and, through "intelligent" interpretation, manage to display the page beautifully, with no indication that anything is awry with the underlying code. As a responsible Web author, however, you should never rely on the kindness of your users' browsers! It's far safer to take the extra time to validate the correctness of your code than to risk having a browser be less forgiving than you had hoped.

Fortunately, Dreamweaver MX can help. You can use its built-in Validator to check a document's code for tag or syntax errors. The Validator supports a gaggle of tag-based languages, including HTML (several versions), XHTML, XML, JSP (JavaServer Pages), CFML (ColdFusion Markup Language), and WML (Wireless Markup Language). And you can customize how the Validator works, as discussed in the next section, "Setting Validator preferences."

To validate your code:

1. Open the document you want to validate.

2. If it is an XML or XHTML file, choose File ➪ Check Page ➪ Validate as XML.

   For all other files, choose File ➪ Check Page ➪ Validate Markup, or press Shift+F6.

   The Validator does its thing and then lists the results in the Validation panel: error descriptions, filenames and line numbers, as shown in Figure 30-9.

File	Line	Description
stackedLayers.htm	9	In HTML 4.0, FONT is deprecated. It may become obsolete in future versions, consider using style sheets instead.
stackedLayers.htm	15	In HTML 4.0, FONT is deprecated. It may become obsolete in future versions, consider using style sheets instead.
stackedLayers.htm	16	In HTML 4.0, FONT is deprecated. It may become obsolete in future versions, consider using style sheets instead.
stackedLayers.htm	28	In HTML 4.0, FONT is deprecated. It may become obsolete in future versions, consider using style sheets instead.
stackedLayers.htm	29	In HTML 4.0, FONT is deprecated. It may become obsolete in future versions, consider using style sheets instead.
stackedLayers.htm	42	In HTML 4.0, FONT is deprecated. It may become obsolete in future versions, consider using style sheets instead.
stackedLayers.htm	43	In HTML 4.0, FONT is deprecated. It may become obsolete in future versions, consider using style sheets instead.

Figure 30-9: The result of the Validator tackling stackedLayers.htm.

3. Double-click an error in the list to display the offending code in the document.

4. To display the error report in your primary browser, click the Browse Report button. To keep a record of the report, print the browser page or click the Save Report button to generate an XML report file.

Tip Right-click (Control+click) in the Validation panel to bring up a context menu that lets you browse the error report, save the report, and more.

Setting Validator preferences

You can customize how the Validator works by changing its preferences. For example, you can specify which languages the Validator should check against and which types of errors the Validator should hunt down. To set your Validator preferences:

1. Choose Edit ➪ Preferences to open the Preferences dialog box (see Figure 30-10) and then click the Validator category to display the Validation options. Alternatively, you can use the keyboard shortcut, Ctrl+U (Command+U).

2. Select the languages you want the Validator to check against.

   When you select some languages, the Validator automatically selects other, related languages. For example, when you select HTML 4.0, the Validator automatically selects HTML 3.2 and HTML 2.0, because the definition for HTML 4.0 includes the definitions of HTML 3.2 and 2.0.

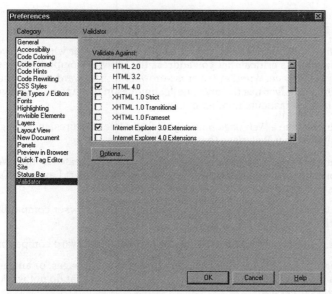

Figure 30-10: You can use the Validator options in the Preferences dialog box to customize the workings of your Dreamweaver Validator.

Caution

If you validate CFML (ColdFusion) and HTML in the same document, the Validator won't be able to assess the number sign (#) correctly. Why not? Because in CFML # is an error and ## is correct; but in HTML, the converse is true: ## is an error and # is correct.

   3. Click Options to open the Validator Options dialog box (see Figure 30-11).

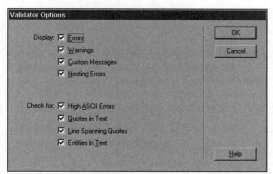

Figure 30-11: Use the Validator Options dialog box to exercise further control over your Validator's personality.

   4. Under Display, select the error types you want the Validator report to display.

   Under Check For, select the items you want the Validator to look for.

   5. Click OK to close the Validator Options dialog box; then click OK to close the Preferences dialog box.

Summary

Unless you're building a Web site for a strictly controlled intranet (for which everyone is using the same browser), it's critical that you address the browser-compatibility issues that your Web site is certain to face. Whether it's cross-browser or backward compatibility you're trying to achieve, Dreamweaver has features and techniques in place to help you get your Web pages viewed by the maximum number of users.

✦ Dreamweaver can take a Web page built with 4.0 and later features, including layers and CSS, and create another Web page that is 3.0-compatible.

✦ Dreamweaver can take a Web page created with layers and create another Web page that uses tables instead. Tools in Dreamweaver, such as Convert Layers to Tables, make it quick and straightforward.

✦ You can use JavaScript within a Web page to handle cross-browser compatibility problems with 4.0 and later browsers.

✦ Careful placement of your DHTML objects can help with backward compatibility.

✦ Dreamweaver enables you to check your Web page, selected pages, or an entire Web site against a browser profile to look for tags and attributes that do not work in a particular browser version.

✦ Browser profiles can be customized or copied and modified for a new browser or browser version.

✦ You can use Dreamweaver's built-in, customizable Validator to check your code for tag or syntax errors.

In the next chapter, you'll learn how to use Dreamweaver for building Web sites in a team environment.

✦   ✦   ✦

Building Web Sites with a Team

Major Web sites that are designed, developed, and maintained by one person are increasingly rare. Once a site has reached a certain complexity and size, it's far more timely and cost effective to divide responsibility for different areas among different people. For all of its positive aspects, team development has an equal number of shortcomings — as anyone who has had his or her work overwritten by another developer working on the same page will attest.

Dreamweaver includes a number of features that make it easy for teams to work together. Team-oriented features have increased significantly in Dreamweaver MX. In addition to the existing Check In/Check Out facility, version control and collaborative authoring have been enabled in Dreamweaver through the connectivity to Microsoft's Visual SourceSafe and the WebDAV (Web Distributed Authoring and Versioning) standard.

In addition to providing a link to industry-standard protocol used in team development, Dreamweaver MX also includes a more accessible Design Notes feature. When custom file columns are set up — which rely on Design Notes to store their information — a project's status is just a glance away. For more detailed feedback, Dreamweaver's Reports command provides an interactive method for uncovering problems and offering a direct link to fixing them. As with many Dreamweaver features, the Reports mechanism is extensible, which means JavaScript-savvy developers can create their own custom reports to further assist their teamwork. This chapter examines the various Dreamweaver tools — both old and new — for developing Web sites with a team. We begin with the essential team-based feature: Check In/Check Out.

Following Check In/Check Out Procedures

Site development can be subdivided in as many different ways as there are site development teams. In one group, all the graphics may be handled by one person or department while layout is handled by another and JavaScript coding by yet another. Or, one team may be given total responsibility over one section of a Web site — the products section, for example — as another team handles the services division. However the responsibilities are shared, there's always the danger of overlap: that two or more team members will unknowingly work on the same page, graphic, or other Web element — and that one person's work will replace the other's when transferred to the remote site. Suddenly, the oh-so-efficient division of labor becomes a logistical nightmare.

Dreamweaver's core protection for team Web site development is its Check In/Check Out system. When properly established and adhered to, the Check In/Check Out system stops files from improperly being overwritten. It also lets everyone on the team know who is working on what file, and provides a direct method of contacting them, right from within Dreamweaver.

As with any team effort, to get the most out of the Check In/Check Out system everybody must follow the rules:

✦ **Rule Number 1:** All team members must have Check In/Check Out set up for their Dreamweaver-defined sites.

✦ **Rule Number 2:** All team members must have Design Notes enabled in their site definition (in order to share Design Notes information).

And, arguably the most important rule:

✦ **Rule Number 3:** All team members must use Dreamweaver to transfer files to and from the remote server.

If the Check In/Check Out systems fails and a file is accidentally overwritten, it is invariably because Rule Number 3 was broken: Someone uploaded or downloaded a file to or from the Web server using a tool other than Dreamweaver.

Check In/Check Out overview

Before discussing the Check In/Check Out setup procedure, let's examine how the process actually works with two fictional team members, Eric and Bella:

1. Eric gets an e-mail with a note to update the content on the About Our Company page with news of the merger that has just occurred.

2. Bella receives a similar note — except Bella is the graphic artist and needs to change the logo to reflect the new organization.

3. Eric connects to the remote site, selects the about.htm file, and chooses the Check Out button on Dreamweaver's Site panel toolbar.

   If Eric had chosen Get instead of Check Out, he would have received a read-only file on his system.

4. Dreamweaver asks Eric if he would like to include dependent files in the transfer. As he doesn't know that Bella needs to work on the site also, he selects OK.

   The file on the remote system is downloaded to Eric's machine and a small green checkmark appears next to the name of each file transferred in both the Remote Site and Local Files views, as shown in Figure 31-1.

5. Bella connects to the remote site in Dreamweaver and sees a red check next to the file she needs to work on, about.htm. Next to the file is the name of the person who currently has the file, Eric, as well as his e-mail address.

6. Bella selects the link to Eric's e-mail address and drops him a note asking him to let her know when he's done.

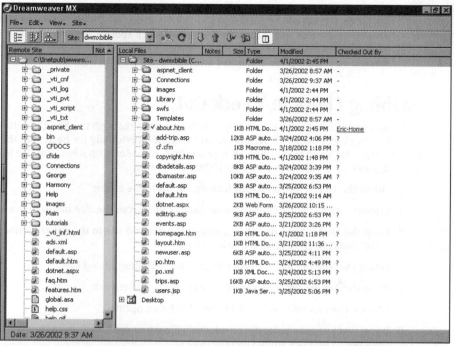

Figure 31-1: For a checked-out file, a checkmark is placed next to the filename on both the local and remote sites. The checkmark is green if you checked it out, and red if someone else checked it out.

7. Eric finishes adding the content to the page and chooses the Check In button to transfer the files back to the remote server.

   The checkmarks are removed from both the Remote and Local views and the local version of about.htm is marked as read-only by Dreamweaver, indicated with a closed padlock symbol. This feature prevents Eric from working on the file without first checking it out.

8. Bella receives Eric's "I'm done!" e-mail and retrieves the file by selecting the Check Out button from the Site panel toolbar.

   Now, on Bella's machine, the transferred files have a green checkmark and her name, while on Eric's screen the checkmarks are displayed in red.

9. After she's finished working on the graphics side of the page, ensuring that Eric's new content wraps properly around her new logo, she's selects the HTML file and then clicks Check In. By opting to transfer the dependent files as well, all of her new graphics are properly transferred. Again, the checkmarks are removed, and the local files are set to read-only.

10. The work is completed without anyone stepping on anyone else's toes — or files.

Caution   Dreamweaver places a small text file with a .lck (lock) extension on both the server and local site for each checked-out document. The .lck file stores the Check Out name of the person transferring the files and, if available, his or her e-mail address. It's important that these files not be deleted from the server, as their existence signals to Dreamweaver that a file has been checked out. After the file is checked back in, the .lck file is deleted from the server.

Enabling Check In/Check Out

Dreamweaver's Check In/Check Out system is activated through the Site Definition dialog box. The Check In/Check Out settings must be input individually for each site; there's no global option for all sites. Although it's generally best to set it up when the site is initially defined, you can enable Check In/Check Out at any time.

To establish the Check In/Check Out feature, follow these steps:

1. Choose Site ➪ Define Sites or select Define Sites from the Site menu in the Site panel.

2. From the Define Sites dialog box, select the desired site in the list and choose Edit or select the New button to define a new site.

3. Select the Remote Info category in the Site Definition dialog box.

4. From the Access list, choose either FTP or Local/Network.

5. Choose the Enable File Check In and Check Out option.

6. If you want to automatically check out a file when opening it from the Site panel, select the Check Out Files when Opening option.

   When the Check Out Files when Opening option is selected, double-clicking a file in the Site panel or selecting it and then choosing File ➪ Open Selection transfers the corresponding remote file to the local system and notes the file as being checked out. Choosing File ➪ Open does not automatically check out a file, whether this option is chosen or not.

7. Enter the name you displayed under the Checked Out By column in the Check Out Name field.

   It's a good idea to use a name that not only identifies yourself, but also the system on which you're working. Thus, `jlowery-laptop` or `jlowery-iMac` is a better choice than just `jlowery`.

8. To enable team members to send you a message from within Dreamweaver, enter your full e-mail address in the E-mail Address field.

   Entering an e-mail address converts the Checked Out By name to an active link. Selecting the link prompts the default e-mail program to display a new message form (the To field contains the supplied e-mail address and the Subject field contains the site name and filename, as shown in Figure 31-2).

9. Make sure that any other necessary information for establishing an FTP or network connection is entered. Select OK to close the Site Definition dialog box.

10. From the Define Sites dialog box, choose Done.

Note   The preceding procedure works for both FTP and network-connected remote sites. If you are working within a Visual SourceSafe or WebDAV environment, see their corresponding sections later in this chapter for enabling Check In and Check Out protocols.

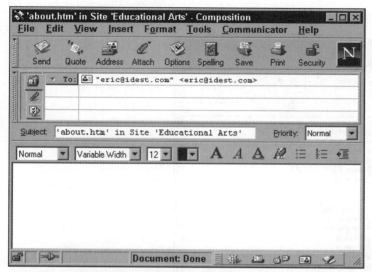

Figure 31-2: Dreamweaver lets you contact the team member working on a file with the e-mail address feature. The subject line is automatically added to reference a particular file and site.

Checking files in and out

Once the Check In/Check Out feature is enabled, additional buttons and commands become available. The Site panel toolbar shows both a Check Out File(s) button and Check In button, as shown in Figure 31-3, and the Site ⇨ Check Out and Site ⇨ Check In commands become active. The redundancy of these commands makes it feasible to check files in and out from wherever you happen to be working in the Dreamweaver environment.

To check out a file or series of files from the Site panel, follow these steps:

1. Choose Window ⇨ Site or click the Show Site button from the Launcher to open the Site panel. If you prefer to use keyboard shortcuts, press F8.

2. If necessary, select the desired site — where Check In/Check Out has been enabled — from the Site drop-down list.

3. Click the Connect button in the Site panel toolbar or choose Site ⇨ Connect.

   If you've chosen Local/Network as your remote access method, you're connected automatically.

4. Choose the HTML or other Web documents you want to check out from the Site panel (it doesn't matter whether you're using Local View or Remote View).

   It's not necessary to select the dependent files; Dreamweaver will transfer those for you automatically.

5. Choose Check Out File(s) from the Site panel toolbar or select Site ⇨ Check Out.

   If you "get" the files instead of checking them out, either by choosing the Get button or by dragging the files from the Remote Site listing to the Local Files listing, the local file will become read-only, but the remote file will not be marked as checked out.

Check Out   Check In

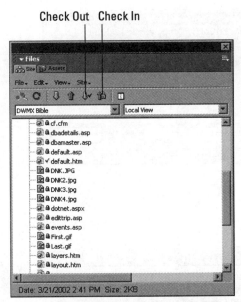

Figure 31-3: The Check In and Check Out buttons
do not appear unless Enable Check In/Check Out
has been selected in the Site Definition.

6. If the Prompt on Get/Check Out option is selected in Preferences, Dreamweaver asks if
   you'd like to transfer the dependent files. Choose Yes to do so or No to transfer only
   the selected files.

   When Dreamweaver has completed the transfer, green checkmarks appear next to each
   primary file (HTML, ASP, ColdFusion, and so on) in both the Remote Site and Local Files
   views; dependent files are made read-only locally, designated by a padlock symbol.

I recommend checking out all the files that you believe you'll need in a work session right at
the start. Although you can check out an open document — by choosing Site ⇨ Check Out or
by selecting Check Out from the File Management button on the toolbar — Dreamweaver
needs to transfer the remote file to your local system, possibly overwriting any changes
you've made. Dreamweaver does ask you if you want to replace the local version with the
remote file; to abort the procedure, choose No.

Tip   If you need to edit a graphic or other dependent file that has been locked as part of the
            check-out process, you can unlock the file from the Site panel. Right-click (Control+click) the
            file in the Site panel and, from the context menu, choose Turn off Read Only. (The Turn off
            Read Only option is called Unlock on the Macintosh.) One related tip: To quickly select the
            file for an image, choose the image in the Assets panel; and from the context menu, choose
            Locate in Site.

Once you've completed your work on a particular file, you're ready to check it back in. To
check in the current file, follow these steps:

1. Choose Site ➪ Check In or select Check In from the Site panel toolbar.

2. If you haven't saved your file and if you've enabled the Save Files Before Putting option from the Site category in Preferences, your file will be automatically saved; otherwise, Dreamweaver asks if you want to store the file before transferring it.

3. If Prompt on Put/Check In is enabled, Dreamweaver will ask if you want to transfer the dependent files as well. If any changes have been made to the dependent files, select Yes.

   Once the files are transferred, Dreamweaver removes the checkmarks from the files and makes the local files read-only.

Note Ever start working on a file only to realize you're working on the wrong one? If you make this or any other mistake that makes you wish you could go back to the original version when working with a checked-out file, don't worry. Even if you've saved your changes locally, you can choose Site ➪ Undo Check Out (or select Undo Check Out from the Site button on the Site panel toolbar) to retransfer the posted file from the remote site. The local file will be made read-only, and the file will no longer be checked out under your name.

Integrating Dreamweaver with Visual SourceSafe

Microsoft's Visual SourceSafe (VSS) is an industrial-strength version-control tool. With VSS, team members can check files in and out just as they can with Dreamweaver. In addition, other valuable features are also available, including the capability to get a history of changes, to compare two or more versions to one another to see the differences, and to restore a previous version. Visual SourceSafe is generally used in larger corporations where many different departments are involved in a Web development project. VSS is bundled with the Enterprise edition of Visual InterDev, as well as being sold separately.

Dreamweaver integrates its own Check In/Check Out system with that of Visual SourceSafe. When a Dreamweaver site is connected to a VSS database, checking out a file in Dreamweaver checks out a file from the VSS project. Likewise, when a file is checked back in Dreamweaver, it is noted as being checked-in in the VSS database. This integration enables Dreamweaver to be smoothly integrated into a large-scale Web development project in which both Dreamweaver users and non-users may be working together, accessing the same files.

Visual SourceSafe is available on both the Macintosh and Windows platforms, and each platform has special requirements:

✦ For Windows systems, the Visual SourceSafe version 6 client must be installed on the local machine.

✦ Macintosh users should have the MetroWerks SourceSafe version 1.1.0 client installed. In addition, you must have the ToolServer utility from the Macintosh Programmer's Workshop installed. ToolServer is found on the Dreamweaver MX CD or it can be downloaded from the Apple Developer's site at http://developer.apple.com/tools/mpw-tools/.

Caution Several versions of ToolServer are available, and you must have the correct version in order for VSS integration to work properly. If you already have ToolServer on your Macintosh, make sure that the file mwcm tool is included in the ToolServer/Tools folder.

Once set up, the Dreamweaver/VSS integration is virtually seamless. Files are checked in and out, just as they would be if VSS were not involved. Dreamweaver performs what SourceSafe sees as an Exclusive file check out; to enable a Multiple Check Out — which enables several people to check out the same file — you must go through VSS. Other VSS administrative features, such as Show History and Differences, must be handled from within SourceSafe by a user with administrator privileges.

Note   Two Dreamweaver site commands are not accessible with a SourceSafe connection: Synchronize and Select Newer. In order to use these commands, Dreamweaver must know how the local system and remote server relate time-wise — are they in the same time zone or is one behind the other? It's not feasible in the current implementation to get time stamp information from a VSS database; consequently, the features that depend on this information are not available.

As noted earlier, the Visual SourceSafe connection is managed through the Site Definition dialog box. To set up VSS connectivity, follow these steps:

1. Choose Site ⇨ Define Sites.

2. From the Define Sites dialog box, choose the site to be connected to the VSS database from the list and select Edit.

3. Select the Remote Info category.

4. From the Access drop-down list, choose SourceSafe Database.

5. Select the Settings button.

    All of the connection information is entered through the displayed Open SourceSafe Database dialog box, shown in Figure 31-4.

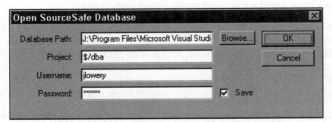

Figure 31-4: Visual SourceSafe projects require a user name and password for access.

6. Enter the path and filename of the SourceSafe database in the Database Path field. Alternatively, select Browse to locate the file.

7. Enter the VSS project name in the Project field.

    The name of every VSS project begins with a $/ prefix — for example, $/bigco — and Dreamweaver supplies this prefix in the Project field.

8. Enter your VSS login name in the Username field.

9. Enter your VSS password in the Password field.

10. To circumvent automatic logon to the VSS database when connecting in Dreamweaver — and cause Dreamweaver to prompt you for a password every time — deselect the Save option.

11. Click OK when you're done to close the Open SourceSafe Database dialog box.

12. If you want to automatically check out a file when opening it from the Site panel, select the Check Out Files when Opening option.

    When this option is enabled, double-clicking a file in the Site panel (or selecting it and then choosing File ➪ Open Selection) automatically performs the check-out procedure.

13. Click OK to close the Site Definition dialog box.

14. Choose Done to close the Define Sites dialog box.

As mentioned earlier, the procedures for checking out and checking in files are almost identical to those described in the "Checking files in and out" section. Simply select the files desired in the Site panel and click the Check Out button or use the menu command, Site ➪ Check Out.

 Note When Multiple Check Out is enabled, the file view column, Checked Out By, displays a list of names separated by commas.

Similarly, you can check a file back in by choosing the Check In button. There is one difference, however: Dreamweaver gives you an opportunity to attach a comment (which will be written into the VSS database) to a file when it is checked in. To view the comments in Visual SourceSafe, select the file and then choose the Show History button; in the History dialog box, choose Details and check the Comments field of the History Details dialog box.

Communicating with WebDAV

Web-based Distributed Authoring and Versioning (WebDAV) is an Internet protocol that enables Web developers to collaborate over the Web itself. Just as Visual SourceSafe enables teams to work together over a network, WebDAV enables developers to log in over the Web to work on a common set of files. Normally, the HTTP protocol, the basis for most Internet communication, only permits files to be read. With the WebDAV set of extensions installed, files may also be written to the server. More important, files may also be locked to prevent multiple, simultaneous edits; in other words, files may be checked out for modification and checked in when the update is complete.

Dreamweaver supports the WebDAV protocol enabling developers and designers around the world to work together on a single site. The WebDAV setup is, as with VSS, handled through the Remote Info category of the Site Definition dialog box. Once established, the Dreamweaver/WebDAV connection is transparent, and the Check In/Check Out features work as they do on a standard FTP or network connection.

Dreamweaver's implementation of WebDAV connectivity is geared toward Microsoft IIS and Apache servers. Both have been fully tested and are supported. WebDAV implementations on other servers may interact erratically, or not at all, with Dreamweaver. For more in-depth information on WebDAV, including a list of publicly available servers, visit www.webdav.org.

To establish a WebDAV connection, follow these steps:

1. Choose Site ⇨ Define Sites.

2. From the Define Sites dialog box, choose the site to be connected to the WebDAV server from the list and select Edit.

3. Select the Remote Info category.

4. From the Access drop-down list, choose WebDAV.

5. Select the Settings button.

   All of the connection information is entered through the displayed WebDAV Connection dialog box, shown in Figure 31-5.

Figure 31-5: Once WebDAV is enabled, team members can collaborate over the Web itself to develop Web sites.

6. Enter the absolute URL to the WebDAV server in the URL field.

7. Enter your WebDAV login name in the Username field.

8. Enter your WebDAV password in the Password field.

9. Enter your e-mail address in the Email field.

   The user name and e-mail address will be displayed for checked-out files.

10. To circumvent automatic logon to the VSS database when connecting in Dreamweaver — and cause Dreamweaver to prompt you for a password every time — deselect the Save option.

11. Click OK when you're done to close the WebDAV Connection dialog box.

12. If you want to automatically check out a file when opening it from the Site panel, select the Check Out Files when Opening option.

    When this option is enabled, double-clicking a file in the Local Files view (or selecting it and then choosing File ⇨ Open Selection) automatically performs the check-out procedure.

13. Click OK to close the Site Definition dialog box.

14. Choose Done to close the Define Sites dialog box.

To use the WebDAV server, select the Connect button on the Site panel toolbar or choose Site ⇨ Connect.

Note   WebDAV is a technology that should definitely remain on every Web developer's radar screen, whether you are currently involved in a WebDAV project or not. WebDAV technology is the underpinnings for Microsoft's Web Folder feature found in Internet Explorer 5 and later and in Office 2000 products.

Keeping Track with Design Notes

When several people are working are on a site, they can't just rely on the Web pages to speak for themselves. In any team collaboration, a great deal of organizational information needs to be communicated behind the scenes: who's working on what areas, the status of any given file, when the project is due, what modifications are needed, and so on. Dreamweaver includes a feature called Design Notes that is designed to facilitate team communication in a very flexible manner.

Dreamweaver Design Notes are small files that, in a sense, attach themselves to the Web pages or objects they concern. A Design Note may be attached to any HTML page, graphic, or media file inserted into a page. Design Notes follow their corresponding file whenever that file is moved or renamed using the Dreamweaver Site panel; moreover, a Design Note is deleted if the file to which it is related is deleted. Design Notes have the same base name as the file to which they are attached — including that file's extension — but are designated with an .mno extension. For example, the Design Note for the file index.html would be called index.html.mno; Design Notes are stored in the _notes subfolder, which is not displayed in the Dreamweaver Site panel.

Design Notes may be entered and viewed through the Design Notes dialog box, shown in Figure 31-6. This dialog box may optionally be set to appear when a file is opened, thus passing instructions from one team member to another automatically. In addition to the Design Notes dialog box, you can configure File view columns to display Design Note information right in the Site panel; the File view columns feature is covered in the "Browsing File View Columns" section.

Setting up for Design Notes

Design Notes are enabled by default but can be turned off on a site-by-site basis. To disable Design Notes, follow these steps:

1. Choose Site ⇨ Define Sites or select Define Sites from the Site listing.

2. In the Define Sites dialog box that opens, select the site you wish to alter and choose Edit.

3. In the Site Definition dialog box, select the Design Notes category (see Figure 31-7).

4. Deselect the Maintain Design Notes option to stop Dreamweaver from creating Design Notes completely.

   Dreamweaver alerts you to the consequences of disabling Design Notes. Click OK to continue.

5. If you want to work with Design Notes locally, but don't want to automatically transfer them to the remote site, leave Maintain Design Notes checked and uncheck Upload Design Notes for Sharing.

6. To remove Design Notes that no longer have an associated file — which can happen if a file is deleted or renamed by a program other than Dreamweaver — click the Clean Up button. Dreamweaver gives you an opportunity to confirm the delete operation.

7. Click OK to close the Site Definition dialog box, and then click Done to close the Define Sites dialog box.

Design Notes serve two different purposes. From a team perspective, they're invaluable for tracking a project's progress and passing information between team members. However, Design Notes are also used by Dreamweaver and other Macromedia products, including Fireworks, to pass data between programs and program commands. For example, Fireworks uses Design Notes to store the location of a Fireworks source file that is displayed in the Image Property inspector when the exported graphic is selected in Dreamweaver.

It's important to realize the dual nature of Design Notes. I strongly recommend — whether you work with a large team or you're a "team of one" — that you keep Design Notes enabled and fully functioning.

Setting the status with Design Notes

What is the one thing a Web site project manager always wants to know? The status of every page under development: What's still in the planning stages, what has been drafted, what has made it to beta, and what's ready to go live? An awareness of each page's status enables the manager to prioritize appropriately and add additional resources to the development of a page if necessary. It's also helpful for individual team members who are working on a page to know how far along that page is.

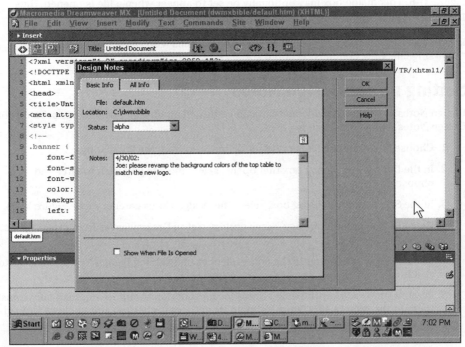

Figure 31-6: You can configure a Design Note to pop up whenever a file is opened to alert a fellow team member of work to be done.

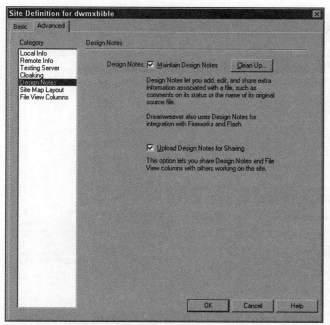

Figure 31-7: Although it's not recommended, you can disable Design Notes through the Site Definition dialog box.

Design Notes put the Status category front and center for all files. It's the one standard field that is always available, and it offers eight different values and one custom value. Entries may be date-stamped in the Notes area to show a history of revisions, as shown in Figure 31-8. Optionally, you can elect to display the Design Note the next time the file is opened by anyone.

To enter the status of a file, follow these steps:

1. Choose File ⇨ Design Notes to open the Design Notes dialog box.

   To insert a Design Note for an object embedded on a Web page, such as a graphic, Flash movie, or other multimedia element, right-click (Control+click) the object and then, from the context menu choose Design Notes.

2. On the Basic Info tab of the Design Notes dialog box, choose one of the following standard options from the Status drop-down list: draft, revision1, revision2, revision3, alpha, beta, final, or needs attention.

3. To add the current date (in m/d/yy format, such as 3/7/01) to the Notes field, click the Calendar icon.

4. Enter any desired text into the Notes field.

   The same Notes text is displayed regardless of which Status option you choose.

5. If you'd like the Design Notes dialog box with the current information to appear the next time the page is loaded, choose the Show When File is Opened option.

   The Show When File is Opened option is only available for Design Notes attached to pages, not for Design Notes attached to page elements such as images.

6. Click OK when you're done.

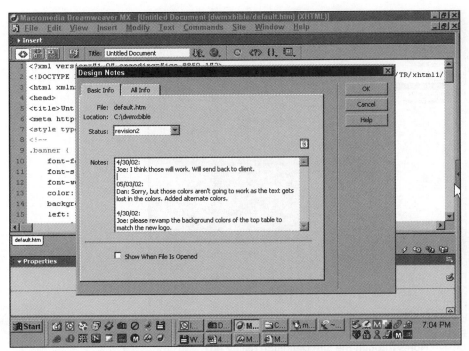

Figure 31-8: Design Notes can maintain a history of revisions for any Web page.

Creating custom Design Notes

Aside from monitoring the status of a project, you can use a Design Note to describe any single item. The All Info tab of the Design Notes dialog box enables you to enter any number of name/value pairs, which can be viewed in the Design Note itself or — more effectively — in the File view columns. This mechanism might be used to indicate which graphic artist in your department has primary responsibility for the page, or how many billable hours the page has accrued. You can also use the All Info tab to set a custom value for the Status list on the Basic Info tab.

To enter a new name/value pair, follow these steps:

1. Choose File ➪ Design Notes to open the Design Notes dialog box.

2. Select the All Info tab.

   If a Status and/or Notes entry has been made on the Basic Info tab, you'll see their values listed in the Info area.

3. Choose the Add (+) button to enter a new name/value pair.

4. In the Name field, enter the term you wish to use.

5. In the Value field, enter the information you want associated with the current term.

6. To edit an entry, select it from the list in the Info area and alter either the Name or Value field.

7. To delete an entry, select it and press the Remove (–) button.

8. Click OK when you're done.

As noted earlier, you can create a custom Status list option in the All Info tab. To do so, just enter **status** in the Name field of a new name/value pair and enter the desired listing in the Value field. If you switch to the Basic Info tab, you'll find your new status entry listed as the last item. You can only add one custom status entry; if you add another, it will replace the previous one.

Viewing Design Notes

To fully view a Design Note, you have several options. You can choose File ➪ Design Notes to open the dialog box; in Windows, this option is available from either the Document window or the Site panel. Another possibility is to right-click (Control+click) the file in either the File or the Site Map view of the Site panel and choose the Design Notes option from the context menu. Finally, if a Design Note is attached to a file, you'll see an icon in the Notes column of the File view, as shown in Figure 31-9. Double-clicking the Notes icon will open the Design Note associated with that file.

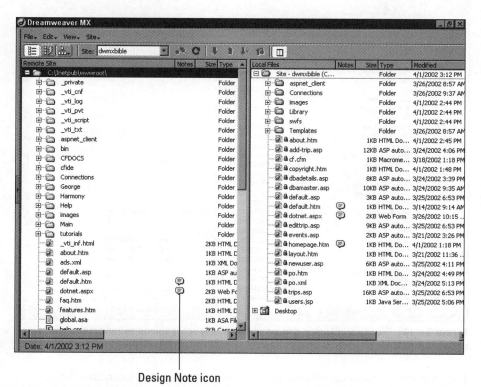

Design Note icon

Figure 31-9: Get immediate access to previously created Design Notes by double-clicking the icon in the Notes column.

Browsing File View Columns

While Design Notes can hold a lot of information about a Web page or element, the details are kept out of sight. With an eye toward heightening the visibility of Design Notes data—thus making them more useful—Dreamweaver has tied the columns of the Site panel's File view directly to Design Notes. In the previous section, you saw how the Notes column indicated that a Design Note existed for a particular file; now you'll learn how to create custom File view columns to display any value stored in a Design Note.

With custom columns in the File view, a quick glance at the Site panel can reveal which files are completed, which are in revision, and which need attention. Moreover, custom columns may be sorted, just as regular columns. You could, for instance, easily group together all the files with the same due date, or those coded by the same programmer. File view columns—even the built-in ones such as Type and Modified—may be re-aligned, re-ordered, or hidden. Only the Name column may not be altered or moved. With this level of customization possible, virtually the entire File view could be reshaped, as the one in Figure 31-10 has been.

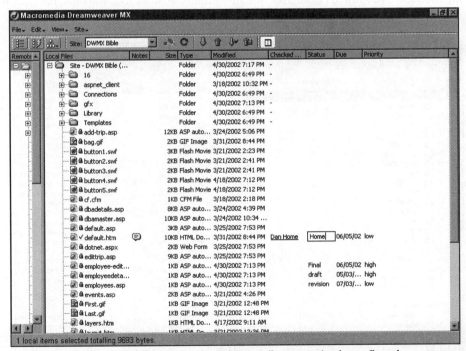

Figure 31-10: File view columns can be substantially reorganized to reflect the concerns of your team on a project-by-project basis.

The six standard columns—Name (which shows the filename), Notes, Size, Type, Modified, and Checked Out By—may be supplemented by any number of custom columns. Modification of the column set-up is handled in the File View Columns category of the Site Definition dialog box. File views are managed on a per-site basis; when defining the file views, you can determine if the views are to be seen by anyone accessing the development site. Likewise, any custom column may optionally be shared among team members.

To create a custom File view, follow these steps:

1. Open the File View Columns category with one of these methods:

   - Choose Define Sites and open the Site Definition for the desired site. Then, select the File View Column option from the category list.

   - Select View ⇨ File View Columns from the Site panel on Windows systems or, on the Macintosh, choose Site ⇨ Site Files View ⇨ File View Columns.

2. If you'd like team members to see the custom columns you're developing, select Enable Column Sharing.

   You also need to choose the Share with All Users of this Site option for each custom column you want to share.

3. To add a custom column, click the Add (+) button.

   A new entry at the end of the list is created.

4. Enter a unique name for the column in the Column Name field.

   If you enter an existing name, Dreamweaver warns you and requests a new name before proceeding.

5. Pick a Design Note field to link to the new column from the Associate with Design Note list.

   You can choose one of the suggested Design Note fields (assigned, due, priority, or status) or you can enter your own. Design Note fields may be uppercase, lowercase, or mixed-case; multiple words are also allowed.

6. Select an Alignment option from the list: Left, Center, or Right.

   Columns that hold numeric or date values should be aligned to the right.

7. Make sure the Show option is selected.

8. To share this column with fellow team members, choose the Share with All Users of this Site option.

   Selecting this option causes Dreamweaver to create a file called dwSiteColumnsAll.xml within the _notes folder on the remote site. When another member of your team connects to the site, Dreamweaver reads this file and incorporates it into that person's site definition. This enables any other user to see the same column set up on his or her system.

9. Use the up and down arrows to reposition the column.

10. To add additional columns, repeat Steps 3 through 9.

11. Click OK when you're done.

How might a team benefit from custom File view columns? Some of the possibilities for custom columns include the following:

- ✦ Project Manager
- ✦ Lead Designer
- ✦ Lead Programmer
- ✦ Template Used

- ✦ Date Created
- ✦ Date Due
- ✦ Percentage Complete
- ✦ Client Contact

Caution   File view columns are sorted alphabetically even if the values are numeric. For example, if you have three files with the numeric values 100%, 50%, and 10%, an ascending sort displays 10%, 100%, 50%. As a workaround, use decimal values (.10, .50, and 1.00) to represent percentages, and the files will sort correctly. If your columns require date values, use leading zeros in dates, such as 01/03, to ensure that the columns are properly sorted.

While having the Design Notes information visible in File view columns is extremely helpful for maintaining an overview of a Web site, Dreamweaver takes the feature a step further. Once a custom file column is established, you can handle additions and modifications to the Design Note from the Site panel. Click in the custom column of the file; the existing information, if any, is highlighted and can be altered. If there is no data in the column, the column becomes editable.

Note   Although the Design Note is actually a separate file, you cannot change File view columns for a locked file. One solution is to temporarily turn off the read-only feature, and then add the File view info and relock if necessary.

To turn off the read-only feature, right-click (Control+click) the file in the Site panel and, from the context menu, choose Turn off Read Only. (The Turn off Read Only option is called Unlock on the Macintosh.)

Generating Reports

Although custom File view columns can present a tremendous degree of detail, the data is only viewable from the Site panel. Often, managers and team members need to extract certain bits of information about a site in order to know where they stand and fix problems in an organized, timely fashion. Some Webmasters use third-party utilities to comb their sites and generate lists of errors, which can then be assigned for resolution. These utilities may also be used to establish workflow patterns as they gather information, such as which pages are currently incomplete, or who is currently working on what site elements.

Dreamweaver reports give the Webmaster and team members a new tool for efficiently building Web sites. The information from a Dreamweaver report may be instantly used — double-clicking any report detail opens the referenced file — or stored as an XML file for later output. Dreamweaver includes seven standard reports that may be generated individually or combined into one. As with many Dreamweaver features, the Reports command is extensible, enabling users to build custom reports.

How do Dreamweaver reports work? The user must first choose from a variety of scopes: the current document, selected files in the site, all the files in a particular folder, or the entire site. Once the scope has been selected, the report elements — what the report will actually cover — are selected. The report is then run, and Dreamweaver outputs the results into a floating panel, as shown in Figure 31-11. Each entry in the Results panel is capable of opening the listed file; in the case of reports querying the underlying HTML, the entries lead directly to the referenced code.

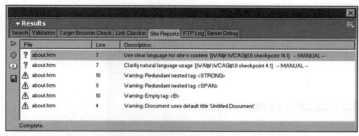

Figure 31-11: Dreamweaver reports return interactive results — just double-click any listed entry to open the related file.

Generated reports may also be saved for later use. The reports are saved in an XML file format that can be imported into a Web page, database, or spreadsheet program. Although this information could be extracted by hand, the structured format of the XML file makes it a perfect candidate for an automated process handled by an extension or other utility.

Two different types of Dreamweaver reports are available: those concerned with the code in the pages themselves and those accessing workflow details.

To access a Dreamweaver report, follow these steps:

1. Choose Site ⇨ Reports or click the Play icon in the Site Reports panel. Windows users may choose the command from either the Document window or the Site panel menus.

2. Select which reports you'd like to include from either the Workflow or HTML Reports categories.

3. If you choose an option from the Workflow category or the Accessibility option in HTML Reports, the Report Settings button activates. Select it to define the report search (see Figure 31-12) for Workflow reports, or the accessibility options (see Figure 31-13) for the Accessibility HTML Report.

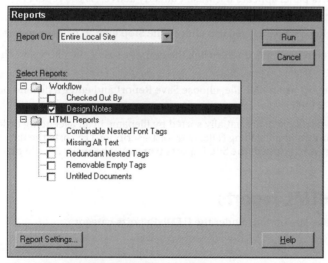

Figure 31-12: The Design Notes report uses the search criteria established in the Report Settings dialog box.

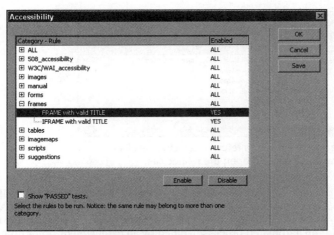

Figure 31-13: The Accessibility report uses the Accessibility options to determine which pieces of your pages to test against Section 508 standards.

Note   Section 508 is the United States government statute concerning accessibility on the Internet and in software development. To learn more about Section 508 standards, see www. section508.gov.

Dreamweaver remembers the Report On setting each time you run this command.

The Report Settings options are covered in detail later, in the section "Using Workflow reports."

4. Click the Run button.

   The Site Reports panel appears if it wasn't already active. As the report is processed, results are listed in the upper window.

5. From the Site Reports panel, you can choose the Stop icon to halt the report.

6. To open any referenced file, double-click the entry or select the entry and choose Open File.

7. To store the report as an XML file, choose Save Report and enter a file and path in the Save File dialog box.

Entries in the Site Reports panel are initially sorted by filename in an ascending order; however, selecting any column heading (File, Line, or Description) re-sorts the list accordingly. If many result listings are returned, the Site Reports panel may be resized to display more of them.

Outputting HTML reports

Dreamweaver includes five options under the HTML Reports category:

✦ **Combinable Nested Font Tags:** This query looks for code in which the font tag has been applied to the same text at different times, as shown in the following example:

```
<font color="#000000"><font size=+1>Monday, December 15th
@7pm</font></font>
```

✦ **Missing Alt Text:** This report searches for <img> tags in which the alt attribute is empty or missing entirely. To comply with accessibility guidelines established by the W3C, all images should have alt attributes that describe the graphic.

✦ **Redundant Nested Tags:** This report identifies tags nested within themselves, as shown in the following example:

```
<b><b>On Sale!</b></b>
```

✦ **Removable Empty Tags:** This search finds non-empty tags (that is, tags with both an opening and closing element) with no content, as in this code:

```
<div align="center"> </div>
```

✦ **Untitled Documents:** This report looks for pages that have no title or use the default "Untitled Document" text.

You can run any or all of the HTML reports at once—just select the desired report(s) from the Reports dialog box. The Site Reports panel lists the name of the file, the line number where the search condition was found, and an error message for each entry. Selecting a file displays the error message with additional detail, if available, in the Detailed Description area. Choosing Open File or double-clicking an entry loads the file, if possible. If the file is currently locked, Dreamweaver asks if you'd like to view the read-only file or unlock it. All HTML report files are displayed in the split-screen Code and Design view.

Using Workflow reports

Workflow reports, unlike HTML reports, don't examine the code of Web pages. They look at the metadata—the information about the information—of a site. Two standard reports are available under the Workflow heading:

✦ **Checked Out By:** This report displays any file checked out by a particular person as designated in the Report Settings dialog box. If nothing is entered in the Report Settings dialog box, a list of all files in the selected scope that have been checked out by anyone is returned.

To run this report, you must be able to connect to your remote site.

✦ **Design Notes:** This report examines the designated files according to search criteria set up in the Report Settings dialog box (refer to Figure 31-12). Searches may be conducted on a maximum of three criteria. If no criterion is entered, a list of all files with Design Notes in the selected scope is returned.

The Report Settings dialog box for the Design Notes reports is relatively flexible, as it enables "and" type searches. To use the Design Notes Report Settings dialog box, follow these steps:

1. In the Reports dialog box, select the Design Notes option under the Workflow category. The Report Settings button is made available.

2. Select Report Settings.

   The Report Settings dialog box opens; the previous Design Notes Settings are restored.

3. In the Report Settings dialog box, enter the name of the Design Notes field in the first column.

   The name of the Design Notes field is case-sensitive: in other words, entering `Status` in the Report Settings dialog box will not match `status` in the Design Note.

4. Choose a criteria type from the middle column drop-down list. The options are as follows: `contains`, `does not contain`, `is`, `is not`, and `matches regex`.

5. In the third column, enter the value of the Design Notes field being sought.

   As with the Design Notes field, the value search is also case-sensitive.

6. To add a second or third condition to the query, repeat Steps 3 through 5 in the second and third line of the Report Settings dialog box.

   Additional conditionals are applied in an "and" type search. For example, settings where the first line reads

   `status is revision3`

   and the second line reads

   `done is 1.00`

   will return all Design Notes for which both conditions are true. Currently, there is no way to perform an "or" type search.

7. Click OK when you're done.

8. Choose Run to execute the search.

Of all the criteria options — `is`, `is not`, `contains`, and so on — available in the Report Settings dialog box for Design Notes, the most powerful is `matches regex`. Regular Expressions are a pattern-matching mechanism and, as such, are extremely flexible. The syntax, however, is unique and requires a bit of use before it becomes second nature. Here are some examples you might find useful:

Regular Expression	Matches
`.*`	Any text
`[^.]`	An empty string
`\d`	Any single number
`[0-5]`	Any digit from 0 to 5
`graphics|code`	Either the word `graphics` or the word `code`

Collaborating with Macromedia Sitespring

Macromedia's Sitespring offers an integrated way to stay on top of your team projects. Sitespring includes client Web sites, task reporting, hour tracking, version control, and a very snazzy way to keep up with all those tasks directly inside Dreamweaver with the Sitespring panel, shown in Figure 31-14.

Figure 31-14: Use the Sitespring panel to log into the Sitespring server for your team.

To begin using Sitespring, simply enter the Sitespring URL and your user name and password. You should have been shown the Sitespring URL once the Sitespring installation completed.

Once you've successfully logged in, you'll see all tasks currently assigned to you, in alphabetical order, as shown in Figure 31-15.

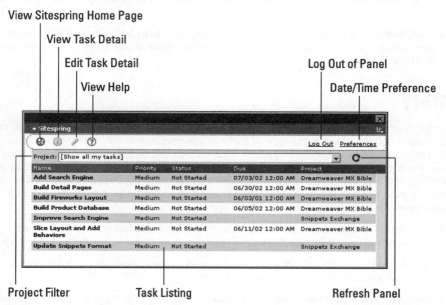

Figure 31-15: After you log in, Sitespring offers you a comperehensive view of all your assigned tasks.

Sitespring offers a lot of information and functionality in a compact space.

✦ **View Sitespring Home Page:** Clicking the globe icon takes you to the Sitespring URL you entered when you logged in to the panel. You may have to log in to the site again.

✦ **View Task Detail:** This option is available only if a task is currently selected. Click a task and then click View Task Detail to open the task on the Sitespring server in a new browser window.

✦ **Edit Task Detail:** This option is available only if a task is currently selected. Click a task and then click Edit Task Detail to open the Edit Task page on the Sitespring server in a new browser window.

✦ **View Help:** The help page in the Sitespring panel gives you a URL to the Sitespring page on Macromedia.com, as well as a link to a detailed help section on Macromedia.com.

✦ **Log Out:** This simply logs you out of the panel and takes you back to the log in screen, where you can log back in as another user if necessary.

✦ **Preferences:** The preferences page allows you to change your date and time preferences, including date format and whether to show standard or 24-hour time.

✦ **Project Filter:** The Project list menu shows you all the projects you currently have access to. Click the list menu and choose a project to filter your task listing to show only tasks associated with that project. Choose [Show all my tasks] to cancel the filter.

✦ **Refresh:** Click Refresh to request an updated list of tasks from the Sitespring server. If you've edited a task on the Sitespring server, you need to click Refresh to update your panel.

✦ **Task Listing:** And finally, the meat of the panel, the Task Listing includes the name of the task, priority, status, due date, and associated project. Click the column headings to sort the listing.

Summary

The expression "many hands make light work" certainly applies to Web site production and maintenance — but without some type of authoring management, the "many hands" may soon create a disaster. Dreamweaver offers both built-in and industry-standard authoring management solutions to aid in the development of Web sites. In addition to the precautions against overwriting files, Dreamweaver includes several other key features to help with team communication and to keep those many hands working together. To get the most out of Dreamweaver for your team, keep the following points in mind:

✦ In order for Dreamweaver's standard Check In/Check Out feature to be effective, everybody on the team must have the system engaged and in use for all file transfers.

✦ Dreamweaver can tie into existing development projects through the Visual SourceSafe integration or the WebDAV standard support.

✦ Metadata — information about information — about a project can be tied to any Web page or Web object through Dreamweaver's Design Notes feature. Again, to get the most out of this feature, it is essential that all team members use Dreamweaver's Site panel to manage their files.

✦ Dreamweaver includes interactive report capabilities that enable team members to quickly check the status of various HTML and workflow conditions, which can, if necessary, enable them to open a file directly for repair.

In the next chapter, you learn about working with XML in Dreamweaver.

✦　　✦　　✦

Integrating with XML

XML, short for Extensible Markup Language, is quickly becoming a powerful force on the Web and an important technology for Web designers to master. XML enables designers to define the parts of any document—from Web page to invoice—in terms of how those parts are used. When a document is defined by its structure, rather than its appearance, as it is with HTML, the same document can be read by a wide variety of systems and put to use far more efficiently.

Dreamweaver adds *Roundtrip XML* as a complement to its Roundtrip HTML core philosophy. Roundtrip HTML ensures that the defined tags of HTML remain just as you've written them. With XML, no one defined set of tags exists—XML tags can be written for an industry, a company, or just a Web site. Roundtrip XML permits Web designers to export and import XML pages based on their own structure.

You can find XML all throughout Dreamweaver, just under the hood. The Design Notes feature is based on XML, as is the completely customizable menu system and even the HTML Styles feature. The Third-party Tags file is pure XML and can describe any kind of tag. In fact, you can use XML to describe most anything, even HTML. This chapter explores the basics of XML, as well as the implementation of Roundtrip XML in Dreamweaver.

Understanding XML

XML is to structure what Cascading Style Sheets (CSS) are to format. Whereas Cascading Style Sheets control the look of a particular document on the Web, XML makes the document's intent paramount. Because there are almost as many ways to describe the parts of documents as there are types of documents, a set language, such as HTML, could never provide enough specification to be truly useful. This is why, with XML, you create your own custom tags to describe the page—XML is truly an extensible language.

XML became a W3C Recommendation in February 1998, after a relatively brief two-year study. The speed with which the recommendation was approved speaks to the need for the technology. XML has been described as a more accessible version of SGML (Standard Generalized Markup Language), the widely used text processing standard. In fact, the XML Working Group that drafted the W3C Recommendation started out as the SGML Working Group.

What can XML do that HTML can't? Suppose you have a shipping order that you want to distribute. With HTML, each of the parts of the document — such as the billing address, the shipping address, and the order details, to name a few — are enclosed in tags that describe their appearance, like this:

```
<h2 align="center"><bold>Invoice</bold></h2>
<p align="left">Ship to:</p>
<p>J. Lowery<br>
101 101st Avenue, Ste. 101<br>
New York, NY 10000</p>
```

With XML, each section of the page is given its own set of tags, according to its meaning, as follows:

```
<documentType>Invoice</documentType>
<ship-toHeader>Ship to:</ship-toHeader>
<customer>J. Lowery<br></customer>
<ship-toAddress>101 101st Avenue, Ste. 101<br>
New York, NY 10000</ship-toAddress>
```

Like HTML, XML is a combination of content and markup tags. Markup tags can be in pairs, such as `<customer>. . .</customer>`, or they can be singular. A single tag is called an *empty tag* because no content is included. Single tags in XML must include an ending slash — as in `<noTax/>`, for example — and are used to mark where something occurs. Here, `<noTax/>` indicates that no sales tax is to be applied to this invoice.

Also like HTML, XML tags can include attributes and values. As with HTML, XML attributes further describe the tag, much like an adjective describes a noun. For example, another way to write the `<ship-toHeader>` tag would be as follows:

```
<header type="Ship To">
```

With a more generalized tag such as this one, you could easily change values, as in `<header type="Bill To">`, rather than include another new tag.

In all, XML recognizes six kinds of markup:

✦ **Elements:** Elements are more commonly known as *tags* and, as in HTML, are delimited by a set of angle brackets `<>`. As noted previously, elements can also have attributes set to particular values.

Caution   While it's possible not to surround values with quotes in HTML — such as in `color=white` — quotes are mandatory in XML.

✦ **Entity references:** Certain characters in XML, such as the delimiting angle brackets, are reserved in order to permit markup to be recognized. These characters are represented by entities in XML. As in HTML, character entities begin with an ampersand and end with a semicolon. For example `&lt;Content&gt;` is XML code to represent `<Content>`.

✦ **Comments:** XML comments are identical to HTML comments; they both begin with `<!--` and end with `-->`.

✦ **Processing instructions:** XML processing instructions are similar to server-side includes in that the XML processor (like the server) passes them on to the application (like the browser).

✦ **Marked sections:** XML can pass blocks of code or other data without parsing the markup and content. These blocks of character data are marked with `<![CDATA[` at the beginning and `]]>` at the end:

```
<![CDATA[If age < 19 and age > 6, then the kids are in ⤶
school]]>
```

Communication between XML and HTML is greatly eased because large blocks of data can be passed in this fashion.

✦ **Document type declarations:** Because every XML document is capable of containing its own set of custom tags, a method for defining these tags must exist. Although a discussion of the formats of such document-type declarations is beyond the scope of this book, it's helpful to know that such declarations can be made for elements, attributes, character entities, and notations. Notations refer to external binary data, such as GIFs, that are passed through the XML parser to the application.

XML documents may begin with an XML declaration that specifies the version of XML being used. The XML declaration for a document compliant with the 1.0 specification looks like the following:

```
<?xml version="1.0"?>
```

A much more detailed document type declaration (DTD), in which each tag and attribute is described in SGML, is also possible. XML documents including these types of DTDs are labeled *valid XML documents*. Other documents that respect the rules of XML regarding nesting of tags and other matters, but don't include DTDs for the elements, are known as *well-formed XML*. Dreamweaver exports well-formed XML documents, but can import either well-formed or valid XML.

Exporting XML

How do you make an XML page? Well, you can use File ➪ New and choose XML from the Basic category, or you can convert an existing document into XML format with one command. Currently, Dreamweaver creates its XML pages based on a template's editable regions. With this approach, the true content of a page — what distinguishes it from all other pages of the same type — can be separated and applied independently of the original Web page. In other words, once the XML information is gathered from a Web page, it can be imported into any other application to be displayed, read, spoken, translated, or acted upon.

Cross-Reference To get a better idea of how to use XML, you need to understand Dreamweaver templates, which are discussed in Chapter 28.

Dreamweaver templates are composed of *locked* and *editable* regions; the locked regions are repeated for each page created from the template, whereas the content in the editable regions is added per page. The connection between XML and templates is similar to the relationship between a database form and its data. In a database, each field has a unique name, such as LastName, FirstName, and so on. When you create a database form to present the data, the placeholders for the data use the same field names. Then, when data from one record flows into the form, the information from the field goes into the areas with the corresponding field names. Likewise, each editable region has a unique name — in essence, a field name. The content within the editable region is the field's data. When exported as an XML file, the name of the editable region is converted to an XML tag that surrounds its data.

For example, Figure 32-1 shows a Dreamweaver template for a purchase order. On the left are the headings (To, Company, Address, and so on) for the information in a locked area, while the specific shipping data on the right resides in a series of editable regions, each with its own name.

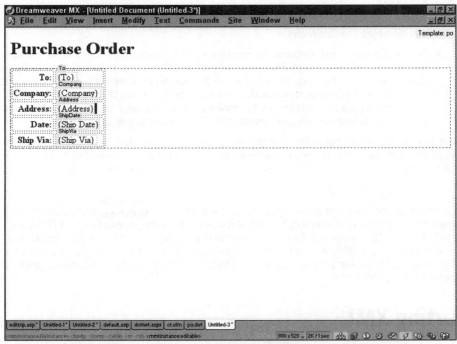

Figure 32-1: Dreamweaver MX creates XML pages based on templates and editable regions. This template is now ready to be exported as an XML file.

When exported as XML by Dreamweaver, the resulting XML file looks like the following:

```
<?xml version="1.0"?>
<po template="/Templates/po.dwt" codeOutsideHTMLIsLocked="false">
    <ShipDate><![CDATA[10 Oct 2002]]></ShipDate>
    <doctitle><![CDATA[
<title>Purchase Order</title>
]]></doctitle>
    <head></head>
    <Address><![CDATA[1234 AnyStreet<br>
        Anytown, USA]]></Address>
    <ShipVia><![CDATA[UPS]]></ShipVia>
    <Company><![CDATA[John's Does]]></Company>
    <To><![CDATA[John Doe]]></To>
</po>
```

Note several important items about the XML file. First, notice the use of self-evident labels for each of the tags, such as <Company> and <ShipVia>; such names make it easy to understand an XML file. Even the one tag not based on a user-defined name, <doctitle>, is straightforward. Second, all the data included in the XML tags is marked as a CDATA area; this ensures that the information is conveyed intact, just as it was entered. Finally, if you look at the <Address> tag data, you see that even HTML tags (here, a <br> tag) are included in the CDATA blocks. This practice enables basic formatting to be carried over from one page to the next. You can avoid this by selecting just the inner content — without any of the formatting tags — to be marked as an editable region.

Dreamweaver can create one of two different types of XML tags during its export operation. The first is referred to as *Dreamweaver Standard XML* and uses an <item> tag with a name attribute set to the editable region's name. For example, if the editable region were named ShipVia, the Dreamweaver Standard tag would be

```
<item name="ShipVia">Content</item>
```

The Dreamweaver Standard XML file has one other distinguishing characteristic. The XML file is saved with a reference to the defining Dreamweaver template, like this:

```
<templateItems template="/Templates/PO.dwt">
```

When importing a Dreamweaver Standard XML file, if the specified template cannot be found, a dialog box appears asking that you select another template.

The other option is to use what Dreamweaver refers to as *Editable Region Name tags*. This method uses the editable region names themselves as tags. In the case of the editable region name ShipVia, the tag pair under this method would be <ShipVia>. . .</ShipVia>.

To create an XML file from within Dreamweaver, follow these steps:

1. Open a Dreamweaver document based on a template that has at least one editable region.

2. Choose File ➪ Export ➪ Export Editable Regions As XML.

   The Export Template Data as XML dialog box opens, as shown in Figure 32-2.

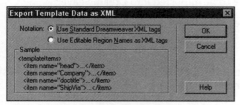

Figure 32-2: Convert any template-based page to an XML document with the Export Template Data as XML dialog box.

3. Choose the format for the XML tags by selecting one of the Notation options:

   • **Use Standard Dreamweaver XML tags:** Select this option to produce <item> tags with name attributes set to the names of the editable regions.

   • **Use Editable Region Names as XML tags:** Select this option to produce XML tags that use the editable region names directly.

   Selecting either option displays sample tags in the Sample area of the dialog box.

4. Select OK when you're done.

An Export Editable Regions as XML Save File dialog box appears.

5. Enter the path and name of the XML file you wish to save in the File Name text box. Click Save when you're done.

Importing XML

As part of Roundtrip XML, Dreamweaver MX includes an Import XML command. Like the Export XML command, Import XML works with Dreamweaver templates. The content information in the XML document fills out the editable regions in the template, much as data fills out a form in a database.

With this import capability, content can be independently created and stored in an XML file and then, to publish the page to the Web, simply imported into the Dreamweaver template.

To be imported, XML files must follow one of the two structures used when exporting a template to XML: Standard Dreamweaver XML or Editable Region Names used as XML tags. Although it's a matter of personal preference, I find the Editable Region Names format to be easier to read and, in general, simpler to work with.

Note When you're importing XML files, make sure that the XML files you're importing have the necessary template declarations in order for Dreamweaver to find the appropriate template it needs to format the incoming data.

How does one create a file from the XML? Naturally, you could open a template for your XML document and fill in the data by hand—but that, in a sense, defeats the purpose of automating your workflow via XML. A more efficient scenario is to use a database to accept and store content; the database entry form could easily be accessible over a network or over the Internet. A report, generated by the database application, blends the content data and the XML structure, resulting in an XML file to be imported into Dreamweaver.

To import an XML file into a Dreamweaver template, follow these steps:

1. If desired, open a file based on a Dreamweaver template.

Tip You don't have to have a page created from a template open in order to access the XML information—Dreamweaver automatically opens one for you.

2. Choose File ➪ Import XML into Template.

The Import XML dialog box opens.

Caution Any existing information in the Dreamweaver document in the editable regions is replaced by the information in the corresponding tags of the XML document.

3. Select an XML file from the Import XML dialog box.

4. Choose Open when you're done.

The XML file is imported into Dreamweaver, and the editable region placeholder names are replaced with the data in the XML document.

Building Your Own XML Files

Dreamweaver now supports editing XML files directly in the Dreamweaver interface. There is no Design view, but Dreamweaver code coloring and syntax checking can make writing your own XML files much easier.

In order to take full advantage of Dreamweaver's code editing features, you should set up all the tags you'll need to create your XML files using Tag Libraries. If you use the last template file as an example, you could define a set of XML tags for describing your purchase order details.

Cross-Reference   To find out how to define your own tag libraries, see the section on the Tag Library Editor in Chapter 33.

Figure 32-3 shows the XML tags defined for the Purchase Order XML files. You can even specify attributes for each of the tags. Now typing <address in Code view will bring up the attributes you've defined, and adding the trailing > will add the closing </address> tag.

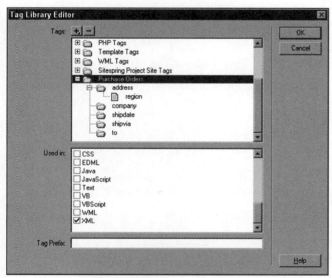

Figure 32-3: With Dreamweaver's Tag Library Editor, you can completely customize the crafting of new XML files.

Summary

XML is a vital future technology that is knocking on the door of virtually every Web designer in business. As the development tools become more common, the Roundtrip XML capability within Dreamweaver makes interfacing with this new method of communication straightforward and effortless. Keep the following points in mind:

✦ XML (Extensible Markup Language) enables content to be separated from the style of a Web page, creating information that can be more easily used in various situations with different kinds of media.

✦ Tags in XML reflect the nature of the content, rather than its appearance.

✦ Dreamweaver includes a Roundtrip XML facility that makes it possible to export and import XML files through Dreamweaver templates.

✦ Use Tag Libraries to create custom XML tags and take advantage of Dreamweaver's Code Hints and Code Completion.

In the next chapter you'll learn about customizing Dreamweaver, including the new tag libraries.

✦　　✦　　✦

Extending
Dreamweaver

Customizing Dreamweaver

◆ ◆ ◆ ◆

In This Chapter

Automating Web development with commands

Including custom XML tags

Examining new Property inspectors

Dreamweaver Techniques: Useful command routines

Modifying keyboard shortcuts

Expanding Dreamweaver's core functionality

Translating server-side content

◆ ◆ ◆ ◆

The Web is a dynamic environment, with new technologies continually emerging. Until recently, HTML standards were changing every year or so, and even now, products are routinely introduced that use the Web as a jumping-off place for new methods and tools. Keeping pace with the constantly shifting work environment of the Web was beyond the capabilities of any suite of Web authoring tools, much less a single one — until Dreamweaver debuted, of course.

The initial version of Dreamweaver had a high degree of extensibility built right in, with its customizable HTML objects and JavaScript behaviors. Macromedia continues to enhance this flexibility with each release. With the implementation of the W3C Document Object Model and a tremendous number of new API functions, objects and behaviors have been beefed up so that they are much more powerful than ever. In addition, Dreamweaver presents a host of ways to extend its power. Here are just some of the options:

- ✦ **Menus:** The entire Dreamweaver menu system is completely customizable. You can add context menu items, rearrange the main menu, and even add completely new menus, all by modifying a single XML file.

- ✦ **Keyboard shortcuts:** Macromedia makes it easy to use the same keyboard shortcuts across its product line — even extending that ease to other products — with the Keyboard Shortcut editor. In addition to adopting the most comfortable set of key combinations, shortcuts for individual commands can be personalized.

- ✦ **Commands:** Commands are JavaScript and HTML code that manipulate the Web page during the design phase, much as behaviors are triggered at runtime.

- ✦ **Custom tags:** With the rapid rise of XML, custom tag support becomes essential in a professional Web authoring tool. Dreamweaver gives you the power to create any custom tag and control how it displays in the Document window.

- ✦ **Property inspectors:** Custom Property inspectors go hand-in-hand with custom tags, enabling the straightforward entry of attributes and values in a manner consistent with the Dreamweaver user interface.

✦ **Custom panels:** Dreamweaver enables you to create custom panels that supplement its panoply of built-in panels.

✦ **Translators:** Translators enable server-side content to be viewed in the Document window at design time, as well as in the browser at runtime.

✦ **C-level extensions:** Some special uses require a root-level addition to Dreamweaver's capabilities. Macromedia's engineers have "popped the hood" on Dreamweaver and made it possible for a C or C++ language library to interface with it through C-level extensions.

✦ **Custom toolbars and objects:** The Document toolbar and Insert bar are now fully extensible, enabling quick and easy access to your most frequently used Dreamweaver objects and commands.

✦ **Tag libraries:** Dreamweaver enables you to create, edit, and delete tag libraries.

Although a few of these extension features require programming skills beyond those of the typical Web designer, most are well within the reach of an HTML- and JavaScript-savvy coder. Moreover, the Keyboard Shortcut editor employs a graphical user interface, making it accessible to all. As with behaviors and objects, the source code for all but the C-level extensions is readily available and serves as an excellent training ground. This chapter, combined with these standard scripts, provides all the tools you need to begin carving out your own personalized version of Dreamweaver.

Adding New Commands

By their very nature, objects and behaviors are single-purpose engines. A custom object inserts a single block of HTML into the `<body>` of a Web page, while custom behaviors add JavaScript functions to the `<head>` and attributes of one tag. Commands, on the other hand, are multifaceted, multipurpose, go-anywhere and do-anything mechanisms. Commands can do everything objects and behaviors can do — and more. In fact, commands can even masquerade as objects.

For all their power, however, commands are one of the most accessible of the Dreamweaver extensions. This section describes the basic structure of commands, as well as how to use the standard commands that ship with Dreamweaver. You can also find information about how to create your own commands and control their integration into Dreamweaver.

Understanding Dreamweaver commands

When I first encountered commands, I thought, "Great! Dreamweaver now has a macro language." I envisioned instantly automating simple Web design tasks. Before long, I realized that commands are even more powerful — and a bit trickier — than a macro recorder. Dreamweaver's adoption of the W3C Document Object Model (DOM) is one of the factors that make commands feasible. The DOM in Dreamweaver makes available, or *exposes*, every part of the HTML page — every tag, every attribute, every bit of content — which can then be read, modified, deleted, or added to. Moreover, Dreamweaver commands can open, read, and modify other files on local systems.

A command can have a parameter form or not, depending on how the command was written. Generally, commands are listed in the Commands menu, but by altering the menus.xml file (as discussed later on in this chapter under "Adjusting the menus.xml file"), you can cause your command to appear as part of any other menu — or to not appear at all. Because one command can call another, such hidden commands are more easily modified.

My original vision of a macro recorder came true with the commands Start Recording and Play Recorded Command. Now, any onscreen action can be instantly logged and replayed—and through the History panel, even converted into a permanent, repeatable command.

So how, specifically, are commands being used? The following list describes some of the commands that have been built by Web designers outside of Macromedia:

- ✦ **Tag Stripper:** Removes all instances of any tag from a Web page. By Massimo Foti.

- ✦ **Breadcrumbs:** Automatically adds navigation elements on a page. By Paul Davis.

- ✦ **Borderless Frames:** Sets all frames in a frameset to no borders. By Massimo Foti.

- ✦ **Add Old Browser Message:** Inserts a message that can be seen only by browsers that do not support the W3C DOM. By Rachel Andrews.

- ✦ **Replicator:** Duplicates any selected element any number of times. By this book's author, Joseph Lowery.

As should be obvious from this list, commands come close to being limited only by the author's imagination.

For further evidence of just how useful commands can be, we'll look at a few of Dreamweaver's standard commands next.

Dreamweaver MX comes with 11 standard commands that, in addition to adding some extra functionality, give you a taste of just how powerful commands can be. You can find a full description of them in Chapter 3.

The Apply Source Formatting and Apply Source Formatting to Selection commands

All the code created by Dreamweaver is structured according to the current Tag Library settings. The Tag Library identifies which codes are indented and which are on their own line, as well as numerous other specifications regarding HTML writing. Occasionally, a Web designer must work with Web pages created earlier or by other designers using other programs, or even by hand. The Apply Source Formatting and Apply Source Formatting to Selection commands can rewrite the original code—of an entire Web page or selected part of the page, respectively—so that it is structured according to the current Tag Library settings. The more accustomed your eye is to following Dreamweaver-style HTML, the more you value this command.

You'll learn more about the Tag Library feature later in this chapter.

The Apply Source Formatting and Apply Source Formatting to Selection commands are examples of Dreamweaver commands that don't display dialog boxes to gather the user's selected parameters—because there are no parameters to set. To invoke the commands, choose Commands ➪ Apply Source Formatting or Commands ➪ Apply Source Formatting to Selection. The commands are applied immediately, with no confirmation or feedback indicating that they are complete. To verify their execution, you have to sneak a peek at your source code.

The Clean Up HTML and Clean Up XHTML commands

Dreamweaver tends to produce compact, uncluttered HTML/XHTML code, which is not always the case for other HTML/XHTML editors and hand-coded efforts. One of the most common problems is redundant <font> tags, which can result when you select some text, change the font, change the font size, and, finally, change the font color. The resulting code is likely to resemble the following:

```
<font face="Arial"><font size="4"><font color="green">
Bonanza!</font></font></font>
```

The Clean Up HTML and Clean Up XHTML commands are custom made to consolidate redundant tags and to remove some of the code clutter that can accumulate during a page's design. In all, you have seven different cleaning operations from which to choose. Note that the Clean Up HTML and Clean Up XHTML commands are applicable only to the current page and cannot be applied sitewide.

XHTML syntax is much less forgiving than HTML; your XHTML code must be nearly perfect to work correctly. The Clean Up XHTML command fixes XHTML code syntax errors, lowercases all tag attributes, and adds (or reports) missing required tag attributes.

To use the Clean Up HTML or Clean Up XHTML commands, follow these steps:

1. Load the desired HTML or XHTML document in your Dreamweaver workspace.

2. Choose Commands ➪ Clean Up HTML (for an HTML document) or Commands ➪ Clean Up XHTML (for an XHTML document).

   The Clean Up HTML / XHTML dialog box appears, as shown in Figure 33-1.

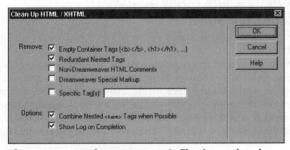

Figure 33-1: Reduce your page's file size and make your HTML more readable with the Clean Up HTML / XHTML command.

3. Choose from these options in the dialog box:

   • To delete empty tag pairs with no code between them (such as <b></b>), select the Remove: Empty Container Tags option.

   • To eliminate superfluous tags that repeat the same code as the tags surrounding them, as in this example

   ```
   <font color="white">And the <font color=
   "white">truth</font>
   is plain to see.</font>
   ```

   select the Remove: Redundant Nested Tags option.

- To delete any HTML comments that were not created by Dreamweaver to mark a Library or Template item, select Remove: Non-Dreamweaver HTML Comments.

- To clear all Dreamweaver-specific comments, such as

  ```
  <!-- #BeginEditable "openingPara" -->
  ```

  select the Remove: Dreamweaver Special Markup option.

- To erase any specific tag(s) and all its attributes, select the Remove: Specific Tag(s) option and type the tag name(s) in the text box.

Note

Enter tag names without angle brackets; separate multiple tags with a comma. For example: `font, blink`.

- To consolidate `<font>` tags, select the Combine Nested `<font>` Tags when Possible option.

- To view a report of the changes applied to your document, select the Show Log on Completion option.

4. Click OK when you're finished.

Dreamweaver performs the actions requested on the current document. If the Show Log option has been selected, an alert displays the changes made, if any.

Recording and replaying commands

I'm a big fan of any kind of work-related automation, and consider myself a power user of word processing macros, so you can imagine my delight when a similar capability was added to Dreamweaver. The capability to record your onscreen actions and then replay them instantly—with the option of saving them as a command or simply pasting them into another document—is a tremendous work-saver. Nearly every onscreen action can be replicated.

How could you use such a macro-like capability in Dreamweaver? Suppose you have a series of 10 images on a page, and you want to give each of them a vertical space of 10, a horizontal space of 8, and a 2-pixel border. You could perform each of these actions one at a time, entering in the same border value and selecting the center alignment button, but it would get rather tedious after the third or fourth image. With Dreamweaver, you can easily automate the procedure:

1. Select the first image.

2. Choose Commands ➪ Start Recording or use the keyboard shortcut, Ctrl+Shift+X (Command+Shift+X).

   The cursor changes to a recording tape symbol, indicating you're in recording mode.

3. Enter the new values in the Property inspector.

4. Choose Commands ➪ Stop or the same keyboard command again: Ctrl+Shift+X (Command+Shift+X). The cursor changes back to its normal state.

5. Select another image.

6. Choose Commands ➪ Play Recorded Command.

7. Repeat Steps 5 and 6 for every image you want to change, as shown in Figure 33-2.

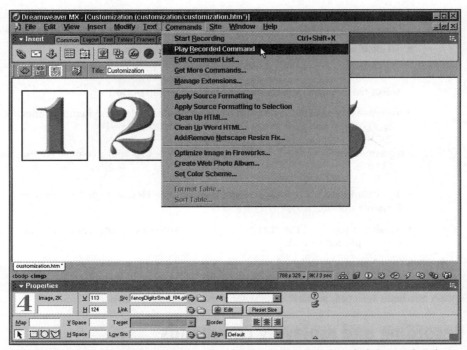

Figure 33-2: After the steps for formatting the first image are recorded, formatting the other images is a one-step process with Dreamweaver's command recorder.

Most of the commands and onscreen moves can be replicated in this manner, but not always. The major exception is the use of the mouse. Dreamweaver cannot repeat mouse moves and selections. You could not, for example, begin to create a drop-cap by recording the drag selection of the first letter in each paragraph. You can, however, use the arrow keys and any keyboard-related combination.

For example, suppose that you have this standard list of names in your document:

```
Joseph Lowery
Andrew Wooldridge
Al Sparber
Simon White
Derren Whiteman
```

You want to change these names to a *Lastname, Firstname* format. To make this change with command recording, use the following procedure:

1. Position your cursor at the beginning of the first name.

2. Choose Commands ⇨ Start Recording.

3. Press Ctrl+Shift+right arrow (Command+Shift+right arrow) to select the first word.

   Dreamweaver highlights the first word and the following space.

4. Press Ctrl+X (Command+X) to cut the selected word.

5. Press End to move to the end of the line.

6. Type a comma and a space.

7. Press Ctrl+V (Command+V) to paste the previously cut word.

8. Press the backspace key to remove the trailing space.

    Now that the first line is complete, it's important to position the cursor to perform the recorded command again.

9. Press the right arrow to move to the start of the next line.

    Because the cursor was left at the end of the last line, the right-arrow key moves it to the front of the following line.

10. Choose Commands ⇨ Stop Recording.

11. Choose Commands ⇨ Play Recorded Command for each name in the list.

If you try to include a mouse move or selection when recording a command or playing back a recorded command, Dreamweaver issues a warning and asks if you'd like to stop recording. If you choose to continue, Dreamweaver ignores the attempted mouse move and resets the pointer in its previous position.

Tip   If you try to record your navigations around a table, Dreamweaver does not record the Tab or Shift+Tab keys. However, you can still record your table moves by using Home and End in combination with the arrow keys; note that this works in Standard view only, not in Layout view. To move from cell to cell, from left to right, press End and then the right arrow. To move right to left, press Home and then the left arrow. You can also move up and down columns by pressing Home or End and then either the up or the down arrow.

Recorded actions are maintained in memory, and when you issue the Start Recording command again, the previously recorded steps are replaced. You can, however, convert recorded steps to a command to use repeatedly in any document or site you'd like by using the History panel:

1. Record a series of actions as described previously.

2. Play the recorded actions at least once by choosing Commands ⇨ Play Recorded Command.

    On the History panel, the collective recorded actions are displayed as a single step, Run Command.

3. In the History panel, select the desired Run Command item. (There might be more than one Run Command in your History list; if so, make sure you select the right one.)

4. Select the Save Selected Steps as a Command button from the bottom of the History panel.

New commands saved in this manner are dynamically added to the Commands menu.

Multiuser System Customization

Starting with the MX version, Dreamweaver is compatible with multiuser operating systems including Windows NT, 2000, and XP, as well as Macintosh OS X. This compatibility means that multiple users can work with a single installation of the program yet maintain their own preferences and configuration. Moreover, network administrators can maintain a group of common settings for all Dreamweaver users on the network.

To achieve such flexibility, Dreamweaver maintains customized files in a special folder for each user. These folders are stored in different locations according to the operating system. Under multiuser systems, the folders are within the specified user folder, designated by the user's ID or login name as shown in the following examples:

- ✦ **Windows 98 and Windows ME, multiuser system:** C:\Windows\Profiles*User ID*\ Application Data\Macromedia\Dreamweaver MX

- ✦ **Windows NT 4:** C:\WINNT\Profiles*User ID*\Application Data\Macromedia\ Dreamweaver MX

- ✦ **Windows 2000 and Windows XP:** C:\Documents and Settings*User ID*\ Application Data\Macromedia\Dreamweaver MX

- ✦ **Windows 98 and Windows ME, single-user system:** C:\Windows\Application Data\ Macromedia\Dreamweaver MX

- ✦ **Mac OS X:** Macintosh HD/Users/*User ID*/Library/Application Support/Macromedia/ Dreamweaver MX

- ✦ **Mac OS 9.1 or later, single-user system:** Macintosh HD:System Folder:Application Support:Macromedia:Dreamweaver MX

- ✦ **Mac OS Mac 9.1 or later, multiuser system, regular user:** Macintosh HD:Users: *User ID*:Preferences:Macromedia:Dreamweaver MX

- ✦ **Mac OS Mac 9.1 or later, multiuser system, administrator (Owner):** Macintosh HD:System Folder:Application Support:Macromedia:Dreamweaver MX

In these examples, Windows systems are shown using drive C:, whereas Macintosh users use the Macintosh HD drive; naturally, the drive letter or name may be different if another system drive is used.

All custom extensions installed by Dreamweaver — either by the features in the program itself, such as the History panel's Save Selected Steps as a Command feature, or by the Extension Manager — are automatically inserted in the proper multiuser folder. Folders are created on an as-needed basis; you won't see an Inspectors folder in your multiuser Configuration folder unless an inspector extension is installed.

In fact, you may need to take one additional step before any user folders are visible. Certain folders — particularly those dealing with system administration — are hidden by default in Windows operating systems. To gain access to such files, open Windows Explorer and set the Folder Options to show hidden files and folders.

Scripting commands

Commands, as with most behaviors, are a combination of JavaScript functions and HTML forms; the HTML provides the user interface for any parameters that need to be set, and JavaScript carries out the particular command. Although you can combine both languages in a single HTML file, many programmers, including those from Macromedia, keep the JavaScript in a separate .js file that is incorporated in the HTML file with a `<script>` tag, as shown in the following example:

```
<script language="javascript" src="Clean Up HTML.js">
```

This separation enables easy modification of the user interface and the underlying code, and the sharing of the JavaScript functions.

Commands are very open-ended. In fact, only two Dreamweaver functions are specific to commands — `canAcceptCommand()` and `commandButtons()` — and neither function is required. Two other command-oriented functions, `receiveArguments()` and `windowDimensions()`, are also used elsewhere, but again, neither is required.

Cross-Reference The DOM in Dreamweaver is covered in great detail in Chapter 35.

The `canAcceptCommand()` function controls when the command is active in the menus and when it is dimmed. If `canAcceptCommand()` is not defined, the command is always available. This function returns true or false; if false is returned, the command is dimmed in the menus.

You can see `canAcceptCommand()` in action in both the Sort Table and Format Table commands. For either of these commands to be effective, a table must be indicated. Rather than require that a table be selected, the `canAcceptCommand()` function calls a subroutine, `findTable()`, which returns true if the user's cursor is positioned inside a table:

```
function canAcceptCommand(){
  if (dw.getDocumentDOM() == null)
    return false;
  else if (dw.getDocumentDOM().getShowLayoutView())
    return false;
  else if (findTable())
    return true;
  else
    return false;
}

function findTable(){
  var tableObj="";
  var selObj = dw.getDocumentDOM().getSelectedNode();

  while (tableObj=="" && selObj.parentNode){
    if (selObj.nodeType == Node.ELEMENT_NODE && selObj.tagName=="TABLE")
    tableObj=selObj;
  else
    selObj = selObj.parentNode;
  }
  return tableObj;
}
```

Macromedia recommends that the `canAcceptCommand()` function not be defined unless at least one case exists in which the command should not be available. Otherwise, the function is asked to run for no purpose, which degrades performance.

The `commandButtons()` function defines the buttons that appear on the parameter form to the right. This expanded functionality is extremely useful when developing commands. Some commands require that an operation be enabled to run repeatedly and not just the one time an OK button is selected. As noted earlier, you don't have to declare the function at all, in which case the form expands to fill the dialog box entirely. If you do not use this standard Dreamweaver method for creating your command buttons, in most cases you'll need to define them yourself.

Each button that is declared has a function associated with it, which is executed when the user selects that particular button. All the buttons for a command are listed in an array, returned by `commandButtons()`. The following example declares three buttons: OK, Cancel, and Help:

```
function commandButtons() {
    return new Array("OK","goCommand()","Cancel",
                    "window.close()","Help","displayHelp()")
}
```

Notice that two of the buttons, OK and Help, call user-defined functions, but the Cancel button simply calls a built-in JavaScript function to close the window. While there are no limitations on the number of buttons a parameter form can hold, you should always strive to keep your parameter forms as simple and uncluttered as possible.

The `receiveArguments()` function is used in conjunction with `runCommand()`. Whenever `runCommand()` calls a specific command—from a behavior, object, or other command—it can pass arguments. If `receiveArguments()` is set up, that is the function executed, and the arguments are read into `receiveArguments()`. This function enables the same command to be called from different sources and have different effects, depending on the arguments passed. The `receiveArguments()` function is used extensively in menu commands and is explained more fully later in this chapter under "Building menu commands."

As with behaviors and objects, you can use the `windowDimensions()` function with commands to set a specific size for the associated dialog box. If `windowDimensions()` is not defined, the size of the dialog box is set automatically. Macromedia recommends that `windowDimensions()` not be used unless your parameter form exceeds 640 × 480.

The remainder of the user interface for a command—the parameter form—is constructed in the same manner, using the same tools that are used for objects and behaviors. A command parameter form or dialog box uses an HTML `<form>` in the `<body>` of the file. If no `<form>` is declared, the command executes without displaying a dialog box. All of the form elements used in objects—text boxes, radio buttons, checkboxes, and lists—are available in commands.

Cross-Reference   For detailed information about how to retrieve information in a parameter form, see Chapter 35.

Dreamweaver Techniques: Useful command routines

When programming a command, I often get stuck on one small point. "If only I knew how to _____, I'd be home free," is my usual refrain. The following routines and explanations will help you "fill in the blank" as you begin to construct your own custom commands.

Getting a user's selection

Although many commands work with the entire HTML document, some require just a portion of text or an object that has been selected by the user. While it seems a simple task, some quirks in the API make getting a selection a little tricky.

Selecting text

The usual method for determining — and acting on — what the user has selected requires the getSelection() function. As discussed in Chapter 35, getSelection() returns two-byte offsets that mark the beginning and end of the user's selection. The difficulty appears when you try to extract the character data that corresponds to those byte offsets. The offsetsToNode() function, which is used to make this translation, expands the offsets to the nearest tag — the innerHTML, in other words. For example, the following function attempts to get the user's selection and report it in an alert:

```
function testCase() {
    var theDom = dreamweaver.getDocumentDOM("document");
    var offsets = dreamweaver.getSelection();
    var theNode =
        dreamweaver.offsetsToNode(offsets[0],offsets[1]);
    var nodeText = theNode.data;
    alert(nodeText);
}
```

If a user selects the word "gray" in the line "The old gray mare just ain't what she used to be," the function returns the entire line. To get just what is selected, you need to use the nodeToOffsets() function in combination with offsetsToNode() and the JavaScript substring() function.

The example code in Listing 33-1 demonstrates the proper substring technique; it is taken from the Change Case command.

Listing 33-1: **Getting Selected Text**

```
function lowerCase(){
  var theDom = dreamweaver.getDocumentDOM("document");
  var offsets = dreamweaver.getSelection();
  var theNode =
      dreamweaver.offsetsToNode(offsets[0],offsets[1]);
  if (theNode.nodeType == Node.TEXT_NODE) {
    var nodeOffsets = dreamweaver.nodeToOffsets(theNode);
    offsets[0] = offsets[0] - nodeOffsets[0];
    offsets[1] = offsets[1] - nodeOffsets[0];
    var nodeText = theNode.data;
    theNode.data = nodeText.substring(0,offsets[0]) +
      nodeText.substring(offsets[0],offsets[1]).toLowerCase()
      + nodeText.substring(offsets[1], nodeText.length);
    window.close();
  }
  else { //it's not a TEXT_NODE
```

Continued

Listing 33-1: *(continued)*

```
    var nodeOffsets = dreamweaver.nodeToOffsets(theNode);
    offsets[0] = offsets[0] - nodeOffsets[0];
    offsets[1] = offsets[1] - nodeOffsets[0];
    var nodeText = theNode.innerHTML;
    theNode.innerHTML = nodeText.toLowerCase();
    window.close();
  }
}
```

Notice two conditions in the example lowerCase() function—either the selected string is text (a TEXT_NODE), or it's not. If the node is something other than a TEXT_NODE, the data property is not available, and innerHTML must be used instead. This situation occurs when a user selects an entire paragraph. In fact, all the user has to select is the last character before the closing tag—such as a period at the end of a paragraph—and the node type switches to ELEMENT_NODE.

Selecting objects

By comparison, you have far fewer hoops to jump through to reference a selected object: You only have to get its outerHTML property, as shown in Listing 33-2.

Listing 33-2: Getting a Selected Object

```
function replicate() {
  var theDom = dreamweaver.getDocumentDOM("document");
  var offsets = dreamweaver.getSelection();
  var selObj =
      dreamweaver.offsetsToNode(offsets[0],offsets[1]);
  if (selObj.nodeType == Node.TEXT_NODE) {
    helpMe2();
    window.close();
    return;
  }
  var theCode = selObj.outerHTML;
}
```

Listing 33-2 also includes a small error routine that checks whether the user's selection is text (selObj.nodeType == Node.TEXT_NODE) and, if so, uses helpMe2() (a custom function that must be defined elsewhere in the script) to put up an advisory and then closes the window to enable the user to reselect.

Using a command as an object

Commands offer a tremendous range of power and can perform actions not available to behaviors or objects. To take advantage of this power with a point-and-click interface, it's best to "disguise" your command as an object. As an object, your command appears in both the Insert bar and the Insert menu.

A Dreamweaver object usually consists of two files: an HTML file for the code and a GIF image for the button, all in the Configuration\Objects*Category* folder (the value of *Category* is the name of the folder that corresponds to the Insert bar category in which the object resides). When using a command as an object, however, you can have as many as five files split between the Configuration\Objects*Category* and Configuration\Commands folders. The standard Rollover object is a good example: three associated rollover files are in the Objects\Common folder, and two are in the Commands folder. (The Objects\Common subfolder alerts you to the fact that the Rollover object resides in the Common category of the Insert bar.) Here is how they are used:

✦ **Objects\Common\Rollover.gif:** The image for the Rollover button that appears in the Common category of the Insert bar

✦ **Objects\Common\Rollover.htm:** A shell file (called by the Rollover button) that reads Objects\Common\Rollover.js

✦ **Objects\Common\Rollover.js:** Contains the objectTag() function, which references the Commands\Rollover.htm file

✦ **Commands\Rollover.htm:** Builds the user interface for the "object" and reads all external JavaScript files, including Commands\Rollover.js

✦ **Commands\Rollover.js:** Contains the actual code for the function that performs the required operations, which returns its value to the Objects\Common\Rollover.htm file by way of the Objects\Common\Rollover.js file

The key to understanding how to use a command as an object is the code linking the two. In the Objects\Common\Rollover.js file is the objectTag(), which is used to write an object into an existing Web page with its return value. In this case, the function first gets the Document Object Model of the relevant command file (Commands\Rollover.htm); this procedure enables the current function to reference any variable set in the other file. Then the popupCommand is executed, which runs Commands\Rollover.htm — which, in turn, launches the dialog box and gets the user parameters. Finally, a result from that command is set to the return value of objectTag() and written into the HTML page. Here's the objectTag() function in its entirety from Objects\Common\Rollover.js:

```
function objectTag() {
  var rolloverTag = callCommand("Rollover.htm");
  if (rolloverTag) { //if inserting call, update behavior funcs as needed
  updateBehaviorFns("MM_findObj","MM_swapImgRestore",
                    "MM_preloadImages","MM_swapImage");
  }
  else {
    rolloverTag = '';
  }
  return(rolloverTag);
}
```

Some custom commands disguised as objects make the DOM connection in the command file, rather than the object file. All iCat objects (written to integrate a shopping cart into Dreamweaver), for example, establish the link in the primary functions of their command JavaScript files, in the following manner:

```
var dom = dreamweaver.getDocumentDOM("../Objects/iCat/Add To Cart.htm");
dom.parentWindow.icatTagStr = icatTagStr;
```

Then, the corresponding objectTag() function simply returns the icatTagStr variable.

Placing code in the <head> section

It's relatively straightforward to insert text wherever the cursor has been set in the document—you just set a text string equal to the [innerHTML | data] property of the DOM at that point. However, how do you insert code in the <head> section of a Web page, where the cursor is generally not found? Certain code, such as <script> tags that hold extensive JavaScript functions, must be inserted in the <head>. By design, behaviors return code specifically intended for the <script> tag—except you can't easily use a behavior to include a line such as the following:

```
<script language="Javascript" src="extend.js"></script>
```

You can insert such a line with commands, however, and this technique, developed by Dreamweaver extensions author Massimo Foti, shows the way.

Unfortunately, no equivalent to the body property exists in the Dreamweaver DOM for the <head> section. The way around this minor limitation is to first locate the sole <head> tag in the document. This task can be accomplished in two lines of JavaScript code:

```
theDom = dreamweaver.getDocumentDOM("document");
theHeadNode = theDom.getElementsByTagName("HEAD");
```

Now the script variable needs to be set. Whenever Dreamweaver encounters a closing </script> tag in a JavaScript function, the tag is flagged because it seems to be missing a mate. To avoid this problem, split the tag into two concatenated strings, as follows:

```
theScript = '<script language="Javascript" src="extend.js"><' + '/script>';
```

Finally, find the first item in the <head> section and append the script to its innerHTML property:

```
theHeadNode.item(0).innerHTML = theHeadNode.item(0).innerHTML + theScript;
```

The full function looks like the following:

```
function insertScript() {
  var theDom, theHeadNode, theScript;
  theDom = dreamweaver.getDocumentDOM("document");
  theHeadNode = theDom.getElementsByTagName("HEAD");
  theScript = '<script language="Javascript" src="extend.js"><' + 'script>';
}
```

On the CD-ROM You can find numerous examples of Massimo Foti's commands and other extensions on the CD-ROM that accompanies this book. Just look in the Additional Extensions folder under his name.

Using commands to call other commands

In the earlier section "Scripting commands," the runCommand() function plays a key role. It's worth emphasizing that this same function is used when you want one command to invoke another command. The proper syntax is

```
var doNew = dw.runCommand("commandFileName");
```

where *commandFileName* is the name of an HTML file in the Configuration\Commands folder. No value is returned with `runCommand()`; the function executes whatever command is called, passing any optional arguments. The function takes the following format:

```
dreamweaver.runCommand("myCommand.htm","argument01","argument02");
```

The called command's dialog box is presented and must be completed or canceled before the originating command is able to continue.

Tip Many commands—especially those disguised as objects—are not intended to be directly accessed by the user. However, Dreamweaver lists any valid command found in the Commands folder on the menu—unless you add a comment as the first line of your HTML file in the following format:

```
<!-- MENU-LOCATION=NONE -->
```

This code line inhibits the command name from being automatically displayed in the Commands menu list.

Creating a blank document

Commands aren't limited to working on the current document—you can use a command to read, modify, and even create new files. Any new file created using `createDocument()` or `createXHTMLDocument()` is an HTML or XHTML page based on the Default.html or Default.xhtml file found in the ConfigurationDocumentTypes\NewDocumentsfolder.

Occasionally, however, a command needs to make a new non-HTML/XHTML document, such as an XML or SMIL file or other file type that doesn't use the `<html>` . . . `</html>` structure. To accomplish this task, you first create an HTML file and then replace its entire contents with your own data—or nothing at all. The following custom function, developed by Andrew Wooldridge, makes and saves a new, blank text file:

```
function doNew() {
  var newDOM = dreamweaver.createDocument();
  var theDoc = newDOM.documentElement;
  theDoc.outerHTML = ".";
  theDoc.innerHTML = " ";
  dreamweaver.saveDocument(newDOM, '../../empty.txt');
}
```

Remember that all the Dreamweaver document functions—such as `saveDocument()`—use addresses relative to the file calling them. For example, if the `doNew()` function just described is included in a command, and therefore stored in the Commands folder, the empty.txt document is saved two folders above the Commands folder or in the Dreamweaver root directory, as the full path to the Commands folder is Dreamweaver MX\Configuration\Commands.

Commands from a Developer's Developer

Hava Edelstein, a JavaScript engineer with Macromedia, has contributed several commands especially valuable for developers. You can find them on the Dreamweaver Exchange at www. macromedia.com/exchange/dreamweaver. Here is an overview of these commands:

✦ **Eval:** This command enables you to quickly spot-check JavaScript statements and perform one-time alterations to your document. A must-have for the serious command developer. The Eval command has been reworked by Mark Erickson and is available on the Exchange as Evaluate JavaScript.

✦ **Show Browser References:** Navigator and Internet Explorer handle object references — especially those objects in layers — quite differently. This command enables you to select any object on the page and then find its proper JavaScript reference, which can be easily cut and pasted into your code.

✦ **Show Document Tree:** Want to see how the current document is structured from a DOM point of view? Run this command to create a new document with all the details, most notably the Node_Type of each node. Included in this command is a useful subroutine, traverseNodes(), which travels recursively through a document's nodes. Recursion is a key programming technique.

Managing Menus and Keyboard Shortcuts

Dreamweaver offers numerous ways to perform most every task: through the Property inspector, context menus, keyboard shortcuts, and even entering code directly. However, in the search for ever-faster, more efficient ways of working, it's often desirable to take control of the menus and other command methods and make them work the way you or your team prefers to work. If, for example, you insert a great number of layers and always define your links via the Property inspector, you'd probably be better off redefining Ctrl+L (Command+L) to Insert Layer, rather than its default, Insert Link.

Dreamweaver places all menus and keyboard shortcuts under your control. Not only can you add new items, but you can also rename menu items, change their keyboard shortcuts, determine when a menu item is active or dimmed — and even add entirely new menu strips. Moreover, all of this functionality is available with the context menus as well.

One file — menus.xml, found in the Configuration\Menus folder — is responsible for menu and keyboard shortcut set-up. While you have to edit the XML file by hand to reconfigure the menus, Dreamweaver includes a Keyboard Shortcut editor for modifying the keystroke commands. Details on using the Keyboard Shortcut editor are found later in this chapter, under "Using the Keyboard Shortcut editor."

This menu customization brings a whole new level of functionality to Dreamweaver. It's entirely possible for a company to create custom subsets of a program for certain departments. For example, let's assume each of several departments in a large firm is responsible for its own section of the Web site. A customized version of Dreamweaver could include a predefined site and disable the Define Site commands in the Site menu. It could also offer a specialized menu for calling up Help screens, tied to the standard F1 keyboard shortcut for Help.

In addition to the fully open architecture of the menus.xml file, command menu items, created by the History panel, can be managed right in the Document window. Before we delve into the relatively complex structure of menus.xml, let's take a look at the Edit Command List feature.

Handling History panel commands

Whenever you save a series of History panel steps as a command, it is instantly added to the bottom of the Commands menu list. Dreamweaver enables you to manage these custom added items—renaming them or deleting them—through the Edit Command List feature.

To manage History panel recorded commands, follow these steps:

1. Choose Commands ➪ Edit Command List.

   The Edit Command List dialog box appears, as shown in Figure 33-3.

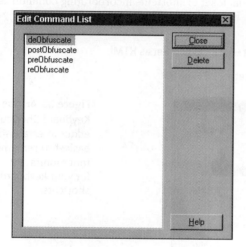

Figure 33-3: Manage your recorded commands through the Edit Command List dialog box.

2. To remove a command, select it and choose Delete.

3. To rename a command, select it and enter the new name or alter the existing one.

Using the Keyboard Shortcut editor

Whenever I'm learning a new program, one of the tasks I set for myself is to memorize the half-dozen or so essential keyboard shortcuts of the software. Keyboard shortcuts are terrific for boosting productivity—so terrific, in fact, that almost every program uses them. While this is a good thing from a single-program user's perspective, in reality no Web designer uses just one program, and having to remember the keyboard shortcuts for every needed program can be an absolute nightmare.

New Feature

To put the brakes on keyboard shortcut overload, Macromedia has implemented a standard keyboard shortcut editor for its key Web products—Flash, Fireworks, and Dreamweaver. Where possible, common features share the same shortcut across the product line. For example, opening the Behaviors panel is accomplished with the same keyboard shortcut in Dreamweaver and Fireworks, Shift+F3. Dreamweaver also includes a set of shortcuts matching those from HomeSite and BBEdit to smooth your transition from those text-based editors. Best of all, you can personalize any existing set of shortcuts to truly work with the way you work best.

To access the Keyboard Shortcut editor, shown in Figure 33-4, choose Edit ➪ Keyboard Shortcuts. The standard Keyboard Shortcut editor includes four different sets of shortcuts:

✦ **BBEdit:** Keyboard shortcut set matching those found in BBEdit.

✦ **Dreamweaver 3:** This set uses the standard shortcuts found in Dreamweaver 3, supplemented with additional shortcuts for Dreamweaver 4+ features, such as the Assets panel. These additional shortcuts will not necessarily be the same as those in the Macromedia Standard set.

✦ **HomeSite:** Keyboard shortcut set matching those found in HomeSite.

✦ **Macromedia Standard:** The default set of shortcuts incorporating common keyboard combinations in Dreamweaver, Fireworks, and Flash.

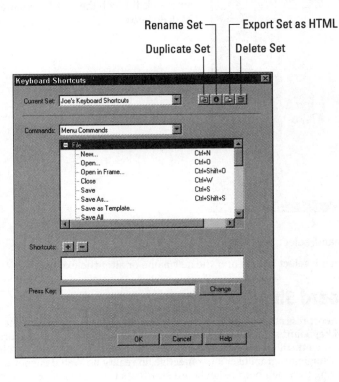

Figure 33-4: Use the Keyboard Shortcut editor to establish the easiest-to-remember mnemonics for your keyboard shortcuts.

To change from one set to another, open the Keyboard Shortcut editor and choose the desired set from the Current Set drop-down list. The changes take effect immediately upon closing the dialog box; there's no need to relaunch Dreamweaver.

The standard sets are locked and cannot be altered — you can only customize a copy of one of the standard sets. Dreamweaver provides all the controls you need to accomplish this on top of the Keyboard Shortcut editor. The four buttons are as follows:

✦ **Duplicate Set:** Copies the current set (standard or custom) and appends the word "copy." The duplicate set can be fully customized.

✦ **Rename Set:** Renames the current shortcut set.

✦ **Export Set as HTML:** Saves a list of the current set of keyboard shortcuts in an HTML format that can be viewed or printed in a browser.

✦ **Delete Set:** Removes a keyboard shortcut set. When Delete Set is chosen, a list of all custom sets is displayed, and any set except the active one may be removed. To remove a sole custom set, select any of the standard shortcut sets prior to choosing Delete Set.

Each command has up to two shortcuts assigned to it. This facility makes it possible to retain the originally assigned keyboard shortcut and to add a more personal one. Use the following steps to create a custom keyboard shortcut set:

1. Choose Edit ➪ Keyboard Shortcuts to open the editor. Note that the Keyboard Shortcut editor might take a few moments to load your current keyboard shortcuts.

A brief note from the Department of Pointless Nonsense, Irony Division: the Keyboard Shortcuts feature is one of the few commands without a keyboard shortcut.

2. Select a standard keyboard shortcut set upon which to base your custom set from the Current Set drop-down list.

3. Click the Duplicate Set button and type in an appropriate name for your custom shortcut set and click OK.

When the duplication is finished, select your new shortcut set from the Current Set list.

4. Choose the type of commands you wish to modify from the Commands drop-down list.

Dreamweaver has five different command types in Windows — Menu, Site Panel, Code Editing, Document Editing, and Site Window — and three under the Macintosh system (Menu, Code Editing, and Document Editing).

5. Select the specific command whose keyboard shortcut you want to modify.

If you've chosen Menu or Site Panel from the Commands list (Windows only), select the plus (+) sign next to the menu heading containing the command. The listing expands to show the first level of menu items. If the command you want to alter is contained within a submenu, click the plus (+) sign next to the submenu. Select the minus (–) sign to collapse an expanded listing.

6. With the desired command selected, click the Add (+) button in the Shortcuts section.

The cursor moves into the Press Key field.

7. Press the keyboard combination you want to assign to the command.

If Dreamweaver detects a conflict with an existing keyboard shortcut, an alert is displayed beneath the Press Key field telling you which command that shortcut is currently assigned to.

8. Select Change to confirm your choice.

If the shortcut you selected is already in use, Dreamweaver brings up an alert dialog box warning you that the shortcut is currently assigned, tells you which command is using it, and asks if you want to reassign it to the command you are editing. To reassign the keystroke, click OK. To choose a new keyboard shortcut, click Cancel.

9. Click OK when you're done to save your keyboard shortcut set.

If a command already has two shortcuts assigned to it, you need to select the one you want to change.

Tip   The personalized keyboard shortcut files are stored in the Configuration\Menus\Custom Sets folder as XML files. To make a keyboard shortcut set available on another system, copy the appropriate XML file to the corresponding folder in the user's Configuration\Menus\ Custom Sets folder. For more details on the location of the user's folders, see the "Multiuser System Customization" sidebar earlier in this chapter.

Adjusting the menus.xml file

When Dreamweaver is launched, the menus.xml file is read by the program, and the menu system is built. You can even customize menus.xml and then reload the file from within Dreamweaver — and instantly update your menu and shortcuts. The key, of course, is editing the XML file.

Caution   There are two points to be aware of when tackling the menus.xml file. First, you have to make sure you're editing the correct version of the file. If you are using a multiuser operating system (Windows NT, Windows 2000, Windows XP, or Mac OS X), you'll find the file in your user Configuration folder. System administrators and users of older systems — Windows 98, Windows ME, and Mac OS 9.x — should use the menus.xml file found in the program's Configuration folder. Second, the syntax for menus.xml is quite complex. Dreamweaver ignores any syntactically incorrect entries and disables their corresponding menu items. So take great care when you edit menus.xml to use proper syntax, and make sure you create a backup of the file *before* you begin editing.

The typical procedure for changing an existing menu item or shortcut is to open the file in a text editor (after backing up the original) and make the necessary changes. When adding menus or menu items, you need to follow the file's syntax exactly, as described in the following sections.

Generic shortcuts

Although Dreamweaver now provides a user interface for editing the keyboard shortcuts, sometimes power-users need to go to the source for major modifications — and the source for shortcuts is menus.xml. The menus.xml file is divided into two main sections: `<shortcutlist>` and `<menubar>`. The `<shortcutlist>` divisions are, as you might suspect, a list of keyboard shortcuts. The `<menubar>` areas are concerned with the various menu bars — in the main Document window, in the Site panel (Windows only), and in the numerous context menus. `<shortcutlist>` and `<menubar>` share several characteristics. They both follow the same basic structure:

```
<shortcutlist id="shortcutListID" [platform="win|mac"]>
  <shortcut attributeName="value" attributeName="value" ... />
  <shortcut attributeName="value" attributeName="value" ... />
  other shortcut items...
</shortcutlist>

<menubar name="menubarname" id="menubarID" [platform="win|mac"]>
  <menu name="menuname" id="menuID">
    <menuitem attributeName="value" attributeName="value" ... />
    <menuitem attributeName="value" attributeName="value" ... />
    other menuitem items...
  </menu>
  other menu items...
</menubar>
```

Shortcuts for menu items are primarily defined within the <menubar> code; the <shortcut-list> is mainly concerned with those shortcuts that do not have a menu item associated with them, such as moving from one word to another. By default, Dreamweaver defines seven <shortcutlist> sections: the Document window menu, the Site panel menu (Windows only), the Timelines panel context menu, the Code inspector context menu, the Server Behaviors panel context menu, the Bindings panel context menu, and the Components panel context menu.

Note   The key difference between the <shortcutlist> and the <menubar> sections is that while you can define new menu items or change existing ones in the <menubar> portion of the code, you can only alter existing shortcuts — you cannot add new shortcuts.

Each <shortcutlist> tag has one required attribute, the ID. The ID refers to a specific window or panel and must be unique within the <shortcutlist> section. The same ID is repeated in the <menubar> section to refer to the same window or panel. For example, the Document window ID is DWMainWindow, whereas the one for the context menu of the Timelines panel is DWTimelineContext. The <shortcutlist> tag takes one optional attribute, platform, which must be set to either win or mac, for Windows and Macintosh systems, respectively. (Note that in syntax statements, optional attributes are enclosed in [brackets].) If no platform attribute is listed, the <shortcutlist> described applies to both platforms. Here, for example, is the beginning of the <shortcutlist> definition for the Site panel, which only appears in the Windows version of the software:

```
<shortcutlist id="DWMainSite" platform="win">
```

A separate <shortcut> tag exists for every keystroke defined in the <shortcutlist>. The <shortcut> tag defines the key used, the tag's ID, the command or file to be executed when the keyboard shortcut is pressed, and the applicable platform, if any. Shortcuts can be defined for single special keys or key combinations using modifiers. The special keys are as follows:

✦ F1 through F12

✦ PgDn, PgUp, Home, End

✦ Ins, Del, BkSp, Space

✦ Esc and Tab

Modifiers can be used in combination with standard keys or special keys, or by themselves. A combination keyboard shortcut is indicated with a plus sign between keys. Available modifiers include those described in Table 33-1.

Table 33-1: Dreamweaver Shortcut Modifier Keys

Key	Example	Use
Alt or Opt	Alt+V; Option+V	Indicates the Alt (Windows) or Option (Macintosh) key modifier
Cmd	Command+S	Indicates the Ctrl (Windows) and the Command (Macintosh) key modifier
Ctrl	Ctrl+U	Indicates the Ctrl (Windows) or Control (Macintosh) key modifier
Shift	Shift+F1	Indicates the Shift key on both platforms

You can also combine multiple modifiers, as in this example:

Command+Shift+Z

The format of the `<shortcut>` tag is identical to that of the `<menuitem>` tag, as described in the following section.

Menubar definitions

Each `<menubar>` section of the menus.xml file describes a different menu strip, either on a window or on the context menu associated with a panel. Nested within the `<menubar>` tag are a series of `<menu>` tags, each detailing a drop-down menu. The individual menu items are defined in the `<menuitem>` tags contained within each set of `<menu>` . . . `</menu>` tags. Here, for example, is the context menu for the HTML Styles panel (I've abbreviated the complete `<menuitem>` tag for clarity):

```
<menubar name="" id="DWHtmlStyleContext">
  <menu name="HTML Style Popup" id="DWContext_HTMLStyle">
    <menuitem name="Edit..." />
    <menuitem name="Duplicate..." />
    <menuitem name="Delete" />
    <menuitem name="Apply" />
    <separator />
    <menuitem name="New..." />
  </menu>
</menubar>
```

The `<menubar>` and `<menu>` tags are alike in that they both require a name—which is what appears in the menu system—and an ID. The ID must be unique within the `<menubar>` structure to avoid conflicts. If a conflict is found (that is, if one item has the same ID as another), the first item in the XML file is recognized, and the second item is ignored.

Note   You can put a dividing line between your menu items by including a `<separator id="idname" />` tag between any two `<menuitem>` tags. (*idname* is any legal, unique XML name string.)

Numerous other attributes exist for the `<menuitem>` tag. The required attributes are name, ID, and either file or command, as marked with an asterisk in Table 33-2.

Tip   The menus.xml file is quite extensive. The main menu for Dreamweaver—the one you most likely want to modify—can be found by searching for the second instance of its ID, `DWMainWindow`. The first instance is used by the corresponding `<shortcutlist>` tag.

You can create submenus by nesting one set of `<menu>` tags within another. For example, here's a simplified look at the File ⇨ Import commands, as structured in menus.xml:

```
<menu name="_File" id="DWMenu_File">
  other menu items...
  <menu name="_Import" id="DWMenu_File_Import">
    <menuitem name="_XML into Template..." />
    <menuitem name="_Word HTML..." />
    <menuitem name="_Tabular Data..." />
  </menu>
  other menu items...
</menu>
```

Table 33-2: Menuitem Tag Attributes

Attribute	Possible Value	Description
name*	Any menu name	The name of the menu item as it appears on the menu. An underscore character causes the following letter to be underlined for Windows' shortcuts—for example, "_Frames" becomes "Frames."
id*	Any unique name	The identifying term for the menu item.
key	Any special key or keyboard key plus modifier(s)	The keyboard shortcut used to execute the command.
platform	win or mac	The operating system valid for the current menu item. If the platform parameter is omitted, the menu item is applicable for both systems.
enabled	JavaScript function	If present, governs whether a menu item is active (the function returns true) or dimmed (the function returns false). Including enabled=true ensures that the function is always available.
command* (required if file is not used)	JavaScript function	Executed when the menu item is selected. This inline JavaScript function capability is used for simple functions.
file* (required if command is not used)	Path to a JavaScript file	The JavaScript file is executed when the menu item is selected; the path is relative to the Configuration folder.
checked	JavaScript function	Displays a checkmark next to the menu item if the function returns true.
dynamic	N/A	Specifies that the menu item is set dynamically by the getDynamicContent() function, which resides in the Menu Commands file specified by the file attribute.

Note how within the ⟨menu⟩ tag that defines the File menu, another ⟨menu⟩ tag defining the Import submenu is nested.

Building menu commands

When examining the menus.xml file, notice that many of the menu items have JavaScript functions written right into the ⟨menuitem⟩ tag, such as this one for File ⇨ New:

```
<menuitem name="New _Window" key="Cmd+N" enabled="true"
        command="dw.newDocument()" id="DWMenu_MainSite_File_New" />
```

Here, when the user selects File ⇨ New, Dreamweaver executes the API function dw.newDocument(),in what is referred to as a *menu command*. Menu commands are used to specify the action of every menu item; what makes them unique is that you can use them to create and activate dynamic menus. Dynamic menus update according to user selections; the Preview in Browser list and HTML Styles menu items are both dynamic menus.

A menu command, as with most of the other Dreamweaver extensions, is a combination of HTML and JavaScript. If the menu command is extensive and cannot be referenced as one or two functions directly in the menus.xml file, it is contained in an HTML file, stored in the Configuration\Menus folder. Menu commands can even use a dialog box, such as standard commands for accepting user input.

Tip   You can find many examples of menu commands, written by the Dreamweaver engineers, in the Configuration\Menus\Mm folder.

Menu commands have access to all of the Dreamweaver API functions and a few of their own. None of the seven menu command API functions, listed in Table 33-3, are required, and three are automatically called when the menu command is executed.

Table 33-3: Command Menu API Functions

Function	Returns	Description
canAcceptCommand()	Boolean (true or false)	Determines whether the menu item is active or dimmed
commandButtons()	An array of labels and functions, separated by commas	Sets the name and effect of buttons on the dialog box
getDynamicContent()	An array of menu item names and unique IDs, separated by a semicolon	Sets the current listing for a menu
isCommandChecked()	Boolean	Adds a checkmark next to the item if true is returned
receiveArguments()	Nothing	Handles any arguments passed by the <menuitem> tag
setMenuText()	A text string	Sets the name of the menu item according to the given function; not to be used in conjunction with getDynamicContent()
windowDimensions()	"Width,Height" (in pixels)	Determines the dimensions of the Parameters dialog box

Working with Custom Tags

With the advent of XML—in which no standard tags exist—the capability to handle custom tags is essential in a Web authoring tool. Dreamweaver incorporates this capability through its third-party tag feature. After you've defined a third-party tag, Dreamweaver displays it in the Document window by highlighting its content, inserting a user-defined icon, or neither. Third-party tags are easily selected through the Tag Selector below the Document window; therefore, they are easy to cut, copy, and paste or otherwise manipulate. Perhaps most important, once a third-party tag is defined, you can apply a custom Property inspector that enables tag attributes to be entered in a standardized user interface.

Third-party tags can be defined directly within Dreamweaver. Just as object files use HTML to structure HTML code for easy insertion, Dreamweaver uses XML to make an XML definition for the custom tag. A custom tag declaration consists solely of one tag, `<tagspec>`, with up to seven attributes. The following list describes each of the legal `<tagspec>` attributes:

✦ **tag_name:** Defines the name of the tag as used in the markup. Any valid name — no spaces or special characters are allowed — is possible. A tag with the attribute `tag_name="invoice"` is entered in the document as `<invoice>`.

✦ **tag_type:** Determines whether the tag has a closing tag (`nonempty`) and is thus capable of enclosing content or if the tag describes the content itself (`empty`). For example, the `<invoice>` tag could have a `tag_type="nonempty"` because all the content is between `<invoice>` and `</invoice>`.

✦ **render_contents:** Sets whether the contents of a non-empty type tag are displayed or not. The `render_contents` attribute value is either true or false; if false, the tag's icon is displayed instead of the contents.

✦ **content_model:** Establishes valid placement and content for the tag in the document. The possible options are as follows:

• **block_model:** Tags defined with `content_model="block_model"` only appear in the `<body>` section of a document and contain block-level HTML tags, such as `<p>`, `<div>`, `<blockquote>`, and `<pre>`.

• **head_model:** Defines a tag that appears in the `<head>` section and can contain text, for example: `content_model="head_model"`.

• **marker_model:** Tags with the attribute `content_model=marker_model` can be placed anywhere in the document with no restrictions on content. The `marker_model` value is most often used for inline tags that are placed within a paragraph or division.

• **script_model:** Like the `marker_model` tag, `script_model` tags can be placed in either the `<head>` or `<body>` section. All content within a `script_model` tag is ignored by Dreamweaver, which enables server-specific scripts to be included without alteration.

✦ **start_string:** The initial delimiter for a custom string-delimited tag; `start_string` and `end_string` must both be defined if one is declared. Lasso tags, for example, use a `start_string` of a left bracket, [.

✦ **end_string:** The closing delimiter for a custom string-delimited tag. The `end_string` for a Lasso tag is the right bracket,].

✦ **detect_in_attribute:** A Boolean value that determines whether Dreamweaver should ignore string-delimited tags used as attributes in other tags. The the default is `false`, but for most string-delimited functions, the `detect_in_attribute` value should be set to `true`.

✦ **parse_attributes:** A Boolean value that determines if Dreamweaver should inspect and parse the attributes within string-delimited tags. By default, Dreamweaver parses all attributes; set `parse_attribute` to `false` to force Dreamweaver to ignore the attributes.

✦ **icon:** Empty tags or non-empty custom tags with `render_content` disabled require a GIF file to act as an icon in the Document window. The icon attribute should be set to any valid URL, relative or absolute (as in `icon="images/invoice.gif"`).

✦ **icon_width:** Sets the width, in pixels, of the icon used to represent the tag. The value can be any positive integer.

✦ **icon_height:** Sets the height, in pixels, of the icon used to represent the tag. The value can be any positive integer.

✦ **is_visual:** Sets whether the tag is rendered in the Design view; either a true or false value is acceptable.

Here's the complete code for a sample custom tag, the Template Expressions tag (which, although created by Macromedia, is technically a third-party tag):

```
<tagspec tag_name="dwtemplate" start_string="@@(" end_string=")@@"
detect_in_attribute="true" icon="TemplateExpr.gif" icon_width="18"
icon_height="18"></tagspec>
```

You can see an example of the Template Expressions custom tags in Figure 33-5.

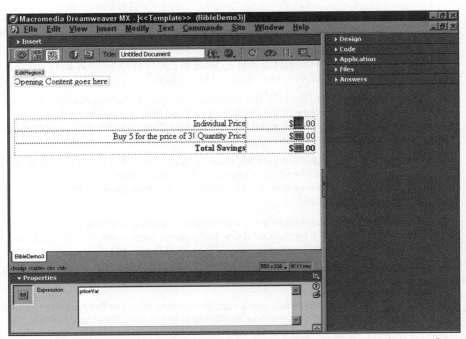

Figure 33-5: Third-party tags, such as these representing template expressions, can be displayed — and manipulated — in Design view.

Tip

If the content is to be rendered for a custom tag, you can easily view it in the Document window by enabling the Third-Party Tags Highlighting option in the Highlighting panel of the Preferences dialog box. Make sure that View ➪ Invisible Elements is enabled.

Once a custom tag is defined, the definition is saved in an XML file in the ThirdPartyTags folder, in Dreamweaver's Configuration folder. If you are establishing a number of custom tags, you can place all the definitions in the same file. Macromedia refers to this as the Tag DB or Database.

Customizing Property Inspectors

Property inspectors are used throughout Dreamweaver to display the current attributes of many different types of tags: text, images, layers, plugins, and so on. Not only do Property inspectors make it easy to see the particulars for an object, they make it a snap to modify those parameters. With the inclusion of custom tags in Dreamweaver, the capability to add custom Property inspectors is a natural parallel. Moreover, you can create custom Property inspectors for existing tags, and the custom Property inspectors will be displayed in place of the built-in Property inspectors.

As with objects, commands, and behaviors, custom Property inspectors are composed of HTML and JavaScript; the Property inspector HTML file itself is stored in the Configuration\Inspectors folder. However, the layout of the Property inspector is far more restrictive than it is with the other Dreamweaver extensions. The dialog box for an object, command, or behavior can be any size or shape desired — any custom Property inspector must fit the standard Property inspector dimensions and design. Because of the precise positioning necessary to insert parameter form items such as text boxes and drop-down menu lists, layers are used extensively to create the layout.

Quite elaborate Property inspectors are possible. The XSSI IF Property inspector built by Webmonkey, shown in Figure 33-6, has three separate tabs (Browser, Basic, and Advanced) based on layers for accessing different possible parameters of an object. Property inspectors, like other extension types, can also incorporate CSS styles, Flash movies, and Shockwave files.

Coding a Property inspector

As with many of the other standard extension files, most of the Property inspector files that ship with Dreamweaver are composed of an HTML file that calls a separate JavaScript file. It is entirely possible, however, to combine HTML and JavaScript into a single file. No matter how it's structured, a custom Property inspector HTML file requires the following four key elements:

✦ An initial DTD (Document Type Definition) line for custom Property inspectors:

```
<!DOCTYPE HTML SYSTEM "-//Macromedia//DWExtension ↩
layout-engine 5.0//pi">
```

✦ An HTML comment line immediately preceding the opening <html> tag that identifies which tag the Property inspector is for; here's the HTML comment line for a META tag Property inspector:

```
<!-- tag:META,priority:5,selection:within,vline,hline -->
<html>
```

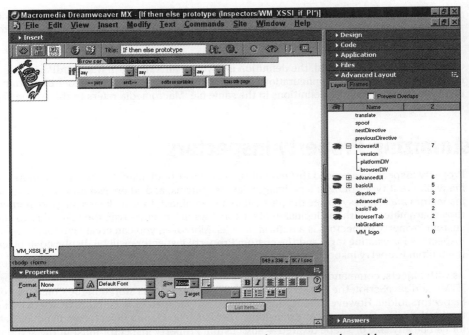

Figure 33-6: The code for some custom Property inspectors, such as this one from Webmonkey, takes advantage of Dreamweaver's layer and CSS styles support.

✦ The function canInspectSelection(), which determines whether the Property inspector should be displayed according to the current selection

✦ A second function, inspectSelection(), that updates the tag's HTML when new values are entered in the Property inspector

If any of these elements is missing or incorrectly declared, Dreamweaver ignores the file and does not display the Property inspector.

Cross-Reference

In addition to the mandatory functions and definitions, custom Property inspectors are capable of using any of the other Dreamweaver JavaScript functions described in Chapter 35, with the exception of the getBehaviorTag() and getBehaviorElement functions. If you include the displayHelp() function, a small question mark in a circle appears in the upper-right corner of your custom Property inspector, which, when selected by the user, executes whatever routines your Help function has declared.

The Property inspector definition

Two main items define a custom Property inspector:

✦ The custom Property inspector DTD, which must be the first line in the file

✦ An HTML comment line, which must immediately precede the opening <html> tag

More than one Property inspector can be defined for a particular tag, making it possible for separate inspectors to be used if different attributes are specified. Therefore, each Property inspector is assigned a priority that determines the one to be displayed. Property inspectors are further defined by whether the current selection is within the tag indicated or contains the entire tag; this feature enables two different Property inspectors to be defined, as with the `<table>` tag. Finally, optional graphic elements are definable: a horizontal line to delineate the upper and lower portions of the Property inspector, and a vertical line to separate the object's name from the other parts of the Property inspector.

Here is the custom Property inspector DTD:

```
<!DOCTYPE HTML SYSTEM "-//Macromedia//DWExtension ⊃
layout-engine 5.0//pi">
```

The HTML comment line uses the following syntax:

```
<!-- tag:ID,priority:1-10,⊃
selection:exact|within,hline,vline,serverModel -->
```

(Note that the last three values of the selection attribute, `hline`, `vline`, and `serverModel`, are all optional.) For example, the Property inspector for the `<link>` tag (a `<head>` element) is defined as follows:

```
<!-- tag:LINK,priority:5,selection:within,vline,hline -->
```

The individual sections of the definition are as follows:

✦ **tag:** The name of the tag for which the Property inspector is intended. Although it's not mandatory, the tag name is customarily uppercased. The tag ID can also be one of three keywords: *COMMENT*, when a comment class tag is indicated; *LOCKED*, when a locked region is to be inspected; or *ASP*, for all ASP elements.

Note The asterisks on either side of the tag keywords are mandatory.

✦ **priority:** The priority of a Property inspector is provided as a number from 1 to 10. The highest priority, 10, means that this Property inspector takes precedence over any other possible Property inspectors. The lowest priority, 1, marks the Property inspector as the one to use when no other Property inspector is available.

Note An example of how `priority` is used can be found in the `<meta>` tag and the `Description` and `Keywords` objects. The Property inspectors for Description and Keywords have a higher priority (6) than the one for the basic `<meta>` tag (5), which enables those inspectors to be shown initially if the proper criteria are met; if the criteria are *not* met, the Property inspector for the `<meta>` tag is displayed.

✦ **selection:** Depending on the current selection, the cursor is either within a particular tag or exactly enclosing it. The selection attribute is set to within or exact, according to the condition under which the Property inspector should be displayed.

✦ **hline:** Inserts a 1-pixel horizontal gray line (see Figure 33-7) dividing the upper and lower halves of the expanded Property inspector.

✦ **vline:** Places a 1-pixel vertical gray line (see Figure 33-7) between the tag's name field and the other properties on the upper half of the Property inspector.

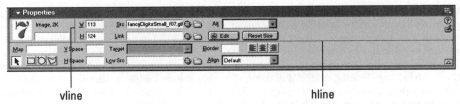

vline   hline

Figure 33-7: The Property inspector for the `<img>` tag uses both the `hline` and `vline` attributes.

The canInspectSelection() function

To control the circumstances under which your custom Property inspector is displayed, use the `canInspectSelection()` function. Like `canAcceptBehavior()` and `canAcceptCommand()` for behaviors and commands, respectively, if `canInspectSelection()` returns true, the custom Property inspector is shown; if it returns false, the Property inspector is not shown.

As noted earlier, the `canInspectSelection()` function is mandatory. If no conditions exist under which the Property inspector should not be displayed, use the following code:

```
function canInspectSelection() {
  return true;
}
```

Several of the standard Dreamweaver `<head>` elements have Property inspector files that use the `canInspectSelection()` function to limit access to specific tags. In this example, from the `<meta>` Description object, the current selection is examined to see if a `<meta>` tag is selected, and the `name` attribute is set to `description`:

```
function canInspectSelection() {
  var dom = dw.getDocumentDOM();
  var metaObj = dom.getSelectedNode();
  if (!metaObj || !metaObj.getAttribute) return false;
  return (metaObj.tagName && metaObj.tagName == "META" &&
   metaObj.getTranslatedAttribute("name") &&
   metaObj.getTranslatedAttribute("name").toLowerCase()=="description");
}
```

The inspectSelection() function

The `inspectSelection()` function is the workhorse of the custom Property inspector code and is responsible for pulling the information from the selected tag for display in the various Property inspector fields. Depending on the code design, the `inspectSelection()` function can also be used to update the HTML code when the attribute values are modified in the Property inspector.

Here's an excerpt of the `inspectSelection()` function from the Link Property inspector file:

```
function inspectSelection() {
  TEXT_HREF = findObject("Href");

  ...
  if (linkObj.getAttribute("href"))
    TEXT_HREF.value = linkObj.getAttribute("href");
```

```
else
    TEXT_HREF.value = "";
  ...
}
```

In this example, if an attribute (href) exists, its value is assigned to the Property inspector's appropriate text box value (TEXT_HREF.value). The remainder of the inspectSelection() function for the <link> tag consists of a series of statements such as those shown in the example code.

 Tip You can design a Property inspector that displays a different interface depending on whether or not it is expanded, as the Keywords Property inspector does. If an inspector is not expanded, the argument(0) property is set to the value min; when it is expanded, argument(0) is equal to the value max.

Many Property inspectors update their HTML tags when a change occurs in one of the input boxes. No real standard method exists to accomplish this, due to the many possible variations with Property inspectors. However, one of the most commonly used events is onBlur(), as in the following example, taken from the Keywords Property inspector file:

```
var minText = '<textarea name="Keywords" onBlur="setMetaTag()" '
  + 'style="width:350;height:32" rows="2" wrap="virtual"></textarea>'
```

The setMetaTag() function that is called is a local one that assigns whatever is currently in the textarea of the Property inspector to the content attribute.

Designing a Property inspector

All the attributes for a Property inspector must fit into a tightly designed space. While it's helpful to look at examples found in the Inspectors folder, many of the standard Property inspectors are built in to the core functionality of the program and are not immediately accessible on the design level. The following specifications and tips should make it easier to design your own custom Property inspectors:

✦ An expanded Property inspector is 86 pixels high: 42 pixels for the top portion and 44 pixels for the bottom portion.

✦ If the hline attribute is specified in the Property inspector definition, a 1-pixel-high line is drawn the entire width of the inspector, 43 pixels from the top (reducing the bottom portion's height to 43 pixels).

✦ If the vline attribute is specified, a single-pixel line is drawn across the top half of the Property inspector, 118 pixels from the left.

✦ The image placed on the upper-left corner of the Property inspector is generally sized at 36 pixels square and placed 3 pixels from the top and 2 pixels from the left. Although you are not required to keep this size image — or its placement — following these guidelines helps make your custom Property inspectors resemble the standard Dreamweaver ones.

✦ It's a good idea to lay out your Property inspector with the View ⇨ Invisible Elements command disabled. The small icons that indicate layers can alter the perceived spacing.

✦ Keep the Layers panel visible. Many custom Property inspectors use multiple layers to position the elements exactly — several of the Webmonkey-designed XSSI Property inspectors employ upwards of 20 layers, as shown in Figure 33-8 — and the Layers panel makes selecting individual layers for adjustment a snap.

✦ Use nested layers to position and group associated items in the Property inspector. Almost all form objects used in Property inspectors for user input, such as text boxes and drop-down lists, are identified by labels. Placing both the label and text boxes in their own layers, while grouping them under one parent layer, provides maximum flexibility and ease of placement.

✦ Apply CSS styles within the Property inspector to easily manage font sizes and design your Property inspector in a WYSIWYG environment.

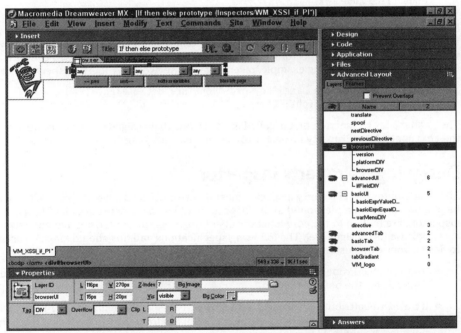

Figure 33-8: Property inspectors, such as Webmonkey's custom XSSI IF inspector, use parent and child layers to position layout components and toggle different options.

Making Custom Floating Panels

Property inspectors are an excellent way to manage the attributes of most elements in a single, consistent user interface. The Property inspector user interface, however, is not the best solution for all situations. Recognizing this, the Macromedia engineers have added another extension type for Dreamweaver: floating panels.

A *floating panel* is a cross between a Property inspector and a command. As with Property inspectors, floating panels can stay on the screen while you work on the Web page; as with commands, floating panels are not restricted to a set size and shape. Custom floating panels have the same basic interface as standard Dreamweaver panels. Any floating panel can be resized or grouped with other floating panels, standard or custom. Once grouped, a custom floating panel also has a tab that, when selected, brings the floating-panel interface to the front. There are only a couple of noteworthy differences between built-in and custom floating panels:

✦ Built-in floating panel tabs can display names and icons; custom floating panel tabs can only display names.

✦ Built-in floating panels can be assigned a minimum size; custom floating panels cannot (that is, the user can shrink them down to about 100 × 100 pixels).

Floating panels, like most other extensions, are a combination of HTML and JavaScript. HTML is the main file that is called; it provides the user interface via an HTML form. JavaScript provides the functionality from the <head> of the HTML page.

Note   Like Property inspectors, floating panels have their own DTD that you must include as the first line in your custom floating panel files: `<!DOCTYPE HTML SYSTEM "-//Macromedia// DWExtension layout-engine5.0//floater">`.

Floating panels are stored in the Configuration\Floaters folder. However, unlike commands or objects, you can't just save your custom floating panel in a particular folder to make it accessible. You must call a function that displays the floating panel, either `dw.setFloaterVisibility(floaterName,true)` or `dw.toggleFloater(floaterName)`. Most often, these functions are called from a `<menuitem>` tag in the menus.xml file, as with the following custom floating panel:

```
<menuitem name="HelpBuilder" enabled="true"
 command="dw.toggleFloater('helpBuilder')"
 checked="dw.getFloaterVisibility('helpBuilder')" />
```

The `checked` attribute ensures that a checkmark is displayed next to the menu item if the floating panel is visible.

Caution   When naming your custom floating panel, be sure to avoid names reserved for Dreamweaver's built-in elements: assets, behaviors, codesnippet, CSS styles, dataSource, documenttype, frames, helpbook, HTML styles, HTML, insertbar, launcher, layers, library, objects, or history properties, reference, samplecontent, serverBehavior, serverFormat, serverModel, site, taglibrary, site files, site map, templates, timelines, timelines, or toolbar.

As indicated in the preceding paragraphs, floating panels have their own API functions, and several methods of the Dreamweaver object are applicable. The floating panel API functions, none of which are required, are described in Table 33-4.

Caution   Macromedia strongly cautions programmers from using `documentEdited()` and `selectionChanged()` unless absolutely needed. Both functions — because they constantly monitor the document — can have an adverse effect on performance if implemented. Macromedia suggests that programmers incorporate the `setTimeout()` method to temporarily pause these functions so that the user can continue to interact with the program.

Table 33-4: Floating Panel API Functions

Function	Returns	Use
displayHelp()	Nothing	Specifies whether a Help button should appear beneath the OK and Cancel buttons
documentEdited()	Nothing	Executes after the current document has been edited
getDockingSide()	A string containing "left", "right", "top", and/or "bottom"	For Dreamweaver MX (Windows only) Specifies where a floating panel can dock
initialPosition(platform)	A string in the form at "left,top"	Sets the position of the floating panel onscreen when it is first called; if left onscreen when Dreamweaver quits, it reopens in the last location
initialTabs()	A string in the format "floatingPanel1, floatingPanel2,..."	Indicates what other floating panels are grouped with the current floating panel when it first appears
isATarget()	Boolean	For Dreamweaver MX (Windows only) Specifies if other panels can dock to this panel
IsAvailableInCodeView()	Boolean	Determines if the floating panel is enabled when Code view is active
isResizable	Boolean	Specifies whether the floating panel can be user-resized
selectionChanged()	Nothing	Executes after the current selection has been altered

Within the Dreamweaver API are two pairs of methods and a single function, which relate to floating panels as follows:

✦ getHideAllFloaters(): Reads the state of the Show/Hide Floating Panel menu option to determine if all floating panels should be hidden (true) or shown (false)

✦ setHideAllFloaters(): Sets the Show/Hide Floating panel to a particular state, to Hide (true) or Show (false)

✦ getFloaterVisibility(floaterName): Reads whether the given floating panel is currently displayed and frontmost (true) or hidden (false)

✦ setFloaterVisibility(floaterName,isVisible): Brings the named floating panel forward if the isVisible argument is true

✦ toggleFloater(floaterName): Toggles the visibility state of the given floating panel between hiding and bringing to the front

Floating panels have a great deal of potential with their flexible interface and constant onscreen presence. The example shown in Figure 33-9, built by the author, scans an entire Web site looking for items marked with a custom table of contents tag, and then lists the object, with its corresponding link.

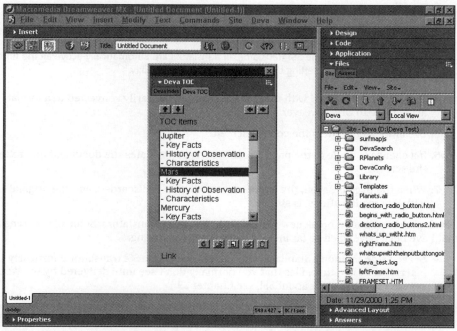

Figure 33-9: The custom floater, built for the Deva help authoring extension, lists phrases marked with a `<toc>` tag.

Developing Translators

In order for any markup tag to be depicted in the Document window — whether it's `<b>` for bold or a custom third-party tag such as Tango's `<@cols>` — it must be translated. Dreamweaver's built-in rendering system translates all the standard HTML code, along with a few special custom tags such as those for ASP and ColdFusion. However, in order to display any other custom tags, or those that perform special functions such as server-side includes, the tag developer must build a custom translator.

As part of its expansion efforts, Dreamweaver supports custom *translators*. This enhancement enables programs that output nonstandard HTML to be displayed onscreen integrated with the regular code. One of Dreamweaver's main claims to fame is its capability to accept code without rewriting it. With Dreamweaver translators, you can visually insert, show, and edit your custom code.

Here's a brief overview of how translators work:

1. When Dreamweaver starts, all the properly coded translators in the Configuration\Translators folder are initialized.

2. If a document is loaded with nonstandard HTML, the code is checked against the installed translators.

3. The translators are enabled.

Note With the exception of the SSI translator, all translators are automatically active all the time — there is no preference setting that determines their availability.

4. The code is processed with the translator and temporarily converted to a format acceptable to Dreamweaver.

5. Dreamweaver renders the code onscreen.

6. If a change is made to the page, Dreamweaver retranslates the document and refreshes the screen.

7. When the page is saved, the temporary translation is discarded, and the original code, with any modifications, is stored.

Developers continue to break new ground with the use of translators. Some of the translators that have been developed so far include those for the following:

✦ **Server-side includes:** Standard with Dreamweaver, the SSI translator effortlessly inserts, at design time, files that you normally don't see until delivered by the Web server. (To learn more about SSI, see Chapter 29.)

✦ **XSSI:** The Extended Server-Side Include (XSSI) extension, developed by Webmonkey authors Alx, Nadav, and Taylor for Macromedia, includes a translator that brings the Apache-served code right in the Document window.

✦ **Tango:** Developed by Pervasive Software, the Tango translator compensates for differences between database-oriented code and standard HTML. Additionally, Tango includes a manually controlled Sample Data translator that enables the Web designer to view the page complete with an example database.

Translator functions

As with other Dreamweaver extensions such as behaviors and commands, translators are HTML files with JavaScript. Translators have no user interface. Other than deciding when to invoke it, you have no parameters to set or options to choose from; all the pertinent code is in a script located in the `<head>` of a translator. In the translator's `<head>`, along with any necessary support routines, you can find two essential JavaScript functions: `getTranslatorInfo()` and `translateMarkup()`. Any other Dreamweaver JavaScript API functions not specific to behaviors can be used in a translator as well.

Note Due to the limitations of JavaScript, much of the heart of custom translation is handled by specially written C-level extensions. These compiled code libraries enhance Dreamweaver's capabilities so that new data types can be integrated. C-level extensions are covered later in this chapter, under "Extending C-Level Libraries."

The getTranslatorInfo() function

The `getTranslatorInfo()` function simply sets up and returns an array of text strings that are read by Dreamweaver during initialization.

The structure of the array is relatively rigid. The number of array elements is specified when the `Array` variable is declared, and a particular text string must correspond to the proper array element. The array order is as follows:

✦ **translatorClass:** The translator's unique name used in JavaScript functions. The name has to begin with a letter and can contain alphanumeric characters as well as hyphens or underscores.

✦ **title:** The title listed in the menu and the Translation category. This text string can be no longer than 40 characters.

✦ **nExtensions:** The number of file extensions, such as .cfml, to follow. This declaration tells Dreamweaver how to read the next portion of the array. If this value is set to zero, all files are acceptable.

✦ **extension:** The actual file extension without the leading period.

✦ **nRegExps:** The number of regular expressions to be declared. Should this value be equal to zero, the array is closed.

✦ **RegExps:** The regular expression to be searched for by Dreamweaver.

✦ **runDefault:** Specifies when the translator executes (always, never, or conditionally).

The number of array elements — and thus, the detail of the function — depends entirely on the translator. Here, for example, is the code for `getTranslatorInfo()` from Live Picture's translator, where a file must have a particular `<meta>` tag to be translated:

```
function getTranslatorInfo(){
  returnArray = new Array( 5 );
  returnArray[0] = "FPX";      // translatorClass
  returnArray[1] = "Flashpix Image Translator";    // title
  returnArray[2] = "0";        // number of extensions
  returnArray[3] = "1";        // number of expressions
  returnArray[4] = "<meta http-equiv=\"refresh\" content=\"0;url=http://";
  return returnArray;
}
```

By comparison, the standard SSI translator's `getTranslatorInfo()` function has 10 array elements, and Webmonkey's XSSI has 17.

The translateMarkup() function

While the `getTranslatorInfo()` function initializes the translator, the `translateMarkup()` function actually does the work. As noted earlier, most of the translators rely on a custom C-level extension to handle the inner workings of the function, but `translateMarkup()` provides the JavaScript shell.

The `translateMarkup()` function takes three arguments, which must be declared but whose actual values are provided by Dreamweaver:

✦ **docName:** The file URL for the file to be translated.

✦ **siteRoot:** The site root of the file to be translated. Should the file be outside the current site, the value would be empty.

✦ **docContent:** A text string with the code for the page to be translated.

Typically, the *docContent* text string is parsed using either JavaScript or a C-level extension within the `translateMarkup()` function that returns the translated document. This translated document is then displayed by Dreamweaver.

Here's an excerpt of the `translateMarkup()` function from the ColdFusion translator:

```
function translateMarkup(docNameStr, siteRootStr, inStr) {
  var outStr = "";
  ...
  // translate
  if (inStr.indexOf("<cf") != -1 || inStr.indexOf("<CF") != -1) {
    var TM =
      new TranslationManager(TRANSLATOR_CLASS, SERVER_MODEL_FOLDER, "");
    TM.serverModelAlwaysCheckTag = myAlwaysCheckTag;
    TM.serverModelAlwaysCheckAttribute = myAlwaysCheckAttribute;

    var split = TranslationManager.splitBody(inStr);
    outStr = TM.translate(split.inStr);
    if (outStr != "")
      outStr = split.preInStr + outStr + split.postInStr;
  }
  ...
  return outStr;
}
```

In this example, notice that the translated document in the form of `outStr` is built by creating a `TranslationManager` object named `TM`, and then calling this object's `translate()` method: `TM.translate(split.inStr)`.

Locking code

Translations are generally intended for onscreen presentation only. Although there's no rule prohibiting translated content from being written out to disk, most applications need the original content to run. To protect the original content, Dreamweaver includes a special locking tag. This XML tag pair, `<MM:BeginLock>`...`<MM:EndLock>`, stops the enclosed content (the translation) from being edited, while simultaneously storing a copy of the original content in a special format.

The `<MM:BeginLock>` tag has several attributes:

✦ **translatorClass:** The identifying name of the translator as specified in `getTranslatorInfo()`.

✦ **type:** The type or tag name for the markup to be translated.

✦ **depFiles:** A comma-separated list of any files on which the locked content depends. If any of the listed dependent files are altered, the page is retranslated.

✦ **orig:** A text string with the original markup before translation. The text string is encoded to include four standard HTML characters:

< becomes %3C;
> becomes %3E;
" becomes %22;
% becomes %25;

To see how the special locking tag works, look at an example taken from the Tango Sample Data translator. Tango uses what are called *meta tags,* which begin with an @ sign, such as the <@TOTALROWS> tag. The Tango Sample Data translator replaces what will be a result drawn from a database with a specified sample value. The original code is

```
<@TOTALROWS samptotalrows=23>
```

After the code is translated, Dreamweaver refreshes the screen with the following code:

```
<MM:BeginLock translatorClass="TANGO_SAMPLEDATA" type ="@TOTALROWS"
    orig="%3C@TOTALROWS samptotalrows=23%3E">23<MM:EndLock>
```

The 23 in bold is the actual translated content that appears in Dreamweaver's Document window.

Note   You don't actually see the locking code — even if you open the Code inspector when a page is translated. To view the code, select the translated item, copy it, and then paste it in another text application, or use the Paste As HTML feature to see the results in Dreamweaver.

Extending C-Level Libraries

All programs have their limits. Most limitations are intentional and serve to focus the tool for a particular use. Some limitations are accepted because of programming budgets — for both money and time — with the hope that the boundaries can be exceeded in the next version. With Dreamweaver, one small section of those high, sharply defined walls has been replaced with a doorway: C-level extensions. With the proper programming acumen, you can customize Dreamweaver to add the capabilities you need.

As with most modern computer programs, the core of Dreamweaver is coded in C and C++, both low-level languages that execute much faster than any noncompiled language, such as JavaScript. Because C is a compiled language, you can't just drop in a function with a few lines of code and expect it to work — it has to be integrated into the program. The only possible way to add significant functionality is through another compiled component called a *library*. With the C-level extensions capability, Dreamweaver enables the incorporation of these libraries, known as DLLs (Dynamic Link Libraries) on Windows systems, and as CFMs (Code Fragment Managers) on Macintosh systems.

One excellent example of the extended library is DWfile. This C-level extension is used by several Dreamweaver partners, including RealNetworks and iCat, to perform tasks outside the capabilities of JavaScript; namely, reading and writing external text files. By adding this one library, Dreamweaver can now work with the support files necessary to power a wide range of associated programs. DWfile is described in detail in the following section.

C-level extensions are also used in combination with Dreamweaver's translator feature. As discussed earlier in this chapter, translators handle the chore of temporarily converting nonstandard code to HTML that Dreamweaver can present onscreen — while maintaining the original code in the file. Although much of this functionality isn't impossible for JavaScript, the conversion would be too slow to be effective. C-level extensions are definitely the way to go when looking for a powerful solution.

Note   A discussion of programming in C or C++, as required by C-level extensions, is beyond the scope of this book. Developers are encouraged to scour the Dreamweaver Support Center for relevant information: www.macromedia.com/support/dreamweaver/.

Calling C-level extensions

C-level extensions, properly stored in the Configuration\JSExtensions folder, are read into Dreamweaver during initialization when the program first starts. The routines contained within the custom libraries are accessed through JavaScript functions in commands, behaviors, objects, translators, and other Dreamweaver extensions.

Let's take a look at how Macromedia's C-level extension DWfile is used. DWfile has 14 main functions:

✦ copy(): Copies a file from one file URL (the first argument) to another (the second argument). DWfile.copy() may be used to copy any type of file, not just text files.

✦ createFolder(): Creates a folder, given a file URL.

✦ listFolder(): Lists the contents of a specified folder in an array. This function takes two arguments: the file URL of the desired folder (required) and a keyword, either "files" (which returns just filenames) or "directories" (which returns just directory names). If the keyword argument is not used, you get both files and directories.

✦ exists(): Checks to see if a specified filename exists. This function takes one argument, the filename.

✦ getAttributes(): Returns the attributes of a specified file or folder. Possible attributes are R (read-only), D (directory), H (hidden), and S (system file or folder).

✦ setAttributes(): Sets the attributes of a specified file.

✦ getCreationDate(): Returns the date when the file was initially created.

✦ getCreationDateObj(): Returns the JavaScript object that represents the date when the file was initially created.

✦ getModificationDate(): Returns the date a specified file or folder was last modified.

✦ getModificationDateObj(): Returns the JavaScript object that represents the date a specified file or folder was last modified.

✦ getSize(): Gets the size of a specified file.

✦ read(): Reads a text file into a string for examination. This function also takes one argument, the filename.

✦ `write()`: Outputs a string to a text file. This function has three arguments; the first two — the name of the file to be created and the string to be written — are required. The third, the mode, must be the word "append." This argument, if used, causes the string to be added to the end of the existing text file; otherwise, the file is overwritten.

✦ `remove()`: Places the referenced file in the Recycling Bin (Windows) or Trash (Macintosh) without requesting confirmation.

The following JavaScript function, which could be included in any Dreamweaver extension, uses DWfile to determine whether theFile, named in a passed argument, exists. If it does, the contents are read and presented in an alert box; if theFile doesn't exist, the function creates it and outputs a brief message.

```
function fileWork(theFile) {
  var isFile = DWfile.exists(theFile);   // does theFile exist?
  if (isFile) {
    alert(DWfile.read(theFile));          // yes: display it in an alert box
  }
  else {                                  // no: create it and display msg
    DWfile.write(theFile,"File Created by DWfile");
  }
}
```

Note how the C-level extension name, DWfile, is used to call the library and its internal functions. Once the library has been initialized, it can be addressed as any other internal function, and its routines are simply called as methods of the function using JavaScript dot notation, such as DWfile.exists(theFile).

Building C-level extensions

You must follow strict guidelines to enable Dreamweaver to recognize a C-level extension. Specifically, you must include two files in the library, and you must declare each function for correct interpretation by Dreamweaver's JavaScript interpreter.

Macromedia engineers have developed a C-Level Extension API in the form of a C header, mm_jsapi.h. This header contains definitions for over 20 data types and functions. To insert mm_jsapi.h in your custom library, add the following statement:

```
#include "mm_jsapi.h"
```

Tip You can find the latest version of mm_jsapi.h on the Dreamweaver Exchange, which you can get to by choosing Help ➪ Dreamweaver Exchange in Dreamweaver or by loading the URL www.macromedia.com/exchange/dreamweaver in your browser.

After you've included the JavaScript API header, you need to declare a specific macro, MM_STATE. This macro, contained within the mm_jsapi.h header, holds definitions necessary for the integration of the C-level extension into Dreamweaver's JavaScript API. You must define MM_STATE only once.

Each library can be composed of numerous functions available to be called from within Dreamweaver. For Dreamweaver's JavaScript interpreter to recognize the functions, each one must be declared in a special function, JS_DefineFunction(), defined in the library. All of the JS_DefineFunction() functions are contained in the MM_Init() function. The syntax for JS_DefineFunction() is as follows:

```
JS_DefineFunction(jsName, call, nArgs)
```

where *jsName* is the JavaScript name for the function, *call* is a pointer to a C-level function, and *nArgs* is the number of arguments that the function can expect. For example, the MM_Init() function for DWfile might appear as follows:

```
void
MM_Init() {
   JS_DefineFunction("exist", exist, 1);
   JS_DefineFunction("read", exist, 1);
   JS_DefineFunction("write", exist, 2);
}
```

Because MM_Init() depends on definitions included in the C header, mm_jsapi.h, it must be called after the header is included.

Tip   If you're building cross-platform C-level extensions, consider using Metrowerks CodeWarrior integrated development environment. CodeWarrior can edit, compile, and debug C, C++, and even Java or Pascal for both Windows and Macintosh operating systems. Perhaps, most importantly, Macromedia engineers used CodeWarrior to test C-level extensions.

Customizing Your Tag Libraries

Previous versions of Dreamweaver required you to manually edit the sourceformat.txt file in order to change code formatting, including tag case, attributes, indentation, and line wrapping. Dreamweaver MX gives you a well-designed dialog box called the Tag Library Editor to make all of those changes for you. By using the Tag Library Editor, you can customize every single tag you place in Dreamweaver, and you can even add additional tags if you're using a proprietary server or design XML files with commonly used tag sets.

New Feature   All tag-related attributes and color code settings are stored in a tag database (the Tag Library), which is manipulated through the Tag Library Editor. Click the Tag Library Editor link in the preferences or choose Edit ⇨ Tag Libraries.

Editing tag libraries, tags, and attributes

To edit the properties for a tag library, follow these steps:

1. Choose Edit ⇨ Tag Libraries to open the Tag Library Editor dialog box, and select the tag library whose properties you want to set, as shown in Figure 33-10.

2. In the Used In list box, choose every type of document that should use the selected tag library. Note that the tags in the selected library will be available only in the document types you've chosen.

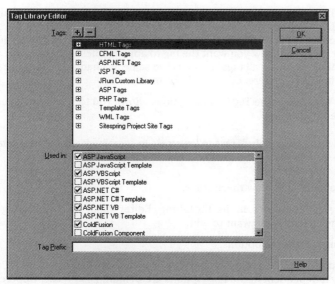

Figure 33-10: You use the Tag Library Editor to customize Dreamweaver's tag libraries.

3. If the tags in the selected tag library require a prefix, enter this prefix in the Tag Prefix field.

   The Tag Prefix box allows you to add a prefix to the beginning of every tag in that particular library. For example, if you developed a tag library for XSL documents, you would add xsl: as the tag prefix to add the prefix to the beginning of every tag.

4. When you are finished, click OK to close the Tag Library Editor dialog box.

To edit a tag in a tag library, follow these steps:

1. Choose Edit ➪ Tag Libraries. In the Tag Library Editor dialog box, open a tag library and select the tag you want to edit.

2. Set your desired Tag Format options:

   • **Line Breaks:** Changing the line breaks option changes where Dreamweaver places lines breaks in your code. Choose between No Line Breaks, Before and After Tag, Before, Inside, After and After Tag Only. This option is great for preventing line breaks after <td> tags and before </td> tags to ensure that no unwanted whitespace shows up in your code.

   • **Contents:** This setting affects how the content inside your tags is formatted. The indentation settings are based on your code format preferences. Choose between Not Formatted, Formatted But Not Indented and Formatted and Indented.

- **Case:** The case settings affect how the tag and its attributes are capitalized. XHTML for example requires that everything be lowercase. Options are Default, Lowercase, Uppercase and Mixed Case. Choosing Mixed Case gives you a prompt to type in exactly how you want the tag to appear. Clicking Set Default allows you to set the default for all tags, which is the same as changing your tag case preferences in Edit ➪ Preferences ➪ Code Format.

The Preview area below the Tag Format options allows you to see exactly how your tag will be written to the page.

Tip I recommend setting your default case to lowercase to comply with XML/XHTML standards.

To edit an attribute for a tag, follow these steps:

1. Choose Edit ➪ Tag Libraries. In the Tag Library Editor dialog box, open a tag library and select the attribute you want to edit.

2. Set your desired attribute options:

   - **Attribute Case:** This option sets the case of your attribute. Attribute Case is completely independent of the tag. Options are Default, Lowercase, Uppercase, or Mixed Case. Choosing Mixed Case allows you to enter exactly how you want the attribute formatted. Clicking Set Default alerts you to return to the Code Format category of Preferences.

   - **Attribute Type:** There are 10 different attributes types for your tag: Text, Enumerated, Color, Directory, File Name, File Path, Flag, Font, Relative Path, and Style. Setting the type affects how Dreamweaver asks for information when using Code Hints in Code view or the Quick Tag Editor. Choosing color for an attribute will cause a color palette to appear if you add the attribute in Code view. Setting the Type to Relative Path will give you a Select File dialog box.

   - **Values:** The Values field is used only for the enumerated attribute type and gives you a list of valid values for a particular attribute.

Creating and deleting tag libraries, tags, and attributes

To create a new tag library, add a tag to an existing library, or add an attribute to an existing tag, follow these steps:

To add a new tag library, follow these steps:

1. Choose Edit ➪ Tag Libraries.

2. Select the Add (+) button and choose New Tag Library.

3. Enter a name for your new tag library and click OK.

4. Your new tag library will now show at the bottom of the list. You're ready to start adding new tags.

To add new tags to one of your tag libraries, follow these steps:

1. Choose Edit ➪ Tag Libraries.

2. Select the Add (+) button and choose New Tags.

3. Choose the Tag Library to add to in the list menu.

4. Enter one or more tags to add.

   If you want to add a large number of tags at one time, simply enter a comma-separated list of tags into the dialog. This method enables you to add a large number of tags very quickly.

5. Choose whether your tag requires matching end tags.

   Choosing matching end tags would give you tags like `<a>text</a>`. Choosing not to have matching end tags would give you tags like `<br>` and `<img>`.

To add a new tag to one of your tag libraries, follow these steps:

1. Choose Edit ➪ Tag Libraries.

2. Select the Add (+) button and choose New Attributes.

3. Choose the Tag Library that contains the tag you want to add attributes to from the first list menu.

4. Choose the tag you want to add attributes to from the second list menu.

5. Enter one or more attributes to add. If you want to add a large number of attributes at one time, simply enter a comma-separated list of attributes into the dialog. This enables you to add a large number of attributes very quickly.

To delete a tag library, tag, or attribute, follow these steps:

1. Choose Edit ➪ Tag Libraries.

2. In the Tag Library Editor dialog box, select the tag library, tag, or attribute you want to delete.

3. Click the Remove (–) button. If you are asked to confirm the deletion, do so.

4. To make your deletions permanent, choose OK. To discard your deletions, click Cancel.

Caution   Once you click that OK button, your deletions are permanent. You cannot undo them, so ponder deeply before clicking that mouse!

Importing a DTD or schema to create a new tag library

Dreamweaver MX enables you to create a new tag library by importing tags from an existing XML Document Type Definition (DTD) file or schema. There are many instances where you may want to add a new tag library. If you're working on a proprietary server or a language that's not supported by Dreamweaver, you can add all the necessary tags into a new Tag Library.

To create new tag library by importing a DTD file or schema, follow these steps:

1. Choose Edit ➪ Tag Libraries.

2. In the Tag Library Editor dialog box, click the Add (+) button and choose DTDSchema ➪ Import XML DTD or Schema File.

3. In the File or Remote URL field, enter the file or URL of the DTD or schema file.

4. In the Tag Prefix field, enter the prefix to be used with the tags you're importing, to identify the tags as part of this tag library.

5. When you're done, click OK to create your new tag library.

Summary

Dreamweaver's commitment to professional Web site authoring is most evident when examining the program's customization capabilities. Virtually every Web site production house can benefit from some degree of personalization — and some clients absolutely require it. As you examine the ways in which you can make your productive life easier by extending Dreamweaver, keep the following points in mind:

✦ Dreamweaver includes a full range of customizable features: objects, behaviors, commands, third-party tags, Property inspectors, and translators. You can even extend the program's core feature set with the C-Level Extensibility option.

✦ You can use commands to affect any part of your HTML page and automate repetitive tasks.

✦ In addition to accessing custom commands through the Command menu, you can configure them as objects for inclusion in the Insert bar. You can also make a command appear in any other standard Dreamweaver menu by altering the menus.xml file.

✦ To make it easy to work with XML and other non-HTML tags, Dreamweaver enables you to create custom tags complete with individual icons or highlighted content.

✦ Attributes for third-party tags are viewable — and modifiable — by creating a custom Property inspector.

✦ Dreamweaver's C-Level Extensibility feature enables C and C++ programmers to add new core functionality to a program.

✦ Tags from server-side applications can be viewed in the Document window, just as they would be when browsed online, when a custom translator is used. A custom translator often requires a C-level extension.

✦ You can use the Tag Library Editor to customize your Dreamweaver MX tag libraries.

In the next chapter, you learn how to create and use Dreamweaver MX objects.

✦　　✦　　✦

Creating and Using Objects

Sometimes the simplest ideas are the most powerful. The Dreamweaver development team had a simple idea: Why not code the insertable objects in HTML? After all, when you choose to insert anything into a Web page—from a horizontal rule to a Shockwave movie—you are just putting HTML in the page. If the objects are just HTML files, what are the possible benefits? For one, the objects can be easily modified. Also, HTML requires no special program to code, and coding the language itself is not extraordinarily difficult. In addition, the core users of Dreamweaver are experts in HTML. Now, a simple idea is turned into a powerful tool.

All the objects included with Dreamweaver can be modified and customized to fit any Web designer's working preferences. Furthermore, custom objects can easily be created. This capability not only enables you to include regular HTML tags that repeatedly occur in your designs, but also opens the door to an impressive new level of expandability. Dreamweaver's capability to accommodate any number of custom objects means you can take advantage of new technologies immediately.

Building a site that needs the latest tags just released by the W3C? Go right ahead—make an object that inserts any or all the tags. You may not be able to see the result in Dreamweaver, but if your browser can handle the tags, you can preview them there.

Find yourself including the same ActiveX control over and over again with only one change in the parameters? Create a custom object that inserts that control with all the constant attributes—and add a parameter form to enter the variable attributes.

This chapter shows you the tremendous potential of Dreamweaver objects. After studying the use of the standard objects, you learn how you can customize your object working environment. Then, you find out how to create your own objects and take advantage of the extensibility features in Dreamweaver.

Inserting Dreamweaver Objects

If you've been using Dreamweaver, you've been using objects. Even if your first exposure to Dreamweaver has been working through the first half of this book, you've already used several types of objects.

Aside from text, everything inserted in a Web page can be considered an object: images, comments, plugins, named anchors — they're all objects that are all extremely easy to use.

Dreamweaver offers several ways to include any object. For a few objects, you even have as many as four different techniques from which to choose:

✦ From the menu, choose Insert and then any of the listed objects.

✦ From the Insert bar (see Figure 34-1), click any button in the standard categories to insert an object at the current cursor position.

✦ Drag any button off the Insert bar and drop it next to any existing content on your Web page.

✦ Many objects have a keyboard shortcut, such as Ctrl+Alt+I (Command+Option+I) for Image or Ctrl+Alt+F (Command+Option+F) for a Flash movie. Keyboard shortcuts insert the chosen object at the current cursor location.

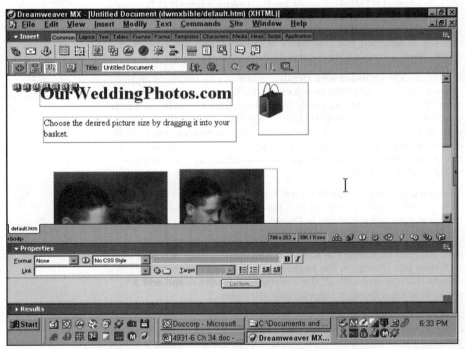

Figure 34-1: You'll find yourself returning to the Insert bar as an easy way to include HTML elements.

Tip

When you insert one of the objects that is classified as Invisible — such as a Comment or Named Anchor — Dreamweaver by default inserts an icon to show the object's placement. If you find these icons distracting, you can turn them all off by choosing the toggle command, View ⇨ Visual Aids ⇨ Invisible Elements. If an invisible element is turned off in Preferences, you never see the icon, regardless of the status of the View menu command.

Modifying the Insert Bar

The Insert bar is one of the most customizable of all Dreamweaver's features. In addition to the flexibility of having it "float" anywhere on the screen, you can also resize and reshape the panel to your liking. Most important, you can rearrange its contents, add new categories, and, as noted earlier, include custom objects.

Reorganizing the objects and adding categories

Dreamweaver organizes the Insert bar based in a file called insertbar.xml located in the Objects folder of the Dreamweaver configuration folder. This XML file contains all the tab and object information for each category of the Insert bar. To rearrange or create new categories, you have to manually edit the file. Dreamweaver picks up and shows all the objects inside a category's folder, so you don't need to manually add new objects to the insertbar.xml file.

You're not limited to the default categories on the Insert bar. If you want to add another category, simply add a new subfolder and the necessary entries to the insertbar.xml file (which I cover next). For example, I've developed a number of custom objects for inserting sound and digital video files, and I wanted to group them on a new category of the Insert bar. In my file management program, I created a folder called Media within the Dreamweaver MX\Configuration\Objects folder and moved all my special object files into the new folder. After editing the insertbar.xml file and restarting Dreamweaver, Media appears on the Insert bar in the order I placed the entry in insertbar.xml.

 Caution   Dreamweaver recognizes only one level of subfolders within the Objects folder as new Insert bar categories. You cannot, for instance, create a subfolder called Videos within the Media subfolder that will be recognized by Dreamweaver as a submenu.

Adding new categories

The only time you have to edit the insertbar.xml file is when you want to add a new category to the Insert bar. Like any other XML file, insertbar.xml is a tag-based file, and the tags accurately describe the data. Look at this portion of the insertbar.xml file as an example:

```
<insertbar>
<category id="DW_Insertbar_Common" folder="Common">
        <BUTTON id="DW_Hyperlink"
        image="Common\Hyperlink.gif"
        enabled=""
        showIf=""
        file="Common\Hyperlink.htm"/>

        <BUTTON id="DW_Email"
        image="Common\E-Mail Link.gif"
        enabled=""
...
</category>
</insertbar>
```

The <insertbar> tag opens your XML file, and the trailing </insertbar> tag closes it at the very end of insertbar.xml. The <category> tag defines the tabs in the Insert bar. Each <category> tag contains a <BUTTON> tag that defines each of the buttons in the category in the Insert bar.

Note If you make any changes to insertbar.xml that affect category names or positions, you must restart Dreamweaver for the changes to take effect. If you're simply moving or adding objects, then Ctrl+Click (Command+Click) on the options menu in the Insert bar and choose Reload Extensions.

Each <category> tag has two attributes, id and folder. The id attribute must be a unique identifier for each element, so you can't have the same identification for a category and a button. The folder attribute is the name of the folder inside the Configuration\Objects folder. The category in the Insert bar will take the name of the category from the name of the folder; or if there is a folderinfo.txt file in the folder, the category will take the name from the first line of that .txt file. The folderinfo.txt file is not required. So this example creates a category called My Objects:

```
<category id="DW_InsertBar_MyObjects" folder="My Objects">
</category>
```

That's all it takes to create a new category on the Insert bar. You can start placing objects in the folder you just created. Dreamweaver orders the categories in the order they're listed in insertbar.xml. If you want your new custom category to appear first on the Insert bar, simply add it to the very beginning of insertbar.xml.

Cross-Reference You can customize not only the Insert bar but also the menus. All menus are controlled via the menus.xml file found in the Configuration\Menus folder. For an in-depth look at how you can change your Insert — or any other — menu, as well as keyboard shortcuts, see Chapter 33.

Moving existing objects

Each of the categories of the Insert bar, which change depending on the particular server model you're working in, have a corresponding folder in the Program Files\Macromedia\Dreamweaver MX\Configuration\Objects\ directory. Each folder has a minimum of two items for each object: an HTML file and a GIF file. The HTML file is the source code for the object, and the GIF file is the button image. Some of the objects also have a JavaScript file, with a .js extension associated with it. If you want to move an item from one Insert bar tab to another, just transfer the files related to that object from one folder to the other.

For example, let's say you're doing a lot of JavaScript work and you want to move the Insert Script object from the Invisibles category to the Common category. To accomplish this task, you need to move Script.htm, Script.js, and Script.gif from the Invisibles folder to the Common folder. You can click and drag the files or cut and paste them (Windows only). You must restart Dreamweaver to see the changes.

Adding Other Objects

Before you begin building your own custom objects, you may want to look around and see if someone else has already created something similar. In addition to having the standard objects that ship with Dreamweaver, numerous Web sites have objects (and behaviors) that are available for download. Macromedia sponsors one of the largest collections at the Macromedia Exchange. You can also search another database of Dreamweaver objects (as well as behaviors, commands, and so on) at the Dreamweaver Extension Database, located on my site, Dreamweaver etc. (`www.idest.com/dreamweaver`). Of course, a variety of objects are available on the CD-ROM accompanying this book.

To facilitate the process of adding new objects and other extensions, Macromedia developed the aptly named Extension Manager. The Extension Manager is a cross-product utility that works with Dreamweaver, Fireworks, and Flash. The Extension Manager works with extensions created in a special format, Macromedia Exchange Package or MXP. MXP files contain the necessary files for the extension, all the required information on where the files should be installed, how to access the extension, who the author is, and more, as shown in Figure 34-2. With a properly formatted MXP file, the Extension Manager can even adjust your menu and keyboard shortcut settings.

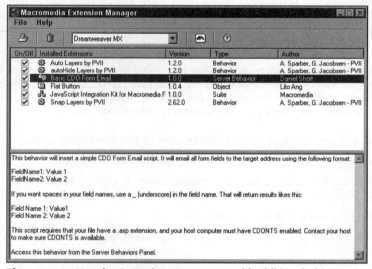

Figure 34-2: Use the Extension Manager to add additional objects without copying files.

The primary source for Macromedia Extension Package files is the Macromedia Exchange (`www.macromedia.com/exchange/`), but you can also retrieve these files from other sources such as developers' sites or this book's CD-ROM. If you've located the MXP file from the Internet, your browser may offer you alternative methods to start the installation:

✦ Download the file to your system and complete the installation after that process is complete.

✦ Install the file directly from the Internet.

Tip

It's a matter of personal preference, but I prefer to store all the extensions locally. The vast majority of them tend to be fairly small and if I need to install them again or on a different machine, I don't have to go through the download process again. Macromedia recommends that you maintain your extensions in the Configuration\Downloaded Extensions folder, but there's no real benefit to doing so if you'd prefer to store them elsewhere.

To complete the installation, follow these steps:

1. If you chose to open the extension from the Internet, the Extension Manager is automatically launched. If you downloaded the extension, double-click the .mxp file to launch the Extension Manager. In either case, the Macromedia Exchange legal disclaimer is presented.

2. Select the Accept button to continue with the installation or Decline to cancel it.

   After you accept the disclaimer, the Extension Manager informs you whether the installation is successful or alerts you to any errors it encounters, such as existing files with the same name.

If the installation succeeds, the extension is added to your list. The list displays the name of the installed extension, its version number, the type, and the author. Selecting the extension will give you a description of the extension, how to access the extension in the Dreamweaver interface, and usually a bit of help on how to use it or how to find help.

Tip   If you have a great number of extensions, you can sort the list in the Extension Manager by selecting the column heading. To change the display order from ascending to descending (to show, for example, the highest version numbers first) click the heading again under Windows; on Macintosh systems, select the sort-order button on top of the scroll bar.

You can also install an extension from within Dreamweaver by following these steps:

1. Choose Commands ➪ Manage Extensions to open the Extension Manager.

2. Select File ➪ Install Extension or use the keyboard shortcut, Ctrl+I (Command+O). Alternatively, Windows users can also select the Install New Extension button.

   The Select Extension to Install dialog box opens.

3. In the Select Extension dialog box, locate the desired .mxp file on your system and choose Install.

   The legal disclaimer is presented.

4. Select the Accept button to continue with the installation or Decline to cancel it.

5. After the installation is complete, choose File ➪ Exit (File ➪ Quit) to close the Extension Manager or click the Close button.

Caution   Some extensions require Dreamweaver to be relaunched in order to take effect.

Even though the Extension Manager is an integral part of the Dreamweaver toolbox, many older extensions, although perfectly usable, may not have been converted to the MXP format. To incorporate objects not in the Extension Manager format into your Dreamweaver system, follow these steps:

1. Uncompress the files if necessary. Object files come with an HTML file and a GIF file, and the two files are usually compressed for easy download or transfer.

2. If necessary, make a new folder for your objects and modify the insertbar.xml as noted in the previous section. All objects must be stored in a subfolder of the Dreamweaver MX\Configuration\Objects folder. You can either store the object files in a standard subfolder (Characters, Common, Forms, Frames, Head, Invisibles, or Special, for instance) or in a new folder that you create.

3. Transfer the object files to the desired folder. Be careful: Make sure you transfer both the HTML and the GIF file together.

Note The new object is automatically added as the last item on the Insert menu. If you want to customize the Insert menu to list the new object in a different location, you change the menus.xml file found in the Configuration\Menus folder.

4. Restart Dreamweaver.

Creating Custom Objects

Each custom object, like each standard object, is made from at least two files: an HTML file describing the object and a GIF file depicting the button. The complexity of the HTML depends on the complexity of the object. You can build just about anything—from a simple object that replicates a repeatedly used item to a high-end object that uses advanced JavaScript techniques for creating special function layers and windows. You can even make objects that create other objects.

To support the "higher end" of the custom object scale, Dreamweaver includes proprietary extensions to JavaScript and a Document Object Model (DOM), which combines a subset of Netscape Navigator 4.0's DOM, a subset of the DOM Level 1 established by the W3C, and a host of custom Dreamweaver extensions. You study these techniques later in this chapter. As the following section shows, however, many objects don't require any JavaScript and are easy to construct.

Note Although it's possible to split off the bulk of the JavaScript functionality into an included .js file, as Macromedia does for many objects, it's not absolutely necessary. This separation of the user interface (the HTML file) and the underlying code (the JavaScript file) is usually undertaken for localization purposes and to allow one developer to work on the interface while another works on the code.

Making simple objects

To make a simple object that inserts any HTML-created item, put only the code necessary to create the object into a file and then save the file in one of the object folders. The key phrase in the preceding sentence is *only the code necessary*. Unlike a regular Web page, you don't have to include the framing <html>...<body>...</body>...</html> sections for a simple custom object—all you need is the essential code necessary to make the object.

For example, let's say you are asked to enhance 100 Web pages and make each page capable of showing a different QuickTime movie. Each of the .mov files is different, so you can't use Dreamweaver's Library feature. The easiest way to handle this situation is to create a dummy version of what you need and then turn that dummy into an object.

The whole process involves these four steps:

✦ Creating the item

✦ Creating the object

✦ Saving the object

✦ Creating a button for the object

Online Sources for Dreamweaver Extensions

You can find new objects and behaviors at numerous online sources aside from the Macromedia Exchange. However, like traditional Web development, creating Dreamweaver extensions is an ever-growing affair—if you can't find what you're looking for at any one site, visit the Dreamweaver Extension Database hosted by Dreamweaver etc.

Dwfile

www.dwfile.com

Run by Paul Boon, dwfile.com is the place to go if you're looking to start building your own extensions. The site has an abundant amount of information on how to build extensions and a number of commercial extensions geared specifically to extension developers.

DWZone

www.dwzone.com

DWZone is part of a larger family of "Zone" sites, including FLZone (Flash) and FWZone (Fireworks). The site contains news articles, extensions and discussion forums, and you can even submit your own articles or extensions to the site.

Massimo's Corner of the Web

www.massimocorner.com

Massimo Foti produces high-quality extensions that fulfill many specific functions faced by a Web developer. For example, his site features extensions devoted to redirecting browsers as well as controlling remote windows and scrolling layers.

Webmonkey Editor Extensions Collection

www.hotwired.com/webmonkey/javascript/code_library/ed_ext

Although this area on the Hot Wired site could potentially hold other Web authoring tools' extensions, Dreamweaver is currently the only one on the market with the capability. You can find several professional-quality objects and behaviors, both cross-browser and browser-specific ones.

Yaromat

www.yaromat.com

Featuring objects, commands, and behaviors by Jaro von Flocken, Yaromat houses some of the most creative Dreamweaver extensions on the Web. His Layer f(x) behavior brings mathematical precision to layer movements, and his other creations are equally dramatic.

Dreamweaver etc.

www.idest.com/dreamweaver

Maintained by yours truly, Joseph Lowery, the Dreamweaver etc. site includes all the objects found on this book's CD-ROM, plus new ones posted after this book's publication.

DreamweaverFAQ

www.dreamweaverfaq.com/Resources/Extensions

Maintained and operated by Angela Buraglia, lead technical editor of this book, and Daniel Short, contributing author, the DreamweaverFAQ site is a wealth of information on all things Dreamweaver, including a large list of extensions and links to other developer sites. The site also sells a number of commercial extensions from leading extension developers.

Step 1: Creating the item

First, create your item as you normally would in Dreamweaver. For this example, insert a plugin and add all the standard attributes: name, height and width, pluginspage, border, v space, and h space—and even a few special parameters such as autostart and stretch. The only attribute that the example omits is the attribute that changes: the file source. You also want the movie to be centered wherever it's located, and you center the plugin. When finished, the complete code for the page and plugin, as generated by Dreamweaver, looks like the following:

```
<html>
<head>
<title>Untitled Document</title>
<meta http-equiv="Content-Type" content="text/html; charset=iso-8859-1">
</head>
<body bgcolor="#FFFFFF">
<div align="center">
  <embed src="" width="135" height="135" name="qtMovie" ⊃
pluginspage="http://www.apple.com/quicktime/" vspace="5" hspace="5" ⊃
border="5" stretch="true" autostart="false"></embed>
</div>
</body>
</html>
```

Step 2: Creating the object

The absolute simplest method available is to skip this step entirely and proceed to saving the HTML in an Objects subfolder as described in Step 3. Dreamweaver ignores the outer code and just inserts whatever is in the <body> tag. However, this technique might be confusing for future development of your object. I recommend that, if you have the time, you complete this step and remove the unnecessary code.

To create a simple object from the preceding, just cut everything in the code but the item (or items) you want repeated. In Code view, or using the Code inspector, select all the code from the opening <html> tag up to and including the <body> tag and then delete. Then delete the closing tags, </body> and </html>. The only remaining code is the following:

```
<div align="center">
  <embed src="" width="135" height="135" name="qtMovie" ⊃
pluginspage="http://www.apple.com/quicktime/" vspace="5" hspace="5" ⊃
border="5" stretch="true" autostart="false"></embed>
</div>
```

In previous Dreamweaver versions, removing the <body> tag would turn the page background to a dark-gray. In order to get the standard extension interface dark gray color, add the new extension DOCTYPE at the very beginning of the document:

```
<!DOCTYPE HTML SYSTEM "-//Macromedia//DWExtension ⊃
layout-engine 5.0//dialog">
```

Step 3: Saving the object

Now your object is ready to be saved. For Dreamweaver to recognize this or any other bit of code as an object, the file must be saved in the Configuration\Objects folder. You can choose to save your object in any of the existing subfolders or you can create a new subfolder within the Objects folder. For this example, place the object in the Media folder.

Caution You must save your new object in a subfolder within the Objects folder. Dreamweaver doesn't recognize objects saved individually in the Objects folder.

After the file is saved, you can restart Dreamweaver to test your object.

Step 4: Creating a button for the object

As shown in Figure 34-3, Dreamweaver displays an "unknown object" placeholder in the Insert bar because you haven't yet made a button image for the qtMovie object. In addition, unless you specifically include the new object in the menu configuration file, menus.xml, the object is listed in the bottom portion of the Insert menu. This arrangement is fine for debugging, but if you want to continue using your object, it's more efficient to create a button image for it and revise the menus.xml file to include it. The following section shows you how to complete this task.

The "unknown object" placeholder

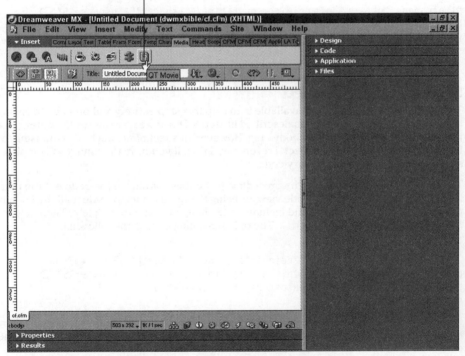

Figure 34-3: You can create custom objects such as the qtMovie object shown here.

Building an object button

Object buttons are GIF files, ideally sized at 18 pixels square. To make the object button, you can use any graphics-creation program that can save GIF files. If your button image file is not 18 pixels by 18 pixels, Dreamweaver resizes it to those dimensions. Your button can be as colorful as you want—as long as it can still fit in an 18-pixel square.

Tip   To create an object button, you can open and modify any of the existing GIF files for the standard buttons. Just be sure to use the Save As command of your graphics program — and not the Save command — to save your modified version.

After you've created your button image, save the GIF file in the same folder as the HTML file for the new object. To get the icon to display correctly, be sure to name the GIF file exactly the same as the HTML file for the object.

Putting JavaScript to Work in Custom Objects

The remaining sections of this chapter deal with using JavaScript to create more complex objects.

Tip   If you're totally unfamiliar with JavaScript, you might want to review this section with a good supporting resource at hand. An excellent choice is Danny Goodman's *JavaScript Bible,* published by Hungry Minds, Inc.

Using the objectTag() function

When Macromedia built a JavaScript interpreter into Dreamweaver, a number of custom DOM functions were included to facilitate object and behavior creation. One of these functions, `objectTag()`, is the key to building advanced objects. All the standard Dreamweaver-built objects use the `objectTag()` function. This function has a single purpose: It writes any specified value into the HTML document.

New Feature   If you need to do any validation inside your objects or create more complex objects, check out Dreamweaver's new `insertObject()` function. The `insertObject()` function enables you to insert code into more than one place, insert code somewhere other than the insertion point, and validate user input. See the extending Dreamweaver documents under Help ⇨ Extending Dreamweaver for more information.

The `objectTag()` is multifunctional; it can insert code in the <head> as well as the <body>. Moreover, the function handles the placement intelligently; `objectTag()` knows which tags should be placed where. Consequently, you don't have to make any special declarations to place code in the <head> section.

You can see a simple use of the `objectTag()` function by looking at the source code for Dreamweaver's Insert Line-Break object. In the Objects\Characters folder, open Line Break.htm and look at the code for this object in Code view. Just like most JavaScript functions that can affect any portion of the page, the `objectTag()` function is written in the <head> section. Here's the function in its entirety:

```
function objectTag() {
  // Return the html tag that should be inserted
  return "<BR>";
}
```

Tip   You should designate a ToolTip to appear when your mouse passes over your new object's button. Enter the desired name in the <title> section of the HTML object file. The designated <title> also appears on any dialog boxes used by the object. If there is no title, then "Untitled Document" will be displayed in the ToolTip.

Aside from the comment line, `objectTag()` returns only one value. In the preceding example, the value happens to be `"<BR>"`. You can insert any HTML code as the return value. However, because JavaScript formats any value as a string, you need to apply JavaScript string-formatting syntax, as follows:

✦ To use the `objectTag()` function to return an HTML tag and a variable, use quotes around each string literal, but not around the variable, and join the two with a plus sign. For example, the following `objectTag()` function code inserts `<img src=images/whatzit.gif>` in the current cursor position:

```
nada = "images/whatzit.gif"
return "<img src=" + nada + ">";
```

✦ To make an object that returns separate lines of code, put each tag on its own line with the symbol for a newline, `\n`, at the end of the string, surrounded by quotes; then add a plus sign at the end of the line. For example, the following `objectTag()` function inserts a Flash movie of a particular size and shape:

```
function objectTag() {
    // Return the html tag that should be inserted
    return '\n' +
'<object classid="clsid:D27CDB6E-AE6D-11cf-96B8-444553540000"
codebase="http://active.macromedia.com/flash2/cabs/swflash.
cab#version=4,0,0,0". "width="145" height="135"> \n' +
' <param name="movie" value="newMovie.swf"> \n' +
' <param name="PLAY" value="false"> \n' +
' <embed src="newMovie.swf" \n' +
'pluginspage="http://www.macromedia.com/shockwave/download/
index.cgi?P1_Prod_Version=ShockwaveFlash" width="145" height="135"
play="false"></embed> \n' +
'</object>'
}
```

Some developers prefer to set the entire collection of strings to a variable and return that variable. In this case, you'd be better served by using JavaScript's add-by-value operator (+=), as in this example:

```
var retval = '';
retval += '<table width="' + newWidth + '" height="' + newHeight +
'" border="0" cellspacing="0" cellpadding="0">\n';
retval += '  <tr>\n';
retval += '    <td>' + newCode + '</td>\n';
retval += '  </tr>\n';
retval += '</table>\n';
return retval;
```

✦ Use single quotes to surround the return values that include double quotes. For every opening quote of one kind, make sure a matching closing quote exists of the same kind. For example:

```
return '<img src="images/eiffel.jpg">';
```

✦ Use the backslash character, \, to display special inline characters such as double and single quotes or newline.

```
return "<strong>You\'re Right!</strong>";
```

Tip

Unless you're mixing variables with the HTML you're using for your object, you should use the "object-only" method described in the earlier section, "Making simple objects." Reserve the `objectTag()` function for your intermediate-to-advanced object-creation projects.

Offering help

As features are added, objects often grow in complexity. An object with multiple parameters — especially if it is intended for public release — could potentially benefit from a Help button. Dreamweaver offers just such a button to aid custom-object builders and their users.

Including the `displayHelp()` function causes Dreamweaver to display a Help button, directly beneath the OK and Cancel buttons found to the right of a user-created parameter form. When selected, this button calls whatever is defined in the function.

For example, to define a Help button that would put up an informative message within Dreamweaver, you might code the `displayHelp()` function this way:

```
displayHelp() {
   alert("Be sure to name all your layers first")
}
```

You're not restricted to in-program alerts. If you have a much larger help file, you can display it in your primary browser by using Dreamweaver's built-in `browseDocument()` function. With the following definition, when the Help button is selected, Dreamweaver first opens the primary browser (if it's not already running) and shows the object-specific help file:

```
displayHelp() { dreamweaver.browseDocument⤵
("http://www.idest.com/dreamweaver/help/entitiesHelp.htm")
}
```

Note that the preceding code includes an absolute URL that pulls a page off the Web. You can also reference a file locally. The best way to do this is to use another Dreamweaver JavaScript function, `getConfigurationPath()`. Just as it sounds, this function returns the current path to the Configuration folder. Using this as a base, you can reference other files installed on the system. In this example, the help file is stored in a folder called HelpDocs, which in turn is stored within the Configuration folder:

```
function displayHelp() {
   var helpPath = dreamweaver.getConfigurationPath() + ⤵
"/Configuration/ExtensionsHelp/Replicator/replicatorHelp.htm"
   dreamweaver.browseDocument(helpPath)
}
```

Attaching a parameter form

To be truly useful, many objects require additional attributes. Several of the standard objects in Dreamweaver use parameter forms to simplify entry of these attributes. A *parameter form* is the portion of the object code that creates a dialog box. Dreamweaver uses the HTML form commands for handling the parameter form duties.

To see how a parameter form is structured, look at the parameter forms used in the standard objects. Select the Insert Script button in the Script category of the Insert bar. The Script dialog box that appears on the screen is a basic parameter form.

Next, open the Script object source file (Objects\Script\Script.htm) in Dreamweaver to see how the parameter form is built. As shown in Figure 34-4, the `<body>` of the file consists of a single `<form>` element with two items inside, a text field and a menu list.

Insert Script dialog box   Parameter form

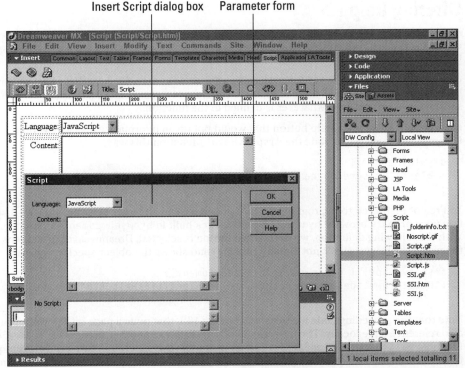

Figure 34-4: To see how the parameter form is used, compare the Script source file to its completed object.

The `<body>` section of the HTML source code for the Script object contains only the `<form>` with three fields: a `<select>` field (the menu list used to select the language), a `<textarea>` field for the actual script, and a `<textarea>` field for the No Script content:

```
<form name="theform">
  <table>
    <tr>
      <td align="right" nowrap>Language:</td>
      <td colspan="4"> <select name="Language">
          <option value="JS" selected>JavaScript</option>
          <option value="JS11">JavaScript1.1</option>
          <option value="JS12">JavaScript1.2</option>
          <option value="VB">VBScript</option>
        </select> </td>
    </tr>
    <tr>
      <td align="right" height="5"></td>
```

```
        <td colspan="4" rowspan="2"> <textarea name="script" cols="50" ⊃
rows="8"></textarea>
        </td>
    </tr>
    <tr>
        <td align="right" valign="top" nowrap>Content:</td>
    </tr>
    <tr>
        <td align="right" height="5"></td>
        <td colspan="4" rowspan="2"><textarea name="noscript" ⊃
cols="50"></textarea></td>
    </tr>
    <tr>
        <td align="right" valign="top" nowrap>No Script:</td>
    </tr>
  </table>
</form>
```

Sizing the Parameter Form Dialog Box

Although you cannot control all aspects of your parameter form—Dreamweaver automatically inserts the OK and Cancel buttons on the upper right—you can designate the dimensions of the parameter's dialog box. Generally, Dreamweaver sizes the dialog box automatically, but for a complex object, you can speed up the display by using the `windowDimensions()` function. Moreover, if your object is intended for general distribution, you can set different window dimensions for the Macintosh and Windows platforms.

The `windowDimensions()` function takes one argument, `platform`, and returns a string in the following form:

```
"width_in_Pixels,height_in_Pixels"
```

The size specified should not include the area for the OK and Cancel buttons. If the dimensions offered are too small to display all the options in the parameter form, scroll bars automatically appear.

The following example of the `windowDimensions()` function creates a parameter form dialog box 650 × 530 pixels if viewed on a Macintosh and 670 × 550 pixels if viewed on a Windows system:

```
function windowDimensions(platform){
    if (platform.charAt(0) == 'm'){ // Macintosh
      return "650,530";
    }
    else { // Windows
      return "670,550";
    }
}
```

Macromedia recommends that you not use the `windowDimensions()` function unless you want your dialog box to be larger than 640 × 480 pixels. Like all Dreamweaver extensions to the Application Programming Interface (API), the `windowDimensions()` function can be used to build both objects and actions.

When the parameter form is displayed as an object, Dreamweaver automatically adds the OK and Cancel buttons; a Help button is added if the `displayHelp()` function is defined. When you select the OK button, the `objectTag()` function combines the values in the `<select>` and `<textarea>` tags with the necessary HTML tags to write the `<script>` code.

Using the form controls

Dreamweaver uses the HTML `<form>` tag and all its various input types to gather attribute information for objects. To use the form elements in a parameter form, their input data must be passed to the JavaScript functions. Because Dreamweaver uses a subset of the Navigator 4.0 Document Object Model (DOM), as shown in Table 34-1, you are restricted to using specific methods for the various input types to gather this information. Properties marked with an asterisk are read-only.

Table 34-1: Form Elements in the Dreamweaver Document Object Model

Object	Properties	Methods	Events
form	elements* (an array of button, checkbox, password, radio, reset, select, submit, text, and text area objects); child objects by name	None	None
Button reset submit	form*	blur() focus()	OnClick
checkbox radio	checked form*	blur() focus()	OnClick
password	value	blur()	OnBlur
text Textarea	form*	focus() select()	OnFocus
select	form*	blur() (Windows only)	onBlur (Windows only)
	options[n].defaultSelected*	focus() (Windows only)	OnChange
	options[n].index*		onFocus() (Windows only)
	options[n].selected*		
	options[n].text*		
	options[n].value		
	selectedIndex		

Note JavaScript uses a hierarchical method of addressing the various elements on any given Web page. Moving from most general to most specific, each element is separated by a period. For example, the background color property of a page is `document.bgColor`. The status of a checkbox named "sendPromo" on a form called "orderForm" is `document.orderForm.sendPromo.checked`. The more complex your objects, the more important it is for you to master this syntax.

Input fields: Text, textarea, password, file, image, and hidden

When information is entered in one of the input type fields, the data is stored in the value property of the specific object. For example, look again at the code for the Plugin object and notice the text field where the selected file's name is displayed:

```
<INPUT TYPE="text" name="pluginfilename" size="30">
```

When the `objectTag()` function is run, the contents of that text box are assigned to a variable, and that variable is included in the output written to the Web page:

```
function objectTag() {
  // Return the html tag that should be inserted
  var retval = '<EMBED SRC="' +
escape(document.forms[0].pluginfilename.value) + '"></EMBED>';

  // clear the field for next insertion
  clearForm();
  return retval;
}
```

In the preceding case, the input filename is located in:

```
document.forms[0].pluginfilename.value
```

Because the form was also named ("theForm"), this same value could also be written as follows:

```
document.theForm.pluginfilename.value
```

Note The "escape" function is an internal JavaScript function that converts a text string so that it can be read by a Web server. Any special characters are encoded into their hexadecimal ASCII equivalents. A single space between words, for instance, is converted to %20.

The text input types recognize two events in the Dreamweaver DOM: `onBlur` and `onFocus`. When a user selects a text field, either by tabbing to or clicking it, that text field is said to have focus — and the `onFocus` event is fired. When the user leaves that field, the field loses focus or blurs — and the `onBlur` event is triggered. Because the DOM does not recognize the `onChange` event handler with text fields, you can use a combination of `onFocus` and `onBlur` to check for changes and act accordingly.

Submit, Reset, and Command buttons

The button input types are used in parameter forms to trigger custom JavaScript functions. Instead of sending data to an external server, the data is sent to a specified internal function. The buttons respond only to `onClick` events and cannot pass any particular properties of their own, such as value or name.

Command buttons are used extensively in the Character Entities object shown in Figure 34-5. (The object was developed before Dreamweaver's Other Characters object was created.) Each character entity is a separate Command button, written in the following form:

```
<input type="BUTTON" value="&#161;"
onClick="getChar('&amp;#161;','&#161;')">
```

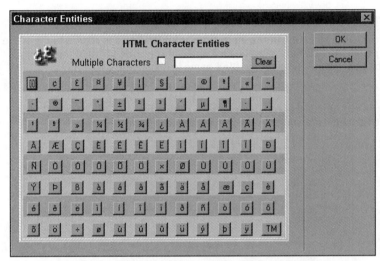

Figure 34-5: This custom Character Entities object uses 97 separate Command buttons.

Each character entity symbol in each line has a specific purpose. The value is the character displayed on the button; the first argument in the getChar() function is written to a hidden field and eventually sent to the Web page; and the second argument is used to display the selected character in a text box.

```
function getChar(val,val2) {
  document.theForm.charValue.value=val
  document.theForm.txChar.value=val2
}
```

When this object is at work, the user makes a selection, clicks OK, and the objectTag() function reads the value from the hidden field and writes it into the Web page:

```
function objectTag() {
  return document.theForm.charValue.value;
}
```

Command buttons can be used to fire any custom JavaScripts and pass any necessary information to be processed eventually by the objectTag() function.

Checkboxes

Checkboxes enable an option to be selected or deselected, so the only information that a function needs from a checkbox is whether it has been selected. Dreamweaver's DOM enables you to read the checked property of the Checkbox object and act accordingly. The Character

Entities object discussed in the preceding section, for instance, uses a checkbox to turn on and off the Multiple Characters option. If the checkbox (named cbMultiple) is selected, `document.theForm.cbMultiple.checked` is true, and one set of statements is executed; otherwise, the second set of statements is run. The code for checkboxes follows:

```
function getChar(val,val2) {
if(document.theForm.cbMultiple.checked) {
  document.theForm.charValue.value=
  document.theForm.charValue.value+val
  document.theForm.txChar.value=
  document.theForm.txChar.value+val2
  } else {
  document.theForm.charValue.value=val
  document.theForm.txChar.value=val2
  }
}
```

Checkboxes are excellent for setting up yes/no situations. You can also use checkboxes to set (turn on) particular attributes. You may, for instance, use a checkbox to make it possible for the user to enable an automatic startup for a QuickTime movie or to turn the control panel on or off.

Radio buttons

Radio buttons offer a group of options from which the user can select only one. The group is composed of `<input type=radio>` tags with the same name attribute; there can be as few as two in the group or as many as necessary.

The input type `radio`, like `checkbox`, makes use of the checked property to see which option was selected. The method used to figure out which of the radio buttons was chosen depends on the number of buttons used on the form:

✦ With just two or three buttons, you may want to use a simple if-else construct to determine which radio button was selected.

✦ If you are offering many options, you can use a loop structure to look at the checked property of each radio button.

With only a couple of radio buttons in a group, you can examine the one radio-type item in the array (starting with 0) to see if it was checked. In the following code, if one radio button is selected, the variable (theChoice) is set to one value — otherwise, it is set to the other value:

```
if (document.forms[0].comm[0].checked == "1")
    theChoice = "left";
  else
    theChoice = "right";
```

When you have many radio buttons, or you don't know how many radio buttons you will have, use a counter loop such as the one shown in this next example from the Enhanced LineBreak object:

```
for (var i = 0; i < document.theForm.lbreak.length; i++) {
    if (document.theForm.lbreak[i].checked) {
        break
    }
}
```

In this example, `lbreak` is the name of the group of radio buttons on the parameter form, and the `length` property tells you how many radio buttons are in the group. When the loop finds the selected radio button in the array, the loop is broken, and the program proceeds to the next group of statements.

Unfortunately, after you know which radio button is checked, there's no easy way to get its value. The Dreamweaver DOM doesn't support the value property for the radio input type. As a result, you have to assign the value to a variable based on which radio button was selected. You can complete this task in a simple series of if-else statements:

```
if (i == 0){
val = ""
      } else {
      if (i == 1) {
      val = "left"
            } else {
            if (i == 2) {
            val = "right"
                 } else {
                 val = "all"
                 }
            }
      }
}
```

Alternatively, you can put all the values in an array and assign them in a statement like the following:

```
return "<br clear=" + newValue[i].name + ">"
```

List boxes and drop-down menus

List boxes and drop-down menus are perfect for offering a variety of options in a compact format. Drop-down menus enable the user to choose an option from a scrolling list; list boxes offer multiple choices from a similar list. Both use the `<select>` tag to set up their available options. When you include a list box or drop-down menu from Dreamweaver, you enter the options by selecting the List Value button and entering the item labels and their associated values in the dialog box. The code for the Direction list box — taken from Matthew David's Marquee object, which is shown in Figure 34-6 — is written as follows:

```
<select name="direction">
     <option value="LEFT" selected>LEFT</option>
     <option value="RIGHT">RIGHT</option>
     <option value="UP">UP</option>
     <option value="DOWN">DOWN</option>
</select>
```

Each list box or drop-down menu must have a unique name — in the preceding code, that name is "direction," given in the `<select>` tag. To discover which option the user selected when working with a drop-down menu, you need to examine the selected Index property of the named `<select>` object. Each `<option>` in a `<select>` tag is placed in an array in the order listed in the displayed menu. Remember, arrays always start with a zero in JavaScript.

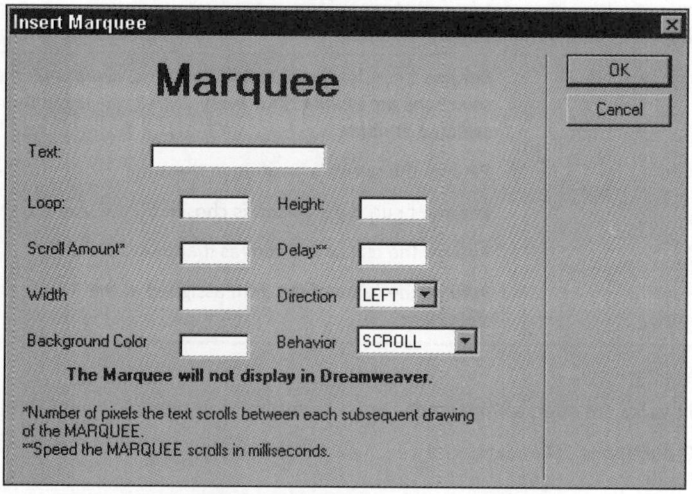

Figure 34-6: The Marquee custom object is designed to take advantage of an Internet Explorer special function: the capability to make a scrolling text display.

The following code looks at each member of the array; if that option is the one in which the selectedIndex property is true, the proper value is assigned to a variable:

```
if(document.forms[0].direction.selectedIndex == 0) {
  direct_choice = 'LEFT'
  } else {
  if(document.forms[0].direction.selectedIndex == 1) {
  direct_choice = 'RIGHT'
  } else {
      if(document.forms[0].direction.selectedIndex == 2) {
      direct_choice = 'UP'
  } else {
      if(document.forms[0].direction.selectedIndex == 3) {
      direct_choice = 'DOWN'
  }
  }
 }
 }
```

The process is slightly different when you have multiple options in a list box. In this situation, you should set up a loop to examine the options[n].selected property. All the options in a <select> tag set have additional properties that can be read by Dreamweaver's DOM, as follows:

Select Option	Description
options[n].defaultSelected	Returns true for the option (or options, when multiple selections are enabled) for every <option> tag with a selected attribute
options[n].index	Returns the option's position in the array
options[n].selected	Returns true if the option is chosen by the user
options[n].text	Returns the text of the item as it appears in the list
options[n].value	Returns the value of the item assigned in the <option> statement

The following method cycles through all the <options> to find which one(s) were selected:

```
for (var i = 0; i < document.theForm.optList.length; i++) {
  if (document.theForm.optList.options[i].selected) {
      result += "\n " + document.theForm.optList.options[i]. ⤶
      value
      }
  }
return result
}
```

Adding images to your objects

Custom objects don't have to be just text, of course. You can include images in your object, just as you would in a regular Web page — with one catch: Dreamweaver has to be able to find your image files. If you are not distributing your custom object, you can use images from any folder on your system. On the other hand, if your objects are going out to other users, you have to either include the image files with the object or use existing graphics stored in known locations.

What existing graphics are on every Dreamweaver system in specific locations? The GIF files for each object, of course. The button for the custom Character Entities object (previously shown in Figure 34-5) is used in the dialog box for the object itself. Because the two files always have to be in the same folder, you can include the image file on the same level. The size of the GIF files is fairly small (18 pixels by 18 pixels), so you can simply double the size of the image and have Dreamweaver rescale it.

Tip   The opposite approach for using one image for both the Insert bar and your dialog box is to make a larger image, say 32 × 32. Often this results in a better looking graphic in both places.

Of course, you can create your own custom graphics for your objects and include those files with the associated HTML and GIF button files. You can even spice up your Dreamweaver standard objects, as shown in Figure 34-7.

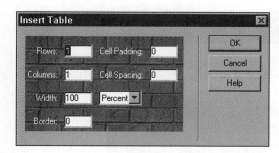

Figure 34-7: You can include graphics in custom objects; in this Insert Table dialog box, the standard Dreamweaver object is altered to add a brick background.

Tip You can count on several other useful graphical objects, all found in the Configuration\ Shared\MM\Images folder. In addition to the plus and minus buttons used in the Dreamweaver dialog boxes for behaviors and parameters, there are GIF files for standard up and down arrows, a transparent 1-pixel image to use for spacing, and more.

Using layers and Flash movies in objects

Standard HTML layout options are fairly limiting. You can, however, use layers in your custom Object dialog boxes. With the expansive possibilities of layers, you can build a Wizard-type object that leads users through a series of complex steps with instructions on every screen. You can also use layers to describe the effect of the user's choices.

For an excellent example of the use of layers to create a Dreamweaver extension, take a look at the Drag Layer behavior, discussed in Chapter 23. This behavior uses five different layers to reveal new options as the user makes certain choices; there's even an error layer to inform the user of a precondition to using the object.

Note Layers enable you to pack in a lot of information — and amass a great deal of input — in a single parameter form. One of the best examples of a multilayered object is Dreamweaver CourseBuilder Knowledge Object. CourseBuilder is a version of the program customized for Web learning, and the Knowledge object is the primary interface. Amazingly enough, all the key functionality of the program is contained in the one object.

Another available option in Dreamweaver objects is the capability to use Flash movies — or any plugin on the system — within the parameter form. All that's required is that the user has the same plugin available on his system.

With Flash's scalable vector graphics, animation capabilities, and interactivity, user interfaces have the potential to take a tremendous leap forward. Instead of a Help message, you can build in a training video that demonstrates particularly difficult concepts.

Incorporating a Flash file in your object's parameter form is no different from using it in your Web page. Just choose Insert ➪ Flash or select the Insert Flash button from the Insert bar. Dreamweaver automatically reads the correct size from the Flash file. Make sure any other parameters you desire are set, and you've just created an advanced user interface! To get an idea of what's possible, take a look at Figure 34-8, which shows a Dreamweaver command that uses Flash as the interface, playing in Dreamweaver.

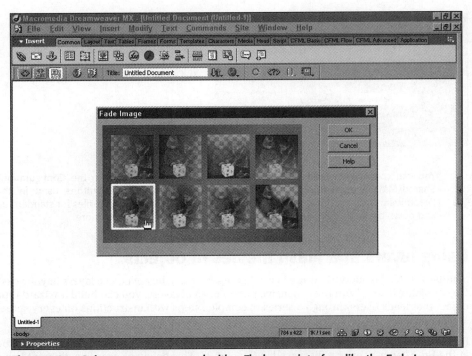

Figure 34-8: Spice up your command with a Flash user interface like the Fade Image command from the author.

Summary

In one sense, objects are analogous to the macros in a word processing program that enable repetitive work to be greatly simplified. Objects can be so much more than just duplication tools, however — they can extend the reach of Dreamweaver's power and instantly incorporate new standards and technology. The standard Dreamweaver objects can be used effortlessly. Just like all objects, they are simply HTML files, and thus provide excellent examples for creating custom objects.

✦ Objects can be inserted from either the Insert bar or the Insert menu.

✦ Both the Insert bar and the Insert menu can be easily modified by adjusting the menus.xml file.

✦ Simple objects can be created by inserting the HTML code necessary to make the object into a file and then saving the file in one of the object's subfolders.

✦ More complex objects can take advantage of Dreamweaver's built-in JavaScript interpreter, its Document Object Model (DOM), special JavaScript functions, and enhanced Application Programming Interface (API). In Dreamweaver, you can even use layers to construct custom objects.

In the next chapter, you learn how to use Dreamweaver behaviors.

✦   ✦   ✦

Creating a Behavior

The technology of Dreamweaver client-side behaviors is open, and anybody with the requisite JavaScript and HTML skills can write one. To talk about *writing* a behavior, however, is a bit of a mistake. You never actually touch the event portion of the behavior — you work only on the action file. To help the creation process, Dreamweaver provides a comprehensive Extending Dreamweaver document, which covers all the custom functions, JavaScript extensions, and the Document Object Model (DOM) that Dreamweaver recognizes.

The functionality and implementation of behaviors in Dreamweaver have greatly expanded since the original release. By incorporating a much broader DOM, Dreamweaver can now read and affect virtually any element on the current HTML page. You can even use behaviors to open other existing documents or create new Web pages from scratch. Perhaps more importantly, the JavaScript API (that is, the set of JavaScript functions built into Dreamweaver) is extremely comprehensive, offering over 600 functions affecting virtually every area of extensibility.

This chapter covers the primary features pertaining directly to behaviors, but the majority of the JavaScript API is beyond the scope of this book. Before delving into the nuts-and-bolts of behavior building, here's an overview of the process of creating a behavior.

Creating a Behavior from Scratch

Writing a behavior is not so complex when you take it one step at a time. In all, you need to follow just six basic steps to create a behavior from scratch:

✦ **Step 1: Define your behavior.** A behavior is an automatic method of incorporating a particular JavaScript function. The best way to begin building your behavior is to write — and, of course, debug — that function. When you create the Dreamweaver behavior, the function will be incorporated into its action file.

✦ **Step 2: Create the action file.** One of the key functions in Dreamweaver behaviors is, aptly enough, `behaviorFunction()`, which inserts your function into the `<head>` section of the Web page. Dreamweaver enables you to include multiple functions as well as single ones.

✦ **Step 3: Build the user interface.** As you look through the standard Dreamweaver behaviors, you see a dialog box that acts as the user interface in all but a few instances. The user interface that you create is based on HTML forms and is alternately referred to as a *parameter form* and seen by the user as a dialog box.

✦ **Step 4: Apply the behavior.** Both an event and an action are required to make up a behavior. The `applyBehavior()` function ties your new function to a specific tag and event. `applyBehavior()` also passes the necessary arguments to the function in the `<head>` section.

✦ **Step 5: Inspect the behavior.** From a user's point of view, building a Web page is often a trial-and-error process. You try one setting and if it doesn't work, you try another. To modify settings for a particular behavior, the user double-clicks the behavior name to reopen the dialog box and change the settings. The `inspectBehavior()` function handles the restoration of the previous values to the parameters form for easy editing.

✦ **Step 6: Test your behavior.** The final step, as in any software development, is testing. You need to try out your new behavior in a variety of Web browsers and debug it, if necessary (and believe me . . . it's always necessary).

To demonstrate the process of creating a behavior, the next few sections take you through a real-world example: the construction of a Set Layer Z Index action by Massimo Foti, esteemed Dreamweaver/Fireworks maven and extension developer (see www.massimocorner.com/). Although it's easy to change the depth of a layer — its Z index — in the design phase, having a layer pop to the front is also a desirable dynamic effect. Massimo has designed a cross-browser behavior that enables Web designers to control layer depth interactively. Set Layer Z Index is a relatively simple but elegant behavior and, as such, perfect for understanding how behaviors in general are constructed.

Note Dreamweaver includes a standard behavior — Change Property — that can also change the Z index of a layer, but it doesn't work across browsers. To get the same effectiveness as Massimo's behavior, you'd have to apply Change Property twice: once for Netscape browsers and again for Internet Explorer.

Step 1: Define your behavior

Behaviors are born of need, desire, or a combination of both. After repeating a single operation a thousand times, you probably find yourself thinking "There's got to be a better way." The better way usually automates the process in any possible way. In the case of inserting JavaScript functions into Web pages, the better way is to create a behavior.

Starting from this vantage point already accomplishes the first phase of behavior creation: defining the behavior. If you were to add the necessary code to a single page to change the Z index of a layer dynamically, it would look like the following code.

Note The lines appearing in boldface type in the following code are the key parts of the file: the function in the `<script>` section (the action) and the runtime function call attached to the text link (the event). After being tested in several browsers, the function is judged to be sound and can be made into a behavior.

```
<html>
<head>
<title>Set Layer Z Index, Massimo Foti</title>
```

```
<meta http-equiv="Content-Type" content="text/html; charset=iso-8859-1">
<script language="JavaScript">
<!--
function tmt_LayerIndex(theTarget, theValue) {
    if (document.layers) {
        target = eval(theTarget);
        target.zIndex = theValue;
    }
    if (document.all) {
        eval("theTarget=theTarget.replace(/.layers/gi, '.all')");
        eval(theTarget + ".style.zIndex = theValue");
    }
}
//-->
</script>
</head>
<body bgcolor="#FFFFFF">
<a href="#" onClick="tmt_LayerIndex('document.layers[\'backLayer\']','4')">
 Click to Bring Layer to Front</a>
<div id="backLayer" style="position:absolute; left:125px; top:95px;
 width:327px; height:142px; z-index:1; background-color: #CCCCFF;
 layer-background-color: #CCCCFF; border: 1px none #000000">
  <p>Back layer</p>
</div>
<div id="frontLayer" style="position:absolute; left:238px; top:45px;
 width:162px; height:258px; z-index:2; background-color: #FFCCCC;
 layer-background-color: #FFCCCC; border: 1px none #000000">
  <p>Front Layer</p>
</div>
</body>
</html>
```

When you define your behavior in this manner, it tells you the arguments you need to generalize. In this example, two exist: theTarget and theValue. Ideally, your action should be flexible enough to enable any argument to be user-defined. Here there are at most two attributes to take in through your parameter form and pass to the function.

After you've created and tested your function in Dreamweaver, save it. I've found it helpful to go back to the original file as I build my action and verify that I have everything in working order.

If you'd like to look at the Set Layer Z Index behavior code in full, you'll find it in the Chapter 35 Examples folder on the CD-ROM that accompanies this book. If you'd like to install the Set Layer Z Index behavior, use the Extension Manager (Help ➪ Manage Extensions) to install the behavior from the CD-ROM's Additional Extensions\Massimo Foti\Behaviors folder.

Step 2: Create the action file

In the next phase of behavior creation, you build the skeleton of the action file and begin filling in the necessary JavaScript functions. Each action file must have, at a minimum, the following four functions:

✦ `canAcceptBehavior()`: Determines if the behavior should be available. If not available, the entry in the Add Action (+) drop-down list is not selectable.

✦ `behaviorFunction()`: Inserts the general function in the `<head>` section of the Web page.

✦ `applyBehavior()`: Attaches the runtime function to the selected tag and inserts the chosen event.

✦ `inspectBehavior()`: Enables the user to reopen the parameter form and make modifications to the original settings.

Note   One of the easiest ways to start an action file is to adapt one that is already built. You can open and modify any of the existing Dreamweaver standard action files, as long as you remember to use the File ➪ Save As feature command and give your file a new name.

Behaviors and other extensions can include external JavaScript files through the `<script language="javascript" src="script.js"></script>` construct. All the Dreamweaver behaviors take advantage of this facility. Its key benefit is to enable easy sharing of JavaScript code among different functions. Although you can still combine the user interface and JavaScript aspects of a behavior in one file, the standard practice is to store your parameter form instructions in the HTML file, such as Play Sound.htm, and the JavaScript in a JS file with an identical name, such as Play Sound.js. We'll use it to make commonly used functions in our script.

Here are the steps to follow in the initial behavior creation phase:

1. Choose File ➪ New to open a new HTML file.

2. Select Modify ➪ Page Properties to change the title of your action file.

3. Choose File ➪ Save to save the HTML file under a new name in the Configuration\Behaviors\Actions folder.

4. Switch to Code view, open the Code inspector, or use your favorite text editor to work on the code for your new action.

Tip   It's best to work on the parameter form — the user interface — in Dreamweaver's Design view and, if your function code is extensive, work on your JavaScript file in Code view.

5. Insert the code to include external JavaScript in the `<head>` of the document.

   For this example, Massimo's uses a series of his own JavaScript functions — and borrows one or two of Macromedia's — in three separate files:

```
<script language="javascript"
src="../../../Shared/Tmt/Scripts/TMT_doc.js"></script>
<script language="javascript"
src="../../../Shared/Tmt/Scripts/TMT_strings.js"></script>
<script language="javascript"
src="../../../Shared/Tmt/Scripts/TMT_UI.js"></script>
```

6. Enter a new `<script language='javascript'>...</script>` tag pair in the `<head>` section of the document.

7. Open your original function test file.

8. Copy the function from the original file to the new behavior file. In our Set Layer Z Index example, the function `tmt_LayerIndex()` is copied.

Caution

Make sure that your behavior name is unique. Whenever you first open the Behaviors panel, Dreamweaver checks to see if multiple function names exist. In the case of repetitive function names, Dreamweaver recognizes the earlier file but not the later one.

9. Add the following functions to the body of the `<script>` tag:

```
function canAcceptBehavior() {
   return true;
}
function behaviorFunction() {
   return tmt_LayerIndex;
}
function applyBehavior() {
   return "";
}
function inspectBehavior(msgStr) {
}
```

Only one function, `behaviorFunction()`, is completed at this time; the rest are place-holders for required functions that you'll code later.

Tip

The `behaviorFunction()` returns just one function, `tmt_LayerIndex`. `behaviorFunction()` can, however, return multiple functions. For more on this capability, see the section "Dreamweaver Behavior Techniques," later in this chapter.

After you've laid out the basic behavior structure, the next step is to define when the behavior can be used. You use the `canAcceptBehavior()` function for this step. If the behavior has no special requirements — such as needing one or more images on the page — you can leave the `canAcceptBehavior()` function as is. Our example behavior uses layers, so the behavior should be available only if layers exist on the current page. To check for layers, use this code:

```
function canAcceptBehavior() {
  var nameArray = getObjectRefs("NS 4.0","document","LAYER");
  return (nameArray.length > 0);
}
```

Here, if the Dreamweaver function `getObjectRefs()` finds any layer objects, the `nameArray` length is greater than zero, and the `canAcceptBehavior` function returns true; otherwise, false is returned, and the behavior name in the Add Action (+) list of the Behaviors panel is dimmed and inactive.

Step 3: Build the user interface

The user interface of a behavior is a parameter form, constructed with HTML form elements. The key indicator of what you need to include in your action's parameter form is the number and type of arguments required by your completed function.

In the Set Layer Z Index example, the function requires two primary arguments: `theTarget` and `theValue`. The interface needs to enable the user to choose the target parameter — the layer being affected — and the value of the Z index. To be useful, the action should list all available layers by name.

Note   Dreamweaver recommends using a specific DOCTYPE statement for different types of extension user interfaces (UIs). For example, when creating a dialog box, you should use: `<!DOCTYPE HTML SYSTEM "-//Macromedia//DWExtension layout-engine 5.0//dialog">`. For more information, look up DOCTYPE in the index of Extending Dreamweaver MX documentation.

All user interface constructions are contained in the `<body>` section of your HTML action file. You can use Dreamweaver's design editor to create and modify your form quickly.

Caution   Many Web designers use tables to line up the various form elements; if you use this approach, be sure to place the table inside the form and not the other way around. Although you can insert a form in the cell of a table, you are limited to just entering form elements in that cell — and you return to no structure at all.

Follow these steps to create your user interface:

1. Open your HTML action file in Dreamweaver.

2. In Design view, choose Insert ➪ Form or select the Form button from the Forms category of the Insert bar. Name the form in the Property inspector for easy JavaScript identification. In this example, you should name the form `theForm`.

3. For better alignment, place a table inside your form by choosing Insert ➪ Table or by selecting the Table button from the Common category of the Insert bar.

   Make sure to place the table *inside* the form, not vice-versa! It's much easier to do this if the form is visible. If your form is invisible, choose View ➪ Visual Aids ➪ Invisible Elements to make it visible.

4. Enter your form elements as needed. Be sure to name each one individually (with the exception of a radio button grouping) for JavaScript purposes.

   Be sure to use JavaScript friendly names: no spaces or special characters and always start the name with a letter.

Note   As with Dreamweaver objects, you don't see the OK, Cancel, and Help buttons that appear when the parameter form is actually used. Dreamweaver displays these buttons to the upper-right part of your interface.

The interface for the Set Layer Z Index action, as shown in Figure 35-1, uses a drop-down list form element to list all available layers and a text box to get the desired Z index from the user.

The Main panel uses a drop-down list and a text box to gather the user input. The last part of setting up the user interface requires a function that initializes the interface and sets the cursor in the right field. To complete this task, you use the `initializeUI()` function. For the Set Layer Z Index action, all the layers in the current page must be displayed in the drop-down list. To display the layers in this way, the `initializeUI()` function includes a number of specialized functions:

```
function initializeUI() {
   var niceNamesArray;
   //Get all the layers available including parent frames
   //Then turn those objects references into nice names
```

```
niceNamesArray = niceNames(getAllObjectRefs("NS 4.0","LAYER"),TYPE_Layer);
//Populate the select element
populateSelect("LAYER_LIST",niceNamesArray);
//Set focus on textbox
findObject("Z-INDEX").focus();
//Set insertion point into textbox
findObject("Z-INDEX").select();
}
```

Massimo uses a combination of Macromedia functions and his own to initialize the dialog box. The Macromedia-designed `niceNames()` function changes JavaScript object references such as `document.layers['onLayer'].document.theForm` to a more readable format such as `form "theForm" in layer "onLayer"`. The results of the `niceNames()` function then is used to fill a drop-down list via Massimo's own `populateSelect()` function, found in the DW_UI.js file included in our opening step. The remaining two lines that start with the `findObject()` function are used to place the user's cursor in the text field when the dialog box opens — a nice touch that demonstrates Massimo's professionalism. Both `niceNames()` and `findObject()` are found in the external JavaScript files included earlier.

Finally, you need to attach the `initializeUI()` to `<body>` with an `onLoad` event in the HTML file. Locate the `<body>` tag and amend it so that it reads as follows:

```
<body onLoad="initializeUI()">
```

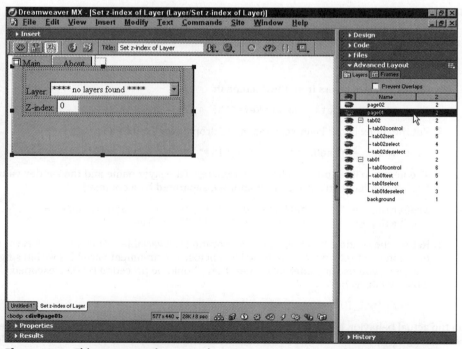

Figure 35-1: This parameter form uses layers to create a two-panel tabbed interface.

Step 4: Apply the behavior

Now you can write the code that links your function to a specific tag and event. You can think of this process in three steps:

1. Make sure that the user entered information in the right places.

2. Organize the user's parameter-form input into a more usable format.

3. Return the runtime function call.

All these steps are executed in the applyBehavior() function, whose placeholder you included in your action file.

You gather information from an action's parameter form in the same way that you gather data from a custom object. Using the same techniques discussed in Chapter 34, you receive the input information and usually convert it to local variables that are easier to handle. The number of variables is equal to the number of arguments expected.

Tip　Potentially, if any of the input from the parameter form might be sent out to a Web server — say, as a URL or a file — you need to encode the text string so that UNIX servers can read it. Use the built-in JavaScript escape() function to convert space and special characters in the URL to UNIX-friendly strings. The companion unescape() function reverses the process and is used in the inspectBehavior() function.

Follow these steps to build your applyBehavior() function:

1. Declare the necessary variables inside the function:

```
var layersArray, layerIndex;
var argString = "";
```

2. Get an array of layers from the document:

```
layersArray = getAllObjectRefs("NS 4.0","LAYER");
```

3. Put the index of the layer selected in the drop-down list into a variable:

```
layerIndex = findObject("LAYER_LIST").selectedIndex;
```

4. The next two lines put the chosen parameters (the layer name and the z-index value) into an argument string, one after another, separated by a comma:

```
argString += "'" + getNameFromRef(layersArray[layerIndex]) + "',";
argString += "'" + findObject("Z-INDEX").value + "'";
```

5. Return the runtime function call, incorporating the variables. The applyBehavior() function must return a complete string. Enclose the argument variables within single quotes. If you use any internal quotes, they should be preceded by (i.e., escaped with) a backslash, as in: \" or \'.

```
return "tmt_DivIndex(" + argString + ")";
```

In the actual behavior, it's a good idea to add error checking to prevent the user from entering something other than an integer in the z-index field. Check the code in the Examples folder of the CD-ROM to see how Massimo handled this issue.

Only one more step remains before you're ready to begin testing your action.

Step 5: Inspect the behavior

Now it's time to add the `inspectBehavior()` function to the JavaScript file. Basically, this function is called when the user double-clicks the action in the Behaviors panel. It restores the information already entered through the parameter form and enables the user to change the parameters. In many ways, `inspectBehavior()` can be considered the reverse of the `applyBehavior()` function: Rather than reading the form and writing the information to the Web page, `inspectBehavior()` reads the information and writes it back to the form.

Interpreting the user-input string of information from a form is referred to as *parsing the string*. Dreamweaver offers several built-in functions to aid the parsing process most of which are collectively called with `extractArgs()`. The `extractArgs()` function is a good example of the powerful code snippets available in the Configuration\Shared folder.

Another key function used in `inspectBehavior()` is `findObject()`. The `findObject()` function – Massimo calls it "the smartest piece of Javascript ever written" – returns an object given the object's name. Sounds simple, but when you consider that an object (such as a form text field or layer) could be almost anywhere in the realm of the document DOM, you see what a daunting prospect that is and how helpful this function can be. Here, `findObject()` is initially used to get the `Layer_List` object, the drop-down list in the dialog box, which is populated programatically. After the string arguments are in an array, they can be extracted and placed back in the parameter form. Follow these steps to write the `inspectBehavior()` function:

1. Declare several basic variables: `argArray`, `layerMenu`, `layersArray`, `menuLength`, and `found`.

   ```
   var argArray,layerMenu,layersArray,menuLength,found;
   ```

2. Use the `extractArgs()` function to separate the arguments passed in `msgStr` and set them equal to a variable, `argArray`.

   ```
   argArray = extractArgs(msgStr);
   ```

3. Get the drop-down menu object by using `findObject()`.

   ```
   layerMenu = findObject("LAYER_LIST");
   ```

4. Examine the user's document, find all the layers, and put them in an array.

   ```
   layersArray = getAllObjectRefs("NS 4.0","LAYER");
   ```

5. Now you're ready to loop through all the layers on the page and look for the name of the one passed in the argument. Once found, that layer is selected and its z-index is displayed in the other field of the dialog box, if the z-index was passed in with the arguments.

   ```
   for(var i=0;i<menuLength;i++){
           if(getNameFromRef(layersArray[i]) == argArray[1]){

                   layerMenu.selectedIndex = i;
                   found = true;
                   break;
           }
   }
   if(argArray[2]){
           findObject("Z-INDEX").value = argArray[2];
   }
   ```

The complete `inspectBehavior()` function, with a little added error checking, looks like the following:

```
function inspectBehavior(msgStr){
    var argArray,layerMenu,layersArray,menuLength,found;
    argArray = extractArgs(msgStr);
    layerMenu = findObject("LAYER_LIST");
    //Get all layers references including parent frames
    layersArray = getAllObjectRefs("NS 4.0","LAYER");
    menuLength = layerMenu.options.length;
    //Loop trought all the <select> options
    for(var i=0;i<menuLength;i++){
        //If the layer reference is same as the argument, got the layer
        if(getNameFromRef(layersArray[i]) == argArray[1]){
            layerMenu.selectedIndex = i;
            //Set the flag and stop looping
            found = true;
            break;
        }
    }
    //If the layer is not found, alert!
    if(!found){
        alert(argArray[1] + " could not be found")
    }
    //Populate the rest of the UI with remaining arguments
    if(argArray[2]){
        findObject("Z-INDEX").value = argArray[2];
    }
}
```

> **Tip**
>
> This example is a fairly simple `inspectBehavior()` function. Keep in mind that the more input you allow from your user, the more complicated it is to restore the information through this function. As with many aspects of building behaviors, one of the best ways to construct your `inspectBehavior()` function is by examining the code of working examples provided in the Macromedia-built behaviors, as well as examples contributed by other developers.

Step 6: Test your behavior

Testing and debugging is the final, necessary phase of building an action. To test your behavior, follow these steps:

1. Quit and restart Dreamweaver.

2. Insert an image or a link in a blank Web page.

3. Select the element to use as your trigger.

4. Open the Behaviors panel.

5. Select the Add Action (+) button and choose your desired behavior.

6. Fill out the parameters form as required.

Your action's name appears in the Actions column, as shown with the Set Layer Z Index example in Figure 35-2.

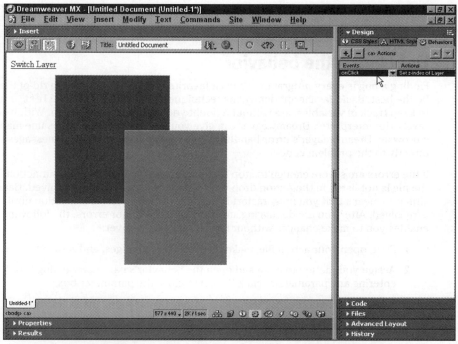

Figure 35-2: Even custom behaviors appear in the Behaviors panel when created properly.

7. Change the event by clicking first on the currently assigned event, then selecting onClick from the drop-down list.

8. Double-click the action to verify that your prior choices have been restored.

9. Test the output of the extension in various Web browsers.

Caution When you first select an event to add, Dreamweaver examines all the actions in the Actions folder. If a problem is found, such as two files having the same function name, you are alerted to the conflict, and the list displays only the older file. You have to correct the problem with the other action and restart Dreamweaver before the file appears in the list again.

If your action is intended for distribution and not your own personal use, you should expand your testing considerably, especially on the user-interface side. As the action programmer, you know what values are expected and you also know — often subconsciously — how to avoid the pitfalls into which a new user may easily stumble. Be especially mindful of accepting input through a text box. Unless you're just passing a message to be displayed onscreen or in the browser status bar, you often have to validate the incoming text string: Is it a number, a word without any special characters, a single name? And so on. Telling the user to enter a number in a particular range doesn't guarantee correct results.

Note   If you intend to distribute the extension publicly, do not assume that it will work in all Dreamweaver versions (3.x, 4.x, MX, and so on) and platforms (Windows, Mac). Always test on different platforms/versions before distributing!

Debugging the behavior

Finding a bug is every programmer's least favorite moment — but getting rid of that bug can be the best. Basic JavaScript debugging techniques, including using the `alert()` function to keep track of variables, are without a doubt your first course of action. With its built-in JavaScript interpreter, Dreamweaver can give you error messages in the same manner as a browser. Dreamweaver's error handling is very good with many error messages pointing directly to the problem code.

If the errors are severe enough to stop Dreamweaver from recognizing your action file as such, the file is not listed in the Action drop-down list until the problem is resolved. Generally this situation means that you must restart Dreamweaver after each modification until the problem is resolved. After you are debugging and modifying the minor errors, the following technique enables you to make changes without restarting Dreamweaver:

1. First, open your action file, make the necessary changes, and resave the file.

2. Assign your action to a tag and open the behavior's parameter dialog box. Without entering any parameters, click Cancel to close the parameter box.

3. Remove the action from the Actions column by selecting the Delete button.

4. Reassign your action, and Dreamweaver loads the new version.

Tip   Remember, JavaScript is case sensitive: The variable myVar is not the same as myvar or MyVar or MYVAR; the function doSomething() is not the same as dosomething() or DoSomething(); and so on. If you get a message that a variable or function cannot be found, make sure you have spelled the variable/function name exactly as it was defined.

The Extending Dreamweaver Documentation

To help developers create behaviors, Macromedia provides the Extending Dreamweaver documentation. Extending Dreamweaver is the background documentation of the various functions available for building behaviors. As such, it provides a useful framework for discussing the underpinnings of Dreamweaver behaviors and how you can use the extensions and built-in functions. The Extending Dreamweaver documentation can be found by choosing Help ➪ Extending Dreamweaver.

Although Extending Dreamweaver covers all types of Dreamweaver extensions, behavior developers will be interested in three main sections: the Dreamweaver Document Object Model, the Dreamweaver JavaScript API, and Behaviors. If your behavior is intended to interact with Fireworks, you'll want to study the Fireworks Integration API section. The more you understand about the various components and their included functions, the more flexibility you'll have in building your behaviors.

 Caution The material in this section is intended for programmers familiar with JavaScript and, as such, is fairly advanced.

Document Object Model

JavaScript is an interpreted programming language that addresses elements in the browser and on the Web page in a hierarchical fashion. To access the properties of any object on the page, JavaScript employs a Document Object Model (DOM). The DOM breaks down the page into successively smaller parts until each element and its specific properties are identified.

Dreamweaver MX integrates a subset of objects, properties, and methods from the W3C DOM Level 1 with a subset of properties from the Internet Explorer 4.0 DOM. The resultant Dreamweaver DOM also includes some useful features not implemented in either of the other DOMs.

Understanding nodes

Dreamweaver's DOM makes available, or *exposes*, virtually every element on a Web page. The DOM is often described using a tree metaphor, with the HTML document as the trunk. Instead of regarding the <head> and the <body> as the major branches, however, Dreamweaver's DOM, like the W3C DOM, uses four separate branches, or *nodes*, to divide the document:

✦ DOCUMENT_NODE: Enables access to objects directly relating to the overall document

✦ ELEMENT_NODE: Contains references to all tags in the HTML document

✦ TEXT_NODE: Describes the contiguous block of text within tags

✦ COMMENT_NODE: Represents the comments within an HTML document and the text strings they contain

Just as one tree branch can lead to another, nodes can contain other nodes. For example, a layer can contain a table that holds table rows that, in turn, hold table data. One node containing another is said to be in a *parent-child* relationship, and a node that cannot contain any other nodes is referred to as a *leaf node* because it is incapable of supporting any more "branches." Figure 35-3 illustrates the node concept.

DOM properties

When referencing a specific tag, the DOM syntax goes from the most general to the most specific. For example, suppose you want to find out what a user entered into a specific text field, a property called *value*. You need to start from the document itself and work your way down through the form and text-box objects, as follows:

```
var theText = document.formName.textboxName.value;
```

The DOM dictates what properties are accessible and in what form. Not all properties and methods are supported. You can't, for instance, directly reference the value of a button in a form. Instead, you have to assign that value to a hidden or other text field and access that value.

Cross-Reference The portion of the DOM relating directly to forms and form elements is discussed in Chapter 34.

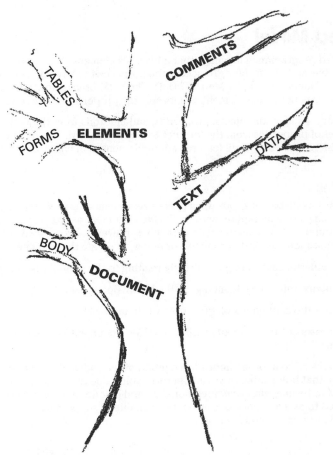

Figure 35-3: Nodes are used to express the structure of the HTML document and its relationship to the browser.

The same rules of use and the same restrictions for implementing forms in objects apply likewise to implementing forms in behaviors. Additionally, the Dreamweaver DOM addresses other major objects as outlined in Table 35-1. Read-only properties are marked with an asterisk (*); otherwise, properties can be both read and set.

Table 35-1: Dreamweaver DOM Properties

Property	Nodes	Returns	Description
nodeType*	all	Node.DOCUMENT_NODE Node.ELEMENT_NODE Node.TEXT_NODE Node.COMMENT_NODE	Returns the node of the specified selection
parentNode*	all	string (HTML tag), document object, or null	Returns null for the document object; returns the parent tag for element, text, and comment objects; if an HTML tag is selected, returns the document object
parentWindow*	DOCUMENT_NODE	parent window object	Returns the JavaScript object corresponding to the document's parent window
childNodes*	all	NodeList	Returns a NodeList array of the immediate children of the current selection.
documentElement*	DOCUMENT_NODE	HTML tag of current document	Returns the JavaScript object corresponding to the HTML tag of the current document
body*	DOCUMENT_NODE	BODY tag of current document	Returns the JavaScript object corresponding to the BODY tag of the current document
URL*	DOCUMENT_NODE	file://URL	Returns the file://URL for the current document
tagName*	ELEMENT_NODE	IMG TABLE	Returns the HTML name (in CAPS) for the current tag
attrName	ELEMENT_NODE	grey #33CC66	Returns the value of the specified tag attribute

Continued

Table 35-1: *(continued)*

Property	Nodes	Returns	Description
innerHTML	ELEMENT_NODE	for \<p>Hello \<i>world!\</i>\</p> p.innerHTML would return: Hello \<i>world!\</i>	Returns the HTML source for a tag, without the tag code itself
outerHTML	ELEMENT_NODE	for \<p>Hello \<i>world!\</i>\</p> p.outerHTML would return: \<p>Hello \<i>world!\</i>\</p>	Returns the HTML source for a tag, including the tag code
data	TEXT_NODE COMMENT_NODE	"J. Lowery" where the tag reads \<p>J. Lowery\</p>	Returns the text string contained within a contiguous block of text or a comment

* Read-only

DOM methods

Methods, in programming, are functions attached to a particular object, such as the document object. Dreamweaver includes several methods in the DOM to help manipulate the HTML page. With the node structure, you can apply these methods to the current document, frameset, frame, or selected object.

Using these methods, your behaviors can inspect the current page and, if desired, change or even delete any attributes found. Table 35-2 outlines the methods contained in the Dreamweaver DOM.

Table 35-2: Dreamweaver DOM Methods

Method	Nodes	Returns	Description
`hasChildNodes()`*	all	true or false	Determines if current selection has children
`getElementsByTagName(tagName)`	DOCUMENT_NODE ELEMENT_NODE	NodeList	Returns a `NodeList` array of all instances of the specified tag on the current page
`getTranslatedAttribute(attrName)`	ELEMENT_NODE	string or null	Gets the translated value of the specified attribute; used in conjunction with Dreamweaver translators
`hasTranslatedAttributes()`	ELEMENT_NODE	true or false	Determines if the tag has translated attributes; used in conjunction with Dreamweaver translators
`getAttribute(attrName)`	ELEMENT_NODE	string or null	Gets the value of the specified attribute
`setAttribute(attrName,attrValue)`	ELEMENT_NODE	nothing	Sets the specified attribute to a specified value
`removeAttribute(attrName)`	ELEMENT_NODE	nothing	Deletes the specified attribute

Dreamweaver JavaScript API extensions

The Dreamweaver JavaScript API is vast, with more than 600 custom JavaScript functions, enabling the savvy behavior programmer to use JavaScript to accomplish almost any task that the user can perform in Dreamweaver. Although in-depth discussion of the Dreamweaver JavaScript API is beyond the scope of this book, I strongly recommend that behavior programmers take the time to familiarize themselves with what this deep API has to offer.

The JavaScript API functions are grouped into the following categories:

Assets panel functions	Live data functions
Behavior functions	Menu functions
Clipboard functions	Path functions
Code hints functions	Print functions
Command functions	Quick Tag Editor functions
Conversion functions	Report functions
CSS Styles functions	Results window functions
Data source functions	Selection functions
Enablers	Server behavior functions
External application functions	Server model functions
File manipulation functions	Site functions
Find/Replace functions	Snippet panel functions
Frame and frameset functions	Source view functions
General editing functions	String manipulation functions
Global document functions	Table editing functions
History functions	Tag Editor and tag library functions
HTML style functions	Tag Inspector functions
JavaScript debugger functions	Timeline functions
Keyboard functions	Toggle functions
Layer and image map functions	Toolbar functions
Layout environment functions	Translation functions
Library and template functions	Window functions

Tip   Behavior programmers will find the API functions under Behavior, File Manipulation, Global Document, Path, Selection, and String Manipulation to be of particular interest.

The Dreamweaver engineers didn't stop with the aforementioned JavaScript APIs; there are additional APIs for file input/output, source control integration, JavaBean management, design notes, Fireworks integration, Flash objects, and more. Extending Dreamweaver has basic documentation about them all.

To make the behavior programmer's life a little easier, I've included coverage of some of the most often used API functions. Although the following sections are in no way exhaustive, they do give a good example of how API functions work in Dreamweaver in general and in behaviors in particular.

Note The Dreamweaver API functions have a prefix of dreamweaver, dom, or site. The dreamweaver prefix can also be abbreviated as dw as in dw.getDocumentDOM(). The dom functions refer to the DOM of a document returned by the getDocumentDOM() function (as explained in the next section). The site functions refer to selections in the Site panel.

The dreamweaver.getDocumentDOM() function

The getDocumentDOM() function is the starting point for many Dreamweaver JavaScript manipulations. It returns the entire DOM for the specified document, thus enabling the document to be read and manipulated. Generally, getDocumentDOM() is used in this fashion:

```
var theDom = dreamweaver.getDocumentDOM("document");
```

theDom holds the DOM of the current document and, by extension, everything connected to it.

Tip Because many behaviors require repeated access to the DOM, it's good practice to assign it to a global variable (such as theDOM) early on in your script.

After you have accessed the document DOM in this manner, you need to request more specific information. If, for example, you want to examine the <body> of the current document, you can code it this way:

```
var theDom = dreamweaver.getDocumentDOM("document");
var theBody = theDom.body;
```

You could also use JavaScript dot notation to shorten the code:

```
var theBody = dreamweaver.getDocumentDOM("document").body;
```

The getDocumentDOM() function requires one argument, *sourceDoc*, which refers to the source document. The argument must be one of the following:

✦ **"document"**: Sets the reference to the current document. Although the "document" argument can be used from anywhere to read the DOM, any edits applied using it must be ultimately called from within the applyBehavior(), deleteBehavior(), or objectTag() functions—or any function in a command or Property inspector file.

✦ **"parent"**: Sets the source document to the parent of the current document. This argument is generally used to determine if a document is within a frameset, like this:

```
var frameset = dreamweaver.getDocumentDOM("parent");
if (frameset) { ... do code ... }
```

✦ **"parent.frames[number]" or "parent.frames['framename']"**: To access another document in the frameset of which the current document is a member, use one of these two argument forms. The first, "parent.frames[number]", is usually used when the names of the current frames are unknown or to cycle through any number of frames. The second, "parent.frames['framename']", is applied in specific cases where the names of the other frames are known and modifications need to be made to them only.

✦ **URL**: Occasionally, the behavior builder needs to reference existing documents, either locally or on the Web. Using a URL—either absolute or relative—as an argument enables you to retrieve information on almost any document you can specify. When using a relative URL, such as this one from Dreamweaver's Untitled Documents.js file, the URL is relative to the location of the behavior or other extensibility file:

```
var curDOM = dw.getDocumentDOM('../../Templates/Default.html');
```

Note Whenever API functions require the DOM object, such as the `dom.getSelection()` function and others discussed in the following sections, you must first get the DOM of the current document. In all the examples that follow, the variable `theDOM` is understood to have been established early on, like this:

```
var theDOM = dreamweaver.getDocumentDOM("document");
```

The dom.getSelection() function

How a behavior performs is quite often dictated by what tag the user selects prior to attaching the behavior. The `getSelection()` function is the *first step* toward getting all the information necessary to control your behavior based on a user selection. I emphasize "first step" because this function returns the selection in the form of *byte offsets in memory*. A *byte offset* is a number that points to a memory address. In the case of the `getSelection()` function, the two byte offsets that are returned mark the beginning and end of the selection in memory. For example, you open a new page in Dreamweaver, type in a phrase such as "The Key Points," and then select the first word, "The." If you used the `getSelection` function like this:

```
var selArray = theDOM.getSelection();
alert(selArray);
```

the alert box would return `161,164`, which denotes the beginning byte (161) and the ending byte (164) offset of the selected word, "The." If your beginning and ending byte offsets are the same (as in `164,164`), then nothing is selected. This fact comes in handy when you want to make sure that the user has selected something before proceeding. To examine what is contained within the byte offsets returned by the `getSelection()` function, you have to use the `offsetsToNode()` function, explained later in this section.

The dom.setSelection() function

Just as `getSelection()` retrieves the memory offsets of the current selection, the `setSelection()` function sets a new pair of memory offsets and thus a new selection. The `setSelection()` function takes two arguments: *offsetBegin* and *offsetEnd*.

`setSelection()` is most often used to restore a user's selection after various document manipulations have taken place. In this example, the selection is first stored in a variable via `getSelection()` and then, after much document modification, restored by `setSelection`:

```
var currSelection = theDOM.getSelection();
// document altering code goes here
theDom.setSelection(currSelection[0],currSelection[1]);
```

Note If the new setting does not conform to a valid HTML selection, such as the attributes within a tag, the selection expands to include the entire tag.

You can also use `setSelection` to deselect anything on the page after completing a behavior. All that's required is that the two arguments be equal. Using the preceding example, the following code:

```
theDOM.setSelection(currSelection[1],currSelection[1]);
```

places the cursor after the previous selection, whereas

```
theDOM.setSelection(currSelection[0],currSelection[0]);
```

places it before the selection.

The dom.offsetsToNode() function

The offsetsToNode() function serves as a translator, converting the byte memory offsets retrieved by getSelection() into readable data. For this reason, you often see the following code combination:

```
selArr = theDOM.getSelection();
selObj = theDOM.offsetsToNode(selArr[0],selArr[1]);
```

where getSelection() returns the array of the selection and the object referenced by that array. As indicated, offsetsToNode() takes two arguments: *offsetBegin* and *offsetEnd*, usually expressed as the initial (0) and next (1) array elements.

After you've used offsetsToNode to get the selected object, you can examine or manipulate it. For example, in the custom Replicator command (included on the CD-ROM that accompanies this book), I used offsetsToNode to see if the selection made was appropriate (text only) and, if not, to call a help function:

```
var offsets = theDOM.getSelection();
var selObj = theDOM.offsetsToNode(offsets[0],offsets[1]);
if (selObj.nodeType != Node.TEXT_NODE) {
  helpMe2();
}
```

The dom.nodeToOffsets() function

As the name indicates, nodeToOffsets() is the inverse of offsetsToNode(). Instead of converting memory offsets to an object, nodeToOffsets takes an object reference and returns its memory offsets. This is useful when you need to manipulate a substring of the selection, usually text.

For example, in the custom command Change Case (included on the CD-ROM that comes with this book), after the selected object is retrieved via getSelection and offsetsToNode, nodeToOffsets expresses it in an array that can be uppercased or lowercased at the click of a button. Here's a fragment of the code from the custom upperCase() function:

```
var theDom = dreamweaver.getDocumentDOM("document");
var offsets = theDom.getSelection();
var theNode = theDom.offsetsToNode(offsets[0],offsets[1]);
if (theNode.nodeType == Node.TEXT_NODE) {
  var nodeOffsets = theDom.nodeToOffsets(theNode);
  offsets[0] = offsets[0] - nodeOffsets[0];
  offsets[1] = offsets[1] - nodeOffsets[0];
  var nodeText = theNode.data;
  theNode.data = nodeText.substring(0,offsets[0]) +
    nodeText.substring(offsets[0], offsets[1]).toUpperCase() +
    nodeText.substring(offsets[1], nodeText.length);
}
```

Because nodeToOffsets returns two memory offsets, you can use these as the arguments in setSelection to choose an object on the page. If, for instance, you wanted to select the first link on the page, you use the code as follows:

```
var theDom = dreamweaver.getDocumentDOM("document");
var theLink = theDom.links[0];
var offsets = theDom.nodeToOffsets(theLink);
```

theDom.setSelection(offsets[0],offsets[1]);The dreamweaver.getTokens() function

The `getTokens()` function is often used in the `inspectBehavior()` function because it does such a good job of parsing a string. A *token* is a group of text characters that do not contain any of the specified separators. Generally, the *separators* in a function are the parentheses that surround the arguments and the commas that separate them. The `getTokens()` function takes two arguments — the string to be parsed and the separators — and puts the results in an array. For example, note the following string

```
doGroovoid('false','Fanfare-Arrival');
```

To extract the two arguments from this statement, use the `getTokens()` function as follows:

```
getTokens("doGroovoid('false','Fanfare-Arrival')","'(),");
```

If you set this function equal to an array called `argArray`, you get the following results:

```
argArray[0] = 'doGroovoid';
argArray[1] = 'false';
argArray[2] = 'Fanfare-Arrival';
```

Usually the first element of the array, the function name, is ignored.

The dreamweaver.getElementRef() function

The `getElementRef()` function is used to gather browser-specific references to a particular object and place them into an array.

The `getElementRef()` function takes two arguments: The first argument is either *NS 4.0* or *IE 4.0*, which reference the Netscape and Internet Explorer formats, respectively; and the second argument is the tag being examined. The string returned puts the specified tag in the format of the named browser. If, for example, `getElementRef()` is used to get the object reference to a specific layer in Netscape terms, like

```
var theObjNS = dreamweaver.getElementRef("NS 4.0", tagArr[i]);
```

the variable, `theObjNS`, is set to something like

```
document.layers['newLayer'];
```

On the other hand, the same layer, in Internet Explorer terms, like this

```
var theObjIE = dreamweaver.getElementRef("IE 4.0", tagArr[i]);
```

returns a string like `document.all.newLayer1`.

Both `getElementRef()` and `getObjectRefs()` return browser-correct references for both browsers for the following tags: `<a>`, `<area>`, `<applet>`, `<embed>`, `<select>`, `<option>`, `<textarea>`, `<object>`, and `<img>`. Additionally, references for the tags `<div>`, `<span>`, and `<input>` are returned correctly for Internet Explorer, as `<layer>` and `<ilayer>` are for Netscape. Absolutely positioned `<div>` and `<span>` tags are also returned correctly for Netscape, but others return the message `"cannot reference <tag>"`.

Caution   Naming objects and layers is often critical in JavaScript, as it certainly is with `getElementRef()` and `getObjectRefs()`. Dreamweaver can't return references for unnamed objects; you get back an `"unnamed <tag>"` message for those. Furthermore, Dreamweaver can't handle references to a named object if it is in an unnamed layer or form. To help with the naming task, Dreamweaver automatically assigns a `name` attribute to forms and an `ID` attribute to layers as they are created.

The dreamweaver.getBehaviorTag() function

The `getBehaviorTag()` function returns the tag selected to implement the current behavior. The `getBehaviorTag()` function can also be incorporated into the behavior setup code to steer the user in the appropriate direction.

The `getBehaviorTag()` function returns the entire tag—name, attributes, values, and any text selected—exactly as it is written (capitalization, spaces, etc.). In most situations, you need to find only the relevant portion of the tag, its name (`img`), for example. You can find the relevant portion of a tag by using JavaScript's `indexOf()` method to search a string (the entire tag) for a specified substring. The following code looks to see if the tag selected for the behavior is an `<img>` tag and, if it's not, alerts the users to what's required:

```
function initializeUI() {
  // uppercase the tag to make indexOf() searching easier
  var theTag = dreamweaver.getBehaviorTag().toUpperCase();
  if (theTag.indexOf('IMG') != -1)) {
    // Behavior UI initilaization goes here
  }
  else {
    alert("This behavior requires you select an IMAGE to proceed.");
  }
}
```

Note   Using the `initializeUI()` function to block access to a behavior is different from using the `canAcceptBehavior()` function to block access. With the `getBehaviorTag()` technique, the user is informed of what the problem is, rather than simply denied access.

The dreamweaver.getBehaviorElement() function

Another method to discover which tag was selected for the invoked behavior is the `getBehaviorElement()` function. The major difference between this function and the `getBehaviorTag()` function is that the former returns the DOM reference to the tag, whereas the latter returns the tag itself. After you have the DOM reference of the behavior tag, you can uncover a terrific amount of information about the tag and its attributes.

Like `getBehaviorTag()`, `getBehaviorElement()` is most often used to determine if the user has selected an appropriate tag for the chosen behavior. If the tag is inappropriate, a helpful message can be displayed to guide the user to a better option. The `getBehaviorElement()` function returns either a DOM reference or `null`. Circumstances under which `null` is returned by `getBehaviorElement()` are as follows:

✦ The function was not invoked from a script called by the Behaviors panel.

✦ The behavior called is part of a timeline.

✦ The function was invoked from a script called by `dreamweaver.popupAction()`.

✦ The function was invoked as part of a Behaviors panel that is attaching an event to a link wrapper (`<a href="#">...</a>`), and the link wrapper has not yet been created.

✦ The function is called outside of a behavior.

The following example assumes that the required tag must be an embedded plugin that is visible on the page:

```
function initializeUI() {
  var theTag = dreamweaver.getBehaviorElement();
```

```
    var tagGood = (theTag.tagName == "EMBED" &&
                   theTag.getAttribute("HIDDEN") == null);
  if (tagGood) {
    // Behavior User Interface code goes here
  }
  else {
    alert("This behavior can not be applied to hidden plug-ins");
  }
}
```

The dreamweaver.browseForFileURL() function

The browseForFileURL() function enables the user, instead of entering an entire path by hand, to locate a file via a dialog box. You can specify whether you want an Open, Save, or Select style dialog box, as well as the label in the title bar. You can even enable the Preview panel for images. No matter which options you choose, the browseForFileURL() function returns the pathname of the file expressed as a file://URL.

The browseForFileURL() function follows this syntax:

```
browseForFileURL('Open'|'Save'|'Select', 'Title Bar Label', true|false);
```

The first argument, either Open, Save, or Select, specifies the type of dialog box. The Select File dialog box displays additional local root information in its lower portion. The second argument is displayed in the title bar of the dialog box; if you don't want to insert your own title, you must specify an empty string '' (two single quotes, with nothing in-between) for the argument, as in this example:

```
browseForFileURL('open','',false);
```

The final argument is a Boolean and indicates whether the Preview dialog box for selecting images is to be displayed. If no title bar label is given and the Preview dialog argument is true, the title displayed is Select Image Source.

The browseForFileURL() function is generally called by a secondary function that is triggered by an onClick event attached to a Browse (Choose) button, which in turn is next to a text field that enables the user to enter the path by hand. Typically this secondary function is called browseFile() and takes one argument, fieldToStoreURL. For instance, the code for a Browse (Choose) button often reads as follows:

```
<input type="text" name="textFile">
<input value="Browse..." type="button" name="button"
       onClick="browseFile(document.theForm.textFile.value)">
```

The browseFile() function then calls the built-in browseForFileURL() function, which opens the Select File dialog box and, if the dialog box is returned with a filename, assigns that filename to a variable. In the standard browseFile() function, shown here, the returned filename is then assigned to a text box value for the given field, which makes the name appear in the text box:

```
function browseFile(fieldToStoreURL) {
  var fileName = "";
  fileName = browseForFileURL()  //returns a local filename
  if (fileName)
    fieldToStoreURL.value = fileName;
}
```

The dreamweaver.getDocumentPath() function

Dreamweaver includes several local document functions that aid in the reading, editing, and storing of current and external documents. The `getDocumentPath()` function is one of these; as the name states, this function returns the path of the specified document. The path returned is in the file://URL format, so that a file located at `c:\sites\index.html` returns `file://c|/sites/` as its path.

The `getDocumentPath()` function takes one argument: the source document. This argument can be `"document"`, `"parent"`, `"parent.frames[number]"`, or `"parent.frames ['framename']"` as described earlier in the `getDocumentDOM()` function. If the document specified has not been saved, `getDocumentPath()` returns an empty string.

The dreamweaver.getConfigurationPath() function

The Configuration folder can be considered the hub of Dreamweaver extensibility. It contains not only all the standard HTML files, such as the behaviors and objects, that are read into the system when Dreamweaver starts, but also various other files that control the look and feel of the menus in other areas. As such, it's often useful to be able to find the path to the Configuration folder so that other files can be created, read, edited, and stored. And that's exactly what `getConfigurationPath()` does.

One sample use of this function, included with Dreamweaver, is part of the secret behind the Rollover object. To a trained eye, the Rollover object is unlike any other — in fact, it's not really an object at all; it's a command masquerading as an object. The `getConfigurationPath()` function plays a key role in the JavaScript file, rollover.js, with this code:

```
var rolloverCmdURL = dreamweaver.getConfigurationPath() +
                     "/Commands/Rollover.htm";
var rolloverDoc = dreamweaver.getDocumentDOM( rolloverCmdURL );
```

In the first line, `getConfigurationPath` is used to locate the Rollover.htm file in the Configuration\Commands subfolder and assign it to a variable. This enables the object to retrieve the DOM for manipulation with the `getDocumentDOM()` function.

Note Like `getDocumentPath()`, `getConfigurationPath()` formats the path as file://URL.

The dreamweaver.getSiteRoot() function

Dreamweaver depends on the establishment of a local site root for much of its Web site management facility: All site-root–relative links and references are based upon the location of the site root folder. The capability to uncover its file location is important for any behaviors or other extensibility files that work on the site root level. Dreamweaver supplies such a capability with the `getSiteRoot()` function.

Very straightforward to use, `getSiteRoot()` does not take an argument; and it returns a file://URL format reference to the local site root of the currently selected document. If an empty string is returned, it means that the file has not been saved.

The dreamweaver.releaseDocument() function

If you're working with a complex document with a lot of images, layers, tables, and text, you're going to have a lot of HTML to deal with. Accessing the DOM for that page can take up a significant chunk of your memory. If you're working with multiple pages, you could begin to run low on memory before the behavior closes and the memory is automatically freed. With the `releaseDocument()` function, you can get back the memory as soon as possible, whenever you request it.

The `releaseDocument()` function's one argument is the DOM of the document in question. You obtain the DOM argument by using the `getDocumentDOM()` function. You can see this function demonstrated in Dreamweaver's displayHelp.js file, which is used to direct all the help requested, contextually.

The dreamweaver.browseDocument() function

Should a help file get too big for an alert dialog box, you might need to provide access to a larger file. Dreamweaver enables you to open any specified file — including an expanded help file — within the primary browser. The `browseDocument()` function takes one argument, the path to the required file (an absolute URL):

```
dreamweaver.browseDocument("http://www.idest.com/help/etable.htm");
```

As noted in Chapter 34, you can use `browseDocument()` to access an absolute URL from the Web or a file from a local drive. To display a local file, you need to combine `browseDocument()` with another function such as `getConfigurationPath()`. The example offered here shows how to use the two functions together to programmatically display Dreamweaver's InsertMenu.htm file:

```
function displayMenu() {
  var menuPath = dreamweaver.getConfigurationPath() + ⤶
"/Objects/InsertMenu.htm";
  dreamweaver.browseDocument(menuPath);
}
```

The dreamweaver.openDocument() and dreamweaver.createDocument() functions

The `openDocument()` and `createDocument()` functions provide similar capabilities although they possess similar restrictions. The `openDocument()` function is equivalent to selecting File ➪ Open and selecting a file from the Open dialog box. The `createDocument()` function, as the name implies, creates a new, blank document, based on the standard default.htm file. In either case, the document loads into a Dreamweaver window and is brought forward.

The `createDocument()` function does not need an argument to work and automatically returns the DOM of the new document. For example, the following code

```
var theNewDoc = dreamweaver.createDocument();
```

is the same as using `getDocumentDOM()` for a new page.

The `openDocument()` function requires an argument in the form of a file://URL. If the URL is given in relative terms, the file is relative to the extensibility file calling the function. For instance, to open a file located one directory up from the Commands folder, you need to refer to it as follows in a custom command:

```
dreamweaver.openDocument("../Extensions.txt");
```

You can also use the same technique referred to earlier in the `browseDocument()` function to access files with the Configuration folder as a base.

Note

Although the twin functions, openDocument and createDocument(), cannot be used within a behavior, they can be called from a custom command or Property inspector. Therefore, it's possible to use the popupCommand() function to access a command that employs openDocument() or createDocument().

The dreamweaver.saveDocument() function

After all your edits and modifications have been finished, you need a way to store the file. The aptly named saveDocument() function performs just that chore for you. This function takes two arguments, *documentObject* and *fileURL*; the first corresponds to the DOM of the file to be saved, and the second to the location where this file is to be saved. Again, fileURL is relative to the extensibility file.

Note

If you omit the fileURL argument in Dreamweaver 4+, the file is saved to its current location if it has already been saved; if not, a Save dialog box is displayed.

The saveDocument function returns true if successful and false if the file-storing attempt fails. If the file specified is noted as read-only, Dreamweaver attempts to check it out; if it is unsuccessful, an error message appears.

The dreamweaver.editLockedRegions() function

Dreamweaver templates are based on a combination of locked and editable regions. Normally, these regions are designated in the Document window, but you can use the editLockedRegions() function to lock and unlock a template's regions programatically. The editLockedRegions() function works by entering true as the function's argument if you want to unlock all the current document's locked regions, and false to lock them again. After the routine calling editLockedRegions() ends, all regions revert to their default status.

Caution

Due to potentially undesirable results from using this function, Macromedia recommends that only custom data translators use editLockedRegions().

The dreamweaver.popupAction() and dreamweaver.runCommand() functions

Although the popupAction() and runCommand() functions are not directly useful to behavior creators because they cannot be called from within a behavior, they do enable considerable cross-pollination of Dreamweaver extensible objects. Invoking these functions calls an existing behavior or command and presents its dialog box to the user—except you use these functions to call the behaviors or commands from within a custom object, command, or Property inspector.

The popupAction() function takes two arguments: the name of the action file and the general function call of the action. The action chosen must be in Dreamweaver's Configuration\Behaviors\Actions subfolder. For example, code to call the Play Sound behavior could look like this:

```
var goPS = dreamweaver.popupAction("Play Sound.htm","MM_controlSound(,,)");
```

Tip

To call an action in a subfolder of the Actions folder, you need to specify the path. For example, if you want to call one of the standard Timeline actions — these actions reside in the Actions\Timeline subfolder — it's necessary to state the action name as `Timeline\Go to Timeline Frame.htm`.

The general function call can be found near the end of the `applyBehavior()` function, where the return value is specified, or as the `behaviorFunction()` return value. The `popupAction()` function returns the completed function call, including whatever parameters are selected by the user. In the previous example, if the user had chosen "Play" and selected "brazil.mid" as the file, the result (`goPS`) would be similar to the following:

```
"MM_controlSound('play',document.CS911946210190.'brazil.mid')";
```

Note

The second argument is a unique name generated by Dreamweaver as part of the function.

Everything is written into the user's page, except the event handler and its corresponding function call, both of which are handled by the calling object, command, or Property inspector.

The `runCommand()` function is a bit simpler; this function requires only one argument: the name of the command file. Any file named must be located in the Configuration\Commands folder. The `runCommand()` function does not return a value but simply executes the specified command.

The dreamweaver.latin1ToNative() and dreamweaver.nativeToLatin1() functions

Dreamweaver provides two functions to help with the localization of your behaviors around the globe. Many countries use font encodings other than Latin 1, which is standard in the United States and several Western European countries. To convert a string of text for a user interface from Latin 1 encoding to that of the user's machine, use the `latin1ToNative()` function. The argument, a text string, should be already translated into the other language. To convert a text string from the user's encoding system to Latin 1, use the inverse function, `nativeToLatin1()`.

Note

Neither of these functions has an effect in Windows systems, which are already based on Latin 1.

The dreamweaver.relativeToAbsoluteURL() function

As more programs such as Fireworks and Director are capable of outputting HTML, behaviors and other extensions are being employed to access their documents. It's often necessary to find the absolute URL of a selected file in order to get the document's DOM or open it. The `relativeToAbsoluteURL()` function returns this needed information, given three arguments:

✦ **docPathURL:** The portion of the current document's relative pathname excluding the filename. For example, if the file in question were to be found at `images\austria.gif`, the docPathURL would be `images/`.

✦ **siteRootURL:** The file://URL of the current site root, as returned from the `getSiteRoot()` function.

✦ **relativeURL:** The full relative pathname of the selected file (for example, `images/austria.gif`).

The syntax for the function is as follows:

```
var absoluteURL =
    dreamweaver.relativeToAbsoluteURL(docPathURL,siteRootURL,relativeURL);
```

Of the three arguments, only docPathURL is a little tricky. After you have the relativeURL, which can be returned from the browseForFileURL() function, you need to examine the pathname and extract the first part of the path leading up to the actual filename. To do so, use the JavaScript function lastIndexOf to find the final "/" character and extract the previous substring. For example:

```
function docBase() {
  var docURL = dreamweaver.getDocumentPath("document");
  var index = docURL.lastIndexOf('/');
  if ( index == -1 ) {  // If there is no additional path, return nothing
    return "";
  }
  else {
    return docURL.substring(0, index);
  }
}
```

Behavior API

You've seen most of the behavior API functions applied in a previous section, "Step 2: Create the action file." You use the behavior API to create behaviors. Its primary functions are as follows:

Function	Role
canAcceptBehavior()	Determines whether an action is allowed for the selected HTML element
windowDimensions()	Sets the width and height of the parameter form dialog box; only define this function if you are creating a Parameters dialog box larger than 640 × 480 pixels
applyBehavior()	Attaches the behavior function to the selected tag
inspectBehavior()	Restores user-selected values to the parameter form for re-editing
behaviorFunction()	Writes a function within <script>...</script> tags in the <head> of the HTML file
deleteBehavior()	Removes a behavior from the HTML file
identifyBehaviorArguments()	Notes the behavior arguments that need to be altered if the file is moved
displayHelp()	Attaches a Help button to the behavior's parameter form dialog box

For discussions of the uses of the `canAcceptBehavior()`, `applyBehavior()`, `inspectBehavior()`, and `behaviorFunction()` functions, see the preceding sections. Following are discussions of the other behavior API functions.

The windowDimensions() function

To speed display, the `windowDimensions()` function sets specific dimensions for the parameters form that the user sees as the dialog box. If this function is not defined, the window dimensions are computed automatically. This function takes one argument, *platform*, which is used to specify whether the user's system is Macintosh or Windows. The legal values for platform are: `"macintosh"` and `"windows"`. `windowDimensions()` returns a string with the width and height in pixels. For example:

```
function windowDimensions(platform) {
  if (platform.charAt(0) == 'm') {   // Macintosh
    return "650,500";
  }
  else {                             // Windows
    return "675,525";
  }
}
```

You can see this function in some of the standard behaviors. However, Macromedia recommends that it be used only when you need the behavior's dialog box to be larger than 640 × 480.

The deleteBehavior() function

Normally, Dreamweaver automatically handles removal of a behavior's event handler and associated JavaScript when the user chooses the Remove (–) button in the Behaviors panel. However, as behaviors grow in complexity and become capable of adding additional support code to the HTML document, it becomes necessary to use the `deleteBehavior()` function on a case-by-case basis. To better understand how `deleteBehavior()` is used, it's best to look at a couple of examples.

Two standard behaviors, Play Sound and Swap Image, use the `deleteBehavior()` function. Play Sound inserts an `<embed>` tag that contains a unique ID. To remove the code, `deleteBehavior()` first reads a function call string, just like the one returned by `applyBehavior()`. If the function finds an `<embed>` tag with the matching ID that is not referenced elsewhere on the page, the code is deleted. Here's the implementation of `deleteBehavior()` for Play Sound:

```
function deleteBehavior(fnCallStr) {
  var argArray,sndName,doc,tagArray,i,embedName;
  argArray = extractArgs(fnCallStr);
  if (argArray.length > 3) {
    //remove "document.", use unique name
    sndName = dreamweaver.getTokens(argArray[2],".")[1];
    //Find all EMBED calls that we created (name starts with "CS"),
    doc = dreamweaver.getDocumentDOM("document"); //get all
    tagArray = doc.getElementsByTagName("EMBED");
    for (i=0; i<tagArray.length; i++) {  //with each EMBED tag
      embedName = tagArray[i].name;
      if (embedName == sndName) { //if same embed
```

```
         if (numOccurences(sndName)<2) { // and embed ref'd no where else
            tagArray[i].outerHTML = ""; //delete the embed
            break;
   } } } }
}
```

Swap Image doesn't insert additional <embed> or other tags; it inserts additional event handlers to make implementing rollovers a one-step process. When a Swap Image behavior is deleted from the page, all the additional event handlers must be stripped out as well. To do so, the deleteBehavior() function first reads in the behavior function call string and then searches for the *Preload ID*. This is a unique name inserted by Dreamweaver if the user checked the Preload option when running the behavior. If the preloadID is found, the preload handler, such as onLoad = MM_preloadImages(), is removed. Next, the Swap Image deleteBehavior() searches to see if the Swap Image Restore code was added — and if so, deletes that event handler as well.

The identifyBehaviorArguments() function

If you've ever had to relocate a Web site from one directory to another, you know the laborious job of making sure all your references are intact. Dreamweaver takes some of the tedium out of this chore. When you use Save As from Dreamweaver, all of the file paths within HTML attributes, such as the image source files and link href files, are automatically updated. Dreamweaver extends the same functionality to URLs contained within behaviors.

For example, suppose that you have constructed a Web page that uses the Check Browser action to route users to various URLs, depending on the browser they are using. Should you elect to save your Web page in a different folder, for whatever reason, Dreamweaver automatically updates the referenced URLs.

For this property to work correctly, a new function must be included in the behavior. The function, identifyBehaviorArguments(), passes the argument structure to Dreamweaver so it can update the URLs, if necessary. The function also identifies the layer objects in the behavior that Dreamweaver must correct if the Convert Layers to Tables command is used.

The identifyBehaviorArguments() function accepts a string that contains the behavior function call, with arguments. The function then extracts the arguments into an array and identifies which arguments in the array are URLs, which ones are layer objects, and which ones are neither. There are four main return values:

✦ **URL:** When the argument is a file or file path

✦ **NS4.0ref:** When the argument identifies a layer in Netscape syntax, such as document.layers[\'Layer1\']

✦ **IE4.0ref:** When the argument identifies a layer in Internet Explorer syntax, such as document.all[\'Layer1\']

✦ **other:** When the argument is none of the preceding

You can see an example of the identifyBehaviorArguments() function in the Check Plugin action:

```
function identifyBehaviorArguments(fnCallStr) {
  var argArray;
  argArray = extractArgs(fnCallStr);
  if (argArray.length == 5) {
```

```
    return "other,URL,URL,other";
  }
  else {
    return "";
  }
}
```

As with the `inspectBehavior()` function, the array for the function call string is one element longer than the number of arguments — the initial array element is the function name itself.

The displayHelp() function

The `displayHelp()` function inserts a Help button on your custom behavior dialog boxes, below the standard OK and Cancel buttons. This function takes no arguments and is usually defined to display a help message or file. The two typical techniques, depending on what you want to accomplish, are the `alert()` method or the Dreamweaver JavaScript extension, `browseDocument()`. To display a brief message, use the `alert()` method, as in the following code:

```
function displayHelp() {
  alert("This behavior works only with .rmf files.");
}
```

When you need to bring up a much longer file, use the `browseDocument()` function:

```
function displayHelp() {
  dreamweaver.browseDocument("http://www.idest.com/dreamweaver/");
}
```

You can also reference local files using `browseDocument()`. See the `browseDocument()` description in the section "Dreamweaver JavaScript API extensions," earlier in this chapter.

Caution   Do not include the JavaScript file displayHelp.js in your behaviors. This is the Dreamweaver file used for calling its own Help pages.

Useful Common Functions

As with most other object-oriented programming languages, it's good programming practice to build a function once and recall it when needed. Dreamweaver includes a large library of such useful functions, which are maintained in the Configuration\Shared\Mm\Scripts\Cmn folder. The functions are grouped by category into JavaScript files; currently 18 such files exist, including docInfo.js, DOM.js, file.js, and string.js. Although they are used extensively throughout the standard behaviors, nothing prevents you from using them in your own routines. To access them, you need to insert only one line in your behavior JavaScript file, as shown the following:

```
<SCRIPT SRC="../../Shared/Mm/Scripts/Cmn/string.js"></SCRIPT>
```

Table 35-3 shows some of the most commonly used functions available in the Shared folder and the file in which they can be found.

Table 35-3: Useful Common Functions

Function	File	Description
getAllObjectRefs()	**docInfo.js**	Returns an array of object references for any specified tag in the current document or, if the document is in a frameset, in all frames.
getAllObjectTags()	**docInfo.js**	Returns an array of tags for any specified tag in the current document or, if the document is in a frameset, in all frames.
browseFile()	**file.js**	Opens the Select File dialog box and inserts the results into a specified text box.
stripStar()	**menuItem.js**	Removes the " *" from the end of a "myObject *" string.
stripValue()	**menuItem.js**	Removes the " (value)" from the end of a "someProperty (value)" string.
addStarToMenuItem()	**menuItem.js**	Adds " *" to the end of a selected menu item, as in Swap Image.
addValueToMenuItem()	**menuItem.js**	Adds a specified value formatted as " (value)" to the end of a selected menu item; for example, " (show)", " (hide)", and " (default)" are added in Show/Hide Layers.
niceNames()	**niceName.js**	Changes JavaScript object references such as document.layers['onLayer'].document. theForm to a more readable format such as form "theForm" in layer "onLayer".
nameReduce()	**niceName.js**	Extracts object names and array numbers/names and encloses them in quotes, if necessary.
badChars()	**string.js**	Removes inappropriate characters such as ~!@#$%^&*()_+|`-=\\{}[]:\";'<>,./ and space.
errMsg()	**string.js**	Concatenates strings given in an argument. For example, errMsg("Now is the %s for %s to band together.", var1, var2) returns "Now is the time for all men to band together." if var1 is set to "time" and var2 is set to "all men". However, if var1 is set to "not the time" and var2 is set to "anyone", then errMsg returns "Now is not the time for anyone to band together."

Continued

Table 35-3: *(continued)*

Function	File	Description
escQuotes()	string.js	Reviews a string and adds the escape character (\) in front of any single quote, double quote, or backslash found.
unescQuotes()	string.js	Removes any escape characters (\) found in a string.
extractArgs()	string.js	Takes a function call and extracts the arguments into an array without quotes.
getParam()	string.js	Returns an array of named objects within a given tag found on the current page.
findObject()	UI.js	Returns the JavaScript object reference for any named object. For example, if you have an image named imgOne in a form in a layer, findObject("imgOne") returns document.layers['onLayer'].imgOne.

Dreamweaver Behavior Techniques

Creating a behavior is often far more than just stringing together a number of predefined functions. Specific techniques exist for many special needs, and if you don't know them, you can spend many hours redeveloping the wheel. In this section, you learn several methods that can help you streamline your work.

Specifying an event

In Dreamweaver, every tag capable of being used to launch a behavior has a default event. Although you can alter the default events for various tags by editing the HTML files in the Events folder, as described in Chapter 23, these changes affect only your own system, not those of other users. You can, however, specify the desired event on a behavior-by-behavior basis — in fact, you can specify a series of desired events.

The event specification takes place in the canApplyBehavior() function. Usually, this function returns either true or false, depending on whether the proper conditions for implementing the behavior have been met. If, however, the conditions have been met *and* you want to specify an event to use, canApplyBehavior() can be set to return a string of acceptable events.

In the following example, the page is inspected, and if a layer is found, the default event is overridden in favor of onKeyDown:

```
function canAcceptBehavior() {
  var nameArray = dreamweaver.getObjectRefs("NS 4.0","document","LAYER");
  if (nameArray.length > 0) {
    return "onKeyDown";
  }
```

```
    else {
      return false;
    }
}
```

It's also possible to specify a series of preferred events, in reverse order of preference, like this:

```
return "onKeyDown, onKeyPress, onKeyUp";
```

If one event handler is not available — perhaps because the user specified an older browser — the next is selected.

Returning a value

Most event handlers don't require a return value to be implemented, but some, such as onMouseOver and onMouseOut, do. Generally, Dreamweaver behaviors don't take this into account, but you can by declaring a special variable, document.MM_returnValue. You can see the return value variable in operation in the standard Display Status Message behavior.

The document.MM_returnValue variable is declared as the last line in the function definition. Thus, Display Status Message reads as follows:

```
function MM_displayStatusMsg(msgStr) { //v2.0
  status = msgStr;
  document.MM_returnValue = true;
}
```

Naturally, the return value could also be false.

Including multiple functions

Although little known, the capability to return multiple functions began in Dreamweaver 1.2. Previously, all behavior functions had to be self-contained, and one could not call on any helper functions. Now, however, multiple functions can easily be defined and returned via behaviorFunction(). Once written into the user's page, all the returned functions are stored in a single <script>...</script> tag pair.

The technique for inserting multiple functions is fairly straightforward. First, list your defined functions in a comma-delimited string in behaviorFunction(). The one trick is to make sure that your primary function — the one called by the event handler — is listed, not first, but *last*. This technique is illustrated in the following code for my custom Resize Layer Patch behavior:

```
function behaviorFunction() {
  return 'reDo,resizePatch';
}
```

Here, my primary function is resizePatch() and is used as such in applyBehavior():

```
function applyBehavior() {
  return 'resizePatch()';  //return fn call with args
}
```

Summary

Although creating a custom behavior is not a simple task, it is a vastly rewarding one—both from the programmer's and the user's perspectives. Dreamweaver gives you tremendous power to automate advanced Web page techniques with access to the Document Object Model. As you ponder building your own behaviors, remember the following:

✦ If you can achieve a result in JavaScript, chances are good you can create a behavior to automate that task.

✦ Dreamweaver includes an expanded Document Object Model (DOM) that enables the programmer to examine and modify virtually every aspect of an HTML page.

✦ You can use Dreamweaver's built-in JavaScript extensions and API functions to build your own actions.

✦ Dreamweaver's JavaScript extensions enable you to open existing documents, as well as create and save new ones.

✦ Many useful functions can be found in the Shared\Mm\Scripts\Cmn folder.

In the next chapter, you learn how Dreamweaver's server behaviors work and how to build your own custom ones.

✦   ✦   ✦

Handling Server Behaviors

Server behaviors are the heart of Dreamweaver, the essential engine that puts the "dynamic" in dynamic Web applications. Server behaviors insert server-model–specific code that handles everything from displaying dynamic data to authenticating users. Even the basic data source connection and the establishment of a recordset are, in reality, server behaviors. Without server behaviors, there would be no dynamic capabilities in Dreamweaver.

Server behaviors are valuable for novices and veteran coders alike. They enable designers who have never heard of an ASP Request collection to gather information from a form — a procedure that utilizes the ASP Request collection — with point-and-click ease. Even serious code jockeys can appreciate the productivity potential of server behaviors, especially the capability to create their own. With the Server Behavior Builder, programmers can build a library of their custom functions, complete with fully functional dialog boxes for maximum flexibility. Once crafted, you can drop any of the custom server behaviors directly onto the page — and, if need be, easily alter the parameters.

This chapter includes an overview of server behaviors as well as basic information about their use and management. You'll also find a detailed description of each of the standard Dreamweaver server behaviors for your reference. Finally, you'll look at ways to extend Dreamweaver's core functionality with the Server Behavior Builder.

Understanding Server Behaviors

In contrast to Dreamweaver's JavaScript behaviors — with their numerous required functions and many more optional ones — a server behavior may be as simple as one line of code. The difference, and it's a key one, is that the code is intended to be executed by the application server, not the browser.

Another difference between server behaviors and JavaScript behaviors is that server behavior code may exist outside the bounds of the HTML page. Any page with a recordset has a section of code before the opening `<html>` tag, and a smaller block of code after the closing `</html>` tag. Dreamweaver automatically places the code in the proper place—and code placement is very important on the server side—when any of its standard server behaviors are used. Dreamweaver includes over 25 standard server behaviors; the exact number varies for each server model. Figure 36-1 displays the available server behaviors for ASP.

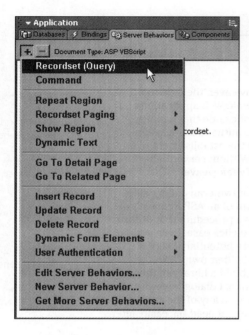

Figure 36-1: Apply any server behavior from the Server Behaviors panel.

The Server Behaviors panel is the focal point for inserting, removing, and managing server behaviors. Unlike the Behaviors panel, which only displays the JavaScript behaviors attached to the selected tag, the Server Behaviors panel displays all the server behaviors included in the current page, in the order in which they were applied. Selecting a specific server behavior listed in the Server Behaviors panel highlights the attached page element, if visible in the Document window. Some server behaviors, such as Recordset, have their own Property inspector, while others display dynamic code as an attribute in a text or other Property inspector.

Although the simplest server behaviors can insert code without any additional user input, all of the built-in server behaviors have a dialog box for specifying parameters. These vary in complexity from a single drop-down list to multiple-section dialog boxes with every type of input element available. As you'll learn in the next section, once you have inserted a server behavior, you can easily modify its parameters.

Applying and Managing Server Behaviors

If you have ever completed any Web applications in Dreamweaver, you've likely already discovered how to apply and update a server behavior. The Server Behaviors panel is the primary tool for inserting, modifying, and removing server behaviors. You can display the Server Behaviors panel in several ways:

✦ Choose Window ➪ Server Behaviors.

✦ Select the Server Behavior icon from either the Launcher panel or the Launcher in the status bar.

✦ Use the keyboard shortcut, Ctrl+F9 (Command+F9).

The Server Behaviors panel remains available regardless of whether you are in Design view, Code view, or the split-screen Design and Code view.

Inserting and removing server behaviors

To add a particular server behavior to your page, choose the Add (+) button from the Server Behaviors panel and select the desired behavior from the list. Many of the server behaviors have prerequisites that must be in place — such as a recordset, form, or selected element — before they can be installed, but these requirements vary from server behavior to server behavior. If you attempt to insert a server behavior and some precondition has not been met, Dreamweaver alerts you to the missing element; and you are prevented from inserting the server behavior until all the required pieces are in place.

Once you select the server behavior from the Add drop-down list, a dialog box appears to enable you to select or enter the needed parameters. Each dialog box is specific to the chosen server behavior, and they vary widely in terms of parameters offered and complexity. For information about a specific server behavior, see the corresponding section for that server behavior later in this chapter. Each section provides step-by-step explanations about completing the pertinent dialog box.

Removing an existing server behavior is simple. Select the entry for the server behavior in the Server Behaviors panel and choose the Remove (–) button. Dreamweaver immediately removes all the associated code without requesting confirmation.

Caution

With JavaScript behaviors, if you delete a page element that has a client-side behavior attached, you'll automatically delete that behavior. This is not always the case with server behaviors, and it's best to always use the Server Behaviors panel's Remove (–) button before deleting any associated text, graphics, or form elements.

Editing the parameters

To modify the attributes or parameters of an inserted server behavior, double-click its entry in the Server Behaviors panel. You can differentiate between multiple applications of the same server behavior in two ways. First, the entry for each server behavior lists one or two of its key attributes in parentheses. For example, a Dynamic Text server behavior applied to the LastName column in the rsMaillist recordset is displayed as follows:

```
Dynamic Text(rsMaillist.LastName)
```

Second, you can tell which server behavior is associated with which page element by selecting the server behavior — the associated text, graphic, or other page element is also selected in Design or Code view.

When the dialog box for a server behavior reopens, you may alter any of the parameters that remain active. In some situations, as with the Go To Detail Page server behavior shown in Figure 36-2, one or more fields may be disabled and unable to be changed. If you need to alter a disabled parameter, delete the server behavior and reapply it.

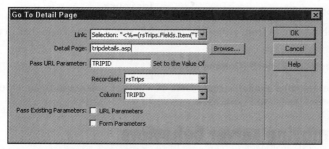

Figure 36-2: When modifying certain server behaviors, some fields, such as the Link field in this Go To Detail Page dialog box, are disabled and cannot be changed.

Standard Server Behaviors

Dreamweaver ships with over 25 server behaviors, and offers the option for adding many more. The default server behaviors are geared toward handling basic Web application tasks such as repeating an area and inserting records in a data source.

In the following sections, each server behavior is briefly described, along with any prerequisites. Step-by-step instructions for including the server behavior are provided; for more contextual information on using the particular server behavior, see the cross-referenced chapter in each section.

Recordset (Query)

To create a simple recordset, follow these steps:

1. From the Server Behaviors panel, select the Add (+) button and choose Recordset (Query) from the drop-down list.

   The Recordset dialog box, shown in Figure 36-3, is displayed.

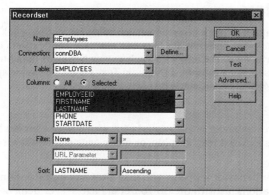

Figure 36-3: You can add recordsets from either the Server Behaviors panel or the Bindings panel.

2. In the Recordset dialog box, enter an identifying label for your recordset in the Name field.

   It's considered good practice to prefix your recordset name with rs — as in rsDBA. This prefix quickly identifies the recordset in the code.

3. Select a connection from the drop-down list of that name.

4. If the desired connection has not been declared, choose Define to open the Connections dialog box.

   After a connection has been selected, the available tables are shown.

5. Select a table to work with from the Tables drop-down list.

   The chosen table's fields are displayed in the Columns list.

6. By default, all of the columns are included in the recordset. To specify certain columns, choose the Selected option and then choose any desired field.

   Shift+click to select contiguous columns, and Ctrl+click (Command+click) to select noncontiguous columns.

7. By default, all of the records in the selected columns will be available. To limit the recordset further, use the four Filter drop-down lists as follows:

   • Choose the field you want to base your filter on from the first drop-down list. This list changes dynamically according to which table you've selected.

   • Select from the second drop-down list the expression with which to compare the data from the selected column in the first drop-down list. Available expressions are =, >, <, >=, <=, <>, begins with, ends with, and contains.

   • Choose the type of value to compare to the selected field from the third drop-down list. Available types are URL Parameter, Form Variable, Cookie, Session Variable, Application Variable, and Entered Value.

   • Enter the value to compare to the selected field in the fourth input field. Values entered are not case-sensitive.

8. To sort the data, select a column from the first drop-down list under Sort and then choose either Ascending or Descending from the second list.

9. At any time, you can see what results will be returned for the recordset by choosing Test.

Tip

To see how your simple recordset translates into SQL, choose the Advanced button. You can return to the original dialog box by selecting Simple on the advanced Recordset dialog box.

10. Click OK when you're done.

Cross-Reference

For more information on defining recordsets, see Chapter 15.

Repeat Region

The Repeat Region server behavior replicates a selected page area as many times as specified. If the Repeat Region surrounds dynamic data, the record pointer advances for each repetition. A tab and highlight note the boundaries of the Repeat Region when Invisible Elements is enabled.

Requirements: One or more selected page elements, such as a table row or a line ending in a line break tag (<br>).

To implement a Repeat Region, follow these steps:

1. Select the dynamic data and the surrounding code you'd like to repeat.

2. From the Server Behaviors panel, choose the Add (+) button and select Repeat Region from the list.

   The Repeat Region dialog box, shown in Figure 36-4, appears.

Figure 36-4: With the Repeat Region server behavior, you can show some or all of the records in the chosen recordset.

3. From the Repeat Region dialog box, choose the recordset you want to work with from the Recordset list.

4. If you want to display a subset of the recordset, enter the number of records you'd like to display in the Show Records field.

5. If you want every record in the recordset to be displayed, choose the Show All Records option.

6. Click OK when you're done.

Cross-Reference   For more information on the Repeat Region server behavior, see Chapter 17.

Recordset Paging

The Recordset Paging server behaviors move the record pointer to the indicated data record in a given recordset. They are frequently used in combination to navigate through a recordset. In all, there are five Recordset Paging server behaviors; however, you insert the following four in an identical fashion:

✦ Move To First Record

✦ Move To Previous Record

✦ Move To Next Record

✦ Move To Last Record

The fifth server behavior in this category, Move To Specific Record, uses a different procedure, which is covered in the following section.

Requirements: A selected page element and at least one recordset with more than one returned row.

To use any of the four basic Recordset Paging server behaviors, follow these steps:

1. Select the text or image to which you'd like to attach the server behavior.

2. From the Server Behaviors panel, select the Add (+) button and choose the desired behavior from the Recordset Paging submenu.

   The appropriate Recordset Paging dialog box appears. Your selection is highlighted in the Link list, as shown in Figure 36-5.

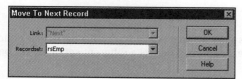

Figure 36-5: The Recordset Paging server behaviors (such as Move To Next Record) identify your selected target, which may be an image or text.

3. Make sure that the link selected is one of those showing in the Link list.

4. Choose the recordset you want to work with from the Recordset drop-down list.

5. Click OK when you're done.

Cross-Reference

For more information on these Recordset Paging server behaviors, see Chapter 17.

Move To Specific Record

The Move To Specific Record server behavior isn't available in ColdFusion or PHP. To use the Move To Specific Record server behavior, follow these steps:

1. Select the text or image to which you'd like to attach the server behavior.

2. From the Server Behaviors panel, choose Move To Specific Record from the Recordset Paging submenu.

   The Move To Specific Record dialog box is displayed, as shown in Figure 36-6.

3. Select the desired recordset from the list labeled Move To Record In.

4. Choose the field referenced in the URL parameter from the Where Column field.

5. Enter the variable in the URL parameter in the Matches URL Parameter field.

6. Click OK when you're done.

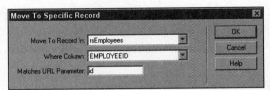

Figure 36-6: An alternative method for creating a detail page uses the Move To Specific Record server behavior.

For more information on the Move To Specific Record server behavior, see Chapter 19.

Show Region

The Show Region server behavior displays an area of the screen if a particular condition is true. These are often called conditional regions. There is a different set of server behaviors for each server model:

ColdFusion and PHP:

✦ Show if Recordset is Empty

✦ Show if Recordset is Not Empty

✦ Show if First Page

✦ Show if Not First Page

✦ Show if Last Page

✦ Show if Not Last Page

ASP.Net C# and ASP.Net VB

✦ Show if DataSet is Empty

✦ Show if DataSet is Not Empty

✦ Show if First Page

✦ Show if Not First Page

✦ Show if Last Page

✦ Show if Not Last Page

JSP

✦ Show Region if Recordset is Empty

✦ Show Region if Recordset is Not Empty

✦ Show Region if First Record

✦ Show Region if Not First Record

✦ Show Region if Last Record

✦ Show Region if Not Last Record

ASP Javascript and ASP VBscript

  ✦ Show Region if Recordset is Empty

  ✦ Show Region if Recordset is Not Empty

  ✦ Show Region if First Record

  ✦ Show Region if Not First Record

  ✦ Show Region if Last Record

  ✦ Show Region if Not Last Record

Requirements: One or more selected page elements and at least one recordset.

Applying a Show Region server behavior is straightforward:

  1. Select the page area you'd like to show conditionally.

  2. From the Server Behaviors panel, choose the Add (+) button and select one of the server behaviors from the Show Record submenu.

     The dialog box for the specific Show Record server behavior you chose is displayed, like the one shown in Figure 36-7. The dialog boxes for all the Show Record server behaviors are identical.

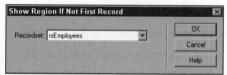

Figure 36-7: To use a Show Record server behavior, just choose a recordset.

  3. Select the recordset on which to base the Show Record condition from the Recordset list.

  4. Click OK when you're done.

For more information on the Show Region server behavior, see Chapter 17.

Go To Detail Page

The Go To Detail Page server behavior is used in master-detail Web applications to navigate from a chosen link on the master page to a designated detail page. This server behavior passes a unique record ID via the URL query string method. The Go To Detail Page server behavior isn't available in ColdFusion, .NET or PHP.

For more on master-detail Web applications, see Chapter 19.

Requirements: A selected page element and at least one recordset.

To attach a Go To Detail Page server behavior, follow these steps:

1. Select the page element—text, graphic, or dynamic data—you'd like to use as the link to the detail page.

2. From the Server Behaviors panel, choose the Add (+) button and then select Go To Detail Page from the drop-down list.

   The Go To Detail Page dialog box, shown in Figure 36-8, is displayed.

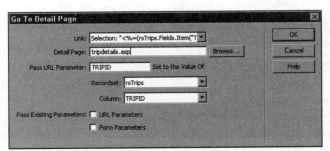

Figure 36-8: Specify the linking parameter sent from the master page in the Go To Detail Page server behavior.

3. Make sure that the page element selected is represented in the Link field.

   If no selection was made, Dreamweaver will create a new Detail text link.

4. Enter the path to the detail page in the Detail Page field or use Browse to locate the file in the Select File dialog box.

5. Enter the variable name you'd like to be sent in the Pass URL Parameter field.

   You can use a name of your own choosing or the name of the field in the database; whichever name you decide upon, make a note of it somewhere, as you'll need to reference it when the detail page itself is constructed.

6. Select the recordset the URL parameter is in from the Recordset list.

7. Choose the field the URL parameter's value is related to from the Column list.

8. Unless you have preexisting URL or Form parameters to send to the detail page, leave the Pass Existing Parameters options unchecked.

9. Click OK when you're done.

Cross-Reference

For more information on the Go To Detail Page server behavior, see Chapter 19.

Go To Related Page

The Go To Related Page server behavior links to a new page that conveys the form and/or URL variables previously passed to the current page.

Requirements: A selected page element and at least one recordset. The page on which the server behavior is inserted must have had form or URL values passed to it.

To attach a Go To Related Page server behavior, follow these steps:

1. Select the page element — text, image, or dynamic data — you'd like to use as the trigger for your behavior.

2. From the Server Behaviors panel, choose the Add (+) button and then select Go To Related Page from the list.

   The Go To Related Page server behavior dialog box appears, as shown in Figure 36-9.

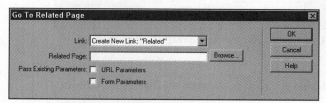

Figure 36-9: The Go To Related Page server behavior can convey form values, URL values, or both to another dynamic page.

3. In the dialog box, verify that the text or code for the selected element displayed in the Link field is correct.

4. Enter the path to the target page in the Related Page field or choose Browse to locate an existing dynamic page.

5. If you want to carry over values received from a query string, select the URL Parameters option.

6. If you want to pass values received from a form, select the Form Parameters option.

7. Click OK when you're done.

For more information on the Go To Related Page server behavior, see Chapter 19.

Insert Record

The Insert Record server behavior adds a new record to a chosen table in a data source.

Requirements: A form with form elements and a Submit button.

To add the Insert Record server behavior, follow these steps:

1. From the Server Behaviors panel, choose the Add (+) button and then select Insert Record.

   The Insert Record dialog box appears, as shown in Figure 36-10.

2. From the Insert Record dialog box, choose the connection from the drop-down list.

   If you need to establish a new connection, select Define.

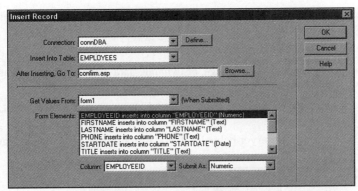

Figure 36-10: Users may add new data directly to a connected data source.

3. Select the data table you want to use from the Insert Into Table list.

4. Enter the path to the destination page in the After Inserting, Go To field, or choose the Browse button to locate the file.

   It's important that you select a confirmation or other page to go to after the form is submitted. If you don't, no feedback is provided to the user, and no change will be apparent.

5. Select the name of the form to be used from the Get Values From list.

   If there is only one form on the page, the form will be preselected.

6. For each object listed in the Form Elements area:

   • Select the data source field the form object's value is to be inserted into from the Column list.

   • Choose the data source type for the data from the Submit As list. The options are Text; Numeric; Date; Date MS Access; Checkbox Y, N; Checkbox 1,0; Check -1,0; and Checkbox MS Access.

Be sure to give your form fields meaningful names so you can easily choose which form field goes into each database column.

7. Click OK when you're done.

For more information on the Insert Record server behavior, see Chapter 19.

Update Record

Use the Update Record server behavior to modify existing records in a data source.

Requirements: A recordset, a form with form elements linked to the dynamic data, and a Submit button.

To insert an Update Record server behavior, follow these steps:

1. From the Server Behaviors panel, choose Update Record.

   The Update Record dialog box appears, as shown in Figure 36-11.

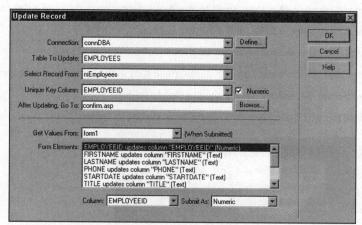

Figure 36-11: With an Update Record server behavior, you can modify your data source remotely.

2. From the Update Record dialog box, choose a connection from the drop-down list.

   If you need to establish a new connection, select Define.

3. Select the data table you want to use from the Table to Update list.

4. Choose the data source on which to base your update from the Select Record From list.

5. Select the key field from the Unique Key Column list.

   Dreamweaver attempts to detect whether the field is a number type and, if so, selects the Numeric option.

6. Enter the path to the destination page in the After Updating, Go To field or choose the Browse button to locate the file.

7. Select the name of the form to be used from the Get Values From list.

   If there is only one form on the page, the form will be preselected.

8. For each object listed in the Form Elements area:

   • Select the data source field into which the form object's value is to be inserted from the Column list.

   • Choose the data source type for the data from the Submit As list. The options are Text; Numeric; Date; Date MS Access; Checkbox Y, N; Checkbox 1,0; Check -1,0; and Checkbox MS Access.

9. Click OK when you're done.

For more information on the Update Record server behavior, see Chapter 19.

Delete Record

The Delete Record server behavior is used to remove existing records from a data source.

Requirements: A recordset, a form, and a Submit button.

To attach a Delete Record server behavior to a form, follow these steps:

1. Make sure that a form exists on a dynamic page that includes at least one recordset.

2. From the Server Behaviors panel, choose Delete Record.

   The Delete Record dialog box is displayed, as shown in Figure 36-12.

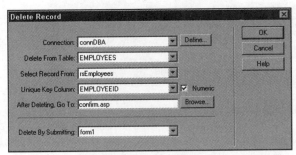

Figure 36-12: Maintain an up-to-date data source with the Delete Record server behavior.

3. From the Delete Record dialog box, choose a connection from the drop-down list.

   If you need to establish a new connection, select Define.

4. Select the data table you want to modify from the Delete From Table list.

5. Choose the data source to base your update on from the Select Record From list.

6. Select the key field from the Unique Key Column list.

   Dreamweaver attempts to detect whether the field is a number type and, if so, selects the Numeric option.

7. Enter the path to the destination page in the After Deleting, Go To field or choose the Browse button to locate the file.

8. Choose the form that contains the Delete button.

9. Click OK when you're done.

For more information on the Delete Record server behavior, see Chapter 19.

User authentication

The World Wide Web is all about accessing information from anywhere in the world. Sometimes, however, you need to restrict access to certain areas of your site to authorized users. Dreamweaver supplies a full complement of server behaviors to support authenticating the user against a specified data source. The user authentication server behaviors are not available for PHP or .NET.

Log In User

The Log In User server behavior redirects authorized users to one page and unauthorized users to another and creates a session variable for the user name.

Requirements: A recordset, a form, appropriate form elements for a user name and a password, and a Submit button.

1. From the Server Behaviors panel, select the Add (+) button and choose User Authentication ⇨ Log In User.

   The Log In User dialog box is displayed, as shown in Figure 36-13.

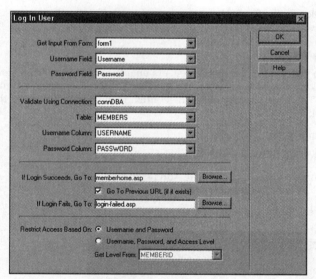

Figure 36-13: The Log In User server behavior verifies that the user may be granted access.

2. If there is more than one form on the page, select the form containing the user name and password fields from the Get Input From Form list.

3. Select the form element used to gather the user name from the Username Field list.

4. Select the form element used to gather the password from the Password Field list.

5. Choose a connection to the data source containing the table of registered users from the Validate Using Connection list.

6. Select the table of registered users from the Table list.

7. Choose the field containing the user name from the Username Column list.

8. Choose the field containing the password from the Password Column list.

9. Enter the path to the page for the authorized user in the If Log In Succeeds, Go To field.

10. If you want the user to proceed to the previously selected link, rather than the page entered in Step 9, select the Go To Previous URL option.

11. Enter the path to the page for the unauthorized user in the If Log In Fails, Go To field.

12. If access levels should be evaluated as part of the authentication:

   • Select the Restrict Access Based On Username, Password, and Access Level option.

   • Choose the data source field containing the access level data from the Get Level From list.

13. Click OK when you're done.

Cross-Reference For more information on the Log In User server behavior, see Chapter 19.

Restrict Access To Page

The Restrict Access To Page server behavior prevents unauthorized users from viewing specific pages by checking a session variable. Once defined, the server behavior may be copied and pasted onto another page by using the context menu commands from the Server Behaviors panel.

Requirements: A dynamic page.

To apply the Restrict Access To Page server behavior, follow these steps.

1. In the Server Behaviors panel, choose the Add (+) button and select User Authentication ➪ Restrict Access To Page.

   The Restrict Access To Page dialog box, shown in Figure 36-14, is displayed.

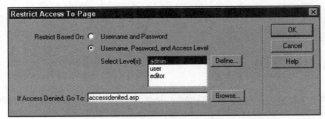

Figure 36-14: Any dynamic page can be protected against unauthorized viewing with the Restrict Access To Page server behavior.

2. If you don't wish to restrict admission by access levels, make sure the Restrict Based On Username and Password option is selected.

3. To set group permissions for the page:

- Choose the Restrict Based On Username, Password, and Access Level option.

- Choose one or more groups from the Select Level(s) area.

4. To add new groups to the Select Level(s) list:

- Choose Define.

  The Define Access Levels dialog box opens.

- Enter the name for the access level in the Name field.

  The name must match a value stored in your data source in whichever column is designated for the group access levels.

- To add additional levels, select the Add (+) button and enter another name.

- To delete any levels, choose the level in the list area and select the Remove (–) button.

- Click OK to close the Define Access Levels dialog box.

5. Enter the path to the file you want to redirect unauthorized users to in the If Access Denied, Go To field. Alternatively, select the Browse button to locate the file.

6. Click OK when you're done.

Cross-Reference   For more information on the Restrict Access To Page server behavior, see Chapter 19.

Log Out User

The Log Out User server behavior clears the user name session variable established by the Log In User server behavior and redirects the user to an exit page. You can set up the Log Out User server behavior so that a user selects a link to log out or is automatically logged out when a particular page, such as one confirming the completion of an order, is viewed.

Requirements: A Log In User server behavior on another page.

To use the Log Out User server behavior, follow these steps:

1. To apply the server behavior to a specific link on the page, select that link.

2. From the Server Behaviors panel, select the Add (+) button and choose User Authentication ⇨ Log Out User.

   The Log Out User dialog box is displayed, as shown in Figure 36-15.

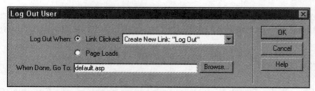

Figure 36-15: You can log a user out automatically by choosing the Log Out When Page Loads option on a order confirmation page.

3. To trigger the server behavior with a link, choose the Log Out When Link Clicked option and make sure your selected link is chosen in the list.

If no link was preselected, Dreamweaver offers to apply the server behavior to a new link, Log Out.

4. To automatically log out users when the current page is viewed, select the Log Out When Page Loads option.

5. If you're using a link as a trigger, enter the path to the destination page in the When Done, Go To field. Alternatively, select the Browse button to locate the file.

Caution

Do not use the When Done, Go To option if you are automatically logging out a user when the page loads. If you do, the user will never see the current page.

6. Click OK when you're done.

Cross-Reference

For more information on the Log Out User server behavior, see Chapter 19.

Check New Username

The Check New Username server behavior verifies that the requested user name is not already in the data source, redirecting the user if it is.

Requirements: An Insert Record server behavior, a form, and appropriate form elements.

1. From the Server Behaviors panel, select the Add (+) button and choose User Authentication ➪ Check New Username.

The Check New Username dialog box is displayed, as shown in Figure 36-16.

Figure 36-16: Make sure a requested user name is not already taken with the Check New Username server behavior.

2. Select the form element that contains the requested user name from the Username Field list.

If a form element is called USERNAME, Dreamweaver automatically selects that entry.

3. Enter the path to the file you want users to see if their requested name is already stored in the data source in the If Already Exists, Go To field or select Browse to locate the file.

4. Click OK when you're done.

Cross-Reference

For more information on the Check New Username server behavior, see Chapter 19.

Dynamic elements

With one exception, dynamic elements in Dreamweaver refer to form elements, linked to a data source field. Data-connected form elements are typically used in Web applications that update records. The single exception is Dynamic Text, which is described in the following section. Dynamic Form Elements (which aren't available in .NET) are covered afterwards.

Dynamic Text

Inserting a Dynamic Text server behavior is the same as dragging a field from a recordset on the Bindings panel onto the page. It's a matter of individual preference which technique you use; personally, I find dragging-and-dropping from the Bindings panel much faster and more intuitive than using the Dynamic Text server behavior.

Requirements: A dynamic page.

To use the Dynamic Text server behavior, follow these steps:

1. Place your cursor on the page where you'd like the dynamic text to appear.

2. From the Server Behaviors panel, choose Dynamic Elements ➪ Dynamic Text.

   The Dynamic Text dialog box is displayed, as shown in Figure 36-17.

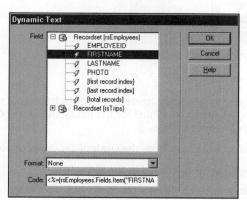

Figure 36-17: You can insert dynamic text through either the Server Behaviors panel or the Bindings panel.

3. If necessary, expand the recordset or other data source to select the desired dynamic data.

4. Choose any necessary server format from the Format list.

5. Enter any required adjustments to the dynamic data in the Code field.

   In most situations, no changes are necessary.

6. Click OK when you're done.

Cross-Reference

For more information on adding dynamic text, see Chapter 16.

Dynamic List/Menu

To link a drop-down list to dynamic data, follow these steps:

1. Insert a list/menu form element on a dynamic page with a recordset.

2. If you have more than one list/menu on the page, select the one you want to convert.

3. From the Server Behaviors panel, choose Dynamic Form Elements ⇨ Dynamic List/Menu.

   The Dynamic List/Menu dialog box, shown in Figure 36-18, is displayed.

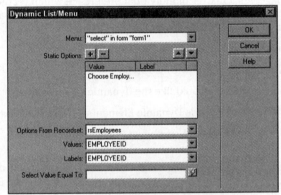

Figure 36-18: Lists give the user a distinct series of items from which to choose.

4. In the Static Options box, add any nondynamic items you want to the top of your list menu. This could be something as simple as a label for the list menu, or as complicated as a full URL with query strings for search pages.

5. Choose the recordset you want to work with from the Options From Recordset list.

6. Verify that the desired drop-down list is displayed in the Menu list.

7. Choose the field from your data source containing the items you want displayed to the user from the Labels list.

8. Choose the field from your data source containing the items you want submitted by the user from the Values list.

9. To preselect an item, enter its value in the Select Value Equal To field or use the lightning bolt icon to choose a value from the established data sources.

10. Click OK when you're done.

Cross-Reference   For more information on the Dynamic List/Menu server behavior, see Chapter 19.

Dynamic Text Field

To link a text field or text area to dynamic data, follow these steps:

1. Insert a text field into a form on a page with a recordset or other data source.

   It's a good idea to name the text field and form at this point. Although you can always change the names later, naming the elements early on avoids problems later.

2. Select the text field.

3. From the Server Behaviors panel, choose Dynamic Form Elements ➪ Dynamic Text Field.

Caution   Be sure to choose Dynamic Text Field and not Dynamic Text from the Dynamic Elements submenu. If you select Dynamic Text while your text field is highlighted, the form element will be replaced.

4. In the Dynamic Text Field dialog box that appears (see Figure 36-19), verify that the correct form element was chosen in the Text Field list. If necessary, choose a different text field.

Figure 36-19: You can make a data field editable by connecting it to a Dynamic Text Field.

5. Select the Set Value To lightning bolt icon to display the available data sources.

6. Choose a field from the Dynamic Data dialog box.

7. If desired, you can apply a server format to the data by choosing an entry in the Format list.

8. Click OK to close the Dynamic Data dialog box and, after reviewing your choices, click OK again to close the Dynamic Text Field dialog box.

Cross-Reference   For more information on the Dynamic Text Field server behavior, see Chapter 19.

Dynamic CheckBox

To convert a static checkbox to a dynamic one, follow these steps:

1. Select a checkbox in a form on a page with a recordset.

2. From the Server Behaviors panel, choose Dynamic Form Elements ➪ Dynamic CheckBox.

   The Dynamic CheckBox dialog box appears, as shown in Figure 36-20.

3. Verify that your selected checkbox is correctly named in the CheckBox list.

4. Select the Check If lightning bolt icon to display the available data sources.

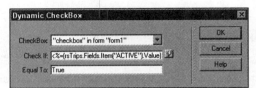

Figure 36-20: Checkboxes can depict whether a particular field of a recordset is True or False.

5. Choose a field from the Dynamic Data dialog box.

6. If desired, you can apply a server format to the data by choosing an entry in the Format list. Click OK when you're done to close the Dynamic Data dialog box.

7. Enter the value expected for a selected checkbox in the Equal To field.

   This value is data source–dependent. For many data sources, 1 is used to represent true; for others, a –1 is used. When working with Yes/No fields from Access databases, enter **True**; be sure to capitalize the word, as lowercase will not work properly.

8. Select OK when you're done.

For more information on the Dynamic CheckBox server behavior, see Chapter 19.

Dynamic Radio Buttons

To link radio buttons to dynamic data, follow these steps:

1. Select a group of radio buttons on a dynamic page with an available data source.

2. From the Server Behaviors panel, choose Dynamic Form Elements ➪ Dynamic Radio Buttons.

   The Dynamic Radio Buttons dialog box appears, as shown in Figure 36-21.

Figure 36-21: Radio buttons can reflect a limited number of choices within a data source field.

3. Verify that your selected form element is displayed in the Radio Button Group list.

4. In the Radio Button Values area, choose the first entry shown and, if necessary, change the Value field to reflect the expected data.

5. Repeat Step 4 for every radio button in the group.

6. Select the Select Value Equal To lightning bolt icon to display the available data sources.

7. Choose a field from the Dynamic Data dialog box.

   Be sure to select a data source field with values parallel to those entered in the radio button group.

8. If desired, you can apply a server format to the data by choosing an entry in the Format list. Click OK when you're done to close the Dynamic Data dialog box.

9. When you're done, click OK to close the Dynamic Radio Buttons dialog box.

Cross-Reference

For more information on the Dynamic Radio Button server behavior, see Chapter 19.

Stored Procedure/Command/Callable

Many advanced Web applications use a stored procedure application object. Stored procedures are known under a variety of names: ASP users call them *commands,* whereas JSP developers know them as *callables;* only ColdFusion users refer to them solely as stored procedures. Stored procedures are complete SQL queries that may return recordsets or other data. Stored procedures are often used for complex data source management such as inserting new tables on the fly.

Stored procedures are created and compiled in the data source itself, such as Microsoft's SQL Server. Because they are precompiled, they execute faster than similar SQL statements entered directly into the Web application. Stored procedures, like recordsets, may be defined as a data source through either the Bindings panel or the Server Behaviors panel.

To define a stored procedure as a data source through the Server Behaviors panel, follow these steps:

1. From the Server Behaviors panel, select the Add (+) button and, depending on your server model: for ASP, choose Command (Stored Procedure); for ColdFusion, choose Stored Procedure; and for JSP, choose Callable (Stored Procedure).

   The stored procedure dialog box for the appropriate server model is displayed; for example, Figure 36-22 shows the Command dialog box seen by JSP users.

Note

Stored procedures and the variables necessary to use them are database- and server model–dependent. A stored procedure on SQL server will be completely different than a ColdFusion stored procedure or another SQL-type database. The Stored Procedure/Command/Callable dialog box may change based on the type of database you're connecting to, as well as the server model.

2. In the Command/Callable/Stored Procedure field, enter a unique name.

3. From the Connection list, choose the connection in which your stored procedure may be found.

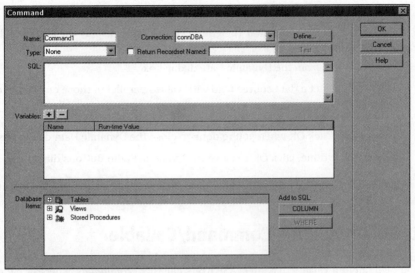

Figure 36-22: Stored procedures must be included in the data source before they can be added as a data source in Dreamweaver.

4. ASP users should choose Stored Procedure from the Type list.

Note   The ASP Command (Stored Procedure) server behavior includes additional types: Insert, Update, and Delete. These work identically to the Prepared (Insert/Update/Delete) server behavior described in the following section on JSP server behaviors.

5. If the stored procedure returns a recordset, choose the Return Recordset option and enter a name in the Returned Recordset Named field.

6. From the Database Items area, expand the Stored Procedure list and choose the desired stored procedure.

    It's a good idea to choose Test to make sure your connection is working properly at this point.

7. To modify the stored procedure, select any other element in the Database Items area and choose the Column or Where button.

8. Enter any necessary variables by clicking the Add (+) button in the Variables area and entering the values under each column: Name, Type, Direction, Size, Default Value, and Run-time Value.

9. Click OK when you're done.

Special JSP server behaviors

A number of server behaviors are only available for sites based on the JSP server model. An important feature of JavaServer Pages is the capability to use *JavaBeans*. JavaBeans are Java components or classes that process events and transmit results to the calling program and other JavaBeans. Dreamweaver offers two JavaBean–related server behaviors: JavaBean and JavaBean Collection.

Prepared (Insert/Update/Delete)

JSP users may employ what's referred to as a Prepared command to insert, update, or delete data sources.

To use a Prepared command, follow these steps:

1. From the Server Behaviors panel, select the Add (+) button and choose Prepared (Insert/Update/Delete) from the list.

   The Prepared (Insert/Update/Delete) dialog box, shown in Figure 36-23, is displayed.

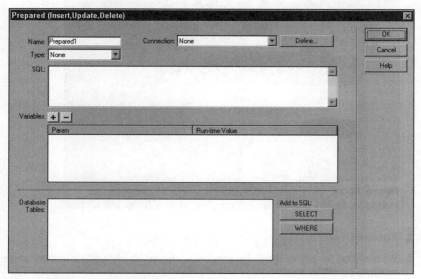

Figure 36-23: You can include three different types of Prepared statements — Insert, Update, or Delete — as a JSP data source.

2. In the Name field, enter a unique name that will appear in the Server Behaviors panel.

3. From the Connection list, choose the connection in which your stored procedure may be found.

4. Choose the prepared statement you want to insert from the Type list: Insert, Update, or Delete.

   Dreamweaver inserts appropriate code into the SQL area for each selection.

5. Complete the SQL code manually by entering columns and values in the SQL area.

6. As an alternative to manually entering the column names in the SQL statement, you can select any other element in the Database Items area and choose the SELECT or WHERE button to insert them.

7. Enter any necessary variables by clicking the Add (+) button in the Variables area and entering the values under each column: Param and Run-time Value.

8. Click OK when you're done.

JavaBean

To insert a JavaBean as a data source, follow these steps:

1. From the Server Behaviors panel, select the Add (+) button and choose JavaBean from the list.

   The JavaBean dialog box, shown in Figure 36-24, is displayed.

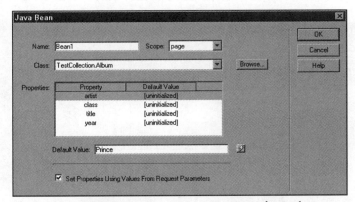

Figure 36-24: Dreamweaver supports JavaBean classes in an individual CLASS (.class) file or compressed in a ZIP or JAR archive.

2. If desired, enter a unique name in the Name field.

3. Set how the JavaBean variables may be accessed by choosing a Scope: page, request, session, or application.

4. Select a JavaBean class from the Class field or click the Browse button to locate the file.

   JavaBeans may be in CLASS (.class), ZIP (.zip), or JAR (.jar) files.

5. To set the default value of any of the bean's properties, select the item from the Properties area and enter a new value in the Default Value field.

   To set the default value to dynamic value, choose the lightning bolt icon.

6. Click OK when you're done.

JavaBean Collection

To insert a JavaBean Collection as a data source, follow these steps:

1. From the Server Behaviors panel, select the Add (+) button and choose JavaBean Collection from the list.

   The JavaBean Collection dialog box, shown in Figure 36-25, is displayed.

Figure 36-25: Dreamweaver automatically reads the indexed property for a selected JavaBean Collection data source.

2. Select a JavaBean class from the Class field or click the Browse button to locate the file.

3. Select an Indexed Property to use from the list.

4. Make sure the Item Class entered by Dreamweaver is correct, modifying it if necessary.

5. Set how the JavaBean variables may be accessed by choosing a Scope: page, request, session, or application.

6. Click OK when you're done.

ASP.NET server behaviors

Two special server behaviors make displaying dynamic data quick and easy: DataGrid and DataList.

DataGrid

The DataGrid server behavior enables you to rapidly add an editable DataGrid to your page. The DataGrid can also include Insert, Update, and Delete buttons.

Requirements: One DataSet on the current page.

To add a DataGrid, follow these steps:

1. From the Server Behaviors panel, select the Add (+) button and choose DataGrid from the list.

   The DataGrid dialog box, shown in Figure 36-26, is displayed.

2. In the ID field, enter a unique name that will appear in the Server Behaviors panel.

3. From the DataSet list, select the DataSet you want to display.

4. Enter the number of records to display in the Show box.

5. Choose the type of navigation from the Navigation list: Links to Previous and Next pages, or Numbered Links to Every Page.

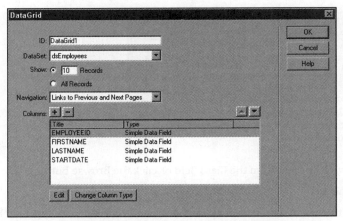

Figure 36-26: DataGrids cover all the necessary functions of inserting, updating, and deleting records.

6. In the Columns area, use the Add (+) and Remove (–) buttons to change the columns displayed in the DataGrid. You can add five different types of fields:

   - Simple Data Field
   - Free Form
   - Hyperlink
   - Edit, Update, Cancel Buttons
   - Delete Button

7. Click Edit to change the way a specific column is submitted to the database and displayed in the grid.

8. Click Change Column Type to change the type of a column already in the Columns list.

9. Click OK when you're done.

DataList

Using the .NET DataList provides a quick way to add columnar or repeating data to your page.

Requirements: One DataSet on the current page.

To add a DataList, follow these steps:

1. From the Server Behaviors panel, select the Add (+) button and choose DataList from the list.

   The DataList dialog box, shown in Figure 36-27, is displayed.

2. In the ID field, enter a unique name that will appear in the Server Behaviors panel.

3. From the DataSet list, select the DataSet you want to display.

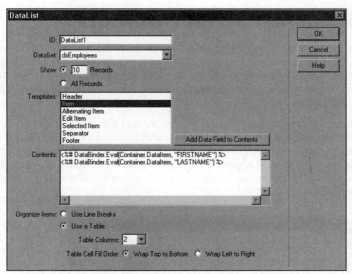

Figure 36-27: DataLists enable you to display repeating data in easy-to-define template regions.

4. Enter the number of records to display in the Show box.

5. The templates box contains the seven template regions of the DataList. Select each region and enter the content to be displayed in the Contents box. Click the Add Data Field to Contents button to add data from your DataSet. The seven template regions are as follows:

   - **Header:** The style for the header at the beginning of the list (if any)

   - **Item:** The style for individual items

   - **Alternating Item:** The style for every other item (alternating item)

   - **Edit Item:** The style for the item being edited

   - **Selected Item:** The style for the selected item

   - **Separator:** The style for the separator between each item

   - **Footer:** The style for the footer at the end of the list (if any)

6. Use the Organize Items radio buttons to specify how to organize your list, either using line breaks or a table. Choosing Use a Table enables the table controls at the bottom of the dialog box.

7. If you've chosen Use a Table, specify a number of table columns and how to wrap the cell contents.

8. Click OK when you're done.

Installing Additional Server Behaviors

Although Dreamweaver's standard server behaviors perform many important functions, they're just the tip of the iceberg in terms of what's possible. You can add additional server behaviors — whether created by Macromedia, yourself, or a third party — at any time. Although you can transfer files to the appropriate places in the Dreamweaver Configuration folder, most custom server behaviors rely on the Extension Manager for installation.

The Extension Manager is an auxiliary program that installs files compressed in the Macromedia Extension Program format; such files carry an .mxp file extension. To access the Extension Manager, choose Commands ➪ Manage Extensions or Help ➪ Manage Extensions. The Extension Manager, shown in Figure 36-28, displays all the extensions — including server behaviors — installed in your system. It also includes information about each extension, such as its type and creator.

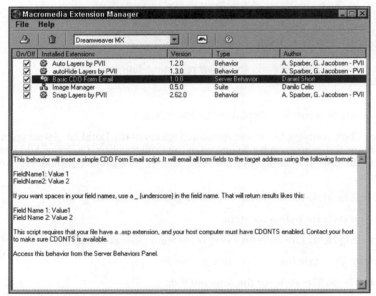

Figure 36-28: The Extension Manager greatly simplifies the process of installing new server behaviors and other extensions.

The Web offers numerous sources for MXP files, but perhaps the best known is the Dreamweaver Exchange, located on the Macromedia site. Once you've downloaded the file, you can install it by following these steps:

1. From Dreamweaver, choose Commands ➪ Manage Extensions to open the Extensions Manager.

Tip You don't even need Dreamweaver open to install an extension — just double-click the MXP file to invoke the Extension Manager and begin the installation process. However, if you have multiple Macromedia products on your system, it's better to open the Extension Manager before beginning the installation.

2. From the Extension Manager, choose File ⇨ Install Extension or use the keyboard shortcut, Ctrl+I (Command+O). You can choose the Install New Extension button from the Extension Manager toolbar.

3. Use the Select Extension to Install dialog box to locate the desired MXP file.

4. When you've located the file, click Install.

   As part of the installation process, Dreamweaver displays the Macromedia Extensions disclaimer.

5. Choose Accept in the Macromedia Extensions Disclaimer dialog box to continue.

   Dreamweaver continues to install the extension, and alerts you if a problem is encountered or if the procedure was successful.

6. Dreamweaver notifies you if the installed extension requires you to restart Dreamweaver before it can be used.

After the server behavior has been properly installed, it appears in the standard list found under the Add (+) button of the Server Behaviors panel, and can be applied like other server behaviors. Any special requirements or directions are noted in the bottom pane of the Extension Manager.

Editing Existing Server Behaviors

One of the wonders of Dreamweaver is the ability to extend every piece of the program. This includes making new server behaviors and editing existing ones. Out of the box, Dreamweaver allows you to edit only those server behaviors you've personally created. This is controlled by an XML attributed in the .edml file for each individual server behavior. We can gain access to these server behaviors by changing that XML attribute.

Before you continue though, please understand that many of the Dreamweaver server behaviors are extremely complex and may not work correctly if edited using the Server Behavior Builder. Instead, create a new server behavior, and copy an existing server behavior to make sure you don't break anything beyond repair.

In order to show a server behavior in the Server Behavior Builder follow these steps:

1. Locate the necessary server behavior .edml file. These are located in your Configuration directory. On a PC the default location is c:\Program Files\Macromedia\Dreamweaver MX\Configuration\{Datasource or Server Behavior}\{server model}\{server behavior name}.edml. For this example, open the Datasources\ASP_VB\Request Variable.edml file.

2. The first line of the .edml file should look like this:

   ```
   <group serverBehavior="Dynamic Data.htm" hideFromBuilder="true">
   ```

3. Change hideFromBuilder="true" to hideFromBuilder="false".

4. Restart Dreamweaver.

The Request Variable server behavior will now be available in the edit list of the Server Behavior Builder.

Creating Custom Server Behaviors

Dreamweaver provides a very sophisticated tool for creating custom server behaviors, the Server Behavior Builder. With the Server Behavior Builder, you can modify an existing server behavior you've created or create a new one from scratch. You can use the Server Behavior Builder in any server model configuration supported by Dreamweaver.

Tip   By default, you're not allowed to edit or copy the default Dreamweaver server behaviors. See the sidebar "Editing Existing Server Behaviors" to learn how to access all the built-in server behaviors.

The Server Behavior Builder breaks up any server behavior into discrete segments called *code blocks*. Each code block is surrounded by the delimiters for the particular server model: `<%. . .%>` for ASP, .NET and JSP; `<cftag>. . .</cftag>` for ColdFusion; and `<?. . .?>` for PHP. Each code block may contain one or more user-supplied parameters. The user enters the parameters in a dialog box; the Server Behavior Builder will even create the dialog box for you.

The Server Behavior Builder can also control the positioning of any individual code block. On the server side, code is executed from the top of the page to the bottom, and it is often critical that a particular code segment follows another in order to be processed properly.

You have the option of modifying an existing server behavior, modifying a copy of an existing server behavior, or creating an entirely new server behavior. The process is about the same for all three methods:

✦ Choose your server behavior. If it already exists, select it from the list, if it's new, give it a name.

✦ Work in the Server Behavior Builder to modify and create code blocks and parameters. The Server Behavior Builder is also used for code block positioning.

✦ Set up the dialog box for any parameters. The Generate Server Behavior Dialog Box command enables you to determine the type and order of any parameter elements.

To modify an existing server behavior, follow these steps:

1. From the Server Behaviors panel, choose the Add (+) button and select Edit Server Behaviors from the list.

   The Edit Server Behaviors dialog box, shown in Figure 36-29, appears.

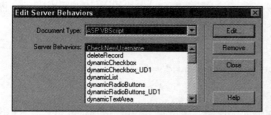

Figure 36-29: You can create server behaviors for different server models, regardless of the server model of the current site.

If you want to create a new server behavior, choose New Server Behavior instead of Edit Server Behaviors and skip to Step 4.

2. From the Server Model list, choose the type of code you want to modify.

3. From the Server Behaviors list, select the specific server behavior you want to adapt.

Dreamweaver posts a warning that if you are modifying a server behavior, the Server Behaviors panel may not be able to identify any instances of it already inserted into the current page. In this situation, it is strongly recommended that you choose New Server Behavior (see Figure 36-30) instead and create a different server behavior based on an existing server behavior.

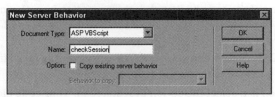

Figure 36-30: When creating a new server behavior, you can either model it on an existing one or start fresh.

After selecting the desired server behavior, the Server Behavior Builder opens, as shown in Figure 36-31.

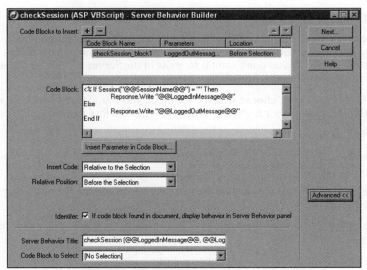

Figure 36-31: Dreamweaver's Server Behavior Builder offers tremendous flexibility in positioning code blocks.

4. Highlight the code block you want to change.

5. Modify the code as desired in the Code Block area.

6. To insert a new parameter, place your cursor in the Code Block area where you'd like the variable and choose Insert Parameter in Code Block.

Tip

To replace a value with a variable, select the value in the Code Block before choosing Insert Parameter in Code Block.

7. Enter a unique name for the variable in the Parameter Name field of the Insert Parameter in Code Block dialog box. Click OK when you're done.

   The new parameter is inserted in the following format: @@parametername@@.

8. Determine the positioning of the code by first choosing an option from the Insert Code list: Above the <html> tag, Below the </html> tag, Relative to a Specific Tag, or Relative to the Selection.

9. If you've chosen Insert Code: Relative to a Specific Tag, select the tag name from the Tag list that appears.

10. From the Relative Position list, select the option best suited for your code block.

11. If you've chosen Relative Position: Custom Position, enter a numeric value in the Custom Position field.

Caution

Positioning of code blocks is very important. In particular, make sure you don't insert code that depends upon a recordset above the code that creates that recordset.

12. Repeat Steps 4 through 11 for every code block you need to modify.

13. Click the Advanced button, and choose how you want the server behavior to be displayed in the Server Behaviors panel. You can add or remove parameters to customize the display. If you don't want it to show in the Server Behaviors panel at all, uncheck the Identifier checkbox.

14. In the Code Block area, choose which code block you want Dreamweaver to select when the server behavior is chosen in the Server Behaviors panel.

15. Click Next to proceed.

   If there are parameters in your server behavior, the Generate Behavior Dialog Box dialog box appears.

16. Set the position of your parameters by selecting an item in the list and using the up and down arrows.

17. Set the type of control for the parameter by choosing the down arrow next to the Display As column.

   Dreamweaver offers 17 controls to choose from:

   - Recordset Menu
   - Recordset Field Menu
   - Editable Recordset Menu
   - Editable Recordset Field Menu
   - CF DataSource Menu

- Connection Menu
- Connection Table Menu
- Connection Column Menu
- Text Field
- Dynamic Text Field
- URL Text Field
- Numeric Text Field
- Recordset Fields Ordered List
- Text Field Comma Separated List
- List Menu

Note If you choose List Menu, you must manually open the created server behavior file to populate the list menu.

- Checkbox
- Radio Group

The Text Field control is the default.

18. Click OK when you're done.

Dreamweaver will build your new or modified server behavior and include it in the Server Behaviors panel.

Summary

Server behaviors are, quite literally, essential to building dynamic pages in Dreamweaver. Without the server-side code that they insert, Web pages would just be static HTML. As you begin to investigate all that server behaviors can do for you, keep the following points in mind:

✦ While Dreamweaver provides many of the same server behaviors for ASP, ColdFusion, JSP, ASP.NET, and PHP, each server behavior outputs code specific to the site's chosen server model.

✦ The Server Behaviors panel is the primary conduit for applying, removing, and modifying server behaviors.

✦ Once a server behavior has been inserted, you can modify the user parameters at any time by double-clicking the item in the Server Behaviors panel.

✦ Server behaviors often have requirements — such as forms or other server behaviors — that must be in place on the page before they can be inserted.

✦ Dreamweaver enables you to modify standard server behaviors. You can also create new ones based on the standard server behaviors or build them from the ground up with the Server Behavior Builder.

✦   ✦   ✦

What's on the CD-ROM

The CD-ROM that accompanies *Dreamweaver MX Bible* contains the following:

◆ Fully functioning trial versions of Macromedia products Dreamweaver MX, Fireworks MX, Flash MX, FreeHand 10, Sitespring 1.2, JRun Server and ColdFusion MX.

◆ Code examples used in the book.

◆ A vast array of Dreamweaver extensions from the leaders in the Dreamweaver community, designed to make your work more productive. The types of extensions include

  • Behaviors

  • Server behaviors

  • Objects

  • Commands

  • Inspectors

  • Floaters

Using the Accompanying CD-ROM

The CD-ROM is what is known as a *hybrid CD-ROM*, which means it contains files that run on more than one computer platform—in this case, both Windows and Macintosh computers.

Several files, primarily the Macromedia trial programs and the other external programs, are compressed. Double-click these files to begin the installation procedure. Most other files on the CD-ROM are uncompressed, and you can simply copy them to your system by using your file manager. A few of the Dreamweaver extensions with files that must be placed in different folders are also compressed.

In the Configuration folder, the file structure replicates the structure that Dreamweaver sets up when it is installed. For example, objects found in the Dreamweaver\Configuration\Objects folder should be in that location for both the CD-ROM and the installed program. One slight variation: In the Additional Extensions folder, you'll find the various behaviors, objects, and so on, filed under their authors' names.

System Requirements

Be sure that your computer meets the minimum system requirements listed in this section. If your computer doesn't match up to most of these requirements, you may have a problem using the contents of the CD.

Macintosh

Macromedia recommends the following minimum requirements for running Dreamweaver on a Macintosh:

✦ Macintosh PowerPC (G3 or higher recommended)

✦ Mac OS 9.1 or higher or Mac OS 10.1 or higher

✦ 96MB of available RAM

✦ 275MB of available disk space

✦ 256-color monitor capable of 800 × 600 resolution (OS X requires thousands of colors)

✦ CD-ROM drive

Windows

Macromedia recommends the following minimum requirements for running Dreamweaver on a Windows system:

✦ Intel Pentium II processor, 300MHz or equivalent

✦ Windows 98, ME, NT, 2000, or XP

✦ 96MB of available RAM

✦ 275MB of available disk space

✦ 256-color monitor capable of 800 × 600 resolution

✦ CD-ROM drive

Files and Programs on the CD-ROM

Dreamweaver MX Bible contains a host of programs and auxiliary files to assist your exploration of Dreamweaver, as well as your Web page design work in general. The following is a description of the files and programs on the CD-ROM that accompanies this book.

Macromedia demos

If you haven't had a chance to work with Dreamweaver (or Fireworks or Flash), the CD-ROM offers fully functioning trial versions of key Macromedia programs for both Macintosh and Windows systems. Each of the demos will run for 30 days; they cannot be reinstalled in order to gain additional time. The following trial programs are included:

✦ Dreamweaver MX

✦ Fireworks MX

✦ Flash MX

✦ FreeHand 10

✦ JRun Server (Windows only)

✦ ColdFusion MX Server (Windows only)

To install any of the programs, just double-click the program icon in the main folder of the CD-ROM where the programs are located and follow the installation instructions on your screen.

Caution   The trial versions of Macromedia programs are very sensitive to system date changes. If you alter your computer's date, the programs will time-out and no longer function. It is a good idea to check your system's date and time before installing them. Moreover, if you've previously run the trial version of the same program from another source (such as downloading it from the Internet), you won't be able to run the trial version again.

Dreamweaver extensions

Dreamweaver is extremely extendible, and the Dreamweaver community has built some amazing extensions. In the Additional Extensions folders of the CD-ROM, you'll find hundreds of behaviors, server behaviors, objects, commands, inspectors, and more. The extensions are grouped according to author, and within each author's folder, they are organized by function.

Where available, extensions are packaged in an .mxp file, which can easily be installed using the Extension Manager. To run the Extension Manager from Dreamweaver, choose Commands ➪ Manage Extensions. Then choose File ➪ Install Extension and browse to the location of the extension's .mxp file.

Note   A small number of extensions were written prior to the availability of the Extension Manager and do not require that program for installation. Extensions that contain files that must be placed in different folders, such as the Commands and Inspectors directories, are compressed in a WinZip format. In those instances, a ReadMe file explains where the files must be placed.

You'll find a ReadMe.htm file in each author's folder, with links to the author's Web site and more information about his or her creations.

Dreamweaver MX Bible code examples

You can find sample code used in *Dreamweaver MX Bible* in the Examples folder of the CD-ROM. Also included are some of the Dreamweaver Techniques used in the book. You can easily view the files through Dreamweaver or your browser without transferring the files to your system. If you do wish to transfer the files, copy the entire folder over to your system.

To incorporate the external style sheets in your Web sites, copy files with .css extensions into your local site's root folder. Then follow the instructions in the "Attaching an external style sheet" section found in Chapter 20.

Web resource directory

The World Wide Web is a vital resource for any Web designer, whether a seasoned professional or a beginner. The CD-ROM contains an HTML page with a series of links to resources on the Web; the series contains general as well as Dreamweaver-specific references.

Dreamweaver MX Bible in PDF format

Can't find the exact reference that you know you read earlier? Search for it in *Dreamweaver MX Bible* in PDF format located on the CD-ROM. You'll need Adobe Acrobat Reader to view the PDF files; if you don't have it installed on your system, you'll find it on the CD-ROM also.

Troubleshooting

If you have difficulty installing or using any of the materials on the companion CD, try the following solutions:

✦ Turn off any anti-virus software that you may have running. Installers sometimes mimic virus activity and can make your computer incorrectly believe that it is being infected by a virus. (Be sure to turn the anti-virus software back on later.)

✦ Close all running programs. The more programs you're running, the less memory is available to other programs. Installers also typically update files and programs; if you keep other programs running, installation may not work properly.

✦ Reference the ReadMe.txt: Please refer to the ReadMe file located at the root of the CD-ROM for the latest product information at the time of publication.

If you still have trouble with the CD, please call the Wiley Customer Care phone number: (800) 762-2974. Outside the United States, call 1 (317) 572-3994. You can also contact Wiley Customer Service by e-mail at techsupdum@wiley.com. Wiley will provide technical support only for installation and other general quality control items; for technical support on the applications themselves, consult the program's vendor or author.

✦ ✦ ✦

Index

Continued

Wiley Publishing, Inc.
End-User License Agreement

5. Limited Warranty.

(a) WPI warrants that the Software and Software Media are free from defects in materials and workmanship under normal use for a period of sixty (60) days from the date of purchase of this Book. If WPI receives notification within the warranty period of defects in materials or workmanship, WPI will replace the defective Software Media.

(b) **WPI AND THE AUTHOR OF THE BOOK DISCLAIM ALL OTHER WARRANTIES, EXPRESS OR IMPLIED, INCLUDING WITHOUT LIMITATION IMPLIED WARRANTIES OF MERCHANTABILITY AND FITNESS FOR A PARTICULAR PURPOSE, WITH RESPECT TO THE SOFTWARE, THE PROGRAMS, THE SOURCE CODE CONTAINED THEREIN, AND/OR THE TECHNIQUES DESCRIBED IN THIS BOOK. WPI DOES NOT WARRANT THAT THE FUNCTIONS CONTAINED IN THE SOFTWARE WILL MEET YOUR REQUIREMENTS OR THAT THE OPERATION OF THE SOFTWARE WILL BE ERROR FREE.**

(c) This limited warranty gives you specific legal rights, and you may have other rights that vary from jurisdiction to jurisdiction.

6. Remedies.

(a) WPI's entire liability and your exclusive remedy for defects in materials and workmanship shall be limited to replacement of the Software Media, which may be returned to WPI with a copy of your receipt at the following address: Software Media Fulfillment Department, Attn.: *Dreamweaver MX Bible*, Wiley Publishing, Inc., 10475 Crosspoint Blvd., Indianapolis, IN 46256, or call 1-800-762-2974. Please allow four to six weeks for delivery. This Limited Warranty is void if failure of the Software Media has resulted from accident, abuse, or misapplication. Any replacement Software Media will be warranted for the remainder of the original warranty period or thirty (30) days, whichever is longer.

(b) In no event shall WPI or the author be liable for any damages whatsoever (including without limitation damages for loss of business profits, business interruption, loss of business information, or any other pecuniary loss) arising from the use of or inability to use the Book or the Software, even if WPI has been advised of the possibility of such damages.

(c) Because some jurisdictions do not allow the exclusion or limitation of liability for consequential or incidental damages, the above limitation or exclusion may not apply to you.

7. U.S. Government Restricted Rights. Use, duplication, or disclosure of the Software for or on behalf of the United States of America, its agencies and/or instrumentalities "U.S. Government" is subject to restrictions as stated in paragraph (c)(1)(ii) of the Rights in Technical Data and Computer Software clause of DFARS 252.227-7013, or subparagraphs (c) (1) and (2) of the Commercial Computer Software - Restricted Rights clause at FAR 52.227-19, and in similar clauses in the NASA FAR supplement, as applicable.

8. General. This Agreement constitutes the entire understanding of the parties and revokes and supersedes all prior agreements, oral or written, between them and may not be modified or amended except in a writing signed by both parties hereto that specifically refers to this Agreement. This Agreement shall take precedence over any other documents that may be in conflict herewith. If any one or more provisions contained in this Agreement are held by any court or tribunal to be invalid, illegal, or otherwise unenforceable, each and every other provision shall remain in full force and effect.